Northwest & Great Plains

Idaho, Iowa, Montana, Nebraska, North Dakota, Oregon, South Dakota, Washington, and Wyoming

MACMILLAN • USA

Frommer's America on Wheels: Northwest & Great Plains

Regional Editor: Risa R Weinreb, assisted by Alan David (Deputy Editor), Elizabeth Arenson (Editorial Assistant), J C Gilland (Computer Software Consultant)
Inspections Coordinator: Laura Van Zee

Contributors: Sue Bailey, Michael Bennett, Wendy Bennett, Sylvia Blishak, Andrea Carlisle, Rebecca Christian, Providence Cicero, Brian Clark, Kathy Craigo, Linda Curtis, Larry Earl, Julie Fanselow, Bob Fischer, Kim Guilford, Bonnie Henderson, Terry Henderson, Mary Heng, Sara Jameson, Leslee Jaquette, Judy Jewell, Kim Johnson, Patricia Kuhn, Serena Lesley, Scott Maben, Katie MacKenzie, Marilyn McFarlane, Robin McMacken, Myrna Oakley, Geoffrey O'Gara, Rodney Orosco, Mark Palmberg, Lorry Patton, Lenore Puhek, Kevin Remillard, Tom Roseliep, Karl Samson, Lin Sanford, Eric Seyfarth, Steve Stuebner, Sarah Thomas, Jean Tiedtke, Dianna Troyer, Katherine Tweed, Loralee Wenger, Leslie Westbrook, Kathy Witkowsky, John Wolcott, Roberta Wolcott, Enid Yurman

Frommer's America on Wheels Staff
Project Director: Gretchen Henderson
Senior Editor: Christopher Hollander
Database Editor: Melissa Klurman
Assistant Editor: Marian Cole

Macmillan Travel
A Simon & Schuster Macmillan Company
1633 Broadway
New York, NY 10019-6785

Manufactured in the United States of America

ISSN: 1082-0841
ISBN: 0-02-860931-X

SPECIAL SALES
Bulk purchases (10+ copies) of Frommer's and selected Macmillan travel guides are available to corporations, organizations, mail-order catalogs, institutions, and charities at special discounts, and can be customized to suit individual needs. For more information write to Special Sales, Macmillan General Reference, 1633 Broadway, New York, NY 10019.

Contents

Nebraska

North Dakota

Oregon

South Dakota

Washington

Wyoming

Introduction

America on Wheels introduces a brand-new lodgings rating system—one that factors in the latest trends in travel preferences, technologies, and amenities and is based on thorough inspections by experienced travel professionals. We rate establishments from one to five flags, plus a unique rating we call Ultra, a special award reserved for only a handful of outstanding properties in each category. Our restaurant selections represent the ethnic diversity of today's dining scene and are categorized with symbols according to their special features, ambience, and services available. In addition, the series provides in-depth sightseeing information, including driving tours and best-of-the-state highlights.

State Introductions

Coverage of each state in the *America on Wheels* series begins with background information that will help familiarize you with your destination. Included is a summary of the state's history and an overview of its geography, followed by practical tips that we hope you will find useful in planning your trip—what kind of weather to expect, what to pack, sources of information within the state, driving rules and regulations, and other essentials.

The "Best of the State" section provides you with a rundown of the top sights and attractions and the most popular festivals and special events around the state. It also includes information on spectator sports and an A-to-Z list of recreational activities available to you.

Driving Tours

The scenic driving tours included guide you along some of the most popular sightseeing routes. Every tour is keyed to a map and includes mileage information and precise directions, refreshment stops, and, for longer tours, recommended places to stay.

The Listings

The city-by-city listings of lodgings, dining establishments, and attractions together make up the bulk of the book. Cities are organized alphabetically within each state. You will find a brief description or "profile" for most cities, including a source to contact for additional information. Any listings will follow.

Types of Lodgings

Here's how we define the lodging categories used in *America on Wheels.*

Hotel

A hotel usually has three or more floors with elevators. It may or may not have parking, but if it does, entry to the guest rooms is likely to be through the lobby rather than directly from the parking lot. A range of lodgings is available (such as standard rooms, deluxe rooms, and suites), and a range of services is available (such as bellhops, room service, and a concierge). Many hotels have a restaurant or coffee shop open for breakfast, lunch, and dinner; they may have a cocktail lounge/bar. Recreational facilities may be available (such as a swimming pool, fitness center, and tennis courts).

Motel

A motel usually has one to three floors, and many of the guest rooms have doors facing the parking lot or outdoor corridors. A motel may only have a small, serviceable lobby and usually offers only limited services; the nearest restaurant may be down the street. A motel is most likely to be located alongside a highway or in a resort area.

Inn

An inn is a small-scale hotel or lodge, usually in an older building that may or may not have been designed for lodgings, and it is often located in scenic surroundings. An inn should have a warm, welcoming atmosphere, with a more homelike quality to its furnishings and facilities. The guest rooms may be individually decorated in a style appropriate to the inn's age and location, and the rooms may or may not have telephones, televisions, or private bathrooms. An inn usually has a lounge or sitting room for guests (with parlor games and perhaps a television) and a small dining room that may or may not be open to the public. Breakfast, however, is almost always served.

Lodge

A lodge is essentially a small hotel in a rural, remote, or mountainous location. The atmosphere, service, and furniture may be more casual than you'd find in a regular hotel, and there may not be televisions or telephones in every guest room. The facilities usually include a coffee shop or restaurant, bar or cocktail lounge, games room, and indoor or outdoor swimming pool or hot tub. In ski areas, the lounge usually has a fireplace and facilities for storing ski gear.

Resort

A resort usually has more extensive facilities and recreational activities than a hotel, and offers three meals a day. The atmosphere is generally more informal than at comparable hotels.

How the Lodgings Are Rated

Every hotel, motel, resort, inn, and lodge rated in this series has been subjected to a thorough hands-on inspection by our team of accomplished travel professionals. We ask the kinds of questions that readers would ask if they could inspect the rooms in advance for themselves (How good is the soundproofing? How firm is the bed? What condition are the room furnishings in?). Then all of the inspection reports are reviewed by regional editors who are experts on their territories. The top-rated properties are then rechecked by a special consultant who has been reviewing and critiquing luxury hotels around the world for almost 25 years. *Establishments are not charged to be included in our series.*

Our ratings are based on *average* guest rooms—not lavish suites or concierge floors—so they're not artificially high. Therefore, in some cases a hotel rated four flags may indeed have individual rooms or suites that might fall into the five-flag category; conversely, a four-flag hotel may have a few rooms in its lowest price range that might otherwise warrant three flags.

The detailed ratings vary by category of lodgings—for example, the criteria imposed on a hotel are more rigorous than those for a motel—and some features that are considered essential in, for example, a four-flag city hotel are relaxed for a resort that offers alternative attractions, sporting facilities, and/or beautiful and spacious grounds. Likewise, amenities such as telephones and televisions—essential in hotels and motels—are not required in inns, whose guests are often seeking peace and quiet. Instead, the criteria take into account such features as individually decorated rooms and complimentary afternoon tea.

There are, of course, several basic attributes that apply to all lodgings across the board: the cleanliness and maintenance of the building as a whole; the housekeeping in individual rooms; safety, both indoors and out; the quality and practicality of the furnishings; the quality and availability of the amenities; the caliber of the facilities; the extent and/or condition of the grounds; the ambience and cleanliness in the dining rooms; and the caliber and professionalism of the service in relation to the rates and types of lodging. Since the *America on Wheels* rating system is highly rigorous, just because a property has garnered only one flag does not mean it is inadequate or substandard.

What the Individual Ratings Mean

One Flag

These properties have met or surpassed the minimum requirements of cleanliness, safety, convenience, and amenities. The staff may be limited, but guests can generally expect a friendly, hospitable greeting. Rooms will have basic amenities, such as air conditioning or heating where appropriate, telephones, and televisions. The bathrooms may have only showers rather than tubs, and just one towel for each guest, but showers and towels must be clean. The one-flag properties are by no means places to avoid, since they can represent exceptional value.

Two Flags

In addition to having all of the basic attributes of one-flag lodgings, these properties will have some extra amenities, such as bellhops to help with the luggage, ice buckets in each room, and better-quality furnishings. Some extra services may include availability of cribs and irons, and wake-up service.

Three Flags

These properties have all the basics noted above but also offer a more generous complement of amenities, such as firmer beds, larger desks, more drawer space, extra blankets and pillows, cable or satellite TV, alarm clock/radios, room service (although hours may be limited), and dry cleaning and/or laundry services.

Four Flags
This is the realm of luxury, with refinements in amenities, furnishings, and service—such as larger rooms, more dependable soundproofing, two telephones per room, in-room movies, in-room safes, thick towels, hair dryers, twice-daily maid service, turndown service, concierge service, and 24-hour room service.

Five Flags
These properties have everything the four-flag properties have, plus a more personal level of service and more sumptuous amenities, among them bathrobes, superior linens, and blackout drapes for lightproofing. Facilities normally include a business center and fitness center. Generally speaking, guests pay handsomely to stay in these properties.

Ultra
This crème-de-la-crème rating is reserved for those rare hotels and resorts, possibly also motels and inns, that are truly outstanding in every or almost every department—places with a "grand hotel" presence, an almost flawless level of service, and a standard of dining equal to that of the finest restaurants.

UNRATED

In the few cases where an inspector was not able to make a detailed inspection, the property is listed as unrated. Also, in some cases where a property was in the process of changing owners or managers, or if the property was undergoing the kind of major renovations that made formal evaluation impossible, then, again, it is listed as unrated.

Types of Dining

Restaurant
A restaurant serves complete meals and almost always offers seating.

Refreshment Stop
A refreshment stop serves drinks and/or snacks only (such as an ice cream parlor, bakery, or coffee bar) and may or may not have seating available.

How the Restaurants Were Evaluated

All of the restaurants reviewed in this series have been through the kind of thorough inspection described above for lodgings. Our inspectors have evaluated everything from freshness of ingredients to noise level and spacing of tables.

Unique to the *America on Wheels* series are the easy-to-read symbols that identify a restaurant's special features, its ambience, and special services. (See the inside front cover for the key to all symbols.) With them you can determine at a glance whether a place is a local favorite, offers exceptional value, or is "worth a splurge."

How to Read the Listings

LODGINGS

Introductory Information
The rating is followed by the establishment's name, address, neighborhood (if applicable), telephone number(s), and fax number (if there is one). Where appropriate, location information is provided. In the resort listings, the acreage of the property is indicated. Also included are our inspector's comments, which provide some description and discuss any outstanding features or special information about the establishment. You can also find out whether an inn is unsuitable for children, and if so, up to what age.

Rooms
Specifies the number and type of accommodations available. If a hotel has an "executive level," this will be noted here. (This level, sometimes called a "concierge floor," is a special area of a hotel. Usually priced higher than standard rooms, accommodations at this level are often larger and have additional amenities and services such as daily newspaper delivery and nightly turndown service. Guests staying in these rooms often have access to a private lounge where complimentary breakfasts or snacks may be served.) Check-in/check-out times will also appear in this section, followed by information on the establishment's smoking policy ("No smoking" for properties that are entirely nonsmoking, and "Nonsmoking rms avail" for those that permit smoking in some areas but have rooms available for nonsmokers). This information may be followed by comments, if the inspector noted anything in particular about the guest rooms, such as their size, decor, furnishings, or window views.

Amenities
If the following amenities are available in the majority of the guest rooms, they are indicated by symbols

(see inside front cover for key) or included in a list: telephone, alarm clock, coffeemaker, hair dryer, air conditioning, TV (including cable or satellite hook-up, free or pay movies), refrigerator, dataport (for fax/modem communication), VCR, CD/tape player, voice mail, in-room safe, and bathrobes. If some or all rooms have minibars, terraces, fireplaces, or whirlpools, that will be indicated here. Because travelers usually expect air conditioning, telephones, and televisions in their guest rooms, we specifically note when those amenities are not available. If any additional amenities are available in the majority of the guest rooms, or if amenities are outstanding in any way, the inspector's comments will provide some elaboration at the end of this section.

Services

If the following services are available, they are indicated by symbols (see inside front cover for key) or included in a list: room service (24-hour or limited), concierge, valet parking, airport transportation, dry cleaning/laundry, cribs available, pets allowed (call ahead before bringing your pet; an establishment that accepts pets may nevertheless place restrictions on the types or size of pets allowed, or may require a deposit and/or charge a fee), twice-daily maid service, car-rental desk, social director, masseur, children's program, babysitting (that is, the establishment can put you in touch with local babysitters and/or agencies), and afternoon tea and/or wine or sherry served. If the establishment offers any special services, or if the inspector has commented on the quality of services offered, that information will appear at the end of this section. Please note that there may be a fee for some services.

Facilities

If the following facilities are on the premises, they are indicated by symbols (see inside front cover for key) or included in a list: pool(s), bike rentals, boat rentals (may include canoes, kayaks, sailboats, powerboats, jet-skis, paddleboats), fishing, golf course (with number of holes), horseback riding, jogging path/parcourse (fitness trail), unlighted tennis courts (number available), lighted tennis courts (number available), waterskiing, windsurfing, fitness center, meeting facilities (and number of people this space can accommodate), business center, restaurant(s), bar(s), beach(es), lifeguard (for beach, not pool), basketball, volleyball, board surfing, games room, lawn games, racquetball, snorkeling, squash, spa, sauna, steam room, whirlpool, beauty salon, day-care center, playground, washer/dryer, and guest lounge (for inns only). If cross-country and downhill skiing facilities are located within 10 miles of the property, then that is indicated by symbols here as well. Our "Accessible for People With Disabilities" symbol appears where establishments claim to have guest rooms with such accessibility. If an establishment has additional facilities that are worth noting, or if the inspector has commented about the facilities, that information appears at the end of this section.

Rates

If the establishment's rates vary throughout the year, then the rates given are for the peak season. The rates listed are EP (no meals included), unless otherwise noted. We'll tell you if there is a charge for an extra person to stay in a room; if children stay free, and if so, up to what age; if there are minimum stay requirements; and if AP (three meals) and/or MAP (breakfast and dinner) rates are also available. The parking rates (if the establishment has parking) are followed by any comments the inspector has provided about rates.

If the establishment has a seasonal closing, this information will be stated. A list of credit cards accepted ends the listing.

DINING

Introductory Information

If a restaurant is a local favorite, an exceptional value (one with a high quality-to-price ratio for the area), or "worth a splurge" (more expensive by area standards, but well worth it), the appropriate symbol will appear at the beginning of the listing (see inside front cover for key to symbols). Then the establishment's name, address, neighborhood (if applicable), and telephone number are listed, followed by location information when appropriate. The type of cuisine appears in boldface type and is followed by our inspectors' comments on everything from decor and ambience to menu highlights.

The "FYI" Heading

"For your information," this section tells you the reservations policy ("recommended," "accepted," or "not accepted"), and whether there is live entertainment, a children's menu, or a dress code (jacket required or other policy). If the restaurant does not have a full bar, you can find out what the liquor policy is ("beer and wine only," "beer only," "wine only," "BYO," or "no liquor license"). This is also where you can check to see if there's a no-smoking policy for the entire restaurant (please note that smoking policies are in flux throughout the country; if smoking—or avoiding smokers—is important to you, it's a good idea to call ahead to verify the policy). If the restaurant is part of a group or chain, address and phone information will be provided for additional locations in the area. This section does not appear in Refreshment Stop listings.

Hours of Operation

Under the "Open" heading, "Peak" indicates that the hours listed are for high season only (dates in parentheses); otherwise, the hours listed apply year-round. If an establishment has a seasonal closing, that information will follow. It's a good idea to call ahead to confirm the hours of operation, especially in the off-season.

Prices

Prices given are for dinner main courses (unless otherwise noted). If a prix-fixe dinner is offered throughout dinner hours, that price is listed here, too. This section ends with a list of credit cards accepted. Refreshment Stop listings do not include prices.

Symbols

The symbols that fall at the end of many restaurant listings can help you find restaurants with the features that are important to you. If a restaurant has romantic ambience, historic ambience, outdoor dining, a fireplace, a view, delivery service, early-bird specials, valet parking, or is family-oriented, open 24 hours, or accessible to people with disabilities (meaning it has a level entrance or an access ramp, a doorway at least 36 inches wide, and restrooms that are on the same floor as the dining room, with doorways at least 36 inches wide and properly outfitted stalls), then these symbols will appear (see inside front cover for key to symbols).

ATTRACTIONS

Introductory Information

The name, street address, neighborhood (if located in a major city), and telephone number are followed by a brief rundown of the attraction's high points and key attributes so you can quickly determine if it's worth a full day of exploration or just a brief detour.

Hours of Operation & Admission

Service information includes hours of operation ("Peak" indicates that the hours listed are for high season only) and the cost of admission. The cost is

ABBREVIATIONS

A/C	air conditioning
AE	American Express (charge card)
AP	American Plan (rates include breakfast, lunch, and dinner)
avail	available
BB	Bed-and-Breakfast Plan (rates include full breakfast)
bkfst	breakfast
BYO	bring your own (beer or wine)
CC	credit cards
CI	check-in time
CO	check-out time
CP	Continental Plan (rates include continental breakfast)
ctr	center
D	double (indicates room rate for two people in one room (one or two beds))
DC	Diners Club (credit card)
DISC	Discover (credit card)
EC	EuroCard (credit card)
effic	efficiency (unit with cooking facilities)
ER	En Route (credit card)
info	information
int'l	international
JCB	Japanese Credit Bureau (credit card)
ltd	limited
MAP	Modified American Plan (rates include breakfast and dinner)
MC	MasterCard (credit card)
Mem Day	Memorial Day
mi	mile(s)
min	minimum
MM	mile marker
refrig	refrigerator
rms	rooms
S	single (indicates room rate for one person)
satel	satellite
stes	suites (rooms with separate living and sleeping areas)
svce	service
tel	telephone
V	Visa (credit card)
w/	with
wknds	weekends

indicated by one to four dollar signs (see inside front cover for key to symbols). It's a good idea to call ahead to confirm the hours.

Special Information

Disabled Traveler Information

The Americans with Disabilities Act (ADA) of 1990 required that all public facilities and commercial establishments be made accessible to disabled persons by January 26, 1992. Any property opened after that date must be built in accordance with the ADA Accessible Guidelines. Note, however, that not all establishments have completed their renovations to conform with the law; be sure to call ahead to determine if your specific needs can be met.

Taxes

State and city taxes vary widely and are not included in the prices in this book. Always ask about the taxes when you are making your reservations. State sales tax is given under "Essentials" in the introduction to each state.

A Disclaimer

Readers are advised that prices fluctuate in the course of time, and travel information changes under the impact of the varied and volatile factors that affect the travel industry. The publisher cannot be held responsible for the experiences of readers while traveling. Readers are invited to send ideas, comments, and suggestions for future editions to: *America on Wheels,* Macmillan Travel, 1633 Broadway, New York, NY 10019-6785.

TOLL-FREE NUMBERS/WORLD WIDE WEB SITES

The following toll-free telephone numbers and URLs for World Wide Web sites were accurate at press time; *America on Wheels* cannot be held responsible for any number or address that has changed. The "TDD" numbers are answered by a telecommunications service for the deaf and hard-of-hearing. Be sure to dial "1" before each number.

Lodgings

Best Western International, Inc
800/528-1234 North America
800/528-2222 TDD

Budgetel Inns
800/4-BUDGET Continental USA and Canada

Budget Host
800/BUD-HOST Continental USA

Clarion Hotels
800/CLARION Continental USA and Canada
800/228-3323 TDD
http://www.hotelchoice.com/cgi-bin/res/webres?clarion.html

Comfort Inns
800/228-5150 Continental USA and Canada
800/228-3323 TDD
http://www.hotelchoice.com/cgi-bin/res/webres?comfort.html

Courtyard by Marriott
800/321-2211 Continental USA and Canada
800/228-7014 TDD
http://www.marriott.com/lodging/courtyar.html

Days Inn
800/325-2525 Continental USA and Canada
800/325-3297 TDD
http://www.daysinn.com/daysinn.html

DoubleTree Hotels
800/222-TREE Continental USA and Canada
800/528-9898 TDD

Drury Inn
800/325-8300 Continental USA and Canada
800/325-0583 TDD

Econo Lodges
800/55-ECONO Continental USA and Canada
800/228-3323 TDD
http://www.hotelchoice.com/cgi-bin/res/webres?econo.html

Embassy Suites
800/362-2779 Continental USA and Canada
800/458-4708 TDD
http://www.embassy-suites.com

Exel Inns of America
800/356-8013 Continental USA and Canada

Fairfield Inn by Marriott
800/228-2800 Continental USA and Canada
800/228-7014 TDD
http://www.marriott.com/lodging/fairf.html

Fairmont Hotels
800/527-4727 Continental USA

Forte Hotels
800/225-5843 Continental USA and Canada

Four Seasons Hotels
800/332-3442 Continental USA
800/268-6282 Canada

Friendship Inns
800/453-4511 Continental USA
800/228-3323 TDD
http://www.hotelchoice.com/cgi-bin/res/webres?friendship.html

Guest Quarters Suites
800/424-2900 Continental USA

Hampton Inn
800/HAMPTON Continental USA and Canada
800/451-HTDD TDD
http://www.hampton-inn.com

Hilton Hotels Corporation
800/HILTONS Continental USA and Canada
800/368-1133 TDD
http://www.hilton.com

Holiday Inn
800/HOLIDAY Continental USA and Canada
800/238-5544 TDD
http://www.holiday-inn.com

Howard Johnson
800/654-2000 Continental USA and Canada
800/654-8442 TDD
http://www.hojo.com/hojo.html

Hyatt Hotels and Resorts
800/228-9000 Continental USA and Canada
800/228-9548 TDD
http://www.hyatt.com

Inns of America
800/826-0778 Continental USA and Canada

Intercontinental Hotels
800/327-0200 Continental USA and Canada

ITT Sheraton
800/325-3535 Continental USA and Canada
800/325-1717 TDD

La Quinta Motor Inns, Inc
800/531-5900 Continental USA and Canada
800/426-3101 TDD

Loews Hotels
800/223-0888 Continental USA and Canada
http://www.loewshotels.com

Marriott Hotels
800/228-9290 Continental USA and Canada
800/228-7014 TDD
http://www.marriott.com/MainPage.html

Master Hosts Inns
800/251-1962 Continental USA and Canada

Meridien
800/543-4300 Continental USA and Canada

Omni Hotels
800/843-6664 Continental USA and Canada

Park Inns International
800/437-PARK Continental USA and Canada
http://www.p-inns.com/parkinn.html

Quality Inns
800/228-5151 Continental USA and Canada
800/228-3323 TDD
http://www.hotelchoice.com/cgi-bin/res/webres?quality.html

Radisson Hotels International
800/333-3333 Continental USA and Canada

Ramada
800/2-RAMADA Continental USA and Canada
http://www.ramada.com/ramada.html

Red Carpet Inns
800/251-1962 Continental USA and Canada

Red Lion Hotels and Inns
800/547-8010 Continental USA and Canada

Red Roof Inns
800/843-7663 Continental USA and Canada
800/843-9999 TDD
http://www.redroof.com

Renaissance Hotels International
800/HOTELS-1 Continental USA and Canada
800/833-4747 TDD

Residence Inn by Marriott
800/331-3131 Continental USA and Canada
800/228-7014 TDD
http://www.marriott.com/lodging/resinn.html

Resinter
800/221-4542 Continental USA and Canada

Ritz-Carlton
800/241-3333 Continental USA and Canada

Rodeway Inns
800/228-2000 Continental USA and Canada
800/228-3323 TDD
http://www.hotelchoice.com/cgi-bin/res/webres?rodeway.html

Scottish Inns
800/251-1962 Continental USA and Canada

Shilo Inns
800/222-2244 Continental USA and Canada

Signature Inns
800/822-5252 Continental USA and Canada

Super 8 Motels
800/800-8000 Continental USA and Canada
800/533-6634 TDD
http://www.super8motels.com/super8.html

Susse Chalet Motor Lodges & Inns
800/258-1980 Continental USA and Canada

Travelodge
800/255-3050 Continental USA and Canada

Vagabond Hotels Inc
800/522-1555 Continental USA and Canada

Westin Hotels and Resorts
800/228-3000 Continental USA and Canada
800/254-5440 TDD
http://www.westin.com

Wyndham Hotels and Resorts
800/822-4200 Continental USA and Canada

Car Rental Agencies

Advantage Rent-A-Car
800/777-5500 Continental USA and Canada

Airways Rent A Car
800/952-9200 Continental USA

Alamo Rent A Car
800/327-9633 Continental USA and Canada
http://www.goalamo.com

Allstate Car Rental
800/634-6186 Continental USA and Canada

Avis
800/331-1212 Continental USA
800/TRY-AVIS Canada
800/331-2323 TDD
http://www.avis.com

Budget Rent A Car
800/527-0700 Continental USA and Canada
800/826-5510 TDD

Dollar Rent A Car
800/800-4000 Continental USA and Canada

Enterprise Rent-A-Car
800/325-8007 Continental USA and Canada

Hertz
800/654-3131 Continental USA and Canada
800/654-2280 TDD

National Car Rental
800/CAR-RENT Continental USA and Canada
800/328-6323 TDD
http://www.nationalcar.com

Payless Car Rental
800/PAYLESS Continental USA and Canada

Rent-A-Wreck
800/535-1391 Continental USA

Sears Rent A Car
800/527-0770 Continental USA and Canada

Thrifty Rent-A-Car
800/367-2277 Continental USA and Canada
800/358-5856 TDD

U-Save Auto Rental of America
800/272-USAV Continental USA and Canada

Value Rent-A Car
800/327-2501 Continental USA and Canada
http://www.go-value.com

Airlines

American Airlines
800/433-7300 Continental USA and Western Canada
800/543-1586 TDD
http://www.americanair.com/aahome/aahome.html

Canadian Airlines International
800/426-7000 Continental USA and Canada
http://www.cdair.ca

Continental Airlines
800/525-0280 Continental USA
800/343-9195 TDD
http://www.flycontinental.com

Delta Air Lines
800/221-1212 Continental USA
800/831-4488 TDD
http://www.delta-air.com

Northwest Airlines
800/225-2525 Continental USA and Canada
http://www.nwa.com

Southwest Airlines
800/435-9792 Continental USA and Canada
http://iflyswa.com

Trans World Airlines
800/221-2000 Continental USA
http://www2.twa.com/TWA/Airlines/home/home.html

United Airlines
800/241-6522 Continental USA and Canada
http://www.ual.com

USAir
800/428-4322 Continental USA and Canada
http://www.usair.com

Train

Amtrak
800/USA-RAIL Continental USA
http://amtrak.com

Bus

Greyhound
800/231-2222 Continental USA
http://greyhound.com

The Top-Rated Lodgings

Five Flags

Four Seasons Olympic Seattle, Seattle, WA
Salishan Lodge, Gleneden Beach, OR

Four Flags

Alexis Hotel Seattle, Seattle, WA
Ann Starrett Mansion, Port Townsend, WA
The Campbell House, Eugene, OR
Coeur d'Alene Resort, Coeur d'Alene, ID
Cornhusker Hotel, Lincoln, NE
Crater Lake Lodge, Inc, Crater Lake, OR
Friday Harbor House, Friday Harbor, WA
Gaslight Inn, Seattle, WA
Governor Hotel, Portland, OR
Green Gables Inn, Walla Walla, WA
Grouse Mountain Lodge, Whitefish, MT
Hannah Marie Country Inn, Spencer, IA
The Harrison House Inn, Langley, WA
The Heathman Hotel, Portland, OR
Heron Haus, Portland, OR
Holiday Inn Crowne Plaza, Seattle, WA
Hotel Vintage Park, Seattle, WA
Hotel Vintage Plaza, Portland, OR
Hyatt Regency Bellevue, Bellevue, WA
Idaho Country Inn, Ketchum, ID
Inn at Langley, Langley, WA
Inn at Ludlow Bay, Port Ludlow, WA
Inn at the Market, Seattle, WA
The Inn at Semi-ah-moo, Blaine, WA
The James House, Port Townsend, WA
Knob Hill Inn, Ketchum, ID
Little America Hotel and Resort, Cheyenne, WY
Lost Creek Ranch, Moose, WY
Marina Village Inn, Everett, WA
Moose Head Dude Ranch, Moose, WY
Redstone Inn, Dubuque, IA
River Rock Lodge, Big Sky, MT
RiverPlace Hotel, Portland, OR
Salish Lodge, Snoqualmie, WA
Shelburne Country Inn, Seaview, WA
Shumway Mansion, Kirkland, WA
Skamania Lodge, Stevenson, WA
The Sorrento Hotel, Seattle, WA
Spring Creek, Jackson, WY
Stephanie Inn, Cannon Beach, OR
Sun Mountain Lodge, Winthrop, WA
Sun Valley Lodge, Sun Valley, ID
Triple Creek Ranch, Darby, MT
The Warwick Hotel, Seattle, WA
Tu Tu' Tun Lodge, Gold Beach, OR
Westin Hotel Seattle, Seattle, WA
The Winchester Country Inn, Ashland, OR
The Woodmark Hotel at Carillon Point, Kirkland, WA

IDAHO

The Gem of the Rockies

STATE STATS

CAPITAL
Boise

AREA
83,337 square miles

BORDERS
Washington, Oregon, Nevada, Utah, Wyoming, Montana British Columbia

POPULATION
1,006,749 (1990)

ENTERED UNION
July 3, 1890 (43rd state)

NICKNAME
Gem State

STATE FLOWER
Syringa

STATE BIRD
Mountain bluebird

FAMOUS NATIVES
Ezra Pound, Lana Turner, Jerry Kramer, Frank Church

For years, Idaho was the land of "Famous Potatoes"—as proclaimed right on state license plates. But as Idaho is discovered by more and more people, it is becoming known less as the home of tater tots and more for its bounty of rugged landscapes and recreational opportunities. Huge wilderness areas and miles of wild rivers are the obvious glories, but a little exploration reveals the deserts and lava lands that also dot the landscape.

There's an astounding variety of geographical features in Idaho: In the Panhandle, dense Pacific forests break open to reveal glacial lakes, while the southwestern part of the state contains North America's highest sand dunes—leftovers from a giant Ice Age flood. Where bone-dry soil once barely supported sagebrush, irrigation has turned much of southern Idaho into agricultural land. (Witness the potato.) The wide variety of habitats means that Idaho is a great place to spot wildlife, from bald eagles to trumpeter swans to moose.

The people who live in Idaho are as unpredictable as the geography. Urban refugees, especially Californians, have invaded Boise; Hollywood types have been hanging out in Sun Valley and Ketchum for decades. Mormons have long settled the southern part of the state. Rugged individualists of all types have claimed the Panhandle as their own. Idaho is not quite like the rest of the country, and even your average Idahoan tends to have a distinctly libertarian bent.

Though there's a bit more big-city excitement now—world-class cuisine and entertainment are showing up in Boise and a luxurious resort atmosphere predominates in Sun Valley and Coeur d'Alene—most people still visit Idaho for its vast areas of untamed wilderness and its superb recreation. From a jet boat ride up Hells Canyon, to a weeklong backpacking trip in the Sawtooth Range, to fly fishing on Henry's Fork of the Snake River, the state offers boundless opportunities. Idaho's appeal is easy to understand: As some here are fond of saying, "Idaho is what America was."

Frommer's #1

A Brief History

A Horse Culture Native Americans—most notably the Shoshone and the Nez Perce—introduced the widespread use of horses in the area. Traditionally, the Nez Perce had relied on salmon and camas-lily bulbs for the bulk of their food. By the 1700s, they had obtained horses, which gave them the ability to travel greater distances to fish for salmon and to hunt buffalo in the faraway hunting grounds of the Great Plains. The Shoshone and Bannock—migratory peoples who lived in the southeastern part of the state—also used horses for hunting. The Kalispel and Kootenai traveled around the Panhandle's lakes and rivers in canoes, and shared fishing, hunting, and gathering grounds with their neighbors, the Coeur d'Alenes. The richness of Idaho's hunting grounds, which supported these tribes for many years, eventually contributed to the natives' downfall as white hunters and trappers moved into the territory.

Trails Across the Wilderness Lewis and Clark's expedition crossed the Continental Divide at Lemhi Pass in late August 1805, as snow was beginning to fall in the Bitterroot Range. After several false starts down wild rivers (including the Salmon River, which they dubbed the "River of No Return"), they met up with friendly Nez Perce, who helped guide them to the Clearwater River, which led them to the Snake River and then the Columbia, which finally empties into the Pacific Ocean.

Trappers responded eagerly to Lewis and Clark's reports of rampant wildlife in the West, establishing trading posts on the West Coast (most notably at Astoria and Fort Vancouver). Once these commercial trading posts were established, overland travel became more common, and by the mid-1850s Idaho was on the route of Oregon Trail migrants. Catholic and Protestant missionaries began to establish themselves just off the main migration route in the southern part of the state, while Mormons established Idaho's first permanent white settlement in 1860, when a small party of emigrants founded the town of Franklin, just north of the Utah border.

As traffic through the territory increased, so did the amount of poking around for gold. When Orofino Creek, on the newly formed Nez Perce reservation, panned out in 1860, the area experienced its first real growth spurt—at the expense of the Nez Perce.

Nez Perce War Though one band of Nez Perce signed on to a treaty allowing for the removal of gold-rich land from the reservation, another group, represented by Old Joseph, refused to abide by the new treaty. For 10 years, Joseph's band remained in their homeland, but by 1877, the government was ready to enforce its rules. Old Joseph's son, (also named Joseph) had succeeded his father and was resigned to a move onto the reservation. But as the band was moving from their eastern Oregon home to the Idaho reservation, three young Nez Perce lashed out and killed several white settlers. The violence escalated quickly, leaving over a dozen whites dead.

The US Army attacked the Nez Perce in retaliation for these killings, but the tribe foiled the attack, killing 34 soldiers with no losses of their own. By then it was evident to the Nez Perce that they must flee. Joseph's band of about 750 men, women, and children began moving east, with the Army in hot pursuit. The Army trailed the Nez Perce across Idaho and Montana, overtaking them just short of the Canadian border. Chief Joseph is best remembered for his surrender speech, in which he said, ". . . from where the sun now stands I will fight no more forever."

Development After the Nez Perce were sent to reservations, there was more room for miners to dig their way through Idaho's deposits of gold and thick veins of silver and lead. Along with the gold rush came territorial status, granted in 1863. (Idaho became the nation's 43rd state in 1890.)

Before Idahoans could begin serious farming,

Fun Facts

- Idaho is often called the Gem State because it produces some of the finest garnets, opals, sapphires, and rubies in the world.
- Craters of the Moon National Monument, located in southern Idaho, is a region of volcanic craters that was used by NASA as a training ground for Apollo astronauts.
- During winter, highway travel between northern and southern Idaho is nearly impossible because the state's only major north–south road is blocked.
- The first full-term Jewish governor in the United States was Moses Alexander, who was Idaho's governor from 1915 to 1919.
- Idahoans use more water per capita than the citizens of any other state.

irrigation projects needed to be set in place. Although small-scale projects came as early as the missionaries' gardens, it took two acts of Congress—the 1894 Carey Act (granting large tracts of federal land to the states) and the 1902 Reclamation Act (which fostered dam-building and irrigation)—to turn arid southern Idaho green. Agriculture is now Idaho's economic mainstay; besides the famous potatoes, the state produces bountiful crops of mint, alfalfa, and beets.

New Ways to Boom After the end of World War II, the Atomic Energy Commission deemed eastern Idaho a barren-enough spot to house a small city of nuclear reactors. The Idaho National Engineering Laboratory (INEL), home to 52 nuclear reactors, is west of Idaho Falls.

A more visitor-friendly boom was started by statesman and railroad tycoon Averell Harriman, who oversaw the development of Sun Valley, the nation's first destination ski resort and, in 1936, the site of the world's first chairlift. In the 1940s, Hollywood stars came to Sun Valley in droves, thereby helping to popularize both the state and the sport.

In recent years, the telecommuting boom has arrived in Idaho. Former urbanites have been flocking to the state (particularly the Boise area), bringing their laptops, cellular phones, and modems with them. Only time will tell how much the Gem State will be transformed by this influx.

DRIVING DISTANCES

Boise

106 mi S of McCall
153 mi SW of Sun Valley
234 mi NW of Pocatello
336 mi NW of Salt Lake City, UT
391 mi S of Coeur d'Alene

Coeur d'Alene

33 mi E of Spokane, WA
44 mi S of Sandpoint
87 mi N of Moscow
150 mi NW of Missoula, MT
285 mi N of McCall

Pocatello

49 mi SW of Idaho Falls
158 mi SW of West Yellowstone, MT
161 mi N of Salt Lake City, UT
171 mi SE of Sun Valley
209 mi SE of Salmon

A Closer Look

GEOGRAPHY

Just about every geological force imaginable had a hand in creating Idaho's landscape—mountains were pushed up by pressure from colliding tectonic plates, lava blanketed the entire state, glaciers chiseled high mountain cirques and arretes, and floodwaters cut deep canyons and deposited piles of sand. The state's highest mountains rise up to 12,000 feet and its lowest point—8,000-foot-deep Hells Canyon—drops to 738 feet above sea level.

Idaho's **Panhandle** is forested with cedar, hemlock, and Douglas fir, and dotted with glacial lakes. The three largest—Lake Coeur d'Alene, Lake Pend Oreille, and Priest Lake—are popular vacation destinations.

Hells Canyon, carved out by the mighty Snake River, traces the edge of **north-central Idaho.** (Lewiston, at the northern edge of Hells Canyon, is used as an inland seaport—thanks to the downstream dams that control the level and flow of the river.) The Clearwater and Lochsa Rivers form a scenic corridor (followed by US 12) east from Lewiston through the Bitterroot Mountains, paralleled to the south by the wilderness-flanked Salmon River, the "River of No Return." Just north of Lewiston, near the university town of Moscow, the wild rivers and soaring mountains are replaced by the soft rolling hills and rich soils of the Palouse region, a prime place to grow wheat and legumes.

Central Idaho's wild heart has few roads, but lots of rivers and mountains—most notably the jagged, forested Sawtooth Mountains and the Lost River Range (with the state's highest peaks) and the Salmon and Middle Fork of the Salmon River. Not far east of the resorts of Sun Valley and Ketchum and the lush forests of the Sawtooth National Recreation Area, Craters of the Moon National Monument—a huge, relatively fresh lava flow—stretches almost all the way to the dry sagebrush plain where the Idaho National Engineering Laboratory's reactors churn away.

Even the tourism department lets slip a line about the "bleak sagebrush plains" of **south-central Idaho.** And though this does, at first glance, sum up the region's geography, the area is actually full of surprises. The high Snake River Plain gathers water from nearby mountains, percolates it through volcanic soil, and spews it into the Snake River. In the **Hagerman Valley,** incredibly pure water gushes out of a steep canyon wall into the Snake River. Although many of the springs have been diverted for crop irrigation, trout farming, and hydroelectric power, the remaining ones are still an impressive sight.

Eastern Idaho, which roughly extends from Idaho Falls north and east to the state's edges, includes two of the West's most spectacular national parks—**Yellowstone** and **Grand Teton.** In addition to eastern Idaho's mountain views and big rivers, there are sand dunes stretching for 50 miles north of St Anthony. At the region's northern edge, the continental divide traces the boundary between Idaho and Montana.

Far **southeastern Idaho** is dry, except within reach of irrigation water, where potato plants flourish. Even where the land is bone dry, some big lakes offer respite from the summer heat. American Falls Reservoir is backed-up waters of the Snake behind American Falls Dam and, down in the far southeast corner, lovely blue Bear Lake straddles the Idaho-Utah border. Other water sources in the desert are mineral springs, both hot and carbonated, concentrated in the far southeast corner of the state. Pocatello is southeastern Idaho's population hub. The Fort Hall Reservation, near Pocatello, is home to Shoshone-Bannock people. In **southwestern Idaho,** agricultural areas (irrigated by the Boise River) give way to high desert, including the continent's tallest sand dunes. North of Boise, the Payette River flows down from Payette Lake.

AVG MONTHLY TEMPS (°F) & RAINFALL (IN)

	Boise	Idaho Falls
Jan	30/1.3	18/0.8
Feb	37/1.0	26/0.7
Mar	43/1.3	35/0.8
Apr	49/1.4	43/0.8
May	57/0.8	53/1.2
June	66/0.6	61/0.8
July	74/0.2	69/0.5
Aug	72/0.2	67/0.8
Sept	63/0.7	57/0.7
Oct	52/0.6	46/0.7
Nov	41/1.4	33/0.8
Dec	31/1.3	21/0.9

CLIMATE

No matter the season, it's best to come to Idaho prepared for a little bit of winter. Though summer weather is generally very pleasant in the mountains, it can snow almost any time of year. The state's varied topography means that a full gamut of weather can happen simultaneously; while the Panhandle may be cloudy and the Sawtooths blustery, the Snake River basin may have unrelenting sunshine and high temperatures. Fall days are usually warm and dry through October, with cool evenings and cold early mornings. Skiers appreciate Idaho's fairly dependable snowfall, as well as the fact that winter temperatures are not so low as to make outdoor activity a struggle.

WHAT TO PACK

Casual clothing is absolutely all you will see in Idaho; if you hit a party in Sun Valley, expensive casual clothing will fit right in. Don't forget to bring sunglasses and sunscreen, and, if you're at all inclined, hiking boots, a day pack, and a water bottle.

Winter travelers should carry tire chains, even if they have a four-wheel drive vehicle. It's also prudent to pack along a sleeping bag, a small cache of food and water, and a good flashlight. During the summer, carry extra water and some food.

TOURIST INFORMATION

The **Idaho Travel Council** will send a copy of the current *State Travel Guide* and a road map upon request (tel 800/VISIT-ID). The *Travel Guide* includes information on arranging guided white-water rafting, fishing, hunting, or pack trips. For more information on guide services, contact the **Idaho Outfitters and Guides Association,** PO Box 95, Boise, ID 83701 (tel 208/342-1919). The state's **Department of Fish and Game,** Box 25, 600 S Walnut St, Boise, ID 83707 (tel 208/334-3700 or toll free 800/635-7820) can provide information on fishing and hunting regulations. A wealth of information on all Idaho's national forests is dispensed by the **Boise National Forest** office at 1750 Front St, Boise, ID 83702 (tel 208/364-4100).

DRIVING RULES AND REGULATIONS

Idaho's driving laws are consistent with those in other western states. The speed limit is 65 mph on freeways, except in metropolitan areas, where it slows to 55. On state and US highways, the speed limit is 55 mph unless otherwise posted. There is no law prohibiting the use of radar detectors. All passengers must wear seat belts, and children under 4 years old or under 40 pounds must be in a child car seat. Right turns after a stop at red lights are permitted unless posted otherwise.

RENTING A CAR

Though it's possible to rent a car in just about any Idaho town, the best deals are out of Boise or, if you're headed to the northern part of the state, Spokane, WA. Salt Lake City, 161 miles from Pocatello, often has good deals on car rentals.

The following rental companies have offices in Idaho:

- **Alamo** (tel toll free 800/327-9633)
- **Avis** (tel 800/831-2847)
- **Budget** (tel 800/527-0700)
- **Dollar** (tel 800/800-4000)
- **Hertz** (tel 800/654-3131)
- **National** (tel 800/227-7368)
- **Payless** (tel 800/729-5377)
- **Thrifty** (tel 800/367-2277)

ESSENTIALS

Area Code: The area code for all of Idaho is **208.**

Emergencies: Dial 911 for police, ambulance, or fire department services.

Liquor Laws: The drinking age in Idaho is 21. Beer and wine are sold in grocery stores and other outlets, including most gas stations. Hard liquor is sold in state stores.

Road Info: During the winter months, call 208/336-6600 for a statewide road report.

Smoking: No smoking is permitted in public buildings; cigarettes are not sold to people under 18 years old.

Taxes: Idaho charges a 5% sales tax, and an additional 2% lodging tax. In many resort areas, there's an additional lodging tax.

Time Zones: Most of Idaho falls into the Mountain time zone, two hours behind the East Coast and an hour ahead of the West Coast. The Panhandle goes by Pacific time, an hour behind the rest of the state.

Best of the State

WHAT TO SEE AND DO

Below is a general overview of some of the top sights and attractions in Idaho; to find out more detailed information, look under "Attractions" under individual cities in the listings portion of this chapter.

Natural Wonders Magnificent **Hells Canyon,** along the Idaho-Oregon border, is not much more than 100 feet across, but in places it's more than 9,000 feet deep. On the west side of the canyon are Oregon's Wallowa Mountains, while the jagged Seven Devils Mountains rise as high as 8,000 feet above the river's Idaho bank. There's not much road access to Hells Canyon; the main access points are near Lewiston, Riggins, or Oxbow Dam. Drive along the canyon rim on Rd 420, also known as Rim Drive.

There's more to the Snake River than Hells Canyon. In the south-central part of the state, just west of Twin Falls, the **Thousand Springs** pour water from the Snake River Plain Aquifer down the canyon cliffs. At **Malad Gorge State Park,** the Malad River cuts a deep and impressive canyon on its way to the Snake, and Niagara Springs feeds water into it. Near the town of Hagerman, the **Hagerman Fossil Beds National Monument** chronicles the prehistoric life of zebralike horses whose fossils were found in the area. South of the Thousand Springs area, west of Castleford, **Balanced Rock** is a geological curiosity—a 40-foot-high rock, perched mushroom-like on a narrow base. The Snake River crashes over **Shoshone Falls** just east of Twin Falls. To the north, past the town of Shoshone on ID 75, the lava tubes forming **Shoshone Ice Caves** have a thick, year-round coat of ice on one wall.

Between Carey and Arco, on a stark stretch of US 20, the 2000-year-old lava flows at **Craters of the Moon National Monument** are indeed weirdly lunar. A loop road and hiking trails pass blown-out cinder cones and vast lava flows.

At **Bruneau Dunes State Park,** 20 miles south of Mountain Home, a 470-foot high mound of bare sand is surrounded by grass-covered dunes. The big dune dates back 11,000 years to the Bonneville Flood, when a huge lake that once covered Utah broke through a range of hills near Pocatello and gushed across southern Idaho, depositing piles of sand.

Wildlife Idaho's varied geography and vast tracts of wild lands make for an abundance of wildlife. A particularly rewarding area for wildlife seekers is the area around Henry's Fork and the Island Park region, considered part of the **Greater Yellowstone Ecosystem,** and home to a wide variety of wildlife, including moose, trumpeter swans, bald eagles, osprey, and wild trout. Big Springs (north of Island Park) and Harriman State Park (north of Ashton) are fine wildlife viewing areas.

The Snake River's various canyons shelter a huge variety of birds, especially raptors. Watch nesting eagles, hawks, and prairie falcons at the **Snake River Birds of Prey Area,** an hour south of Boise. In northern Idaho, Lake Coeur d'Alene is a veritable winter resort for bald eagles, who plunge into the lake after kokanee salmon. The lake's northeast shores, particularly Beauty and Wolf Lodge bays, are good places to see the action.

Historic Trails On their trip to the Pacific, Lewis and Clark crossed into Idaho at Lolo Pass, picked their way through the Bitterroot Mountains, and made their way down the Clearwater River to the Snake, a route now roughly paralleled by US 12. Travelers can learn about both the Lewis and Clark expedition and the eastbound flight of the Nez Perce from the many historical signs along US 12.

The **Nez Perce/Nee-Me-Poo trail** runs from northeastern Oregon's Wallowa Mountains to the Bear's Paw Battlefield in northern Montana, with many important sites located along and near the Clearwater and Lochsa Rivers in Idaho. Significant places along the trail are marked by roadside markers (many along US 12). Visitors can pick up a map of the other Nee-Me-Poo trail sites at the **Nez Perce National Historical Park Museum** in Spalding.

Oregon Trail emigrants passed through southern Idaho on their way from Independence, MO to Oregon's Willamette Valley. A couple of sites are near small towns just east of Twin Falls. The weathered, hewn-log **Stricker Rock Creek Store,** south of Hansen, was a place for wagon-train travelers to stock up on supplies. You can walk in ruts carved by wooden wagon wheels at the **Milner Interpretive Area** near Murtaugh. Further east, **Massacre Rocks State Park** marks the spot where 11 emigrants were killed by Indians. A more upbeat Oregon Trail stop was Soda Springs, where naturally carbonated spring water still bubbles up at **Hooper Springs Park.**

Museums In Boise, the **Idaho State Historical Museum** sums up the state's history and reconstructs the culture of gold miners, Oregon trail emigrants, and Native Americans. The **Mission of the Sacred Heart** is Idaho's oldest building, and a lovely one to boot. It's just south of I-90 in Cataldo. The **Appaloosa Museum,** at the western edge of Moscow almost to the Washington state line, celebrates the official state horse and portrays its cultural significance to the Nez Perce, who developed the breed. In the agricultural town of Blackfoot, the **World Potato Exposition** exalts the spud, and offers "free taters for out-of-staters."

Family Favorites **Silverwood Theme Park**, south of Coeur d'Alene, is part frontier town, part amusement park. Tourists in downtown **Wallace** can take a tram ride to an old silver mine, where an underground walking tour recreates the typical miner's life. Would-be miners can search for Idaho's state rock—the glassy, deep-purple star garnet—along the banks of **Emerald Creek,** south of Coeur d'Alene near Clarkia. The Forest Service issues permits and provides instruction. Amateur paleontologists can search for fossilized leaves at the **Fossil Bowl,** a privately operated motorcycle racetrack and dig site on ID 3 at the southern edge of Clarkia. The **Boise Tour Train** pulls out of Julia Davis Park, home of Zoo Boise (known for its birds of prey), a pioneer village, the Boise Art Museum, and the Idaho Historical Museum.

EVENTS AND FESTIVALS

- **Winter Carnival,** McCall. Snow sculpting, cross-country skiing, dogsled races, and more. Late January. Call 208/634-7631.
- **Lionel Hampton Jazz Festival,** Moscow. University of Idaho campus. Late February. Call 208/882-1800.
- **Idaho Shakespeare Festival,** Boise. Performances all summer long. Call 208/336-9221 for schedule and ticket information.
- **Boise River Festival.** River parade, balloon fest, air show, and other events. June. Call 208/344-7777 or 383-7318 for schedule.
- **National Old-Time Fiddlers Contest,** Weiser. Top country fiddlers play informally and in competition. June. Call 208/549-0450.
- **Sun Valley Ice Show.** World famous skaters perform at the outdoor ice rink. Mid-June through mid-September. Call toll free 800/635-8261.

- **Salmon River Days,** Salmon. Festivities revolve around white water. Early July. Call 208/756-4935.
- **Idaho International Folk Dance Festival,** Rexburg. Dance troupes from around the world. July. Call 208/356-5700.
- **Sun Valley Music Festival.** Classical and jazz at the Sun Valley Center for the Arts and Humanities. July–August. Call 208/726-9491.
- **Festival at Sandpoint,** on Lake Pend Oreille at Sandpoint Memorial Field. Concert series, blending genres from classical to pop. Late July through mid-August. Call 208/263-2161.
- **Shoshone-Bannock Indian Festival and Rodeo,** Fort Hall Reservation. A mix of traditional and contemporary Native American culture. August. Call 208/237-9791.

SPECTATOR SPORTS

Auto Racing Watch stock-car racing from April to September at **Stateline Stadium & Speedway** in Post Falls, right where I-90 crosses from Idaho to Washington. Call 208/773-5019 for schedule.

Baseball The **Boise Hawks** (tel 208/322-5000) and the **Idaho Falls Braves** (tel 208/522-8363) play minor-league ball at Memorial Stadium and McDermott Field, respectively.

College Athletics Idaho doesn't have professional football or basketball teams, but university teams are followed closely in Moscow, Boise, and Pocatello. In Moscow, the **University of Idaho Vandals** (tel 208/885-6466) play in the Kibbie Dome. Pocatello's **Idaho State Bengals** (tel 208/236-2831) call the Holt Arena home. The **Boise State Broncos** (tel 208/385-1011) hit the gridiron at Bronco Stadium.

Greyhound Racing The dogs run year-round at the **Coeur d'Alene Greyhound Park,** which is actually west of Coeur d'Alene in the town of Post Falls (tel 208/733-0545).

Horse Racing Thoroughbred racing and pari-mutuel wagering are the attraction at **Les Bois Park** (tel 208/376-7223), from May to August.

Rodeos Pocatello hosts the **Dodge National Circuit Finals Rodeo** at Idaho State University in March (tel 208/233-1546). The **Lewiston Roundup** (tel 208/743-3531), a Professional Rodeo Cowboys Association event, takes place in early September, and the **Snake River Stampede** (tel 208/466-8497), mid-July in Nampa, features lots of country music after the day's rodeo events end.

ACTIVITIES A TO Z

Ballooning The Teton Hot Air Balloon Race & Great American Outdoor Festival takes place in early July in the town of Teton Valley. Contact the **Grand Targhee Resort** (tel toll free 800/443-8146) for information. Balloons soar over central Idaho in mid-August, when Salmon holds its Balloon Fest (tel 208/774-3411).

Bicycling The 10-mile-long Wood River Trail System links the resorts in Ketchum and Sun Valley. More adventurous types can head off into the nearby Sawtooths on a mountain bike. Forest Service roads are often good mountain bike trails; stop by a bike shop or ranger station to learn the locals' favorite routes. A number of outfitters run mountain bike trips throughout the state; contact the **Idaho Outfitters and Guides Association,** PO Box 95, Boise, ID 83701 (tel 208/342-1919), for more information.

Bird Watching Trumpeter swans winter on the Henry's Fork of the Snake River, and eagles dive into Lake Coeur d'Alene on winter fishing binges, but the state's prime bird-watching is south of Boise at the **Snake River Birds of Prey Area** (tel 208/384-3300), where the riverside cliffs support the densest nesting concentration of falcons, eagles, hawks, and owls in North America.

Camping The Idaho State Parks and Recreation Department operates 25 campgrounds, and even more are on Forest Service or Bureau of Land Management land. Private campgrounds tend to have more luxuries (such as flush toilets, rather than pits) and may also offer rental cabins.

Fishing Idaho's rivers and streams harbor legendary numbers of feisty trout. Henry's Fork of the Snake River, a nine-mile meander just west of Yellowstone National Park, is known for its great fly fishing and abundant wild trout. Silver Creek, near Sun Valley, was one of Ernest Hemingway's favorite fishing spots. It's open to catch-and-release fly fishing only. The nearby Big and Little Wood Rivers are also eminently fishable. Try the Salmon or the lower Clearwater River for steelhead (sea-run rainbow trout). Another spectacular steelhead spot is Niagara Springs, in the Hagerman Valley. Fish the Panhandle's big lakes (especially Lake Pend Oreille) for kokanee, a landlocked variety of salmon. For more information, contact the **Department of Fish and Game,** Box 25, 600 S Walnut St, Boise, ID 83707 (tel 800/635-7820 or 208/334-3700).

Golf It should come as no surprise that Idaho's best golfing is to be found in resort communities. Sun Valley boasts two 18-hole courses and Coeur d'Alene has three (most notably the course at the Coeur d'Alene Resort), but there are also good courses in Boise and Twin Falls, and almost every town has at least a 9-hole course.

Guided Outdoor Adventures The **Idaho Outfitters & Guides Association** puts out a brochure with general information and ads for guided trips. Write to them at PO Box 95, Boise, ID 83701 or call 208/342-1919. Many guides run white-water rafting, hunting, fishing, and horse packing trips; more specialized offerings include llama treks or hut-to-hut cross-country skiing.

Hiking Stop for a hike in the **Sawtooth National Recreation Area** (tel 208/726-7672) or the Seven Devils Mountains, south of Riggins. (Windy Saddle Trailhead is a good starting point.) **Craters of the Moon National Monument** is good for a short hike, but wear sturdy shoes—the sharp *a'a* lava can tear up sneakers in no time. Rangers lead nature walks here during the summer; call 208/527-3257 for details.

Hot Springs Idaho's hot springs run the gamut from undeveloped, clothing-optional soaking pools to full-fledged resorts. **Lava Hot Springs** (tel toll free 800/423-8597 or 208/776-5221), in southeastern Idaho, is a town built around its natural hot water. There's a large outdoor swimming pool (not too hot and open only in the summer) as well as several hot soaking pools. A few miles east, at **Soda Springs** (tel 208/547-4470), carbonated water bubbles up in the city park (and just north of town at Hooper Spring Park). Not surprisingly, the **Thousand Springs** area of the Snake River is home to several hot springs resorts: **Banbury Hot Springs** (tel 208/543-4098), **Sligar's Thousand Springs Resort** (tel 208/837-4987), and **Miracle Hot Springs** (tel 208/543-6002); all are on US 30 in the Hagerman Valley. In central Idaho, the hot water at **Salmon Hot Springs** (tel 208/756-4449) is piped into a large swimming pool.

Rock Climbing At the **City of Rocks National Reserve** (tel 208/824-5519), near the Utah border south of Burley, the same granite spires that once excited Oregon Trail pioneers' imaginations are now a climbing mecca.

Skiing **Sun Valley** (tel 208/622-4111 or toll free 800/635-8261), the nation's first ski resort, is still

Selected Parks & Recreation Areas

- **Craters of the Moon National Monument,** PO Box 29, Arco, ID 83213 (tel 208/527-3257)
- **Hagerman Fossil Beds National Monument,** PO Box 570, Hagerman, ID 83332 (tel 208/837-4793)
- **City of Rocks National Reserve,** PO Box 169, Alma, ID 83312 (tel 208/824-5519)
- **Hells Canyon National Recreation Area,** 88401 OR 82, Enterprise, OR 97828 (tel 541/426-4978)
- **Sawtooth National Recreation Area,** Star Rte, ID 75, Ketchum, ID 83340 (tel 208/726-7672)
- **Nez Perce National Historical Park,** PO Box 93, Spalding, ID 83551 (tel 208/843-2261)
- **Bear Lake State Park,** PO Box 297, Paris, ID 83261 (tel 208/945-2790)
- **Bruneau Dunes State Park,** HC 85, Box 41, Mountain Home, ID 83647 (tel 208/366-7919)
- **Dworshak State Park,** PO Box 2028, Orofino, ID 83544 (tel 208/476-5994)
- **Eagle Island State Park,** 2691 Mace Rd, Eagle, ID 83616 (tel 208/939-0696 in summer; 208/939-0704 in winter)
- **Farragut State Park,** E 13400 Ranger Rd, Athol, ID 83801 (tel 208/683-2425)
- **Harriman State Park,** HC 66, Box 500, Island Park, ID 83429 (tel 208/558-7368)
- **Hells Gate State Park,** 3620A Snake River Ave, Lewiston, ID 83501 (tel 208/799-5015)
- **Henrys Lake State Park,** HC 66, Box 20, Island Park, ID 83429 (tel 208/558-7532)
- **Heyburn State Park,** Rte 1, Box 139, Plummer, ID 83851 (tel 208/686-1308)
- **Malad Gorge State Park,** 1074 E 2350 S (south of I-84 exit 147), Hagerman, ID, 83332 (tel 837-4505)
- **Massacre Rocks State Park,** 3592 N Park Lane, American Falls, ID, 83211 (tel 208/548-2672)
- **Old Mission State Park,** PO Box 30, Cataldo, ID 83810 (tel 208/682-3814)
- **Ponderosa State Park,** PO Box A, McCall, ID 83638 (tel 208/634-2164)
- **Priest Lake State Park,** ID 57, Indian Creek Bay #423, Coolin, ID 83821 (tel 208/443-2200)

one of the finest. Its 75 runs are well serviced by lifts, and the vertical drop of 3,400 feet is as good as it gets in the Northwest. Cross-country skiing, both on groomed trails and in the back country, is great here too. Up in the Panhandle, Sandpoint's **Schweitzer Ski & Summer Resort** (tel 208/263-9555) has a lovely setting above Lake Pend Oreille, and catches lots of good snow as Pacific fronts slam into the Selkirk Mountains. Schweitzer has long been popular with the locals, and recent expansions have made it into more of a destination resort. Though there are some cross-country ski trails near the resort, cross-country skiers should check out the trails at **Priest Lake State Park. Bogus Basin Ski Area** (tel 208/336-4500), 16 miles from Boise, is a popular night-skiing spot. Way over on the Idaho-Wyoming border, **Grand Targhee Ski Resort** (tel toll free 800/827-4433) has spectacular views of the Tetons, deep powdery snow, and acres of skiing in a relatively no-frills environment. For a truly unique experience, try cross-country skiing across the jagged lava at Craters of the Moon.

Water Sports Try wind surfing or sailing on the Snake River at Lewiston. The river opens up here, and dams make it more lakelike. It's also possible to catch a breeze on any of the Panhandle's big lakes, or on Payette Lake near McCall. Jet boats zip up and down the Snake River through Hells Canyon; Lewiston is a good place to catch a ride.

White-Water Rafting Strung together, Idaho's white-water rivers would stretch for over 3,000 miles, providing opportunities for some absolutely spectacular raft trips. The Middle Fork of the Salmon River, the state's preeminent stretch of white water, empties into the main Salmon River. Lewis and Clark's River of No Return is still a wild ride today. Salmon River trips run out of several towns along the river, including Stanley, Salmon, and Riggins.

THE IDAHO ROCKIES

Start	Twin Falls
Finish	Stanley
Distance	Approximately 225 miles
Time	2–3 days
Highlights	Shoshone Falls, Craters of the Moon National Monument, resort towns of Ketchum/Sun Valley, Sawtooth National Recreation Area, Galena Summit overlook, Sawtooth Mountains, old-time Western town of Stanley

The American West is a laboratory for geology on the grand scale, and few places demonstrate this as abundantly as south-central Idaho. From the spectacular chasm of the Snake River Canyon to desolate lava beds to the peaks of the Sawtooth Range, Idaho's landscape remains a place where Earth's forces are still very much at work. This tour takes the traveler from the high desert to the mountains, with stops including one of the most unusual national monuments in the United States, the lively ski towns of Sun Valley and Ketchum, and the adventure-packed Sawtooth National Recreation Area.

This driving tour is best savored over two to three days. Despite the Gem State's growing popularity, you'll find little traffic along the tour's mostly two-lane highways. Travelers should note that while there's a wide selection of restaurants and accommodations in the larger or more tourist-oriented towns along the route (Twin Falls and Ketchum, in particular), the smaller settlements may have nothing more than a convenience store. Keep an eye on your gas gauge, too; it can be 50 miles or more between filling stations in much of Idaho.

For additional information on lodgings, restaurants, and attractions in the region covered by the tour, look under specific cities in the listings portion of this chapter.

The north side of Twin Falls is the jumping-off spot for this tour. To get there from the south, take US 93 and turn right when the highway merges with US 30. Follow US 30 east 6 miles into Twin Falls, then turn left on Blue Lakes Blvd and head north to the city limits. If you're coming from the east or west via I-84, take exit 173 and drive south 4 miles to the south rim of the:

1. **Snake River Canyon,** known to most people as the gorge that daredevil Evel Knievel tried to leap across on a rocket-powered motorcycle in 1974. You can see Knievel's launching ramp from the parking lot of the Buzz Langdon Visitor Center, which also overlooks the Perrine Bridge. This 1,500-foot-long span sits a head-spinning 486 feet above the Snake River, making it the highest bridge in the state.

   The Snake River Canyon was created about 15,000 years ago when Utah's prehistoric Lake Bonneville burst through its northern reaches, sending a massive flood toward the Snake River. The Snake bulged to more than 1,000 times its present flow, ripping through porous basalt rocks to create the gorge we see today.

   Take the walkway across Perrine Bridge and enjoy the view below. A road leading into the canyon from the south rim allows access to Centennial Park, which offers picnicking and wildlife viewing. (Bald eagles are occasionally sighted in the area.) In summer, scenic boat trips leave from here. Ask at the visitor center for more information.

   From the visitor center, backtrack south on Blue Lakes Boulevard to Falls Avenue (the second stoplight, a little more than 1½ miles from the visitor center). Turn left here and drive 3 miles east, then 2 winding miles north into the canyon for:

2. **Shoshone Falls.** The 212-foot-tall Shoshone are sometimes called "the Niagara of the West," even though they are actually taller than the more-famous Niagara. Shoshone Falls are typically at their best in early spring, before local irrigation companies harness the flow to provide water for south-central Idaho's many acres of farmland. But even if the flow has slowed to a trickle, the plunge remains an impressive sight.

   Shoshone Falls is bordered by parkland. **Dierkes Lake,** just upriver, is a favorite spot for swimming, fishing, and waterskiing. (A trail east of Dierkes Lake's picnic and playground area leads to several hidden lakes.) Shoshone Falls and Dierkes Lake parks are open 7am–9pm, with a nominal per-vehicle fee charged during summer. The steep and narrow canyon road is suitable for all vehicles, but take care negotiating its zig-zag route.

   From Shoshone Falls/Dierkes Lake, retrace your route back into Twin Falls. Upon returning to Blue Lakes Blvd, continue north across the Perrine Bridge; this city street turns back into US 93. Follow US 93, past the I-84 junction and across 21 miles of farmland and rolling sage-covered range, to:

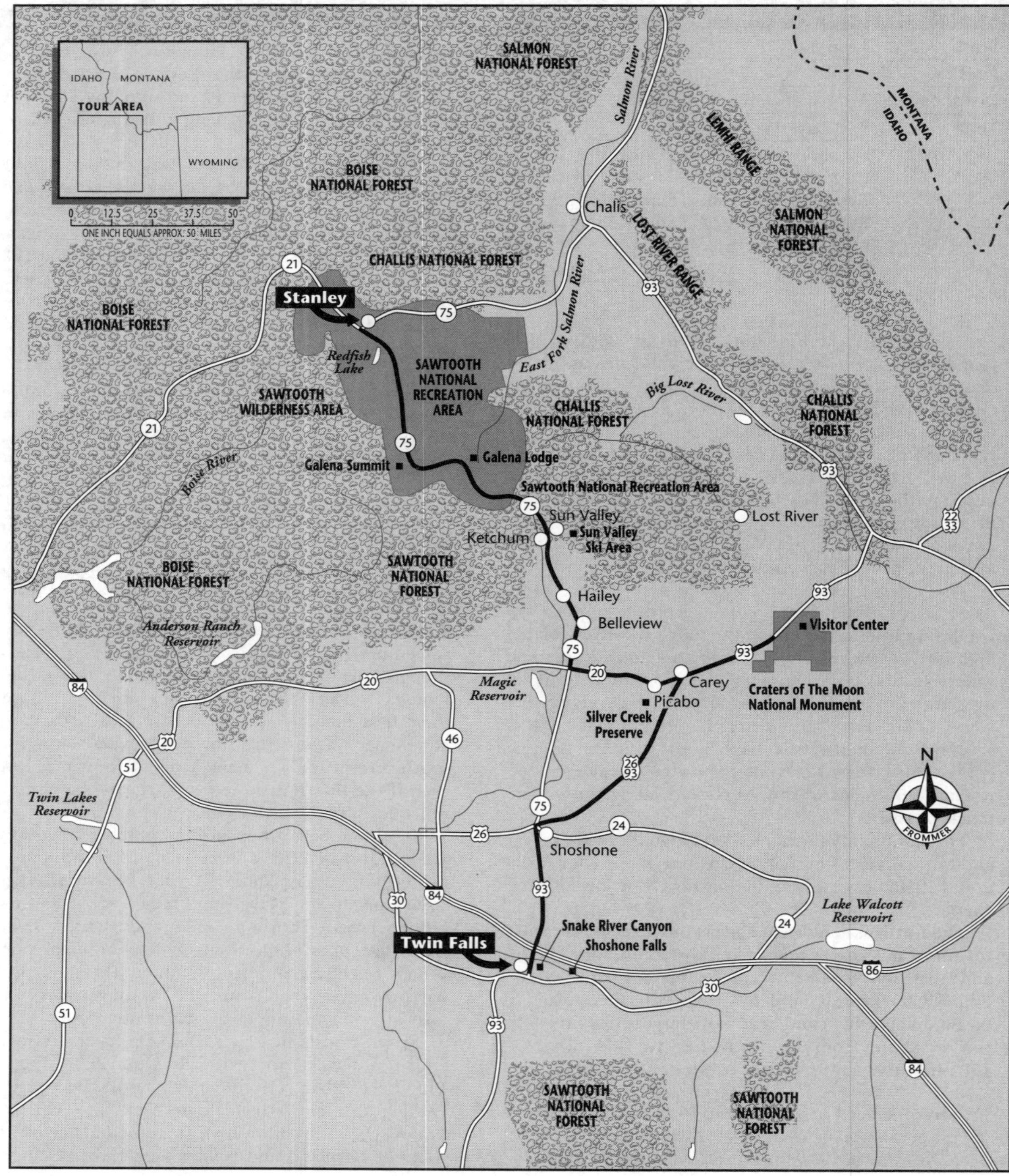

IDAHO
MONTANA
TOUR AREA
WYOMING
0 12.5 25 37.5 50
ONE INCH EQUALS APPROX. 50 MILES
SALMON NATIONAL FOREST
Salmon River
MONTANA
IDAHO
LEMHI RANGE
BOISE NATIONAL FOREST
Chalis
LOST RIVER RANGE
SALMON NATIONAL FOREST
CHALLIS NATIONAL FOREST
Stanley
East Fork Salmon River
BOISE NATIONAL FOREST
Redfish Lake
SAWTOOTH NATIONAL RECREATION AREA
Big Lost River
SAWTOOTH WILDERNESS AREA
CHALLIS NATIONAL FOREST
CHALLIS NATIONAL FOREST
Galena Summit
Galena Lodge
Boise River
Sawtooth National Recreation Area
Sun Valley
Lost River
Ketchum
Sun Valley Ski Area
BOISE NATIONAL FOREST
SAWTOOTH NATIONAL FOREST
Hailey
Belleview
Visitor Center
Anderson Ranch Reservoir
Carey
Magic Reservoir
Picabo
Craters of The Moon National Monument
Silver Creek Preserve
Twin Lakes Reservoir
Shoshone
N
FROMMER
Lake Walcott Reservoirt
Snake River Canyon
Shoshone Falls
Twin Falls
SAWTOOTH NATIONAL FOREST
SAWTOOTH NATIONAL FOREST

3. **Shoshone,** which, although rather sleepy today, was a hell-raising railroad town in Idaho's pioneer days. Gambling parlors, dance halls, and dens of ill-repute lined the streets. One early visitor remarked that 10 to 15 arrests a day weren't uncommon and that vagrants were tossed into a "jail" that was nothing more than a hole in the ground surrounded by guards.

   Stop in Hoyt and Carol Pugh's **Moon Creek Store** (tel 208/886-2004) for a peek at an authentic Western saddlery. Located at the intersection of US 93 and S Rail St, Moon Creek typically has 100 saddles on display, along with blankets, turquoise jewelry, coffee beans, and firewater (the shop doubles as Shoshone's local Idaho Liquor Store). The family-run **Shoshone Showhouse** (tel 208/886-2332) and **Sundae Matinee Ice Cream and Pizza Parlor,** located in a former opera house just down the street, serve up bargain movies and snacks on weekend evenings (tel 208/886-2306).

   Depending on the time of day you hit Shoshone, you might want to have a meal or get a lunch to go. There are no dining or grocery facilities at the tour's next stop—Craters of the Moon National Monument—so plan accordingly.

Take a Break

Grab a quick bite or a carryout picnic lunch at the **Manhattan Cafe,** 133 S Rail St W, in Shoshone (tel 208/886-2142). The Manhattan's wide menu features down-home cooking with prices to match. Chicken-fried steaks and hand-dipped milkshakes are among the specialties; dinner specials (usually about $6 to $7) even include beverage and dessert.

From Shoshone, head northeast on US 26/93. It's 62 miles to:

4. **Craters of the Moon National Monument,** home to one of the world's strangest landscapes. The monument's lava beds are mainly of two types: the rough, broken *aa* (pronounced "ah-ah," Hawaiian for "hard on the feet") and the smooth, ropelike *pahoehoe* (pronounced "pa-ho-ee-ho-ee"). You can get a good look at both kinds along the North Crater Flow Trail, a short hiking route near the visitor center (tel 208/527-3257).

   Plan to spend a minimum of two hours exploring the monument's many features. A seven-mile loop road gives access to several short trails that lead to such features as the Big Crater, Spatter Cones, and Indian Cave. The monument is especially beautiful around mid-June, when a colorful assortment of wildflowers springs forth from the chunky black lava. Camping is available.

   From Craters of the Moon, backtrack southwest on US 26/93 to Carey. Just past Carey, bear right (following the signs for Sun Valley and Boise) onto US 20 and drive west. In 7 miles, you'll skirt the tiny hamlet of Picabo (the word, pronounced "peek-a-boo," is a Native American word meaning "shining waters"). Picabo achieved recent fame through its namesake, top US skier Picabo Street (who actually was raised some 25 miles due north in Triumph). From Picabo, drive another 4 miles west and look for the signs for:

5. **Silver Creek,** considered one of the West's top fly-fishing streams. To reach The Nature Conservancy's Silver Creek Preserve, turn south and follow the dirt road for 1½ miles to the log cabin–style visitor center. Silver Creek is among Idaho's most scenic spots, and it's easy to see why fish, people, and countless other creatures like to slow down and spend some time here. Visitors can explore a short, self-guiding nature trail; watch for some of the more than 150 species of birds living in the area (including bald and golden eagles); or put on waders and do some catch-and-release fly-fishing. Check locally for more detailed fishing regulations.

   From Silver Creek Preserve, return to US 20 and turn left. Drive west 7½ miles to ID 75. (A state rest area is located just across the highway.) From here, it's 26 miles north to:

6. **Ketchum/Sun Valley,** which bills itself as America's first destination ski resort. In the 1930s, railroad executive Averell Harriman sent Austrian count Felix Schaffgotsch to seek out an ideal spot for a European-style winter resort. The mountains surrounding Ketchum reminded Schaffgotsch of his homeland, and before long, all of Hollywood was in love with Sun Valley.

   Despite (or maybe because of) its remote location, the Ketchum/Sun Valley area continues to appeal to celebrities. Actor Bruce Willis recently bought and renovated the **Mint Lounge and Restaurant** in Hailey, a decidedly nontouristy town 11 miles south of Ketchum. He's been known to show up there for jam sessions with his band, the Accelerators.

   Sun Valley has grown from a winter resort to a year-round destination in recent years. You may want to rent a bicycle or in-line skates and set off on the **Wood River Trails System** (an extensive network of paved paths weaving throughout the area), or take a drive into the backcountry: Trail Creek Road east of Sun Valley or Warm Springs Road west of Ketchum are both excellent, scenic choices and are accessible by most vehicles.

Sun Valley and Ketchum are also noted for outstanding shopping, dining, and accommodations. In fact, this is a good—although somewhat pricey—place to spend the night. Upscale choices include the venerable **Sun Valley Lodge,** in Sun Valley Village (tel 208/622-4111), or the **Knob Hill Inn** at 961 N Main in Ketchum (tel 208/726-8010). Also in Ketchum, the **Best Western Kentwood Lodge,** 180 S Main (tel 208/726-4114), is among the area's more moderately priced lodgings. **Felix,** at the Knob Hill Inn, and **Michel's Christiania,** 303 Walnut Ave N in Ketchum (tel 208/726-3388), rank among the classiest spots for fine dining.

Take a Break

After a day on Sun Valley's bike paths or ski slopes, locals and visitors alike often head for **Louie's Pizza and Italian Restaurant,** located at 331 Leadville Ave N in Ketchum. A valley favorite for more than 30 years, Louie's creative menu features pizza, pasta, chicken, and veal. Meals cost $7 to $13, with several family-style combos available.

Self-guided tour tapes for points north of Ketchum may be borrowed free at the Sawtooth National Forest's Ketchum Ranger District office (206 Sun Valley Rd) or the Sawtooth National Recreation Area headquarters north of town (see below). The tapes guide visitors along ID 75 to Stanley and can be returned at the Stanley Ranger Station or Redfish Lake Visitor Center. Before leaving Ketchum/Sun Valley, you may want to pay homage to famous former resident Ernest Hemingway. A memorial to the writer sits along the south side of Trail Creek Road (almost 3 miles east of the downtown Ketchum stoplight) and the author is buried in the Ketchum Cemetery (just north of town on ID 75).

From Ketchum, head north on ID 75. The mountains loom ahead, and you're just 8 miles from the:

7. **Sawtooth National Recreation Area,** a spacious preserve that's nearly as big as Rhode Island. The SNRA encompasses the White Cloud, Boulder, and Sawtooth mountain ranges; its boundaries also include the 340-square-mile **Sawtooth Wilderness Area** and its more than 200 alpine lakes. The SNRA's headquarters (tel 208/726-7672) can provide maps and information on the area's many recreational facilities and attractions, including hot springs, hiking, camping, fishing, cross-country skiing, horseback riding, and more. From the SNRA headquarters, it's 16 miles north to:

8. **Galena Lodge** (tel 208/726-4010), located on the right side of the road just as ID 75 starts the climb to Galena Summit. Long known as a winter recreation spot, the recently renovated Galena Lodge is now open in summer, too, with mountain bike rentals, weekly wildflower walks, and about 30 miles of hiking and biking terrain ranging from easy to expert. Winter visitors will find excellent cross-country skiing and wood-heated yurts (circular domed tents) available for overnight stays. The lodge (open Thanksgiving–March and June–mid-September) also serves snacks and meals. From Galena Lodge, continue north on ID 75 almost 6½ miles to:

9. **Galena Summit,** and one of Idaho's best views. Actually, you'll want to drive a mile past the 8,701-foot summit to a sweeping overlook of the Sawtooth Mountains and the headwaters of the Salmon River, one of North America's top white-water rafting rivers.

From here, it's apparent how the glacier-carved Sawtooths got their name: The range—with 42 peaks topping 10,000 feet—really does look something like a crosscut saw reclining across the horizon. As for the Salmon River, often called the "River of No Return," it's the longest river within one state in the continental United States and is over 420 miles long. From the overlook, it's hard to imagine that the Salmon's tiny trickle winds up a raging river, but it does.

From the Galena overlook, ID 75 winds down the mountain to the broad Stanley Basin. Access signs point the way to such recreational spots as Alturas Lake and Fourth of July Creek, but for the SNRA's most beloved attraction, you'll want to drive 27 miles north to the turnoff for:

10. **Redfish Lake,** where stunning, close-up mountain vistas provide the backdrop for a wide range of recreational activities. Check at the Redfish Lake Visitor Center (tel 208/774-3376) for information on hiking, boating, camping, horseback riding, fishing, mountain biking, and more. Try the Bench Lakes or Fishhook Creek trails for good family hiking, or take the shuttle boat across four-mile-long Redfish Lake to access more remote and challenging trails in the Sawtooth Wilderness Area.

After you return to ID 75, drive another 4½ miles north to reach:

11. **Stanley,** one of the most thoroughly Western towns you'll find anywhere. This is an outfitting spot for summer Salmon River floats and winter snowmobiling, and local folks can tell you where

you might find some great hot springs just a few miles downriver. Stanley is also another likely overnight stopping point, with lodging options that include the **Mountain Village Resort,** at ID 75/21 (tel 208/774-3661), and **Danner's Log Cabin Motel,** 1 Wall St (tel 208/774-3539).

From the Stanley Basin, travelers can choose to retrace their drive back to Twin Falls and I-84 (which heads west to Boise and the Pacific Northwest or southeast to Utah); continue on the Salmon River Scenic Byway northeast to Challis (where ID 75 rejoins US 93); or perhaps take the back road to Boise via ID 21 west of Stanley. Whichever route you choose, expect more outstanding scenery amid Idaho's rugged Rockies.

Idaho Listings

Boise

See also Caldwell, Nampa

Although it is the state capital and Idaho's largest city, Boise retains the feel of a small town. Known as the City of Trees, Boise is full of parks and green neighborhoods—all abutting the scenic Rocky Mountains. It has resident companies in opera and ballet, as well as a philharmonic orchestra. Golf is plentiful, horse racing and championship drag racing are popular attractions, and skiing and white-water rafting opportunities abound nearby. **Information:** Boise Convention and Visitors Bureau, 168 N 9th St #200, Boise, 83702 (tel 208/344-7777).

PUBLIC TRANSPORTATION

Boise Urban Stages (The Bus) (tel 208/336-1010) services the greater Boise area with 16 routes. Fares: adults 75¢, seniors and persons with disabilities 35¢, children 6–18 50¢; children under 6 ride free. All Saturday fares 35¢. Transfers are free. Exact change required.

HOTELS

Boise Park Suite Hotel

424 E Parkcenter Blvd, 83706 (East Boise); tel 208/342-1044 or toll free 800/342-1044; fax 208/342-2763. Broadway exit off I-84. This all-suite establishment has a plain exterior but is quite pleasant inside. Close to Boise River Greenbelt for walking, bicycling, and in-line skating. **Rooms:** 130 stes. CI 2pm/CO noon. Nonsmoking rms avail. Accommodations have a small refrigerator, microwave, kitchen and sitting areas. **Amenities:** A/C, cable TV w/movies, refrig, dataport. All units w/minibars. Popcorn and coffee in the rooms. **Services:** Fax, computer, and printer available. **Facilities:** 98 1 bar, whirlpool, washer/dryer. Outdoor pool is secluded. **Rates (CP):** $115 ste. Extra person $10. Children under age 12 stay free. Parking: Outdoor, free. AE, CB, DC, DISC, MC, V.

DoubleTree Club Hotel at Parkcenter

475 W Parkcenter Blvd, 83706; tel 208/345-2002 or toll free 800/222-TREE; fax 208/345-8354. I-84 to Broadway exit 54; take Broadway to Parkcenter. Attractive hotel that's a favorite with corporate travelers because of its proximity to businesses in east Boise. **Rooms:** 158 rms and stes. CI open/CO 1pm. Nonsmoking rms avail. Charming and well-decorated rooms. **Amenities:** A/C, cable TV w/movies, dataport, voice mail. **Services:** Babysitting. **Facilities:** 75 1 restaurant (bkfst and dinner only), 1 bar, whirlpool. Lap pool in lushly landscaped courtyard. **Rates (CP):** $102–$112 S; $112–$122 D; $165–$175 ste. Extra person $10. Children under age 12 stay free. Parking: Outdoor, free. AE, CB, DC, DISC, EC, ER, JCB, MC, V.

Downtowner

1800 Fairview Ave, 83702; tel 208/344-7691 or toll free 800/RED-LION; fax 208/336-3652. Take I-84 exit into Boise; take Fairview to hotel. Deluxe hotel near downtown Boise, with fetching views of the mountains from the high-rise rooms. Very spacious and attractive lobby. **Rooms:** 182 rms and stes. CI 3pm/CO 1pm. Nonsmoking rms avail. Rooms are attractive but somewhat small. Ask for a mountain-view room. **Amenities:** A/C, satel TV, dataport. Some units w/terraces, some w/whirlpools. **Services:** **Facilities:** 400 1 restaurant, 1 bar, sauna, whirlpool. Downstairs pub with sports-bar atmosphere and some special brews on tap. **Rates:** $85–$105 S; $100–$120 D; $195 ste. Extra person $15. Children under age 18 stay free. Parking: Outdoor, free. AE, CB, DC, DISC, JCB, MC, V.

Holiday Inn

3300 Vista Ave, 83705 (Boise Airport); tel 208/344-8365 or toll free 800/HOLIDAY; fax 208/343-9635. Top-notch Holiday Inn at convenient location near I-84 and airport. Superior accommodations justify higher rates. **Rooms:** 266 rms and stes. CI noon/CO noon. Nonsmoking rms avail. Spacious and comfortable, with nice decorations. **Amenities:** A/C, cable TV w/movies, dataport, voice mail. Some units w/terraces. **Services:** Car-rental desk, children's program, babysitting. **Facilities:** 250 1 restaurant, 1 bar, games rm, sauna, steam rm, whirlpool, playground, washer/dryer. Excellent "playport" for kids in Holidome area. **Rates:** Peak (summer) $80–$120 S; $90–

$130 D; $195–$240 ste. Children under age 19 stay free. Lower rates off-season. Parking: Outdoor, free. AE, CB, DC, DISC, MC, V.

The Idanha
928 Main St, 83702; tel 208/342-3611 or toll free 800/714-7346, 800/798-3611 in ID; fax 208/383-9690. At 10th St. For historic charm, this 94-year-old hotel with turrets and bay windows is the premier place to stay downtown. Prices competitive with other luxury hotels in area. **Rooms:** 45 rms and stes. CI 2pm/CO noon. Nonsmoking rms avail. Rooms are big; suites are extremely spacious and elegant. **Amenities:** A/C, cable TV w/movies. **Services:** Babysitting. **Facilities:** 150 2 restaurants (*see* "Restaurants" below), 2 bars (1 w/entertainment). No garage directly attached to the hotel, so parking is a bit of a hassle. **Rates (CP):** $60–$75 S; $66–$81 D; $110 ste. Extra person $6. Children under age 18 stay free. Parking: Outdoor, free. AE, DC, DISC, JCB, MC, V.

Marriott Residence Inn
1401 Lusk, 83706 (Near Boise State University); tel 208/344-1200 or toll free 800/331-3131; fax 208/384-5354. West of Capitol Blvd. Charming all-suite hotel in quietest part of downtown Boise. A good deal for folks who like to cook for themselves and prefer larger quarters. Popular with business travelers. **Rooms:** 104 effic. CI 3pm/CO noon. Nonsmoking rms avail. All units have complete kitchenettes. Accommodations have comfortable sitting areas and TV viewing space. Guests can move furniture around as they like. **Amenities:** A/C, cable TV w/movies, refrig, dataport, voice mail. Some units w/terraces, some w/fireplaces. **Services:** Babysitting. **Facilities:** 25 Basketball, volleyball, whirlpool, playground, washer/dryer. Large city park is directly behind hotel. Near Boise River Greenbelt. **Rates (CP):** $120–$150 effic. Children under age 18 stay free. Parking: Outdoor, free. Rates drop for stays of 30 days or longer. AE, CB, DC, DISC, JCB, MC, V.

The Owyhee Plaza
1109 Main St, 83702 (Downtown); tel 208/343-4611 or toll free 800/233-4611, 800/821-7500 in ID; fax 208/336-3860. Between 12th and 11th Sts. The Owyhee, with its mix of historical flavor and contemporary luxury, is one of Boise's finest hotels. Good value. **Rooms:** 100 rms and stes. CI 3pm/CO 1pm. Nonsmoking rms avail. Rooms are spacious and well decorated. **Amenities:** A/C, cable TV w/movies, dataport. Some units w/minibars, some w/terraces, some w/whirlpools. Small refrigerators in many units. **Services:** VP Babysitting. **Facilities:** 300 2 restaurants, 1 bar (w/entertainment), beauty salon. **Rates:** $49–$93 S; $59–$103 D; $125–$175 ste. Extra person $10. Children under age 18 stay free. Parking: Outdoor, free. AE, CB, DC, DISC, EC, MC, V.

The Red Lion Riverside
2900 Chinden Blvd, 83714; tel 208/343-1871 or toll free 800/RED-LION; fax 208/344-1079. Take I-84 into Boise; get off on Garden St. Beautiful, sprawling property on the banks of the Boise River. **Rooms:** 304 rms and stes. CI 3pm/CO 1pm. Nonsmoking rms avail. Large, elegant, and well-decorated. Riverside rooms are the best. **Amenities:** A/C, satel TV, dataport. Some units w/terraces, 1 w/fireplace, some w/whirlpools. **Services:** **Facilities:** 1000 2 restaurants, 2 bars (1 w/entertainment), spa, sauna, steam rm, whirlpool. Spacious courtyard for sunning or reading. **Rates:** $99–$109 S; $114–$124 D; $165–$395 ste. Extra person $15. Children under age 18 stay free. Parking: Outdoor, free. AE, CB, DC, DISC, JCB, MC, V.

The Statehouse Inn
981 Grove St, 83702; tel 208/342-4622 or toll free 800/243-4622; fax 208/344-5751. Clean and elegant hotel in the heart of downtown Boise. Popular among business travelers. **Rooms:** 88 rms and stes. CI 2pm/CO 1pm. Nonsmoking rms avail. Extra charm provided by colorful bedspreads and nice furniture. **Amenities:** A/C, cable TV w/movies, dataport, VCR. Some units w/whirlpools. Complimentary Calistoga mineral water in rooms. **Services:** Babysitting. **Facilities:** 100 1 restaurant, 1 bar, sauna, whirlpool. Very spacious fitness center. **Rates:** $60–$71 S; $70–$81 D; $145 ste. Extra person $10. Children under age 12 stay free. Parking: Indoor/outdoor, free. Suite rates include full breakfast. AE, CB, DC, DISC, MC, V.

MOTELS

Best Western Airport Inn
2660 Airport Way, 83705 (Boise Airport); tel 208/384-5000 or toll free 800/758-5004; fax 208/384-5566. Exit 53 off I-84. Clean, comfortable, and convenient, but noisy. Sandwiched between the freeway and the airport. Prices are fair and competitive with surrounding properties. **Rooms:** 50 rms. CI 2pm/CO 1pm. Nonsmoking rms avail. **Amenities:** A/C, cable TV w/movies, dataport. **Services:** **Facilities:** Washer/dryer. Outdoor pool has large patio seating area with lounge chairs. **Rates (CP):** $46 S; $51 D. Extra person $6. Children under age 18 stay free. Parking: Outdoor, free. AE, CB, DC, DISC, MC, V.

Cabana Inn
1600 Main St, 83702; tel 208/343-6000; fax 208/343-6000. On western edge of downtown Boise. An attractive Spanish-style building. Rooms are "no frills" but clean, and among the cheapest in Boise. A better value than other similarly priced motels. **Rooms:** 46 rms and stes. CI noon/CO 11am. Nonsmoking rms avail. Rooms have concrete-block walls. **Amenities:** A/C. Some units w/terraces. **Services:** **Facilities:** **Rates:** Peak (June–Labor Day) $40–$48 S or D; $55 ste. Children under age 12 stay free. Lower rates off-season. Parking: Outdoor, free. AE, DC, DISC, MC, V.

Flying J Motel

8002 Overland Rd, 83709 (West Boise); tel 208/322-4404 or toll free 800/733-1418; fax 208/322-7487. Take Overland/South Cole exit off I-84. Clean, basic motel with competitive rates and plenty of parking space for RVs and other large vehicles, right next to I-84 at the edge of Boise. Across the freeway from the Temple of Latter Day Saints. **Rooms:** 86 rms. CI 4pm/CO 11am. Nonsmoking rms avail. **Amenities:** A/C, VCR. **Services:** **Facilities:** 1 restaurant, games rm, whirlpool, beauty salon, washer/dryer. **Rates (CP):** Peak (May 1–Sept 1) $40–$45 S; $50–$53 D. Children under age 16 stay free. Lower rates off-season. Parking: Outdoor, free. Special rates for Latter Day Saints church groups. AE, DC, DISC, MC, V.

Motel 6

2323 Airport Way, 83705 (Boise Airport); tel 208/344-3506; fax 208/344-6264. Exit 53 off I-84; left on Airport Way. Solid, no-frills property close to airport and freeway. **Rooms:** 91 rms. CI 7am/CO noon. Nonsmoking rms avail. **Amenities:** A/C, cable TV w/movies. **Services:** **Facilities:** **Rates:** $35 S; $41 D. Extra person $3. Children under age 17 stay free. Parking: Outdoor, free. AE, CB, DC, DISC, MC, V.

Quality Inn Airport Suites

2717 Vista Ave, 83705 (Boise Airport); tel 208/343-7505 or toll free 800/221-2222; fax 208/342-4319. Exit 53 off I-84; head north on Vista. No-frills motel with large rooms and surprisingly nice furnishings, considering the drab concrete exterior. Very competitive rates. **Rooms:** 79 rms and effic. CI 11am/CO noon. Nonsmoking rms avail. All rooms are mini-suites with separate sitting area. **Amenities:** A/C, cable TV w/movies, refrig, dataport. Some units w/terraces. Kitchen facilities limited to microwave, small sink, and small refrigerator. **Services:** Free beverage and snack service Tues–Sat 5–7pm includes beer and wine. **Facilities:** Washer/dryer. **Rates (CP):** Peak (summer) $56 S; $59 D; $44–$62 effic. Extra person $6. Children under age 18 stay free. Lower rates off-season. Parking: Outdoor, free. AE, DC, DISC, MC, V.

Ramada Inn

1025 S Capitol Blvd, 83706 (Near University); tel 208/344-7971 or toll free 800/2 RAMADA; fax 208/345-6846. Just south of downtown. Renovated in 1994, this clean and basic property enjoys a central downtown location next to the Boise River. Rates are slightly higher than at other motels across the street. **Rooms:** 127 rms and stes. CI 3pm/CO noon. Nonsmoking rms avail. **Amenities:** A/C, dataport. Some units w/whirlpools. **Services:** Masseur, babysitting. **Facilities:** 60 1 restaurant, 1 bar (w/entertainment), spa, sauna, whirlpool. **Rates (BB):** $49–$67 S; $57–$75 D; $85 ste. Extra person $8. Children under age 18 stay free. Parking: Outdoor, free. AE, CB, DC, DISC, MC, V.

Rodeway Inn

1115 N Curtis Rd, 83706; tel 208/376-2700 or toll free 800/228-2000; fax 208/377-0324. Take Curtis Road exit off I-84. Next to St Alphonsus Medical Center. Well-kept motel on outskirts of Boise. A favorite of business travelers and sports teams. **Rooms:** 98 rms and stes. CI 2pm/CO noon. Nonsmoking rms avail. **Amenities:** A/C, cable TV w/movies, dataport. All units w/terraces. **Services:** Babysitting. All guests receive coupons for free cocktails and dessert for each day of stay. **Facilities:** 100 1 restaurant, 1 bar (w/entertainment), sauna, whirlpool. Putting green at side of pool. **Rates (BB):** $60–$72 S; $70–$75 D; $68–$78 ste. Extra person $10. Children under age 17 stay free. Parking: Outdoor, free. Discounts available for school groups, sports teams, and seniors. AE, CB, DC, DISC, MC, V.

Safari Motor Inn

1070 Grove St, 83702 (Downtown); tel 208/344-6556 or toll free 800/541-6556; fax 208/344-7240. At 11th St. Probably the best value in downtown Boise. **Rooms:** 103 rms and stes. CI 3pm/CO 1pm. Nonsmoking rms avail. Bright and spacious. **Amenities:** A/C, cable TV w/movies, refrig, dataport. 1 unit w/whirlpool. **Services:** **Facilities:** 50 Sauna, whirlpool. Rather limited fitness center includes a treadmill and an exercise bike. **Rates (CP):** $43–$63 S; $48–$68 D; $63–$120 ste. Extra person $5. Children under age 18 stay free. Parking: Outdoor, free. AE, DC, DISC, MC, V.

University Inn

2360 University Dr, 83706; tel 208/345-7170 or toll free 800/345-7170; fax 208/345-5118. Very clean and reasonably priced independent motel that wraps around outdoor pool and features some charming rooms. Located at edge of Boise State University campus and near Boise River Greenbelt. **Rooms:** 81 rms and stes. CI 1:30pm/CO noon. Nonsmoking rms avail. **Amenities:** A/C, cable TV w/movies, dataport. **Services:** Social director. **Facilities:** 75 1 restaurant, 1 bar, whirlpool. **Rates (BB):** $44–$48 S; $52–$56 D; $66–$74 ste. Extra person $8. Children under age 18 stay free. Parking: Outdoor, free. AE, DC, DISC, MC.

RESTAURANTS

★ Amoré

921 W Jefferson (Downtown); tel 208/343-6435. At 10th St. **Italian/Mediterranean.** Amoré was a hit from the first minute it opened; the lusty food, chic atmosphere, and top-notch service still pack them in. The vast choice of pastas runs from basic lasagna al forno to seafood-veggie fettucine. Daily specials, many salads, great bread, and a nice wine list and selection of microbrews round out the menu. **FYI:** Reservations recommended. Jazz/classical. Children's menu. Beer and wine only. Additional location: 904 Main St (tel

342-3230). **Open:** Peak (June 15–Sept) lunch Mon–Fri 11:30am–2pm; dinner Mon–Sat 5:30–10pm, Sun 5:30–9pm. **Prices:** Main courses $3–$18. DC, DISC, MC, V.

Chart House Restaurant
2288 N Garden; tel 208/336-9370. At Main St. **American.** This restaurant, known for its scenic views of the nearby Boise River and its wildlife, features an extensive salad bar, juicy steaks, and generous portions. A bit pricey, but you receive good value. **FYI:** Reservations recommended. Children's menu. **Open:** Daily 5:30–10pm. **Prices:** Main courses $11–$31. AE, CB, DC, MC, V.

Harrison Hollow Brewhouse
2455 Harrison Hollow Lane (Highlands); tel 208/343-6820. **American/Cajun.** This brewpub draws an eclectic mix of patrons, from "suits" to cyclists. Five brews are always available. For eats there's a surprising amount of fish, and large portions. An excellent deal. **FYI:** Reservations not accepted. Blues/rock. Children's menu. Beer and wine only. **Open:** Mon–Thurs 11am–10pm, Fri–Sat 11am–11pm–Sun 11am–9pm. **Prices:** Main courses $5–$12. AE, MC, V.

Peter Schott's
In the Idanha, 928 Main St (Downtown); tel 208/336-9100. At 10th St. **New American.** Owner/chef Peter Schott opened this elegant Boise restaurant in 1977. Crystal chandeliers, candlelit tables with fine table linens and tableware, and soft decorative tones set the mood for intimate celebrations. Diners can start with seafood-stuffed mushrooms or one of the many salads, then move on to entrees like marinated, grilled buffalo steak or rack of lamb. Lots of fresh seafood specials are offered daily. **FYI:** Reservations recommended. **Open:** Mon–Sat 6–10pm. **Prices:** Main courses $16–$23. AE, CB, DC, DISC, MC, V.

Renaissance Ristorante Italiano
110 S 5th (Downtown); tel 208/344-6776. At Main St. **Italian.** Located in a dark, quiet, downstairs corner of a historic building. Owner/chef Victor Aspiazu will prepare food to accommodate dietary or taste preferences. Starters include smoked trout in a red bell-pepper sauce over linguine; and shiitake mushrooms in a demiglace with Chianti sauce. Entrees might feature seafood prima (chunks of snapper, scallops, prawns, and rock shrimp with vegetables in a light broth over pasta), sautéed salmon, or New York steak. The bread comes from a top-notch bakery in Boise; vegetarian items always available. **FYI:** Reservations recommended. Beer and wine only. No smoking. **Open:** Peak (Nov–Jan) Mon–Thurs 5:30–9:30pm, Fri–Sat 5:30–10pm, Sun 5–9pm. **Prices:** Main courses $12–$22. AE, DC, DISC, MC, V.

Table Rock Brew Pub & Grill
705 Fulton St; tel 208/342-0944. At Capitol Blvd, south of downtown. **American/Cajun/Kosher.** When Table Rock opened in 1991, it was an instant hit among brew aficionados. There are always five custom beers and, generally, five additional "brewer's whim" choices, all made by brewmaster Terry Dennis from Idaho spring water, Camas Prairie barley, and Southern Idaho hops. As for the food choices, the smoked chicken ravioli, Louisiana hot Cajun sausages, and Reuben sandwich are all excellent. **FYI:** Reservations not accepted. Children's menu. Beer and wine only. **Open:** Mon–Sat 11:30am–midnight, Sun noon–11pm. **Prices:** Main courses $5–$14. AE, DC, DISC, MC, V. 

ATTRACTIONS

Boise Art Museum
670 S Julia Davis Dr; tel 208/345-8330. Idaho's largest visual arts institution, consisting of 10 galleries, an atrium, and an outdoor sculpture garden. Permanent collection includes works by regional artists as well as internationally known masters, including Auguste Rodin, Francisco Goya, and Ansel Adams. **Open:** Tues–Fri 10am–5pm, Sat–Sun noon–5pm. Closed some hols. **$**

Basque Museum and Cultural Center
611 Grove St; tel 208/343-2671. Boise is the center of one of the largest Basque colonies outside Spain, a settlement that began in the late 19th century when young Basque men were recruited to herd sheep in the West. This museum focuses on the past and present of Basques in Idaho via paintings by contemporary Basque artists, historical displays, and photographs. **Open:** Tues–Fri 10am–4pm, Sat 11am–3pm. Closed some hols. **Free**

Idaho State Historical Museum
610 Julia Davis Dr; tel 208/334-2120. Objects in the museum narrate the history of Idaho from prehistoric times through the days of fur trading, the gold rush, and pioneer settlement. Ten richly detailed interiors show how natives of the state lived and conducted business in the late 19th and early 20th centuries. Other exhibits highlight the state's Native American, Basque, and Chinese populations. **Open:** Mon–Sat 9am–5pm, Sun 1–5pm. Closed some hols. **Free**

The Discovery Center of Idaho
131 Myrtle St; tel 208/343-9895. Hands-on science museum with over 100 permanent interactive exhibits, including a bubble-maker. **Open:** June–Aug, Tues–Sat 10am–5pm, Sun noon–5pm; Sept–May, Tues–Fri 9am–5pm, Sat 10am–5pm, Sun noon–5pm. Closed some hols. **$$**

Old Idaho Penitentiary
2445 Old Penitentiary Rd; tel 208/368-6080. Completed in 1870, this building served as Idaho's prison for over a century. A museum includes photos of the famous outlaws and gunmen who spent time here, exhibits of contraband prisoner weapons (ball and chain, the "Oregon boot"), and a slide show on the history of the penitentiary. Self-guided walking tours (allow 90 minutes) cover the cellhouses, the punishment block, and the death row and gallows area. Admission includes History of Electricity and Idaho Transportation exhibits. **Open:** Mem Day–Sept, daily 10am–6pm. **$**

Morrison Knudsen Nature Center
600 S Walnut; tel 208/334-2225. Situated in a bend of the Boise River, this 4½-acre complex opened in 1990. Inside the visitors center are two aquariums housing cold- and warm-water fish, a video display explaining fish habitat, a topographic model of the river, and a touch-feel gallery with pelts, skulls, and horns. An outdoor nature walk winds along a 550-foot river stream, where four underground viewing stations provide visitors a glimpse of the fish, insects, and aquatic plants beneath the surface. **Open:** Grounds, daily sunrise–sunset; office, Tues–Sun 10am–5pm. Closed some hols. **$**

World Center for Birds of Prey
5666 W Flying Hawk Lane; tel 208/362-3716. Originally founded to prevent the extinction of the peregrine falcon, the world's fastest bird (capable of speeds in excess of 200 mph), the center is now dedicated to the conservation of all birds of prey and their environments. Visitors touring the facilities can see falcons and eagles up close, and can also visit the Tropical Raptor Building, where exotic species such as the giant harpy eagle, with a wing-span of nearly seven feet, are studied to learn how to prevent their extinction. Spring is the best time so see young peregrine falcons and incubated eggs, which can be viewed through one-way mirrors. **Open:** Daily 8am–5pm. **$$**

Bogus Basin Ski Area
2405 Bogus Basin Rd; tel 208/336-4500. The varied 500 acres of terrain (Idaho's largest ski area) contains an 1,800 foot vertical drop, 10 lifts, and 46 trails. With 5 miles of lighted nightskiing runs, this is the second-largest nightskiing facility in the United States. Also popular with snowboarders. **Open:** Nov 25–Apr 5, daily 9am–10pm. **$$$$**

Bonners Ferry

This picturesque town near the Canadian border owes its origins to the ferry service that was provided from here across the Kootenai River for California gold miners bound for British Columbia. The nearby Kootenai National Wildlife Refuge attracts migrating waterfowl. **Information:** Greater Bonners Ferry Chamber of Commerce, PO Box 375, Bonners Ferry, 83805 (tel 208/267-5922).

MOTELS

Bonners Ferry Log Inn Motel
US 95 N, 83805 (North Hill); tel 208/267-3986. 2 miles N of town. This new and unique motel, housed in a log building and designed like a country inn, reflects a labor of love. Its entrance, lobby, walkways, and rooms are adorned with handcrafted items ranging from flower baskets to bird houses. Municipal airport located just across the highway. **Rooms:** 22 rms. CI open/CO 11am. Nonsmoking rms avail. Each room has handmade white-lacquered, pine-log posted beds with quilted bedspreads. **Amenities:** TV, voice mail. No A/C. **Facilities:** Whirlpool. **Rates (CP):** Peak (June 1–Sept 30) $46–$52 S; $58–$63 D. Extra person $6. Children under age 12 stay free. Lower rates off-season. Parking: Outdoor, free. Wedding, group, and outdoor recreation packages available. Senior and commercial discounts. AE, DC, DISC, MC, V.

Bonners Ferry Resort
6438 US 95 S, 83805 (South Hill); tel 208/267-2422. Bare basics offered here to budget-minded families who desire a children's play area. Check-in desk is located in the adjoining cafe. **Rooms:** 24 rms and effic. CI open/CO 11am. Nonsmoking rms avail. Varnished knotty pine walls. Most rooms have showers only; some have refrigerators. **Amenities:** A/C. **Services:** **Facilities:** 1 restaurant, 1 bar, games rm, whirlpool, playground, washer/dryer. Full hookups for 60 RVs. Tent sites available. Dog-walk area. On-premises bar has big-screen TV for sporting events. **Rates:** Peak (June 1–Aug 31) $36 S; $40–$58 D; $42–$52 effic. Children under age 2 stay free. Lower rates off-season. Parking: Outdoor, free. Weekly and monthly rates available. DISC, MC, V.

Kootenai Valley Motel
US 95 S, 83805 (South Hill); tel 208/267-7567 or toll free 800/341-8000; fax 208/267-7567. S end of town on US 95 S. For budget-minded travelers and families looking for accommodations with cooking facilities. **Rooms:** 22 rms, stes, and effic; 2 cottages/villas. CI 2pm/CO 11am. Nonsmoking rms avail. Two cottages have full kitchens. **Amenities:** A/C. Some units w/fireplaces, 1 w/whirlpool. Seven units have refrigerators. One room has a wet bar. **Services:** Babysitting. Fax, message, and typing services available for business travelers. Refundable $10 pet deposit. **Facilities:** 1 restaurant (*see* "Restaurants" below), volleyball, lawn games, whirlpool, playground. Large yard for children to run and play in. Barbecue area. **Rates:** Peak (June 1–Aug 31) $65–$85 S; $75–$95 D; $100–$150 ste; $90–$110 effic; $100–$150 cottage/villa. Extra person $10. Children under age 18 stay free. Lower rates off-season. Parking: Outdoor, free. Golf, ski, and lake cruise packages available. Weekly and monthly rates offered. AARP, military, government, and commercial discounts. MC, V.

RESTAURANT

★ Chic 'N Chop
US 95 S (South Hill); tel 208/267-2431. Next to Kootenai Valley Motel. **American.** A small, country town cafe decorated with wildlife paintings, it's a favorite of locals for its friendly service, excellent food, and large portions at good prices. **FYI:** Reservations accepted. Children's menu. No liquor license. **Open:** Sun–Mon 4:30am–7pm, Tues–Sat 4:30am–8pm. **Prices:** Main courses $3.95–$9.95. CB, DISC, MC, V.

Burley

This southern Idaho city is a half-hour drive from some of the state's most popular attractions: the Pomerelle ski area, Massacre Rocks State Park, Minidoka National Wildlife Refuge, and Sawtooth National Forest. Many rock climbers come through here on their way to the City of Rocks formations, and an annual boat regatta on the Snake River draws big crowds. **Information:** Burley Chamber of Commerce, 324 Scott Ave, Rupert, 83350 (tel 208/436-4793).

MOTEL

Best Western Burley Inn
800 N Overland Ave, 83313; tel 208/678-3501 or toll free 800/599-1849; fax 208/678-9532. At exit 208 off I-84. Just off the interstate, this place is popular with business travelers year-round. Summer brings vacationers and others coming to nearby Snake River Recreation Area. **Rooms:** 128 rms and stes. Executive level. CI 2pm/CO noon. Nonsmoking rms avail. **Amenities:** A/C, cable TV w/movies, dataport. Some units w/terraces, some w/whirlpools. **Services:** Children's program, babysitting. Pets allowed at discretion of the manager. **Facilities:** 800 1 restaurant, 1 bar (w/entertainment), basketball, volleyball, playground, washer/dryer. Spacious courtyard; nearby health club offers guest passes. **Rates:** Peak (May–Oct) $58 S; $62–$66 D; $78 ste. Extra person $4. Children under age 18 stay free. Lower rates off-season. Parking: Outdoor, free. Ski, honeymoon, and holiday packages avail. AE, CB, DC, DISC, MC, V.

ATTRACTIONS

City of Rocks
Almo; tel 208/824-5519. ID 77 to Almo; continue 2 mi W and follow signs. A landmark for emigrants on the California Trail, the granite spires of this 25-square-mile national reserve give the appearance of a Stone Age city. Grounds offer scenic walks near the historic California Trail; wildlife watching for elk, deer, eagles, falcons, and hawks; world-class technical rock climbing; and picnicking and camping. **Open:** Park, daily 24 hours; visitors center, daily 8am–5:30pm. **Free**

Minidoka National Wildlife Refuge
ID 24, Rupert; tel 208/436-3589. 12 mi NE of Rupert, in the Snake River Valley. The refuge encompasses over 20,000 acres, including manmade Lake Walcott, and is home to ducks, geese, mallards, pintails, wigeons, cormorants, great blue herons, and many other types of waterfowl. (Bald eagles are also common during winter months.) Recreational activities include hunting (in season), fishing, and wildlife photography. Although there are no established hiking trails, visitors are free to hike on refuge property. **Open:** Refuge: daily dawn–dusk. Refuge office: Mon–Fri 8am–4:30pm, closed some hols. **Free**

Caldwell

Located west of Boise along the Boise and Snake Rivers, Caldwell is an agricultural community that turns its attention to rodeo each summer. The Caldwell Night Rodeo in mid-August is usually broadcast nationally, while the Little Britches Rodeo in early July remains a popular kids' event. **Information:** Caldwell Chamber of Commerce, 300 Frontage Rd, PO Box 819, Caldwell, 83606 (tel 208/459-7493).

HOTEL

Comfort Inn
901 Specht Ave, 83605; tel 208/454-2222 or toll free 800/221-2222; fax 208/454-9334. Take exit 29 off I-84; left on Specht; left on Hospitality Way. Clean and attractive property with a historic flavor. **Rooms:** 65 rms, stes, and effic. CI 3pm/CO 1pm. Nonsmoking rms avail. Rooms feature bright decor and artwork on the walls. **Amenities:** A/C, satel TV w/movies. Some units w/whirlpools. Suites have hot tub, VCR, coffeemaker, refrigerator, and hairdryer. Microwave and small refrigerator available upon request. **Services:** Babysitting. Free fax and copy services available. **Facilities:** 70 1 restaurant, basketball, volleyball, sauna, whirlpool, playground. Well-landscaped lawn area in back features a large barbecue. **Rates (CP):** Peak (May–Sept) $49–$65 S; $59–$85 D; $90–$105 ste; $84–$94 effic. Extra person $8. Children under age 18 stay free. Lower rates off-season. Parking: Outdoor, free. AE, CB, DC, DISC, JCB, MC, V.

MOTEL

Sundowner Motel
1002 Arthur St, PO Box 1055, 83606; tel 208/454-1585 or toll free 800/454-9487; fax 208/454-9487. Exit 28 to 10th Ave. Small, family-owned, no-frills hotel located in downtown Caldwell. **Rooms:** 64 rms. CI 2pm/CO 11am. Nonsmoking rms avail. Concrete walls, but attractive bedspreads. **Amenities:** A/C, satel TV. Some units w/terraces. **Services:** **Facilities:** Small, plain pool, but heavily used. **Rates (CP):** $39–$44 S; $39–$48 D. Extra person $2. Children under age 8 stay free. Parking: Outdoor, free. AE, CB, DC, MC, V.

Coeur d'Alene

A booming tourist town on the shores of Lake Coeur d'Alene. Art galleries, antique book stores, and restaurants are among 350 businesses thriving downtown. Rugged Tubbs Hill Park offers nature trails and beautiful views. **Information:** Greater Coeur d'Alene Convention and Visitors Bureau, PO Box 1088, Coeur d'Alene, 83816 (tel 208/664-0587).

MOTELS

Bennet Bay Inn

E 5144 Coeur d'Alene Lake Dr, 83814; tel 208/664-6168 or toll free 800/368-8609. Exit 15 off I-90, 3.5 miles E on Coeur d'Alene Lake Dr. Located on the southeast outskirts of town, overlooking Lake Coeur d'Alene. **Rooms:** 21 rms and effic. CI 3pm/CO noon. Local appeal for romantic interludes because of seven theme rooms with mirrored four-person hot tubs and decor keyed to names like Victorian, Ocean, Fantasy, Galaxy, Montana, Garden, and Hawaiian. **Amenities:** A/C, TV w/movies, VCR. 1 unit w/fireplace, some w/whirlpools. Refrigerators and 25-inch TVs in theme rooms. **Services:** Movie library has 150 selections. **Facilities:** **Rates:** Peak (June 15–Oct 1) $45–$65 S or D; $45–$65 effic. Lower rates off-season. Parking: Outdoor, free. Theme rooms $60–$120 in winter, $90–$150 in summer. AE, DISC, MC, V.

Boulevard Motel

2400 Seltice Way, 83814; tel 208/664-4978. Exit 11 off I-90, 1 block W. Older hotel nestled among tall ponderosa pines. Borders the freeway and has no sound buffering, so noise level is high. **Rooms:** 10 rms and effic. CI open/CO 11am. Small, clean, woodsy rooms with lacquered lodgepole-pine decor. **Amenities:** A/C. No phone. **Services:** No cats, but small dogs OK. **Facilities:** Playground. **Rates:** Peak (June–Sept) $38–$60 S or D; $47–$57 effic. Lower rates off-season. Parking: Outdoor, free. AE, CB, DC, DISC, MC, V.

Comfort Inn

280 W Appleway, 83814; tel 208/765-5500 or toll free 800/221-2222; fax 208/664-0433. Junction of US 95 and I-90. Easy access to shopping centers, restaurants, attractions, and business centers draws seniors, families, and business people. **Rooms:** 51 rms, stes, and effic. Executive level. CI open/CO noon. Nonsmoking rms avail. **Amenities:** A/C. Some units w/terraces, some w/whirlpools. About half the rooms have full kitchens. Eight have a separate hot tub room. **Services:** VCR and movie rentals at front desk. Complimentary newspaper in the morning and coffee, tea, and cocoa in lobby 24 hours. **Facilities:** 20 Volleyball, sauna, whirlpool, playground, washer/dryer. Planned renovations to include fitness center, steam room, and enclosed pool. **Rates (CP):** Peak (June 15–Oct 20) $46–$86 S or D; $109–$179 ste; $69–$103 effic. Extra person $10. Children under age 16 stay free. Lower rates off-season. Parking: Outdoor, free. Sweetheart, golf, and Silverwood Theme Park packages avail. AE, CB, DC, DISC, MC, V.

Days Inn

2200 Northwest Blvd, 83814; tel 208/667-8668 or toll free 800/325-2525; fax 208/765-0933. Exit 11 off I-90, 2 miles N of City Center. Two miles from city beach and park and North Idaho College, which has theater performances and hosts sporting competitions. **Rooms:** 61 rms and stes. CI noon/CO noon. Nonsmoking rms avail. **Amenities:** A/C. **Services:** Children's program. Movies and VCRs available for rent at front desk. Large separate seating area in lobby. **Facilities:** 30 Steam rm, whirlpool. **Rates (CP):** Peak (July 1–Aug 31) $70 S; $75 D; $125 ste. Extra person $5. Children under age 12 stay free. Lower rates off-season. Parking: Outdoor, free. Seniors and commercial discounts; family packages avail. AE, CB, DC, DISC, JCB, MC, V.

El Rancho Motel

1915 E Sherman Ave, 83814 (East Coeur d'Alene); tel 208/664-8794 or toll free 800/359-9791. 1 mile E of Coeur d'Alene Resort. Typical mom-and-pop older budget motel, situated on a busy street. Close to recreation, shopping, and restaurants. **Rooms:** 14 rms and effic. CI 2pm/CO 11am. Nonsmoking rms avail. Clean, tidy rooms with knotty pine interiors and flower pictures. **Amenities:** A/C. Microwaves available. **Services:** Nonrefundable pet fee of $3. **Rates:** Peak (June 16–Sept 16) $52 S; $59 D; $66 effic. Extra person $6. Children under age 12 stay free. Lower rates off-season. Parking: Outdoor, free. Senior and commercial rates available. AE, CB, DC, DISC, MC, V.

Garden Motel

1808 Northwest Blvd, 83814; tel 208/664-2743; fax 208/664-2743. Exit 11 off I-90, ½ mile NW of downtown center and lake. Affordable older motel near North Idaho College and the city beach and marina area. **Rooms:** 23 rms, stes, and effic. CI 2pm/CO 11am. Nonsmoking rms avail. Clean, basic rooms. **Amenities:** A/C. **Services:** **Facilities:** Whirlpool, washer/dryer. An atrium near the pool room has a large rubber tree plant and seating for guests. Lots of grass where children can run and play. **Rates:** Peak (May 1–Sept 15) $70–$100 S or D; $79–$100 ste; $79–$100 effic. Extra person $6. Children under age 18 stay free. Lower rates off-season. Parking: Outdoor, free. AE, CB, DC, DISC, MC, V.

Holiday Inn

414 W Appleway, 83814; tel 208/765-3200 or toll free 800/HOLIDAY; fax 208/664-1962. Junction of US 95 and I-90. Centrally located, with an inviting lobby. **Rooms:** 122 rms and stes. CI 3pm/CO noon. Nonsmoking rms avail. **Amenities:** A/C, dataport, voice mail. 1 unit w/terrace. Suites have two TVs, entertainment system, wet bar, refrigerator, large bathtub, and robes. **Services:** Children's program, babysitting. **Facilities:** 200 1 restaurant, 1 bar (w/entertainment). Planned renovations include indoor pool, fitness center, and added meeting space for 500 people. **Rates:** Peak (June 1–Sept 30) $99 S; $109 D; $245 ste. Extra person $10. Children under age 19 stay free. Lower rates off-season. Parking: Outdoor, free. Senior discounts for rooms and meals. Golf, ski, shopping, and B&B packages avail. AE, CB, DC, DISC, JCB, MC, V.

Red Rose Motel

621 Sherman Ave, 83814 (Downtown); tel 208/664-3167; fax 208/667-4949. 5 blocks E of Coeur d'Alene Resort.

Appropriately named—rose bushes beautify the grounds—and popular because of its convenient location three blocks from beach, city park, and marina. Within easy walking distance to shopping complexes and a variety of restaurants. **Rooms:** 17 rms. CI 2pm/CO 11am. Nonsmoking rms avail. **Amenities:** A/C. **Services:** Free coffee in lobby in morning. **Facilities:** **Rates:** Peak (July 1–Aug 31) $72 S; $76 D. Extra person $5. Children under age 18 stay free. Lower rates off-season. Parking: Outdoor, free. AE, CB, DC, DISC, MC, V.

Rodeway Inn Pines Resort
1422 Northwest Blvd, 83814; tel 208/664-8244 or toll free 800/651-2510; fax 208/664-5547. Exit 11 off I-90. Located near city beach and park, and North Idaho College campus **Rooms:** 65 rms. Executive level. CI 2pm/CO noon. Nonsmoking rms avail. **Amenities:** A/C. Some units w/terraces, 1 w/whirlpool. Refrigerators available upon request. Guest rooms for people with disabilities offer closed-caption TV and audio-visual doorbell/telephone. **Services:** Babysitting. **Facilities:** 80 1 restaurant, 1 bar, whirlpool, playground, washer/dryer. Centennial Trail for in-line skating, biking, and walking passes in front of property. Most rooms offer park-at-your-door convenience. Large complex with lots of room for children to run and play. **Rates:** Peak (June 15–Sept 10) $62–$82 S or D. Extra person $5. Children under age 18 stay free. Lower rates off-season. Parking: Outdoor, free. AE, CB, DC, DISC, MC, V.

Sundowner Motel
2113 Sherman Ave, 83814 (East Coeur d'Alene); tel 208/667-9787 or toll free 800/717-9787. 1 mile E of downtown center and Coeur d'Alene Resort. Clean, competitively priced property. **Rooms:** 22 rms and effic. CI 2pm/CO 11am. Nonsmoking rms avail. **Amenities:** A/C. Some units w/whirlpools. Two suites with mirrored four-person hot tub and VCR. **Services:** **Rates:** Peak (mid-June–Sept 1) $62 S; $67 D; $70 effic. Extra person $10. Children under age 18 stay free. Lower rates off-season. Parking: Outdoor, free. AE, DC, DISC, MC, V.

Suntree Inn
W 3705 Fifth Ave, Post Falls, 83854 (Flying J Travel Plaza); tel 208/773-4541 or toll free 800/888-6630; fax 208/773-0235. Exit 2 off I-90, N side of fwy. Near the Flying J Travel Plaza, Greyhound Race Track, and Post Falls factory outlet mall. Popular with businesspeople because of nearby Riverbend Commerce Park. **Rooms:** 100 rms and stes. Executive level. CI 3pm/CO 1pm. Nonsmoking rms avail. Pleasing flower decor in rooms. **Amenities:** A/C. Some units w/whirlpools. **Services:** Free local calls. **Facilities:** Games rm, whirlpool, washer/dryer. **Rates (CP):** Peak (May 1–Sept 30) $50 S; $65 D; $75–$95 ste. Extra person $5. Children under age 14 stay free. Lower rates off-season. Parking: Outdoor, free. "Getaway to the Dogs" package for Greyhound Race Track. Discounts for frequent guests. Canadian dollar accepted at par. AE, DC, DISC, MC, V.

Super 8 Motel
505 W Appleway, 83814; tel 208/765-8880 or toll free 800/800-8000; fax 208/765-8880. Junction of US 95 and I-90. Clean and comfortable **Rooms:** 95 rms. Executive level. CI 2pm/CO 11am. Nonsmoking rms avail. **Amenities:** A/C. **Services:** Refundable pet fee deposit is $20. Coffee, hot cocoa, and tea available in lobby 24 hours. **Facilities:** 15 Guests may use nearby Ironwood Athletic Club for $10. **Rates:** Peak (June 1–Oct 31) $60 S; $74 D. Extra person $5. Children under age 12 stay free. Lower rates off-season. Parking: Outdoor, free. Frequent guest program avail. AE, CB, DC, DISC, MC, V.

RESORT

Coeur d'Alene Resort
2nd and Front Sts, PO Box 7200, 83816 (Downtown); tel 208/765-4000 or toll free 800/688-5253; fax 208/667-0217. On Lake Coeur d'Alene. 200 acres. Noted for its elegance, it's a landmark in Coeur d'Alene. Locals bring their guests here for meals, walks on the floating boardwalk, lake cruises, and browsing through the spectacular lobby and the art and gift shops. Within walking distance of city beach and park, Tubbs Hill Nature Area, and downtown stores and restaurants. **Rooms:** 337 rms and stes. Executive level. CI 4pm/CO noon. Nonsmoking rms avail. Lake Tower rooms and suites are large, two-tiered, with over-size bathrooms, two dressing areas, and balconies with seating that have magnificent views of the lake. Condo units also available. **Amenities:** A/C, cable TV w/movies, voice mail, bathrobes. All units w/minibars, some w/terraces, some w/fireplaces, some w/whirlpools. Lighted "Do Not Disturb" signs are room-switch activated. Lake Tower rooms have fireplaces and jet tubs. **Services:** VP Car-rental desk, social director, masseur, children's program, babysitting. Very Important Kids (VIK) program of horseback rides, movies, ice skating, and more for ages 5–11, with options for children under 5. Newspapers delivered every morning. **Facilities:** 18 4 500 4 restaurants (*see* "Restaurants" below), 3 bars (2 w/entertainment), games rm, racquetball, spa, sauna, steam rm, whirlpool, day-care ctr, playground. World's longest (¾ mile) floating boardwalk surrounds marina. Guests with boats can reserve a slip during stay, and public docking is available for resort visitors. Resort has the world's first and only floating green (14th hole) on a course designed by Scott Miller; marine shuttle service to golf course. Shopping complex, indoor computer golf course, bowling lane, and both poolside and marina bars. Lake Coeur d'Alene cruises available daily for lunch, dinner, and charters. **Rates:** Peak (May 1–Aug 31) $80–$295 S or D; $200–$400 ste. Extra person $10. Children under age 17 stay free. Min stay wknds. Lower rates off-season. Parking: Indoor/outdoor, $9/day. Rates vary by view and location. Wedding, golf, and ski packages avail. AE, CB, DC, MC, V.

RESTAURANTS

Beverly's
In Coeur d'Alene Resort, 2nd and Front Sts (Downtown); tel 208/765-4000. **Regional American/French/Seafood.** In addition to spectacular views of Lake Coeur d'Alene, this restaurant is noted for prime rib and peppered NY steak with roasted shallots and balsamic vinegar sauce. Wine list has more than 700 selections. There are personal wine storage bins for frequent customers. **FYI:** Reservations recommended. Guitar/jazz. Children's menu. Dress code. **Open:** Peak (May 1–Oct 31) lunch Mon–Sat 11am–2:30pm; dinner daily 5–10pm; brunch Sun 9am–2:30pm. **Prices:** Main courses $13.95–$26.95. AE, CB, DC, DISC, MC, V.

The Cedar's
S end of US 95 Bridge (on Lake Coeur d'Alene); tel 208/664-2922. ½ mile off US 95, south of Spokane River Bridge. **Seafood/Steak.** This floating restaurant on the border of Lake Coeur d'Alene and the Spokane River has been a local favorite for 30 years. There is not a bad view from the place. True to its name, the interior is cedar finished, which lends a northwestern, woodsy ambience to the romantic river setting. The menu offers recommended wines for each entree. One of the specialties is biergarten steak, a filet mignon marinated in beer and spices. **FYI:** Reservations recommended. No smoking. **Open:** Mon–Sat 5:30–11pm, Sun 5–11pm. **Prices:** Main courses $10.25–$23. AE, DC, MC, V.

Cricket's Restaurant and Oyster Bar
424 Sherman Ave (Downtown); tel 208/765-1990. 2 blocks E of Coeur d'Alene Resort. **American/Seafood.** One look at the 1955 Buick and 1940s-era gas pumps on the roof tells you that you are in for a fun time. Daily deliveries of fresh fish and live lobster tanks ensure satisfaction and return visits from locals. The menu changes twice weekly, according to the availability of fresh fin fish. The oyster bar features daily shellfish specialties, which can be washed down with imported beers or regional microbrews. **FYI:** Reservations accepted. **Open:** Daily 11am–9:30pm. **Prices:** Main courses $12.95–$17.95. CB, DC, DISC, MC, V.

Wilson Frank's Restaurant and Bakery
501 Sherman Ave (Downtown); tel 208/667-9459. At 5th St. **Regional American.** Antique farm implements on unfinished red cedar walls and high-backed wooden chairs give a rustic, western feeling to this family-style restaurant. Noted for its good, hearty fare and large selection of homemade pies, which can also be purchased to go. **FYI:** Reservations accepted. Children's menu. No liquor license. **Open:** Peak (June 1–Sept 15) Sun–Thurs 6am–10pm, Fri–Sat 6am–11pm. **Prices:** Main courses $6.25–$10. DISC, MC, V.

ATTRACTIONS

Museum of North Idaho
115 Northwest Blvd; tel 208/664-3448. Located on the campus of North Idaho College. Native American artifacts and exhibits on steamboats, railroads, and the local logging industry. Admission includes entrance to the nearby Fort Sherman Museum. **Open:** Apr–Oct, Tues–Sat 11am–5pm. Also open Sun July–Aug. Closed some hols. **$**

Farragut State Park
13400 E Ranger Rd, Athol; tel 208/683-2425. 25 mi N of Coeur d'Alene. Nestled at the foot of the Coeur d'Alene and Bitteroot Mountain ranges, this park is situated on the shore of the state's largest lake, Lake Pend Oreille. Several day-use areas feature picnic areas with shelters. There's also a manmade swimming beach; hiking, biking, and horse trails; two year-round campgrounds. Wintertime activities include cross-country skiing, snowmobiling, and sledding. **Open:** Visitor center Apr–Sept, sunrise–sunset. Park open year-round **$**

Craters of the Moon National Monument

Established in 1924 by President Calvin Coolidge, this 53,000-acre monument is a vast plain of lava flows, cinder cones, and other volcanic formations. (As its name indicates, the area would probably look more at home on the surface of the moon.) There's not a single volcano here, but instead a "Great Rift Zone" that began erupting 15,000 years ago and only stopped 2,000 years ago. Geologists predict it will someday erupt again.

As desolate as the landscape looks, and despite an average July rainfall of only one-half inch, an amazing variety of wildlife exists here: more than 2,000 insect species, 148 birds, 47 mammals, 8 reptiles, and over 200 species of plants. The **visitors center** has displays identifying the wildflowers and animals in the area, as well as a video about erupting volcanoes and how lava flows created the volcanic features in the park. Guided walks and tours are sometimes offered; ask at the visitors center for a schedule. A 52-site campground is located near the visitors center building.

Eight hiking trails, ranging from ½ to six miles, wind through lava tubes, splatter cones, and craters. (Backcountry permits available at the visitors center.) Drivers may follow the **self-guided tour** along the seven-mile-long loop road, which is open to cars from late April to mid-November. In winter, the loop road is transformed into a groomed cross-country skiing trail, and no-fee winter camping is available in the North Crater parking lot.

For further information, contact PO Box 29, Arco, ID 83213 (tel 208/527-3257).

Driggs

A seasonal resort. Driggs is only a few miles from the Wyoming border and Grand Teton National Park, with

Yellowstone National Park just a bit farther to the north. **Information:** Teton Valley Chamber of Commerce, PO Box 250, Driggs, 83422 (tel 208/354-2500).

HOTEL

Best Western Teton West

476 N Main St, 83422; tel 208/354-2363 or toll free 800/252-2363; fax 208/354-2962. On ID 33. Low rates and close proximity to superb skiing, along with breathtaking views of the Teton Mountains and Big Hole Mountain Range, are this property's main assets. The lobby and corridors have a mildew odor. **Rooms:** 41 rms. CI 3pm/CO noon. Nonsmoking rms avail. Decor and furnishings are minimal and drab. **Amenities:** A/C, cable TV w/movies. Pool towels, alarm clocks available. **Services:** Babysitting. **Facilities:** 30 Whirlpool, washer/dryer. Wax room for skis. **Rates (CP):** Peak (June 15–Sept 15/Dec 20–Mar) $42 S; $58 D. Extra person $4. Children under age 12 stay free. Lower rates off-season. Parking: Outdoor, free. Ski package avail. AE, CB, DC, DISC, MC, V.

RESTAURANTS

Knight's British Rail

65 Depot St; tel 208/354-8365. Off Main St. **Eclectic.** Located in a 1916 house, this eatery and pub is a favored local place to socialize. The menu offers a diverse range of Italian, Chinese, American, and vegetarian dishes; highlights include teriyaki chicken satay with creamy peanut sauce, whiskey chicken, pasta Alfredo, and spicy Thai fry. All breads, desserts, dressings, and sauces are homemade, and only fresh vegetables are used. **FYI:** Reservations recommended. Blues/dancing/guitar/singer. Children's menu. Beer and wine only. No smoking. **Open:** Peak (June 15–Sept) daily 6–10pm. **Prices:** Main courses $8–$17. AE, DISC, MC, V.

Teton Bakery and Cafe

68 N Main; tel 208/354-8116. **American.** Delicious homebaked breads, pastries, bagels, brownies, and muffins make up for nondescript decor. The breakfast/lunch menu features Create-Your-Own Omelettes, the Hungry Man Breakfast (hash browns topped with onions, eggs, and ham, bacon, or sausage), and omelette burritos. **FYI:** Reservations not accepted. No liquor license. **Open:** Mon–Fri 6am–2pm, Sat 7am–1pm, Sun 7am–3pm. **Prices:** Lunch main courses $2.25–$4.95. No CC.

Hagerman

A popular launching point for white-water rafting on the Snake River—abundant springs in the Hagerman Valley provide a near-constant flow for the river. Visitors also are drawn to the Hagerman Fossil Beds National Monument. **Information:** Hagerman Valley Chamber of Commerce, PO Box 599, Hagerman, 83332 (tel 208/837-9131).

RESTAURANT

The Riverbank

191 State St; tel 208/837-6462. **Regional American/Cajun.** Fresh, tasty food in a no-frills atmosphere. The Ozark-style catfish and southern Idaho fried trout are favorites. All entrees come with hush puppies and green-tomato pickles. Pies can be as diverse as kiwi-cheese, sweet potato, and lemon shaker. **FYI:** Reservations not accepted. Children's menu. No liquor license. No smoking. **Open:** Thurs–Sat 4–9pm, Sun noon–8pm. **Prices:** Main courses $8–$17. MC, V.

ATTRACTIONS

Hagerman Fossil Beds National Monument

221 N State St (visitors center); tel 208/837-4793. 7 mi W of Hagerman. During the late Pliocene period, 3½ million years ago, early species of horse, beaver, otter, mastodon, pelican, swan, and many other animals and birds lived along the edge of the ancient Lake Idaho. Their remains eventually became fossilized in the sediment; the Snake River then carved away at the sedimentary rock, leaving many of the fossils exposed. The famous **Hagerman Horse Quarry** (the source of more than 20 complete prehistoric horse fossils) even inspired the Idaho legislature to name the Hagerman horse as the official state fossil.

The Hagerman area was designated as a national monument in 1988, and the Park Service has only recently begun offering boat tours of the fossil beds along the Snake River, bus rides to the Horse Quarry, bird-watching walks, and guided walking tours of the monument. The visitors center, located in downtown Hagerman, offers fossil displays and an orientation film. **Open:** June–Sept, daily 8:30am–5pm; Oct–May, Thurs–Sat 8:30am– 5pm, Sun 1–5pm. **Free**

Malad Gorge State Park

1074 E 2350 S; tel 208/837-4505. Established in 1975, this 652-acre park features a 3½-mile scenic loop road, picnic areas with shelters, hiking trails, and scenic views of the Malad Gorge and the Malad River. Fishing and hunting in season. **Open:** Daily 7:30am–8pm. **Free**

Idaho Falls

Idaho's second-largest city, located near the Wyoming border. Gateway to the Targhee National Forest just to the east. **Information:** Eastern Idaho Visitors Info Center, 505 Lindsay Blvd, PO Box 50498, Idaho Falls, 83405 (tel 208/523-2255).

HOTELS

Best Western AmeriTel Inn

900 Lindsay Blvd, 83402; tel 208/523-6000 or toll free 800/600-6001; fax 208/523-0000. Exit 119 off I-15; exit 307 off US 20. Attractive, well-maintained, and quiet, the AmeriTel stands at one end of the greenbelt along the Snake River. Just

a short walk from the waterfalls, restaurants, and boutiques. **Rooms:** 94 rms, stes, and effic. CI 2pm/CO noon. Nonsmoking rms avail. Pleasant decor, firm and comfortable mattresses, generously sized pillows. **Amenities:** A/C, cable TV w/movies, dataport. Some units w/whirlpools. Refrigerators on request. **Services:** **Facilities:** Whirlpool, washer/dryer. **Rates (CP):** Peak (May–Sept) $79 S or D; $139–$169 ste; $139–$169 effic. Extra person $8. Children under age 12 stay free. Lower rates off-season. Parking: Outdoor, free. Discounts for seniors. AE, CB, DC, DISC, MC, V.

Holiday Inn Westbank
475 River Pkwy, 83402; tel 208/523-8000 or toll free 800/432-1005; fax 208/529-9610. This eight-floor cylindrical stucco building is across the street from the Falls as well as the Greenbelt, which runs along the Snake River. **Rooms:** 142 rms and stes. CI 2pm/CO noon. Nonsmoking rms avail. Spacious, quiet, and comfortable accommodations with a subdued and pleasing decor. Several rooms overlook the Snake River and waterfalls. **Amenities:** A/C, cable TV w/movies, dataport, VCR. Some units w/terraces, 1 w/whirlpool. **Services:** Babysitting. Masseur available on request. **Facilities:** 1 restaurant, 1 bar, sauna, whirlpool, beauty salon, washer/dryer. Guests get free passes to Downtown athletic club. Nearby greenbelt good for jogging, walking, bicycling, and rollerblading. **Rates:** $75–$95 S or D; $250 ste. Extra person $10. Children under age 17 stay free. Parking: Outdoor, free. Honeymoon packages avail. AE, CB, DC, DISC, JCB, MC, V.

Littletree Inn
888 N Holmes, 83401; tel 208/523-5993 or toll free 800/521-5993; fax 208/523-7104. At Elva St. Pleasant hotel located on a main street. Beautiful golf course located across the street. **Rooms:** 92 rms, stes, and effic. CI 1pm/CO noon. Nonsmoking rms avail. Rooms line a courtyard with a large grassy area, flowers, and trees. Corridor is a bit gloomy, with stained and worn carpeting. Some accommodations have an alarm clock and radio. **Amenities:** A/C, cable TV w/movies. Some units w/terraces, some w/whirlpools. **Services:** **Facilities:** 1 restaurant, 1 bar (w/entertainment), sauna, whirlpool, washer/dryer. **Rates (BB):** Peak (May–Aug) $49–$69 S; $59–$69 D; $79–$99 ste; $69 effic. Extra person $10. Children under age 18 stay free. Lower rates off-season. Parking: Outdoor, free. Golf package avail. Frequent guest program offers every 13th night free. AE, DC, DISC, MC, V.

MOTEL

Best Western Stardust
700 Lindsay Blvd, PO Box 51420, 83402; tel 208/522-2910 or toll free 800/527-0274; fax 208/529-8361. Off W Broadway. Clean and comfortable, the Stardust offers many amenities and recently underwent an exterior facelift. The major asset is its location—along the Snake River greenbelt and near the waterfalls. A pretty and lively area, with several restaurants and boutiques nearby. **Rooms:** 248 rms and stes. CI 1pm/CO noon. Nonsmoking rms avail. Comfortable, with coordinated but minimal decor. Some rooms have river views. Standard doubles are small; deluxe doubles are bigger and offer extra counter space in the bathroom. **Amenities:** A/C, cable TV w/movies. Some units w/minibars. Refrigerators and microwaves available for small rental fee. **Services:** Pleasant staff. **Facilities:** 1 restaurant, 1 bar (w/entertainment), sauna, whirlpool, washer/dryer. Small but well-equipped fitness center. **Rates:** Peak (July–Aug) $65–$85 S; $75–$95 D; $89–$109 ste. Extra person $10. Children under age 12 stay free. Lower rates off-season. Parking: Outdoor, free. Corporate rates avail. AE, DC, DISC, MC, V.

RESTAURANTS

Garcia's
2180 E 17th St; tel 208/522-2000. At Channing Way, adjacent to Grand Teton Mall. **Mexican.** Garcia's, housed in a Southwest-style building, has a welcoming and casual atmosphere and a bold and festive decor. Dinners feature fajitas, burritos, tacos, and some traditional American entrees. Sunday brunch offers an all-you-can-eat buffet; on other days, a social, margarita-drinking crowd gathers around the attractive bar. **FYI:** Reservations accepted. Children's menu. **Open:** Mon–Thurs 11am–10pm, Fri–Sat 11am–11pm, Sun 10am–9pm. **Prices:** Main courses $4–$12. AE, DC, DISC, MC, V.

Jake's
851 Lindsay Blvd; tel 208/524-5240. Off W Broadway. Exit 119 off I-15, or exit 307 off US 20. **American.** The casual yet elegant atmosphere of this bistro—accented with wood and brass fixtures and subdued lighting—lends itself to both business and social get-togethers, as well as to quiet, romantic evenings out for couples. Dinner fare includes fine prime rib, pan-fried shrimp, barbecued ribs, and fajitas. **FYI:** Reservations recommended. Children's menu. **Open:** Lunch Mon–Fri 11:30am–2pm; dinner Mon–Thurs 5:30–10pm, Fri–Sat 5:15–10:30pm. **Prices:** Main courses $11–$17. AE, DISC, MC, V.

La Yaquesita
110 Science Center Dr; tel 208/523-1779. Exit 308 off US 20. **Mexican.** This friendly place is known locally for its tasty authentic cuisine, made by the owner/chefs who prepare their own sauces and tamales. In the Sonoran tradition, specialty dishes include chorizo (ground pork sausage), chile rellenos (stuffed peppers), and mole poblano (thick chile sauce served over chicken). The food doesn't burn, but hot sauces are available on the side. Ceiling fans and air conditioning on both floors keep it cool in the summer. **FYI:** Reservations accepted. Children's menu. Beer and wine only.

No smoking. **Open:** Lunch daily 11am–3pm; dinner Mon–Thurs 5–9pm, Fri 5–10pm, Sat 3–10pm. **Prices:** Main courses $7–$15. DISC, MC, V.

Lost Arts Brew & Bread Works
298 D St; tel 208/528-9288. At Shoup Ave. **New American/Pub.** This funky coffeehouse/pub presents a wide variety of live entertainment, ranging from Peruvian folk music and Jewish klezmer to Chicago blues and one-act plays. The menu features gourmet pizzas, deli sandwiches, home-baked breads, and 25 microbrewed beers. Lost Arts attracts a lively, well-educated crowd, with many regulars, who don't mind putting up with crowded quarters and noise. Out-of-towners will have no trouble finding the building—painted pink with rose awnings and sponge-painted doors. Inside are solid walnut, handcrafted tables, batik curtains, and Native American blankets and rugs on the walls. **FYI:** Reservations not accepted. Folk/jazz. Beer and wine only. No smoking. **Open:** Mon–Thurs 11am–11pm, Fri 11am–1am, Sat noon–1am. **Prices:** Main courses $6–$9. MC, V.

Mona Lisa's at the Falls
325 River Pkwy (Greenbelt); tel 208/528-7655. Off W Broadway. **French/Italian.** Pretty little spot offering lovely views of the falls. Menu favorites include manicotti stuffed with chicken, stuffed pork tenderloin with Basque-style sausage, fresh pastas, and Chicago-style pizzas. **FYI:** Reservations recommended. Jazz/classical. **Open:** Peak (Mem Day–Labor Day) Mon–Thurs 11am–10pm, Fri–Sat 11am–11pm, Sun 1–8pm. **Prices:** Main courses $9–$19. AE, DISC, MC, V.

★ **Smitty's Pancake House Restaurant**
645 W Broadway; tel 208/523-6450. At Lindsay Blvd. **American.** The ambience here evokes old-world Europe, with high-beamed white ceilings, antique plates, and oil paintings in ornate gold frames adorning the walls. It's also a home-away-from-home type place: Service is polite and prompt; portions are generous; and diners can order breakfast, lunch, or dinner throughout the day. Menu specialties include Swedish and Bavarian pancakes and hearty sandwiches served with soup or salad. **FYI:** Reservations not accepted. Children's menu. No liquor license. **Open:** Daily 6am–9pm. **Prices:** Main courses $7–$14. No CC.

Westbank Restaurant
475 River Pkwy (Greenbelt); tel 208/528-6332. Off W Broadway. **American.** Spacious and attractive dining room located at the city greenbelt along the Snake River. Windows spanning the entire front of the building afford diners a wonderful view of the waterfalls across the street. The menu features varied entrees, including New York steak, chicken Florentine, and salmon steak. **FYI:** Reservations accepted. Children's menu. **Open:** Sun–Thurs 6am–10pm, Fri–Sat 6am–midnight. **Prices:** Main courses $9–$16. AE, CB, DC, DISC, MC, V.

ATTRACTIONS

EBR-1: Experimental Breeder Reactor #1
US 20/26; tel 208/526-0050. The site where electricity was first generated from nuclear energy in 1951. Visitors can tour two nuclear reactors and a reactor control room. Numerous displays and exhibits explain nuclear fission. Guided tours available. **Open:** Mem Day–Labor Day, daily 8am–4pm. **Free**

Kelly Canyon Ski Area
706 S Bellin; tel 208/538-6261. 25 mi NE on ID 26, the mountain offers a 938 foot vertical drop, 20 trails, and 5 ski lifts. This is also a popular cross-country skiing area. **Open:** Dec 10–Apr 10, Tues–Sun. **$$$$**

Kellogg

Site of Bunker Hill, once the world's largest silver-producing mine, Kellogg is now a ski resort town with the world's largest single-stage gondola. Visitors can ride the gondola to reach a year-round recreational playground, including an outdoor amphitheater that hosts a summer concert series. **Information:** Greater Kellogg Chamber of Commerce, 608 Bunker Ave, Kellogg, 83837 (tel 208/784-0821).

MOTEL

Silverhorn Motor Inn
699 W Cameron Ave, 83837; tel 208/783-1151 or toll free 800/437-6437; fax 208/784-5081. 1 block N of I-90 at exit 49. Easy access off I-90. Located just six blocks from gondola base station at Silver Mountain Ski Resort. **Rooms:** 40 rms. CI open/CO noon. Nonsmoking rms avail. **Amenities:** A/C, cable TV. **Services:** Babysitting. Fax and copier service available. **Facilities:** 1 restaurant, whirlpool, washer/dryer. Located one block from jogging and walking paths. Free shuttle service to county airport for private-plane travelers. **Rates:** Peak (Mem Day–Labor Day) $51 S; $56–$61 D. Extra person $4. Children under age 12 stay free. Lower rates off-season. Parking: Outdoor, free. Ski packages avail. AE, CB, DC, DISC, MC, V.

ATTRACTIONS

Old Mission State Park
I-90, Cataldo; tel 208/682-3814. 15 mi W of Kellogg. The Old Mission for which this park is named is the oldest standing building in Idaho, built in 1853 by Catholic missionaries to the Coeur d'Alene tribe. The Greek Revival–style building, constructed partly with Native American labor, has 18-inch-thick walls. Today, the park offers guided tours of the mission and its surrounding historic cemeteries, as well as a picnic area, nature/historical walking trail, and a tourist information center. **Open:** June–Aug, daily 8am–6pm; Sept–May, daily 9am–5pm. Closed some hols. Park visitor center closed Nov–Feb. **$**

Silver Mountain Ski and Summer Resort
610 Bunker Ave; tel 208/783-1111. Fifty named trails, offering challenges for all ability levels, are accessible by five lifts, a surface tow, and a gondola. Vertical lift of 2,300 feet. Silver Mountain backs up their resort with a "money back guarantee"—if you're not happy with snow conditions, you can return to the base within 1½ hours and get a pass good for another day of free skiing. Kids six and under ski free when accompanied by an adult.

Summer activities include gondola and chairlift rides, mountain biking, hiking, and an outdoor concert series. The resort's several restaurants are open all year. **Open:** Winter, daily 8am–5pm; summer, daily 10am–6pm. Closed mid-Apr–Mem Day, mid-Oct–Thanksgiving. **$$$$**

Ketchum

See Sun Valley

Lava Hot Springs

This southeastern Idaho village sprung up around a series of hot springs once frequented by Native Americans. Public and private springs attract visitors year-round. Others take to tubing down the Portneus River or attending the annual mountain men rendezvous or one of two annual peddler's fairs. **Information:** Lava Hot Springs Chamber of Commerce, PO Box 238, Lava Hot Springs, 83246 (tel 208/776-5500).

INNS

Lava Hot Springs Inn
5 Portneuf Ave, 83246; tel 208/776-5830 or toll free 800/527-5830 in ID. ⅛ mi S of US 30. 1 acre. Built in 1924 as a hospital, the inn has been renovated by spouses George Katsilometes and Fran Brady. It overlooks the river, which provides a soothing backdrop. Two cats greet guests and, if invited, might sleep at the foot of your bed. (The cats are kept away from people who are allergic to them.) **Rooms:** 23 rms (15 w/shared bath); 1 cottage/villa. CI 3pm/CO noon. No smoking. Rooms are cozy, some with antique dressers. **Amenities:** VCR. No A/C, phone, or TV. Some units w/whirlpools. Two rooms for honeymooners feature marble baths with Roman-style whirlpool tubs plus TV and VCR. **Services:** Masseur, babysitting, wine/sherry served. The stout buffet breakfast might include blueberry pancakes, scrambled eggs, freshly ground coffee, muffins, and granola. Various massages (Swedish, shiatsu, etc.) available on premises. **Facilities:** 25 Spa, sauna, whirlpool, washer/dryer, guest lounge w/TV. Two large outdoor hot tubs are along the Portneuf River. **Rates (BB):** Peak (Mem Day–Labor Day) $49–$54 S w/shared bath, $79–$89 S w/private bath; $54–$59 D w/shared bath, $79–$95 D w/private bath; $89–$95 cottage/villa. Extra person $10. Children under age 5 stay free. Lower rates off-season. Parking: Outdoor, free. AE, DISC, MC, V.

Riverside Inn and Hot Springs
255 Portneuf Ave, 83246; tel 208/776-5504 or toll free 800/733-5504; fax 208/776-5504. Just off Main Street; along Portneuf River. Built in 1914 on the banks of the Portneuf River, the Riverside was dubbed "The Honeymoon Hotel" for its elegance. White lace curtains, an antique couch, and a moose head on the wall add atmosphere to the lobby, where the owners' friendly bull mastiff greets visitors. Recently renovated. **Rooms:** 16 rms (12 w/shared bath). CI 3pm/CO 11am. No smoking. Cozy, country feel, with quilts on the beds. **Amenities:** No A/C, phone, or TV. **Services:** Babysitting, afternoon tea served. White limo for transfers to the airport. Acupuncture available. **Facilities:** 49 Whirlpool. Three indoor, two outdoor hot tubs. **Rates (CP):** Peak (Mem Day–Labor Day) $35–$50 S w/shared bath, $45–$55 S w/private bath; $38–$50 D w/shared bath, $45–$60 D w/private bath. Extra person $5.50. Lower rates off-season. Parking: Outdoor, free. Honeymoon specials avail. DISC, MC, V.

RESTAURANTS

Chateau Portneuf
305 W Main St; tel 208/776-5509. **International.** This 1914 house with a southwestern-accented interior is the setting for chef Gary Barnett's eclectic cuisine: teriyaki beef meatballs in a marmalade glaze; apricot-curry quail; blackened catfish; filet mignon sauced with chokecherry demi-glacé or brandied peppercorns. **FYI:** Reservations recommended. Harp. Beer and wine only. No smoking. **Open:** Thurs–Sun 5–9pm. Closed Jan 1–5. **Prices:** Main courses $11–$19; prix fixe $10–$18. DISC, MC, V.

★ **Silver Grill Cafe**
78 E Main St; tel 208/776-5562. **American.** This western cafe—a local favorite—has fast, friendly service and a menu that covers the range from omelettes to T-bone steak. **FYI:** Reservations not accepted. Children's menu. Dress code. No liquor license. **Open:** Peak (June–Aug) Sun–Thurs 6:30am–10pm, Fri–Sat 6:30am–11pm. **Prices:** Main courses $7–$13. MC, V.

★ **Steak and Stein**
89 1st St; tel 208/776-5607. At the Bannock County Historical Center, 1 block off Main St. **American.** Decorated by murals of elk and eagles as well as wildlife prints, the dining room decor reflects area residents' passion for the outdoors. The varied menu encompasses lobster, prime rib, and vegetarian pasta, with plenty of other options. The adjoining Blue Moon restaurant is your basic burger place, enlivened by pool tables, video poker, pinball, and live entertainment on weekends. **FYI:** Reservations accepted. Country music/karaoke/rock. Children's menu. **Open:** Peak (May–Sept) Wed–Sun 5–11pm. **Prices:** Main courses $12–$19. DISC, MC, V.

ATTRACTION

Idaho's World Famous Hot Pools and Olympic Swimming Complex
430 E Main; tel 208/776-5221 or toll free 800/423-8597. These mineral-laden waters race out of natural underground springs at an average of 3.3 million gallons a day. Five hot pools, with temperatures ranging from 104°F to 112°F. World-class Olympic AAU swimming pool, the only facility of its kind in the inter-mountain area, features a 10-meter diving tower. There's also a smaller 25-meter pool. Park, picnic area. **Open:** Hot baths, Apr–Sept, daily 8am–11pm; Oct–Mar, daily 9am–10pm; swim complex, Mem Day–Labor Day, daily 10am–8pm. Closed some hols. **$$**

Lewiston

A town defined by its rivers: the Clearwater, Snake, and Salmon all mingle here. Geese flock here, as do rodeo fans for the Lewiston Roundup, one of the four biggest events on the Western Rodeo Circuit. Hydroplane racing is a popular pastime. **Information:** Lewiston Chamber of Commerce, 2207 E Main, Lewiston, 83501 (tel 208/743-3531).

HOTEL

Ramada Inn
621 21st St, 83501; tel 208/799-1000 or toll free 800/232-6730. Part of the Ramada Inn and Convention Center, which sits on a hill overlooking the Clearwater River. Attracts conventioneers, businesspeople, and event participants. The inviting lobby features a small waterfall, fresh flowers, and overstuffed chairs. **Rooms:** 136 rms. Executive level. CI 2pm/CO noon. Nonsmoking rms avail. Some standard tower rooms have river views. **Amenities:** A/C, cable TV w/movies. Some units w/whirlpools. Executive rooms include microwaves, refrigerators, coffeemakers. **Services:** Car-rental desk. Fax, copying, and typing service available. **Facilities:** 500 1 restaurant, 2 bars, games rm, whirlpool, washer/dryer. Guests can use adjacent Adcope Athletic Center. Banquet facilities. A microbrewery and brewpub is on premises. **Rates:** Peak (Mar 15–Nov 1) $76–$86 S; $86–$96 D. Extra person $10. Children under age 18 stay free. Lower rates off-season. Parking: Outdoor, free. Senior, commercial, and government discounts. Honeymoon, anniversary, golf, and Hells Canyon jet-boat river tour packages avail. AE, CB, DC, DISC, EC, JCB, MC, V.

MOTELS

Pony Soldier Motor Inn
1716 Main St, 83501 (Downtown); tel 208/743-9526 or toll free 800/634-PONY; fax 208/746-6212. Located downtown on US 12 business route. Popular with repeat visitors because of its location near the commercial district and within walking distance of shops and restaurants. **Rooms:** 66 rms and effic. Executive level. CI 2pm/CO noon. Nonsmoking rms avail. Larger, executive rooms available; with choice of king- or queen-size beds. **Amenities:** A/C, cable TV w/movies, refrig, dataport. Recliners and bathrobes are offered in executive rooms. **Services:** Complimentary newspaper and 24-hour coffee, teas, cocoa, and cider. **Facilities:** 20 Whirlpool, washer/dryer. Free laundry facilities. **Rates (CP):** $56–$59 S; $64 D; $66–$69 effic. Extra person $5. Children under age 12 stay free. Parking: Outdoor, free. Various packages and discounts avail. AE, DC, DISC, MC, V.

Sacajawea Motor Inn
1824 Main St, 83501 (Downtown); tel 208/746-1393 or toll free 800/333-1393; fax 208/743-3620. Located downtown on US 12 business route. Near the Dike Bypass and Walk, a paved recreation trail used for walking, biking, in-line skating, and waterfowl viewing. **Rooms:** 90 rms. CI noon/CO noon. Nonsmoking rms avail. Most rooms open to parking area. **Amenities:** A/C, cable TV w/movies, refrig, dataport. Some units w/whirlpools. Deluxe rooms have whirlpool, microwave, and wet bar. **Services:** **Facilities:** 280 1 restaurant (*see* "Restaurants" below), 1 bar, whirlpool, washer/dryer. **Rates:** $46 S; $54 D. Extra person $3. Parking: Outdoor, free. Children are $3 each. Senior, commercial, government, and group rates avail. AE, CB, DC, DISC, MC, V.

Super 8 Motel
3120 North-South Hwy, 83501; tel 208/743-8808 or toll free 800/800-8000; fax 208/743-8808. Just off US 12 E and 95 S, adjacent to Flying J Travel Plaza. Overlooks the Clearwater River, noted for its steelhead fishing. Clean rooms and good security—no doors opening to the parking lot. Easy highway access. **Rooms:** 62 rms and stes. CI open/CO 11am. Nonsmoking rms avail. All rooms have queen beds. **Amenities:** A/C, cable TV w/movies. Five business rooms offer large work area and recliner. **Services:** VCRs and movies for rent in lobby. Free local calls; no charge for operator access. Guests can book Hells Canyon jet-boat tours. **Facilities:** 20 Washer/dryer. Public boat launch near motel. Complimentary use of nearby fitness center. **Rates:** Peak (May 1–Sept 15) $50 S; $55 D; $95 ste. Extra person $5. Children under age 12 stay free. Lower rates off-season. Parking: Outdoor, free. Several packages and discounts avail. AE, CB, DC, DISC, MC, V.

RESTAURANTS

★ Bojack's
311 Main St (Downtown); tel 208/746-9532. Off US 12 Business, 4 blocks E of Snake River Bridge. **Seafood/Steak.** Located in a farming and ranching community, this restaurant meets the demands of locals and out-of-towners alike for excellent food, large portions, and fair prices. The dining area is located downstairs under a bar, so the atmosphere can be noisy. Noted for charbroiled steaks and seafood entrees,

the menu is limited because the staff "believes in fixin' a few things right, rather than many items just so-so." Few desserts are offered because the meals are so hearty that there's little room left for them. **FYI:** Reservations not accepted. **Open:** Mon–Thurs 5–10pm, Fri–Sat 5–10:30pm. **Prices:** Main courses $8–$16. AE, DISC, MC, V.

The Helm
In Sacajawea Motor Inn complex, 1824 Main St (Downtown); tel 208/746-1393. Off US 12 Business. **Regional American.** Located in a riverside town, this restaurant offers a nautical and historical atmosphere. The Coffee Shop section, which appeals to families, has paper placemats relating the shipping, mining, and Native American history of the region. The more formal Captain's Table section appeals to businesspeople and couples. Both sections offer the same menu, with popular entrees such as yacht club steak (marinated and deep-fried bite-size pieces), and salmon with an Indian barbecue sauce. **FYI:** Reservations accepted. Children's menu. **Open:** Mon–Sat 6am–10pm, Sun 6am–9pm. **Prices:** Main courses $7–$19. AE, CB, DC, DISC, MC, V.

ATTRACTIONS

Nez Perce National Historical Park
Spalding; tel 208/843-2261. Park headquarters located at Spalding, 11 mi E of Lewiston. When this expansive park was created in 1965, it consisted of 24 sites scattered across north central Idaho. In 1992 an additional 14 sites were added in the adjoining states of Oregon, Washington, and Montana. All the sites celebrate the history and culture of the Nez Perce tribe and their struggle for freedom under legendary Chief Joseph.

Driving tour brochures and park maps are available at the **visitors center,** which maintains a museum containing Nez Perce artifacts and an auditorium where films are shown and interpretive talks are given. Staff can answer questions about the history of the region, the Nez Perce, and how to get around the park.

Some of the more popular sites in the Idaho section of the park include **Buffalo Eddy,** which has a large collection of petroglyphs; the **Camas Meadows Battle Site,** where the Nez Perce stopped the advance of US troops who were forcibly trying to move the tribe from their land (see Big Hole National Battlefield, Montana, for more information on the battle); and **Weis Rockshelter,** built more than 8,000 years ago and inhabited until about 600 years ago.

Major highways leading into the area include US 2 and US 12 (the major east-west routes), US 89, US 93, US 95, and US 195 (the major north-south route). For more information contact: Superintendent, Nez Perce National Historical Park, PO Box 93, Spalding, ID 83551. **Free**

Dworshak Fisheries Complex
ID 7, Ahsahka; tel 208/476-4591. 35 mi NE of Lewiston. One of the largest producers of steelhead trout and spring chinook salmon in the world. Visitors are welcome to tour the facilities at 7:30am and 4pm daily. Exhibits describe hatchery activities. **Open:** Daily 7:30am–4pm. **Free**

McCall

A quaint alpine community (5,021 feet above sea level) located at the south end of Payette Lake. Abundant lakes make this a vacationer's paradise. Cold weather brings the annual Winter Carnival festival and related snow sports. **Information:** McCall Area Visitors Bureau, 1001 State St, PO Box D, McCall, 83683 (tel 208/634-7631).

HOTEL

Hotel McCall
3rd and Lake Sts, PO Box 1778, 83638; tel 208/634-8105. A cozy mountain hotel with a bed-and-breakfast feel. Located near Payette Lake and downtown McCall, but better accommodations are available locally for less. **Rooms:** 22 rms and stes. CI 2pm/CO 11am. No smoking. Very quiet and spacious. **Amenities:** Cable TV, bathrobes. No A/C. **Services:** **Facilities:** 1 beach (lake shore), lifeguard, games rm, washer/dryer. Guests have to cross the street to get to beach. **Rates (CP):** $57–$82 D; $99–$120 ste. Extra person $15. Children under age 3 stay free. Parking: Outdoor, free. AE, MC, V.

LODGE

Shore Lodge
501 W Lake St, PO Box 1006, 83638; tel 208/634-2244 or toll free 800/657-6464; fax 208/634-7504. Located in the "Switzerland of Idaho," this spacious lodge offers gorgeous views of Payette Lake and the nearby mountains. Because of the lodge's popularity, it's best to make reservations early. Very good value. **Rooms:** 116 rms and stes. CI 3pm/CO noon. Nonsmoking rms avail. Lakeside accommodations have either patios or balconies, and offer the best views. **Amenities:** Cable TV, voice mail. No A/C. Some units w/minibars, some w/terraces, some w/fireplaces. **Services:** Masseur, children's program, babysitting. **Facilities:** 2 restaurants, 2 bars (w/entertainment), 1 beach (lake shore), basketball, volleyball, games rm, racquetball, spa, sauna, whirlpool. Spacious deck and lounging area near lakeshore. **Rates:** Peak (June–Sept) $104–$139 ste. Extra person $10. Children under age 12 stay free. Lower rates off-season. MAP rates avail. Parking: Outdoor, free. AE, CB, DISC, MC, V.

RESTAURANT

★ The Pancake House
201 N 3rd St; tel 208/634-5849. **American.** A place where you'll see rustic wood decor and smiling folks with forks constantly in motion. Although known for their plate-size

sourdough pancakes (you might get detoured by the huckleberry pancakes), the breakfast menu stretches in all directions. Beyond king-size omelettes lies the trencherman's special treat — an 8-oz sirloin steak, pork chops, hash browns and gravy, two eggs and toast. If you need lunch after that, come back for chili, soups, burgers, and plates of meat, potatoes, and vegetables. **FYI:** Reservations not accepted. Children's menu. Dress code. No liquor license. **Open:** Daily 6am–2pm. **Prices:** Lunch main courses $3–$6. AE, CB, DC, DISC, ER, MC, V.

ATTRACTIONS

Brundage Mountain
Tel 208/634-4151. Surrounded by Boise and Payette National Forests, Brundage Mountain offers year-round recreation. From mid-November to mid-April, skiers and snowboarders can take advantage of 38 downhill trails (10% black diamond, 70% intermediate, 20% beginner), 4 chairlifts, and 3 tows. Children's Ski Center and daycare facilities for kids up to eight years old. Rental equipment, ski school, restaurant. For the latest information on snow conditions, call 208/634-5650.

Summer at Brundage is dedicated to mountain biking and hiking, with bikes available for rent. The chairlift is open regularly on weekends from July 2 to Labor Day for sightseers who want to check out the view or have a high-altitude picnic. **Open:** Ski season, daily 9am–4pm. Call ahead for summer hours. **$$$$**

Ponderosa State Park
Miles Standish Rd; tel 208/634-21644. Situated on a peninsula that juts into Payette Lake, this 1,000-acre park contains every type of topography, from sagebrush flats to lakeside marshes to rocky cliffs. Facilities include a 170-site campground, nature trails (for hiking in summer and cross-country skiing in winter), boating ramps, lake fishing, and a picnic area. **Open:** Daily 9am–10pm. **$**

Montpelier

Set along the Oregon Trail, Montpelier is the center of the Bear Lake Recreational Area. Boating, fishing, and scuba diving are key activities. **Information:** Greater Bear Lake Valley Chamber of Commerce, 904 Washington, PO Box 265, Montpelier, 83254 (tel 208/847-3717).

ATTRACTION

Bear Lake State Park
Bear Lake, Paris; tel 208/945-2790. 12 mi S of Montpelier. Bear Lake is 20 miles long, 8 miles wide, and at least 28,000 years old. For 8,000 of those years, the lake was cut off from the Bear River by earthquake activity. The lake's unique water chemistry has given rise to many rare species of fish, making it a very popular fishing site. The North Beach area of the park has picnic facilities, a swimming beach, and a boat ramp; East Beach area is comprised of the same amenities plus a campground. (Separate fees charged for each area.) In wintertime, the park offers groomed snowmobiling trails, cross-country skiing, and ice fishing. **Open:** Daily dawn–dusk. **$**

Moscow

In the rolling hills of the Palouse area, 283 miles north of Boise. Home to the University of Idaho. Of interest are the Fort Russell Historic District and the abundant outdoor recreational opportunities. **Information:** Moscow Chamber of Commerce, 411 S Main St, PO Box 8936, Moscow, 83843 (tel 208/882-1800).

MOTELS

Mark IV Motor Inn
414 N Main, 83843 (Downtown); tel 208/882-7557 or toll free 800/833-4240; fax 208/883-0684. On US 95 N. Within walking distance of downtown. Five minutes from University of Idaho campus; 20 minutes from Washington State University at Pullman, WA. Location attracts families attending university functions. **Rooms:** 86 rms and stes. CI 3pm/CO noon. Nonsmoking rms avail. Recently upgraded rooms with queen-size beds, carpeting, and pastel colors. Commercial-rate rooms are smaller, but have same amenities. In summer, four RV sites (with electrical hook-up) rent for $12/night. **Amenities:** A/C, cable TV w/movies. 1 unit w/minibar. Dataport equipment available. **Services:** Complimentary coffee in lobby 24 hours. **Facilities:** 1 restaurant (*see* "Restaurants" below), 1 bar, whirlpool. **Rates:** $32–$41 S; $37–$51 D; $50–$87 ste. Extra person $5. Children under age 10 stay free. Min stay special events. Parking: Outdoor, free. Senior and commercial rates avail. One child under 10 stays free with parents; two children are charged the same rate as one adult. AE, CB, DC, DISC, MC, V.

Motel 6
101 Baker, 83843 (West End); tel 208/882-5511; fax 208/882-9475. 1 mi W of downtown on ID 8 W. Across from the University of Idaho campus. Popular with budget-minded travelers. Within walking distance of Palouse Empire Mall (with 62 shops) and lots of fast-food and casual restaurants. **Rooms:** 110 rms. CI open/CO noon. Nonsmoking rms avail. Plain, painted rooms with showers only. **Amenities:** A/C, satel TV. **Services:** Complimentary morning coffee in lobby. **Facilities:** Washer/dryer. **Rates:** Peak (May 25–Dec 21) $27 S; $33 D. Extra person $3. Children under age 17 stay free. Lower rates off-season. Parking: Outdoor, free. Senior discounts avail. AE, CB, DC, DISC, MC, V.

University Inn
1516 Pullman Rd, 83843; tel 208/882-0550 or toll free 800/325-8765; fax 208/883-3056. ID 8 W, 1½ mi W of down-

town. Located across from the University of Idaho campus and a few miles from Washington State University in Pullman, WA. Popular with visiting professors and families. **Rooms:** 173 rms and stes. Executive level. CI 3pm/CO noon. Nonsmoking rms avail. 64 rooms face beautifully landscaped courtyard. All suites have king-size beds. **Amenities:** A/C, cable TV w/movies, voice mail. 1 unit w/terrace, some w/whirlpools. Complimentary in-room coffee. Suites have wet bars, refrigerators, and king-size beds; honeymoon suite has large whirlpool and wet bar. **Services:** Nonrefundable pet fee of $10/night. Accommodations for corporate travelers offer fax, copy, and modem services. **Facilities:** 400 2 restaurants (*see* "Restaurants" below), 2 bars (1 w/entertainment), games rm, steam rm, whirlpool. Guests may use recreation facilities at the university's Kibbie Activity Center for $3/day. Well-manicured courtyard has barbecue area and lots of tables and chairs. One of the restaurants is open 24 hours; one of the lounges offers stand-up comedy three nights a week. **Rates (CP):** $76–$103 S; $88–$103 D; $175–$375 ste. Extra person $10. Children under age 18 stay free. Parking: Outdoor, free. Commercial, senior, government, and group discounts. AE, CB, DC, DISC, MC, V.

RESTAURANTS

The Broiler
In University Inn, 1516 Pullman Rd; tel 208/882-0550. **American.** A small, quiet place with soft lighting and decor. Visitors enjoy the relaxed atmosphere and personalized service while dining on charbroiled steaks, seafood, and pasta entrees, as well as specialty luncheon salads. **FYI:** Reservations recommended. **Open:** Lunch Mon–Fri 11:30am–2pm; dinner Mon–Thurs 5:30–10pm, Fri–Sat 5:30–11pm; brunch Sun 9am–2pm. **Prices:** Main courses $10–$19. AE, CB, DC, DISC, MC, V.

Mark IV Restaurant and Lounge
In Mark IV Motor Inn, 414 N Main (Downtown); tel 208/882-7557. **American.** A no-frills, family-style atmosphere with no special decor—just large portions of good, wholesome food served up at budget prices. Standard menu includes burgers, salads, pastas, seafood, chicken, and beef. **FYI:** Reservations accepted. Children's menu. **Open:** Daily 6am–10pm. **Prices:** Main courses $6–$13. AE, CB, DC, DISC, MC, V.

Mountain Home

Site of Mountain Home Air Force Base and a High Desert landscape of unique canyonlands and pristine wilderness. Some of the Gem State's most fascinating geologic wonders make this a boundless playground for the outdoors-oriented. **Information:** Mountain Home Chamber of Commerce, 165 E 2nd, PO Box 3, Mountain Home, 83647 (tel 208/587-4334).

MOTELS

Best Western Foothills Motor Inn
1080 US 20, 83647; tel 208/587-8477 or toll free 800/528-1234; fax 208/587-5774. Exit 95 off I-84. This property attracts a mix of businesspeople and vacationers. **Rooms:** 76 rms, stes, and effic. Executive level. CI 2pm/CO noon. Nonsmoking rms avail. Queen deluxe rooms; some king-size beds available. **Amenities:** A/C, cable TV, dataport. 1 unit w/whirlpool. Queen rooms have microwaves and refrigerators. **Services:** Car-rental desk, children's program, babysitting. Safety deposit boxes on request. Fax service available, free copying, overnight delivery service pick-ups and drop-offs. **Facilities:** 50 Volleyball, lawn games, sauna, whirlpool. **Rates (CP):** Peak (May–Sept) $57 S; $65 D; $125 ste; $85 effic. Extra person $5. Children under age 12 stay free. Lower rates off-season. Parking: Outdoor, free. Honeymoon packages avail. AE, CB, DC, DISC, JCB, MC, V.

Sleep Inn
1180 US 20, 83647; tel 208/587-9743 or toll free 800/4-CHOICE; fax 208/587-7382. Exit 95 off I-84. Good choice for budget-minded travelers. **Rooms:** 60 rms. Executive level. CI 2pm/CO noon. Nonsmoking rms avail. Very small bathrooms. **Amenities:** A/C, satel TV w/movies, refrig, dataport, VCR. Some units w/minibars. **Services:** Babysitting. Free fax service. **Facilities:** 40 Pool privileges at Best Western Foothills Motor Inn, two doors away. **Rates (CP):** Peak (May 1–Aug 31) $49–$54 S; $54–$59 D. Extra person $5. Children under age 18 stay free. Lower rates off-season. Parking: Outdoor, free. AE, CB, DC, DISC, EC, ER, JCB, MC, V.

ATTRACTION

Bruneau Dunes State Park
HC 85; tel 208/366-7919. Rugged 4,800-acre park centered around a 15,000-year-old group of sand dunes. Park facilities include campground with tent and trailer sites, picnic area, hiking and nature trails, equestrian trail. Fishing for bass and bluegill in nearby lakes (nonmotorized boats only). **Open:** Visitor center, Mar–Oct daily 8am–5pm. $

Nampa

This city of 32,000 people is the site of the annual Snake River Stampede rodeo. Visitors are invited to take a driving tour of area wineries and orchards. **Information:** Nampa Chamber Commerce, 1305 3rd St S, PO Box A, Nampa, 83653 (tel 208/466-4641).

HOTEL

Shilo Inn Nampa Blvd
617 Nampa Blvd, 83687; tel 208/466-8993 or toll free 800/222-2244; fax 208/465-3239. Exit 35 off I-84. Solid, older

property with convenient freeway access. **Rooms:** 61 rms and stes. CI 2pm/CO noon. Nonsmoking rms avail. **Amenities:** A/C, satel TV w/movies, refrig. All rooms have microwaves. **Services:** **Facilities:** Sauna, steam rm, whirlpool, washer/dryer. Small outdoor pool. **Rates (CP):** Peak (June–Aug) $40–$55 S; $49–$59 D; $65–$69 ste. Extra person $9. Children under age 12 stay free. Lower rates off-season. Parking: Outdoor, free. AE, CB, DC, DISC, ER, JCB, MC, V.

MOTELS

Alpine Villa Motel

124 3rd St S, 83651 (Downtown); tel 208/466-7819. Exit 35 off I-84. Take Nampa Blvd to 3rd St S. Funky old hotel with low-budget, apartment-like rooms. Cheapest place in town. **Rooms:** 11 rms and effic. CI 1pm/CO 11am. Nonsmoking rms avail. Tacky but huge. Efficiencies have full, separate kitchen. **Amenities:** A/C, cable TV w/movies, refrig. **Services:** **Rates:** $32 S; $35 D; $40–$50 effic. Extra person $5. Parking: Outdoor, free. MC, V.

Desert Inn

115 9th Ave S, 83651; tel 208/467-1161 or toll free 800/588-5268; fax 208/467-5268. At 2nd St. This small, family-owned, downtown motel is a favorite stopping place for country music acts with gigs in Nampa. Very quiet, with nice antiques and an atrium. Rates are a bit high given the simplicity of the place. **Rooms:** 40 rms. CI 2pm/CO 11am. Nonsmoking rms avail. **Amenities:** A/C, satel TV w/movies. **Services:** **Facilities:** Small pool, no landscaping. **Rates (CP):** $42–$44 S; $44–$46 D. Extra person $5. Children under age 12 stay free. Parking: Outdoor, free. AE, DC, DISC, MC, V.

Pocatello

One of the state's largest cities and home of Idaho State University, Pocatello is adjacent to Fort Hall Indian Reservation, where the public may tour the fort and view authentic Oregon Trail wagon ruts. Shoshone-Bannock tribes host an annual festival featuring dance competitions and an all–Native American rodeo. Pebble Creek and Caribou ski areas are also nearby. **Information:** Greater Pocatello Convention and Visitors Bureau, 343 W Center, PO Box 626, Pocatello, 83204 (tel 208/233-1525).

PUBLIC TRANSPORTATION

Pocatello Urban Transit (tel 208/234-A BUS) provides bus service throughout the Pocatello area. Fares: 60¢; students, seniors, and persons with disabilities 30¢ (9am–3pm only). Transfers are free; Idaho State University campus is Free Fare Zone. **Special Services Transportation** (tel 208/232-0111) provides door-to-door service on lift-equipped minibuses for seniors and riders with disabilities, Mon–Fri.

HOTELS

AmeriTel Inn–Pocatello

1500 N Bench Rd, 83204; tel 208/234-7500 or toll free 800/600-6001; fax 208/234-0000. Off I-15 at exit 71. Very attractive, modern property. New lobby with green-marble counter and burgundy and tan decor. Slated to add 39 new rooms. **Rooms:** 110 rms, stes, and effic. Executive level. CI 2pm/CO 11am. Nonsmoking rms avail. Nicely outfitted rooms feature light-brown wood furniture and prints on the walls. **Amenities:** A/C, cable TV, dataport. Some units w/whirlpools. **Services:** **Facilities:** 100 Spa, washer/dryer. **Rates (CP):** Peak (June–Aug) $61–$74 S; $61–$79 D; $89–$139 ste; $89–$110 effic. Extra person $5. Children under age 18 stay free. Lower rates off-season. Parking: Outdoor, free. AE, DC, DISC, MC, V.

Best Western Cotton Tree Inn

1415 Bench Rd, 83201; tel 208/237-7650 or toll free 800/662-6686; fax 208/238-1355. Exit 71 off I-15. Fairly new brick building conveniently located about four miles from downtown Pocatello. **Rooms:** 149 rms, stes, and effic. Executive level. CI 2pm/CO noon. Nonsmoking rms avail. Comfortable accommodations have a country decor with golden-colored pine and nice views of the foothills and mountains. **Amenities:** A/C, cable TV, dataport. Some units w/whirlpools. Some have VCRs; rooms for honeymooners have Roman baths. **Services:** Staff very willing to help guests. **Facilities:** 70 1 restaurant, 1 bar (w/entertainment), racquetball, whirlpool, washer/dryer. **Rates:** Peak (Mem Day–Labor Day) $56–$62 S; $61–$67 D; $77–$159 ste; $77–$83 effic. Extra person $5. Children under age 18 stay free. Lower rates off-season. Parking: Outdoor, free. Discounts for business people, seniors, and groups avail. AE, DC, DISC, MC, V.

RESTAURANTS

($) The Golden Wheel Grill

In Yellowstone Hotel, 230 W Bonneville; tel 208/233-1613. Historic downtown Pocatello, one block off Main Street. **Eclectic/International.** A tasty treasure in downtown Pocatello, the restaurant is located in the historic Yellowstone Hotel. Manager/chef Frances Lyle presents diverse menu choices such as Japanese soba with prawns, Thai beef and shrimp, pecan-crusted catfish, chicken mole, steak Sinatra, and grilled halibut with cilantro-lime crème fraîche. Selection of microbrewed beers and wine. **FYI:** Reservations accepted. Beer and wine only. **Open:** Lunch Mon–Fri 11am–2pm; dinner Tues–Sat 5–10pm. **Prices:** Main courses $9.95–$16.50. MC, V.

★ Remo's

160 W Cedar; tel 208/233-1710. 1 block W of Yellowstone Ave. **Italian.** The eclectic fare includes carpaccio, shrimp Louie, veal piccata, rack of lamb, pastas, and pizza, as well as escargots and a hot Peking chicken salad. Desserts range

from spumoni to chocolate raspberry cheese pie. **FYI:** Reservations recommended. Children's menu. **Open:** Lunch Mon–Sat 11:30am–3pm; dinner Mon–Sat 3–10pm, Sun 4–9pm. **Prices:** Main courses $6–$20. AE, DC, DISC, V.

The Sandpiper Restaurant
1400 Bench Rd; tel 208/233-1000. Exit 71 off I-15. **American.** Good seafood, beef, and spirits restaurant with a nautical decor and nice view of the foothills. The salad bar is playfully-placed behind a row of vertical oars. Appetizers include Thai prawns and oyster shooters. Featured entrees are tournedos of beef tenderloin, black and blue prime rib, brandied pork, and smoked chicken linguine. **FYI:** Reservations recommended. Blues/folk/singer. Children's menu. Additional locations: 1309 Blue Lakes Road, Twin Falls (tel 734-7079); 750 Lindsay Blvd, Idaho Falls (tel 524-3722). **Open:** Dinner Mon–Thurs 5:30–10pm, Fri–Sat 5:30–10:30pm, Sun 4:30–9pm. **Prices:** Main courses $13.95–$21.95. AE, DC, DISC, MC, V.

ATTRACTION

Massacre Rocks State Park
3592 N Park Lane, American Falls; tel 208/548-2672. 35 mi SW of Pocatello. This 900-acre park was named after an 1862 battle between Native Americans and two pioneer wagon trains in which 10 settlers were killed. One of the park's picnic areas surrounds Register Rock, where many Oregon Trail pioneers carved their names. The park offers a 52-unit campground, visitors center, hiking trails, self-guided nature trail, and boating and fishing on nearby Snake River. **Open:** Mem Day–Labor Day, daily 8:30am–8:30pm. **$**

Post Falls

See Coeur d'Alene

Rexburg

This potato-farming town with strong Mormon roots hosts an international folk festival each summer. Ricks College (named for town founder Thomas Ricks), the largest privately owned junior college in the United States, is located here. **Information:** Rexburg Chamber of Commerce, 420 W 4th S, Rexburg, 83440 (tel 208/852-5700).

HOTEL

Best Western Cottontree Inn
450 W 4th St S, 83440; tel 208/356-4646 or toll free 800/662-6886; fax 208/356-7461. Ricks College exit off US 20; left after railroad tracks. Clean and quiet. Dramatic, pyramid-shaped windows on either side of the entrance let light into the attractive lobby. Beautifully landscaped indoor courtyard with lush plants and small swimming pool. **Rooms:** 100 rms and stes. CI 2pm/CO noon. Nonsmoking rms avail. **Amenities:** A/C, cable TV. Some units w/terraces, 1 w/whirlpool. **Services:** Movie and VCR rentals available. **Facilities:** Whirlpool, washer/dryer. **Rates:** Peak (June 15–Aug) $62–$72 S or D; $250 ste. Extra person $5. Children under age 18 stay free. Lower rates off-season. Parking: Outdoor, free. AE, DC, DISC, MC, V.

RESTAURANT

Frontier Pies Restaurant & Bakery
460 W 4th St S; tel 208/356-3600. US 20 to Ricks College exit. **American.** When you see the old pioneer wagon out front, you have arrived. The interior is decorated with antiques and collectibles; and booths afford diners a measure of privacy. Many menu items (including soups, sauces, and baked goods) are made from scratch daily. Specialties include grilled or broiled burgers, teriyaki chicken salad, and shrimp stir-fry. Prompt, friendly service. **FYI:** Reservations not accepted. Children's menu. No liquor license. No smoking. Additional location: 201 E 1st St, Idaho Falls (tel 528-6300). **Open:** Mon–Thurs 7am–10pm, Fri–Sat 7am–11pm. **Prices:** Main courses $7–$11. DC, DISC, MC, V.

St Anthony

A small farming community in eastern Idaho, perhaps best known for its annual snowmobile races. In the fair-weather months, recreationists head north of town to tear around sprawling sand dunes. **Information:** South Freemont Chamber of Commerce, 110 W Main St, St Anthony, 83445 (tel 208/624-3775).

MOTEL

Weston Inn Best Western
115 S Bridge, 83445; tel 208/624-3711 or toll free 800/528-1234; fax 208/624-3711. St Anthony exit off US 20. Located adjacent to the North Fork of the Snake River, this motel is clean and comfortable. **Rooms:** 30 rms. CI open/CO noon. Nonsmoking rms avail. **Amenities:** A/C, cable TV. Some units w/terraces. **Services:** **Rates:** Peak (June–Aug) $45–$48 S or D. Extra person $5. Children under age 13 stay free. Lower rates off-season. Parking: Outdoor, free. AE, CB, DISC, MC, V.

RESTAURANT

The Relay Station
593 N 2600 E; tel 208/624-4640. 2 mi N of St Anthony exit on US 20. **American.** Located in a log cabin–style building, this restaurant's name refers to a between-town stopover point for stagecoach travelers. The cozy, clean interior features a high white ceiling with wood beams, some hanging plants, and a pellet stove. Menu offerings include prime-rib sandwiches, charbroiled burgers, chicken-fried steak, and grilled halibut. Friendly service. **FYI:** Reservations accepted.

Children's menu. Beer and wine only. **Open:** Peak (June–Aug) Mon–Sat 8am–10pm, Sun 10am–5pm. **Prices:** Main courses $8–$14. MC, V.

Sandpoint

Between Bonners Ferry and Coeur d'Alene in Idaho's panhandle, this resort community sits on the western shore of Lake Pend Oreille and is surrounded by the Selkirk Mountains. Winter sports figure prominently. **Information:** Greater Sandpoint Chamber of Commerce, 100 US 95 N, PO Box 928, Sandpoint, 83864 (tel 208/263-2161).

MOTELS

Edgewater Resort Motor Inn
Bridge St, PO Box 128, 83864 (Downtown); tel 208/263-3194 or toll free 800/635-2534; fax 208/263-3194. Located adjacent to City Beach, the motel's beach is reserved for guests only. City Beach has a designated, safe swim area, separated from the public boat launch, jet skiing, windsurfing, sailing, and waterskiing. **Rooms:** 55 rms. CI 3pm/CO noon. Nonsmoking rms avail. Condo units available. All rooms face beach and Lake Pend Oreille. **Amenities:** A/C. 1 unit w/minibar, all w/terraces, 1 w/fireplace, some w/whirlpools. **Services:** Babysitting. Pet fee deposit is $100. **Facilities:** 200 1 restaurant, 1 bar, 1 beach (lake shore), sauna, steam rm, whirlpool, playground. Paved path nearby for biking, walking, and in-line skating. **Rates:** Peak (May 15–Sept 30) $104–$160 S; $104–$170 D. Extra person $6. Children under age 10 stay free. Lower rates off-season. Parking: Outdoor, free. Golf, ski, and "romantic rendezvous" packages available. AE, CB, DC, DISC, MC, V.

Quality Inn
807 N 5th Ave, PO Box 128, 83864; tel 208/263-2111 or toll free 800/635-2534; fax 208/263-3289. N edge of town off US 95 N. Attracts families and general travelers because of its reputation for service, friendliness, and amenities. Twelve corporate full-service meeting rooms a boon for business conferees. **Rooms:** 57 rms and effic. CI 3pm/CO noon. Nonsmoking rms avail. Pool-side rooms available. **Amenities:** A/C, voice mail. Some units w/terraces, some w/whirlpools. **Services:** Coffee and newspapers in lobby each morning. **Facilities:** 35 1 restaurant, 1 bar, whirlpool, washer/dryer. Inviting pool area with skylight, lounge chairs, and lots of green plants. Well-kept courtyard for pets. **Rates:** Peak (July 1–Aug 31) $56–$76 S; $66–$92 D; $96–$104 effic. Extra person $6. Children under age 17 stay free. Min stay special events. Lower rates off-season. Parking: Outdoor, free. Golf and ski packages available. AE, CB, DC, DISC, ER, JCB, MC, V.

Super 8 Motel
3245 US 95 N, 83864; tel 208/263-2210 or toll free 800/800-8000; fax 208/263-2210. Near Bonner Mall. In a central location near the US 95 turn-off for the Schweitzer Mountain resort, which is noted for its summer and winter recreational activities. **Rooms:** 61 rms. CI 2pm/CO 11am. Nonsmoking rms avail. Family suites sleep up to 6. **Amenities:** A/C. Refrigerators and microwaves available. **Services:** Coffee in lobby 24 hours. **Facilities:** Whirlpool. **Rates:** Peak (mid-June–mid-Sept) $51–$60 S; $61–$85 D. Extra person $5. Children under age 12 stay free. Lower rates off-season. Parking: Outdoor, free. Special packages for golf, ski, and Silverwood Theme Park (30 mi S on US 95). AE, CB, DC, DISC, JCB, MC, V.

LODGE

Green Gables Lodge
Schweitzer Mountain Ski Resort, PO Box 815, 83864; tel 208/265-0257 or toll free 800/831-8810; fax 208/263-7961. 9 miles NW of town. Five-year-old lodge located at the Schweitzer mountain resort, which offers year-round recreational opportunities and is a regional favorite for alpine skiing. Popular for group retreats in summer. The lodge's large lobby features overstuffed chairs, a fireplace, and jigsaw puzzles for guests' enjoyment. **Rooms:** 82 rms, stes, and effic. CI 4pm/CO 11am. Nonsmoking rms avail. Northwest-side rooms have views of mountain; southeast-facing rooms look out to Lake Pend Oreille. Adjoining rooms and Northwest-styled suites available. **Amenities:** A/C. Some units w/whirlpools. **Services:** Social director, masseur, children's program, babysitting. Masseur available for winter season only. **Facilities:** 60 1 restaurant, 1 bar, games rm, whirlpool, day-care ctr, washer/dryer. The Lodge shares facilities in resort complex. For winter season, child-care facilities available for all ages, including infants. Additional meeting space for 300 persons available at day lodge. **Rates:** Peak (Dec 20–Jan 2/Feb 1–Mar 15/July 1–Aug 25) $59–$155 S or D; $125–$230 ste; $69–$145 effic. Extra person $10. Children under age 12 stay free. Lower rates off-season. Parking: Indoor/outdoor, free. Winter recreation packages can include alpine and nordic skiing, dog sledding, horse-drawn sleigh rides, and snowshoeing. Summer recreation packages can include golf (with preferred tee times), llama treks, and mountain biking. Closed Apr 7–May 26/Oct 10–Nov 24. AE, CB, DC, DISC, MC, V.

ATTRACTION

Schweitzer Mountain Resort
Off US 95; tel 208/263-9555 or toll free 800/831-8810. 11 mi NW of Sandpoint. An average of 300 feet of natural snow fall on Schweitzer's 48 downhill ski trails and 8 cross-country trails every winter. Six lifts are in operation during day hours; two lifts are available for weekend night skiing (mid-December–mid-March). A "skier guarantee" policy allows visitors to

receive a voucher for another day if ski conditions are not to their liking. Ski and snowboard rentals, ski school, horse-drawn sleigh rides (must reserve 24 hours in advance, tel 208/265-0257), and snowmobile tours are offered during winter months. For the latest information on snow conditions, call 208/263-9562.

Summertime visitors can enjoy horseback riding, scenic chairlift rides, mountain biking, llama trekking, hiking, and an outdoor concert series. **Open:** Call ahead for specific hours. Closed Apr–mid-May, mid-Oct–Thanksgiving. **$$$$**

Sawtooth National Recreation Area

See also Sun Valley

Sawtooth covers an impressive 765,000 acres of mountain meadows and granite peaks of the rugged Sawtooth Mountains, and contains within it more than 300 pristine mountain lakes. Hiking is a popular way to see the landscape, and the grounds are traversed with 750 miles of trails for this purpose. Within the wilderness area, trail use is restricted to horseback riding and hiking. Mountain bikers can take advantage of primitive roads and tracks left behind by a mining boom, as well as dirt and gravel roads. Another popular activity in the recreation area are whitewater and raft trips down the Salmon River.

Along ID 75 is the **Sawtooth National Fish Hatchery**, which produces more than three million chinook salmon each year. During the summer months the facility offers a tour three times daily. Also on ID 75, north from Ketchum, is the SNRA Headquarters. Visitors can obtain maps and instructions here, as well as a self-guided mile-post tour of the area on cassette. For more information contact Sawtooth NRA, Star Route, Ketchum, ID 83340 (tel 208/726-7672).

MOTELS

Danner's Log Cabin Motel

1 Wall St, PO Box 196, Stanley, 83278; tel 208/774-3539. On ID 21. In 1906, the office of this place was used a ranger station; 30 years later, cabins were built to house gold miners. The frontier atmosphere still prevails, with dirt streets and nearby jagged mountain peaks providing the backdrop for this collection of converted rustic cabins. One of the best buys in town—book ahead, especially for weekends. **Rooms:** 9 cottages/villas. CI 5pm/CO 11am. Cabins have log furniture, a porch with chairs and table, and log railings. **Amenities:** Refrig. No A/C, phone, or TV. **Services:** Social director, babysitting. Information about hiking and recreational activities (including free maps) available in office. Horseback riding and mountain hiking tours arranged. **Facilities:** Picnic table and barbecue available. A short walk away from a city park with a playground and fine views of the Sawtooth Mountains. **Rates:** Peak (Mem Day–Labor Day) $40–$90 cottage/villa. Extra person $5. Lower rates off-season. Parking: Outdoor, free. Closed Nov–Apr. MC, V.

Mountain Village Resort

Jct ID 75 and ID 21, PO Box 150, Stanley, 83278; tel 208/774-3661 or toll free 800/843-5475; fax 208/774-3761. Lodgepole-pine posts give a rustic feeling to this property located on the edge of the Sawtooth National Recreation Area. Incredible views of Sawtooth Mountains make up for commonplace facilities. **Rooms:** 61 rms, stes, and effic. CI 3pm/CO 11am. Nonsmoking rms avail. **Amenities:** Satel TV, VCR. No A/C. **Services:** Car-rental desk. **Facilities:** 30 1 restaurant (*see* "Restaurants" below), 1 bar (w/entertainment), whirlpool, washer/dryer. Large parking lot, good for vehicles towing snowmobiles. Private, enclosed natural hot springs with clothes-changing area. Hiking, cross-country skiing, and river rafting available nearby. **Rates:** Peak (Mem Day–Oct) $50–$60 S; $55–$65 D; $70–$85 ste; $110–$117 effic. Extra person $5. Children under age 4 stay free. Lower rates off-season. Parking: Outdoor, free. AE, DC, DISC, MC, V.

LODGE

Idaho Rocky Mountain Ranch

HC64 Box 9934, Stanley, 83278; tel 208/774-3544; fax 208/774-3477. Off ID 75, 10 mi S of Stanley. A modernized log lodge, complete with a huge porch filled with rockers facing the Sawtooth Mountains. Go for the privacy and the experience. **Rooms:** 4 rms; 9 cottages/villas. CI 3pm/CO 11am. No smoking. The rustic, one-bedroom cabins are simple and clean. **Amenities:** No A/C, phone, or TV. Some units w/fireplaces. **Services:** Babysitting. Will book raft trips and hikes. **Facilities:** 1 restaurant (bkfst and dinner only), volleyball, lawn games, whirlpool. Hot-springs pool, mountain bike rentals. **Rates (MAP):** $119–$179 S; $156–$216 D; $74–$92 cottage/villa. Extra person $68. Children under age 2 stay free. Min stay peak. Parking: Outdoor, free. Closed Oct–May. MC, V.

RESTAURANT

Mountain Village Restaurant and Saloon

In the Mountain Village Resort, Jct ID 75 and ID 21, Stanley; tel 208/774-3317. **American.** The log decor, rock fireplace, and stuffed elk and bear remind you that this place is in the Sawtooth National Recreation Area. Breakfast consists of the usual eggs and pancakes; lunch moves on to soups, salads, and sandwiches. Dinner offers chicken, steak, and trout. Ice cream and pie for dessert. **FYI:** Reservations accepted. Children's menu. Dress code. **Open:** Peak (Mem Day–Labor Day) daily 6am–11pm. **Prices:** Main courses $7–$17. AE, DISC, MC, V.

Shoshone

See Twin Falls

Stanley

See Sawtooth National Recreation Area

Sun Valley

America's first destination ski resort, founded in 1936. Average annual snowfall is 10 feet. The resort communities of Sun Valley, Ketchum, Warm Springs, and Elkhorn all serve this skier's paradise. **Information:** Sun Valley–Ketchum Chamber of Commerce, PO Box 2420, Sun Valley, 83353 (tel 208/726-3423).

PUBLIC TRANSPORTATION

Ketchum Area Rapid Transit (KART) (tel 208/726-7140) provides bus service throughout the Warm Springs, Ketchum, Sun Valley, and Elkhorn area. Door-to-door service is available for the elderly and persons with disabilites with 24-hour advance notice; call 208/726-7576.

HOTELS

Knob Hill Inn

960 N Main St, PO Box 800, Ketchum, 83340; tel 208/726-8010 or toll free 800/526-8010; fax 208/726-2712. ½ mi N of Ketchum on ID 75. Outstandingly impressive four-story hotel on a hill just outside Ketchum, offering both European flair and American convenience. The beautiful lobby features an open-beam and stucco ceiling, handsome furnishings, plus flowers, trees, and statues of cherubs. Bald Mountain views, too. **Rooms:** 24 rms and stes. Executive level. CI 3pm/CO 11am. No smoking. Decorated with custom furniture, rooms are large and glamorized with Italian marble shower stalls. **Amenities:** Cable TV, refrig, VCR, in-rm safe, bathrobes. No A/C. All units w/minibars, all w/terraces, some w/fireplaces, some w/whirlpools. **Services:** VP Twice-daily maid svce, social director, masseur, babysitting. Evening turndown includes cookies. **Facilities:** 40 2 restaurants (bkfst and dinner only; *see* "Restaurants" below), spa, sauna, whirlpool. Enjoy the views of Bald Mountain ski hill from the swimming pool. Austrian-style pastries are made on-site at the cafe. Lovely garden area with pond and terraces. **Rates (BB):** Peak (Christmas–Easter) $150–$300 S or D; $200–$300 ste. Extra person $25. Min stay wknds. Lower rates off-season. Parking: Outdoor, free. AE, MC, V.

UNRATED **Premier Resorts at Sun Valley**

500 S Main St, Devil's Bedstead Bldg, Ketchum, PO Box 659, Sun Valley, 83353; tel 208/727-4000 or toll free 800/635-4444; fax 208/726-8387. Off ID 75. This property management company offers over 450 different accommodations, ranging from studios at the base of the ski mountain to luxury homes renting for $15,000 per month. **Rooms:** 450 rms, stes, and effic; 125 cottages/villas. Executive level. CI 4pm/CO 10am. Nonsmoking rms avail. **Amenities:** Refrig, VCR, CD/tape player. No A/C. Some units w/terraces, some w/fireplaces, some w/whirlpools. **Services:** Babysitting. **Facilities:** 55 **Rates:** Peak (Dec 19–Jan 4/Feb–Apr 15/July–Sept) $60–$95 S; $95–$175 D; $175–$500 ste; $175–$500 effic; $250–$2,000 cottage/villa. Min stay. Lower rates off-season. Parking: Indoor/outdoor, free. AE, DISC, MC, V.

Private Idaho of Sun Valley

660 N Main St, Suite C3, PO Box 1934, Ketchum, 83340; tel 208/726-7722 or toll free 800/249-7722; fax 208/726-1201. Off ID 75. Property management company that can arrange for accommodations ranging from a studio to a five-bedroom apartment, mostly in the Elkhorn resort area. **Rooms:** 60 stes and effic; 3 cottages/villas. CI 4pm/CO 11am. Nonsmoking rms avail. Standard to luxury accommodations, some decorated with western motif. **Amenities:** Cable TV, refrig. No A/C. Some units w/terraces, some w/fireplaces, some w/whirlpools. **Services:** Children's program, babysitting. **Facilities:** 150 Sauna, whirlpool. Tennis, sauna, hot tub, and private 18-hole golf course are available. **Rates:** Peak (Christmas weeks/June–Sept/Dec–Apr) $108–$225 ste; $108–$225 effic; $350–$600 cottage/villa. Min stay. Lower rates off-season. Parking: Outdoor, free. No CC.

MOTELS

Bald Mountain Lodge

151 S Main St, Ketchum, PO Box 2000, Sun Valley, 83353; tel 208/726-9963 or toll free 800/892-7407. Three blocks from ski lifts. Clean but rustic. Lovely flowers at entrance in spring/summer. **Rooms:** 30 rms, stes, and effic. CI open/CO noon. Nonsmoking rms avail. Very dark cabin atmosphere, with knotty-pine walls. **Amenities:** Cable TV. No A/C. **Services:** **Facilities:** **Rates:** Peak (Dec 15–Apr 1/June 1–Sept 15) $45–$65 S; $55–$65 D; $65–$105 ste; $75–$105 effic. Extra person $5. Lower rates off-season. Parking: Outdoor, free. AE, CB, DC, DISC, MC, V.

Clarion Inn of Sun Valley

600 N Main St, Ketchum, PO Box 660, Sun Valley, 83353; tel 208/726-5900 or toll free 800/262-4833; fax 208/726-3761. One block from center of Ketchum. Conveys the atmosphere of a small bed-and-breakfast, even though it's part of a chain. The lobby has a fireplace at its center surrounded by big couches. Ketchum's art galleries and shops are just two blocks away. **Rooms:** 58 rms. CI 3pm/CO 11am. Nonsmoking rms avail. Clean, spacious, and bright. **Amenities:** Cable TV. No A/C. Some units w/terraces, some w/fireplaces, some w/whirlpools. **Services:** Masseur, babysitting. **Facilities:** 75 2 restaurants (lunch and dinner only), whirlpool. A second-floor reading nook offers comfort-

able chairs and a stocked bookshelf. Behind the inn, a complex contains a large whirlpool and excellent restaurant, Jack's Appaloosa, which serves southwest and wild-game specialties. Plenty of parking in a private lot, with free KART bus stop nearby. **Rates (CP):** Peak (mid-June–mid-Sept; Christmas–Apr) $54–$94 S; $59–$129 D. Children under age 18 stay free. Lower rates off-season. Parking: Outdoor, free. AE, DC, DISC, MC, V.

Heidelberg Inn

Warm Springs Rd, PO Box 5704, Ketchum, 83340 (Warm Springs); tel 208/726-5361 or toll free 800/284-4863; fax 208/726-2084. 2½ mi from Ketchum. Ski-lodge atmosphere. Good value. **Rooms:** 30 rms and effic. CI 3pm/CO 11am. Nonsmoking rms avail. **Amenities:** Cable TV w/movies, refrig, dataport, VCR, CD/tape player. No A/C. Some units w/terraces, all w/fireplaces, 1 w/whirlpool. Units have river-rock fireplace. **Services:** Continental breakfast can be served in guests' rooms. **Facilities:** Spa, sauna, whirlpool, playground, washer/dryer. Picnic tables on the lawn. **Rates (CP):** Peak (Dec 23–Jan 1/Feb 3–Apr 1/June 16–Oct 21) $55–$90 S; $65–$105 D; $55–$90 effic. Extra person $8. Children under age 12 stay free. Lower rates off-season. Parking: Outdoor, free. AE, DC, DISC, MC, V.

Kentwood Lodge Best Western

180 S Main St, PO Box 2172, Ketchum, 83340; tel 208/726-4114 or toll free 800/805-1001; fax 208/726-2417. In the center of Ketchum; at River St. Impressive building made of stucco, river rock, and lodgepole-pine logs. Carved wood elk and bear statues at entrance. **Rooms:** 55 rms, stes, and effic. CI 2pm/CO 11am. No smoking. Western decor accented with log furniture. Honeymoon suite has heart-shaped whirlpool tub. **Amenities:** A/C, cable TV, refrig. Some units w/terraces, some w/fireplaces, some w/whirlpools. All accommodations have microwaves; several have kitchens. **Services:** Babysitting. **Facilities:** 1 restaurant (bkfst and lunch only), 1 bar, games rm, whirlpool, washer/dryer. Indoor parking is first-come, first-served; another small lot is within walking distance. **Rates (CP):** Peak (mid-June–Sept; Christmas–Apr) $75–$135 S or D; $195–$135 ste; $115–$135 effic. Extra person $10. Children under age 12 stay free. Min stay peak. Lower rates off-season. Parking: Indoor/outdoor, free. AE, DC, DISC, MC, V.

Ketchum Korral Motor Lodge

310 S Main St, PO Box 2241, Ketchum, 83340; tel 208/726-3510 or toll free 800/657-2657; fax 208/726-5287. ID 75, ⅛ mi from center of Ketchum. Set on a small hill, this property has an immaculately groomed lawn with lots of flowers. Before he bought a house in Ketchum, Ernest Hemingway stayed in cabin #38 during his fall hunting trips. Good value. **Rooms:** 17 rms, stes, and effic; 8 cottages/villas. CI 2pm/CO 11am. No smoking. Rooms are clean but nothing special. **Amenities:** Cable TV, refrig. No A/C. Some units w/terraces, some w/fireplaces. **Services:** **Facilities:** Volleyball, whirlpool. Short drive to River Run ski lift. **Rates:** Peak (Christmas–Jan) $50–$65 S; $55–$85 D; $65–$115 ste; $75–$115 effic; $75–$115 cottage/villa. Extra person $10. Children under age 12 stay free. Min stay peak. Lower rates off-season. Parking: Outdoor, free. AE, DISC, MC, V.

Lift Tower Lodge

703 S Main St, PO Box 185, Ketchum, 83340; tel 208/726-5163 or toll free 800/462-8646; fax 208/726-2614. Basic accommodations, but with a great location—with the old exhibition chair out front, and the ski mountain to the back. Long walk to ski lifts, but quick drive to River Run chairlift. **Rooms:** 14 rms. CI 2pm/CO 11am. Nonsmoking rms avail. Rooms facing the back have good views; those to the front are dark, small, noisy, and lacking in atmosphere. **Amenities:** Cable TV, refrig. No A/C. 1 unit w/whirlpool. **Services:** **Facilities:** Whirlpool. **Rates:** Peak (June–Sept/Dec–Mar) $42–$46 S; $54–$62 D. Extra person $10. Children under age 10 stay free. Lower rates off-season. Parking: Outdoor, free. AE, DISC, MC, V.

Tamarack Lodge

500 Sun Valley Rd, Ketchum, PO Box 2000, Sun Valley, 83353; tel 208/726-3344 or toll free 800/521-5379. ½ mi from downtown Ketchum, heading toward Sun Valley. Standard motel with some Tyrolean motifs. **Rooms:** 26 rms and stes. CI 2pm/CO 11am. Nonsmoking rms avail. Spacious and light, all have open-beamed ceilings. Most rooms have a view of Bald Mountain; others open onto a courtyard. **Amenities:** A/C, cable TV w/movies, refrig. All units w/terraces, some w/fireplaces. **Services:** KART free bus stops across the street. **Facilities:** Whirlpool. Private courtyard with off-street parking, enclosed pool, lawn, and a majestic blue spruce. **Rates:** Peak (July–Sept/Christmas–mid-Mar) $59–$92 S or D; $79–$134 ste. Extra person $10. Children under age 14 stay free. Lower rates off-season. Parking: Outdoor, free. AE, DC, MC, V.

Tyrolean Lodge Best Western

260 Cottonwood, PO Box 802, Ketchum, 83340 (River Run); tel 208/726-5336 or toll free 800/333-7912; fax 208/726-2081. ¾ mi from center of Ketchum. Cozy lobby with fireplace and many couches. **Rooms:** 57 rms and stes. CI 2pm/CO 11am. Nonsmoking rms avail. Some rooms have views. **Amenities:** Cable TV, refrig. No A/C. Some units w/minibars, some w/terraces, some w/whirlpools. **Services:** **Facilities:** Volleyball, sauna, whirlpool. Guests can walk to ski lift. **Rates (CP):** Peak (June 2–Oct 19; Dec 23–Jan 1; Feb 2–Apr 5) $55–$75 S; $65–$95 D; $115–$150 ste. Extra person $8. Children under age 11 stay free. Lower rates off-season. Parking: Outdoor, free. AE, DC, DISC, MC, V.

INN

Idaho Country Inn

134 Latigo Lane, Ketchum, PO Box 2355, Sun Valley, 83353; tel 208/726-1019; fax 208/726-5718. The inn sits on a hill with a superb view of Bald Mountain Ski Area. Very attractive, built of river rock and clapboard, and surrounded by lots of flowers in the summer. **Rooms:** 10 rms. CI 3pm/CO 11:30am. No smoking. Each of the large rooms has a name like Wagon Days, Bear Tracks, or Willow. Individually decorated with custom furnishings, and all have excellent views of the ski hill. Big bathrooms, too. **Amenities:** A/C, cable TV, refrig. All units w/terraces. **Services:** Social director, afternoon tea served. **Facilities:** Whirlpool, guest lounge w/TV. Large outdoor deck; an eight-person hot tub on the hill with mountain views; cozy guest lounge with fireplace; gift shop featuring handmade Idaho items. **Rates (BB):** Peak (June–Sept/Dec–Mar) $95–$185 S or D. Min stay peak. Lower rates off-season. Parking: Outdoor, free. AE, MC, V.

RESORTS

Elkhorn Resort and Golf Club

1 Elkhorn Rd, PO Box 6009, 83354 (Elkhorn); tel 208/622-4511 or toll free 800/355-4676; fax 208/622-3261. 3 mi from ID 75/Sun Valley Rd intersection. 15 acres. Lots to see and do at this resort located a half-mile from the Dollar Mountain ski area, a favorite of kids and beginners. In winter, Elkhorn has more sunlight than many other areas, where the sun sets earlier. The setup creates a bit of Tyrolean village atmosphere, built around a central plaza where free jazz concerts are held in the summer. **Rooms:** 132 rms, stes, and effic. Executive level. CI 4pm/CO noon. Nonsmoking rms avail. Rooms have western decor. **Amenities:** Cable TV w/movies, refrig, VCR. No A/C. Some units w/fireplaces, some w/whirlpools. **Services:** Car-rental desk, masseur, children's program, babysitting. Free buses run to Ketchum and Sun Valley. **Facilities:** 18 18 300 4 restaurants, 6 bars (2 w/entertainment), volleyball, lawn games, spa, sauna, steam rm, whirlpool, day-care ctr, washer/dryer. The Robert Trent Jones–designed 18-hole golf course is challenging and beautiful, ringed by hills where Native Americans gathered some 10,000 years ago. For kids, a fishing pond is stocked with trout. Trail riding is available in summer, and hiking trails are nearby. Most nights, the Atrium bar headlines live music. **Rates:** Peak (June–Oct/Christmas–April) $118–$128 S; $128 D; $225 ste; $225 effic. Extra person $10. Children under age 12 stay free. Min stay peak. Lower rates off-season. Parking: Outdoor, free. AE, DISC, MC, V.

Sun Valley Inn

1 Sun Valley Rd, PO Box 10, 83353; tel 208/622-4111 or toll free 800/786-8259; fax 208/622-2030. 1 mi E of ID 75 in Ketchum. 3,888 acres. The less expensive hotel of two comprising the Sun Valley Company Resort, this overlooks a series of duck ponds and tall evergreens. An outdoor patio is open in summer; in winter, sleigh rides leave from here. Large rooms for the money—good for families. **Rooms:** 113 rms and effic; 5 cottages/villas. CI 4pm/CO 11am. Nonsmoking rms avail. Some rooms have views. The double rooms are large. Condominiums, cottages, and three-bedroom apartments available. **Amenities:** Cable TV w/movies, voice mail. No A/C. Some units w/terraces, some w/fireplaces. **Services:** Twice-daily maid svce, car-rental desk, social director, masseur, children's program, babysitting. Free buses to ski mountain and Ketchum. **Facilities:** 18 18 800 1 restaurant, volleyball, games rm, lawn games, spa, beauty salon, day-care ctr, playground, washer/dryer. Lovely heated outdoor pool overlooking Bald Mountain Ski Area. Several convention rooms. Tennis courts and golf a short walk. Cafeteria off lobby serves breakfast, lunch, and dinner. Small adjacent Tyrolean-style mall has three restaurants, deli, ski shop, bookstore, gift shop, and drugstore. Sun Valley village has many ponds, trees, and a walkway; there is a movie theater in the village and kids can walk or ride on a bus to activities without parental supervision. **Rates:** Peak (Dec 15–Apr 18) $69–$99 S or D; $350–$370 effic; $550–$800 cottage/villa. Extra person $15. Lower rates off-season. Parking: Outdoor, free. AE, DISC, MC, V.

Sun Valley Lodge

1 Sun Valley Rd, PO Box 10, 83353; tel 208/622-4111 or toll free 800/786-8259; fax 208/622-2030. 1 mi E of ID 75 in Ketchum. 3,888 acres. Sun Valley is America's first-destination ski resort, and this elegant lodge was built in 1936. The resort is in its own separate world, one mile from Ketchum. Famous guests have included Ernest Hemingway and the Shah of Iran. The large lobby overlooks the ice rink. Good value for the money. **Rooms:** 148 rms and stes; 5 cottages/villas. CI 4pm/CO 11am. Nonsmoking rms avail. Small rooms with very high-quality furnishings. Some rooms have excellent views of the ice rink and ski hill. Condominiums, cottages, and three-bedroom apartments available. **Amenities:** Voice mail. No A/C. Some units w/terraces, some w/fireplaces. **Services:** Twice-daily maid svce, car-rental desk, social director, masseur, children's program, babysitting. Free buses to Ketchum. **Facilities:** 18 18 75 2 restaurants (*see* "Restaurants" below), 1 bar (w/entertainment), volleyball, games rm, lawn games, spa, sauna, beauty salon, day-care ctr, playground. Two excellent public areas include the Sun Room on the second floor complete with a piano, two fireplaces, and a view of the ice rink; the Hall of Photos in the main lobby features pictures of famous visitors from 1936 to the present. The property has a small Tyrolean-style mall with restaurants, ski shops, gift shops, bookstore, deli, drugstore, and post office. **Rates:** Peak (Dec 15–Apr 18) $69–$129 S or D; $249–$309 ste; $550–$800 cottage/villa. Extra person

$15. Lower rates off-season. Parking: Outdoor, free. Condos cost $110–$280 standard, $150–370 deluxe. AE, DISC, MC, V.

RESTAURANTS

★ Baldy Base Club
Warm Springs Village, Ketchum; tel 208/726-3838. At Bald Mountain's Warm Springs lifts. **American.** Eat while looking out at the Warm Springs side of Bald Mountain. Basic pasta, fish, soup, and salads. Great après-ski place in winter—a real hotspot. **FYI:** Reservations accepted. Children's menu. Dress code. No smoking. **Open:** Daily 11:30am–10pm. Closed May, Oct. **Prices:** Main courses $6–$18. AE, MC, V.

Evergreen Bistro
Rivers St and 1st Ave, Ketchum; tel 208/726-3888. 2 blocks from stoplight in Ketchum, near movie theater. **New American/Continental.** Located in a large house with several intimate rooms. The basically French-country menu is accented by more exotic items like Vietnamese spring rolls. Other choices include Molly's Caesar salad, with sun-dried tomatoes, and salmon with dill. **FYI:** Reservations recommended. Dress code. Beer and wine only. No smoking. **Open:** Daily 6–10pm. Closed May–June; Oct–Nov. **Prices:** Main courses $9–$25. AE, MC, V.

Felix's Restaurant
In Knob Hill Inn, 960 N Main, Ketchum; tel 208/726-1166. ½ mi from Ketchum Center, ID 75 N. **Continental.** Chef/owner Felix Gonzalez greets patrons and makes everyone feel at home at this intimate restaurant, known for its excellent food and attention to detail. Subtle decor lets the food shine. Notable dishes include rack of lamb, veal scaloppine, and paella. Excellent, extensive wine list. **FYI:** Reservations recommended. Beer and wine only. No smoking. **Open:** Daily 6–9:30pm. **Prices:** Main courses $16–$25; prix fixe $14–$20. AE, MC, V.

Gretchen's
In Sun Valley Lodge, 1 Sun Valley Rd; tel 208/622-4111. 1 mi E of Ketchum. **American.** A light, cheery room, overlooking the ice rink where Olympic skaters practice for the nightly Sun Valley Ice Show, where meals are presented at big tables surrounded by comfortable chairs. Adding to the European flavor of Sun Valley Resort, waitresses wear dirndls and aprons imported from Bavaria. The selection of good salads and sandwiches should please kids and adults alike. **FYI:** Reservations accepted. Children's menu. Dress code. **Open:** Daily 7am–9pm. **Prices:** Main courses $10–$18. AE, DC, DISC, MC, V. VP

★ The Kneadery
260 Leadville Ave, Ketchum; tel 208/726-9462. 1 block E of jct ID 75 and Sun Valley Rd. **American.** The fun atmosphere is congenial to children and, apparently, celebrities alike. Mismatched chairs, a wooden carousel horse, and oak tables create the setting for breakfast specials like trout and eggs, eggs Benedict, French country frittata, and homemade corned beef hash. Great club sandwich, variety of vegetarian sandwiches at lunch. Outdoor deck open in summer. **FYI:** Reservations not accepted. Children's menu. Dress code. Beer and wine only. No smoking. **Open:** Daily 7:30am–2pm. **Prices:** Lunch main courses $3–$7. AE, MC, V.

Louie's Pizza & Italian Restaurant
331 Leadville Ave N, Ketchum; tel 208/726-7775. 1 block from ID 75/Ketchum Main St. **Italian/Pizza.** Many of the booths in this busy restaurant (located in a former church) are large enough to accommodate entire families tanking up on pizza and pasta. **FYI:** Reservations not accepted. Children's menu. Beer and wine only. No smoking. **Open:** Daily 4–10:30pm. **Prices:** Main courses $9–$14. AE, MC, V.

Michel's Christiania Restaurant
303 Walnut Ave N, Ketchum; tel 208/726-3388. At Sun Valley Rd, ½ mi from Ketchum stop light. **Continental.** In the great upstairs dining area, try appetizers like Michel's escargots or homemade pheasant pâté. Fish and seafood entrees include salmon, mussels, rock shrimp, and squid; meat fanciers will like the venison chops or roast rack of lamb. The adjoining Olympic Bar has pictures of famous skiers. **FYI:** Reservations accepted. Jazz. Dress code. No smoking. **Open:** Daily 6–10pm. Closed May; Oct–Nov. **Prices:** Main courses $11–$24. AE, MC, V.

Perry's
131 W 4th St, Ketchum; tel 208/726-7703. 2 blocks from ID 75. **Deli.** Sandwiches like turkey-bacon-provolone and albacore tuna with water chestnuts are served here on freshly baked bread. Six to eight soups are made fresh every day and desserts are homemade. **FYI:** Reservations not accepted. Children's menu. Beer and wine only. No smoking. **Open:** Daily 7am–5:30pm. **Prices:** Lunch main courses $3–$7. MC, V.

Peter's
180 6th St, Ketchum; tel 208/726-9515. 3 blocks NW of ID 75. **International.** The art on the walls and the carved armoires give a Bavarian feeling to Peter Weisz's restaurant. The owner/chef brings Austrian and German influences to his menu with choices like Wiener schnitzel and spaetzle, but also look for alternative selections such as Chinese chicken salad—the house favorite. **FYI:** Reservations recommended. Dress code. Beer and wine only. No smoking. **Open:** Peak (June 20–Sept 30/Dec 20–Apr 5) lunch daily 11:30am–2:30pm; dinner daily 6–10pm. Closed Apr 15–30. **Prices:** Main courses $12–$26. AE, DISC, MC, V.

★ Pioneer Saloon
308 Main St N, Ketchum (Downtown); tel 208/726-3139. **Regional American.** Hearty Idaho food—prime rib, huge baked potatoes, and rainbow trout. The rustic lodge decor has mounted animals (including "Fred," a 43-point buck), plus pictures of miners, skiers, and historic Ketchum. Chips and salsa served with your drinks in the bar. **FYI:** Reserva-

tions not accepted. Dress code. No smoking. **Open:** Peak (July–Sept/Christmas–Apr) daily 5:30–10:30pm. **Prices:** Main courses $6–$21. AE, MC, V.

Smoky Mountain Pizza
200 Sun Valley Rd, Ketchum; tel 208/622-5625. At ID 75; W of Main St light. **Italian/Pizza.** This boisterous, friendly place is a favorite with kids, who can enjoy video games and a pool table in the separate kids' room. The red-and-white checked table cloths offer an appropriate setting for pizzas made with any of 15 various toppings. Crust options include honey-wheat, deep dish, and extra thin. **FYI:** Reservations not accepted. Children's menu. Dress code. Beer and wine only. No smoking. Additional location: 34 E State St, Eagle (tel 939-0212). **Open:** Peak (Christmas–Apr; July–Sept) daily 11:30am–10pm. **Prices:** Main courses $4–$9. DISC, MC, V.

Sun Valley Lodge Dining Room
In Sun Valley Lodge, 1 Sun Valley Rd; tel 208/622-4111. 1 mi E of Ketchum. **Continental.** This elegant dining room features a piano player and views of the ski hill. Starters include venison ravioli, baked oysters, and various salads. Entree picks on the ever-changing menu might be sesame-marinated salmon, or lamb chops with sun-dried tomatoes and port-wine sauce. Buffet-style Sunday brunch features individually made crepes and a large assortment of seafood, meat, salad, and dessert choices. Nice wine list. **FYI:** Reservations accepted. Jazz/piano. Dress code. **Open:** Dinner Tues–Sat 6–9:30pm; brunch Sun 9am–2pm. **Prices:** Main courses $18–$28. AE, DISC, MC, V. VP

Warm Springs Ski Lodge
At the base of Warm Springs ski lift, Ketchum; tel 208/622-2306. **American.** Styled after the grand National Park hotels, this elegant mountain ski lodge boasts upholstered dining chairs, three fireplaces, and marble bathrooms with gold-plated fixtures. The food is also several cuts above the usual ski fare, with choices such as fettuccine, baked potatoes with various toppings, and gourmet pizzas. Cappuccino, caffe lattes, and other warm drinks available. **FYI:** Reservations not accepted. Rock. No smoking. **Open:** Daily 7:30am–5pm. Closed May–Nov. **Prices:** Lunch main courses $6–$12. MC, V.

ATTRACTIONS

Soldier Mountain
ID 20, Fairfield; tel 208/764-2300 or 764-2260. 60 mi SW of Sun Valley and 12 mi N of Fairfield along ID 20. The mountain has the reputation of being both affordable and having good powder runs. Vertical drop of 1,400 feet, 36 trails, and three lifts. **Open:** Nov 25–Apr, Thurs–Sun. **$$$$**

Sun Valley Resort
Tel 208/622-4111 or toll free 800/635-8261. A massive 3,400-foot vertical drop, 16 lifts, and more than 70 runs are just a few of the reasons that this is one of the premier skiing facilities in the country. Another factor in the resort's popularity is that the Bald Mountain and Dollar Mountain runs can handle more than 26,000 skiers an hour. Since skiers can spread out over 2,000 acres, and some runs are up to 3 miles long, there are rarely lift lines and slopes don't seem crowded even at capacity. **Open:** Nov 25–May 1. **$$$$**

Wood River Trails
ID 75, between Ketchum and Bellevue, Hailey; tel 208/788-2117. This 10-mile recreational trail system links the communities of the Wood River Valley, including Bellevue, Hailey, Bald Mountain, and Ketchum. A paved road, dedicated to walkers, bicyclists, and in-line skaters, is paralleled by an equestrian trail. In winter, the trail is dominated by cross-country skiers. There are many public access points to Big Wood River for those who want to fish. **Open:** Daily 24 hours. **Free**

Twin Falls

A city of 30,000 in southern Idaho, this is where daredevil Evel Knievel attempted his infamous motorcycle jump across the Snake River Canyon. Nearby Shoshone Falls is known as the Niagara of the West. **Information:** Twin Falls Area Chamber of Commerce, 858 Blue Lakes Blvd N, Twin Falls, 83301 (tel 208/733-3974).

MOTELS

AmeriTel Inn
1377 Blue Lakes Blvd, 83301; tel 208/736-8000 or toll free 800/822-8946; fax 208/734-7777. 4 mi S of exit 173 off I-84. Pleasant, newer motel with a largely corporate clientele. **Rooms:** 118 rms, stes, and effic. CI 2pm/CO 11am. Nonsmoking rms avail. Rooms are well designed for business travelers. **Amenities:** A/C, cable TV, dataport. Some units w/whirlpools. Some rooms have three phones, most have recliners; microwaves, and small refrigerators available. Special "spa" suites. **Services:** Free morning newspaper; expanded continental breakfast. Fax and copy service. Twice-daily maid service and express checkout available on request. **Facilities:** 75 Whirlpool, washer/dryer. Indoor pool open 24 hours. **Rates (CP):** Peak (May–Sept) $70 S; $75 D; $110 ste; $90 effic. Extra person $5. Children under age 12 stay free. Lower rates off-season. Parking: Outdoor, free. Honeymoon packages avail. AE, CB, DC, DISC, MC, V.

Best Western Apollo
296 Addison Ave W, 83301; tel 208/733-2010 or toll free 800/528-1234; fax 208/734-0748. 4 miles E of jct US 93/30. The only major chain motel along Addison Ave W; fine for overnight stay. **Rooms:** 50 rms and stes. CI 3pm/CO noon. Nonsmoking rms avail. **Amenities:** A/C, cable TV. **Services:** Coffee and doughnuts in lobby. Small pets OK at manager's discretion. **Facilities:** Whirlpool.

Rates: Peak (May 14–Oct 16) $43–$48 S; $52 D; $68–$89 ste. Children under age 12 stay free. Lower rates off-season. Parking: Outdoor, free. AE, CB, DC, DISC, EC, ER, JCB, MC, V.

Best Western Canyon Springs Inn

1357 Blue Lakes Blvd, 83301; tel 208/734-5000 or toll free 800/727-5003; fax 208/734-5000 ext 350. Exit 173 off I-84; 4 mi S. Busy motel mainly attracting a business crowd. Located on Twin Falls' commercial strip. **Rooms:** 112 rms. Executive level. CI 2pm/CO 1pm. Nonsmoking rms avail. **Amenities:** A/C, cable TV w/movies, dataport. Some units w/terraces. **Services:** VCRs available. Complimentary cocktails. **Facilities:** 2 restaurants, 1 bar (w/entertainment), games rm. **Rates:** $69–$75 S; $75–$81 D. Extra person $6. Children under age 12 stay free. Parking: Outdoor, free. Wedding and group rates avail. AE, DISC, MC, V.

Weston Plaza

1350 Blue Lakes Blvd N, 83301; tel 208/733-0650 or toll free 800/333-7829; fax 208/733-8272. 4 mi S of exit 173 on I-84. Rather spartan rooms with few frills. **Rooms:** 200 rms, stes, and effic. CI 2pm/CO noon. Nonsmoking rms avail. **Amenities:** A/C, cable TV. Some rooms have desks and alarm/clock radios. **Services:** Fax and copy service available. **Facilities:** 1 restaurant, 1 bar (w/entertainment), sauna, whirlpool, washer/dryer. **Rates:** $46–$52 S; $50–$56 D; $85 ste; $85 effic. Extra person $4. Children under age 18 stay free. Parking: Outdoor, free. Special winter rates, honeymoon package avail. AE, CB, DC, DISC, MC, V.

RESTAURANTS

★ Buffalo Cafe

218 4th Ave W; tel 208/734-0271. 1½ blocks W of Shoshone Street, on the edge of downtown. **Regional American/Cafe.** This out-of-the-way western cafe offers good, basic food (and plenty of it), and a breakfast menu considered the best around. Favorites include "Buffalo Chips" (fried spuds layered with veggies, bacon, sour cream, cheese, and two eggs) and a 9-oz hamburger. **FYI:** Reservations not accepted. Children's menu. No liquor license. No smoking. **Open:** Daily 6am–2pm. **Prices:** Lunch main courses $4–$8. MC, V.

Grandma's Deli

109 N Greenwood (ID 75), Shoshone; tel 208/886-2105. **Deli.** The simple menu includes sandwiches, soups, salads, and cookies. A few tables are available for eating in. A good spot to grab a lunch-to-go en route to Craters of the Moon National Monument, about an hour's drive to the northeast (via US 93). **FYI:** Reservations not accepted. No liquor license. No smoking. **Open:** Tues–Sat 11am–6pm. **Prices:** Lunch main courses $2–$4. MC, V.

Manhattan Cafe

133 S Rail St W, Shoshone; tel 208/886-2142. S side of the railroad tracks, W of US 93. **American.** A quintessential small town restaurant, where tourists rub elbows with farmers, ranchers, and even the mayor. Specialties include chicken-fried steak and hand-dipped milk shakes. A restaurant has been operating on this site since the 1890s. **FYI:** Reservations not accepted. Children's menu. No liquor license. **Open:** Peak (Apr–Sept) daily 6am–10pm. **Prices:** Main courses $6–$10. AE, CB, DC, DISC, MC, V.

Rock Creek

200 Addison Ave W; tel 208/734-4154. West of the city center. **Seafood/Steak.** In a town full of chain restaurants, this locally owned place stands out. Specialties are prime rib and fresh seafood, and there is a large salad bar. The sourdough bread is flown in from California. A lower-priced "cafe menu" is also available in the dining room, bar, and on the small outdoor deck. **FYI:** Reservations not accepted. **Open:** Mon–Sat 5:30–11pm, Sun 5–10pm. **Prices:** Main courses $8–$26. AE, MC, V.

ATTRACTIONS

Shoshone Ice Cave

1561 ID 75 N, Shoshone; tel 208/886-2058. 45 mi W of Twin Falls. Unique three-block-long cave formed by the lava from a now-extinct volcano. The cave acts as a natural refrigerator, and is home to an underground glacier that is 1,000 feet long and 8–30 feet deep, depending upon the season. (Cave temperature hovers around 30°F year-round.) Guided tours last approximately 40 minutes and cover 3½ miles. Free museum containing Native American artifacts and cave minerals; picnic area. **Open:** May–Sept, daily 8am–8pm. **$$**

Twin Falls County Museum

21337 US 30, Kimberly; tel 208/423-5907. 5 mi W of Twin Falls. Displays of interest in this historical museum feature pioneer fashions, 19th-century photographs, antique dolls, and agricultural equipment. Re-created interiors give visitors a glimpse at a typical early 20th century pioneer house, a barbershop, and a grocery store. **Open:** Tues–Sat noon–5pm. Closed Sept 1–May 15. **Free**

Shoshone Falls

Falls Ave; tel 208/733-3974. Whitewater here plunges more than 212 feet, bathing the area in a cool rainbow mist. Shoshone actually plummets 52 feet farther than Niagara Falls, earning the falls the nickname "Niagara of the West". For the best view of the falls try to visit in early spring when water flow is at its peak. **Open:** Daily dawn–dusk. **$**

Wallace

Billing itself as the silver capital of the world, Wallace has surrendered more than one billion ounces of silver in more than a century of mining. Tourists come for the Sierra Silver mine tour and the Wallace District Mining Museum. **Information:** Wallace Chamber of Commerce, PO Box 1167, Wallace, 83873 (tel 208/753-7151).

MOTEL

The Wallace Inn

100 Front St, 83873; tel 208/752-1252 or toll free 800/N-IDA-FUN; fax 208/753-0981. 1 block S of I-90 at exit 61. Located in a historic mining town near Silver Mountain Ski Resort and Lookout Ski Area. The area is a popular snowmobiling destination; you can drive your machine from the motel parking lot to the trail head. Silver mine tours and mining museum two blocks away. **Rooms:** 63 rms and stes. Executive level. CI 3pm/CO noon. Nonsmoking rms avail. Flower decor in rooms. **Amenities:** A/C, TV, voice mail. 1 unit w/whirlpool. Suites have two phones, refrigerators, wet bars, vanities, and hair dryers. **Services:** VCRs and movies for rent. Complimentary morning coffee and newspaper in lobby. **Facilities:** 100 1 restaurant, 1 bar, sauna, steam rm, whirlpool. **Rates:** $69 S; $79 D; $200 ste. Extra person $8. Children under age 12 stay free. Parking: Outdoor, free. Senior, commercial, and government rates; ski, snowmobile, golf, and Silver Mountain concert packages avail. AE, CB, DC, DISC, MC, V.

RESTAURANT

Jameson Dining Room and Saloon

In the Jameson Building, 304 6th St (downtown); tel 208/556-1554. Across from train depot. **Eclectic.** The Jameson building started out in 1889 as a steak house and billiard hall, and the restaurant tradition continues today. Menu offerings include excellent steaks as well as pasta, chicken, and seafood dishes. An all-you-can-eat barbecue beef-rib dinner on Saturday nights is a local crowd pleaser. The third floor of the building serves as a B&B and patrons are welcome to take a look around the historic building. **FYI:** Reservations accepted. Children's menu. **Open:** Tues–Sat 11:30am–8pm. Closed mid-Nov–mid-Apr. **Prices:** Main courses $7–$14. AE, DC, DISC, MC, V.

ATTRACTIONS

Wallace District Mining Museum

509 Bank St; tel 208/556-1592. Over one billion ounces of silver have been taken from this region's silver mines in the last century. This fascinating museum captures the tremendous impact of mining on the local economy and culture, with artifacts depicting the both the hardships and the riches involved. Photographs and paintings illustrate early mines, while the 20-minute film "North Idaho's Silver Legacy" depicts modern mining techniques. The museum lobby houses one of the world's largest silver dollars, at 3 feet in diameter and weighing 150 pounds. **Open:** June–Aug, daily 8am–8pm; May and Sept, daily 8am–6pm; Oct–Apr, Mon–Fri 9am–4pm, Sat 10am–4pm. Closed some hols. **$**

Sierra Silver Mine Tour

420 Fifth St; tel 208/752-5151. Visitors ride a trolley from the visitors center to the mine entrance, where they are issued hard hats and given a brief overview of mining techniques. Hourly tours of the now-depleted mine are given by actual miners. Children under age 4 are not allowed on the tour. **Open:** Mid-May–June, daily 9am–4pm; July–Aug, daily 9am–6pm; Sept–mid-Oct, daily 9am–4pm. **$$$**

IOWA

America's Heartland

STATE STATS

CAPITAL
Des Moines

AREA
56,276 square miles

BORDERS
Minnesota, South Dakota, Nebraska, Missouri, Wisconsin, and Illinois

POPULATION
2,814,064 (1993)

ENTERED UNION
December 28, 1846 (29th state)

NICKNAME
Hawkeye State

STATE FLOWER
Wild rose

STATE BIRD
Eastern goldfinch

FAMOUS NATIVES
William "Buffalo Bill" Cody, Herbert Hoover, Grant Wood, John Wayne, George Gallup

Iowa is a place of quiet and gentle beauty. Because it is the big buckle in America's corn belt, the state is often though of as a flat stretch of land covered with neat rows of corn. Visitors soon learn, however, that much of Iowa consists of gently rolling countryside. Row after row of gold and green stalks of corn; a wide open, brilliant blue sky; herds of sheep grazing on deep green grass sprinkled with red barns and white farm houses—these are the sights of Iowa. In Iowa you can watch eagles soar over steep bluffs, swim in silver lakes, visit butterfly preserves, motor down miles of rivers, tiptoe through the Pella tulip gardens, and hike trails through woodlands and verdant prairie. You will discover covered bridges, brick streets in old villages, Mormon frontier towns, and some of the finest Victorian-era homes in the country.

Of course it was the rich black earth that drew smart farmers to settle here. Iowa evolved into a lot of small towns surrounded by farmland. If the early pioneers had known about "wind-chill factor," it's doubtful many of them would have stayed. Winters can be brutally cold, and hearing that it's actually -47°F "considering the wind-chill" can be dispiriting. On the other hand, the highest recorded temperature in Iowa was 118°F. To say that Iowa's temperatures run to extremes is an understatement.

The state's major cities—Des Moines, Davenport, Cedar Rapids, and the college towns of Ames and Iowa City—offer a blend of small-town intimacy and big-city cultural opportunities. Iowa also has two large universities and several small, fine colleges. Iowa City (home to the University of Iowa) is filled with writers, philosophers, linguists, musicians, filmmakers, and students of medicine from all over the world. Ames is home of the sprawling Iowa State University, a beautiful campus with its own small lake and tree-lined walks.

Iowans are more amused or turned off than impressed by "sophisticates" who expect to find them a dull people. Pretty much everything that happens here—that is, everyone's fortunes from day to day—

Frommer's #1

depends upon the weather and the land. Those two basic, real-life factors keep most minds quite literally down to earth. If what you eat, drive, wear, and do depends upon the fortunate coming together of sun, rainfall, seeds, and soil, then you live in a very elemental world. People in Iowa accept the whims and graces of nature, and they are proud of that way of life. This close association with the earth gives the people of Iowa a frank, friendly, open style with little pretension. The gentleness of the natives, and the surprising beauty of the landscape, make Iowa both a good place to live and a good place to visit.

A Brief History

An Iowa Lesson in Humility In the 1880s, group of rich Englishmen settled into western Iowa. They came out of a sort of romantic colonialism—they would help settle the Wild West. Educated at Oxford and Cambridge, they decided to try their hands at being gentlemen farmers, having read about the challenge and adventure of the region and believing they could become even richer. They built grand houses, held foxhunts and horse races, played polo, outfitted themselves in the latest fashions from London and Paris, and held regular balls. For a time, English-speaking butlers and nannies abounded.

But things fell apart: The Scandinavian, German, Czech, and Dutch pioneers didn't take to the English class system and neither, after a while, did the butlers and nannies. The nannies received proposals from men with their own farms, and the butlers decided to take on the West themselves, either as farmers or businessmen. Labor was hard to come by, since everyone wanted to have his own farm—not work for landed gentry—so the Englishmen found themselves doing their own work. Those who could take the rigorous field work, not to mention doing their own laundry and cooking, eventually became part of the fabric of American life. Those who couldn't went back to England.

The Mound Builders Long before the Englishmen arrived, Iowa was the home of the "mound builders." Archeologists believe that these people were a branch in the family of Asians who crossed the Bering Sea and who, over many thousands of nomadic years of hunting and gathering, settled into various regions of the North American continent and evolved into distinct, linguistic tribes. In the region now known as Iowa, their cultures broke into groups numbering 17 tribes, including the Iowa, the Fox, the Potawatomi, the Sauk, and Winnebago. Various scholars have tried to reconstruct the movements of these peoples, but details are sketchy. What is known is that the Sauk and Fox tribes of the Algonquin migrated into the Iowa from neighboring Wisconsin. Others, such as the Winnebago, were moved into the area by the federal government. But it was the often warlike Sioux, from what is now Missouri and points south, who dominated the area.

Enter the French French explorers Jacques Marquette and Louis Joliet entered the area in 1673, spoke with the native people, and recorded their findings. They were followed by other French explorers, traders, and settlers. The lands bounded by the Mississippi and Des Moines Rivers proved especially profitable for fur traders, and many of the trading posts they established evolved into important Iowa towns and cities.

By the late 18th century, French-Canadian Julien Dubuque and his men were busy mining lead along the Catfish Creek in the eastern part of the state on land leased from Native Americans. (The city of Dubuque was to arise from these early mining camps.)

Birth of a State The gunshot that could be produced from Iowa lead was very much in demand as pioneers and homesteaders expanded westward into tribal territory, particularly after the acquisition of Iowa as part of the Louisiana Purchase of 1803. The Black Hawk War that erupted in 1832 saw the Sauk and Fox fighting to retake their former lands in Illinois along the Mississippi River. Defeated by the US Army, the tribes were compelled to cede most of their land on the Iowa side of the river; before long, all native lands had been ceded to the United States.

Meanwhile, the continuing influx of settlers were changing the surrounding landscape entirely and permanently from prairie to farmland. In 1838, Iowa was organized as a territory and Iowa City became the capital. By 1846, Iowa had been granted statehood and Des Moines, near the state's center, was named its capital city.

The advent of railroad construction brought great prosperity to the state; in 1855, the first line was laid down between Davenport and Muscatine along Iowas's eastern border. By the time of the Civil War, most Iowans were sympathetic to the antislavery cause, and many fought for the Union. The Underground Railroad, which aided fugitive slaves in their flight to freedom, had stations in Iowa, and abolitionist John Brown was headquartered there for a while.

Farmers prospered during the immediate aftermath of the Civil War but fell upon hard times during the currency and financial crises that plagued the nation in the 1870s. Many farmers supported populist reform movements that sought, among other things, to regulate the steep railroad and grain-storage rates that were the bane of small farmers. Economic conditions did improve by the end of the century, though, and large-scale farming and rapid mechanization ushered in a new era of high productivity and relative prosperity.

Religious Refuge Iowa has been the site of several religion-based communities, notably the Mormons and the Amana Colonies . In the 1880s, the Reorganized Church of Jesus Christ of Latter-Day Saints, under the leadership of Joseph Smith III, established its headquarters in Lamoni. The headquarters later moved to Missouri, and the Smith family's former home is now a museum. The Amana Colonies, a group of seven small villages in east-central Iowa, were founded in 1855 by German Pietists who had fled religious persecution in Germany. Members strived for a communal way of living. Although communal ownership is a thing of the past, museums and shops provide a window into the Amana way of life—showing both those aspects that were left behind and those, such as the making of fine woolens, that still endure.

Iowa Today Modern-day Iowa remains largely an agricultural state. It is a leader in the production of corn, hogs, pigs, and cattle, and raises large crops of soybeans, oats, and hay. Industries such as home appliance and cereal manufacturing as well as tourism add their share to the state's coffers. The constant fluctuation in farm prices in addition to the steady nationwide decline in manufacturing over the past two decades has rendered Iowa susceptible to economic downturns. But the state has managed to partially rebound from the particularly hard times brought on by the recessions of the 1980s.

DRIVING DISTANCES

Des Moines

120 mi E of Omaha, NE
170 mi N of Kansas City, MO
197 mi SW of Dubuque
258 mi S of Minneapolis, MN
350 mi W of Chicago
350 mi NE of Tulsa, OK

Dubuque

86 mi E of Waterloo
90 mi SW of Madison, WI
175 mi NW of Chicago
225 mi E of Sioux City
278 mi SE of Minneapolis, MN
345 mi NE of Omaha, NE

Sioux City

95 mi N of Omaha, NE
100 mi SE of Sioux Falls, SD
213 mi NW of Des Moines
225 mi NW of Kansas City, MO
297 mi NW of Cedar Rapids
400 mi NW of Branson, MO

A Closer Look

GEOGRAPHY

Iowa's gradually changing topography becomes most visible as one drives across the state. The differences in the three great regions of Iowa—north, northeast, and south—are related to the movements of glaciers. Once completely covered with forests and grasslands, Iowa changed with the coming of these giant ice blankets. They covered most of the forests and, as they melted, carved out rivers and streams, bluffs and valleys, and ground some of the highest points down to flatness. Between these gargantuan land shifts, *loess* formed and blew across the land. (Loess is the common term for the mix of silt, sand, and clay that forms the richness of the earth from which plants so easily grow in this part of the country.) Less than 5% of the forest that stood after the glaciers remains today. While the state was once 85% virgin prairie, now only 10% of it has not been cultivated and the marshes in the northeast section have all but vanished.

Iowa is located between two of America's mightiest rivers. The **Mississippi** carves the eastern border of Iowa and it is flanked by steep bluffs, green valleys, and rolling hills; the **Missouri** forms the western border with Nebraska. Meandering at an angle across central Iowa is the Des Moines River. Corn is the stable crop for the north-central plains region because the land is perfect for it, a rich black loam that lays mostly flat and is easily tilled. Dairy farmers prefer the so-called northeast dairy area because the rising bluffs, woodlands, and valleys make it better pasture area than tilling land. Of course, farming is prevalent all over the state because of that abundant rich, black soil. More cattle and sheep tend to be raised in the hilly southern pasture region where they graze on land that gently swells and falls.

CLIMATE

Although seasonal temperatures are extreme, Iowans are used to them; if you hear them complaining, it's probably only to make conversation. Summer—even with the heat and humidity, sudden thunderstorms, and tornado sightings—is still the favorite season of most Iowa residents, followed by a deep appreciation for the lingering Indian summers that sometimes stretch well into November. Winters can be hard, with winds that blow painfully cold and snow that piles up overnight. Spring is usually very short; as they say in Iowa, if you take a nap on an April afternoon, you might miss it altogether.

AVG MONTHLY TEMPS (°F) & RAINFALL (IN)

	Davenport	Des Moines
Jan	19/1.0	21/1.4
Feb	25/1.1	26/1.1
Mar	37/2.3	36/2.4
Apr	51/3.4	51/3.5
May	62/3.7	62/3.8
June	72/4.7	72/3.8
July	77/3.8	76/4.0
Aug	74/4.2	74/4.3
Sept	65/3.5	66/3.3
Oct	54/2.6	55/2.5
Nov	39/1.8	40/1.9
Dec	24/1.3	27/1.7

WHAT TO PACK

If you come to Iowa in the spring, be sure to bring a raincoat and a sweater or jacket for cool days. However, keep in mind that a spring day can be extremely warm so pack summer clothes too. Once it's June, forget the sweater, but a long-sleeved shirt will keep off the chill—and mosquitoes—of a summer evening. In the fall the brilliant Indian summer days can be bright but are not really all that warm, especially when you get into October. A light jacket is usually necessary for day, and a sweater worn under the same jacket in the evenings. Wintertime means bundling up, and the best advice is to wear layers so you can find your own comfort level inside well-heated houses and buildings. You will most definitely need boots, a warm coat, a scarf, and mittens or gloves.

TOURIST INFORMATION

The **Iowa Division of Tourism** (tel 515/242-4705 or toll free 800/345-IOWA) will provide you with maps and a packet of information on Iowa events, attractions, and festivals. Each region of the state also has a tourism office. The Western Iowa regional office is in Red Oak (tel 712/623-4232), the Central Iowa office is in Webster City (tel 515/832-4808), and the Eastern Iowa office is in Vinton (tel 319/472-5135).

Iowa also has several **Welcome Centers** located in each region. Welcome Centers supply visitors with maps, directions, and travel guides as well as regional event calendars. Western Iowa Welcome Centers are located in Elk Horn, Emmetsburg, Missouri Valley, Sergeant Bluff, Sioux City, and Underwood. Central Iowa centers are in Bloomfield, Clear Lake, Davis City, Des Moines, Dows, and Lamoni. In eastern Iowa you will find centers in Amana Colonies, Burlington, Dubuque, Elkader, Le Claire, Victor, and Wilton. Welcome Centers in each city are listed in the phone book.

DRIVING RULES AND REGULATIONS

Drivers must be 16 if they have successfully completed an approved course in driver education; 18 otherwise. The speed limit on rural interstates is 65 mph, and on the urban interstates it is 55 mph. Aircraft and radar are used to enforce speed limits. Driver and front seat passengers are required to wear seat belts, and child restraints are mandatory for children under three. A right turn on a red light is permitted after a complete stop, unless a sign prohibits it. Motorcyclists are not required to wear a helmet but they must use a headlight during daylight hours. It is illegal in Iowa to have an open container of alcohol in the car, and refusal to take a chemical blood alcohol test is grounds for revoking a driver's license.

RENTING A CAR

The following car rental agencies have offices in Iowa. Their age requirements begin at 19 and vary for each company. Be sure to ask your insurance agent if your personal car insurance covers rental cars. If not, the rental car agency will sell you insurance.

- **Alamo** (Des Moines only; tel toll free 800/327-9633)
- **Avis** (tel 800/331-1212)
- **Budget** (tel 800/527-0700)
- **Hertz** (tel 800/654-3131)
- **National** (tel 800/328-4567)

ESSENTIALS

Area Codes: The state has three area codes. In the east, it is **319;** in central Iowa, **515;** and in the west, **712.**

Emergencies: If you need assistance on the road, call the Iowa State Patrol (tel toll free 800/525-5555).

Gambling: Gambling on any of the Iowa touring riverboats is restricted to those who are over 21.

Liquor Laws: People who purchase or consume alcohol in the state of Iowa must be over 21 years of age.

Road Info: Call 515/288-1047 for winter road conditions (November 15–April 15) and detour information (April 16–November 14).

Smoking: Smoking is restricted to smoking areas in most restaurants, and some restaurants are entirely nonsmoking. No smoking is allowed in state office buildings or in Des Moines International Airport.

Taxes: Iowa has a statewide sales tax of 5%; locally, an optional 1% may be added.

Time Zone: Iowa is in the Central time zone.

Best of the State

WHAT TO SEE AND DO

Below is a general overview of some of the top sights and attractions in Iowa. To find out more detailed information, look under "Attractions" under individual cities in the listings portion of this book.

Parks & Recreation Areas Thomas H MacBride was an Iowa conservationist who envisioned and helped to create a statewide system of "rural parks": beautiful, quiet places for Iowans and their visitors to enjoy clear lakes and streams, the prairie, and woodlands. The first state park, **Backbone,** was formed in 1920 and others soon followed—Dolliver, Lacey-Keosauqua, and Maquoketa Caves. Today, Iowa has 76 state parks, with a total of over 5,000 campsites. Recreation areas—which offer state park facilities and activities, as well as fishing—entered the park system in the 1960s. **Brushy Creek Recreation Area** is Iowa's largest, consisting of 6,000 acres of prairies, streams, woodlands, and valleys.

Burial and ceremonial mounds, some in the shape of animals or birds, are preserved in the **Effigy Mounds National Monument**. The mounds, which date from 500 BC to AD1300, are located on the Mississippi River Bluffs just north of Marquette. A museum on the site tells the history of the mounds and the surrounding prairies and wetlands, and there are 11 miles of hiking trails.

Historic Sites & Special Places John Wayne was born in Winterset, and in the Madison County countryside are six historic **covered bridges** listed in the National Register of Historic Places. The romance of a movie star and of the very romantic book and movie, *The Bridges of Madison County,* have made this area quite popular. Just an hour and a half away, a different kind of romance blooms with the tulips at the **Pella Historical Village,** a collection of 21 buildings (including an opera house, bakeries, and markets) all nestled in a courtyard and connected by red brick walkways. Fine Dutch laces, treats, music, dancing, and food are all available in these quaint buildings.

West Branch is the site of the **Herbert Hoover Presidential Library and Museum,** a 186-acre site with a working blacksmith shop. The land also contains Hoover's gravesite and the cabin in which he was born. The town of Lewis in eastern Iowa is the site of the **Hitchcock House,** an 1856 home built by Rev George Hitchcock and used as part of the Underground Railroad. In its basement is a hiding place for men and women fleeing Southern slavery.

In Council Bluffs, the wealthy Civil War Gen Grenville M Dodge constructed a lavish 14-room home for his family. The **Historic General Dodge House,** which is on the National Register of Historic Places, hosts a Victorian-style Christmas celebration each year, complete with special trees, candles and decorations in every room. A more grim reminder of Victorian times can be seen in the **Historic Squirrel Cage Jail,** a three-story brick structure with a rotating "cage" so jailers could view all cells from a single vantage point.

Museums For historic riverboat cruises, cable car rides, and strolls through antique shops, old churches, and the waterfront district, Dubuque is the place. The galleries and exhibits of the **Mississippi River Museum** in Dubuque tell the tales of the gamblers, explorers, and pilots who were part of the great river's history. One of the chief attractions is the ***William M Black,*** a 277-foot side-wheeler (and a

National Historic Landmark) that is docked outside the museum complex.

You can get a complete sense of rural life in 19th-century Iowa by strolling through the **Humboldt County Historical Museum** in Dakota City. **Mill Farm** was built in 1878 and includes a schoolhouse, restored farm buildings, blacksmith and tinsmith shops, a jail, doctor's office, post office, and Native American artifacts. Another view of Victorian life can be seen in Cedar Falls at the **Victorian Home & Carriage House Museum,** where gowned mannequins display the elegance of the wealthier Iowans' Victorian lifestyles. The **Historic and Coal Mining Museum** has exhibits depicting a pioneer farm and village and artifacts from the Mormon Trail of 1846, as well as a coal mine replica on the lower level showing mining tools and equipment. The **Confederate Air Force Museum** in Council Bluffs displays World War II airplanes.

Family Favorites Catch a ride on the **Boone & Scenic Valley Railroad,** an excursion train that travels 12 miles into the beautiful Des Moines River Valley and over two great bridges. The train is based in the town of Boone in Boone County, long the railroad hub of Iowa. Displays of historic railroad items and equipment should please train enthusiasts visiting the area.

In 1876, Laura Ingalls Wilder, author of the tremendously popular *Little House* series of children's books, moved to a large house in the town of Burr Oak. The building, now a National Historic Landmark, has since been turned into the **Laura Ingalls Wilder Museum.** The **Belinda Toy Museum** in Knoxville was originally built in 1846 as a church; today it holds collections of airplanes, dolls, trains, and tin and cast-iron toys. **Living History Farms,** in Urbandale, is a 600-acre agricultural museum with a 1700 Ioway Indian village, a pioneer farm, a horse farm, and lots of family activities, including a sports weekend where merchants suit up for an authentic 1870 baseball game, traditional music, and old-time crafts. **Adventureland** in Altoona boasts four huge roller coasters and over 100 other rides.

The **National Balloon Museum,** in Indianola, houses a collection of ballooning artifacts that show the history of hot-air ballooning. (Ballooning is very popular in Iowa, and Indianola hosts the annual National Balloon Classic.) Families can also tour the seven authentic German villages of the **Amana Colonies** to see working artisans, museums, and specialty shops selling everything from antique furniture and handmade quilts to oven-fresh breads and local fruit wines. Enjoy great old-world cooking and tour Iowa's only woolen mill.

Architecture Iowa's architectural highlight is **Cedar Rock,** a Frank Lloyd Wright–designed residence on the Wapsipinicon River near Quasqueton. Wright designed the house and its interior furnishings in the late 1940s, in his "Usonoian" style. Both the house and grounds were donated to the state in 1981 by the original owners. All are now open for public tours May through October.

One of only 33 basilicas in the United States, the **Basilica of St Francis Xavier** in Dyersville is also one of the few examples of medieval Gothic architecture in the country. Its spires rise 212 feet.

EVENTS AND FESTIVALS

- **Lake Red Rock Eagle Days.** Live eagles and other birds of prey in the wild at winter roosting sites. Late February or early March. Call 515/828-7522.
- **Morningside Days,** Sioux City. Features a parade, craft fair, and carnival. Late May. Call 800/593-2228.
- **Folk Trade Weekend,** Urbandale. Artists from all over the Midwest come to Living History Farms to teach doll making, spinning, and woodcarving. June. Call 515/278-5286 or 515/278-2400.
- **Bluegrass Music Festival,** Amana Colonies. June. Call 800/245-5465.
- **Summerfest,** Eagle Grove. Crafts, quilts, stage entertainment, street dances and games for kids. Third or fourth weekend in June. Call 515/448-4821.
- **Annual Folk Festival,** Hinton. Music, arts and crafts, and children's activities including nature walks and wagon rides. Last weekend in June. Call 712/947-4270.
- **Western Days.** Includes a rodeo, parade, craft fair, draft horse pull, and fireworks. July. Call 712/464-7611.
- **Riverboat Days, Clinton. Carnival, pageant, tractor pulls.** July. Call 800/457-9975 or 800/395-7277.
- **Iowa Games Qualifying Festival,** Waterloo. An Olympic-style sportsfest for athletes of all ages and abilities. Mid-July. Call the Waterloo Convention & Visitors Bureau at 800/728-8431.
- **Lewis and Clark White Catfish Camp and Public Festival,** Council Bluffs. This celebration on the

banks of the Missouri River includes campfire programs, games, wood walks, and a pioneer fashion show. Fourth weekend in July. Call 712/328-5638.

- **Bix Beiderbecke Jazz Festival,** Davenport. Late July. Call 319/324-7170.
- **Ghost Baseball Players,** Dyersville. Players dress in vintage uniforms to appear in Farmer Lansing's magical Field of Dreams. Labor Day weekend. Call 319/875-2311.
- **Madison County Covered Bridge Festival,** Winterset. October. call 515/462-1185.

SPECTATOR SPORTS

Archery Clear days and broad, level fields make Iowa a natural for archers. A statewide archery tournament is held in La Porte City in Hickory Hills Park. Call 319/296-2180 for information.

Auto Racing The Sprint Car Championship is held every August at the **Knoxville Speedway National** (tel 515/842-5431). For a 1.8-mile street course, go to the **Des Moines Street Circuit** at Abuts Veterans Auditorium, 4th and Crocker in Des Moines (tel 515/243-5518). The **Greater Des Moines Grand Prix** (SCAA Trans-Am Championship) is held in July; call the Abuts Auditorium number for ticket information.

Ballooning Held annually in Indianola, the **National Balloon Classic** features 100 hot air balloons in competition for money and prizes. Skydivers and stunt planes are also part of the show. Call 515/961-8415 for additional information.

Baseball The **Iowa Cubs** (American Association, Class AAA) draw crowds at the Sec Taylor Stadium in Des Moines (tel 515/243-6111). Veterans Memorial Ball Park in Cedar Rapids hosts the **Cedar Rapids Reds** (Midwest League, Class A). Call 319/363-3887 for Reds ticket info.

Basketball There may be no NBA franchise in Iowa, but fans have plenty to cheer about when it comes to the college game. The **University of Iowa Hawkeyes** take to the court at Carver-Hawkeye Arena in Iowa City; call 319/335-9327 for ticket and schedule information. Cross-state rival **Iowa State University Cyclones** make their run for glory at Hilton Coliseum (515/294-1816) in Ames.

Football The **Iowa State Cyclones** play at Jack Trice Field in Ames (tel 515/294-1816). Across the state to the east in Iowa City, you'll meet the **University of Iowa Hawkeyes.** Streets are filled with cheering fans and traffic jams before and after games are a given. Call 319/335-9327 for ticket information.

Greyhound Racing Greyhounds run at **Dubuque Greyhound Park and Casino** (tel toll free 800/373-3647). The track's on-site casino has more than 500 slot machines, concession stands, and an entertainment center for children.

Horse Racing Thoroughbred racing is held at **Prairie Meadows** (tel 515/967-1000) in Altoona. The season runs from March to September.

Softball It may not be held on a field of dreams, but lots of people find the ISC World Fast Pitch Softball Tournament in Sioux City just as exciting. It is held in August at the Penn Corp Park. Call 800/593-2228 or 712/279-4800.

ACTIVITIES A TO Z

Bicycling You'll appreciate those long, flat stretches as you ride your bike from park to park for a big Iowa bike adventure. Numerous parks are interconnected by four bike routes around the state. Contact the Division of Tourism for detailed bike route brochures. You're also welcome to join the increasingly popular, weeklong bike race extravaganza known as RAGBRAI (*Register's* Annual Great Bicycle Ride Across the State—sponsored by the *Des Moines Register*), held every summer.

Boating Iowa has 9,000 miles of streams and rivers, along with plenty of natural and artificial lakes. There are more than 1,000 public boat launch sites. You can use any sized boat motor (operated at a no-wake speed) on any Iowa lake of 100 acres or more. Both Lake Macbride and Big Creek require a maximum boat motor size of 10 horsepower between May 21 and September 7. Otherwise, any size motor can be used at a no-wake speed. Smaller lakes require use of electric motors, not exceeding 1½ hp. Natural lakes, rivers, and federal impoundments do not have a boat-motor size restriction.

Butterfly Watching Bellevue State Park is home to Iowa's largest butterfly garden. The **Garden Sanctuary for Butterflies** was designed to provide habitat for a wide spectrum of butterflies. Plants provide food and shelter for the beautiful insects while visitors can look on. The sanctuary is near the park's Nelson Unit, south of Bellevue, where visitors can also tour the South Bluff Nature Center. Call 319/872-4019 for details.

Camping Camping is popular in Iowa. State parks, recreation areas, and forests contain 58 campgrounds with a total of 5,700 campsites. No reservations are taken for these sites, which are available on a first-come, first-served basis. In state forests, campground facilities are available at Stephens, Shimek, and Yellow River. Nine of the state parks have family cabins, each accommodating four people. Reservations can be made for overnight group camps at Dolliver, Lake Keomah, and Springbrook State Parks. Call the park ranger for details.

Fishing Iowa's Great Lakes region and the state's many miles of rivers and streams contain bass, trout, pike, bluegill, catfish, and many more kinds of fish. You can pick up a fishing license at most state parks. Call the **Department of Natural Resources** (tel 515/281-5145) for details on sites and fishing regulations.

Golf All that green—a golfer's dream! Iowa is heaven for golfers. Call the **Iowa Golf Association** (tel 319/378-9142) for the names and locations of Iowa's many golf courses.

Hiking Almost every park in Iowa has hiking trails. The **Department of Natural Resources** (tel 515/281-5145) will gladly send you a list of them all, or you can contact the **Iowa Sierra Club** (tel 515/277-9868).

Horseback Riding Horseback riding is popular in the recreation areas, state forests, and state parks. You can camp with your horse and follow trails at Waubonsie and Elk Rock State Parks, Brushy Creek, and Volga River State Recreation Areas, as well as Stephens, Shimek, and Yellow River State Forests. Stone State Park has 15 miles of trails for the rider.

Picnicking Back in the 1930s, the WPA and CCC constructed dozens of enclosed shelters at state parks for group events. The **Division of Natural Resources** (tel 515/242-5967) will provide you with a list of these parks. Shelters have electricity, water, toilets, cooking stoves, and refrigerators. Open shelters are also available for picnics and group outings at state parks. You can either take a chance and count on a first-come, first-served arrangement, or make a reservation through the park ranger.

Water Sports Windsurf, sail, and water-ski at West Okoboji Lake, a glacial "blue water" lake located in Dickinson County in northwest Iowa, or any of Iowa's other great lakes or rivers. The **Department of Natural Resources** will provide you with information on Iowa's waterways. Call 515/242-5967, or write to them at DNR, 900 E Grand, Des Moines, IA 50319-0034.

Winter Sports Iowans are used to enjoying the outdoors, and cold temperatures don't stop them. The resort at **Sundown Mountain** (tel 319/556-6676), with a 475-foot vertical drop, is a popular spot for downhill skiing. State parks and recreation areas also sponsor lots of cold weather fun. You can ski, sled, snowmobile, ice skate, or cross-country ski at the **Eagle Point Nature Center** in Clinton (tel 319/242-9088) or the **E B Lyons Nature Center,** adjacent to the Mines of Spain State Recreation Area in Dubuque (tel 319/556-0620). Contact the Iowa Department of Natural Resources for a list of winter recreation areas with designated trails and routes.

Selected Parks & Recreation Areas

- **Effigy Mounds National Monument,** RR 1, Box 25A, Harpers Ferry, IA 52146 (tel 319/873-3491)
- **Herbert Hoover National Historic Site,** PO Box 607, West Branch, IA 52538 (tel 319/643-2541)
- **Bellevue State Park,** 21466 429th Ave, Bellevue, IA 52031 (tel 319/872-3243)
- **Bob White State Park,** RR 1, Box 124A, Allerton, IA (tel 515/873-4670)
- **Clear Lake State Park,** 2730 S Lakeview Dr, Clear Lake, IA 50428 (tel 515/357-4212)
- **Elk Rock State Park,** Red Rock Reservoir, 811 146th St, Knoxville, IA 50138 (tel 515/842-6008)
- **Geode State Park,** RR 2, Danville, IA 52623 (tel 319/392-4601)
- **Lake Ahquabi State Park,** 1650 118th Ave, Indianola, IA 50125 (tel 515/961-7101)
- **Lake Keomah State Park,** RR 1, Oskaloosa, IA 52577 (tel 515/673-6975)
- **Ledges State Park,** 1519 250th St, Madrid, IA 50156 (tel 515/432-1852)
- **Maquoketa Caves State Park,** RR 2, Maquoketa, IA 52060 (tel 319/652-5833)
- **Pine Lake State Park,** RR 3, Box 45, Eldora, IA 50627 (tel 515/858-5832)
- **Springbrook State Park,** 2437 160th Rd, Guthrie Center, IA 50115
- **Viking Lake State Park,** RR 1, Box 191, Stanton, IA 51573 (tel 712/829-2235)
- **Waubonsie State Park,** RR 2, Box 66, Hamburg, IA 51640 (tel 712/382-2786)
- **Wildcat Den State Park,** 1884 Wildcat Den Rd, Muscatine, IA (tel 319/263-4337)

MISSISSIPPI RIVER ROAD

Start	Marquette
Finish	Keokuk
Distance	Approximately 215 miles
Time	1 day
Highlights	A quiet, scenic stretch of the first river you learned how to spell; prehistoric burial mounds; bald eagle sighting; a pearl button museum; the nation's crookedest street; riverboat gambling

Identified by green-and-white signs marked with a pilot's wheel, the Great River Road parallels the Mississippi River—the nation's vast, central, watery highway. Glaciers bypassed much of the Iowa section of this 3,000-mile network of federal, state, and county roads, leaving hills and bluffs that some call "Little Switzerland."

Here in the heart of America, the river that "just keeps rolling along" (as per Jerome Kern and Oscar Hammerstein's *Showboat*) guides visitors along a 215-mile stretch from Marquette to Keokuk. In between, the road climbs up hills to follow the river's banks, winds past hospitable small towns and tidy farmhouses, and widens out on blufftops that afford panoramic views. This tour starts in the Upper Iowa River Valley, near the Minnesota border, and then threads its way downriver and past the old harbor towns of Dubuque, Clinton, and Burlington before finishing at Keokuk, just north of the Missouri border. There will be time to explore Native American burial mounds, ethnic settlements and river museums, try your luck at riverboat gambling, and ride a cable car.

For additional information on lodgings, restaurants, and attractions in the region covered by the tour, look under specific cities in the listings portion of this chapter.

From Marquette, it's just a short 3-mile drive to the first stop of the tour:

1. **Effigy Mounds National Monument,** on IA 76 (tel 319/873-3491), which preserves 191 examples of prehistoric Native American burial mounds, some estimated to be up to 2,500 years old. The monument's 11 miles of trails lead up to 300-foot-high bluff tops, with trailside exhibits and markers explaining how the mounds were built. As the surrounding maple, oak, and walnut trees suggest, a steep and rocky section of the Marching Bear Trail was once a logging road. A one-hour walk on the self-guided Fire Point Trail leads to representative examples of several types of mounds and scenic viewpoints. Guided walks along the trail by park rangers are given on a scheduled basis from Memorial Day to Labor Day.

Next, take IA 76 south for a little over 2 miles to US 18E at Marquette; continue south 2½ miles to McGregor, which was established in 1837 as a ferryboat landing. The **River Junction Trade Co,** at 312 Main St in McGregor (tel 319/873-2387), is located in a century-old building with tin ceilings; a black, potbellied stove; and wooden floors. Frontier-style clothing, including long johns, military shirts, paper collars, and hats from straw sombreros to wool felt derbies, are the store's specialty.

Follow IA 340 at the junction of US 18 from the south end of Main St and wind upward 1½ miles to **Pikes Peak State Park** (tel 319/873-2341). From atop this 500-foot bluff (the tallest on the Mississippi), you can see the twin suspension bridges connecting Iowa and Wisconsin, and the confluence of the Mississippi and Wisconsin Rivers.

Return to the junction of IA 340 and Main St in McGregor, and take the Great River Road (County Road X56) for about 16 miles, until it swoops dramatically into:

2. **Guttenberg,** a mile-long German village with streets named after Goethe and Schiller. Guttenberg has a bed-and-breakfast and an art gallery, the **Old Brewery,** 402 S Bluff St (tel 319/252-2094), in a caveside building made from native stone. At Lock and Dam No 10, you can watch barges "lock through" the river. (The locks you'll see on this tour are like a series of stair steps that keep the Mississippi's water level. If it was too shallow, barges couldn't make it south to wider, deeper water.) If you stop in at **Kann Imports,** 530 S River Park Dr (tel 319/252-2072), located in an unassuming white frame building, you will find an inventory of distinct and exotic items unexpected in a small Iowa town: Lalique crystal, Meissen figurines, Swiss music boxes, German clocks, Russian religious icons.

Take the Great River Road (US 52) south out of Guttenberg for almost 6 miles, until it separates from the highway to follow the river and directs you to follow C9Y for 15 miles to Balltown. Some international travelers say the panoramic view outside Balltown—puffy quilts of rolling green hills dotted by barns—reminds them of Ireland. A ferry crosses the river at Cassville, WI, a few miles away.

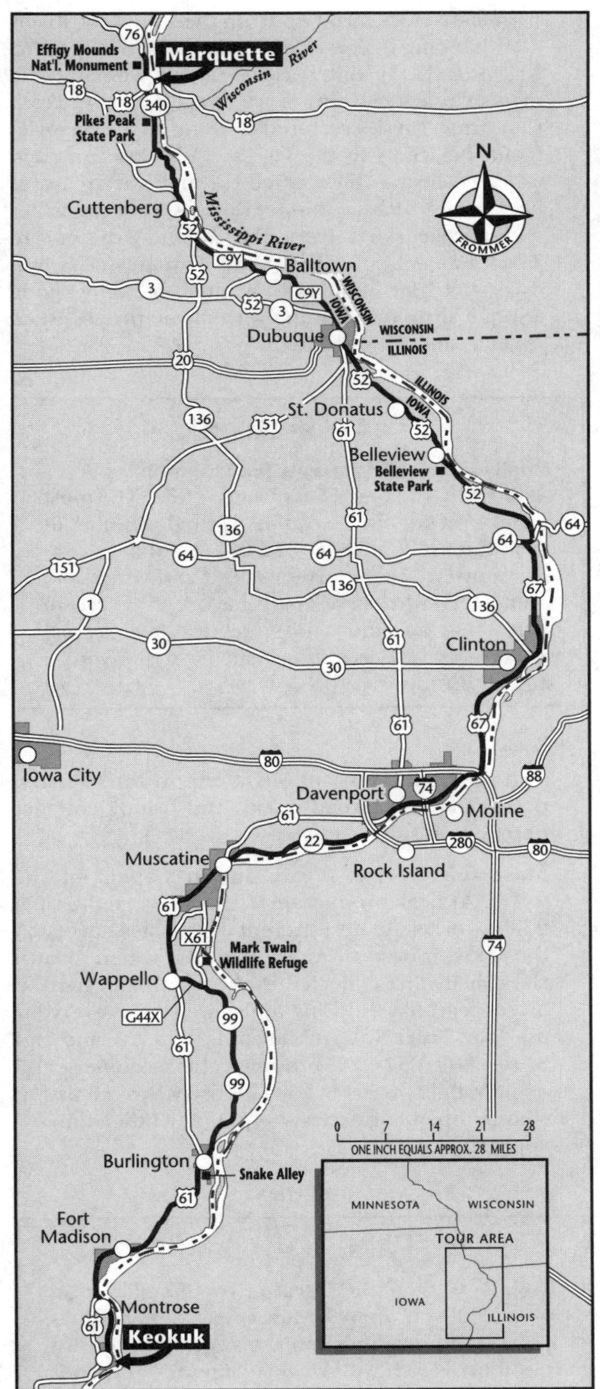

Continue on the Great River Road, taking the turn east onto US 52 (as directed by the pilot's wheel sign) for 15½ miles to:

Take a Break

Iowa's oldest bar and restaurant, **Breitbach's Country Dining** on the Great River Road in Balltown (tel 319/552-2220) is quite likely the only restaurant in the country that can claim to have served both Jesse James and Brooke Shields. Set in a ramshackle, antique-filled white frame building and operated by a big, exuberant German family, it offers down-home food such as pies, roasts, soups, breads, and real mashed potatoes. If you don't see it on the menu, try asking for it. Open 8am–9pm daily March 15–November 1; closed Mondays November 2–March 14. Dinner entrees are $6 to $15.

3. **Dubuque,** where needle-thin church steeples rise over blocks of vintage red brick and limestone buildings. This river port (population 60,000) is Iowa's oldest city. The slender arrow of the Shot Tower, where hundreds of workers turned lead into ammunition during the Civil War, is a local landmark. At the **Mississippi River Museum,** on 3rd St in Ice Harbor (tel toll free 800/226-3369), visitors can turn a pilot's wheel, play a Mesquakie dice game, and go aboard the *William M Black,* a channel dredger that looks as if the original crew still lives there.

   The **Cable Car Square** area at 4th and Bluff Streets is a neighborhood of gift, import, food, and antique shops located at the base of **Fenelon Place Elevator,** 512 Fenelon Place (tel 319/582-6496). The cable car, which bills itself as the world's shortest and steepest scenic railway, was built by a banker in 1882 as a shortcut from his blufftop home to his bank 2½ blocks away. Open 8am–10pm daily, April–October.

   Return to US 52 and follow it south for some 13 miles to tiny:

4. **St Donatus,** a Luxembourg enclave. The entire village is listed as a historic district on the National Register. Stone masons from the old country built the distinctive limestone buildings here. **Kalmes Store,** a gas station and cafe on 100 N Main St (US 52), serves Luxembourger specialties (tel 319/773-2480). On a hill behind the store is **St Donatus Catholic Church** (tel 319/773-2293), where you can hike up a trail called the **Outdoor Way of the Cross,** with grazing sheep keeping you company. Follow the cubicles all the way to the tiny, hilltop Pieta Chapel for a spectacular view of the surrounding countryside.

   Return to US 52 (you're still on the Great River Road) and follow it almost 8 miles south to one of Mark Twain's favorite places, the pretty little town of:

5. **Bellevue.** Bellevue has a dramatic layout: the shops occupy one side of the main drag and the river sprawls along the other. The riverfront is uncommonly accessible here, its banks dotted with gazebos, gliders, bird houses, and a public dock. **Bellevue State Park,** on US 52 at the south end of town (tel 319/872-4019), occupies a blufftop from which you get a bird's eye view of barge traffic. The park also has a butterfly garden, planted and maintained by community volunteers.

Continue south on US 52 and watch for the junction of US 52 and IA 64. Take IA 64 west to US 67 south, traveling a total of 33 miles to the old river town of:

6. **Clinton,** once a railroad and milling center. Today it has a gambling boat, a nature center, and a stadium that is home to the Clinton LumberKings, a Class-A baseball club of the San Diego Padres. One of the town's most familiar landmarks is the **Clinton Area Showboat Theatre,** on Riverview Dr at the riverfront (tel 319/242-6760), a restored paddlewheeler that presents a lively roster of summer stock shows. The 14-acre **Bickelhaupt Arboretum,** 340 S 14th St (tel 319/242-4771), has outstanding collections of lilacs and miniature trees set in a narrow, wooded valley.

For a genuine slice of American pie, don't miss the vintage red brick **Smith Brothers General Store** at 1016 4th St. With rubber chickens hanging in the windows beneath green striped awnings, the overflowing stock inside includes lariats, pictures of Elvis, and packages of rat poison—and you can help yourself to bottled soda from an upright, cylindrical, Depression-era cooler. A trip down these crowded aisles and you'll understand why locals say, "If they don't have it, you don't need it."

Traveling south on US 67 from Clinton for 29 miles takes you to:

7. **Davenport.** Davenport and Bettendorf (in Iowa) and Moline and Rock Island (in Illinois) make up the Quad Cities, a metropolitan area with a total population of 400,000 people. The **President Riverboat Casino,** at the junction of US 67 and 61 on River Dr (tel toll free 800/262-8711), claims to be the Midwest's largest casino, with five decks sitting above the water. One of a trio of riverboats in the area, its hull was originally part of the *Cincinnati,* a famous overnight packet boat and luxury sidewheeler that operated on the Mississippi in the 1920s and '30s. Designated a National Landmark, the Victorian-style boat has more than 750 slot machines, a poker parlor, and table games such as blackjack and roulette.

A four-block stroll up from the President Riverboat Landing is **Trash Can Annie,** 421 Brady St (tel 319/322 5893). Billed as the largest women's and men's vintage clothing store in the country, Trash Can Annie carries restored clothing and accessories from the 1850s to the 1970s. TV's Roseanne and other celebrities have sifted through the treasures here, which include flapper dresses from the 1920s and poodle skirts from the 1950s. Adjacent to Trash Can Annie is **Riverbend Antiques,** 425 Brady St (tel 319/323-8622), a huge, half-block-long antique store overflowing with movie props, estate jewelry, and art deco items.

Take a Break

Family-operated **Whitey's Ice Cream** has been a tradition in the Quad Cities since 1933. The most popular of its nine locations is in Davenport at 1230 Locust St (tel 319/322-0828). All the stores are staffed by courteous red-and-white-clad youngsters, who serve up 36 flavors of ice cream with "less air and more cream." For a real splurge, try a Boston—a malt or shake with a sundae on top.

Take US 22 west out of Davenport for 19 miles, past quarries, railroad tracks, and fishing cottages perched on stilts, to:

8. **Muscatine,** former Pearl Button Capital of the world. At peak production in the 1890s, more than 2,500 workers in 43 different companies harvested the shiny, iridescent interiors of the rough, brown clam shells that collected in the river bend here to make pearl-like buttons and jewelry for everyday use. The **Pearl Button Museum,** Iowa Ave and 2nd St (tel 800/257-3275) displays the machinery and memorabilia of this bygone industry. No admission charge; open Saturdays 1–4pm, any other time by appointment.

Take a Break

Take US 61 S out of Muscatine for 2½ miles to an area lined with **open-air markets.** These markets showcase the region's renowned produce, grown in soil made rich with river sediment. The stands sell melon, sweet corn, potatoes, tomatoes, and locally made crafts, and most are open Memorial Day through October. A popular one is **Hoopes Melon Shed** (tel 319/263-7302).

Continue south on US 61 for 8 miles to Wappello; then east for about 6 miles on County Road G44X and follow signs for the Louisa Division of the **Mark Twain National Wildlife Refuge Complex** (tel 319/523-6982). The refuge is part of a chain of migratory bird refuges linking northern breeding grounds to southern wintering areas. During the fall migrations, populations of more than 100,000 ducks and 6,000 geese are common. Bald eagles gather at the refuge to feed on fish and injured waterfowl.

When you leave the refuge, take County Road X61 south for approximately 6 miles to IA 99; then travel south 28 miles to a nostalgic port of call:

9. Burlington, once the territorial capital of Iowa. Stop at the **Port of Burlington Welcome Center,** in a former municipal dock at 400 N Front St (tel 319/752-8731), to get brochures for two self-guided driving tours through historic neighborhoods. Your tour will include a vertiginous drive down **Snake Alley,** between Washington and Columbia Sts on 6th St, which is proclaimed by Ripley's *Believe It Or Not* as the most crooked street in the world. This landmark consists of five half-curves and two quarter-curves, and drops 58 feet over a distance of 275 feet.

Leaving Burlington, take US 61 south, past county cemeteries and farms on a stretch of the River Road that runs parallel to the Hiawatha Pioneer Trail, for 16½ miles to:

10. Fort Madison. Here the river widens, and you can walk along it at Riverview Park, downtown on the riverfront. **Old Fort Madison** (tel 319/372-6318), an outdoor museum that is the focal point of the riverfront, is a reconstruction of the first US military post on the upper Mississippi River. Among the historical buildings to explore are blockhouses with shooting platforms, officers' quarters, a factory where manufactured goods were exchanged with Native Americans for furs and hides, and enlisted men's barracks. Open Wednesday–Sunday, Memorial Day through August.

Return to US 61 south for 8 miles to Montrose, where you'll turn left. Continue on the River Road for 13 miles until you reach:

11. Keokuk, founded in the 1820s at the place where the Des Moines River flows into the Mississippi. Keokuk was once home to Mark Twain, who lived here for a couple of years with his brother, Orion, and worked as a typesetter. The town played an important role in Civil War history as a swearing-in place and medical center. Soldiers wounded in Southern battlefields were transported upriver to Keokuk. Many of those who died were laid to rest in **National Cemetery** at 18th and Ridge Sts (tel 319/524-1304). Founded at the same time as Arlington National Cemetery, it was the first national cemetery west of the Mississippi.

Iowa Listings

Algona

Located in the heart of Kossuth County, on US 169 in the northwest sector of Iowa. **Information:** Algona Area Chamber of Commerce, 123 E State St, Algona, 50511 (tel 515/295-7201).

MOTELS

The Burr Oak Motel
US 169 S, 50511; tel 515/295-7213 or toll free 800/341-8000; fax 515/295-2979. 1 mi S of Algona. Safe and quiet facility—a terrific deal. **Rooms:** 42 rms and stes. CI noon/CO 10am. Nonsmoking rms avail. Large, modern rooms come with choice of king, queen, or waterbeds. **Amenities:** A/C, cable TV w/movies. **Services:** Popcorn in lobby. **Facilities:** 25 1 restaurant. Adjacent supper club/lounge serves good food. **Rates (CP):** $27–$35 S; $34–$45 D; $35–$40 ste. Extra person $3. Children under age 6 stay free. Parking: Outdoor, free. AE, DC, DISC, MC, V.

Candlelite Motel
US 169, 50511; tel 515/295-2441. Located on the south end of town near Kossuth County Fairgrounds. Rooms are dark, but clean and comfortable. **Rooms:** 18 rms. CI noon/CO 10:30am. **Amenities:** A/C, cable TV. **Services:** Free drink in lounge for guests. **Facilities:** 1 bar. Truck parking. **Rates (CP):** $28 S; $32–$35 D. Extra person $5. Children under age 12 stay free. Parking: Outdoor, free. 11th-night-free program. AE, DISC, MC, V.

Super 8 Motel
210 E Norwood Dr, 50511; tel 515/295-7225 or toll free 800/800-8000; fax 515/295-7225 ext 101. 1 block S of US 18 on US 169. Located within two blocks of shops and restaurants. **Rooms:** 30 rms. CI open/CO 11am. Nonsmoking rms avail. Single rooms offer queen beds and recliners. Waterbeds available. **Amenities:** A/C, cable TV w/movies. **Services:** Free local calls. **Facilities:** Parking for trucks and buses. **Rates (CP):** $33–$37 S; $39–$48 D. Extra person $4. Children under age 12 stay free. Parking: Outdoor, free. AE, DISC, MC, V.

Altoona

See Des Moines

Amana Colonies

Founded as a religious commune nearly 150 years ago, the seven villages that form the Amana Colonies have been designated a National Historic Landmark. Old World–style craft shops, artisans, wineries, and restaurants make the Colonies one of Iowa's most popular tourist sites. Just south—in Williamsburg—is the famous Tanger Factory Outlet, home of over 60 designer and brand-name manufacturer outlet stores.

MOTELS

Guest House Motel Inn
4712 220th Trail, Amana, 52203; tel 319/622-3599. Off Main St. Situated in the middle of the Amana colonies, the motel's older building dates to the 19th century. Best suited for short stays; other accommodations in the area offer more for the money. **Rooms:** 38 rms. CI open/CO 11am. Nonsmoking rms avail. Plainly decorated and clean. **Amenities:** A/C, cable TV. **Services:** **Facilities:** **Rates:** $35–$40 S; $58–$68 D. Extra person $4. Children under age 10 stay free. Parking: Outdoor, free. AE, DISC, MC, V.

Holiday Inn
I-80, exit 225, PO Box 187, Amana, 52203; tel 319/668-1175 or toll free 800/633-9244; fax 319/668-2853. Surprisingly quiet, though right alongside interstate. **Rooms:** 155 rms. Executive level. CI 3pm/CO 11am. Nonsmoking rms avail. Very comfortable. **Amenities:** A/C, cable TV w/movies, dataport. **Services:** **Facilities:** 400 1 restaurant, 1 bar, sauna, whirlpool. **Rates:** Peak (May–Oct) $74 S; $82 D. Extra person $6. Children under age 19 stay free. Lower rates off-season. Parking: Outdoor, free. AE, CB, DC, DISC, JCB, MC, V.

RESTAURANTS

Amana Barn Restaurant
4709 220th Trail, Amana; tel 319/622-3214. 10 miles N of I-80 exit 225. **German.** One of the premier restaurants in the Amana Colonies, the Amana Barn offers family-style dinners of schnitzel, sauerbraten, and pork and beef entrees. Can accommodate bus groups; has large banquet facilities. Sunday brunch is a local favorite. **FYI:** Reservations accepted. Guitar/zither. Children's menu. **Open:** Lunch Mon–Sat 11am–4pm; dinner Mon–Sat 4–8:30pm, Sun 10am–8pm; brunch Sun 10am–1pm. **Prices:** Main courses $10–$17. AE, DISC, MC, V.

Colony Inn Restaurant
741 47th Ave, Amana; tel 319/622-6270. 7 blocks E of IA 151. **German.** Housed in an 1860 building, the wide-open dining rooms have antique chairs and tables. Family-style meals start with fried potatoes, salads, corn, sauerkraut, fresh cottage cheese and move on to the likes of Swiss steak and smoked pork. **FYI:** Reservations accepted. Beer and wine only. **Open:** Peak (May–Sept) breakfast daily 7–11am; lunch daily 11am–8pm; dinner daily 11am–8pm. **Prices:** Main courses $10–$16. AE, DISC, MC, V.

Ox Yoke Inn
4420 220th Trail, Amana; tel 319/622-3441. 10 miles N of I-80, exit 225. **German.** Here the family-style meals consist of salads, relishes, breads, main courses such as fried chicken or ham, and dessert. Located in a 125-year-old building, the restaurant has been run by the same family for more than 50 years. For groups of 20 or more, the staff will provide a tour guide for the historic Amana Colonies free of charge. **FYI:** Reservations recommended. Piano/accordion. Children's menu. No smoking. **Open:** Lunch Mon–Sat 11am–2pm; dinner Sun 11am–7pm, Mon–Sat 5–8pm; brunch Sun 9am–noon. **Prices:** Main courses $8–$17; prix fixe $13–$14. AE, CB, DC, DISC, MC, V.

The Ronneburg
Main St, Amana; tel 319/622-3641. Two blocks E of US 151. **German.** Another of the Amana's traditional family-style dining establishments with checked tablecloths in a homey communal dining area. Large variety of salads and relishes, followed by ham, Swiss steak, chicken. **FYI:** Reservations accepted. **Open:** Daily 11am–8pm. **Prices:** Main courses $2–$17. AE, CB, DC, MC, V.

ATTRACTIONS

Museum of Amana History
4310 220th Trail, Amana; tel 319/622-3567. The village of Amana was founded in 1855 by colonists from the Community of True Inspiration, a religious group founded in 18th-century Germany. The Inspirationists emphasized personal religious experience and communal property; eventually, their holdings in Amana included a school, several communal kitchens, and worker-run factories (including the home of the original Amana refrigerator). The current Museum, comprising three village buildings, includes displays of local crafts, a re-creation of a church interior, a Kinderschule, and audio-visual presentations. A washhouse/woodshed, an integral part of communal Amana, houses winemaking and garden displays. **Open:** Apr–mid-Nov, Mon–Sat 10am–5pm, Sun noon–5pm. $

Communal Kitchen and Coopershop Museum
1003 26th Ave, Amana; tel 319/622-3567. Communal kitchens were an integral part of daily life for the True Inspirationists religious sect, whose members settled here in the mid-19th century. In this museum, housed in the only remaining kitchen building, visitors can see the large brick hearth, the huge sink with its wooden tubs, and all the original implements used to prepare meals. (Each kitchen in the village would serve three daily meals for 30 to 40 people.) In the adjoining dining room, long tables are set with period china and silver.

The colony's coopershop provided the large wooden barrels and other containers used to store these vast amounts of food. The Coopershop Museum's interpretive exhibits illustrate the craft of barrel-making. **Open:** May–Oct, Mon–Sat 9am–5pm, Sun noon–5pm. $

Ames

Home of Iowa State University, founded in 1858 as Iowa's land-grant university. ISU's spacious campus features the Iowa State Center, a four-building complex that is the site for athletic and educational activities as well as a full array of cultural events. **Information:** Ames Chamber of Commerce, 213 Duff, Ames 50010 (tel 515/232-2310).

HOTEL

Holiday Inn Gateway Center
US 30 and Elwood Dr, 50010; tel 515/292-8600 or toll free 800/HOLIDAY; fax 515/292-4446. Set in a very attractive area—complete with acres of trees, trails, and landscaping—this property also offers a beautiful, spacious lobby. **Rooms:** 188 rms. Executive level. CI 3pm/CO noon. Nonsmoking rms avail. Accommodations are clean, bright, and modern. **Amenities:** A/C, cable TV w/movies. 1 unit w/minibar. **Services:** Car-rental desk, children's program. Very pleasant staff. **Facilities:** 600 1 restaurant, 2 bars, games rm, sauna, whirlpool. **Rates:** $69 S or D. Extra person $10. Children under age 12 stay free. Parking: Outdoor, free. Corporate, government, B&B rates; romance and family packages avail. AE, CB, DC, DISC, MC, V.

MOTELS

Budgetel Inn
2500 Elwood Dr, 50010; tel 515/296-2500 or toll free 800/488-3438; fax 515/296-2500. Exit 146 from US 30. Located in an open area outside of town, this property has a large, attractive lobby with a balcony and library. **Rooms:** 89 rms and stes. Executive level. CI 3pm/CO noon. Nonsmoking rms avail. Accommodations are clean and bright. **Amenities:** A/C, cable TV w/movies, dataport, VCR. 1 unit w/terrace, some w/whirlpools. Continental breakfast delivered to room. **Services:** Complimentary fax and copy service. **Facilities:** Whirlpool, washer/dryer. **Rates (CP):** $59 S; $71 D; $100 ste. Extra person $5. Parking: Outdoor, free. AE, DISC, MC, V.

Comfort Inn
1605 S Dayton Ave, 50010; tel 515/232-0689 or toll free 800/221-2222; fax 515/232-0689. Exit 111B off I-35. Simple property situated in a concrete parking lot east of town. **Rooms:** 52 rms and effic. CI 3pm/CO 11am. Nonsmoking rms avail. Rooms are clean, bright, and plainly decorated. **Amenities:** A/C, cable TV w/movies, refrig. **Services:** **Facilities:** Games rm, whirlpool. **Rates (CP):** Peak (Mar–Sept) $53 S; $57 effic. Extra person $5. Children under age 12 stay free. Lower rates off-season. Parking: Outdoor, free. AE, DISC, MC, V.

Hampton Inn
1400 S Dayton Ave, 50010; tel 515/239-9999 or toll free 800/426-7866; fax 515/239-6015. At 16th. New facility located in a business district east of town. Priced a bit higher than competitors, but worth the difference. **Rooms:** 57 rms. Executive level. CI 2pm/CO 11am. Nonsmoking rms avail. Large, well-furnished rooms feature wardrobe dressers and reclining chairs. **Amenities:** A/C, cable TV w/movies, dataport, voice mail. Some units w/whirlpools. **Services:** **Facilities:** Washer/dryer. **Rates (CP):** Peak (June 1–Sept 3) $52–$80 S or D. Children under age 18 stay free. Lower rates off-season. Parking: Outdoor, free. AE, CB, DC, DISC, MC, V.

RESTAURANTS

★ The Broiler Steak House
6008 W Lincoln Way; tel 515/292-2516. **American.** This long-time hometown favorite serves a wide variety of seafood, steaks, prime rib, and vegetarian platters. Banquet facilities for 200. **FYI:** Reservations recommended. Children's menu. Dress code. **Open:** Lunch Sun 11:30am–2pm; dinner Mon–Thurs 5:30–9:30pm, Fri–Sat 5:30–10:30pm, Sun 5–9pm. **Prices:** Main courses $9–$16. AE, DC, DISC, MC, V.

($) ★ Hickory Park Restaurant Company
121 S 16th St; tel 515/232-8940. Duff Ave exit off US 30; N 2 blocks. **Barbecue.** A local landmark known for great food, casual atmosphere, and tremendous value. Superb hickory-smoked barbecue features beef and pork ribs, while a sandwich of sliced barbecued meat with all the fixings makes a satisfying, substantial meal. Choose from more than 100 ice cream desserts. **FYI:** Reservations accepted. Children's menu. Beer and wine only. **Open:** Sun–Thurs 10am–9:30pm, Fri–Sat 10am–10pm. **Prices:** Main courses $4–$13. No CC.

($) ★ Lucullan's on the Park
400 Main St (Historic District); tel 515/232-8484. **Coffeehouse/Italian.** Known throughout the region as a good bet for its freshly made pastas and bread. Selections include calzone rustica, lemon or Cajun pasta, and the herb-cheese bread. Lunch portions available. **FYI:** Reservations accepted. Children's menu. **Open:** Sun 11am–9pm, Mon–Thurs 11am–10pm, Fri–Sat 11am–11pm. **Prices:** Main courses $6–$15. AE, DC, DISC, MC, V.

ATTRACTIONS

Mamie Doud Eisenhower Birthplace
709 Carroll St, Boone; tel 515/432-1896. 15 mi NW of Ames. Restored birthplace of the former First Lady, wife of 34th president Dwight Eisenhower. The five-room, Victorian-style clapboard house features an heirloom chandelier brought from Sweden in 1868 by Doud's grandfather, family portraits, and an Ansonia mantel clock. A basement museum displays personal memorabilia, while an adjacent barn houses a 1949 Chrysler Windsor Sedan used by the Eisenhowers and a two-seated buggy used by Doud's parents. **Open:** Apr–May, Tues–Sat 1–5pm; June–Oct, daily 10am–5pm. Open other times by appointment. Closed some hols. **$**

Boone and Scenic Valley Railroad
11th and Division Sts, Boone; tel 515/432-3519 or toll free 800/626-0319. 15 mi NW of Ames. Diesel-powered trains make a 12-mile, 1½-hour run several times daily through the scenic Des Moines River valley. On weekends, a 104-ton Chinese steam locomotive—the only one in the United States—and an Iowa steam locomotive are added to the schedule. Call for reservations and specific departure times. **Open:** Mem Day–Oct. **$$$**

Anita

Small town situated three miles south of I-80 on IA 83, near Lake Anita, in Iowa's southwestern sector. Close by is the historic site of the first train robbery committed west of the Mississippi River.

RESTAURANT

($) ★ Redwood Steakhouse
1808 W Main; tel 712/762-3530. On IA 83, W of downtown. **Regional American.** Over 25 years old. Noted for terrific food and a comfortable, traditional setting. The hot, golden onion rings are regarded by many Redwood fans as the best

in the state. Popular entrees include the Redwood Special rib-eye steak and pork fillet. Private room can accommodate up to 85 people. **FYI:** Reservations accepted. Children's menu. **Open:** Daily 5–10pm. **Prices:** Main courses $7–$13; prix fixe $6–$17. MC, V.

Atlantic

A quaint, quiet town containing many well-restored Victorian homes; located between Omaha and Des Moines, just south of I-80. **Information:** Atlantic Area Chamber of Commerce, 614 Chestnut St, Atlantic, 50022 (712/243-3017).

MOTEL

Best Western Country Squire Inn
1902 E 7th, 50022; tel 712/243-4723 or toll free 800/528-1234; fax 712/243-2864. 1 block W of US 71. A meeting and convention center located close to highways, shopping, and the hospital. **Rooms:** 44 rms. Executive level. CI 3pm/CO 11am. Nonsmoking rms avail. Accommodations are nicely decorated, and all have queen-size beds. **Amenities:** A/C, cable TV w/movies. 1 unit w/whirlpool. Large (25") TV. **Services:** **Facilities:** 250 Spa, sauna, whirlpool. **Rates:** $35–$59 S or D. Extra person $3. Children under age 18 stay free. Parking: Outdoor, free. AE, CB, DC, DISC, MC, V.

INN

Chestnut Charm Bed and Breakfast
1409 Chestnut St, 50022; tel 712/243-5652. 7 blocks S of downtown. 2 acres. An 1898 Victorian mansion featuring a garden/patio area with fountain and wrought-iron gazebo, and a piano in the front parlor. Good for a romantic getaway. Unsuitable for children under 18. **Rooms:** 5 rms and stes. CI 4pm/CO 11am. No smoking. Richly decorated theme rooms have names like Gatsby Room, Tabitha's Quarters, and Fireside Room. All have private baths and brass beds. **Amenities:** A/C. No phone or TV. Thick comforters. **Services:** Beverages at check-in; evening gourmet dinners by advance reservation. **Facilities:** 1 restaurant (bkfst and dinner only), guest lounge w/TV. **Rates (BB):** $55–$70 S; $65–$85 D; $85–$95 ste. Parking: Outdoor, free. MC, V.

RESTAURANT

★ The Pines Restaurant
1500 E 7th St; tel 712/243-3606. IA 83. **Regional American/Steak.** Known for serving "broasted" chicken. Other menu offerings are steaks, seafood, and sandwiches. Fresh fish might be red snapper, walleye, or catfish. Prime rib is highlighted on Thursday, Friday, and Saturday. **FYI:** Reservations recommended. Children's menu. **Open:** Mon–Sat 5–10:30pm. **Prices:** Main courses $10–$16. AE, DISC, MC, V.

Bettendorf

Part of the Quad Cities metropolitan area, which also includes Davenport, IA, and Moline and Rock Island, IL. Sprawling along the Mississippi River on Iowa's eastern border, the area blends historic significance as a river commerce hub with the modern flavor of metropolitan attractions. Historic riverboats and railroad depots beckon along with new shopping, dining, nightclub, and casino locales. **Information:** Quad City Convention and Visitors Bureau, 2020 3rd Ave, Moline, IL 61265 (tel 309/788/7800).

HOTELS

The Abbey Hotel
1401 Central Ave, 52722; tel 319/355-0291 or toll free 800/438-7535. State St/Riverfront exit off I-74 N. Situated atop a bluff overlooking the Mississippi, this castlelike brick and stone structure was built in 1917 as a Carmelite convent. Listed on the National Register of Historic Places, the property was converted to a hotel in 1990 featuring such luxurious touches as an Italian marble lobby and crystal chandeliers. **Rooms:** 19 rms. CI 2pm/CO noon. Nonsmoking rms avail. As many as five of the original "cells" have been combined to create each of the spacious guest accommodations (which include marble bathrooms). Antiques enhance the period atmosphere. Most rooms have a view of the river. **Amenities:** A/C, cable TV. All units w/minibars, all w/terraces. **Services:** X **Facilities:** 50 A museum room on the third floor preserves the history of the Carmelite Sisters and contains many original furnishings. The Gothic chapel is often used for weddings. **Rates (BB):** $75–$125 S or D. Extra person $6. Children under age 10 stay free. Parking: Outdoor, free. AE, DC, DISC, MC, V.

Heartland Inn
815 Golden Valley Rd, 52722; tel 319/355-6336 or toll free 800/334-3277. Spruce Hills/Kimberly Rd exit off I-74 at Utica Ridge. Very service-oriented hotel. **Rooms:** 87 rms. CI 3pm/CO 11am. Nonsmoking rms avail. **Amenities:** A/C, cable TV w/movies. 1 unit w/whirlpool. **Services:** Morning coffee delivered to guest rooms on weekdays. Weekly manager's social. **Facilities:** Whirlpool. 24-hour coffee bar. **Rates (CP):** Peak (Apr–Oct) $41–$125 S or D. Extra person $9. Children under age 16 stay free. Lower rates off-season. Parking: Outdoor, free. Frequent travelers' program avail. AE, CB, DC, DISC, MC, V.

Holiday Inn Bettendorf
909 Middle Rd, 52722; tel 319/355-4761 or toll free 800/626-0780. Off I-74. Older, two-story hotel. **Rooms:** 159 rms. CI 3pm/CO noon. Nonsmoking rms avail. Ask for one of the recently refurbished rooms. **Amenities:** A/C, cable TV w/movies. **Services:** **Facilities:** 1 restaurant, games rm, whirlpool. Games room with table tennis, miniature golf, and more. **Rates:** $49–$81 S or D. Extra person $8.

Children under age 18 stay free. Parking: Outdoor, free. Riverboat gambling and concert packages avail. AE, CB, DC, DISC, MC, V.

Jumer's Castle Lodge
900 Spruce Hills Dr, 52722; tel 319/359-7141 or toll free 800/285-8637. Directly off of I-80 and I-74. Full-service hotel with a European-Bavarian theme, complete with antiques and oil paintings. **Rooms:** 210 rms and stes. Executive level. CI 2pm/CO noon. Nonsmoking rms avail. Tower room has spiral staircase leading down to an atrium with chairs, desk, and armoire. **Amenities:** A/C, cable TV w/movies, refrig, in-rm safe. All units w/minibars, some w/terraces, some w/fireplaces, 1 w/whirlpool. Complimentary box of chocolates in each room. **Services:** VP Twice-daily maid svce, masseur. Free local calls. **Facilities:** 200 1 restaurant, spa, sauna, whirlpool. Dining room serves German-American cuisine. **Rates:** $76–$138 S or D; $133 ste. Extra person $7. Children under age 18 stay free. AP and MAP rates avail. Parking: Outdoor, free. AE, CB, DC, DISC, MC, V.

MOTELS

Days Inn
3202 E Kimberly Rd, 52722; tel 319/355-1190 or toll free 800/329-7466. Off I-74. Two-story motel with rooms reached via interior corridors. **Rooms:** 65 rms. CI 2pm/CO 11am. Nonsmoking rms avail. **Amenities:** A/C, cable TV w/movies. **Services:** **Facilities:** Whirlpool. **Rates (CP):** $40–$60 S or D. Extra person $6. Children under age 18 stay free. Parking: Outdoor, free. 13th-night-free program. AE, CB, DC, DISC, MC, V.

El Rancho Inn
2205 Kimberly Rd, 52722; tel 319/355-6471 or toll free 800/397-0299. Close to John Deere Center, River Bandits baseball, and Thunder basketball venues, as well as the convention center/concert arena. Adjacent to golf course and bike/jogging path. **Rooms:** 65 rms. CI 3pm/CO noon. Nonsmoking rms avail. Early check-in sometimes available. **Amenities:** A/C, cable TV w/movies. **Facilities:** 1 restaurant. **Rates (CP):** $34–$49 S or D. Extra person $4. Children under age 18 stay free. Parking: Outdoor, free. AE, DISC, MC, V.

RESTAURANT

Jumer's Restaurant
In Jumer's Castle Lodge, 900 Spruce Hills Dr; tel 319/359-1607. **American/German.** Dark woodwork and mounted deer and moose heads characterize this restaurant, which makes an attempt at a Bavarian castle motif. Tables are prettily arrayed with flowers and candles. Different choices of schnitzel and sausage. **FYI:** Reservations recommended. Guitar/piano. Children's menu. **Open:** Breakfast Mon–Sat 6–11am, Sun 6:30–11am; lunch daily 11:30am–4pm; dinner Sun–Thurs 4:30–10pm, Fri–Sat 4:30–11pm; brunch Sun–10am–2pm. **Prices:** Main courses $7–$29. AE, DC, DISC, MC, V.

ATTRACTION

The Children's Museum
533 16th St; tel 319/344-4106. Permanent exhibits allow kids to journey through the human circulatory system via virtual reality, learn about optical illusions and kaleidoscopes in the Mirror Magic area, explore the physical properties of soap bubbles, and investigate early 19th-century Iowa farm life. Recent traveling exhibits have included a profile of the Exxon Valdez oil spill and a display of Chinese friendship scrolls. **Open:** Tues–Wed 10am–5pm, Thurs–Fri 10am–8pm, Sat 10am–5pm, Sun noon–5pm. Closed some hols. **$**

Burlington

Scenic bluffs overlook this river city and Iowa's first territorial capital (1838–1840). Today's visitors come for antique shopping, boat racing, and riverboat gambling. **Information:** Burlington/W Burlington Area Chamber of Commerce, 807 Jefferson St, PO Box 6, Burlington, 52601 (tel 319/752-6365).

MOTELS

Arrowhead Motel
2520 Mt Pleasant St, 52601; tel 319/752-6353 or toll free 800/341-8000; fax 319/752-6353. 1 mile E of jct US 61. Accommodations in one recently constructed building are OK, though other rooms are a little dated. Try to get one of the newer rooms; otherwise, you might consider looking elsewhere. **Rooms:** 30 rms and stes. CI open/CO 11am. Nonsmoking rms avail. Most rooms need renovation, though management does a nice job with what they have. **Amenities:** A/C, cable TV, refrig. Suites have full kitchens. **Services:** **Facilities:** Washer/dryer. **Rates:** $32–$38 S; $36–$42 D; $38–$54 ste. Extra person $6. Parking: Outdoor, free. AE, CB, DC, DISC, MC, V.

Best Western Pzazz Motor Inn
3001 Winegard Dr, 52601; tel 319/753-2223 or toll free 800/373-1223; fax 319/753-2223. E of US 61. Just a few blocks from US 34, with easy access to downtown. **Rooms:** 151 rms and stes. CI 1pm/CO noon. Nonsmoking rms avail. Spacious rooms. **Amenities:** A/C, cable TV w/movies, VCR. Some units w/terraces, some w/whirlpools. **Services:** Masseur, babysitting. **Facilities:** 750 3 restaurants, 3 bars (1 w/entertainment), games rm, sauna, whirlpool, beauty salon, washer/dryer. **Rates:** $58 S; $66 D; $105 ste. Extra person $4. Children under age 18 stay free. Parking: Outdoor, free. Winter weekend packages avail Oct 1–May 20. AE, CB, DC, DISC, MC, V.

Comfort Inn
3051 Kirkwood, 52601; tel 319/753-0000 or toll free 800/221-2222; fax 319/753-0000. Off US 34 at jct US 61. Rather quiet given its location just off a busy road. **Rooms:** 52 rms. CI noon/CO 11am. Nonsmoking rms avail. Clean and tastefully appointed. **Amenities:** A/C, cable TV w/movies. 1 unit w/whirlpool. **Services:** **Facilities:** **Rates (CP):** Peak (Oct–Apr) $45 S; $50 D. Extra person $5. Children under age 18 stay free. Lower rates off-season. Parking: Outdoor, free. AE, CB, DC, DISC, MC, V.

RESTAURANT

Big Muddy's
710 Front St; tel 319/753-1699. On the riverfront just N of the bridge. **American.** Housed in an old railroad station on at the edge of the Mississippi River, this basic eatery offers a great view of the river, especially from the outside patio. Salads and sandwiches are served at lunch, while the dinner choices are predominantly steak and seafood. Prime rib is the house specialty. **FYI:** Reservations recommended. Blues. Children's menu. **Open:** Mon–Sat 11am–2am, Sun 10am–2am. **Prices:** Main courses $9–$29. AE, DISC, MC, V.

ATTRACTIONS

Phelps House Museum
512 Columbia (Snake Alley); tel 319/753-5880. Former home (originally built in 1851) of three generations of one of Burlington's most prominent families. The nine rooms open to the public feature such treasures as marble fireplaces, mahogany and walnut furniture, and oriental rugs. The dining room is graced with a collection of family tableware, including a set of rare yellow Wedgwood china. From 1894 to 1899, Phelps House served as Burlington's first Protestant hospital, and part of the third floor houses a collection of antique medical equipment. **Open:** Wed and Sun 1:30–4:30pm. Closed Nov–Apr. $

Log Cabin Museum
Crapo Park; tel 319/753-5981. Cabin built on the bluff where Lt Zebulon Pike first raised the American flag on what would later become Iowa soil. Hanging on the walls are the hand tools used to build the cabin, along with pioneer household implements such as the cradle and flail for grain harvesting, the wheel for yarn spinning, and many others. **Open:** Wed and Sun 1:30–4:30pm. Closed Oct 1–May 1.

The Apple Trees Museum
1616 Dill St (Perkins Park); tel 319/753-2449. Housed in an 1899 addition to the Charles E Perkins mansion, this collection recalls the lavish lifestyle of a rags-to-riches Midwest railroad man. Carved oak woodwork, imposing fireplaces, and an outstanding array of Native American pottery and beadwork reflect Perkins's immaculate taste. The former billiard room is now decorated with Victorian antiques, glassware, china, and dolls; the Tools & Trades room features 19th-century tools and machinery. **Open:** Wed and Sun 1:30–4:30pm. Closed Nov–Apr.

Carroll

This bustling town is nestled in Iowa's west-central plains at the intersection of US 30 and US 71. Named for Maryland lawyer Charles Carroll, one of the signers of the Declaration of Independence. **Information:** 223 W 5th St, PO Box 307, Carroll, 51401 (tel 712/792-4383).

HOTEL

Carrollton Inn
US 71 N, 51401; tel 712/792-5600 or toll free 800/798-3535; fax 712/792-5600. 1 block N of US 30. Located on the edge of town (adjacent to a city park), this property boasts a convention complex and ballroom. **Rooms:** 89 rms and stes. Executive level. CI 2pm/CO noon. Nonsmoking rms avail. Rooms are large and comfortable. Two executive suites available. **Amenities:** A/C, cable TV w/movies, dataport. Some units w/whirlpools. Bridal suite features a heart-shaped whirlpool. **Services:** Babysitting. Movie rentals, including selections for children. **Facilities:** 1 restaurant, 1 bar, games rm, sauna, steam rm, whirlpool, beauty salon, washer/dryer. **Rates:** $45 S; $55 D; $90 ste. Extra person $5. Children under age 12 stay free. Parking: Outdoor, free. AE, DC, DISC, MC, V.

MOTEL

Econo Lodge
1225 Plaza Dr, 51401; tel 712/792-5156 or toll free 800/424-4777; fax 712/792-6674. On US 30, E of Carroll. A new facility, clean but stark. **Rooms:** 41 rms and stes. CI 11am/CO 11am. Nonsmoking rms avail. Bright and nicely decorated. **Amenities:** A/C, cable TV w/movies. **Services:** Babysitting. **Facilities:** Games rm, sauna, steam rm. Truck parking. **Rates (CP):** $37–$40 S; $46–$59 D; $43–$51 ste. Extra person $3. Children under age 16 stay free. Parking: Outdoor, free. AE, DISC, MC, V.

Cedar Falls

See also Waterloo

Site of the University of Northern Iowa's 850-acre campus. Naturalists will enjoy the Harman Reserve Nature Center, an 80-acre woodland with an extensive trail system. **Information:** Cedar Falls Tourism and Visitors Bureau, PO Box 367, Cedar Falls, 50613 (tel 319/266-3593).

RESTAURANT

The Olde Broom Factory

110 N Main St; tel 319/268-0877. Near Chamber of Commerce office, just off US 218. **American.** Offers an eclectic menu with nightly Cajun specials and reasonable prices, as well as views of the Cedar River. The 133-year-old building once housed one of the largest wooden pump works in the world. More recently, brooms were made here until vacuum cleaners took the lead in the 1940s. **FYI:** Reservations recommended. Jazz. Children's menu. Dress code. **Open:** Lunch Mon–Fri 11am–2:30pm, Sat 11am–2pm; dinner Mon–Thurs 5–10pm, Fri 5–11pm, Sat 4:30–11pm, Sun 2–10pm; brunch Sun 10am–2pm. **Prices:** Main courses $6–$18. AE, CB, DC, DISC, MC, V.

ATTRACTIONS

Victorian Home Museum

303 Franklin St; tel 319/277-8817 or 266-5149. Built in the Italian revival style popular during the Civil War, this mansion is furnished with 1890s Victorian antiques and household goods. The house's cupola (open to the public) offers a view of the Cedar River to the north and the sweeping prairies to the south and west. A collection of mannequins dressed in period gowns is also on display. Guided tours available by appointment. **Open:** Wed–Sun 2–4pm. Closed some hols. **$**

The Little Red School

First and Clay Sts; tel 319/277-8817 or 266-5149. Built in 1909, this fully restored one-room school is equipped with a bell tower and bell, pot-bellied stove, blackboards, desks, and other furnishings typical of the turn-of-the-century schoolhouse. Guided tours available by appointment. **Open:** May–Oct, Wed & Sat–Sun 2–4:30pm. **$**

Cedar Rapids

Iowa's second-largest city, with attractions ranging from the 21-room Queen Anne–style Brucemore mansion to the ethnic bakeries and crafts shops of Czech Village. **Information:** Cedar Rapids Area Convention and Visitors Bureau, 119 1st Ave SE, PO Box 5339, Cedar Rapids, 52406 (tel 319/398-5009).

PUBLIC TRANSPORTATION

EAGL city bus service (tel 319/398-5335) connects downtown area to shopping malls and many hotels. Fares: adults 50¢, seniors and persons with disabilities 25¢, students 30¢; children under 5 ride free. Transfers are 10¢. Exact change required. Paratransit service provided door-to-door for 85¢; call 319/398-3625 for reservations. Cedar Rapids also has downtown trolley route that operates in am and pm rush hours; call 319/398-5367 for schedule.

HOTELS

Five Seasons Hotel

350 1st Ave NE, 52401; tel 319/363-8161 or toll free 800/282-4692; fax 319/363-3804. ½ mi NE of jct I-380 and US 151. Full-service, modern high-rise in the heart of downtown. **Rooms:** 275 rms and stes. Executive level. CI 3pm/CO noon. Nonsmoking rms avail. Comfortably appointed rooms with an emphasis on attractive utility rather than overbearing lavishness. **Amenities:** A/C, cable TV w/movies, dataport. Some units w/minibars. Deluxe rooms on concierge floor have bathrobes and padded hangers. **Services:** Twice-daily maid svce, babysitting. Concierge-level guests receive complimentary continental breakfast and evening hors d'oeuvres and cocktails. **Facilities:** 2000 1 restaurant, 1 bar, games rm, sauna, whirlpool. Enclosed skywalk connects hotel with nearby parking garage and adjacent shopping district. **Rates:** $69–$109 S; $79–$119 D; $175–$325 ste. Extra person $10. Children under age 12 stay free. Parking: Indoor, $3/day. Weekend packages avail. AE, CB, DC, DISC, MC, V.

Sheraton Inn

525 33rd Ave SW, 52404; tel 319/366-8671 or toll free 800/325-3535; fax 319/362-1420. Exit 17 off I-380, ½ mi W. Located in a quiet area, slightly away from the town's main motel strip. Good for the traveler seeking something a little more than the usual motel. **Rooms:** 157 rms and stes. Executive level. CI 3pm/CO noon. Nonsmoking rms avail. Larger than average. **Amenities:** A/C, cable TV w/movies. Some units w/whirlpools. Suites offer complimentary champagne and fruit. **Services:** Social director, babysitting. **Facilities:** 1550 1 restaurant, 1 bar (w/entertainment), games rm, sauna, whirlpool, washer/dryer. **Rates:** Peak (Feb–Nov) $57–$67 S; $67–$77 D; $185 ste. Extra person $10. Children under age 18 stay free. Lower rates off-season. Parking: Outdoor, free. AE, CB, DC, DISC, MC, V.

MOTELS

Cedar Rapids Village Inn

100 F Ave NW, 52405; tel 319/366-5323 or toll free 800/858-5511; fax 319/366-5323. Just N of the I-380 overpass on IA 94. Located at the junction of three busy thoroughfares, close to downtown and the river. **Rooms:** 87 rms and stes. CI noon/CO noon. Nonsmoking rms avail. Clean and reasonably quiet given the location; all rooms have been remodeled in the last few years. **Amenities:** A/C, cable TV. **Services:** Social director. **Facilities:** 140 1 restaurant, 1 bar, washer/dryer. **Rates:** $35–$40 S; $37–$46 D; $70–$80 ste. Extra person $5. Children under age 12 stay free. Parking: Outdoor, free. AE, CB, DC, DISC, MC, V.

Comfort Inn North

5055 Rockwell Dr, 52402; tel 319/393-8247 or toll free 800/228-5150; fax 319/393-8247. 1.25 miles E of jct I-380/IA

100. New building in a quiet location; short drive to shopping. **Rooms:** 59 rms. CI 2pm/CO 11am. Nonsmoking rms avail. **Amenities:** A/C, cable TV w/movies. Deluxe rooms have refrigerators and microwaves. **Services:** **Facilities:** Whirlpool. **Rates (CP):** $47–$53 S; $52–$61 D. Extra person $5. Children under age 18 stay free. Parking: Outdoor, free. AE, CB, DC, DISC, ER, MC, V.

Country Inn by Carlson
4747 1st Ave SE, 52403; tel 319/393-8800 or toll free 800/456-4000; fax 319/378-3505. 4 mi NE of downtown. Completely renovated in 1994; a bit pricey for the location, 15 minutes from downtown. **Rooms:** 50 rms and stes. CI 2pm/CO noon. Nonsmoking rms avail. Suites consist of single rooms with larger-than-standard beds and additional seating. Units for guests with disabilities have roll-in showers. **Amenities:** A/C, cable TV, dataport. **Services:** Babysitting. **Facilities:** 16 Whirlpool. **Rates (CP):** $49–$54 S; $56–$62 D; $98 ste. Extra person $7. Children under age 18 stay free. Parking: Outdoor, free. AE, CB, DC, DISC, MC, V.

Days Inn
3245 Southgate Place SW, 52404; tel 319/365-4339 or toll free 800/325-2525; fax 319/365-4339. I-380 exit 17, ½ mi W. Very clean rooms. Located in a busy neighborhood. **Rooms:** 40 rms and stes. CI 1pm/CO 11am. Nonsmoking rms avail. Average in size and appointments. **Amenities:** A/C, cable TV. **Services:** **Facilities:** Whirlpool. **Rates (CP):** Peak (May–Sept) $44–$53 S; $55–$65 D; $60–$70 ste. Extra person $5. Children under age 18 stay free. Lower rates off-season. Parking: Outdoor, free. Weekend specials avail. AE, CB, DC, DISC, MC, V.

Econo Lodge
622 33rd Ave SW, 52404; tel 319/363-8888 or toll free 800/424-4777; fax 319/363-8888. Exit 17 off I-380. Standard rooms here are clean and fairly large, but there's lots of traffic noise from the interstate. **Rooms:** 50 rms and stes. CI 2pm/CO 11am. Nonsmoking rms avail. Suites are deluxe one-room units. **Amenities:** A/C, cable TV. Some units w/whirlpools. **Services:** **Facilities:** Whirlpool. **Rates (CP):** Peak (Apr–Nov) $43–$53 S; $56–$58 D; $70–$100 ste. Extra person $5. Children under age 17 stay free. Lower rates off-season. Parking: Outdoor, free. Group rates avail. AE, CB, DC, DISC, MC, V.

Exel Inn
616 33rd Ave SW, 52404; tel 319/366-2475 or toll free 800/356-8013; fax 319/366-2475. Exit 17 off I-380; ½ mi W. Located near the interstate for easy access to downtown or the University of Iowa in nearby Iowa City. **Rooms:** 103 rms. CI 3pm/CO noon. Nonsmoking rms avail. Rooms are smallish and well-worn, but very clean. **Amenities:** A/C, cable TV w/movies, dataport. 1 unit w/whirlpool. **Services:** Pets in smoking rooms only. **Facilities:** Barbecue grill on sundeck. **Rates (CP):** $29–$42 S; $38–$48 D. Extra person $5. Children under age 17 stay free. Parking: Outdoor, free. Standard rates may increase on weekends. Senior rates avail. AE, CB, DC, DISC, MC, V.

Heartland Inn
3315 Southgate Court SW, 52404; tel 319/362-9012 or toll free 800/334-3277; fax 319/362-9694. Exit 17 off I-380, ½ mi W. The building is in good shape, but is situated in a high-traffic area. **Rooms:** 116 rms, stes, and effic. CI 4pm/CO noon. Nonsmoking rms avail. Small but nicely decorated rooms. **Amenities:** A/C, cable TV w/movies. Some units w/fireplaces, some w/whirlpools. Deluxe one-room units have whirlpools. **Services:** **Facilities:** 30 Sauna. **Rates (CP):** $42–$56 S; $43–$52 D; $58–$150 ste; $58–$67 effic. Extra person $8. Children under age 16 stay free. Parking: Outdoor, free. Lower rates for extended stays. Honeymoon and anniversary packages avail. AE, CB, DC, DISC, MC, V.

Holiday Inn
2501 Williams Blvd SW, 52404; tel 319/365-9441 or toll free 800/465-4329; fax 319/365-0255. 1½ mi NE of jct US 151 and US 30. An almost secluded property off the highway a few miles from downtown. **Rooms:** 186 rms and stes. CI 2pm/CO noon. Nonsmoking rms avail. Rooms appear a bit threadbare in spots; larger rooms have sofas. **Amenities:** A/C, satel TV w/movies. **Services:** Babysitting. **Facilities:** 300 1 restaurant, 1 bar, games rm, sauna, whirlpool, washer/dryer. Small putting green, pool tables. Guest privileges at nearby fitness center. **Rates:** $50–$80 S or D; $95–$125 ste. Children under age 16 stay free. Parking: Outdoor, free. AE, CB, DC, DISC, MC, V.

Red Roof Inn
3325 Southgate Court SW, 52404; tel 319/366-7523 or toll free 800/843-7663; fax 319/366-7639. ¼ mi W of I-380 exit 17. Located very near the interstate, it's rather noisy, and the exterior needs work. Rates are reasonable, though there are better bargains around. **Rooms:** 108 rms. CI 2pm/CO noon. Nonsmoking rms avail. **Amenities:** A/C, satel TV. **Services:** **Facilities:** **Rates:** Peak (Aug–Sept) $37–$45 S; $45–$53 D. Extra person $7. Children under age 18 stay free. Lower rates off-season. Parking: Outdoor, free. Rates increase for University of Iowa football weekends. AE, CB, DC, DISC, MC, V.

RESTAURANTS

The Amalgamated Spirit & Provision Co
3320 Southgate Court; tel 319/363-2031. Take I-38 to exit 17. **American.** The frumpy exterior belies a cozy interior. Prime rib is king here, but fresh seafood specials are likewise available, with a different fish offered each week. Reservations accepted only for 10 or more, but you can wait the short time in the plush bar. **FYI:** Reservations not accepted. Children's menu. Additional location: 4407 1st Ave NE (tel

393-9727). **Open:** Lunch Mon–Fri 11:30am–2pm; dinner Mon–Thurs 5–10pm, Fri–Sat 5–11pm, Sun 5–9pm. **Prices:** Main courses $10–$20. AE, CB, DC, DISC, MC, V.

The Dragon
329 2nd Ave SE; tel 319/362-9716. 1 block E of Five Seasons Center. **Chinese.** Located in the heart of downtown, the Dragon has been a local institution for 40 years. In the lavishly decorated rear dining room, diners can choose a favorite like sweet and sour pork or opt for a plain ol' burger and fries. Extensive wine list. **FYI:** Reservations accepted. **Open:** Lunch Tues–Fri 11am–2:30pm; dinner Tues–Thurs 4:30–10pm, Fri–Sat 11am–11pm, Sun 11:30am–9pm. **Prices:** Main courses $6–$13. AE, CB, DC, DISC, MC, V.

The Springhouse Restaurant
3980 Center Point Rd; tel 319/393-4995. 2 mi N of downtown. **Diner.** Located well outside the downtown area, this sparsely decorated eatery has all the classic greasy-spoon favorites—from grilled cheese sandwiches to Salisbury steak. Stick-to-the-ribs food for breakfast, lunch, or dinner. Reservations accepted for groups. **FYI:** Reservations accepted. Children's menu. No liquor license. **Open:** Mon–Sat 6am–9pm, Sun 7:30am–8pm. **Prices:** Main courses $6–$11. DISC, MC, V.

ATTRACTIONS

Cedar Rapids Museum of Art
410 3rd Ave SE; tel 319/366-7503. Housed in a restored 1905 beaux arts building and a newly constructed wing, separated by a lush Winter Garden, this distinguished regional collection features the works of two native sons: Marvin Cone and *American Gothic* painter Grant Wood. Highlights include Wood's *Young Gordon* and Cone's *Anniversary*; other regional artists are shown as well. **Open:** Tues–Wed and Fri–Sat 10am–4pm; Thurs 10am–7pm; Sun noon–3pm. Closed some hols. **$**

Brucemore
2160 Linden Dr SE; tel 319/362-7375. A classic example of Queen Anne architecture, this 21-room mansion was built in 1886 for $55,000. Over the next century, Brucemore was owned by three prominent families of America's industrial middle class: the Sinclairs (meat packing), the Douglases (Quaker Oats), and the Halls (steel and manufacturing). Each succeeding generation left its imprint on the house, adding rooms, porches, and interior wall murals. Today, much of the original furniture remains: mahogany furniture, crystal chandeliers, even a "Tahitian Room" with bamboo furniture and hula dolls. The furniture in the 1935 Swan Room is graced by 20 swans; the sunroom was decorated by Grant Wood.

Other fixtures on the 26-acre estate include six outbuildings, pool, duck pond, orchard, and formal gardens. Fairs, fine arts performances, Christmas pageants, and garden walks are held throughout the year; call for schedule. **Open:** Tues–Sat 10am–3pm; tours on the hour. Closed Jan and some hols. **$$**

National Czech and Slovak Museum and Library
30 16th Ave SW; tel 319/362-8500. Housed in a restored two-room immigrant home, this museum celebrates the contributions of the Czechs, Slovaks, and Moravians who immigrated here in the late 19th and early 20th centuries. Over 40 national costumes made from handmade lace, embroidery, and beadwork are on display, as are ethnic crafts such as hand-carved pipes, hand-painted porcelains, and lead crystal. The museum's oldest artifact is a Czech Bible printed in 1587. Guided tours, gift shop. **Open:** Tues–Sat 9:30am–4pm. Closed some hols. **$**

Science Station
427 First St SE; tel 319/366-0968. Three floors of interactive exhibits allow visitors to surround themselves in giant soap bubbles, step into the middle of a giant kaleidoscope, or broadcast from a real TV weather studio. Science Station Store sells lab kits, books, and souvenirs. **Open:** Tues–Sat 9am–5pm, Sun 1–4pm. Closed some hols. **$**

Indian Creek Nature Center
6665 Otis Rd SE; tel 319/362-0664. Within this 140-acre nature preserve are a beaver colony and herds of white-tailed deer, as well as wildflowers and prairie grasses. An old dairy barn now serves as an interpretive center, with displays on natural habitats, a demonstration bee hive, and an observation tower. Nature trails are open to cross-country skiers in winter. **Open:** Mon–Fri 9am–4pm, Sat 11am–4pm, Sun 1–4pm. Closed some hols. **$**

Charles City

This north-central Iowa town is the home base of the Hart-Parr Company, manufacturer of the 1st gasoline-powered tractor. Thirty minutes south of Charles City on US 218 is Nashua's famous Little Brown Church in the Vale, a popular wedding site. **Information:** Charles City Area Chamber of Commerce, 610 S Grand Ave, Charles City, 50616 (tel 515/228-4234).

MOTELS

Hartwood Inn
1312 Gilbert St, 50616; tel 515/228-4352 or toll free 800/972-2335; fax 515/228-2672. ½ mi E of jct US 218 N/US 18 W. A well-kept budget motel. **Rooms:** 35 rms. CI 11am/CO 11am. Nonsmoking rms avail. Some rooms open onto a nice deck overlooking a nearby river. **Amenities:** A/C, cable TV, refrig, dataport. Some units w/terraces. **Services:** Babysitting. **Facilities:** Washer/dryer. **Rates:** $32–$45 S; $42–$60 D. Extra person $5. Children under age 16 stay free. Parking: Outdoor, free. AE, CB, DC, DISC, MC, V.

Lamplighter Motel
1416 Gilbert St, 50616; tel 515/228-6711 or toll free 800/341-8000; fax 515/228-7203. 1 mi NW of jct US 218N/US

18W. Economical lodging with clean, neat rooms. **Rooms:** 47 rms. CI 2pm/CO 11am. Nonsmoking rms avail. **Amenities:** A/C, cable TV. **Services:** **Facilities:** Games rm, whirlpool. **Rates:** $31–$34 S; $37–$42 D. Extra person $6. Parking: Outdoor, free. AE, CB, DC, DISC, MC, V.

ATTRACTION

The Little Brown Church
IA 346, Nashua; tel 515/435-2027. 10 mi SE of Charles City. Built in the mid-19th century by pioneers, this church is the subject of the gospel song "The Church in the Wildwood," by William Pitts. More than 67,000 weddings have been held here since World War I, an Annual Wedding Reunion is held at the church every August. The parish maintains a 10-acre park with picnic tables, rest rooms, parking, and a gift shop. **Open:** Daily sunrise–sunset. **Free**

Clear Lake

See also Mason City

Perhaps best known as the site of the 1959 plane crash that killed rockers Buddy Holly, Richie Valens, and J P "the Big Bopper" Richardson; the town hosts an annual tribute to these musical legends. Fishing and boating on nearby Clear Lake is extremely popular throughout the summer season. **Information:** Clear Lake Area Chamber of Commerce, 205 Main Ave, PO Box 188, Clear Lake, 50428 (tel 515/357-2159).

MOTELS

Best Western Holiday Lodge
US 18, PO Box J, 50428; tel 515/357-5253 or toll free 800/528-1234; fax 515/357-8153. W of I-35. Basic motel offering tidy rooms, located just off the interstate in a lake resort area. **Rooms:** 144 rms and stes. Executive level. CI 3pm/CO 11am. Nonsmoking rms avail. **Amenities:** A/C, satel TV w/movies, refrig, dataport, VCR. Some units w/terraces. **Services:** Twice-daily maid svce, babysitting. **Facilities:** 1 restaurant, 1 bar (w/entertainment), games rm, sauna, whirlpool. **Rates (CP):** $47–$67 S; $55–$68 D; $60–$120 ste. Extra person $8. Children under age 18 stay free. Parking: Outdoor, free. AE, CB, DC, DISC, MC, V.

Budget Inn
US 18 and I-35, 50428; tel 515/357-8700 or toll free 800/341-8000; fax 515/357-8811. Adjacent to the interstate, this bare-bones property is fine for a good night's sleep. **Rooms:** 60 rms and stes. CI noon/CO noon. Nonsmoking rms avail. Nothing fancy, but the beds work. **Amenities:** A/C, satel TV, dataport. **Services:** **Facilities:** Playground. **Rates (CP):** $37–$51 S or D; $40–$46 ste. Extra person $6. Children under age 16 stay free. Parking: Outdoor, free. AE, DC, DISC, MC, V.

Heartland Inn
1603 S Shore Dr, 50428; tel 515/357-5123 or toll free 800/334-3277; fax 515/357-2228. A well-maintained property facing Clear Lake, with easy access to water sports. **Rooms:** 18 rms. CI 3pm/CO 11am. Nonsmoking rms avail. All rooms face lake. **Amenities:** A/C, cable TV w/movies, refrig. Some units w/terraces, some w/whirlpools. **Services:** **Facilities:** **Rates (CP):** Peak (May 1–Labor Day) $75–$125 S or D. Extra person $8. Children under age 16 stay free. Lower rates off-season. Parking: Outdoor, free. AE, DC, DISC, MC, V.

Super 8 Motel
I-35, exit 193 E, 50428; tel 515/357-7521 or toll free 800/800-8000; fax 515/357-5999. Basic, predictable, no-frills. **Rooms:** 60 rms. CI 2pm/CO 11am. Nonsmoking rms avail. **Amenities:** A/C, satel TV. **Services:** **Facilities:** **Rates (CP):** $35–$46 S or D. Parking: Outdoor, free. Special rates for seniors, truckers, and repeat guests. AE, DC, DISC, MC, V.

ATTRACTION

Surf Ballroom
460 N Shore Dr; tel 515/357-6151. On February 2, 1959, Buddy Holly, Ritchie Valens, and J P "the Big Bopper" Richardson played their last performances here before their plane crashed nearby, killing all three of them. A monument to their memory is erected outside the concert hall and a memorial concert is held each year. At other times visitors can hear a wide variety of music including country, big band, and classics of the '50s and '60s.

Clinton

Situated on the banks of the Mississippi River, just north of the Quad City area. Clinton's attractions include several floating casinos and a showboat theater. Baseball fans can watch the Class-A Clinton Lumber Kings play. **Information:** Clinton Convention and Visitors Bureau, 333 4th Ave S, PO Box 1024, Clinton, 52733 (tel 319/242-5702).

MOTELS

Best Western Frontier Motor Inn
2300 Lincolnway, 52732; tel 319/242-7112 or toll free 800/728-7112; fax 319/242-7117. At jct US 30/US 67. Close to riverboat/showboat area, with winter dock and excursions available. **Rooms:** 117 rms and stes. CI 2pm/CO noon. Nonsmoking rms avail. Nicely appointed, rooms are pleasant and bright. **Amenities:** A/C, cable TV w/movies, refrig, VCR. Some units w/terraces, 1 w/whirlpool. **Services:** Car-rental desk, children's program. Courtesy car

available by appointment. **Facilities:** 1 restaurant (dinner only), spa, whirlpool, washer/dryer. **Rates:** Peak (Apr–Jan) $42–$67 S; $50–$75 D; $95–$140 ste. Extra person $6. Children under age 12 stay free. Lower rates off-season. Parking: Outdoor, free. AE, CB, DC, DISC, MC, V.

Ramada Inn
1522 Lincolnway, 52732; tel 319/243-8841 or toll free 800/232-0044; fax 319/242-6202. At jct US 30/US 67. Close to riverboat gambling casinos. **Rooms:** 103 rms, stes, and effic. Executive level. CI 3pm/CO noon. Nonsmoking rms avail. Tidy and clean moderate-size rooms. **Amenities:** A/C, cable TV w/movies, refrig, dataport. **Services:** Children's program. Free shuttle to casinos. **Facilities:** 250 Games rm, whirlpool. **Rates (CP):** $50 S; $56 D; $75 ste; $85 effic. Extra person $6. Children under age 18 stay free. Parking: Outdoor, free. AE, CB, DC, DISC, MC, V.

Super 8 Motel
1711 Lincolnway, 52732; tel 319/242-8870 or toll free 800/800-8000; fax 319/242-8870. At 17th St. Sparsely landscaped property with small and barren, but tidy, rooms. **Rooms:** 63 rms. CI 2pm/CO 11am. Nonsmoking rms avail. **Amenities:** A/C, cable TV w/movies. **Services:** Complimentary continental breakfast is just toast and coffee. **Facilities:** Truck parking available. **Rates (CP):** $40 S; $49 D. Extra person $3. Children under age 12 stay free. Parking: Outdoor, free. Ask about Travelers Advantage Club offering special services. AE, CB, DC, DISC, MC, V.

Timber Motel
2225 Lincolnway, 52732; tel 319/243-6901. At jct US 67/US 30. Clean and pleasant enough, although motel is small and sparsely furnished. A cheap place for a short stay. **Rooms:** 32 rms. CI open/CO 11am. Nonsmoking rms avail. Some rooms have refrigerators. **Amenities:** A/C, cable TV w/movies. **Services:** Juice, coffee, donuts offered in lobby for breakfast. **Facilities:** **Rates (CP):** $33 S; $39 D. Extra person $6. Children under age 12 stay free. Parking: Outdoor, free. AE, CB, DISC, MC, V.

RESTAURANT

The Unicorn
1004 N 2nd St; tel 319/242-7355. **American/Continental.** This attractive red brick Victorian home offers four different rooms for dining, as well as a boutique and gift shop. For the most romantic locale, ask for a table by a window. The menu features choices chicken dijonnaise, prime rib, and coquilles St Jacques. Chocolate souffle cake for dessert. **FYI:** Reservations recommended. **Open:** Lunch Mon–Sat 11am–2pm; dinner Fri–Sat 6–9pm; brunch. **Prices:** Main courses $11–$20. AE, DISC, MC, V.

Clive

See Des Moines

Coralville

See Iowa City

Council Bluffs

See also Omaha (NE)

Located across the Missouri River from Omaha, Council Bluffs was an early connection on America's first transcontinental railroad. At the height of the rail era, eight different rail lines passed through town. **Information:** Council Bluffs Chamber of Commerce, 7 N 6th St, PO Box 1565, Council Bluffs, 51502 (tel 712/325-1000).

MOTELS

Best Western Crossroads of the Bluffs
2216 27th Ave, 51501; tel 712/322-3150 or toll free 800/528-1234; fax 712/322-6233. Exit 1B off I-29/80. Plain but clean property. Near dog track and casino. **Rooms:** 108 rms. CI 11am/CO 2pm. Nonsmoking rms avail. Pluses include flowered-chintz sofas and better-quality furnishings. **Amenities:** A/C, cable TV w/movies. Some units have coffeemakers. **Services:** **Facilities:** 650 1 restaurant, 1 bar (w/entertainment), games rm, sauna, whirlpool, playground, washer/dryer. Pool has a bricked deck area. **Rates:** $54–$59 S or D. Extra person $2. Children under age 18 stay free. Parking: Outdoor, free. Reservations are a must. Zoo packages ($90) include kids' meals and zoo passes. Romance package ($75) includes steak dinner for two. AE, CB, DC, DISC, MC, V.

Fairfield Inn
520 30th Ave, 51501; tel 712/366-1330 or toll free 800/228-2800; fax 712/366-1330. Exit 3 off I-29/80. An immaculate new motel, close to several fast-food outlets. Lobby is attractive and breezy. **Rooms:** 62 rms and stes. CI 2pm/CO 11am. Nonsmoking rms avail. **Amenities:** A/C, cable TV w/movies. **Services:** Pets allowed in smoking rooms only. **Facilities:** 35 Games rm, whirlpool. **Rates (CP):** Peak (mid-May–Sept) $47–$60 S; $57–$80 D; $60–$90 ste. Extra person $5. Children under age 18 stay free. Lower rates off-season. Parking: Outdoor, free. AE, DC, DISC, MC, V.

Heartland Inn
1000 Woodbury Ave, 51503; tel 712/322-8400 or toll free 800/334-3277 ext 21; fax 712/322-4022. Exit 5 off I-80. Neat motel with bright rooms. Located near a shopping mall. **Rooms:** 89 rms. CI 3pm/CO noon. Nonsmoking rms avail. Deluxe accommodations have two phones. **Amenities:** A/C, cable TV w/movies. Some rooms have dataports. **Services:** Pet fee $10/night. **Facilities:** 15

Sauna, whirlpool. **Rates:** $43–$50 S; $50–$57 D. Extra person $7. Children under age 16 stay free. Parking: Outdoor, free. AE, CB, DC, DISC, MC, V.

RESTAURANTS

Szechwan Chinese Restaurant
2612 W Broadway; tel 712/325-1782. Off I-29. **Chinese.** Serves fairly standard Chinese fare, like crab rangoon and Hunan chicken, plus a few original dishes like "Triple Delight" (shrimp, chicken, and beef served in a potato-noodle nest). **FYI:** Reservations accepted. Beer and wine only. **Open:** Fri–Sat 11am–10pm, Sun–Thurs 11am–9pm. **Prices:** Main courses $6–$15. AE, MC, V.

Tish's
1207 S 35th; tel 712/323-5456. 12 blocks S of Broadway. **Burgers.** Office workers from Omaha cross the bridge at lunch for pork tenderloin, hamburgers, and grilled-cheese sandwiches at this combination restaurant/ice cream stand in the middle of its own sand volleyball complex. The new dining room has vaulted ceilings and old-fashioned, darkwood office chairs. **FYI:** Reservations not accepted. Children's menu. **Open:** Sun–Sat 11am–10pm. **Prices:** Main courses $5–$12. No CC.

ATTRACTIONS

RailsWest Railroad Museum
1512 S Main St; tel 712/323-5182. Museum, housed in the historic 1899 Rock Island depot, includes displays of timetables, passes, historic photos, uniforms, and other memorabilia documenting the role of the railroads in America's westward expansion. HO gauge model railroad re-creates the railroad operations of the surrounding region. **Open:** Mem Day–Labor Day, Mon–Tues and Thurs–Sat 10am–4pm, Sun 1–5pm; Thanksgiving–Jan 1, Sat and Sun 1–5pm. Closed Dec 25. $

Historic General Dodge House
605 3rd St; tel 712/322-2406. Elegant 14-room Victorian house listed as a National Historic Landmark. Originally built in 1869 by Civil War general Grenville Dodge, the mansion is now open as a museum and is decorated with period furnishings. Guided tours available. **Open:** Tues–Sat 10am–5pm, Sun 1–5pm. Closed some hols. $

Historic Rotary "Squirrel Cage" Jail
226 Pearl; tel 712/323-2509. Built in 1885 at a cost of $30,000, this unique jail was built to minimize the need for personal contact between prisoners and their jailer. Its rotary design consists of a metal drum with three levels, each divided into 10 pie-shaped cells; a cell could be entered or exited only when the drum was rotated to align its door with the outside doorway. Visitors can tour the cells and view displays of prison artifacts, handcuffs, and shackles. **Open:** June–Aug, Fri–Sat 10am–4pm, Sun noon–4pm; Apr–May and Sept, Sat–Sun noon–4pm. Closed some hols.

Creston

The cattle and railroad hub of southern Iowa, located on US 34. Green Valley State Park, two miles north of town, attracts boaters and fishing enthusiasts. **Information:** Creston Chamber of Commerce, 116 W Adams, PO Box 471, Creston, 50801 (tel 515/782-7021).

MOTELS

Berning Motor Lodge
301 W Adams St, 50801 (Downtown); tel 515/782-7001; fax 515/782-7415. Huge place, covering nearly an entire city block. Located near an old train depot and antique mall. **Rooms:** 47 rms and stes. Executive level. CI open/CO 11am. Nonsmoking rms avail. Honeymoon suites and a penthouse apartment available. **Amenities:** A/C, cable TV. 1 unit w/whirlpool. **Services:** Car-rental desk. **Facilities:** 350 2 restaurants, 1 bar, spa, beauty salon. Two beauty salons; well-equipped fitness center. **Rates (AP):** $35 S; $40 D; $75 ste. Extra person $5. Children under age 12 stay free. Parking: Outdoor, free. AE, MC, V.

Super 8 Motel
804 W Taylor, 50801; tel 515/782-6541 or toll free 800/800-8000; fax 515/782-6541. Near jct US 34 and IA 25. Modestly priced property close to the airport. **Rooms:** 83 rms. CI 3pm/CO 11am. Nonsmoking rms avail. Queen and king rooms offer recliners. **Amenities:** A/C, cable TV w/movies. **Services:** Free local calls. **Facilities:** Truck parking. **Rates (CP):** Peak (Apr–Sept) $38–$45 S; $47–$53 D. Extra person $6. Children under age 12 stay free. Lower rates off-season. Parking: Outdoor, free. AE, CB, DC, DISC, MC, V.

Davenport

Part of the Quad Cities metropolitan area, which also includes Bettendorf, IA and Moline and Rock Island, IL. Sprawling along the Mississippi River on Iowa's eastern border, the area blends historic significance as a river commerce hub with the modern flavor of metropolitan attractions. Historic riverboats and railroad depots beckon along with new shopping, dining, nightclub, and casino locales. **Information:** Quad City Convention and Visitors Bureau, 2020 3rd Ave, Moline, IL 61265 (tel 309/788/7800).

HOTELS

Best Western Riverview Inn
227 LeClaire St, 52801; tel 319/324-1921 or toll free 800/553-1879. At River Dr. Six-story hotel right on the Mississippi. **Rooms:** 150 rms. CI 3pm/CO 11am. Nonsmoking rms avail. Some accommodations have river views. Rooms on the nonsmoking floor have been recently redone. **Amenities:** A/C, cable TV w/movies. **Services:** **Facilities:** 1

restaurant, whirlpool. **Rates:** Peak (Apr–Jan) $46–$59 S or D. Extra person $6. Children under age 12 stay free. Lower rates off-season. Parking: Outdoor, free. AE, CB, DC, DISC, MC, V.

Best Western Steeple Gate Inn
100 W 76th St, 52801; tel 319/386-6900 or toll free 800/528-1234. At jct US 61/I-80. Features a beautiful tree-lined atrium and fun night club. **Rooms:** 121 rms. CI 2pm/CO noon. Nonsmoking rms avail. **Amenities:** A/C, cable TV w/movies. **Services:** **Facilities:** 1 restaurant, whirlpool. **Rates:** Peak (Apr–Jan) $64–$105 S or D. Extra person $6. Children under age 12 stay free. Lower rates off-season. Parking: Outdoor, free. AE, CB, DC, DISC, MC, V.

Blackhawk Hotel
200 E 3rd St, 52801; tel 319/328-6000 or toll free 800/553-1173. Exit US 61 S off I-80 E. Known as the "Grand Dame" of the Quad Cities, this elegant hotel built in 1915 is listed on the National Register of Historic Places. A recent renovation has restored the original marblework and decor of the lobby. An atrium joins the hotel to the adjacent RiverCenter and Adler Theater; the affiliated President Riverboat Casino (the biggest on the Mississippi Strip) is two blocks away. **Rooms:** 187 rms. CI 3pm/CO noon. Nonsmoking rms avail. Many rooms have superb views of the river. **Amenities:** A/C, cable TV w/movies. **Services:** **Facilities:** 1 restaurant (*see* "Restaurants" below). Seven meeting/banquet rooms. **Rates:** $50–$69 S or D. Extra person $8. Children under age 12 stay free. Parking: Outdoor, free. AE, DC, DISC, MC, V.

Comfort Inn
7222 Northwest Blvd, 52806; tel 319/391-8222 or toll free 800/272-1779. I-80, exit 292. Close to Wacky Waters theme park and seven miles from Mississippi Valley fairgrounds. **Rooms:** 89 rms. CI 2pm/CO 11am. Nonsmoking rms avail. Later check-out sometimes available on weekends. **Amenities:** A/C, cable TV w/movies. **Services:** **Facilities:** 1 restaurant. **Rates (CP):** $40–$125 S or D. Extra person $4. Children under age 18 stay free. Parking: Outdoor, free. AE, CB, DC, DISC, MC, V.

MOTELS

Days Inn
101 W 65th St, 52806; tel 319/388-9999 or toll free 800/329-7466. Exit 295A off I-80. Fairly new two-story motel across from multiplex cinemas. **Rooms:** 64 rms. CI 3pm/CO noon. Nonsmoking rms avail. **Amenities:** A/C, cable TV w/movies, VCR. **Services:** Free local calls. Complimentary continental breakfast includes muffins, donuts, fresh orange juice. **Facilities:** Sauna, whirlpool. Winter plug-ins available. **Rates (CP):** $44–$70 S or D. Extra person $6. Children under age 18 stay free. Parking: Outdoor, free. 13th-night-free program. AE, CB, DC, DISC, MC, V.

Excel Inn of Davenport
6310 N Brady St, 52806; tel 319/386-6350. At jct I-80/US 61. Two-story motel with rooms reached by interior corridors. **Rooms:** 103 rms. CI 3pm/CO noon. Nonsmoking rms avail. Recently refurbished with new drapes, bedspreads, and carpets. **Amenities:** A/C, cable TV w/movies. **Services:** Fax and modem available. **Facilities:** Washer/dryer. **Rates (CP):** $29–$100 S or D. Children under age 18 stay free. Parking: Outdoor, free. Truck rates avail. DISC, MC, V.

Fairfield Inn
3206 E Kimberly Rd, 52807; tel 319/355-2264 or toll free 800/228-2800; fax 319/355-2264. US 6 exit off I-79. Located in an attractive setting. Very neat. **Rooms:** 62 rms and stes. CI 3pm/CO 11am. Nonsmoking rms avail. Small, bright rooms with modern furnishings. **Amenities:** A/C, cable TV w/movies. **Services:** Babysitting. **Facilities:** Games rm, whirlpool. Attractive indoor pool. Guests can use facilities at local health club three blocks away. **Rates (CP):** $50 S; $56 D; $66 ste. Extra person $6. Children under age 17 stay free. Parking: Outdoor, free. 13th-night-free program. AE, CB, DC, DISC, MC, V.

Hampton Inn
3330 E Kimberly Rd, 52807; tel 319/359-3921 or toll free 800/HAMPTON; fax 319/359-1912. Off I-74. Located next to the convention center, it was undergoing some remodeling. Pleasant staff. **Rooms:** 134 rms, stes, and effic. Executive level. CI 2pm/CO noon. Nonsmoking rms avail. Honeymoon suites available. Four rooms designed for guests with disabilites. **Amenities:** A/C, cable TV w/movies, dataport. 1 unit w/minibar, some w/whirlpools. **Services:** Car-rental desk. **Facilities:** Whirlpool. Pool area was being enclosed. **Rates (CP):** $52 S; $56 D; $70–$90 ste; $100–$150 effic. Extra person $6. Children under age 18 stay free. Parking: Outdoor, free. AE, CB, DC, DISC, MC, V.

Heartland Inn
6605 N Brady St, 52806; tel 319/386-8336 or toll free 800/334-3277 ext 15; fax 319/386-6005. At jct US 61/I-80. Newish motel with spacious, bright facilities. **Rooms:** 86 rms and stes. Executive level. CI 3pm/CO 11am. Nonsmoking rms avail. Clean and large, rooms offer recliners and desks. **Amenities:** A/C, cable TV w/movies. 1 unit w/whirlpool. **Services:** Babysitting. Free local calls. "Manager's Social" on Wednesday evenings features free hors d'oeuvres and beverages. **Facilities:** Sauna. **Rates (CP):** Peak (Apr–Oct) $42–$45 S; $51–$54 D; $90–$140 ste. Extra person $9. Children under age 16 stay free. Lower rates off-season. Parking: Outdoor, free. Frequent-guest programs avail. AE, CB, DC, DISC, MC, V.

Ramada Inn
6263 N Brady St, 52806; tel 319/386-1940 or toll free 800/272-6232; fax 319/386-1940. At jct I-88/US 61. Clean, spacious rooms in a nicely landscaped motel with a large lobby. **Rooms:** 178 rms and stes. Executive level. CI 3pm/CO

noon. Nonsmoking rms avail. **Amenities:** A/C, cable TV w/movies, refrig. 1 unit w/whirlpool. **Services:** Car-rental desk, children's program. **Facilities:** 1 restaurant, 1 bar (w/entertainment), sauna, steam rm, whirlpool. **Rates:** Peak (Nov–Apr) $38 S; $50 D; $75 ste. Extra person $6. Children under age 12 stay free. Lower rates off-season. Parking: Outdoor, free. AE, CB, DC, DISC, MC, V.

INN

Bishop's House Inn of St Ambrose University
1527 Brady St, 52803; tel 319/322-8303. 5 blocks S of University at Kirkwood. Beautiful Italianate home built in the 1870s offering spacious and beautifully decorated accommodations in a residential area. A good deal. Unsuitable for children under 12. **Rooms:** 5 rms. CI 4pm/CO 11am. No smoking. **Amenities:** A/C. No TV. 1 unit w/fireplace, 1 w/whirlpool. **Services:** Twice-daily maid svce, afternoon tea served. Delicious breakfast buffet. Sandy Krueger, the very gracious innkeeper, can help guests with all details of their stay. **Facilities:** Guest lounge w/TV. **Rates (BB):** $65–$140 D. Parking: Outdoor, free. MC, V.

RESTAURANTS

Butch Cassidy's
In Blackhawk Hotel, 200 E 3rd St; tel 319/328-6080. **American.** A casual, Western-themed eatery serving filet mignon, prime rib, shrimp scampi, and lighter fare like the chicken-walnut salad. **FYI:** Reservations recommended. Children's menu. **Open:** Daily 6am–10pm. **Prices:** Main courses $6–$14. AE, DC, DISC, MC, V.

Iowa Machine Shed
7250 Northwest Blvd; tel 319/391-2427. Exit 292 off I-80. **American.** Housed in a barnlike structure, this restaurant dedicated to the American farmer lives up to its name—antique farm equipment hangs on the walls and a vintage tractor (which kids can ride in during summer) sits out front. Here they cut their own beef and prepare specialties in their own smoker. Big steaks, prime rib, and stuffed Iowa pork chops are served with scalloped potatoes and other hearty side dishes; Wednesday features smokehouse specials. Apple dumplings are one of the special desserts. Tuesday nights, children eat for 99¢. **FYI:** Reservations not accepted. Children's menu. **Open:** Mon–Sat 6am–10pm, Sun 7am–9pm. **Prices:** Main courses $8–$12. AE, CB, DC, DISC, MC, V.

River City Cafe
6511 N Brady St; tel 319/386-2722. **American.** Casual restaurant with river theme and bright furnishings. Pasta, fresh seafood, a few Cajun dishes. **FYI:** Reservations accepted. Jazz/piano. Children's menu. **Open:** Mon–Thurs 6am–10pm, Fri–Sat 6am–11pm, Sun 7am–9pm. **Prices:** Main courses $9–$11. AE, CB, DC, DISC, MC, V.

ATTRACTION

Putnam Museum of History and Natural Science
12th and Division Sts; tel 319/324-1933. Historical artifacts and specimens from around the world, hands-on and multisensory activities, and live theatrical performances. The award-winning "River, Prairie, and People" exhibit offers visitors the opportunity to explore the people, culture, and wildlife of the Mississippi Valley, while mummies and fossil displays represent the ancient world. **Open:** Tues–Fri 9am–5pm, Sat 10am–5pm, Sun noon–5pm. Closed some hols. **$$**

Decorah

Norwegian heritage blends with a beautiful natural landscape in Decorah, home of the nation's oldest and largest immigrant/ethnic museum. Just north of town, in Burr Oak, is the restored home of author Laura Ingalls Wilder (famous for the *Little House on the Prairie* books). Spillville, a few miles southwest of Decorah, was the summer home of Czech composer Antonin Dvorak and the headquarters of famed clock makers Joseph and Frank Bily. **Information:** Decorah Area Chamber of Commerce, 111 Winnebago, Decorah, 52101 (tel 319/382-3990).

MOTELS

Cliff House Motel and Restaurant
IA 9 and US 52, PO Box 49, 52101; tel 319/382-4241 or toll free 800/632-5980; fax 319/382-4152. The most interesting aspect of this motel is its built-into-the-hillside construction. Hard-to-please travelers should look elsewhere. **Rooms:** 110 rms and stes. Executive level. CI 2pm/CO 11am. Nonsmoking rms avail. Unappealing decor/furnishings. **Amenities:** A/C, cable TV w/movies, VCR. Some units w/terraces, some w/whirlpools. **Services:** Babysitting. **Facilities:** 1 restaurant, 1 bar (w/entertainment), games rm, whirlpool. **Rates (BB):** $24–$44 S; $32–$52 D; $44–$75 ste. Extra person $8. Children under age 16 stay free. Parking: Outdoor, free. AE, CB, DC, DISC, MC, V.

Heartland Inn
705 Commerce Dr, 52101; tel 319/382-2269 or toll free 800/334-3277; fax 319/382-4767. 1½ mi E of jct US 52 and IA 9. Better-than-average motel with easy access from highway. **Rooms:** 58 rms and stes. Executive level. CI 2pm/CO 11am. Nonsmoking rms avail. Attractive and neat. **Amenities:** A/C, cable TV w/movies, refrig, dataport. Some units w/whirlpools. **Services:** **Facilities:** **Rates (CP):** Peak (Apr–Oct) $48–$57 S; $55–$64 D; $90–$110 ste. Extra person $7. Children under age 16 stay free. Lower rates off-season. Parking: Outdoor, free. AE, DC, DISC, MC, V.

ATTRACTIONS

Laura Ingalls Wilder Park and Museum
3603 236th Ave, Burr Oak; tel 319/735-5916. One of the childhood homes of *Little House on the Prairie* author Laura Ingalls Wilder—the Ingalls family managed a hotel here from 1876 to 1877. Today, the former Masters Hotel is a museum filled with Wilder family artifacts and period antiques. **Open:** May–Sept, daily 10am–4pm. **$**

Bily Clocks Museum/Antonin Dvorak Exhibit
Main St, Spillville; tel 319/562-3569. 13 mi SW of Decorah. Museum highlights the clockbuilding and woodcarving talents of the Bily brothers, Spillville natives who have attracted worldwide attention for their craftsmanship and decorative clocks. The collection is held in the former summer home of Antonin Dvorak, the world-famous composer, who composed part of the quartette "Humoresque" here, as well as a portion of his famous *New World* symphony. **Open:** May–Oct, daily 8:30am–5pm; Mar–Nov, Sat–Sun 10am–4pm; Apr, daily 10am–4pm. Closed some hols. **$**

Denison

Seat of Crawford County, and the birthplace of TV and film star Donna Reed. **Information:** Denison Chamber of Commerce, 109 N 14th St, Dension, 51442 (tel 712/263-5621).

MOTEL

Best Western Denison's Inn
502 Boyer Valley Rd, 51442; tel 712/263-5081 or toll free 800/428-0684. Jct US 30/59. Bright and comfortable rooms. Located outside of town, near several historic sites. **Rooms:** 40 rms. CI 2pm/CO 11am. Nonsmoking rms avail. **Amenities:** A/C, cable TV w/movies. **Services:** **Facilities:** 10 Truck parking. **Rates (CP):** \$32–\$38 S; \$40–\$48 D. Extra person \$5. Children under age 12 stay free. Parking: Outdoor, free. AE, CB, DC, DISC, MC, V.

Des Moines

See also Altoona, Johnston

Iowa's largest city rests in the junction of I-80 and I-35, and encompasses contingent cities of Altoona, Ankeny, Clive, Johnston, Urbandale and West Des Moines. Founded in 1843 and the state capital since 1858, Des Moines is the industrial, financial, and cultural center of the state. **Information:** Greater Des Moines Convention and Visitors Bureau, 601 Locust #222, Des Moines, 50309 (tel 515/286-4960).

PUBLIC TRANSPORTATION

The Des Moines Metropolitan Transit Authority (the Metro) (tel 515/283-8100) serves the cities of Des Moines, Clive, Windsor Heights, West Des Moines, and Urbandale. Buses offer route service Mon–Sat. Paratransit available. Fares: adult 75¢, seniors and persons with disabilities 35¢, children 6–10 50¢; children under 6 free. Express routes are \$1. Des Moines also has downtown lunch hour trolley (Ollie the Trolley) serving Court Ave, Kaleidoscope, and Locust Mall.

HOTELS

Best Western Des Moines International Hotel
1810 Army Post Rd, 50312 (Des Moines Int'l Airport); tel 515/287-6464 or toll free 800/383-6462; fax 515/287-5818. Located in the airport flight pattern, so it can get noisy. Rates are very competitive for area. **Rooms:** 145 rms. CI 1pm/CO noon. Nonsmoking rms avail. **Amenities:** A/C, cable TV w/movies. **Services:** **Facilities:** 350 1 restaurant, 1 bar, games rm, washer/dryer. **Rates (CP):** Peak (Feb–Aug) \$54–\$70 S; \$64–\$75 D. Extra person \$5. Children under age 12 stay free. Lower rates off-season. Parking: Outdoor, free. AE, DC, DISC, MC, V.

Embassy Suites on the River
101 East Locust St, 50309 (Downtown); tel 515/244-1700 or toll free 800/EMBASSY; fax 515/244-2537. Take I-235 and exit on 3rd St or 6th St. This all-suite property, with a beautiful atrium lobby, is one of the nicest hotels downtown. **Rooms:** 234 stes and effic. Executive level. CI 3pm/CO noon. Nonsmoking rms avail. Each generous-size suite has a view of the river or the Capitol. **Amenities:** A/C, cable TV w/movies, refrig, voice mail, bathrobes. All units w/terraces, 1 w/whirlpool. **Services:** Babysitting. Complimentary cocktails 5–7pm. Meeting planning services available. **Facilities:** 1000 2 restaurants, 1 bar (w/entertainment), games rm, spa, sauna, whirlpool, washer/dryer. Outdoor amphitheater under construction. **Rates (BB):** \$109–\$149 ste; \$109–\$149 effic. Extra person \$10. Children under age 12 stay free. Parking: Indoor/outdoor, \$3/day. Corporate, government, and group rates avail. AE, DC, DISC, MC, V.

Fort Des Moines Hotel
1000 Walnut, 50309; tel 515/243-1161 or toll free 800/532-1466; fax 515/243-4317. S edge of downtown. Charming old hotel. **Rooms:** 242 rms and stes. CI 3pm/CO noon. Nonsmoking rms avail. Clean and quiet. **Amenities:** A/C, satel TV w/movies, refrig. 1 unit w/fireplace, some w/whirlpools. **Services:** Babysitting. **Facilities:** 1000 2 restaurants, 2 bars (1 w/entertainment), games rm, sauna, whirlpool, washer/dryer. **Rates:** \$59–\$114 S; \$59–\$124 D; \$69–\$300 ste. Extra person \$10. Children under age 16 stay free. Parking: Indoor/outdoor, \$2–\$4/day. AE, CB, DC, DISC, MC, V.

Hampton Inn
5001 Fleur Dr, 50321; tel 515/287-7300 or toll free 800/HAMPTON; fax 515/287-6343. Across from Des Moines International Airport. Clean and quiet. **Rooms:** 122 rms. CI 2pm/CO 11am. Nonsmoking rms avail. Small but well-decorated. **Amenities:** A/C, cable TV w/movies,

dataport. **Services:** Facilities: **Rates (CP):** $55–$63 S or D. Children under age 18 stay free. Parking: Outdoor, free. AE, CB, DC, DISC, MC, V.

Holiday Inn Airport
6111 Fleur Dr, 50321 (Des Moines Int'l Airport); tel 515/287-2400 or toll free 800/248-4013; fax 515/287-4811. Located on a busy commercial street. **Rooms:** 220 rms and stes. CI 3pm/CO noon. Nonsmoking rms avail. Rooms are well appointed and the suites are lovely. **Amenities:** A/C, satel TV w/movies, refrig, dataport, voice mail. Some units w/terraces, some w/whirlpools. **Services:** Children's program. Downtown shuttle available 24 hours. **Facilities:** 2 restaurants, 1 bar, spa, sauna, whirlpool, washer/dryer. "Holidome" covered swimming pool area with whirlpool, greenery, and activities for kids. Kids eat free with parents in hotel restaurant. **Rates (BB):** $82 S or D; $225 ste. Children under age 18 stay free. Parking: Outdoor, free. AE, CB, DC, DISC, MC, V.

Holiday Inn Downtown
1050 6th Ave, 50314; tel 515/283-0151 or toll free 800/HOLIDAY; fax 515/283-0151. N of I-235. Located on the north edge of downtown, near I-235. Priced a bit high. **Rooms:** 253 rms and stes. CI 3pm/CO noon. Nonsmoking rms avail. Fairly standard. **Amenities:** A/C, satel TV w/movies, dataport. Some units w/whirlpools. **Services:** Social director. **Facilities:** 2 restaurants, 1 bar. Top-floor restaurant offers great views. **Rates:** Peak (Sept–Oct) $79 S or D; $175–$225 ste. Extra person $10. Children under age 20 stay free. Lower rates off-season. Parking: Indoor/outdoor, free. AE, DC, DISC, MC, V.

Holiday Inn University Park
1800 50th St, 50266; tel 515/223-1800 or toll free 800/HOLIDAY; fax 515/223-0894. From I-80 take Univ Park exit. Just off the interstate in a commercial area, this well-landscaped property is in a beautiful setting. **Rooms:** 288 rms and stes. CI 3pm/CO noon. Nonsmoking rms avail. Accommodations are very quiet and well appointed. **Amenities:** A/C, satel TV w/movies. 1 unit w/whirlpool. **Services:** Twice-daily maid svce, babysitting. Guest admission to 7 Flags fitness center $5. **Facilities:** 2 restaurants, 1 bar, spa, sauna, whirlpool, washer/dryer. Children under 12 eat free with adults in hotel restaurant. **Rates:** Peak (Sept–Nov) $99 S or D; $120 ste. Extra person $10. Children under age 18 stay free. Lower rates off-season. Parking: Outdoor, free. AE, CB, DC, DISC, MC, V.

Marriott Hotel
700 Grand Ave, 50309 (Downtown); tel 515/245-5500 or toll free 800/228-9290; fax 515/245-5567. Located in the heart of downtown on the city's skywalk system. **Rooms:** 415 rms and stes. Executive level. CI 4pm/CO noon. Nonsmoking rms avail. Rooms are spacious and nicely furnished, with king or double beds available. **Amenities:** A/C, cable TV w/movies, dataport, voice mail. 1 unit w/whirlpool. Iron and ironing board in each room. Accommodations on the concierge level include perks such as bathrobes and coffeemakers. **Services:** Twice-daily maid svce, babysitting. Concierge-level guests receive complimentary continental breakfast and afternoon hors d'oeuvres. **Facilities:** 2 restaurants, 2 bars, spa, sauna, steam rm, whirlpool, beauty salon. **Rates:** $49–$117 S or D; $250–$500 ste. Children under age 16 stay free. Min stay special events. Parking: Indoor, $7–$9/day. AE, CB, DC, DISC, JCB, MC, V.

Ramada Inn–Westmark Convention Center
1250 74th St, 50266; tel 515/223-6500 or toll free 800/2-RAMADA; fax 515/223-1687. Exit 121 off I-80. Older facility located on the edge of the city, with easy access to the interstate. Plenty of space for kids to play. **Rooms:** 153 rms and stes. CI 2pm/CO 11am. Nonsmoking rms avail. **Amenities:** A/C, satel TV. Some units w/minibars. **Services:** **Facilities:** 1 restaurant, 1 bar (w/entertainment), basketball, games rm, sauna, whirlpool. **Rates:** $45–$55 S; $57–$65 D; $80–$120 ste. Extra person $6. Children under age 12 stay free. Parking: Outdoor, free. AE, CB, DC, DISC, MC, V.

Rodeway Inn
4995 NW Merle Hay Rd, 50322; tel 515/278-2381 or toll free 800/237-7633. At exit 131 off I-80. Located close to interstate and large shopping mall. **Rooms:** 120 rms. Executive level. CI 3pm/CO noon. Nonsmoking rms avail. **Amenities:** A/C, cable TV w/movies, dataport. **Services:** **Facilities:** 1 restaurant, 1 bar, sauna, whirlpool, washer/dryer. **Rates (CP):** Peak (May–Aug) $59–$75 S or D. Extra person $6. Children under age 18 stay free. Lower rates off-season. Parking: Outdoor, free. AE, CB, DC, DISC, JCB, MC, V.

MOTELS

Best Western Colonial Inn
5020 NE 14th St, 50313; tel 515/265-7511 or toll free 800/528-1234; fax 515/265-7511. Exit 136 off I-35; go 1 block N. Located close to a major highway and a busy street, but the rooms in the rear of the building are relatively quiet. Restaurant next door. **Rooms:** 62 rms and stes. CI 2pm/CO 11am. Nonsmoking rms avail. **Amenities:** A/C, cable TV. All units w/terraces. **Services:** **Facilities:** **Rates:** Peak (Apr–Oct) $35–$45 S; $39–$49 D; $95 ste. Extra person $4. Lower rates off-season. Parking: Outdoor, free. AE, CB, DC, DISC, MC, V.

Best Western Executive Center
11040 Hickman Rd, 50325; tel 515/278-5575 or toll free 800/722-IOWA; fax 515/278-4078. Located across the road from Living History Farms and close to the interstate. The interior is much nicer than the exterior. **Rooms:** 157 rms. CI 3pm/CO noon. Nonsmoking rms avail. Nicely decorated. **Amenities:** A/C, satel TV w/movies, refrig, dataport. **Services:** Twice-daily maid svce,

babysitting. **Facilities:** 1 restaurant, 1 bar, games rm, spa, sauna, whirlpool, washer/dryer. **Rates:** Peak (June–Aug) $67–$73 S; $74 D. Extra person $5. Children under age 18 stay free. Lower rates off-season. Parking: Outdoor, free. AE, CB, DC, DISC, MC, V.

Budget Host Inn

7625 Hickman Rd, 50322; tel 515/276-5401 or toll free 800/BUD-HOST. Hickman Road exit off I-80/35; 2 mi E. An older, basic property. **Rooms:** 52 rms. CI open/CO 11am. Nonsmoking rms avail. Rooms feel small and cramped. **Amenities:** A/C, cable TV w/movies. Some units w/terraces. **Services:** **Facilities:** **Rates:** Peak (June–Aug) $30–$38 S; $38–$45 D. Extra person $5. Children under age 12 stay free. Lower rates off-season. Parking: Outdoor, free. AE, CB, DC, DISC, MC, V.

Days Inn Capitol City

3501 E 14th St, 50316; tel 515/265-2541 or toll free 800/325-2525; fax 515/263-1151. Exit 136 off I-80; 2 mi S. Pleasing hostelry close to the state fairgrounds. The beautiful courtyard is home to some very friendly squirrels. **Rooms:** 143 rms. CI 3pm/CO noon. Nonsmoking rms avail. Rooms are small but clean. **Amenities:** A/C, cable TV. Some units w/terraces. **Services:** **Facilities:** 1 restaurant, 1 bar, games rm, washer/dryer. **Rates:** Peak (May–Sept) $45–$60 S or D. Extra person $6. Children under age 16 stay free. Lower rates off-season. Parking: Outdoor, free. AE, CB, DC, DISC, JCB, MC, V.

The Drake Inn

1140 24th St, 50311; tel 515/255-4000 or toll free 800/252-7838; fax 515/255-1192. Located near Drake University, in a quiet residential neighborhood, this property has a very attractive exterior and well-landscaped grounds. **Rooms:** 52 rms. CI 3pm/CO noon. Nonsmoking rms avail. **Amenities:** A/C, cable TV w/movies. Some units w/terraces. **Services:** **Facilities:** **Rates:** Peak (May–Apr; Sept) $45–$55 S; $48–$58 D. Extra person $5. Children under age 16 stay free. Lower rates off-season. Parking: Outdoor, free. AE, DC, DISC, MC, V.

Econo Lodge

5626 Douglas Ave, 50310; tel 515/278-1601 or toll free 800/55-ECONO; fax 515/278-1602. By Merle Hay Mall. Located on a heavily trafficked street one block from a large shopping mall, this property is stark on the outside, but clean and comfortable on the inside. **Rooms:** 48 rms. CI noon/CO 11am. Nonsmoking rms avail. **Amenities:** A/C, cable TV. **Services:** **Rates:** Peak (Apr–Aug) $30–$45 S; $40–$55 D. Extra person $5. Children under age 18 stay free. Lower rates off-season. Parking: Outdoor, free. AE, CB, DC, DISC, MC, V.

Fairfield Inn

1600 NW 114th St, Clive, 50325; tel 515/226-1600 or toll free 800/228-2800; fax 515/226-1600. Take I-80 and 35 to University Ave exit. Located on a quiet side street near the interstate, this well-maintained, nicely decorated property offers good value. **Rooms:** 135 rms. CI 3pm/CO noon. Nonsmoking rms avail. **Amenities:** A/C, cable TV w/movies. **Services:** **Facilities:** **Rates (CP):** Peak (May–Aug) $45–$64 S or D. Extra person $7. Children under age 18 stay free. Lower rates off-season. Parking: Outdoor, free. AE, CB, DC, DISC, MC, V.

Fourteenth Street Inn

4685 NE 14th St, 50313; tel 515/265-5671; fax 515/262-7469. I-80 to exit 136. This attractive, clean, well-kept property offers good value. Plenty of space outside for kids to play. Two restaurants nearby. **Rooms:** 135 rms. CI 2pm/CO noon. Nonsmoking rms avail. **Amenities:** A/C, satel TV w/movies. **Services:** Masseur. **Facilities:** **Rates:** Peak (June–Aug) $34–$55 S or D. Extra person $6. Children under age 17 stay free. Lower rates off-season. Parking: Outdoor, free. AE, DISC, MC, V.

Heartland Inn

5000 NE 56th St, Altoona, 50009; tel 515/967-2400 or toll free 800/334-3277; fax 515/967-0150. Spacious new facility near Prairie Meadows casino and raceway, as well as Adventureland amusement park. **Rooms:** 86 rms and stes. Executive level. CI 3pm/CO 11am. Nonsmoking rms avail. **Amenities:** A/C, cable TV w/movies. Some units w/whirlpools. **Services:** Car-rental desk. **Facilities:** Sauna, steam rm, whirlpool. **Rates (CP):** Peak (June–Aug) $53–$60 S; $63–$70 D; $90–$150 ste. Extra person $8. Children under age 16 stay free. Lower rates off-season. Parking: Outdoor, free. AE, DC, DISC, MC, V.

Hickman Motor Lodge

6500 Hickman Rd, 50322 (Windsor Heights); tel 515/276-8591. An economical, clean, recently remodeled property near shopping and restaurants. **Rooms:** 41 rms. CI 11am/CO 11am. Nonsmoking rms avail. Large comfortable rooms with minimal furnishings; three small apartments also available. **Amenities:** A/C, cable TV w/movies. **Services:** Babysitting. **Facilities:** 1 bar (w/entertainment). Clean, well lighted, nicely landscaped outdoor areas. **Rates:** $32–$35 S; $39–$41 D. Extra person $5. Children under age 12 stay free. Parking: Outdoor, free. Group rates avail. AE, DC, MC, V.

RESTAURANTS

$ Bishop's Cafeteria

In Southridge Mall, 111 E Army Post Rd; tel 515/287-1273. **Cafeteria.** One of America's oldest cafeteria chains, Bishop's has been operating since the 1920s and has nine locations in Iowa. There's a sandwich line and an entree line, as well as a kids' area where a low-level counter enables children to serve themselves. Special menu items for diabetics. **FYI:** Reservations not accepted. Children's menu. No liquor license. **Open:** Mon–Sat 11am–8pm, Sun 11am–7pm. **Prices:** Main courses $5–$7. Lunch main courses $4–$6. AE, DISC, MC, V.

Christopher's
2616 Beaver Ave; tel 515/274-3694. At Urbandale Ave off Merle Hay Rd. **American/Italian/Vegetarian.** A Des Moines favorite since it opened in 1963, Christopher's is known for its great food and especially attentive wait staff, many of whom have worked for this family eatery for years. The bar area features a big-screen TV and free appetizers, while the wood-paneled dining room offers tables and booths. Italian chicken, seafood, and beef specialties dominate the menu, and the wine list is one of the best in town. **FYI:** Reservations accepted. Children's menu. Dress code. **Open:** Mon–Thurs 3–10:30pm, Fri–Sat 3–11:30pm. **Prices:** Main courses $8–$18. AE, CB, DC, DISC, MC, V.

Crimmins Cattle Company
4901 Fleur Dr; tel 515/287-6611. Near airport. **American/Seafood.** An intimate dining room, decorated western-style and affording much privacy. The menu emphasizes beef (prime rib is the specialty), but seafood is also offered. Appetizers and sandwiches are also available on the bar menu. **FYI:** Reservations accepted. Country music/rock/dixieland. Children's menu. **Open:** Sun–Thurs 4–10pm, Fri–Sat 4–11pm. **Prices:** Main courses $11–$21. AE, DISC, MC, V.

8th Street Seafood Bar & Grill
1261 8th St; tel 515/223-8808. Off I-235. **Seafood/Steak.** One of Des Moines' best restaurants. Fresh fish and seafood, including Maine lobster, are flown in daily. Each week the chef creates six different featured entrees. **FYI:** Reservations recommended. Jazz/piano. **Open:** Mon–Thurs 5–10pm, Fri–Sat 5–11pm. **Prices:** Main courses $15–$42. AE, CB, DC, DISC, MC, V.

Garcia's of Scottsdale
6116 Douglas Ave (Shopping District); tel 515/270-0800. South of Merle Hay Mall. **Mexican.** Dishes are made from original family recipes, using 100% natural cheeses and dairy products. New and most popular are the shrimp fajitas, tacos, and chimichangas. Most meals can be prepared using low-fat methods and ingredients. All items on the children's menu cost a penny per pound of the child's weight. **FYI:** Reservations accepted. Children's menu. **Open: Prices:** Main courses $6–$10. AE, CB, DC, DISC, MC, V.

Greenbriar Restaurant and Bar
5810 Merle Hay Road, Johnston; tel 515/253-0124. 1 mi N of I-80, next to Village Square Mall. **Eclectic.** This place offers a wide variety of menu choices like burgers, prime rib, seafood, rack of lamb, and pasta; then comes the full dessert tray. Extensive wine list. **FYI:** Reservations accepted. Folk. Children's menu. **Open:** Lunch Mon–Fri 11:30am–2pm; dinner Mon–Thurs 5–9:30pm, Fri–Sat 5–10:30pm. **Prices:** Main courses $9–$20. AE, DISC, MC, V.

Iowa Machine Shed Restaurant
11151 Hickman Rd; tel 515/270-6818. Take I-80/35 to exit 125; adjacent to the Living History Farms. **American/German.** Located on the property of Iowa's Living History Farms, this restaurant serves large, family-style meals. The emphasis is on beef (steaks and prime rib) and pork chops. Other entrees include chicken and fish, either broiled or fried. Typical vegetables are dilled carrots and cheesy hash browns. **FYI:** Reservations not accepted. Children's menu. Beer and wine only. **Open:** Mon–Sat 6am–10pm, Sun 7am–9pm. **Prices:** Main courses $5–$18. AE, CB, DC, DISC, ER, MC, V.

Mustards Restaurant
6612 University Ave; tel 515/274-9307. Take I-235 N to 63rd St exit. **Eclectic/Vegetarian.** Award-winning barbecue ribs are the draw here, but you can also choose burgers, pizza, Polish-style sausage, salads, and pasta. **FYI:** Reservations not accepted. Children's menu. Beer and wine only. Additional locations: 2923 SW 9th St (tel 283-2696); 1904 Forest Ave (tel 282-8078). **Open:** Daily 11am–10pm. **Prices:** Main courses $5–$12. DISC, MC, V.

North End Diner
5055 Merle Hay Road; tel 515/276-5151. Off I-80. **New American.** Daily blue-plate specials in this funky 1950s-style diner include meatloaf with mashed potatoes, "wets" (french fries with gravy), thick malted milks, and other traditional fare. Great breakfasts, burgers, salads, and deli sandwiches, as well as full dinners. **FYI:** Reservations accepted. Children's menu. **Open:** Mon–Thurs 6:30am–11pm, Fri–Sat 6:30am–midnight, Sun 6:30am–10pm. **Prices:** Main courses $5–$15. AE, DC, DISC, MC, V.

ATTRACTIONS

State Capitol
E 9th St and Grand Ave; tel 515/281-5591. The century-old landmark building features a 275-foot 22-karat gold-leafed dome flanked by four smaller domes. Tours highlight the legislative and Supreme Court chambers, governor's office, law library, and a scale model of the battleship *Iowa*. **Open:** Daily 8am–4pm. **Free**

State of Iowa Historical Building
600 E Locust St; tel 515/281-5111. Housed in a modern granite-and-glass structure, the museum focuses on Iowa's heritage and history and how people, animals, and the land have coexisted throughout the state's history. A permanent exhibit on the settlement of Iowa invites visitors to churn butter, scrape animal hides, and play Native American games. **Open:** Tues–Sat 9am–4:30pm, Sun noon–4:30pm. **Free**

Terrace Hill Historic Site/Governor's Residence
2300 Grand Ave; tel 515/281-3604. 2 mi W of downtown Des Moines. One of the finest examples of Second Empire architecture west of the Hudson, this historic 1880s house has been used as the governor's mansion since 1971. Collections include a silver-and-crystal chandelier, a 9-by-13-foot stained-glass window, eight marble fireplaces, several Ming

vases, and dozens of paintings and sculptures. Guided tours available. **Open:** Mar–Dec, Tues–Sat 10am–1:30pm. Closed some hols. **$**

Hoyt Sherman Place
1501 Woodland Ave; tel 515/243-0913. Former residence of Hoyt Sherman, brother of Gen William Tecumseh Sherman and prominent Des Moines businessman. The Italianate home, completed in 1877, is graced with hand-carved wainscoting, marble fireplaces, and etched-glass windows. Two large upstairs rooms exhibit collections of decorative and fine arts, including a 1796 handcrafted sampler, an Inca collar, black basalt Wedgwood vases, and a Chippendale game table. Adjacent art gallery features works by Frederick E Church, George Innes, and Thomas Moran. Guided tours of the house given by reservation only; fee charged. **Open:** Mon–Fri 8am–4pm. Closed some hols, last 2 weeks in Aug. **Free**

Salisbury House
4025 Tonawanda Dr; tel 515/279-9711. Situated on 11 wooded acres, this 42-room English Tudor mansion is a replica of the King's House in Salisbury, England, complete with authentic furnishings of the Tudor period, paintings, tapestries, oriental rugs, and stained glass. Guided tours are given Mon–Fri at 2pm and last approximately 1½ hours. **$**

Science Center of Iowa
4500 Grand Ave; tel 515/274-4138. Located in Greenwood Park, this museum has exhibitions on mechanics, astronomy, chemistry, and life science. The **Sargent Space Theater** features a computer-generated Digistar planetarium system that simulates riding on a roller coaster and flying past high-rise buildings, as well as gazing at the stars. Evening laser shows Fri and Sat (additional fee). **Open:** Mon–Sat 10am–5pm, Sun noon–5pm. Closed some hols. **$$**

Des Moines Art Center
4700 Grand Ave; tel 515/277-4405. Built atop a hill in Greenwood Park, this center is almost as well known for its unique contemporary architecture—by Eliel Saarinen, I M Pei, and Richard Maier—as for the art inside. The permanent collection includes 19th- and 20th-century paintings by Monet, Cassatt, Sargent, Rauschenberg, and Stella, along with sculptures by Rodin, Moore, Arp, and Brancusi. Admission is free 11am–1pm daily and all day on Thursdays; scheduled docent tours are available. **Open:** Tues–Wed 11am–5pm, Thurs 11am–9pm, Fri–Sat 11am–5pm, Sun noon–5pm. Closed some hols. **$**

Living History Farms
2600 NW 111th St; tel 515/278-2400. A 600-acre agricultural museum dedicated to preserving pioneer farming skills. Featured are an Ioway Indian Village (circa 1700), an 1850 pioneer farm, and a horse farm (circa 1900). **Walnut Hill,** a re-created 1875 town, is centered around Victorian-style Flynn Mansion. Costumed guides work in the general store, blacksmith shop, potters, and doctor's office. Special events include crafts demonstrations, traditional music, and a 1900 farm supper program with authentic meals based on turn-of-the-century recipes. **Open:** May–Oct, Mon–Sat 9am–5pm, Sun 11am–6pm. **$$$**

Adventureland Park
Exit 142 off US 65; tel 515/266-2121. Theme park with more than 100 rides, shows, and attractions, including four giant roller coasters and white-water rapids. **Open:** Mem Day–Labor Day, daily 10am–close; Sept–Oct, Sat–Sun 10am–8pm. **$$$$**

White Water University Fun Park
5401 E University; tel 515/265-4904. Water park featuring a wave pool, hot tub, and various tube rides and water slides. Lockers, showers, and changing rooms available. Miniature golf course (with waterfalls), figure-8 go-kart track, picnic area. **Open:** Mem Day–Labor Day, daily 11am–8pm. **$$$$**

Dubuque

Etched into towering limestone bluffs on the edge of the Mississippi River is this city of charming vintage, with its classic Victorian mansions, riverboat cruises, waterfront district, and Cable Car Square. Dubuque is celebrated for its historic preservation, delightful eateries, and comfortable bed-and-breakfast inns. **Information:** Dubuque Area Chamber of Commerce, 770 Town Clock Plaza, PO Box 705, Dubuque, 52004 (tel 319/557-9200).

HOTEL

Holiday Inn Dubuque Five Flags
450 Main St, 52001; tel 319/556-2000 or toll free 800/421-1213; fax 319/556-2303. Across from civic center. An underground tunnel connects this hotel with the civic center building. From here, it's also an easy walk to downtown offices and historical district and also close to riverboat gambling. **Rooms:** 193 rms and stes. CI 2pm/CO noon. Nonsmoking rms avail. Some rooms have nice view of the river. **Amenities:** A/C, cable TV w/movies, dataport, voice mail. Some units w/whirlpools. **Services:** Babysitting. **Facilities:** 1 restaurant, 2 bars (1 w/entertainment), games rm, spa, whirlpool. **Rates:** Peak (May–Oct) $67–$77 S or D; $128–$138 ste. Extra person $10. Children under age 18 stay free. Lower rates off-season. Parking: Indoor/outdoor, free. AE, CB, DC, DISC, MC, V.

MOTELS

Best Western Dubuque Inn
3434 Dodge St, 52003; tel 319/556-7760 or toll free 800/747-7760; fax 319/556-4003. 2½ miles from Julien Dubuque Bridge. Easy access to US 20 and convenient to shopping areas and attractions. With the pool-recreation area and spacious meeting rooms, the motel is a good bet for both families and business travelers. **Rooms:** 155 rms and stes. CI

2pm/CO 11am. Nonsmoking rms avail. Clean, spacious rooms. **Amenities:** A/C, dataport. Some units w/minibars, 1 w/terrace, 1 w/whirlpool. **Services:** Social director. Vans available for local transportation. **Facilities:** 2 restaurants, 1 bar (w/entertainment), sauna, whirlpool. **Rates:** Peak (May 5–Nov 12) $74–$150 S or D; $125 ste. Extra person $4. Children under age 18 stay free. Lower rates off-season. Parking: Outdoor, free. AE, CB, DC, DISC, JCB, MC, V.

Best Western Midway Hotel
3100 Dodge St, 52003; tel 319/557-8000 or toll free 800/33-MIDWAY; fax 319/557-7692. US 20, west 2 miles from Julien Dubuque Bridge. Conveniently located adjacent to shopping area. Large indoor pool/recreation area make this an attractive stop for families. **Rooms:** 151 rms and stes. Executive level. CI 3pm/CO 1pm. Nonsmoking rms avail. Tastefully furnished, many face indoor pool (closed at night). **Amenities:** A/C, cable TV w/movies, dataport, VCR. Some units w/whirlpools. **Services:** Car-rental desk, babysitting. **Facilities:** 1 restaurant, 1 bar (w/entertainment), games rm, sauna, whirlpool. **Rates:** Peak (June 1–Oct 31) $56–$66 S; $70–$80 D; $100–$125 ste. Extra person $5. Children under age 18 stay free. Lower rates off-season. Parking: Outdoor, free. AE, CB, DC, DISC, MC, V.

Days Inn
1111 Dodge St, 52003; tel 319/583-3297 or toll free 800/772-3297; fax 319/583-5900. ¾ mi W of Mississippi River on US 20. Set against a bluff just off highway. A good homebase from which to visit area attractions. **Rooms:** 156 rms and stes. CI 2pm/CO 11am. Nonsmoking rms avail. **Amenities:** A/C, satel TV w/movies, dataport. **Services:** **Facilities:** 1 restaurant (lunch and dinner only), 1 bar. **Rates (CP):** Peak (May 1–Nov 7) $42–$62 S; $52–$62 D; $125–$150 ste. Extra person $5. Children under age 18 stay free. Lower rates off-season. Parking: Outdoor, free. AE, CB, DC, DISC, EC, ER, JCB, MC, V.

Dodge House
701 Dodge St, 52003; tel 319/556-2231 or toll free 800/942-0009; fax 319/556-2231. 2 blocks W of Julien Dubuque Bridge. Well-maintained property, convenient to highway and local attractions. **Rooms:** 85 rms. CI open/CO 11am. Nonsmoking rms avail. Rooms are clean, neat, and attractive—but nothing fancy. **Amenities:** A/C, cable TV w/movies, refrig. **Services:** **Facilities:** 1 restaurant, 1 bar, games rm, washer/dryer. **Rates:** Peak (Apr–Oct) $26 S; $36–$45 D. Extra person $2. Children under age 12 stay free. Lower rates off-season. Parking: Outdoor, free. AE, CB, DC, DISC, MC, V.

Fairfield Inn
3400 Dodge St, 52003; tel 319/588-2349 or toll free 800/228-2800; fax 319/588-2349. On US 20 about 3 miles from Julien Dubuque Bridge. Good place for families as well as business travelers. **Rooms:** 56 rms and stes. Executive level. CI 2pm/CO 11am. Nonsmoking rms avail. Comfortable and tastefully furnished. **Amenities:** A/C, cable TV, refrig. **Services:** **Facilities:** Games rm, whirlpool. Nice meeting room with coffee always available. **Rates (CP):** Peak (Apr 1–Nov 12) $45–$63 S or D; $52–$63 ste. Extra person $6. Children under age 18 stay free. Lower rates off-season. Parking: Outdoor, free. AE, CB, DC, DISC, MC, V.

Heartland Inn
4025 McDonald Dr, 52003; tel 319/582-3752 or toll free 800/334-3277 code 12; fax 319/582-0113. 4 miles from downtown. Clean and neat and convenient to US 20 on west edge of town. A good place for the budget-conscious traveler. **Rooms:** 88 rms. Executive level. CI 3pm/CO 11am. Nonsmoking rms avail. **Amenities:** A/C, cable TV w/movies. **Services:** Friendly staff is knowledgeable about area attractions. **Facilities:** Sauna, whirlpool. **Rates (CP):** Peak (May 1–Nov 13) $46–$55 S; $54–$63 D. Extra person $8. Children under age 16 stay free. Lower rates off-season. Parking: Outdoor, free. AE, CB, DC, DISC, MC, V.

Motel 6
2670 Dodge St, 52001; tel 319/556-0880; fax 319/582-0190. 2 miles from Julien Dubuque Bridge. Convenient to US 20. Basic, no frills. **Rooms:** 98 rms. CI 6pm/CO noon. Nonsmoking rms avail. **Amenities:** A/C, dataport. Some units w/terraces. **Services:** **Facilities:** **Rates:** $28 S; $34 D. Extra person $3. Children under age 17 stay free. Parking: Outdoor, free. AE, DC, DISC, MC, V.

Super 8 Motel
2730 Dodge St–US 20, 52003; tel 319/582-8898 or toll free 800/800-8000; fax 319/582-8898. 2 miles from Julien Dubuque bridge. Good for families and business travelers. Close to restaurants, shopping, and attractions. **Rooms:** 62 rms and stes. CI 1pm/CO 11am. Nonsmoking rms avail. Clean, neat, simply furnished rooms. **Amenities:** A/C, cable TV. **Services:** Babysitting. Friendly staff. **Facilities:** **Rates (CP):** Peak (Apr 1–Sept 30) $39–$54 S or D; $59 ste. Extra person $3. Children under age 18 stay free. Lower rates off-season. Parking: Outdoor, free. AE, CB, DC, DISC, MC, V.

INNS

The Hancock House
1105 Grove Terrace, 52001; tel 319/557-8989. 5 blocks W of US 52/151/61. This sumptuous Victorian home features several rooms with period furnishings and antiques. **Rooms:** 9 rms and stes. CI 3pm/CO 11am. No smoking. **Amenities:** A/C, cable TV, bathrobes. Some units w/fireplaces, some w/whirlpools. One room has a whirlpool overlooking the city. **Services:** Babysitting, afternoon tea and wine/sherry served. **Facilities:** Washer/dryer, guest lounge. **Rates (BB):** Peak (Apr–Sept) $75–$125 S;

$95–$150 D; $125–$150 ste. Extra person $10. Children under age 3 stay free. Min stay wknds. Lower rates off-season. Parking: Outdoor, free. AE, DISC, MC, V.

Redstone Inn
504 Bluff St, 52001; tel 319/582-1894; fax 319/582-1893. Adjacent to Post Office downtown. 1 acre. An intimate Victorian mansion in the historic downtown district that's worth a splurge. **Rooms:** 15 rms and stes. CI 2pm/CO noon. Nonsmoking rms avail. Rooms reflect a bygone era; they're filled with an exquisite, eclectic array of antiques. **Amenities:** A/C, cable TV, refrig, bathrobes. Some units w/minibars, some w/fireplaces, some w/whirlpools. **Services:** Afternoon tea and wine/sherry served. Eager, helpful staff. **Facilities:** 75 1 restaurant (bkfst only), 1 bar, washer/dryer, guest lounge. **Rates (BB):** Peak (May 1–Oct 31) $49–$175 S; $59–$175 D; $102–$175 ste. Extra person $10. Min stay peak. Lower rates off-season. Parking: Outdoor, free. AE, MC, V.

The Richards House Bed and Breakfast Inn
1492 Locust St, 52001; tel 319/557-1492. 15 blocks north of Julien Dubuque Bridge and US 20. Elegant 1883 Victorian mansion converted to an inn. Luxurious appointments include 90 stained-glass windows, eight ornate fireplaces, and embossed wall coverings. **Rooms:** 5 rms (2 w/shared bath). CI 3pm/CO 11am. No smoking. Rooms furnished with fine Victorian antiques. **Amenities:** A/C, cable TV, bathrobes. Some units w/fireplaces. **Services:** Babysitting, afternoon tea and wine/sherry served. **Facilities:** 14 Games rm, washer/dryer, guest lounge w/TV. **Rates (BB):** Peak (Nov–Apr) $55–$65 S or D w/shared bath, $75–$95 S or D w/private bath; $130–$150 ste. Extra person $25. Children under age 1 stay free. Min stay special events. Lower rates off-season. Parking: Outdoor, free. AE, CB, DC, DISC, MC, V.

RESTAURANTS

★ Pasta O'Shea's
395 Bluff St; tel 319/582-7057. 9 blocks N and 1 block W of Julien Dubuque Bridge. **American/Italian.** Located in a former church, this eatery specializes in seafood/pasta combinations like shrimp, scallops, crab, and lobster over linguine with garlic and olive oil. The obliging staff will let you put together almost any combination of seafood and pasta. Fresh fish, chicken Marsala, and steaks, too. **FYI:** Reservations recommended. Piano. **Open:** Lunch Mon–Fri 11am–2pm; dinner daily 5–10pm. **Prices:** Main courses $10–$17. AE, MC, V.

$ The Ryan House
1375 Locust St; tel 319/556-5000. 14 blocks N of Julien Dubuque Bridge. **American.** You don't have to be rich to eat in this impressive mansion. Dine on moderately priced pastas and stir-fried dishes at lunch, or filet mignon and lobster in the evening. Entree-size salads are available at both meals. **FYI:** Reservations recommended. Children's menu. **Open:** Lunch Mon–Sat 11am–2pm; dinner Mon–Sat 5–10pm; brunch Sun 10am–2pm. **Prices:** Main courses $9–$18. MC, V.

Tollbridge Inn
2800 Rhomberg Ave; tel 319/556-5566. Near the Hawthorne St Harbor, about 2 miles from Downtown, overlooking US Lock & Dam #11. **American.** The Tollbridge overlooks a lock and a dam on the river and bills itself as the "Finest Dining by a Dam Site." Menu specialties are beef Wellington and prime rib. Other choices include pork, seafood, and pasta. **FYI:** Reservations recommended. Guitar/piano/singer. Children's menu. **Open:** Lunch Mon–Sat 11am–2pm; dinner daily 5–10pm; brunch Sun 9am–2pm. **Prices:** Main courses $11–$17. AE, DISC, MC, V.

ATTRACTIONS

Mississippi River Museum
3rd St Ice Harbor; tel 319/557-9545 or toll free 800/226-3369. Six sites, located in a two-block area along the Mississippi waterfront, focus on Dubuque's role as a riverport. The **Riverboat Museum's** displays include a genuine riverboat paddle wheel, a simulated log raft, and Native American and fur-trade artifacts. Two 19th-century rivercraft—the sidewheeler ***William M Black*** and the towboat ***Logsdon***—are open to tours. (Visitors who climb up to the riverboat's pilot house can even ring the pilot's bell.) There's a boatyard with examples of fishing skiffs, clamming boats, and pleasure craft of all types, as well as a Dubuque Heritage Center on the third floor of the Iowa Welcome Center. Two-day pass includes admission to all River Adventure sites. **Open:** Daily 10am–5:30pm. Closed some hols. **$$$**

Matthias Ham House
2241 Lincoln Ave; tel 319/557-9545. Italianate villa built in 1856 by wealthy lead miner Mathias Ham. Furnishings were shipped to Dubuque by steamboat from New Orleans and St Louis; Victorian antiques, fine china, and a collection of dolls are among the highlights. An 1833 log cabin—Iowa's oldest building—is also on the grounds. **Open:** June–Oct, daily 10am–5pm; May, Sat–Sun 10am–5pm. **$**

Crystal Lake Cave
7699 Crystal Lake Cave Dr; tel 319/556-6451. Named for a crystal-clear underground lake formed through seepage from the nearby Mississippi River. The cave's many unusual formations include St Peter's Dome, the Chandelier, the Chapel, and the Pipe Organ. Guided tours follow a lit, ¾-mile trail; last tour leaves 45 minutes before closing time. **Open:** Mem Day–Labor Day, daily 9am–6pm. Call for schedule at other times of year. **$$$**

Sundown Mountain
17017 Asbury Rd; tel 319/556-6676 or toll free 800/397-6676. The state's largest ski area, with six lifts serving 20 downhill slopes (including several black double-diamonds).

Runs are up to 4,000 feet long and include a 475-foot vertical drop. Two cross-country trails, snowboarding, ski school, lodge. Call 800/634-5911 for updated information on snow conditions. **Open:** Mid-Nov–mid-Mar, daily 9am–10pm. Closed some hols. **$$$$**

Dyersville

Perhaps most famous as the backdrop for the film *Field of Dreams,* Dyersville is also the home of one of only 33 basilicas in the United States (the Basilica of St Francis Xavier). **Information:** Dyersville Area Chamber of Commerce, 1410 9th St SE, PO Box 187, Dyersville (tel 319/875-2311).

ATTRACTIONS

Basilica of St Francis Xavier

Corner of 1st Ave W and 2nd St SW; tel 319/875-7325. One of the finest examples of Gothic architecture in the Midwest, and one of only 33 basilicas in the United States. Frescoes representing the Lamb of God line the side arches of the central ceiling, and 64 stained-glass windows depict the life of Christ, biblical scenes, and the saints. Other highlights include a rose window with an unusual Native American motif (in recognition of the area's heritage) and a main altar made of Italian marble and Mexican onyx. **Open:** Daily 6am–6pm. **Free**

Field of Dreams Movie Site

28963 Lansing Rd; tel 319/875-8404. 3 mi E of Dyersville. Since 1989—the year after the Kevin Costner movie *Field of Dreams* was shot here—visitors have been coming to this Iowa corn field to toss a few baseballs, walk the bases, and just sit and relax on the bleachers. For information about the baseball fantasy camp that takes place here every Labor Day weekend, call 800/336-2267. Gift shop. **Open:** Apr–Nov, 9am–6pm. **Free**

Fairfield

This small southeast Iowa town, home of the Maharishi International University, rests at the intersection of US 34 and IA 1. **Information:** Fairfield Area Chamber of Commerce, 204 W Broadway, PO Box 945, Fairfield, 52556 (tel 515/472-2111).

MOTEL

Super 8 Motel

3001 W Burlington Ave, 52556; tel 515/469-2000 or toll free 800/800-8000; fax 515/469-2000. Off US 34, west edge of town. This two-year-old property is a bit noisy because of its proximity to the highway. Rates are competitive with other area motels. **Rooms:** 45 rms and stes. CI 1pm/CO 11am. Nonsmoking rms avail. Average-size, standard rooms. **Amenities:** A/C, cable TV w/movies. Some units w/whirlpools. Suites have whirlpools next to the beds and are a bit cramped. **Services:** Pet deposit of $50 plus $5/night charge. **Facilities:** Whirlpool, washer/dryer. **Rates (CP):** $39 S; $48 D; $69–$89 ste. Extra person $3. Children under age 12 stay free. Parking: Outdoor, free. AE, CB, DC, DISC, MC, V.

Fort Dodge

Founded on the site of the original Fort Dodge, built in 1862 to protect emigrants heading west. The modern-day city is a focal point for education and industry in north-central Iowa. **Information:** Fort Dodge Chamber of Commerce, 1406 Central Ave, PO Box T, Fort Dodge, 50501 (tel 515/955-5500).

MOTELS

Budget Host Inn

116 Kenyon Rd, 50501; tel 515/955-8501 or toll free 800/BUD-HOST; fax 515/955-4968. At US 169 and US 20. Located south of Fort Dodge, this is a basic and economical place to stay. **Rooms:** 111 rms, stes, and effic. Executive level. CI open/CO noon. Nonsmoking rms avail. Nonsmoking room available **Amenities:** A/C, cable TV, refrig. Some units w/terraces. Some rooms have special telephones for the deaf and hard-of-hearing. **Services:** **Facilities:** 150 1 restaurant (dinner only), 2 bars, games rm, whirlpool, washer/dryer. Restaurant/lounge features homemade pizza. **Rates:** $36–$50 S; $43–$57 D; $50–$67 ste; $50–$67 effic. Extra person $5. Children under age 14 stay free. Parking: Outdoor, free. Senior rates. AE, CB, DC, DISC, ER, JCB, MC, V.

Holiday Inn

2001 US 169 S, 50501; tel 515/955-3621 or toll free 800/HOLIDAY; fax 515/955-3643. Attracts businesspeople and families. Spacious lobby. **Rooms:** 102 rms. CI 3pm/CO 1pm. Nonsmoking rms avail. **Amenities:** A/C, cable TV w/movies, dataport. **Services:** Children's program. Coffee in lobby. **Facilities:** 500 1 restaurant, 1 bar. **Rates:** $49–$58 S or D. Children under age 12 stay free. Parking: Outdoor, free. Corporate rates. AE, CB, DC, DISC, JCB, MC, V.

ATTRACTIONS

Blanden Memorial Art Museum

920 Third Ave S; tel 515/573-2316. Built in 1930 as Iowa's first art museum, the Blanden's permanent collection is especially strong in early 20th-century American paintings and prints, European prints from the 16th century to the present, Asian textiles, and African sculpture. Two galleries are given over to special exhibits and traveling exhibitions. **Open:** Tues–Fri 10am–5pm, Sat–Sun 1–5pm. Closed some hols. **Free**

Fort Museum and Frontier Village
Jct Bus 20 and Museum Rd; tel 515/573-4231. Housed in a reconstruction of Fort Williams (a Civil War militia fort built and operated by citizens of the town), the Fort Museum contains Native American artifacts, military memorabilia, and period furniture and clothing. Frontier Village re-creates the sights and sounds of the area's pioneer days. A General Store sells stick candy and souvenirs, and a Blacksmith Shop offers metalworking demonstrations; there's also a drugstore, newspaper office, and jail. **Open:** Daily 9am–6pm. Closed mid-Oct to May 1. **$$**

Grinnell

Home of Grinnell College, founded in 1846—eight years before the city itself. Located in a primarily agricultural area. **Information:** Grinnell Area Chamber of Commerce, 1010 Main St, PO Box 538, Grinell, 50112 (tel 515/236-6555).

MOTELS

Best Western Grinnell
2210 West St S, 50112; tel 515/236-6116 or toll free 800/252-9781; fax 515/236-6199. Exit 182 off I-80; 2 mi S of Grinnell. Stark, small building on a concrete frontage road. Adequate for a one-night stay, although it's priced a bit high. **Rooms:** 38 rms. CI open/CO 11am. Nonsmoking rms avail. Although they're clean, rooms are small, dark, and old. **Amenities:** A/C, cable TV w/movies. Free newspaper and coffee. **Services:** **Facilities:** Discount at lounge/restaurant next door. **Rates:** Peak (May 1–Nov 5) $38–$60 S; $44–$70 D. Extra person $4. Children under age 11 stay free. Lower rates off-season. Parking: Outdoor, free. AE, DC, DISC, MC, V.

Days Inn
IA 146 and I-80, 50112; tel 515/236-6710 or toll free 800/329-7466; fax 515/236-5783. Exit 182 off I-80; 2 mi S of Grinnell. A fairly new facility—bright and well decorated. Close to Grinnell College. **Rooms:** 41 rms. CI 4pm/CO 11am. Nonsmoking rms avail. **Amenities:** A/C, cable TV w/movies. **Services:** Children's program. Free local calls. Coffee in lobby 24 hours. **Facilities:** **Rates (CP):** Peak (Apr–Sept) $41–$46 S; $51–$66 D. Extra person $5. Children under age 12 stay free. Lower rates off-season. Parking: Outdoor, free. AE, DC, DISC, MC, V.

Iowa City

The first state capital from 1841 until 1847; when the capital was moved to Des Moines, Iowa City was compensated by being named the home of the new University of Iowa. Eight miles east is West Branch, birthplace of President Herbert Hoover and site of the Hoover Presidential Library. **Information:** Iowa City/Coralville Convention and Visitors Bureau, 408 1st Ave, Iowa City, 52241 (tel 319/337-6592).

HOTELS

Highlander Inn
2525 N Dodge, 52240; tel 319/354-2000 or toll free 800/728-2000; fax 319/354-7506. I-80 exit 246. An older property, but all rooms were remodeled in 1994. **Rooms:** 95 rms and stes. CI 2pm/CO noon. Nonsmoking rms avail. **Amenities:** A/C, cable TV w/movies, dataport. Some units w/terraces. **Services:** Babysitting. The quality-conscious staff caters to special needs. **Facilities:** 600 2 restaurants, 2 bars, sauna, steam rm, whirlpool. Plenty of space for special events and conferences. Spotless pool and sun deck. **Rates:** Peak (Sept–Oct) $67–$85 S; $74–$92 D; $160–$165 ste. Extra person $7. Children under age 18 stay free. Lower rates off-season. Parking: Outdoor, free. Anniversary, honeymoon, and other packages available. Rates increase during college football season (Sept–Nov). AE, DC, DISC, MC, V.

Holiday Inn
210 S Dubuque St, 52240; tel 319/337-4058 or toll free 800/848-1335; fax 319/337-9045. 2 blocks SE of Old Capitol building. Located in the middle of downtown, it isn't a bargain, but it is worth the price. Easy access to area shopping, restaurants, and entertainment. **Rooms:** 236 rms and stes. Executive level. CI 3pm/CO noon. Nonsmoking rms avail. **Amenities:** A/C, cable TV w/movies, refrig. Some units w/whirlpools. **Services:** **Facilities:** 500 1 restaurant, 1 bar (w/entertainment), games rm, sauna, steam rm, whirlpool. **Rates:** $76–$86 S or D; $135–$150 ste. Extra person $10. Children under age 19 stay free. Min stay special events. Parking: Indoor/outdoor, free. Rates increase during college football season, (Sept–Nov). AE, CB, DC, DISC, MC, V.

MOTELS

Country Inn
2216 N Dodge, 52240; tel 319/351-1010 or toll free 800/456-4000; fax 319/351-1802. I-80 exit 246. Just off I-80 with quick access to downtown and university campus. **Rooms:** 80 rms. CI 2pm/CO noon. Nonsmoking rms avail. All recently renovated, tastefully decorated. **Amenities:** A/C, cable TV w/movies, dataport. All units w/terraces. **Services:** Babysitting. **Facilities:** 30 1 restaurant, whirlpool. **Rates (CP):** $50–$57 S or D. Extra person $7. Children under age 18 stay free. Min stay special events. Parking: Outdoor, free. Rates increase during college football season (Sept–Nov). AE, DC, DISC, MC, V.

Heartland Inn
87 2nd St, Coralville, 52241; tel 319/351-8132 or toll free 800/334-3277 ext 19; fax 319/351-2916. I-80 exit 242. Intersection 1st Ave and US 6. Five-year-old motel near

shopping and sports facilities. Good deal for anyone visiting the University of Iowa campus. **Rooms:** 171 rms. CI 3pm/CO 11am. Nonsmoking rms avail. **Amenities:** A/C, cable TV w/movies. Some units w/fireplaces, some w/whirlpools. Deluxe rooms boast a fireplace and a whirlpool, although everything is in a single room. **Services:** Staff will cater to special requests for honeymoons and anniversaries. **Facilities:** Steam rm. **Rates:** $44–$54 S; $54–$70 D; $105–$165 ste. Extra person $8. Children under age 16 stay free. Parking: Outdoor, free. Rates increase during college football season (Sept–Nov). AE, CB, DC, DISC, MC, V.

RESTAURANTS

The Highlander Inn Restaurant
2525 N Dodge; tel 319/351-3150. Exit 246 off I-80. **American.** A long-time local favorite, featuring surf-and-turf classics with particular emphasis on Iowa's famed beef. Nice wine list. Call early for reservations during college football season (Sept–Nov). **FYI:** Reservations recommended. Children's menu. **Open:** Breakfast daily 6–11am; lunch daily 11am–5pm; dinner Mon–Sat 5–10pm, Sun 4:30–9:30pm; brunch Sun 9am–2pm. **Prices:** Main courses $9–$30. AE, CB, DC, DISC, MC, V.

Iowa River Power Company
501 1st Ave, Coralville; tel 319/351-1904. 1 mile S from I-80 exit 242. **American.** Housed in an old hydroelectric plant on the bank of the Iowa River, this local institution features prime rib and beef tenderloin. **FYI:** Reservations recommended. Children's menu. **Open:** Peak (Aug–Dec) lunch Mon–Fri 11:30am–2:15pm; dinner Mon–Sat 5–10:30pm, Sun 4–10pm; brunch Sun 10:30am–2pm. **Prices:** Main courses $13–$25. AE, CB, DC, MC, V.

ATTRACTION

Herbert Hoover National Historic Site
Parkside Dr and Main St, West Branch; tel 319/643-2541. 8 mi E of Iowa City. Set aside by Congress to preserve several historically significant properties associated with the 31st president. The 14-by-20 foot Hoover birthplace cottage, the Quaker meetinghouse where Hoover worshipped, and a blacksmith shop similar to the one owned by Hoover's father are all open for public viewing. President and Mrs Hoover are both buried here, on a hillside overlooking his birthplace.

The **Hoover Presidential Library & Museum,** one of nine presidential libraries operated by the National Archives, includes multimedia exhibits on Hoover and his era (including World War I and the Great Depression); there's also a re-creation of the President's fishing cabin and an eight-foot slab from the Berlin Wall. Admission to the museum is included in historic site fee. **Open:** Daily 9am–5pm. Closed some hols. **$**

Johnston

See Des Moines

Keokuk

A former fur-trading post near the borders of Illinois and Missouri, Keokuk is the site of Iowa's only Civil War cemetery. Keokuk was the hometown of Samuel F Miller, named to the Supreme Court Justice by President Abraham Lincoln. **Information:** Keokuk Area Chamber of Commerce, 401 Main St #1, Keokuk, 52632 (tel 319/524-5055).

MOTELS

Days Inn
4th and Main Sts, 52632; tel 319/524-8000 or toll free 800/329-7466; fax 319/524-4114. Off US 61. This property is located only minutes from the river, in the heart of downtown. **Rooms:** 84 rms. CI 2pm/CO noon. Nonsmoking rms avail. **Amenities:** A/C, cable TV. **Services:** Babysitting. **Facilities:** 1 restaurant (bkfst and dinner only), 1 bar (w/entertainment). Pool needs better maintenance. **Rates (BB):** $42–$44 S; $48–$52 D. Extra person $5. Children under age 16 stay free. Parking: Outdoor, free. AE, CB, DC, DISC, MC, V.

Keokuk Motor Lodge
3764 Main St, 52632; tel 319/524-3252 or toll free 800/252-2256; fax 319/524-1582. Off US 61 Business Route. Located just outside of downtown, this property has several acres worth of attractive, well-cared-for grounds. **Rooms:** 60 rms. CI noon/CO 11am. Nonsmoking rms avail. Rooms are clean but need upgrading. **Amenities:** A/C, cable TV, dataport, voice mail, in-rm safe, bathrobes. **Services:** Small pets allowed. **Facilities:** Pool is a tad shabby. **Rates (CP):** $37 D. Extra person $4. Children under age 8 stay free. Parking: Outdoor, free. AE, CB, DC, DISC, MC, V.

Super 8 Motel
3511 Main St, 52632; tel 319/524-3888 or toll free 800/800-8000; fax 319/524-3888. Just off US 61. Moderately attractive chain motel. **Rooms:** 62 rms. CI 1pm/CO 11am. Nonsmoking rms avail. Larger-than-average rooms are meticulously cared for. **Amenities:** A/C, cable TV. **Services:** **Facilities:** **Rates (CP):** $39–$46 S; $48–$54 D. Extra person $3. Children under age 12 stay free. Parking: Outdoor, free. AE, CB, DC, DISC, MC, V.

Le Mars

A thriving northwest Iowa community with a historic pioneer-era flavor, situated 26 miles northeast of Sioux City. Location of Teikyo Westmar University.

MOTELS

UNRATED **The Amber Inn**
635 8th Ave SW, PO Box 511, 51031; tel 712/546-7066 or toll free 800/338-0298; fax 712/548-4058. ½ mi S of downtown; along US 75. This dated property is in the process of renovation. **Rooms:** 73 rms and stes. CI open/CO 11am. Nonsmoking rms avail. Rooms are very basic, but have new TVs and carpets. **Amenities:** A/C, cable TV. **Services:** **Facilities:** **Rates (CP):** $27–$30 S; $32–$34 D; $55 ste. Extra person $2. Children under age 12 stay free. Parking: Outdoor, free. AE, DISC, MC, V.

Super 8 Motel
1201 Hawkeye Ave SW, 51031; tel 712/546-8800 or toll free 800/800-8000; fax 712/546-8800 ext 403. 1 mi S of downtown; along IA 75. Attractive to business travelers, this basic property is clean and has a friendly staff. **Rooms:** 61 rms and stes. CI 2pm/CO 11am. Nonsmoking rms avail. **Amenities:** A/C, satel TV. **Services:** Free local calls. **Facilities:** Whirlpool. Parking for large vehicles. **Rates (CP):** $33–$42 S; $38–$42 D; $45–$58 ste. Extra person $1. Parking: Outdoor, free. AE, CB, DC, DISC, MC, V.

Maquoketa

Located midway between Davenport and Dubuque on US 61. Nearby Maquoketa Caves State Park features limestone caves and a natural bridge, while historic stone mills attract the tourists and locals alike. **Information:** Maquoketa Area Chamber of Commerce, 112 N Main, Maquoketa, 52060 (tel 319/652-4602).

MOTELS

Key Motel
119 McKinsey Dr, 52060; tel 319/652-5131 or toll free 800/622-3285. E of US 61 on IA 64. A bare-bones lodging favored by local construction workers. **Rooms:** 30 rms. CI 11am/CO 11am. Nonsmoking rms avail. Clean and well-kept. **Amenities:** A/C, cable TV, refrig. **Services:** **Facilities:** Washer/dryer. **Rates:** Peak (June–Oct) $35–$45 S or D. Extra person $2.50. Children under age 12 stay free. Lower rates off-season. Parking: Outdoor, free. AE, CB, DC, DISC, MC, V.

Super 8 Motel
10021 West Platt St, 52060; tel 319/652-6888 or toll free 800/800-8000; fax 319/652-6888. Off US 61; just 2 blocks E on IA 64. Simple, neat, and clean property convenient to the highway. **Rooms:** 50 rms and stes. CI 1pm/CO 11am. Nonsmoking rms avail. **Amenities:** A/C, cable TV. Some units w/whirlpools. **Services:** **Facilities:** Washer/dryer. **Rates:** Peak (Apr–Sept) $43 S; $46 D; $70 ste. Extra person $5. Children under age 12 stay free. Lower rates off-season. Parking: Outdoor, free. AE, CB, DC, DISC, MC, V.

ATTRACTION

Maquoketa Caves State Park
IA 428; tel 319/652-5833. 6 mi NW of Maquoketa. This 272-acre park is built on top of a series of 16 small caves, some of which are open for exploration. Day-use area includes six picnic areas, playground, and hiking and nature trails; there's also a 28-site campground. Visitor center has displays on Native American history, cave formation, and the history of the park. **Open:** Daily sunrise–sunset. **$**

Marquette

Named for Father Jacques Marquette, the first European to explore Iowa territory (in 1673). Nearby bluffs shelter Effigy Mounds National Monument, site of almost 200 prehistoric Native American burial and ceremonial mounds, dating from 500 BC to AD 1300. **Information:** McGregor/Marquette Chamber of Commerce, 146 Main St, PO Box 105, McGregor, 52157 (tel 319/873-2186).

ATTRACTION

Effigy Mounds National Monument
151 IA 76, Harpers Ferry; tel 319/873-3491. National monument established to preserve 25,000-year-old Native American burial mounds. Within the monument's borders are 191 known prehistoric mounds, many of them built in the shapes of birds and other animals. The monumental Great Bear Mound is 70 feet across the shoulders and forelegs, 137 feet long, and 3½ feet high. Museum exhibits and an audiovisual presentation at the visitors center explain the history of the Effigy Mounds. A one-hour walk on the self-guided Fire Point Trail leads to the Little Bear Mound, Hopewellian mounds, and scenic viewpoints along the 300-foot-high bluff tops. **Open:** Daily 8am–5pm. Closed some hols. **$**

Marshalltown

The location of the Iowa Veterans Home and Marshalltown Community College. **Information:** Marshalltown Convention and Visitors Bureau, 709 S Center St, PO Box 1000, Marshalltown, 50158 (tel 515/752-8373).

MOTELS

Best Western Inn
3303 S Center St, 50158; tel 515/752-6321 or toll free 800/241-2974; fax 515/752-4412. Jct US 30/IA 14. Good for meetings and conventions. **Rooms:** 161 rms, stes, and effic. Executive level. CI 3pm/CO noon. Nonsmoking rms avail. Rooms are fairly large; king rooms offer reclining chairs. Poolside rooms are worth the extra money. **Amenities:** A/C, cable TV w/movies, refrig, dataport. Some units w/terraces. **Services:** Children's program.

Facilities: 1 restaurant, 1 bar, whirlpool. **Rates:** Peak (June–Aug) $53–$63 S; $108 ste; $108 effic. Extra person $7. Children under age 18 stay free. Lower rates off-season. Parking: Outdoor, free. AE, CB, DC, DISC, MC, V.

Comfort Inn
2613 S Center St, 50158; tel 515/752-6000; fax 515/752-8762. ½ mi N of US 30 on IA 14. A new facility that's clean, bright, and comfortable. **Rooms:** 62 rms and stes. Executive level. CI 3pm/CO noon. Nonsmoking rms avail. All nicely decorated. **Amenities:** A/C, cable TV w/movies, dataport. 1 unit w/whirlpool. **Services:** **Facilities:** Whirlpool. **Rates (CP):** Peak (May–Sept) $42–$44 S; $52–$54 D; $90–$140 ste. Extra person $5. Children under age 18 stay free. Lower rates off-season. Parking: Outdoor, free. AE, CB, DC, DISC, MC, V.

Days Inn
403 E Church St, 50158; tel 515/753-7777 or toll free 800/329-7466; fax 515/753-7777. Located in a residential area near a hospital/clinic, it's a convenient place for patients' families to stay. **Rooms:** 30 rms. Executive level. CI 2pm/CO noon. Nonsmoking rms avail. Rooms are cluttered and small. **Amenities:** A/C, satel TV w/movies, dataport. 1 unit w/fireplace. **Services:** Children's program. **Facilities:** Truck parking. **Rates (BB):** $38–$45 S; $45–$65 D. Extra person $5. Children under age 18 stay free. Parking: Outdoor, free. Extended stay rates avail. AE, CB, DC, DISC, EC, JCB, MC, V.

Mason City

See also Clear Lake

Hometown of *Music Man* composer Meredith Willson; the city still hosts the annual North Iowa Band Festival. Frank Lloyd Wright's only Prairie School house in Iowa–the Stockman House–is located downtown. **Information:** Mason City Convention and Visitors Bureau, 15 W State, PO Box 1128, Mason City, 50402 (tel 515/423-5724).

MOTELS

Comfort Inn
410 5th St SW, 50401; tel 515/423-4444 or toll free 800/228-5150; fax 515/424-5358. Exit 194 off I-35, E on US 18. Attractive motel in a relaxing setting. **Rooms:** 60 rms and stes. CI 3pm/CO noon. Nonsmoking rms avail. **Amenities:** A/C, cable TV, dataport, bathrobes. Some units w/whirlpools. **Services:** Babysitting. **Facilities:** Whirlpool. **Rates (CP):** $49–$67 S; $55–$73 D; $84–$90 ste. Extra person $6. Children under age 18 stay free. Min stay special events. Parking: Outdoor, free. AE, CB, DC, DISC, JCB, MC, V.

Days Inn
2301 4th St SW, 50401; tel 515/424-0210 or toll free 800/329-7466; fax 515/424-5284. 6 mi E of I-35 on US 18 E. A good place to stay for the budget-conscious. Close to restaurants and attractions. **Rooms:** 59 rms and stes. Executive level. CI 3pm/CO noon. Nonsmoking rms avail. **Amenities:** A/C, cable TV. **Services:** Babysitting. **Facilities:** **Rates (CP):** $32–$39 S; $45–$49 D; $59 ste. Extra person $5. Children under age 18 stay free. Parking: Outdoor, free. AE, DC, DISC, MC, V.

Holiday Inn
2101 4th St SW, 50401; tel 515/423-1640 or toll free 800/465-4329; fax 515/423-4862. 6 miles E of I-35 on US 18. Better-than-average lodging. Good place for families because of the pool and games for kids. **Rooms:** 135 rms and stes. Executive level. CI 3pm/CO noon. Nonsmoking rms avail. **Amenities:** A/C, dataport. Some units w/whirlpools. **Services:** **Facilities:** 1 restaurant, 1 bar, games rm, sauna, whirlpool. **Rates:** Peak (June–Aug) $59 S; $67 D; $97–$140 ste. Extra person $8. Children under age 19 stay free. Lower rates off-season. Parking: Outdoor, free. AE, CB, DC, DISC, MC, V.

ATTRACTION

Van Horn's Truck Museum
IA 65 N; tel 515/423-0550. This museum contains some of the nation's oldest and most unusual commercial vehicles, with trucks dating back to 1909. Vehicles are displayed in a turn-of-the-century setting, including a store-front street made up of gas stations, general stores, a fire house, and garages. There's also a reconstructed warehouse where mannequins "load" old-fashioned merchandise onto antique trucks. **Open:** May 25–Sept 22, Mon–Sat 9am–4pm, Sun 11am–5pm. **$$**

Missouri Valley

Entrance point for visitors entering from Nebraska on US 30. Adjacent to the DeSoto National Wildlife Refuge, which provides over 7,000 acres for birdwatching and hiking. **Information:** Missouri Valley Chamber of Commerce, 400 E Erie, PO Box 130, Missouri Valley, 51555 (tel 712/642-2553).

ATTRACTION

DeSoto National Wildlife Refuge
US 30; tel 402/642-2772. Each spring and fall, this 7,800-acre park serves as a migratory stopover for thousands of ducks and geese. A 12-mile wildlife drive allows visitors to get a close-up view of the birds; interpretive brochures keyed to numbered stops on the drive are available at the visitors center. Other facilities include four nature trails, eight picnic areas, and three boat ramps. The visitors center also houses

the hull of the 178-ft steamboat *Bertrand,* which was excavated from the nearby Missouri River in 1968. **Open:** Daily 9am–4:30pm. Closed some hols. **$**

Mount Pleasant

A largely agricultural community, located at the crossing of US 34 and US 218 in southeast Iowa. Also the site of the Harlan-Lincoln Home, the former home of President Lincoln's son-in-law and his family; Mrs Lincoln's mourning veil and other Lincoln family possessions are on display. **Information:** Mount Pleasant Area Chamber of Commerce, 124 S Main St, PO Box 109, Mount Pleasant, 52641 (tel 319/385-3101).

MOTELS

Heartland Inn

US 218 N, 52641; tel 319/385-2102 or toll free 800/334-3277; fax 319/385-3223. Set in the middle of an asphalt parking lot; OK for a fast overnight stay. Rates are a bit higher than at similar motels in the area. **Rooms:** 60 rms. CI 2pm/CO 11am. Nonsmoking rms avail. Rooms are clean, basic. **Amenities:** A/C, cable TV w/movies. **Services:** **Facilities:** 30 Sauna, whirlpool. **Rates (CP):** $39 S; $47 D. Extra person $8. Children under age 16 stay free. Parking: Outdoor, free. AE, CB, DC, DISC, MC, V.

Super 8 Motel

US 218 N, 52641; tel 319/385-8888 or toll free 800/800-8000; fax 319/385-8888. An ordinary property a bit away from town. **Rooms:** 55 rms. CI 1pm/CO 11am. Nonsmoking rms avail. Average-size rooms are modestly appointed. **Amenities:** A/C, cable TV. **Services:** **Facilities:** **Rates (CP):** $39 S; $48 D. Extra person $4. Children under age 12 stay free. Parking: Outdoor, free. AE, CB, DC, DISC, MC, V.

Muscatine

An agricultural town, poised on the banks of the Mississippi between the Quad Cities (on the north) and Burlington (on the south). **Information:** Muscatine Chamber of Commerce, 319 E 2nd St, PO Box 297, Muscatine, 52761 (tel 319/263-8895).

ATTRACTION

Muscatine Art Center

1314 Mulberry Ave; tel 319/263-8282. Housed in the 1908 Musser mansion. Paperweights, Oriental carpets, American art pottery, and period antiques offer an exciting contrast to works by noteworthy American artists such as Grant Wood and Georgia O'Keeffe. A recent gift of 27 pieces by Matisse, Degas, Chagall, Renoir, and other European masters rounds out the permanent collection. National traveling exhibitions and shows by contemporary artists are featured in the Stanley Gallery. **Open:** Tues–Fri 10am–5pm, Thurs until 9pm, Sat–Sun 1–5pm. Closed some hols. **Free**

Newton

A frequent stop for University of Iowa football fans traveling from Des Moines to Iowa City on I-80. Corporate headquarters of the Maytag Corporation, the familiar appliance manufacturing firm. **Information:** Newton Visitor and Conference Bureau, 113 1st Ave W, Newton, 50508 (tel 515/792-0299).

MOTELS

Best Western Inn

2000 W 18th St S, 50208; tel 515/792-4200 or toll free 800/373-6350; fax 515/792-0108. S of I-80 on exit 164. Very quiet property set on a hill south of the interstate. **Rooms:** 118 rms. CI 4pm/CO noon. Nonsmoking rms avail. Small rooms; two have queen-size waterbeds. **Amenities:** A/C, cable TV w/movies. 1 unit w/minibar. **Services:** **Facilities:** 1 restaurant (bkfst and dinner only), 1 bar, games rm, spa, sauna, whirlpool. **Rates (BB):** Peak (June–Aug) $37–$63 S; $45–$71 D. Extra person $6. Children under age 12 stay free. Lower rates off-season. Parking: Outdoor, free. AE, CB, DC, DISC, MC, V.

Days Inn

1605 W 19th St S, 50208; tel 515/792-2330 or toll free 800/DAYS-INN; fax 515/792-1045. Located south of the downtown area. Rates are a bit high for the quality. **Rooms:** 59 rms. CI 2pm/CO 11am. Nonsmoking rms avail. Small, dark, quiet. **Amenities:** A/C, cable TV w/movies, VCR. **Services:** Children's program. Free local calls. Video rental. **Rates (CP):** $39–$51 S; $44–$60 D. Extra person $5. Children under age 12 stay free. Parking: Outdoor, free. AE, CB, DC, DISC, JCB, MC, V.

Super 8 Motel Newton

1635 S 12th Ave W, 50208; tel 515/792-8868 or toll free 800/800-8000; fax 515/792-8868. Small, basic facility, looking a bit worn. **Rooms:** 43 rms. CI 2pm/CO 11am. Nonsmoking rms avail. Rooms with choice of king-size, queen-size, or waterbeds. **Amenities:** A/C, cable TV w/movies. **Services:** Fax and copy services. **Facilities:** 15 **Rates (CP):** Peak (Apr–Sept) $38–$44 S; $47–$55 D. Extra person $6. Children under age 12 stay free. Lower rates off-season. Parking: Outdoor, free. AE, DC, DISC, MC, V.

Terrace Lodge

I-80 and IA 14, 50208; tel 515/792-7722 or toll free 800/383-7722; fax 515/792-1787. An older facility set into a hill south of Newton. **Rooms:** 60 rms and stes. Executive level. CI open/CO 11am. Nonsmoking rms avail. Clean but small and dark, and with older furnishings. **Amenities:** A/C, satel TV. **Services:** **Facilities:** 250 1 restaurant, 1 bar (w/entertainment), sauna, whirlpool. **Rates (CP):** $42–$49 S; $48–$56 D; $95–$110 ste. Extra person $6. Children under age 13 stay free. Parking: Outdoor, free. AE, CB, DC, DISC, MC, V.

Okoboji

See Spirit Lake

Osceola

The seat of Clarke County, Osceola is located at the junction of US 69 and US 34. **Information:** Osceola Chamber of Commerce, 100 S Filmore, PO Box 1, Osceola, 50213 (tel 515/342-4200).

MOTELS

Best Western Regal Inn
1520 Jeffrey's Dr, PO Box 238, 50213; tel 515/342-2123 or toll free 800/252-2289. 2 blocks E of I-35 on US 3A. Located close to golf and tennis. **Rooms:** 35 rms. CI 11am/CO 11am. Nonsmoking rms avail. Nice-size rooms. **Amenities:** A/C, cable TV w/movies. **Services:** Babysitting. **Facilities:** **Rates:** $36–$50 S; $39–$52 D. Extra person $3. Parking: Outdoor, free. AE, CB, DC, DISC, MC, V.

Super 8 Motel
Jimmy Dean Ave, 50213; tel 515/342-6594 or toll free 800/800-8000; fax 515/342-6594. A clean, economical place to stay. **Rooms:** 53 rms. CI open/CO 10:30am. Nonsmoking rms avail. Smallish rooms. **Amenities:** A/C, cable TV w/movies. **Services:** Fax service. **Facilities:** Truck and bus parking. **Rates (CP):** $38–$41 S; $43–$49 D. Extra person $6. Children under age 12 stay free. Parking: Outdoor, free. AE, CB, DC, DISC, MC, V.

Oskaloosa

Nelson Pioneer Farm, listed in the National Register of Historic Places, is located in Oskaloosa, a thriving Mahaska County community in southeast Iowa. **Information:** Oskaloosa Area Chamber of Commerce, 124 N Market St, Oskaloosa, 52577 (tel 515/672-2591).

MOTELS

Friendship Inn
1315 A Ave E, 52577; tel 515/673-8351 or toll free 800/453-4511; fax 515/673-8351. Off US 63 E. Rambling structure located just off the highway, in the middle of an asphalt parking lot. **Rooms:** 42 rms. CI 2pm/CO 11am. Nonsmoking rms avail. Rooms are clean and modestly appointed. **Amenities:** A/C, cable TV. **Services:** Staff does not seem to be service oriented. **Facilities:** 100 Washer/dryer. **Rates:** $39–$44 S or D. Extra person $3. Children under age 18 stay free. Parking: Outdoor, free. AE, CB, DC, DISC, MC, V.

King Lear Motel
2278 US 63 N, 52577; tel 515/673-8641 or toll free 800/255-2110; fax 515/673-4111. Older property needing renovation; although cheap, rates are no bargain relative to other nearby motels. **Rooms:** 40 rms and stes. CI 3pm/CO 11am. Nonsmoking rms avail. Bedspreads and linen need upgrading. **Amenities:** A/C, cable TV. **Services:** **Facilities:** 35 Washer/dryer. **Rates (CP):** $28 S; $35 D; $45 ste. Extra person $3. Children under age 5 stay free. Parking: Outdoor, free. AE, DISC, MC, V.

Super 8 Motel
306 S 17th St, 52577; tel 515/673-8481 or toll free 800/800-8000. Just off US 63. Located near restaurants and shopping; easy access to highway. Rates are average for area and level of accommodations. **Rooms:** 51 rms and stes. CI noon/CO 11am. Nonsmoking rms avail. Standard rooms are small but clean; suites are somewhat larger and have additional seating. **Amenities:** A/C, cable TV w/movies. **Services:** **Facilities:** 20 **Rates:** $38–$45 S or D; $50 ste. Extra person $3. Children under age 12 stay free. Parking: Outdoor, free. AE, CB, DC, DISC, MC, V.

ATTRACTION

Nelson Pioneer Farm
2294 Oxford Ave; tel 515/672-2989. An active farm for more than 100 years, today the museum focuses on pioneer life through 14 original buildings from the late 1800s, including a log cabin, a post office, school (circa 1861), a lumber yard office (circa 1864), and a country store. **Open:** May 1–Oct 12, Tues–Sat 10am–4:30pm, Sun 1–4pm. **$**

Ottumwa

Roughly 30 miles from Iowa's southern border, Ottumwa rests at the junction of US 34, US 63, and IA 23. **Information:** Ottumwa Area Convention and Visitors Bureau, 108 E 3rd St, PO Box 308, Ottumwa, 52501 (tel 515/682-3465).

MOTELS

Days Inn
206 Church St, 52501; tel 515/682-8131 or toll free 800/329-7466; fax 515/682-5902. At jct of US 34 and US 63. Located near downtown, the structures are not particularly attractive. Better rooms nearby can be had for less. **Rooms:** 134 rms. CI 2pm/CO noon. Nonsmoking rms avail. Rooms need renovation; appointments are worn and dated. **Amenities:** A/C, cable TV. Some units w/terraces. **Services:** **Facilities:** 1 restaurant. Pool somewhat rundown. Free YMCA passes for guests. **Rates:**

Peak (Apr–Sept) $54–$60 S or D. Extra person $6. Children under age 18 stay free. Lower rates off-season. Parking: Outdoor, free. AE, CB, DC, DISC, MC, V.

Heartland Inn
125 W Joseph St, 52501; tel 515/682-8526 or toll free 800/334-3277; fax 515/682-7124. On US 63. This property is just far enough off the road to be quiet. Across from the Greyhound Park Racetrack. **Rooms:** 90 rms. CI 3pm/CO noon. Nonsmoking rms avail. Bigger-than-average rooms. **Amenities:** A/C, cable TV w/movies, dataport. **Services:** Free dinner on Wednesday nights. Pet fee $10. **Facilities:** Sauna, whirlpool, washer/dryer. Free passes to the YMCA. **Rates (CP):** $39 S; $47 D. Extra person $8. Children under age 16 stay free. Parking: Outdoor, free. Romance packages avail. AE, CB, DC, DISC, MC, V.

ATTRACTIONS

Exploratorium of Iowa
104 S Market; tel 515/682-0921. Hands-on science museum that provides children with an opportunity to explore science, art, and history. Exhibits include a space room with moon walk, a display on the human body, and a light and sound demonstration **Open:** Sun–Fri 1–5pm, Sat 10am–5pm. Closed some hols. **$**

Airpower Museum
22001 Bluegrass Rd; tel 515/938-2773. Thirty-acre complex featuring restored antique airplanes (from 1903 to World War II); plane models, engines, and propellers; hot-air balloons; exhibits on military aircraft; and displays dedicated to the accomplishments of famous aviators like Charles Lindbergh and Amelia Earhart. **Open:** Mon–Fri 9am–5pm, Sat 10am–5pm, Sun 1–5pm. Closed some hols.

The Beach Ottumwa
101 Church St; tel 515/682-SURF. Family-oriented water park offers 200-foot speed slide, a wave pool with sandy beach, an indoor pool, a lagoon with paddleboats, and a kiddie wading pool. There's also a picnic area and volleyball and basketball courts **Open:** Outdoor park Mem Day–Labor Day, indoor park year-round; call ahead for hours. Closed some hols. **$$$**

Pella

Iowa's other true "Holland alternative" (the other being Orange City) is Pella, home of Old World charm, wooden shoes, and Dutch architecture. **Information:** Pella Chamber of Commerce, 518 Franklin St, Pella, 50219 (tel 515/628-2626).

MOTEL

Pella Super 8 Motel
105 E Oskaloosa, 50219; tel 515/628-8181 or toll free 800/800-8000; fax 515/628-8181. On IA 163. Likable, basic property decorated in a Dutch motif. Near restaurants and shopping. **Rooms:** 41 rms and stes. CI 2pm/CO 11am. Nonsmoking rms avail. **Amenities:** A/C, cable TV w/movies. **Services:** Fax and copy services. **Facilities:** **Rates (CP):** $39–$46 S; $48–$51 D; $44–$51 ste. Extra person $3. Children under age 12 stay free. Parking: Outdoor, free. Rates rise during the tulip festival. AE, CB, DC, DISC, MC, V.

Quad Cities

See Bettendorf, Davenport

Shenandoah

Established near the early Mormon settlement of Manti, in the southwest corner of the state. Today, Shenandoah is the site of several large seed companies. **Information:** Shenandoah Chamber of Commerce, 614 W Sheridan, PO Box 38, Shenandoah, 51601 (tel 712/246-3260).

MOTEL

Days Inn
108 N Fremont, 51601; tel 712/246-5733 or toll free 800/329-7466; fax 712/246-2230. At jct IA 48 and US 59. Comfortable lodgings, close to restaurants, golf, and tennis. **Rooms:** 33 rms and stes. Executive level. CI open/CO 11am. Nonsmoking rms avail. **Amenities:** A/C, cable TV w/movies, refrig. **Services:** **Facilities:** **Rates (CP):** Peak (Apr–Sept) $32–$42 S; $44–$48 D; $44–$54 ste. Extra person $4. Children under age 12 stay free. Lower rates off-season. Parking: Outdoor, free. AE, CB, DC, DISC, MC, V.

Sioux City

See also South Sioux City (NE)

Sioux City was made famous when the Lewis and Clark expedition passed through in 1804. Perched on the Missouri River, modern-day Sioux City offers sports, arts, theater, and more. **Information:** Sioux City Convention and Tourism Bureau, 801 4th St, PO Box 3183, Sioux City, 51102 (tel 712/279-4800).

PUBLIC TRANSPORTATION

Sioux City Transit (STC) (tel 712/279-6404) provides bus service throughout the greater Sioux City area. Tickets and tokens can be purchased at local banks. Fares: adults 85¢, seniors and persons with disabilities 40¢, children 5–11 45¢; children under 5 ride free. Transfers are free.

HOTEL

Hilton Hotel
707 4th St, 51101; tel 712/277-4101 or toll free 800/HILTONS; fax 712/277-3168. Exit 130 off I-29. At 12 stories, this is the closest thing to a big-city hotel in western Iowa. The main floor hums with a large check-in area, restaurant, and gift shop, plus a skyway leading to a mini-mall. **Rooms:** 193 rms and stes. Executive level. CI 2pm/CO noon. Nonsmoking rms avail. Clean and large. **Amenities:** A/C, cable TV. Some units have microwaves. **Services:** Car-rental desk. Transportation available to airport, casino, and riverfront. **Facilities:** 1 restaurant, 1 bar (w/entertainment), games rm, sauna, whirlpool. Popular banquet facilities. **Rates:** Peak (June–Aug) $89–$104 S; $99–$114 D; $104–$114 ste. Extra person $10. Children under age 18 stay free. Lower rates off-season. Parking: Indoor, free. Romance package and senior discounts avail. AE, CB, DC, DISC, MC, V.

MOTELS

Best Western City Centre
130 Nebraska St, 51101 (Downtown); tel 712/277-1550 or toll free 800/528-1234; fax 712/277-1120. Exit 147B off I-29. Although it is showing signs of wear, this place fills fast on weekends. Located near Civic Center and riverboat gambling. **Rooms:** 115 rms and stes. CI 2pm/CO noon. Nonsmoking rms avail. Room furnishings and carpets need attention. **Amenities:** A/C, cable TV. Hair dryers available. **Services:** Car-rental desk. Free local calls. Complimentary coffee, tea, and cocoa all day; free cocktails 5–8pm. Shuttle to restaurants, riverboats, hospitals, and airport. **Facilities:** 1 bar. **Rates (BB):** $49–$52 S; $54–$59 D; $70 ste. Extra person $10. Children under age 12 stay free. Parking: Outdoor, free. AE, DC, DISC, MC, V.

Comfort Inn
4202 S Lakeport St, 51106; tel 712/274-1300 or toll free 800/228-5150; fax 712/274-1300. Exit 144B off I-29. This neat and clean motel with spacious rooms is close to the airport and across the road from a shopping mall. **Rooms:** 70 rms and stes. CI 2pm/CO 11am. Nonsmoking rms avail. **Amenities:** A/C, cable TV. Some units w/whirlpools. **Services:** **Facilities:** Games rm, whirlpool. Glassed-in pool area. Within a half-mile of minor league baseball stadium. **Rates (CP):** Peak (June–Aug 19) $52–$76 S; $52–$81 D; $65–$75 ste. Extra person $5. Children under age 18 stay free. Lower rates off-season. Parking: Outdoor, free. AE, CB, DC, DISC, MC, V.

Fairfield Inn
4716 S Hills Dr, 51106; tel 712/276-5600 or toll free 800/228-2800; fax 712/276-5600. I-29 to US 20; take Lakeport Rd exit. Located across the road from a large shopping mall and close to the airport. Rates are a bit high for size of rooms. Minor league baseball park within half-mile. **Rooms:** 62 rms and stes. CI noon/CO 11am. Nonsmoking rms avail. Rooms are very neat, but small. **Amenities:** A/C, cable TV. **Services:** **Facilities:** Whirlpool. **Rates (CP):** $47–$71 S; $49–$71 D; $63 ste. Extra person $6. Children under age 16 stay free. Parking: Outdoor, free. AE, DC, DISC, MC, V.

Holiday Inn
1401 Zenith Dr, 51103; tel 712/277-3211 or toll free 800/HOLIDAY; fax 712/277-1410. Exit 149 off I-29. Although this motel is dated, it offers many facilities: both indoor and outdoor pools, a play area, and more. **Rooms:** 156 rms and stes. CI 3pm/CO noon. Nonsmoking rms avail. **Amenities:** A/C, cable TV. 1 unit w/whirlpool. **Services:** Babysitting. Transportation available to casinos and downtown. **Facilities:** 1 restaurant, 1 bar, games rm, sauna, whirlpool, playground. **Rates:** $57–$58 S; $57–$58 D; $125 ste. Extra person $6. Children under age 12 stay free. Parking: Outdoor, free. AE, CB, DC, DISC, MC, V.

RESTAURANT

The First Edition Beef, Seafood & Spirits
416 Jackson (Downtown); tel 712/277-3200. Next to Hilton Inn. **American/Southwestern/Steak.** Simply decorated restaurant where the main draw is hand-cut steaks; each variety of meat is offered in three sizes and arrives at the table on wooden platters. **FYI:** Reservations accepted. Blues/rock. **Open:** Lunch Mon–Fri 11am–2pm; dinner Mon–Thurs 5:30–9:30pm, Fri–Sat 5:30–10:30pm. **Prices:** Main courses $9–$17. AE, DC, MC, V.

Spencer

Located on the spacious plains of northwest Iowa, Spencer is a popular stopover for visitors to Iowa's upper lakes region. **Information:** Spencer Area Association of Business and Industry, 122 W 5th St, PO Box 3047, Spencer, 51301 (tel 712/262-5680).

HOTEL

The Hotel
605 Grand Ave, 51301 (Downtown); tel 712/262-2010; fax 712/262-5610. Historical landmark built in 1920 and last renovated in 1986. **Rooms:** 40 rms and stes. Executive level. CI 1pm/CO 11am. Nonsmoking rms avail. All rooms—from economy to executive—are comfortable and tastefully furnished. **Amenities:** A/C, cable TV. Some units w/minibars. **Services:** Complimentary evening hors d'oeuvres in cocktail lounge. **Facilities:** 1 restaurant, 1 bar. **Rates:** $29–$39 S; $29–$45 D; $49 ste. Children under age 10 stay free. Parking: Outdoor, free. AE, DISC, MC, V.

MOTELS

AmericInn Motel

1005 13th St W, 51301; tel 712/262-7525 or toll free 800/634-3444; fax 712/262-7514. On US 71. This clean, bright, and attractive property opened in May 1995. **Rooms:** 46 rms, stes, and effic. Executive level. CI 3pm/CO 11am. Nonsmoking rms avail. Rooms have excellent soundproofing. Suites, with whirlpools, are an exceptional value. **Amenities:** A/C, cable TV. Some units w/whirlpools. Two-room suites have refrigerator and microwave **Services:** **Facilities:** 15 Games rm, whirlpool, washer/dryer. **Rates (CP):** $43 S; $47 D; $60 ste; $86 effic. Extra person $6. Children under age 12 stay free. Parking: Outdoor, free. Senior and frequent-guest rates avail. AE, DC, DISC, MC, V.

Super 8 Motel

209 11th St SW, 51301; tel 712/262-8500 or toll free 800/843-1991; fax 712/262-8500 ext 125. 2 blocks W of jct US 18/71. Small motel, close to restaurants and shopping mall. Rates are high for the area. **Rooms:** 31 rms. CI open/CO 11am. Nonsmoking rms avail. Cramped rooms. Single rooms have queen or king beds. **Amenities:** A/C, cable TV w/movies. **Services:** **Facilities:** Truck parking. **Rates (CP):** Peak (Apr–Sept) $39 S; $49 D. Lower rates off-season. Parking: Outdoor, free. AE, CB, DC, DISC, MC, V.

INN

Hannah Marie Country Inn

4020 US 71, 51301; tel 712/262-1286 or toll free 800/712/972-1286; fax 712/262-3294. 200 acres. Made up of two houses connected by a veranda, this charming B&B is located on a 200-acre farm. The garden courtyard is perfect for weddings. **Rooms:** 5 rms. CI 5pm/CO 11am. Nonsmoking rms avail. Each room offers touches like feather beds and is beautifully decorated with antiques in keeping with a theme, such as the Teddy Roosevelt safari room. **Amenities:** A/C, TV. No phone. Some units w/whirlpools. Chocolates on pillows each evening. **Services:** Afternoon tea served. Welcome beverage upon arrival. **Facilities:** 50 Whirlpool, guest lounge w/TV. The herb gardens and small bistro cafe are available for lunch or dinner by appointment. **Rates (BB):** $50–$87 S or D. Parking: Outdoor, free. Rates include full breakfast and evening dessert. Closed mid-Dec–Apr. AE, MC, V.

RESTAURANTS

The Prime Rib Restaurant and Lounge

1205 S Grand Ave; tel 712/262-4625. 1 block S of US 71. **Seafood/Steak.** Although the menu focuses on prime rib and steak, it also offers a variety of less-filling appetizers, sandwiches, and burgers, plus pasta and seafood entrees. Fun and casual atmosphere. **FYI:** Reservations accepted. Children's menu. Additional location: US 71, Milford, IA (tel 338-4202). **Open:** Mon–Thurs 5–10pm, Fri–Sat 5–11pm. **Prices:** Main courses $6–$14. AE, DC, DISC, MC, V.

$ Stub's Ranch Kitchen

US 71 S; tel 712/262-2154. **American.** It has become a local tradition to stop here for a meal of salads, entrees, vegetables, relishes, and desserts—all served buffet-style. The decor is rustic and the staff is friendly. **FYI:** Reservations recommended. Children's menu. Beer and wine only. **Open:** Lunch Mon–Sat 11:30am–1:30pm; dinner Tues–Sat 5:30–8:30pm, Sun 11am–8pm; brunch. **Prices:** Main courses $8; prix fixe $8. MC, V.

Spirit Lake

One of the towns in Iowa's Great Lakes area, which also includes Okoboji, Arnolds Park, and Milford. The area, once a Native American tribal meeting ground, is now popular with summertime swimmers and boaters.

HOTEL

Village East Resort and Conference Center

US 71 N, PO Box 499, Okoboji, 51355; tel 712/332-2161 or toll free 800/727-4561; fax 712/332-7727. Located on 100 acres overlooking Brooks Golf Course, near East Lake Okoboji. **Rooms:** 97 rms and stes. Executive level. CI 4pm/CO 11am. Nonsmoking rms avail. Rooms have an elegant decor, separate sitting area, and balcony or patio. Double, queen, and king rooms, as well as two-story suites, are available. **Amenities:** A/C, cable TV w/movies. Some units w/terraces, 1 w/whirlpool. **Services:** Masseur, babysitting. Transportation to beach and tropical indoor pool and spa at Village West. **Facilities:** 18 2 2 250 1 restaurant (*see* "Restaurants" below), 1 bar, games rm, lawn games, racquetball, spa, sauna, whirlpool, beauty salon. Village Princess yacht for lake excursions. **Rates:** Peak (mid-May–Sept) $115–$125 S; $139–$159 D; $185 ste. Extra person $10. Children under age 16 stay free. Min stay peak. Lower rates off-season. Parking: Outdoor, free. Seasonal, holiday, and event packages avail. AE, DC, DISC, MC, V.

MOTEL

Shamrock Motel

2231 18th St, 51360; tel 712/336-2668; fax 712/336-1007. Jct IA 9 and US 71, N of Lake Okobaji. Located just north of Iowa's Great Lakes area. No children are permitted in the new, 12-unit addition to main building. **Rooms:** 36 rms. Executive level. CI 2pm/CO 11am. No smoking. Nonsmoking rms avail. Clean and comfortable, decorated with a country motif. **Amenities:** A/C, cable TV w/movies. Rooms with two beds have small refrigerators. **Services:** Free coffee and tea in lobby. **Facilities:** **Rates:** Peak

(June 15–Sept 3) $58 S; $71 D. Extra person $5. Children under age 12 stay free. Min stay special events. Lower rates off-season. Parking: Outdoor, free. AE, CB, DC, DISC, MC, V.

RESTAURANT

Minerva's Restaurant and Bar
In Village East Resort, US 71 N, Okoboji; tel 712/332-5296. **New American/Italian.** Overlooking a beautiful golf course, Minerva's is attractively furnished in brass, leather, and wood. Try one of the ample entree salads, such as Minerva's caesar or the southwest fajita salad; other specialties include fresh salmon with angel-hair pasta. All-you-can-eat Sunday brunch offers an array of egg dishes, fresh fruits, meats, and glorious desserts for $5.95. **FYI:** Reservations accepted. Children's menu. Additional location: 2901 Hamilton Blvd, Sioux City (tel 252-1012). **Open:** Breakfast daily 6–10:30am; lunch daily 11am–4:30pm; dinner daily 4:30–10pm; brunch. **Prices:** Main courses $9–$15. AE, CB, DC, DISC, MC, V.

Storm Lake

Located on the northern shore of Storm Lake. Both lake and town are sites for summer water sports and winter sports alike. **Information:** Storm Lake Chamber of Commerce, 119 W 6th, PO Box 548, Storm Lake, 50588 (tel 712/732-3780).

MOTELS

The Palace Motel
E Lake Shore Dr, 50588; tel 712/732-5753. Small mom 'n' pop motel across from a golf course. A good deal. **Rooms:** 23 rms. CI 2pm/CO 11am. Nonsmoking rms avail. Each of the small but pleasant rooms contains a large desk. **Amenities:** A/C, cable TV. **Services:** **Facilities:** **Rates:** $30 S; $40 D. Extra person $5. Parking: Outdoor, free. MC, V.

Sail Inn Motel
1015 E Lakeshore Dr, 50588; tel 712/732-1160. off US 71. Very relaxed motel directly facing the shores of Storm Lake. **Rooms:** 94 rms. CI open/CO 11am. Nonsmoking rms avail. Small and clean. **Amenities:** A/C, cable TV w/movies. **Services:** Coffee and rolls in lobby each morning. **Facilities:** Bike/walking path in front of property. **Rates (CP):** Peak (Apr–Sept) $34–$35 S; $38–$42 D. Children under age 16 stay free. Lower rates off-season. Parking: Outdoor, free. AE, DISC, MC, V.

Storm Lake Super 8
101 W Milwaukee Ave, 50588; tel 712/732-3063 or toll free 800/800-8000; fax 712/732-3063. New facility located near a busy intersection. Reasonable rates for a resort area. **Rooms:** 59 rms. CI open/CO 11am. Nonsmoking rms avail. Rooms are fresh and bright. Single and king rooms feature recliners. **Amenities:** A/C, cable TV w/movies. **Services:** Free local calls. Copy service. **Facilities:** **Rates (CP):** Peak (Apr–Sept) $39–$46 S; $48–$54 D. Children under age 12 stay free. Lower rates off-season. Parking: Outdoor, free. AE, DISC, MC, V.

RESTAURANT

Lakeshore Family Cafe
1520 N Lake Ave; tel 712/732-9800. Off US 71. **American.** Known for homestyle recipes. Typical offerings include chicken strips, shrimp baskets, stuffed baked potatoes, and charbroiled sandwiches and steaks. Each of the five separate dining areas is uniquely decorated. Save room for dessert—the ice-cream buffet is a must. **FYI:** Reservations recommended. Children's menu. Beer and wine only. **Open:** Sun–Thurs 6am–9pm, Fri–Sat 6am–11pm. **Prices:** Main courses $5–$9. DISC, MC, V.

ATTRACTION

Sanford Museum and Planetarium
117 E Willow St, Cherokee; tel 712/225-3922. 20 mi NW of Storm Lake. Exhibits highlighting the history of Northwest Iowa, from prehistoric fossils to mid-19th century artifacts. An Art Wall in the East Gallery displays works by local artists. Planetarium presents programs on the last Sunday on each month, beginning at 2pm. **Free**

Waterloo

See also Cedar Falls

The sister city of Cedar Falls. Waterloo's economy is driven by industry, including the John Deere Works manufacturing plant. **Information:** Waterloo Convention and Visitors Bureau, 215 E 4th St, PO Box 1587, Waterloo, 50704 (tel 319/233-8350).

MOTELS

Comfort Inn
1945 LaPorte Rd, 50702; tel 319/234-7411 or toll free 800/221-2222; fax 319/234-7411. Exit 72 off I-380; go west. Simple, neat, and comfortable. **Rooms:** 56 rms, stes, and effic. CI 3pm/CO 11am. Nonsmoking rms avail. **Amenities:** A/C, cable TV w/movies, refrig, dataport. **Services:** **Facilities:** Games rm, spa, whirlpool. **Rates (CP):** Peak (May–Aug) $47–$60 S; $52–$69 D; $52–$69 ste; $47–$60 effic. Extra person $5. Children under age 18 stay free. Lower rates off-season. Parking: Outdoor, free. AE, DC, DISC, MC, V.

Exel Inn
3350 University Ave, 50701; tel 319/235-2165 or toll free 800/356-8013; fax 319/235-7175. 2 mi W of US 63. Basic, clean lodging. **Rooms:** 104 rms. CI noon/CO noon. Nonsmoking rms avail. **Amenities:** A/C, cable TV w/movies, dataport. 1 unit w/whirlpool. **Services:** **Facilities:**

Games rm, washer/dryer. **Rates (CP):** $26–$40 S; $31–$45 D. Extra person $4. Children under age 17 stay free. Parking: Outdoor, free. AE, CB, DC, DISC, MC, V.

Fairfield Inn
2011 LaPorte Rd, 50702; tel 319/234-5452 or toll free 800/228-2800; fax 319/234-5452. Exit 72 off I-380; just W of exit. Attractive and clean, located near restaurants. **Rooms:** 57 rms and stes. CI 3pm/CO 11am. Nonsmoking rms avail. **Amenities:** A/C, cable TV w/movies, refrig. **Services:** **Facilities:** Games rm, spa, whirlpool. **Rates (CP):** Peak (May 26–Aug 19) $53–$60 S or D; $58–$66 ste. Extra person $7. Children under age 18 stay free. Lower rates off-season. Parking: Outdoor, free. AE, DC, DISC, MC, V.

Heartland Inn
3052 Marnie Ave, 50701; tel 319/232-7467 or toll free 800/334-3277; fax 319/232-0403. 1 mi N of US 20 on US 63. Better than average, especially at these rates. **Rooms:** 55 rms and stes. CI 2pm/CO noon. Nonsmoking rms avail. **Amenities:** A/C, cable TV w/movies, refrig. Some units w/whirlpools. **Services:** Babysitting. **Facilities:** 25 Sauna, whirlpool. **Rates (CP):** $40–$49 S; $47–$56 D; $80–$125 ste. Extra person $7. Children under age 17 stay free. Parking: Outdoor, free. AE, CB, DC, DISC, MC, V.

ATTRACTIONS

Waterloo Museum of Art
225 Commercial St; tel 319/291-4491. Located in the Waterloo Recreation and Arts Center. The museum's permanent collection is especially strong in Midwestern paintings, drawings, and prints; American decorative arts including pottery, jewelry, and glass; and Caribbean and American folk art. The museum also owns a small collection of drawings and paintings by Grant Wood (of *American Gothic* fame). Museum shop sells work by artists from all over the Midwest, as well as Haitian objets d'art. Guided tours. **Open:** Mon 10am–9pm, Tues–Fri 10am–5pm, Sat–Sun 1–4pm. Closed some hols. **Free**

Rensselaer Russell House Museum
520 W 3rd St; tel 319/233-0262. Fully restored Italianate mansion built by the son of an immigrant carpenter. Guided tours lead visitors into the interior, with its authentic mid-Victorian furnishings and family belongings. Formal gardens, gift shop. **Open:** Apr–May and Sept–Oct, Tues–Sat 1–4:30pm; June–Aug, Tues–Fri 10am–4:30pm, Sat 1–4:30pm. Open Fri–Sat in Dec; call for hours. Closed some hols. **$**

Webster City

This comfortable town in north-central Iowa is the home of Iowa Central Community College. **Information:** Webster City Area Association of Business and Industry, PO Box 310, Webster City, 50595 (tel 515/832-2564).

MOTELS

Executive Inn
1700 Superior St, 50595; tel 515/832-3631 or toll free 800/322-3631; fax 515/832-6830. Superior St exit off US 20; ¾ mi N. Good value for the in-town location. **Rooms:** 39 rms. Executive level. CI 2pm/CO 11am. Nonsmoking rms avail. King rooms offer a work/desk area and a recliner; double rooms have combo game/dining tables. **Amenities:** A/C, cable TV w/movies, refrig, dataport. **Services:** Free local calls. Secretarial and copy services. **Facilities:** 10 Games rm, sauna. **Rates (CP):** $32–$40 S; $35–$48 D. Extra person $4. Children under age 13 stay free. Parking: Outdoor, free. AE, CB, DC, DISC, MC, V.

Super 8 Motel
305 Closz Dr, 50595; tel 515/832-2000; fax 515/832-3547. Just S of US 20 on IA 17. This place has parking for large vehicles, and is across the street from a truckstop/restaurant. **Rooms:** 44 rms and stes. CI 2pm/CO 11am. Nonsmoking rms avail. Small but clean. Rollaway beds available. **Amenities:** A/C, satel TV, in-rm safe. **Services:** Free local calls. **Facilities:** Washer/dryer. Close to golf and fishing. **Rates (CP):** $39 S; $46 D; $50–$60 ste. Extra person $4. Children under age 12 stay free. Parking: Outdoor, free. AE, DC, DISC, MC, V.

ATTRACTION

Country Relics Village
IA 17 N, Stanhope; tel 515/826-3491. Seven buildings furnished with small-scale collectibles and authentic artifacts of the early 1900s. The complex also includes the original 1882 Stanhope–Chicago Northwestern Railway Depot and a McCormick Machines Dealership with antique tractors, gasoline engines, and horse-drawn vehicles. **Open:** May–Oct, daily 9am–5pm; Dec, daily 5–8pm. Closed some hols. **$$**

Winterset

Made internationally famous by *The Bridges of Madison County,* the town was already known to serious film buffs as the birthplace of actor John Wayne. All six of the famous covered bridges here are listed in the National Register of Historic Places. **Information:** Madison County Chamber of Commerce, 73 Jefferson, PO Box 55, Winterset, 50273 (tel 515/462-1185).

MOTEL

Super 8 Motel

IA 92 and 10th St, 50273 (Downtown); tel 515/462-4888 or toll free 800/800-8000; fax 515/462-8888. Located near the covered bridges featured in the book and film *The Bridges of Madison County*. **Rooms:** 31 rms. CI open/CO 11am. Non-smoking rms avail. **Amenities:** A/C, cable TV w/movies. **Services:** Free local calls. **Facilities:** Truck and bus parking. **Rates (CP):** Peak (Apr–Sept) $33–$45 S; $41–$55 D. Extra person $4. Children under age 10 stay free. Lower rates off-season. Parking: Outdoor, free. Rates rise during the covered bridge festival. AE, CB, DC, DISC, MC, V.

ATTRACTION

Birthplace of John Wayne

216 S 2nd St; tel 515/462-1044. This modest, four-room frame house in central Iowa was the birthplace of Marion Robert Morrison, later to become internationally famous as John Wayne. The museum illustrates typical early 20th-century midwestern life, with its period furnishings and other family heirlooms, and there's also an impressive collection of movie-star memorabilia. Hundreds of rare photos of the Duke are on display, as well as the eyepatch from the movie *True Grit* and hundreds of letters to Wayne from Lucille Ball, Gene Autry, Jimmy Stewart, Kirk Douglas, Bob Hope, and other screen legends. **Open:** Daily 10am–5pm **$**

MONTANA

The Last Best Place

STATE STATS

CAPITAL
Helena

AREA
148,000 square miles

BORDERS
Idaho, Wyoming, North Dakota, and South Dakota; Saskatchewan, Alberta, and British Columbia, Canada

POPULATION
850,000 (1994)

ENTERED UNION
November 8, 1889

NICKNAMES
Treasure State, Big Sky Country

STATE FLOWER
Bitterroot

STATE BIRD
Western meadowlark

FAMOUS NATIVES
Gary Cooper, Chet Huntley, Myrna Loy, Charles M Russell, Mike Mansfield

Montana has become known as the Last Best Place, which explains why newcomers and old-timers alike feel so strongly about their home. People live in Montana by choice, not by necessity. We eat scenery, Montanans joke—which is a good thing, because while it's a great place to visit, it's a tough place to make a living. Whether fourth-generation or recent transplant, this commitment to their home lends Montanans common ground, even when—as is often the case—they can't agree on anything else. The best way you can show respect for Montanans is to show respect for the land, because above all it is the land that drew them there and keeps them from leaving.

With a total population of less than 800,000 spread over its 93 million acres, Montana remains essentially a state of small towns and ranching communities, where individuality is prized but neighborliness expected. The nation's fourth-largest state is so sparsely populated (there are four times as many cows as people) that it's allowed only one representative in Congress—a tricky job indeed, considering the political spectrum runs the gamut from the Democratic stronghold of Butte (mother of Local Miners Union Number 1) to the right-wing Montana Militia of Noxon and Hamilton. Montana is perceived as a scenic refuge from the rest of the world, a place where you can be who you are and do what you want with little interference. Montanans don't like to be told what to do: They have repeatedly rejected a state sales tax and vociferously opposed the idea of zoning. In previous decades, such a live-and-let-live attitude attracted rugged individualists willing and eager to take risks—ranchers, miners, and loggers. More recently, Montana's relative isolation has attracted urban refugees, telecommuters, and movie stars seeking privacy with a view.

The state's motto, *Ora y Plata,* (Gold and Silver) reflects the importance of mining to Montana's history (though in fact copper became the more lucrative metal). Traditionally, Montana's economy has relied on natural resources—mining, timber, agricul-

Frommer'

#1

ture, and oil and gas still play a large role. But with stricter environmental regulations and a changing global economy, Montana is becoming more reliant on tourism for its bread and butter. A record 7.7 million people showed up in the state in 1994, more than eight times the state's indigenous population.

Montana's growth—as a hip hideaway and as a vacation destination—has been a mixed blessing. On the one hand, the state is becoming decidedly more culturally sophisticated: By day, you can see a rodeo or powwow, raft white-water rapids, or ski fresh powder, and that same night you can treat yourself to a gourmet dinner and a foreign film or even some decent theater. And of course, the roadside latté stand is now de rigeur. On the other hand, many Montanans are wondering what price the state will pay for "Californication," the local term for the influx of out-of-staters that some say waters down the real flavor of the West.

Despite it all, tourists will still find a warm welcome in Montana, because Montanans remain tremendously proud of the state's spectacular beauty and outdoor recreational opportunities. But nowadays, the hospitality often comes with a farewell plea: "Thanks for coming. Now—shhh!—keep it to yourself."

Fun Facts

- Many may be familiar with such Montana nicknames as Big Sky Country and the Mountain State. But did you know that Montana is also known as the Stub Toe State?
- George Custer, popularly known as General Custer, was actually not a general when he and his troops were defeated by the Sioux at the battle of Little Big Horn in southern Montana in 1876. He was only a lieutenant-colonel.
- The first woman elected to Congress was Montanan Jeannette Rank, who won her seat in the House of Representatives in 1917.
- Great Falls, in central Montana, should be called the "Windy City," the title commonly associated with Chicago. The wind blows there an average of 13 miles per hour all day long.
- Although most people think of Yellowstone National Park as part of Wyoming, three of the park's five entrances are actually in Montana.

A Brief History

Dinosaur Heaven Seventy million years ago, there was an enormous ocean covering the center of North America—and central Montana was on its western shore. Dinosaurs thrived in these swampy coastlands, and when they died, their remains were covered with sediments washing down from the newly formed Rocky Mountains. Millions of years later, the sediments were eroded away by the Ice Age glaciers, leaving the bones near the surface.

In 1978, Montana native Jack Horner, a largely self-taught paleontologist, made a startling discovery near Choteau, on the eastern front of the Rockies: He found evidence of a giant dinosaur nest. Horner began to challenge the previously held notion that dinosaurs were cold-blooded amphibians who deserted their young. Horner's theory that the dinosaurs were warm-blooded ancestor's of today's birds is still debated within scientific circles, but it provided fodder for the book and movie *Jurassic Park.*

The First Hikers Humans showed up in Montana long after the dinosaurs were fossilized. Asiatic peoples are believed to have entered North America between 10,000 and 30,000 years ago, over the Bering Strait land bridge and into Alaska. From there they headed south along the eastern front of the Rockies, some all the way to Central and South America. Remnants of the so-called "Great North Trail" can be seen today, and there are plans to restore it and erect interpretive signs for modern-day hikers.

Today, Montana is home to 11 Native American tribes—the descendants of those original settlers. For thousands of years, these people flourished on the Plains and in the western valleys, until they were displaced by the white settlers who descended upon the state in the latter half of the 19th century.

Now *That's* a Party In 1805, the explorers Meriwether Lewis and William Clark and their party of four dozen soldiers, guides, and interpreters became the first whites to set foot in Montana. From their start in St Louis, the expedition poled up the Missouri River to its Montana headwaters near the present-day town of Three Forks. Enlisting the help of the Shoshone, including the famed guide Sacajawea, they then crossed the Rocky Mountains. From there they followed the Clearwater, Snake, and Columbia Rivers west to the Pacific, returning back through Montana the following year. A "Lewis and Clark Trail" map put out by the National Park Service traces the expedition's route through the state.

Native Americans Paid the Price In the 1800s, fur traders arrived in the newly charted territory. They were after beaver, whose pelts were in high demand by hatmakers. From the Fort Union Trading Post on the Montana–North Dakota border, thousands of beaver pelts were floated down the Missouri to St Louis. Eventually demand for beaver declined when fashion dictated silk over fur, but not before the fur trade hurried the demise of the Native Americans. Many Indians trapped and sold beavers in exchange for whiskey, which killed them slowly. Others died faster deaths, after being exposed to the deadly smallpox virus (for which they had no immunity) or during battles with the US Cavalry. The final blow came with the near-extinction of the Plains buffalo, the Native Americans' major source of food. Ostensibly, the buffalo were slaughtered for their hides. But the US government, knowing that starvation would bring the tribes into submission, did nothing to regulate the killing. By 1883, the buffalo were gone, and by 1890 wholesale resettlement of Montana's Plains Indians onto federally managed reservations had been completed.

Good Diggings By the 1860s, the hunt was on for a different prey: gold. Over $240 million worth of the precious metal was eventually taken out of the state, but the living conditions weren't exactly golden. "If there is such a place as hell," wrote an observer about the mining town of Bannack, "this must be the back door to it." Still, newcomers in search of their fortunes flocked to Montana: In 1867, 10,000 optimistic souls disembarked at Fort Benton.

But it was copper that would put Montana on the map with "the richest hill on earth": the colorful town of Butte, host to the infamous Copper King wars between the notoriously unscrupulous mining barons—and bitter political rivals—William A Clark and Marcus Daly. Butte became home of the world's largest open-pit mine, where employment was so steady that Butte was known as "an island surrounded by land."

Whoever wasn't coming for metals was coming for cows, or more specifically, for free government grazing land for their cowherd. Open-range ranching boomed after the Civil War, particularly with the arrival of the railroad in the 1880s. But the winter of 1886–87 was even harsher than usual, with temperatures plummeting to −55°F in Havre. Combined with drought and depressed cattle prices, many cattlemen were ruined. Montana cattle-ranching was by no means eradicated, but it was significantly downsized by the turn of the century.

DRIVING DISTANCES

Missoula

116 mi NW of Helena
119 mi W of Butte
129 mi S of Whitefish
201 mi NW of Bozeman
269 mi NW of West Yellowstone
340 mi NW of Billings

Bozeman

82 mi SE of Butte
90 mi N of West Yellowstone
95 mi SE of Helena
142 mi W of Billings
201 mi SE of Missoula
306 mi SE of Whitefish

Billings

142 mi E of Bozeman
217 mi NE of West Yellowstone
224 mi E of Butte
224 mi SE of Helena
340 mi SE of Missoula
435 mi SE of Whitefish

The Homestead Years It sounded great: 320 acres, practically free for the taking, as long as you cultivated at least half the acreage. Tens of thousands of easterners flooded into Montana after passage of the Enlarged Homestead Act of 1909. Lured by state and railroad propaganda that promised fertile land and mild climates, these would-be farmers faced a serious reality check upon arriving in the harsh plains of eastern Montana. It has been estimated that between the turn of the century and the drought of 1917, three-quarters of the 80,000 homesteaders left the state for more fertile ground.

Land Reliant As the 20th century progressed, Montana continued to rely on what the land grew (wheat, hay, foodstuffs, and timber) as well as what lay underneath it (gold, silver, copper, and oil and gas) for its major income. That has left the state with a boom-and-bust economy, and a people somewhat resentful of what they see as exploitation by outside interests. Only recently have Montanans begun to look elsewhere—to tourism and telecommuting and retirees—for their future. It's unlikely that Montanans would ever give up their high-paying natural-resource industries. But many Montanans are learning that, in a sense, they *can* eat scenery, in which case they are some of the best-fed folks in the world.

A Closer Look

GEOGRAPHY

Montana is the fourth-largest state (after Alaska, Texas, and California), and one of the most sparsely populated. While the state's name is derived from the Latin word for "mountain," it is only the western third of the state that is covered with mountains, where the plains meet the Rockies and the Continental Divide wends its way from Wyoming to Canada. The eastern two-thirds of the state is real Big Sky country, with enormous sheep and cattle ranches, and dryland wheat and barley farms stretching as far as the eye can see. Here is the scenery and wildlife that has made the state famous, the stuff often seen in the movies: endless snowcapped mountain ranges that provide habitat for black bear, deer, and elk; rivers abundant with rainbow and cutthroat trout; and crystal-clear glacial lakes.

AVG MONTHLY TEMPS (°F) & RAINFALL (IN)

	Missoula	Billings
Jan	22/1.1	23/0.7
Feb	28/0.8	28/0.6
Mar	36/0.9	35/1.1
Apr	45/1.0	46/1.5
May	53/1.8	55/2.2
June	60/2.0	64/2.3
July	68/0.9	73/1.0
Aug	66/0.9	71/0.9
Sept	56/1.2	60/1.3
Oct	45/1.0	50/1.1
Nov	33/1.0	36/0.8
Dec	25/1.1	27/0.7

Northwestern Montana, a region of lush mountains, teeming rivers and wide open valleys, best lives up to the state's reputation. Its defining topographical feature is the **Continental Divide,** which serves as the boundary between southwestern Montana and central Idaho. Covered with forests thick with lodgepole and Ponderosa pine and larch, these mountains are the birthplace of the nation's rivers. Courtesy of the glaciers that drifted through during the Ice Age, the mountain ranges are dotted with numerous glacial lakes and separated by wide, fertile valleys.

Southwestern Montana is so-called "Gold-West Country," for obvious reasons. Beneath the arid, sagebrush-covered foothills and on into the mountains lay rich veins of gold and other precious metals. The ghost town of Bannack, site of the first major gold discovery in the state, has been turned into a state park.

North-central Montana is where a north-south wall of mountains announces an abrupt end to the Great Plains. Digging here has extracted a different sort of reward: dinosaur remains discovered at **Egg Mountain,** along the Rocky Mountain Front near Choteau. Just east of the Rockies is Montana's so-called **"Golden Triangle,"** covering a fertile area from the agricultural trading center of Great Falls to Havre to Cutbank, which supplies half the state's wheat and barley crop. The "sublimely grand spectacle" of the Missouri River's waterfalls that greeted Meriwether Lewis at the future site of **Great Falls** have long since been dammed for hydroelectric power; the dam itself has become a tourist attraction.

High mountain peaks and plateaus, the famed fishing of the Madison River, the remote alpine mountains of the Absaroko-Beartooth Wilderness, the mountain-ringed Paradise Valley and three entrances to Yellowstone National Park distinguish **south-central Montana,** an outdoor-lovers' playground. Undoubtedly the most spectacular route to Yellowstone—only passable during summer, and then not for the faint of heart–is along the spectacular 68-mile Beartooth Highway (US 212), which wends through the mountains from the former coal-mining camp of Red Lodge to the 11,000-foot Beartooth Plateau and on to the park's northeastern entrance. (Beware: Snow can close the Beartooth Highway anytime of year.)

"Remote" would be an understated description of **northeast Montana,** where ranches are measured in miles. In the midst of this prairie sits 134-mile-long **Fort Peck Lake,** a popular summertime destination that is the manmade result of the Missouri River's Fort Peck Dam, part of Franklin Roosevelt's New Deal project. The grizzly and elk that once populated the prairie have long since been forced into the mountains, but the prairie still provides great bird-watching habitat.

Largely wide-open cattle country, **southeastern Montana's** bottomlands along the Yellowstone River also lends this region distinction as a prime producer of sugar beets. The 1951 discovery of the Williston Basin, a rich oil field that underlies eastern Montana and part of North Dakota and Saskatchewan, helped fund the modernization of Montana's largest city, Billings.

CLIMATE

The watchword for Montana weather is unpredictable, particularly anywhere near the mountains. The backpacker could set out on a cloudless morning only to be ambushed in the afternoon by a hailstorm or, in high altitudes, a snow squall and even the occasional blizzard. In general, the weather west of the Divide tends to be less extreme than on the east side, where the wind, which blows unhindered across the plains, also may exacerbate matters. Humidity throughout the state, however, tends to be low, which makes the extreme hot or cold easier to take.

Winters anywhere in Montana are long. While the valleys often go weeks in winter without significant snowfall accumulation, the mountains get tremendous amounts of the stuff, keeping ski season going until well into April (and sometimes beyond) and high mountain roads impassable until June or after. Glacier National Park's famed Going-to-the-Sun Road and the Beartooth Highway leading to Yellowstone National Park, for instance, usually don't open until early June, and sometimes snowstorms shut them down temporarily even during the summer. Real summer doesn't begin until July, and sometimes not even then. But when it finally does arrive, it can do so with a vengeance: Temperatures often reach the high 80s or low 90s, with very little rain as respite. As a rule, however, nights are blessedly cool. September is many people's favorite month in Montana, after most of the tourists have cleared out but before snow season.

WHAT TO PACK

Bring a little of everything—with the exception of formal wear, since Montanans are extraordinarily casual. (You'll see jeans at even the fanciest restaurants.) A baseball cap and sunglasses are useful for shielding the high-altitude sun, and comfortable shoes are paramount, since many activities in Montana revolve around the outdoors. Everyone should bring a wool sweater or fleece jacket, which retain heat even when wet. Obviously, winter visitors should come prepared with tire chains and sunscreen, but so, however, should spring, summer, and fall visitors. With luck, you'll need only the latter.

TOURIST INFORMATION

Travel Montana, Department of Commerce, 1424 9th Ave, PO Box 200533, Helena, MT 59620-0533 (tel 406/444-2654 in MT; toll free 800/VISIT-MT out-of-state) is the state's tourist information agency. On request, they will send a packet with maps and comprehensive information about accommodations and recreational opportunities. More specific information about activities and events can be obtained from the six regional tourist offices listed below.

- **Glacier Country** (Northwestern Montana): 945 4th Ave E, Kalispell, MT 59901 (tel 406/756-7128 or toll free 800/338-5072).
- **Gold West Country** (Southwest Montana): 1155 Main St, Deer Lodge, MT 59722 (tel 406/846-1943).
- **Russell Country** (North Central Montana): PO Box 3166, Great Falls, MT 59403 (tel 406/761-5036 or toll free 800/527-5348).
- **Yellowstone Country** (South Central Montana): PO Box 1107, Red Lodge, MT 59068 (tel 406/446-1005 or toll free 800/736-5276).
- **Missouri River Country** (Northeast Montana): Box 874, Wolf Point, MT 59201 (tel 406/653-3600).
- **Custer Country** (Southeast Montana): Rte 1, Box 1206A, Hardin, MT 59034 (tel 406/665-1671).

DRIVING RULES AND REGULATIONS

The minimum age for drivers is 15 with driver's training, 16 without. The use of seat belts for driver and all passengers is mandatory. Children under 4 years old or under 40 pounds must be secured in an approved child safety seat. Motorcyclists and motorcycle passengers under 18 must wear helmets. Liability insurance is mandatory; the car's registration and proof of insurance must be carried in the car. Right turns are allowed after stops at a red light.

General speed limits are 25 to 45 mph in towns and cities, 15 mph in school zones, and 55 mph on highways (except on rural interstates, where the speed limit is 65 mph). Weather conditions sometimes dictate mandatory use of chains or studded snow tires.

RENTING A CAR

The minimum age to rent a car is 25, and a major credit card is necessary. If the town you're in doesn't have a rental agency, check with a local car dealer: They sometimes have rentals. Montana car rental rates are relatively high and rarely include unlimited mileage, although they tend to be competitive throughout the state. Opting for a weekly rate is generally a good idea.

Major rental companies with offices in Montana include:

- **Avis** (tel toll free 800/331-1212)
- **Budget** (tel 800/527-0700)
- **Dollar** (tel 800/800-4000)
- **Hertz** (tel 800/654-3131)
- **Enterprise** (tel 800/325-8007)
- **Payless** (tel 800/237-2804)

ESSENTIALS

Area Code: The area code for all of Montana is **406.**

Emergencies: For police, fire, or ambulance services, call 911.

Gambling: Electronic gaming machines and some card games are legal in Montana; small casinos—each establishment is limited to 20 machines—are littered throughout the state. You must be 18 to play.

Liquor Laws: You must be 21 years old and have proper identification to purchase alcoholic beverages. Licensing hours are 8am–2am.

Road Info: For updated information on road conditions, call toll free 800/332-6171.

Taxes: Montana has no sales tax. However, there is a 4% accommodations tax at hotels, motels, and campgrounds. West Yellowstone, Big Sky, and St Regis have imposed a local 3% resort tax on luxury items.

Time Zone: Montana is in the Mountain time zone, one hour ahead of the West Coast and two hours behind the East Coast.

Best of the State

WHAT TO SEE AND DO

Below is a general overview of some of the top sights and attractions in Montana. To find out more detailed information, look under "Attractions" under individual cities in the listings portion of this book.

Glacier National Park Long held sacred by the Blackfeet, whose reservation borders the park to the east, the so-called Crown of the Continent is now treasured by people the world over. Nestled up against the Canadian border in the northwest corner of Montana, adjacent to Alberta's Waterton Lakes National Park, Glacier boasts 1,500 square miles of craggy mountains peaks, alpine meadows, and impossibly blue glacier lakes. Native wildlife includes bighorn sheep, mountain goats, bald eagles, elk, black bear, and some of the last grizzly bear in the lower 48 states. Glacier also boasts 750 miles of hiking trails, more than enough to keep even the hardiest of backpackers happy for many seasons. There are also horseback trips, rafting and guided boat tours, and scenic overflights. Lodging and camping facilities are available, but reservations go quickly.

The 52-mile long **Going-to-the-Sun Road** bisects the park, switchbacking up the mountains to 6,680-foot Logan Pass, on the Continental Divide, and offering spectacular views. The road was considered an engineering marvel upon its completion in 1932, and it's still worthy of admiration. Travelers should know that Going-to-the-Sun Road generally isn't open until the second week in June, sometimes experiences closures during the summer due to weather conditions, and usually closes for winter in mid-October. Anyone planning on driving the road should come prepared with chains. There are seasonal restrictions on vehicle size; check with the National Park Service.

Yellowstone National Park In 1807, when mountain man Jim Colter described Yellowstone's "hidden fires, smoking pits, noxious steams, and smell of brimstone," no one believed him. But Colter's tales proved true, and in 1872 "Colter's Hell," as skeptics had nicknamed the place, became the nation's first national park. (Although Montana claims only the top edge of the park, three of Yellowstone's five entrances are located in the state.)

Yellowstone occupies a high-altitude basin located over a hot spot in the earth, which explains why Yellowstone claims more geothermal features than in all the rest of the world, the most famous of which is Old Faithful. Yellowstone's protected environment also serves as a haven for wildlife, which seem completely unbothered by human observers—as long as they keep their distance.

Other Natural Wonders Many people would claim that the entire state is a natural wonder; 13 roadless wilderness areas help keep it that way. Two of the most popular areas for backcountry experiences are the **Bob Marshall Wilderness,** south of Glacier National Park, where the Continental Divide is demarcated by massive vertical cliffs called the Chinese Wall, and the **Absaroka-Beartooth Wilderness,** on the north edge of Yellowstone National Park, which claims the largest single expanse of 10,000-plus feet elevation in the Lower 48, including Montana's highest point, Granite Peak (elevation 12,799 feet).

Montana has plenty of water for water enthusiasts; among the prettiest is 28 mile-long **Flathead Lake,** the largest natural body of freshwater west of the Mississippi, which lies just south of Glacier National Park. Fisherpeople and boaters alike choose **Bighorn Canyon National Recreation Area,** southeast of Billings on the Montana-Wyoming border, for its spectacular setting (in a deep gorge between the Pryor and Bighorn Mountains) and its renowned walleye fishing.

Wildlife Wildlife is one of Montana's claims to fame, and if you keep your eyes open you'll see a lot of it. Glacier National Park and Yellowstone National Park are good places to begin, but you're also likely to spot wildlife from just about anywhere, including the highways and rural backroads.

The American bison, nearly hunted to extinction, has made a comeback. The **National Bison Range** in Moiese is a fine place to see the wooly creatures in their historic habitat. With any luck, a self-guided auto tour will earn you views of at least a few of the 300–500 bison who live there, as well as pronghorn, elk, bighorn sheep, and white-tailed and mule deer.

Birding fans won't want to miss **Freezeout Lake Wildlife Management Area,** 10 miles south of Choteau, which often claims the largest concentration of waterfowl in Montana—up to a million birds during peak migration (March–May and September –November), including as many as 300,000 snow geese and 10,000 tundra swans. Up to 200 bald eagles congregate between November and December to eat spawning kokanee salmon at **Canyon Ferry Wildlife Management Area,** located east of Helena.

The **Charles M Russell National Wildlife Refuge,** in north-central Montana, may be the wildest remnant left in the northern Great Plains. During the September mating season, you can witness mating rituals of the nation's largest remaining prairie elk herd—nearly 1,000 strong.

Historic Sites Montana hosted a number of important battles between the US government and Native Americans. The **Little Bighorn Battlefield National Monument** in south-central Montana commemorates one of the worst defeats in US military history—and one of the largest Native American victories: the 1876 routing of Lieutenant Colonel George A Custer and 260 of his men by Sioux and Northern Cheyenne warriors. The following year, after a 1,700-mile flight, Chief Joseph of the Nez Perce made his famous "I will fight no more forever" surrender speech at **Bear's Paw Battlefield,** in north-central Montana. Happier times for Native Americans are recalled at **Pictograph Cave State Park** near Billings, where a series of three caves display faded pictographs from as many as 500 years ago.

Montana's fur-trading days are preserved for visitors to the **Fort Union Trading Post,** a National Historic Site on the Montana–North Dakota border. The National Park Service has reconstructed the fort to its original condition, and visitors can buy such period goods as blankets, trading beads, and smoking pipes.

There are plenty of mining ghost towns dotted through the foothills and mountains of western Montana. Long since abandoned for better diggings, **Bannack** was the site of Montana's first major gold discovery in 1862 and the territory's first capital. Today it's a state park. The only authentic thing missing from the streets of the former mining towns of **Virginia City** and nearby **Nevada City,** southeast of Butte, are the vigilantes: Both have been restored to their former lively selves, especially during summer nights, when the Virginia City Players perform 19th-century melodrama at the Virginia City Opera House.

The role of ranching in Montana has been well-preserved at the **Grant-Kohrs Ranch National Historic Site,** just west of Deer Lodge. Visitors can tour the original ranch house, so lavishly decorated that it was considered the finest in the Territory, as well as the barns and outbuildings.

Museums Thanks in part to paleontologist Jack Horner, the dinosaur exhibit at the **Museum of the Rockies** in Bozeman ranks among the nation's best. The **C M Russell Museum** in Great Falls is largely devoted to works by adopted son and cowboy artist Charlie Russell, whose log cabin studio is next door and whose paintings, sketches, bronzes, and illustrated letters captured the settling of the West and the last days of the Plains Indians. Butte's **World Museum of Mining** showcases a reconstructed, turn-of-the-century mining camp on the site of the Hell Roarin' Gulch mine. Exhibits at the **Museum of the Plains Indian and Craft Center** in Browning, on the east edge of Glacier National Park, focus on the history and culture of Northern Plains Indians, particularly that of the Blackfeet. The **Montana Historical Society** in Helena concentrates on the history of the state; exhibits at the **Historical Museum at Fort Missoula** explore more local history. The summertime museum-without-walls program at the **Western Heritage Center** in Billings takes you around the Billings area for a day to explore native culture with a Crow guide.

Powwows These traditional social gatherings include song, games, and dance, and provide a unique opportunity to witness Native American culture. You'll find a powwow somewhere in Montana just about every summer weekend. Two of Montana's biggest are North American Indian Days in Browning (held on the Blackfeet Reservation during the second week in July) and the Crow Fair Powwow and Rodeo (held the third week of August on the Crow Agency southeast of Billings).

Family Favorites Kids of all ages will enjoy the **Gates of the Mountains** boat tour, a two-hour trip out of Helena that traces one of the most scenic parts of Lewis and Clark's route up the Missouri River, while dinosaur fanatics gravitate toward tours of **Egg Mountain,** near Choteau, where paleontologist Jack Horner made his historic finds. Claustrophobics and the bat-shy (western big-eared bats live there) aside, a favorite sidelight is a tour of the enormous limestone caves at **Lewis and Clark Caverns State Park,** about an hour's drive east of Butte.

Western Montana is blessed with numerous hot springs, some of which have been developed into small resorts: Among the best-loved is **Chico Hot Springs Resort** near Livingston, where you can swim outdoors year-round. At the **Sapphire Gallery** in Philispburg, around twelve dollars will get you tweezers and a bucket of gravel from the nearby Sapphire Mountains—then it's up to you to find the green, red, and white sapphires hidden in it.

EVENTS AND FESTIVALS

- **Professional Rodeo Cowboys Association Circuit Finals,** Great Falls. The state's top cowboys shoot for the championship. January. Call 406/727-8115.
- **Race to the Sky Sled Dog Race,** Helena to Holland Lake. It takes mushers and their dogs nearly a week to cross the mountains in Montana's version of the Iditarod. February. Call 406/442-4008 or 442-2335.
- **C M Russell Auction of Original Western Art,** Great Falls. Named for the cowboy artist, this four-day event is one of the largest of its kind. March. Call 406/761-6452.
- **St Patrick's Day,** Butte. Thousands of people—Irish and would-be Irish—converge on the mile-high city for the parade and post-parade shenanigans. Contact the Butte Chamber of Commerce (tel 406/494-5595).
- **International Wildlife Film Festival,** Missoula. A weeklong screening of the world's best nature films. April. Call 406/728-9380.
- **Miles City Bucking Horse Sale,** Miles City. Cowboys compete for prizes; bucking horses strut their stuff for rodeo stock buyers. Third weekend in May. Call 406/232-6585.
- **College National Finals Rodeo,** Bozeman. A crash course in roping and riding. June. Call 406/585-2215 or toll free 800/432-3408.
- **Red Bottom Celebration,** on the Fort Peck Indian Reservation in Frazer. A powwow celebrating the Lower Band of the Assiniboine. June. Call 406/768-5155.
- **Bannack Days,** Bannack State Park. A historical re-creation of life in one of Montana's old gold-mining towns. Third weekend in July. Call 406/834-3413.
- **Flathead Festival,** various locations in the Flathead Valley. Two weeks of concerts featuring jazz, classical, folk, rock, and country music. July. Call 406/257-0787.
- **Montana Cowboy Poetry Gathering,** Lewistown. The real thing—in rhyme. Third weekend in August. Contact the Lewistown Chamber of Commerce (tel 406/538-5436).
- **Crow Fair Powwow and Rodeo,** Crow Agency. One of Montana's largest powwows. August. Call 406/638-2601.
- **Nordicfest,** Libby. Community celebration of Scandinavian heritage. Third weekend in September. Call 406/293-6838.
- **The Running of the Sheep,** Reedpoint. Eight thousand people show up for this sheep drive, eastern Montana's answer to Pamplona, Spain's Running of the Bulls. Sunday of Labor Day weekend. Call 406/326-9911.

- **Flathead International Balloon Festival,** Flathead Valley. Twenty-five balloons light up the skies. First weekend in October. Call 406/756-9191.
- **Annual Griz-Bobcat Football Game,** alternates between Missoula and Bozeman. The state's most famous sports rivalry. November. Call the University of Montana (tel 406/243-4051) or Montana State University (tel 406/994-4221) for tickets.
- **Annual Bald Eagle Migration,** Canyon Ferry Lake east of Helena. As many as 200 bald eagles come to eat the spawning salmon. November to mid-December. Call 406/444-4720.
- **Kick Out the Kinks Benefit Ski Race,** Izaak Walton Inn, on US 2 south of Glacier National Park. A weekend of cross-country ski racing and festivities to benefit local emergency services. December. Call 406/888-5700.

SPECTATOR SPORTS

Baseball Minor-league teams play in Helena, Butte, Billings, and Great Falls, offering a great chance to see major league prospects against a beautiful backdrop. Call local chambers of commerce for scheduling and ticket information.

College Athletics Montana has no professional teams; instead, sports fans rally around the **University of Montana Grizzlies,** in Missoula, or **Montana State University's Bobcats,** who play in Bozeman. Both schools' basketball and football teams play in the Big Sky conference; the schools are serious rivals. The U of M women's basketball team (known as the Lady Griz) have developed a loyal following as well, due to their fine record: they've won the Big Sky title 10 out of the past 13 years. For Grizzly tickets, call the University of Montana (tel 406/243-4051); call Montana State University (tel 406/994-4221) for tickets to Bobcat games.

Rodeo Rodeos, one of the classic western get-togethers, take place all over the state during the summer and fall. The season opener is the Bucking Horse Sale in Miles City, devoted solely to bronco riding. The College National Finals are held every June in Bozeman; in July, Great Falls hosts the Montana Pro Rodeo Finals; also in July, old-timers strut their stuff for the Hall of Champions Rodeo in Red Lodge. Most county fairs also include some rodeo events. For more information, contact the Northern Rodeo Association, Box 1122, Billings, MT 59103 (tel 406/252-1122).

ACTIVITIES A TO Z

Bicycling While Montana certainly has the space and scenery for quality day-cycling, it's actually not a great state in which to do a lot of bicycle touring. Many of the highways are narrow and, particularly in western Montana, heavily trafficked, because they provide the only route from Point A to Point B. Fortunately, there are ways around the trouble spots if you know how to plan. The Missoula-based **Adventure Cycling Association** (tel 406/721-1776) has become a sort of AAA for cyclists, and can provide route information for trips anywhere in the nation. In September, the Association hosts Cycle Montana, a 13-day trip from Glacier National Park to Yellowstone; only hardcore cyclists need apply.

Montana also has plenty of off-road mountain biking opportunities. Many of the ski resorts allow mountain biking in the off-season. The Adventure Cycling Association is working on a Great Divide Mountain Bike Route that will run from Roosville, MT to Antelope Well, NM. The Montana section is already open.

Camping Montana has thousands of campsites, from sites in private campgrounds with all the modern amenities to primitive spots in wilderness areas. The *Montana Travel Planner,* published by Travel Montana (tel 406/444-2654 in MT; or toll free 800/VISIT-MT out of state), lists the state's private and public campgrounds, organized alphabetically by county.

Climbing No surprise here—there's plenty of it. Popular climbing spots include the Bitterroot Mountains (south of Missoula), Humbug Spires (south of Butte), the Little Belt Mountains (southeast of Great Falls), and the Beartooth Plateau (north of Yellowstone). **Pipestone Mountaineering,** with locations in Missoula (tel 406/721-1670) and Butte (tel 406/782-4994), offers climbing classes.

Fishing Times have changed since Norman Maclean, author of *A River Runs Through It,* fished the Blackfoot River outside of Missoula, but flyfishing is more popular than ever in Montana. Ennis, located on the renowned Madison River, has become the state's unofficial flyfishing capital; other world-class trout streams include the Gallatin, Jefferson, and Big Hole Rivers, as well as sections of the Missouri and the Smith. Flathead Lake is well-known for its lake trout. There's good salmon fishing at Hauser and Canyon Ferry Lakes outside Helena;

and plenty of walleye at Fort Peck Lake, in northeast Montana, and Bighorn Lake in southeast Montana. There's no shortage of fishing guides, either. Contact the **Fishing Outfitters Association of Montana (FOAM),** PO Box 67, Gallatin Gateway, MT 59730. Travel Montana, in conjunction with Montana Fish, Wildlife and Parks, publishes a fishing guide with a list of fishable rivers, streams, and lakes, as well as an explanation of state fishing regulations.

Golf Despite the short season, golf is the fastest-growing sport in Montana; you'll see courses throughout the state. In 1991, *Golf* magazine selected Bigfork's Eagle Bend Golf Course as the nation's best new course. The Old Works Golf Course, a Jack Nicklaus–designed project on the site of the former smelting operations in Anaconda, has just recently opened.

Hiking With literally thousands of miles of trails, Montana is a hiker's paradise. The **Montana Wilderness Association** (Box 635, Helena, MT 59624, tel 406/443-7350) offers guided day trips during the summer. Lots of people like to hike all or part of the Continental Divide Trail, which continues all the way to Mexico. You can purchase trail maps through the US Forest Service or at area sporting goods stores.

Hunting Fall in Montana means hunting, and hunters converge on Montana for elk and deer or even bear. For license and permit information, contact **Montana Fish, Wildlife and Parks,** 1420 E 6th Ave, Helena, MT 59620 (tel 406/444-2535).

Kayaking Kayaking has been increasing in popularity in recent years. There are kayaking schools in Missoula, Bozeman, and Billings. Contact a local sporting goods store for specifics.

Pack Trips On horsepack trips, you can sit back and enjoy the ride. For a list of licensed outfitters, contact the **Montana Outfitters and Guides Association,** PO Box 1248, Helena, MT 59624 (tel 406/449-3578). Llama pack trips, in which the gentle animals carry everything but you, are becoming increasingly popular as well, but few llama companies are members of MOGA; contact a regional tourist office or a sporting goods store in the area you want to travel.

Rafting Montana has water to suit every person's comfort zone, from Class I flatwater to heavy-duty Class IV rapids, and guided trips to get you through them in high style. Generally, rafting season runs from May through September. *The River Wild* was filmed on the Middle Fork of the Flathead River in Glacier National Park. Other popular white-water routes include the Alberton Gorge on the Clarkfork River near Missoula; the Yellowstone River near Gardiner; and the Gallatin River near Big Sky. Popular flatwater trips include the Upper Missouri River near Great Falls, the Madison River through Beartrap Canyon near Ennis; and the Smith River in remote central Montana.

Skiing Hitting the slopes is one way to stay sane in a state with winters as long as Montana's. Montana has 14 downhill ski resorts and 10 cross-country areas, and virtually limitless backcountry terrain.

Selected Parks & Recreation Areas

- **Yellowstone National Park,** Superintendent, Yellowstone National Park, WY 82190 (tel 307/344-7381)
- **Glacier National Park,** Superintendent, West Glacier, MT 59936 (tel 406/888-5441)
- **National Bison Range,** US 212, Moiese, MT (tel 406/644-2211)
- **Charles M Russell National Wildlife Refuge,** 55 mi S of Malta on US 191 (tel 406/538-8706)
- **Big Springs Trout Hatchery,** 7 mi S of Lewistown (tel 406/538-5588)
- **Bighorn Canyon National Recreation Area,** Box 458, Fort Smith, MT 59035 (tel 406/666-2412)
- **Little Bighorn Battlefield National Monument,** 15 mi SE of Hardin (tel 406/638-2621)
- **Grant-Kohrs Ranch National Historic Site,** PO Box 790, Deer Lodge, MT 59722 (tel 406/846-2070)
- **Fort Union Trading Post and National Historic Site,** RR 3, Box 71, Williston, ND 58801 (tel 701/572-9083)
- **Bannack State Park,** off MT 278, W of Dillon (tel 406/834-3413)
- **Canyon Ferry State Recreation Area,** 18 mi NE of Helena (tel 406/475-3310)
- **Freezeout Lake Wildlife Management Area,** 10 mi S of Choteau on US 89 (tel 406/467-2646)
- **Lewis and Clark Caverns,** 19 mi W of Three Forks off MT 2 (tel 406/287-3541)
- **Giant Springs Heritage State Park,** 3 mi E of US 87 on River Dr in Great Falls (tel 406/454-3441)
- **Missouri Headwaters State Park,** 3 mi N of Three Forks (tel 406/994-4042)
- **Pictograph Cave State Park,** 7 mi SE of Billings off I-90 (tel 406/252-4654)

The alpine season generally runs from Thanksgiving until mid-April; backcountry skiing goes well into June. You'll find a complete listing of all the state's ski resorts, as well as other winter opportunities, in the *Montana Winter Guide,* put out by Travel Montana. Travel Montana also maintains a ski report and travel information line (tel 406/444-2654 in MT; toll free 800/VISIT-MT ext 4WG out of state).

Snowmobiling With 1,600 miles of maintained trails all over Montana, there's plenty of snowmobiling opportunities. West Yellowstone claims to be the snowmobile capital of the world. Snowmobiles on public land must display a current registration decal. Snowmobile users not currently registered must obtain a nonresident, temporary-use permit from the Department of Fish, Wildlife and Parks. Contact the Montana Snowmobile Association (Box 3202, Great Falls, MT 59403) for information.

Water Sports In addition to its world-famous rivers, Montana has plenty of lakes on which to boat and canoe and waterski and swim. The biggest are northwestern Montana's Flathead Lake and northeastern Montana's Fort Peck Lake. Resorts often rent equipment. Check with regional tourist offices.

GLACIER COUNTRY

Start	Missoula
Finish	Glacier National Park
Distance	Approximately 280 miles
Time	2–3 days
Highlights	Wildlife viewing opportunities—from waterfowl and raptors to big game animals; glacial lake valley and majestic mountains; Native American and early pioneer heritage sites and museums; lakeside communities and recreation; historic railroad hotels

Montana's name is derived from a Spanish word meaning "mountainous region"—a very appropriate moniker considering the numerous mountain ranges within view of this driving tour around the northwestern part of the state. The route will lead you through the pastoral landscapes of Mission and Flathead Lake Valleys and into the snow-capped mountains forming the Continental Divide, with the showcase being the Waterton/Glacier International Peace Park. A large part of the valley lands and mountains are home to the Confederated Salish and Kootenai Tribes and the Blackfeet Nation. A multitude of recreational opportunities is available on the tribal lands (tribal recreation permits are required) and in the bordering state and national forests. Nearby Flathead Lake, the largest body of fresh water west of the Mississippi River, offers all forms of water sports and recreation.

The region's diversity of habitats means visitors will likely see hundreds of wildlife species. The large stick nests of bald eagles and osprey are commonly sighted on the tops of utility poles and ponderosa pine trees, while the nests of great blue heron can be spotted in cottonwood trees. Raptors perch on fence posts, mountain bluebird boxes form "bluebird trails" along fence rows, and the melodious song of the state bird—the distinctively marked western meadowlark—is heard throughout the region. (Bird and flower identification field guides will enhance your viewing and photographing pleasure.) Soft evening breezes often carry the coyote's tune and the gray wolf's howl.

The driving tour follows one of the routes of The Trail of the Great Bear, a scenic corridor linking America's first national park (Yellowstone) to the world's first international peace park (Waterton/Glacier) and to Canada's first national park (Banff). The region's mountainous terrain is still home to the grizzly bear, the trail's symbol. It is the spirit of this great bear that prevails in the wild lands along the corridor.

For additional information on lodgings, restaurants, and attractions in the region covered by the tour, look under specific cities in the listings portion of this chapter.

I-90 gives easy access to the first stop:

1. **Missoula,** the largest city in western Montana and the educational, recreational, and entertainment hub of the region. The city is home to the University of Montana, which offers a wide range of sporting events and theatrical performances.

   From Missoula, take exit 96 off I-90 and follow US 93 north. You will travel through a canyon and over a low-elevation pass, forested on both sides with thick stands of evergreens. This area is the last remaining natural wildlife corridor for grizzlies, wolves, and other wildlife species. The animals use the corridor to travel between the high-elevation mountain habitats located on the west and east sides of US 93.

   As you drive north through the small town of Ravalli, you'll see a large tree-covered hill directly in front of you; this is your next stop. Drive 6 miles west of Ravalli on MT 200 to its junction with MT 212. Then follow MT 212 north for 5 miles to the entrance of:

2. **The National Bison Range,** a wildlife refuge for a free-roaming herd of 300–500 American bison. Numerous other big game animals (such as deer and elk) and large populations of song birds and raptors also inhabit the refuge, which was established in 1908 when the bison was nearly extinct. The refuge has a visitors center (tel 406/664-2211) with exhibits and displays, two scenic drives, a nature trail and picnic area (both accessible for guests with disabilities), and a bison paddock for close-up viewing and photos. The most scenic and interesting option is the 19-mile, self-guided **Red Sleep Mountain Drive.** It climbs 2,000 feet through four types of habitat (grassland, riparian, wetland, montane forest) on a winding, narrow gravel road with tight turns, no guard rails, and a long, steep downgrade. (Trailers and towed units are not allowed on the mountain drive; bicycles and motorcycles are prohibited on the driving loops.)

   The best time to visit the refuge is early morning and late evening, when the animals are most likely to be moving around and feeding. Bring binoculars

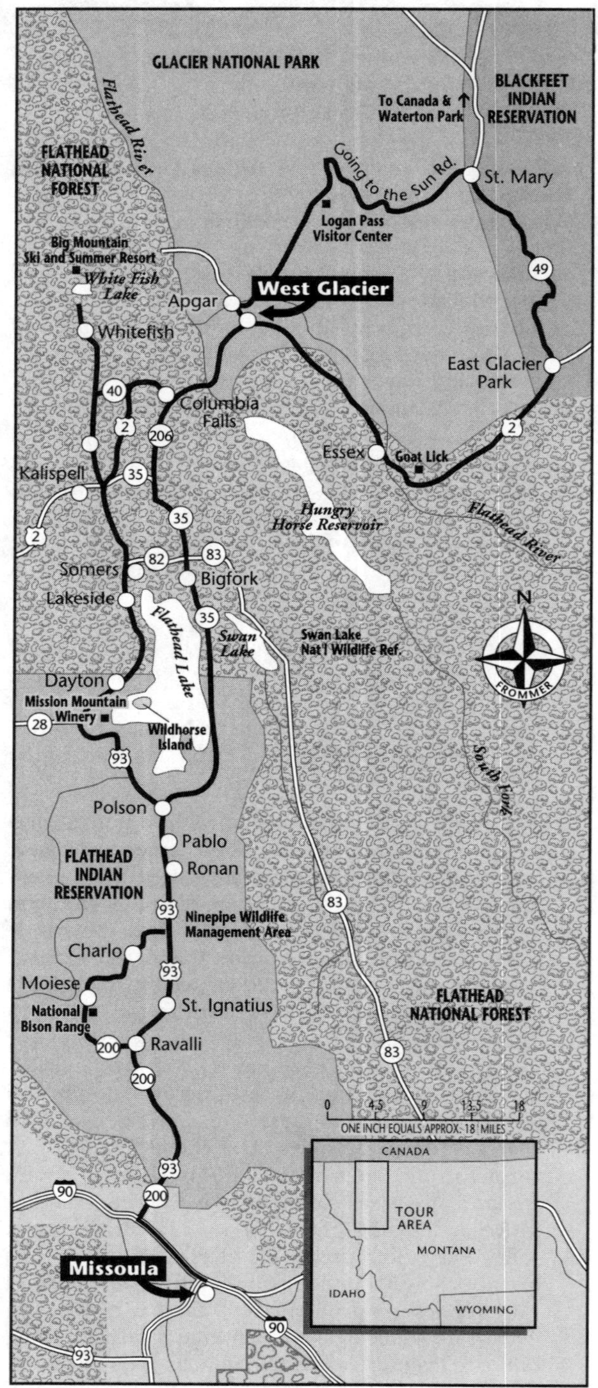

and a telephoto lens for your camera. Entry fee is $4 per car (during the dry summer months when the Red Sleep Mountain Drive is open). The visitor center is open 8am–4:30pm daily. The refuge itself is open dawn to dusk.

Take a Break

You can sample a low-fat, low-cholesterol buffalo burger at the **Burger "B"** (tel 406/644-2385) in Moiese, on MT 212 near the entrance to the Bison Range. It offers walk-up window service only and has a couple of picnic tables. Most travelers prefer to take their burgers and beverages to the refuge's shaded picnic area. Lunch items cost $2 to $5. Open daily 11:30am–7:30pm.

From the Bison Range, backtrack 11 miles to Ravalli and drive 5 miles north on US 93 to:

3. **St Ignatius Mission** (tel 406/745-2768), a historic church with 58 frescos and murals painted by an Italian Jesuit priest/cook, Brother Joseph Carignano, who had no formal art schooling. The beautifully colored murals tell various stories from the Old and New Testaments. The mission and town was founded in 1854 by Jesuit missionaries. Parking for large RV units; wheelchair access available.

From St Ignatius, continue your drive north on US 93. The majestic Mission Mountains will be on your right (to the east). There are several scenic, wildlife, and historical interpretive sites along the side of the highway. The route also passes through the **Ninepipe Wildlife Management Area,** a collection of glacial pothole lakes and ponds surrounded by native grassland. The refuge is home to a large variety of wildlife, waterfowl, and songbirds.

Continue driving north on US 93 for 19 miles to Pablo. On the west side of the highway at the northern edge of Pablo is:

4. **The People's Center,** an educational and cultural center of the Confederated Salish and Kootenai Tribes of the Flathead Reservation (tel 406/675-2700). The center's goal is to preserve and promote the Salish and Kootenai cultures. Guided tours are offered daily 9am–9pm during the peak tourist season. Admission is $2 for adults, $1 for seniors, and $5 for families. Pablo is the tribal headquarters, so tribal land recreation permits may be acquired here.

From The People's Center, drive 7 miles north on US 93 to:

5. **Polson,** the outdoor recreation and vacation hub for the south end of Flathead Lake. Water sports

are the main focus at the 23-mile-long and 15-mile-wide lake, but the area offers golf and summer theater performances as well.

At MP 59 at Polson, travelers have two route choices. Both routes pass by several state parks offering public access to the lake. US 93 follows the west shore of the lake to Kalispell, while MT 35 follows the east shore to Bigfork. Both routes include connecting highways to Glacier National Park. For the east shore drive, skip to Bigfork (Stop 7).

Travelers going up (north) the west side of Flathead Lake will pass through several small lakeside towns with marinas offering boat rentals. According to Native American legend, **Wild Horse Island** got its name because local tribes swam their horses out to the island for safe-keeping from raiding parties. (Today, several horses are allowed to roam the island as a reminder of its heritage.) The island, now managed by the state as a day-use park, is a popular picnicking, hiking, and wildlife-viewing location. A large population of deer and bighorn sheep—popular photo subjects—make their home here.

Continue driving north on US 93. In Dayton, watch for the Mission Mountain Winery (tel 406/849-5524) on the east side of the highway. Montana's only winery, Mission Mountain offers complimentary tastings of its award-winning varietals. Tastings and tours are available May–October, 10am–5pm daily.

From the winery, drive 27 miles north on US 93 to:

6. Kalispell, the northern gateway to Flathead Valley and the surrounding mountains. The town—a popular shopping, dining, and lodging stop—could be your first overnight stay on the tour. The modern, full-service **Cavanaugh's at Kalispell Center,** 20 N Main (tel 406/752-6660 or toll free 800/843-4667), and the historic **Kalispell Grand Hotel,** 8 First St W (tel 406/755-8100 or toll free 800/858-7422), are good choices for downtown lodging close to specialty stores and restaurants.

Travelers may want to make a 20-mile side trip to Big Mountain Ski and Summer Resort (tel 406/862-2918 or toll free 800/858-5439), located north of Whitefish. It is noted for its views of Glacier National Park, summer festivals, alpine nature trails, guided trail rides and dinners, and mountain biking (rentals available). Lodging options on the mountain range from family budget accommodations (Alpinglow Inn) to more luxurious accommodations (Kandahar Lodge) offering a quiet romantic ambience.

If you are heading directly to Glacier National Park, follow US 2 from Kalispell for 32 miles to West Glacier (Stop 8).

7. Bigfork is the summer playground for the north end of Flathead Lake. The drive along the eastern shoreline from Polson to Bigfork on MT 35 passes through fruit orchards and small lakeside communities. Roadside stands with seasonal fresh fruit, berries, and farm produce dot the scenic route. Bigfork has a renowned theater (Bigfork Summer Playhouse), a golfing and yachting community (Eagle Bend), and a well-known dude ranch (Flathead Lake Lodge). The town offers easy access to mountain getaways.

From Bigfork, follow the combination of MT 35 and MT 206 north for 22 miles to Columbia Falls, and then follow US 2 north for 15 miles to:

8. West Glacier, the west entrance to Glacier National Park (tel 406/888-5441 in the US or 403/859-2224 in Canada). The West Glacier area is a good place to make some outdoor adventure plans. Llama-trekking into national forest lands and designated wilderness areas is available in the region, and fly-fishing float trips and white-water rafting adventures on the branches of the Flathead River are very popular. Several companies, situated along both sides of US 2, offer helicopter sightseeing flights over Glacier National Park; the views are breathtaking. For information on these and other treks, call Glacier Country (tel toll free 800/338-5072) and ask for a free Glacier Country Guide.

The designated 141-mile Glacier Park driving loop will take you along famous **Going-to-the-Sun Rd** to St Mary, then south on US 89 and MT 49 through the Blackfeet Indian Reservation to East Glacier Park, and back on US 2 to West Glacier, with a stop at the historic Izaak Walton Inn at Essex. This scenic drive lets you experience the climatic differences of the landscape and habitat on both sides of the Continental Divide. The west side of the Divide features dense forests of evergreens clinging to the steep mountainsides, while the east side consists of a dryer climate of rolling grasslands and deciduous trees. The park has over 700 miles of hiking trails, which connect pristine alpine lakes and meadows, cascading waterfalls, scenic viewpoints, and backcountry campsites. The park entrance kiosk is about 1 mile north off US 2. A seven-day vehicle pass costs $5; hikers and cyclists pay $3.

Apgar Village (about 1 mile from the kiosk) is the first building complex you will see. The village visitors center can provide information on narrated lake cruises, driving tours aboard historic red jammer buses, guided trail rides, and educational field trips. Seeing the park and experiencing its grandeur takes more than a day, so it makes sense to plan an overnight stay at one of the park's lodges. Glacier Park, Inc. (tel 602/207-6000) is the concessioner for seven properties. For lodging selections in the park or near the park entrances, look under the specific towns in the listings portion of this guide.

From Apgar Village, follow the Going-to-the-Sun Rd, a 50-mile-long highway that bisects the park and connects the towns of West Glacier and St Mary. Completed in 1932 and listed on the National Register of Historic Places, this narrow and winding road is considered a great feat of engineering because of the steep and rocky terrain. Some portions have vehicle size limitations and bicycling restrictions. (The road is closed by snow October–June.)

Take a Break

The **Cedar Dining Room** (tel 406/888-5431) is located in the historic Lake McDonald Lodge on the northeastern shore of Lake McDonald. Even if you aren't hungry, stop and marvel at the interior cedar-log architecture of the lobby. Lunch specials cost under $7, while dinner entrees are $11 to $18.

Follow the serpentine road through the western side of the park up to the Logan Pass visitor center, taking time to stop at the scenic overlooks. The road crosses the Continental Divide at Logan Pass (at an elevation of 6,648 feet). Continuing down the east side, stop to view the roadside waterfalls, flora and fauna, and regal mountains. (You'll know when wildlife is on or near the road because of the traffic jams.) The road will take you to:

9. **St Mary,** a small tourist town located just outside the park's main east entrance. It is a popular stop for food, fuel, and shopping before heading into the remote east side locations of the park.

From St Mary, you can drive 33 miles north on US 89, MT 17, and Canada 6 to reach the Waterton entrance of the international peace park. The US/Canada border is located 17 miles north of St Mary. Be sure to carry proof of citizenship (birth certificate, voter's registration card). A state drivers license is *not* proof of US citizenship.

To complete the Glacier Park loop, leave St Mary and drive 31 miles south on US 89 and MT 49 to:

10. **East Glacier Park,** a small town located outside the park's boundary. As an Amtrak stop, the town continues to serve rail travelers arriving to see the park.

Take a Break

The Goat Lick Steak & Rib House (tel 406/226-5551) is located in the grand, historic Glacier Park Lodge. Lunch items include soups, salads, and burgers for under $6, while dinner entrees —mostly steak and ribs—are $12 to $20. Sixty immense ponderosa logs support the structure of the huge lobby, which is worthy of a photo stop and tour even if you are not hungry.

From East Glacier Park, follow US 2 for a 56-mile drive back to West Glacier via the 5,216-foot Marias Pass at the Continental Divide. US 2 loops around the southern boundary of the park. There are several roadside turnoffs for wildlife viewing; the most popular is Goat Lick (near MP 182), a natural mineral salt lick along the Middle Fork of the Flathead River that attracts mountain goats.

From Goat Lick, continue west on US 2 for about 2 miles to Essex turnoff (near MP 180) to reach the:

11. **Izaak Walton Inn,** on US 2 (tel 406/888-5700), a historic railroad hotel currently served by Amtrak. The Inn is about a half-mile south of the highway. Built in 1939 by the Great Northern Railroad and filled with railroad memorabilia, the Izaak Walton is a popular vacation destination for rail fans. Besides the hotel rooms, guests can stay in refurbished cabooses. In the winter, the Inn is a highly rated cross-country ski destination; summer guests can go mountain biking, horseback riding, hiking, and wildlife watching. The appropriately decorated Dining Car restaurant offers breakfast, lunch, and dinner.

From Izaak Walton Inn, drive 27 miles west on US 2 to West Glacier to complete the Glacier Park loop.

Montana Listings

Anaconda

Historic mining town founded by copper king Marcus Daly. Today, Anaconda attracts outdoor enthusiasts who come for the nearby lakes and mountains; Anaconda Pintler Wilderness is a popular destination. Fairmont Hot Springs is located southeast of town. **Information:** Anaconda Chamber of Commerce, 306 E Park St, Anaconda, 59711 (tel 406/563-2400).

MOTELS

Marcus Daly Motel
119 W Park, 59711 (Downtown); tel 406/563-3411 or toll free 800/535-6528 in MT; fax 406/563-2268. Located near shopping. Popular lodging for construction workers. **Rooms:** 19 rms. CI open/CO 11am. Nonsmoking rms avail. Rooms are clean and adequate. **Amenities:** A/C, cable TV. **Services:** **Facilities:** **Rates:** Peak (June–Oct) $30–$36 S; $38–$45 D. Extra person $5. Children under age 10 stay free. Lower rates off-season. Parking: Outdoor, free. Senior, government, construction worker, as well as weekly rates avail. AE, CB, DC, DISC, MC, V.

Vagabond Lodge Motel
1421 E Park, 59711; tel 406/563-5251 or toll free 800/231-2660; fax 406/563-3356. Edge of town, near shelter area. A well-kept, older motel, with antiques in lobby. Located near shops and restaurants. **Rooms:** 19 rms. CI open/CO 11am. Nonsmoking rms avail. Very clean and spacious; some rooms are furnished with antiques. **Amenities:** A/C, cable TV. **Services:** **Facilities:** 15 **Rates:** $39 S; $45–$62 D. Parking: Outdoor, free. MC, V.

RESORT

Fairmont Hot Springs Resort
1500 Fairmont Rd, 59711; tel 406/797-3241 or toll free 800/332-3272; fax 406/797-3337. Take I-90 to exit 211. 300 acres. This expanded, motel-like property offers many resort and convention facilities. Native Americans used the mineral springs here before the springs were developed commercially in 1869. Guided horseback rides at nearby stable. **Rooms:** 135 rms, stes, and effic. CI 3pm/CO 11am. Nonsmoking rms avail. Some rooms overlook the golf course. Time-share condos available. **Amenities:** A/C, satel TV w/movies. All units w/terraces, some w/whirlpools. **Services:** Social director, masseur, children's program. **Facilities:** 4 18 2 500 2 restaurants, 1 bar (w/entertainment), basketball, volleyball, games rm, lawn games, spa, steam rm, playground, washer/dryer. Mineral water soaking pools fed by hot springs. Swimming pool has 350-foot waterslide. Casino. **Rates:** Peak (May 19–Sept) $74–$86 S or D; $95–$275 ste; $95–$275 effic. Extra person $10. Children under age 12 stay free. Min stay special events. Lower rates off-season. Parking: Outdoor, free. Seasonal events packages avail. AE, DC, DISC, MC, V.

RESTAURANT

Donivan's Family Restaurant
211 E Park; tel 406/563-6241. **Cafe.** Friendly hangout with a small-town atmosphere. Varied cafe-style menu ranges from sandwiches and fish-and-chips to rib eye steak. **FYI:** Reservations not accepted. Children's menu. **Open:** Daily 6am–midnight. **Prices:** Main courses $2–$9. AE.

ATTRACTIONS

Copper Village Museum & Arts Center
401 E Commercial; tel 406/563-2422. Housed in the 100-year-old former City Hall building. Museum contains exhibits, photos, and artifacts dealing with Anaconda's history as a copper-mining town, while the arts center displays artwork by local and national artists. Film series, occasional concerts. **Open:** Museum: Tues–Sat 1–4pm. Gallery: summer, Tues–Sat 10am–5pm; winter, Tues–Sat noon–5pm. Closed some hols. **Free**

Lost Creek State Park
Off MT 273; tel 406/542-5500. 10 mi NE of Anaconda. The park has been kept in a relatively primitive condition; several wildlife viewing sites provide visitors with glimpses of the mountain goats and bighorn sheep that populate the bluffs. A short nature trail, leading to a scenic overlook near Lost Creek Falls, is equipped with interpretive displays describing the geology of the area. Campground with 25 sites. **Open:** May–Nov, daily dawn–dusk. **Free**

Bigfork

See Flathead Lake

Big Sky

A year-round mountain resort village, conceived and developed by the late newsman Chet Huntley. Home of Big Sky Ski and Summer Resort; 10 miles NW of the main entrance to Yellowstone National Park.

HOTEL

River Rock Lodge

3080 Pine Dr, PO Box 160700, 59716; tel 406/995-2295 or toll free 800/995-9966; fax 406/995-2727. A luxurious, beautiful retreat built from river rock and huge timber logs. **Rooms:** 29 rms and stes. Executive level. CI 2pm/CO 11am. No smoking. Rooms have fabulous mountain views. Vista suite has private balcony and a huge walk-in closet. **Amenities:** Cable TV, refrig, VCR. No A/C. All units w/minibars, some w/fireplaces, some w/whirlpools. Vista suite features fireplace, whirlpool, marble wet bar, and fluffy robes. Down comforters (in linen duvet covers) and down pillows. Large armoires house TV, VCR, and a copy of the film *A River Runs Through It* (which was filmed nearby). Hair dryers available. **Services:** Twice-daily maid svce, social director, masseur, babysitting. Ski shuttle. **Facilities:** 50 Games rm. Books and board games available. **Rates (CP):** Peak (Dec 23–Jan 2/Jan 20–Mar 22) $70–$145 S; $85–$160 D; $175–$260 ste. Extra person $15. Children under age 12 stay free. Min stay special events. Lower rates off-season. Parking: Outdoor, free. Seasonal and group rates avail. AE, CB, DC, DISC, MC, V.

MOTEL

Best Western Buck's T-4

US 191, PO Box 160279, 59716; tel 406/995-4111 or toll free 800/822-4484; fax 406/995-2191. 1 mile S of Big Sky. Better-than-average and well-maintained, this motel began as a hunting lodge in 1946. The decor is accented with warm wood tones and native stone. **Rooms:** 75 rms, stes, and effic. CI 3pm/CO 11am. Nonsmoking rms avail. All of the large, recently redecorated rooms have great views. **Amenities:** A/C, satel TV. Some units w/whirlpools. Some rooms have hair dryers. **Services:** Babysitting. Extra charge for pets. VCR and movies for rent. **Facilities:** 200 2 restaurants (bkfst and dinner only), 2 bars, games rm, whirlpool, washer/dryer. Ski lockers available. Snowmobiling on property. Laundry facilities in summer only. **Rates:** Peak (July–Aug/Jan 15–Apr 30) $54–$76 S; $69–$89 D; $125–$150 ste; $150 effic. Extra person $6. Children under age 12 stay free. Lower rates off-season. Parking: Outdoor, free. Various packages avail. Closed Apr 15–May 20/Nov 1–Nov 15. AE, CB, DC, DISC, JCB, MC, V.

RESORTS

Huntley Lodge at Big Sky Resort and Shoshone Condominiums

PO Box 160001, 59716; tel 406/995-4211 or toll free 800/548-4486; fax 406/995-5003. From US 19, take Big Sky turnoff. 10,000 acres. Scenic family vacation spot in the Montana mountains, great for winter or summer vacations. A larger-than-life bronze sculpture entitled *Sitting Bear* adorns the rock and log lobby, which features western decor. Walk to the ski lifts. **Rooms:** 200 rms. CI 5pm/CO noon. Nonsmoking rms avail. Warm colors, attractive bedspreads, and softly carved wooden furniture enhance the accommodations. Almost every room offers a beautiful mountain view. Condos also available. **Amenities:** A/C, cable TV, dataport, voice mail. Mini-fridges and hair dryers in some rooms. **Services:** VP Masseur, children's program, babysitting. Friendly staff. **Facilities:** 18 2 4 1000 10 restaurants, 5 bars (3 w/entertainment), volleyball, games rm, lawn games, racquetball, spa, sauna, steam rm, whirlpool, beauty salon, day-care ctr, playground, washer/dryer. **Rates (BB):** Peak (Feb 4–Mar 24/Dec 24–Jan 1) $108–$115 S; $118–$125 D. Extra person $10. Children under age 10 stay free. Min stay peak. Lower rates off-season. Parking: Outdoor, free. Group rates and packages avail. Closed Oct–Thanksgiving/mid-Apr–May. AE, CB, DC, DISC, MC, V.

Lone Mountain Ranch

MT 64 off US 191, PO Box 160069, 59716; tel 406/995-4644; fax 406/995-4670. 150 acres. The resort operates as a ranch in summer and a cross-country ski resort in winter. **Rooms:** 6 rms; 23 cottages/villas. CI 3pm/CO 11am. No smoking. Modern cabins with western decor, plump sofas and chairs in living rooms, and large closets. **Amenities:** No A/C, phone, or TV. All units w/terraces, all w/fireplaces, 1 w/whirlpool. Nice, thick towels and pretty linens. Wood-burning stoves and fireplaces. **Services:** Social director, masseur, babysitting. Children's program in summer. Naturalist-guided hiking. Tours available for nordic skiers. Snowcoach tours into Yellowstone Park. **Facilities:** 1 restaurant, 2 bars (1 w/entertainment), whirlpool, playground, washer/dryer. Sleigh ride dinners in winter; Orvis-endorsed fly-fishing lodge; ski shop and wax room; white-water rafting available in summer. **Rates (AP):** Peak (June–Oct 15) $1,450 S; $2,300 D; $1,900–$3,100 cottage/villa. Extra person $650–$850. Children under age 2 stay free. Min stay. Lower rates off-season. AP rates avail. Parking: Outdoor, free. Weekly stays only. Advanced reservations required. Closed Oct 15–Dec 3/Apr–May. DISC, MC, V.

RESTAURANTS

★ Allgood's Bar & Grill
In West Fork Meadow Mall, Unit 7; tel 406/995-2750. **Barbecue.** This light and airy restaurant isn't fancy, but the food is good, the portions are large, and the drinks are generous. Friendly proprietor Dick Allgood makes sure no one leaves a stranger. Breakfast offerings include familiar egg, omelet, french toast, and waffle combinations. Home-smoked barbecue specialties are served the rest of the day. Try the ribs, pork, chicken, turkey, or combo plate. Salads, soups, and sandwiches also available. **FYI:** Reservations accepted. **Open:** Breakfast daily 7–11:30am; lunch daily 11:30am–2:30pm; dinner daily 6–10pm. **Prices:** Main courses $6–$17. AE, MC, V.

★ First Place Restaurant
Meadow Village Shopping Center; tel 406/995-4244. Take US 191 to Big Sky exit; 2 mi up US 191 spur. **New American.** Situated in the corner of a small shopping center, First Place offers a menu with French and Italian inflections. Starters include Brie baked in puff pastry with a red-wine butter sauce. Entree choices might be fettuccine with shrimp and sun-dried tomatoes in a champagne sauce; rack of baby lamb, charbroiled with rosemary and garlic; or twin filet mignons served with two sauces—red wine and béarnaise. **FYI:** Reservations recommended. **Open:** Daily 6–10pm. Closed Apr 15–May 25. **Prices:** Main courses $12–$20; prix fixe $17–$20. AE, DISC, MC, V.

ATTRACTION

Big Sky Ski and Summer Resort
Tel 406/995-5000. 18 mi N of Yellowstone National Park, off US 191. Big Sky's 61 named runs offer something for everyone, from beginners to "black double diamond" experts, while 9 lifts ensure short or nonexistent lift lines. Big Sky is very family-oriented: All children 10 or under ski free (with a limit of two children per paying adult), and there's a Ski Day Camp for youngsters 6–14. Ski and snowboarding lessons are taught by professional instructors, and cross-country skiers can enjoy 45 miles of groomed ski trails at Lone Mountain Ranch. Call 406/995-4211 for information on current snow conditions.

During summer months, the resort offers opportunities for white-water rafting, fishing, golf (on an 18-hole course designed by Arnold Palmer), tennis, horseback riding, and mountain biking. **Open:** Mid-Nov–mid-Apr, daily 9am–4pm. **$$$$**

Big Timber

A small rural town at the foot of the Crazy Mountains. Home of Greycliff Prairie Dog Town State Park and the Absaroka-Beartooth Wilderness. **Information:** Sweet Grass County Chamber of Commerce, 219 McLeod St, PO Box 1012, Big Timber, 59011 (tel 406/932-5131).

MOTEL

CM Russell Lodge and Motel
Hwy 10 W (Old I-90), PO Box 670, 59011; tel 406/932-5245 or toll free 800/279-6113; fax 406/932-5243. On the west edge of town. A clean and well-maintained older motel located near the Boulder River. **Rooms:** 41 rms and stes. CI noon/CO 11am. Large rooms, average decor. **Amenities:** A/C, cable TV. **Services:** Babysitting. **Facilities:** 75 1 restaurant, 1 bar, washer/dryer. Private fishing access to Boulder River. Golf and water slide nearby. **Rates:** $36 S; $39–$48 D; $60–$80 ste. Extra person $6. Children under age 10 stay free. Parking: Outdoor, free. Closed Dec 26–Mar. AE, MC, V.

INN

The Grand Bed and Breakfast
139 McLeod St, PO Box 1242, 59011; tel 406/932-4459. This 1890 hotel was a favorite stopping place for frontier travelers and it's still a good deal. Antique furnishings and fine details. **Rooms:** 10 rms, stes, and effic (5 w/shared bath). CI 2pm/CO 11am. No smoking. Each room is uniquely appointed with period wardrobes, dressers, and nice linens. Several accommodations share a large complex with separate shower- and tub-rooms and a sauna. **Amenities:** A/C, bathrobes. No phone or TV. Some rooms have telephones. Thick, colorful towels. **Services:** Babysitting. Coffee in Commons Room on second floor. Pets allowed at manager's discretion. **Facilities:** 80 1 restaurant, 1 bar, sauna, washer/dryer, guest lounge w/TV. **Rates (BB):** $55 D w/shared bath, $75–$125 D w/private bath; $95–$125 ste; $95 effic. Extra person $15. Parking: Outdoor, free. Romance packages avail. DISC, MC, V.

ATTRACTION

C Sharps Arms Company/Montana Armory
100 Centennial Dr; tel 406/932-4353. This unique facility, which manufactures replica Sharps and Winchester rifles, features displays of antique and specialty firearms and other shooting supplies. **Open:** Mon–Fri 8am–5pm. Closed some hols. **Free**

Billings

This historic railroad city—Montana's largest city—is located in the valley of the Yellowstone River. Billings is bordered on its northern edge by sandstone rimrocks—a popular place for hiking and mountain biking. **Information:** Billings Convention and Visitors Bureau, 815 S 27th St, PO Box 31177, Billings, 59107 (tel 406/245-4111).

PUBLIC TRANSPORTATION

Billings Metropolitan Transit (MET) (tel 406/657-8218) provides 10 routes serving the greater Billings area. **MET Plus** serves the elderly and persons with disabilities. Peak hours are 6:40–9:45am and 3:15–6:15pm weekdays. Fares: adults and children 6 and older 75¢, seniors and persons with disabilities 25¢; children under 6 ride free. Transfers are free. To schedule paratransit rides, call 406/248-8805.

HOTELS

The Billings Inn

880 N 29th St, 59101; tel 406/252-6800 or toll free 800/ 231-7782; fax 406/252-6800. Homey, charming, and well appointed, this hotel located in the so-called "medical corridor" specializes in taking care of families in medical crisis. Above average for any traveler, it is one of the best deals in Billings. **Rooms:** 60 rms, stes, and effic. CI 2pm/CO 11am. Nonsmoking rms avail. Beautiful colonial-style furniture in pleasant rooms with nice views. **Amenities:** A/C, cable TV. All suites, and some regular rooms, have microwaves and refrigerators. Every room has a reclining chair. **Services:** Babysitting. Evening meals can be catered. Newspapers and coffee in lobby. Wheelchairs can be provided. **Facilities:** Washer/dryer. **Rates (CP):** $39 S; $43 D; $49 ste; $44–$54 effic. Extra person $5. Children under age 12 stay free. Parking: Outdoor, free. AE, CB, DC, DISC, MC, V.

Radisson Northern Hotel

19 N 28th St, 59101; tel 406/245-5121 or toll free 800/ 333-3333; fax 406/259-9862. On a busy corner in the heart of Billings, this elegant historical landmark has been renovated with classic western and Native American themes. **Rooms:** 160 rms and stes. CI 3pm/CO noon. Nonsmoking rms avail. Beautiful cherry-wood doors in every room and great views of the city and surrounding areas from large windows. The older-style bathrooms have sparkling white tile. **Amenities:** A/C, cable TV w/movies, refrig, dataport, bathrobes. Fluffy robes and towels. **Services:** VP Babysitting. Coffee and newspapers available in lobby from 5am. Very attentive staff with "Yes, I can" attitude. **Facilities:** 500 1 restaurant (*see* "Restaurants" below), 1 bar. Golf privileges at the championship Briarwood Golf Club. Large banquet facility. **Rates:** $84 S; $94 D; $99–$109 ste. Extra person $10. Children under age 17 stay free. Parking: Indoor, free. Corporate rates avail. AE, CB, DC, DISC, JCB, MC, V.

Sheraton Billings Hotel

27 N 27th St, 59101 (Downtown); tel 406/252-7400 or toll free 800/588-7666; fax 406/252-2401. Better-than-average high-rise hotel located in the heart of Billings, 1½ miles from the airport. Traditionally furnished and sumptuously decorated lobby features a "water wall." **Rooms:** 286 rms and stes. Executive level. CI 2pm/CO noon. Nonsmoking rms avail. Nice, large rooms; those on the west side of the building have views of the Pryor Mountains. **Amenities:** A/C, satel TV w/movies. Some units w/minibars, 1 w/whirlpool. Suites have refrigerators, bathrobes. **Services:** Executive Travelers Club offers special services for corporate guests, including continental breakfast, health club privileges, and a private lounge. **Facilities:** 1000 1 restaurant, 1 bar, games rm, spa, sauna, whirlpool. **Rates:** $86–$105 S; $96–$115 D; $130–$190 ste. Extra person $10. Children under age 18 stay free. Parking: Indoor/outdoor, free. Weekend, holiday, and hunting packages avail. AE, CB, DC, DISC, MC, V.

MOTELS

Airport Metra Inn

403 Main St, 59105 (Heights); tel 406/245-6611 or toll free 800/234-6611. Located next to Metra Event center, fairgrounds, and airport. **Rooms:** 105 rms and effic. CI 3pm/CO 11am. Nonsmoking rms avail. Rooms could be better maintained. **Amenities:** A/C, satel TV, refrig. Some units w/whirlpools. **Services:** Complimentary coffee in lobby. **Facilities:** 100 1 restaurant (lunch and dinner only), 1 bar. Casino. **Rates:** $37 S; $45 D; $41–$46 effic. Extra person $4. Children under age 18 stay free. Parking: Outdoor, free. Senior and corporate rates. AE, CB, DC, DISC, MC, V.

Comfort Inn

2030 Overland Ave, 59102; tel 406/652-5200 or toll free 800/221-2222; fax 406/652-5200. Southwest Billings off I-90, exit 446. Newer property near restaurants, mall, business park, and I-90. Fairly quiet despite proximity to railroad and freeway. **Rooms:** 60 rms and stes. CI 3pm/CO 11am. Nonsmoking rms avail. Lovely rooms with nice oak furniture. Some kings have pull-out couch. **Amenities:** A/C, cable TV. Some kings have microwaves and refrigerators. **Services:** Babysitting. "Guest-of-the-day" service includes in-room treats and privileges at Billings Athletic Club. **Facilities:** Games rm, whirlpool. **Rates (CP):** Peak (June 1–Sept 30) $46–$60 S; $54–$70 D; $57–$79 ste. Extra person $10. Children under age 18 stay free. Lower rates off-season. Parking: Outdoor, free. Corporate and group rates available. AE, DC, DISC, MC, V.

Dude Rancher Lodge

415 N 29th, 59101; tel 406/252-2584 or toll free 800/ 221-3302; fax 406/259-5561. Center of Billings. Far from a generic motel, this charming, older hostelry with distinctive western decor and hospitality is so comfortable, it's like staying with an old friend. An excellent value. Within walking distance of Alberta Bair theater and downtown. **Rooms:** 55 rms and stes. CI 1pm/CO 11am. Nonsmoking rms avail. Cozy rooms with pine paneling and refinished oak western furniture from the '50s. Armoires provide lots of space for clothing and gear. **Amenities:** A/C, cable TV. **Services:** Exceptionally accommodating staff. **Facilities:** 25 1 restaurant. The restaurant is a popular local gathering place and will cater dinner parties and lunch-

eons in the Fireside lobby. **Rates:** Peak (Apr–Sept) $36–$50 S; $40–$55 D; $65 ste. Extra person $4. Children under age 17 stay free. Lower rates off-season. Parking: Outdoor, free. AE, DC, MC, V.

Ponderosa
2511 1st Ave N, PO Box 1791, 59103; tel 406/259-5511 or toll free 800/628-9081; fax 406/245-8004. This newly decorated, better-than-average motel is within walking distance of Yellowstone Art Center, Western Heritage Center, and the Alberta Bair Theater. **Rooms:** 130 rms and stes. CI 3pm/CO 11am. Nonsmoking rms avail. "King rooms," with separate sitting area and pullout sofa, are comparable to suites elsewhere. **Amenities:** A/C, cable TV. 1 unit w/whirlpool. Dataports in some rooms. **Services:** **Facilities:** 1 restaurant, 1 bar (w/entertainment), sauna, washer/dryer. Vehicle plug-ins for winter. Pool area landscaped with flowers and trees. **Rates:** Peak (May–Sept) $47–$59 S; $57–$70 D; $80–$150 ste. Extra person $5. Children under age 18 stay free. Lower rates off-season. Parking: Outdoor, free. Senior, corporate, and military rates. AE, CB, DC, DISC, ER, JCB, MC, V.

Quality Inn Homestead Park
2036 Overland Ave, 59102 (Homestead Park); tel 406/652-1320 or toll free 800/228-5151; fax 406/652-1320. Exit 446 off I-90; follow King Ave W to Homestead Business Park. This motel, near a mall, restaurants, and theater, has a large, inviting lobby. **Rooms:** 120 rms and stes. CI 3pm/CO noon. Nonsmoking rms avail. Upscale furnishings and decor. **Amenities:** A/C, cable TV. Refrigerator, wet bar, queen-size fold-out sofas in some suites. Dataports in some rooms. **Services:** Car-rental desk, babysitting. Fax service available. **Facilities:** Whirlpool. Club room features full breakfasts and late-night snacks. Guest privileges at Billings Athletic Club and nearby private golf course. **Rates:** Peak (June–Sept 15) $45–$54 S; $52–$72 D; $52–$76 ste. Extra person $5. Children under age 18 stay free. Lower rates off-season. Parking: Outdoor, free. Corporate rate includes full breakfast. AE, CB, DC, DISC, ER, JCB, MC, V.

Rimrock Inn
1203 N 27th St, 59101; tel 406/252-7107 or toll free 800/624-9770; fax 406/252-7107 ext 305. North central Billings. Very well maintained older property within walking distance of Montana State University and close to downtown and the airport. **Rooms:** 83 rms. CI 1pm/CO 11am. Nonsmoking rms avail. Nicely decorated; live plants. **Amenities:** A/C, cable TV. **Services:** Car-rental desk, babysitting. Movie rentals available at desk. **Facilities:** 1 restaurant (lunch and dinner only), 1 bar, games rm, spa, sauna. Barber shop on premises. **Rates (CP):** $35 S; $35 D. Parking: Outdoor, free. Rates determined by number of beds used, not number in party. Corporate rates available. AE, CB, DC, DISC, JCB, MC, V.

Rimview Inn
1025 N 27th, 59101; tel 406/248-2622 or toll free 800/551-1418; fax 406/248-2622. North central Billings. The largest saltwater aquarium in Montana is in the lobby of this older motel, located in the "medical corridor" of downtown Billings. Close to airport and Montana State University. **Rooms:** 54 rms and effic. CI 2pm/CO 11am. Nonsmoking rms avail. Clean and well-kept large rooms. **Amenities:** A/C, cable TV, refrig. Some units w/terraces, some w/whirlpools. Most rooms have kitchenettes and recliners. Waterbeds available. **Services:** **Facilities:** Whirlpool, washer/dryer. Free extended parking for guests who fly out of Billings. **Rates (CP):** Peak (May 15–Oct 15) $32–$42 S or D; $34–$50 effic. Extra person $2. Lower rates off-season. Parking: Outdoor, free. Weekly rates avail. AE, CB, DISC, MC, V.

RESTAURANTS

The Athenian
18 N 29th; tel 406/248-5681. Downtown. **Greek.** Owner/chef Nick Rentzio presents the cuisine of his homeland, with many ingredients imported from Greece. You may wish to try the northern Greek chicken with six different sauces, the layered eggplant and ground beef dish called moussaka, or a large salad, and finish with one of the honey-graced desserts like baklava. **FYI:** Reservations recommended. Children's menu. Beer and wine only. **Open:** Mon–Sat 11am–10pm. **Prices:** Main courses $5–$15; prix fixe $5–$13. MC, V.

★ **The Cattle Company**
In Rimrock Mall, 300 S 24th St W; tel 406/656-9090. West Billings. **American.** Reflects an Old West atmosphere thanks to appropriate memorabilia. The large menu offers steak kabob, rotisserie chicken, seafood, and fresh-water fish such as walleyed pike and trout. **FYI:** Reservations not accepted. Children's menu. **Open:** Lunch Mon–Thurs 11am–2pm, Fri–Sat 11am–3pm; dinner Mon–Thurs 5–10pm, Fri–Sat 5–11pm, Sun 5–9pm. **Prices:** Main courses $8–$14. AE, DC, DISC, MC, V.

$ ★ **Fuddruckers**
2011 Overland Ave; tel 406/656-5455. Southwest edge of city, off I-90. **Burgers.** Burgers are the specialty in this fun and casual place that's friendly to families. Customize your food at the toppings bar and eat on the patio overlooking a pond filled with ducks and geese. Bakery on premises. **FYI:** Reservations not accepted. Children's menu. Beer and wine only. **Open:** Peak (Mem Day–Labor Day) Mon–Thurs 10:30am–10pm, Fri–Sat 10:30am–11pm, Sun 10:30am–10pm. **Prices:** Main courses $3–$6. AE, CB, DC, DISC, MC, V.

★ **Golden Belle**
In Radisson Northern Hotel, 19 N 28th St (Downtown); tel 406/245-2232. **American.** Plush, with crystal chandeliers and a baby grand piano, this is a real favorite of families celebrat-

ing special occasions. Chef Ross Nicholson specializes in Montana beef and flaming desserts. Heart-healthy meals available. **FYI:** Reservations recommended. Piano. Children's menu. **Open:** Breakfast Mon–Sat 6:30–11am, Sun 7am–2pm; lunch daily 11am–2:30pm; dinner Mon–Sat 4:30–10pm, Sun 4:30–9pm; brunch Sun 9:30am–2pm. **Prices:** Main courses $8–$20; prix fixe $12–$18. AE, CB, DC, DISC, MC, V.

★ Granary
1500 Poly Dr; tel 406/259-3488. West Billings near "the Rims". **Seafood/Steak.** Housed in a historic mill filled with antique machinery. Locals gather for drinks and hors d'oeuvres on large outdoor deck under gracious elm trees. Entrees of beef are the top draw here, with fillet teriyaki the house specialty. **FYI:** Reservations recommended. No smoking. **Open:** Peak (May 15–Sept 1) Mon–Thurs 5:30–9pm, Fri–Sat 5:30–10pm, Sun 5:30–10pm. **Prices:** Main courses $14–$20; prix fixe $18. AE, DISC, MC, V.

$ Jade Palace
2021 Overland Ave; tel 406/656-8888. Southwest Billings. **American/Chinese.** Beautiful, spacious, and quiet. There are fresh flowers in the sun room. Chef Edward Tam prepares sautéed stir-fry or Kung Pao shrimp, and his restaurant is known for consistent quality and great prices. **FYI:** Reservations accepted. Children's menu. **Open:** Mon–Thurs 11am–10pm, Fri–Sat 11am–10:30pm, Sun 11am–9pm. **Prices:** Main courses $7–$15; prix fixe $10–$12. AE, DISC, MC, V.

$ Le Croissant
2711 1st Ave N; tel 406/245-8885. Downtown. **Cafe/French.** Sparkling and casual, this small eatery boasts homemade bagels and croissants along with many salads and sandwiches. Chef Nancy Patch-Sasse provides a unique-for-the-area selection of French fare. Fresh ground coffee and a good choice of jams and jellies present a good way to begin your morning. **FYI:** Reservations not accepted. No liquor license. No smoking. **Open:** Mon–Sat 7am–4pm. **Prices:** Lunch main courses $2–$4; prix fixe $3–$5. MC, V.

$ ★ Torres Cafe
6200 S Frontage Rd; tel 406/652-8426. **Mexican.** This very popular, family-run Mexican restaurant is somewhat off the main beat. For 32 years, Urbano and Hermilia Torres, with their 11 children, have been serving tasty beef and cheese enchiladas and specialty burritos. Fresh tortillas, salsa picante, Mexican spices, and gifts are for sale. **FYI:** Reservations accepted. Children's menu. No liquor license. No smoking. **Open:** Tues–Sat 11am–9pm. **Prices:** Main courses $3–$7. AE, DISC, MC, V.

$ Walkers Grill
In Historic Chamber of Commerce Building, 301 N 27th (Downtown); tel 406/245-9291. **American Bistro.** The contemporary, eclectic bistro food served here is sometimes prepared with Asian or south-of-the-border spices. Specialties include Montana meats like antelope or rabbit. Smaller dishes, specialty pizzas, pastas, and salads are also offered. Small, well-chosen wine list. **FYI:** Reservations accepted. Children's menu. Dress code. **Open:** Mon–Sat 5:30–10:30pm. **Prices:** Main courses $8–$17; prix fixe $8–$15. AE, DISC, MC, V.

ATTRACTIONS

Billings Area Visitor Center
815 S 27th St; tel 406/245-4111 or toll free 800/735-2635. In front of this downtown visitor center, the Cattle Drive Monument stands in tribute to the centennial of the Great Montana Cattle Drive of 1889. Brochures, information, and assistance regarding all area attractions are available inside. **Open:** May–Sept, daily 8:30am–6pm; Oct–Apr, Mon–Fri 8:30am–5pm. Closed some hols. **Free**

Moss Mansion Museum
914 Division St; tel 406/256-5100. On the National Register of Historic Places. Built between 1901 and 1903, the mansion features many Eastern and European influences: a Moorish-style entryway patterned after the Alhambra in Spain, Persian and Aubusson carpets, and a Louis XIV–style parlor. Original furnishings, light fixtures, carpets, draperies, and family mementos are on permanent display. Guided tours through two of the house's three floors include stops in the Shakespeare library (with stained-glass windows depicting scenes from his plays) and the English Tudor dining room. **Open:** June–Aug, daily 10am–5pm; Sept–May, daily 1–3pm. Closed some hols. **$$**

Peter Yegen Jr Yellowstone County Museum
Off MT 3 at Billings Logan International Airport; tel 406/256-6811. Depicts frontier life through dioramas and Native American, pioneer, and cowboy relics such as a Northern Pacific steam engine and a sheepherder's wagon. Excellent views of Billings and Yellowstone Valley. Picnic area. **Open:** Mon–Fri 10:30am–5:30pm, Sun 1–5pm. Closed some hols. **Free**

Western Heritage Center
2822 Montana Ave; tel 406/256-6809. Housed in the original Parmly Billings Library (circa 1901). Historical photos, period clothing, art, western crafts, and historic artifacts are featured in the exhibits, which explore the history and culture of the Yellowstone River region. Donation requested. **Open:** Tues–Sat 10am–5pm, Sun 1–5pm. Closed some hols. **Free**

Pompeys Pillar National Historic Landmark
I-94; tel 406/657-6262. 1 mi N of Billings. The site of the only remaining physical evidence of the Lewis and Clark expedition in Montana. In July 1806, William Clark and his party were traveling down the Yellowstone River when they sighted this 200-foot-high sandstone outcropping in the middle of the wide valley. Clark carved his name in the rock, where it is still visible today. Other petroglyphs also remain,

believed to be the work of the Shoshone, who used the pillar as a lookout and for sending smoke signals. A steep trail to the top offers a vista of the Yellowstone Valley and the surrounding area. Picnic area. **Open:** Mem Day–Labor Day, daily sunrise–sunset. **Free**

Black Eagle

See Great Falls

Bozeman

Named for John Bozeman, the man who brought the first wagon train to the Gallatin Valley. Today, Bozeman is best known as the home of Montana State University. **Information:** Bozeman Area Chamber of Commerce, 1205 E Main, PO Box B, Bozeman, 59715 (tel 406/586-5421).

MOTELS

Best Western City Center Motor Inn
507 W Main St, 59715 (Downtown); tel 406/587-3158 or toll free 800/528-1234. Located within walking distance of historic downtown shopping and restaurants. **Rooms:** 64 rms and stes. CI 2pm/CO 11am. Nonsmoking rms avail. **Amenities:** A/C, cable TV. **Services:** **Facilities:** 100 2 restaurants, 1 bar, whirlpool. **Rates:** Peak (June–Sept) $45–$65 S; $60–$80 D; $80–$95 ste. Extra person $5. Children under age 12 stay free. Lower rates off-season. Parking: Outdoor, free. AE, CB, DC, DISC, MC, V.

Best Western Grantree Inn
1325 N 7th Ave, 59715; tel 406/587-5261 or toll free 800/624-5865; fax 406/587-9437. Exit 306 off I-90. Located on a busy motel strip close to highway interchange. Pleasant rooms. **Rooms:** 103 rms and stes. Executive level. CI 4pm/CO 11am. Nonsmoking rms avail. **Amenities:** A/C, cable TV w/movies, VCR. 1 unit w/whirlpool. **Services:** **Facilities:** 250 1 restaurant, 1 bar, spa, whirlpool, washer/dryer. **Rates:** Peak (June–Sept 15) $58–$88 S; $66–$92 D; $68–$125 ste. Extra person $4. Children under age 17 stay free. Lower rates off-season. Parking: Outdoor, free. AE, CB, DC, DISC, EC, ER, JCB, MC, V.

Comfort Inn
1370 N 7th Ave, 59715; tel 406/587-2322 or toll free 800/587-3833; fax 406/587-2423. Near I-90 interchange, S on N 7th Ave. Nicer and newer than most motels in the area. **Rooms:** 87 rms and stes. Executive level. CI 4pm/CO 11am. Nonsmoking rms avail. Attractively decorated, spacious rooms. **Amenities:** A/C, cable TV w/movies, refrig, dataport, VCR. Some units w/whirlpools. **Services:** **Facilities:** 70 Games rm, sauna, whirlpool, washer/dryer. **Rates (CP):** Peak (May–Sept) $58–$99 S; $75–$99 D; $85–$99 ste. Extra person $4. Children under age 16 stay free. Lower rates off-season. Parking: Outdoor, free. AE, CB, DC, DISC, MC, V.

Fairfield Inn
828 Wheat Dr, 59715; tel 406/587-2222 or toll free 800/228-2800; fax 406/587-2222. Exit 306 off I-90. Clean and friendly property located in a cluster of similar accommodations near a highway interchange. **Rooms:** 57 rms and stes. CI 2pm/CO 11am. Nonsmoking rms avail. Basic motel decor. **Amenities:** A/C. **Services:** **Facilities:** 12 Whirlpool. **Rates (CP):** Peak (June–Sept) $53–$78 S; $88–$105 D; $88–$110 ste. Extra person $6. Children under age 18 stay free. Lower rates off-season. Parking: Outdoor, free. Discount for frequent guests. AE, DC, DISC, MC, V.

Holiday Inn
5 Baxter Lane, 59715; tel 406/587-4561 or toll free 800/366-5101; fax 406/587-4413. S of I-90 Interchange. On the plus side, there are lots of conference facilities; on the minus, room renovation is needed, and hallways are dimly lit and gloomy. **Rooms:** 178 rms. CI 3pm/CO 11am. Nonsmoking rms avail. **Amenities:** A/C, cable TV w/movies, dataport. Some units w/whirlpools. **Services:** Masseur, babysitting. **Facilities:** 400 1 restaurant, 1 bar, games rm, whirlpool, washer/dryer. **Rates:** Peak (June–Sept) $58–$88 S; $58–$99 D. Children under age 18 stay free. Lower rates off-season. Parking: Outdoor, free. AE, CB, DC, DISC, JCB, MC, V.

INNS

UNRATED **Lindley House**
202 Lindley Place, 59715; tel 406/587-8403 or toll free 800/787-8404; fax 406/582-8112. 1 block S of historic downtown. Beautifully renovated Victorian manor house (1898) listed on the National Register of Historic Places. (Not rated because there are fewer than 10 rooms.) Unsuitable for children under 10. **Rooms:** 7 rms and stes (2 w/shared bath). CI 4pm/CO 11am. No smoking. Wonderful attention to detail, reflected in dramatic French wall coverings and antique beds with down pillows and comforters. The suites are especially sumptuous: One has a sunken tub and shower with two heads. **Amenities:** Cable TV, CD/tape player, bathrobes. No A/C or phone. Some units w/terraces, 1 w/fireplace, 1 w/whirlpool. **Services:** Social director, masseur, afternoon tea and wine/sherry served. Arrangements can be made for scenic day trips. **Facilities:** 12 Guest lounge w/TV. Beautifully landscaped patio with hot tub. **Rates (BB):** Peak (May–Nov) $75 S w/shared bath; $90 D w/shared bath, $110–$130 D w/private bath; $175–$195 ste. Extra person $15. Children under age 2 stay free. Lower rates off-season. Parking: Outdoor, free. Valentine's Day and ski packages avail. MC, V.

UNRATED **The Voss Inn**
319 S Willson, 59715; tel 406/587-0982. Willson Historic District. This renovated Victorian home located in a beauti-

fully maintained historic district draws many repeat guests. (Not rated because there are fewer than 10 rooms.) Unsuitable for children under 6. **Rooms:** 6 rms. CI 2pm/CO 11am. No smoking. Individually decorated with coordinated wall papers and period antiques. **Amenities:** A/C. No TV. 1 unit w/terrace, 1 w/fireplace. **Services:** Afternoon tea and wine/sherry served. **Facilities:** Guest lounge w/TV. Large veranda with outdoor seating. **Rates (BB):** $70–$80 S; $80–$90 D. Parking: Outdoor, free. AE, MC, V.

RESORT

Mountain Sky Guest Ranch

Big Creek Rd on US 89, PO Box 1128, 59715; tel 406/587-1244 or toll free 800/548-3392. In Gallatin Mountains; 30 mi SW of Livingston. This all-cabin guest ranch sits on its own 4,000 acres of breathtaking scenery. Entire facility available for rent to one group. **Rooms:** 27 cottages/villas. CI noon/CO noon. Nonsmoking rms avail. One-, two-, and three-bedroom cabins offer a variety of accommodations; cabins have a country decor with wicker and split-pine log furniture. **Amenities:** Refrig, bathrobes. No A/C, phone, or TV. All units w/terraces, some w/fireplaces. Down comforters and beautiful, thick towels. **Services:** Masseur, children's program, babysitting. Comprehensive kid's program—must be 7 years old to ride horses. **Facilities:** 2 70 1 restaurant, 2 bars (1 w/entertainment), basketball, volleyball, games rm, sauna, whirlpool, playground, washer/dryer. New outdoor pool; nature room for resource materials; baby grand in main lodge; barbecues on lawn; softball field. **Rates (AP):** Peak (June 15–Aug) $1,715–$1,995 cottage/villa. Lower rates off-season. Parking: Outdoor, free. Rates are per person per week. Closed Oct–May. MC, V.

RESTAURANTS

Bighorn Café and Restaurant

1216 W Lincoln St; tel 406/585-1106. Between S 11th and S 19th. **Eclectic.** Chef/owner Eric Stenberg presents simple food creatively. Look for pizzas, sandwiches, and salads at lunch; dinner entrees might be smoked pork, venison, seafood ravioli, smoked chicken with linguine, or a mixed grill. There's a bakery and espresso bar on premises. **FYI:** Reservations recommended. Guitar. Children's menu. No liquor license. No smoking. **Open:** Mon–Fri 6:30am–10pm, Sat 8am–11pm, Sun 9am–9pm. **Prices:** Main courses $12–$17. MC, V.

✱ John Bozeman's Bistro

242 E Main St (Downtown); tel 406/587-4100. **Eclectic.** Eclectic cuisine served in a rustic but comfortable atmosphere. Menu emphasizes fresh seafood and wild game dishes; vegetarians are catered to as well. **FYI:** Reservations recommended. Guitar. Children's menu. Beer and wine only. No smoking. **Open:** Lunch Tues–Sat 11am–4pm; dinner Tues–Sun 5–9:30pm; brunch Sat 8–11:30am, Sun 8am–1pm. **Prices:** Main courses $12–$20. AE, DC, DISC, MC, V.

✱ O'Brien's Restaurant

312 E Main St; tel 406/587-3973. **Continental.** Intimate dining and friendly service. Elegantly prepared dishes include tournedos, shrimp, chicken, veal, and fresh seafood specials. **FYI:** Reservations recommended. No smoking. **Open:** Daily 5–9pm. **Prices:** Main courses $15–$18. DISC, MC, V.

✱ Spanish Peaks Brewery and Italian Cafe

120 N 19th Ave; tel 406/585-2296. 1 block N of Main St. **Italian.** Menu specialties include brick oven–baked, California-style pizzas and sundry other pasta and Italian dishes. Lunch is served in the bar or on the outside patio; dinner is served in the dining room. Visible through windows in the bar is the microbrewery, heralded for its Black Dog Ale. **FYI:** Reservations recommended. Beer and wine only. No smoking. **Open:** Lunch daily 11:30am–2:30pm; dinner daily 5:30–10:30pm. **Prices:** Main courses $8–$17. DISC, MC, V.

ATTRACTIONS

Gallatin County Pioneer Museum

317 W Main St; tel 406/585-1311. Collections here include Native American artifacts, a barbed wire exhibit, and 19th-century household items, all displayed among jail cells and a gallows at the former local jail. **Open:** June–Sept, Mon–Fri 10am–4:30pm, Sat 1–4pm; Oct–May, Mon–Thurs 11am–4pm. Closed some hols. **Free**

Museum of the Rockies

Kagy Blvd S; tel 406/994-2251. Located on the campus of Montana State University, the museum houses an extensive display of dinosaur bones, as well as exhibits on pioneer history and astronomy. **Open:** Mem Day–Labor Day, daily 9am–9pm; Labor Day–Mem Day, Mon–Sat 9am–5pm, Sun 12:30–5pm. Closed some hols. **$$**

Butte

Butte's famous "richest hill on earth" yielded over nine million tons of gold, silver, and copper ore. When the high-grade copper ore was almost gone, the Berkeley Open Pit Mine was established to extract low-grade copper ore. Today, an interpretive site overlooks the gigantic pit. **Information:** Butte-Silver Bow Chamber of Commerce, 2950 Harrison Ave, Butte, 59701 (tel 406/494-5595).

HOTELS

Best Western Copper King Inn

4655 Harrison Ave S, 59701; tel 406/494-6666 or toll free 800/332-8600; fax 406/494-3274. Exit 127 or 127A off I-90; S on Harrison Ave 13 blocks. Nicely renovated property with a very spacious lobby. **Rooms:** 150 rms and stes. Executive level. CI 3pm/CO 11am. Nonsmoking rms avail.

Rooms are large; some open onto pool area, some have recliners and sofas. **Amenities:** A/C, cable TV w/movies. Some units w/terraces, some w/whirlpools. **Services:** Fax, copier, and business services available. **Facilities:** 3500 2 restaurants, 1 bar (w/entertainment), basketball, spa, sauna, whirlpool, washer/dryer. **Rates:** Peak (June–Sept) $60–$76 S; $60–$76 D; $125–$175 ste. Extra person $8. Children under age 18 stay free. Lower rates off-season. Parking: Outdoor, free. AE, CB, DC, DISC, MC, V.

War Bonnet Inn
2100 Cornell Ave, 59701; tel 406/494-7800 or toll free 800/443-1806; fax 406/494-2875. Exit 127 off I-90 W, turn right; exit 127B off I-90 E, go north. Located near the popular World Museum of Mining and the Montana College of Mineral Science and Technology. **Rooms:** 134 rms and stes. CI 3pm/CO noon. Nonsmoking rms avail. **Amenities:** A/C, cable TV w/movies. Some units w/terraces. **Services:** Babysitting. **Facilities:** 450 1 restaurant, 1 bar, games rm, sauna, steam rm, whirlpool. **Rates:** Peak (May 15–Sept 15) $72–$85 S or D; $125–$150 ste. Children under age 16 stay free. Lower rates off-season. Parking: Outdoor, free. Senior rates. AE, CB, DC, DISC, MC, V.

MOTEL

Best Western Butte Plaza Inn
2900 Harrison Ave, 59701; tel 406/494-3500 or toll free 800/543-5814; fax 406/494-7611. Take I-90 to exit 127; turn left on Harrison Ave. Contemporary yet folksy motel, run by an Austrian couple who grew up in the hotel business. **Rooms:** 134 rms, stes, and effic. Executive level. CI noon/CO noon. Nonsmoking rms avail. All rooms have one king or two queen beds. **Amenities:** A/C, cable TV w/movies, dataport. 1 unit w/whirlpool. **Services:** Babysitting. Extended continental breakfast includes European-style baked goods. Boxed lunches to go. Fax, copier, and typing services available. Deposit for pets. **Facilities:** 100 1 restaurant, 1 bar, sauna, steam rm, whirlpool, washer/dryer. **Rates (CP):** Peak (June–Aug) $68–$88 S; $79–$99 D; $125–$175 ste; $125–$175 effic. Extra person $8. Children under age 12 stay free. Lower rates off-season. Parking: Outdoor, free. Senior rates avail. AE, CB, DC, DISC, MC, V.

RESTAURANTS

Metals Banque
8 W Park St (Uptown); tel 406/723-6160. **American.** Visitors to this recently restored Butte bank (built in 1906) can have a drink at the marble tellers' counter, then eat lunch or dinner in the former vault. The menu offers steak, seafood, pasta, and some Tex-Mex selections. There are no gambling machines on premises, which is unusual for Butte. **FYI:** Reservations accepted. Children's menu. **Open:** Peak (July–Sept/Dec/Mar) Mon–Thurs 11am–10pm, Fri–Sat 11am–11pm, Sun 4–10pm. **Prices:** Main courses $5–$15. DISC, MC, V.

Pork Chop John's
8 W Mercury St; tel 406/782-0812. Montana St exit off I-90. **Fast food.** In 1920, John Burkland started selling pork-chop sandwiches to copper miners from the back of his wagon at each shift change. Twelve years later, he opened his first sandwich shop with a counter, eight stools, and a walk-up window. Today's owner, John Orizotti, uses the same recipe in his 50-seat restaurant, and proudly sells half a million sandwiches annually. **FYI:** Reservations not accepted. Children's menu. No liquor license. Additional location: 2400 Harrison Ave (tel 782-0812). **Open:** Mon–Sat 10:30am–1am. **Prices:** Main courses $3–$7. No CC.

ATTRACTIONS

World Museum of Mining
Park St; tel 406/723-7211. Located at an inactive silver and zinc mine, this museum is the centerpiece of Hell Roarin' Gulch, a 22-acre re-creation of a typical 1899 Montana mining camp. The museum has exhibits of underground firefighting equipment, gold bullion scales, mining cars, and a stage coach. Other village buildings include an assay office, Old West saloon, general store, soda fountain, and 33 other businesses. Picnic area, gift shop. **Open:** Apr–May, Tues–Sun 10am–5pm; June–Labor Day, daily 9am– 9pm; Labor Day–late Nov, Tues–Sun 10am–5pm. **$**

Mineral Museum at Montana Technical College
Park St; tel 406/496-4414. Displays more than 1,300 mineral specimens including what is considered to be the largest gold nugget found in Montana. Also, housed in a special darkened room is an exhibit of fluorescent minerals. **Open:** Daily 8am–4:30pm. Closed some hols. **Free**

US High Altitude Sports Center
1 Olympic Way; tel 406/723-7060. A designated training site for the US national speed-skating team. When world-class skating events are not being held here, the center is open to the general public for skating and other indoor sports. **Open:** Daily 24 hrs. Closed mid-Mar–mid-Oct.

Chinook

Named for the Native American word for the warm, dry winds that quickly raise temperatures and melt snow, allowing cattle to graze in the wintertime. The Fort Belknap Indian Reservation, home of the Gros Ventre and Assiniboine tribes, is nearby. **Information:** Chinook Chamber of Commerce, PO Box 744, Chinook, 59523 (tel 406/357-2236).

MOTEL

Chinook Motor Inn
100 Indiana Ave, PO Box 1418, 59523; tel 406/357-2248 or toll free 800/603-2864. In an unassuming two-story, white-brick building, this place caters to business travelers and groups, but families will feel welcome here too. **Rooms:** 38 rms and stes. CI 6pm/CO 11am. Nonsmoking rms avail. **Amenities:** A/C, cable TV. **Services:** **Facilities:** 235 1 restaurant (*see* "Restaurants" below), 1 bar, games rm. **Rates:** $39–$43 S; $42–$54 D; $42–$54 ste. Extra person $5. Children under age 12 stay free. Parking: Outdoor, free. AE, DISC, MC, V.

RESTAURANT

Morgan's Family Restaurant
In Chinook Motor Inn, 100 Indiana Ave; tel 406/357-2548. **American.** Sandwiched between the bar and lobby, this restaurant is simple and unpretentious. Large portions of traditional, mostly American fare. Fajitas (unusual for the area) are a specialty. Lunch and dinner specials. **FYI:** Reservations accepted. Children's menu. **Open:** Peak (Mem Day–Labor Day) Mon–Sat 6am–10pm, Sun 7am–10pm. **Prices:** Main courses $6–$18. AE, DISC, MC, V.

Columbia Falls

See also Kalispell, Whitefish

This small community located just outside Glacier National Park is also a gateway to the Bob Marshall and Great Bear Wilderness Areas. **Information:** Columbia Falls Area Chamber of Commerce, 233 13th St E, PO Box 312, Columbia Falls, 59912 (tel 406/892-2072).

MOTEL

Ol' River Bridge Inn
7358 US 2 E, PO Box 969, 59912 (Columbia Heights); tel 406/892-2181 or toll free 800/845-3411; fax 406/892-2166. Near jct of US 2 E and MT 206. Conveniently located on direct route to Glacier National Park (13 miles to west entrance) and 15 miles from Big Mountain Ski and Summer Resort. Appeals to families on a budget and outdoor enthusiasts. Discounted passes to waterslide park (one mile away). **Rooms:** 31 rms. CI 3pm/CO 11am. Nonsmoking rms avail. All rooms have two queen-size beds; family unit can sleep up to eight. **Amenities:** A/C, cable TV w/movies. **Services:** Babysitting. Shuttle services for special events. Fax and copying services available. **Facilities:** 400 1 restaurant (*see* "Restaurants" below), 1 bar (w/entertainment), whirlpool. **Rates:** Peak (May–Oct 15) $49–$52 S or D. Extra person $3. Lower rates off-season. Parking: Outdoor, free. Senior and commercial rates; golf, snowmobile, and holiday packages avail. AE, DISC, MC, V.

RESORT

Meadow Lake Golf and Ski Resort
100 St Andrews Dr, 59912; tel 406/892-7601 or toll free 800/321-4651; fax 406/892-0330. 300 acres. A full-service golfing and cross-country skiing resort located near Glacier National Park and Big Mountain Ski and Summer Resort. Lodging choices include motel-style rooms housed in a central lodge, or privately owned condos, villas, and townhouses bordering the golf course. **Rooms:** 24 rms and stes; 90 cottages/villas. Executive level. CI 3pm/CO 11am. Nonsmoking rms avail. All units offer views of golf course and surrounding mountain landscape. Condos, villas, and townhouses have full kitchens. **Amenities:** A/C, cable TV w/movies, VCR, voice mail. All units w/terraces, some w/fireplaces, some w/whirlpools. Condos, villas, and townhouses feature laundries, fireplaces, barbecue grills, private decks, TVs, VCRs, and covered or garage parking. **Services:** Car-rental desk, social director, children's program, babysitting. Fax, copier, computer/modem, limited currency exchange, secretarial service, and overnight courier service. Complimentary shuttle to Glacier International Airport, Amtrak station, and Big Mountain. Special excursions to Big Sky Waterslide Park and Glacier National Park. Masseur available on request. **Facilities:** 18 1 125 1 restaurant, 1 bar (w/entertainment), volleyball, games rm, whirlpool, playground. Casino lounge. Direct access to Flathead National Forest for hiking and mountain biking. Ice-skating pond. **Rates:** Peak (mid-June–mid-Sept/Christmas–Jan 1) $119 S or D; $119 ste; $149–$429 cottage/villa. Extra person $15. Children under age 16 stay free. Lower rates off-season. MAP rates avail. Parking: Outdoor, free. No minimum stay at Inn, but two-night minimum stay at condos, villas, and townhouses. Guests receive 25% discount on greens fees. Seasonal vacation packages include river rafting, golfing, skiing, and snowmobiling. Senior, group, and commercial rates avail. AE, DISC, MC, V.

RESTAURANT

The Ol' River Bridge Restaurant
In the Ol' River Bridge Inn, 7358 US 2 E (Columbia Heights); tel 406/892-2181. Near jct US 2 E and MT 206. **Eclectic.** A lively local favorite, decorated with red carpeting and red velvet wall coverings, plus early American signs and prints. The Montana breakfast includes two nine-inch pancakes, a chunk of ham, and two eggs for less than $5. Salads, sandwiches, and burgers is the lunch fare. Dinner entrees include steak and seafood, plus the house specialty, prime rib. **FYI:** Reservations not accepted. Country music/dancing/karaoke. Children's menu. **Open:** Peak (May–Oct 15) daily 6am–11pm. **Prices:** Main courses $6–$16. AE, DISC, MC, V.

ATTRACTIONS

Amazing Fun Center
US 2, Coram; tel 406/387-5902. 7 mi SW of West Glacier entrance to Glacier National Park. Entertainment complex with a 1½-mile-long three-dimensional maze, bumper boats equipped with electric squirt guns, and an 18-hole miniature golf course. "Bankshot basketball" challenges players to sink baskets from three different points. Snack bar and picnic area. **Open:** Mem Day–Labor Day, daily 9:30am–8:30pm.

Big Sky Waterslide
7954 MT 2E; tel 406/892-5025. 10 mi SW of Glacier National Park. All kinds of watery fun: nine water slides, Bullet water roller coaster, Big Splash river ride, and the Geronimo free-fall thrill ride. If you'd rather not get wet, there's also a miniature golf course, video arcade, and picnic area. **Open:** Mem Day–Labor Day, daily 10am–8pm. **$$$$**

Cooke City

The northeast entrance to Yellowstone National Park and the western terminus of the 64-mile-long Beartooth Scenic Highway. Built on the site of a former gold-mining camp; visitors can try gold panning in the local streams.

MOTEL

Alpine Motel
Main St (US 212), PO Box 1030, 59020; tel 406/838-2262. Spotless and well maintained. **Rooms:** 27 rms and stes. CI 2pm/CO 11am. Nonsmoking rms avail. Charming older rooms have pine furniture and wall paneling. Newer section has two-bedroom apartments in addition to standard rooms. All accommodations have view of mountains. **Amenities:** Satel TV. No A/C or phone. **Services:** Portable wheelchair ramp provided on request. **Facilities:** **Rates:** Peak (June 15–Sept 7) $35–$50 S; $40–$60 D; $80 ste. Extra person $10. Lower rates off-season. Parking: Outdoor, free. AE, CB, DC, DISC, MC, V.

RESTAURANT

★ **Pine Tree Cafe**
US 212; tel 406/838-2213. E end of Main St/US 212. **American/Cafe.** American breakfast favorites like omelettes, pancakes, and french toast start the day here. Familiar lunch and dinner choices such as burgers (beef or buffalo), chicken-fried steak, meat loaf, and chicken are joined by various Mexican offerings. **FYI:** Reservations not accepted. No liquor license. **Open:** Peak (June–Aug) daily 7am–9pm. Closed Oct 15–Dec 26/Apr–May 15. **Prices:** Main courses $4–$9; prix fixe $5–$9. No CC.

Darby

Small Bitterroot Valley town in western Montana, settled about 1800. The Darby Pioneer Memorial Museum depicts the town's early history. The Alta Ranger Station near Painted Rocks Reservoir (the first US Forest Service ranger station in the United States) provides visitors with a wealth of information on outdoor recreational opportunities in the surrounding mountains.

LODGE

Triple Creek Ranch
5551 W Fork Stage Rte, 59829; tel 406/821-4664 or toll free 800/654-2943; fax 406/821-4666. 7½ mi W on MT 473, off US 93 S. Full-service guest ranch tucked away in a very quiet mountain setting; recently named a member of the prestigious Relais & Chateaux association. Three creeks cross the property, with wooden walkways running along the creek beds. The hand-hewn log lodge and cabins attract professional people looking for a relaxed or romantic getaway. Exclusively for adults; children under age 16 permitted only when the entire ranch is reserved by a group. **Rooms:** 17 stes. Executive level. CI 3pm/CO noon. All accommodations feature the highest quality mattresses, linen, and bedding. Wildlife art prints and photos decorate the rooms and lodge, which feature Native American fabric designs. Super-deluxe log cabins, laid out to provide privacy on at least two sides, have two-person showers and steamers and his-and-hers vanities and toilets. **Amenities:** A/C, satel TV w/movies, refrig, dataport, VCR, CD/tape player, bathrobes. All units w/minibars, all w/terraces, all w/fireplaces, some w/whirlpools. Jet tubs, wet bars, whole bean coffee and grinders, stocked refrigerators in each cabin. 27-inch TVs. Some cabins have outdoor hot tubs on private decks; others offer indoor whirlpools. **Services:** Social director, masseur. One-to-one staff/guest ratio means exquisite, personalized service. All meals are available in-cabin or in the beautiful, well-appointed dining room. Fresh fruit, snacks, and chips and salsa placed in cabin daily. Two-way radio provided for convenience of people leaving the property on hikes or rides. **Facilities:** 1 restaurant, 1 bar (w/entertainment), games rm, lawn games, whirlpool, washer/dryer. Guest lounge with board games; video and book library. Hiking and biking trails, Frisbee golf course, stocked trout pond. Private trail rides are offered when guests want to ride, not at designated group-ride times. **Rates (AP):** Peak (mid-May–mid-Oct/mid-Dec–mid–Feb) $425–$765 ste. Lower rates off-season. MAP rates avail. Parking: Outdoor, free. Peak season Mountain Hideaway package ($475–$765 per couple per night, American Plan) includes cabin, stocked minibar, cocktails in lounge, wine with meals, three full meals, snacks in cabin, and all on-premise recreational facilities. Off-season B&B package ($150–$175 per couple per night, avail mid-Oct–mid-Dec

and mid-Feb–early May) includes cabin and an elaborate continental breakfast brought to cabin in a picnic basket. Fly-fishing, snowmobiling, and ATV ride packages avail. AE, DISC, MC, V.

Dayton

See Flathead Lake

Deer Lodge

Site of early Montana's territorial prison, which is open for self-guided tours. Grant-Kohrs Ranch, a National Historic Site, is located to the north of town. **Information:** Powell County Chamber of Commerce, 1171 Main St, PO Box 776, Deer Lodge, 59722 (tel 406/846-2094).

MOTELS

Deer Lodge Super 8

1150 N Main St, 59722; tel 406/846-2370 or toll free 800/800-8000; fax 406/846-2373. Exit 184 off I-90. Basic motel with adequate rooms near historic area. **Rooms:** 54 rms, stes, and effic. CI noon/CO 11am. Nonsmoking rms avail. **Amenities:** A/C, cable TV w/movies. **Services:** **Facilities:** **Rates:** Peak (June–Oct) $34–$40 S; $55–$70 D; $45–$85 ste; $60–$100 effic. Extra person $4. Children under age 5 stay free. Lower rates off-season. Parking: Outdoor, free. Senior rates avail. AE, DC, DISC, MC, V.

Scharf's Motor Inn

819 Main St, 59722; tel 406/846-2810 or toll free 800/341-8000; fax 406/846-3412. Adequate and clean accommodations; good for families. **Rooms:** 42 rms and effic. CI open/CO 11am. Nonsmoking rms avail. **Amenities:** A/C, cable TV. **Services:** **Facilities:** 1 restaurant (*see* "Restaurants" below), playground, washer/dryer. **Rates:** Peak (June–Sept) $32–$37 S; $37–$41 D; $37–$41 effic. Extra person $4. Children under age 10 stay free. Lower rates off-season. Parking: Outdoor, free. AE, DC, DISC, MC, V.

RESTAURANTS

Country Village

141 I-90 N; tel 406/846-1443. **Cafe.** Very pleasant hangout offering all the usual breakfast options: eggs, pancakes, and breakfast meats. The featured lunch special might be beef stir-fry, and pork cutlet is a typical dinner entree. Convenience store, gas, and gift shop available nearby. **FYI:** Reservations not accepted. Children's menu. Beer and wine only. **Open:** Daily 7am–9pm. **Prices:** Main courses $5–$7. AE, DISC, MC, V.

Scharf's Restaurant

819 Main St; tel 406/846-3300. Off I-90. **Cafe.** A small-town family cafe serving sandwich specials such as a German sausage sandwich with sauerkraut, Philly steak, and chicken Malibu (with ham and cheese). **FYI:** Reservations not accepted. Children's menu. Beer and wine only. **Open:** Peak (July–Aug) daily 6am–10pm. **Prices:** Main courses $4–$8. AE, CB, DC, DISC, MC, V.

ATTRACTIONS

Powell County Museum and Arts Foundation

1106 Main St; tel 406/846-3111. Housed in the old prison Mule Barn, the museum boasts one of the largest collections of Old West guns, cowboy artifacts, and saloon memorabilia in Montana. The Desert John's Saloon collection features 19th-century whiskey bottles, an old-style standing bar, and antique advertising signs. **Open:** Mem Day–Labor Day, daily 8am–9pm. **$$$**

Grant-Kohrs Ranch National Historic Site

Off I-90; tel 406/846-2070. Former headquarters of a mid-19th-century ranch that grazed more than one million acres in Montana, Wyoming, Idaho, Colorado, and Canada. Park rangers give guided tours of the 23-room ranch house, furnished with period antiques. Self-guided tours include the bunkhouse, blacksmith shop, wagon collection, and livestock. Craft demonstrations are given during the summer months. **Open:** Summer, daily 8am–5:30pm; rest of year, daily 9am–5pm. Closed some hols. **$**

Dillon

Located at the center of five stock-raising valleys, as evidenced by the large cattle herds and numerous hay-producing fields. Recreation opportunities range from fishing to rockhounding; Bannack State Park, site of the state's first major gold strike and first territorial capital, is a short drive away. **Information:** Beaverhead Chamber of Commerce, 125 S Montana, PO Box 425, Dillon, 59725 (tel 406/683-5511).

MOTELS

Sacajawea Motel

775 N Montana St, 59725; tel 406/683-2381. An older motel with a pleasant exterior. The lobby is filled with antiques and potted geraniums. **Rooms:** 15 rms and effic. CI open/CO 11am. Nonsmoking rms avail. Rooms have large tiled showers but no tubs. Accommodations for guests with disabilities are very spacious. **Amenities:** A/C, cable TV. No phone. **Services:** **Facilities:** Playground. **Rates:** $22 S; $28 D; $32 effic. Extra person $2. Children under age 2 stay free. Parking: Outdoor, free. DISC, MC, V.

Sundowner Motel

500 N Montana St, 59725; tel 406/683-2375 or toll free 800/524-9746. Exit 63 off I-15. Located near the college and

restaurants, this place garners repeat business from tournament-goers, families, businesspeople, and the fishing crowd. **Rooms:** 32 rms. CI open/CO 11am. Nonsmoking rms avail. Single rooms have king beds; other rooms have two queen beds. **Amenities:** A/C, cable TV w/movies. **Services:** Toiletries available at front desk. **Facilities:** Playground. Vehicle plug-ins in winter. **Rates (CP):** Peak (June–Oct) $33–$36 S; $39–$45 D. Extra person $3. Children under age 2 stay free. Lower rates off-season. Parking: Outdoor, free. AE, CB, DC, DISC, MC, V.

Super 8
550 N Montana St, 59725; tel 406/683-4288 or toll free 800/800-8000; fax 406/683-4288 ext 101. Exit 63 off I-15. Located near restaurants and downtown. **Rooms:** 47 rms and effic. CI 3pm/CO 11am. Nonsmoking rms avail. Accommodations for guests with disabilities feature two phones, shower chair, and removable, handheld shower head. **Amenities:** A/C, cable TV, refrig. Some rooms have microwaves. **Services:** **Facilities:** **Rates:** Peak (June–Sept) $40–$45 S; $50–$65 D; $55–$70 effic. Extra person $5. Children under age 12 stay free. Lower rates off-season. Parking: Outdoor, free. AE, CB, DC, DISC, MC, V.

The Town House Inn
450 N Interchange, 59725; tel 406/683-6831 or toll free 800/442-4667; fax 406/683-2021. Exit 63 off I-15. Lots of visual stimulation in the lobby, since the motel's pool, casino, and lounge are all open to the central area. **Rooms:** 46 rms and stes. CI open/CO 11am. Nonsmoking rms avail. Spacious rooms. **Amenities:** A/C, cable TV w/movies. **Services:** **Facilities:** 1 bar, playground, washer/dryer. **Rates (CP):** Peak (June–Sept) $49 S; $58 D; $62–$66 ste. Extra person $3. Children under age 12 stay free. Lower rates off-season. Parking: Outdoor, free. AE, DC, DISC, MC, V.

RESTAURANTS

Pappa T's Family Restaurant
10 N Montana; tel 406/683-6432. **Cafe.** Located in an old building with a tin ceiling, this eatery dishes up burgers of many varieties, pizzas, chicken, deli sandwiches, and salads. The walls are decorated with photographs of Montana. **FYI:** Reservations not accepted. Children's menu. **Open:** Daily 11am–10pm. **Prices:** Main courses $5–$10. AE, MC, V.

Wern Wok
17 E Bannack; tel 406/683-2356. **American/Chinese.** A small but clean place, with a nice atmosphere and over 100 items on its menu. Familiar dishes like fried rice and egg foo yung share table space with combination dinners. Steaks are also available. **FYI:** Reservations accepted. Children's menu. **Open:** Lunch Mon–Sat 11am–2pm; dinner Mon–Thurs 4–9:30pm, Fri–Sat 4–10pm, Sun 4–9pm. **Prices:** Main courses $4–$11. MC, V.

East Glacier

See Glacier National Park

Ennis

Located on the Madison River, which has an international reputation for excellent trout fishing. Good wildlife viewing at Cliff and Wade Lakes. **Information:** Ennis Chamber of Commerce, PO Box 291, Ennis, 59729 (tel 406/682-4388).

MOTEL

Riverside Motel and Outfitters
346 E Main St, PO Box 688, 59729; tel 406/682-4240 or toll free 800/535-4139; fax 406/682-7727. On MT 287. Simple, cabin-style motel, with large shade trees, near trout streams, as well as downtown and restaurants. Very friendly owners. **Rooms:** 12 rms and effic. CI 2pm/CO 11am. Nonsmoking rms avail. Flower boxes at each cabin door. Kitchenette units are fully stocked. **Amenities:** Cable TV w/movies, refrig. No A/C. **Services:** Babysitting. Licensed fishing guides available; guided river-float trips. **Facilities:** Playground. Barbecue area. **Rates:** Peak (June–Aug) $38 S; $50 D; $60–$75 effic; $75 cottage/villa. Extra person $5. Children under age 6 stay free. Lower rates off-season. Parking: Outdoor, free. Closed Dec–mid-May. DISC, MC, V.

RESTAURANTS

Ennis Cafe
Main St (Downtown); tel 406/682-4442. **American/Cafe.** A clean, spacious spot with a varied menu, best known for buffalo burgers and "secret ingredient" strawberry pie. **FYI:** Reservations not accepted. Children's menu. No liquor license. **Open:** Peak (June–Sept) daily 6am–11pm. **Prices:** Main courses $6–$13. No CC.

The Wild Rose Bistro
213 E Main; tel 406/682-4717. **New American.** The chef is a Los Angeles transplant, so expect a West Coast spin on the food. Breakfast choices feature prime rib hash with poached eggs, and smoked trout omelet. Lunch soups might be turkey wild rice, or roasted corn chowder with salmon. For dinner starters, there's flash-fried salmon cakes with béarnaise sauce, and sautéed mushrooms in a demiglacé. Among the entree picks are New York steak with cabernet reduction, and cappellini with snow crab sauced with a Parmesan cream. **FYI:** Reservations accepted. Children's menu. No liquor license. No smoking. **Open:** Peak (June–Aug) lunch daily 11:30am–2:30pm; dinner daily 5:30–10pm. Closed Oct–May. **Prices:** Main courses $11–$20. DISC, MC, V.

Essex

See Glacier National Park

Flathead Lake

See also Kalispell

The largest fresh-water lake west of the Mississippi River, Flathead attracts all types of water-sports enthusiasts. Wild Horse Island, maintained by the state as a day-use park, provides opportunities for hiking and picnicking. The town of Bigfork, located on the northeastern shore of the lake, is a popular hub for boaters and Rocky Mountain trekkers. On the opposite shore of the lake is Polson, which is close to wildlife refuges and Native American cultural centers.

MOTELS

Port Polson Inn

502 US 93, PO Box 1411, Polson, 59860 (Downtown); tel 406/883-5385 or toll free 800/654-0682; fax 406/883-3998. Located across the highway from the south end of Flathead Lake, this property provides unobstructed views of the water and the surrounding mountain landscape. **Rooms:** 44 rms, stes, and effic. CI noon/CO noon. Nonsmoking rms avail. Most rooms offer full view of the lake; ceiling fans and screened air vents facing the lake cool the rooms naturally. High-quality bedspreads and thick towels. Suites have recliners and large vanity areas. Honeymoon suite available. Two fully furnished apartments have private patio decks, complete kitchens, and separate bedroom with two queen beds. **Amenities:** Cable TV w/movies. No A/C. 1 unit w/terrace. Apartments are air conditioned; hair dryers in suites. **Services:** Car-rental desk. **Facilities:** Sauna, whirlpool, washer/dryer. Vehicle plug-ins in winter. Indoor and outdoor hot tubs. Public dock and beach a half-mile away. Public park adjacent to property. **Rates (CP):** Peak (mid-June–mid-Sept) $56 S; $66 D; $100–$150 ste; $66–$84 effic. Extra person $5. Children under age 16 stay free. Lower rates off-season. Parking: Outdoor, free. Commercial rates avail. Golf packages avail for eight area courses. AE, DC, DISC, MC, V.

Timbers Motel

8540 MT 35 S, PO Box 757, Bigfork, MT; tel 406/837-6200 or toll free 800/821-4546; fax 406/837-6200. ½ mi S of Bigfork. Popular with families and leisure travelers on a budget. Located a half-mile from a public lakeside park with a boat launch and areas for picnicking and swimming. **Rooms:** 40 rms. CI 2pm/CO 11am. Nonsmoking rms avail. **Amenities:** A/C, cable TV. **Services:** Babysitting. Complimentary morning coffee in lobby. Free local calls. Free, regularly scheduled, public trolley service in summer to/from local attractions. Pet fee $5. **Facilities:** Sauna, whirlpool, washer/dryer. Guests can use local health club. Premiere Eagle Bend 27-hole golf course is two miles away. **Rates:** Peak (mid-June–mid-Sept) $48–$55 S; $53–$58 D. Extra person $5. Lower rates off-season. Parking: Outdoor, free. MC, V.

RESORTS

Eagle Bend Golf and Yacht Community

279 Eagle Bend Dr, PO Box 960, Bigfork, 59911; tel 406/837-7333 or toll free 800/255-5641; fax 406/837-7347. On Flathead River, about 2 miles W of town. 400 acres. A full-service golfing and yachting community; rated the #2 new golf course in the nation by *Golf Digest.* This district, located at the north end of Flathead Lake and at the edge of a federally protected waterfowl area, has become a popular year-round vacation destination for all types of outdoor recreation. **Rooms:** 26 cottages/villas. CI 3pm/CO 11am. Nonsmoking rms avail. Accommodations are primarily townhouses, with one house available. Each unit is individually owned and decorated, generally with a western motif. **Amenities:** Refrig, VCR. No A/C. All units w/terraces, some w/fireplaces, some w/whirlpools. Each unit equipped with iron, ironing board, and microwave. Complimentary coffee and fruit basket for arriving guests. **Services:** Masseur, babysitting. Free, regularly scheduled summertime trolley service to most area attractions. **Facilities:** 27 4 30 1 restaurant, 1 bar, basketball, volleyball, racquetball, squash, spa, sauna, steam rm, whirlpool, washer/dryer. Trails through waterfowl refuge offer wildlife watching and photo opportunities. **Rates:** Peak (mid-June–mid-Sept) $936–$1,932 cottage/villa. Min stay. Lower rates off-season. Parking: Indoor/outdoor, free. Rates are weekly, and vary with size of unit. Three-day minimum stay during peak season; two-day during off season. Off-season long-term rates avail. MC, V.

Flathead Lake Lodge

MT 35, PO Box 248, Bigfork, 59911; tel 406/837-4391; fax 406/837-6977. 2,000 acres. Located on the north end of Flathead Lake, this full-service dude ranch has been in operation since 1945. Fun-filled, relaxing activities are centered on horses and ranching routines. Guests can join in as many ranch duties as they desire. **Rooms:** 17 rms; 20 cottages/villas. CI 2pm/CO 11am. Accommodations in two log lodges and 20 log cabins. Each individually decorated unit has a log-post bed. **Amenities:** No A/C, phone, or TV. **Services:** Car-rental desk, social director, children's program, babysitting. Staff teaches general horsemanship and rodeo skills. Evening campfires, and barn dances where visitors can learn how to line dance. Shuttle service to Glacier International Airport and Whitefish Amtrak station. **Facilities:** 4 90 1 restaurant, 1 beach (lake shore), lifeguard, basketball, volleyball, games rm, lawn games, snorkeling, playground, washer/dryer. On-premises activities include trail rides, overnight camping in teepees, chuck wagon breakfasts, lake cruises, and guest-participant rodeos. River rafting, flyfishing, and the 27-hole Premier Eagle Bend golf course are all nearby. **Rates (AP):** $1,456 S; $1,456 cottage/villa. Min stay. Parking: Outdoor, free. Weekly American Plan packages cover all on-premises recreation, activities, and meals. Adults, $1,456 per week; teens (age 13–19), $1,092; children (age 6–12), $952; children (age 3–5), $721; children (under age 3), $96. Closed Oct–May. AE, MC, V.

KwaTaqNuk Resort
303 US 93 E, Polson, 59860; tel 406/883-3636 or toll free 800/882-6363; fax 406/883-5392. 25 acres. Located on Flathead Lake, a few blocks from the center of town, this opened in 1992. Owned and operated by local confederated Salish and Kootenai Tribes. Nearby sporting clay facilities, river rafting, horseback riding, bike rentals, tennis, and golf. **Rooms:** 112 rms and stes. CI 3pm/CO 11am. Nonsmoking rms avail. Cityside and lakeside rooms available, all decorated with southwestern motif. King- or queen-size beds available. **Amenities:** A/C, cable TV. Some units w/terraces, 1 w/whirlpool. **Services:** Car-rental desk, social director. VCR and video rentals. Flathead Lake cruises from public dock. **Facilities:** 400 1 restaurant (*see* "Restaurants" below), 1 bar, 1 beach (lake shore), volleyball, games rm, whirlpool. Covered parking available. Restaurant has patio deck overlooking lake. Art gallery, plus large gift shop specializing in Native American and western art. **Rates:** Peak (June 16–Sept 15) $81–$96 S; $89–$104 D; $150 ste. Extra person $10. Children under age 16 stay free. Lower rates off-season. Parking: Outdoor, free. Lakeside rooms are $15 more. Senior and corporate rates, holiday and golf packages avail. AE, CB, DC, DISC, MC, V.

Marina Kay Resort
180 Vista Lane, Bigfork, 59911; tel 406/837-5861 or toll free 800/433-6516; fax 406/837-1118. On Bigfork Bay; ¼ mi from town center. 4 acres. A family resort complex located on waterfront, a few blocks from the town center. **Rooms:** 125 rms, stes, and effic. Executive level. CI 3pm/CO 11am. Nonsmoking rms avail. Offers accommodations ranging from one-bedroom units to three-bedroom condos. **Amenities:** A/C. All units w/terraces, some w/fireplaces, some w/whirlpools. Most units have two phones and refrigerators. All individually owned and decorated condo units have fireplaces; some have private hot tubs. **Services:** Car-rental desk, social director, masseur, babysitting. Free, regularly scheduled public trolley service to most area attractions during the summer months. **Facilities:** 180 2 restaurants, 2 bars (1 w/entertainment), volleyball, whirlpool, washer/dryer. Marina with charter fishing boat and watercraft rentals. Casual pub-style lounge has entertainment and dining; poolside Tiki Bar offers beverages and food. Family barbecue and live music every Sunday during the summer. Premier Eagle Bend 27-hole golf course is two miles away; public tennis courts are across street. **Rates:** Peak (June 22–Sept 16) $66–$100 S or D; $96 ste; $110–$266 effic. Extra person $5. Children under age 18 stay free. Lower rates off-season. Parking: Outdoor, free. Holiday, event, murder-mystery weekend, golf, snowmobiling, and "suite-deal" packages avail. AE, MC, V.

RESTAURANTS

★ Bigfork Inn
604 Electric Ave, Bigfork (Downtown); tel 406/837-6680. Corner of Grand. **Eclectic.** Once a country inn, this historic landmark now offers family dining in a western-style atmosphere incorporating rough cedar wood, exposed logs, and wildlife art. You'll find a good assortment of appetizers and entrees ranging from pasta to chicken-fried steak. Two favorites are the twice-roasted duck served with pecan, bing-cherry, and red-currant sauce; and the Cajun shrimp pasta with grilled red bell peppers, sautéed with angel-hair pasta in an Italian-style cream sauce. **FYI:** Reservations recommended. Dancing/jazz. Children's menu. **Open:** Daily 5–10pm. **Prices:** Main courses $10–$16. DISC, MC, V.

★ Pemmican Restaurant
In KwaTaqNuk Resort, 303 US 93 E, Polson (Downtown); tel 406/883-3636. **Eclectic.** Natural wood and earth-tone colors predominate the decor at this Native American–owned restaurant. Indian tacos and salads are typical lunch offerings, while dinner includes a nightly fresh-fish special, prime rib, and Cajun entrees—all served with traditional Indian fry bread. The children's menu features a coloring book. A private dock allows Flathead Lake boaters to dock and dine. **FYI:** Reservations recommended. Children's menu. **Open:** Peak (June–Sept 15) breakfast daily 6–11am; lunch daily 11am–2pm; dinner Sun–Thurs 5–10pm, Fri–Sat 5–11pm; brunch Sun 10am–2pm. **Prices:** Main courses $13–$16. AE, CB, DC, DISC, MC, V.

★ Show Thyme
548 Electric Ave, Bigfork (Downtown); tel 406/837-0707. **Eclectic.** Located in an old bank built in 1908, this casual hangout is noted for exceptional value and quality food and has many loyal patrons. Red-brick walls, lots of green plants, and natural lighting create a relaxing, gardenlike atmosphere. The lunch menu offers sandwich, burger, fish, and chicken specials; the signature dish on the dinner menu is rack of lamb with sun-dried sour cherries and rosemary-port demi-glacé, served with garlic mashed potatoes. **FYI:** Reservations recommended. Children's menu. No smoking. **Open:** Peak (June–Sept) Mon–Sat 11:30am–10pm. **Prices:** Main courses $10–$20. AE, DISC, MC, V.

Tuscany's Ristorante
331 Bridge St, Bigfork (Downtown); tel 406/837-6065. ½ block N of Swan River Bridge. **Italian.** Superb northern Italian dining in an elegant, warm, country atmosphere. The converted house is shaded by birch trees and has lots of flowers and an herb garden in front. Dining rooms are decorated with lace curtains and dried flower arrangements. From the outdoor dining patio, you can hear the rushing

waters of the nearby Swan River. The signature dishes include osso buco Milanese and veal scaloppine. Seafood specials complement the large selection of pasta entrees. Desserts include a double-chocolate flourless cake with brandy-whipped cream. **FYI:** Reservations recommended. Guitar/harp. Beer and wine only. No smoking. **Open:** Peak (June 1–Sept 15) daily 5–10pm. **Prices:** Main courses $10–$19. AE, MC, V.

REFRESHMENT STOP

Mission Mountain Winery
In Mission Mountain Vineyard, US 93 N, Dayton; tel 406/849-5524. **Winery.** Mission Mountain, Montana's only winery, has won many awards. The tasting room, with both a bar and tables, offers a nice lakeside view; a private dock allows Flathead Lake boaters to make a port call to sample the wines. Tours available. **Open:** Daily 10am–5pm. Closed Nov–Apr. MC, V.

ATTRACTIONS

National Bison Range
US 212, Moiese; tel 406/644-2211. 25 mi S of Flathead Lake. This federally protected 18,000-acre range is home to sheep, deer, elk, and antelope, as well as the rare bison. A 19-mile self-guided driving tour allows visitors a close-up look at the herds and scenic views of Mission Valley. Visitors center (located near Moiese), nature trails, picnic area. **Open:** Daily dawn–dusk. **$$**

Bigfork Art and Cultural Center
Village Sq, Bigfork; tel 406/837-6927. Nonprofit center providing space for lectures and classes as well as displays of works by local and regional artists. Gift shop sells local crafts. **Open:** Tues–Sat 11am–5pm. Closed some hols; Jan–Feb. **Free**

Fort Peck

See also Glasgow

A small town by the Fort Peck Dam on the Missouri River and the Fort Peck Indian Reservation. The dam's reservoir attracts boaters and fishing enthusiasts.

HOTEL

The Fort Peck Hotel
175 S Missouri St, PO Box 168, 59223; tel 406/526-3266 or toll free 800/560-4931; fax 406/526-3446. Listed on the National Register of Historic Places, this well-maintained 60-year-old hotel is within two blocks of historic Fort Peck Theater. **Rooms:** 38 rms. CI open/CO noon. Nonsmoking rms avail. Some rooms have shared bath. Chenille bedspreads, ceiling fans. Some rooms have antique furniture **Amenities:** No A/C, phone, or TV. Alarm clocks available. Old-fashioned bed warmers to take off the chill. **Services:** Babysitting. Complimentary shoe shine. **Facilities:** 1 restaurant, 1 bar. TV and phone in lobby. Guest privileges at local gym. Snowmobiling and ice fishing within 2 miles. **Rates (CP):** $36–$42 S or D. Children under age 12 stay free. Parking: Outdoor, free. AE, DISC, MC, V.

Gallatin Gateway

A small community located south of Bozeman on US 191. As its name implies, it is the gateway to Gallatin River and Gallatin National Forest. The river, noted for its fine trout fishing, was one of the filming sites for the movie *A River Runs Through It.*

HOTEL

Gallatin Gateway Inn
76405 Gallatin Rd, PO Box 376, 59730; tel 406/763-4672 or toll free 800/676-3522. 4 acres. A grand hotel of the railroad era, this authentically renovated property is listed on the National Register of Historic Places. Located in a country setting, just off the highway to Yellowstone National Park. **Rooms:** 35 rms and stes. CI 4pm/CO 11am. Nonsmoking rms avail. Spacious, comfortably appointed accommodations; some rooms are located in a carriage house annex. Bathrooms have pedestal sinks, which suit the time period but offer little counter space. Two rooms with shared bath are perfect for families. **Amenities:** Cable TV. No A/C. **Services:** Masseur. **Facilities:** 1 1 restaurant (dinner only; *see* "Restaurants" below), 2 bars, whirlpool, washer/dryer. **Rates (CP):** Peak (June–Sept) $60–$75 S; $65–$80 D; $85–$100 ste. Extra person $5. Children under age 12 stay free. Lower rates off-season. Parking: Outdoor, free. AE, DISC, MC, V.

RESTAURANT

Dining Room
In the Gallatin Gateway Inn, 76405 Gallatin Rd; tel 406/763-4672. Center of Gallatin Gateway. **New American.** Chef Erik Carr melds his classical training and European and California cooking experiences with fresh Montana ingredients to create marvelous dishes. Starters might be smoked trout cakes with cabbage-apple slaw and lemon-caper aioli, or grilled lamb chop with a lavender-thyme-honey-mustard glaze served with soft polenta and mint jus. Entree choices include corkscrew pasta with braised buffalo pancetta, caramelized mushrooms, and game broth; and sherry-braised rabbit with lentils, leeks, garlic, and sage. Winemaker dinners offered. **FYI:** Reservations recommended. Children's menu. No smoking. **Open:** Peak (June–Sept 15) dinner daily 6–9:30pm; brunch Sun 10am–2pm. **Prices:** Main courses $13–$28. DISC, MC, V.

Gardiner

Small tourist town at the north entrance to Yellowstone National Park. Various businesses cater to park visitors' recreational desires, ranging from rafting to snowmobiling. **Information:** Gardiner Chamber of Commerce, PO Box 81, Gardiner, 59030 (tel 406/228-2244).

MOTELS

Absaroka Lodge
US 89, PO Box 10, 59030; tel 406/848-7414 or toll free 800/755-7414; fax 406/848-7560. At the Yellowstone River Bridge. Newer, clean, simple property in the center of town. **Rooms:** 41 rms and stes. CI 2pm/CO 11am. Nonsmoking rms avail. Rooms have plain decor. **Amenities:** A/C, cable TV. Some units w/terraces. Balconies overlook Yellowstone River and Gallatin Mountains. Suites have refrigerators, coffeemakers, and microwaves **Services:** Masseur. Coffee available in small lobby. **Facilities:** On-site whitewater rafting. **Rates:** Peak (June 12–Sept 17) $40–$80 S; $40–$80 D; $50–$90 ste. Extra person $5. Children under age 12 stay free. Lower rates off-season. Parking: Outdoor, free. Cross-country ski and snowmobile packages available. AE, CB, DC, DISC, MC, V.

Best Western by Mammoth Hot Springs
US 89, PO Box 646, 59030; tel 406/848-7311 or toll free 800/828-9080; fax 406/848-7120. 1 mi from the N entrance of Yellowstone Nat'l Park. Clean and comfortable with newly decorated rooms. **Rooms:** 85 rms, stes, and effic. CI 4pm/CO 11am. Nonsmoking rms avail. Done in cheerful western decor, most rooms have beautiful views of the mountains and the Yellowstone River. **Amenities:** A/C, cable TV, dataport. Some units w/terraces, some w/whirlpools. **Services:** **Facilities:** 40 1 restaurant, 1 bar, sauna, whirlpool, washer/dryer. Outdoor deck with fine views. **Rates:** Peak (June 15–Sept 30/Dec 25–Mar 30) $43–$76 S; $45–$99 D; $80–$155 ste; $70–$145 effic. Extra person $5. Lower rates off-season. Parking: Outdoor, free. Snowmobiling and cross-country ski packages avail. AE, CB, DC, DISC, MC, V.

Westernaire Motel
US 89, PO Box 208, 59030; tel 406/848-7397. Well-maintained older motel; clean and quiet with a big repeat business. **Rooms:** 11 rms. CI noon/CO 10am. Nonsmoking rms avail. Large rooms with pine furniture; all have mountain views and a covered front porch with lawn chairs. **Amenities:** Cable TV. No A/C or phone. **Services:** **Facilities:** 1 restaurant (lunch and dinner only). Large lawn, barbecue patio. **Rates:** Peak (June 1–Sept 15) $32–$77 S; $32–$77 D. Extra person $5. Children under age 3 stay free. Lower rates off-season. Parking: Outdoor, free. MC, V.

Wilson's Yellowstone River Motel
14 Park St, PO Box 223, 59030; tel 406/848-7322. 2 blocks from Roosevelt Arch. Small, clean property in a quiet area at the edge of the Yellowstone River. It's an easy walk to restaurants, gift shops, and art gallery. **Rooms:** 38 rms and effic. CI 11am/CO 11am. Nonsmoking rms avail. Nice view of the mountains on the west side. **Amenities:** A/C, cable TV. Some rooms have refrigerators. **Services:** **Facilities:** Barbecue and picnic area on rear patio, overlooking the river. **Rates:** Peak (June 15–Sept 30) $30–$69 S; $30–$70 D; $65–$80 effic. Extra person $3. Lower rates off-season. Parking: Outdoor, free. Closed Nov–Apr. AE, CB, DC, DISC, MC, V.

Yellowstone Village Motel
US 89, PO Box 297, 59030; tel 406/484-7417 or toll free 800/228-8158; fax 406/848-7418. One mi from N entrance of Yellowstone Nat'l Park. A homey, comfortable, better-than-average motel. Very competitive rates. **Rooms:** 43 rms, stes, and effic. CI 3pm/CO 11am. Nonsmoking rms avail. Nice clean rooms. Accommodations on west side have great views of mountains. One- and two-bedroom condos and suites available. **Amenities:** A/C, cable TV w/movies. Fluffy towels and pretty linens. Condos and suites have refrigerators. **Services:** Babysitting. **Facilities:** Basketball, sauna, washer/dryer. Amazing view of mountains from indoor pool with adjoining deck. **Rates:** Peak (May 26–Sept 15) $34–$64 S; $38–$79 D; $50–$125 ste; $65–$150 effic. Extra person $5. Children under age 6 stay free. Lower rates off-season. Parking: Outdoor, free. AE, DISC, MC, V.

RESTAURANT

($) ★ Cecil's Restaurant
Park and 3rd St; tel 406/848-7561. Across from Roosevelt Arch and N entrance to Yellowstone Nat'l Park. **Eclectic.** Healthy dining is encouraged in this fun, casual place, with simple decor and an entertaining staff. Several vegetarian choices are included among the buffalo burgers and wild game specialties. Fresh trout and Mexican food are big hits here. Box lunches available. **FYI:** Reservations not accepted. Children's menu. Beer and wine only. **Open:** Daily 7am–10pm. Closed Oct 15–May 7. **Prices:** Prix fixe $6–$15. MC, V.

ATTRACTION

Yellowstone National Park
The original entrance to the park, this is the only one open to cars year-round. See "Yellowstone National Park" in the Wyoming chapter for full description.

Glacier National Park

See also Browning

So named because of the 48 slow-moving glaciers that continue to carve the valleys throughout an incredible expanse of over one million acres, Glacier National Park stands as the result of the efforts of naturalist George Bird Grinnell, co-founder of the Audubon Society. Established in 1910, it became the first international park in 1931. (Its official name is Waterton-Glacier International Peace Park, since it spills over into part of Alberta, Canada.) **Going-to-the-Sun Road,** a 50-mile drive traversing the park from West Glacier to St Mary, offers splendid views of glaciers, waterfalls, lakes, wildflowers, and wildlife; moose, elk, and grizzly bear can be found virtually anywhere along the route. Points of interest and overlooks are clearly marked along the road, and there is plenty of interpretive signage. The Loop, at the midpoint of the road, offers an excellent vantage point for views of 9,000-foot Heaven's Peak. (Note that Going-to-the Sun Road is open seasonally—usually early June to mid-October—and that park regulations exclude any vehicles over 20 feet long.)

Recreational opportunities in the park abound. **Lake McDonald,** the lagest of the park's 200 lakes, is teeming with trout (especially cutthroat, bull, rainbow, and brook) and pygmy whitefish. Glacier Park Boat Co (tel 406/752-5488) offers narrated boat tours. There are over 700 miles of hiking trails, ranging from easy nature walks to brutally steep backcountry treks. "Nature for Kids" activities (offered daily in summer) include evening campfire talks, slide show programs, and guided hikes. There are seven modern and 63 backcountry campgrounds scattered throughout the park; inquire at any visitors center about backcountry passes. In winter months, the park is taken over by snowshoers and cross-country skiers.

There are park entrances at West Glacier, Camas Road, St Mary, Many Glacier, Two Medicine, and Polebridge; visitors centers at Apgar, Logan Pass, and St Mary; and a ranger station at Many Glacier. For more information, contact Superintendent, Glacier National Park, West Glacier, MT 59936 (tel 406/888-5441)

HOTELS

Glacier Park Lodge

MT 49, East Glacier, 59434; tel 602/207-6000; fax 406/226-4404. Near jct US 2 and MT 49; across from Amtrak station. 600 acres. Built in 1913 by the Great Northern Railroad to entice wealthy travelers to visit the park via rail. The huge lobby, framed by massive log uprights and beams, is decorated with lots of live plants and wildlife art. Portraits of Blackfeet adorn the walls—part of the Native American motif that runs throughout. **Rooms:** 161 rms and stes. CI 3pm/CO 11am. Nonsmoking rms avail. Various accommodations available, with garden or mountain views. Economy rooms in the main lodge are small and have showers only; they're noisy because they open onto balconies overlooking the lobby. Suites in the main lodge have a private deck, king-size beds, and upgraded furnishings, while rooms in the annex are generally larger and offer tub/shower combinations. (Rooms are assigned at check-in, so special accommodations requests are subject to availability at that time.) **Amenities:** No A/C or TV. Some units w/terraces. **Services:** Car-rental desk, social director, babysitting. Will arrange river-rafting trips and tours. **Facilities:** 1 restaurant, 1 bar, basketball, volleyball, lawn games, washer/dryer. Bike rentals available two blocks away. Evening entertainment might feature a cabaret, Native American fireside talks, hayrides, or barbecues. **Rates:** $99–$145 S; $105–$151 D; $187 ste. Extra person $6. Children under age 12 stay free. Parking: Outdoor, free. Group rates avail through central reservations. Closed late Sept–mid-May. DISC, MC, V.

Lake McDonald Lodge

Going-to-the-Sun Rd, West Glacier, 59434; tel 602/207-6000; fax 406/226-4404. 11 mi from W entrance of park. Located on the eastern shore of Lake McDonald, this historic lodge has a large lobby with cedar-trunk beams and peeled-post balcony railings. Wildlife art, native-wood chairs, a stone fireplace, and a chandelier decorated with Native American symbols enhance the sublime natural setting. **Rooms:** 100 rms. CI 3pm/CO 11am. No smoking. Rooms carry through the Native American motif, with earth-tone colors and wooden walls. Accommodations are assigned at check in, so special requests are subject to availability at that time. **Amenities:** No A/C or TV. **Services:** **Facilities:** 1 restaurant (*see* "Restaurants" below), 1 bar, 1 beach (lake shore), volleyball, lawn games. Scenic coach tours on Going-to-the-Sun Rd depart from lodge, while narrated boat cruises on Lake McDonald depart from lodge's dock. **Rates:** $55–$100 S; $61–$106 D. Extra person $6. Children under age 12 stay free. Parking: Outdoor, free. Group rates avail through central reservations. Closed late Sept–early June. DISC, MC, V.

UNRATED Many Glacier Hotel

Swiftcurrent Lake, East Glacier, 59434; tel 602/207-6000; fax 406/226-4404. 12 mi W of Babb, off US 89. One of the grand hotels built by Great Northern Railroad to service wealthy travelers. No elevators. **Rooms:** 208 rms and stes. CI 3pm/CO 11am. Nonsmoking rms avail. Rooms are assigned at check in, so special requests are subject to availability at that time. **Amenities:** No A/C or TV. **Services:** Social director. **Facilities:** 1 restaurant, 1 bar (w/entertainment), 1 beach (lake shore). Scenic coach tours on Going-to-the-Sun Road depart from hotel, while narrated boat cruises on Swiftcurrent and Josephine Lakes depart from hotel's dock. **Rates:** $81–$146 S; $96–$146 D; $156 ste. Extra person $6. Children under age 12 stay free. Parking: Outdoor, free. Group rates avail through central reservations. Closed mid-Sept–early June. DISC, MC, V.

MOTELS

Mountain Pine Motel

MT 49 N, PO Box 260, East Glacier, 59434; tel 406/226-4403; fax 406/226-9290. ½ mi N of US 2. A small motel on direct route to east entrance to Glacier National Park. Clean, safe accommodations for budget-minded travelers. Lots of outdoor recreation opportunities plus evening entertainment at nearby Glacier Park Lodge. **Rooms:** 26 rms and effic. CI 2pm/CO 11am. Two family units sleep up to eight. Also, two houses have complete kitchens and two or three bedrooms—minimum stay of three-nights required. **Amenities:** Satel TV. No A/C. 1 unit w/terrace, 1 w/fireplace. **Services:** Babysitting. Complimentary shuttle to Amtrak station and car rental agencies. **Facilities:** **Rates:** Peak (June 15–Sept 15) $47 S; $52–$56 D; $60–$175 effic. Extra person $3. Children under age 5 stay free. Lower rates off-season. Parking: Outdoor, free. Closed Oct–Apr. AE, DC, DISC, MC, V.

Village Inn Motel

Apgar Village, West Glacier, 59434; tel 602/207-6000; fax 406/226-4404. About 2 mi off US 2 (follow signs). Located on the southern shore of Lake McDonald, near the West Glacier entrance to the park. **Rooms:** 36 rms, stes, and effic. CI 3pm/CO 11am. Nonsmoking rms avail. Guests on the first floor can park at their door. All rooms offer views of lake and surrounding mountains, and feature natural wood and earth-tone decor. Range of accommodations includes 12 economy rooms (no kitchen); 12 efficiencies (full kitchen); and 12 family units (that sleep up to 6). Rollaway beds available. Rooms are assigned at check-in; special requests (specific views, floor, cribs, etc.) are subject to availability at that time; special requests cannot be guaranteed by the reservations office. **Amenities:** No A/C, phone, or TV. **Services:** **Facilities:** 1 beach (lake shore). Scenic coach tours on Going-to-the-Sun Road, narrated boat cruises on Lake McDonald, Glacier Institute field classes given at various locations in the park. Nature trails and lake swimming available. **Rates:** $74 S; $80 D; $111 ste; $94–$112 effic. Extra person $6. Children under age 12 stay free. Parking: Outdoor, free. Group rates avail through central reservations. Closed late Sept–mid-May. DISC, MC, V.

INN

Izaak Walton Inn

Izaak Walton Inn Rd, PO Box 653, Essex, 59916; tel 406/888-5700; fax 406/888-5200. ½ mi off US 2; at milepost 180. 80 acres. Listed on the National Register of Historic Places, this property was built in 1939 at the southern tip of Glacier National Park as a hotel for rail crews on the Great Northern Railroad, and for tourists arriving at the park by train. Filled with railroad memorabilia, the knotty-pine-paneled lodge has an inviting lobby with a large, stone fireplace. Located at an elevation of 3,860 feet and surrounded by wilderness, the inn receives over 20 feet of snow a year and is internationally known as a cross-country ski destination. **Rooms:** 37 rms, stes, and effic. CI 3pm/CO 11am. No smoking. 1995 remodeling provided all accommodations with private bathrooms. Lodge rooms are decorated with period furnishings and quilted bedspreads. Four renovated cabooses (with outside decks) serve as efficiency suites. **Amenities:** No A/C, phone, or TV. Some units w/terraces, 1 w/fireplace. **Services:** Car-rental desk, social director, children's program, babysitting. Masseur available on request. Shuttle service to Amtrak station. In winter, ski instruction and rental equipment is available. **Facilities:** 1 restaurant (*see* "Restaurants" below), 1 bar, games rm, lawn games, sauna, washer/dryer, guest lounge. Recreation room offers table tennis, pool table, puzzles, and board games. Wildlife viewing area nearby. Groomed, partially lighted 33-km cross-country ski trail system; ski-waxing room. Hiking and mountain-biking trails in summer. **Rates:** $92 S or D; $126 ste; $425 effic. Extra person $5. Children under age 6 stay free. Min stay peak. AP rates avail. Parking: Outdoor, free. Three-night minimum stay in lodge rooms during holidays; three-night minimum stay in cabooses year-round. Various packages avail. MC, V.

RESTAURANTS

Cedar Dining Room

In Lake McDonald Lodge, Going-to-the-Sun Rd, West Glacier; tel 406/888-5431. About 10 mi from W entrance. **Regional American.** Diners get a majestic view of the lake and mountain peaks of Glacier National Park. Breakfast varies from continental style to a full buffet. Lunch offers traditional favorites—soups, salads, and burgers—as well as complete meals of meat loaf, salmon, pasta, and baked Montana whitefish. Dinner entrees feature roast duck, trout, steaks, and pasta. "Wellness Connection" choices are highlighted on the menu. Popular desserts include cinnamon ice cream and old-fashioned apple bread pudding with caramel sauce. **FYI:** Reservations not accepted. Children's menu. No smoking. **Open:** Breakfast daily 6:30–9:30am; lunch daily 11:30am–2pm; dinner daily 5:30–9:30pm. Closed late Sept–early June. **Prices:** Main courses $11–$19. DISC, MC, V.

★ The Dining Car

In Izaak Walton Inn, Izaak Walton Inn Rd, Essex; tel 406/888-5700. ¼ mi off US 2; near MP 180. **Regional American.** Diners at this unique eatery, located in a historic railroad hotel, have a clear view of the rail yard and passing trains. The menu continues the "train of thought" with appropriately named entrees such as the famous "Shortline," the restaurant's signature dish of huckleberry chicken served with fettuccine Alfredo. Lunch includes a good selection of soups, sandwiches, and burgers. **FYI:** Reservations not accepted. Children's menu. No smoking. **Open:** Daily 7am–8pm. **Prices:** Main courses $13–$20. MC, V.

★ Glacier Village Restaurant

304–308 US 2 E, East Glacier; tel 406/226-4464. At jct of US 2 and MT 49. **Cafeteria.** Home-cooked meals served in generous portions at modest prices are emphasized at this 40-year-old mainstay. Breakfast features apple-granola pancakes, European porridge, and glacier fried pie, while chicken pot pie and lasagna rank among the local dinner favorites. Pies and pastries are made on the premises. Lunch and dinner are available with self service or table service. **FYI:** Reservations not accepted. Children's menu. Beer and wine only. **Open:** Peak (mid-June–Labor Day) daily 6am–9pm. Closed Oct–Apr. **Prices:** Main courses $3–$8. MC, V.

($) The Restaurant Thimbleberry
MT 49 N, East Glacier; tel 406/226-5523. ½ mi off US 2 on MT 49. **Regional American.** Set in a log building with tables and benches made of logs, this small country eatery features a natural-wood-finished interior enhanced by wildlife and Native American art. It prides itself on serving typical home-style meals such as liver and onions, chicken-fried steak, and meatloaf, along with the usual chops, steaks, and roasts. Well known for St Mary's whitefish and Navajo fry bread. **FYI:** Reservations accepted. Children's menu. Beer and wine only. **Open:** Daily 7am–9:30pm. Closed Labor Day–Mothers Day. **Prices:** Main courses $5–$15. No CC.

✱ Villager Dining Room
304–308 US 2 E, East Glacier; tel 406/226-4464. At jct of US 2 and MT 49. **Continental.** A family-owned restaurant complex for over 40 years. The dining room offers a casual, fine-dining atmosphere, where specialties include lamb loin chops and Flathead Lake whitefish. Vegetarian and low-fat entrees are noted on the menu. Good selection of wines and microbrews. **FYI:** Reservations accepted. Children's menu. Beer and wine only. **Open:** Peak (mid-June–Labor Day) daily 5–9:30pm. Closed Oct–Apr. **Prices:** Main courses $8–$18. MC, V.

ATTRACTION

Museum of the Plains Indian and Crafts Center
Jct of MT 2 and MT 89 W, Browning; tel 406/338-2230. Exhibits highlight the creative achievements of Native American artists and craftsmen. Among the displays of costumes, ceremonial items, and tribal art is *Winds of Change,* a five-screen multimedia presentation about the evolution of tribal cultures on the Northern Plains. **Open:** June–Sept, daily 9am–5pm; Oct–May, Mon–Fri 10am–4:30pm. Closed some hols. **Free**

Glasgow

See also Fort Peck

Located in the Missouri River Valley in northeastern Montana. Fort Peck Dam is a half-hour drive from town. **Information:** Glasgow Area Chamber of Commerce and Agriculture, 740 E US 2, PO Box 832, Glasgow, 59230 (tel 406/228-2222).

MOTEL

Cottonwood Inn
US 2 E, PO Box 1240, 59230; tel 406/228-8213 or toll free 800/321-8213; fax 406/228-8248. Well-maintained, clean motel near railroad tracks. **Rooms:** 92 rms. CI noon/CO 11am. Nonsmoking rms avail. Large rooms are decorated in soft colors. **Amenities:** A/C, cable TV. Some units w/whirlpools. Refrigerators in some rooms. **Services:** **Facilities:** 1 restaurant, 1 bar, sauna, whirlpool, washer/dryer. Casino. **Rates:** $43 S; $58 D. Extra person $5. Children under age 12 stay free. Parking: Outdoor, free. Rooms with hot tub $70. AE, CB, DC, DISC, MC, V.

RESTAURANT

($) ✱ Sam's Supper Club
307 1st Ave N; tel 406/228-4614. **Mexican/Steak.** A casual, friendly eatery featuring Mexican dishes at lunch and steak and seafood for dinner. One specialty is walleye stuffed with seafood and baked in a wine sauce. Turtle cheesecake is a favorite for dessert, and there's a selection of blender drinks and imported beers. **FYI:** Reservations recommended. Children's menu. **Open:** Lunch Mon–Fri 11am–2pm; dinner Tues–Sat 5–10pm. **Prices:** Main courses $7–$12; prix fixe $11. MC, V.

Glendive

Located on the banks of the Yellowstone River, Glendive is a popular destination for fishing enthusiasts (paddlefish are especially plentiful), and rockhounds looking for moss agate and fossils. Nearby attractions include the Frontier Gateway Museum and the badlands of Makoshika State Park. **Information:** Glendive Chamber of Commerce and Agriculture, 200 N Merrill, PO Box 930, Glendive, 59330 (tel 406/365-5601).

HOTEL

Best Western Jordan Inn and Conference Center
223 N Merrill Ave, PO Box 741, 59330; tel 406/365-5655 or toll free 800/528-1234. A sky bridge connects a historic hotel to a more modern motel at this elaborate complex of hotel rooms, motel rooms, meeting rooms, banquet rooms, restaurants, and casino. **Rooms:** 95 rms and stes. CI noon/CO noon. Nonsmoking rms avail. Motel rooms are newly decorated, hotel rooms were being updated. **Amenities:** A/C, cable TV. Most units have hair dryers; suites offer microwave, wet bar, and refrigerator. **Services:** Babysitting. **Facilities:** 2 restaurants, 2 bars, games rm, sauna, washer/dryer. Guest privileges at local gym. Vehicle plug-ins in winter. 15 miles from fishing on the Yellowstone River. **Rates:** Peak (May–Sept) $42–$55 S; $46–$57 D; $59–$99 ste. Extra person $5. Children under age 12 stay free. Lower rates off-season. Parking: Outdoor, free. AE, CB, DC, DISC, MC, V.

MOTEL

Days Inn
2000 N Merrill Ave, 59330; tel 406/365-6011 or toll free 800/329-7466; fax 406/365-2876. Exit 215 off I-94, 2 blocks N. An exceptionally clean, quiet property on the east edge of town. Very competitive rates. Within walking distance to water slide, restaurant, bar, and casino. **Rooms:** 59 rms. CI 1pm/CO 11am. Nonsmoking rms avail. Large rooms with average decor. **Amenities:** A/C, cable TV. **Services:** Masseur. Hair dryers available at front desk. **Facilities:** **Rates (CP):** Peak (May–Sept) $28–$37 S; $38–$46 D. Extra person $5. Children under age 12 stay free. Lower rates off-season. Parking: Outdoor, free. AE, CB, DC, DISC, MC, V.

Great Falls

Montana's second-largest city, located at the falls of the Missouri River. Home of Malmstrom Air Force Base and the College of Great Falls. **Information:** Great Falls Area Chamber of Commerce, PO Box 2127, Great Falls, 59403 (tel 406/761-4434).

HOTELS

Best Western Heritage Inn
1700 Fox Farm Rd, 59404; tel 406/761-1900 or toll free 800/548-0361 in the US, 800/548-8256 in Canada; fax 406/761-0136. 1 block N of 10th Ave. A well-appointed, classy place with a festive atmosphere. New Orleans–style decorations feature lots of wrought iron, and huge skylights cover indoor pools. Ideal for families. **Rooms:** 239 rms and stes. CI 2pm/CO noon. Nonsmoking rms avail. **Amenities:** A/C, satel TV w/movies. Suites have wet bar. **Services:** Babysitting. **Facilities:** 1 1 1200 1 restaurant, 1 bar (w/entertainment), games rm, racquetball, sauna, washer/dryer. Casino. **Rates:** Peak (June–Aug) $53–$83 S; $69–$89 D; $80–$125 ste. Extra person $6. Children under age 12 stay free. Lower rates off-season. Parking: Outdoor, free. AE, CB, DC, DISC, MC, V.

Holiday Inn Great Falls
400 10th Ave S, 59405; tel 406/727-7200 or toll free 800/HOLIDAY, 800/257-1998, 800/626-8009 in MT. At 4th St. A three-story hotel best suited for meetings and business travelers. **Rooms:** 173 rms and stes. CI 2pm/CO noon. Nonsmoking rms avail. **Amenities:** A/C, cable TV w/movies, dataport. Some units w/terraces, 1 w/whirlpool. Nintendo. **Services:** **Facilities:** 600 1 restaurant, 1 bar. **Rates:** Peak (June–Sept 15) $54–$64 S; $59–$69 D; $125 ste. Extra person $5. Children under age 18 stay free. Lower rates off-season. Parking: Outdoor, free. AE, CB, DC, DISC, JCB, MC, V.

MOTELS

Best Western Ponderosa Inn
220 Central Ave, 59401 (Downtown); tel 406/761-3410 or toll free 800/266-3410; fax 406/761-3410. Located two blocks from Civic Center, this no-frills property offers adequate accommodations. **Rooms:** 105 rms and stes. CI 2pm/CO noon. Nonsmoking rms avail. **Amenities:** A/C, cable TV w/movies, refrig, dataport. 1 unit w/minibar. Microwave. **Services:** Car-rental desk. **Facilities:** 200 1 restaurant, 1 bar, games rm, sauna, washer/dryer. Rooftop pool. **Rates:** Peak (June–Aug) $48–$51 S; $53–$56 D; $100 ste. Extra person $5. Children under age 12 stay free. Lower rates off-season. Parking: Indoor, free. AE, CB, DC, DISC, ER, JCB, MC, V.

Comfort Inn of Great Falls
11 9th St Sq, 59403; tel 406/454-2727 or toll free 800/221-2222; fax 406/454-2727 ext 405. Built in 1993, this clean, neat, white-stucco building is across the street from a shopping mall and within a block of six movie screens. **Rooms:** 64 rms and stes. CI 1pm/CO 11am. Nonsmoking rms avail. One floor of this three-story building contains only nonsmoking rooms. **Amenities:** A/C, cable TV w/movies, dataport. Coffeemakers available upon request. **Services:** Babysitting. Pet fee $5/night. **Facilities:** 15 Games rm, whirlpool. **Rates (CP):** Peak (July–Sept) $54–$58 S; $65–$73 D; $65–$75 ste. Extra person $5–$10. Children under age 18 stay free. Lower rates off-season. Parking: Outdoor, free. AE, DC, DISC, MC, V.

Days Inn
101 14th Ave NW, 59404; tel 406/727-6565 or toll free 800/329-7466; fax 406/727-6308. Built in 1993, this small, clean motel is near the state fairgrounds. **Rooms:** 62 rms. CI 2pm/CO 11am. Nonsmoking rms avail. **Amenities:** A/C, cable TV w/movies. **Services:** **Facilities:** 15 Washer/dryer. **Rates (CP):** Peak (May–Aug) $35–$55 S; $35–$65 D. Extra person $5. Children under age 13 stay free. Lower rates off-season. Parking: Outdoor, free. AE, CB, DC, DISC, JCB, MC, V.

Super 8 Lodge
1214 13th St S, 59405; tel 406/727-7600 or toll free 800/800-8000; fax 406/727-7600. Economy-class motel with a Tudor-style exterior. Located near the biggest shopping center in town. **Rooms:** 117 rms and stes. CI 2pm/CO 11am. Nonsmoking rms avail. Some rooms have waterbeds. **Amenities:** A/C, cable TV w/movies. **Services:** **Facilities:** 10 **Rates (CP):** Peak (June–Aug) $36–$46 S; $44–$57 D; $36–$66 ste. Extra person $4. Children under age 12 stay free. Lower rates off-season. Parking: Outdoor, free. Weekly rates avail in off season. AE, CB, DC, DISC, MC, V.

RESTAURANTS

★ Borries
1800 Smelter Ave, Black Eagle; tel 406/761-0300. **Italian.** Located on the north side of the Missouri River, this no-frills restaurant is known for its pasta, steaks, and seafood. The Tuesday night special is prime rib; giant lobster dinners are offered occasionally. Separate bar has tables for dining. **FYI:** Reservations accepted. **Open:** Mon–Thurs 5–10pm, Fri 5–11pm, Sat 4–11pm, Sun 3–10pm. **Prices:** Main courses $5–$38. DISC, MC, V.

Jaker's
1500 10th Ave S; tel 406/727-1033. **American.** A classy, low-key spot, with lots of oak—the ideal venue for a power lunch. The lower deck area has a great view of 10th Ave S, supposedly the busiest street in Montana. Steak and seafood are the mainstays; ostrich is offered occasionally. **FYI:** Reservations recommended. Children's menu. **Open:** Lunch Mon–Fri 11:30am–2:30pm; dinner Mon–Thurs 5–10pm, Fri–Sat 5–11pm, Sun 4–10pm. **Prices:** Main courses $10–$37. AE, DISC, MC, V.

3–D International
1825 Smelter Ave, Black Eagle; tel 406/453-6561. **International.** 1996 marked the 50th anniversary of this inviting, friendly place. The wide-ranging menu offers a long list of Chinese, Thai, American, and Italian choices. Prime rib is the specialty Fri–Sun. In addition to French, Italian, and West Coast labels, the wine list boasts choices from Idaho and Montana's own Mission Mountain Johannesburg Riesling. **FYI:** Reservations accepted. Children's menu. **Open:** Mon–Thurs 5–10pm, Fri 5–10:30pm, Sat 4:30–10:30pm, Sun 4–10pm. **Prices:** Main courses $9–$33. DISC, MC, V.

ATTRACTIONS

C M Russell Museum Complex
400 13 St N; tel 406/727-8787. Charles Marion Russell, "America's Cowboy Artist," lived and worked in Great Falls. His hometown museum has a complete collection of original Russell paintings, bronzes, art, and personal memorabilia, in addition to works by his contemporaries. **Open:** May–Sept, Mon–Sat 9am–6pm, Sun 1–5pm; Oct–Apr, Tues–Sat 10am–5pm, Sun 1–5pm. Closed some hols. **$$**

Giant Springs State Park
4600 Giant Springs Rd; tel 406/454-3441. Each day, Giant Springs deposits almost 400 million gallons of water into the Roe River, making it the largest freshwater spring in the United States. An interpretive trail (which is wheelchair accessible) explains the natural wonder of the springs and details the local explorations of Lewis and Clark, who came through the area in 1805. Picnic area, playground, and neighboring trout hatchery. **Open:** Daily 7am–dusk. **$**

Ulm Pishkun State Park
Ulm-Vaughn Rd; tel 406/454-3441. Former site of buffalo jumping, the ritual in which ancient Native Americans ran thousands of bison off the cliffs of the Pishkun. The mass slaughter would usually occur in the fall, to provide buffalo meat for the winter. An interpretive trail atop the plateau describes the ceremony and the songs and dances that accompanied it. Picnic area. **Open:** Daily 7am–dusk. Closed to vehicles Oct 15–Apr 15. **Free**

Hamilton

Seat of Ravalli County, Hamilton is a rural community located in the scenic Bitterroot Valley of western Montana. **Information:** Bitterroot Valley Chamber of Commerce, 105 E Main St, Hamilton, 59840 (tel 406/363-2400).

MOTELS

City Center Motel
415 W Main St, 59840; tel 406/363-1651. 4 blocks W of US 93 S. Flower boxes and flower pots on walkway lend an attractive touch to this motel that draws budget-minded travelers for sporting events and festivals. Gets lots of repeat business. Also popular for family reunions. Public outdoor pool four blocks away. **Rooms:** 14 rms, stes, and effic. CI open/CO 11am. Nonsmoking rms avail. One suite is set up like an apartment. **Amenities:** A/C, cable TV. Seven efficiencies offer coffee machines, refrigerators, stoves with ovens, microwaves, and complete kitchen setups. **Services:** Coffee in lobby. Deposit required for male cats. **Facilities:** **Rates:** Peak (June–Aug) $36 S; $40–$46 D; $45 ste; $45 effic. Extra person $4. Children under age 6 stay free. Lower rates off-season. Parking: Outdoor, free. Group and commercial rates avail. AE, CB, DC, DISC, MC, V.

Hamilton's Comfort Inn
1113 N First St, 59840; tel 406/363-6600 or toll free 800/442-INNS; fax 406/363-5644. N edge of town on W side of US 93 S. Central location attracts fair and festival participants and spectators. Also popular for weddings and family reunions. **Rooms:** 65 rms. CI 2pm/CO 11am. Nonsmoking rms avail. Contemporary decor. Some rooms have recliners and sofas; king and queen beds available. **Amenities:** A/C, cable TV w/movies, voice mail. Dataports in some rooms. Two minisuites have wet bars, microwaves, refrigerators, and coffeemakers. **Services:** Free local calls. Fax and copying available. Pet fee $4/night. **Facilities:** 30 1 bar, sauna, whirlpool, washer/dryer. Casino and convenience store next door. Truck parking. Vehicle plug-ins in winter. **Rates (BB):** Peak (June 15–Sept 15) $48 S; $53–$55 D. Extra person $5. Children under age 12 stay free. Lower rates off-season. Parking: Outdoor, free. Senior, corporate, and trucker rates avail. AE, DC, DISC, MC, V.

Sportsman Motel
410 N First St, 59840 (Downtown); tel 406/363-2411. E side of US 93 S. Clean, safe rooms for budget-minded travelers. Attracts seniors, families, and truckers. **Rooms:** 19 rms. CI

2pm/CO 10am. Nonsmoking rms avail. Western-style decor in rooms. **Amenities:** A/C, cable TV. Six rooms have microwaves and refrigerators. **Services:** **Facilities:** Washer/dryer. Truck parking. **Rates:** Peak (June 1–Sept) $30 S; $35–$39 D. Extra person $5. Children under age 6 stay free. Lower rates off-season. Parking: Outdoor, free. Commercial rates avail. AE, CB, DC, DISC, MC, V.

RESTAURANTS

La Trattoria Italian Restaurant
315 S Third St (Downtown); tel 406/363-5030. 3 blocks W of US 93 S; between Bedford and Madison. **Italian.** Following Italian tradition, this family-run restaurant is also the owners' home; the decor of the 1909 house includes family photos as well as Italian country prints and stained-glass windows. The menu features classic, southern Italian cuisine with an emphasis on fresh, homemade pastas, including many recipes that have been in the family for generations. **FYI:** Reservations recommended. Children's menu. Wine only. No smoking. **Open:** Peak (June–Sept 3) Mon–Thurs 11:30am–9pm, Fri 11:30am–10pm, Sat 5–10pm. **Prices:** Main courses $7–$16. AE, DISC, MC, V.

Second Street Grill and Bar
163 S 2nd St (Downtown); tel 406/363-4433. Half block S of Main St. **Eclectic.** A small, casual place with a loyal local following. The wide variety offered here ranges from prime rib and swordfish to Cajun and Thai dishes. Swordfish tacos, salads, and small-portion plates offer grazing possibilities. Good selection of regional microbrews. **FYI:** Reservations not accepted. Jazz. Children's menu. Beer and wine only. No smoking. **Open:** Daily 11am–10pm. **Prices:** Main courses $5–$18. AE, DISC, MC, V.

ATTRACTION

Daly Mansion
251 Eastside Hwy; tel 406/363-6004. Built in 1910 as a summer home for the family of Irish immigrant and "copper king" Marcus Daly, this 24-bedroom Georgian revival mansion features Victorian-period antiques and several Italian marble fireplaces. The grounds include a tennis court, swimming pool, children's playhouse, and greenhouse. Tours can be arranged by appointment during the winter off-season. **Open:** Apr 15–Oct 15, daily 11am–4pm. Closed Oct 16–Apr 14 except by appointment. **$$**

Hardin

A ranching community bordering the Crow Indian Reservation. Site of the Little Bighorn Battlefield National Monument and the annual Custer's Last Stand Reenactment each June. **Information:** Hardin Area Chamber of Commerce and Agriculture, 219 N Center Ave, Hardin, 59034 (tel 406/665-1672).

MOTEL

The American Inn
1324 N Crawford, 59034; tel 406/665-1870 or toll free 800/582-8094; fax 406/665-1615. North edge of city. Located 12 miles from Custer Battlefield and Montana's largest gambling casino. Big Horn River, famous for fly fishing, and Yellowtail Dam are 45 miles away. **Rooms:** 42 rms. CI 11am/CO 11am. Nonsmoking rms avail. Pleasant rooms done in warm colors. The honeymoon suite has a heart-shaped hot tub. **Amenities:** A/C, cable TV w/movies. Some have refrigerators. **Services:** Friendly staff is knowledgeable on the history of the area. **Facilities:** Games rm, whirlpool, playground, washer/dryer. Good facilities for people with disabilities include well-maintained outdoor pool with lift, text phones for the hearing impaired; beds and door alarms are also appropriate for travelers with disabilities. Barbecue area. Nintendo available. **Rates (CP):** Peak (June 1–Sept 1) $30–$65 S; $35–$75 D. Extra person $5. Children under age 12 stay free. Lower rates off-season. Parking: Outdoor, free. Higher rates for Custer Reenactment and the Crow Fair. AE, DC, DISC, MC, V.

ATTRACTIONS

Big Horn County Historical Museum
Exit 497 off I-90; tel 406/665-1671. Fourteen-building complex includes a 1911 farmhouse, a barn and blacksmith shop, a county store, a one-room schoolhouse, and a post office. Farm exhibit with tractors, horse-drawn wagons, and other historic equipment; Native American artifacts and beadwork, locally made crafts for sale. Picnic area and self-guided tours. **Open:** May–Sept, daily 8am–8pm; Oct–Apr, Mon–Sat 9am–5pm. Closed some hols. **Free**

Bighorn Canyon National Recreation Area
MT 313, Fort Smith; tel 406/666-2412. See Lovell, WY for full description.

Havre

Historic railroading town, best known for Havre Beneath the Streets, a tour of the historic underground "city" comprising a bordello, opium den, bakery, and other merchants. **Information:** Havre Area Chamber of Commerce, 518 1st St, PO Box 308, Havre, 59501 (tel 406/265-4383).

MOTELS

Havre Super 8 Motel
166 19th Ave W, 59501; tel 406/265-1411 or toll free 800/800-8000; fax 406/265-1411 ext 200. Three-story, Tudor-style motel set back from main highway, across from Holiday Village Mall. **Rooms:** 64 rms and stes. CI 1pm/CO 11am. Nonsmoking rms avail. No dressers with drawers. **Amenities:** A/C, cable TV w/movies. **Services:** **Facilities:** **Rates:** Peak (June–Sept 5) $35–$41 S; $45–$49 D; $41–$69

ste. Extra person $3. Children under age 12 stay free. Lower rates off-season. Parking: Outdoor, free. Good deals in the off season on longer stays. AE, CB, DC, DISC, JCB, MC, V.

Havre Townhouse Inn
601 W 1st St, 59501; tel 406/265-6711 or toll free 800/442-INNS; fax 406/265-6213. Modern, two-story property located on the main highway through town. **Rooms:** 105 rms, stes, and effic. CI 2pm/CO 11am. Nonsmoking rms avail. Special accommodations include two honeymoon suites (one with free-standing hot tub, the other with whirlpool) and a three-bedroom town house with large fenced yard. Several suites have kitchenettes. **Amenities:** A/C, cable TV. 1 unit w/fireplace, some w/whirlpools. **Services:** Pet fee $3/night. **Facilities:** 150 1 bar, games rm, sauna, whirlpool, washer/dryer. Adjacent casino. **Rates:** Peak (May 15–Sept) $54 S; $56–$60 D; $74–$135 ste; $74–$135 effic. Extra person $4. Children under age 13 stay free. Lower rates off-season. Parking: Outdoor, free. AE, DC, DISC, MC, V.

RESTAURANTS

Andy's Supper Club
658 W 1st St; tel 406/265-9963. **Steak.** Sizzling steaks, steaks, and more steaks are served in this smartly appointed, red-and-black dining room. Prime rib is featured on Wednesday and Sunday nights. Comfortable seating at the semicircular bar. **FYI:** Reservations accepted. **Open:** Daily 5–11:30pm. **Prices:** Main courses $6–$22. MC, V.

Uncle Joe's Steakhouse
1400 1st St; tel 406/265-5111. **Steak.** Silver-painted tin ceilings and some tin paneling on the lower walls are about the only concessions to interior decoration at Uncle Joe's. Tables start where the bar stools end. Locals come here for good steak. **FYI:** Reservations accepted. **Open:** Tues–Sun 11am–11pm. **Prices:** Main courses $5–$40. MC, V.

ATTRACTIONS

Havre Beneath The Streets
100 3rd Ave; tel 406/265-8888. The businesses of early Havre were connected by underground tunnels. Stops on these historical underground tours include the Sporting Eagle Saloon (a turn-of-the-century honky tonk), a blacksmith shop, a Chinese laundry, and the post office, along with other stores that provided provisions for the people of this typical mining town. Reservations required. **Open:** Peak (June–Aug) Mon–Sat 9am–5pm, Sun 1–4pm. Closed some hols, Sun in off-season. **$$**

Fort Assinniboine National Historic Site
US 2; tel 406/265-4000. 6 mi SW of Havre on US 87. The fort was constructed in 1879 and served as the pioneer outpost of north central Montana. Today it is the home of the Northern Agricultural Research Center and its surviving buildings are open to visitors during guided tours. **Open:** June–Aug, daily, call for schedule. **$**

Helena

Former gold-mining town and present-day capital of Montana. Two local mines allow visitors to sift for sapphires and other gems. Nearby Canyon Ferry Recreation Area offers excellent fishing and wildlife viewing; migrating bald eagles are plentiful in late fall. **Information:** Helena Area Chamber of Commerce, 225 Cruse Ave, Helena, 59601 (tel 406/442-4120).

HOTELS

Best Western Colonial Inn
2301 Colonial Dr, 59601; tel 406/443-2100 or toll free 800/422-1002; fax 406/442-0301. Exit US 12 W (Prospect Ave) off I-15; turn left at light; 11th Ave becomes Colonial Dr. Spacious and well-kept; close to Capitol Complex and airport. Past guests have included John F Kennedy, Bob Dole, and Joan Baez. **Rooms:** 149 rms and stes. Executive level. CI 4pm/CO 11am. Nonsmoking rms avail. **Amenities:** A/C, cable TV, refrig, dataport, CD/tape player. Some units w/terraces, some w/fireplaces, some w/whirlpools. **Services:** Car-rental desk, babysitting. Very helpful front desk staff; 24-hour road condition information. **Facilities:** 350 1 restaurant, 1 bar, sauna, whirlpool, beauty salon, washer/dryer. **Rates:** Peak (June–Aug) $66–$69 S; $75–$82 D; $88–$99 ste. Extra person $7. Children under age 18 stay free. Lower rates off-season. Parking: Outdoor, free. AE, DC, DISC, MC, V.

Holiday Inn Express
701 Washington Ave, 59601; tel 406/449-4000 or toll free 800/HOLIDAY; fax 406/449-4522. Capitol Complex exit off I-15; W on US 12. Very nice hotel opened in 1995; located near Capitol Complex. **Rooms:** 75 rms, stes, and effic. CI 3pm/CO noon. No smoking. **Amenities:** A/C, cable TV, refrig, dataport. Some units w/minibars. **Services:** **Facilities:** 30 Washer/dryer. **Rates (CP):** Peak (June–Aug) $59 S; $65 D; $75–$85 ste; $75–$85 effic. Extra person $6. Children under age 19 stay free. Lower rates off-season. Parking: Outdoor, free. Corporate and government rates avail. AE, CB, DC, DISC, JCB, MC, V.

Park Plaza Hotel
22 N Last Chance Gulch, 59601 (Downtown); tel 406/443-2200; fax 406/442-4030. Attracts businesspeople because of downtown location. Close to walking mall, historic section, and cathedral. **Rooms:** 71 rms and stes. CI 3pm/CO 3pm. Nonsmoking rms avail. Spacious accommodations. **Amenities:** A/C, cable TV. Some units w/terraces. **Services:** Babysitting. **Facilities:** 200 1

restaurant, 2 bars (1 w/entertainment). **Rates:** $60–$65 S; $66–$72 D; $76–$120 ste. Extra person $6. Children under age 12 stay free. Parking: Outdoor, free. Corporate and government rates. AE, DC, DISC, MC, V.

MOTELS

Aladdin Motor Inn

2101 E 11th Ave, 59601; tel 406/443-2300 or toll free 800/541-2743; fax 406/442-7057. Attractive to business travelers and corporate groups. Near the Capitol Complex. **Rooms:** 72 rms and stes. CI 2pm/CO noon. Nonsmoking rms avail. Spacious and clean. **Amenities:** A/C, cable TV w/movies, refrig, dataport. Some units w/fireplaces. **Services:** **Facilities:** 1 restaurant (dinner only), 1 bar, sauna, steam rm, whirlpool, washer/dryer. Surveillance monitors in stairwells. **Rates:** $45 S; $58 D; $60 ste. Extra person $5. Children under age 10 stay free. Parking: Outdoor, free. AE, DC, DISC, MC, V.

Comfort Inn

750 Fee St, 59623; tel 406/443-1000 or toll free 800/228-5150; fax 406/443-1000. Exit US 12 off I-15 N or S to Prospect Ave. Located near Capitol Complex and museum, with easy access to airport and downtown. **Rooms:** 56 rms. CI 2pm/CO 11am. Nonsmoking rms avail. **Amenities:** A/C, cable TV. Some units have microwave, refrigerator, fold-out sofa. **Services:** Pets permitted in smoking rooms only. **Facilities:** Games rm, whirlpool. **Rates (CP):** Peak (Apr–Oct) $46–$58 S; $59–$66 D. Children under age 18 stay free. Lower rates off-season. Parking: Outdoor, free. Senior, corporate, government, and tour-group rates avail. AE, DC, DISC, MC, V.

Jorgenson's Holiday Motel

1714 11th Ave, PO Box 857, 59624; tel 406/442-1770; fax 406/449-0155. Capitol exit off I-15 N or S; take US 12 W, turn left at 3rd light. Three-section motel located near the Capitol Complex. **Rooms:** 117 rms and stes. CI open/CO noon. Nonsmoking rms avail. **Amenities:** A/C, cable TV w/movies. Some units w/whirlpools. Some rooms have refrigerators and microwaves. **Services:** **Facilities:** 1 restaurant, 1 bar, washer/dryer. **Rates:** Peak (June 12–Sept 31) $48–$56 S; $49–$61 D; $86–$95 ste. Extra person $4. Children under age 10 stay free. Lower rates off-season. Parking: Outdoor, free. AE, DC, DISC, MC, V.

Shilo Inn

2020 Prospect Ave, 59601; tel 406/442-0320 or toll free 800/222-2244; fax 406/449-4426. Off US 12 E. Located near Capitol Complex. **Rooms:** 47 rms and effic. CI 2pm/CO noon. Nonsmoking rms avail. **Amenities:** A/C, satel TV w/movies, refrig, VCR. All rooms include microwave. **Services:** **Facilities:** Sauna, steam rm, whirlpool, washer/dryer. **Rates (CP):** Peak (May 15–Oct 15) $69 S or D; $85 effic. Extra person $9. Children under age 12 stay free. Lower rates off-season. Parking: Outdoor, free. AE, CB, DC, DISC, EC, ER, JCB, MC, V.

RESTAURANTS

Ice Cream Parlor

718 Logan; tel 406/442-0117. North edge of Historical Helena. **American/Ice cream.** Once a family dairy, it now sells the ultimate cow end-product—40 flavors of it, to be exact. Booths, wire chairs, and antique decorative accents provide that old-fashioned ice cream parlor feel. If you aren't quite ready for sweets, you can order sandwiches, salads, burgers, or hot dogs. **FYI:** Reservations not accepted. Children's menu. No liquor license. **Open:** Peak (June–Sept) Sun–Wed 8am–10pm, Thurs–Sat 8am–10:30pm. **Prices:** Main courses $4–$7. No CC.

Queen City

42 S Park Ave; tel 406/443-3354. Historic Helena area; S end of town. **Seafood/Steak.** One of Helena's best places to celebrate a special occasion, Queen City offers a Victorian garden setting decorated with antiques and old silver serving pieces. Entree favorites are the fresh king salmon or cowboy steak. Children are welcome. Banquet room can accommodate tour groups. **FYI:** Reservations recommended. Children's menu. Beer and wine only. **Open:** Mon–Thurs 5:30–9pm, Fri–Sat 5:30–10pm. **Prices:** Main courses $8–$16. AE, DISC, MC, V.

Stonehouse

120 Reeder's Alley; tel 406/449-2552. South Park, historical area. **Regional American/American.** Located in an 1874 building that was originally a boarding house for miners. House specialties include prime rib au jus with a creamy horseradish sauce and vegetables Wellington (encased in pastry) served with a Mornay sauce. **FYI:** Reservations recommended. Children's menu. Beer and wine only. No smoking. **Open:** Peak (summer) lunch Mon–Fri 11:30am–2pm; dinner Mon–Sat 5–10pm, Sun 5–9pm. **Prices:** Main courses $12–$15. AE, CB, DC, DISC, MC, V.

Yat Son's Restaurant

2 S Last Chance Gulch; tel 406/442-5405. **American/Chinese.** Located in historic part of Helena near downtown. Chinese decor and music are background for generous portions of traditional, familiar menu choices. The bar serves wine and beer. **FYI:** Reservations accepted. Children's menu. Beer and wine only. **Open:** Peak (summer) dinner Tues–Sat 4–10pm, Sun 4–9pm. **Prices:** Main courses $4–$12. AE, DC.

ATTRACTIONS

Montana State Capitol

1301 6th Ave; tel 406/444-4794. Begun in 1899, the neoclassical building is made of Montana sandstone and granite with a dome of Montana copper. Historical paintings and statues decorate the interior; the House Chambers is adorned by the Charley Russell mural *Lewis and Clark Meeting the Flathead Indians at Ross' Hole*. **Open:** Mon–Sat 9am–5pm, Sun 11am–4pm. **Free**

Montana Historical Society
224 N Roberts; tel 406/444-4710. The Society's **Historical Museum,** founded in 1865, is dedicated to preserving Montana's heritage. The museum features the work of cowboy artist Charles M Russell and Yellowstone National Park photographer F Jay Haynes, in addition to Native American artifacts and archives on the Lewis and Clark expedition.

The Society also provides guided tours of the State Capitol (Mon–Sat, 10am–4pm; Sun, 11am–3pm) and manages a history library, temporary exhibits, photograph archives, a press, museum store, and education program. **Open:** Mem Day–Labor Day, Mon–Fri 8am–6pm, Sat–Sun 9am–5pm; Labor Day–Mem Day, Mon–Fri 8am–5pm, Sat 9am–5pm. Closed some hols. **Free**

Original Governor's Mansion
304 N Ewing; tel 406/444-4710. In 1888, entrepreneur William A Chessman originally built this 22-room home for his wife and their two children. The state of Montana acquired the handsome brick mansion in 1913 to serve as the first official governor's residence, and Montana's governors lived here until 1959. Today, the Queen Anne–style house's beautiful interiors are open to the public. All visitors must be on guided tours, which start on the hour from noon to 4pm. **Open:** June–Aug, Tues–Sun noon–5pm; Sept–Dec and Apr–May, Tues–Sat noon–5pm. Closed some hols. **Free**

Kalispell

See also Columbia Falls, Whitefish

Northern entrance to the Flathead Valley, nearby Big Mountain Ski and Summer Resort, and Glacier National Park. **Information:** Kalispell Area Chamber of Commerce, 15 Depot Park, Kalispell, 59901 (tel 406/752-6166).

HOTELS

Cavanaugh's at Kalispell Center
20 N Main St, 59901 (Downtown); tel 406/752-6660 or toll free 800/THE-INNS; fax 406/752-6628. 2 blocks S of jct of US 93 and US 2. Centrally located downtown next to convention center and adjacent to Kalispell Center Mall. Bike rentals one block away. Tennis courts within walking distance. **Rooms:** 132 rms, stes, and effic. Executive level. CI 4pm/CO noon. Nonsmoking rms avail. Rooms have dried flower arrangements and live plants, and most have chairs and ottomans. **Amenities:** A/C, cable TV w/movies. 1 unit w/fireplace, some w/whirlpools. Mini-suites have wet bars, refrigerators, and microwaves; two suites have fireplaces and hot tubs. Half the accommodations have dataports. Fluffy bathrobes in suites and mini-suites. **Services:** Car-rental desk, babysitting. Free ski shuttle to Big Mountain Ski Resort. **Facilities:** 1000 1 restaurant, 1 bar (w/entertainment), sauna, whirlpool. Indoor and outdoor hot tubs, as well as an indoor solarium lap pool. Casino. Sunday champagne brunch served in atrium. Discounted passes offered to local health club. **Rates:** Peak (May 16–Sept) $87 S; $97 D; $95–$140 ste; $95–$140 effic. Extra person $12. Children under age 18 stay free. Lower rates off-season. Parking: Outdoor, free. Senior, corporate, and government rates; golf, ski, river rafting, horseback riding, and fall foliage packages avail. AE, CB, DC, DISC, MC, V.

Kalispell Grand Hotel
100 Main St, PO Box 986, 59903 (Downtown); tel 406/755-8100 or toll free 800/858-7422; fax 406/752-8012. Corner of 1st St W. A historic landmark, this red-brick building retains its original stately decor with oak staircase, pressed-tin ceilings, and terrazzo floor. **Rooms:** 40 rms. CI 3pm/CO 11am. Nonsmoking rms avail. Richly appointed with dark cherry furnishings. Two-room family units available. **Amenities:** A/C, cable TV. Some units w/whirlpools. **Services:** Car-rental desk, babysitting. Pet deposit is $25. Complimentary 24-hour coffee and tea. **Facilities:** 25 2 restaurants (lunch and dinner only), 1 bar (w/entertainment), beauty salon. **Rates (CP):** Peak (July–Sept) $60–$72 S; $67–$84 D. Extra person $7. Children under age 12 stay free. Lower rates off-season. Parking: Outdoor, free. Senior, corporate, and group rates avail. AE, DISC, MC, V.

Ramada Klondike Inn
4834 US 93 S, 59901; tel 406/857-2200 or toll free 800/2-RAMADA; fax 406/857-2221. Jct US 93 and MT 82, 7 mi S of Kalispell. Full-service hotel/convention complex opened in 1994. Victorian-style lobby with beautiful chandeliers. Popular with golfers, conventioneers, leisure travelers, and families. **Rooms:** 102 rms and stes. Executive level. CI 3pm/CO 11am. Nonsmoking rms avail. Decorated with oak furniture and landscape prints, rooms have views of Flathead Lake, Glacier National Park, and adjacent mountain ranges. Family units sleep up to eight. **Amenities:** A/C, cable TV, voice mail. Some units w/terraces, some w/whirlpools. Executive suites are larger and offer dataports and more work space. Suite options include sauna, jet tubs, wet bars, refrigerators, and balconies. **Services:** Car-rental desk. VCRs, Nintendo games, and movies for rent. **Facilities:** 1000 1 restaurant, 1 bar, sauna, whirlpool. Indoor and outdoor pools and hot tubs. Elevated, indoor running track circles pool. Casino, grocery store, gas station, banquet rooms. Quarter-mile to public beach and boat launch. **Rates:** Peak (June 1–Sept 15) $59–$89 S or D; $85–$159 ste. Extra person $10. Children under age 16 stay free. Lower rates off-season. Parking: Outdoor, free. AE, CB, DC, DISC, JCB, MC, V.

Red Lion Inn
1330 US 2 W, 59901; tel 406/755-6700 or toll free 800/547-8010; fax 406/755-6717. 1 mi W of downtown. Located on the west side of town, this motel, restaurant, casino, and lounge complex offers easy access to main attractions of Big Mountain Ski and Summer Resort, Glacier National Park, and Flathead Lake. Fairgrounds a half-mile away. Golf course nearby. **Rooms:** 64 rms. CI 3pm/CO noon. Nonsmoking rms avail. **Amenities:** A/C, cable TV w/movies, dataport, voice mail. Some units w/terraces. All rooms have ski racks, irons, and ironing boards. Deluxe rooms are poolside and feature mountain views and private balconies. **Services:** Car-rental desk, babysitting. Fax and copying service available. Complimentary morning pastry and newspaper in lobby. **Facilities:** 1 restaurant, 1 bar (w/entertainment), whirlpool. Free pass to local full-service health club. **Rates:** Peak (June–Aug) $79 S; $84–$89 D. Extra person $10. Children under age 18 stay free. Lower rates off-season. Parking: Outdoor, free. Senior, commercial, government, and group rates avail. AE, DC, DISC, ER, JCB, MC, V.

MOTELS

Aero Inn
1830 US 93 S, 59901 (Kalispell City Airport); tel 406/755-3798 or toll free 800/843-6114; fax 406/752-1304. 1 mi S of downtown. Located adjacent to the city airport, this property attracts families on a budget and businesspeople. **Rooms:** 62 rms and effic. CI 3pm/CO 11am. Nonsmoking rms avail. Commercial-rate rooms are smaller, but have a desk area. One apartment unit has a kitchenette. **Amenities:** A/C, cable TV w/movies. 1 unit w/terrace, 1 w/fireplace. Apartment unit has fireplace. Roll-in showers for guests with disabilities. **Services:** **Facilities:** Games rm, sauna, whirlpool. Microwave in lobby. **Rates (CP):** Peak (June 11–Sept 11) $59 S; $64–$68 D; $98–$123 effic. Extra person $5. Children under age 5 stay free. Lower rates off-season. Parking: Outdoor, free. Senior, commercial, and pilot rates avail. AE, CB, DC, DISC, MC, V.

Best Western Outlaw Inn
1701 US 93 S, 59901; tel 406/755-6100 or toll free 800/237-7445; fax 406/756-8994. 10 blocks S of downtown. A large motel, restaurant, and entertainment lounge centrally located at the south end of Kalispell. City center 10 blocks away. Many repeat guests because of location and facilities. **Rooms:** 220 rms and stes. CI 2pm/CO 11am. Nonsmoking rms avail. Executive suites offer vaulted ceilings, king-size beds, and sofas. **Amenities:** A/C, cable TV w/movies, dataport, voice mail. Some units w/terraces, some w/whirlpools. Honeymoon suite has private hot tub and balcony. **Services:** Car-rental desk, babysitting. **Facilities:** 1 1000 1 restaurant, 1 bar, games rm, racquetball, sauna, whirlpool, beauty salon, playground, washer/dryer. Casino, tanning salon, two sun decks, two indoor pools, one indoor children's wading pool, four indoor hot tubs, sauna. **Rates:** Peak (June–Sept 15) $77–$114 S; $87–$134 D; $104–$124 ste. Extra person $10. Children under age 12 stay free. Lower rates off-season. Parking: Outdoor, free. Ski, golf, and other packages avail. AE, CB, DC, DISC, ER, JCB, MC, V.

Days Inn Kalispell
1550 US 93 N, 59901; tel 406/756-3222 or toll free 800/DAYS-INN; fax 406/756-3277. 1 mi N of jct US 93/US 2. Opened in 1991, but rooms and furnishings still look new. Attracts leisure travelers and businesspeople. **Rooms:** 53 rms. CI 2pm/CO 11am. Nonsmoking rms avail. Deluxe accommodations, equipped with a queen bed and a hide-a-bed, are larger than standard rooms. **Amenities:** A/C, cable TV w/movies. **Services:** Car-rental desk. **Facilities:** Free guest passes to local athletic club. **Rates (CP):** Peak (June 15–Sept) $59 S; $64–$69 D. Extra person $5. Children under age 12 stay free. Lower rates off-season. Parking: Outdoor, free. Golf packages and various discounts avail. AE, DC, DISC, JCB, MC, V.

Friendship Inn
1009 US 2 E, 59901; tel 406/257-7155 or toll free 800/424-4777, 800/759-2576 in the US, 800/477-2622 in Canada; fax 406/257-7170. 1 mi E of jct US 93 and US 2. Centrally located motel for budget-minded travelers. Public pool and park two blocks away. **Rooms:** 30 rms, stes, and effic. CI open/CO 11am. Nonsmoking rms avail. Half of rooms have showers only. **Amenities:** A/C, cable TV w/movies. Efficiency units offer kitchenettes or full kitchens. **Services:** Fax and copying available. 24-hour coffee and microwave in lobby. Movie selection at front desk for viewing in room. **Facilities:** Whirlpool, washer/dryer. Winter plug-ins available. **Rates (CP):** Peak (June 15–Sept 15) $45–$85 S; $55–$125 D; $55–$100 ste; $55–$100 effic. Extra person $10. Children under age 12 stay free. Lower rates off-season. Parking: Outdoor, free. Senior, commercial, and group rates avail. AE, CB, DC, DISC, MC, V.

RESTAURANTS

★ Dos Amigos
25 2nd Ave W (Downtown); tel 406/752-2711. At corner of 1st St W. **Mexican/Southwestern.** Built around an existing 1912 brick house, earth-tone colors and log cathedral ceiling add to the festive, southwestern ambience of this popular eatery. The menu features over 40 entrees ranging from Baja shrimp to Mexicali ribs. The cowboy caviar appetizer (layers of jalapeño cream cheese, black beans, monterey jack and cheddar cheeses, olives, onions, tomatoes, and sour cream) is a house favorite; other vegetarian dishes are also highlighted. Desserts might be fried ice cream or strawberry chimichangas. **FYI:** Reservations accepted. Children's menu. Beer and wine only. Additional location: Wisconsin Ave at Reservoir Rd, Whitefish (tel 862-9994). **Open:** Peak (June–Sept) Mon–Thurs 11am–10pm, Fri–Sat 11am–11pm, Sun 11:30am–10pm. **Prices:** Main courses $6–$14. AE, DISC, MC, V.

1st Avenue West
139 1st Ave W (Downtown); tel 406/755-4441. 2 blocks S of Kalispell Center Mall. **New American.** This casual fine-dining establishment specializes in corn-fed beef, seafood flown in from both coasts, and a variety of pasta entrees. Soups, salads, and sandwiches are also available, while appetizers and light snacks can be had throughout the day at the Montana version of an oyster bar. In addition to a large selection of wines by the glass, there are a dozen northwest microbrews. **FYI:** Reservations accepted. Children's menu. No smoking. **Open:** Lunch Mon–Fri 11am–3pm; dinner daily 5:30–10pm. **Prices:** Main courses $6–$15. AE, MC, V.

ATTRACTION

Conrad Mansion National Historic Site Museum
Fourth St E; tel 406/755-2166. A preserved, pre-1900 mansion with an original collection of period furniture, toys, and clothing displayed throughout its 23 rooms. Landscaped gardens; Christmas Victorian holiday bazaar. **Open:** May 15–June 14 and Sept 16–Oct 15, daily 10am–5:30pm; June 15–Sept 15, daily 9am–8pm. **$$**

Lewistown

Located at the geographical center of the state. Attractions include several wildlife management refuges and the ice caves and fossils of the Crystal Lake area. **Information:** Lewiston Area Chamber of Commerce, 408 NE Main St, PO Box 818, Lewiston, 59457 (tel 406/538-5436).

HOTELS

Historic Calvert Hotel
216 7th Ave S, 59457; tel 406/538-5411. This most unusual lodging was built in 1917 as a dormitory for Fergus County High School students unable to negotiate the roads by sleigh in winter. The two-story brick building with a central courtyard became a hotel in 1928 and is now on the National Register of Historic Places. It remains much the way it was when it was built. **Rooms:** 45 rms and effic. CI open/CO 11am. There are 6 apartments; 19 rooms with private bath (tub or shower or combo); and 19 rooms sharing a hall bath. Some accommodations have the original dormitory beds and wallpaper; all have antique furnishings. **Amenities:** Cable TV. No A/C or phone. **Services:** **Facilities:** The second-story fire escape is a metal-lined chute leading to a door that pops open on impact—quite marvelous. **Rates:** $15–$21 S; $28 D; $175–$225 effic. Parking: Outdoor, free. Apartments rented by the month only. Special room, pay 5 nights/stay 2 free; pay 9 nights/stay 5 free; pay 12 nights/stay 18 free. MC, V.

Yogo Inn of Lewistown
211 E Main St, 59457; tel 406/538-8721 or toll free 800/860-9646; fax 406/538-8969. Nice combination of hotel amenities, such as full bar and room service, and motel conveniences, such as self-parking. Large, sprawling building provides several quiet nooks with tables and chairs. Geared to groups and business travelers, but families will be comfortable here. **Rooms:** 124 rms. CI 1pm/CO noon. Nonsmoking rms avail. **Amenities:** A/C, cable TV. Some units w/terraces. **Services:** Car-rental desk, babysitting. **Facilities:** 300 1 restaurant (*see* "Restaurants" below), 1 bar (w/entertainment), games rm, whirlpool, beauty salon, washer/dryer. Banquet facilities. **Rates:** $49–$55 S; $59–$65 D. Extra person $7. Children under age 12 stay free. Parking: Outdoor, free. AE, CB, DC, DISC, MC, V.

MOTEL

Lewistown Super 8 Motel
102 Wendell, PO Box 616, 59457; tel 406/538-2581 or toll free 800/800-8000; fax 406/538-2702. Right on US 87 and MT 200, this Tudor-style motel has few extras, but offers clean accommodations. Cafe, restaurant, and casino across the street. **Rooms:** 44 rms. CI 2pm/CO 11am. Nonsmoking rms avail. **Amenities:** A/C, cable TV w/movies. **Services:** **Facilities:** Washer/dryer. **Rates:** $38 S; $44 D. Extra person $3. Children under age 6 stay free. Parking: Outdoor, free. AE, CB, DC, DISC, MC, V.

RESTAURANTS

Pete's Drive Inn and Fireside Restaurant
1308 W Main; tel 406/538-9400. **Diner.** For 1950s nostalgia, this is the place. Converted from an old A&W, it still has working speakers on the drive-in side, but you have to go inside to pick up the food. You might try the fries with triple-patty hamburgers or their specialty, marinated "broasted" chicken. **FYI:** Reservations not accepted. No liquor license. **Open:** Peak (June–Sept) daily 5:30am–10pm. **Prices:** Main courses $2–$8. No CC.

The Whole Famdamily
206 W Main St; tel 406/538-5161. **Deli.** Deli sandwiches with a health-food inclination and fresh-baked breads made from Montana wheat are the ticket on this menu. Two dinner specials are served after 5pm. Lunch is generally crowded. **FYI:** Reservations accepted. Dress code. Beer and wine only. No smoking. **Open:** **Prices:** Main courses $6–$8. AE, DISC, MC, V.

Yogo Garden
In Yogo Inn of Lewistown, 211 E Main St; tel 406/538-8721. **American.** Hotel restaurant with bar across the lobby and several dining areas and a counter. A few booths afford some privacy, but since the dining room opens to the lobby, passers-by can watch you eat. Known primarily for steak dinners, there is also a children's menu, and a small wine list. **FYI:** Reservations accepted. Piano. Children's menu. Dress code. **Open:** Peak (June–Sept) daily 6am–10pm. **Prices:** Main courses $9–$14. AE, CB, DC, DISC, MC, V.

Little Bighorn Battlefield National Monument

15 mi S of Hardin, 1 mi E of MT 90. This site memorializes one of the last armed efforts of Northern Plains Indians to preserve their traditional way of life against the encroachment of white settlers. On June 25, 1876, more than 200 US soldiers of the 7th Cavalry were killed by an overwhelming number of Sioux and Cheyenne warriors at this location. Among the dead was Lt-Col George Armstrong Custer.

At the site is a national cemetery, monuments, memorials, a visitors center, and a historical museum with maps, photographs, and dioramas depicting the battle. The park is open year-round, park rangers and Native American guides give free tours and programs on various topics relating to the battle. For more information, contact Box 39, Crow Agency, MT 59022 (tel 406/638-2622).

Livingston

A historic railroad and cattle ranching town located in the Paradise Valley. The Yellowstone River flows through the valley, which is nearly surrounded by the Gallatin and Absaroka Ranges of the Rocky Mountains. **Information:** Livingston Chamber of Commerce, 212 W Park, Livingston, 59047 (tel 406/222-0850).

HOTEL

Murray Hotel

201 W Park St, 59047; tel 406/222-1350; fax 406/222-6745. Built in 1904 for East Coast visitors wanting to experience the Wild West. The hotel has its original 1905 Otis elevator (still in fine working order) in case you choose to not use the marble stairs. Film director Sam Peckinpah lived here in the 1970s, and his suite is available. **Rooms:** 32 rms, stes, and effic. CI 2pm/CO 11am. Nonsmoking rms avail. Individually decorated rooms are tastefully old fashioned; most have a separate living area. **Amenities:** A/C, cable TV. Most rooms have refrigerators; suites have coffeemakers and wet bars. **Services:** **Facilities:** 150 1 restaurant, 1 bar (w/entertainment), whirlpool. Espresso bar with fresh pastries in lobby; hot tub on the roof; guest privileges at the Firehall Athletic Club. **Rates:** Peak (June–Oct) $39–$49 S; $46–$56 D; $65–$150 ste; $60–$70 effic. Extra person $3. Lower rates off-season. Parking: Outdoor, free. Airline employee and group discounts. Weekend and ski packages avail. AE, DISC, MC, V.

RESTAURANT

Livingston Bar and Grill

130 N Main St; tel 406/222-7909. **American.** Housed in the original "Bucket of Blood Bar," where Calamity Jane entertained upstairs, this eatery is steeped in history. Check out the antique French backbar while you dine on Rocky Mountain oysters, buffalo burgers, or Louisiana-style seafood gumbo. Don't expect any fancy decor here, but do come for the good food. **FYI:** Reservations recommended. **Open:** Peak (Mem Day–Sept) Mon–Sat 11:30am–10pm, Sun 5–10pm. **Prices:** Main courses $11–$40; prix fixe $13–$20. MC, V.

Lolo

Located about 10 miles south of Missoula, at the crossroads of US 90, US 93, and US 12. Lolo Hot Springs Resort is west of town.

LODGE

Fort Lolo Hot Springs

38500 US, 12 W, PO Box 386, 59870; tel 406/273-2201; fax 406/777-5844. 7 mi E of Lolo Pass on US 12; 25 mi W of Lolo. Located against a backdrop of lodgepole pines, this property adjoins LoLo Hot Springs Resort on the Lewis & Clark Expedition Trail. The building is screened from the highway by pointed upright logs, log and rail fencing is used for walkways, and wood chips provide general ground cover. **Rooms:** 34 rms. CI open/CO 11am. Natural peeled-log decor and oak furnishings embellish 12 deluxe rooms, which are twice the size of the motel-like rooms in the Old Town section. The six executive rooms offer better views. Hot water comes from the natural hot springs. **Amenities:** No A/C, phone, or TV. **Services:** **Facilities:** 30 1 restaurant, 1 bar (w/entertainment), volleyball. Complimentary access to mineral hot-springs pool complex. The Eatery and Saloon offers casino games for adults and video games for kids. Guided horse trail rides and hiking and mountain biking trails nearby. Snowmobilers and cross-country skiers can leave right from their rooms. **Rates:** $36–$59 S; $42–$69 D. Extra person $12. Parking: Outdoor, free. MC, V.

RESORT

Lolo Hot Springs Resort

38500 US 12 W, 59847; tel 406/273-2294 or toll free 800/273-2290; fax 406/273-3677. 7 miles E of Lolo Pass. 112 acres. Situated in an alpine setting, this all-teepee property offers a rather unique sleeping experience. **Rooms:** 10 cottages/villas. CI open/CO noon. 18-foot diameter teepees with cedar-chip floors sleep six to eight people. **Amenities:** No A/C, phone, or TV. **Services:** Social director, children's program. **Facilities:** 1 restaurant (*see* "Restaurants" below), 1 bar (w/entertainment), volleyball, games rm, lawn games, playground. The hot mineral springs–

pool complex consists of picnic area, indoor pool, and outdoor pool; daily pool passes cost $4/adult, $2/children under 12. The full-service Eatery and Saloon offers video games for children, casino machines for adults. 80 RV sites with full hook-ups and unlimited tent camping area; dump stations, showers, and lawn games available. Trout fishing in adjacent stream; hiking and mountain biking trails. Guided horse trail rides, plus a horse corral. **Rates:** $25 cottage/villa. Parking: Outdoor, free. RV sites with full hook-ups $18. Tenting $13. Closed Oct–May. DISC, MC, V.

RESTAURANTS

Guy's Lolo Creek Steakhouse
6600 US 12 W; tel 406/273-2622. ¼ mi W of US 93 S on US 12 W. **Steak.** This steakhouse has a large local following and an excellent reputation. Each of the almost 200 logs used in the construction of the building was hand-hewn and fitted; wagon-wheel-and-antler chandeliers and wildlife art complete the western atmosphere. The menu specializes in Montana products, which means lots of beef. Steaks are cooked over a wood-fueled, open-pit fire; seafood, chicken, and pork entrees are also available. **FYI:** Reservations not accepted. **Open:** Tues–Thurs 5–10pm, Fri–Sat 5–10:30pm, Sun 5–10pm. **Prices:** Main courses $10–$25. AE, DISC, MC, V.

Lolo Hot Springs Eatery and Saloon
In Lolo Hot Springs Resort, 38500 US 12 W; tel 406/273-2290. 25 mi W of Lolo; 7 mi E of Lolo Pass. **Regional American.** Named for the natural mineral springs where the Lewis & Clark Expedition stopped on their trip out west (in 1805) and again on their eastbound return (in 1806). The signature entree here is meaty barbecue pork. The popular half-pound LoLo burger is typical of the large portions served here. Catering is available. Guests can take a dip in the mineral springs. **FYI:** Reservations accepted. Country music/dancing. Children's menu. **Open:** Peak (mid-May–Sept) daily 8am–10pm. **Prices:** Main courses $9–$20. DISC, MC, V.

Miles City

Site of historic Fort Keogh (once the largest army post in the state), Miles City has a large historic district and is a major livestock center. **Information:** Miles City Area Chamber of Commerce, 901 Main St, Miles City, 59301 (tel 406/232-2890).

MOTELS

Best Western War Bonnet Inn
1015 S Haynes Ave, PO Box 1055, 59301; tel 406/232-4560 or toll free 800/528-1234; fax 406/232-0363. Exit 138 off I-94. Clean and cheerful rooms. Property has been newly decorated in bright colors. **Rooms:** 54 rms and stes. CI noon/CO noon. Nonsmoking rms avail. **Amenities:** A/C, cable TV. Suites have minibar, microwave, and hair dryer. **Services:** **Facilities:** Sauna, whirlpool. **Rates (CP):** Peak (May–Sept) $46–$71 S; $52–$79 D; $95 ste. Extra person $5. Children under age 12 stay free. Lower rates off-season. Parking: Outdoor, free. Senior and commercial rates avail. AE, CB, DC, DISC, MC, V.

Comfort Inn
1615 S Haynes Ave, 59031; tel 406/232-3141 or toll free 800/228-5150; fax 406/232-2924. Exit 138 off I-94. New, sparkling, pleasant facility boasts oak furniture and cheerful colors. **Rooms:** 49 rms and stes. CI noon/CO 11am. Nonsmoking rms avail. Light, clean rooms. **Amenities:** A/C, cable TV. Suite has VCR and refrigerator. **Services:** Babysitting. Coffee available in lobby 24 hours; complimentary newspapers. **Facilities:** 35 Games rm, whirlpool, washer/dryer. Truck parking. **Rates (CP):** $44 S; $49–$54 D; $57–$62 ste. Extra person $5. Children under age 15 stay free. Parking: Outdoor, free. AE, DC, DISC, MC, V.

Super 8 Motel
I-94 and MT 59, 59301; tel 406/232-5261 or toll free 800/800-8000; fax 406/232-5262. Exit 138 off I-94, 1 mi S. Clean and adequate. On south edge of town; adjacent to miniature golf. **Rooms:** 58 rms. CI 2pm/CO 11am. Nonsmoking rms avail. **Amenities:** A/C, cable TV. **Services:** **Facilities:** Truck parking. **Rates (CP):** Peak (June 1–Sept 15) $34 S; $45 D. Extra person $5. Children under age 12 stay free. Lower rates off-season. Parking: Outdoor, free. AE, DC, DISC, MC, V.

RESTAURANT

$ Hole In The Wall
602 Main St; tel 406/232-9887. **Seafood/Steak.** Housed in an 1875 building, the decor includes historic pictures of the Hole-In-The-Wall Gang, and the 19th-century bar has an actual bullet hole in it. Owned and operated by the same family since 1947, this hangout now specializes in Montana beef and freshly baked breads and pies. **FYI:** Reservations accepted. Children's menu. **Open:** Breakfast daily 5–10am; lunch daily 11am–5pm; dinner daily 5–10pm. **Prices:** Main courses $6–$12; prix fixe $9. MC, V.

ATTRACTION

Range Riders Museum
W Main St; tel 406/232-6146. This wide-ranging museum, consisting of nine buildings, houses everything from a 400-piece gun collection to a restored Indian Wars–era fort. A one-room school is furnished with pioneer-period furniture, a heritage center displays mid- to late-19th-century photographs of local ranches, and the Charles M Russell Gallery contains nearly 200 Western prints. The Coach House is home to collections of antique wood planes, livestock brands, and early telegraph equipment. **Open:** Apr–Oct, daily 8am–8pm. **$**

Missoula

See also Lolo

Surrounded by mountains and situated along the banks of the Clark Fork River, Missoula is the third-largest city in Montana. Missoula is bordered by national forests to the north, south, and west; the National Bison Range is 30 miles north of town. Home of the University of Montana. **Information:** Missoula Area Convention and Visitors Bureau, 825 E Front, PO Box 7577, Missoula, 59807 (tel 406/543-6623).

PUBLIC TRANSPORTATION

The Missoula Urban Transportation District (the Mountain Line) (tel 406/721-3333) serves Missoula with 12 routes. Fares: adults 65¢, seniors/disabled/children age 5 and older 35¢; children under 5 ride free. Exact change required.

HOTELS

Holiday Inn Parkside
200 S Pattee St, 59802 (Downtown); tel 406/721-8550 or toll free 800/399-0402; fax 406/721-7427. On N side of Clark Fork River; 1 block E of Higgins Ave. Located five blocks from the University of Montana, this property attracts families and groups attending university events. River trails adjacent to property for walking, biking, and in-line skating. **Rooms:** 200 rms and stes. CI 4pm/CO noon. Nonsmoking rms avail. **Amenities:** A/C, cable TV w/movies, dataport. Some units w/terraces. All interior rooms have private balconies overlooking the atrium. **Services:** Car-rental desk. Fax and copy services. **Facilities:** 600 2 restaurants, 1 bar (w/entertainment), games rm, sauna, whirlpool. Casino. **Rates:** $78–$82 S; $85–$89 D; $110–$200 ste. Extra person $7. Children under age 19 stay free. MAP rates avail. Parking: Outdoor, free. River-view rooms $4 extra. Ski, honeymoon, and bed-and-breakfast packages avail. AE, CB, DC, DISC, ER, JCB, MC, V.

Village Red Lion Inn
100 Madison Ave, 59802 (Downtown); tel 406/728-3100 or toll free 800/RED-LION; fax 406/728-2530. 1 block S of Broadway Ave; across from Clark Fork River. Located across the Clark Fork River from the University of Montana campus, it's convenient for families attending university events. **Rooms:** 172 rms and stes. CI 3pm/CO noon. Nonsmoking rms avail. Rooms are larger than typical motel room. Family units available. **Amenities:** A/C, cable TV w/movies, dataport, voice mail. Some units w/terraces, some w/whirlpools. Iron. Suites have wet bars, refrigerators, and two TVs **Services:** Car-rental desk. Complimentary newspapers. **Facilities:** 1000 2 restaurants, 1 bar (w/entertainment), whirlpool, beauty salon. **Rates:** Peak (May–Oct) $72–$82 S; $85–$95 D; $100–$200 ste. Extra person $5–$10. Min stay special events. Lower rates off-season. MAP rates avail. Parking: Outdoor, free. Riverside rooms cost $10 more. Golf, ski, fishing, and romance packages avail. AE, CB, DC, DISC, MC, V.

MOTELS

Best Western Executive Inn
201 E Main St, 59802 (Downtown); tel 406/543-7221 or toll free 800/528-1234; fax 406/543-7225. Between Pattee and Main; 1 block E of Higgins Ave. Located near the center of town and within walking distance of restaurants and stores; close to University of Montana. **Rooms:** 51 rms and stes. Executive level. CI 1pm/CO noon. Nonsmoking rms avail. Most rooms overlook pool. **Amenities:** A/C, cable TV w/movies, voice mail. Suites offer king-size beds, refrigerators, microwaves, skylights, and more table space with chairs. **Services:** Car-rental desk. **Facilities:** 1 restaurant (bkfst and lunch only). Covered parking. **Rates:** Peak (mid-May–mid-Oct) $50–$55 S; $55–$65 D; $77–$85 ste. Extra person $5. Children under age 12 stay free. Lower rates off-season. Parking: Outdoor, free. Senior and commercial rates avail. Off-season plan offers third night free. AE, CB, DC, DISC, EC, ER, JCB, MC, V.

Days Inn Westgate
8600 Truck Stop Rd, 59802; tel 406/721-9776 or toll free 800/DAYS-INN; fax 406/721-9781. Take I-90 to exit 96, at US 93 N and MT 200 W. Located on the access route to Flathead Lake and Glacier National Park, it's adjacent to a truck plaza served by several 24-hour restaurants and gas stations. **Rooms:** 69 rms. CI open/CO 11am. Nonsmoking rms avail. Pleasing floral design in rooms. **Amenities:** A/C, satel TV. **Services:** Twice-daily maid svce, car-rental desk. VCRs and movies for rent; complimentary morning coffee, juice, and doughnuts in lobby. Pet fee $5/night. **Facilities:** 16 1 restaurant, 1 bar, whirlpool, beauty salon, washer/dryer. Parking for large trucks. **Rates (CP):** Peak (May 15–Oct 15) $56–$62 S; $66–$80 D. Extra person $5. Children under age 12 stay free. Lower rates off-season. Parking: Outdoor, free. Senior, trucker, military, government, and corporate rates avail. AE, DC, DISC, MC, V.

Econo Lodge
1609 W Broadway, 59802; tel 406/543-7231; fax 406/728-1930. 2 blocks W of Russell Ave, on Business MT 200 E. Located across from the Greyhound bus station, it attracts budget-minded travelers looking for a clean, safe place for the night. **Rooms:** 79 rms. CI 2pm/CO 11am. Nonsmoking rms avail. Some accommodations offer king-size beds and over-stuffed chairs with foot stools. Deluxe room is larger, with king-size bed and sofa bed. **Amenities:** A/C, cable TV. Deluxe room offers wet bar. **Services:** Poolside beverage service available. Pet deposit is $25. **Facilities:** 1 restaurant, 1 bar (w/entertainment), washer/dryer. Large courtyard with pool area, plus safe play area for children. Casino. **Rates (CP):** Peak (May–Sept) $50–$75 S; $60–$85 D. Extra person $10. Children under age 18 stay free. Lower rates off-season. Parking: Outdoor, free. Senior, commercial, government, and long-term rates avail. AE, CB, DC, DISC, MC, V.

4B's Inn Motel and Conference Center
3803 S Brooks St, 59801 (South End); tel 406/251-2665 or toll free 800/272-9500; fax 406/251-5733. On Business US 93 S and US 12 W. Contemporary, inviting property. Lobby features a fireplace, lots of seating, and wildlife art. **Rooms:** 90 rms. CI 2pm/CO 11am. Nonsmoking rms avail. **Amenities:** A/C, cable TV, dataport, voice mail. **Services:** Car-rental desk. Complimentary shuttle (four scheduled runs daily) to airport, mall, and hospital; unscheduled runs are $5 for first person and $2 for each additional. Free local calls. Meals at adjacent restaurant can be charged to room; complimentary coffee and newspaper in lobby. **Facilities:** 450 1 restaurant, whirlpool, washer/dryer. Complimentary guest passes for local health club. **Rates:** Peak (mid-May–mid-Sept) $50–$60 S or D. Lower rates off-season. Parking: Outdoor, free. Rates determined by number of beds in room. Senior and commercial rates; ski and shopping packages avail. AE, DISC, MC, V.

Orange St Budget Motor Inn
801 N Orange St, 59802 (North Side); tel 406/721-3610 or toll free 800/328-0801; fax 406/721-8875. Exit 104 off I-90; 1 block S. Budget motel located four blocks from the center of town, within walking distance of restaurants and stores and 1½ miles from University of Montana. **Rooms:** 81 rms and effic. CI 6pm/CO 11am. Nonsmoking rms avail. One apartment with complete kitchen and separate living room is available for long-term lease. **Amenities:** A/C, cable TV. Third-floor rooms designed for businesspeople (dataports, recliners, large work tables). Some rooms have water beds. **Services:** Car-rental desk. VCRs and movies for rent. Complimentary coffee, tea, and cocoa in lobby 24-hours; iced tea in afternoon during summer; hot cider in winter; newspapers. Fax and copy services available. Pet fee $10/night. **Facilities:** 30 **Rates (CP):** Peak (May 1–Oct) $51 S; $53–$58 D; $80 effic. Extra person $3. Children under age 12 stay free. Lower rates off-season. Parking: Outdoor, free. Senior, commercial, government rates avail. AE, DC, DISC, MC, V.

Red Lion Inn
700 W Broadway St, 59802 (West Broadway); tel 406/728-3300 or toll free 800/RED-LION; fax 406/728-4441. I-90 exit 104 (Orange St); 4 blocks W of Orange St on Business US 200 W. Located near the highway and the University of Montana, the property features attractive landscaping. Public recreation facilities across street (tennis, pool, basketball, playground, picnic area, and walking paths). **Rooms:** 76 rms. CI 3pm/CO noon. Nonsmoking rms avail. Rooms, larger than average, open to covered walkways. Half of rooms have showers only; half have tub/shower combo. **Amenities:** A/C, cable TV, dataport. Irons and ironing boards. **Services:** Car-rental desk, social director, babysitting. Fax, copying, secretarial, and computer services available. Free local calls. Fresh cookies in lobby. **Facilities:** 60 1 restaurant, whirlpool. Guest passes to local full-service athletic club cost $5. **Rates:** Peak (May 15–Sept 15) $59–$86 S; $69–$96 D. Extra person $10. Children under age 18 stay free. Lower rates off-season. Parking: Outdoor, free. Off-season program offers third night free. Senior and corporate rates, winter sports packages avail. AE, CB, DC, DISC, MC, V.

Rodeway Inn Southgate
3530 Brooks St, 59801 (South Side); tel 406/251-2250 or toll free 800/247-2616; fax 406/251-2006. On Business US 93; 1 block N of Reserve St. Located near the south end of town, across from the Southgate Mall. **Rooms:** 81 rms. Executive level. CI 3pm/CO noon. Nonsmoking rms avail. Family suites are large, and sleep up to six. **Amenities:** A/C, cable TV. 1 unit w/whirlpool. Some rooms have dataports and coffeemakers. Family suites have large-screen TVs with VCRs. Honeymoon suite has red, heart-shaped, two-person jet tub and complimentary champagne and red rose. **Services:** Car-rental desk, social director. Complimentary 24-hour coffee, tea, and cocoa; newspaper; and use of microwave. Shuttle service to hospital, golf courses, and to/from car dealerships and car rental agencies. Designated pick-up point for river-rafting trips. **Facilities:** 20 Sauna, whirlpool, washer/dryer. **Rates (CP):** Peak (May 1–mid-Sept) $62 S; $58–$69 D. Extra person $6. Children under age 18 stay free. Lower rates off-season. Parking: Outdoor, free. Senior and commercial rates; ski, golf, and shopping packages avail. AE, CB, DC, DISC, MC, V.

RESTAURANTS

Alley Cat
125½ W Main St (Downtown); tel 406/728-3535. Off Higgins Ave and W Front St. **Regional American/French.** French cafe style and atmosphere enhance the French-influenced menu choices at this casual restaurant. Entrees range from fresh salmon with white-mushroom sauce to breast of duck with apricot-and-cherry chutney. Fresh herbs and spices are used in the creative sauces. Gourmet desserts. **FYI:** Reservations recommended. Beer and wine only. No smoking. **Open:** Mon–Sat 5–9:30pm. **Prices:** Main courses $14–$19. AE, MC, V.

★ The Depot
201 W Railroad (Downtown); tel 406/728-7007. 1 block W of Higgins Ave. **Eclectic.** The red-brick walls, wood-mosaic tables, fireplace, and oak decor conjure up an old-world feeling in this casual eatery noted for prime rib and fresh seafood. An open-air garden bar offers appetizers and light fare. **FYI:** Reservations recommended. **Open:** Daily 5:30–11pm. **Prices:** Main courses $10–$21. AE, DC, DISC, MC, V.

★ Goldsmith's Premium Ice Cream
809 E Front St; tel 406/721-6732. Across from University of MT. **Cafe.** This old-fashioned, soda fountain–style cafe is especially noted for its 24 flavors of homemade ice cream. It also offers great omelettes and pancakes for breakfast; burg-

ers and sandwiches for lunch; and popular vegetarian entrees for dinner. An outside patio overlooks the Clark Fork River. **FYI:** Reservations not accepted. Children's menu. No liquor license. No smoking. **Open:** Peak (June–Sept) Sun–Thurs 7am–10:30pm, Fri–Sat 7am–11pm. **Prices:** Main courses $5–$8. No CC.

Greenleaf Cafe and Restaurant
In Hammond Arcade Building, 101 S Higgins Ave (Downtown); tel 406/728-5969. Corner of Front St and Higgins Ave. **Mediterranean.** Filled with live plants, this casual cafe has nice natural lighting. The continental/Mediterranean cuisine focuses on pasta, seafood, lamb, veal, and chicken entrees. Traditional favorites are lamb kabob, hummus, marinated lentil salad, and kibbeh (ground lamb with spices and herbs). Dinners-to-go are available for local hotel and motel guests. **FYI:** Reservations recommended. Children's menu. No liquor license. No smoking. **Open:** Peak (May–Aug) Tues–Sun 10am–9pm. **Prices:** Main courses $6–$17. AE, CB, DC, MC, V.

The Lily Restaurant
515 S Higgins Ave (Downtown); tel 406/542-0002. Above the Crystal Theatre; ½ block S of Higgins Ave Bridge. **New American/Thai.** This small restaurant, upstairs from the Crystal Theatre, is known to locals for its quiet ambience. Seasonal favorites include the pan-seared breast of duck served on fricassee of snow peas, wild mushrooms, and homemade fettucine with orange bourbon reduction; roasted corn crab cakes (fresh crab meat tossed with roasted corn, bell peppers and goat cheese, then served with a chipotle-cream sauce); and Thai pineapple-prawns served with jasmine rice. The in-house bakery is noted for its tasty desserts. A stair-climber provides access for diners with disabilities. **FYI:** Reservations accepted. Beer and wine only. No smoking. **Open:** Tues–Sat 5–9:30pm. **Prices:** Main courses $10–$19. AE, MC, V.

The Mustard Seed
419 W Front St (Downtown); tel 406/728-7825. ½ block W of Orange St Bridge. **American/Japanese.** An Oriental cafe-style restaurant with a casual family atmosphere. Individual servings and family-style portions of dishes like spring rolls, chicken teriyaki, and shrimp-fried rice are reasonably priced. Vegetarian choices are also available. **FYI:** Reservations not accepted. Children's menu. Beer and wine only. No smoking. Additional location: Southgate Mall (tel 542-7333). **Open:** Peak (May–Sept) lunch Mon–Fri 11am–2:30pm, Sat–Sun noon–5pm; dinner Mon–Thurs 5–9:30pm, Fri–Sat 5–10pm, Sun 5–9:30pm. **Prices:** Main courses $9–$11. AE, DC, DISC, MC, V.

★ Zimorino's Red Pies Over Montana
424 N Higgins Ave (Downtown); tel 406/549-7434. Between Pine and Spruce. **Italian.** The name comes from the 1950s movie *Red Skies Over Montana,* with Richard Widmark, but the food comes from old family recipes perfected in the Italian bakeries and pizzerias of New York. Pizzas are hand-tossed in view of patrons, and sausages and meatballs are made on the premises. Servers move quickly through the place, which has a festive, noisy atmosphere. Very popular—there is generally a waiting line of 20 minutes on weekdays and 40 minutes on weekends in the summer. An espresso bar and selection of microbrews round out the offerings. **FYI:** Reservations not accepted. Children's menu. Beer and wine only. No smoking. **Open:** Sun–Thurs 5–10pm, Fri–Sat 5–10:30pm. **Prices:** Main courses $8–$15. MC, V.

ATTRACTIONS

Historical Museum at Fort Missoula
Building 322, off South Ave; tel 406/728-3476. Located on 32 acres at the site of historic Fort Missoula (1877–1947). The museum comprises 12 historic structures containing over 15,000 artifacts. At the visitors center (formerly the quartermaster's storehouse), there are exhibits on the fort's history as 19th-century pioneer outpost, World War I training center, and World War II alien detention center. Other buildings include a carriage house, a church, a schoolhouse, and a guard cabin; all have indoor galleries. Self-guided tour maps; guided tours available with advance notice. **Open:** Mem Day–Labor Day, Mon–Sat 10am–5pm, Sun noon–5pm; Labor Day–Mem Day, Tues–Sun noon–5pm. Closed some hols. **$**

University of Montana
Arthur Ave; tel 406/243-0211. Established in 1893, the campus combines traditional brick buildings and tree-lined walks with modern facilities such as the Maureen and Mike Mansfield Library, the Montana Theatre (with two stages), and Washington-Grizzly Stadium. The **Museum of Fine Arts/ Paxon Gallery** features contemporary visual arts.

Missoula Museum of the Arts
335 N Pattee; tel 406/728-0447. Permanent collection of 19th- and 20th-century Northwest art displayed in what was once the city's Carnegie Library. Donation requested. **Open:** Mon–Fri noon–5pm. Closed some hols.

Moiese

One of western Montana's smallest rural ranching towns, located on MT 212 at the entrance to the National Bison Range.

RESTAURANT

Burger "B"
4924 MT 212; tel 406/644-2385. **Burgers.** This small walk-up/dine-out burger place is located at the entrance to the National Bison Range. The lean buffalo burger is especially popular. Although the layout offers a couple of picnic tables, most patrons drive the quarter-mile to the Range's nature trail and picnic area, where there's ample room for a picnic

amid the sights and sounds of nature. A small convenience store adjoins Burger "B"; the nearest restrooms are at the Range's visitor center or its picnic area. **FYI:** Reservations not accepted. No liquor license. **Open:** Daily 11:30am–7:30pm. **Prices:** Lunch main courses $3–$5. No CC.

Nevada City

HOTEL

Nevada City Hotel

MT 287, PO Box 338, 59755; tel 406/843-5377 or toll free 800/648-7588. Looks like a movie set, with boardwalks running in front of the cabins and two-story log hotel in this re-created western town. Check out the two-story outhouse in the back. **Rooms:** 14 rms; 17 cottages/villas. CI 4pm/CO 10am. Everything is clean but old, with some period antiques in the smallish accommodations. **Amenities:** No A/C, phone, or TV. **Services:** Social director. **Facilities:** 1 restaurant (bkfst and lunch only). **Rates:** $45–$60 S or D; $45–$60 cottage/villa. Extra person $5. Children under age 12 stay free. Parking: Outdoor, free. Closed Oct–May. AE, DISC, MC, V.

Polson

See Flathead Lake

Red Lodge

At the foot of the Beartooth Mountains and the north end of the Beartooth Scenic Byway. Legend says its name comes from the Red Lodge Clan of the Crow tribe, who covered their teepees with the local red clay. **Information:** Red Lodge Chamber of Commerce, 601 N Broadway, PO Box 988, Red Lodge, 59068 (tel 406/446-1718).

HOTEL

Pollard Hotel

2 N Broadway, 59068 (Downtown); tel 406/446-0001 or toll free 800/POLLARD; fax 406/446-3733. Listed on the National Register of Historic Places, this elegant and quiet 100-year-old hotel has been recently renovated for $3.5 million. Buffalo Bill Cody, Calamity Jane, and Jeremiah Johnson were guests here. Very good rates. **Rooms:** 36 rms and stes. CI 4pm/CO noon. No smoking. Exquisite appointments in every individually decorated room. A few suites have stained-glass windows above the whirlpool. Huge closets. Beautiful mountain views from west side of building; some rooms overlook atrium. **Amenities:** A/C, cable TV. Some units w/terraces, some w/whirlpools. Down pillows are standard but may be replaced with non-allergenic ones. **Services:** Masseur, babysitting. Turndown service with chocolates or cookies. **Facilities:** 50 1 restaurant (*see* "Restaurants" below), 1 bar, racquetball, sauna, steam rm, whirlpool. **Rates (BB):** Peak (June 15–Sept/Dec 15–Mar) $75–$150 S; $85–$115 D; $115–$200 ste. Extra person $10. Children under age 2 stay free. Lower rates off-season. Parking: Outdoor, free. AE, MC, V.

MOTEL

Best Western LuPine Inn

702 S Hauser, 59068; tel 406/446-1321 or toll free 800/528-1234; fax 406/446-1465. Located on quiet street one block from Rock Creek. **Rooms:** 46 rms, stes, and effic. CI 3pm/CO noon. Nonsmoking rms avail. Wardrobes in rooms. West-facing rooms have mountain views. **Amenities:** A/C, cable TV. Some units w/terraces, some w/whirlpools. Dataports available on request. **Services:** Masseur, babysitting. **Facilities:** 100 Games rm, sauna, whirlpool, playground, washer/dryer. Ski wax rooms. **Rates:** Peak (June–Aug) $36–$57 S; $41–$57 D; $45–$61 ste; $61–$71 effic. Extra person $5. Children under age 12 stay free. Lower rates off-season. Parking: Outdoor, free. Ski club and group rates. AE, CB, DC, DISC, MC, V.

RESORT

Rock Creek Resort

Rte 2, PO Box 3500, 59068; tel 406/446-1111; fax 406/446-3688. 4½ mi S of Red Lodge on US 212. 20 acres. Located in a beautiful canyon just below Beartooth Pass on the way to Yellowstone Park. **Rooms:** 88 rms, stes, and effic. CI 3pm/CO 11am. Nonsmoking rms avail. Most rooms have kitchen facilities and balconies with views of Rock Creek or the mountains. Lots of storage space. New apartments (one, two, and three bedrooms) have plush Spanish decor with antique and contemporary furnishings. **Amenities:** Cable TV, refrig. No A/C. Some units w/terraces, some w/fireplaces, some w/whirlpools. **Services:** Masseur, babysitting. **Facilities:** 4 300 2 restaurants, 2 bars, basketball, volleyball, lawn games, sauna, whirlpool, playground, washer/dryer. Stocked fishing pond in center of complex; cross-country ski and snowshoe rentals; soccer field. **Rates:** Peak (May 15–Sept) $65–$195 S; $82–$195 D; $115–$195 ste; $115–$195 effic. Extra person $20. Children under age 10 stay free. Lower rates off-season. Parking: Outdoor, free. Group rates avail. AE, DC, DISC, MC, V.

RESTAURANTS

The Dining Room at the Pollard

In Pollard Hotel, 2 N Broadway (Downtown); tel 406/446-0001. **Regional American/French.** Local artwork and turn-of-the-century furnishings are the backdrop for the game specialties (such as venison and ostrich) offered here by chef R Scott Greenlee. Try the braised pheasant chasseur with white wine and wild mushrooms, or many other seafood, fowl, lamb, and beef entrees. Crusty sourdough breads and rich desserts are always available. **FYI:** Reservations recommended. No smoking. **Open:** Breakfast daily 7am–10:30pm; lunch Mon–Sat 10:30am–2pm; dinner daily 5:30–9:30pm; brunch Sun 7am–2pm. **Prices:** Main courses $9–$20; prix fixe $29. AE, MC, V.

Pius' International Room
In Pius and Karin's Place, 115 S Broadway; tel 406/446-3333. Downtown. **American/Continental.** Burgundy velvet booths and German table linen set the tone for house specialties like jaeger schnitzel (a veal steak with chanterelle mushrooms), pepper steak, and duck with Grand Marnier sauce. Collectors will enjoy seeing one of the largest collections of Jim Beam bourbon bottles around. Outside beer garden. **FYI:** Reservations recommended. **Open:** Wed–Sat 5–10pm, Sun 3:30–9pm. **Prices:** Main courses $10–$15; prix fixe $11–$12. AE, DISC, MC, V.

Willy Pitcher's Pub & Grill
17 Broadway; tel 406/446-1717. Downtown. **New American.** It resembles an outdoor Parisian alleyway brought indoors, yet manages not to be too cute. The lunch menu features salads, burgers, and sandwiches. Dinner picks are charbroiled beef tenderloin topped with mushrooms and Gorgonzola cheese, and large prawns sautéed in tequila, lime, fresh tomatoes, garlic, pineapple, and Mexican spices. **FYI:** Reservations recommended. Folk/guitar. **Open:** Peak (June–Oct) lunch daily 11am–2pm; dinner Mon–Sat 5–10pm, Sun 4–9pm; brunch Sun 9am–1pm. **Prices:** Main courses $10–$17; prix fixe $11–$14. MC, V.

ATTRACTIONS

Carbon County Museum
1007 S Broadway; tel 406/446-3914. Started in 1959 as a collection of rodeo memorabilia, this small local museum now includes exhibits on all aspects of Montana's pioneer heritage: homesteading, mining, Native Americans, cowboys, moonshining, and more. The town's first telephone switchboard and the original homesteading cabin of Jeremiah Johnston are among the most popular displays. **Open:** Mem Day–Labor Day, daily 10am–6pm. **Free**

Red Lodge Mountain Resort
101 Ski Run Rd; tel 406/446-2610 or toll free 800/444-8977. During winter, the ski area boasts an average snowfall of more than 250 inches, 25 miles of runs, a vertical drop of 2,016 feet, and 6 chairlifts. The resort operates an 18-hole public golf course from May to October. **Open:** Dec–Apr, daily 9am–4pm; May–Oct, daily 8am–dusk. **$$$$**

Three Forks

Discovered in 1805 by the Lewis and Clark expedition, Three Forks is located at the site where the Gallatin, Jefferson, and Madison Rivers join to form the headwaters of the Missouri River. **Information:** Three Forks Chamber of Commerce, PO Box 1103, Three Forks, 59752 (tel 406/285-3198).

HOTEL

The Sacajawea Inn
5 N Main St, PO Box 648, 59752; tel 406/285-6515 or toll free 800/821-7326; fax 406/285-4210. Exit 278 off I-90, on MT 2. Various wings of this historic inn were built in 1882 and 1910; a restoration in 1992 made everything sparkle. The long, colonnaded front porch features a line of rocking chairs, perfect for enjoying the view. **Rooms:** 33 rms. CI open/CO 11am. No smoking. Cozy, uniquely decorated rooms. **Amenities:** Cable TV. No A/C. **Services:** Babysitting. **Facilities:** 150 1 restaurant (*see* "Restaurants" below), 1 bar, whirlpool, playground. **Rates (CP):** Peak (June–Sept) $69–$119 S or D. Extra person $5. Children under age 12 stay free. Lower rates off-season. Parking: Outdoor, free. AE, DISC, MC, V.

RESTAURANT

Sacajawea Inn Restaurant
5 N Main St; tel 406/285-6515. MT 2; off I-90. **Regional American.** If river watching makes you hungry (three rivers—Madison, Gallatin, and Jefferson—join here to form the headwaters of the Missouri), stop by this restored inn for traditional breakfast and lunch favorites and dinners that include prime rib and salmon. A specialty is halibut with raspberry–macadamia nut sauce. **FYI:** Reservations accepted. Children's menu. Beer and wine only. No smoking. **Open:** Peak (June–Sept) breakfast daily 7am–noon; lunch daily noon–2pm; dinner daily 5–9pm; brunch Sun 9am–2pm. **Prices:** Main courses $5–$20. AE, DISC, MC, V.

ATTRACTIONS

Madison Buffalo Jump State Monument
Buffalo Jump Rd; tel 406/285-3198. 5 mi E on I-90, then 7 mi S. This 618-acre site offers demonstrations of an ancient hunting technique used by Native Americans as long as 2,000 years ago. Picnic area, hiking trails. **Open:** May–Sept, daily sunrise–sunset. **$**

Missouri River Headwaters State Park
Tel 406/285-3431. Approximately 3 mi E, then 3 mi N of US 10. Discovered in 1805 by Lewis and Clark, the headwaters are formed by the joining of the Madison, Gallatin, and Jefferson Rivers. Activities at the 527 acre park include fishing, birdwatching, camping, and picnicking. **Open:** May–Sept, daily sunrise–sunset. **$**

Virginia City

One of Montana's oldest cities—founded during the gold rush of 1863—Virginia City served as the territorial capital from 1865 to 1876. Today, many buildings have been restored, and the ghost town is a popular tourist attraction. A narrow-gauge train carries visitors between Virginia City and Nevada City, a restored gold mining camp 1½ miles away.

MOTEL

Fairweather Inn
305 W Wallace, PO Box 338, 59755; tel 406/843-5377 or toll free 800/648-7588; fax 406/843-5377. Dusty, old hotel in a historic mining town. Many repairs needed. **Rooms:** 15 rms. CI 4pm/CO 10am. Narrow stairways and halls lead to the accommodations, most of which share baths, rooming-house style. Not recommended for families. **Amenities:** No A/C, phone, or TV. 1 unit w/terrace. **Services:** Social director, masseur. **Rates:** $37–$45 S or D. Extra person $5. Children under age 12 stay free. Closed Sept–May. AE, DISC, MC, V.

RESTAURANT

Morning Sun Restaurant
118 W Wallace; tel 406/843-5418. **American/Cafe.** Set in an 1864 building, this eatery serves good meals, from sandwiches at lunch to chicken, roast beef, and steak for dinner. Fast, though sometimes brusque, service. **FYI:** Reservations not accepted. Children's menu. No liquor license. **Open:** Daily 7am–8pm. Closed Oct–Apr. **Prices:** Main courses $6–$10. No CC.

West Glacier

See Glacier National Park

West Yellowstone

A small tourist town at the west entrance to Yellowstone National Park, with plenty of local businesses catering to the needs of park visitors. West Yellowstone is the departure point for cross-country skiing and snowmobiling treks into the park. Nearby Earthquake Lake was formed by a 1959 quake. **Information:** West Yellowstone Chamber of Commerce, 30 Yellowstone Ave, PO Box 458, West Yellowstone, 59758 (tel 406/646-7701).

HOTELS

A Holiday Inn Sunspree Resort and Conference Hotel
315 Yellowstone Ave, PO Box 459, 59758; tel 406/646-7365 or toll free 800/646-7365; fax 406/646-4433. Located three blocks from the west entrance to Yellowstone National Park, this major convention center can accommodate 400 guests. Mission-style furniture and rich colors throughout the building. **Rooms:** 123 rms and stes. Executive level. CI 3pm/CO 11am. Nonsmoking rms avail. Rooms are large and attractively decorated; all have sofas, and some have beautiful views of the park. Family suites have separate king bedroom, two standard beds, plus pullout couch. **Amenities:** A/C, cable TV w/movies, refrig, dataport. Some units w/fireplaces, some w/whirlpools. All units have microwaves. Suites have wet bars, whirlpools, and robes. **Services:** Social director, children's program, babysitting. **Facilities:** 1 restaurant, 1 bar, sauna, whirlpool, daycare ctr, washer/dryer. Restored 1903 railroad car located in hotel is walk-through museum. Antique luggage rack from railroad serves as snack bar in lobby. **Rates:** Peak (Dec 22–Mar 17/June 10–Sept 2) $79–$200 S or D; $150–$200 ste. Extra person $8. Children under age 18 stay free. Lower rates off-season. Parking: Indoor/outdoor, free. Snowmobile packages include on-site rental of clothing. Standard rates are $10 higher on weekends. AE, CB, DC, DISC, JCB, MC, V.

Stage Coach Inn
209 Madison Ave, PO Box 160, 59758; tel 406/646-7381 or toll free 800/842-2882; fax 406/646-9575. This charming, older, upscale hotel is homey and comfortable. **Rooms:** 88 rms. CI 5pm/CO 11am. Nonsmoking rms avail. Renovated, older rooms have contemporary log furniture, antler lamps, beautiful armoires, luxurious bedspreads, and original artwork. **Amenities:** Cable TV. No A/C. 1 unit w/minibar. **Services:** Twice-daily maid svce, masseur. **Facilities:** 1 restaurant, 2 bars (1 w/entertainment), games rm, sauna, whirlpool, washer/dryer. Some vehicle plug-ins available during winter. **Rates:** Peak (June 6–Sept 22/Dec 21–Mar 21) $44–$107 S; $49–$107 D. Extra person $6. Children under age 12 stay free. Lower rates off-season. Parking: Indoor/outdoor, free. Summer and winter packages avail. AE, CB, DC, DISC, MC, V.

MOTELS

Best Western Executive Inn
286 Dunraven, PO Box 1280, 59758; tel 406/646-7681 or toll free 800/528-1234; fax 406/646-9549. 2 blocks from center of West Yellowstone. This older property is reasonably maintained. **Rooms:** 81 rms and stes. CI 3pm/CO 11am. Nonsmoking rms avail. Average rooms. **Amenities:** A/C, cable TV. 1 unit w/fireplace. Some rooms have refrigerators. **Services:** **Facilities:** 1 restaurant (bkfst and dinner only), 1 bar, whirlpool, washer/dryer. The new exercise room overlooks outdoor pool. **Rates:** Peak (May 28–Sept 10/Dec 28–Mar 15) $45–$67 S; $55–$82 D; $100–$140 ste. Extra person $8. Children under age 12 stay free. Lower rates off-season. Parking: Outdoor, free. Group rates avail. AE, DC, DISC, MC, V.

Best Western Weston Inn
103 Gibbon St, 59758; tel 406/646-7373 or toll free 800/528-1234. A quiet location 3½ blocks from the west entrance to Yellowstone National Park. A good place for families. **Rooms:** 65 rms. CI 3pm/CO 11am. No smoking. Well-maintained, clean rooms with new bedspreads and drapes.

Amenities: A/C, cable TV. Some accommodations have dataports. Refrigerators available upon request. **Services:** Complimentary coffee in lobby. **Facilities:** Whirlpool. **Rates:** Peak (Dec 25–Mar 20/Mem Day–Sept) $30–$75 S; $35–$85 D. Extra person $5. Children under age 12 stay free. Lower rates off-season. Parking: Outdoor, free. AE, DC, DISC, MC, V.

Big Western Pine Motel

234 Firehole Ave, PO Box 67, 59758; tel 406/646-7622 or toll free 800/646-7622; fax 406/646-9443. Center of town. This older property is well maintained and family oriented. **Rooms:** 45 rms and effic. CI 3pm/CO 11am. Nonsmoking rms avail. Newly remodeled large rooms decorated in warm, soft tones. One- and two-bedroom efficiencies are completely stocked. One large cabin sleeps 20. Pretty linens. **Amenities:** A/C, cable TV, voice mail. **Services:** Babysitting. Elderhostel program for seniors. **Facilities:** 60 1 restaurant, 1 bar, whirlpool. **Rates:** Peak (June 15–Sept 15/Dec 25–May 20) $33–$60 S; $45–$80 D; $55–$100 effic. Extra person $5. Lower rates off-season. Parking: Outdoor, free. Snowmobile, honeymoon, and spring rendezvous packages avail. AE, CB, DC, DISC, MC, V.

The Hibernation Station

212 Gray Wolf Ave, PO Box 821, 59758; tel 406/646-4200 or toll free 800/580-ELKS; fax 406/646-4200. Two blocks SW of Imax and Grizzly Discovery Center. A first-class, all-cabin property located three blocks from the west gate to Yellowstone National Park. Craftsman Bill Oldroyd built these sturdy cabins from massive logs. **Rooms:** 30 cottages/villas. CI 2pm/CO 11am. Nonsmoking rms avail. New, luxurious cabins have hand-painted armoires, log-frame beds, and great views. **Amenities:** Cable TV. No A/C. Some units w/terraces, some w/fireplaces, some w/whirlpools. Goosedown comforters and pillows, fluffy towels, and fine linens. **Services:** Babysitting. **Facilities:** Whirlpool. **Rates (CP):** Peak (Dec–Mar/May 28–Sept 25) $65–$145 cottage/villa. Children under age 12 stay free. Lower rates off-season. Parking: Outdoor, free. Honeymoon and snowmobiling packages avail. AE, CB, DC, DISC, MC, V.

RESTAURANTS

($) ★ Alice's Restaurant

In Lionshead Resort, 1545 Targhee Pass Hwy; tel 406/646-7296. 7½ mi SW of W Yellowstone on US 20. **German.** Housed in a large log cabin, this simple dining room serves good, basic meals. Homemade pies, cinnamon rolls, and potato pancakes tempt diners in the morning, while fresh trout dishes are the specialty at dinner. Lunch served in winter only. **FYI:** Reservations recommended. Singer. **Open:** Peak (Dec 15–Mar 20/May 15–Oct 15) breakfast daily 6:30–10:30am; dinner daily 5–9:30pm. **Prices:** Main courses $7–$13. AE, CB, DC, MC, V.

★ Cappy's Bistro

In The Book Peddler, 108 Canyon St; tel 406/646-9537. **Coffeehouse.** If you're looking for a book on the geology, archeology, or history of the local region, you'll find it here. You can also enjoy espresso bar coffees and teas along with pastries, soups, breads, and sandwiches served by a friendly, young, energetic staff. **FYI:** Reservations not accepted. Children's menu. No liquor license. No smoking. **Open:** Peak (June 15–Labor Day) Tues–Sun 7am–4pm. **Prices:** Lunch main courses $3–$8. AE, DISC, MC, V.

($) ★ Three Bears Restaurant

205 Yellowstone Ave; tel 406/646-7811. **Seafood/Steak.** Set in a rustic log structure and decorated with sportsman memorabilia and three stuffed black bears. Prime rib and steaks are the main fare, but also a favorite is rainbow trout with shrimp, crab meat, mushrooms, and onions. Apple brown Betty for dessert. **FYI:** Reservations accepted. Children's menu. No smoking. **Open:** Breakfast daily 7–11am; dinner daily 5–10pm. Closed Oct 15–Dec 15/Mar 20–May 1. **Prices:** Main courses $9–$19; prix fixe $13–$17. DISC, MC, V.

ATTRACTION

Yellowstone National Park

West entrance to the park. See "Yellowstone National Park" in the Wyoming chapter for full description.

Whitefish

See also Columbia Falls, Kalispell

Scenic resort town located on Whitefish Lake, at the base of Big Mountain Ski and Summer Resort. Its location makes it a short drive for visitors going east to Glacier National Park, south to Flathead Lake, and north to Canada. **Information:** Whitefish Area Chamber of Commerce, PO Box 1120, Whitefish, 59937 (tel 406/862-3548).

HOTEL

Best Western Rocky Mountain Lodge

6510 US 93 S, 59937; tel 406/862-2569 or toll free 800/237-8433; fax 406/862-1154. ½ mi S of downtown. European-style hotel opened in 1995. Beautifully appointed lobby with slate floor, rock fireplace, stone columns, and natural wood decor. Flower boxes in every window. **Rooms:** 79 rms and stes. Executive level. CI 3pm/CO 11am. Nonsmoking rms avail. **Amenities:** A/C, dataport, voice mail. Some units w/terraces, some w/fireplaces, some w/whirlpools. 12 suites have fireplaces and other amenities including wet bars, jet tubs, microwaves, and refrigerators. **Services:** Car-rental desk, social director, babysitting. Masseur available on request. Fax and copy service. Pet fee $50. **Facilities:** 200 Whirlpool, washer/dryer. Game tables in common area. **Rates (BB):** Peak (July–Aug/

Dec 22–Jan 1) $85–$119 S or D; $149 ste. Extra person $10. Children under age 12 stay free. Lower rates off-season. Parking: Outdoor, free. Senior and commercial rates; ski and golf packages avail. AE, CB, DC, DISC, EC, ER, JCB, MC, V.

INN

Good Medicine Lodge

537 Wisconsin Ave, PO Box 562, 59937; tel 406/862-5488 or toll free 800/860-5488; fax 406/862-5489. ½ mi N of town. 1 acre. A warm, inviting country-inn atmosphere pervades this "Green Hotel," which prides itself on recycling. The original portion of the lodge features cedar post and beam construction, while the newer lounge has a 30-foot cathedral ceiling and two fireplaces. Within walking distance of stores and restaurants; snowmobiling, snowshoeing, and ice skating nearby. **Rooms:** 11 rms and stes. CI 3pm/CO 11am. No smoking. Custom-made lodgepole-pine beds and vaulted red-fir ceilings. Most rooms have tub/shower units. **Amenities:** Dataport. No A/C or TV. Some units w/terraces. **Services:** Babysitting, afternoon tea served. Complimentary soft drinks, coffee, cocoa, and cookies available in lobby. **Facilities:** 10 Lawn games, whirlpool, washer/dryer, guest lounge w/TV. Refrigerator, microwave, icemaker, and recycling center available for guest use. Heated ski and boot room with a boot and glove dryer. One block to ski, bike, kayak, canoe, and powerboat rentals. **Rates (BB):** Peak (May 15–Oct 15/Dec 21–Jan 3) $65 S; $85–$95 D; $125–$170 ste. Extra person $30. Children under age 10 stay free. Lower rates off-season. Parking: Outdoor, free. $5 discount for seniors. Ski packages avail. Closed Oct 15–Nov/Apr 15–May 15. MC, V.

LODGES

Alpinglow Inn

3900 Big Mountain Rd, PO Box 1770, 59937; tel 406/862-6966 or toll free 800/754-6760; fax 406/862-0076. Located at Big Mountain Ski and Summer Resort, with direct access to lifts and ski trails (guests can ski in/ski out). Typical ski-lodge lobby decor with fireplace and lots of seating. As the name implies, guests have spectacular views of mountain peaks at sunset, when a warm glow lights up the peaks. **Rooms:** 54 rms. CI 4pm/CO 11am. Nonsmoking rms avail. All rooms overlook mountains or valley, and have one queen-size bed and two bunk beds. Family units sleep up to eight. **Amenities:** A/C. **Services:** Car-rental desk, babysitting. Masseur available on request. Pet fee $25. **Facilities:** 100 1 restaurant, sauna, whirlpool, washer/dryer. Ski and boot storage; luggage storage and separate showers for late-departing guests who want to ski in the morning. Resort's children's programs and day care are located across the street. Horse-drawn sleigh rides, ice skating, and a tubing hill. Summer activities also include guided horse trail rides, mountain biking, hiking on nearby nature trails, berry picking, gondola rides. **Rates:** Peak (mid-June–early Sept; mid-Dec–early Jan) $68–$90 S; $78–$110 D. Extra person $5-20. Children under age 13 stay free. Lower rates off-season. AP rates avail. Parking: Outdoor, free. Ski and snowmobiling packages avail. Closed mid-Apr–mid-June; mid-Oct–Nov. AE, DISC, MC, V.

Grouse Mountain Lodge

1205 US 93 W, 59937; tel 406/862-3000 or toll free 800/321-8822; fax 406/862-0326. ¾ mi W of town on US 93. Located next to Whitefish Golf Course and 10 miles from Big Mountain Ski and Summer Resort. The lobby of this elegant lodge is a "must-see," even if you don't plan to stay here. The floor is made from 100-year-old slate tiles taken off the roofs of old barns and houses, and there's a huge stone fireplace. A large etched-glass mural of Glacier National Park graces the hallway, while wagon-wheel and antler chandeliers complete the theme. **Rooms:** 144 rms, stes, and effic. CI 4pm/CO 11am. Nonsmoking rms avail. Rooms have mountain views. **Amenities:** A/C, voice mail. Some units w/terraces, some w/whirlpools. Some rooms have dataports; some have private hot tubs, full kitchens, and sleeping lofts. Corner suites have large desks. **Services:** Car-rental desk, social director, children's program, babysitting. Complimentary shuttle to Big Mountain Ski Resort. Bar service on outdoor patio. Group barbecues in summer; sleigh and dog-sled rides in winter. **Facilities:** 18 350 1 restaurant, 1 bar, volleyball, games rm, sauna, whirlpool, day-care ctr, washer/dryer. Three hot tubs. Adjacent to soccer field and tennis courts. Golf course groomed for cross-country skiing in winter. Storage area for ski equipment. Discount pass to local fitness center. **Rates:** Peak (June–Sept; Dec 23–Jan 2) $119 S; $119–$139 D; $149–$189 ste; $159–$189 effic. Extra person $10. Children under age 12 stay free. Lower rates off-season. Parking: Outdoor, free. Ski, golf, wedding, and holiday packages avail. AE, CB, DC, DISC, MC, V.

Kandahar Lodge

3824 Big Mountain Rd, PO Box 1659, 59937; tel 406/862-6098 or toll free 800/862-6094; fax 406/862-6095. At Big Mountain Ski and Summer Resort. An intimate, European-style lodge in an alpine setting, with accent on relaxation and romantic interludes. Beautiful lobby with huge rock fireplace and overstuffed sofas and chairs. Thirty-foot vaulted ceiling, slate floors, stained-glass windows, and antique furnishings complete the feeling. Within walking distance of ski lifts. **Rooms:** 50 rms, stes, and effic. CI 4pm/CO 11am. Nonsmoking rms avail. Accommodations include small studio apartments with kitchenettes; plus upstairs and downstairs sleeping lofts, some with kitchenettes. **Amenities:** A/C, cable TV. Down comforters. **Services:** Car-rental desk, babysitting. Ski shuttle. Masseur available on request. Staff will go grocery shopping in town for guests. Fax and copier service. **Facilities:** 20 1 restaurant (bkfst and dinner only), games rm, sauna, whirlpool, washer/dryer. Heated ski and boot room. Dog sledding, cross-country skiing, horse-drawn sleigh rides, ice skating, tubing hill. Summer activities include guided horse trail rides, mountain biking, nature and hiking trails, berry picking, gondola rides, tennis, and volleyball. **Rates:** Peak (June 23–Sept 4/mid-Dec–early Jan) $82–$92 S or D; $152 ste; $92–$132 effic. Extra person $10. Children under age 13 stay free. Lower rates off-season. Parking: Outdoor, free. Weekly and group rates, ski and golf packages avail. Closed mid-Apr–mid-May/mid-Oct–mid-Nov. AE, DISC, MC, V.

North Forty Resort
3765 MT 40 W, PO Box 4250, 59937; tel 406/862-7740 or toll free 800/775-1740; fax 406/862-7741. 2½ mi from US 93; on MT 40. 40 acres. An inviting and relaxing property, opened in 1993. High-quality, log-constructed lodge and cabins are set in a lodgepole-pine forest filled with native shrubs and wildflowers. Located near river rafting, hiking, and snowmobiling. **Rooms:** 22 cottages/villas. CI 4pm/CO 11am. Nonsmoking rms avail. Earth-tone decor and log furnishings. Beautiful, deluxe log cabins come with kitchenettes and picnic tables. **Amenities:** Cable TV w/movies, refrig. No A/C. All units w/terraces, all w/fireplaces. Down comforters and pillows (synthetics available on request). Deluxe log cabins are equipped with refrigerators, microwaves, and outdoor barbecue grills. **Services:** Car-rental desk, babysitting. **Facilities:** Volleyball, lawn games, sauna, whirlpool, playground. **Rates:** Peak (mid-June–mid-Sept/mid-Dec–early Jan) $79–$179 cottage/villa. Extra person $10. Children under age 14 stay free. Lower rates off-season. Parking: Outdoor, free. Weekly discounts. Golf, ski, and snowmobiling packages avail. AE, DISC, MC, V.

Ptarmigan Village
3000 Big Mountain Rd, PO Box 458, 59937; tel 406/862-3594 or toll free 800/552-3952; fax 406/862-6664. 5 mi from downtown. Condo complex located only minutes from recreational activities at Big Mountain Ski and Summer Resort. **Rooms:** 44 cottages/villas. CI 3pm/CO 10am. Nonsmoking rms avail. Individually owned rental units are decorated mostly with an outdoors motif and wildlife art. **Amenities:** Cable TV, refrig, dataport. No A/C. All units w/terraces, 1 w/whirlpool. Most units have decks and gas barbecue grills. **Services:** Free ski-shuttle service. **Facilities:** 4 Basketball, sauna, whirlpool, playground, washer/dryer. On-mountain winter recreation includes dog sledding, alpine and cross-country skiing, horse-drawn sleigh rides and dinners, and ice skating. In summer, options include guided trail rides on horseback, mountain biking, hiking, gondola rides. **Rates:** Peak (Dec 25–Mar; June–Aug) $70–$145 cottage/villa. Extra person $10. Min stay. Lower rates off-season. Parking: Outdoor, free. Minimum stay of two nights required. Discounts on stays of five nights or more. MC, V.

RESTAURANTS

★ The Place
845 Wisconsin Ave; tel 406/862-4500. Near Big Mountain Ski and Summer Resort; 1 mi from downtown. **American.** Home cooking is the trademark of this eatery decorated with wildlife art and Northwest pioneer memorabilia. An on-site smokehouse is used to crank out the signature barbecue ribs. The Place is also noted for its pizzas, and there's a selection of 10 microbrews on tap. Everything on the menu is available for take-out. **FYI:** Reservations not accepted. Children's menu. Beer and wine only. **Open:** Peak (May–mid-Sept) Sun–Thurs 11:30am–10:30pm, Fri–Sat 11:30am–11:30pm. **Prices:** Main courses $5–$15. AE, MC, V.

★ Whitefish Lake Restaurant
Whitefish Golf Club; tel 406/862-5285. On US 93. **Seafood/Steak.** The hand-hewn log building was constructed as a WPA project in 1936. Originally designed as a plane hangar, it later wound up as a golf clubhouse. Today, the restaurant's western decor is accented by wildlife art. Each spring and fall the menu changes, but traditional favorites are prime rib and smoked trout. Also known for fresh seafood. **FYI:** Reservations recommended. Children's menu. No smoking. **Open:** Daily 5:30–10pm. Closed Nov 6–Thanksgiving. **Prices:** Main courses $11–$20. AE, MC, V.

Wisdom

A high-elevation ranching town, perhaps best-known for a local factory that manufactures custom-made cowboy hats for country music and Hollywood stars. Big Hole National Battlefield is 12 miles west of town.

ATTRACTION

Big Hole National Battlefield
MT 43; tel 406/689-3155. 12 mi W of Wisdom. Site of an 1877 battle between the Nez Perce tribe and troops from the US Army, who were under orders to place the fleeing Nez Perce on a reservation. Approximately 60 to 90 Native Americans were ultimately killed, along with 29 soldiers.

Today, a visitors center (overlooking the main battlefield) features an 18-minute video program and a museum of photos and mementos of those who fought here. There's also a picnic area, self-guided walking tour, and fishing (only where permitted; ask at visitor center). Cross-country skiing in winter. **Open:** Daily 8am–4:30pm. Closed some hols. $$

NEBRASKA

Where the Prairie Meets the West

STATE STATS

CAPITAL
Lincoln

AREA
77,335 square miles

BORDERS
South Dakota, Wyoming, Colorado, Kansas, Missouri, and Iowa

POPULATION
1,578,400 (1990)

ENTERED UNION
March 1, 1867

NICKNAME
Cornhusker State

STATE FLOWER
Goldenrod

STATE BIRD
Western meadowlark

FAMOUS NATIVES
Fred Astaire, Marlon Brando, Henry Fonda, Gerald Ford, Malcolm X

The Old West lives on in Nebraska's many restored log cabins, sod houses, and one-room schoolhouses. Whole villages are preserved to honor the prairie's past. Trips along the Oregon Trail are still available (complete with chuck-wagon meals), and you can still ride in a stagecoach, ascend piney hills on horseback, admire herds of buffalo, and camp out on the prairie.

Old West figures Buffalo Bill and Wild Bill Hickok spent time in Nebraska and the great novelist Willa Cather, born in Virginia, moved to Red Cloud when she was eight years old. (The whole town of Red Cloud is now a museum.) Some of painter George Catlin finest works were inspired by the Nebraska landscape, and influential artist Robert Henri spent his youth here.

Sterling Morton, the founder of Arbor Day, was born in Nebraska City and his home is now a state historical park, so it is perhaps fitting that Nebraska offers so many opportunities for outdoor recreation. Visitors can sail on shimmering, 35,000-acre Lake McConaughy, canoe on the Niobrara River, or ride down the Missouri River on the *Spirit of Brownville*. Many visitors come to see hundreds of thousands of sandhill cranes announce the arrival of spring by returning to the North Platte River and adjoining wetlands.

Today, Nebraska is the buckle of America's farm belt, producing a bounty of soybeans, wheat, sugar beets, corn, sorghum, and alfalfa. Cattle may outnumber humans 3 to 1, but the 20th century has not passed the state by. Omaha is home to the Strategic Air Command, one of the military's most top-secret posts, and several major insurance companies.

Frommer' #1

A Brief History

Earliest Times Around 8000 BC, after the volcanic eruptions and the melting of the glaciers, the Paleo-Indians made their way across the Bering Strait from Asia, and down to the Great Plains. These peoples eventually evolved into nomadic tribes (the Sioux, Cheyenne, Potawatome, and Arapaho) and agricultural tribes (the Ponca, Pawnee, Omaha, and Otoe). For centuries, the nomadic groups moved their teepees across the Great Plains, following the buffalo herds. Buffalo provided their food, clothing, and shelter, while the agricultural tribes lived in earth lodges and grew (or gathered) most of their food. By the early 16th century, horses arrived on the Plains from Spanish settlements to the south. This made the lives of the Native Americans considerably easier, and the earth lodge people in east and northeast Nebraska began to hunt buffalo in addition to their farming.

In the 1700s, fur traders in canoes rowed up the Platte River to trade beads and shells for the furs and pelts harvested by the native peoples. These beads and shells began to be utilized in the artwork of these tribes, but this new beauty in their art marked, of course, the end of their way of life. The next outsiders to enter the area were the French and the Spanish, who brought not only alcohol (and alcoholism) with them, but diseases —such as smallpox—from which the native people had no immunity.

Pathway to the West One could almost write the story of Nebraska by writing about every one of its trails: the Villasur Trail of 1732, carved into the terrain by the Spanish; the Mallet Brothers Trail (French), started in 1739; the Astoria Brothers Trail in 1812; the Sidney Black Hills Gold Trail of 1849 (and for 30 years after); the Mormon Trail in the 1830s, and other less famous trails such as Freighters Trail and the Shawnee Cattle Trails. Lewis and Clark made their way up the Missouri to the region in 1804. But of course it's the Oregon Trail that everyone knows. Beginning in 1812, this trail was used by the settlers heading west to homestead or to try their luck in the Gold Rush. Over 350,000 people passed this way on wagon trains, and in many areas you can still see the wagon-wheel ruts.

But nobody traveled these trails easily at first. Threatened by encroachment, the natives—particularly the Sioux and Cheyenne—fought hard. Crazy Horse, the great Oglala Sioux leader, was killed while under arrest at Fort Robinson. By 1854, Nebraska became a territory of the United States and the eastern tribes were subdued and "resettled" on reservations.

It was clear to all that this territory was excellent farmland. The railroad laid tracks and created advertisements to entice German and Scandinavian immigrants to homestead. (The state attracted so many German settlers that it even has a "sausage capital," Eustis.) The pockets of railroad owners were lined and relined each day, and each day their land holdings grew until at one point they owned almost a fifth of Nebraska. The territory became a state in 1867.

Fun Facts

- Nebraska's state government is the only one with a unicameral (one-house) legislature.
- Promotional slogans for Omaha have ranged from "Agricultural Capital of the World" to "The Nation's Largest Producer of Quick-Frozen Meat and Fruit Pies."
- Chimney Rock, the 475-foot-high narrow column of stone located near Scottsbluff, is visible for 40 miles. It served as a landmark and guidepost for pioneers headed for the Oregon Territory.
- The city of Lincoln is the only Plains state capital that is not a river port.
- Chadron was the starting point for a grueling 1,000-mile horse race held in 1898. The winner, who wore out 2 horses on the journey, crossed the finish line in Chicago after 15 days, 4 hours.

Harvest & Home Today, 23 million acres of the state is agricultural cropland, while 20 million is used for range and cattle pastures (mostly in the western part of the state). Corn, alfalfa, soybeans, sorghum, fruit, wheat, sugar beets, and popcorn are some of the state's most lucrative harvests. Nebraska is also rich in oil, natural gas, gravel and stone, potash, pumice, and gypsum.

Nebraska has contributed many important people to history, including Malcolm X (born in Omaha); the first Native American doctor, Susan Picotte; and anthropologist, philosopher, and Nobel Prize winner Loren Eisely. Many personalities in film and television hail from Nebraska as well: Fred Astaire, Marlon Brando, Johnny Carson, Dick Cavett, Henry Fonda, Sandy Dennis, and Montgomery Clift, among others.

A Closer Look

GEOGRAPHY

If you're driving across the flatlands or sandhills of Nebraska today, it takes a lot of imagination to believe that this state was once subtropical with patches of jungle. The **Ashfall Fossil Beds,** near Royal, help the imagination along with displays of the intact skeletons (preserved by volcanic ash) of the four-tusked elephants and three-toed horses who once lived here. Volcanoes and glaciers and inland seas did not leave Nebraska quite bereft of trees, but almost. The 90,000-acre **Nebraska National Forest,** in the central part of the state, is a mostly manmade forest.

Eastern Nebraska is known as the Till Plains, with land composed of a rich mixture of clay, rock, and sand created as a result of glacial melting and animal and plant deposits. When combined with loess (the dust blown in by winds), the Till Plains make perfect farmland. The hilly nature of this region is due to clay and clay shell beds that have eroded over millennia. The **Missouri River** flows along Nebraska's eastern border, carving its way through the hilly, rich soil.

People tend to think of Nebraska as a "dry plains" area, but it actually has 11,000 miles of flowing streams. The **Platte River** cuts across the southern half of the state and feeds into the Missouri. In general, Platte River valley land is flat and composed of silt, clay, sand, and gravel. The **Niobrara River** valley, east of Valentine, is a point where six ecological systems meet and bring together a diverse assortment of plant and animal life. The Niobrora, with its serene surroundings, is especially popular with canoeists and kayakers.

About 8,000 years ago, sand blown in by strong winds created the **Sandhills,** the middle section of the state's Great Plains; they comprise 20,000 square miles, or onefourth of the state. The rolling sandhills are actually covering a sand sea, the largest in the western hemisphere. Only the Sahara and Arabian deserts exceed it in size—the difference is that this sand is held in place by a grassy blanket. However, it's not as dry as it might at first appear and there are lots of small streams to keep the cows satisfied.

In contrast to the east, where the state is pastoral with green pastures, deep woods, and hilly land, **western Nebraska** consists of grasslands and high plains where pine and yucca grow. The working together of the ash, wind, clay, and sandstone formed odd rocky buttes and towers, such as **Chimney Rock,** a landmark for the men and women of the Oregon Trail as they came across western Nebraska, and the aptly named **Toadstool Park,** where swirls of sandstone slabs sit on stems of clay in the state's "little bad lands" section. In the western part of the state, the land is used mostly for cattle ranching and growing sugar beets and wheat.

DRIVING DISTANCES

Lincoln

55 mi SW of Omaha
97 mi E of Grand Island
192 mi W of Des Moines, IA
277 mi E of North Platte
394 mi SW of Minneapolis, MN
523 mi SE of Rapid City, SD

Omaha

55 mi NE of Lincoln
137 mi W of Des Moines, IA
146 mi NE of Grand Island
282 mi E of North Platte
373 mi SW of Minneapolis, MN
529 mi SE of Rapid City, SD

Scottsbluff

99 mi S of Chadron
175 mi NW of North Platte
230 mi NW of McCook
317 mi NW of Grand Island
396 mi NW of Lincoln
452 mi W of Omaha

CLIMATE

These rolling plains are a land of weather extremes: frigidly cold days in the winter, blustery springs, and long, hot summers. The wintertime can bring blizzards, spring can mean severe hailstorms, and every summer, tornadoes skim the skies and sometimes even hit. It tends to be dry year-round, and droughts are a constant threat to the state's farmers. Spring is always uncertain and it comes late, and the occasional warm March day is only a signal of good things to come. Crisp fall days may look warm because the sun is shining but the temperature can drop quickly at night, and you may need a winter coat.

WHAT TO PACK

Nebraska is not really a dress-up state, and it has a Western flavor once you leave its largest cities. (Some not-too-fancy evening clothes will make you feel less out of place at a symphony concert or gallery opening in Lincoln or Omaha.) People like to wear cowboy boots on rugged terrain, or sturdy shoes for camping or fishing. Light, loose clothing in summer keeps the mosquitoes at bay and keeps you cool. The cold winters are blustery and can be snowy, so bring gloves and wool sweaters for layering up outdoors.

TOURIST INFORMATION

For general information, contact the **Nebraska Division of Travel and Tourism,** PO Box 94666, Lincoln, NE 68509 (tel toll free 800/228-4307). Recreation information is available from the **Nebraska Game and Parks Commission,** PO Box 30370, Lincoln, NE 68503 (tel 402/471-0641). The **US Forest Service** in Colorado will provide regulations and information for use of all Rocky Mountain region forests they govern. They can be reached at US Forest Service, Rocky Mountain Region, 11177 W 8th St, Lakewood, CO 80225 (tel toll free 800/280-CAMP).

DRIVING RULES AND REGULATIONS

The minimum age for a learner's permit is 15; 16 for a driver's license. Speed limits are 65 mph on interstates, and 55 mph for rural highways. Radar and other devices are used to check speeds. Seat belts are mandatory for the driver and front seat passengers. Children must wear restraints if they are under 4 years old or under 40 pounds. Children between four and five must wear a safety belt or be secured in a safety seat. A right turn is permitted after a complete stop at a red light, unless otherwise posted. Motorcycle helmets are required.

AVG MONTHLY TEMPS (°F) & RAINFALL (IN)

	Omaha	Scottsbluff
Jan	21/0.7	25/0.5
Feb	27/0.8	30/0.5
Mar	39/2.0	36.1.1
Apr	52/2.7	47/1.6
May	62/4.5	56/2.8
June	72/3.9	67/2.6
July	77/3.5	74/2.1
Aug	74/3.2	72/1.0
Sept	65/3.7	61/1.1
Oct	53/2.2	50/0.8
Nov	39/1.5	36/0.6
Dec	25/1.0	26/0.6

RENTING A CAR

The following rental agencies have offices in Nebraska. Check with your insurance company to determine whether you are insured while driving a rental car. If not, the agencies can sell you insurance.

- **Alamo** (Omaha only; tel toll free 800/327-9633)
- **Avis** (Lincoln, North Platte, and Omaha, tel 800/331-1212)
- **Budget** (tel 800/527-0700)
- **Dollar** (Omaha and Lincoln; tel 800/327-7607 or 800/421-6868)
- **Hertz** (tel 800/654-3131)
- **National** (tel 800/328-4567)
- **Thrifty** (Omaha only; tel 800/367-2277)

ESSENTIALS

Area Codes: Nebraska has two area codes: **402** in the east (including Omaha and Lincoln) and **308** in the west (Grand Island, North Platte).

Emergencies: In case of emergency, call toll free 800/525-5555.

Liquor Laws: You must be 21 to buy or consume alcoholic beverages in Nebraska.

Road Info: For a report of statewide road conditions, call 800/906-9069 (in-state only). For Omaha conditions, call 402/553-5000 (in-state) or 402/471-4533 (out-of-state).

Smoking: Smoking is restricted in gymnasiums, arenas, and health facilities, and at public meetings, restaurants, and retail and grocery stores.

Taxes: Nebraska has a 6.5% sales tax and some cities have an option for a local sales tax as well.

Time Zone: Nebraska is split between the Central and Mountain time zones, with the more populated eastern two-thirds of the state (including Omaha, Lincoln, Grand Island, and North Platte) falling within Central time.

Best of the State

WHAT TO SEE AND DO

Below is a general overview of some of the top sights and attractions in Nebraska. To find out more detailed information, look under "Attractions" under individual cities in the listings portion of this book.

Parks & Recreation Areas Public lands in Nebraska include areas where you can view wildlife and birds, watch the buffalo roam, take your mountain bike up a rugged trail, fish, and enjoy the state's primitive grassland and pastoral beauty. The **Pine Ridge National Recreation Area** is a perfect example of the dramatic western Nebraska landscape, full of sandstone cliffs and deep-green pine trees. The **Bessey Ranger District,** in central Nebraska, has

22,000 acres of planted pines and cedar with a campground and tennis courts, a canoe launch, and hiking trails.

Fort Robinson State Park, west of Crawford, provides a bit of everything. You can fish, picnic, swim, camp, look at exhibits of harness and blacksmith shops, visit a 1908 veterinary hospital, and see where German World War II prisoners were kept. This huge complex, which covers 22,000 acres of Nebraska's dramatically beautiful Pine Ridge area, is one of the most popular stops for visitors to Nebraska, so call ahead for reservations.

Eugene T Mahoney State Park, near Ashland, is a popular spot for horseback riding, softball, fishing, and hiking, as well as wintertime sledding and ice skating. The mineral springs at **Victoria Springs Recreation Area,** near Broken Bow, are renowned for their healing qualities.

Manmade Wonders Almost every tree in the **Nebraska National Forest** was planted. The forest is composed of jack pine, ponderosa pine, and eastern red cedar and includes 90,000 acres of sandhills prairie and forest. Another spectacular manmade wonder in the state is **Lewis and Clark Lake,** which is now a State Recreation Area. Gavins Point Dam keeps this 32,000 acres of water in place.

Wildlife One of the biggest draws to the state is the sight of half a million sandhill cranes returning to the Platte River and adjoining wetlands every spring. The endangered whooping crane also passes through in the spring, and bald eagles are often seen flying over the Platte. Special bird watching sites have been set aside at **Lake McConaughy,** and thousands of snow geese are seen every year at the **De Soto National Wildlife Refuge** along the Missouri River. Besides magnificent birds, Nebraska boasts a hearty supply of antelope, deer, hares, some buffalo (at **Fort Niobrara National Wildlife Refuge** near Valentine), prairie dogs, and a variety of snakes.

Historic Areas, Sites & Monuments Windlass Hill, at the Ash Hollow Historical Park, is a living monument to the travelers on the Oregon Trail. (It is the steepest incline their wagons had to descend.) **Chimney Rock,** a towering sandstone butte that stands over 500 feet tall, was used as a landmark and meeting place by the travelers; it is now a National Historic Site. For another sense of travel along the old Trail, visitors can walk in the ruts of wagon trains and view the high plains from atop the **Scotts Bluff National Monument,** rising some 800 feet above the plains.

In Scottsbluff, a marker at the southeast corner of town points to the grave of Rebecca Winters, one of the women who died on the Oregon Trail. Set in the rolling hills near Beatrice are nature trails and a furnished pioneer cabin. Both are part of the **Homestead National Monument,** which commemorates the Homestead Act of 1862.

Gordon, 135 miles northeast of Scottsbluff, is the site of the grave of Great Plains writer Mari Sandoz, author of *Old Jules.* The Mari Sandoz Room in the home of her sister, Caroline, contains her typewriter and books. In Nebraska City, you can visit **Arbor Lodge,** the home of Arbor Day founder Sterling Morton. In Gothenburg, you can view two original Pony Express stations, take a walk through a historic depot, and visit a sod house with a barbed-wire buffalo in its yard. The flour mill at **Champion Mills State Historical Park,** on the banks of Frenchman Creek, ran from 1884 until 1969, making it the last water-powered flour mill to cease operation in the state.

The art deco–style capitol building in Lincoln, with a statue of a grain sower at its top, is one of the buildings Nebraska is most proud of. William Jennings Bryan's home, **Fairview,** is also in Lincoln.

Museums The complex of buildings and historical sites at the **Stuhr Museum of the Prairie Pioneer** in Grand Island evokes pioneer life in a 19th-century railroad town. Henry Fonda's home is one of four historic homes in the complex. Pioneer clothing, household goods, and a complete pharmacy are part of the collection at the **Museum of the High Plains** in McCook. The **Knight Museum** in Alliance displays Native American artifacts and equipment used by the cavalry. The **Trailside Museum** at Fort Robinson State Park features a mammoth skeleton and fossils dating back 200 million years. If you want to learn more about how the railroad crossed the west, check out the **Union Pacific Museum** in Omaha. The **Museum of Nebraska Art** in Kearney features Nebraska artists dating back to 1819.

The entire town of **Red Cloud,** the Nebraska hometown of Willa Cather, is a museum. The town, located 60 miles south of Grand Island, served as a setting for at least three of Cather's novels. Lots of Cather memorabilia is on display at the **Cather Historical Center,** and tours can be taken through her childhood home.

Family Favorites Ashfall Fossil Beds State Historical Park features 10 million year old skeletons of saber-toothed deer, rhinos, and bone-crushing dogs. The animals were trapped under volcanic ash when a volcano erupted all those millions of years ago in the region we now know as Idaho. The **Northeast Nebraska Zoo** in Royal is the home of Reuben, a chimp who speaks to humans using sign language. The **Riverside Zoo** in Scottsbluff is western Nebraska's largest zoo. Regional animals such as otters and prairie dogs live here, as well as some exotics. In Omaha, children love the **Henry Doorly Zoo,** with its tubby penguins and shark aquarium.

Since Nebraska soil doesn't erode much, the entire state is almost like one big fossil bed. Most of the soil in the state's 93 counties have yielded up the bones of ancient elephants and other prehistoric animals. You can dig for fossils, pet snakes and lizards, and view dinosaur skeletons at the **Nebraska State Museum** in Lincoln. Its Hall of Elephants contains complete skeletons of all North American elephants.

An hour's drive from North Platte, in the hills along the banks of Medicine Creek, is **Dancing Leaf Earth Lodge.** Visitors interested in Native American history can step into an igloo-shaped lodge, enjoy a sweat lodge, walk nature trails, and learn about regional plant life.

EVENTS AND FESTIVALS

- **Heritage Doll Auction/Antique Auction,** Geneva. Dolls, quilts, and other antiques. March. Call the Geneva Chamber of Commerce (tel 402/993-6659).
- **Cinco de Mayo,** Scottsbluff. Mexican dancing, good food, and crafts. Early May. Call toll free 800/788-9475.
- **Square and Round Dance Festival,** Lincoln. Held annually in Pershing Auditorium. May. Call toll free 800/423-8212.
- **Santa Lucia Festival,** Omaha. Street parade to Rosenblatt Stadium to celebrate Italian heritage in Nebraska. Summer. Call 402/346-3251.
- **Wurst Tag,** Eustis. German heritage celebration in Nebraska's sausage capital. June. Contact the Eustis Chamber of Commerce, PO Box 173, Eustis, NE 69028-0173.
- **John C Fremont Days Festival,** Fremont. Hot-air balloon races, sporting events, antique and collectors' shows, children's activities. July. Call toll free 800/228-4307.
- **Victorian Garden Walk,** Omaha. Sponsored by the General Crook House Museum. Cutting garden, herb garden, guides. August. Call toll free 800/332-1819.
- **Czech Festival,** Wilber. Costumes, Queen Pageant, children's activities, music, even a duck and dumpling run. August. Call 402/821-2732.
- **Thayer County Fair,** Deshler. Agricultural shows, speedway races, volleyball, dancing, parades. third week of August. Call toll free 800/228-4307.
- **Annual Heritage Days Festival,** McCook. Arts and crafts fair, bandshell entertainment, and parades. September. Call toll free 800/657-2179.
- **Threshers Bee,** Pierce. Annual baling and threshing event, followed by a parade. September. Call toll free 800/228-4307.
- **Fort Sidney Old Fashioned Christmas,** Sidney. In late November, the Post Commander's home and the museum are dressed up for Christmas. Tours. Refreshments. Call toll free 800/421-4769.

SPECTATOR SPORTS

Archery Every summer, the Nebraska Bowman State Field Archery Tournament is held at the **Republican Valley Archers Outdoor Range,** near Indianola. Call 308/364-2362 for information.

Auto Racing Car races are held at the **I-80 Speedway** in Greenwood (tel 402/944-2233). The Eagle National Spring Car Race takes place in Lincoln; call 402/464-8118 for information.

Baseball The **NCAA College Baseball World Series** takes place in Omaha's Rosenblatt Stadium every June. The same stadium plays host to Omaha's triple-A baseball team, the **Omaha Royals.** Call Rosenblatt Stadium (tel 402/444-4750) or the Greater Omaha Convention and Visitors Bureau (tel toll free 800/332-1819) for schedule and ticket information.

Basketball The **Omaha Racers** of the Continental Basketball Association are the team to watch. Call Ak-Sar-Ben Field (tel 402/444-1888) for ticket information.

Football The 1995 NCAA national champion and consistently top-ranked **University of Nebraska Huskers** draw throngs of gung-ho fans to Lincoln's Memorial Stadium. Call the Lincoln Convention Center and Visitors Bureau (tel toll free 800/423-8212) for information.

Hockey The **Omaha Lancers** of the United States Hockey League face off at Ak-Sar-Ben Field. Call 402/444-1888 for information.

Horse Racing Thoroughbred racing takes place February through December at **Fonner Park** in Grand Island (tel 308/382-4515). There's also racing at Omaha's **Ak-Sar-Ben Field** from May to August. Call 402/444-1888 for ticket information.

Sailing The **Annual Sailing Regatta** is held every July in McCook. Contact the McCook Chamber of Commerce for exact dates. The **Governor's Regatta Sailboat Cup,** one of the biggest inland regattas in the country, takes place on Lake Ogallala on Labor Day weekend.

Tractor Pulls Nebraskans love a good tractor pull, and the Antique Tractor Pull in Leigh is one of the best. Call 402/487-3303 for more information.

ACTIVITIES A TO Z

Bicycling Mountain biking is popular in the scenic Pine Ridge area south of the Black Hills. These are steep trails in places, with lots of challenges. If you're looking for something a little less daunting, there are lots of great bike paths in Lincoln that are mostly flat and easy to ride. Lewis and Clark Lake has a bike trail on its south shore.

Bird Watching The most popular bird watching event in Nebraska is the springtime return of the sandhill cranes to the Platte. Contact **Wings Over the Platte** (tel toll free 800/658-3178), the organizer of the event, for more information. Wings Over the Platte sponsors sunrise and sunset crane tours, an early bird tour, a rainwater basin tour, a nature hike, and much more. The National Audubon Society's **Rowe Sanctuary** (tel 308/468-5282) can advise about viewing sites throughout the state.

Camping Smith Falls State Park, home of the state's highest waterfall (at 75 feet), is a popular spot for camping. The white sand beaches of Lake McConaughy is another great place to camp, as is the Nebraska National Forest. For maps and information about camping in national forests, call the **US Forest Service** (tel toll free 800/280-CAMP). For maps and a list of all 72 state camping areas, contact the **Nebraska Travel and Tourism Division** (tel toll free 800/228-4307).

Canoeing The Niobrara River, in northern Nebraska, was named by *Backpacker* magazine as one of the top 10 canoeing rivers in the nation. The gentle river winds through oak and maple forests. If you didn't bring your gear, there are lots of places to rent canoes in Valentine. For information on canoeing in this beautiful river, call **Smith Falls State Park** (tel 402/376-1306).

Cross-Country Skiing Nebraska—with its gently rolling terrain and snowy winters—is perfect for cross-country skiing. One of the top spots in the state is **Mahoney State Park** (tel 402/944-2523), southwest of Omaha. There's a lighted run for tobogganers, in addition to the groomed cross-country trails. **Platte River State Park** (tel 402/234-2217) provides similar opportunities; the trails at **Indian Cave State Park** (tel 402/883-2575) are more rigorous.

Fishing The Snake River is best for trout, while the Merrit and Calamus Reservoirs are full of walleye, bass, crappie, and catfish. Smallmouth bass are plentiful in several lakes along I-80 between Grand Island and Hershey. If it's rainbow trout you're after, go to Keller Park, a rare spot for this lovely fish and other warm-water species. Call the **Nebraska Game and Parks Commission** (tel 402/471-0641) for information on license requirements.

Golf You can golf to your heart's content on this gentle rolling landscape. One of the most beautiful courses in the Nebraska sandhills is at **Sandhills Golf Club,** an hour north of North Platte. This 18-hole, 7,200 yard championship course was designed with input from pro golfer Ben Crenshaw. Call 308/546-2237 for information.

Hiking Quiet hiking trails are in nearly every state park, but one of the prettiest is at **Indian Cave State Park,** where you can wind through the oak and aspen on over 3,000 rugged acres along the shady bluffs that flank the Missouri River. Duck into caves and watch wild turkey and white-tailed deer along the way. Call 402/883-2575 for information.

Powwows These Native American gatherings are a great way to get a feel for the traditional cultures of the Great Plains through dance, food, crafts, and artwork. Powwows are held all year, all over the state. Some of the more prominent ones are the Omaha Tribe's **Harvest Celebration Powwow,** in Macy (tel 402/837-5391); the **Winnebago Powwow,** in Winnebago (tel 402/878-2272); and the **Santee Sioux Powwow,** in Santee (tel 402/857-2302).

Selected Parks & Recreation Areas

- **Nebraska National Forest,** Forest Headquarters, Chadron, NE 69337 (tel 308/432-0300)
- **Arbor Lodge State Historical Park,** Box 15, Nebraska City, NE 68410-0015 (tel 402/873-7222)
- **Ashfall Fossil Beds State Historical Park,** PO Box 66, Royal, NE 68773 (tel 402/893-2000)
- **Buffalo Bill Ranch State Historical Park,** RR 1, Box 229, North Platte, NE 69101 (tel 308/535-8035)
- **Chadron State Park,** HC 75, Box 33, Chadron, NE 69337 (tel 308/432-6167)
- **Eugene T Mahoney State Park,** 28500 W Park Hwy, Ashland, NE 68003-3508 (tel 402/944-2523)
- **Fort Atkinson State Historical Park,** Box 240, Fort Calhoun, NE 68023 (tel 402/468-5611)
- **Fort Hartsuff State Historical Park,** RR 1, Box 37, Burwell, NE 68823-9801 (tel 308/346-4715)
- **Fort Kearny State Historical Park and Recreation Area,** RR 4, Box 59, Kearney, NE 68847 (tel 308/234-9513)
- **Fort Robinson State Park,** PO Box 392, Crawford, NE 69339 (tel 308/665-2660)
- **Indian Cave State Park,** RR 1, Box 30, Shubert, NE 68347 (tel 402/883-2575)
- **Niobrara State Park,** PO Box 226, Niobrara, NE 68760-0226 (tel 402/857-3373)
- **Platte River State Park,** 14421 346th St, Louisville, NE 68037-3001 (tel 401/234-2217)
- **Ponca State Park,** PO Box 688, Ponca, NE 68770-0688 (tel 402/755-2284)
- **Rock Creek Station State Historical Park,** RR 4, Box 36, Fairbury, NE 68352-9413 (tel 402/729-5777)
- **Smith Falls State Park,** HC 13, Box 38, Sparks, NE 69220 (tel 402/376-1306)

Water Sports Both Lewis and Clark Lake and Big Mac (Lake McConaughy) are popular for sailing. Big Mac is 36,000 acres of emerald lake with sandy shorelines. Windsurfing, boating, and swimming are the order of the day. The **Lake McConaughy State Recreation Area** (tel 308/284-3542) can give you more information on the best places to swim, fish, sail, or windsurf, or call the Keith County/Ogallala Chamber of Commerce and Tourism (tel toll free 800/658-4390).

Wildflower Viewing One of the best places to see wildflowers is in the **Wildcat Hills State Recreation Area** (tel 308/436-2383), located 20 miles south of Scottsbluff in western Nebraska. These natural gardens provide dramatic color for Nebraska's "little badlands." Dozens of species grow along the North Platte River, especially in Morrill County. Starry white flowers called Hooker's Sandwort grow all summer in **Toadstool Park** and the **Ogallala National Grasslands.**

THE GREAT PLATTE RIVER ROAD

Start	Aurora
Finish	Ogallala
Distance	265 miles
Time	2–3 days
Highlights	Snapshots of the Old West; prairie and Western museums; Pony Express stations; Buffalo Bill's Ranch; the glorious spectacle of cranes in season; pioneer landmarks; virgin prairie and river hikes

The modern-day routes of I-80 and US 30 take you across Nebraska's flat prairies via trails used a century ago by explorers, settlers, and traders pushing west. The Pony Express, Oregon Trail, and early major railroad lines paralleled the Platte River, bringing with them settlers who came for rich farmland and plentiful water. When white settlers first arrived in the valley, the shallow Platte River was up to two miles wide and laced with wide sandbars. The river is visible for parts of the tour, but the flat prairie terrain makes drive-by viewing difficult, since the river is essentially at road level.

Today, the valley's single largest attraction is the annual migration of a half-million sandhill cranes, the largest crane migration site in the world. This spectacle occurs in February and March, but interstate traffic has encouraged a robust development of historical attractions and nature trails open year-round.

For specific information about lodgings and restaurants on the tour route, look under individual cities in the listings portion of this chapter.

I-80, US 30, and NE 14 all provide easy access to the first stop:

1. **Aurora,** a city founded in 1871 and, like many prairie towns, named for the Illinois home town an early settler left behind.

   If there are children in your group, you should begin your tour at the **Edgerton Educational Center,** 208 16th St (tel 402/694-4032). To get there, take exit 332 off I-80 and go 3 miles north on NE 14. The center pays tribute to Harold Edgerton, the father of electronic strobe photography. (Edgerton's invention captured, for the first time, the sight of a bullet shooting through an apple and other high-speed phenomena.) Children teach themselves about scientific principles via hands-on displays, such as bubble races.

   Next door is the **Plainsman Museum** (tel 402/694-6531), a collection of artifacts (including more than 1,200 dolls) donated by county residents. The adjacent **Plainsman Agricultural Museum** houses vintage implements and a complete 1881 homestead.

   From Aurora, on either I-80 or US 34, head 19 miles west to:

2. **Grand Island,** a city named for its placement between two channels of the Platte River. The site was known to fur traders as early as 1820 as "La Grande Isle," which at the time was one of the most conspicuous features of the valley. The **visitors information center,** just off exit 312, is housed in a train caboose. Four miles north on US 281 is the **Stuhr Museum,** 3133 W US 34 (tel 308/381-5316), a 200-acre complex that offers a broad view of prairie settlement via year-round exhibits of typical pioneer furniture and equipment.

   One of the town's seasonal highlights (May–mid-Oct) is **Railroad Town,** a replica of the mainline towns that fed Plains development. Over 50 shops in the village are staffed by working craftspeople who sell their wares. Several period homes (including the birthplace of Henry Fonda) have been moved to the site, and costumed guides are on hand to answer any questions.

   If you will be staying the night, Grand Island offers a number of motels, as well as the **Kirschke House,** 1124 W 3rd St (tel 308/381-6851), a vine-covered bed-and-breakfast in the center of town.

   From Grand Island, return to US 281 and go 21 miles south to:

3. **Hastings,** a town founded in the 1870s by a group of Englishmen lured to America by the promise of free land.

   The principal stop as you enter town is the **Lied IMAX Theatre,** 1330 N Burlington Ave (tel toll free 800/508-4629). The theater uses a screen 70 feet wide and 5 stories tall for spectacular images of natural phenomena such as the Grand Canyon. The **Hastings Museum** and the **J M McDonald Planetarium** are in the same building.

   Return to I-80 and head west to:

4. **The crane watch areas at Alda and Gibbon.** The sandhills cranes descend on the Platte River Valley en masse from mid-February to mid-April, but several watch areas make attractive stops any time of the year and offer a chance to see the prairie as it once was. One such stop is ½ mile south of I-80 exit 305: **Crane Meadows,** 9775 S Alda Rd. Self-guided hiking tours feature native prairie, river, and wood-

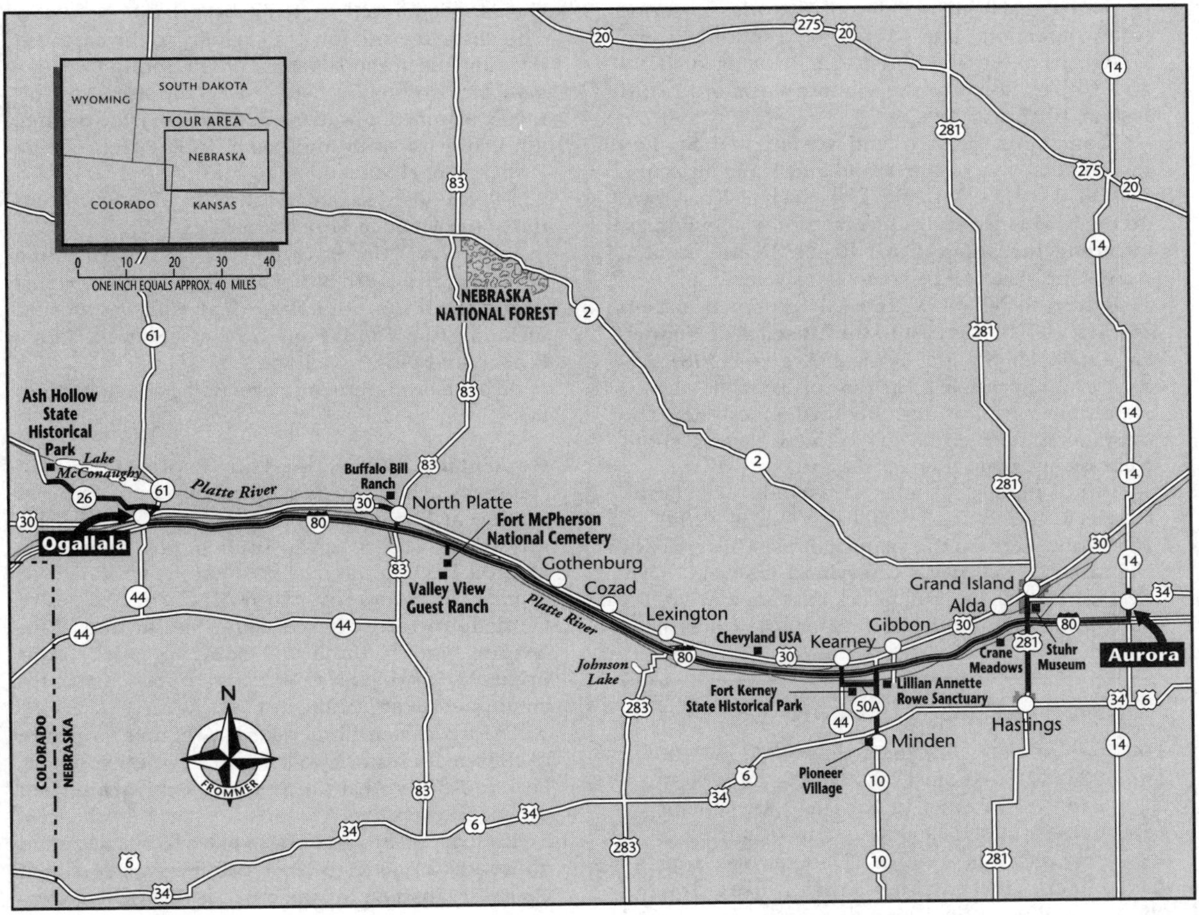

land trails with glimpses of endangered species such as piping plovers, least terns, and prairie white-fringed orchids. Tall-grass species are waist high by midsummer and tower over walkers by fall. Bring your own wading shoes, inner tubes, and cross-country skis to use in shallow waters or on trails.

Return to I-80 and go west 20 miles to exit 285. Head south 2 miles and west 2 miles to the **Lillian Annette Rowe Sanctuary** of the National Audubon Society, a 1,100-acre preservation site. At the main office, the society manages a small access site to the Platte River and two nature-viewing blinds. Guides educate visitors on river species.

A larger trail can be accessed from the interstate by taking exit 279, going 1 mile south on NE 10 and 1½ miles east on a gravel road to the **Mark Bolin Trail,** which is open seven days a week.

From the Bolin trail, return to NE 10 and go 12 miles south to:

5. **Pioneer Village** (tel 308/832-1181) in Minden: the result of one man's effort to collect anything and everything to do with prairie progress. More than 50,000 items and buildings are crammed onto a 20-acre site. Holdings include 300-plus vehicles, numerous one-of-a-kind antiques, and a steam-operated carousel with its original animals.

From Minden, return to NE 10 and go 9 miles north to NE 50A. Go west 7 miles, which is the back way into:

6. **Kearney,** named for Fort Kearny, a military post that guarded the passing of the gold prospectors, west-bound wagon trains, Pony Express riders, and other traffic along the Platte from 1847 to 1871.

Before entering the city on NE 50A, you'll pass by **Fort Kearny State Historical Park,** an excavated archeological site with education markers where structures once stood. Several buildings have been recreated, including a replica of a powder magazine (where ammunition was kept) and a split-log livery.

Return to NE 50A and go 2 miles west to NE 44 and 3 miles north to the **visitors bureau,** just off I-80 at 1007 2nd Ave.

From there, return to 2nd Ave and 11th St, then go 5 blocks west to the **Trails and Rails Museum,** 710 W 11th St (tel 308/234-3041). This town green is rimmed with several historic buildings, including the 1850s Boyd Ranch House, once a main supply station to Western travelers.

Return to NE 44 or 2nd Ave, go north to 24th St, then go 2 blocks east to the **Museum of Nebraska Art,** 24th St and Central Ave (tel 308/234-8559), an impressive 1911 post office made of New Hampshire granite and Bedford limestone. The museum is devoted to art created by and about Nebraskans, from pioneer days to the present.

Other points of interest include the **Frank House,** 19th Ave and US 30 (tel 308/234-8284), an 1889 showpiece on the campus of the University of Nebraska at Kearney. **Chevyland USA,** 14 miles west on I-80 at the Elm Creek exchange or via US 30 (tel 308/856-4208), features classic Chevrolets.

Take a Break

Habetat and **Bazooka Joe's** (tel 308/237-2405 and 308/237-2910), just off 2nd Ave on W 46th St, on the north edge of Kearney. Two theme restaurants—at the same location—catering to distinctly different crowds. Habetat has four different environmental-motif dining areas, from the Platte River Room (with hand-painted wildlife murals) to a fireside room with rustic, woodsy furniture. Menu prices range from $6 to $17. Bazooka Joe's is a rock 'n' roll diner with 1950s-style chrome and vinyl furniture. Sandwiches and burgers cost $4 to $7.

From Kearney, return to I-80 and travel 32 miles west (or upstream) to:

7. **Lexington,** a town that sprang up in 1874 from a nearby Pony Express station. During its wild and woolly days, Lexington was a favorite haunt of thieves and scalawags who were later driven out by vigilantes.

Local attractions include a number of antique shops; **Johnson Lake,** 9 miles south of Lexington on US 283; the **Heartland Museum of Military Vehicles,** exit 237 off I-80; and the **Dawson County Museum,** 805 N Taft (tel 308/324-5340).

From Lexington, return to I-80 and go west 13 miles to:

8. **Cozad,** established in 1873 by a land speculator who chose the site for its proximity to the east-west dividing line at the 100th meridian. John J Cozad, a gambler, eventually had to flee the area and his family assumed new identities; his son later became a noted artist using the name Robert Henri. The **Robert Henri Museum,** 220 E 8th St (tel 308/784-4154), is housed in one of John Cozad's old properties—the Hendee Hotel, built in 1875.

Just down the street is the **100th Meridian Museum,** 206 E 8th St (tel 308/784-1100), and just to the north is a brief **Historical Walkway** of sites including an 1848 Pony Express Station and a century-old pioneer school.

From Cozad, return to I-80 and go west 10 miles to:

9. **Gothenburg,** dubbed the Pony Express Capital of Nebraska. The 1860 **Sam Macchette Pony Express Station** in Ehmen Park, 2 miles north of exit 211, was once used as a fur-trading post along the Oregon Trail. It was moved to Ehmen Park from its original site southwest of town. Carriage rides of Gothenburg are offered here. A second Pony Express Station, south of Lexington, is still on its original site (which is now a private ranch). Ask for an appointment at Ehmen Park.

Before leaving Ehmen Park, pick up a brochure of the town's historic walking tour, or on your way back to I-80, stop at the **Sod House Museum** right off the interstate.

Return to I-80, go west 22 miles to exit 190, and go south 2 miles to **Fort McPherson National Cemetery,** named for the outpost that once guarded the Oregon Trail.

From the cemetery, go ½ mile west and ½ mile south to **Valley View Guest Ranch** (tel 308/582-4320), a working ranch that offers trail rides, Platte River views, and evening campfires.

From the ranch, return to I-80 and go 11 miles west ("upriver") to:

10. **North Platte,** founded in 1866 as a trading post; it later evolved into a rough, raw Western town. Take exit 179 off I-80, go north on US 83 through town to Rodeo Dr and then go west on US 30 to Buffalo Bill Ave, where you'll go north about 4 blocks to your next stop: the **Buffalo Bill Ranch** (tel 308/535-8035), the original home of William Frederick "Buffalo Bill" Cody.

Cody—already famous as a guide, buffalo hunter, and scout—found his lasting niche in 1882, when locals asked him to design a July 4th shebang. His "Old Glory Blowout," an extravaganza of the vanishing West, was so successful he turned it into a go-for-broke traveling show known as "Buffalo

Bill's Wild West Show and Congress of Rough Riders of the World," which toured the United States and Europe. The ranch is the resting place of much of the show's memorabilia; trail rides are available.

From the ranch, backtrack on Buffalo Bill Ave to the **Lincoln Historical Society** (tel 308/534-5640). The grounds of this county museum contain several historic buildings moved to the site, including the county's first homestead log house (1869) and the Fort McPherson headquarters building (1863).

Take a Break

Ole's Big Game Lounge (tel 308/239-4500), on the main street in Paxton. This campy small-town bar sports more than 200 wildlife mounts, courtesy of a previous owner who loved big game hunting. Menu prices range from $3 to $15.

From North Platte, head west for 53 miles on I-80 or US 30 to your final stop. If you are hungry, you might want to make a stop in Paxton, about 30 miles west of North Platte.

11. **Ogallala,** a cow town clinging to its cowboy ways, is the end of the tour.

From exit 126 off I-80, take NE 61 north through town to US 26, and go west 24 miles to **Ash Hollow,** a state historical park emphasizing geology, paleontology, and Nebraska's pioneer legacy. Ash Hollow Cave drew early peoples for thousands of years before white settlers first came to the valley in 1811; the area later hosted wagon trains and fur traders drawn to the best stop along the Overland Trail.

Windlass Hill, 2 miles south on US 26, has a walkway from which hikers can still see deep ruts carved in the hillsides by thousands of westward-bound wagons.

Other area sights include **Lake McConaughy,** 9 miles north of town on NE 61, Nebraska's largest reservoir; the **Mansion on the Hill,** NE 61 and N Spruce St, a history house devoted to the cattle drivers who put the city on the map; and **Boot Hill,** a cemetery for cowboys who never returned to Texas.

To follow the Platte River westward as you leave Nebraska, leave the interstate and follow US 26, where you may consider two other stops, the first being **Chimney Rock** near Bayard, a 500-foot-tall sandstone cone that marked the trail for early wagoneers, and **Scotts Bluff National Monument** near Gering, another natural formation that called to early travelers.

Nebraska Listings

Alliance

This midsize ranching town was founded in 1887 and renamed in 1888 by the Chicago, Burlington and Quincy Railroad so it could be closer to the top of the state's alphabetical list. The seat of Box Butte County is in the heart of the sandhills and is home to Carhenge, a whimsical tribute to Stonehenge. **Information:** Alliance Area Chamber of Commerce, 215 Box Butte Ave, PO Box 571, Alliance, 69301 (tel 308/762-1520).

MOTELS

Sunset Motel
1210 E NE 2, 69301; tel 308/762-8660 or toll free 800/767-8660; fax 308/762-4914. On E side of town. The big attraction here is the 40-foot swimming pool. **Rooms:** 19 rms. CI 2pm/CO 11am. Nonsmoking rms avail. Neat and comfortable. **Amenities:** A/C, cable TV, dataport. **Services:** **Facilities:** Games rm, whirlpool, playground, washer/dryer. Grounds also include RV hook-ups. **Rates (CP):** Peak (Apr–Sept) $55–$70 S; $60–$80 D. Extra person $5. Children under age 12 stay free. Lower rates off-season. Parking: Outdoor, free. AE, CB, DC, DISC, MC, V.

West Way Motel
1207 W 3rd St, PO Box 0, 69301; tel 308/762-4040 or toll free 800/722-4041; fax 308/762-4082. 4 acres. Typical brick structure, set in a rural area, offers both character and a feeling of security. **Rooms:** 44 rms. CI 2pm/CO 11am. Nonsmoking rms avail. Clean and tidy. **Amenities:** A/C, cable TV w/movies, refrig. **Services:** **Facilities:** 1 restaurant, playground, washer/dryer. **Rates:** Peak (May–Sept) $43–$52 S; $57–$72 D. Extra person $5. Lower rates off-season. Parking: Outdoor, free. AE, CB, DC, DISC, MC, V.

Ashland

A small agricultural town located squarely between Omaha and Lincoln, making it a favorite commuter town. Founded in 1866 and named for Ashland, Kentucky. **Information:** Ashland Chamber of Commerce, 1501 Silver St, Ashland, 68003 (tel 402/944-2050).

RESORT

Mahoney State Park
28500 W Park Hwy, 68003-3508; tel 402/944-2523; fax 402/944-7604. Exit 426 off I-80. 720 acres. Very popular state-owned resort overlooking the Platte River. Make reservations a year in advance. **Rooms:** 40 rms; 41 cottages/villas. CI 4pm/CO 11am. Nonsmoking rms avail. Spacious cabins, with wrap-around decks and vaulted ceilings, have a master bedroom and a bunk room and are outfitted with family den–type furnishings. Many lodge rooms overlook the Platte River. Everything's clean, but facilities reflect the wear common to this type of family resort. **Amenities:** A/C, TV. Some units w/terraces, some w/fireplaces. **Services:** Pets allowed in cabins only (not in lodge). Shuttle to other nearby state parks. **Facilities:** 1 restaurant, basketball, volleyball, games rm, lawn games, playground, washer/dryer. Water slides, miniature golf, trail rides, and horseshoe pits. Campgrounds and RV hookups available. Walking trails available at nearby parks. **Rates:** $55–$65 S or D; $80–$190 cottage/villa. Min stay peak. Parking: Outdoor, free. Two-night stay required during summer and weekends year-round. MC, V.

Beatrice

A farming and industrial community established on the Blue River in 1857 and named for a founder's daughter. **Information:** Gage County Visitors Commission, 226 S 6th St, Beatrice, 68310 (tel 402/223-2338).

MOTELS

Holiday Villa
1820 N 6th St, 68310; tel 402/223-4036. A typical small-town motel, reasonably priced. **Rooms:** 52 rms, stes, and effic. CI 11am/CO 11am. Nonsmoking rms avail. Rooms are large, and currently undergoing renovation, including new carpets and couches. **Amenities:** A/C, cable TV. 1 unit

w/fireplace. **Services:** VCRs for rent. **Facilities:** 35 Playground. **Rates:** $24–$26 S; $28–$32 D; $34–$36 ste; $37–$41 effic. Extra person $4. Children under age 10 stay free. Parking: Outdoor, free. AE, DC, MC, V.

Super 8
3210 N 6th St, 68310; tel 402/223-3536 or toll free 800/800-8000; fax 402/223-3536. A straightforward, no-frills wayside stop with an abundance of friendly service. **Rooms:** 40 rms. CI 11am/CO 11am. Nonsmoking rms avail. Although outdated, rooms are very clean and outfitted with new 25-inch TVs with remotes. **Amenities:** A/C, cable TV. **Services:** **Facilities:** 20 **Rates (CP):** Peak (Mar–Nov 15) $28–$34 S; $34–$44 D. Children under age 5 stay free. Lower rates off-season. Parking: Outdoor, free. AE, DC, DISC, MC, V.

ATTRACTIONS

Homestead National Monument of America
NE 4; tel 402/223-3514. 4 mi W of Beatrice. Created to honor the settlers who came west after the passage of the Homestead Act in 1862. Families from the eastern United States, and even from other countries, came to Nebraska and the surrounding states on the basis of a government promise: homesteaders who worked their 160-acre plot of government land could claim it as their own after five years. The monument is on the site of one of the first such parcels of land to be given away.

A visitors center offers a slide program, historical exhibits, a farm implements display, and self-guided tour brochures for the park's 2½ miles of trails. Restored buildings open to the public include the **Palmer-Epard Cabin,** a homesteader's cabin built in 1867 and furnished in 1880s style, and the **Freeman School,** a one-room schoolhouse that was in use until 1967. Picnic area. **Open:** Summer, daily 8am–6pm; fall and spring, daily 8:30am–5pm. Closed Dec 25. **Free**

Rock Creek Station State Historical Park
57425 710 Rd, Fairbury; tel 402/729-5777. 20 mi NE of Beatrice. Rock Creek was the Pony Express station where James Butler "Wild Bill" Hickok began his career as a gunfighter, when he killed local rancher David McCanles in 1861. Today's 350-acre park offers a picnic area, a modern campground, walking trails, horseback riding, and covered-wagon rides. McCanles's buildings and corrals have been reconstructed and are open to the public. The Burlington Northern Foundation visitors center features displays on Hickok, the Oregon Trail (which passed through here; some of the tracks are still visible), and the Pony Express. **Open:** Daily dawn–dusk. **$**

Bellevue

The oldest town in the state, Bellevue was established around 1832 as a fur-trading post just north of the junction of the Platte and Missouri Rivers, and was formally declared a municipality in 1855. Now home to StratCom, the nation's strategic air command center. **Information:** Bellevue Chamber of Commerce, 1620 Wilshire Dr, Bellevue, 68005 (tel 402/291-5216).

MOTEL

UNRATED **Best Western White House Inn**
305 N Fort Crook, 68005; tel 402/293-1600 or toll free 800/528-1234; fax 402/293-1600. Exit Fort Crook Rd, off Kennedy Fwy. A clean, well-maintained property near air base. **Rooms:** 58 rms. CI noon/CO 11am. Nonsmoking rms avail. **Amenities:** A/C, satel TV, refrig, dataport. **Services:** **Facilities:** Sauna, whirlpool, washer/dryer. **Rates:** $38–$41 S; $50 D. Extra person $3. Children under age 12 stay free. Parking: Outdoor, free. AE, CB, DC, DISC, MC, V.

Broken Bow

The seat of Custer County was established in 1870 and named for Indian artifacts found nearby. The ranching and farming town lies at the southeast entrance to the sandhills. **Information:** Broken Bow Chamber of Commerce, 444 S 8th Ave, Broken Bow, 68822 (tel 308/872-5691).

HOTEL

Arrow Hotel
509 S 9th Ave, 68822 (Downtown); tel 308/872-6662; fax 308/872-6208. On NE 2; across from town square. An older, renovated hotel that offers spacious suites at bargain prices. **Rooms:** 22 rms and effic. CI 11am/CO 11am. Nonsmoking rms avail. Some suites have two bathrooms. **Amenities:** A/C, cable TV, refrig. Rooms still have rotary phones. **Services:** **Facilities:** 120 1 restaurant (*see* "Restaurants" below), 1 bar, beauty salon, washer/dryer. **Rates:** $33 S; $37 D; $31–$39 effic. Extra person $4. Children under age 3 stay free. AE, DISC, MC, V.

MOTEL

UNRATED **Super 8**
215 ES "E" St, 68822; tel 308/872-6428 or toll free 800/800-8000; fax 308/872-5031. On NE 2; on S edge of town. Clean and small chain motel books solid on summer weekends. **Rooms:** 33 rms and stes. CI 1pm/CO 11am. Nonsmoking rms avail. **Amenities:** A/C, cable TV, dataport. Some units w/whirlpools. **Services:** Dogs under 15 pounds only. **Facilities:** 20 Whirlpool. **Rates (CP):** $32–$36 S; $40–$45 D; $39–$44 ste. Extra person $3. Parking: Outdoor, free. AE, DC, DISC, MC, V.

RESTAURANT

The Lobby Restaurant

In Arrow Hotel, 509 S 9th Ave; tel 308/872-3363. On NE 2; across from downtown square. **American.** The specialty of this hotel dining room is prime rib; other typical offerings include chicken, fried shrimp, and chicken-fried steak. Booths are made from old wooden hotel-room doors left over after a 1986 remodeling. **FYI:** Reservations accepted. **Open:** Mon–Sat 7am–10pm, Sun 8am–2pm. **Prices:** Main courses $4–$15. AE, DISC, MC, V.

Chadron

Chadron, established circa 1885 and named for a French-Indian trapper, is located on the border of the White River Valley at the edge of the scenic Pine Ridge area. The city is surrounded by buttes and canyons. Home to Chadron State College. **Information:** Chadron-Dawes County Area Chamber of Commerce, 706 W 3rd, PO Box 646, Chadron, 69337 (tel 308/432-4401).

MOTELS

UNRATED **Best Western Inn**

1100 W 10th St, 69337; tel 308/432-3305 or toll free 800/528-1234; fax 308/432-5990. ½ mi S of jct US 385/US 20. Definitely the nicest motel in Chadron. **Rooms:** 53 rms, stes, and effic. Executive level. CI 1pm/CO 11am. Nonsmoking rms avail. Rooms accessible from the inside and from the parking lot. **Amenities:** A/C, cable TV, dataport. Some units w/terraces, some w/fireplaces, some w/whirlpools. **Services:** Babysitting. Helpful, friendly staff. **Facilities:** 50 Whirlpool, washer/dryer. Scheduled renovation will add courtyard, heated indoor pool, and whirlpool. **Rates (CP):** Peak (June–Aug) $55 S; $65 D; $70–$110 ste; $70–$110 effic. Extra person $7. Children under age 12 stay free. Lower rates off-season. Parking: Outdoor, free. AE, DC, DISC, MC, V.

Super 8

US 20 W, PO Box 843, 69337; tel 308/432-4471 or toll free 800/800-8000; fax 308/432-3991. 2½ mi E of jct US 385/US 20. Standard rooms. A recent renovation added new units, including a whirlpool suite, plus an indoor, heated pool. **Rooms:** 45 rms and stes. CI 2pm/CO 11am. Nonsmoking rms avail. **Amenities:** A/C, cable TV w/movies. 1 unit w/whirlpool. Good-quality, thick towels in the bathrooms. **Services:** **Facilities:** 12 Whirlpool, washer/dryer. **Rates (CP):** Peak (June 15–Sept) $37 S; $45–$51 D; $51–$55 ste. Children under age 4 stay free. Lower rates off-season. Parking: Outdoor, free. AE, CB, DC, DISC, MC, V.

RESTAURANTS

Chuck Wagon Restaurant

806 E 3rd St; tel 308/432-3391. **American.** There's something for everyone at this friendly place, from plain hamburgers to the "Saint and Sinner" dinner—lobster and steak—for $25. **FYI:** Reservations accepted. Children's menu. **Open:** Sun 6am–9:30pm, Mon–Sat 6am–10pm. **Prices:** Main courses $6–$25. AE, DISC, MC, V.

★ **South 40 Steakhouse**

1250 W 10th St; tel 308/432-5111. Off US 385. **American.** The large dining room feels cozy with its dark tablecloths and candles. On the menu, you'll find plenty of variety: from peanut-butter pancakes for breakfast, to healthy stir-fry plates for dinner and a buffet brunch on Sunday. **FYI:** Reservations accepted. Children's menu. Dress code. **Open:** Mon–Sat 6am–10pm, Sun 6am–2pm. **Prices:** Main courses $10–$11. MC, V.

ATTRACTIONS

Museum of the Fur Trade

6321 US 20; tel 308/432-3843. 5 mi E of Chadron. Exhibits devoted to the story of the North American fur trade from colonial times to the present. Among the items on display are trade goods from the 16th century, such as beads, kettles, knives, and silverworks; weapons, including a collection of Northwest guns and Hawken rifles; and all types of American furs, such as buffalo, beaver, badger, and mink. There's also a trading post and Native American garden. **Open:** June–Aug, daily 8am–5pm. **$**

Chadron State Park

15951 NE 385; tel 308/432-6167. 9 mi S of Chadron. With the majestic Pine Ridge as its backdrop, Chadron State Park covers 974 acres. Summertime activities include horse trail rides, Jeep rides, paddleboats, and nightly campfire film screenings. Swimming pool open Memorial Day–Labor Day. Nature trails are used as cross-country skiing trails in winter. Modern housekeeping cabins and a campground are open year-round. **Open:** Mem Day–Labor Day, daily 8am–noon, 1pm–5pm; rest of year, daily 6am–10pm. Closed some hols. **$**

Fort Robinson State Park

3200 US 20, Crawford; tel 308/665-2900. 20 mi NE of Chadron. Built on the site of a former military post (1874–1948), this 22,000-acre park blends historical displays with natural beauty. Six reconstructed buildings includes officers' quarters and veterinary hospital; guided tours available. Amenities and activities include an indoor swimming pool, snack bar, museum, self-guided nature trail, river and lake fishing, Jeep and stagecoach rides, mountain-biking trails, and a nine-hole golf course. Eight-mile-long Smiley Canyon Scenic Drive wends its way through a herd of buffalo. Post Playhouse presents theater during summer months. **Open:** Visitor center: summer, daily 8am–7:30pm. Call ahead for fall hours. **$**

Columbus

The seat of Platte County was established in 1856 by former residents of Columbus, OH. A growing industrial center, Columbus is noted for its agricultural businesses and for one of the state's two largest power companies. **Information:** Columbus Area Chamber of Commerce, 764 3rd Ave, PO Box 515, Columbus, 68602-0515 (tel 402/564-2769).

MOTELS

Days Inn

371 33rd Ave, PO Box 1024, 68601; tel 402/564-2527 or toll free 800/329-7466; fax 402/562-6356. Jct US 30 and 81. Reasonably priced, all-brick motel. **Rooms:** 44 rms. CI 2pm/CO noon. Nonsmoking rms avail. **Amenities:** A/C, cable TV w/movies. **Services:** Babysitting. **Facilities:** **Rates:** $34 S; $40 D. Extra person $6. Children under age 18 stay free. Parking: Outdoor, free. AE, CB, DC, DISC, MC, V.

Eco-Lux Lodge

3803 23rd St, 68601; tel 402/564-9955; fax 402/564-9436. On US 30; on E side of town. Clean, new brick building, with an aquarium and Frederic Remington sculptures adding a nice touch to the lobby. Well located for shopping and restaurants. **Rooms:** 39 rms and stes. CI 3pm/CO 11am. Nonsmoking rms avail. **Amenities:** A/C, cable TV w/movies. The honeymoon suite offers a hot tub and whirlpool. **Services:** **Facilities:** 20 Washer/dryer. Microwave in lobby. **Rates:** $36–$50 S; $43–$60 D; $45–$60 ste. Extra person $4. Children under age 18 stay free. Parking: Outdoor, free. AE, CB, DC, DISC, JCB, MC, V.

New World Inn

265 33rd Ave, PO Box 1024, 68601; tel 402/564-1492 or toll free 800/433-1492; fax 402/563-3989. With its white stones and tall pines, this motel offers a touch of class. Inside, the decor includes a marble fireplace, paintings, and a stately grandfather clock. **Rooms:** 155 rms and stes. Executive level. CI 2pm/CO noon. Nonsmoking rms avail. **Amenities:** A/C, cable TV w/movies. **Services:** Babysitting. **Facilities:** 500 1 restaurant, 1 bar (w/entertainment), whirlpool, playground, washer/dryer. Good security, with cameras in hallways. Pool is framed with wrought iron and has its own little bridge. **Rates:** $49 S; $53 D; $100 ste. Extra person $6. Children under age 18 stay free. Parking: Outdoor, free. AE, CB, DC, DISC, MC, V.

Rosebud Motel

922 E 23rd St, 68601; tel 402/564-3256. E edge of town on US 30. Set off the highway for privacy, this location is nearly rural. Clean and serviceable and near the Ag-Park; attracts horse racing fans. **Rooms:** 11 rms. CI 3pm/CO 11am. Nonsmoking rms avail. Decorated with geometric wallpaper and tweed carpets. **Amenities:** A/C, cable TV w/movies. Rollaways available. **Services:** **Facilities:** **Rates:** $28 S; $32 D. Extra person $5. Children under age 10 stay free. Parking: Outdoor, free. AE, DISC, MC, V.

RESTAURANTS

★ Husker House

1754 33rd Ave; tel 402/564-4121. 4 blocks N of US 30. **American.** Steak, seafood, and chicken entrees highlight the menu offerings here. A nicely remodeled room decorated with grapevine wreaths is available for private parties of up to 40 people. **FYI:** Reservations recommended. Children's menu. **Open:** Mon–Sat 5–10pm. **Prices:** Main courses $6–$14. MC, V.

($) Johnnie's Steakhouse & Lounge

US 30 E and 3rd Ave; tel 402/563-3434. **American.** The name says it all—come for the steak. The dining room, with a knotty-cedar arched ceiling, can accommodate up to 400 people. **FYI:** Reservations accepted. Country music/dancing/jazz. Children's menu. **Open:** Lunch Sun–Fri 10:30am–2:30pm; dinner Sun–Fri 5–10pm, Sat 5–11pm. **Prices:** Main courses $7–$19; prix fixe $11. AE, DISC, MC, V.

Fremont

This agricultural and college town was founded in 1856 and named for Col John C Fremont, then a candidate for president. The seat of Dodge County has a variety of industries, many of them in food production. **Information:** Dodge County Convention and Visitors Bureau, 92 W 5th St, PO Box 182, Fremont, 68025 (tel 402/721-2641).

MOTELS

Budget Host Relax Inn

1435 E 23rd St, 68025; tel 402/721-5656 or toll free 800/616-9966; fax 402/721-5656. E US 30. New brick building located near restaurants **Rooms:** 35 rms. CI noon/CO 11am. Nonsmoking rms avail. Double rooms have two counters and two sinks. **Amenities:** A/C, cable TV w/movies, dataport. Alarm clocks available. **Services:** **Facilities:** Truck parking available. **Rates:** $32 S; $37–$41 D. Extra person $4. Children under age 10 stay free. Parking: Outdoor, free. AE, DISC, MC, V.

Comfort Inn

1649 E 23rd St, 68025; tel 402/721-1109 or toll free 800/228-5150; fax 402/721-1109. E US 30. New property; ultramodern and clean. **Rooms:** 48 rms and stes. CI 2pm/CO 11am. Nonsmoking rms avail. Single accommodations offer recliners; suites have couch. **Amenities:** A/C, cable TV w/movies. Suites have microwaves and refrigerators. **Services:** **Facilities:** Games rm, sauna, whirlpool.

Rates (CP): $44 S; $50 D; $52–$68 ste. Extra person $5. Children under age 18 stay free. Parking: Outdoor, free. AE, DC, DISC, JCB, MC, V.

UNRATED **Holiday Lodge**
1220 E 23rd St, PO Box 409, 68025; tel 402/727-1110 or toll free 800/743-ROOM; fax 800/743-1631. US 30 and Yeager Ave. Very pleasant motel. **Rooms:** 100 rms. CI 3pm/CO noon. Nonsmoking rms avail. **Amenities:** A/C, cable TV w/movies. **Services:** Sunday brunch is served poolside. **Facilities:** 200 1 restaurant, 1 bar (w/entertainment), games rm, whirlpool. Excellent pool area, with exercise loft above. **Rates:** $40–$63 S or D. Extra person $6. Parking: Outdoor, free. AE, CB, DC, DISC, MC, V.

RESTAURANTS

Al's Cafe
207 S Bell St; tel 402/721-5700. US 275; on S edge of town. **American.** Genuine family-style cafe in business for more than 60 years. Friendly, old-time hospitality brings folks back for cafe favorites like hamburgers, sandwiches, and the locally famous chicken-fried steaks. **FYI:** Reservations recommended. Children's menu. **Open:** Mon–Sat 6am–10pm. **Prices:** Main courses $4–$9. No CC.

K C's Cafe & Bar
In Downtown Shopping Center, 631 Park Ave; tel 402/721-3353. US 77 to 1st St. **American.** Filled with memorabilia from Fremont's past, this humble spot has a warm atmosphere. In addition to the antiques, people come for the old-fashioned favorites like homemade fried chicken and gravy. **FYI:** Reservations recommended. Children's menu. **Open:** Lunch Mon–Sat 11am–2pm; dinner Mon–Sat 5–9:30pm. **Prices:** Main courses $3–$10; prix fixe $5. AE, MC, V.

ATTRACTION

May Museum
1643 N Nye; tel 402/721-4515. Italianate revival mansion built in 1874 by Fremont's first mayor, Theron Nye. Of primary interest are the numerous mantels, the richly carved paneling of oak and mahogany, the art-glass windows, and the exceptional tile work of the master bath. A log house, Victorian garden, and gazebo (where concerts are often held during summer months) are also on the grounds. **Open:** Jan–Mar by appointment only; Apr–Dec, Wed–Sun 1:30–4:30pm. Closed some hols. **$**

Grand Island

Union Pacific Railroad founded the city—today the seat of Hall County—in 1866, although the island between two channels of the Platte River was well known to fur traders as early as 1820 as La Grande Isle. At the time, it was one of the most conspicuous features of the Platte River valley. Today, Grand Island's midstate placement makes it a popular convention center and industrial site. **Information:** Grand Island Convention and Visitors Bureau, 309 W 2nd St, PO Box 1486, Grand Island, 68802 (tel 308/382-4400).

MOTELS

Conoco Motel
2107 W 2nd St, 68803; tel 308/384-2700. An inexpensive motor lodge that has seen better days. Located on a busy street, and surrounded by cement. **Rooms:** 38 rms. CI noon/CO noon. Nonsmoking rms avail. **Amenities:** A/C, cable TV. **Services:** Small pets OK at manager's discretion. **Facilities:** 20 1 restaurant. **Rates:** Peak (June–Aug) $27–$30 S; $36 D. Extra person $2. Lower rates off-season. Parking: Outdoor, free. AE, CB, DC, DISC, MC, V.

Holiday Inn
US 281 and I-80, 68802; tel 308/384-7770 or toll free 800/465-4329. Exit 312 off I-80. A modestly appointed but well-maintained motel. **Rooms:** 214 rms and stes. CI 4pm/CO noon. Nonsmoking rms avail. **Amenities:** A/C, satel TV w/movies, dataport. Some units w/terraces, 1 w/whirlpool. **Services:** Car-rental desk, babysitting. **Facilities:** 500 1 restaurant, 1 bar, games rm, sauna, whirlpool, playground, washer/dryer. **Rates:** Peak (mid-June–Aug) $57–$64 S; $62–$69 D; $99 ste. Extra person $5. Children under age 21 stay free. Lower rates off-season. Parking: Outdoor, free. AE, CB, DC, DISC, JCB, MC, V.

RESTAURANTS

Dreisbach's
1137 S Locust St; tel 308/382-5450. 2 blocks N of US 30 on Locust. **Steak.** This long-time favorite of beef lovers continues to dish out its own cuts of sirloin, fillets, and prime rib (the latter offered in a blackened-Cajun version). Family-style dinners of ham, chicken, and roast beef are served tableside, and all meals come with an unlimited supply of baking-powder biscuits and Nebraska honey. Often packed on weekends. **FYI:** Reservations accepted. Children's menu. **Open:** Lunch Mon–Fri 11am–1:30pm; dinner Mon–Sat 4:30–10pm, Sun 4:30–9pm; brunch Sun 11am–1:30pm. **Prices:** Main courses $9–$26. AE, CB, DC, DISC, MC, V.

Yen Ching
610 W 2nd St; tel 308/384-3020. On US 30. **Chinese.** Splashes of red enliven the ambience of this Chinese restaurant, which offers a choice of over 60 entrees. One of the favorites is the "Happy Family," a sizzling blend of seafood, beef, and vegetables. Several low-fat and low-sodium items available. **FYI:** Reservations accepted. Additional location: 2623 S Locust (tel 384-8298). **Open:** Mon–Sat 11:30am–9:30pm. **Prices:** Main courses $7–$11. AE, DC, MC, V.

ATTRACTION

Heritage Zoo
2103 W Stolley Park Rd; tel 308/385-5416. Small zoo specializing in local and migratory Nebraska wildlife, such as bobcats, sandhill cranes, prairie dogs, and eagles. Herpatarium, waterfowl pond, petting zoo. Weekend animal demonstrations are offered in an outdoor amphitheater. **Open:** Daily 10am–6pm. Closed Sept–Apr. $

Harrison

The seat of Sioux County, established in 1886 and named for President Benjamin Harrison.

RESTAURANT

Sioux Sundries
201 Main St; tel 308/668-2577. **American.** Hidden inside an old-fashioned dime store, this eatery is best-known for its 28-oz hamburger, reputed to be the largest burger served in America. Homemade cinnamon rolls and peanut-butter shakes are also popular. Nebraska governors and legislators make a point of stopping in for oversize meals. **FYI:** Reservations accepted. Children's menu. No liquor license. **Open:** Mon–Fri 6:30am–5:30pm, Sat 6:30am–7pm. **Prices:** Lunch main courses $4–$7. MC, V.

ATTRACTION

Agate Fossil Beds
301 River Rd; tel 308/668-2211. Some 19 million years ago, dinosaurs and many other now-extinct creatures lived on this Miocene savanna. Here at Agate Fossil Beds, their fossils are concentrated in beds of sedimentary rock formed by the deposition of silt and volcanic ash in an ancient river valley. The visitors center (about 3 mi E of Agate Springs Ranch) has self-guided tour maps to areas of exposed fossils. The center also has exhibits depicting what these prehistoric creatures may have looked like, as well as the **Cook Collection of Oglala Lakota artifacts.** (Please keep in mind that everything here is protected by the Federal government; do *not* remove any fossils you may find.) For further information, contact the Superintendent, Scotts Bluff National Monument, Box 27, Gering, NE 69341 (tel 308/436-4340). **Open:** Daily 8:30am–5:30pm. Closed some hols.

Hastings

Established in 1872 by English immigrants lured by propaganda boasting of rich farmland. The county seat of Adams County is home to Hastings College. **Information:** Hastings/Adams County Convention and Visitors Bureau, 220 N Hastings Ave, PO Box 941, Hastings, 69802 (tel 402/461-2370).

MOTELS

Holiday Inn
2205 Osborne Dr E, 68901; tel 402/463-6721 or toll free 800/465-4329. On US 281 on N side of town. Clean motel with nice family restaurant on-site. **Rooms:** 101 rms and stes. CI 3pm/CO 11am. Nonsmoking rms avail. All rooms have two vanities—one inside bathroom and one outside. **Amenities:** A/C, satel TV w/movies, dataport. **Services:** Babysitting. **Facilities:** 1 restaurant, 1 bar, games rm, sauna, whirlpool, washer/dryer. Large, central recreation area around pool. **Rates:** Peak (mid-May–mid-Sept) $56–$63 S; $66–$73 D; $75 ste. Extra person $5. Children under age 12 stay free. Lower rates off-season. Parking: Outdoor, free. AE, CB, DC, DISC, MC, V.

Midlands Lodge
910 W J St, 68901; tel 402/463-2428 or toll free 800/237-1872; fax 402/463-2411. Jct US 281/US 6. Surprising quality for the price. **Rooms:** 47 rms. CI noon/CO 11am. Nonsmoking rms avail. Rooms done in sturdy tweeds and light grays; all have double vanities (one inside bathroom, one outside). Oversize suites with four double beds are a great value. **Amenities:** A/C, cable TV, refrig. **Services:** **Facilities:** **Rates:** Peak (May 15–Sept 15) $27–$32 S; $32–$37 D. Extra person $4. Children under age 12 stay free. Lower rates off-season. Parking: Outdoor, free. AE, CB, DC, DISC, MC, V.

Super 8
2200 N Kansas Ave, 68901; tel 402/463-8888 or toll free 800/800-8000; fax 402/463-8899. On US 281 in N end of city. A new facility. **Rooms:** 50 rms and stes. CI 3pm/CO 11am. Nonsmoking rms avail. Attractive bedspreads and framed prints match the color scheme and woodwork. **Amenities:** A/C, cable TV, dataport. Some units w/whirlpools. **Services:** Babysitting. **Facilities:** Games rm. **Rates (CP):** Peak (mid-May–mid-Sept) $39–$42 S; $44–$49 D; $75 ste. Extra person $5. Children under age 12 stay free. Lower rates off-season. Parking: Outdoor, free. AE, CB, DC, DISC, MC, V.

RESTAURANT

Bernardo's
1109 S Baltimore; tel 402/463-4666. US 281 S to US 6, W ½ mi. **Steak.** The decor is typical of a small-town steak house—dark colors and rather blasé furniture—but the steaks are worth coming for, particularly the prime rib. Small eaters might try ordering the prime-rib sandwich, which offers the same quality (but less quantity) of the full cut. Senior discounts. **FYI:** Reservations accepted. Children's menu. **Open:** Lunch Mon–Fri 11am–1:30pm; dinner daily 5–11pm. **Prices:** Main courses $6–$27. AE, DISC, MC, V.

ATTRACTION

Hastings Museum/Lied IMAX Theatre
14th St and Burlington Ave; tel 402/461-IMAX. Museum contains permanent exhibits on the culture of the Plains Native Americans; fossil records of the prehistoric West; and birds, rocks, and minerals. Third floor features a transportation exhibit and an extensive collection of firearms. J M McDonald Planetarium offers four different sky shows, while the Lied IMAX theater uses its five-story tall screen to bring the natural world to life. (Separate admission fee for IMAX theater; combination tickets available.) **Open:** Museum: Mon–Sat 9am–5pm, Sun 10am–5pm. Call for planetarium and IMAX schedules. Closed some hols. **$$**

Kearney

Seat of Buffalo County. Named for the nearby Fort Kearny, an active military fort between 1847 to 1871; the town was established somewhat later (about 1873). Today, the city is home to the University of Nebraska at Kearney and is a midstate business center. **Information:** Kearney Area Chamber of Commerce, 1007 2nd Ave, PO Box 607, Kearney, 68848-0607 (tel 308/237-3101).

MOTELS

Best Western Inn
1010 3rd Ave, 68847; tel 308/237-5185 or toll free 800/359-1894; fax 308/234-1002. Exit 272 off I-80. Exterior has recently been spruced up. **Rooms:** 69 rms. CI 2pm/CO noon. Nonsmoking rms avail. Attractive burgundy decor and better-quality furnishings. **Amenities:** A/C, cable TV. **Services:** **Facilities:** 1 restaurant (bkfst and dinner only), basketball, sauna, whirlpool. **Rates (BB):** Peak (June–Aug) $49–$62 S; $54–$72 D. Extra person $5. Children under age 13 stay free. Lower rates off-season. Parking: Outdoor, free. AE, CB, DC, DISC, MC, V.

Budget Host Motel
1401 2nd Ave, 68847; tel 308/237-3153 or toll free 800/333-1401; fax 308/234-6073. Exit 272 off I-80; 1 mi N on NE 10. A tidy little motor court with geraniums planted outside the rooms. **Rooms:** 34 rms. CI 2pm/CO 11am. Nonsmoking rms avail. **Amenities:** A/C, cable TV, dataport. Some units w/terraces. **Services:** **Facilities:** 1 restaurant, 1 bar. **Rates:** Peak (June–Aug) $35–$36 S; $43–$46 D. Extra person $4. Children under age 12 stay free. Lower rates off-season. Parking: Outdoor, free. AE, DISC, MC, V.

Comfort Inn
903 2nd Ave, 68847; tel 308/237-5858 or toll free 800/221-2222; fax 308/237-5858. Exit 272 off I-80. Bright, cheery, economy motel that's well cared for. **Rooms:** 66 rms and stes. CI 3pm/CO 11am. Nonsmoking rms avail. Whirlpool suites are small, but attractive. **Amenities:** A/C, cable TV w/movies. Some units w/whirlpools. **Services:** **Facilities:** Whirlpool. **Rates (CP):** Peak (May–Sept) $38–$60 S; $42–$70 D; $77–$87 ste. Extra person $5. Children under age 17 stay free. Lower rates off-season. Parking: Outdoor, free. Group rates avail. AE, DC, DISC, MC, V.

Holiday Inn
301 2nd Ave, PO Box 1118, 68848; tel 308/237-3141 or toll free 800/465-4329, 800/652-1909 in NE; fax 308/234-4675. Exit 272 off I-80. A good choice for families with kids. **Rooms:** 209 rms and stes. CI 3pm/CO noon. Nonsmoking rms avail. Some rooms open onto pool area. **Amenities:** A/C, cable TV, dataport. Some units w/terraces. Suites have coffeemakers, hair dryers, and mini-refrigerators. **Services:** **Facilities:** 1 restaurant, 2 bars (1 w/entertainment), games rm, sauna, whirlpool, washer/dryer. Dome-covered pool has swim-under bridge, waterfall, lots of greenery, and a tree-house bar in the center. An oversized hot tub is in a separate room. **Rates:** Peak (Mem Day–Labor Day) $81–$86 S; $86–$91 D; $99 ste. Children under age 20 stay free. Lower rates off-season. Parking: Outdoor, free. Kids younger than 12 eat free. AE, CB, DC, DISC, JCB, MC, V.

Ramada Inn
110 2nd Ave, 68847; tel 308/237-5971 or toll free 800/272-6232, 800/248-4460 in NE; fax 308/236-7549. Exit 272 off I-80; N 1 mi on NE 10. Large convention-oriented hotel with an attractive restaurant and lounge. **Rooms:** 151 rms and stes. CI 4pm/CO 11am. Nonsmoking rms avail. All rooms have dual vanities. Some accommodations overlook pool. **Amenities:** A/C, cable TV w/movies, dataport. Some units w/whirlpools. Suites offer mini-refrigerators. **Services:** **Facilities:** 1 restaurant, 1 bar, volleyball, games rm, whirlpool, washer/dryer. Sand-lot volleyball. **Rates:** $49–$56 S; $59–$76 D; $110 ste. Children under age 18 stay free. Parking: Outdoor, free. AE, CB, DC, DISC, MC, V.

Super 8
15 W 8th St, 68847; tel 308/234-5513 or toll free 800/800-8000; fax 308/234-3835. Exit 272 off I-80. A clean, neat, plain-Jane motel. **Rooms:** 61 rms. CI 1pm/CO 11am. Nonsmoking rms avail. Some rooms have full-length mirrors. **Amenities:** A/C, cable TV. **Services:** Complimentary morning coffee and doughnuts. **Facilities:** **Rates:** Peak (Apr–Oct) $42–$47 S; $52–$62 D. Children under age 12 stay free. Lower rates off-season. Parking: Outdoor, free. Rates determined by number of people staying in room. AE, CB, DC, DISC, MC, V.

Western Inn South
510 3rd Ave, 68847; tel 308/234-1876 or toll free 800/437-8457; fax 308/237-0543. Exit 272 off I-80. Newly redone rooms are airy and clean. **Rooms:** 45 rms. CI 2pm/CO 11am. Nonsmoking rms avail. **Amenities:** A/C, cable

TV, dataport. **Services:** **Facilities:** Sauna, whirlpool. **Rates:** Peak (June–Aug) $47–$50 S; $48–$59 D. Extra person $5. Children under age 12 stay free. Lower rates off-season. Parking: Outdoor, free. Free breakfast during winter. Group rates avail. AE, DC, DISC, MC, V.

RESTAURANTS

Bazooka Joe's

121 W 46th St; tel 308/237-2910. Exit 272 off I-80; 3 mi N on 2nd Ave. **Burgers.** A full-tilt salute to the 1950s, with metal-tube chairs and neon lights. There's even a black-and-white tiled dance floor where you can step out while waiting for your burgers and sandwiches. Soda-fountain treats include the "Green River Float," with ice cream, lime syrup, and phosphate. Menus are on old records, with kids' menus inscribed on 45s. **FYI:** Reservations accepted. Comedy/karaoke. Children's menu. Beer and wine only. **Open:** Breakfast Sat–Sun 7–10:30am; lunch Mon–Fri 11am–2pm, Sat–Sun 10:30am–2pm; dinner Sun–Thurs 5–9pm, Fri–Sat 5–10pm. **Prices:** Main courses $4–$8. AE, DISC, MC, V.

Grandpa's Steakhouse

13 Central Ave; tel 308/237-2882. Exit 272 off I-80; S 2 blocks. **Steak.** The dining room presents a motley mix of Victoriana and steak-house furnishings, (from velvet-tufted chairs to a campy painting of a hillbilly grandpa), but there's little confusion about the favorite entree: steak, featuring prime cuts like T-bones, filet mignon, and others. Fish and chicken selections also available. **FYI:** Reservations accepted. Children's menu. **Open:** Mon–Sat 5–11pm, Sun 11am–2pm. **Prices:** Main courses $7–$19. AE, CB, DC, DISC, MC, V.

Habetat

121 W 46th St; tel 308/237-2405. Exit 272 off I-80, 3 mi N on 2nd Ave. **Eclectic.** A pleasant surprise in western Nebraska. Hand-painted murals in the Crane Room celebrate the wildlife of the Platte River, while the Bird Room faces an urban pond that attracts 15 kinds of finches, as well as ducks and swans. The outdoorsy theme even carries to the menu, which is bound with small sticks. House specialties include pecan chicken; mixed-grill skewers of shrimp, chicken, and beef; and a full selection of steaks. **FYI:** Reservations accepted. Children's menu. **Open:** Lunch Mon–Sat 11am–4pm; dinner Mon–Thurs 4–9:30pm, Fri–Sat 4–10:30pm, Sun 5–9:30pm; brunch Sun 10–2:30am. **Prices:** Main courses $5–$17. AE, DISC, MC, V.

ATTRACTIONS

Museum of Nebraska Art

2401 Central Ave; tel 308/865-8559. Collections that reveal the range of Nebraska's history, from the artist/explorers to the pioneer years and on through the contemporary scene. Major strengths are in the works of George Catlin, Robert Henri, and Thomas Hart Benton. The Grant Reynard Collection documents the entire career of the Nebraska native. **Open:** Tues–Sat 11am–5pm; Sun 1–5pm. Closed some hols. **Free**

Fort Kearny State Historical Park

NE 4; tel 308/865-5305. The first fort to protect travelers on the Oregon Trail, Fort Kearny (built in 1848) also acted as a Pony Express station and gold miner's outfitting depot during its 23-year history. Restored buildings now open to the public include the stockade and blacksmith/carpenter shop; self-guided tours are based around interpretive plaques explaining the fort's history.

Fort Kearny State Recreation Area (2 mi NE of the park) offers a campground, picnic shelters, a hike/bike trail, fishing—bass, bluegill, catfish, and crappie are plentiful—and a beach (tel 308/234-9513). **Open:** Mem Day–Labor Day, daily 9am–5pm. **$**

Lexington

The seat of Dawson County evolved in 1889 from a nearby Pony Express station at Plum Creek. Antique shops abound. **Information:** Lexington Area Chamber of Commerce, 200 W US 30, PO Box 97, Lexington, 68850 (tel 308/324-5504).

MOTELS

Comfort Inn

2810 Plum Creek Pkwy, 68850; tel 308/324-3747 or toll free 800/221-2222; fax 308/324-2590. Exit 237 off I-80. Care has been taken in designing all aspects of this new motel, which is neat as a pin. **Rooms:** 49 rms and stes. CI open/CO 11am. Nonsmoking rms avail. Queen rooms have recliners. **Amenities:** A/C, cable TV. 1 unit w/whirlpool. **Services:** **Facilities:** 30 Whirlpool, washer/dryer. **Rates (CP):** Peak (June–Aug) $50–$55 S; $55–$70 D; $70–$90 ste. Extra person $5. Children under age 18 stay free. Lower rates off-season. Parking: Outdoor, free. AE, CB, DC, DISC, JCB, MC, V.

Econo Lodge

I-80 Exchange and US 283, 68850; tel 308/324-5601 or toll free 800/424-4777; fax 308/324-4284. Exit 237 off I-80, N on NE 21. Showing signs of wear and tear. **Rooms:** 50 rms. CI 2pm/CO noon. Nonsmoking rms avail. Institutional-type metal doors; some rooms have peeling wallpaper. **Amenities:** A/C, satel TV. **Services:** **Rates (CP):** Peak (May–Oct) $30–$40 S; $36–$46 D. Extra person $5. Children under age 18 stay free. Lower rates off-season. Parking: Outdoor, free. AE, CB, DC, DISC, MC, V.

Minute Man Motel—Budget Host

801 Plum Creek Pkwy, 68850; tel 308/324-5544 or toll free 800/973-5544. Exit 237 off I-80; N on NE 21. An older, well-maintained motor lodge. **Rooms:** 36 rms. CI 11am/CO 11am. Nonsmoking rms avail. Adequate, with brown carpeting and cheap paneling. **Amenities:** A/C, cable TV.

Services: Dogs allowed in designated rooms only; cats not permitted. **Facilities:** Small basketball court—bring your own ball. **Rates:** $28–$30 S; $36 D. Extra person $2. Children under age 12 stay free. Parking: Outdoor, free. Rates are a bargain. AE, CB, DC, DISC, MC, V.

RESTAURANT

Valentino's
601 N Grant; tel 308/324-4617. Exit 237 off I-80, NE 21 N to downtown. **Pizza.** Part of a popular statewide pizza chain. The lunch and dinner buffets offer good values for families and include a selection of pizzas, pastas, and "dessert" pizzas—a lighter dough topped with fruit and icing. **FYI:** Reservations not accepted. Children's menu. Beer and wine only. **Open:** Daily 11am–10pm. **Prices:** Main courses $3–$6; prix fixe $6. No CC.

ATTRACTIONS

Dawson County Museum
805 N Taft St; tel 308/324-5340. The largest exhibit in this local museum details the early days of the Union Pacific Railroad. Other displays showcase quilts and Native American artifacts. An 1860 log cabin, 1888 schoolhouse, 1903 Baldwin locomotive engine, and 1919 biplane are kept on the grounds. **Open:** Mon–Sat 9am–5pm, Sun 1–5pm. **Free**

Robert Henri Museum and Historical Walkway
218 E 8th, Cozad; tel 308/784-4154. 12 mi SE of Lexington. This museum, located in the home of native son and artist Robert Henri, is furnished with period antiques and displays both original works and reproductions by the artist. Other late 19th-century buildings on the grounds include a church, a school, and an original Pony Express station. **Open:** Mon–Sat 9am–5pm, Sun 1–5pm. **$**

Lincoln

The state's capital and home to the University of Nebraska at Lincoln, the state's largest campus. Founded in 1854 as the city of Lancaster and the seat of the county by the same name, the name was changed in the 1860s after the city won a nasty battle to be the state's capital. The university endows the city with a youthful makeup and a pool of engineers around whom the city has built a small, thriving base of electronic and communications companies. The city's top draw is the university's top-ranked football team, the Huskers; lodging and dining choices narrow considerably in season. The annual state fair reminds visitors of the city's lasting agricultural ties. **Information:** Lincoln Convention and Visitors Bureau, 1221 N St #320, PO Box 83737, Lincoln, 68501 (tel 402/434-5335).

PUBLIC TRANSPORTATION

StarTran (tel 402/476-1234) provides service with over 20 routes throughout the greater Lincoln area. Stops are marked by blue and green signs, but buses will stop at any corner outside of the downtown loop. All of StarTran's regular bus routes are wheelchair accessible. Fares: adults 75¢, children 5–11 40¢, elderly and persons with disabilities 35¢; children under 5 ride free. Transfers are free.

HOTELS

Cornhusker Hotel
333 S 13th St, 68508 (Downtown); tel 402/474-7474 or toll free 800/793-7474; fax 402/474-1847. I-80 downtown to M St; E 4 blocks. A sumptuous downtown hotel. The lobby, decorated with rich brocades and Oriental rugs, is dominated by a sweeping oak staircase. Walkways connect building to downtown shopping. **Rooms:** 290 rms and stes. Executive level. CI open/CO noon. Nonsmoking rms avail. **Amenities:** A/C, satel TV w/movies, dataport, in-rm safe. Some units w/minibars. Suites have two phones, plus refrigerator and hair dryer. **Services:** Twice-daily maid svce, babysitting. Refundable $250 pet deposit. **Facilities:** 2 restaurants (*see* "Restaurants" below), 1 bar (w/entertainment). Restaurants are excellent. **Rates:** $115 S; $125 D; $175–$450 ste. Extra person $10. Children under age 5 stay free. Parking: Indoor, $4/day. AE, CB, DC, DISC, MC, V.

Ramada Hotel
141 N 9th St, 68508 (Haymarket); tel 402/475-4011 or toll free 800/432-0002; fax 402/475-9011. At the end of I-80. A quality hotel at the foot of Lincoln's historic Haymarket district, also close to downtown and the university. Potted plants in the lobby add a nice touch. **Rooms:** 233 rms and stes. CI 3pm/CO noon. Nonsmoking rms avail. Second-floor rooms have a balcony. Minisuites offer couches that fold out into double beds. **Amenities:** A/C, satel TV w/movies, dataport. **Services:** Babysitting. **Facilities:** 1 restaurant, 1 bar, games rm, sauna, whirlpool. Large ballroom facilities. **Rates:** $70–$90 S; $80–$100 D; $90–$100 ste. Extra person $5. Children under age 16 stay free. Parking: Indoor, free. Romance and bed-and-breakfast packages avail. AE, CB, DC, DISC, ER, MC, V.

MOTELS

Best Western Villager Motor Inn
5200 O St, 68510; tel 402/464-9111 or toll free 800/356-4321; fax 402/467-0505. Exit 405 off I-80. The outside looks fairly ordinary, but the rooms are a nice surprise, with good-quality furnishings. **Rooms:** 187 rms and stes. CI 2pm/CO noon. Nonsmoking rms avail. Decorated with dark woods, and pretty, formal upholstery, plus bed skirts in floral prints. **Amenities:** A/C, satel TV w/movies. Some units w/whirlpools. **Services:** Babysitting. **Facilities:** 2 restaurants (*see* "Restaurants" below), 2 bars, whirlpool, washer/dryer. **Rates:** Peak (Apr–Oct) $54–

$58 S; $60–$64 D; $85–$150 ste. Extra person $6. Children under age 18 stay free. Lower rates off-season. Parking: Outdoor, free. AE, CB, DC, DISC, MC, V.

Budget Host Motel
2732 O St, 68510; tel 402/476-3253 or toll free 800/283-4678; fax 402/476-7546. Exit 403 off I-80. Older motor court; pretty far down the totem pole. **Rooms:** 42 rms and stes. Executive level. CI 2pm/CO noon. Nonsmoking rms avail. Room decor consists of yesterday's earth tones and blond-finished furniture. **Amenities:** A/C, cable TV, refrig. **Services:** **Rates:** Peak (Mar–Oct) $32–$37 S; $38–$45 D; $34–$47 ste. Extra person $5. Children under age 12 stay free. Lower rates off-season. Parking: Outdoor, free. AE, CB, DC, DISC, ER, MC, V.

Cobbler Inn
4808 W O St, 68528; tel 402/475-4800 or toll free 800/777-4808. Exit 395 off I-80. This adequate motel on the outskirts of Lincoln is parked next to a truck stop with a small display of antique trucks and old-time gas pumps. In keeping with the "cobbler" theme, the attractive exposed-beam lobby is decorated with antique shoes. **Rooms:** 49 rms. CI open/CO noon. Nonsmoking rms avail. Clean, neat, and generally quiet. **Amenities:** A/C, satel TV w/movies. **Services:** **Facilities:** 75 1 restaurant, games rm, washer/dryer. **Rates:** $39–$42 S; $45 D. Extra person $3. Children under age 12 stay free. Parking: Outdoor, free. AE, DISC, MC, V.

Days Inn
2920 NW 12 St, 68521 (Lincoln Municipal Airport); tel 402/475-3616 or toll free 800/329-7466; fax 402/475-4356. Exit 399 off I-80. Unremarkable but clean property. **Rooms:** 84 rms. CI 3pm/CO noon. Nonsmoking rms avail. **Amenities:** A/C, satel TV. **Services:** Pet fee $5/night. **Facilities:** Nearby chain restaurants give discounts to guests. **Rates (CP):** Peak (May–July) $35–$43 S; $52 D. Extra person $5. Children under age 12 stay free. Lower rates off-season. Parking: Outdoor, free. Rates rise on Husker football weekends. AE, CB, DC, DISC, MC, V.

Hampton Inn
1301 W Bond Circle, 68521 (Lincoln Municipal Airport); tel 402/474-2080 or toll free 800/426-7866; fax 402/474-3401. Exit 399 off I-80. Well-maintained property convenient to airport. The nicely appointed lobby and breakfast area are furnished in colonial American style. **Rooms:** 111 rms and stes. CI 2pm/CO noon. Nonsmoking rms avail. **Amenities:** A/C, cable TV, dataport. Some units w/terraces, 1 w/whirlpool. Two-room suites have refrigerator. **Services:** **Facilities:** 75 Games rm. **Rates (CP):** $54 S; $59–$66 D; $59–$67 ste. Children under age 18 stay free. Parking: Outdoor, free. Third or fourth person stays free. AE, DC, DISC, MC, V.

Harvester Motel
1511 Center Park Rd, 68512; tel 402/423-3131 or toll free 800/500-1366; fax 402/423-3155. 3 blocks S of NE 2 on 14th St. Clean, pleasant facility on city's south side. **Rooms:** 80 rms and stes. CI 2pm/CO 11am. Nonsmoking rms avail. **Amenities:** A/C, satel TV, dataport. Some units w/terraces, some w/whirlpools. Suites have refrigerators. **Services:** Babysitting. **Facilities:** 200 1 restaurant (*see* "Restaurants" below), 1 bar, games rm, day-care ctr, washer/dryer. **Rates (CP):** $40–$45 S; $50–$55 D; $125–$130 ste. Extra person $3. Children under age 12 stay free. Parking: Outdoor, free. Group rates avail. AE, CB, DC, DISC, MC, V.

Holiday Inn Airport
1101 W Bond, 68521 (Lincoln Municipal Airport); tel 402/475-4971 or toll free 800/465-4329; fax 402/475-0606. Exit 399 off I-80. Basic airport accommodations, though slightly frayed around the edges. **Rooms:** 105 rms and stes. CI 3pm/CO noon. Nonsmoking rms avail. **Amenities:** A/C, satel TV w/movies, dataport. "Female traveler" rooms include hair dryer and wash line. Refrigerator available on request. **Services:** Free transportation anywhere in town. **Facilities:** 200 1 restaurant, 1 bar, games rm, washer/dryer. Nice restaurant with linen tablecloths and a kids-eat-free policy. **Rates:** $54–$89 S; $61–$95 D; $89 ste. Extra person $7. Children under age 16 stay free. Parking: Outdoor, free. AE, CB, DC, DISC, JCB, MC, V.

Sleep Inn
3400 NW 12th St, 68521; tel 402/475-1550 or toll free 800/627-5337; fax 402/475-1550. Exit 399 off I-80. A new motel radiating fresh appeal and cleanliness. The open staircase in the lobby is unusually attractive for an economy motel. **Rooms:** 80 rms. CI 1pm/CO noon. Nonsmoking rms avail. **Amenities:** A/C, cable TV w/movies, dataport. **Services:** **Facilities:** 30 Washer/dryer. **Rates (CP):** Peak (July–Sept) $49–$64 S; $54–$69 D. Extra person $6. Children under age 18 stay free. Lower rates off-season. Parking: Outdoor, free. AE, CB, DC, DISC, JCB, MC, V.

RESTAURANTS

Harvester Restaurant
In Harvester Motel, 1501 Center Park Rd; tel 402/420-2494. 3 blocks S of NE 2 on 14th St. **German/Czechoslovakian.** This traditional spot on the city's far south side has carved a niche for itself with Czech and German specialties like svickova (marinated beef with creamed vegetables and gravy), and roast duck with potato dumplings. Kolaches, rye bread, strudel, and pies baked fresh daily. **FYI:** Reservations accepted. Children's menu. **Open:** **Prices:** Main courses $3–$14. MC, V.

Inn Harms Way
In Lincoln Station, 7 P St (Haymarket); tel 402/438-3033. I-80 to downtown. **Seafood.** Housed in an elegantly renovated train station, with salvaged depot benches used as seating. Seafood is flown in daily for dishes ranging from English-style fish-and-chips (wrapped in the local newspaper) to mahimahi and shark. During summer, diners can sit on the depot platform, which is just off the still-functional train tracks.

FYI: Reservations accepted. Children's menu. **Open:** Mon–Fri 11am–10pm, Sat 5–10pm. **Prices:** Main courses $7–$33. AE, DC, DISC, MC, V.

Lazio's

710 P St (Haymarket District); tel 402/474-2337. Take I-80 until it becomes 9th St. **American/Steak.** This microbrewery churns out a small river of suds, ranging from pale ale to a hearty Black Jack stout. Food choices feature burgers and chicken grilled over a lively hickory flame. Original antique photos of Lincoln sites and vintage carousel animals dot the dining room. **FYI:** Reservations not accepted. Children's menu. **Open:** Mon–Sat 11am–1am, Sun 11am–10pm. **Prices:** Main courses $5–$15. AE, DISC, MC, V.

★ Misty's

6235 Havelock Ave; tel 402/466-8424. 56th St exit off I-80. **Steak.** Old-fashioned, red-tufted booths and soft lighting make Misty's an elegant steak house. Known for sterling-quality beef cuts—including filet mignon, New York strip, and fork-tender prime rib–plus the popular Cajun-blackened prime rib. Seafood and combination platters also available. **FYI:** Reservations accepted. Children's menu. Additional location: 5508 S 56th St (tel 423-2288). **Open:** Mon–Thurs 11am–11pm, Fri–Sat 11am–midnight, Sun 4–10pm. **Prices:** Main courses $9–$30. AE, DC, MC, V.

The Renaissance

In Cornhusker Hotel, 333 S 13th (Downtown); tel 402/474-7474. I-80 to downtown; E on M St. **French.** The decor of this genteel dining room is defined by oak paneling, oversize windows, and brocade-upholstered chairs. The menu lists elegant, French-accented dishes such as breast of duck in a blueberry-merlot sauce; grilled beef tenderloins with five-onion butter is a lunchtime favorite. Jackets recommended but not required. **FYI:** Reservations recommended. Children's menu. Dress code. **Open:** Lunch Mon–Fri 11:30am–2pm; dinner Mon–Sat 5:30–10:30pm; brunch Sun 10am–1:30pm. **Prices:** Main courses $19–$28. AE, CB, DC, DISC, MC, V. VP

★ Rock'n Roll Runza

210 N 14th St (Downtown); tel 402/474-2030. I-80 to downtown; E on O St to 14th St; N 2 blocks. **Burgers.** This blast from the past aims to re-create the 1950s, with red-vinyl booths, Formica tables, and wait staff dressed as poodle-skirted cheerleaders or Fonzie-style hunks. On the soda fountain–style menu, you'll find chili dogs, meatloaf dinners, and ice-cream desserts, plus the chain's trademark "runzas": beef and cabbage sandwiches baked in their own bread. Ask for special glasses so you can check out the 3-D menu. **FYI:** Reservations not accepted. Children's menu. No smoking. **Open:** Peak (June–Aug) Mon–Thurs 10:30am–10:30pm, Fri–Sat 10:30am–midnight, Sun 10am–9pm. **Prices:** Main courses $3–$6. MC, V.

Spike & Olly's

In Best Western Villager, 5200 O St; tel 402/467-0560. 4 blocks E of 48th St. **American.** The huge brass espresso machine dominating the bar is for looks only, but everything else is for real at this restaurant, where the bread and pies are made on-site. Popular entrees include smoked-chicken fettuccine and Cajun jambalaya (a blend of ham, sausage, chicken, and peppers served over rice). **FYI:** Reservations accepted. Children's menu. **Open:** Mon–Sat 6am–10pm, Sun 6am–9:30pm. **Prices:** Main courses $6–$15. AE, DC, DISC, MC, V.

Terrace Grille

In Cornhusker Hotel, 333 S 13 St (Downtown); tel 402/474-7474. I-80 to downtown; E on M St. **Eclectic.** At this eclectic and sophisticated restaurant, hand-painted murals depicting a variety of scenes—from Venice gardens to Nebraska sunflowers—cover each wall, fiber-optic lights decorate part of the ceiling, and faux-marble pillars support the bar. The diverse decor is matched by the variety of the entrees, which range from Reuben sandwiches to Caribbean grilled swordfish. **FYI:** Reservations accepted. **Open:** Sun–Thurs 6:30am–10pm, Fri–Sat 6:30am–11pm. **Prices:** Main courses $8–$17. AE, CB, DC, DISC, MC, V.

Valentino's

3457 Holdrege; tel 402/467-3611. Across from University of Nebraska E campus. **Pizza.** The original Valentino's proved so popular with the students at nearby U of N that it spawned a statewide chain of more than 30 pizzerias. An all-you-can-eat buffet includes pizza, pasta dishes, and "dessert pizza" (a lighter dough topped with fruit and icing). A very good value for families. **FYI:** Reservations accepted. Children's menu. Beer and wine only. Additional locations: 10190 Maple, Omaha (tel 571-1400); 2245 N Webb Rd, Grand Island (tel 308/382-7711). **Open:** Daily 11am–10pm. **Prices:** Main courses $3–$8; prix fixe $7. AE, DISC, MC, V.

ATTRACTIONS

Museum of Nebraska History

15th and P Sts; tel 402/471-3270. Three floors of exhibits tell the tale of the plains people from pre-historic times through the 1950s. Period settings include a Pawnee earthlodge, a Winnebago Reservation house, a Victorian parlor, an 1880s sod house, and a walk-through general store. **Open:** Mon–Sat 9am–5pm, Sun 1:30–5pm. Closed some hols. **Free**

University of Nebraska State Museum and Ralph Mueller Planetarium

14th and O Sts; tel 402/472-2641. Natural history museum features dinosaur skeletons, rocks and minerals, and animal fossils. Planetarium offers astronomy programs and laser light shows. **Open:** Planetarium show: summer, Tues–Sun at 2pm; rest of year, Sat–Sun at 2pm. Closed some hols. **$**

National Museum of Roller Skating
4730 South St; tel 402/483-7551. A nonprofit educational institution where visitors can learn about roller skating as sport, recreation, entertainment, and business. The museum houses one of the world's largest collections of roller skates as well as the roller-skating amateur athlete hall of fame. **Open:** Mon–Fri 9am–5pm. Closed some hols. **Free**

Lincoln Children's Zoo
27th and B Sts; tel 402/475-6741. Small-scale, kid-oriented zoo with over 200 animals, including camels, crocodiles, baboons, and a rare red panda. Exhibits are all close-up, for good viewing. The Critter Encounter Area features a petting zoo, pony rides, and free entertainment in the Bird Cage Theater (summer months only). Iron Horse Railroad runs around the perimeter of the park. **Open:** May–Sept, daily 10am–5pm. **$$**

Historic Haymarket
Between 7th and 9th Sts and O and S Sts; tel 402/434-6900 or toll free 800/423-8212. This renovated and revitalized turn-of-the-century warehouse district now houses a variety of unique shops and quaint boutiques selling antiques, books, clothing, and crafts. In summer, the area plays host to street fairs, dances, and a Saturday morning farmer's market. Restaurants are scattered throughout. **Open:** Daily 10am–5pm, open until 9pm on Fri. **Free**

McCook

Established in 1882 as the seat of Red Willow County. Named for Alexander McCook, a Union general in the Civil War. **Information:** McCook Convention and Visitors Bureau, 305 E 1st St, PO Box 337, McCook, 69001 (tel 308/345-3200).

MOTELS

Chief Motel Best Western
612 W B St, 69001; tel 308/345-3700 or toll free 800/528-1234; fax 308/345-7182. On US 6/34/83. Simple but clean, with a pleasant staff. **Rooms:** 111 rms and stes. CI open/CO 11am. No smoking. Suites sleep four to six people. **Amenities:** A/C, cable TV, dataport. Some units w/terraces, some w/whirlpools. **Services:** **Facilities:** 1 restaurant, 1 bar, games rm, whirlpool. **Rates:** $39–$46 S; $50–$56 D; $72–$80 ste. Extra person $7. Children under age 12 stay free. Parking: Outdoor, free. AE, DC, DISC, MC, V.

Super 8 Motel
1103 E B St, 69001; tel 308/345-1141 or toll free 800/800-8000; fax 308/345-1141. ½ mi E on US 6 and 34. Run-of-the-mill motel just off the highway. **Rooms:** 40 rms. CI 1pm/CO 11am. Nonsmoking rms avail. **Amenities:** A/C, cable TV w/movies. **Services:** **Facilities:** **Rates:** $33–$38 S; $38–$41 D. Extra person $4. Children under age 12 stay free. Parking: Outdoor, free. Senior discounts avail. AE, CB, DC, DISC, MC, V.

ATTRACTION

Senator George Norris State Historic Site
706 Norris Ave; tel 308/345-5293. Senator George W Norris was the father of the Rural Electrification Act and a powerful political maverick in the early 1900s. Original family furnishings and memorabilia from Norris's 40 eventful years in Washington are featured in this restored two-story gray stucco house (circa 1886), a registered National Historic Landmark. **Open:** Wed–Sat 10am–noon, 1–5pm, Tues and Sun 1:30–5pm. Closed some hols. **$**

Minden

For lodgings and dining, see Hastings

Seat of Kearney County. Founded around 1876 and best known for the large history theme park, Pioneer Village. **Information:** Minden Chamber of Commerce, PO Box 375, Minden, 68959 (tel 308/832-1811).

ATTRACTION

Harold Warp Pioneer Village
Jct US 6 and NE 10; tel 308/832-1181 or toll free 800/445-4447. A 20-acre "museum of progress," with 50,000 items covering every field of human endeavor from music to flying machines to antique tractors. The complex's 28 buildings include a railroad depot, a re-creation of a Nebraska general store, a fire house with antique and modern firefighting equipment, an authentically restored Pony Express station, and a log fort. One two-story building houses over 50 automobiles of all eras, as well as one floor full of antique motorcycles, bicycles, and snowmobiles. A steam-powered carousel is located on the grounds, and rides cost just a nickel. Restaurant, campground. **Open:** Daily 8am–sunset. **$$$**

Nebraska City

Home of Arbor Day founder J Sterling Morton, whose legacy remains in his mansion-turned-park, the National Arbor Day Foundation, and numerous apple orchards. Before the Civil War, Nebraska City was a prominent stop on the Underground Railroad; John Brown built a cave and small tunnel to a nearby creek. Seat of Otoe County. **Information:** Nebraska City Chamber of Commerce, 806 1st Ave, Nebraska City, 68410 (tel 402/873-6654).

HOTEL

Lied Conference Center
2700 Sylvan Rd, 68410; tel 402/873-8733 or toll free 800/546-5433; fax 402/873-4999. From jct of NE 2 and US 75, go E to Steinhardt Rd. A small-town conference facility that doubles as a pastoral weekend getaway. Environmental awareness prevails, from the lobby colonnaded with 35-foot high Douglas fir timbers to the carpet made from recycled pop bottles. Voluntary recycling by guests and water conservation are also in place. **Rooms:** 96 rms. CI 3pm/CO noon. Nonsmoking rms avail. Rooms feature mission-style furniture and Native American–print bedspreads; each room has two desks. **Amenities:** A/C, cable TV, dataport, voice mail. **Services:** Babysitting. **Facilities:** 1 restaurant (*see* "Restaurants" below), 1 bar, sauna, whirlpool. Terrace overlooks property's own orchard. **Rates:** Peak (Sept–Oct) $99 S or D. Extra person $10. Children under age 18 stay free. Min stay peak. Lower rates off-season. AP and MAP rates avail. Parking: Outdoor, free. Weekend packages avail. AE, CB, DC, DISC, MC, V.

RESTAURANT

Lied Restaurant
In Lied Conference Center, 2700 Sylvan Rd; tel 402/873-8733. NE of jct US 75 and NE 2. **American.** Massive Douglas fir timbers stand guard in this dining room located in an old timber-and-stone lodge. The terrace overlooks an orchard owned by Arbor Day Farm, the showpiece of the National Arbor Day Foundation. Varied dinner choices include chicken-fried steak, honey-mustard chicken, veal chops, and shrimp scampi. Buffets are offered for breakfast and lunch. **FYI:** Reservations accepted. Children's menu. No smoking. **Open:** Peak (May–Oct) breakfast Mon–Sat 6:30–10:30am; lunch Mon–Fri 11:30am–2pm, Sat–Sun 10:30am–5pm; dinner Sun–Sat 5–9pm; brunch Sun 10am–2pm. **Prices:** Main courses $10–$20. AE, CB, DC, DISC, MC, V.

ATTRACTION

Arbor Lodge State Historical Park
2300 W 2nd Ave; tel 402/873-7222. Encompassing 65 acres of hilly, wooded land a few miles west of the Missouri River, this land was part of the estate of J Sterling Morton, founder of Arbor Day. Arbor Lodge, the 52-room neocolonial mansion located on the grounds, boasts Victorian and Empire furnishings and a Tiffany skylight in its sun parlor. Other points of interest include a carriage house, Italian terraced garden, an 1890 log cabin, a pine grove planted by Morton in 1891, and a ½-mile tree trail that winds through the original arboretum area. **Open:** Grounds, daily 8am–sunset. Closed some hols. $

Norfolk

Norfolk lies in the low hills of the Elkhorn River valley and was founded in 1866 by a group of German farmers from Wisconsin who came for the fertile farm ground. This large industrial center is the hometown of Johnny Carson. **Information:** Madison County Convention and Visitors Bureau, 405 Madison Ave, PO Box 386, Norfolk, 68702 (tel 402/371-0182).

MOTELS

Capri Motor Hotel
211 E Norfolk Ave, 68701; tel 402/371-4550. E side of town; on US 275B. Basic lodging located near colleges and businesses. Comparable to other motels in the same area. **Rooms:** 13 rms. CI open/CO 10:30am. Nonsmoking rms avail. Balconies offer a pleasant view of a stream. Concrete-block walls are painted pale blue and pink. **Amenities:** A/C, cable TV w/movies. Some units have radios. **Services:** **Facilities:** Empty lot on grounds set up for horseshoe games. **Rates:** $25 S; $33 D. Extra person $5. Parking: Outdoor, free. AE, DISC, MC, V.

Days Inn
1001 Omaha Ave, 68701; tel 402/379-3035 or toll free 800/329-7466; fax 402/371-1307. On US 275; 3 blocks E of US 81. Fresh, new-looking property. Pleasing lobby decor features an open oak staircase, couches, and overstuffed chairs. **Rooms:** 61 rms and stes. CI 2pm/CO 11am. Nonsmoking rms avail. Suites offer two phones. **Amenities:** A/C, cable TV w/movies, refrig, dataport. Some units w/whirlpools. **Services:** **Facilities:** Spa, sauna, steam rm, whirlpool, washer/dryer. Exceptionally clean, clear pool. **Rates (CP):** $33–$105 S or D; $105 ste. Extra person $6. Children under age 12 stay free. Parking: Outdoor, free. AE, CB, DC, DISC, MC, V.

Eco-Lux Inn
1909 Krenzien, 68701; tel 402/371-7157; fax 402/371-7157. Near US 275. New, two-story brick structure. Restaurant within walking distance. **Rooms:** 44 rms. CI 2pm/CO 11am. Nonsmoking rms avail. Larger rooms have couches. **Amenities:** A/C, cable TV w/movies, dataport. 30″ TVs. **Services:** **Facilities:** **Rates (CP):** Peak (June–Sept) $34 S; $50 D. Extra person $4. Children under age 12 stay free. Lower rates off-season. Parking: Outdoor, free. AE, CB, DC, DISC, MC, V.

RESTAURANTS

★ Brass Lantern
1018 S 9 St; tel 402/371-2500. 4 blocks E of jct US 275 and US 81. **American.** Steak—in all its forms—is the star of the menu. Established almost 60 years ago, this restaurant features a historic mural of Norfolk, painted by a local artist over a span of many years. **FYI:** Reservations recommended.

Children's menu. **Open:** Lunch Sun–Fri 11am–2pm; dinner daily 5–10pm; brunch. **Prices:** Main courses $5–$22; prix fixe $6. AE, CB, DC, DISC, MC, V.

The Granary
922 S 13 St; tel 402/371-5334. On US 81; 5 blocks N of jct US 275. **Regional American.** Decorated in an Americana motif, with pioneer memorabilia, paintings, and wagon wheels. Fried chicken and fish dominate the menu. Excellent prices. **FYI:** Reservations not accepted. Children's menu. **Open:** Mon–Wed 10:45am–9:30pm, Thurs–Sat 10:45am–10:30pm. **Prices:** Main courses $3–$7; prix fixe $3–$5. No CC.

Valentino's
1025 S 13th St; tel 402/379-2500. On US 81; 2 blocks N of jct US 27 S. **Italian.** Decked out in clean black and red, this remodeled member of the state's popular pizza chain is a good choice for families. Buffet lunches and dinners are a good value. **FYI:** Reservations accepted. Children's menu. Beer and wine only. **Open:** Mon–Sat 11am–11pm, Sun 9am–11pm. **Prices:** Main courses $6–$9; prix fixe $5–$7. MC, V.

North Platte

Founded about 1866 on the north fork of the Platte River and incorporated in 1871, North Platte was the home of Buffalo Bill Cody and his Wild West Show. Its wild and woolly ways have not been forgotten. In June, Nebraskaland Days, a statewide celebration of rodeo and western attractions, fills the town. **Information:** North Platte/Lincoln City County Convention and Visitors Bureau, 502 S Dewey, PO Box 1207, North Platte, 69103 (tel 308/532-4729).

MOTELS

Camino Inn
2102 S Jeffers, PO Box 430, 69101; tel 308/532-9090 or toll free 800/760-3333; fax 308/532-0165. Exit 177 off I-80. This former chain motel has kept itself up well. **Rooms:** 226 rms and stes. CI 3pm/CO noon. Nonsmoking rms avail. Some rooms face pool. **Amenities:** A/C, cable TV, dataport. **Services:** **Facilities:** 1 restaurant, 1 bar (w/entertainment), games rm, whirlpool, washer/dryer. **Rates:** Peak (mid-May–Sept 1) $65–$70 S; $70–$75 D; $75–$80 ste. Extra person $5. Children under age 18 stay free. Lower rates off-season. Parking: Outdoor, free. AE, CB, DC, DISC, MC, V.

Comfort Inn
2901 S Jeffers St, 69101; tel 308/532-6144 or toll free 800/221-2222; fax 308/532-6144. Exit 177 off I-80, S on US 83. A tidy and clean place just off I-80, near a small lake. Bright common areas. **Rooms:** 94 rms. CI 2pm/CO 11am. Nonsmoking rms avail. **Amenities:** A/C, cable TV, dataport. Some units w/whirlpools. **Services:** **Facilities:** Games rm, whirlpool. **Rates (CP):** Peak (mid-May–Sept) $55–$60 S or D. Children under age 18 stay free. Lower rates off-season. Parking: Outdoor, free. AE, CB, DC, DISC, MC, V.

Days Inn
3102 S Jeffers St, 69101; tel 308/532-9321 or toll free 800/329-7466; fax 308/534-9203. Exit 177 off I-80; N on US 83. A well-run motel managed by a cheery retired couple. **Rooms:** 29 rms. CI open/CO 11am. Nonsmoking rms avail. **Amenities:** A/C, cable TV. **Services:** Only "nonexotic" pets weighing under 15 pounds are permitted. **Facilities:** **Rates (CP):** Peak (Apr–Sept) $34–$44 S; $40–$50 D. Extra person $5. Children under age 13 stay free. Lower rates off-season. Parking: Outdoor, free. AE, CB, DC, DISC, MC, V.

Hampton Inn
200 Platte Oasis Pkwy, 69101; tel 308/534-6000 or toll free 800/426-7866; fax 308/534-3415. Exit 177 off I-80. Opened in 1995, this property offers an attractive lobby and pool area. Located near several restaurants and fast-food outlets. **Rooms:** 111 rms and stes. CI 2pm/CO 11am. Nonsmoking rms avail. Rooms feature reproduction colonial headboards and well-upholstered furniture. **Amenities:** A/C, cable TV, dataport. Some units w/whirlpools. **Services:** **Facilities:** 50 Whirlpool. **Rates (CP):** Peak (June–Aug) $59–$79 S; $65–$85 D; $85 ste. Children under age 18 stay free. Lower rates off-season. Parking: Outdoor, free. AE, CB, DC, DISC, MC, V.

Rambler Motel
1420 Rodeo Rd, 69101; tel 308/532-9290. Exit 177 off I-80; N on US 83, W on Rodeo Rd. The furniture is dated, but this little motel near Buffalo Bill's Ranch is a bargain for a night's stay. **Rooms:** 25 rms. CI open/CO 11am. Mix 'n' match decor, with 1950s-era furniture (in good repair) and new carpeting. All rooms face onto a grassy center yard. **Amenities:** A/C, cable TV, refrig. TVs are mostly new. **Services:** Car-rental desk. **Facilities:** Washer/dryer. Used-car rental business on site. **Rates:** Peak (June–Aug) $22 S; $25–$28 D. Extra person $3. Children under age 4 stay free. Lower rates off-season. Parking: Outdoor, free. AE, DISC, MC, V.

Stanford Motel
1400 E 4th St, 69101; tel 308/532-9380 or toll free 800/743-4934; fax 308/532-9634. Exit 177 off I-80, N on US 83 to E 4th, E on US 30. A tidy and economical place for a night's stay, though some furnishings are a bit dated. **Rooms:** 31 rms. CI open/CO 11am. Nonsmoking rms avail. Decor is a hodge-podge of faux–French provincial (done in white and gold), and other motley pieces dating back to the 1960s. One room with three beds is popular for large families or groups. **Amenities:** A/C, cable TV, refrig. Half of the accommodations have refrigerator and microwave. **Services:** Small pets permitted in some rooms. Friendly staff. **Facili-**

ties: Washer/dryer. Free passes to North Platte City recreation center, which has a pool. **Rates:** Peak (May 1–mid-Sept) $30–$35 S; $35–$39 D. Extra person $4. Children under age 12 stay free. Lower rates off-season. Parking: Outdoor, free. AE, DISC, MC, V.

The Stockman Inn

1402 S Jeffers St, PO Box 1303, 69103; tel 308/534-3630 or toll free 800/624-4643; fax 308/534-0110. Exit 177 off I-80; N on US 83. A bland motel near the interstate. Lobby and common areas look pretty worn out—chipped paint, older furniture, outdated brown tones. **Rooms:** 150 rms and stes. CI 3pm/CO 11am. Nonsmoking rms avail. Half the rooms have doors opening to the parking lot. **Amenities:** A/C, cable TV. Suites have refrigerators. **Services:** **Facilities:** 1 restaurant (*see* "Restaurants" below), 1 bar (w/entertainment). **Rates:** Peak (May–Aug) $43–$47 S; $49–$53 D; $87–$93 ste. Extra person $7. Children under age 18 stay free. Lower rates off-season. Parking: Outdoor, free. AE, CB, DC, DISC, MC, V.

Travelers Inn

602 E 4th St, 69101; tel 308/534-4020 or toll free 800/341-8000. Exit 177 off I-80, US 83 N to E US 30, E 5 blocks. A respectable motor lodge with brown and tan furniture. **Rooms:** 33 rms. CI open/CO 11am. Nonsmoking rms avail. Some units have tub-and-shower combination. **Amenities:** A/C, cable TV. Refrigerators available. **Services:** **Facilities:** **Rates:** Peak (Mem Day–Labor Day) $32 S; $40 D. Extra person $3. Children under age 12 stay free. Lower rates off-season. Parking: Outdoor, free. AE, CB, DC, DISC, MC, V.

RESTAURANTS

Fireplace Dining Room

In Stockman Inn, 1402 S Jeffers St; tel 308/534-3630. Exit 177 off I-80, N on US 83 to W Leota. **American.** A favorite with area seniors, who come here for the prime rib and roast-beef and BLT sandwiches. Predictable, older western decor. **FYI:** Reservations accepted. Children's menu. **Open:** Daily 6am–10pm. **Prices:** Main courses $4–$17. AE, CB, DC, DISC, MC, V.

Golden Dragon Chinese Restaurant

120 W Leota; tel 308/532-5588. Exit 177 off I-80; N on US 83. **Chinese.** Although the decor here is schizophrenic—Oriental lanterns and western-style red-and-white gingham tablecloths—the food is all Chinese. More than 100 entrees are offered, including the usual Cantonese and Szechuan favorites along with some territorial improvisations such as crispy steak cubes: squares of browned, shredded beef served with peppers and carrots. **FYI:** Reservations accepted. Beer and wine only. Additional location: 320 3rd Ave, Kearney (tel 234-3333). **Open:** Peak (Apr–Oct) **Prices:** Main courses $6–$16. AE, DISC, MC, V.

ATTRACTIONS

Lincoln County Museum

2403 N Buffalo; tel 308/534-5640. Local history museum contains pioneer-era artifacts and exhibits, including furniture, quilts, clothing, a re-created doctor's office, and a model railroad. The new Frank & Fred Leu Memorial Wing contains four mounted longhorn steers, a buffalo, and a collection of Western art and photographs. In addition to the museum, there are 10 preserved buildings on the grounds. A Pony Express station (1860), railroad depot (1866), country school (1903), and barber shop (1900) are among the restored buildings which are open to the public. **Open:** Mem Day–Sept, daily 9am–8pm. **Free**

Buffalo Bill Ranch State Historical Park

Buffalo Bill Ave; tel 308/532-4803. The remains of Buffalo Bill's ranch, including the restored 18-room ranch house, barn, and an interpretive center showing a film on the man's life. In summer, trail rides and buffalo stew cookouts are held here. **Open:** Summer, daily 10am–8pm; fall and spring, Mon–Fri 9am–5pm; closed Nov 1–Apr 1. **$**

Ogallala

This cowtown named for the Oglala branch of Sioux remains famous as the end of the trail for the cattle drives that once moved up the Plains from Texas. Once called the Gomorrah of the Plains, Ogallala has settled down in recent years. Close to Lake McConaughy, Nebraska's largest reservoir. Seat of Keith County. **Information:** Ogallala/Keith County Convention and Visitors Bureau, 204 E A, PO Box 628, Ogallala, 69153 (tel 308/284-4066).

MOTELS

Comfort Inn

110 Pony Express Rd, 69153; tel 308/284-4028 or toll free 800/222-2222; fax 308/284-4028. Exit 126 off I-80. Bright and cheerful. **Rooms:** 49 rms and stes. CI 1pm/CO 11am. Nonsmoking rms avail. Suites have two phones. **Amenities:** A/C, cable TV. 1 unit w/whirlpool. **Services:** **Facilities:** Games rm, whirlpool, washer/dryer. **Rates (CP):** Peak (June–Sept) $45–$50 S; $50–$65 D; $57–$82 ste. Extra person $5. Children under age 18 stay free. Lower rates off-season. Parking: Outdoor, free. AE, CB, DC, DISC, MC, V.

Days Inn

601 Stagecoach Trail, 69153; tel 308/284-6365 or toll free 800/329-7466; fax 308/284-2153. Exit 126 off I-80. Clean and bright rooms, but the common areas are uncared for, even though the motel is just 2½ years old. **Rooms:** 31 rms. CI open/CO 11am. Nonsmoking rms avail. **Amenities:** A/C, cable TV. **Services:** No cats; $5 fee for dogs. **Facilities:** **Rates:** Peak (Mem Day–Labor Day) $36–$45 S;

$40–$55 D. Extra person $5. Children under age 12 stay free. Lower rates off-season. Parking: Outdoor, free. AE, DISC, MC, V.

Ramada Limited

201 Chuckwagon Rd, 69153; tel 308/284-3623 or toll free 800/573-7148; fax 308/284-4949. Exit 126 off I-80. Remodeled exterior, simple but clean rooms. **Rooms:** 152 rms. CI 2pm/CO noon. Nonsmoking rms avail. **Amenities:** A/C, cable TV. **Services:** Babysitting. Continental breakfast arranged with more flair than ordinary economy motels (muffins and croissants in napkin-lined baskets). Pet fee $5/night. **Facilities:** 300 1 restaurant, 1 bar, games rm, washer/dryer. **Rates (CP):** Peak (Mem Day–Labor Day) $43–$59 S; $49–$66 D. Extra person $6. Children under age 19 stay free. Lower rates off-season. Parking: Outdoor, free. AE, CB, DC, DISC, MC, V.

RESTAURANT

★ Ole's Big Game Steakhouse and Lounge

Main St, Paxton; tel 308/239-4500. Exit 145 off I-80. **Steak.** Original owner Rosser "Ole" Herstedt was an avid hunter who had to find a place to display his larger trophies. Housed in this rough-hewn, small-town bar, his 200 mounts include a 1,500-pound polar bear, a baboon, and an iguana. The menu features burgers, steaks, and Rocky Mountain oysters. **FYI:** Reservations not accepted. Children's menu. **Open:** Mon–Sat 8am–1am, Sun 10am–10pm. **Prices:** Main courses $3–$15. MC, V.

ATTRACTION

Lake McConaughy State Recreation Area

1500 NE 61N; tel 308/284-3542. 8 mi NE of Ogallala. Nebraska's largest reservoir, the 35,000-acre "Big Mac" is a favorite of boaters, divers, windsurfers, swimmers, and water-skiers. For the fishermen, the lake is stocked with game fish including rainbow trout, channel catfish, walleye, white bass, and smallmouth bass. (A 24-hour fishing report is available at 308/355-FISH.) Ice fishing and geese hunting are popular during the winter months. The coastline is dotted with 3 lodges, 4 restaurants, 10 picnic areas, and 11 campgrounds. **Open:** Daily dawn–dusk. $

Omaha

See also Bellevue, Council Bluffs (IA)

The seat of Douglas County was founded in 1854 by land sharks greedy to jump the Missouri River after a treaty opened Nebraska for settlement. Its place on the "Muddy Mo" and on the way west quickly established Omaha as a trading and commercial center. (In the 1990s, Omaha remains an east-west gateway because of coast-to-coast I-80, one of the most heavily traveled interstates in the country.) Until the 1970s, Omaha was best known for its livestock slaughteryards; today's primary industries include food production, railroads, insurance, credit-card processing, and telemarketing. Omaha is known nationally for Boys Town, the orphanage founded by Father Flanagan. For two weeks every June, Omaha hosts the College World Series. **Information:** Greater Omaha Convention and Visitors Bureau, 6800 Mercy Rd #202, Omaha, 68106 (tel 402/444-4660).

PUBLIC TRANSPORTATION

Metro Area Transit (MAT) buses (tel 402/341-0800). Route #2 provides service every day between downtown Omaha and Westroads along the busy Dodge St corridor and runs through the Downtown, Midtown, Crossroads, and Westroads transit centers. During rush hours on weekdays, it provides service to Oakview Mall, Regency, and One Pacific Place. Route #2 provides transfers to most other routes in the MAT system. MAT does not operate on major holidays. Fares: adults $1; seniors, persons with disabilities, and children 5–11 50¢; students with photo ID 75¢; children under 5 ride free. Exact change required.

HOTELS

Clarion Carlisle Hotel

10909 M St, 68137; tel 402/331-8220 or toll free 800/526-6242; fax 402/331-8729. Exit 445 off I-80, L St E to 108th St. A tastefully decorated hotel on the west side of city. **Rooms:** 138 rms and stes. CI 2pm/CO noon. Nonsmoking rms avail. Outfitted in tones of deep berry, gray, and cream, accented with brass fixtures. **Amenities:** A/C, cable TV w/movies, dataport. Some rooms have hair dryers. Crown rooms have irons and ironing boards. **Services:** Deposit for pets $30. **Facilities:** 300 1 restaurant, 1 bar, whirlpool, washer/dryer. **Rates (CP):** $59–$89 S or D; $129 ste. Extra person $6. Children under age 19 stay free. Parking: Outdoor, free. AE, CB, DC, DISC, JCB, MC, V.

Embassy Suites

7270 Cedar St, 68164; tel 402/397-5141 or toll free 800/362-2779; fax 402/397-1623. Exit 72nd St N. Combines fun for the kids with a touch of southwestern-style refinement for mom and dad. The hotel is built around a central courtyard with a Spanish motif, including a terra-cotta fountain, tiles, adobe walls, and 40-foot ficus trees. **Rooms:** 188 effic. CI 3pm/CO noon. Nonsmoking rms avail. Accommodations feature full kitchens and two TVs. **Amenities:** A/C, cable TV w/movies, refrig, dataport, voice mail. Some units w/terraces. **Services:** Children's program, babysitting. Complimentary cocktails each evening. On weekends, a magician entertains kids during cocktail hour. $25 deposit for pets. **Facilities:** 150 1 restaurant (lunch and dinner only), games rm, sauna, steam rm, whirlpool, washer/dryer. Pool and sauna accented with Mexican-style blue tiles. **Rates (BB):** Peak (June–Sept) $99–$119 effic. Extra person $10. Children under age 16 stay free. Lower rates off-season. Parking: Outdoor, free. AE, DISC, MC, V.

Holiday Inn Old Mill
655 N 108th St, 68154; tel 402/496-0850 or toll free 800/465-4329; fax 402/496-3839. Exit 3 W off I-680, W to Old Mill Rd. Near several shopping areas; a good overnighter. **Rooms:** 214 rms and stes. Executive level. CI 2pm/CO noon. Nonsmoking rms avail. **Amenities:** A/C, cable TV w/movies, dataport, voice mail. Some units w/whirlpools. Suites have refrigerators, some have coffeemakers. **Services:** Executive-level guests receive complimentary breakfast. **Facilities:** 1200 1 restaurant, 1 bar, games rm, sauna, steam rm, whirlpool, washer/dryer. Executive level features tasteful TV lounge and business center. **Rates:** $61–$63 S; $68–$96 D; $89–$175 ste. Extra person $7. Children under age 18 stay free. Parking: Outdoor, free. AE, CB, DC, DISC, JCB, MC, V.

Homewood Suites
7010 Hascall St, 68106; tel 402/397-7500 or toll free 800/225-5466; fax 402/397-4281. Exit 72nd St N off I-80. Extraordinarily quiet, all-suite property. Common areas reflect a colonial-inn theme, with faux-oak beams and an oversize fireplace, and feature well-upholstered furniture. **Rooms:** 116 stes and effic. CI 2pm/CO noon. No smoking. Nicely appointed with stylish, white-washed pine furniture. **Amenities:** A/C, cable TV, refrig, dataport, VCR, voice mail. Some units w/terraces, some w/fireplaces, some w/whirlpools. Suites with sunken whirlpools are a top choice for romantic getaways. **Services:** Babysitting. A local service delivers takeout from area restaurants. **Facilities:** 25 Sauna, whirlpool, washer/dryer. Full business facilities include fax, copy machines, computers. **Rates (CP):** $83–$175 ste; $83–$175 effic. Parking: Outdoor, free. AE, CB, DC, DISC, MC, V.

Marriott
10220 Regency Circle, 68114; tel 402/399-9000 or toll free 800/228-9290; fax 402/399-0223. Exit Dodge St E off I-680. Located just off the interstate in the business area of the upscale Regency neighborhood, this property attracts business clientele during the week and leisure travelers on weekends. **Rooms:** 301 rms and stes. Executive level. CI 3pm/CO noon. Nonsmoking rms avail. Attractive—but not lavish—furnishings, done in dark woods. **Amenities:** A/C, cable TV w/movies, dataport, voice mail. All units w/terraces. Irons and ironing boards in each room. Hair dryers and robes in executive suites. **Services:** Babysitting. **Facilities:** 600 2 restaurants (*see* "Restaurants" below), 1 bar, spa, sauna, whirlpool, washer/dryer. Impressive workout center with new Lifecycles, treadmills, and free weights. Tree-shaded pool courtyard open for special events. **Rates:** $79–$117 S or D; $250 ste. Children under age 18 stay free. Parking: Outdoor, free. Honeymoon packages avail for $99, including breakfast and champagne. AE, CB, DC, DISC, JCB, MC, V.

Radisson Redick Tower Hotel
1504 Harney St, 68102 (Downtown); tel 402/342-1500 or toll free 800/333-3333; fax 402/342-5317. 1 block E of 16th St Mall. Located in a 1929 building, this elegantly refurbished hotel is convenient to downtown businesses, Orpheum theater events, and trips to the Old Market area. **Rooms:** 89 rms and stes. CI 3pm/CO noon. Nonsmoking rms avail. Tastefully furnished. **Amenities:** A/C, cable TV w/movies, dataport. Some units w/whirlpools. **Services:** VP Babysitting. Deposit required for pets. **Facilities:** 80 1 restaurant, 1 bar, sauna, whirlpool. **Rates (BB):** $115–$185 S or D; $129–$275 ste. Children under age 18 stay free. Parking: Indoor, $4/day. Honeymoon package includes suite, champagne, and breakfast for $160/night. Zoo package offers room, breakfast, and zoo passes for four for $99. AE, CB, DC, DISC, MC, V.

UNRATED **Westin Aquila Court**
1615 Howard St, 68102; tel 402/342-2222 or toll free 800/228-3000; fax 402/342-2569. Lavish renovation of a 1923 building on the National Register of Historic Places. Opened in October 1995. **Rooms:** 146 rms, stes, and effic. Executive level. CI 1pm/CO noon. Nonsmoking rms avail. All ground-level rooms open onto a fountain terrace. Bathrooms all feature granite floors and vanities. Many accommodations have a fireplace room downstairs and a bedroom on the second level. The Presidential Suite ($425 per night) is palatial, with hardwood floors, a whirlpool, and hand stenciling over the french doors leading to the terrace. **Amenities:** A/C, cable TV w/movies, refrig, dataport, voice mail, bathrobes. All units w/minibars, some w/terraces, some w/fireplaces, some w/whirlpools. Security drawer in each room. On the concierge level, rooms have fax machines and duvet comforters. **Services:** VP Car-rental desk, masseur, children's program, babysitting. 15-pound maximum for pets. **Facilities:** 500 1 restaurant, 1 bar (w/entertainment), sauna, steam rm, washer/dryer. **Rates (CP):** $149–$169 S or D; $169–$425 ste; $239–$249 effic. Extra person $10. Children under age 18 stay free. Min stay special events. Parking: Outdoor, $3–$6/day. AE, CB, DC, DISC, ER, JCB, MC, V.

MOTELS

Best Western Omaha Inn
4706 S 108th St, 68137; tel 402/339-7400 or toll free 800/528-1234; fax 402/339-5155. Exit 446 off I-80. A blasé motel close to fast food restaurants and the interstate. **Rooms:** 102 rms. CI 3pm/CO noon. Nonsmoking rms avail. **Amenities:** A/C, cable TV w/movies. Some units w/whirlpools. **Services:** **Facilities:** 100 1 bar (w/entertainment), games rm, sauna, whirlpool. **Rates (CP):** $56 S; $64–$74 D. Children under age 18 stay free. Parking: Outdoor, free. AE, CB, DC, DISC, MC, V.

Best Western Regency West
909 S 107th Ave, 68114; tel 402/397-8000 or toll free 800/228-9414; fax 402/397-8000. Exit 2 off I-680; E 2 blocks. A well-maintained motel near several shopping malls. **Rooms:** 150 rms and stes. CI noon/CO noon. Nonsmoking rms avail. **Amenities:** A/C, satel TV w/movies. Some units w/whirlpools. Some rooms have hair dryers; many king rooms offer microwaves and refrigerators. **Services:** Babysitting. Free shuttle service is offered. **Facilities:** 300 1 restaurant, 1 bar, games rm, sauna, whirlpool, washer/dryer. **Rates:** Peak (June–Sept 5) $62–$67 S; $67–$72 D; $125–$150 ste. Extra person $5. Children under age 18 stay free. Lower rates off-season. Parking: Outdoor, free. Honeymoon package avail: room with whirlpool, welcome basket, and breakfast, for $125–$150. AE, CB, DC, DISC, JCB, MC, V.

Clubhouse Inn
1151 Miracle Hills Dr, 68154; tel 402/496-7500 or toll free 800/258-2466; fax 402/496-0234. Take I-680 to exit 3; Dodge St W to 114th, N 6 blocks. A compromise between an economy motel and a suite hotel. **Rooms:** 137 rms and stes. CI 3pm/CO noon. Nonsmoking rms avail. **Amenities:** A/C, cable TV. Some units w/terraces, some w/whirlpools. Suites are equipped with two TVs and refrigerator. **Services:** Complimentary cocktail hour. **Facilities:** 40 Whirlpool, washer/dryer. Attractive pool and patio area. **Rates (BB):** $69 S; $79 D; $85–$150 ste. Extra person $5. Children under age 16 stay free. Parking: Outdoor, free. AE, CB, DC, DISC, MC, V.

Comfort Inn
9595 S 145th St, 68138; tel 402/896-6300 or toll free 800/544-4444; fax 402/896-6300. Exit 440 off I-80. New motel close to Millard and nearby lake park. Immaculately maintained rooms. **Rooms:** 50 rms and stes. CI 2pm/CO 11am. Nonsmoking rms avail. Furnishings are in excellent condition. Nicely coordinated decor, with attractive headboards and wallpaper borders that match the green flowered bedspreads. **Amenities:** A/C, cable TV, dataport. Some units w/whirlpools. **Services:** **Facilities:** **Rates (CP):** Peak (mid-May–Sept) $51–$55 S; $58–$68 D; $131 ste. Extra person $5. Children under age 16 stay free. Lower rates off-season. Parking: Outdoor, free. Whirlpool suites go for half price Sun–Thurs. AE, DC, DISC, JCB, MC, V.

Econo Lodge West Dodge
7833 Dodge St, 68114; tel 402/391-7100 or toll free 800/541-2435; fax 402/391-7100. Exit Dodge St E off I-680. A clean facility adjacent to a residential area. Near restaurants, two shopping malls, and two hospitals. **Rooms:** 48 rms and effic. CI open/CO noon. Nonsmoking rms avail. Nicely furnished, well-kept rooms. **Amenities:** A/C, cable TV. **Services:** Pet fee $5/day for dogs. **Facilities:** Washer/dryer. **Rates:** Peak (May–Sept) $43–$48 S; $48–$53 D; $85–$90 effic. Extra person $5. Children under age 18 stay free. Lower rates off-season. Parking: Outdoor, free. Group and hospital-visitor rates avail. AE, CB, DC, DISC, JCB, MC, V.

Hampton Inn
3301 S 72nd St, 68124; tel 402/391-8129 or toll free 800/426-7866; fax 402/391-7998. Exit 72nd St N off I-80. Pleasant accommodations. Cafe-style lobby features well-upholstered furniture. **Rooms:** 133 rms and stes. CI noon/CO noon. Nonsmoking rms avail. **Amenities:** A/C, cable TV. Some units w/whirlpools. Some rooms have coffeemakers, refrigerators, alarms clocks, and radios. **Services:** **Facilities:** 15 **Rates (CP):** $53 S; $59 D; $130–$170 ste. Children under age 18 stay free. Parking: Outdoor, free. AE, DC, DISC, MC, V.

Hawthorn Suites Hotel
11025 M St, 68137; tel 402/331-0101 or toll free 800/527-1133; fax 402/331-2782. Exit 445 off I-80, E to 108th, S to M St. These full living quarters are a good choice for families who need space to cook meals. **Rooms:** 88 effic. CI 2pm/CO noon. Nonsmoking rms avail. High-quality, apartment-grade furniture; some units have loft bedrooms and Murphy beds; decks overlook courtyards. **Amenities:** A/C, cable TV w/movies, refrig, dataport. All units w/terraces, some w/fireplaces. Icemakers and irons in all suites. **Services:** Babysitting. Private service delivers take-out from restaurants. **Facilities:** 15 Basketball, volleyball, whirlpool, washer/dryer. Free passes to two nearby gyms. **Rates (CP):** $69–$140 effic. Min stay special events. Parking: Outdoor, free. Honeymoon and zoo packages avail. AE, CB, DC, DISC, JCB, MC, V.

Holiday Inn Express
3001 Chicago St, 68131; tel 402/345-2222 or toll free 800/465-4329; fax 402/345-2501. Popular with people who have business at nearby Creighton University or hospitals. Common areas are brightly decorated. **Rooms:** 123 rms and stes. CI 2pm/CO noon. Nonsmoking rms avail. **Amenities:** A/C, cable TV, refrig. Some units w/terraces, some w/whirlpools. **Services:** Pet fee varies with pet size, usually running about $20. **Facilities:** 50 Sauna, whirlpool, washer/dryer. Breakfast room more attractive than at most economy hostelries. **Rates (CP):** $58 S; $64 D; $80–$120 ste. Extra person $6. Children under age 19 stay free. Parking: Outdoor, free. AE, DC, DISC, JCB, MC, V.

La Quinta Inn
3330 N 104th Ave, 68134; tel 402/493-1900 or toll free 800/531-5900; fax 402/496-0757. Exit 4 off I-680, W on 108th, N to Bedford. Motel with a southwestern decor and a small, but attractive and exceptionally well-maintained, lobby. Near fast-food outlets. **Rooms:** 129 rms and stes. CI 3pm/CO noon. Nonsmoking rms avail. **Amenities:** A/C, cable TV w/movies. King rooms have dataports. **Services:** **Facilities:** 30 Washer/dryer. **Rates (CP):** $51–

$58 S; $57–$64 D; $68–$80 ste. Extra person $6. Children under age 18 stay free. Parking: Outdoor, free. AE, DC, DISC, MC, V.

Oak Creek Inn

2808 S 72nd St, 68124; tel 402/397-7137 or toll free 800/228-9669; fax 402/397-3492. Exit 72nd St N off I-80, N 6 blocks. Clean, well-maintained rooms and a spacious pool make this motel inviting for families. **Rooms:** 102 rms and stes. CI 2pm/CO 11am. Nonsmoking rms avail. Accommodations currently being refurbished. Some face the parking lot, others the pool. **Amenities:** A/C, satel TV w/movies. Some units w/terraces, some w/whirlpools. Some rooms have tape players and refrigerators. **Services:** Can arrange bicycle rentals for access to nearby Keystone Trail. **Facilities:** 350 1 restaurant (lunch and dinner only), 1 bar (w/entertainment), games rm, sauna, whirlpool. **Rates (CP):** $45–$50 S; $55–$60 D; $80–$175 ste. Extra person $5. Children under age 12 stay free. Parking: Outdoor, free. Group rates avail; ninth-night-free program. AE, DC, DISC, MC, V.

Park Inn International

NE 50 and I-80, 68138; tel 402/895-2555 or toll free 800/437-7275; fax 402/895-1565. Exit 440 off I-80, N 3 blocks. A well-kept, bright, utilitarian property. **Rooms:** 56 rms. CI 1pm/CO noon. Nonsmoking rms avail. **Amenities:** A/C, cable TV w/movies. Some units w/whirlpools. All rooms have microwaves. **Services:** **Facilities:** 1 bar, whirlpool, washer/dryer. **Rates (CP):** $42–$45 S; $45–$50 D. Extra person $5. Children under age 18 stay free. Parking: Outdoor, free. AE, CB, DC, DISC, JCB, MC, V.

Ramada Inn Airport

Abbott Dr and Locust St, 68110; tel 402/342-5100 or toll free 800/999-1240; fax 402/342-5100. ½ mile S of Eppley Airfield. A fading motel with tired decor. **Rooms:** 149 rms and stes. CI 1pm/CO 1pm. Nonsmoking rms avail. **Amenities:** A/C, satel TV, dataport. All units w/terraces. **Services:** **Facilities:** 400 1 restaurant, 1 bar, sauna, whirlpool. Video games in lobby. Dead plants and mold problems in the pool area. **Rates:** $56–$65 S; $63–$70 D; $95 ste. Extra person $7. Children under age 12 stay free. Parking: Outdoor, free. AE, CB, DC, DISC, ER, JCB, MC, V.

Residence Inn by Marriott

6990 Dodge St, 68132; tel 402/553-8898 or toll free 800/331-3131; fax 402/553-8898. At 72nd St. A practical, comfortable choice for longer stays. Interior courtyards have superior landscaping. **Rooms:** 80 stes. CI 3pm/CO noon. Nonsmoking rms avail. All accommodations have two closets, iron, full kitchenettes, and small dining area. **Amenities:** A/C, cable TV w/movies, refrig, dataport, voice mail. All units w/terraces, some w/fireplaces. **Services:** Babysitting. Light dinner included in rates Mon–Thurs. Local firm will deliver meals from area restaurants by arrangement. **Facilities:** Basketball, volleyball, whirlpool, washer/dryer. **Rates (CP):** Peak (May–Sept) $100–$150 ste. Lower rates off-season. Parking: Outdoor, free. Honeymoon package avail. AE, CB, DC, DISC, MC, V.

Sleep Inn

2525 Abbott Dr, 68110; tel 402/342-2525 or toll free 800/424-6223; fax 402/342-2525. A clean, spartan property near airport. **Rooms:** 93 rms and stes. CI 2pm/CO noon. Nonsmoking rms avail. Showers only—no tubs. **Amenities:** A/C, satel TV w/movies, voice mail. **Services:** **Facilities:** 25 **Rates (CP):** Peak (May 1–Sept) $40–$45 S; $45–$49 D; $45–$49 ste. Extra person $4. Children under age 12 stay free. Lower rates off-season. Parking: Outdoor, free. AE, CB, DC, DISC, JCB, MC, V.

RESTAURANTS

Bohemian Cafe

1406 S 13th St; tel 402/342-9838. Off I-80. **Czechoslovakian.** A Czech-style cafe, where waiters in traditional costumes dish up selections such as jaeger schnitzel, svickova, and roast pork loin. Most dinners include dumplings. Specials include hasenpfeffer (braised rabbit) served with sour-cream gravy (offered Thurs and Sat). Strudel and kolacky desserts. **FYI:** Reservations not accepted. Accordian. Children's menu. **Open:** Daily 11am–10pm. **Prices:** Main courses $7–$11. DISC, MC, V.

Chardonnay

In Marriott Hotel, 10220 Regency Circle (Regency); tel 402/399-9000. Exit 3 off I-680, E on Dodge to Regency Pkwy. **New American.** An intimate, 50-seat bistro, lit by modern Scandinavian fixtures and oil lamps, where dishes are served on Wedgwood china. The superb beef dishes include twin beef medallions with Madeira-morel sauce; and tournedos with bordelaise sauce, Stilton cheese, and walnuts. Lamb chops and rack of lamb with mint sauce are among other favorites. Gourmet coffees are served with white and dark chocolate shavings and a demitasse of whipped cream. Extensive wine collection. Not truly wheelchair accessible, but a small ramp is available. **FYI:** Reservations recommended. Dress code. **Open:** Mon–Thurs 6–10pm, Fri–Sat 6–11pm. **Prices:** Main courses $18–$55; prix fixe $33. AE, CB, DC, DISC, MC, V.

Di Coppia

In Regency Court, 120 Regency Pkwy (Regency); tel 402/392-2806. Exit 3 off I-680 to Dodge St. **Continental.** Casual elegance in an understated setting. Breezy, distinctive dishes include Mediterranean chicken with leeks, capers, and sun-dried tomatoes; and pan-seared prime filet of beef rubbed with cracked pepper and covered in brandy-cream sauce. The most popular pasta dish is the cappellini gamberetti (angel-hair pasta in lobster-cream sauce, with shrimp and fresh tomatoes). **FYI:** Reservations recommended. Piano. **Open:**

Lunch Mon–Sat 11:30am–2pm; dinner Mon–Thurs 5:30–9pm, Fri–Sat 5:30–10pm. **Prices:** Main courses $10–$23. AE, DC, DISC, MC, V.

The Food Gallery
In Cedarnole Center, 312 S 72nd St; tel 402/393-4168. Dodge St. **Middle Eastern.** This small restaurant offers vegetarian dishes like hummus, yubrak (cabbage rolls), fava pottage, and potato kibbe (stuffed with spinach, onion, pine nuts, and parsley) as well as the likes of chicken in a cream-lobster-sherry sauce; and lamb kabobs in demiglacé with almonds and onions. **FYI:** Reservations recommended. Dress code. **Open:** Mon–Thurs 9am–9pm, Fri–Sat 9am–10pm. **Prices:** Main courses $6–$19. CB, DC, DISC, MC, V.

French Cafe
1017 Howard St (Old Market); tel 402/341-3547. 5 blocks S of Dodge. **New American/French.** Long-time favorite, with worn wooden floors and black-painted walls. Menu selections include filet mignon with a black-peppercorn and brandy sauce, salmon piccata, and pan-seared game hen with chanterelle-mushroom sauce and fried leeks. Roasted rack of pork is served on pasta in a rosemary demiglacé. A limited menu of light dishes is offered between lunch and dinner. **FYI:** Reservations recommended. **Open:** Lunch Mon–Sat 11am–2pm; dinner Mon–Thurs 5:30–9pm, Fri–Sat 5:30–10pm; brunch Sun 10:30am–2pm. **Prices:** Main courses $15–$32. AE, CB, DC, DISC, MC, V.

Garden Cafe
In Rockbrook Village, 108th and Center Streets; tel 402/393-0252. Exit 2 off I-680. **American.** What started as a single restaurant serving up homey favorites like potato-and-meat casseroles has quickly mushroomed into a dozen area cafes. A garden theme carries throughout, with white woodwork, trellises, and gazebos. The cafe is especially known for its sandwiches, salads, and baked goods, with 35 sweets—typically including muffins, lemon-meringue pie, zebra brownies, and lemon bars—made daily on site. **FYI:** Reservations not accepted. Children's menu. Beer and wine only. Additional locations: 1212 Harney St (tel 422-1574); 6891 A St, Lincoln (tel 434-3750). **Open:** Peak (Mem Day–Labor Day) daily 6am–11pm. **Prices:** Main courses $5–$13. AE, DC, DISC, MC, V.

Gorat's
4917 Center St; tel 402/551-3733. Exit 450 off I-80; N on 60th St. **Steak.** For more than 50 years, the Gorat family has been aging, cutting, trimming, and serving steaks. The signature cut is the 14-oz Omaha sirloin (with the bone left in for extra flavor); if you want a bigger steak, just ask. All meat is cut on site and can be grilled or charbroiled. Separate wheelchair entrance. **FYI:** Reservations recommended. Piano. Children's menu. Dress code. **Open:** Lunch Mon–Fri 11am–2pm; dinner Mon–Tues 5–10pm, Wed–Thurs 5–10:30pm, Fri–Sat 5pm–midnight. **Prices:** Main courses $7–$31. AE, MC, V.

Imperial Palace
11201 Davenport St; tel 402/330-3888. Exit 3 off I-680, Dodge St W. **Chinese.** As much care has been lavished on the restaurant's design as on the over 150 Szechuan and Cantonese dishes on its menu: The exterior is built to resemble an Oriental palace, while a cobblestoned "river" stocked with 100 koi flows through the dining room. Selections range from the typical sweet-and-sour entrees and Peking duck to beggar's chicken (a whole fowl stuffed with black mushrooms and other seasonal vegetables, then baked in clay). Advance notice required for the elaborate specialty dishes. **FYI:** Reservations not accepted. Additional location: 27th and Vine Streets, Lincoln (tel 474-2688). **Open:** Lunch Mon–Sat 11:30am–2:30pm; dinner Mon–Thurs 5–9:30pm, Fri–Sat 5–10:30pm, Sun noon–9pm. **Prices:** Main courses $6–$25. AE, MC, V.

Jams
In Beverly Hills Shopping Center, 7814 Dodge St; tel 402/399-8300. At 78th. **New American.** Hip little bar/cafe striving for a New York feel, complete with black, exposed duct work, a 36-foot mural depicting typical diners, and lighting over the bar held by a line of little tin men. The seasonal menu may include portobello mushrooms with basil aioli (for starters), smoked pork tenderloin with a sauce of sun-dried cherries and cracked pepper, or angel-hair pasta with pancetta, eggplant, grilled chicken, and crimini mushrooms. Reservations accepted for parties of six or more. **FYI:** Reservations not accepted. **Open:** Mon–Thurs 11am–10pm, Fri 11am–11pm, Sat 5–11pm. **Prices:** Main courses $13–$16. AE, DC, MC, V.

Joe Tess' Place
5424 S 24 St; tel 402/731-7278. Take Kennedy Fwy to Q St exit; E to 24th St. **Seafood.** Fried carp and catfish put this fish-fry place on the map, although they've recently started to accommodate leaner tastes by adding grilled salmon, carp, and chicken fillets (the last is served with a honey-mustard sauce) to their menu. Side dishes include traditional options such as coleslaw and jacket fries (sliced potatoes with skins left on). **FYI:** Reservations not accepted. Children's menu. No smoking. Additional location: 6572 Ames Ave (tel 451-8580). **Open:** Sun–Thurs noon–10pm, Fri–Sat 11am–11pm. **Prices:** Main courses $4–$9. AE, MC, V.

La Casa
4432 Leavenworth; tel 402/556-6464. Exit 451 off I-80, N on 42nd. **Pizza.** Although this 40-year-old institution serves lasagna, manicotti, and cannelloni, the house specialty is Neapolitan-style thin-crust pizza. The crust is *so* thin that there's a limit of five toppings per pie—that's all the crust will support! Take-out available starting at 11am. **FYI:** Reservations not accepted. Children's menu. Additional location: 8216 Grover (tel 391-6300). **Open:** Tues–Thurs 5–10pm, Fri–Sat 5–11pm, Sun 4:30–9:30pm. **Prices:** Main courses $6–$14. DISC, MC, V.

Le Cafe de Paris
1228 S 6th St; tel 402/344-0227. From 10th St go E on Pacific. **French.** Quiet, authentic French restaurant tucked into an older, residential neighborhood. Starters include lobster bisque and fresh asparagus vinaigrette, while a typical offering of entrees might include veal scaloppine served on an onion compote. Finish off with a chocolate soufflé or banana flambé. Only one seating per night per table, so reservations are a must. **FYI:** Reservations recommended. Jacket required. **Open:** Mon–Sat 6–10pm. Closed July 1–15. **Prices:** Main courses $18–$30. AE.

Leonarda's
3854 Leavenworth; tel 402/346-5464. 4 blocks E of 42nd. **Sicilian.** A relative newcomer in Omaha, this small place gained a quick reputation for its authentic Sicilian dishes, such as hearty spaghetti Monalisa, served with a creamy red-wine sauce with mushrooms and chunks of boneless chicken breast. Also often requested is veal scaloppine with sautéed pesto, garlic, and marsala sauce. **FYI:** Reservations not accepted. Children's menu. Beer and wine only. **Open:** Lunch Mon–Fri 11am–2pm; dinner Mon–Thurs 5–9pm, Fri–Sat 5–11pm. **Prices:** Main courses $6–$14. AE, MC, V.

Maxine's Restaurant
In the Red Lion Inn, 1616 Dodge St (Downtown); tel 402/636-4915. At N end of 16 St Mall. **Regional American/Continental.** Long-time downtown favorite, located atop the Red Lion. Probably best known for its steak Diane (tenderloin medallions in a cabernet sauce with mushrooms, garlic, and fresh rosemary taken from the restaurant's own herb garden). Other dishes with regional appeal include blackened catfish, grilled pheasant breast, and honey-mustard Iowa pork chops. Some pasta dishes, including angel-hair pasta with sun-dried tomato and eggplant, are offered as a side dish or appetizer. Parking validated in a nearby garage. **FYI:** Reservations recommended. Children's menu. **Open:** Lunch Mon–Fri 11:30am–1:30pm; dinner Sun–Thurs 5–10pm, Fri–Sat 5–11pm; brunch Sun 9am–2pm. **Prices:** Main courses $11–$19. AE, CB, DC, DISC, MC, V.

Ross's
909 S 72nd St; tel 402/393-2030. Exit 449 off I-80; N on 72nd St. **Steak.** Only USDA choice aged beef is served at this fine steak house, and all of it is cut in-house. Favorites include filet mignon, New York strip steak, plus chateaubriand carved tableside. **FYI:** Reservations recommended. Big band/jazz. Children's menu. Dress code. No smoking. **Open:** Lunch Mon–Fri 11am–2pm; dinner Mon–Sat 5–10:30pm. **Prices:** Main courses $9–$19. AE, CB, DC, DISC, MC, V.

(\$) Spaghetti Works
In Old Market, 502 S 11th St (Old Market); tel 402/422-0770. I-480 to 14th St; S to Howard; E to 11th St. **Italian.** Like all of the Old Market restaurants and shops, this trattoria is located in an old warehouse with high ceilings and labor-worn wooden floors. A favorite with teens and families, as well as those looking for a good value. Patrons can enjoy a traditional spaghetti or lasagna dinner, plus an area favorite: beer-cheese sauce or red sauce with chicken livers. Reservations taken for large parties only. **FYI:** Reservations not accepted. Children's menu. Additional locations: 8531 Park Dr, Ralston (tel 592-1444); 228 N 12th St, Lincoln (tel 475-0900). **Open:** Peak (May–Aug) Mon–Thurs 11am–10pm, Fri 11am–11pm, Sat noon–11pm, Sun noon–10pm. **Prices:** Main courses $5–$7. AE, CB, DC, MC, V.

Spanna
In Westridge Shopping Center, 721 N 132nd St; tel 402/493-7606. At W Dodge Rd. **Californian/Continental.** Euro-style, Swiss-owned bistro, with a contemporary decor featuring exposed duct work and chrome accents. These newcomers carved a solid niche for themselves with dishes like roast whiskey chicken, potato gnocchi, cassoulet, broiled quail, and their signature onion soup with white wine and cream. The menu changes to accommodate seasonal specialties such as burgundy snail stew with wild morel mushrooms. **FYI:** Reservations recommended. **Open:** Lunch Tues–Sat 11am–2pm; dinner Tues–Thurs 5–9:30pm, Fri–Sat 5–10pm. Closed June 23–July 7. **Prices:** Main courses $13–$17. AE, DC, MC, V.

V-Mertz
1022 Howard (Old Market); tel 402/345-8980. 5 blocks S of Dodge. **Continental.** Housed in a former banana warehouse in the Old Market district, this restaurant is known for its casual elegance. Although the menu changes daily, typical dishes include beef medallions with tomato goat-cheese tart, and a juniper-thyme cabernet sauce; or sautéed sweetbreads with marsala cream and grilled mushrooms. **FYI:** Reservations recommended. **Open:** Lunch Mon–Sat 11:30am–2pm; dinner Mon 6–9pm, Tues–Thurs 6–10pm, Fri–Sat 6–11pm. **Prices:** Main courses $22–$31. AE, CB, DC, DISC, MC, V.

ATTRACTIONS

Joslyn Art Museum
2200 Dodge St; tel 402/342-3300. Permanent collection includes works from antiquity to the present, with a special emphasis on 19th- and 20th-century paintings. Among the European artists represented in the collection are El Greco, Delacroix, Courbet, and Corot, as well as impressionists Degas, Monet, Pissarro, and Renoir. The American galleries include a 20th-century area with cubist, fauvist, surrealist, and abstract art, and a western American collection. The museum also contains a 1,000-seat concert hall, a 200-seat lecture hall, and an art reference library. **Open:** Tues–Wed and Fri–Sat 10am–5pm, Thurs 10am–8pm, Sun noon–5pm. Closed some hols. **$$**

Omaha Childrens Museum
500 S 20th St; tel 402/342-6164. Hands-on museum offering exhibits and activities in the arts, humanities, and physical sciences. **Open:** Tues–Sat 10am–5pm, Sun 1–5pm. Closed some hols. **$$**

Union Pacific Museum
1416 Dodge St; tel 402/271-3530. Located in Union Pacific headquarters in downtown Omaha, this museum features original railroad advertising posters, model trains, and other train memorabilia from the mid-18th century to the present. Popular exhibits include a display on the "driving of the golden spike" symbolizing the completion of the Transcontinental Railroad and a model of President Lincoln's funeral car. **Open:** Mon–Fri 9am–3pm, Sat 9am–noon. Closed some hols. **Free**

Omaha's Henry Doorly Zoo
3701 S 10th St; tel 402/733-8401. Home of the world's largest indoor rain forest—1½ acres of palm trees, orchids, and rare plants—as well as the world's only "test-tube" tiger. Other highlights at this 110-acre zoo include a cold-water penguin habitat, a coral reef, a walk-through aviary, and a shark tank with a 70-foot acrylic walk-through tunnel. **Open:** Daily 9:30am–5pm. Closed some hols. **$$$**

Ak-Sar-Ben Aquarium
21502 W NE 31, Gretna; tel 402/332-3901. 6 mi S of Omaha. The only facility of its type in the Great Plains, the center features an extra-large 1,450 gallon tank, and 11 smaller ones. In the tanks are 50 varieties of native Nebraska fish. The large tank houses paddlefish and shovelnose sturgeon; smaller fish, reptiles, and amphibians such as box turtles, bullfrogs, crawdads, and American eels inhabit the smaller tanks. **Open:** Wed–Mon 10am–4:30pm. Closed some hols. **$**

DeSoto National Wildlife Refuge
US 30, Missouri Valley; tel 402/642-2772. 20 mi NW of Omaha. Each spring and fall, this 7,800-acre park serves as a migratory stopover for thousands of ducks and geese. A 12-mile wildlife drive allows visitors to get a close-up view of the birds; interpretive brochures keyed to numbered stops on the drive are available at the visitors center. Other facilities include four nature trails, eight picnic areas, and three boat ramps. The visitors center also houses the hull of the 178-ft steamboat *Bertrand,* which was excavated from the nearby Missouri River in 1968. **Open:** Daily 9am–4:30pm. Closed some hols. **$**

Winter Quarters Historical Site
3215 State St; tel 402/453-9372. More than 3,000 members of the Church of Jesus Christ of Latter-Day Saints (popularly known as Mormons) occupied this site in the winter of 1846, during their migration westward to Utah. More than 600 of their number died here, due to the harsh weather and lack of food. A Mormon pioneer cemetery, replica cabin, water-powered gristmill, and covered wagon are on the grounds, and displays of Mormon crafts are featured in the visitors center. Guided tours are available 8am–sunset. **Open:** Daily 9am–dusk. **Free**

Fort Atkinson State Historic Park
7th and Madison Sts, Fort Calhoun; tel 402/468-5611. The first US military post west of the Missouri River, Fort Atkinson was established in 1819. More than 1,000 soldiers were garrisoned here at the fort's peak, when they were responsible for keeping the peace between fur traders and the surrounding Native American peoples. There are recreated blacksmith, gunsmith, carpenter, and cooper shops on the grounds, and living history demonstrations are staged periodically during the summer. Visitors center and small picnic area near the parking lot. **Open:** Mem Day–Labor Day, daily 9am–5pm. **$**

Ak-Sar-Ben Field and Coliseum
63rd and Center Sts; tel 402/444-1888. Home of the Omaha Lancers (hockey), Omaha Racers (basketball), and horse racing, as well as a wide array of rodeos, festivals, and fairs. **Open:** Call for schedule.

O'Neill

Established in 1874 under the name of Rockford, the seat of Holt County was later renamed for Gen John J O'Neill, who founded an Irish colony here. **Information:** O'Neill Area Chamber of Commerce, 315 E Doublas, O'Neill, 68763 (tel 402/336-2355).

HOTEL

Golden Hotel
402 E Douglas, 68763 (Downtown); tel 402/336-4436 or toll free 800/658-3148; fax 402/336-3549. Jct of US 275/20/281. An older hotel with a comfortable TV-viewing area for conversation and coffee. **Rooms:** 34 rms and effic. CI open/CO 11am. Nonsmoking rms avail. Big-screen TV. **Amenities:** A/C, cable TV w/movies, refrig. **Services:** **Facilities:** Beauty salon, washer/dryer. Downtown street parking only. **Rates (CP):** $21–$27 S; $27–$32 D; $28–$30 effic. Extra person $5. Children under age 12 stay free. Parking: Outdoor, free. AE, DISC, MC, V.

MOTELS

Carriage House Budget Host
929 E Douglas, PO Box 151, 68763; tel 402/336-3403 or toll free 800/234-7989; fax 402/336-3409. 6 blocks E of downtown; on US 20. Likable, clean property surrounded by ornamental plum trees. **Rooms:** 15 rms. CI open/CO noon. Nonsmoking rms avail. Blue floral-print wallpaper and airy windows add freshness. **Amenities:** A/C, cable TV w/movies, dataport. **Services:** **Rates (CP):** $26–$30 S; $32–$36 D. Extra person $3. Parking: Outdoor, free. AE, DISC, MC, V.

Elms Motel
E US 20/275, PO Box 228, 68763; tel 402/336-3800 or toll free 800/526-9052. E edge of town; on US 20 and 275. A

small, airy entryway features seasonal plants in full bloom. **Rooms:** 21 rms. CI open/CO 11am. Nonsmoking rms avail. **Amenities:** A/C, cable TV w/movies. **Services:** **Facilities:** Playground. **Rates:** $25 S; $36–$38 D. Children under age 12 stay free. Parking: Outdoor, free. AE, DC, MC, V.

Inn Keeper
725 E Douglas, 68763; tel 402/336-1640; fax 402/336-1640. This motel with shake shingles has a pleasant exterior, but no room for landscaping. **Rooms:** 40 rms and stes. CI 2pm/CO 11am. Nonsmoking rms avail. Tidy but ordinary, with no special view from the windows. **Amenities:** A/C, cable TV w/movies. 1 unit w/fireplace. **Services:** Babysitting. **Facilities:** 100 1 restaurant (lunch and dinner only), 1 bar. **Rates (CP):** $26–$39 S; $35–$46 D; $46 ste. Extra person $3. Children under age 10 stay free. Parking: Outdoor, free. AE, DC, DISC, MC, V.

Paxton

See Ogallala

Red Cloud

The seat of Webster County was established in 1872 and named for the last warrior chief of the Teton Sioux. Home of the Willa Cather Historical Center, which honors the noted Nebraska author.

ATTRACTION

Willa Cather Pioneer Memorial
326 N Webster St; tel 402/746-2653. Pulitzer Prize–winning novelist Willa Cather (*My Antonia, O Pioneers!*) spent her formative years here in Red Cloud, and much of the town is preserved in the Willa Cather Historic District. Tours of Cather-related sites originate here at the Pioneer Memorial, which houses the largest collection of Cather memorabilia in the country. A research library has collections of Cather's letters and rare first editions of her books. Original oil paintings, visually representing key scenes from her work, line the walls of her restored childhood home. Original furnishings, books, and the family Bible complete the depiction of typical late-19th-century prairie life. Other buildings in the Historic District include Burlington Depot, St Juliana Falconieri Catholic Church, Grace Episcopal Church, and Pavelka Farmstead (the setting for *My Antonia!*). **Open:** Mon–Sat 8am–5pm, Sun 1–5pm. Closed some hols. $

Royal

Established in 1880, this tiny town is perhaps best known for its zoo.

ATTRACTIONS

Ashfall Fossil Beds State Historical Park
Tel 402/893-2000. Located 6 mi N of US 20, between Orchard and Royal, this site call itself "A Prairie Pompeii of Prehistoric Wildlife." Ten million years ago, volcanic ash swept across the subtropical grasslands of Nebraska. Skeletons of the thousands of prehistoric rhinos, three-toed horses, and camels that perished in the storm have been preserved in the resulting bed of volcanic ash and are on display in the "Rhino Barn." **Open:** May and Sept, Wed–Sat 10am–4pm, Sun 1–4pm; June–Aug, Mon–Sat 9am–5pm, Sun 11am–5pm. $

Northeast Nebraska Zoo
3rd and Ponca Sts; tel 402/893-2002. Home to more than 30 kinds of mammals and birds, including brown lemurs, mountain lions, bobcats, snow monkeys, and a chimpanzee named Reuben. Guided tours of the five-acre zoo are available during summer months. **Open:** May–Sept, Mon–Sat 9:30am–5pm, Sun noon–5pm; Oct–Apr, Tues –Sat 10am–4:30pm, Sun noon–4:30pm. Closed Dec 25. $

Scottsbluff

Founded in 1899, Scottsbluff is named for an early traveler whose body was found at the base of the nearby bluffs—the area's predominant feature. **Information:** Scottsbluff/Gering United Chamber of Commerce, 1517 Broadway, Scottsbluff, 69361 (tel 308/632-2133).

MOTELS

Candlelight Inn
1822 E 20th Place, 69361; tel 308/635-3751 or toll free 800/424-2305; fax 308/635-1105. On US 26 E. A charming country-style motel located within walking distance of Monument Mall and restaurants. Good quality accommodations. **Rooms:** 56 rms. CI open/CO 11am. Nonsmoking rms avail. Rooms have a country-accented decor; some have sofas. **Amenities:** A/C, refrig, VCR. Microwave. **Services:** Car-rental desk, social director, babysitting. Complimentary evening hors d'oeuvres. **Facilities:** 75 1 bar, playground, washer/dryer. **Rates (CP):** $48–$52 S; $52–$56 D. Extra person $5. Parking: Outdoor, free. AE, CB, DC, DISC, MC, V.

Capri Motel
2424 Ave I, 69361; tel 308/635-2057 or toll free 800/424-2305; fax 308/635-1990. Located near Scotts Bluff National Monument and Riverside Zoo, this is a clean and comfortable facility. **Rooms:** 30 rms and stes. CI noon/CO 11am. Nonsmoking rms avail. Large desk in each room. **Amenities:** A/C, cable TV w/movies, refrig, dataport. **Services:** **Facilities:** Washer/dryer. **Rates (CP):** Peak (May–Sept) $28–$36 S; $37–$41 D; $58–$70 ste.

Extra person $3. Children under age 11 stay free. Lower rates off-season. Parking: Outdoor, free. AE, CB, DC, DISC, MC, V.

Comfort Inn
2018 Delta Dr, 69361; tel 308/632-7510 or toll free 800/221-2222; fax 308/632-8495. Fairly new and exceptionally clean motel with an inviting, comfortable lobby. **Rooms:** 46 rms and stes. CI 1pm/CO 11am. Nonsmoking rms avail. Spacious accommodations. **Amenities:** A/C, cable TV w/movies. Four rooms have microwave and refrigerator. **Services:** **Facilities:** Whirlpool, washer/dryer. Lots of greenery near the pool. **Rates (CP):** $45–$55 S or D; $67–$82 ste. Extra person $5. Children under age 18 stay free. Parking: Outdoor, free. AE, CB, DC, DISC, EC, ER, JCB, MC, V.

Sands Motel
814 W 27th St, 69361; tel 308/632-6191 or toll free 800/535-1075; fax 308/635-3909. SE corner of US 71 and US 26. A small, charming motel, close to restaurants and a large shopping mall. **Rooms:** 19 rms. CI open/CO 10:30am. Nonsmoking rms avail. Clean and comfortable rooms. **Amenities:** A/C, cable TV. Some rooms have refrigerators; alarm clocks upon request. **Services:** Portable ramp available for guests with disabilities. **Facilities:** **Rates:** $26–$35 S or D. Extra person $4. Children under age 1 stay free. Parking: Outdoor, free. AE, DISC, MC, V.

RESTAURANTS

Bush's Gaslight Restaurant & Lounge
3315 N 10; tel 308/632-7315. S of Main St. **American.** Etchings of local historical landscapes line the walls of four separate, cozy dining rooms (one with a fireplace). In this part of Nebraska, most people come for the steaks, but the menu offers a respectable selection of seafood and chicken dishes as well. **FYI:** Reservations accepted. Children's menu. **Open:** Sun–Thurs 4:30–10:30pm, Fri–Sat 4:30–11:30pm. **Prices:** Main courses $6–$13. DISC, MC, V.

Grampy's Pancake House and Restaurant
1802 E 20th Place; tel 308/632-6906. Off US 26. **American.** Friendly service is the true hallmark of this old-fashioned, family-style restaurant. Known for pancake specialties, the menu also includes a variety of sandwiches and dinners like the fried-shrimp special. The prix-fixe menu is a good choice for families. Senior discounts. **FYI:** Reservations accepted. Children's menu. No liquor license. **Open:** Daily 6am–11pm. **Prices:** Main courses $5–$10. AE, DISC, MC.

ATTRACTIONS

Scotts Bluff National Monument
Gering; tel 308/436-4340. 10 mi SW of Scottsbluff and 3 mi W of Gering. For thousands of years, Native Americans have called this massive 800-foot-tall sandstone and clay formation *Me-a-pa-te,* or "hill that is hard to go around." In the 19th-century, thousands of westward pioneers, Pony Express riders, fur traders, and hunters used the "Nebraska Gibraltar" as a landmark. Even today, their wagon-train trails can still be seen along the ground.

The visitors center features the **Oregon Trail Museum,** which commemorates the massive emigration and includes works by noted pioneer painter and photographer William Henry Jackson. Visitors can reach the top of the bluff by car or by hiking the 1½-mile-long **Saddle Rock Trail** (guide books and self-guided tour maps available at the visitors center). The top of the summit gives excellent views of the unusual landforms (including nearby Chimney Rock) and all varieties of prairie wildlife, such as coyotes, prairie dogs, and gophers.

For further information, contact the Superintendent, Scotts Bluff National Monument, Box 27, Gering, NE 69341 (tel 308/436-4340). **Open:** Mon–Fri sunrise–sunset. **$$**

Chimney Rock National Historic Site
Chimney Rock Rd, Bayard; tel 308/586-2581. 10 mi S of Scottsbluff. Rising 500 feet over the North Platte River Valley in eastern Nebraska, this strangely shaped spire was one of the most welcomed sights on the Oregon Trail. The pioneers knew their journey was at least half over when they caught a glimpse of Chimney Rock. A visitors center at the 83-acre site tells the story of the thousands who trekked through on the Oregon and Mormon Trails. **Open:** Daily 9am–6pm. **$**

Wildcat Hills State Recreation Area
NE 71, Gering; tel 308/436-2383. 20 mi S of Scottsbluff. This 935-acre state recreation area is primarily geared toward day use. Three stone shelters are available on a first-come, first-served basis, and picnic tables and fire grates are scattered throughout the area. A playground is located on the eastern access road. More than three miles of nature trails wind through the canyons and rocky bluffs, providing views of the buffalo and elk that populate the area. Although there is no designated camping area, primitive camping is allowed on several grassed areas; ask at park headquarters. **Open:** Daily dawn–dusk. **$**

Wildlife World
950 U St, Gering; tel 308/436-7104. 10 mi W of Scottsbluff. More than 200 animals from 6 continents are "preserved" here, in lifelike habitats. One of the most popular displays is the 19-foot-tall, 30-foot-long replica baluchithere, a prehistoric rhinoceros. **Open:** June–Aug, Mon–Sat 9am–5pm, Sun 1–5pm; Sept–May, Tues–Sat 9am–noon and 1–4pm. Closed some hols. **$**

North Platte Valley Museum
11th and J Sts, Gering; tel 308/436-5411. 10 mi S of Scottsbluff. Local history museum depicting the settlement of the North Platte Valley, from the hunters of 10,000 years ago to the fur traders, cattle ranchers, and homesteaders of the 19th century. Exhibits include tools, clothing, and home

furnishings of the early white settlers; horse-drawn carriages; houses made of sod and logs; and artifacts from the Sioux, Cheyenne, and Pawnee tribes. **Open:** May 1–Sept 30, Mon–Sat 9am–5pm, Sun 1–5pm. Closed some hols. **$**

Sidney

The seat of Cheyenne County was founded in 1869 and grew up around old Fort Sidney. Home to Cabela's, one of the nation's largest outdoor outfitters, which also has a superstore here. **Information:** Cheyenne County Chamber of Commerce, 740 Illinois, Sidney, 69162 (tel 308/254-5851).

ATTRACTION

Cabela's

115 Cabela Dr; tel 308/254-7889. Here at the corporate headquarters of "the world's foremost outfitter," shoppers can pick up their fishing, hunting, and outdoor gear in a gigantic 73,000-square-foot warehouse filled with more than 60,000 products and 500 wildlife mounts from around the world. The mounts include everything from Canada geese to Alaskan caribou and polar bears. The store also features an 8,000-gallon aquarium filled with warm-water and cold-water fish, an art gallery, and a 27-foot-tall indoor "mountain." **Open:** Mon–Sat 8am–8pm, Sun noon–5:30pm. Closed some hols. **Free**

South Sioux City

See also Sioux City (IA)

A river city essentially split in half from its sister on the Iowa side. Both have become known for leisure boating and for their proximity to nearby Native American casinos. **Information:** South Sioux City Convention and Visitors Bureau, 2700 Dakota Ave, South Sioux City, 68776 (tel 402/494-1307).

MOTELS

Econo Lodge

4402 Dakota Ave, 68776; tel 402/494-4114 or toll free 800/424-4777; fax 402/494-4114. Exit 144B off I-29; US 20, exit 2. A rather well-worn, utilitarian place to sleep. Lobby area decorated in red and white—the state university colors. **Rooms:** 60 rms and stes. CI 2pm/CO 11am. Nonsmoking rms avail. Nonsmokers should beware of taking a smoking room—odors are strong. **Amenities:** A/C, cable TV. Some rooms are being renovated with traveling seniors in mind, and will include coffeemakers and recliners. **Services:** **Facilities:** Whirlpool, washer/dryer. **Rates (CP):** $35–$40 S; $44–$48 D; $57–$67 ste. Extra person $5. Children under age 13 stay free. Parking: Outdoor, free. Group and extended-stay rates avail. AE, CB, DC, DISC, MC, V.

Park Plaza Motel

1201 1st Ave, 68776; tel 402/494-2021 or toll free 800/341-8000; fax 402/494-5998. Exit 148 off I-29, W on US 20 8 blocks. Older but well-kept brick building, tucked between a residential and a business district. **Rooms:** 50 rms. CI 1pm/CO 11am. Nonsmoking rms avail. **Amenities:** A/C, cable TV. **Services:** **Facilities:** 1 restaurant, 1 bar, washer/dryer. **Rates:** Peak (May 15–Aug 31) $31–$35 S; $36–$45 D. Extra person $3. Children under age 6 stay free. Lower rates off-season. Parking: Outdoor, free. AE, CB, DC, DISC, EC, ER, JCB, MC, V.

Travelodge

400 Dakota Ave, 68776; tel 402/494-3046 or toll free 800/578-7878; fax 402/494-8299. Exit 148 off I-29; W on US 20. Basic, rather worn motel. **Rooms:** 61 rms and stes. CI open/CO 11am. Nonsmoking rms avail. Some rooms overlook the Missouri River. **Amenities:** A/C, cable TV. Some units w/terraces. **Services:** **Facilities:** **Rates (CP):** $25–$36 S; $34–$42 D; $34–$42 ste. Extra person $4. Children under age 12 stay free. Parking: Outdoor, free. AE, CB, DC, DISC, EC, ER, JCB, MC, V.

Valentine

Each year, this sandhills town, founded in 1882, draws thousands of letters from cupids sending their heart-felt messages through the town for its distinctive postmark. Surrounded by three national wildlife areas, Valentine is also a popular jumping-off spot for canoers on the scenic Niobrara River and other outdoor enthusiasts. **Information:** Valentine Chamber of Commerce, 239 S Main St, PO Box 201, Valentine, 69201 (tel 402/376-2969).

MOTELS

Dunes Motel

US 20, 69201 (Downtown); tel 402/376-3131. At jct US 83. Located close to downtown, restaurants, and businesses, this motel's most notable feature is its timber arch construction. Canoeing nearby. **Rooms:** 24 rms. CI open/CO 11am. Nonsmoking rms avail. **Amenities:** A/C, cable TV w/movies, dataport. **Services:** **Facilities:** **Rates:** Peak (May 15–Sept 15) $30 S; $38 D. Extra person $3. Lower rates off-season. Parking: Outdoor, free. AE, MC, V.

Motel Raine

US 20 W, PO Box 231, 69201; tel 402/376-2030 or toll free 800/999-3066; fax 402/376-1956. A comfortable motel that serves travelers well. Office is filled with a rainbow of African violets, reflecting the homey attention found throughout the property. Near Niobrara River canoeing. **Rooms:** 34 rms. CI open/CO 11am. Nonsmoking rms avail. Clean, comfortable ambience, with very large double rooms. **Amenities:** A/C, cable TV, dataport. **Services:** **Facilities:**

Playground. **Rates (CP):** Peak (May–Sept) $34 S; $42 D. Extra person $2. Children under age 8 stay free. Lower rates off-season. Parking: Outdoor, free. AE, DISC, MC, V.

Trade Winds Lodge
US 20 E, 69201; tel 402/376-1600 or toll free 800/341-8000. On the east edge of town. Pine trees and flowers present a nice front for this redwood and brick establishment. Interior decor featuring barbed-wire art and lots of leather reflects western ranching environment. **Rooms:** 32 rms. CI open/CO 11am. Nonsmoking rms avail. Rooms surround swimming area for easy access. **Amenities:** A/C, cable TV w/movies. **Services:** **Facilities:** Special pet "exercise" area. **Rates:** Peak (May 15–Sept 15) $40 S; $50 D. Lower rates off-season. Parking: Outdoor, free. AE, CB, DC, DISC, MC, V.

RESTAURANT

Pepper Mill Restaurant and Steakhouse
112 N Main (Downtown); tel 402/376-1440. Off US 275. **Regional American.** Paintings of nearby Smith Falls add a touch of the West to this friendly establishment. Generous-size steaks; some Italian dishes. **FYI:** Reservations accepted. Big band/comedy/country music/dancing/dinner theater/jazz. Children's menu. **Open:** Mon–Sat 6am–10pm. **Prices:** Main courses $6–$16; prix fixe $5. AE, DISC, MC, V.

ATTRACTION

Sandhills Museum
W NE 20; tel 402/376-3293. Unusual collection of antiques includes vintage automobiles (from as far back as 1900), music boxes, firearms, Native American artifacts, a moonshine still, and household items from pioneer days. **Open:** Mem Day–Labor Day, daily 9am–6pm. $

York

Homesteaders from York, PA founded this agricultural town around 1870. Site of York College. **Information:** York County Convention and Visitors Commission, 211 E 6th St, PO Box 448, York, 68467 (tel 402/362-5531).

MOTELS

Best Western Inn
2426 S Lincoln Ave, 68467; tel 402/362-5585 or toll free 800/452-3185; fax 402/362-6053. Exit 353 off I-80; N 1 mi on US 81. An adequate motor court near the interstate. **Rooms:** 41 rms. CI 2pm/CO 11am. Nonsmoking rms avail. **Amenities:** A/C, cable TV, dataport. **Services:** Free breakfast in winter. **Facilities:** Washer/dryer. **Rates (CP):** Peak (June–Oct) $36–$45 S; $47–$49 D. Extra person $4. Children under age 12 stay free. Lower rates off-season. Parking: Outdoor, free. AE, CB, DC, DISC, MC, V.

Comfort Inn
3815 S Lincoln Ave, 68467; tel 402/362-6555 or toll free 800/221-2222. Exit 353 off I-80; N on US 81. An attractive economy property. **Rooms:** 49 rms and stes. CI 1pm/CO 11am. Nonsmoking rms avail. Exceptionally clean rooms. Whirlpool suite features a tiled tub and arched doorways. **Amenities:** A/C, cable TV. 1 unit w/whirlpool. Suites have refrigerators. **Services:** **Facilities:** 25 Whirlpool, washer/dryer. **Rates (CP):** Peak (June–Sept) $40–$45 S; $49–$55 D; $69–$77 ste. Extra person $5. Children under age 18 stay free. Lower rates off-season. Parking: Outdoor, free. AE, CB, DC, DISC, MC, V.

Days Inn
3710 S Lincoln Ave, 68467; tel 402/362-6355 or toll free 800/329-7466; fax 402/362-2827. Exit 353 off I-80; N on US 81. Nice layout for an economy motel. **Rooms:** 39 rms and stes. CI 1pm/CO 11am. Nonsmoking rms avail. **Amenities:** A/C, cable TV. 1 unit w/whirlpool. Suites have refrigerator and wet bar. **Services:** Small pets under 25 pounds only; no cats. **Facilities:** Whirlpool, washer/dryer. **Rates (CP):** Peak (May–Sept) $42 S; $48–$55 D; $71–$85 ste. Extra person $6. Children under age 12 stay free. Lower rates off-season. Parking: Outdoor, free. AE, CB, DC, DISC, MC, V.

RESTAURANT

Chances "R" Restaurant
124 W 5th; tel 402/362-7755. Exit 353 off I-80; US 81 N to downtown. **American.** Dark paneling, custom stained-glass windows and lamps, and collectible knickknacks make a homey backdrop for the house specialties: pan-fried chicken with homemade gravy and mashed potatoes. Other favorites include grilled pork chops or roast beef, both served with gravy and real mashed potatoes. There's also a full selection of hamburgers and steaks. Desserts feature jumbo cookies, cakes, custard pie, and caramel rolls. Prime rib buffet on Saturday nights. **FYI:** Reservations accepted. Children's menu. **Open:** Mon–Sat 6am–midnight, Sun 8am–11pm. **Prices:** Main courses $4–$32. DISC, MC, V.

NORTH DAKOTA

Land of the Unexpected

STATE STATS

CAPITAL
Bismarck

AREA
70,665 square miles

BORDERS
Minnesota, Montana, and South Dakota; Manitoba and Saskatchewan, Canada

POPULATION
638,800 (1990)

ENTERED UNION
November 2, 1889 (39th state)

NICKNAMES
Sioux State, Peace Garden State

STATE FLOWER
Wild prairie rose

STATE BIRD
Western meadowlark

FAMOUS NATIVES
Angie Dickinson, Louis L'Amour, Peggy Lee

You may already know that Theodore Roosevelt loved North Dakota and built a ranch near Medora. You've heard about the blizzards and the hot summers, the wheat fields and the cattle. But perhaps you did not know that North Dakota has more millionaires per capita than any other state. It's had some eccentrics, too, including a farmer who built a 26-foot-high Hereford bull and an 80-foot, Asian-style pagoda out of pieces of an old grain elevator.

There's lots of room here for big things. North Dakota is the site of an International Peace Garden (on the US/Canada border), where art and music festivals draw thousands of visitors each year. There's lots of room for wildlife, too. This peaceful state is a bird watcher's paradise, where meadowlarks seem to be singing from every fence post. Thousands of birds inhabit or migrate through the wetlands, and quiet lakes are full of walleye and perch.

North Dakota natives know how to hunker down and get through blizzards, droughts, and tough times. The native people whose ancestors first came to this area 10,000 years ago invite you to join in their powwows, watch demonstrations of activities that have gone on for centuries (such as quill work and bead making), and visit historic sites that hold much meaning for the original dwellers on this land.

Dakota is a Sioux word meaning "friend." This is a friendly place. It's quiet here, but not too quiet. Just about right.

A Brief History

Home of the Plains Indian Native Americans have been living in the region that is now North Dakota for some 11,000 years. Tribes that lived predominantly by farming included the earthlodge-dwelling Mandan, Arikara, and Hidatsa; nomadic or semi-nomadic tribes, which followed the buffalo across the plains, moving their teepees with them,

Frommer's #1

were the Cheyenne, Cree, Sioux, Crow, Chippewa, and Assiniboin.

Things began to change when fur traders entered the region in the early 18th century, bearing beads and guns to be traded for the tribes' beaver, otter, and fox pelts. The year after the northwestern half of the territory was acquired by the young United States as part of the Louisiana Purchase of 1803 (the southeastern half was gained from the British in 1818), explorers Lewis and Clark journeyed up the Missouri River and wintered in the North Dakota region. They were eventually guided to the Pacific by Sacajawea, a young Shoshone woman who had been raised by members of the Hidatsa. When trading posts were established in the Red River Valley by the North West Company and the Hudson's Bay Company a few years later, it marked the beginning of a half-century of dominance by the fur industry in the region.

It took only another generation of traders and explorers and strongly held forts to open the territory wide enough for homesteaders to make their way in. By the late 1860s, farming settlements were being established, and treaties with the Sioux and Hidatsa were being made and broken. When gold was discovered in the Black Hills—the sacred hunting grounds of the Sioux—in the early 1870s and the whites refused yet again to honor treaty agreements meant to keep them off the Native American land, renewed war broke out. But despite the stunning victory by Sioux and Cheyenne warriors over George Armstrong Custer and his Seventh Cavalry regiment at the Little Bighorn River (in present-day Montana) in 1876, the fate of the Plains Indians was already determined. Faced with railroads, gold prospectors, homesteaders, and the US Army, they were forced onto reservations.

Fun Facts

- The geographic center of North America lies seven miles west of Rugby, ND.
- North Dakota produces 80% of the national supply of durum wheat. That's enough to serve up pasta for 93 nights to every American.
- The tallest manmade structure in the United States is the KTHI-TV tower near Blanchard, ND. It soars 2,063 feet.
- North Dakota ranks third in the nation for acreage farmed organically—108,000 certified organic acres.
- You can now buy microwave lutefisk—a type of dried, salted fish— in North Dakota. Michael's Classic Lutefisk Meals makes this singular Scandinavian dish that appeals to few other nationalities.

Tracks to the Future The Northern Pacific Railroad finished laying down tracks in the region in 1872. The railroad brought settlers from points east as well as many immigrants from the Old World—chiefly Germany, Russia, and Scandinavia. (The capital city changed its name from Edwinton to Bismarck in order to attract German settlers.) The newcomers had been tempted to this inhospitable prairie by the low land prices advertised in newspapers back east and in Europe. Cattle ranchers came too, following Theodore Roosevelt's example and dreaming of a spread of their own. More than 100,000 people arrived between 1879 and 1886, and in 1889 the territory became a state. More than half a million people had moved in by the end of the century.

Standing On Its Own Massive immigration had come at a high cost. The homesteaders had traveled to their destinations under great duress, danger, and sometimes illness, but success was not as easy as advertised in the papers back east. By the turn of the century, bankers and grain-elevator operators in other states (particularly Minnesota) had established control of North Dakota's finances and wheat production. As a result, the early 1900s saw the establishment of the Nonpartisan League, whose purpose was to organize North Dakota farmers to establish their own bank, improve farm conditions in the state, and prevent out-of-state banks and regulators from having any control over North Dakota money and grain.

Drought & Slow Rebuilding The Nonpartisan League was a success, but the whole farming enterprise was nearly wiped out by drought and economic depression in the 1930s. The impoverished, dust-ridden state seemed to have no more to offer and people left by the thousands. Still, those who stayed watched things improve in the 1940s and 1950s and continue to improve for farms and cities alike with each passing decade. The state began to rely on its natural resources—mostly oil and coal—for income. The Garrison Dam diverted water from the Missouri River to irrigate farms, and the lake that formed from the dam's waters, Lake Sakakawea, became a focus for recreation in the state. Farmers still have had to face cycles of flood and drought, but North Dakota continues to grow and to thrive.

A Closer Look

GEOGRAPHY

Think of North Dakota not as a dry flat prairie, but as a place of valleys and rosy bluffs, craggy buttes, and forests. Lakes, wetlands, and rivers are plentiful here. The **Missouri River** flows through the western portion of the state, and the **Red River** carves the border between North Dakota and Minnesota. Spring-fed **Devils Lake** covers 70,000 acres and is the largest natural lake in the state.

North Dakota can be divided into three distinct regions. Eastern North Dakota is famous for the **Red River Valley.** Fargo and Grand Forks (the state's two largest cities) are located in this mostly flat valley—a narrow ribbon of some of the most fertile land in the country. This is where the "bonanza" farms began, where homesteaders felt they had discovered land so rich it was as good as gold. Wheat, beans, sugar beets, and potatoes grow in soil that was once the bottom of a glacial lake, Lake Agassiz, which covered the state's eastern edge 10,000 years ago.

The central region, or **Drift Prairie,** is named for drift (rich soil perfect for raising wheat). Its beginning is marked by the Pembina Escarpment, a dramatic rise onto rolling plains where you will find the famous **Dakota "potholes,"** or small lakes, and the sway of tall prairie grasses in the breeze. The central rolling plains include the pretty city of Bottineau, nestled at the base of the Turtle Mountains (which are green, rolling hills, not actually mountains). The northern part of the Drift Prairie has thousands of depressions in the land, caused by glaciers, which fill with rain and drain slowly. Bismarck and Mandan lie on either side of the Missouri River, which cuts through this section of the state.

The western region of the state is marked by another rise, the Missouri Escarpment, bringing the land up again, to the **Missouri Plateau.** This land once teemed with dinosaurs, who roamed the area after an inland sea receded some 70 million years ago. Over the years, the sediment and plant life left behind by glaciers became deep deposits of coal and oil. The **Badlands** still smolder in places from deep coal burns ignited by lightning; these underground coal fires have given a reddish glow to some of the steep and craggy, or soft and molded, surface rock.

DRIVING DISTANCES

Bismarck

110 mi S of Minot
132 mi E of Medora
178 mi SW of Devils Lake
193 mi W of Fargo
225 mi SE of Williston
250 mi SW of Grand Forks

Fargo

120 mi SE of Devils Lake
76 mi S of Grand Forks
242 mi NW of Minneapolis, MN
268 mi SE of Bottineau
354 mi NE of Pierre, SD
391 mi SE of Williston

Grand Forks

250 mi NE of Bismarck
131 mi NE of Dickinson
149 mi NE of Jamestown
192 mi SE of Bottineau
75 mi E of Devils Lake
267 mi E of Minot

CLIMATE

Winter in North Dakota can be bitterly cold, with a startling brightness on the snowy fields and plains. A haunting wind can whirl in snow from Canada and points north for days on end. Still, North Dakotans go outside in the winter, undaunted, and fortified by their northern European ancestry. The spring rainy season is cool, and things begin to heat up quickly after the last frost. In the summer, the weather is hot and sunny; even if you're staying in northern North Dakota, don't forget to wear sunscreen. The Badlands are subject to sudden summer storms that shower the earth with big pellets of hail. (You should avoid any open stretches of prairie or Badlands during electrical storms.)

WHAT TO PACK

Winters are serious business in North Dakota. Good wool sweaters and a thick, no-nonsense coat are ideal. Bring caps, scarves, gloves, and warm boots, and wear layers so you can adjust your comfort level to well-heated houses and buildings. In summertime it's usually so muggy at night you won't need a jacket, but bring a long-sleeved shirt or light sweater anyway—to keep the mosquitoes away. (Campers should pack insect repellent!) Summer clothing should be light, loose, and cool. Chilly autumn and rainy spring days may require a jacket. Autumn nights can be very nippy, so pack a sweater or two.

TOURIST INFORMATION

Call 800/HELLO-ND for a free state map and a packet of brochures on travel in North Dakota, or contact **North Dakota Parks and Tourism,** 604 E Boulevard Ave, Bismarck, ND 58505 (tel 701/328-2525). The tourism office provides information on the different geographic regions, Native American presentations, state history, and more.

For information on many of the state's parks, accommodations, festivals, and events, contact any North Dakota Welcome Center. They are located in Hankinson, Oriska, Pembina, West Fargo, Bowman, and Williston, and are listed in the municipal phone directories. Recreation information is available from **North Dakota Parks and Recreation,** 1835 E Bismarck Expwy, Bismarck, ND 58504 (tel 701/221-5357).

For information on Native American events and points of interest, contact the following tribes: Turtle Mountain Band of Pembina Chippewa, PO Box 1449, Belcourt, ND 58316 (tel 701/477-6451); Mandan, Hidatsa, and Arikara Three Affiliated Tribes, HC3, Box 2, New Town, ND 58763 (tel 701/627-4781); Devils Lake Sioux Tribe, PO Box 359, Fort Totten, ND 58335 (tel 701/766-4221); Standing Rock Sioux Tribe, PO Box D, Fort Yates, ND 58538 (tel 701/854-7201).

AVG MONTHLY TEMPS (°F) & RAINFALL (IN)

	Bismarck	Fargo
Jan	9/0.5	6/0.7
Feb	16/0.4	12/0.5
Mar	28/0.8	26/1.0
Apr	43/1.7	43/1.8
May	55/2.2	56/2.5
June	64/2.7	66/2.8
July	70/2.1	71/2.7
Aug	68/1.7	69/2.4
Sept	57/1.5	58/2.0
Oct	46/0.9	46/1.7
Nov	29/0.5	28/0.7
Dec	14/0.5	12/0.7

DRIVING RULES AND REGULATIONS

The speed limit is 65 mph on rural interstates; all other interstates are 55 mph unless otherwise posted. Radar and aircraft are used to enforce speeding laws. Nonresident drivers must be licensed in their home state and be at least 16 years old. Front seat passengers must use safety belts. Children under age 3 must be in a car safety seat; those 3–10 must use a car safety seat or a safety belt. A right turn is permitted after a complete stop at a red light unless otherwise prohibited by signs. Helmets are required for motorcyclists under 18.

RENTING A CAR

The following car rental agencies have offices in North Dakota. The minimum age requirement varies with each company, so you should call for details. Before you leave home, check with your insurance company for coverage on rental cars. If you are not covered, the car rental companies will sell you insurance.

- **Avis** (tel toll free 800/331-1212)
- **Budget** (tel 800/527-0700)
- **Dollar** (Grand Forks only; tel 800/421-6868 or 800/327-7607)
- **Hertz** (tel 800/654-3131)
- **National** (tel 800/328-4567)

ESSENTIALS

Area Code: North Dakota has one area code, **701.**

Emergencies: Call 911 for emergencies; for road emergencies, call toll free 800/472-2121.

Gambling: The minimum age for gambling is 21. Be sure to check for local policies concerning admittance of children into parimutuel betting facilities.

Liquor Laws: You must be 21 years old to drink alcoholic beverages in the state.

Road Info: For information on the condition of state roads, call 701/328-2898 or 328-2545 (or 800/472-2686 in ND only). These numbers will give winter road conditions; in summer they provide information about roads under construction.

Smoking: Smoking is restricted in North Dakota at arts and cultural activities, in elevators, government buildings, gymnasiums and arenas, health facilities, restaurants, rest rooms, retail and grocery stores, and in schools. Smoking is prohibited at child care centers.

Taxes: North Dakota has a statewide sales tax of 5%. Locally, there are options for adding 1% or more.

Time Zone: The portion of the state west and south of the Missouri River (including Theodore Roosevelt National Park) is in the Mountain time zone;

the rest of the state (Bismarck, Grand Forks, Fargo, Minot) is in the Central time zone.

Best of the State

WHAT TO SEE AND DO

Below is a general overview of some of the top sights and attractions in North Dakota. To find out more detailed information, look under "Attractions" under individual cities in the listings portion of this book.

National Parks Teddy Roosevelt spent a lot of time hunting and ranching in North Dakota. **Theodore Roosevelt National Park,** in the western part of the state, stands as a legacy of the 26th president's conservation efforts. North Dakota's only national park, it includes 70,000 acres of Badlands and prairie. Roosevelt built a ranch here, on the west bank of the Little Missouri River. Elk, deer, coyotes, bobcats, weasels, and beavers share this big chunk of land with the bison. The visitors center in Medora has Roosevelt's original log cabin on display.

State Parks Over 17,000 acres of North Dakota land is dedicated to state parks and recreation areas, with facilities for camping (over 1,500 campsites in all), hiking, horseback riding, swimming, tennis, and fishing. You can snowmobile in some of the parks, or canoe or water-ski along hundreds of miles of waterways.

In 1873, General Custer came to Fort Abraham Lincoln, where the Heart and Missouri Rivers meet. Today, **Fort Abraham Lincoln State Park,** features a reconstructed Mandan tribal village. Visitors can camp, picnic, or hike at **Fort Stevenson State Park,** near Garrison; and equestrians can rent a horse and ride the riverside trails at **Turtle River State Park,** a 784-acre park near Grand Forks. Turtle River is the only state park equipped with bicycle trails.

Natural Wonders Each year, millions of birds come to nest around the "pothole lakes" in the central part of the state. Estimates claim that over 50 million birds, representing more than 10% of North American bird species, live in North Dakota during warm weather. You can see a lot of them—including herons, white pelicans, geese, and a variety of ducks—at the 58,000-acre **J Clark Salyer National Wildlife Refuge,** south of Bottineau; the **Audubon National Wildlife Refuge,** north of Underwood; the **Long Lake National Wildlife Refuge,** near Moffit; and the **Arrowwood National Wildlife Refuge,** on the banks of the James River.

The multicolored **Badlands,** part of which are located in North Dakota, are a distinctive grouping of buttes and rugged hills. Composed of layers of coal, sandstone, silt-stone, and mudstone, they have streaks of a reddish color caused by deep, ongoing coal fires.

Emerald-green **Devils Lake** is one of the only closed basin lakes in the United States. Flanked by forests of oak and elm, this 700,000-acre spring-fed lake is the largest natural prairie lake in North Dakota. Devils Lake is also the site of an enormous annual waterfowl migration including snow geese, a variety of ducks, and sandhill cranes.

Manmade Wonders **Lake Sakakawea,** a 364,000-acre reservoir on the Missouri River, was formed after the creation of Garrison Dam. Tours of the dam, one of the largest rolled-earth dams in the world, are available throughout the summer.

The **International Peace Garden,** north of Dunseith, is a monument to the harmony shared between the United States and Canada. Nearly 2,300 acres of botanical gardens extend into both countries. The garden contains a large floral clock, wildflower gardens, field crop displays, sunken gardens, cascading waterfalls and fountains, and lots of lakeside picnic areas and hiking trails. The Peace Garden is also the site of a music camp, art festival, and annual fiddle competition. Concerts are held every Sunday in the summer.

Wildlife Look for road signs with binoculars on them—the sign of an area rich in wildlife viewing opportunities. The prairies, lakes, and hilly sections of North Dakota provide homes for mule deer, antelope, big horn sheep, elk, moose, white-tailed deer, prairie dogs, bobcats, mountain lions, bears, eagles, snow geese, and more. *A Wildlife Viewing Guide* (Falcon Press) is available at most bookstores and from state and federal agencies, or call 701/328-2525 and ask for a copy. Buffalo still roam through **Theodore Roosevelt National Park,** while elk and moose inhabit the woodsy Turtle Mountain region. Antelope, coyotes, prairie dogs, and bighorn sheep can be spotted in the Badlands.

Historic Sites & Areas North Dakota is full of historic places of interest. The **Assumption Abbey,** built in 1910, and its 2,000-acre farm are located 75 miles west of Bismarck at Richardton. Tours are guided by Brother Frankenhauser, who shares stories about Benedictine monastic life. Visitors can purchase wine from the abbey's cellars.

Horse and cattle thieves were up to no good all over the west, and Dakota Territory was no exception. The **White Earth Valley,** a peaceful place today, was once the site of outlaws, hangings (some fair and some not), cattle rustling, sharp shooting, and posses. The Maskawapa Historical Society in White Earth operates two museums: the White Earth Jail and the White Earth Presbyterian Church.

Medora, located in the heart of the Badlands, was named for the wife of the Marquis de Mores. The French nobleman and his American wife came here in the 1880s with dreams of building a meat-packing empire. The pair's **Château de Mores** is a 26-room mansion set high above the Missouri River.

The 19-story **state capitol building** in Bismarck, built in the 1930s, is sometimes known as the Skyscraper of the Plains. Marble floors and walls and bronze pillars give the building an austere elegance. If you take the elevator to the 18th floor, you can look out over the city, the Missouri, and far, far across the prairie. A statue of Sacajawea stands at the forefront of the capitol grounds to honor the Shoshone woman who took Lewis and Clark all the way to the Pacific and back.

Museums A collection of state treasures and an extensive display of state history is housed at the **Heritage Center** on the grounds of the state capitol. Here you will find displays featuring the domestic aspects of settlement life, as well as pioneer farming tools, a typical 19th-century schoolroom, and even a one-room house built by a woman homesteader.

Just south of US 2 at Rugby, where the stone cairn marks the geographical center of North America, is the **Pioneer Village Museum,** with displays of Native American artifacts. The village contains a railroad depot, livery stable, blacksmith shop, saloon, and a jail. Three tribes—the Arikara, Hidatsa, and Mandan—own the **Indian Museum** at New Town, while both folk art and fine art are on display at the **E'Lan Gallery,** in the former home of North Dakota poet James W Foley, in Bismarck.

Family Favorites Children will gasp at the enormity of the 37-foot-long allosaurus housed at the spacious **Dakota Dinosaur Museum** in Dickinson. The museum has over 100 exhibits, including several other reconstructed dinosaurs, fossils, seashells, mammals, and fluorescent rocks. You'll also find dinosaurs at **Pioneer Trails Regional Museum** in Bowman and at the **Heritage Center** on the state capitol grounds in Bismarck.

The kids can build a house, watch a puppet show, see amazing bubbles (and blow a few themselves), ride a choo-choo train, and tour a 19th-century farmhouse at the **Children's Museum** at Yunker Farm in Fargo.

EVENTS AND FESTIVALS

- **North Dakota Winter Show,** Valley City. A boot-stomping springtime rodeo, plus square dancing, horse shows, and livestock contests. March. Call 701/845-1401.
- **Native American Days,** Grand Forks. Springtime fun at a multitribe powwow. April. Call 701/777-4291.
- **Scandinavian Hjemkomst Festival,** Fargo. Taste lutefisk and other Scandinavian specialties and see craft demonstrations and the May Pole dance. May. Call 701/282-3653.
- **Syttende Mai,** Towner. A celebration of Norwegian national independence, with parades and lots of Scandinavian crafts and events. May. Call 701/537-5687.
- **Dakota Cowboy Poetry Gathering,** Medora. A star attraction for anyone interested in cowboy poetry and western arts and crafts. May. Call 701/623-4444.
- **North Dakota Chautauqua Festival,** Devils Lake. Remembrance of the educational chautauqua gatherings of the late 19th and early 20th centuries, with plays, workshops, and other events. Summer. Call 701/662-4903.
- **Dinosaur Days,** Dickinson. Dinosaur hollering contest, Stegosaurus Stomp, and bone and dinosaur egg treasure hunt. Hot-air balloon rally, too. June. Call 701/225-4988.
- **Fort Seward Wagon Train,** Jamestown. Annual weeklong wagon train adventure following a historic route. Late June or early July. Call 701/252-6844.
- **Northern Plains Indian Culture Fest,** Knife River Indian Villages. Demonstrations of bead and quill work, Native American dances. Tour an actual earthlodge. July. Call 701/745-3300.
- **Turtle Mountain Mountain Man Rendezvous,** Lake Metigoshe State Park. Celebration of the mountain man, with a re-creation of 19th-century camp life. Tomahawk tossing. July. Call 701/263-4651.

- **Pioneer Days/Bonanzaville USA,** West Fargo. This valley was the site of the early "bonanza farms," and every summer this restored pioneer village comes alive. August. Call 701/282-2822.
- **Folkfest,** Bismarck. Celebration of German history in the region. Folk dancing, German food, parades, river race. September.
- **United Tribes Powwow,** Bismarck. Multitribal event features native costumes, food, crafts, singing, and dancing. Fall. Call 701/255-3285.

SPECTATOR SPORTS

Auto Racing Bottineau, in the heart of the Turtle Mountains, has recently opened the **Thunder Mountain Speedway** (tel 701/263-4801). Speedway racing is also held in Mandan, Fargo, and Grand Forks. Call the local convention and visitors bureau for schedule and ticket information.

Football The **North Dakota State University Bison** play in Fargo, and have been a top program in the country for over two decades. Call 701/237-8981 for ticket information.

Hockey With all those Scandinavian ancestors, hockey is bound to be a Dakota favorite. The **Fighting Sioux** of the University of North Dakota in Grand Forks have won five NCAA Division I national championships. Call 701/777-2234 for tickets.

Horse Racing The Great American Horse Race, inspired by the old Pony Express riders, is held in the fall at Fort Abraham Lincoln State Park. Call 701/663-9571 for info. Thoroughbred horse racing is also happening at the Wells County Fairgrounds in Fessenden. Call 701/547-3555 for tickets.

Rodeos If you like the idea of watching wranglers and thrill riders, you'll have plenty of opportunities all over the state. You can buy tickets for rodeos held at Bismarck's Civic Center by calling 701/222-4308 or 222-6489. Information on rodeo events is available from the North Dakota Office of Tourism (tel toll free 800/435-5663).

ACTIVITIES A TO Z

Bicycling Rolling plains, few hills, and wide roads make bicycling tremendously popular in North Dakota. Each summer, a 414-mile circular bike ride called the CANDISC starts at Fort Stevenson State Park and winds through the Badlands and the old town of Medora. Call 701/337-5576 for details and a map. The State Department of Parks and Recreation (tel 701/221-5357) has maps of other cross-country bike tours.

Bird Watching North Dakota has over 60 national wildlife refuges as well as prairie lake regions and wetlands that are either nesting places or migratory stops for thousands of birds. Plant yourself with a pair of binoculars in one of the wetland areas in the central region of the state and observe white pelicans, great blue herons, sandhill cranes, and the sharp-tailed grouses. Unusual birds such as the piping plover, ferruginous hawk, and Sprague's pipet live in this part of the country, and the rare whooping crane migrates through the state in April and September.

Butterfly Watching Trekking to the sandhills in the **Cheyenne National Grassland** (tel 701/683-4342), about 40 miles southwest of Fargo, allows you to observe some of North Dakota's smallest treasures. The bright yellow prairie ringlet is here, along with the more familiar monarch, the delicate eastern tailed blue, the Edwards fritillary, the black swallowtail, the viceroy, and many more.

Camping North Dakota state parks have a total of 1,300 campsites. A new reservation system, which covers about 30% of the available sites, serves Cross Ranch, Fort Abraham Lincoln, Fort Ransom, Fort Stevenson, Grahams Island, Icelandic, Lake Metigoshe, Lake Sakakawea, Lewis and Clark, Shelvers Grove, and Turtle River State Parks. Call 800/807-4723 to make reservations (at least three days in advance).

Fishing Walleye and bass swim the emerald waters of Devils Lake, where bait-and-tackle shops, plenty of accessible boat ramps, and guide services are available. Locals and visitors alike ice fish for yellow perch in the lake every winter. Contact North Dakota Game and Fish (tel 701/221-6300) for information on fishing regulations.

The **North Dakota Governor's Cup** takes place every year at Fort Stevenson State Park, where several hundred fishing enthusiasts cast their lines into Lake Sakakawea for walleye. Contact the Garrison Chamber of Commerce (tel 701/463-2600) for details.

Golf More than a dozen 18-hole courses and five dozen 9-hole courses put North Dakota close to the top of the list nationwide for number of golf courses

Selected Parks & Recreation Areas

- **International Peace Garden,** Dunseith, ND 58329 (tel 701/263-4390)
- **Theodore Roosevelt National Park (South Unit),** Medora, ND 58645 (tel 701/623-4466)
- **Theodore Roosevelt National Park (North Unit),** Watford City, ND (tel 701/623-4466)
- **Battleview State Park,** east of Bowman (tel 701/523-5641)
- **Beaver Lake State Park,** 3850 70th St SE, Wishek, ND 58495 (tel 701/452-2752)
- **Black Tiger Bay State Park,** Rte 1, Box 165, Devils Lake, ND 58301
- **Cross Ranch State Park,** HC2, Box 152, Sanger, ND 58567 (tel 701/794-3731)
- **Fort Abraham Lincoln State Park,** Rte 2, Box 139, Mandan, ND 58554 (tel 701/663-9571)
- **Fort Ransom State Park,** Rte 1, Box 20A, Fort Ransom, ND 58033 (tel 701/973-4331)
- **Fort Stevenson State Park,** Rte 1, Box 262, Garrison, ND 58540 (tel 701/337-5576)
- **Grahams Island State Park,** Rte 1, Box 165, Devils Lake, ND 58301 (tel 701/766-4015)
- **Icelandic State Park,** HCR3, Box 64A, Cavalier, ND 58220 (tel 701/ 265-4561)
- **Lake Metigoshe State Park,** #2 Lake Metigoshe State Park, Bottineau, ND 58338 (tel 701/263-4651)
- **Lake Sakakawea State Park,** Box 732, Riverdale, ND 58565 (tel 701/487-3315)
- **Lewis and Clark State Park,** Rte 1, Box 13A, Epping, ND (tel 701/859-3071)
- **Little Missouri State Park,** 18 mi N of Killdeer on ND 22 then 2 mi E on Township Rd (tel 701/859-3071)
- **The Narrows State Park,** Rte 1, Box 165, Devils Lake, ND 58301 (tel 701/766-4015)
- **Shelvers Grove State Park,** Rte 1, Box 165, Devils Lake, ND 58301 (tel 701/766-4015)
- **Turtle River State Park,** Rte 1, Box 9B, Arvilla, ND 58214 (tel 701/594-4445)

per person. Check the local phone book for the course nearest you.

Hiking Nineteen state parks and recreation areas have hiking trails. **North Dakota Parks and Recreation** (tel 701/221-5357) can send you information on all park hiking trails. Some perennial favorites include the 85-acre Chahinkapa Park and Zoo in Wahpeton, Mirror Lake Park south of Hettinger, Fort Abraham Lincoln, and Theodore Roosevelt National Park.

Water Sports Swimming, sailing, water skiing, and boating are popular at many of the state's lakes. The **Devils Lake Tourist Information Center** (tel 701/662-4903) will give you information on boat access and the best spots for swimming in the park. **Lake Sakakawea,** with its 1,600 miles of shoreline, is a water lover's paradise. Fishing, water skiing, sailing, boating, swimming, wind surfing, and just floating on the crystal blue waters are all great pleasures to be found on this huge lake. Contact the **Garrison Chamber of Commerce** (tel 701/463-2600) for information about the Lake Sakakawea region.

Winter Sports Downhill skiing is available at **Bottineau Winter Park** (tel 701/263-4556); **Frostfire Mountain** (tel 701/549-3600), near Walhalla; and **Skyline Skiway** (tel 701/766-4035) at Devils Lake. Or you might prefer to join in a cross-country snowmobile race over the snowy plains. The **North Dakota Tourism Department** (tel 800/435-5663) will give you the locations for everything from dogsled races to where to find popular cross-country ski trails.

North Dakota Listings

Amidon

RESTAURANT

✱ Georgia's and the Owl
US 85 and Main; tel 701/879-6289. **American.** Prime rib is the specialty here—weighing in from petite portions to a two-pound extravaganza. Also offered are various fish and seafood dishes as well as homemade desserts. The upper-level dining room is furnished with some charming antiques. **FYI:** Reservations recommended. Country music. Children's menu. **Open:** Peak (June–Sept) Sun–Thurs 11am–9:30pm, Fri–Sat 11am–midnight. **Prices:** Main courses $12–$24. No CC.

Bismarck

Bismarck was settled in 1873 on the site of Camp Greeley, an outpost established to protect railroad crews working their way across the Dakotas. (The railroad named the new town after the German chancellor, in the hope of luring foreign capital.) Even before the railroad, the site was a popular Missouri River crossing for the likes of Sitting Bull and Lewis and Clark. Today, Bismarck is a squeaky-clean and almost spartan city, with wide streets, well-kept lawns and a friendly bearing. The state historical center and capitol buildings are key attractions, as is an attractive bicycling and walking park along the Missouri. **Information:** Bismarck-Mandan Convention and Visitors Bureau, 107 W Main St, PO Box 2274, Bismarck, 58502 (tel 701/222-4308).

HOTELS

Holiday Inn Bismarck
605 E Broadway, 58501 (Downtown); tel 701/255-6000 or toll free 800/465-4329; fax 701/223-0400. Exit 159 off I-94; S on State St to 7th St; W on Broadway. Comfortable, with better-than-average furnishings and carpets. **Rooms:** 215 rms and stes. CI 2pm/CO noon. Nonsmoking rms avail. **Amenities:** A/C, cable TV w/movies, dataport. 1 unit w/whirlpool. Some suites have three phones, refrigerator, stove, and two baths. **Services:** VP Social director, babysitting. Upon request, tours can be arranged to state capitol building and other nearby attractions. **Facilities:** 500 1 restaurant, 1 bar, sauna, whirlpool, beauty salon. Casino. Pool has attractive greenhouse windows. **Rates:** $50–$85 S or D; $85–$250 ste. Extra person $5. Children under age 18 stay free. Parking: Indoor, free. During summer, kids stay and eat free. Weekend packages often avail. AE, CB, DC, DISC, ER, JCB, MC, V.

Radisson Inn Bismarck
800 S 3rd St, 58504; tel 701/258-7700 or toll free 800/333-3333; fax 701/224-8212. Across from Kirkwood Mall. Popular midtown hotel, often booked during conventions. Reservations are a must. **Rooms:** 306 rms and stes. Executive level. CI 3pm/CO noon. Nonsmoking rms avail. Better-than-average furnishings. **Amenities:** A/C, cable TV w/movies. Some units w/terraces, some w/whirlpools. **Services:** Social director. **Facilities:** 1500 1 restaurant (*see* "Restaurants" below), 1 bar, games rm, sauna, whirlpool. Small casino. **Rates:** $52–$66 S; $62–$76 D; $130–$175 ste. Extra person $10. Children under age 18 stay free. Parking: Outdoor, free. AE, CB, DC, DISC, ER, JCB, MC, V.

MOTELS

Best Western Doublewood Inn
1400 E Interchange, 58501; tel 701/258-7000 or toll free 800/554-7077; fax 701/258-2001. Exit 159 off I-94. When the state legislature is in session, this motel books up quickly, so reservations are recommended. **Rooms:** 144 rms and stes. CI 4pm/CO noon. Nonsmoking rms avail. **Amenities:** A/C, cable TV w/movies, dataport. **Services:** **Facilities:** 500 1 restaurant, 1 bar, games rm, sauna, whirlpool. **Rates:** $53–$58 S; $63–$68 D; $90 ste. Extra person $5. Children under age 18 stay free. Parking: Outdoor, free. Weekend packages avail. AE, CB, DC, DISC, ER, MC, V.

Best Western Fleck House
122 E Thayer Ave, 58501 (Downtown); tel 701/255-1450 or toll free 800/528-1234; fax 701/258-3816. Across from federal building. This motel has few amenities, but it's clean and conveniently located for downtown business. **Rooms:** 58

rms, stes, and effic. CI 2pm/CO noon. Nonsmoking rms avail. Plain, but in good repair. **Amenities:** A/C, cable TV. **Services:** **Facilities:** Washer/dryer. Outdoor pool in poor condition. **Rates (CP):** Peak (May 16–Sept 15) $32–$42 S; $38–$44 D; $50–$65 ste; $44–$54 effic. Extra person $2. Children under age 12 stay free. Lower rates off-season. Parking: Outdoor, free. Group rates avail. AE, CB, DC, DISC, MC, V.

Bismarck Ramada Inn
1215 W Main, 58504; tel 701/223-9600 or toll free 800/272-6232; fax 701/224-9210. Bismarck Expwy, just E of Memorial Bridge. Very tired-looking motel, located just off the Missouri River and a riverside park. OK if there's nothing else available. **Rooms:** 256 rms and stes. CI 2pm/CO noon. Nonsmoking rms avail. Furnishings are clean but worn and dated. **Amenities:** A/C, cable TV w/movies. Some units w/minibars. **Services:** **Facilities:** 1 restaurant, 1 bar (w/entertainment), games rm, beauty salon, washer/dryer. **Rates:** $50–$64 S; $57–$67 D; $150 ste. Extra person $5. Children under age 18 stay free. Parking: Outdoor, free. Group and weekend rates avail. AE, DC, DISC, MC, V.

Expressway Inn
200 Bismarck Expwy, 58504; tel 701/222-2900 or toll free 800/456-6588; fax 701/222-2900. Although this property is mostly geared to business and convention travelers, a play area and nearby fast-food restaurants attract families as well. **Rooms:** 163 rms and stes. Executive level. CI 2pm/CO noon. Nonsmoking rms avail. **Amenities:** A/C, cable TV, CD/tape player. **Services:** **Facilities:** Games rm, whirlpool, playground. **Rates (CP):** $30–$36 S; $37–$44 D; $65 ste. Extra person $4. Children under age 14 stay free. Parking: Outdoor, free. Weekly and tour rates avail. AE, DC, DISC, MC, V.

Fairfield Inn
135 Ivy Ave, 58504; tel 701/223-9293 or toll free 800/228-2800; fax 701/223-9293. An economy motel with a sunny disposition as evidenced in the clean, bright common areas. **Rooms:** 63 rms and stes. CI 2pm/CO 11am. Nonsmoking rms avail. Clean furnishings in good repair. Second-floor suite directly above pool. **Amenities:** A/C, cable TV. **Services:** **Facilities:** Games rm, whirlpool, washer/dryer. Small but attractive pool area. **Rates (CP):** $42–$50 S; $48–$56 D; $48–$63 ste. Extra person $6. Children under age 16 stay free. Parking: Outdoor, free. AE, DC, DISC, MC, V.

Kelly Inn
1800 N 12th St, 58501; tel 701/223-8001 or toll free 800/635-3559; fax 701/223-8001. Exit 159 off I-94. This clean motel, just off the interstate, is near the State Capitol and the history center. **Rooms:** 101 rms and stes. CI 2pm/CO noon. Nonsmoking rms avail. Suites are plain. **Amenities:** A/C, cable TV w/movies. 1 unit w/whirlpool. **Services:** **Facilities:** 1 restaurant, 1 bar, games rm, sauna, whirlpool. **Rates:** Peak (June–Sept) $40–$46 S; $46–$51 D; $55–$85 ste. Extra person $5. Children under age 12 stay free. Lower rates off-season. Parking: Outdoor, free. Occasional weekend, rodeo, and hockey special rates. AE, CB, DC, DISC, MC, V.

RESTAURANTS

Captain's Table
In Best Western Seven Seas Inn, 2611 Old Red Trail, Mandan; tel 701/663-7401. **American.** Nautical trappings are a tip-off to the mainly seafood menu available here. Items include poached salmon, walleye fillets, and Alaskan king crab, as well as a variety of surf-and-turf combinations (after all, Plains folk prefer their seafood served with beef). More adventurous entrees include shrimp Creole, and beef tenderloin smothered with snow crab, asparagus, and béarnaise sauce. **FYI:** Reservations recommended. Children's menu. **Open:** Mon–Thurs 6:30am–10pm, Fri–Sat 6:30am–11pm, Sun 7am–9pm. **Prices:** Main courses $9–$25. AE, CB, DC, DISC, MC, V.

★ Caspar's East 40
1401 E Interchange Ave; tel 701/258-7222. Exit 159 off I-94. **Continental.** Casper Borggreve has filled his restaurant with antiques found at auctions. His finds include a bar from an old Montana saloon, a chandelier from Spain, and stained-glass windows from a Methodist church. The rich menu offers milk-fed veal medallions topped with crab meat and hollandaise sauce; and escargots seasoned with garlic and parsley butter. Smaller dining rooms with fireplaces are ideal in cool weather for sipping hot chocolate or spirits. **FYI:** Reservations accepted. Children's menu. Dress code. **Open:** Peak (June–Aug) Mon–Sat 11am–9:30pm. **Prices:** Main courses $9–$16. AE, CB, DC, DISC, MC, V.

Passages
In Radisson Inn Bismarck, 800 S 3rd St; tel 701/258-7700. Across from Kirkwood Mall. **American.** This dark, quiet cafe features a number of staples— like New York strip sirloin and filet mignon—as well as such delightful surprises as baked Brie in puff pastry with raspberry vinaigrette and pears; tequila shrimp served with lime butter; and fettucine with crab, scallops, and shrimp with garlic cream. **FYI:** Reservations accepted. Children's menu. **Open:** Mon–Fri 6am–10:30pm, Sat–Sun 7am–10:30pm. **Prices:** Main courses $11–$24. AE, CB, DC, DISC, MC, V.

ATTRACTIONS

State Capitol
N 6th St; tel 701/328-2480. The 19-story capitol building, commonly referred to as the "Skyscraper of the Prairies," is built of white limestone, and together with other buildings on the 130-acre complex houses the State Legislature, State Supreme Court, Highway Department, State Library, Heritage Center, and Governor's Residence. Located within the

main building is the Rough Rider Gallery, with portraits of famous North Dakotans. To tour the buildings, visitors must take one of the guided tours offered on the hour at the information desk.

The **Arboretum Trail** runs through the middle of the capital city and provides visitors with a unique opportunity to view nature, art, and architecture simultaneously. Posts identify 75 different species of plants on the grounds. The trail passes the statues of Sacajawea, a Shoshone woman who helped guide Lewis and Clark, John Burke, and a Pioneer Family. **Open:** Mem Day–Labor Day, Mon–Fri 8–11am and 1–4pm, Sat 9–11am and 1–4pm, Sun 1–4pm; Labor Day–Mem Day, Mon–Fri 8–11am and 1–4pm. Closed some hols. **Free**

Camp Hancock State Historic Site
Main and 1st Sts; tel 701/328-2464. The site preserves a military camp established in 1872 to protect workers building the Northern Pacific Railroad. On the grounds are a log headquarters building, the "Bread of Life," one of the city's oldest churches, a Northern Pacific Railroad Locomotive, and a museum with historical displays. **Open:** Daily sunrise–sunset. **Free**

Fort Abraham Lincoln State Park
ND 1806, Mandan; tel 701/663-9571. Approximately 8 mi W of Bismarck. A portion of this state historical park features ruins from On-A-Slant Village, which was occupied by the Mandan tribe until they were wiped out by smallpox in the early 19th century. (Historical tours of the village's four reconstructed earthlodges are given 9am–9pm.) Also on site are reconstructed buildings from Fort Abraham Lincoln, the last command post of Gen George Custer before he made his "last stand" at Little Big Horn.

A **visitor center** contains artifacts and exhibits on the Mandan, the Lewis and Clark Expedition (the two explorers camped here in 1804 on their way out west), the early homesteaders, and the Army's campaign against the Plains Indians. Recreational activities include fishing, hiking, picnicking, and camping. Cross-country skiing and snowmobiling are popular with winter visitors. **Open:** June–Aug, daily 9am–9pm; Sept–Oct and Apr–May, daily 9am–5pm. **$$**

Lewis and Clark Riverboat
Exit 35 off I-94; tel 701/255-4233. Port of Bismarck, under Grant Marsh Bridge. Missouri River sightseeing cruises are given aboard this 19th-century-style paddlewheeler. Also dining cruises, moonlight cruises, and excursions to Fort Abraham Lincoln State Park. **Open:** Mem Day–Labor Day, call for schedule. **$$$$**

Cross Ranch State Park
Off US 83, Sanger; tel 701/794-3731. 25 mi NW of Bismarck. The park offers a visitor center, campground, log-cabin rentals, hiking trails, and a boat ramp. In summer, organized activities include weekend campfire programs, interpretive hikes, guided canoe trips, and a children's outdoor adventure program; in winter, hiking trails are groomed for cross-country skiing. **Open:** Park: daily, sunrise–sunset. Closed some hols. **$**

Bottineau

Border town founded in 1884; seat of Bottineau County and home to a state forestry school. Bottineau is located in the Turtle Mountain Recreation Area, which offers a variety of outdoor activities and includes the International Peace Gardens. **Information:** Bottineau Convention and Visitors Bureau, 103 E 11th St, Bottineau, 58318 (tel 701/228-3849).

ATTRACTIONS

International Peace Garden
ND 3, Dunseith; tel 701/263-4390. 18 mi SW of Bottineau, on the Canadian border. Established in 1932 to commemorate the long-lasting peace between Canada and the United States. Three tours—a **Canadian Natural Drive,** the **United States Cultural Drive,** and the **Walking Tour–Formal Garden**— let visitors see some of the 120,000 annuals grown here. There's also a 120-foot Peace Tower, a carillon bell tower, and a Peace Chapel. Picnic area, lodge, campground. **Open:** May–Sept, daily 8am–9pm. **$**

Lake Metigoshe State Park
ND 43; tel 701/263-4651. Located in the scenic Turtle Mountains, just 15 miles from the International Peace Gardens. Recreational activities in the park include boating, fishing, and swimming in Lake Metigoshe; camping, hiking, and picnicking in the woods; and cross-country skiing and snowmobiling in the winter. Theatrical programs are presented in an outdoor amphitheater during summer months. **Open:** Daily sunrise–sunset. **$**

Bowman

Commercial and agribusiness town located at the base of the sandstone-capped Twin Buttes. The seat of Bowman County, Bowman is about 20 miles from the Bowman-Haley Dam. **Information:** Bowman Chamber of Commerce, PO Box 1143, Bowman, 58623 (tel 701/523-5880).

MOTELS

Budget Host 4U Motel
704 US 12 W, PO Box 590, 58623; tel 701/523-3243 or toll free 800/283-4678; fax 701/523-3357. Well-kept building and grounds located in a rural community. Economical. **Rooms:** 40 rms. CI open/CO 11am. Nonsmoking rms avail. Clean and comfortable, nothing fancy. Some rooms have showers with steam capability. **Amenities:** A/C, cable TV. **Services:** **Facilities:** Sauna. **Rates:** $22–$26 S; $32–$40 D. Extra person $4. Children under age 12 stay free. Parking: Outdoor, free. AE, CB, DC, DISC, MC, V.

Super 8 Motel
614 3rd Ave SW, PO Box 675, 58623; tel 701/523-5613 or toll free 800/800-8000. Jct of US 12 and US 85. Clean, well-kept motel in rural community en route to the Black Hills of South Dakota. Economical. **Rooms:** 31 rms. CI open/CO 11am. Nonsmoking rms avail. Cooking odors from manager's apartment on premises. **Amenities:** A/C, cable TV. 1 unit w/whirlpool. **Services:** **Facilities:** Games rm, sauna, whirlpool. **Rates (CP):** Peak (Apr–Sept) $30–$33 S; $39–$43 D. Extra person $5. Children under age 12 stay free. Lower rates off-season. Parking: Outdoor, free. AE, DC, DISC, MC, V.

Cavalier

Agricultural town located near the Tongue River, in the center of what was the largest Icelandic settlement in America in the 1870s. Seat of Pembina County. **Information:** Cavalier Area Chamber of Commerce, PO Box 271, Cavalier, 58220 (tel 701/ 265-8188).

ATTRACTION

Icelandic State Park
13571 ND 5; tel 701/265-4561. Located in North Dakota's Tongue River Valley, this park offers year-round camping and picnicking. In the warmer months, 220-acre Lake Renwick provides excellent boating and fishing facilities as well as a swimming beach, while wintertime's ample snows bring cross-country skiing, ice skating, and snowmobiling.

The park's **Pioneer Heritage Center** uses artifacts, exhibits, and audiovisual programs to depict North Dakota's early homesteading years and the impact of Icelandic immigrants on the area. Nearby are several historic buildings, including a farmhouse, a barn, and a one-room school. Adjacent to the homestead is the 200-acre **Gunlogson Nature Preserve,** with an extensive system of self-guided trails and foot bridges across the Tongue River. **Open:** Summer, daily 9am–10pm; winter, daily 9am–4:30pm. **$**

Devils Lake

The seat of Ramsey County was settled in 1882 on the shores of Devils Lake, a corruption of a Native American name meaning spirit waters. The state's largest natural lake is a popular fishing and water recreation site. **Information:** Devils Lake Convention and Visitors Bureau, PO Box 879, Devils Lake, 58301 (tel 701/662-4903).

MOTEL

Comfort Inn
215 US 2 E, 58301; tel 701/662-6760 or toll free 800/228-5150; fax 701/662-6760. At ND 20. Clean and pleasing facility, opened in 1992. A good deal. **Rooms:** 60 rms. CI 2pm/CO 11am. Nonsmoking rms avail. Very clean and well laid out. **Amenities:** A/C, cable TV. Some units w/minibars, some w/whirlpools. Microwave and refrigerator available for $3 per night. **Services:** Free local calls. **Facilities:** Games rm, whirlpool. **Rates (CP):** $36–$46 S; $42–$52 D. Extra person $5. Children under age 18 stay free. Parking: Outdoor, free. AE, CB, DC, DISC, JCB, MC, V.

ATTRACTIONS 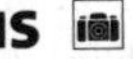

Fort Totten State Historic Site
ND 57; tel 701/766-4441. One of the best preserved frontier military posts in the west. Built in the late 1800s, the site includes 17 original buildings, which originally comprised a military base to protect the overland route to Montana, and then served as an American Indian boarding school. Visitors can learn more about the fort at an interpretive center or the Pioneer Daughters Museum where an audiovisual presentation is shown daily and there are displays on authentic military attire and Indian artifacts. **Open:** Daily 7:30am–dusk. **Free**

Devils Lake State Parks
RR 1; tel 701/766-4015. Four parks—Grahams Island, Black Tiger Bay, The Narrows, and Shelvers Grove—very popular with fishing enthusiasts. (Devils Lake offers some of the best fishing in the area.) Each has slightly different amenities: Grahams Island offers fishing-boat rentals and modern campsites, Black Tiger Bay and The Narrows have picnicking and primitive campsites, and Shelvers Grove has picnic shelters and modern campsites. Ask about the availability of Rent-A-Camp sites, which come complete with tent, cots, cooler, and firewood. **Open:** Mid-May–Sept, dawn–dusk. **$**

Sullys Hill National Game Preserve
Off ND 57; tel 701/766-4272. Located on the south shore of Devils Lake in the heart of the Fort Totten Sioux Reservation, Sullys Hill is one of only four refuges for bison and elk in the United States. Self-guided four-mile auto tour (May–October only) allows visitors to get a look at these rare animals, as well as deer, Canadian geese, eagles, and other wildlife. Mile-long nature trail, waterfowl observation areas, outdoor amphitheater, wintertime cross-country skiing. **Open:** Daily 8am–dusk. **Free**

Dickinson

Settled in 1880 near the Heart River, Dickinson quickly established itself as a retail and accommodations center for area ranchers and farmers. Dickinson's economy was hit hard by falling oil prices in the late 1980s. Seat of Stark County and home of Dickinson State University. **Information:** Dickinson Convention and Visitors Bureau, 314 3rd Ave W, PO Box 181, Dickinson, 58602 (tel 701/225-4988).

HOTELS

Dickinson Inn and Suites—Best Western
71 Museum Dr, 58601; tel 701/225-9510 or toll free 800/285-1122; fax 701/225-9255. Miniature golf is within walking distance. **Rooms:** 123 rms and stes. Executive level. CI 3pm/CO noon. Nonsmoking rms avail. Clean and comfortable rooms are nicely decorated and well laid out. **Amenities:** A/C, cable TV. Some units w/terraces. **Services:** Babysitting. Limousine rental on premises. **Facilities:** 300 1 bar, games rm, whirlpool, beauty salon. **Rates (CP):** Peak (June–Sept) $30–$50 S; $30–$60 D; $50–$79 ste. Extra person $5. Children under age 12 stay free. Lower rates off-season. Parking: Outdoor, free. AE, CB, DC, DISC, JCB, MC, V.

Hospitality Inn
532 15th St W, PO Box 1778, 58601; tel 701/227-1853 or toll free 800/422-0949; fax 701/225-0090. I-94 and ND 22. Clean and comfortable property, with a welcoming fireplace in the lobby. Located near shops and restaurants. **Rooms:** 149 rms and stes. CI 3pm/CO noon. Nonsmoking rms avail. Attractively decorated. **Amenities:** A/C, cable TV. Some units w/terraces, some w/whirlpools. Two units have hot tubs. **Services:** Car-rental desk, social director. **Facilities:** 600 1 restaurant, 1 bar, games rm, sauna, whirlpool, washer/dryer. **Rates:** $45–$51 S; $50–$56 D; $90 ste. Extra person $5. Children under age 18 stay free. Parking: Outdoor, free. DISC, MC, V.

MOTEL

Comfort Inn
493 Elks Dr, 58601; tel 701/264-7300 or toll free 800/221-2222; fax 701/264-7300. Well-maintained property close to shopping and restaurants. **Rooms:** 118 rms. CI open/CO 11am. Nonsmoking rms avail. Nicely decorated, average-size rooms. **Amenities:** A/C, cable TV. **Services:** Babysitting. **Facilities:** 15 Games rm, washer/dryer. **Rates (CP):** Peak (June–Sept) $25–$31 S; $38–$41 D. Extra person $3. Children under age 18 stay free. Lower rates off-season. Parking: Outdoor, free. AE, CB, DISC, MC, V.

ATTRACTION

Dakota Dinosaur Museum
200 Museum Dr; tel 701/225-DINO. Museum's collection contains over 10,000 dinosaur bones and casts from the North Dakota area, including 10 full-scale dinosaurs, a Tyrannosaurus Rex skull cast, and a 37-foot-long Edmontosaurus skeleton. Smaller displays include fossils, rocks, fluorescent minerals, and a collection of seashells. Kids ages 5–12 can dig for "dinosaur bones" in a sandy area next to the museum; advance registration required. **Open:** May–Sept, daily 9am–6pm; Oct–Apr, Tues–Sat 9am–5pm, Sun noon–5pm. Closed some hols. **$$**

Fargo

Founded in 1872 and named for William Fargo, founder of the Wells-Fargo Express. Like many Plains towns, the actual site of the city was determined when a major railroad announced its river crossing site. Fargo, the largest city in North Dakota, remains a center for grain research and marketing, but its reputation as a boomtown comes more from diversified manufacturing and software development industries. Home to State University and numerous casinos, which brings a fair number of Canadians across the border. **Information:** Fargo-Moorhead Convention and Visitors Bureau, 2001 44th St SW, PO Box 181, Fargo, 58103 (tel 701/282-3653).

HOTELS

Holiday Inn
I-29 and 13th Ave, 58106; tel 701/282-2700 or toll free 800/465-4329; fax 701/281-1240. Take I-29 to exit 64. Nice, chain hotel. Welcoming, spacious lobby with tiled-floors and brass-trim accents. **Rooms:** 309 rms and stes. CI 3pm/CO noon. Nonsmoking rms avail. Newly redecorated rooms have dark-wood furnishings, armchairs, and fabric-covered ottomans. **Amenities:** A/C, cable TV w/movies, dataport. Some units w/minibars, some w/whirlpools. **Services:** Children's program, babysitting. Pool area attendant supervises games in an indoor garden. **Facilities:** 2000 2 restaurants, 1 bar (w/entertainment), games rm, sauna, whirlpool, washer/dryer. Pool remodeled in 1995 with water slides and a pirate-ship theme. Small casino. **Rates:** $63–$70 S or D; $90–$125 ste. Children under age 19 stay free. Parking: Outdoor, free. Romance packages avail. AE, CB, DC, DISC, JCB, MC, V.

Radisson Hotel Fargo
201 5th St N, 58102; tel 701/232-7363 or toll free 800/333-3333; fax 701/298-9134. Exit 65 off I-29, E to downtown. Conveniently located. **Rooms:** 151 rms and stes. Executive level. CI 3pm/CO noon. Nonsmoking rms avail. Rather ordinary furnishings. Suites are snazzier, with unique decor, armoires, and larger closets. **Amenities:** A/C, cable TV w/movies. All units w/minibars, some w/whirlpools. Business-class rooms are larger and have dataports, coffeemakers, and ironing board. Whirlpool and bathrobes in all suites. **Services:** Babysitting. **Facilities:** 300 1 restaurant (*see* "Restaurants" below), 1 bar (w/entertainment), sauna, whirlpool. **Rates:** $65–$86 S or D; $125–$150 ste. Children under age 18 stay free. Parking: Indoor, free. Corporate rates and honeymoon, winter, and summer getaway plans avail. AE, CB, DC, DISC, ER, JCB, MC, V.

Scandia Hotel
717 4th St N, 58102; tel 701/232-2661 or toll free 800/223-2913; fax 701/232-3972. Across from Merit Care Medical Center. Popular with travelers visiting the nearby medical center. **Rooms:** 58 rms, stes, and effic. CI noon/CO 11am.

Nonsmoking rms avail. Apartment-size suites, worth the slightly higher price, have a spacious kitchen/dining area. **Amenities:** A/C, cable TV. **Services:** **Facilities:** Washer/dryer. **Rates:** $31 S; $36 D; $41–$49 ste; $41–$46 effic. Extra person $5. Children under age 6 stay free. Parking: Outdoor, free. DISC, MC, V.

MOTELS

Best Western Doublewood Inn

3333 13th Ave S, 58103; tel 701/235-3333 or toll free 800/435-3235; fax 701/280-9482. Exit 64 off I-29; 3 blocks E. Nice, basic chain motel. Located near several restaurants. **Rooms:** 173 rms and stes. Executive level. CI 3pm/CO noon. Nonsmoking rms avail. **Amenities:** A/C, cable TV w/movies, refrig, dataport. Some units w/whirlpools. Microwave. Suites have VCRs. **Services:** Babysitting. **Facilities:** 1200 1 restaurant, 1 bar, games rm, sauna, whirlpool, beauty salon. Free passes to health club next door. **Rates (BB):** Peak (Feb–Oct) $68–$78 S; $78–$88 D; $110–$175 ste. Extra person $5. Children under age 18 stay free. Lower rates off-season. Parking: Outdoor, free. Occasional weekend discounts. Suite packages avail. AE, CB, DC, DISC, MC, V.

Comfort Inn East

1407 35th St S, 58103; tel 701/280-9666 or toll free 800/221-2222; fax 701/280-9666. Exit 64 off I-29; E to 34th St, S 1 block. Clean grounds and a utilitarian lobby. **Rooms:** 66 rms and stes. CI 2pm/CO 11am. Nonsmoking rms avail. **Amenities:** A/C, cable TV. Suites have microwaves and refrigerators. **Services:** **Facilities:** Games rm, whirlpool. **Rates (CP):** Peak (June–Aug) $42–$47 S; $47–$52 D; $52–$62 ste. Extra person $5. Children under age 18 stay free. Lower rates off-season. Parking: Outdoor, free. 13th-night-free program. AE, DC, DISC, MC, V.

Comfort Suites

1415 35th St S, 58103; tel 701/237-5911 or toll free 800/221-2222; fax 701/237-5911. Exit 64 off I-29; E to 34th St; S 1 block. Groups and families will like the larger-than-average accommodations here. Randomly chosen "guest-of-the-day" gets free upgrade to a room with a hot tub. **Rooms:** 66 stes. CI 2pm/CO 11am. Nonsmoking rms avail. **Amenities:** A/C, cable TV, refrig. Some units w/whirlpools. **Services:** **Facilities:** 45 Games rm, whirlpool. **Rates (CP):** Peak (June–Aug) $55–$96 ste. Extra person $5. Children under age 18 stay free. Lower rates off-season. Parking: Outdoor, free. Honeymoon packages avail. AE, DC, DISC, JCB, MC, V.

Country Suites By Carlson

3316 13th Ave S, 58103; tel 701/234-0565 or toll free 800/456-4000; fax 701/234-0565. Exit 64 off I-29; E 2 blocks. Chain motel with country-inn decor. Guests greeted with scent of potpourri as they enter the lobby. **Rooms:** 99 rms and stes. CI 3pm/CO noon. Nonsmoking rms avail. **Amenities:** A/C, cable TV, refrig. Some units w/whirlpools. All rooms have microwaves; some have dataports. **Services:** **Facilities:** 225 1 bar, games rm, whirlpool. **Rates (CP):** $49–$81 S; $53–$74 D; $54–$81 ste. Extra person $10. Children under age 18 stay free. Parking: Outdoor, free. Holiday packages avail. AE, CB, DC, DISC, MC, V.

Days Inn

901 38th St SW, 58103; tel 701/282-9100 or toll free 800/329-7466; fax 701/277-1581. Ordinary economy hotel, but with a friendly staff. **Rooms:** 97 rms. CI 3pm/CO 11am. Nonsmoking rms avail. **Amenities:** A/C, cable TV. **Services:** **Facilities:** Breakfast room in lobby. **Rates (CP):** $29–$42 S; $39–$47 D. Extra person $6. Children under age 18 stay free. Parking: Outdoor, free. AE, DC, DISC, JCB, MC, V.

Econo Lodge

1401 35th St S, 58103; tel 701/232-3412 or toll free 800/427-4777; fax 701/232-3412. Exit 64 off I-29. Nondescript motel; good for overnight stays. **Rooms:** 66 rms. CI open/CO 11am. Nonsmoking rms avail. **Amenities:** A/C, cable TV. **Services:** **Facilities:** **Rates (CP):** $28–$37 S; $39–$45 D. Extra person $5. Children under age 18 stay free. Parking: Outdoor, free. 13th-night-free package avail. AE, DC, DISC, MC, V.

Select Inn of Fargo

1025 38th St SW, 58102; tel 701/282-6300 or toll free 800/641-1000; fax 701/282-6308. Exit 64 off I-29. A property with few amenities, targetted mainly at the overnight business traveler. **Rooms:** 177 rms, stes, and effic. CI 2pm/CO 11am. Nonsmoking rms avail. Clean, but boring furnishings. **Amenities:** A/C, cable TV. Closed-captioned TV in some rooms. **Services:** VCRs for rent. **Facilities:** 16 1 bar, washer/dryer. **Rates (CP):** $28–$36 S; $32–$36 D; $61 ste; $31–$35 effic. Extra person $3. Children under age 13 stay free. Parking: Outdoor, free. Frequent guest program. AE, CB, DC, DISC, ER, MC, V.

RESTAURANTS

The Grainery

West Acres Shopping Center; tel 701/282-6263. I-29 Exit 64, 1 block W on 13 Ave. **American.** 1890s warehouse-style decor. The Teddy Roosevelt room features a fireplace and vintage hunting paraphernalia, including a mounted buffalo head. The house specialties are beer-cheese soup and beef in all forms from burgers to filet mignon. **FYI:** Reservations recommended. Children's menu. Dress code. **Open:** Peak (summer) Sun 11am–6pm, Mon–Thurs 11am–10pm, Fri–Sat 11am–11pm. **Prices:** Main courses $6.50–$18.50. AE, CB, DC, DISC, MC, V.

Historic Conservatory Restaurant

613 1st Ave N; tel 701/241-7080. Exit 65 off I-29 to Main Ave; E to downtown. **New American.** In 1910, this was a piano warehouse; later it became a music conservatory.

Neoclassical columns rise to the 18-foot-high ceiling. On the balcony where music judges once sat, the chairs are now occupied by diners enjoying such seasonal specialties as roast duckling with orange-balsamic glaze, and herb-crusted loin of lamb. Espresso bar. Meeting rooms available. **FYI:** Reservations recommended. Guitar/harp/piano. **Open:** Lunch Mon–Fri 11am–2pm; dinner Mon–Sat 5:30–10pm; brunch Sun 10:30am–2pm. **Prices:** Main courses $11–$21. AE, CB, DC, DISC, MC, V.

Pannekoeken
3340 13th Ave SW; tel 701/237-3559. Exit 64 off I-29; E 3 blocks. **American.** This restaurant is named for the house specialty, pannekoeken, a rich pancake of eggs and butter that's popular in Holland. Lace curtains, stenciled walls, etched glass, and booths put a modern spin on the Dutch cafe decor. Pannekoeken can be served with bacon for breakfast, or teamed with Gouda cheese, meat, and vegetables for other meals. Also served are salads and entrees like pot roast and pork loin ribs. **FYI:** Reservations not accepted. Children's menu. Beer and wine only. **Open:** Sun–Thurs 6am–11pm, Fri–Sat 6am–midnight. **Prices:** Main courses $7–$10. AE, DC, DISC, MC, V.

Passages Cafe
In Radisson Hotel Fargo, 201 5th St N (Downtown); tel 701/293-6717. **American.** Minnesota wild rice soup; fettucine with scallops, crab, and shrimp in cream sauce. Also steaks and smoked pork tenderloin. Extensive Sunday buffet. **FYI:** Reservations recommended. Children's menu. No smoking. **Open:** Sun–Thurs 6:30am–10:30pm, Fri–Sat 6:30am–11:30pm. **Prices:** Main courses $13–$17. AE, CB, DC, DISC, MC, V.

ATTRACTIONS

The Children's Museum at Yunker Farm
1201 28th Ave N; tel 701/232-6102. Calling itself "a hands-on place for discovery," this museum lets children make giant bubbles, whisper to friends through a 60-foot-long tube, and make sculptures with magnets, nuts, and bolts. Other exhibits include a live beehive and medical and dental displays. **Open:** Mon–Sat 10am–5pm, Sun 1–5pm. Closed Mon (Sept–May) and some hols. $

Bonanzaville, USA
Exit 343 off I-94, West Fargo; tel 701/282-2822. Reconstructed pioneer village featuring 45 19th-century farm era buildings such as a sod house, a schoolhouse, a jail, a blacksmith, and a printshop. Separate buildings house an Indian artifacts museum, an antique car and tractor display, an airplane exhibit, and a train depot with locomotives, a steam engine, and model trains. **Open:** June–Oct, daily 9am–5pm; May, Mon–Fri 9:30am–4pm. $$

Garrison

Small town founded in 1903 and named after a nearby creek. Popular for hunting and fishing among those headed to the eastern end of Lake Sakakawea. **Information:** Garrison Chamber of Commerce, PO Box 459, Garrison, 58540 (tel 701/463-2600).

MOTEL

Garrison Motel
ND 37, 58540; tel 701/463-2858. W on ND 37; off US 83. Rather plain-looking property, but the staff is small-town friendly and they know the region inside-out. Most guests come here for nearby hunting and recreation at Lake Sakakawea. **Rooms:** 30 rms. CI 2pm/CO noon. Nonsmoking rms avail. **Amenities:** A/C, cable TV. **Services:** Guide services arranged for hunting and fishing. **Facilities:** 20 **Rates:** Peak (May–Sept) $28 S; $36 D. Extra person $3. Children under age 12 stay free. Lower rates off-season. Parking: Outdoor, free. Senior, ice-fishing, and military rates avail. AE, DISC, MC, V.

ATTRACTIONS

Fort Stevenson State Park
RR 1; tel 701/337-5576. Located on the north shore of Lake Sakakawea, reputed to be the nation's largest manmade reservoir. The 483-acre park is a favorite with boaters, who can enjoy the lake's marina, boat ramp, boat rentals, and fish cleaning station. (Walleye and salmon are especially plentiful.) There's also a swimming beach, campground (with 105 sites), and picnic area. **Open:** Daily 7am–10pm. $

Lake Sakakawea State Park
ND 200, Riverdale; tel 701/487-3315. The lake is one of the top walleye fishing destinations in the nation and host to many wind-surfing and sailing competitions. Visitors can also take advantage of marinas, beaches, swimming, boating, and salmon fishing. **Open:** Daily sunrise–sunset. $

Grand Forks

Settled in 1868 as a fur-trading town at the confluence of the Red and Red Lake Rivers. The city is home to a large US Air Force Base; not surprisingly, the University of North Dakota campus here includes one of the nation's largest pilot training programs and Grand Forks has the only international airport in the state. **Information:** Greater Grand Forks Convention and Visitors Bureau, 202 N 3rd St #200, Grand Forks, 58203 (tel 701/746-0775).

MOTELS

Best Western Fabulous Westward Ho Motel
US 2 W, PO Box 5880, 58206; tel 701/775-5341 or toll free 800/528-1234; fax 701/775-3703. An Old West experience,

from the board-bridge entryway to the brands hanging on the knotty pine walls. There's even a covered wagon parked out front and an outside boardwalk with hitching-post railings. Huge grounds offer plenty of room for families to stretch. **Rooms:** 108 rms and stes. CI 2pm/CO noon. Nonsmoking rms avail. Plain rooms, but with cowboy feel. All accommodations open to the boardwalk. **Amenities:** A/C, cable TV. **Services:** Social director. **Facilities:** 3 restaurants, 3 bars (1 w/entertainment), volleyball, sauna, playground. Swimming pool surrounded by a corral-like fence. **Rates:** Peak (May 15–Oct 15) $40–$45 S; $49–$59 D; $80 ste. Extra person $5. Children under age 12 stay free. Lower rates off-season. Parking: Outdoor, free. AE, DC, DISC, MC, V.

Best Western Town House

710 1st Ave N, 58203; tel 701/746-5411 or toll free 800/867-9797; fax 701/746-1407. A spacious lobby opens to an atrium with pool. Airline crews often stay here. **Rooms:** 103 rms, stes, and effic. Executive level. CI 2pm/CO noon. Nonsmoking rms avail. **Amenities:** A/C, cable TV w/movies. **Services:** Car-rental desk, babysitting. **Facilities:** 9 300 1 restaurant, 1 bar, games rm, sauna, whirlpool. Pool has waterfall and private area for sunbathing; there's also a rose garden and miniature golf. Guests can receive free passes to the neighboring YMCA. **Rates:** $35–$60 S; $35–$70 D; $60–$125 ste; $60–$125 effic. Extra person $5. Children under age 18 stay free. Parking: Outdoor, free. AE, CB, DC, DISC, JCB, MC, V.

C'mon Inn

3051 32nd Ave S, 58201; tel 701/775-3320 or toll free 800/255-2323; fax 701/780-8141. Exit 138 from I-29. Lovely, all-new rooms. Atrium with five semi-private hot tubs; lobby offers generous seating space. **Rooms:** 80 rms and stes. CI 3pm/CO noon. Nonsmoking rms avail. **Amenities:** A/C, cable TV w/movies, dataport, VCR. Some units w/terraces, some w/whirlpools. **Services:** Social director. **Facilities:** 80 Games rm, whirlpool. **Rates (CP):** $40–$48 S; $49–$73 D; $83–$91 ste. Extra person $6. Children under age 12 stay free. Parking: Outdoor, free. AE, DISC, MC, V.

Comfort Inn

3251 30th Ave S, 58201; tel 701/775-7503 or toll free 800/221-2222; fax 701/775-7503. Exit 138 from I-29. Basic chain motel. **Rooms:** 67 rms. CI 3pm/CO 11am. Nonsmoking rms avail. Comfortable rooms. **Amenities:** A/C, cable TV. **Services:** **Facilities:** 20 Games rm, whirlpool. Vehicle plug-ins in winter. **Rates (CP):** Peak (May–Aug) $40–$49 S; $40–$65 D. Extra person $6. Children under age 18 stay free. Lower rates off-season. Parking: Outdoor, free. Free "Room in the Inn" at Thanksgiving and Christmas for people with family members hospitalized nearby. AE, CB, DC, DISC, ER, JCB, MC, V.

Country Inn and Suites by Carlson

3350 32nd Ave S, 58201; tel 701/775-5000 or toll free 800/456-4000; fax 701/775-9073. Exit 138 E. Friendly place. All public areas and the majority of rooms are nonsmoking. **Rooms:** 89 rms, stes, and effic. Executive level. CI 3pm/CO 11am. Nonsmoking rms avail. Pleasant rooms decorated with light-wood furnishings and pastel fabrics. One suite has a full kitchen. **Amenities:** A/C, cable TV w/movies, refrig, VCR. All units w/minibars. **Services:** Car-rental desk, children's program. **Facilities:** Sauna, whirlpool, washer/dryer. Vehicle plug-ins in winter. **Rates (CP):** Peak (May–Oct 1) $37–$120 S; $41–$126 D; $46–$126 ste; $66–$80 effic. Extra person $6. Children under age 18 stay free. Lower rates off-season. Parking: Outdoor, free. AE, DC, DISC, MC, V.

Days Inn

3101 34th St S, 58201; tel 701/775-0060 or toll free 800/329-7466; fax 701/775-0060. Exit 138 E from I-29. Comfortable and welcoming to families. **Rooms:** 52 rms and stes. CI 2pm/CO 11am. Nonsmoking rms avail. **Amenities:** A/C, cable TV. **Services:** Twice-daily maid svce, babysitting. **Facilities:** Games rm, whirlpool. **Rates (CP):** Peak (July–Aug) $49 S; $55 D; $54–$60 ste. Extra person $6. Children under age 18 stay free. Lower rates off-season. Parking: Outdoor, free. Free "Room in the Inn" program at Thanksgiving and Christmas for people with family members hospitalized nearby. AE, DC, DISC, ER, MC, V.

Fairfield Inn by Marriott

3051 S 34th St, 58201; tel 701/775-7910 or toll free 800/228-2800; fax 701/775-7910. Exit 138 from I-29. Comfortable, pleasant, warm, and welcoming, this property attracts lots of business travelers. **Rooms:** 62 rms and stes. CI 2pm/CO 11am. Nonsmoking rms avail. **Amenities:** A/C, cable TV. **Services:** **Facilities:** 15 Games rm, whirlpool. **Rates (CP):** Peak (July–Aug) $43–$48 S; $48–$54 D; $53–$59 ste. Extra person $6. Children under age 18 stay free. Lower rates off-season. Parking: Outdoor, free. "13th Night Free" program. Free "Room in the Inn" program at Thanksgiving and Christmas for people with family members in nearby hospitals. AE, DC, DISC, MC, V.

Holiday Inn

1210 N 43rd St, 58203; tel 701/772-7131 or toll free 800/HOLIDAY; fax 701/780-9112. Exit 141 off I-29. Property with easy access to the interstate, but far enough away to be quiet. **Rooms:** 150 rms and stes. CI 3pm/CO noon. Nonsmoking rms avail. Nicely decorated rooms. **Amenities:** A/C, cable TV w/movies. 1 unit w/whirlpool. **Services:** Car-rental desk, children's program, babysitting. **Facilities:** 400 1 restaurant, 1 bar, games rm, sauna, whirlpool, washer/dryer. "Holidome" covered pool area with lots of greenery and a kids' play area. **Rates:** $60 S; $60 D; $135 ste. Extra person $5. Children under age 19 stay free. Parking: Outdoor, free. AE, DC, DISC, MC, V.

Ramada Inn and Conference Center
1205 N 43rd St, PO Box 13757, 58208; tel 701/775-3951 or toll free 800/570-3951, 800/2-RAMADA in Canada; fax 701/775-9774. Jct I-29 and US 12, exit 141. Generally considered the best lodging in the city. **Rooms:** 100 rms. CI 1pm/CO noon. Nonsmoking rms avail. Rooms are very well kept; housekeeping staff take pride in their job. **Amenities:** A/C, cable TV. **Services:** Car-rental desk, social director, babysitting. Extremely cordial and accommodating staff. **Facilities:** 800 2 restaurants (*see* "Restaurants" below), 1 bar (w/entertainment), games rm, sauna, whirlpool, washer/dryer. **Rates:** Peak (July 1–Sept 1) $53–$58 S; $63–$68 D. Extra person $7. Children under age 18 stay free. Lower rates off-season. Parking: Outdoor, free. AE, CB, DC, DISC, EC, ER, JCB, MC, V.

Road King Inn
1015 N 43rd St, 58203; tel 701/775-0691 or toll free 800/950-0691; fax 701/775-9964. Exit 141 at jct I-29 and US 2. Recently remodeled property attractive to business travelers. Dark woods and paisley fabrics give a warm, cozy feeling. **Rooms:** 98 rms. CI 3pm/CO noon. Nonsmoking rms avail. **Amenities:** A/C, cable TV. **Services:** **Facilities:** Washer/dryer. Lounge with big-screen TV adjacent to lobby. **Rates (CP):** $33–$44 S; $37–$40 D. Extra person $5. Children under age 18 stay free. Parking: Outdoor, free. AE, CB, DC, DISC, MC, V.

Select Inn
1000 N 42nd St, 58203; tel 701/775-0555 or toll free 800/641-1000; fax 701/775-9967. Exit 141 off I-29. Very basic but clean place—nothing fancy. Often used by students who come to town for special courses. **Rooms:** 120 rms. CI 4pm/CO noon. Nonsmoking rms avail. **Amenities:** A/C, cable TV. **Services:** **Facilities:** Washer/dryer. **Rates (CP):** $28 S; $34 D. Extra person $2. Children under age 12 stay free. Parking: Outdoor, free. AE, DISC, MC, V.

RESTAURANTS

The Dining Room at the Ramada
In Ramada Inn and Conference Center, 1205 N 43rd St; tel 701/775-3951. **American.** Standard menu—offering steak, chicken, seafood, and some pasta—is presented very nicely against a background of dark wood and a burgundy and green color scheme. **FYI:** Reservations accepted. Piano. Children's menu. Dress code. **Open:** Lunch daily 11am–2pm; dinner daily 5–10pm. **Prices:** Main courses $9–$25. AE, CB, DC, DISC, ER, MC, V.

★ La Campana-Paradiso
905 S Washington St; tel 701/772-3000. **Mexican.** Good, fresh ingredients are used to make all the usual favorites. Decorated with tiles, statuary, and paintings, the overall feeling is nice and comfortable. **FYI:** Reservations accepted. Children's menu. **Open:** Mon–Thurs 11am–midnight, Fri–Sat 11am–1am, Sun 11am–11pm. **Prices:** Main courses $5–$9. Lunch main courses $5–$6. AE, DISC, MC, V.

ATTRACTIONS

Grand Forks County Historical Society
2405 Belmont Rd; tel 701/775-2216. Dedicated to preserving the heritage of the Red River Valley, the society maintains several restored buildings. The Myra Museum is decorated with period furnishings from the 18th to the early 20th century, the Campbell House (circa 1879) is a log cabin with pioneer family furnishings. A one-room school house, a carriage house and pavilion, a chapel made from pieces of original churches in the Grand Forks area, and a post office/general store are also located on the grounds. **Open:** May 15–Sept 15, daily 1–5pm. $

Dakota Queen Riverboat
67 S Riverboat Rd; tel 701/775-5656. Paddlewheeler offers two types of cruises on the Red River. Sightseeing cruises allow visitors to spot birds, beaver, and fish in their natural habitats; other sights include Alligator Alley and Millionaire's Row. Dinner cruises also available. **Open:** May–Aug, Sat and Thurs, call for schedule. **$$$$**

Jamestown

Founded in 1871 near the convergence of the James and Pipestem Rivers. Both rivers form lakes north of town, either naturally or by dam. Jamestown has its own small buffalo herd and is the birthplace of western writer Louis L'Amour. **Information:** Jamestown Promotion and Tourism Center, 212 3rd Ave NE, PO Box 389, Jamestown, 58402 (tel 701/252-4838).

MOTELS

Best Western Dakota Inn
I-94 and US 281 S, 58401; tel 701/252-3611 or toll free 800/726-7924; fax 701/251-1212. Exit 258 off I-94; US 281 S 1 block. Clean motel designed for the interstate traveler. **Rooms:** 123 rms and stes. CI noon/CO noon. Nonsmoking rms avail. Some rooms have better furniture (such as four-poster beds) than others; apartment-size suite has two bathrooms. **Amenities:** A/C, cable TV. Some units w/minibars, 1 w/whirlpool. Whirlpool in apartment-size suite. **Services:** **Facilities:** 450 1 restaurant (*see* "Restaurants" below), 1 bar (w/entertainment), volleyball, games rm, whirlpool, washer/dryer. **Rates:** Peak (mid-May–mid-Sept) $38–$42 S; $46–$55 D; $55–$120 ste. Extra person $5. Children under age 16 stay free. Lower rates off-season. Parking: Outdoor, free. Group rates and occasional weekend packages avail. AE, DC, DISC, MC, V.

Comfort Inn
811 20th St SW, 58401; tel 701/252-7125 or toll free 800/221-2222; fax 701/252-7125. Exit 258 off I-94. A clean, family-oriented property, located near fast-food outlets. Exceptionally good security for an economy motel. **Rooms:** 52 rms and stes. CI open/CO 11am. Nonsmoking rms avail.

Amenities: A/C, cable TV. **Services:** **Facilities:** 1 restaurant, 1 bar, games rm, whirlpool. **Rates (CP):** Peak (May–Oct) $39–$47 S; $49–$64 D; $45–$65 ste. Extra person $6. Children under age 18 stay free. Lower rates off-season. Parking: Outdoor, free. AE, DC, DISC, ER, JCB, MC, V.

Gladstone Select Inn
111 2nd St NE, 58401; tel 701/252-0700 or toll free 800/641-1000; fax 701/252-0700. Exit 258 off I-94; US 281 N to Main St. This very popular convention center is often booked solid, so reservations are recommended. **Rooms:** 117 rms and stes. CI 2pm/CO 11am. Nonsmoking rms avail. **Amenities:** A/C, cable TV. Some units w/minibars, some w/terraces. **Services:** Staff is practiced at setting up meetings and conventions. **Facilities:** 150 1 restaurant, 1 bar (w/entertainment), games rm, whirlpool. Casino. **Rates:** $42–$44 S; $42–$62 D; $55–$63 ste. Extra person $4. Children under age 12 stay free. Parking: Outdoor, free. Group rates avail. AE, DC, DISC, MC, V.

RESTAURANTS

Firepit
In Best Western Dakota Inn, I-94 and US 281 S; tel 701/252-3611. Exit 258 off I-94. **American.** Meat's the game here—buffalo burgers, beef burgers, steaks, pork chops, and chicken. Buffets at lunch and on Sunday. The circular fireplace in a sunken pit draws the chill off of North Dakota nights. **FYI:** Reservations accepted. Country music. Children's menu. Jacket required. **Open:** Mon–Sat 7am–10pm, Sun 7am–2pm. **Prices:** Main courses $4–$13. AE, DISC, MC, V.

Wagon Masters
805 SW 20th St; tel 701/252-4243. Exit 258 off I-94. **American.** Here's your chance to try a buffalo burger or buffalo steak. If that's a bit too exotic, you can always order what the locals come for: prime rib or barbecued ribs. The diverse menu also includes sandwiches, pasta, and chicken. **FYI:** Reservations accepted. Children's menu. **Open:** Mon–Sat 6am–10pm, Sun 7am–10pm. **Prices:** Main courses $4–$16. AE, CB, DC, DISC, MC, V.

ATTRACTIONS

Frontier Village
Exit 258 off I-94; tel 701/252-4835. It's impossible to miss the enormous bison statue that stands watch over this reconstructed old west town. Visitors can tour a post office, a trading post, a saloon, a barber shop, a jail and sheriff's office, a one-room school house (circa 1883), and a country church (circa 1881). Donation suggested. **Open:** May–Sept, daily 9am–9pm. **Free**

National Buffalo Museum
500 17th St SE; tel 701/252-8648. Museum dedicated to the history of the American bison. Displays show the evolution of the buffalo as well as related Native American artifacts including a 10,000-year-old buffalo skull, and the Bill Freeman painting *Thundering Herd.* **Open:** Mem Day–Labor Day, daily 9am–8pm; Sept–Oct, May, daily 9am–5pm; Nov–Apr, daily noon–5pm. Closed some hols. **$**

Kenmare

This former lignite mining town on Middle Des Lacs Lake is headquarters for the Des Lacs National Wildlife Refuge, a magnet for both snow geese and hunters. **Information:** Kenmare Association of Commerce, PO Box 324, Kenmare, 58746 (tel 701/385-4857).

ATTRACTIONS

Des Lacs National Wildlife Refuge
ND 1A; tel 701/385-4411. Area surrounds the portion of Des Lacs Lake located in the United States and is home to deer, coyote, sharp-tailed grouse, the Baird's sparrow, and a range of waterfowl. The **Taskers Coulee Recreational Area** (3 mi SW on County Rd 1A) offers a picnic area, bird watching area, and hiking trails. **Open:** Mon–Thurs 7am–5pm, Fri 7am–4pm. Closed some hols. **Free**

Lostwood National Wildlife Refuge
RR 2; tel 701/848-2722. Established in 1935 as a breeding ground for migratory birds and other wildlife, this 27,000-acre refuge now houses 3 species of reptiles, 37 mammals, and 226 birds. Blue-winged teal, mallard, gadwall, and wigeon are among the most common birds, while whitetail deer, coyote, badger, mink, and weasel roam the prairie lands.

Car and hiking trails provide access to the refuge spring through fall, and certain portions of the wilderness are open to snowshoers and cross-country skiers during the winter. Check at refuge headquarters for details. **Open:** Apr 15–Sept 30, daily dawn–dusk. **Free**

Mandan

See Bismarck

Medora

Medora was founded in 1883 by the Marquis de Mores, a colorful Frenchman who hoped to establish a cattle shipping empire on the banks of the Little Missouri River. Theodore Roosevelt also figures predominantly in the town's history—Roosevelt once owned the nearby Maltese Cross and Elkhorn ranches. Headquarters for the south unit of Theodore Roosevelt National Park. **Information:** Medora Chamber of Commerce, PO Box 186, Medora, 58645 (tel 701/623-4910).

MOTELS

Badlands Motel
I-94, PO Box 198, 58645; tel 701/623-4422; fax 701/623-4494. Exit 27 off I-94 W; exit 26 off I-94 E. Clean, comfortable, moderately priced motel located near Theodore Roosevelt National Park. Mini-golf adjacent to property; bike rentals and horseback riding nearby. **Rooms:** 116 rms. CI open/CO 11am. Nonsmoking rms avail. Well decorated. **Amenities:** A/C, cable TV, voice mail. **Services:** Babysitting. **Facilities:** 500 **Rates:** Peak (Mem Day–Labor Day) $35–$54 S; $40–$65 D. Extra person $3. Children under age 6 stay free. Lower rates off-season. Parking: Outdoor, free. Closed Oct–Apr. AE, DISC, MC, V.

Sully Inn
4th and Broadway, PO Box 466, 58645; tel 701/623-4455; fax 701/623-4922. The couple who own this older, small motel work hard at making their guests feel at home. **Rooms:** 19 rms and stes. CI 4pm/CO 10am. Nonsmoking rms avail. Each room is uniquely decorated with homey touches. **Amenities:** A/C, cable TV. **Services:** Babysitting. **Facilities:** 1 restaurant, 1 bar, washer/dryer. **Rates:** Peak (May–Oct) $20–$40 S; $30–$55 D; $70–$85 ste. Extra person $5. Children under age 12 stay free. Lower rates off-season. Parking: Outdoor, free. DISC, MC, V.

ATTRACTION

Chateau de Mores State Historic Site
I-94; tel 701/623-4355. French nobleman Antoine de Vallombrosa, the Marquis de Mores, built this 26-room mansion when he moved to the plains to begin a cattle shipping empire and a beef packing plant. Tours of the chateau highlight French furnishings and a gun collection, as well as period decorations and antiques. Visitors can also view the remains of the packing plant. **Open:** May–Sept, daily 8:30am–6pm. **$**

Minot

Settled in 1886, Minot has put down permanent roots with diversified economic interests including ranching, manufacturing, and telecommunications. The town also receives an on-going boost from a major US Air Force base. Each July, Minot hosts the State Fair and in the fall, the Norsk Höstfest, a celebration of Scandinavian heritage. Seat of Ward County and home of Minot State University. **Information:** Minot Convention and Visitors Bureau, 1015 S Broadway, PO Box 2066, Minot, 58702 (tel 701/857-8206).

HOTEL

Holiday Inn Riverside
2200 Burdick Expwy E, 58701; tel 701/852-2504 or toll free 800/468-9968; fax 701/852-2630. Off US 83, E 2 miles on Burdick Expwy. Rooms overlook an attractive courtyard with an open-air bar and potted plants. **Rooms:** 173 rms and stes. CI 3pm/CO noon. Nonsmoking rms avail. Some rooms have sofas. **Amenities:** A/C, cable TV w/movies, dataport. **Services:** Babysitting. **Facilities:** 1200 1 restaurant, 1 bar, games rm, whirlpool, beauty salon. **Rates:** $45–$50 S; $45–$55 D; $88–$150 ste. Extra person $5. Children under age 18 stay free. Parking: Outdoor, free. AE, DC, DISC, MC, V.

MOTELS

Best Western International Inn
1505 N Broadway, 58703; tel 701/852-3161 or toll free 800/735-4493; fax 701/838-5538. Across from Minot Airport. Airport location is convenient, but the dull-brown color scheme is a drawback. **Rooms:** 271 rms and stes. Executive level. CI 3pm/CO 11am. Nonsmoking rms avail. Some rooms face the pool. **Amenities:** A/C, cable TV w/movies. **Services:** **Facilities:** 800 1 restaurant, 1 bar (w/entertainment), games rm, whirlpool, beauty salon. **Rates:** $46–$55 S; $55–$65 D; $125 ste. Extra person $6. Children under age 18 stay free. Parking: Outdoor, free. AE, DC, DISC, MC, V.

Best Western Safari Inn
1510 26th Ave SW, 58701; tel 701/852-4300 or toll free 800/735-5868; fax 701/883-1234. Off US 2 and US 52; Exit 20th Ave SW. A nicer-than-average motel with a jungle-motif courtyard. Lobby is small, but has attractive brass accents. **Rooms:** 100 rms and stes. Executive level. CI 3pm/CO 11am. Nonsmoking rms avail. Furniture has a white-pickled finish. **Amenities:** A/C, satel TV w/movies, dataport. Some units w/whirlpools. TVs hidden away in armoires. **Services:** **Facilities:** 20 1 bar (w/entertainment), games rm, whirlpool. Bar features dancing and a DJ. **Rates:** $43–$48 S; $49–$54 D; $55–$65 ste. Extra person $6. Children under age 18 stay free. Parking: Outdoor, free. Group rates avail. AE, CB, DC, DISC, ER, MC, V.

Days Inn
2100 4th St SW, 58701; tel 701/852-3646 or toll free 800/529-7466; fax 701/852-0501. Off US 83, W 4 blocks on 20th Ave SW. Clean facilities and friendly staff; located near shopping and restaurants. **Rooms:** 82 rms and stes. CI 3pm/CO noon. Nonsmoking rms avail. **Amenities:** A/C, cable TV w/movies, dataport. Many double rooms have two phones. **Services:** **Facilities:** 30 **Rates (CP):** Peak (June–Aug) $38–$49 S; $40–$53 D; $45–$60 ste. Children under age 18 stay free. Lower rates off-season. Parking: Outdoor, free. AE, CB, DC, DISC, JCB, MC, V.

Fairfield Inn
900 24th Ave SW, 58701; tel 701/838-2424 or toll free 800/228-2800; fax 701/838-2424. US 52 and US 83. Bright, clean, exceptionally well-maintained economy motel near several reasonably priced restaurants. **Rooms:** 62 rms and stes. CI 2pm/CO 11am. Nonsmoking rms avail. **Amenities:** A/C, cable TV w/movies. **Services:** **Facilities:** 15 Games rm, whirlpool. Pool area gets lots of sun.

Rates (CP): Peak (June 11–Sept 11) $37–$43 S; $42–$48 D; $45–$51 ste. Extra person $6. Children under age 18 stay free. Lower rates off-season. Parking: Outdoor, free. AE, DC, DISC, MC, V.

Select Inn of Minot
225 22nd Ave NW, 58701; tel 701/852-3411 or toll free 800/641-1000; fax 701/852-3450. Near Minot Airport. Very clean but ordinary motel near airport. **Rooms:** 100 rms and stes. CI 2pm/CO 11am. Nonsmoking rms avail. **Amenities:** A/C, cable TV w/movies. **Services:** **Facilities:** Washer/dryer. **Rates (CP):** $29 S; $33–$36 D; $30–$46 ste. Extra person $3. Children under age 13 stay free. Parking: Outdoor, free. Group, senior, government rates avail. AE, CB, DC, DISC, MC, V.

RESTAURANTS

Field and Stream
US 83 N; tel 701/852-3663. **American.** The owners don't mind if you feed the goldfish in the indoor stream, but please keep the prime rib and Alaskan king crab for yourself. Mounted game carry out the outdoor theme. Limo service available from Minot motels. **FYI:** Reservations recommended. Children's menu. Dress code. **Open:** Mon–Sat 5–9:30pm. **Prices:** Main courses $8–$26. AE, DC, DISC, MC, V.

The Roll'N Pin
2145 N Broadway; tel 701/839-8774. US 83 and 21st Ave on N side of town. **American.** Popular breakfast and lunch spot that bakes its own pies, cookies, and muffins. Come early for the strawberry-rhubarb pie—it goes fast. Entrees include roast turkey, and beef or pork dinners with stuffing, mashed potatoes and gravy. Senior citizen menu available. **FYI:** Reservations not accepted. Children's menu. No liquor license. **Open:** Mon–Sat 6am–11pm, Sun 7am–11pm. **Prices:** Main courses $4–$8. No CC.

Speedway
US 2; tel 701/838-0649. At jct US 52, 5 mi W of Minot. **American.** The parking lot overflows and the decibel level skyrockets at this local nightspot, known for beef cut daily by the staff. Prime rib and sirloin get top billing, but a crowded seafood menu includes lobster, grilled salmon, and "sea pigs" (shrimp wrapped in bacon, then deep-fried). No children. Out-of-area checks accepted. **FYI:** Reservations not accepted. **Open:** Mon–Sat 11am–midnight. **Prices:** Main courses $5–$16. No CC.

ATTRACTIONS

Roosevelt Park and Zoo
1219 Burdick Expwy SE; tel 701/852-2751. The zoo features animals from around the world including Bengal tigers, white tigers, giraffes, monkeys, and penguins. The Magic City Express, a two-fifths scale model replica of a Great Northern steam locomotive, transports visitors from the zoo to a public pool and 360-foot water slide. Gardens, picnic areas. **Open:** May–Aug, daily 10am–8pm; Sept–Apr, daily 8am–4pm. $

Upper Souris National Wildlife Refuge
US 52 via CR 11; tel 701/468-5467. The 32,089 acre refuge contains a 20-mile lake which is home to more than 290 species of birds including Hungarian partridges, ring-necked pheasants, and sharp-tailed grouse. Fishing, ice-fishing, picnicking; self-guiding driving tour south of Lake Darling Dam. **Open:** Daily 5am–10pm. **Free**

New Town

Between two major arms of Lake Sakakawea, this Fort Berthold Reservation town was established in 1952 when previous tribal towns were flooded for the Garrison Dam. Crow Flies High Observation Point, overlooking the lake, offers spectacular photo opportunities. Popular for fishing and home of a large tribal casino. **Information:** New Town Chamber of Commerce, PO Box 422, New Town, 58763 (tel 701/627-4316).

MOTEL

Four Bears Casino and Lodge
4 Bears Bridge, PO Box 579, 58763; tel 701/627-3141 or toll free 800/294-5454; fax 701/627-3714. W side of 4 Bears Bridge, ND 23. If the slot machines are unkind at this full-fledged casino, Lake Sakakawea is a handy diversion. Native American–style furnishings blend with neon lights at this popular motel. Reservations are a must. **Rooms:** 40 rms. CI 3pm/CO noon. Nonsmoking rms avail. **Amenities:** A/C, satel TV w/movies. **Services:** Fishing guide and boat service available. **Facilities:** 1 restaurant (*see* "Restaurants" below), 2 bars (1 w/entertainment), games rm. Adjacent RV park with 85 sites. Casino security includes guards and closed-circuit cameras in all hallways. **Rates (CP):** $55 S or D. Extra person $5. Children under age 17 stay free. Parking: Outdoor, free. Bus tour rates. AE, DISC, MC, V.

RESTAURANTS

Lucky's Cafe
In Four Bears Casino and Lodge, 4 Bears Bridge; tel 701/627-4018. On the west side of 4 Bears Bridge on ND 23. **American.** Slot machine bells ring loud and clear at this reasonably priced cafe. A buffet often includes fried shrimp and roast beef carved to order. Regular menu has sandwiches, steaks, walleye trout. **FYI:** Reservations not accepted. Children's menu. **Open:** Sun–Thurs 7am–9pm, Fri–Sat 7am–10pm. **Prices:** Main courses $6–$17; prix fixe $7–$9. AE, DISC, MC, V.

Scenic 23 Supper Club
Route 1; tel 701/627-3949. 7 miles E of New Town on ND 23. **American.** Seating at the front windows overlooking Lake

Sakakawea is limited, but folks really come for the view on their plates. Thick, fleshy portions of walleye are the main attraction, either grilled or breaded, then wok-fried. Steaks and sandwiches also available. **FYI:** Reservations not accepted. Country music. Children's menu. **Open:** Fri–Sat 5pm–midnight, Mon–Thurs 5–11pm. **Prices:** Main courses $6–$13. No CC.

Rugby

The seat of Pierce County, located near the geographical center of North America. The town, founded in 1886, was one of several railroad towns given English names.

ATTRACTION

Geographical Center Pioneer Village and Museum
1 block E of jct of US 2 and ND 3; tel 701/776-6414. A fieldstone cairn marks the geographical center of North America as determined by the US Department of the Interior. The adjacent pioneer village highlights the daily lives of North Dakotans in the late 1800s. Buildings include a blacksmith, jail, livery, Norwegian pioneer house, church, and schoolhouse. A country fair is held in mid-August with craft demonstrations, entertainment, and ethnic food and crafts. **Open:** May–Sept, daily 8am–7pm. **$$**

Theodore Roosevelt National Park

For lodgings, see Medora, Williston

Set amid the Dakota Badlands, this 70,000-acre park honors the 26th US president for his enduring contributions to the conservation of the nation's resources. Roosevelt tried his hand at ranching here in the 1880s (before he became a full-time politician) and fell in love with the stark beauty of the buttes. Not much has changed since his day—free-roaming wild horses and herds of bison still dot the landscape.

The park is open year-round. From May through September, day-use fees are collected and all facilities are open, including the visitors centers, campgrounds, and 85 miles of backcountry trails. Interpretive services are scheduled daily June–September, with films, talks, campfire programs, nature walks, and other activities. Camping is available year-round, though no services are available November–April. Trail rides of various lengths are offered May–September by the park concessioner (contact Peaceful Valley Trail Rides, PO Box 197, Medora, ND 58645).

The park has three visitors centers: **South Unit** in Medora (open daily except Thanksgiving, Christmas, and New Year's Day), **Painted Canyon** off I-94 (open daily, summer only), and **North Unit** near Watford City (open daily in summer; weekends and most weekdays in winter). Hiking and horseback riding permits are available at either the South or North Unit visitors center. For further information, contact Superintendent, Theodore Roosevelt National Park, PO Box 7, Medora, ND 58645 (tel 701/623-4466).

Wahpeton

Founded in 1869 on the Minnesota border, where the Otter Tail River flows into the Red River of the North to form the Bois de Sioux. Wahpeton is home to the state's Native American school and is a center for high-tech manufacturing companies like 3M. Wahpeton derives its name from the Sioux *wa-qpe-tong-wong* (village of many leaves). **Information:** Wahpeton Convention Center and Visitors Bureau, 118 N 6th St, Wahpeton, 58075 (tel 701/642-8744).

MOTELS

Comfort Inn
209 13th St S, 58705; tel 701/642-1115 or toll free 800/221-2222; fax 701/642-1115. Exit 23 off I-29, E on ND 13. Average but clean motel near downtown. **Rooms:** 46 rms and stes. CI 2pm/CO 11am. Nonsmoking rms avail. **Amenities:** A/C, cable TV. 1 unit w/whirlpool. Suites have refrigerators. Closed-captioned TVs in six rooms. **Services:** **Facilities:** Games rm, whirlpool. **Rates (CP):** $41–$46 S; $46–$51 D; $41–$48 ste. Extra person $5. Children under age 18 stay free. Parking: Outdoor, free. AE, CB, DC, DISC, EC, ER, JCB, MC, V.

Wahpeton Super 8
995 21st Ave N, 58075; tel 701/642-8731 or toll free 800/800-8000; fax 701/642-8733. Exit 23 off I-29; E 10 mi on ND 13. Exceptionally well-kept for an economy motel. Good choice for families. **Rooms:** 58 rms and stes. CI open/CO 11am. Nonsmoking rms avail. **Amenities:** A/C, cable TV, dataport. Some units w/whirlpools. Two rooms have hot tubs; some have refrigerators. Suites have whirlpools and recliners. **Services:** Pets allowed by permission of manager. **Facilities:** 1 restaurant, 1 bar (w/entertainment), games rm, whirlpool, washer/dryer. **Rates:** $32–$39 S; $42–$49 D; $53–$69 ste. Extra person $4. Children under age 18 stay free. Parking: Outdoor, free. Corporate, trucker, and bus tour rates avail. AE, CB, DC, DISC, EC, ER, JCB, MC, V.

Williston

The Williams County seat, Williston was settled in 1870 at the confluence of the Missouri and Yellowstone Rivers. Located near the Fort Union Trading Post, which was the surrender site for Sitting Bull. **Information:** Williston Convention and Visitors Bureau, 10 Main St, Williston, 58801 (tel 701/774-9041).

MOTELS

Airport International Inn
3601 2nd Ave W, PO Box 1800, 58802; tel 701/774-0241; fax 701/774-0318. Attractive, well-kept motel that's close to the north unit of Theodore Roosevelt National Park. Home of the Miss North Dakota Pageant. **Rooms:** 145 rms and stes. CI 1pm/CO noon. Nonsmoking rms avail. Good-size rooms with attractive furnishings. **Amenities:** A/C, cable TV. **Services:** Social director. **Facilities:** 1000 1 restaurant, 1 bar, games rm, whirlpool. **Rates:** $33–$75 S; $38–$80 D; $75–$80 ste. Extra person $5. Children under age 18 stay free. Parking: Outdoor, free. AE, CB, DISC, MC, V.

El Rancho Motel
1623 2nd Ave W, 58801; tel 701/572-6321 or toll free 800/433-8529; fax 701/572-6321. Well-kept property in an attractive building. **Rooms:** 92 rms. CI open/CO noon. Nonsmoking rms avail. Clean, comfortable, and well laid out. **Amenities:** A/C, cable TV, refrig. Some units w/terraces. **Services:** **Facilities:** 150 2 restaurants, 1 bar. **Rates (CP):** $30–$35 S; $34–$39 D. Extra person $4. Children under age 12 stay free. Parking: Outdoor, free. AE, CB, DC, DISC, MC, V.

Select Inn
213 35th St W, 58801; tel 701/572-4242 or toll free 800/641-1000; fax 701/572-4211. Attractive economy motel close to Theodore Roosevelt National Park—North Unit. **Rooms:** 60 rms. CI open/CO noon. Nonsmoking rms avail. Well sized and attractive. **Amenities:** A/C, cable TV w/movies. **Services:** Expanded continental breakfast. **Facilities:** Whirlpool, washer/dryer. **Rates (CP):** $28–$33 S; $33–$47 D. Extra person $4. Children under age 12 stay free. Parking: Outdoor, free. AE, DC, DISC, MC, V.

Super 8 Lodge
2324 2nd Ave W, PO Box 907, 58801-907; tel 701/572-8371 or toll free 800/800-8000. Well-kept building and grounds located close to the north unit of Theodore Roosevelt National Park. Economical. **Rooms:** 82 rms and stes. CI 2pm/CO noon. Nonsmoking rms avail. Rooms are clean, large, and well designed. **Amenities:** A/C, cable TV w/movies. **Services:** VP **Facilities:** 1 bar, games rm, whirlpool. **Rates (CP):** Peak (June–Sept) $27–$37 S; $39–$42 D; $39–$43 ste. Extra person $4. Children under age 12 stay free. Lower rates off-season. Parking: Outdoor, free. AE, CB, DC, DISC, MC, V.

RESTAURANT

El Rancho Dining Room
1623 2nd Ave; tel 701/572-6321. **American.** Nothing elaborate or different—just good, basic American fare: steaks, prime rib, and salmon, served in attractive quarters. **FYI:** Reservations recommended. Children's menu. **Open:** Lunch daily 11:30am–2pm; dinner daily 6–10pm. **Prices:** Main courses $7–$17. AE, CB, DC, DISC, MC, V.

ATTRACTION

Fort Union Trading Post National Historic Site
RR 3; tel 701/572-9083. 24 mi SW of Williston. Built near the confluence of the Yellowstone and Missouri Rivers by John Jacob Astor's American Fur Company, this fur-trading post shaped and controlled the economy of the Northern Plains for much of the 19th century. Today, many of the fort's buildings, palisades, and bastions have been reconstructed; the bourgeois (superintendent's) house contains exhibits on Lewis and Clark, the fur traders, and the neighboring Assinboin, Cree, Crow, Blackfoot, and Sioux peoples. Summertime living history programs; small picnic area near parking lot. **Open:** Mem Day–Labor Day, daily 8am–8pm; Labor Day–Mem Day, daily 9am–5:30pm. Closed some hols. **Free**

Wishek

One of several towns settled by the German Russians who flooded the Dakotas in the 1880s. Wishek retains a distinctly German flair and hosts an annual Sauerkraut Day in October.

ATTRACTION

Beaver Lake State Park
3850 70th St SE; tel 701/452-2752. 15 mi NW of Wishek. This 93-acre park features a campground with 25 fully equipped sites, two picnic shelters, and a playground. Beaver Lake offers opportunities for fishing, boating, and swimming; a self-guided nature trail points out the various plants, wildlife, and geologic features of the area. **Open:** Daily, dawn–dusk. **$**

OREGON

The Lure of the Oregon Trail

STATE STATS

CAPITAL
Salem

AREA
97,073 square miles

BORDERS
California, Washington, Idaho, Nebraska, and the Pacific Ocean

POPULATION
3,038,000 (1993)

ENTERED UNION
February 14, 1859 (33rd state)

NICKNAME
Beaver State

STATE FLOWER
Oregon grape

STATE BIRD
Western meadowlark

FAMOUS NATIVES
Edwin Markham, Linus Pauling, John Reed

If the pioneers who trudged 2,000 miles down the Oregon Trail in the 1840s had known about the rugged mountains, tumultuous rivers, and vast forests awaiting them, would they have come? Perhaps not, but they *did* come and their legacy lives on in Oregon today. The first settlers worked hard to push back nature, but we have changed our minds about nature over the past 150 years. Today, the outdoors are no longer a barrier to overcome—they are a way of life. New immigrants and visitors are still journeying to Oregon, but now they come for the very hurdles that the pioneers struggled to put behind them. People wait expectantly for their favorite times of year—salmon-fishing season, ski season, hiking season, biking season, rafting season.

Despite its seeming plenitude and uncompromised natural beauty, Oregon is struggling to retain its identity. Rapid growth is threatening to take the Oregon out of Oregon. Strawberry fields and hazelnut orchards have become tract houses and shopping malls. The wild salmon have almost disappeared from many of the state's rivers. Environmentalists and the timber industry fight over the remains of the original forests that once covered much of the state. Meanwhile, the state struggles to strike a balance between economic growth and preservation of the environment.

Still, there are few places anywhere in the nation where so much beauty is so close at hand. It is this proximity to nature that keeps Oregon such a special place, one that has captivated so many visitors over the years. Today, as more than a century ago, a diverse and compelling landscape awaits those traveling the new Oregon trails.

Frommer's #1

A Brief History

Turn Back? In 1579, "thicke and

stinking fogges" turned back famed British buccaneer Sir Francis Drake when he sailed the *Golden Hind* as far north as the southern coast of Oregon. The Spanish, who had established themselves in what is today California, had not been interested in exploring this gray and rainy coastline. It took another 200 years for Europeans to finally develop an active interest in this region, when the lucrative trade in sea otter pelts propelled them to claim dominion over Oregon.

Fatal Encounter The earliest traders found friendly Native American tribes willing to barter otter pelts for beads, metal, tobacco, and other goods. Oregon's natives had well-established cultures along both the Pacific Coast and the shores of the Columbia River, where they thrived on such bountiful wild foods as salmon, shellfish, huckleberries, and camas roots. Their rich and complex societies were among the most highly developed in North America. But the Europeans brought with them more than just goods for barter: They carried infectious diseases for which Native Americans had no natural resistance. Within a few decades, the once large population was reduced by smallpox and other afflictions to a fraction of its pre-European contact numbers. Today, Oregon's tribal populations remain small.

Fun Facts

- Crater Lake, which occupies the pit of a volcano whose top was blown off by an eruption some 7,000 years ago, is the deepest lake in the United States. Its intensely blue water plunges to a maximum depth of 1,932 feet.
- Nearly half of Oregon's area is forested, totaling nearly 30 million acres.
- Matt Groening, creator of the hit television series "The Simpsons," got his start in Portland. Giant wall murals of the cartoon family can be seen on different buildings around town.
- Mill Ends Park, in Portland, is the world's smallest park, measuring 24 inches in diameter.
- There are more restaurants per capita in Portland than in any other West Coast city.
- Portland is the only city in America with an extinct volcano within its city limits—Mount Tabor.

Northwest Passage By the late 18th century, the fur trade and the quest for the fabled northwest passage (a water route from the Pacific to the Atlantic) had brought Russian, American, British, and Spanish ships to this region. In 1792, American trader Robert Gray sailed through the mouth of a great river and named it the Columbia after his ship, the *Columbia Rediviva.* Thirteen years later, in late 1805, the Lewis and Clark expedition finally arrived at the Pacific after traveling up the Missouri River, and over the Rockies, and down the Columbia. The expedition spent a cold, wet winter camped near the river's mouth. Five years later, fur traders working for John Jacob Astor established a trading post, called Fort Astoria, near the spot of Lewis and Clark's camp. This was the first permanent settlement in the Northwest.

A Well-Traveled Route In 1829, the British (in the guise of the Hudson's Bay Company), founded Oregon City at the falls of the Willamette River. Over the next decade, a slow trickle of missionaries and settlers began migrating to the Oregon country. By the 1840s, this trickle had become a flood, as families, lured by the promise of free land, journeyed 2,000 miles overland along the Oregon Trail. In 1844, Oregon City became the first incorporated city west of the Rocky Mountains and two years later, with American pioneers pouring into the region, the British finally relinquished claims to Oregon and Washington. It would be only 13 more years before Oregon became the 33rd state in the Union.

Save the Salmon The late 19th century saw the harvesting of massive numbers of the Columbia River's seemingly endless salmon population. Utilizing such highly efficient equipment as fish wheels that literally scooped salmon out of the river, salmon canneries flourished. However, the salmon population dropped so rapidly that the canneries soon put themselves out of business. By the 1930s, dams were being built on the Columbia and Snake Rivers, and salmon populations once again took a beating. Today, Oregon is still trying to work out a way to recover its once-vast salmon populations. However, these dams did provide irrigation water and cheap electricity that fueled both industry and farming.

Toward a Diversified Future Farming and logging were the economic mainstays of Oregon's economy from the middle of the 19th century right up to recent years. However, with the timber industry experiencing frequent ups and downs, the latest caused by a combination of recession and restrictions on logging in spotted owl habitat, the state began encouraging economic diversification. Today, the Portland area is the site of numerous high-tech manufacturing plants, including those of Intel, Epson, and Toshiba. For much of this century, citizens of Oregon have turned to the outdoors as their main source of recreation, so it comes as no surprise that such sportswear manufacturers as Nike and Jantzen are headquartered there.

A Closer Look

GEOGRAPHY

With two mountain ranges running parallel to both each other and the coast for almost the entire length of the state, Oregon is easily divided into distinct geographical regions. The **Oregon coast,** stretching for 400 miles from the mouth of the Columbia River to the California state line, is rivaled only by the coasts of Maine and California for scenic beauty. Here, the **Coast Mountains** meet the sea, creating wind-swept capes, rocky islands, arches, sea caves, sand dunes, and long stretches of sandy beach.

The fertile **Willamette Valley** (the area between the Coast and Cascade Mountains) is the population center of the state, with Portland, Salem, Corvallis, and Eugene all lying along the banks of the Willamette River. The Willamette Valley is still the state's main agricultural region, producing an amazing diversity of crops—grapes, hops, mint, grass seed, hazelnuts, berries, and more.

From the **Columbia Gorge** in the north to the California state line in the south, the **Cascade Mountains** divide the state into the "wet west" and the "dry east." The Cascades include the highest peak in Oregon: 11,235-foot **Mount Hood.** The collapsed volcano that is the focal point of **Crater Lake National Park** is at the southern end of the Cascades.

In striking contrast to Oregon west of the Cascades, **central and eastern Oregon** are characterized by a high desert landscape punctuated by grasslands, small mountain ranges, and large, shallow lakes. In **northeastern Oregon,** the desert gives way to the Wallowa and Blue Mountains, which are separated by the wide, fertile valley of the Grand Ronde River. To the east of the Wallowas lies Hells Canyon; carved by the Snake River, it is the deepest river gorge in the United States.

DRIVING DISTANCES

Bend

125 mi E of Eugene
131 mi SE of Salem
139 mi N of Klamath Falls
160 mi S of The Dalles
182 mi SE of Portland
321 mi W of Boise

Crater Lake

57 mi NW of Klamath Falls
103 mi E of Roseburg
109 mi SW of Bend
127 mi SE of Eugene
245 mi S of Portland
413 mi N of San Francisco

Portland

60 mi S of Mount St Helens, WA
62 mi W of Hood River
79 mi E of Cannon Beach
115 mi N of Eugene
180 mi S of Seattle
182 mi NW of Bend

CLIMATE

Oregon can be broken into several climatological zones. Along the rainy Pacific coast, temperatures rarely drop far below freezing or soar much above 80°F. In the Portland area and the rest of the Willamette Valley, summer temperatures regularly top 100°F and winter temperatures regularly drop into the teens. Here rains fall steadily from October to July, but quantities are less than in most parts of the Eastern Seaboard. In the Cascade Range, heavy snowfalls support numerous ski areas. To the east of the Cascades lies a high desert that receives little rainfall and experiences high summer temperatures and equally extreme winter temperatures.

WHAT TO PACK

A raincoat is an essential for a trip to Oregon, especially between October and June. It can be cool any time of year, so a jacket or warm sweater are also in order. Since summer temperatures can top 100°F in the Portland area, lightweight clothes are in order if you plan to visit the city during the summer.

TOURIST INFORMATION

For information on tourist activities throughout the state, contact the **Oregon Tourism Division,** 775 NE Summer St, Salem, OR 97310 (tel toll free 800/547-7842). If you are visiting the Portland vicinity, contact the **Portland Oregon Visitor Association,** 3 World Trade Center, 26 SW Salmon St, Portland, OR 97204 (tel 503/222-2223 or toll free 800/345-3214). For information on national parks, monuments, and historic sites in Oregon, contact the **National Park Service, Outdoor Recreation**

Information Office, 915 2nd Ave, Rm 442, Seattle, WA 98174 (tel 206/220-7450). The **US Forest Service Recreational Information Office,** 800 NE Oregon St, Portland, OR 97232 (tel 503/326-2877), dispenses information on national forests in the state, while the **Oregon Parks & Recreation Department, Reservation/Information Center,** 3554 SE 82nd Ave, Portland, OR 97266 (tel 503/731-3411 or toll free 800/452-5687) handles state park inquiries.

DRIVING RULES AND REGULATIONS

The driver and all passengers in a vehicle must wear safety belts, and children under one year old must be in car seats. After coming to a complete stop, drivers may make a right turn on a red light (or a left turn, when turning from the left lane of a one-way street into another one-way street). Radar detectors are legal in Oregon.

AVG MONTHLY TEMPS (°F) & RAINFALL (IN)

	Portland	Pendleton
Jan	40/6.2	33/1.7
Feb	43/3.9	39/1.1
Mar	46/3.6	44/1.1
Apr	50/2.3	50/1.0
May	57/2.1	58/1.1
June	63/1.5	66/0.7
July	68/0.5	74/0.3
Aug	67/1.1	72/0.6
Sept	63/1.6	64/0.6
Oct	54/3.1	53/1.0
Nov	46/5.2	41/1.5
Dec	41/6.4	36/1.7

RENTING A CAR

All the major car rental companies have offices in Oregon. You'll find desks for many of these in the arrivals hall of Portland International Airport. The following are national companies with offices in Portland.

- **Alamo** (tel toll free 800/327-9633)
- **Avis** (tel 800/831-2847)
- **Budget** (tel 800/527-0700)
- **Dollar** (tel 800/800-4000)
- **Enterprise** (tel 800/325-8007)
- **Hertz** (tel 800/654-3131)
- **National** (tel 800/227-7368)
- **Thrifty** (tel 800/367-2277)

ESSENTIALS

Area Codes: The area code for Portland and northwestern Oregon is **503.** The area code for the rest of the state is **541.**

Emergencies: For the police, the fire department, or an ambulance, dial 911.

Liquor Laws: The legal age for possession and consumption of alcoholic beverages is 21. Penalties for drunk driving are severe and strictly enforced.

Road Info: For road conditions around the state, phone 541/889-3999.

Smoking: The Oregon Indoor Clean Air Act prohibits smoking in any indoor public area (restaurants, hotel lobbies, shopping malls, theaters), except in designated smoking areas. However, restaurants that seat fewer than 30 people are exempt from this law.

Taxes: There is no sales tax in Oregon. Hotel-room taxes vary with locality. (The Portland hotel room tax is 9%.)

Time Zone: Most of Oregon is in the Pacific time zone. A small section in the eastern part of the state is in the Rocky Mountain time zone.

Best of the State

WHAT TO SEE AND DO

Below is a general overview of some of the top sights and attractions in Oregon. To find out more detailed information, look under "Attractions" under individual cities in the listings portion of this book.

Parks & Recreation Areas

Crater Lake, the flooded caldera of a massive volcano that erupted 7,700 years ago, is the deepest lake in the United States and Oregon's only national park. A rim drive leads to breathtaking viewpoints, and there are trails for hiking and cross-country skiing. A separate volcanic eruption in central Oregon produced what is now the **Newberry Crater National Monument.** Here, fishing lakes and obsidian flows attract visitors. In the northeast corner of the state lies the Snake River and **Hells Canyon National Recreation Area.** In central Oregon, three separate sections of the **John Day Fossil Beds National Monument** are filled with colorful hills and fossilized plants and animals (no dinosaur bones, though). Not far from the California state line, **Oregon Caves National Monument** preserves the marble caves of the Siskiyou Mountains.

Oregon's most popular state parks lie along the state's 400-mile coastline. These parks range in size from scenic picnic spots to miles-long stretches of rugged coastline. From south to north the most scenic parks are almost any of the parks between Brookings and Gold Beach, **Sunset Bay State Park** and **Cape Arago State Park** (near Coos Bay), **Devils Elbow State Park** (north of Florence), **Oswald West State Park,** and **Ecola Beach State Park.** Popular parks located elsewhere in the state include **Silver Falls** (east of Salem), with its numerous waterfalls; **Wallowa Lake,** a picturesque glacial lake at the foot of the Wallowa Mountains; and **Rooster Rock,** a popular beach (known for its clothing-optional area) on the Columbia River.

Natural Wonders Just east of Portland lies the **Columbia Gorge National Scenic Area.** Here in the gorge, which was carved by ancient flood waters, dozens of waterfalls (the tallest being Multnomah Falls) cascade down basalt cliffs. Rising above the gorge is **Mount Hood,** a snow-capped volcanic peak offering year-round skiing.

All up and down the Oregon coast, nature has contrived to produce geological wonders. Rugged, rocky islands—known as haystack rocks or seastacks—dot the coastline, with the most picturesque to be found at Cannon Beach, Bandon, and between Gold Beach and Brookings. Other natural wonders along the coast include miles of huge sand dunes near Florence, blowholes at Cape Perpetua, spouting horns in Depoe Bay, and the Devil's Punchbowl (a collapsed sea cave) north of Newport.

Out in the northeast corner of the state, the glacier-carved Wallowa Mountains attract backpackers and horsepackers. On the north side of these mountains lies the picturesque Wallowa Lake, and to the east lies the Snake River and the Hells Canyon National Recreation Area.

Wildlife Large herds of elk—the largest of Oregon's land mammals—can often be seen at Jewel Meadows, north of US 26 about 40 miles east of Seaside, and at Dean Creek Elk Viewing Area, one mile east of Reedsport. Pronghorn antelope graze on the grasses of the **Hart Mountain National Antelope Refuge,** between Burns and Lakeview in the eastern part of the state. Sharp-eyed wildlife watchers might also spot bighorn sheep in this refuge. The best places to see seals and sea lions are at **Sea Lion Caves** (a huge natural sea cave north of Florence), **Cape Arago State Park** near Coos Bay, the Strawberry Hill wayside south of Yachats, and along the waterfront in Newport. Bird watchers will find the state's best birding at the **Malheur National Wildlife Refuge,** which is frequented by more than 300 species of birds at various times of year.

Historic Sites & Areas History buffs can trace the footsteps of Lewis and Clark at **Fort Clatsop,** a reproduction of the fort that the intrepid explorers built during the winter of 1805–1806. Rock Fort, outside The Dalles, is on another site used by the expedition. In the middle of the 19th century, pioneers crossing Oregon wore wagon-wheel ruts into the landscape; today these ruts can still be seen in various places in eastern Oregon.

Just south of Oregon City is the historic town of **Aurora,** which was founded as a utopian community and now has dozens of antique stores. Other towns with high concentrations of historic homes include Oregon City, Jacksonville (in the southern part of the state), and Albany (south of Salem).

Historic lodges scattered around the state include **Timberline Lodge,** on Mount Hood; **Crater Lake Lodge,** which reopened in 1995 after a complete renovation; **Wolf Creek Tavern,** a former stagecoach stop in southern Oregon; and the **French Glen Hotel,** a small and remote building in central Oregon.

Museums The **Oregon History Center** in Portland chronicles the state's past, while in nearby Oregon City, the **End of the Oregon Trail Center** focuses on 19th-century pioneers. Way out in eastern Oregon, the **Oregon Trail Interpretive Center** in Baker City chronicles the travails of those hardy pioneers who crossed the continent by covered wagon in the 1840s and 1850s.

Most of the museums along the coast are small repositories of local history; however, there are a few exceptions worth noting. Astoria's **Columbia River Maritime Museum** is an old salt's dream come true, with dozens of boats on display. If things that float aren't your forte, how about things that fly? At Tillamook's **World War II Blimp Hangar Museum,** blimps and fighter planes are the focus.

Among the museums that focus on the state's Native American heritage are the **Favell Museum** in Klamath Falls and the **Warm Springs Museum,** in the central part of the state. Ashland's **Pacific Northwest Museum of Natural History** acts as an introduction to diverse natural habitats of the region, while the **High Desert Museum,** just south of Bend, combines aspects of a museum with live animal displays for an informative look at the life and geography of the high desert.

Beaches In addition to the dozens of state parks along the Oregon coast, there are numerous community beaches that each have something different to offer. Seaside, Lincoln City, and Newport are the coast's three most popular family beaches with miles of sand as well as summer traffic jams. Cannon Beach and Bandon offer sand, surf, and art galleries. Gearhart, Manzanita, Neskowin, and Yachats are preferred by people looking for peace and quiet. The **Oregon Dunes National Recreation Area,** south of Florence, offers miles of beach backed by high sand dunes.

Public Gardens An inordinate number of Oregonians are crazy about gardening, so it is should not be surprising that Portland has two famed public gardens. The **International Rose Test Garden** displays thousands of rose plants, while the gardens of the adjacent **Japanese Garden Society of Oregon** are a tranquil retreat renowned as one of the best such gardens outside Japan. On the Oregon coast, outside the town of Coos Bay, a former private formal garden has become **Shore Acres State Park.**

Family Favorites The **Metro Washington Park Zoo** in Portland is known for its elephant herd, but also has excellent rain forest and tundra exhibits. Equally popular is the **Oregon Coast Aquarium** in Newport, where puffins and sea otters steal the show. The adjacent **Mark O Hatfield Marine Science Center** is currently building a tank for the orca whale made famous by the movie *Free Willy.* For a drive-through experience, there is **Wildlife Safari Game Park,** outside Roseburg. Children can even pet baby leopards and the like at **West Coast Game Park Safari,** near Bandon.

There are a couple of children's museums in Oregon, including the **Portland Children's Museum** and the **Gilbert House Children's Museum** in Salem. Interactive science exhibits, a submarine, planetarium, and Omnimax theater keep families busy at Portland's **Oregon Museum of Science and Industry (OMSI).**

Families also enjoy the state's different excursion trains. The **Spirit of Oregon** dinner train chugs along from the tiny farm community of Roy (west of Portland) and up into the Coast Range. In the central part of the state, the **Crooked River Dinner Train** provides a similar experience in a high desert setting. The **Mount Hood Scenic Railroad,** which leaves from Hood River, passes through apple orchards on the flanks of Mount Hood. Another small train, the **Fun Run Express,** runs along the shore of Nehalem Bay between Garibaldi and the Nehalem Winery.

Shopping Oregon's most popular crafts markets, which showcase the creative endeavors of the region's craftspeople, take place on Saturdays in Portland and Eugene. Similar offerings, as well as fine art, are available year-round in the garden-crazy coastal community of Cannon Beach and the Western theme town of Sisters in central Oregon. Few towns in Oregon offer a greater concentration of antiques shops than the historic community of Aurora, just south of Oregon City. The Sellwood neighborhood of Portland also has a dense concentration of shops selling antiques and collectibles.

Cuisine Berries of all types grow well in the Oregon climate, and can show up in every course at some restaurants. They even find their way into several local beers. The region's most famous comestible—salmon—has lately been the focus of conservation efforts but still shows up frequently on menus (much of the salmon served in Oregon actually comes from Alaska, where populations are not endangered). The prolific Willamette Valley produces excellent wines, with the pinot noirs being the most highly acclaimed. Microbreweries are another staple on the Oregon scene, with dozens of breweries producing unusual beers and ales in the Portland area.

EVENTS AND FESTIVALS

- **Oregon Shakespeare Festival,** Ashland. A nine-month-long festival of plays by the Bard and others. February to October. Call 541/482-4331.
- **Cinco de Mayo,** Portland. Celebration of Mexican heritage. Weekend nearest May 5th. Call 503/292-5752.
- **Portland Rose Festival.** The second-largest floral parade in the country, plus lots of other activities. First three weeks of June. Call 503/227-2681.
- **Britt Festivals,** Jacksonville. Music and dance under the stars. June–September. Call 541/773-6077.
- **World Championship Timber Carnival,** Albany. Logging events, parade, fireworks. July 4 weekend. Call 541/928-2391.
- **Oregon Country Fair,** Veneta. A visual and performing arts festival that attracts hippies—young and old—from around the region. Second weekend in July. Call 541/343-4298.
- **Da Vinci Days,** Corvallis. A celebration of science and technology, with lots of performances and interactive exhibits. Mid-July. Call 541/757-6363.

- **Oregon Brewers Festival,** Portland. Microbreweries show off their suds. Waterfront Park. Last weekend in July. Call 503/778-5917.
- **Chief Joseph Days,** Joseph. Rodeo and exhibits by Native Americans. Last full weekend in July. Call 541/432-1015.
- **Mount Hood Festival of Jazz,** Gresham. Features jazz musicians from around the country. First full weekend in August. Call 503/232-3000.
- **Oregon State Fair,** Salem. Agricultural exhibits, horse racing, rodeo, concerts, and a midway. 12 days in late August–early September. Call 503/378-3247.
- **Artquake,** Portland. A huge downtown street fair celebrating the visual and performing arts. Labor Day weekend. Call 503/227-2787.
- **Pendleton Round-Up and Happy Canyon Pageant.** Rodeo, Native American pageant, country-music concert. Mid-September. Call 541/276-2553 or toll free 800/43-RODEO.
- **Winter Solstice Renaissance Festival,** Portland. Renaissance costumes and festivities. Held at OMSI. Late December. Call 503/797-4000.

SPECTATOR SPORTS

Auto Racing The **Portland International Raceway** (tel 503/285-6635) packs in the crowds with a full schedule of drag races and Indy car races during its February–October season.

Baseball With no major-league ball team in the state, baseball isn't as popular as basketball. However, the class A minor-league **Portland Rockies** (tel 503/223-2837) play at Portland's Civic Stadium. Tickets are available through all G I Joe/TicketMaster outlets (tel 503/224-4400).

Basketball The **Portland Trail Blazers** (tel 503/231-8000) have had their ups and downs in recent years but fans remain so loyal that the team got a new arena, the Rose Garden, in 1995. Tickets are available through all G I Joe/TicketMaster outlets (tel 503/224-4400).

Football Oregon doesn't have a pro football franchise, but it does have two major university teams. The **University of Oregon Ducks** (tel 541/346-4461 or toll free 800/WEBFOOT) play at Autzen Stadium in Eugene, while the **Oregon State University Beavers** (tel 541/737-3720) play at Parker Stadium in Corvallis.

Hockey The **Portland Winter Hawks** (tel 503/238-6366), a Western Hockey League team that has its own small following, play at both Memorial Coliseum and at the new Rose Garden arena.

Horse/Greyhound Racing Fans of wagering on the races have two places to place their bets in Portland. Thoroughbreds race at **Portland Meadows** (tel 503/285-9144) from October to April, and greyhounds run at **Multnomah Greyhound Track** (tel 503/667-7700) from April to September.

ACTIVITIES A TO Z

Ballooning Hot-air balloon rides over Oregon wine country leave from McMinnville. There are also hot-air balloon companies operating in the Bend area.

Bicycling The Oregon coast is one of the most popular bicycle touring routes in the country. During the summer months, it is best to travel from north to south, because of the prevailing winds. (The whole trip takes about a week to complete if you are cycling at a leisurely pace.) Another region growing in popularity is the wine country of Yamhill County and other parts of the Willamette Valley. The most popular spots for mountain biking are Crater Lake National Park, Forest Park in Portland, Mount Hood, and the area near Bend. There's also a trail, open to mountain bikes, that runs along the Deschutes River in central Oregon. For a map and information on bicycle routes in Oregon, contact the Bikeway Program Manager, Oregon Department of Transportation, Bicycle/Pedestrian Program, Transportation Building, Rm 200, Salem, OR 97310 (tel 503/378-3432).

Bird Watching **Malheur National Wildlife Refuge,** the state's premier bird-watching area, attracts more than 300 species of birds over the course of the year. Nearby Summer Lake offers good opportunities to view migratory waterfowl and shorebirds. There is also good bird watching on Sauvie Island (outside Portland) and along the coast.

Camping Public and private campgrounds can be found all across Oregon, from the coast to the eastern deserts. However, those along the coast and those in the Cascades are the most popular, with any campground on a lake staying particularly busy. During the summer months, campground reservations are almost a necessity. For more state park campground reservations and information, contact the Oregon Parks & Recreation Department, Reservation/Information Center, 3554 SE 82nd Ave, Portland, OR 97266 (tel 503/731-3411 or toll free 800/452-5687). Summer campsite reservations are taken beginning June 1.

Camping is also very popular in **Crater Lake National Park.** The summer season here is quite short and consequently campgrounds stay filled. Reservations (tel 503/594-2211) are a necessity.

Canoeing & Kayaking A few favorite canoeing lakes include Crescent Lake, Upper Klamath Lake (where there is a canoe trail), Waldo Lake and Crescent Lake southeast of Eugene, and the many lakes of the Cascade Lakes Loop southwest of Bend. White-water kayaking is popular on many of the rivers that flow down out of the Cascade Range, including the Deschutes, the Clackamas, the Mollala, and the Sandy. Down in southern Oregon, the North Umpqua and the Rogue provide plenty of white-water action.

Golf Oregon has nearly 200 private and public golf courses, including several resort courses. The majority of courses are clustered in the Portland metropolitan area and at the resorts in the Bend-Redmond area.

Hang Gliding Lakeview, in south-central Oregon near the California state line, is Oregon's premier hang-gliding location. Strong steady winds and high bluffs provide perfect conditions for experienced hang gliders.

Hiking Thousands of miles of hiking trails criss-cross the state. They tend to be concentrated in national forests, especially in the wilderness areas of the Cascade Range. However, many state parks also have extensive hiking trail systems. Locations on or near the coast with popular hiking trails include Saddle Mountain State Park, Ecola State Park, Oswald West State Park, and Cape Lookout State Park.

For a quick hiking fix, Portlanders often head for the city's Forest Park or out to the many trails of the Columbia Gorge National Scenic Area (Eagle Creek Trail is a long-time favorite). The trails leading out from Timberline Lodge on Mount Hood lead through forests and meadows at treeline and are particularly busy on summer weekends.

The **Pacific Crest Trail** travels the length of the Cascade Range from the Columbia River in the north to the California state line in the south. Along its length are such scenic hiking areas as the Mount Hood Wilderness, the Mount Jefferson Wilderness, the Three Sisters Wilderness, Diamond Peak Wilderness, Mount Thielsen Wilderness, and Sky Lakes Wilderness. The **Oregon Coast Trail** runs the length of the Oregon coast. In most places it travels along the beach, but in other places it climbs up and over capes and headlands through dense forests and wind-swept meadows. The longest stretches of the trail are along the southern coast in Samuel H Boardman State Park. There is also a long beach stretch in the Oregon Dunes National Recreation Area.

Rock Climbing Smith Rocks State Park, near Redmond in central Oregon, is a rock-climbing mecca of international renown. So numerous are the routes that an entire book has been written about Smith Rock climbs, some of which are among the toughest in the world. Many climbers claim that sport climbing got its American start here.

Sailing Though lakes and offshore waters provide sailing opportunities for some, it is the wide waters of the Columbia River around Portland that attract the greatest numbers of weekend sailors.

Skiing The Cascade Range provides ample opportunities for downhill and cross-country skiing. On Mount Hood, ski areas include Mount Hood Meadows, Mount Hood Ski Bowl, and Timberline. Farther south, there are Hoodoo Ski Bowl, east of Salem, and Willamette Pass, east of Eugene. Outside of Bend, there is Mount Bachelor. In the eastern part of the state, Anthony Lakes provides powder skiing. Down in the south, the Mount Ashland ski area is the only option. Teacup Lake, Trillium Basin, and Mount Hood Meadows (all on Mount Hood) offer good groomed trails for cross-country skiiers. There are also plenty of groomed trails near Mount Bachelor.

Swimming The beaches of Oregon are beautiful, but they don't offer much in the way of swimming. The waters of the Pacific Ocean are often rough and always cold, so only the hardiest souls try swimming here and then only on the warmest days of late summer. Likewise, many of the state's rivers are fed by glaciers and snow melt and are far too cold for anything more than a brisk plunge. Consequently, swimmers head for lakes and low-elevation rivers. Rooster Rock State Park (east of Portland) and Sauvie Island (northwest of Portland), both on the Columbia River, offer good swimming, as does Blue Lake in northeast Portland. Other places to cool off include Wallowa Lake in the northeast, Detroit Lake (east of Salem), and the many lakes near the coastal town of Florence.

Water Sports Throughout the state, there are lakes and rivers that are heavily used by boaters, jet skiers, and waterskiers; the Columbia and the Willamette are the most popular water sports areas. Other lakes well known to water sports enthusiasts include Detroit Lake, Fern Ridge Reservoir (west of Eugene), Lake Simtustus (near Madras), Prineville Reservoir (near Prineville), and Wallowa Lake (near Joseph).

Whale Watching Depoe Bay, north of Newport, is not only the smallest harbor in the world, but it is also home port for several whale-watching boats that head out in the late winter and early spring to look for migrating gray whales. It is also possible to whale watch from shore—Cape Lookout and Cape Meares offer the best vantage points.

White-Water Rafting Central Oregon's Deschutes River, and the south's Rogue River (featured in the movie *The River Wild*) are the two most popular rafting rivers in the state. Other popular rafting rivers include the Clackamas outside Portland and the McKenzie outside Eugene. Out in the southeastern corner, the remote Owyhee River provides adventurers with still more white water.

Windsurfing The Columbia River Gorge, with its wind-whipped waves, is one of the most renowned windsurfing spots in the world. Hood River is the center of activity here, with plenty of windsurfing schools and rental companies. The best conditions are in the summer. The south Oregon coast also has some popular spots including Floras Lake (north of Port Orford) and Pistol River beach (south of Gold Beach).

Selected Parks & Recreation Areas

- **Crater Lake National Park,** PO Box 7, Crater Lake, OR 97604 (tel 541/594-2211)
- **Mount Hood National Forest,** 2955 NW Division St, Gresham, OR 97030 (tel 503/666-0771)
- **Deschutes National Forest/Newberry National Volcanic Monument,** 1230 NE 3rd St, Rm A-262, Bend, OR 97701 (tel 541/383-4709)
- **Columbia River Gorge National Scenic Area,** USDA Forest Service, 902 Wasco Ave, Ste 200, Hood River, OR 97031 (tel 541/386-2333)
- **Cape Perpetua Scenic Area,** Siuslaw National Forest, US 101, 3 mi S of Yachats (tel 541/547-3289)
- **Cape Arago State Park,** off US 101, 14 mi SW of Coos Bay (tel 541/888-4902)
- **Cape Lookout State Park,** off US 101, 12 mi S of Tillamook (tel 503/842-4981)
- **Devil's Lake State Park,** off US 101 in Lincoln City (tel 541/994-2002)
- **Ecola State Park,** PO Box 681, Cannon Beach, OR 97110 (tel 503/436-2844)
- **Jessie M Honeyman State Park,** US 101, 3 mi S of Florence (tel 541/997-3851)
- **Oswald West State Park,** US 101, 10 mi S of Cannon Beach (tel 503/368-5153)
- **Samuel H Boardman State Park,** US 101, 4 mi N of Brookings (tel 541/469-2021)
- **Silver Falls State Park,** OR 214, 26 mi E of Salem (tel 503/873-8681)
- **Smith Rock State Park,** off US 97, 9 mi NE of Redmond (tel 541/548-7501)
- **Wallowa Lake State Park,** OR 82, 6 mi S of Joseph (tel 541/432-4185)

THE CENTRAL OREGON COAST

Start	Lincoln City
Finish	Coos Bay
Distance	170 miles
Time	2–3 days
Highlights	Spectacular stretch of the Pacific Coast; state parks with easy access to wide, sandy beaches; short hikes in the coastal hills or along the beach; Oregon Coast Aquarium; wildlife sanctuaries and sea lion viewing areas; fresh seafood restaurants; historic lighthouses; scenic fishing villages of Newport, Yachats, Florence, and Reedsport; microbreweries

Hugging the rustic coastline, scenic US 101 covers some of the most diverse and memorable terrain along the West Coast. The Coast Range Mountains to the east separate the small, oceanside fishing towns from the interior of Oregon, creating an out-of-the-way but friendly atmosphere. State parks offer access to wide, sandy beaches and unlimited strolling aside the crashing surf, while rocky beaches expose some of the best tide-pooling found anywhere. Almost all accommodations, restaurants, and scenic attractions are on, or adjacent to, US 101, and all streets and roads lead back to the highway, creating ample opportunities for relaxed wandering.

For additional information on lodgings, restaurants, and attractions in the region covered by the tour, look under specific cities in the listings portion of this chapter.

Lincoln City is approximately 90 miles from Portland. From the center of Portland take I-5 to OR 99W (follow the signs to Tigard). OR 99W becomes OR 18, which will take you all the way to US 101 and:

1. **Lincoln City.** One of the larger towns on the Oregon coast, the city is actually made up of five communities. Lincoln City is the area's hub for dining, recreation, overnight accommodations, and shoreline activities. During July and August, motels and hotels can fill up and eateries can be crowded. The town's visitors center, US 101 and SW 8th St (tel 503/994-8378), is a good stop on your way out of town to pick up information about places to see and events to attend, particularly during the summer months. Seven miles south of Lincoln City is Siletz (suh-LETS) Bay, a beautiful and protected estuary that offers the tour's first wildlife views.

Take a Break

Perhaps the best restaurant on the coast, the **Bay House,** just south of Lincoln City at 5911 SW US 101 (tel 503/996-3222), is sophisticated and casual at the same time. Carefully prepared seafood and pastas provide a wonderful introduction to Northwest cuisine. Picture windows in the two dining rooms provide views of the wildlife in Siletz Bay, and the wine list is excellent. Entrees range from $13 to $25.

Continuing approximately 14 miles south on US 101 you will find the small town of:

2. **Depoe Bay,** where a tiny but beautiful harbor houses a small fleet of boats and the road winds along bluffs that drop to the Pacific below. Two miles south of town is a short but worthwhile side trip, called the **Otter Crest Loop** (look for the highway signs). An Oregon State Park lookout at **Cape Foulweather** offers stunning coastal vistas and the chance to see blue whales during their migration. The **Lookout Gift Shop** sells knickknacks and dispenses tourist information at 500 feet above the crashing surf; coin-operated binoculars are available.

   Another natural attraction that shouldn't be missed is at the southern end of the Otter Crest Loop where it rejoins US 101. **Devil's Punchbowl State Park** has a marine gardens oceanshore preserve, which can be reached by taking the short path from the parking lot. The preserve allows you to walk among the intertidal zone and see (depending on the tide) purple shore crabs, common sea stars, red sea cucumbers, and gooseneck barnacles, as well as peregrine falcons, western gulls, and black oyster catchers. The main attraction at the park is the Devil's Punch Bowl, a large hole formed in the seaside rock that fills with churning, foaming water at high tide. About 20 miles south of Depoe Bay on US 101, you will discover:

3. **Newport.** Just before entering town, you will find a clearly marked turnoff to the **Yaquina Head Outstanding Natural Area** and its post–Civil War lighthouse. The lighthouse has been carefully restored and maintained, and tours are available. The area, a breeding ground for seabirds, offers excellent bird-watching (especially during the spring and

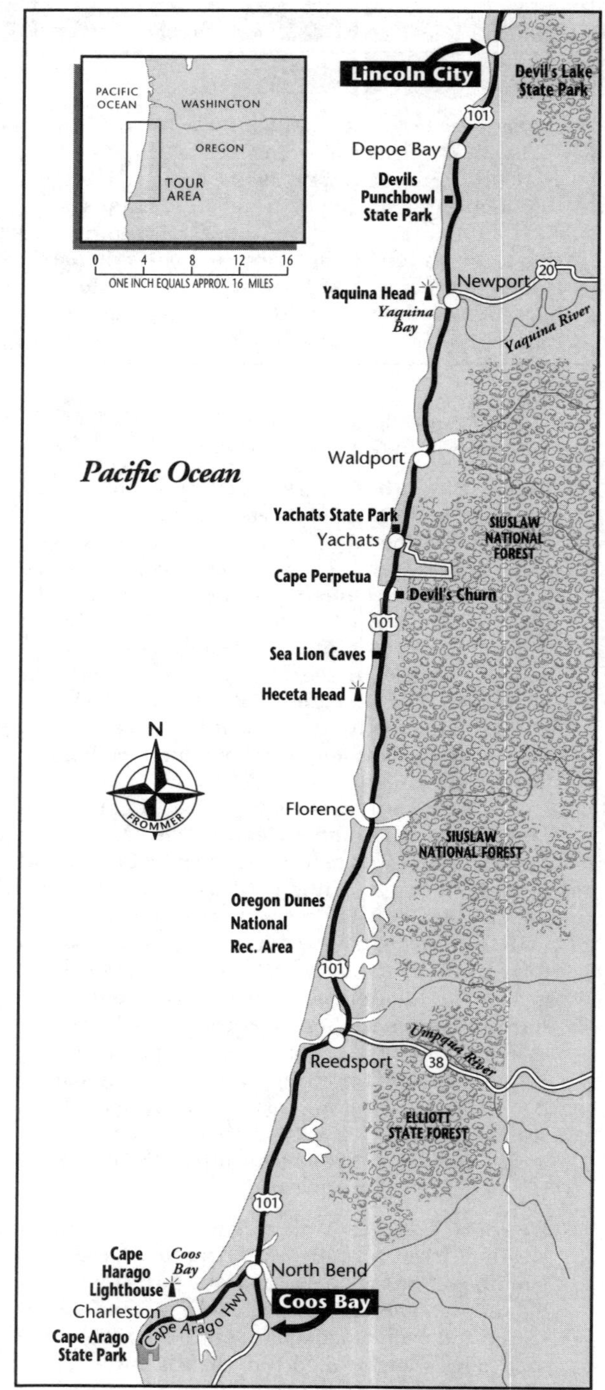

summer months) and outstanding views.

Bay Boulevard, Newport's historic waterfront district off US 101, is lined with shops and restaurants, side-by-side with canneries and working fishing boats. Many of the attractions on Bay Boulevard can be somewhat touristy, but worth noting is the **Wood Gallery,** 818 SW Bay Boulevard (tel 503/265-6843), which displays sculpture, furniture, musical instruments, and jewelry—all made from wood—as well as paintings and metal sculptures. Many local artists are represented in the store's collection. Just south of the impressive bridge that takes US 101 across Yaquina Bay you will find the **Mark O Hatfield Marine Science Center,** which is operated by Oregon State University. The center's aquariums and interpretive displays provide an excellent introduction to the sea's geology, ecology, and wildlife; there's even a tank where kids can touch a sampling of the slithering, swimming, and sticky marine life of the region.

Following a quarter-mile drive back toward US 101, you will find the more high-tech (and more crowded, particularly in the summer) **Oregon Coast Aquarium** (tel 503/867-3474). This well-designed facility includes a small theater that shows a film on whale migration, a display on the ecology of wetlands, a sandy beach with a wave machine, and a touch tank for kids. On the way back to US 101, you will also pass the **Rogue Ale Brewery Tasting Room,** which dispenses a different kind of introduction to the area. The brewery has become an institution along the central coast of Oregon, with its line of imaginatively named microbrews. The tasting room gives visitors a chance to sample standard brews and seasonal specialties.

Continue south on the coast highway until you reach:

4. **Waldport.** The small, unassuming building at the foot of the Alsea Bay Bridge, just as you enter Waldport, is the **Alsea Bay Bridge Interpretive Center.** This delightful center offers a history of the area from its settlement by Native Americans to the arrival of white settlers and the establishment of sawmills, canaries, fishing fleets, rail lines, and bridge construction (the most recent being the rebuilding of the Alsea Bay Bridge in 1991). Here, you can get an idea of the effort that went into creating the roadway that has carried you on your travels. Southbound again, you will enter:

5. **Yachats** (pronounced YAH-hots), a town which calls itself the Gem of the Oregon Coast. Yachats is indeed a fine thing to behold—small but sophisticated, with a great little cove and adjoining beaches. Park your car anywhere; you can walk the length of town in a matter of minutes. Plan to stop in at **Clark's Market,** in the center of the three-block business district on US 101, to pick up picnic supplies and other necessities. While you are there,

you can drop in at the tourist information center next door, where a helpful staffer is on hand to answer questions or dispense information.

One of the best spots to enjoy a picnic lunch is **Yachats State Park,** two blocks toward the sea on Ocean View. You can picnic on the wide lawn overlooking the inlet, or take the stairs to the rocky shoreline and its impressive collection of beached driftwood and tidepools. From this vantage point, you can see the hills above Yachats spill into the coastline, dwarfing the town.

Take a Break

One of the joys of driving the Oregon Coast is finding pleasant surprises where you might not expect them. **La Sere,** 2nd and Beach Sts (tel 503/547-3420), is one of those rare discoveries. A modern but welcoming interior offers a pleasant rest from the road. Seafood dishes are a mainstay, but carefully prepared meats complement the menu. Entrees range from $11 to $21.

Driving south out of Yachats, you are confronted with another set of choices about 2 miles south of town. Your first option is to turn left at the sign for:

6. **Cape Perpetua.** The 1-mile drive leads to a high bluff overlook and a spectacular, hawk's-eye view of the mountain, sea, and coastal terrain. If the coastal clouds have lifted for the afternoon, you can see for miles and miles. Short hiking trails along the cape begin from the parking lot and the overlook.

   Alternately, you can explore the clearly marked 19-mile, 45-minute loop drive that takes you back to Yachats and US 101, through the heart of **Suislaw National Forest,** or turn right off the highway and into the parking lot at the sign for the **Devil's Churn.** At one end of the lot, a paved path leads down the bluff, where a long slit in the rocky coast has created a whirling, frothing "cauldron" of sea water. The end of the trail lands you on a table-flat section of rocky shoreline.

   If you decide to spend the night here, there's a lovely inn about 6 miles south of Devil's Churn (look for the sign at the side of the highway). The **Oregon House,** 94288 US 101 (tel 503/547-3329), is a former estate with 5 buildings and 10 individually decorated and moderately priced units. The secluded grounds offer great views of the shoreline, and a lighted path leads down to the beach.

   Continuing south, you will encounter perhaps the most scenic stretch of the coast—wild and little-developed, with plenty of well-marked vista points to take it all in. On a turnout approximately 10 miles south of Yachats, you will come upon:

7. **Sea Lion Caves** (tel 503/547-3111), the only mainland rookery for the Stellar Sea Lion between central California and the Bering Sea. (Signs proclaim that it is the largest sea cave in North America.) An observation deck allows you to see the animals outside on a rock ledge during the spring and summer, but it's even more fun to take the elevator down to the 125-foot-high sea cave to see the animals nesting on rocks in the cavernous room. The sea-lion bulls can weigh up to 1,500 pounds, and they cut an impressive profile. You can also spot a variety of nesting birds in the cave. From one underground vantage point, you can get a clear view of the **Haceta Head Lighthouse** perched on a sea-coast promontory. The Spanish colonial–style Coast Guard lighthouse was built in 1894 and is said to be the most photographed lighthouse in the world. Southward again on US 101, you continue to:

8. **Florence.** If you are weary of being on the move, the town of Florence is a good spot to recharge. The restaurants and shops along Bay Street are quaint without being too touristy. **Catch the Wind Kite Shop,** 1251 Bay St (tel 503/997-9500), is a good place to find just the right flyer for a sea breeze and a wide beach. All manner of kites, including sporty stunt kites, are available in countless shapes and colors. Down the street, **Incredible, Edible Oregon,** at 1350 Bay Street (tel 503/997-7018), offers made-in-Oregon products and produce including wine, woodcrafted items, clothing, and books.

   In the town of Reedsport, 21 miles south of Florence, you will find the **Oregon Dunes Forest Service Information Center,** at the intersection of US 101 and OR 38 (tel 503/271-3611). This is the gateway to the **Oregon Dunes National Recreation Area.** The center features interpretive exhibits and dispenses information about dune buggy rides, camping, beachcombing, fishing, and hikes in the area as well as interpretive programs offered by the Forest Service.

   In addition, there are great opportunities for bird-watching a few miles east on OR 38. The highway follows the Umpqua River, and just off US 101 you find yourself in a beautiful river valley, with sheer cliffs rising on the other side of the Umpqua. Great blue herons, egrets, and ospreys ply the valley air currents. In addition, stately elk make their home in this area. (Clearly marked wildlife viewing areas with information boards dispense wildlife facts and figures.) Fishermen will find shad, smallmouth bass, steelhead, and coho and chinook salmon in the Umpqua River.

Should you decide to spend the night along the Umpqua, a wonderful place to stay is the **Salbasgeon Inn,** situated 7 miles east on OR 38 (tel 503/271-4831). The moderately priced motel is on the banks of the river, and is a relaxing spot for bird-watching, fishing, or just watching the river flow outside your window.

As you continue south from Reedsport, US 101 leaves the coast to swing around the Oregon Dunes National Recreation Area, so the drive is less scenic along this stretch. About 27 miles south of Reedsport is the town of:

9. **North Bend.** If you choose, you can stop by the visitors center in town at 1380 Sherman Ave (tel 503/756-4613) for directions to the nearby Coos County Historical Museum or to find out where the best antique stores are in the business district, which has retained its small-town character.

Look for the clearly marked signs on Virginia Street and US 101 in North Bend and follow the Cape Arago Hwy to Charleston Harbor. Six miles past Charleston Harbor, along a winding country road, you'll reach **Cape Arago State Park.** The park has a protected beach for swimming (a rarity on the rugged coastline), views of the Cape Arago Lighthouse, a beautiful botanical garden, scenic picnic areas, and short hiking paths. On the horseshoe-shaped reef just offshore, you can see a sea lion breeding and resting ground. The constant barking of the sea lions adds a natural "soundtrack" to the park. From the park follow the Cape Arago Hwy back to US 101 and then south a few miles into:

10. **Coos Bay.** The three cities of North Bend, Coos Bay, and Charleston form the largest metropolitan region on the Oregon Coast. What the area lacks in scenic value, it makes up for with conveniences such as retail stores, coffeehouses, and a good number of restaurants.

Take a Break

A Coos Bay culinary favorite, **Kum Yon's,** 835 S Broadway (tel 503/269-2662), is always bustling. The eclectic marriage of Chinese, Japanese, and American cuisine is pulled off admirably and offers a nice change from the standard seafood served at many restaurants along the coast. Entree prices range from $7 to $14.

Coos Bay is a decades-old working timber and wood town. Some of the original character can be discovered by dropping in the **Bay Area Visitors Center,** Commercial St and US 101 (tel 503/269-0215), to pick up a walking tour map with numbered sites including the Elk's Temple, the Methodist Hospital, several Victorian homes, and the Tioga and Chandler Hotels. The boardwalk in front of the center also has interpretive exhibits.

THE COLUMBIA RIVER GORGE

Start	Portland, OR
Finish	Vancouver, WA
Distance	Approximately 165 miles
Time	1½ days
Highlights	Spectacular waterfalls; volcanic cliffs; forested trails; second-largest river in the United States; highest mountain in Oregon; Bonneville Dam; apple, pear, and cherry orchards; windsurfing; historic towns on the Oregon Trail; Gorge artifacts

It's not hard to understand why much of the Columbia River Gorge has been designated a National Scenic Area. Beautiful trails wind through the shady forests, and waterfalls cascade in profusion as the creeks and streams that flow from Larch Mountain and Mount Hood (at 11,235 feet, the highest point in Oregon) flow toward the broad Columbia. The Columbia is the second-largest river in the country and the only sea-level break in a mountain range that extends from northern California to Canada. The sheer basalt cliffs that rise above the river reveal a dramatic geologic history of volcanic eruptions and immense floods.

I-84 runs beside the river on the Oregon side; WA 14 follows the Washington shore. Historic US Scenic Highway 30, which parallels I-84 for 22 miles, is the preferred route for a more leisurely trip and close views of the falls and greenery. This tour includes all three roads.

For additional information on lodgings, restaurants, and attractions in the region, look under specific cities in the listings portion of this chapter.

From Portland, drive I-84 east about 20 miles to Corbett and exit 22, the turnoff to:

1. **US Scenic Highway 30,** a winding road edged by mossy stone walls. The road, cut into the steep cliffs of the Gorge between 1913 and 1915, is listed on the National Register of Historic Places. Taking exit 22 will place you on a hill road that travels to a fork. Turn left; this road becomes US 30, heading east.

   The Scenic Highway rises from river level up 720 feet to:

2. **Crown Point,** Stop here for a panoramic overview of the river and forest and, on the north side of the Gorge, Mount St Helens and Mount Adams. The stone building on Crown Point is **Vista House,** built in 1918 to honor Oregon pioneers. It has maps, brochures, and a gift shop.

   Continue on the Scenic Highway for a little less than 2½ miles to arrive at the parking area for **Latourell Falls.** A two-mile scenic trail curves up the hill through tall trees and past ferns and wildflowers to the 100-foot falls.

   More accessible from the road is **Shepperd's Dell,** east of Latourell on the Scenic Highway. A paved path, beside a low, moss-covered wall, leads to these pretty falls.

   The next stop along the Scenic Highway is **Bridal Veil Falls State Park,** which is located on a bluff high above the river. In the spring, meadows of blue camas flowers bloom; the roots of these flowers were once a staple of the Native American diet. The park has picnic tables, rest rooms, and a paved trail with wheelchair access.

   You will pass **Wahkeena Falls** on your way to the showpiece of the Gorge:

3. **Multnomah Falls.** With a drop of 620 feet, Multnomah is the fourth-tallest waterfall in the United States. Interpretive signs at the base of the falls explain the history, botany, and geology of the region. A partially paved trail leads to the top of the falls and a dizzying view from an observation platform. (If you're hungry, there are snacks and meals available in Multnomah Falls Lodge.)

   A mile east of Multnomah Falls is the **Oneonta Gorge Botanical Area,** where wildflowers grow on the banks of a narrow ravine. After Oneonta on US 30 you will come to yet another falls, **Horsetail,** and then **Ainsworth State Park,** where the portion of US 30 officially designated as a Scenic Highway ends.

   Join I-84 at this point and drive east for 5 miles to:

4. **Bonneville Dam.** Bonneville is the oldest dam on the river (operating since 1938) and it provides much of the power for the region. There's a visitors center, and self-guided tours are available daily.

   One mile east of Bonneville, **Eagle Creek Trail** rises beside a rippling brook toward the heart of the inner gorge. It's a two-mile walk through the forest to lovely **Punchbowl Falls,** and six miles to **Tunnel Falls,** which drops in a misty veil over a cavern.

   From Eagle Creek Trail, drive 23 miles east on

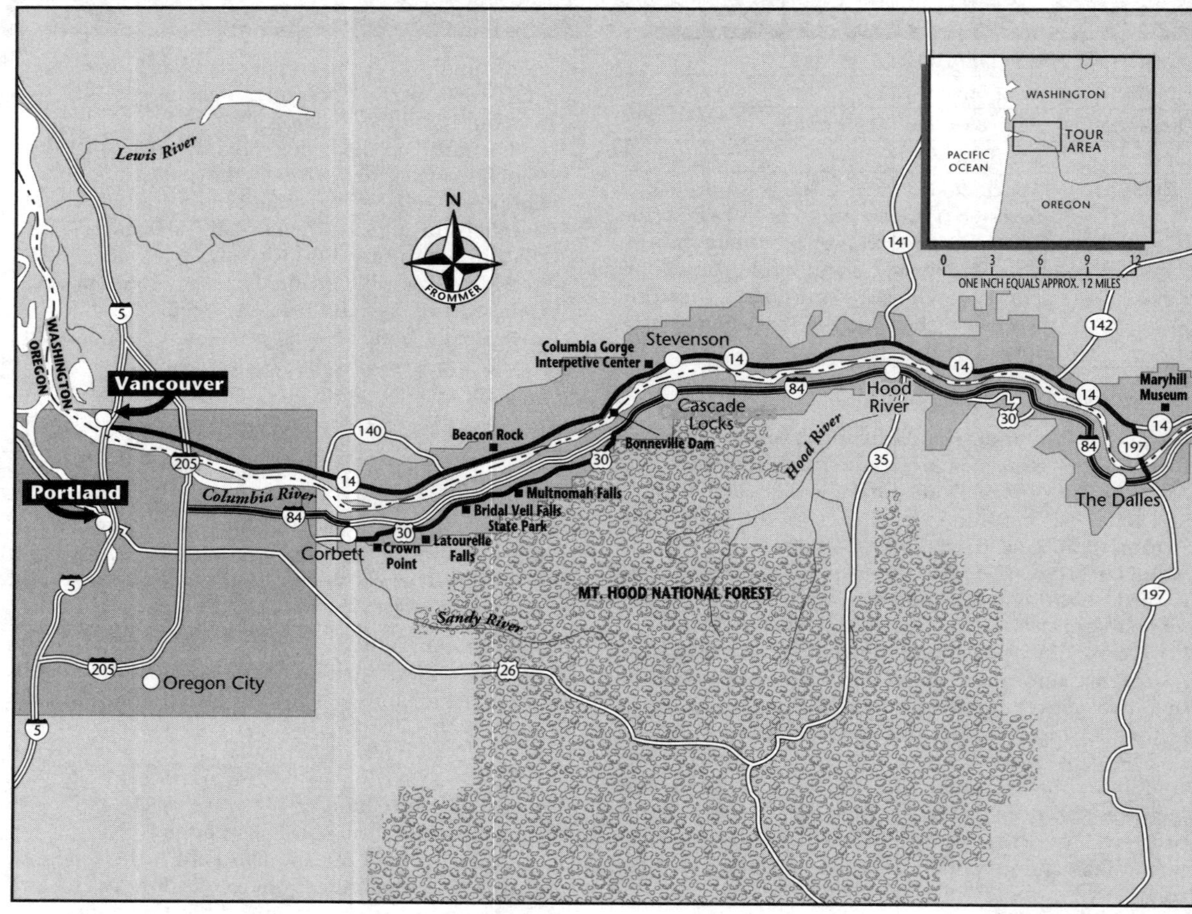

I-84 to the town of Hood River. Along the way you'll pass **Cascade Locks,** which has a historical museum and marine park. Next to the Locks is the **Bridge of the Gods,** which, according to Native American legend, is on the site of an ancient stone bridge used by the gods. The present structure was built in 1926. The town of Cascade Locks was named for the shipping locks that were constructed here in 1896, allowing boats to navigate the river's rapids. The town is now headquarters of the sternwheeler *Columbia Gorge,* which offers narrated river cruises in the summer.

From I-84, take exit 64 at:

5. **Hood River** and follow the signs a short distance to **Port Marina Park.** The **Hood River Visitors Center,** located in the park, offers maps and brochures. Next to the center is the **Hood River County Historical Museum** (tel 503/386-6772), which offers an interesting look at life on the river, from early Native American settlements to pioneer days.

Hood River is a small town with a big reputation. Long known for its apple and pear orchards, in recent years it has gained renown as the windsurfing capital of the world. Thanks to the constant winds of the Columbia Gorge, windsurfers skim the river's waves like hundreds of colorful birds. Port Marina Park is the most popular site. Hood River is also becoming famous for its microbreweries and wineries.

Take a Break

Purple Rocks Art Bar and Cafe, 606 Oak St (tel 503/386-6061), is a casual, light, and airy eatery. The menu features huge salads, sandwiches, soups, and grilled meats. All ingredients are fresh and organically grown, and there's a small patio for outdoor eating. Lunch prices range from $3.25 to $7.50.

The fruit orchards outside of town draw hordes of visitors in spring, when some 15,000 acres of trees explode with pink and white blooms. (With snow-capped Mount Hood rising behind them, they're a photographer's dream.) Festivals take place in spring and fall to celebrate the area's abundant crops. The old-fashioned **Mount Hood Railroad** offers orchard tours in vintage train cars. The refurbished depot is listed on the National Register of Historic Places.

East of Hood River you're on the dry side of the Cascade Range, with the lush green forests behind you; wheat fields and sagebrush lie ahead. From Hood River, drive 24 miles east on I-84 and take exit 84 to:

6. **The Dalles,** a historic town on the Oregon Trail. This was the end of the overland trail, where pioneers were faced with two options, both of them dangerous: Load their covered wagon onto a raft and float it down the Columbia, or take the southern land route around Mount Hood's steep shoulders.

From exit 84, follow 2nd St to **The Dalles Convention and Visitors Bureau,** 404 W 2nd St (tel 503/296-2231), and pick up a walking-tour map and brochures. Adjacent to the Visitors Center is the original **Wasco County Courthouse,** now a museum. The restored building looks as it did in 1858, when Wasco was the largest county in the United States, covering 130,000 square miles from Oregon to Wyoming.

Three blocks away, at W 3rd and Lincoln Sts, stands the historic **St Peter's Landmark.** The steeple on this red-brick Gothic revival church rises 176 feet and is topped by a cross and a rooster weathervane that can be seen from all over town.

In 1850, an Army post was established here (it was later named Fort Dalles); the remains of that post can be seen at 15th and Garrison Sts. The original Surgeon's Quarters, today the **Fort Dalles Museum,** contains memorabilia from those early frontier days.

Cherry orchards thrive near The Dalles, and a cherry festival is held here every spring. The area is also noted for its wildflower displays, especially west of town at Rowena Crest. The Nature Conservancy maintains the **Tom McCall Preserve** on this grassy plateau; there are guided walks when the flowers are in bloom and the hillsides blaze with color. The plateau, high above the river, provides broad views of the Gorge and mountains.

Leaving The Dalles, head north across the bridge that spans the Columbia to Washington State. For an interesting side trip, if additional time is available, turn east on WA 14 and travel 20 miles to **Maryhill Museum.** The museum, perched on a windswept cliff above the river, maintains an excellent collection of sculptures by Auguste Rodin. A nearby replica of England's **Stonehenge,** built as a World War I memorial, is another point of interest.

If not taking the side trip, turn west on WA 14 and drive about 44 miles to Stevenson. One mile west of the town of Stevenson, turn right at the sign to Skamania Lodge and:

7. **Columbia Gorge Interpretive Center.** Stop at the impressive new Center, which overlooks the river and forest, for a glimpse of the history of the Gorge. On display are an immense fishing wheel and a sawmill, a room full of Japanese immigrants' artifacts, petroglyph replicas, a fascinating collection of Asian art and furniture, the world's largest rosary collection, and more.

If you're looking for an overnight stop, you might try the **Skamania Lodge,** PO Box 189, Stevenson, WA 98648 (tel 509/427-7700 or toll free 800/221-7117). Its comfortable and moderately priced rooms have river and forest views and the luxurious lodge/conference center is full of amenities.

Take a Break

The restaurant at **Skamania Lodge** (tel 509/427-7700), on the hillside above the Interpretive Center, overlooks a field of wildflowers and the Columbia River, with the cliffs of Oregon rising beyond. Excellent Northwest cuisine, focusing on fresh local ingredients and prepared in an open kitchen, is featured. Dinner entrees range from $12 to $20.

From Stevenson, head west on WA 14, driving about 45 miles to:

9. **Vancouver, WA.** One of the landmarks you will notice on the way is **Beacon Rock.** A trail winds up to the summit of this 800-foot-high volcanic remnant, where you're rewarded with stunning views up and down the river. **Beacon Rock State Park** has a picnic area and playground.

From WA 14, turn right on Grand Blvd, go about 1 mile to 5th St, and turn left. Continue on 5th St to **Fort Vancouver National Historic Site,** 1501 E Evergreen Blvd. This was the headquarters for the Hudson's Bay Company trading post in the mid-1800s. Visitors may tour the partially reconstructed fort and watch volunteers demonstrate frontier skills. A visitors center and museum stand on the hill above the fort.

Across the road is **Officers' Row,** the oldest neighborhood in the Northwest. This group of 21 gracious Queen Anne–style homes once housed the likes of Ulysses S Grant; now most of them have been turned into condos or office buildings. Top-quality craft items are sold in the Folk Art Center in the Grant House.

Take a Break

Sheldon's Cafe, 1101 Officers' Row (tel 360/699-1213), offers light but filling lunch fare Tues–Fri. Specialties include unusual sandwiches such as fried eggplant and grilled chicken-apple sausage. Several tables on the veranda and garden patio are available in warm weather. Lunch entrees are $4 to $7.

Other points of interest in Vancouver are the **Pearson Air Museum,** 1105 E 5th St; **Covington House,** 4208 Main St (one of the oldest remaining log cabins in the area); **Esther Short Park**, 8th and Esther Sts (Washington's first public square); and **Columbia Arts Center,** 400 W Evergreen Blvd. The Arts Center houses most of the city's visual and performing arts organizations and has a continuing schedule of art exhibits, plays, and concerts.

To return to the starting point of the tour, it's a direct route across the Columbia River on I-5 from Vancouver to Portland.

Oregon Listings

Albany

See also Corvallis

Albany's charms include more than 500 historic homes, churches, and buildings. Visitors can take a tour of 10 covered bridges nearby. **Information:** Albany Visitors Association, 300 SW 2nd Ave, PO Box 965, Albany, 97321 (tel 541/928-0911).

MOTELS

Best Western Pony Soldier Motor Inn
315 Airport Rd SE, 97321; tel 541/928-6322 or toll free 800/528-1234; fax 541/928-8124. Exit 234A off I-5 S, exit 234 off I-5 N. A well-maintained motel convenient to I-5. Caters to business travelers. **Rooms:** 72 rms. CI open/CO noon. Nonsmoking rms avail. Nicely furnished rooms. **Amenities:** A/C, cable TV w/movies, refrig, dataport. Executive rooms offer microwaves, coffeemakers, robes, toiletries, and recliners. Hair dryers available at front desk. **Services:** **Facilities:** 12 Whirlpool, washer/dryer. Pleasant courtyard pool. **Rates (CP):** $59–$75 S; $62–$79 D. Extra person $5. Children under age 12 stay free. Parking: Outdoor, free. AE, DC, DISC, MC, V.

Holiday Inn Express
100 Price Rd SE, 97321; tel 541/928-5050 or toll free 800/928-5657; fax 541/928-4665. Off I-5, exit 233. New, well-furnished property convenient to freeway, downtown, county fairgrounds, and small airport. **Rooms:** 78 rms. Executive level. CI 1pm/CO 1pm. Nonsmoking rms avail. **Amenities:** A/C, satel TV w/movies. Some units w/fireplaces. Executive and king minisuites include wet bars, coffeemakers, and mini-refrigerators; executive suites also have spa tubs. Most rooms have dataports. **Services:** Fax service available. Free morning newspaper in lobby. Free use of bikes. **Facilities:** 75 Whirlpool, washer/dryer. Private aircraft parking. **Rates (CP):** $64–$79 S; $69–$83 D. Extra person $7. Children under age 19 stay free. Parking: Outdoor, free. AE, CB, DC, DISC, ER, JCB, MC, V.

Valu Inn
3125 Santiam Hwy SE, 97321; tel 541/926-1538 or toll free 800/547-0106; fax 541/928-0576. Exit 233 off I-5. Inexpensive, clean motel close to freeway. Good for families on a budget. **Rooms:** 60 rms. CI 1pm/CO 11am. Nonsmoking rms avail. Poor soundproofing in rooms means freeway noise seeps in. **Amenities:** A/C, cable TV w/movies. Clock radios available. **Services:** **Facilities:** Washer/dryer. **Rates:** Peak (June 15–Oct 15) $36 S; $44 D. Extra person $6. Children under age 12 stay free. Lower rates off-season. Parking: Outdoor, free. AE, DISC, MC, V.

Ashland

An eclectic town of Victorian homes and museums, widely known for its Tony Award–winning Oregon Shakespeare Festival (held from mid-February through October). Home of Southern Oregon State College. **Information:** Ashland Convention and Visitors Bureau, 110 E Main St, PO Box 1360, Ashland, 97520 (tel 541/482-3486).

HOTELS

Columbia Hotel
262½ E Main St, 97520; tel 541/482-3726. 1½ blocks from Shakespearean theater. Comfortable and well-maintained 1910 hotel with original architectural features. Congenial owner wants to preserve ambience without gentrification. No elevator. **Rooms:** 24 rms. CI 1pm/CO 11am. No smoking. Sinks in every room. Four rooms have private baths; other accommodations have toilets and showers down the hall. **Amenities:** No A/C, phone, or TV. **Facilities:** Grand piano in lobby for guest use. **Rates:** Peak (June 5–Oct 10) $32–$85 S or D. Extra person $6. Children under age 13 stay free. Min stay peak. Lower rates off-season. Parking: Outdoor, free. Closed Nov 1–20. MC, V.

Mark Antony Hotel
212 E Main St, 97520; tel 541/482-1721 or toll free 800/926-8669; fax 541/488-0649. 1 block from Shakespearean theater. Within walking distance to most Ashland attractions, this nine-story, aging, landmark hotel needs a renovation. Rates are high given the condition of the building and rooms. **Rooms:** 65 rms and stes. CI 4pm/CO noon. Nonsmoking rms avail. Rooms are basic, worn, but clean. **Amenities:** A/C. No TV. **Services:** Masseur. Complimentary

coffee and tea in lobby. On-site restaurant offers guests 15% discounts on meals. **Facilities:** 1 restaurant, 1 bar (w/entertainment). Pool poorly maintained. Bicycles can be delivered to hotel. **Rates:** Peak (June 6–Oct 9) $64–$72 S; $82 D; $82 ste. Children under age 12 stay free. Lower rates off-season. Parking: Outdoor, free. AE, CB, DC, DISC, MC, V.

MOTELS

Ashland Regency Inn

50 Lowe Rd, 97520; tel 541/482-4700 or toll free 800/482-4701. Exit 19 (Valley View Rd) off I-5. Older motel just off interstate has been attractively refurbished by new owner. Rates are a little high for type of accommodations. **Rooms:** 44 rms. CI 2pm/CO 11am. Nonsmoking rms avail. **Amenities:** A/C, cable TV. **Services:** Free local calls. Complimentary coffee and tea. **Facilities:** Full RV hookups. Rose garden. Off-site cottage available in downtown Ashland (five blocks from Shakespeare theater). **Rates:** Peak (May 15–Sept) $55 S; $60 D. Extra person $5. Children under age 6 stay free. Lower rates off-season. Parking: Outdoor, free. DISC, MC, V.

Best Western Heritage Inn

434 Valley View Rd, 97520; tel 541/482-6932 or toll free 800/528-1234; fax 541/482-8905. Exit 19 off I-5; 2 mi N of Ashland. This new, Tudor-style building, in a country setting, has a large and welcoming lobby decorated in a Shakespearean motif. **Rooms:** 53 rms and effic. CI 4pm/CO 1pm. Nonsmoking rms avail. Housekeeping needs attention. South-facing rooms have view of pastures, meadow, and mountains. **Amenities:** A/C, cable TV w/movies. Some units w/whirlpools. **Services:** **Facilities:** Whirlpool, washer/dryer. Festively decorated indoor pool is open 24 hours. Extensive, well-tended flower gardens around parking lot; a few picnic tables and small barbecue grill also on grounds. **Rates (CP):** Peak (June 15–Oct 15) $77–$91 S; $84–$98 D; $73–$91 effic. Extra person $7. Children under age 19 stay free. Lower rates off-season. Parking: Outdoor, free. AE, CB, DC, DISC, JCB, MC, V.

Palm Motel

1065 Siskiyou Blvd, 97520; tel 541/482-2636. Across from Southern Oregon State College. Small mom-and-pop motel with an appropriately funky 1940s green neon sign at entrance. Writers, teachers, playgoers, and artsy types from Ashland hide out here. **Rooms:** 13 rms and effic; 6 cottages/villas. CI 2pm/CO 11am. Nonsmoking rms avail. Thirteen uniquely decorated rooms, two with fully stocked kitchens. Gas odors accumulate in rooms with kitchens when weather precludes opening windows. Tired furnishings. **Amenities:** A/C, cable TV. No phone. 1 unit w/terrace. **Services:** Hosts in residence 24 hours. **Facilities:** Lawn games. Carefully tended lawn and flower beds, including a rose garden. Picnic areas with barbecue grills. **Rates:** Peak (Mem Day–Oct 3) $29–$50 S; $45–$70 D; $56–$76 effic; $85–$140 cottage/villa. Extra person $10. Lower rates off-season. Parking: Outdoor, free. MC, V.

Stratford Inn

555 Siskiyou Blvd, 97520; tel 541/488-2151 or toll free 800/547-4741, 800/452-5319 in OR; fax 541/482-0479. A three-story structure in a residential area adjacent to downtown, this property is well-kept on the exterior, but needs attention on the inside. Somewhat overpriced despite its good location. **Rooms:** 55 rms, stes, and effic. CI 1pm/CO 11am. No smoking. **Amenities:** A/C, cable TV, refrig. 1 unit w/whirlpool. **Services:** Babysitting. Young, generally unprofessional staff. **Facilities:** Whirlpool, washer/dryer. **Rates:** Peak (June 15–Sept) $87 S; $92 D; $135–$145 ste; $100–$110 effic. Extra person $5. Lower rates off-season. Parking: Outdoor, free. Ski packages avail. AE, CB, DC, DISC, MC, V.

Super 8 Motel Ashland

2350 Ashland St, 97520; tel 541/482-8887 or toll free 800/800-8000; fax 541/482-0914. Exit 14 off I-5. Attractive two-story motel with an English Tudor–style exterior and rooms that are better than average for an economy motel. Well-maintained grounds feature flower beds. Located across the road from a new shopping center and about a mile from the Shakespeare Theater. **Rooms:** 67 rms and stes. CI 2pm/CO noon. Nonsmoking rms avail. **Amenities:** A/C, cable TV. **Services:** Babysitting. $25 pet deposit. Copying service. Free local calls. **Facilities:** **Rates:** Peak (May 22–Sept 30) $51–$55 S; $60–$70 D; $86 ste. Extra person $4–$16. Children under age 17 stay free. Lower rates off-season. Parking: Outdoor, free. AE, CB, DC, MC, V.

Timbers Motel

1450 Ashland St, 97520; tel 541/482-4242; fax 541/482-8723. Across from Southern Oregon State College. The managers at this older but meticulously maintained mom-and-pop motel run a tight ship, carefully tending the small gardens and placing bouquets of fresh flowers in the lobby. High-season rates are an especially good value. **Rooms:** 29 rms and effic. CI open/CO 11am. Nonsmoking rms avail. Clean, coordinated decor, with new carpet in some rooms. **Amenities:** A/C. **Services:** Babysitting. **Facilities:** Cross-country and downhill skiing are 14 miles away. **Rates:** Peak (June–Oct 14) $51–$55 S; $60–$70 D; $70–$80 effic. Extra person $5. Children under age 1 stay free. Lower rates off-season. Parking: Outdoor, free. AE, CB, DC, DISC, MC, V.

INNS

Buckhorn Springs

2200 Buckhorn Springs Rd, 97520; tel 541/488-2200. 20 minutes E of Ashland in foothills of Cascade and Siskiyou Mt, exit 14 off I-5. 120 acres. Restored, century-old, rustic, mineral-springs resort listed on National Register of Historic Places. **Rooms:** 8 rms (1 w/shared bath); 6 cottages/villas (2 w/shared bath). CI 3-6pm/CO 11am. No smoking. Generously-sized rooms with claw-foot tubs in open area at side of bedroom. Fresh flowers, armoires, and individual decorations in each accommodation. Lodge rooms and five housekeeping cabins along the creek. **Amenities:** No A/C, phone, or TV. Some units w/terraces. **Services:** Masseur, babysitting, afternoon tea served. Rafting outfitters will pick up guests at lodge. **Facilities:** 1 restaurant (bkfst and dinner only), lawn games, guest lounge. Piano and fireplace in common room; large deck overlooks the creek. An herb/vegetable garden supplies the family-style restaurant. **Rates (BB):** Peak (June–Sept) $70 S w/shared bath, $100–$160 S w/private bath; $130–$170 D w/shared bath, $110–$120 D w/private bath; $330 ste; $150–$330 effic; $95 cottage/villa w/shared bath, $150–$330 cottage/villa w/private bath. Extra person $25. Children under age 8 stay free. Min stay peak. Lower rates off-season. Parking: Outdoor, free. Closed Nov–Mar. DISC, MC, V.

The Winchester Country Inn
35 S 2nd St, 97520; tel 541/488-1113 or toll free 800/972-4991; fax 541/488-4604. 1½ acres. Small, elegant inn occupying a historic residence surrounded by terraced English cottage gardens. Innkeepers Laurie and Michael Gibbs are knowledgeable, and go the extra mile for their guests. Located two blocks from the Shakespearean theaters. **Rooms:** 14 rms and stes; 2 cottages/villas. CI 3pm/CO 11am. No smoking. Accommodations are tastefully decorated with antiques and accented by pastel floral fabrics and coordinating paint and wallpaper. The Queen Anne room features a claw-foot tub. **Amenities:** A/C. No TV. Some units w/minibars, some w/terraces. Sherry in a crystal decanter delivered to each room. Nighttime treats such as chocolate-covered strawberries and chocolate truffles. **Services:** Masseur, babysitting, wine/sherry served. **Facilities:** 1 restaurant (dinner only; *see* "Restaurants" below), guest lounge. The inn has a popular restaurant, where you can dine on the garden terrace. **Rates (BB):** Peak (June–Oct 10) $125–$175 S; $130–$180 D; $180 ste; $180 cottage/villa. Extra person $40. Children under age 7 stay free. Lower rates off-season. Parking: Outdoor, free. Getaway Package (including meals) avail. AE, DISC, MC, V.

RESORT

Windmills Ashland Hills Inn & Suites
2525 Ashland St, 97520; tel 541/482-8310 or toll free 800/547-4747; fax 541/488-1783. Just off I-5 exit 14; go E on Ashland St (OR 66). 14 acres. Despite its semirural setting, with extensive grounds and views of the foothills of the Cascade and Siskiyou Mountains, this property is located just off the I-5 interchange. **Rooms:** 230 rms and stes. CI 4pm/CO 11am. Nonsmoking rms avail. Spacious rooms are decorated with custom floral drapes and bedspreads, lending a country feel. Most standard rooms have a private balcony: some have views of an appealing pool courtyard, others of the mountains. **Amenities:** A/C, cable TV. Some units w/terraces, some w/whirlpools. Coffee and newspaper delivered to rooms daily. **Services:** Babysitting. Full breakfast included for guests staying in the newer suites. **Facilities:** 2 restaurants, 1 bar, whirlpool, beauty salon, washer/dryer. Free use of bicycles. Within walking distance of nine-hole public golf course. **Rates:** Peak (June–Sept) $85–$115 S; $95–$105 D; $130–$250 ste. Extra person $6. Children under age 19 stay free. Lower rates off-season. Parking: Outdoor, free. Ski and romance packages avail. AE, DC, DISC, MC, V.

RESTAURANTS

Alex's Plaza Restaurant & Bar
35 N Main St; tel 541/482-8088. **Continental.** An Ashland institution located in a historic 19th-century building. Choose from several comfortable dining locales: a deck above Lithia Creek, a balcony facing the Plaza, or in front of the fireplace in the dining room. Featured entrees include New Zealand lamb and seafood stew. **FYI:** Reservations recommended. No smoking. **Open:** Mon 5–10pm, Tues–Sun 11:30am–10pm. **Prices:** Main courses $12–$19. AE, MC, V.

Ashland Bakery & Cafe
38 E Main St; tel 541/482-2117. On Ashland Plaza by Shakespearean Theater. **Eclectic.** A simple, no-nonsense cafe that has long been a favorite for breakfast, lunch, and dinner, as well as people-watching. You might encounter actors from the Shakespearean theater reviewing their lines over cappuccino and popular breakfast choices like tofu scramble or huevos rancheros. Fajitas and pastas also help keep the place packed all day. The restaurant is especially child-friendly, with high chairs available and changing tables in both men's and women's rest rooms. **FYI:** Reservations not accepted. Beer and wine only. No smoking. **Open:** Mon 7am–4pm, Tues–Sun 7am–9pm. Closed Feb 1–15. **Prices:** Main courses $9–$10. MC, V.

Chateaulin Restaurant and Wine Shoppe
50 E Main St; tel 541/482-2264. Near Plaza. **French.** Just down the path from the Shakespearean theater, this quaint bistro immerses diners in a French-country setting of exposed brick walls, dark beams, lace curtains, and flower-bedecked tables. The menu features fresh regional ingredients from Pacific salmon to Northwest lamb. A fine wine list features several rare labels from small vineyards. The adjoining full-service wine shop sells cheeses, pâtés, and picnic baskets to go. **FYI:** Reservations recommended. No smoking. **Open:** Peak (June–Oct) daily 5–9:30pm. **Prices:** Main courses $15–$24. AE, DISC, MC, V.

The Firefly
15 N 1st St; tel 541/488-3212. ½ block off Main St. **International.** Two young, innovative chefs from the San Francisco area have captivated diners with their signature cuisine, which chef/owner Tim Keller describes as "a growing garden, all connected, rising to the sun." Popular entrees,

enhanced with fresh spices from the world over, include grilled chipotle-marinated pork chop with yucca cakes and sauce mole, and Japanese-style salmon with soba noodles and vegetable sushi. Generous portions. **FYI:** Reservations recommended. Beer and wine only. No smoking. **Open:** Peak (June 1–Sept 30) dinner Wed–Sun 5–9pm. Closed Jan 21–Feb 7. **Prices:** Main courses $13–$23. MC, V.

Greenleaf Restaurant
49 N Main St; tel 541/482-2808. On Plaza by Ashland Creek. **Mediterranean.** A good choice for casual meals, either on the creekside decks or in the brick-walled dining room. The Greenleaf is known for its extensive breakfast menu—with choices like eggs Benedict or soufflés—as well as dinners featuring homemade soups, sandwiches, and pastas. Choose from one of Ashland's largest selections of microbrews and Oregon wines. Picnic baskets available. **FYI:** Reservations not accepted. Beer and wine only. No smoking. **Open:** Peak (June 1–Sept 7) daily 8am–9pm. Closed Jan 1–Feb 15. **Prices:** Main courses $5–$12. DC, MC, V.

Monet Restaurant and Garden
36 S 2nd St; tel 541/482-1339. **French.** Chef/owner Pierre Verger and his wife Dale created this homage to French painter Claude Monet. Set in a white clapboard house, the decor includes pastel colors, pink floral tablecloths, pink and white striped drapes, and prints of Monet's paintings. Light French cuisine is featured: omelet Niçoise (with eggplant, zucchini, tomatoes, and green pepper); roast duck; fillet of salmon and salmon mousse; and lamb tenderloin with watercress sauce. **FYI:** Reservations recommended. No smoking. **Open:** Peak (mid-June–Sept 30) lunch Tues–Sat 11:45am–1:45pm; dinner daily 5:30–9pm. Closed Jan. **Prices:** Main courses $13–$22. MC, V.

Pinehurst Inn
17250 OR 66; tel 541/488-1002. 23 mi E of Ashland. **Northwest.** This family-run eatery with an unhurried pace can be found in a rustic, secluded 1920s roadhouse on Jenny Creek. Breakfast features unusual omelettes and fresh pastries. Entrees might be sautéed chicken breast stuffed with herbed-cream cheese and toasted almonds, or salmon baked in parchment garnished with smoked tomatoes and rosemary mustard. Homemade jams and salsas. Classic 1930s ragtime plays in the background. **FYI:** Reservations recommended. Children's menu. Dress code. No smoking. **Open:** Daily 8:30am–9pm. **Prices:** Main courses $14–$20. DISC, MC, V.

Primavera Restaurant & Catering
241 Hargadine; tel 541/488-1994. At 1st St. **Eclectic.** Romance reigns supreme in this intimate restaurant located in a former Spanish-style church. A life-size mural of Ballet Russe dancers cavorts across the walls, and piano or harp music provides a soothing backdrop on weekends. The menu, which changes daily, might include thyme-roasted duck or dried tomato and green-olive polenta with vegetable ragout. Lighter fare is offered in the bistro and bar. **FYI:** Reservations recommended. Harp/piano. Children's menu. No smoking. **Open:** Peak (June 14–Oct 31) Wed–Sun 5–10pm. Closed Jan–Feb 15. **Prices:** Main courses $17–$25. MC, V.

Thai Pepper
84 N Main St; tel 541/482-8058. Along Ashland Creek. **Thai.** Located on the creek and across the street from the Shakespeare theaters, this is a popular choice for casual but intimate dining. Favorites include the Thai shrimp, with coconut-peanut sauce and fresh spinach, and any of the curries. **FYI:** Reservations recommended. Beer and wine only. No smoking. **Open:** Peak (June 15–Oct 15) lunch Tues–Sat 11:30am–2pm; dinner daily 5:30–9pm. **Prices:** Main courses $9–$15. MC, V.

The Winchester Country Inn
35 S 2nd St; tel 541/488-1115. 1 block from Shakespeare theaters. **International.** Casual but elegant dining set amid terraced gardens. The menu emphasizes seasonal products, from fresh fish to morels and other veggies. Game dishes—such as quail with fresh blueberry glaze—are highlighted; the signature dish is marinaded filet mignon. **FYI:** Reservations recommended. No smoking. **Open:** Dinner daily 5:30–9pm; brunch Sun 9:30am–1:30pm. Closed Jan 1–15. **Prices:** Main courses $16–$25. AE, DISC, MC, V.

ATTRACTIONS

Oregon Shakespeare Festival
15 S Pioneer St; tel 541/482-4331. Founded in 1935, the **OSF** is one of the oldest and largest professional regional theaters in the country. The company presents an 11-play repertory of Shakespearean, classical, and contemporary plays on three different stages: the outdoor Elizabethan Stage, the modern 600-seat Angus Bowmer Theatre, and the intimate 140-seat Black Swan. A presentation of Renaissance music and dance is given in the courtyard before each Elizabethan Stage performance. A museum houses costumes, props, and other Festival artifacts; in summer, concerts, lectures, and readings are given in adjacent Bankside Park **Open:** Feb 17–Oct 29 Tues–Sun. **$$$$**

Pacific Northwest Museum of Natural History
1500 E Main; tel 541/488-1084. This 300,000-square-foot museum opened in July of 1994. Visitors are given an access code or passport when they enter the exhibit hall; with these passports, they can test their environmental knowledge, touch the natural world through multisensory exhibits (incorporating sound, lighting, and even fragrance), and watch live animal shows. **Open:** Apr–Oct, daily 9am–5pm; Nov–Mar, daily 10am–4pm. Closed some hols. **$$$**

Schneider Museum of Art
1460 Fielder St; tel 541/552-6245. Located on the Southern Oregon State College Campus. Permanent collection includes paintings, drawings, original prints, and an extensive

collection of Native American baskets and ceremonial objects. Guided tours available. **Open:** Tues–Fri 11am–5pm, Sat 1–5pm. Closed some hols. **Free**

Ashland Vineyards and Winery
2775 E Main; tel 541/488-0088 or toll free 800/503-WINE. Sample award-winning cabernet, merlot, chardonnay, sauvignon blanc, Riesling, pinot gris, and Muller-Thurgau in the tasting room of Ashland's first winery. Winery tours and picnic area available. The winery will ship any purchases. **Open:** Tues–Sun 11am–5pm. Closed some hols. **Free**

Lithia Park
Off the downtown plaza; tel 541/488-5340. Wooded 100-acre park with shade trees, lawns, flowers, fountains, and ponds complete with white swans. During summer months, local concerts are presented weekly in the park's bandshell, as are performances of Ballet in the Park. Horse-drawn carriage rides, nature trails, volleyball and tennis courts, picnic area. **Open:** Daily 24 hours. **Free**

Ski Ashland
Exit 6 off I-5; tel 541/482-2897. Nestled in the heart of the Southern Oregon Alps, Mount Ashland offers quality skiing and a friendly, family atmosphere. The mountain features 23 runs (half of them black diamond); four lifts; a lodge complete with a cafeteria, lounge, ski check, and a family deck; a ski school; a rental and retail shop; and a recreational race department. Night skiing and snowboarding also available. Call 541/482-2754 for updates on snow conditions. **Open:** Thanksgiving to Apr 16, Sun–Wed 9am–4pm, Thurs–Sat 9am–10pm. **$$$$**

Astoria

This fishing town at the mouth of the Columbia River was the first permanent settlement west of the Rockies. **Information:** Astoria-Warrenton Area Chamber of Commerce, 111 W Marine Dr, PO Box 176, Astoria, 97103 (tel 503/ 325-6311).

MOTELS

Astoria Dunes Motel
288 W Marine Dr, 97103; tel 503/325-7111 or toll free 800/ 441-3319; fax 503/325-0804. At west end of town near Columbia River bridge. Rather spartan motel located in two adjacent buildings. Close to the highway, so noise is a problem. **Rooms:** 58 rms. CI 2pm/CO 11am. Nonsmoking rms avail. Rooms have river views that also take in the parking lot and boat storage yards. Rooms in the newer building have very pleasant furnishings. **Amenities:** Cable TV w/movies. No A/C. 1 unit w/whirlpool. **Services:** **Facilities:** Whirlpool. **Rates:** Peak (May 15–Sept 30) $48–$80 S; $58–$80 D. Extra person $7. Lower rates off-season. Parking: Outdoor, free. AE, CB, DC, DISC, MC, V.

Bayshore Motor Inn
555 Hamburg, 97103; tel 503/325-2205 or toll free 800/ 621-0641; fax 503/325-5550. North end of Young's Bay Bridge. Fairly ordinary motel with pleasant rooms, about a third of which have good views of the Columbia River. **Rooms:** 37 rms and effic. CI 2pm/CO 11am. Nonsmoking rms avail. One of the rooms overlooking Youngs Bay Bridge has a kitchenette, but no headboard, bathtub, or adequate drawer space. **Amenities:** Cable TV. No A/C. **Services:** Coffee, tea, hot chocolate in lobby all day. **Facilities:** Washer/dryer. Microwave in lobby. **Rates (CP):** Peak (June–Aug) $55–$60 S; $60–$70 D; $70 effic. Extra person $5. Children under age 10 stay free. Min stay special events. Lower rates off-season. Parking: Outdoor, free. Senior rates avail. AE, CB, DC, DISC, MC, V.

Crest Motel
5366 Leif Erickson Dr, 97103; tel 503/325-3141 or toll free 800/421-3141. On US 30 at east end of town. This relatively secluded motel consists of five buildings, ranging from 4 to 23 years old, located on a wooded rise at the far east edge of town. A good choice for a quiet overnight stay. **Rooms:** 40 rms. CI 2pm/CO noon. Nonsmoking rms avail. Many units have views of the river. **Amenities:** Cable TV. No A/C. Some units w/terraces. Most units have microwave and mini-refrigerator. **Services:** **Facilities:** Whirlpool, washer/dryer. **Rates:** Peak (May 15–Oct 15) $46–$83 S or D. Extra person $7. Children under age 10 stay free. Min stay special events. Lower rates off-season. Parking: Outdoor, free. AE, CB, DC, DISC, MC, V.

Red Lion Inn
400 Industry St, 97103; tel 503/325-7373 or toll free 800/ 547-8010; fax 503/325-8727. Overlooking boat basin at south end of Columbia River bridge. This large motel, surrounding a picturesque boat basin, is set far enough off the busy highway to be relatively quiet inside. **Rooms:** 125 rms. CI 3pm/CO noon. Nonsmoking rms avail. Most of the rooms are dark, but have views of the water. **Amenities:** Cable TV w/movies. No A/C. All units w/terraces. **Services:** **Facilities:** 350 1 restaurant, 1 bar (w/entertainment). The Seafarer Lounge, providing a variety of entertainment, is a popular spot. **Rates:** Peak (June–Sept) $69 S; $84 D. Extra person $15. Children under age 18 stay free. Lower rates off-season. Parking: Outdoor, free. AE, CB, DC, DISC, MC, V.

Shilo Inn
1609 E Harbor Dr, Warrenton, 97146; tel 503/861-2181 or toll free 800/222-2244; fax 503/861-2980. Convenient to US 101, this five-year-old motel is 4½ miles from the beach at Fort Stevens State Park. **Rooms:** 62 rms. CI 4pm/CO noon. Nonsmoking rms avail. Some rooms have pleasant view of wetlands off Youngs Bay. **Amenities:** A/C, refrig. Microwave. **Services:** Free morning newspaper. Hats and inexpensive swimsuits for sale in lobby. **Facilities:** 70 1 restaurant, 1 bar, sauna, steam rm,

whirlpool, washer/dryer. **Rates:** Peak (May–Sept) $89–$150 S or D. Extra person $10. Children under age 12 stay free. Min stay special events. Lower rates off-season. Parking: Outdoor, free. AE, CB, DC, DISC, ER, JCB, MC, V.

INN

Rosebriar Motel
636 14th St, 97103; tel 503/325-7427 or toll free 800/487-0224; fax 503/325-6937. Originally built in 1902 and elegantly restored in 1992. An appealing romantic getaway with traditional furnishings, modern (private) baths, and views of the Columbia River. Children are allowed, but not encouraged. **Rooms:** 11 rms and stes; 1 cottage/villa. CI 3pm/CO 11am. No smoking. **Amenities:** Cable TV. No A/C. 1 unit w/terrace, some w/fireplaces, some w/whirlpools. **Services:** Breakfast includes such items as scones, frittata, and quiche. Crib or rollaway bed available for one-time $5 charge. **Facilities:** 70 Guest lounge. **Rates (BB):** Peak (June 16–Sept 9) $65–$85 D; $105–$139 ste; $139 cottage/villa. Extra person $10. Children under age 2 stay free. Lower rates off-season. Parking: Outdoor, free. MC, V.

RESTAURANTS

Pier 11 Feed Store Restaurant
77 11th St; tel 503/325-0279. **American.** Built in a 19th century freight-depot-turned-feed-mill, Pier 11 is literally on the river, with magnificent views. The menu isn't so spectacular; dinners are predictable selection of steaks and seafood, most deep-fried or sautéed. In addition to a children's menu, the main menu listing has "small appetite fare" with smaller portions and prices. No pipes or cigars. **FYI:** Reservations recommended. Children's menu. **Open:** Peak (Mem Day–Oct 1) daily 7am–10pm. **Prices:** Main courses $11–$25. DISC, MC, V.

The Rio Cafe
125 9th St; tel 503/325-2409. **Mexican.** A funky interior—painted wood, floral vinyl tablecloths, and kitschy wall decor from tropical Mexico—adds to the charm. Co-owner Juan Chacon, from Nayarit on Mexico's Pacific coast, ensures the food is authentic (not Americanized) Mexican. Homemade corn tortillas, salsa fresca, lots of seafood specials. Good variety of Mexican beers and sodas. **FYI:** Reservations not accepted. Children's menu. Beer and wine only. No smoking. **Open:** Lunch Mon–Sat 11am–3pm; dinner Thurs–Sat 5:30–9pm. **Prices:** Main courses $7–$8. MC, V.

★ Ship Inn
1 2nd St; tel 503/325-0033. On the Columbia River at west end of town. **Seafood.** Overlooking the broad Columbia River, this busy fish-and-chips restaurant, self-billed as a family pub, is a local institution. Additional menu choices are sandwiches, English pasties, and pork sausages, which you can order à la carte or as a full dinner. **FYI:** Reservations not accepted. **Open:** Daily 11:30am–9:30pm. **Prices:** Main courses $5–$13; prix fixe $9–$17. DISC, MC, V.

ATTRACTIONS

Fort Clatsop National Memorial
OR 101; tel 503/861-2471. A unit of the National Park system, this memorial commemorates the Lewis & Clark Expedition of 1804–1806. The fort served as winter quarters for the corps from December 7, 1805 to March 23, 1806. During their stay the leaders reworked their history-making journals and Clark prepared many of his famous maps. The park staff presents audiovisual programs, exhibits, special talks and walks, and living history demonstrations in the summer. **Open:** Daily 8am–5pm. Closed Dec 25. **$**

Captain George Flavel Museum
441 Exchange St; tel 503/325-2203. Captain George Flavel, who made his fortune operating the first pilot service over the Columbia River Bar, built this Queen Anne Victorian mansion in 1885. Today the Flavel house, still the most elegant mansion in town, is preserved as a museum. The high-ceilinged rooms are filled with period furnishings that accent the home's superb construction. Of particular note is the ornate woodwork throughout the house. Price includes admission to the Heritage Museum and the Uppertown Firefighters Museum (see below). **Open:** Oct–Apr, daily 11am–4pm; May–Sept, daily 10am–5pm. Closed some hols. **$$**

Heritage Museum
1618 Exchange St; tel 503/325-2203. Regional history museum housed in Astoria's former City Hall, built circa 1904. The main gallery covers the Native American and pioneer inhabitants of the area, with an authentic Chinese Tong Altar and the tombstone of one of Oregon's first white inhabitants (an Englishman who died in 1814). The other two galleries look at logging, fishing, and transport in Clatsop County, and the ethnic immigrants who came to the North Coast to work in those industries. **Open:** May–Sept, daily 10am–5pm; Oct–Apr, daily 11am–4pm. Closed some hols. **$$**

Uppertown Firefighters Museum
30th St and Marine Dr; tel 503/325-2203. Housed in an old fire station, built in 1896 by prominent Portland architect Emil Schact. Exhibits include an 1878 Hayes horse-drawn ladder wagon, 1912 American LaFrance Chemical Wagon, and the fire house's original fire pole. **Open:** May–Sept, Fri–Sun 10am–5pm; Oct–Apr, Fri–Sun 11am–4pm. Closed some hols. **$$**

Columbia River Maritime Museum
1792 Marine Dr; tel 503/325-2323. One of the most extensive maritime collections on the West Coast. Visitors can tour the seagoing lighthouse *Columbia,* view the lower Columbia River from an observation deck, and explore the many maritime items and publications at the museum gift store. **Open:** Daily 9:30am–5pm. Closed some hols. **$$**

Baker City

Between the Wallowas and Elkhorns, this once-bustling 1860s gold-rush town still hosts an annual Miner's Jubilee. Home of the National Historic Oregon Trail Interpretive Center. Skiers love the powder at nearby Anthony Lakes Ski Area. **Information:** Baker County Convention and Visitors Bureau, 490 Campbell St, Baker City, 97814 (tel 541/523-3356).

MOTELS

Best Western Sunridge Inn

1 Sunridge Lane, 97814; tel 541/523-6444 or toll free 800/233-2368; fax 541/523-6446. West of city center at exit 304 off I-84. Well-kept motel with view of the Elkhorn Range. Popular with tour groups. **Rooms:** 156 rms and stes. CI 3pm/CO noon. Nonsmoking rms avail. Rooms are solid though not luxurious, and have all the necessary comforts. Some rooms have balconies with mountain views. **Amenities:** A/C, cable TV w/movies. Some units w/terraces, some w/whirlpools. **Services:** Babysitting. **Facilities:** 120 1 restaurant, 1 bar, spa, whirlpool. **Rates:** Peak (Apr–Sept) $56 S; $60 D; $150 ste. Extra person $4. Children under age 3 stay free. Lower rates off-season. Parking: Outdoor, free. AE, CB, DC, DISC, MC, V.

Eldorado Inn

695 Campbell St, 97814; tel 541/523-6494 or toll free 800/537-5756; fax 541/523-6494. In the north end of Baker City; exit 304 off I-84. An unusual Spanish Mission–style motel. The lobby has a colorful, tiled floor and rustic wood beams. Located near truck stop. **Rooms:** 56 rms and stes. CI 1pm/CO noon. Nonsmoking rms avail. The two largest rooms on the second floor, above the pool, are designated as honeymoon suites—mirrored walls and ceilings, dark furniture, noisy air conditioning. **Amenities:** A/C, cable TV w/movies, refrig. **Services:** Coffee and tea available all day. **Facilities:** Whirlpool. Guests can use microwave in lobby. **Rates:** $41 S; $44 D; $50 ste. Extra person $4. Children under age 12 stay free. Parking: Outdoor, free. Senior and corporate rates available. AE, DC, DISC, MC, V.

Friendship Inn

134 Bridge St, 97814; tel 541/523-6571 or toll free 800/932-9220; fax 541/523-9424. At the edge of town by Powder River. Very simple motel with clean, basic rooms. **Rooms:** 40 rms. CI 11am/CO 11am. Nonsmoking rms avail. **Amenities:** Cable TV. No A/C. A few rooms have refrigerators. **Services:** Free coffee in lobby. Free local calls. **Facilities:** Refrigerator and microwave in lobby available for guest use. **Rates:** Peak (June–Oct) $36–$46 S; $41–$51 D. Extra person $5. Children under age 5 stay free. Lower rates off-season. Parking: Outdoor, free. Senior and extended-stay rates avail. AE, DC, DISC, MC, V.

Quality Inn

810 Campbell St, 97814; tel 541/523-2242 or toll free 800/221-2222; fax 541/523-2242. At the edge of Baker City, just off I-84. This coral-stucco motel with red-tile roof has an Old West and Spanish Mission flavor. **Rooms:** 54 rms. CI 1pm/CO noon. Nonsmoking rms avail. Rooms for guests with disabilities have appropriate lift bars, but the door peephole is too high to be used from a wheelchair. **Amenities:** A/C, cable TV. Some rooms have refrigerators. **Services:** Babysitting. Coffee, tea, and fruit in lobby at all times. **Facilities:** 130 Guests have use of pool at Eldorado Inn across the road. Microwave in lobby for guest use. **Rates (CP):** $45 S; $49–$52 D. Extra person $5. Children under age 18 stay free. Parking: Outdoor, free. AE, CB, DC, DISC, JCB, MC, V.

RESTAURANTS

★ Jimmy Chan's Restaurant

1841 Main St; tel 541/523-5230. Downtown. **Chinese.** This unpretentious and popular eatery offers a wide array of Cantonese and Mandarin dishes, as well as some American standards. Both booths and tables are brightly lighted. Daily low-priced specials; children's and seniors' portions available. **FYI:** Reservations accepted. Dress code. Beer and wine only. **Open:** Mon–Thurs 11am–9pm, Fri–Sat 11am–10pm, Sun noon–9pm. **Prices:** Main courses $5–$10. MC, V.

The Phone Company Restaurant

1926 1st St (Downtown); tel 541/523-7997. **Continental.** From 1910 to 1954, the building was home to the telephone company. Today's dining area features high ceilings and white brick walls graced with photos of old Baker City. Service is prompt and helpful, and the clam chowder is outstanding. Specials, like smoked salmon and fettucine or garlic prawns, change daily. **FYI:** Reservations accepted. Dress code. Beer and wine only. No smoking. **Open:** Mon–Sat 11:30am–9pm. **Prices:** Main courses $9–$16. MC, V.

★ Sumpter Junction Restaurant

2 Sunridge Lane; tel 541/523-9437. **American/Mexican.** This old-fashioned country-style restaurant is named for a local mining district's historic railroad. A well-priced breakfast and steak and chicken dinners are brought to your red vinyl booth. It's worth a visit just to see the model train that runs around the entire main room, through miniature tunnels and past a frontier village. **FYI:** Reservations accepted. Children's menu. Dress code. Beer and wine only. No smoking. **Open:** Daily 6am–10pm. **Prices:** Main courses $7–$12. AE, DISC, MC, V.

ATTRACTIONS

Oregon Trail Interpretive Center

Exit 304 off I-84; tel 541/523-1843. Run by the Bureau of Land Management, this impressive center features living history presentations, exhibits, and multimedia displays on the Oregon Trail experience, mining the west, explorers and fur trade, Native American history, and the natural history of northeastern Oregon. The center grounds include an amphitheater, a re-creation of a pioneer encampment, a lode mine, and a 4.2-mile interpretive trail along the sagebrush steppe. **Open:** Daily 9am–5pm. Closed some hols. **Free**

Sumpter Valley Railway Co
Dredge Loop Rd; tel 541/894-2268. Historic Sumpter Valley steam train, complete with a 1915 gear-driven Heisler locomotive, a restored original clear-story coach, two observation cars, and a caboose. On its scenic five-mile run, the woodburning steam-powered train passes through an Oregon Wildlife Game Habitat preserve to the historic gold mining town of Sumpter, where you can see the "old dredging ship." Displays detailing the history of the railroad are at the rail yard. **Open:** Mem Day–Sept, Sat–Sun and hols. **$$$**

Bandon

The stormwatching capital of the world and one of the most charming towns on the coast. The cranberry harvest and festival is a fall highlight. Home of West Coast Game Park Safari, America's largest wild-animal petting park. **Information:** Bandon Chamber of Commerce, 300 SE 2nd, PO Box 1515, Bandon, 97411 (tel 541/347-9616).

MOTELS

Harbor View Motel
355 US 101, PO Box 1409, 97411; tel 541/347-4417 or toll free 800/526-0209; fax 541/347-3616. Located on the edge of the historic old town district, a short walk away from restaurants, shopping, and galleries. **Rooms:** 59 rms and effic. CI 3pm/CO noon. Nonsmoking rms avail. **Amenities:** A/C, cable TV w/movies, refrig. Some units w/terraces. **Services:** **Facilities:** Whirlpool. **Rates (CP):** Peak (July–Sept) $69–$82 S; $81 D; $104 effic. Extra person $5. Children under age 6 stay free. Lower rates off-season. Parking: Outdoor, free. Two-for-one discount in off season. AE, CB, DC, DISC, MC, V.

The Inn at Face Rock
3225 Beach Loop Rd, 97411; tel 541/347-9441 or toll free 800/638-3092; fax 541/347-2532. Off US 101. Although a little worn out, this motel offers solitude near the beach. **Rooms:** 65 rms, stes, and effic; 2 cottages/villas. CI 3pm/CO 11am. Nonsmoking rms avail. **Amenities:** Cable TV. No A/C. All units w/terraces, some w/fireplaces. **Services:** Babysitting. VCRs for rent. Fee for pets. **Facilities:** 9 50 1 restaurant, 1 bar, whirlpool, washer/dryer. The somewhat disheveled golf course is the only set of links in the area. **Rates:** Peak (May–Oct) $69–$99 S; $79–$109 D; $89–$119 ste; $89–$119 effic; $175–$225 cottage/villa. Extra person $10. Children under age 12 stay free. Min stay special events. Lower rates off-season. Parking: Outdoor, free. Golf, shopping packages avail. AE, DC, DISC, MC, V.

Sunset Oceanfront Accommodations
1755 Beach Loop Rd, 97411; tel 541/347-2453. With rooms built into a seaside bluff, this hotel lives up to its name. **Rooms:** 59 rms and effic; 3 cottages/villas. CI 4pm/CO 11am. Nonsmoking rms avail. Balconies offer great views of the setting sun and nearby rock formations. **Amenities:** Cable TV, refrig. No A/C. Some units w/terraces, some w/fireplaces. **Services:** **Facilities:** 1 restaurant (lunch and dinner only), 1 bar (w/entertainment), 1 beach (ocean), sauna, whirlpool, washer/dryer. **Rates:** Peak (May 15–Sept 30) $40–$100 S or D; $66–$100 effic; $110–$220 cottage/villa. Extra person $5. Lower rates off-season. Parking: Outdoor, free. Two-for-one off-season rates. AE, DISC, MC, V.

Table Rock Motel
840 Beach Loop Dr, 97411; tel 541/347-2700. Off US 101. This motel offers seaside lodging at a modest price. **Rooms:** 15 rms and effic. CI 2pm/CO 11am. Nonsmoking rms avail. **Amenities:** Cable TV. No A/C or phone. **Services:** **Rates:** Peak (May–Sept) $32–$63 S or D; $48–$63 effic. Lower rates off-season. Parking: Outdoor, free. DC, DISC, MC, V.

RESTAURANTS

★ **Andrea's**
160 Baltimore Ave; tel 541/347-3022. In Old Town. **Regional American.** With a welcoming cafe atmosphere, this restaurant offers homestyle specialties like potato-cheese enchiladas and feta cheese pizza. Local artists' work is displayed, and a jazz guitarist strums nightly. **FYI:** Reservations recommended. Jazz. Beer and wine only. No smoking. **Open:** Peak (Mem Day–Jan) daily 9am–9:30pm. **Prices:** Main courses $10–$19. No CC.

Bandon Boatworks
275 Lincoln SW; tel 541/347-2111. ½ mi W of Old Town. **Seafood/Steak.** A small two-room restaurant located on a wind-swept point where the Coquille River meets the sea. A salad bar and fresh bread start off the meal; mostly seafood entrees follow. Mexican specialties are featured on Sundays. **FYI:** Reservations recommended. Beer and wine only. **Open:** Lunch Tues–Sat 11:30am–2:30pm; dinner Tues–Sat 5–9pm, Sun noon–8:30pm. Closed Jan–Feb 15. **Prices:** Main courses $11–$24. AE, DC, DISC, MC, V.

★ **Harp's Restaurant**
130 Chicago Ave; tel 541/347-9057. **New American/Continental.** In the heart of Old Town, this eatery offers light treatments of fish, beef, and chicken. A specialty is pasta à la Harp (scampi with hot pepper and lemon sauce). The well-chosen wine list features mostly Oregon wines. **FYI:** Reservations recommended. Beer and wine only. No smoking. **Open:** Peak (June 1–Dec 31) daily 5–9:30pm. **Prices:** Main courses $12–$19. AE, CB, DC, MC, V.

Lord Bennett's Restaurant
1695 Beach Loop Rd; tel 541/347-3663. Off US 101. **Seafood/Steak.** A surprisingly sophisticated oasis on this particular stretch of coast, this restaurant offers unmatched views, prompt service, and delightful variations on the seafood theme. Highlights include sole stuffed with shrimp, ricotta, and herbs; and butter-garlic sautéed shrimp. Imaginative Sunday brunch. **FYI:** Reservations recommended. Country music/jazz. Children's menu. **Open:** Peak (June–Sept) lunch daily 11am–3pm; dinner daily 5–10pm; brunch Sun 11am–3pm. **Prices:** Main courses $12–$16. AE, CB, DC, DISC, MC, V.

ATTRACTION

West Coast Game Park Safari
OR 101; tel 541/347-3106. Billed as America's largest wild animal petting adventure, this outdoor, walk-through animal exhibition center has over 450 animals and birds spanning 75 different species. Visitors can pet baby animals and see an array of lions, tigers, snow leopards, bears, chimps, black panthers, cougars, lynx, bison, camels, zebras, elk and more. Special events and showings are also offered. **Open:** June–Aug, daily 9am–7:30pm; Mar–May and Sept–Nov, daily 9am–5pm. **$$$**

Beaverton

This bustling Portland suburb is called Oregon's Silicon Forest for its high-technology firms. Beaverton is home to Washington Square, one of the Northwest's largest shopping malls. **Information:** Washington County Convention and Visitors Bureau, 5075 SW Griffith Dr #120, Beaverton, 97005 (tel 503/644-5555).

HOTELS

Courtyard by Marriott
8500 SW Nimbus Dr, 97005; tel 503/641-3200 or toll free 800/321-2211; fax 503/641-1287. Elegantly decorated; spacious public areas, including lounge with fireplace. **Rooms:** 149 rms and stes. CI 3pm/CO noon. Nonsmoking rms avail. All rooms look out to a landscaped courtyard and gazebo. **Amenities:** A/C, dataport, voice mail. All units w/terraces. **Services:** Twice-daily maid svce. **Facilities:** 27 1 restaurant (bkfst and dinner only), 1 bar, whirlpool, washer/dryer. Lovely indoor pool has sliding glass doors that open to a grassy area. **Rates:** Peak (May–Sept) $70–$98 S; $78–$108 D; $98–$108 ste. Extra person $10. Children under age 12 stay free. Lower rates off-season. Parking: Outdoor, free. AE, DISC, MC, V.

Greenwood Inn
10700 SW Allen Blvd, 97008; tel 503/643-7444 or toll free 800/289-1300; fax 503/626-4553. Off OR 217. Contemporary Northwest architecture and art enhance this hotel, which recently underwent a $4 million upgrade. **Rooms:** 250 rms, stes, and effic. CI 3pm/CO noon. Nonsmoking rms avail. **Amenities:** A/C, refrig, dataport. Some units w/terraces, some w/fireplaces, some w/whirlpools. **Services:** Car-rental desk, babysitting. Free shuttle service within five-mile radius. **Facilities:** 2 850 2 restaurants (*see* "Restaurants" below), 2 bars (1 w/entertainment), games rm, sauna, whirlpool. Pavilion Bar and Grill offers fine dining and Sunday brunch amid an oasis of greenery and waterfalls, while renovated Wanigan Lounge serves Oregon microbrews on tap plus an eclectic array of pizzas. Beautifully landscaped courtyard swimming pool areas. Privileges at (and transportation to) nearby fully equipped health club. **Rates:** $86–$102 S; $96–$112 D; $170–$400 ste; $150–$220 effic. Extra person $10. Children under age 16 stay free. Parking: Outdoor, free. Special rates and amenities for corporate travelers. AE, DISC, MC, V.

MOTEL

Ramada Inn
13455 SW Canyon Rd, 97005; tel 503/643-9100 or toll free 800/272-6232; fax 503/643-0514. Conveniently located near the high-tech Beaverton area, it's also close to Washington Square mall shops and within 15 minutes of downtown Portland. **Rooms:** 143 rms, stes, and effic. CI 3pm/CO noon. Nonsmoking rms avail. Clean and comfortable rooms. **Amenities:** A/C, dataport, voice mail. **Services:** **Facilities:** 10 Whirlpool. **Rates (CP):** Peak (June–Sept) $65–$86 S or D; $125–$135 ste; $120 effic. Children under age 12 stay free. Lower rates off-season. Parking: Indoor/outdoor, free. AE, DISC, MC, V.

RESTAURANTS

★ **Hall Street Bar & Grill**
3775 SW Hall St; tel 503/641-6161. Corner of Cedar Hills Blvd. **Northwest.** Upscale and casual. You might encounter executives from Nike and Intel making deals here over mesquite-grilled salmon with lemon-vermouth butter, and key lime pie with coconut cream. Barbecued specialties are served on the large patio in summer. Lively bar, where there's Cambazola crostini to nibble. **FYI:** Reservations recommended. Jazz/reggae. Children's menu. Dress code. No smoking. **Open:** Mon–Fri 11:15am–10pm, Sat 5–10pm, Sun 4–9pm. **Prices:** Main courses $10–$18. AE, MC, V.

Pavillion Bar & Grill
In Greenwood Inn, 10700 SW Allen Blvd; tel 503/626-4550. At OR 217. **Northwest.** One of the most beautiful restaurants in the area. Chef Kevin Kennedy wraps prosciutto around sturgeon, sears it, and serves it in pinot noir jus with caramelized shallots, red potatoes, and shredded red chard. Great smoked salmon chowder. Relaxing atmosphere. Good Oregon wines. **FYI:** Reservations recommended. Jazz. Children's menu. **Open:** Mon–Thurs 6:30am–10pm, Fri 6:30am–11pm, Sat 7am–11pm, Sun 7am–10pm. **Prices:** Main courses $12–$22. AE, CB, DC, DISC, MC, V.

Swagat
4325 SW 109th Ave; tel 503/626-3000. Just off Beaverton–Hillside Hwy. **Indian.** Informal, with zero glamour, but serving the wonderful cuisine of India. Many Indian families eat here. Try delicious lamb shanks with eggplant, or a dosa, a long crisp crepe rolled around a vegetable curry—one feeds three people. Vegetarians can choose among nine entrees. **FYI:** Reservations not accepted. Beer and wine only. No smoking. **Open:** Lunch daily 11:30am–2:30pm; dinner daily 5–10pm. **Prices:** Main courses $7–$12; prix fixe $9–$12. AE, CB, DC, DISC, MC, V.

ATTRACTION

Cooper Mountain Vineyards
9480 SW Grabhorn Rd; tel 503/649-0027. Situated on top of an extinct volcano, this 75-acre vineyard enjoys especially rich soil. Although Cooper Mountain's pinot noir, chardonnay, and pinot gris have garnered awards, most of the grapes grown here are sold to other winemakers. Free guided tours and tastings. **Open:** May–Nov, Fri–Sun noon–5pm; Feb–Apr, Sat–Sun noon–5pm; or by appointment. **Free**

Bend

See also Sunriver

The state's fastest-growing city, Bend is at the heart of central Oregon's recreation wonderland: a half-hour from Mount Bachelor (the Pacific Northwest's largest ski resort) and gateway to white-water rafting and fishing on the Deschutes River, wilderness backpacking, snowmobiling, observatory stargazing, golfing, and more. Newberry National Volcanic Monument and the High Desert Museum are south of town. **Information:** Bend Chamber of Commerce, 63085 N US 97, Bend, 97701 (tel 541/382-3221).

MOTELS

Bend Riverside Motel
1565 NW Hill St, 97701; tel 541/389-2363 or toll free 800/228-4019; fax 541/388-4000. 5 blocks N of downtown, on the Deschutes River. Two separately managed motels located on same property and handled out of a shared office. On spacious grounds near scenic Mirror Pond and Deschutes River. **Rooms:** 188 rms, stes, and effic. CI 2pm/CO 11am. Nonsmoking rms avail. Accommodations vary widely from a simple, no-frills room to a kitchen-bedroom combo; some have river views. **Amenities:** A/C, cable TV w/movies. Some units w/terraces, some w/fireplaces. **Services:** **Facilities:** 1 15 Sauna, whirlpool, washer/dryer. **Rates:** $49–$69 S or D; $99–$110 ste; $69–$110 effic. Children under age 2 stay free. Parking: Indoor/outdoor, free. AE, DC, DISC, MC, V.

Best Western Entrada Lodge
19221 Century Dr, 97702; tel 541/382-4080 or toll free 800/528-1234; fax 541/382-4080. About 3½ mi W of Bend. A popular spot for downhill skiers, just 16 miles from Mount Bachelor. Although a 1990 forest fire consumed timber around this property, the Entrada was left standing and the setting is still nice. The lobby features a wood stove in a sunken fire pit. **Rooms:** 79 rms. CI 2pm/CO noon. Nonsmoking rms avail. **Amenities:** A/C, cable TV, dataport. 1 unit w/whirlpool. **Services:** **Facilities:** 25 Whirlpool, washer/dryer. The "skiers' spa" stays open until 10pm. **Rates (CP):** Peak (June–Sept) $49–$59 S; $55–$69 D. Extra person $5. Children under age 12 stay free. Min stay special events. Lower rates off-season. Parking: Outdoor, free. AE, CB, DC, DISC, MC, V.

Hampton Inn Bend
15 NE Butler Market Rd, 97701; tel 541/388-4114 or toll free 800/426-7866; fax 541/389-3261. On US 97 adjacent to Bend River Mall. Clean and comfortable, in a busy section of town. **Rooms:** 99 rms. CI 4pm/CO noon. Nonsmoking rms avail. **Amenities:** A/C, cable TV w/movies, dataport. **Services:** Fresh fruit and hot drinks available in lobby each evening. **Facilities:** 10 Whirlpool. The hospitality suite doubles as a small meeting room or guest room. **Rates (CP):** Peak (July–Sept) $50–$60 S; $55–$65 D. Children under age 18 stay free. Lower rates off-season. Parking: Outdoor, free. AE, CB, DC, DISC, MC, V.

Holiday Motel
880 SE 3rd St, 97702; tel 541/382-4620 or toll free 800/252-0121. On US 97 at Wilson. A friendly, clean, and well-priced motel on a busy highway in south Bend. **Rooms:** 25 rms, stes, and effic. CI 2pm/CO 11am. Nonsmoking rms avail. **Amenities:** A/C, cable TV w/movies. 1 unit w/fireplace. **Services:** Babysitting. **Facilities:** Whirlpool. **Rates (CP):** $30–$34 S; $38–$42 D; $65 ste; $65 effic. Parking: Outdoor, free. AE, DC, DISC, MC, V.

The Riverhouse
3075 N US 97, 97701; tel 541/389-3111 or toll free 800/546-3928; fax 541/389-0870. From the front, the Riverhouse just looks like a better-than-average strip motel, but out its back door, the Deschutes River flows through the property. Conveniently located across from the Bend River Mall and several restaurants. This is Bend's chief convention center. **Rooms:** 220 rms, stes, and effic. CI 4pm/CO noon. Nonsmoking rms avail. They aren't immaculate, but some respectable suites are available for budget-conscious travelers. Try to stay in a room facing the river. **Amenities:** A/C, cable TV w/movies, dataport, VCR, voice mail. All units w/terraces, some w/fireplaces, some w/whirlpools. **Services:** **Facilities:** 2 18 2 400 3 restaurants, 1 bar (w/entertainment), sauna, whirlpool, washer/dryer. Guests have been known to cast a fly and pull a trout out of the river. **Rates:** $53–$70 S or D; $85–$105 ste;

$76–$105 effic. Extra person $5. Children under age 6 stay free. Min stay special events. Parking: Outdoor, free. Rooms with river views cost $5 extra. AE, CB, DC, DISC, MC, V.

Sonoma Lodge
450 SE 3rd St, 97701; tel 541/382-4891 or toll free 800/800-8334. On US 97 5 blocks S of railroad overpass. Simple, reasonably priced single-level strip motel. Accommodating owners work hard at fulfilling guests' requests. **Rooms:** 17 rms, stes, and effic. CI 1pm/CO 11am. Nonsmoking rms avail. The four family units with kitchens are comfortable for up to six people each. **Amenities:** A/C, cable TV w/movies, refrig, dataport. Some units w/terraces, 1 w/fireplace. **Services:** Car-rental desk, babysitting. Continental breakfast includes lodge's freshly baked breads. **Facilities:** **Rates (CP):** Peak (June 15–Sept 15) $32–$45 S; $36–$59 D; $39–$69 ste; $39–$69 effic. Extra person $4–6. Children under age 4 stay free. Lower rates off-season. Parking: Outdoor, free. Bicycling and white-water rafting packages available. AE, CB, DC, DISC, MC, V.

LODGE

Rock Springs Guest Ranch
64201 Tyler Rd, 97701; tel 541/382-1957 or toll free 800/225-DUDE (3833); fax 541/382-7774. 8 miles NW of downtown Bend. 2,500 acres. Set in the beautiful, peaceful foothills of the Cascades, this wonderful guest ranch escape caters to week-long groups—mostly business retreats. Abundant wildlife on property. **Rooms:** 26 rms; 2 cottages/villas. CI 4pm/CO 11am. Nonsmoking rms avail. Clean and comfortable ranch cabins, with multiple units under one roof that can be joined to make larger quarters. **Amenities:** Refrig. No A/C, phone, or TV. All units w/terraces, some w/fireplaces. **Services:** Social director, masseur, children's program, babysitting. **Facilities:** 2 50 1 restaurant, 1 bar, basketball, volleyball, games rm, lawn games, whirlpool, playground, washer/dryer. Entirely retreat-oriented with a conference center. A waterfall pours into a whirlpool in summer, and the natural, spring-fed pond is graced by wild waterfowl. Plenty of fun activities for adults and kids, such as a team-building rope course, trapshooting, and horseshoes. **Rates (AP):** Peak (late June–Sept) $1,325–$1,475 S. Children under age 2 stay free. Min stay peak. Lower rates off-season. Parking: Outdoor, free. Seven-night stay (Sat–Sat) required in summer. Weekly summer rates range from $1,325 to $1,475 for adults, $775 to $975 for children, not including the minimum 8% service charge. Special three-day minimum holiday stays for Thanksgiving and Christmas. AE, DC, DISC, MC, V.

RESORTS

Black Butte Ranch
13653 Hawks Beard Rd, PO Box 8000, Black Butte Ranch, 97759; tel 541/595-6211 or toll free 800/452-7455; fax 541/595-2077. 8 mi NW of Sisters on US 20. 1,840 acres. Lodging choices at this wonderfully scenic destination resort include condos and private home rentals. The close-up view of the Three Sisters, a trio of snow-capped Cascades peaks, is breathtaking, and recreational activities abound. Just 16 miles from Hoodoo Ski Area. **Rooms:** 100 cottages/villas. CI 4pm/CO 11am. Nonsmoking rms avail. Accommodations vary from lodge condos to country-house condos to resort homes—there are 100 in all, and all are privately owned. **Amenities:** A/C, cable TV w/movies, refrig, VCR. All units w/terraces, some w/fireplaces. **Services:** Social director, masseur, children's program, babysitting. Special programs aimed at kids, teens, families, and adults—from "ranch adventures" and wildlife studies to soccer camps and snowmobiling. Also fly-fishing clinics, arts and crafts classes, trail rides. **Facilities:** 36 11 8 24 2 restaurants, 1 bar, basketball, volleyball, games rm, sauna, playground, washer/dryer. Swimming facilities offer lessons and water aerobics. **Rates:** Peak (June–Sept) $80–$250 cottage/villa. Extra person $10. Min stay peak. Lower rates off-season. Parking: Outdoor, free. Two-night minimum stay required. Six-night minimum required July–Aug for rental homes only. AE, DC, DISC, MC, V.

Inn of the Seventh Mountain
18575 SW Century Dr, 97702; tel 541/382-8711 or toll free 800/452-6810; fax 541/382-3517. 7 mi W of Bend. 44 acres. Surrounded by lots of open spaces and situated above the Deschutes River, this is a family- and group-oriented resort centered around lots of outdoor recreation. **Rooms:** 282 rms, stes, and effic. CI 5pm/CO noon. Nonsmoking rms avail. Most rooms have views of the volcanic peaks of the Cascades. The majority of accommodations are individually owned condos, spacious for the most part. Layouts can sleep from 1 to 10 people. **Amenities:** A/C, cable TV, refrig, dataport, VCR, voice mail. Some units w/terraces, some w/fireplaces. Many units have full kitchens. **Services:** Social director, masseur, children's program, babysitting. Video rentals, tennis clinics available. **Facilities:** 7 600 2 restaurants, 1 bar (w/entertainment), basketball, volleyball, games rm, lawn games, squash, sauna, whirlpool, playground. On-site recreation abounds: whitewater rafting tours, on-river patio boats, in-line skating, barbecue hay rides, and something called "pickle ball," all in summer. There's also golf at the adjacent, separately owned Seventh Mountain Golf Village. In winter, there's an ice-skating rink, snowmobiling, sleigh rides, plus a challenging, Army-style rope course. Grocery store/deli on site. Ice/roller rink doubles as a 600-seat meeting facility. **Rates:** Peak (June–Sept) $59–$65 S; $89–$99 D; $99–$285 ste; $99–$285 effic. Min stay special events. Lower rates off-season. Parking: Outdoor, free. Two-night min stay required Mem Day and Labor Day weekends. Deposit required on all advance reservations. AE, CB, DC, MC, V.

Mount Bachelor Village Resort
19717 Mount Bachelor Dr, 97702; tel 541/389-5900 or toll free 800/452-9846; fax 541/388-7820. 170 acres. This resort has its nicest units (all multi-story suites) perched along a cliff with wonderful views of the Deschutes River and nearby national forest lands. Skiing 18 miles away at Mount Bachelor. **Rooms:** 100 rms, stes, and effic. CI 5pm/CO noon. Nonsmoking rms avail. The "ski house" condominiums will do, but for a little more money you can stay in some of the nicest rooms in the area, the "river ridge" condominiums, located above the river. One-, two-, and three-bedroom suites available. The three-bedroom suite sleeps up to eight. **Amenities:** A/C, cable TV w/movies, refrig, voice mail. Some units w/terraces, all w/fireplaces, some w/whirlpools. The decks of the "river ridge" condominiums have private hot tubs. **Services:** Children's program, babysitting. **Facilities:** 4 2 50 Basketball, volleyball, racquetball, squash, spa, whirlpool, washer/dryer. Full access to the Athletic Club of Bend, next door, for $5/day. Nice walking, jogging, and biking paths surround the property. **Rates:** $68–$165 S or D; $68–$285 ste; $97–$285 effic. Min stay. Parking: Outdoor, free. Rates based on number of bedrooms, not number of guests. AE, MC, V.

RESTAURANTS

★ Cafe Paradisio
945 NW Bond St (Downtown); tel 541/385-5931. Between Minnesota and Oregon Ave. **Eclectic.** Bend's most popular coffeehouse is located in a 1918 building that has housed a vaudeville theater, a movie house, and a pool hall at various times in its history. (The movie house's projector room still sits above the front entrance.) A rotating display of works by local artists adds to the comfortable, casual atmosphere. Select from a full range of espresso drinks; mocha almond roca and chocolate malted espresso rank among the most frequent requests. Most dishes—burritos, pasta, chili, casseroles—are vegetarian. Sunday hours vary; call first. **FYI:** Reservations not accepted. Blues/jazz/Latin. Beer and wine only. No smoking. **Open:** Mon–Thurs 8am–11pm, Fri 8am–midnight, Sat 10am–midnight. **Prices:** Main courses $3–$5. No CC.

★ Deschutes Brewery & Public House
1044 Bond St (Downtown); tel 541/382-9242. Between Greenwood Ave and Oregon Ave. **Pub/Northwest.** Deschutes, with its modern brick architecture and smoke-free atmosphere, is probably the most popular watering hole in central Oregon. Its microbrews are crafted on site and are now sold throughout the state, but purists insist on drinking them at "the source." The standard, always-on-tap brews range from Cascade Golden Ale to Obsidian Stout. Accompany your drink with pub-fare favorites such as a garlic burger, cajun burger, and the daily sausage specialty. Fourteen different dinner specials are offered daily, with choices like grilled salmon with fresh-fruit salsa. **FYI:** Reservations not accepted. Children's menu. Beer and wine only. No smoking. **Open:** Mon–Thurs 11am–11:30pm, Fri–Sat 11am–12:30am, Sun 11am–10:30pm. **Prices:** Main courses $6–$13. MC, V.

Giuseppe's
932 NW Bond St (Downtown); tel 541/389-8899. Between Oregon and Minnesota. **Italian.** Bend's original feed and grain shop, dating to 1910, now feeds casual Italian fare to a grateful clientele. Popular dishes include scallops Parmesan, seafood ravioli, chicken Venetian, and Sambuca prawns. There's a quaint lounge in front, a large party room in back, and a dining room featuring a row of high-back wooden booths. **FYI:** Reservations recommended. Children's menu. **Open:** Tues–Thurs 5–9:30pm, Fri–Sat 5–10pm, Sun 5–9pm. **Prices:** Main courses $8–$14. AE, DC, MC, V.

★ McKenzie's Restaurant
1033 NW Bond St (Downtown); tel 541/388-3891. Near Greenwood Ave. **Northwest.** Located in a historic brick building, but the lack of windows makes it a bit claustrophobic. Fresh seafood, pasta, and wild game prevail along with some vegetarian fare such as stuffed Anaheim chiles, lasagna, and sautéed shitake mushrooms. Largest selection of microbrews on tap in central Oregon. **FYI:** Reservations accepted. Children's menu. No smoking. **Open:** Lunch daily 11:30am–5pm; dinner daily 5–9:30pm. **Prices:** Main courses $8–$16. AE, MC, V.

★ Mexicali Rose
301 NE Franklin Ave; tel 541/389-0149. Corner of US 97. **Mexican.** Located in a house built in the early 1900s from local lava rock. Several tables have a view of a "desertarium" scene just outside the window, complete with fake reptiles. Menu highlights are chicken breast baked in an orange-cinnamon-raison-almond sauce, a crab enchilada, and hot-marinated fajitas. **FYI:** Reservations accepted. Children's menu. **Open:** Peak (June–Aug) Sun–Thurs 5–9:30pm, Fri–Sat 5–10pm. **Prices:** Main courses $6–$10. AE, MC, V.

★ Pine Tavern
967 NW Brooks St (Downtown); tel 541/382-5581. At foot of Oregon Ave on Mirror Pond. **Northwest.** This is Bend's oldest restaurant, built in 1936. Two giant ponderosa pine trees shoot up from the center of the main dining room. Dining on the outdoor patio offers a splendid view of the Deschutes River's Mirror Pond with its many geese, swans, and ducks. Prime rib, fresh seafood, chicken, and pasta entrees prevail. A special treat: sourdough scones with honey-butter. **FYI:** Reservations recommended. Children's menu. No smoking. **Open:** Lunch Mon–Sat 11:30am–2:30pm; dinner daily 5:30–9:30pm. **Prices:** Main courses $8–$18. AE, DC, DISC, MC, V.

ATTRACTIONS

The High Desert Museum
59800 S US 97; tel 541/382-4754. Indoor/outdoor 150-acre museum re-creates the legacy of the high desert through pioneer history demonstrations and hands-on exhibits. There are 20 acres of outdoor trails that meander through the forest, passing streams filled with trout, ponds where river otters play, and observation points where visitors can witness a porcupine being hand-fed or a dramatic presentation of live birds of prey. **Open:** Daily 9am–5pm. Closed some hols. **$$$**

Lava Lands Visitors Center
58201 S OR 97; tel 541/593-2421. 11 mi S of Bend. Interpretive trails, historical information, and displays on the geology and archeology of this 50,000-acre area of lakes, volcanoes, and lava flows. Nearby Lava Butte rises 5,000 feet above the visitors center and offers a spectacular view of the Cascades. **Open:** May–mid-June, Wed–Sun 10am–4pm; mid-June–Labor Day, daily 9am–5pm; Labor Day–mid-Oct, Wed–Sun 10am–4pm. **Free**

Brookings

Brookings, at the southernmost tip of Oregon's coastline, has all the beauty of (and a much more temperate climate than) points north. Stunning scenery is punctuated by Samuel H Boardman and Harris Beach state parks to the northwest and the Siskiyou Mountains to the east. **Information:** Brookings-Harbor Chamber of Commerce, 16330 Lower Harbor Rd, PO Box 940, Brookings, 97415 (tel 541/469-3181).

MOTELS

Beaver State Motel
437 Chetco Ave, PO Box 7000, 97415; tel 541/469-5361. This property is adjacent to US 101 and is best suited for road-weary travelers on a budget. **Rooms:** 17 rms. CI noon/CO 11am. Nonsmoking rms avail. The small rooms are well past their prime. **Amenities:** TV. No A/C. **Services:** Small dogs allowed. **Rates:** Peak (May 16–Sept 15) $39–$55 S; $52–$65 D. Extra person $5. Lower rates off-season. Parking: Outdoor, free. AE, CB, DISC, MC, V.

Best Western Brookings Inn
1143 Chetco Ave, PO Box 1139, 97415; tel 541/469-2173 or toll free 800/822-9087; fax 541/469-2996. Conveniently located, clean, and well-kept. **Rooms:** 68 rms and stes. CI 1pm/CO noon. Nonsmoking rms avail. Rooms closest to US 101 are noisy. **Amenities:** Satel TV w/movies. No A/C. 1 unit w/whirlpool. **Services:** **Facilities:** 100 1 restaurant, 1 bar, whirlpool. Has the largest conference room of any property in town; catering available. **Rates:** Peak (May 15–Oct 16) $50–$60 S; $55–$65 D; $75–$90 ste. Extra person $5. Children under age 12 stay free. Lower rates off-season. Parking: Outdoor, free. AE, CB, DC, DISC, MC, V.

Westward Motel
1026 Chetco Ave, PO Box 1079, 97415; tel 541/469-7471. In the center of the business district, on US 101. Generally good value. **Rooms:** 32 rms. CI 2pm/CO 11am. Nonsmoking rms avail. Newer rooms in the back are large and bright, but avoid the accommodations towards the front. **Amenities:** Cable TV w/movies. No A/C. **Facilities:** **Rates:** Peak (Mem Day–Sept) $38–$55 S; $55–$75 D. Children under age 3 stay free. Lower rates off-season. Parking: Outdoor, free. AE, DC, DISC, MC, V.

RESTAURANTS

Great American Smokehouse
15657 S US 101; tel 541/469-6903. 2 mi S of Brookings's business district on US 101. **Seafood.** A locals' hangout. Excellent place for carefully prepared just-caught fish. There's a terrific lunch menu, with a wide variety of fish sandwiches. **FYI:** Reservations accepted. Children's menu. Beer and wine only. **Open:** Peak (June–Sept) Mon–Sat 10:30am–9pm, Sun 10:30am–8pm. **Prices:** Main courses $11–$20. DISC, MC, V.

Mama's Ristorante Italiano
703 Chetco Ave; tel 541/469-7611. Center of town; on US 101. **American/Italian.** Built as a lumber company headquarters in the late 1800s, the building is the oldest in town. The restaurant offers good value for Italian favorites; beer-batter prawns and prime rib are also worthy of note. **FYI:** Reservations recommended. Beer and wine only. No smoking. **Open:** Peak (June–Aug) Mon–Sat 11am–9pm, Sun 4–9pm. **Prices:** Main courses $6–$14. AE, DC, DISC, MC, V.

Rubio's Mexican Restaurant
1136 Chetco Ave; tel 541/469-4919. In the north end of town on US 101. **American/Mexican.** Features traditional homemade Mexican dishes as well as seafood specialties. Look for the filet Veracruz (cod with mild red sauce) and pescaditos (the fresh catch rolled in corn shells with salsa and sour cream). Nice selection of Mexican beers. **FYI:** Reservations recommended. Children's menu. Beer and wine only. **Open:** Peak (June–Aug) Tues–Sun 11am–9:30pm. **Prices:** Main courses $8–$15. AE, DISC, MC, V.

ATTRACTIONS

Harris Beach State Park
1655 OR 101; tel 541/469-2021. This section of the rugged Oregon coastline is a beachcomber's paradise, with a variety of shells, rocks, and semi-precious stones deposited along the sand. Besides sunbathing, kite-flying, rock climbing, and beach walking, park visitors can fish, clam, and crab. Camp and trailer sites with electric hook-up are available, as are yurts—weather-resistant, circular domed tents complete with plywood floors, electricity, bunk beds and a plexiglass skylight. Hiking trails, picnic area. **Open:** Daily 7am–dusk. **$**

Loeb State Park
1655 OR 101; tel 541/469-2021. Set in a beautiful stand of old growth myrtlewood trees on the banks of the Chetco River, this 320-acre state park borders the western boundary of the Siskiyou National Forest. Campsites have electricity and water, plus firewood, picnic tables, flush toilets, and showers. The park provides access to rafting and drift boating, swimming, fishing, and a two-mile nature trail. **Open:** Daily 7am–dusk. $

Burns

This High Desert cattle-country town has suffered economically in recent years, but it remains a friendly place. Burns hosts a migratory-bird festival in the spring, when countless northbound waterfowl descend on nearby marshes. Gateway to Malheur National Wildlife Refuge and the fascinating 9,670-foot Steens Mountain to the south. **Information:** Harney County Chamber of Commerce, 18 W D St, Burns, 97720 (tel 541/573-2636).

MOTELS

Best Western Ponderosa Motel
577 W Monroe, 97720; tel 541/573-2047 or toll free 800/528-1234; fax 541/573-3828. At second light on US 20 in town from either direction. Although functional, this is not one of Best Western's more handsome properties. **Rooms:** 52 rms and stes. CI 3pm/CO 11am. Nonsmoking rms avail. Generally clean. Some family units have three beds. **Amenities:** A/C, cable TV w/movies, dataport. **Services:** **Facilities:** The pool could use a facelift. **Rates (CP):** Peak (May–Sept) $37–$43 S; $48–$58 D; $55 ste. Children under age 16 stay free. Lower rates off-season. Parking: Outdoor, free. AE, CB, DC, DISC, MC, V.

Silver Spur Motel
789 N Broadway, 97720; tel 541/573-2077 or toll free 800/400-2077; fax 541/573-6602. North end of downtown on US 20/US 395. Well-kept motel on the downtown strip. Convenient to shopping. **Rooms:** 26 rms. CI 3pm/CO 11:30am. Nonsmoking rms avail. Rooms have been recently renovated with a knotty-pine decor. **Amenities:** A/C, cable TV w/movies, refrig, dataport. **Services:** **Facilities:** Guests can use health club one block away, free of charge. Small outdoor sitting area (with waterfall) has just been added. **Rates (CP):** $37 S; $41 D. Extra person $5. Children under age 10 stay free. Parking: Outdoor, free. AE, CB, DC, DISC, MC, V.

RESTAURANTS

Burns Powerhouse Restaurant
305 E Monroe; tel 541/573-9060. 2 blocks S of jct US 20 and OR 78. **Seafood/Steak.** Constructed from large blocks of stone, this 1924 building once housed the Burns Power Company. The dark interior is brightened by western art and antiques, with local ranch brands decorating the walls. Menu choices run from cheeseburgers to shrimp Louie to T-bone steaks. **FYI:** Reservations not accepted. Children's menu. **Open:** Daily 9am–9:30pm. **Prices:** Main courses $6–$14. MC, V.

Pine Room Restaurant
Monroe at Egan; tel 541/573-6631. Downtown, at second light from either direction. **Seafood/Steak.** This is the heart of Oregon's cattle ranching country, so plenty of steak can be found on the menu. There are also chicken and seafood choices. Don't let the rather unattractive exterior keep you away. Lounge open Tues–Sat, 4 pm–closing. **FYI:** Reservations recommended. Children's menu. **Open:** Tues–Sat 5–10pm. Closed 9 days each March. **Prices:** Main courses $6–$15. MC, V.

Cannon Beach

A mecca for artists, photographers, writers, and tourists, all drawn to Haystack Rock and the Needles—distinct coastal monoliths gracing the surf. Galleries and shops abound on crowded Hemlock Street. **Information:** Cannon Beach Chamber of Commerce, PO Box 64, Cannon Beach, 97110 (tel 503/436-2623).

MOTELS

Hallmark Resort
1400 S Hemlock St, PO Box 547, 97110; tel 503/436-1566 or toll free 800/345-5676; fax 503/436-0324. In midtown area, on beach. This contemporary wood-shingled motel clings to the hillside overlooking Haystack Rock, the North Coast's most recognizable landmark. Location, fine rooms, and good indoor swimming facilities make this an appealing family-vacation destination year-round. **Rooms:** 134 rms, stes, and effic. CI 4pm/CO noon. Nonsmoking rms avail. Two-bedroom suites accommodate six. **Amenities:** Cable TV w/movies, refrig. No A/C. Some units w/terraces, some w/fireplaces, some w/whirlpools. All oceanfront rooms have gas fireplaces and balconies. **Services:** Masseur, babysitting. Rental VCRs, movies free. **Facilities:** 1 restaurant, 1 bar, 1 beach (ocean), lifeguard, spa, sauna, whirlpool, washer/dryer. Beach accessible by long stairway. **Rates:** Peak (June 15–Oct 1) $99–$189 S or D; $165–$229 ste; $165–$229 effic. Min stay peak and special events. Lower rates off-season. Parking: Indoor/outdoor, free. AE, CB, DC, DISC, JCB, MC, V.

Surfsand Resort
Hemlock and Gower Streets, PO Box 219, 97110; tel 503/436-2274 or toll free 800/547-6100; fax 503/436-9116. On Cannon Beach Loop Road in midtown, adjacent to beach. This pleasant motel offers easy access to a public beach that has a lifeguard during summer. **Rooms:** 75 rms and effic. CI 4pm/CO noon. Nonsmoking rms avail. Rooms are of gener-

ous size. Although many rooms have balconies, some overlook the parking lot—only a few are oceanfront. **Amenities:** Cable TV w/movies, VCR. No A/C. Some units w/terraces, some w/fireplaces, some w/whirlpools. Some rooms have mini-fridges. Bathrobes are in the nicest rooms. **Services:** Masseur. Free hot-dog roast Sun nights in summer. **Facilities:** 1 restaurant, 1 bar, 1 beach (ocean), lifeguard, spa, whirlpool, washer/dryer. **Rates:** Peak (June 6–Labor Day) $124–$139 S or D; $149–$249 effic. Min stay peak and wknds. Lower rates off-season. Parking: Outdoor, free. Romance packages available. Several houses (sleeping up to eight) available for $94–$375. AE, CB, DC, DISC, MC, V.

Tolovana Inn
3400 S Hemlock, Tolovana Park, 97145; tel 503/436-2211 or toll free 800/333-8890; fax 503/436-0134. This wood-shingle condominium complex, with virtually all units available to rent, is located on a wide beach ¾-mile from Haystack Rock. **Rooms:** 178 rms and effic. CI 4pm/CO 11am. Non-smoking rms avail. Accommodations are very simple, small, and pleasant. Suites (efficiencies) have full kitchen and dining facilities. Many have ocean views and a few are actually oceanfront. Efficiencies may be rented with or without an extra bedroom; a Murphy bed pulls down from the living room wall. **Amenities:** Cable TV, voice mail. No A/C. Some units w/terraces, some w/fireplaces. Suites have gas fireplaces. **Services:** Rental VCRs, movies free. **Facilities:** 1 restaurant, 1 beach (ocean), lifeguard, games rm, sauna, whirlpool, washer/dryer. **Rates:** Peak (June 15–Oct 15) $68–$85 S or D; $131–$225 effic. Min stay peak and special events. Lower rates off-season. Parking: Outdoor, free. AE, DISC, MC, V.

INNS

Cannon Beach Hotel Lodgings
1116 S Hemlock St, PO Box 943, 97110; tel 503/436-1392; fax 503/436-2101. On Cannon Beach loop road. 1 acre. Three different lodgings are available: the Cannon Beach Hotel, an elegantly restored 1909 boarding house; the new Courtyard Inn, a wood-shingled building surrounding a private brick courtyard; and the rustic Hearthstone Inn, located in the Cannon Beach midtown area. All three are just a short walk from the beach. **Rooms:** 26 rms and stes. CI 3pm/CO 11am. No smoking. Some units have kitchenettes. **Amenities:** Cable TV. No A/C. Some units w/fireplaces, some w/whirlpools. Some units have whirlpool tubs, VCRs. **Services:** Free hot chocolate, tea, and coffee in lobby. **Facilities:** 1 restaurant, guest lounge. **Rates (CP):** Peak (June 16–Sept) $69–$154 S; $145 ste. Extra person $10. Children under age 2 stay free. Min stay peak and wknds. Lower rates off-season. Parking: Outdoor, free. Wedding and anniversary packages avail. MC, V.

Stephanie Inn
2740 S Pacific, PO Box 219, 97110; tel 503/436-2221 or toll free 800/633-3466; fax 503/436-9711. At the end of Matannska Street, on the beach. 1 acre. This elaborate (by Oregon coast standards) new three-story inn is popular with honeymooners seeking luxury, privacy, and all-inclusive amenities. A slate floor, huge exposed beams, and elegant furnishings characterize the interior. Service is excellent. Unsuitable for children under 12. **Rooms:** 46 rms and stes. CI 3pm/CO noon. No smoking. Rooms are individually decorated in traditional style and vary by size, decor, view (ocean, mountains, parking lot); many four-poster and sleigh beds. **Amenities:** Cable TV w/movies, VCR, bathrobes. No A/C. Some units w/minibars, some w/terraces, all w/fireplaces. Dinner can be served in room by special arrangement. **Services:** Masseur, wine/sherry served. In summer, picnic lunches available to go. Cookies and Starbucks coffee in lobby 24 hours, wine served in oceanfront sitting room every afternoon. **Facilities:** 1 beach (ocean), lifeguard, guest lounge. Free passes to Cannon Beach Athletic Club. **Rates (BB):** $119–$239 D; $260–$360 ste. Extra person $25. Min stay peak, wknds, and special events. MAP rates avail. Parking: Outdoor, free. Midweek off-season specials. Romance, winemaker's dinner, Mother's and Father's Day packages. AE, CB, DC, DISC, MC, V.

RESTAURANTS

The Bistro
263 N Hemlock St; tel 503/436-2661. **Italian.** Situated in a little courtyard off the main street, the Bistro's intimate feel is enhanced by small windows and a dark wood interior. The food here is generally Italian—pasta and seafood are the main offerings—but there are some East Indian accents. Entrees include a seafood stew with fennel, tomato, curry, and saffron; and broiled brochette of lamb on rice with eggplant curry. The modest wine list features Northwest choices. **FYI:** Reservations recommended. Guitar. No smoking. **Open:** Peak (June–Sept) daily 5:30–9:30pm. Closed Jan. **Prices:** Main courses $7–$16; prix fixe $13–$22. MC, V.

Cafe de la Mer
1287 S Hemlock St; tel 503/436-1179. In Cannon Beach's "midtown", on Cannon Beach Loop Rd. **Seafood.** Located in a weather-beaten building, this intimate cafe has a well-established reputation for fine seafood entrees, delicate desserts, and an excellent wine list. Specialties include bouillabaisse and—for landlubbers—rack of lamb. Restaurant hours fluctuate, so call before you head over. **FYI:** Reservations recommended. Beer and wine only. No smoking. **Open:** Peak (summer) daily 5:30–9pm. **Prices:** Main courses $17–$30. AE, MC, V.

Pulicci's Restaurant
988 S Hemlock St; tel 503/436-1279. In midtown area, on Cannon Beach Loop Rd. **Italian.** This small restaurant has fewer than a dozen tables tucked in little nooks. An eclectic

mix of stained glass, original art, house plants, chianti bottles, and kitschy collectibles gives a warm tone. The short menu features mostly standard but well-prepared Italian specialties. Oregon wines predominate. **FYI:** Reservations accepted. Beer and wine only. No smoking. **Open:** Peak (July–Nov 15) Thurs–Mon 5:30–9pm. **Prices:** Main courses $9–$19. MC, V.

Cave Junction

LODGE

Oregon Caves Chateau

20000 Caves Hwy, PO Box 128, 97523; tel 541/592-3400; fax 541/592-6654. 468 acres. Rustic log lodge dating from 1934. Located 4,000 feet up Grayback Mountain, in a thick forest next to Oregon Caves National Monument. The lobby has a huge, two-sided stone fireplace. Allow 30 minutes to drive the 20 miles up the winding, narrow road to the hotel. **Rooms:** 22 rms and stes. CI 4pm/CO 11am. No smoking. All rooms are very clean and have private baths. Accommodations on the second and third floors have original furniture and Pendleton-wool blankets. Since the original wall treatment is dark and the hotel is located in the trees, rooms have a cozy, cavelike feel. **Amenities:** No A/C, phone, or TV. Bathrooms offer a nice selection of toiletries, including sewing kits. **Services:** Shuttle service available to Illinois Valley Airport (private planes only). Free evening lectures by park rangers. **Facilities:** 40 2 restaurants (*see* "Restaurants" below). Old-fashioned, hand-cranked telephone in the hallway. A creek flows right through the dining room. **Rates:** Peak (Mem Day–Labor Day) $69–$70 S or D; $79–$89 ste. Extra person $9. Children under age 6 stay free. Lower rates off-season. Parking: Outdoor, free. Romance package avail. Closed Dec 31–Feb 29. MC, V.

RESTAURANT

Oregon Caves Chateau Dining Room & Coffee Shop

20000 Caves Hwy; tel 541/592-3400. On US 199. **American/Cafe.** One of the most unusual features here is the creek that travels through the restaurant. Entrees include steak, grilled trout, and seafood pasta. Fine chocolate desserts. Good selection of award-winning local Illinois Valley wines. The adjacent Coffee Shop features the original wood fountain counter and offers a classic club sandwich, layered on toasted sourdough bread. **FYI:** Reservations recommended. Children's menu. Dress code. Beer and wine only. No smoking. **Open:** Peak (late May–mid-Sept) daily 7am–9pm. Closed mid-Oct–mid-May. **Prices:** Main courses $8–$16. MC, V.

ATTRACTION

Oregon Caves National Monument

19000 Caves Hwy; tel 541/592-2100. 20 mi SE of Cave Junction. High in the rugged Siskiyou Mountains, the Oregon Caves are one of southern Oregon's oldest attractions. First discovered in 1874, the caves, which stretch for three miles under the mountain and are still growing, are formed by water seeping through marble bedrock. The slight acidity of the water dissolves the marble, which is later redeposited as beautiful stalactites, stalagmites, draperies, soda straws, columns, and flowstone. Guided tours of the cave take about 1½ hours; children under six are not allowed on tours but a nursery is available.

Above ground, there are two wooded picnic areas near the main parking area, several miles of hiking trails, and a lodge/restaurant. **Open:** May–mid-June, daily 8:30am–5pm; mid-June–Labor Day, daily 8:30am–7pm; Labor Day–mid-Oct, daily 8:30am–5pm; mid-Oct–Apr, daily 9:30am–4pm. Closed Dec 25. **Free**

Coos Bay

Built around the largest natural harbor between San Francisco and Puget Sound, this Scandinavian/German town is the state's largest coastal community. **Information:** Bay Area Visitor Bureau, 50 E Central, PO Box 210, Coos Bay, 97420 (tel 541/269-0215).

MOTELS

Best Western Holiday Motel

411 N Bayshore Dr, 97420; tel 541/269-5111 or toll free 800/228-8655. Located near the center of town, this motel offers the conveniences and standards of a property associated with a national chain. **Rooms:** 77 rms, stes, and effic. CI 3pm/CO noon. Nonsmoking rms avail. **Amenities:** A/C, cable TV w/movies, refrig. Some units w/whirlpools. **Services:** Charge for small pets. **Facilities:** 30 Whirlpool, washer/dryer. **Rates (CP):** $69 S; $74 D; $74–$125 ste; $79–$89 effic. Extra person $5. Children under age 12 stay free. Parking: Outdoor, free. AE, CB, DC, DISC, MC, V.

Red Lion Inn

1313 N Bayshore Dr, 97420; tel 541/267-4141 or toll free 800/547-8010; fax 541/267-2884. In the center of town on US 101. The only motel in town that can accommodate large groups. **Rooms:** 142 rms and stes. CI 2pm/CO 1pm. Nonsmoking rms avail. Good-size rooms are tastefully done. **Amenities:** A/C, cable TV w/movies. All rooms have irons and ironing boards. **Services:** Staff is most attentive. **Facilities:** 200 1 restaurant, 1 bar (w/entertainment), washer/dryer. Free guest passes to local health club. **Rates:** Peak (May–Aug) $69 S; $84 D; $98 ste. Extra person $15. Children under age 18 stay free. Lower rates off-season. Parking: Outdoor, free. AE, CB, DC, DISC, MC, V.

RESTAURANTS

★ Blue Heron Bistro

100 Commercial Ave; tel 541/267-3933. Off US 101. **International.** International cuisine includes Cajun, Caribbean, and French creole, with Italian and seafood specials also offered. Lunch features salads and sandwiches. One of the best beer selections around. Settle in with magazines and newspapers or games for the kids. **FYI:** Reservations accepted. Beer and wine only. No smoking. **Open:** Peak (June–Sept) daily 9am–10pm. **Prices:** Main courses $8–$13. MC, V.

★ Kum Yon's

835 S Broadway St; tel 541/269-2662. South end of town center, off US 101. **Chinese/Japanese/Korean.** Bustling, eclectic Asian restaurant serving Japanese, Chinese, and Korean dishes. Top honors go to the sashimi and the chef's special sushi assortment. **FYI:** Reservations accepted. Children's menu. Beer and wine only. No smoking. Additional location: 1006 SW Coast Hwy, Nauport (tel 265-5330). **Open:** Sun–Thurs 11am–9:30pm, Fri–Sat 11am–10pm. **Prices:** Main courses $7–$20; prix fixe $8–$14. AE, MC, V. ♿

Corvallis

See also Albany

This Willamette Valley college town (home of Oregon State University) sets a standard in livability, with continuous performing and visual art displays, folk festivals, and science exhibitions such as July's da Vinci Days. **Information:** Corvallis Convention and Visitors Bureau, 420 NW 2nd St, Corvallis, 97330 (tel 541/757-1544).

MOTELS

Corvallis Ramada Inn and Convention Center

1550 NW 9th St, 97330; tel 541/753-9151 or toll free 800/272-6232; fax 541/758-7089. I-5 exit 228. Full-service motel convenient to the university. **Rooms:** 120 rms, stes, and effic. CI 3pm/CO noon. Nonsmoking rms avail. All suites have cooking facilities. **Amenities:** A/C, cable TV w/movies, dataport. **Services:** Fax service available. **Facilities:** 550 1 restaurant, 1 bar, washer/dryer. Guest passes to nearby health club. **Rates:** $74–$96 S; $82–$100 D; $99–$134 ste; $99–$134 effic. Extra person $8. Children under age 18 stay free. Min stay special events. Parking: Outdoor, free. AE, CB, DC, DISC, ER, JCB, MC, V.

Motel Orleans

935 NW Garfield St, 97330; tel 541/758-9125 or toll free 800/626-1900; fax 541/758-0544. Exit 228 off I-5. Very pleasant budget motel. Convenient to university. **Rooms:** 61 rms. CI 2pm/CO 11am. Nonsmoking rms avail. **Amenities:** A/C, cable TV. **Services:** **Facilities:** ♿ Washer/dryer. Discount at nearby health club. Guests can use outdoor pool at neighboring motel. **Rates:** Peak (May–Oct) $44–$56 S; $48–$56 D. Extra person $4. Children under age 13 stay free. Lower rates off-season. Parking: Outdoor, free. AE, CB, DC, DISC, MC, V.

Shanico Inn

1113 NW 9th St, 97330; tel 541/754-7474 or toll free 800/432-1233; fax 541/754-2437. Located just off a main thoroughfare near downtown, this inexpensive motel offers good service and pleasant accommodations. **Rooms:** 76 rms and stes. CI 2pm/CO noon. Nonsmoking rms avail. **Amenities:** A/C, cable TV w/movies, dataport. Four rooms have mini-refrigerators; guests in other rooms may request one (subject to availability). **Services:** Complimentary coffee in lobby 24 hours. Pet fee $3/night. Typewriters available at front desk. **Facilities:** 25 ♿ Guests have free use of a nearby health club. Microwave in lobby available to guests 24 hours. **Rates (CP):** $42–$47 S; $49–$59 D; $42–$59 ste. Extra person $5. Children under age 12 stay free. Parking: Outdoor, free. AE, CB, DC, DISC, MC, V.

RESTAURANTS

★ Bombs Away Cafe

2527 NW Monroe St; tel 541/757-7221. **Southwestern.** This busy, loud, and frenetic place is popular with university and town crowds for its unusual, eclectic southwestern fare. Try duck chimichangas, goat-cheese and black-bean quesadillas, or braised lamb posole. A good selection of northwestern microbrews is also available. At 10pm, the dinner menu ends (a simple bar menu is in effect until midnight), smoking is allowed, and those under 21 are no longer permitted. **FYI:** Reservations not accepted. Children's menu. No smoking. **Open:** Mon–Fri 11am–10pm, Sat 4–10pm, Sun 4–9pm. **Prices:** Main courses $3–$13. MC, V. ♿

The Gables

1121 NW 9th St; tel 541/752-3364. **American.** Corvallis' fanciest dinner house is dimly lit and sedate, with a decor of dark-wood paneling, wallpaper, carpeted floors, and plush chairs. Menu choices include seafood, steaks, and prime rib, plus a few surprises such as vegetarian ravioli. The wine list emphasizes Northwest vintages. **FYI:** Reservations recommended. Children's menu. No smoking. **Open:** Daily 5–9pm. **Prices:** Main courses $12–$23. AE, DC, DISC, MC, V. ♿

★ Nearly Normal's

109 NW 15th St; tel 541/753-0791. University area. **Eclectic.** Tucked in an older house on a residential street, Nearly Normal's has been serving its self-described "gonzo cuisine" for 14 years. The restaurant, which began life as an outdoor market booth, still has a funky atmosphere complete with wood floors, plants, and white-painted walls hung with eclectic art. The diverse menu features a tempeh reuben and

"nearly Mexican" burritos. Breakfast is served all day. Several microbrews and local root beers are available. **FYI:** Reservations not accepted. Children's menu. Beer and wine only. No smoking. **Open:** Peak (early Apr–early Sept) Mon–Fri 8am–9pm, Sat 9am–9pm. Closed Dec 25–Jan 1. **Prices:** Main courses $5–$8. No CC.

Cottage Grove

A picturesque gold-rush town south of Eugene. Visit the Cottage Grove Hotel, an old miner's haunt restored to house a collection of specialty shops. A scenic drive looping through the mining district showcases covered bridges. **Information:** Cottage Grove Area Chamber of Commerce, 710 Row River Rd, PO Box 587, Cottage Grove, 97424 (tel 541/942-2411).

HOTEL

Best Western—The Village Green Resort Hotel
725 Row River Rd, 97424; tel 541/942-2491 or toll free 800/343-7666; fax 541/42-2386. Well-maintained, well-landscaped property offering some of the amenities of a modest resort. Convenient to I-5. **Rooms:** 96 rms and stes. Executive level. CI 3pm/CO 11am. Nonsmoking rms avail. **Amenities:** A/C, cable TV w/movies. All units w/terraces, some w/fireplaces. **Services:** **Facilities:** 2 250 1 restaurant, 1 bar (w/entertainment), lawn games, whirlpool, playground, washer/dryer. Golf course across street. **Rates:** Peak (June 15–Sept 15) $69 S; $79 D; $99–$109 ste. Extra person $5. Children under age 13 stay free. Lower rates off-season. Parking: Indoor, free. Golf packages avail. AE, CB, DC, DISC, MC, V.

Crater Lake National Park

The crater that holds this serene, sapphire-blue lake was born in the explosive volcanic eruption of Mount Mazama nearly 8,000 years ago. The mountain's summit collapsed, leaving a 4,000 foot hole where the mountain used to be. Thousands of years of rain and melting snow have filled 1,932 feet of the crater, making Crater Lake the deepest lake in the United States and the seventh-deepest in the world. Toward one end of the lake, the cone of Wizard Island rises from the water. This island is the tip of a volcano that has been slowly building since the last eruption of Mount Mazama.

The 286-square-mile park maintains two visitors centers. The **Steel Information Center** is open daily year-round while the **Rim Village Visitors Center** is open only from May to September. Though the park is open all year, Rim Drive is the only park road kept clear of the deep winter snows that blanket the region. During the summer, the Drive provides many viewpoints of the lake as it makes a 39-mile-long circuit of the crater's perimeter.

There are many activities available here—including hiking, cross-country skiing, picnic areas, and camping—but the most popular are the boat trips around the lake. A naturalist on each boat provides a narrative on the ecology and history of the lake, and all tours include a stop on Wizard Island. Tours, which begin at Cleetwood Cove, are offered from late June through mid-September (fee charged).

To reach the park from I-5, take exit 62 in Medford and follow OR 62 for 75 miles, if you are coming from the south. To reach the park from the north, take exit 124 in Roseburg and follow OR 138. For more information, contact the Superintendent, Crater Lake National Park, Box 7, Crater Lake, OR 97604 (tel 541/594-2211).

MOTEL

UNRATED **Mazama Village**
400 Rim Village Dr, PO Box 128, Crater Lake, 97604; tel 541/594-2511; fax 541/594-2622. Just off OR 62, 7 mi S of lake. Basic national park lodgings—no frills. **Rooms:** 40 rms. CI 4pm/CO noon. **Amenities:** No A/C, phone, or TV. **Services:** **Facilities:** **Rates:** $59–$74 S or D. Extra person $10. Children under age 18 stay free. Parking: Outdoor, free. Closed Oct 16–May 18. MC, V.

LODGE

Crater Lake Lodge, Inc
Crater Lake National Park, 400 Rim Village Dr, PO Box 128, Crater Lake, 97604; tel 541/594-2511; fax 541/594-2622. On rim of Crater Lake; OR 62. Reopened in May 1995 after a seven-year, $18 million renovation, this historic lodge dates back to 1909 and is set right on the edge of Crater Lake. It's built in the grand style, with stone walls, a copper roof, Douglas fir floors, and massive columns of unpeeled ponderosa pine. Worth it—a special place. **Rooms:** 71 rms. CI 4pm/CO 11am. No smoking. Although small, the rooms offer plenty of rustic charm combined with the benefits of modern plumbing and electricity. Some accommodations offer spectacular lake views; others overlook the forest or meadow. In keeping with the lodge's history, furnishings are mission-style; lake-view rooms offer window seats. **Amenities:** A/C. No phone or TV. **Services:** **Facilities:** 1 restaurant (*see* "Restaurants" below). Fine restaurant. **Rates:** $99–$119 S or D. Extra person $10. Parking: Outdoor, free. Closed Oct 15–May 17. MC, V.

RESTAURANT

Crater Lake Lodge Restaurant
In Crater Lake Lodge, 400 Rim Village Dr, Crater Lake; tel 541/594-2511. On rim of Crater Lake. **Northwest.** Reopened after a seven-year reconstruction, this historic 1924 dining room boasts a huge stone fireplace, polished hard-

wood floors, natural beamed ceiling, rustic bark molding, oak chairs covered with hunter-green cushions, and windows offering beautiful views of Crater Lake. Chef Wayne Turnipseed features Northwest specialties such as smoked Oregon game sausage with roasted garlic–Dijon sauce, cioppino (seafood cooked in an Oregon white wine and tomato saffron sauce), and broiled salmon with roasted bell peppers and caramelized baby onions drizzled with tarragon-butter sauce. Oregon wines and beers are showcased. Lodge guests have first priority in the 150-seat nonsmoking dining room, so dinner reservations may be hard to secure. Lunch is unreserved. **FYI:** Reservations recommended. No smoking. **Open:** Breakfast daily 7–11am; lunch daily 11–2am; dinner daily 5–10pm. Closed Oct 15–May 17. **Prices:** Main courses $20–$25. MC, V.

Depoe Bay

Sightseeing, charter fishing, and whale-watching excursions depart from Depoe Bay—the world's smallest navigable harbor. Visitors can stroll above the basalt rock cliffs and feel the ocean spray, or explore the gift shops on the promenade. **Information:** Depoe Bay Chamber of Commerce, 630 SE US 101, PO Box 21, Depoe Bay, 97341 (tel 541/765-2889).

INN

Channel House Bed & Breakfast Inn

35 Ellingson St, PO Box 56, 97341; tel 541/765-2140 or toll free 800/447-2140; fax 541/765-2191. At US 101. Romantic retreat features outdoor hot tubs and indoor gas fireplaces. Unsuitable for children under 13. **Rooms:** 12 rms. CI 4pm/CO 11am. Although rooms are larger and provide more privacy than most B&Bs, the setting is less intimate. **Amenities:** Cable TV w/movies, refrig, bathrobes. No A/C. All units w/minibars, some w/terraces, some w/fireplaces, some w/whirlpools. Wet bars are a attractive plus. **Rates (CP):** $60–$200 D. Extra person $20. Parking: Outdoor, free. DISC, MC, V.

Eugene

Oregon's second-largest city is an oasis of public parks, tree-lined streets, and miles of jogging and bike paths. This dynamic, progessive, culturally diverse, and laid-back community is the home of the University of Oregon. On the arts scene, Eugene hosts the nationally acclaimed Oregon Bach Festival and features a city symphony, opera and ballet companies, and the Oregon Mozart Players. Several microbreweries produce and sell handcrafted beers in town. **Information:** Convention and Visitors Association of Lane County, 115 W 8th #190, PO Box 10286, Eugene, 97440 (tel 541/484-5307).

PUBLIC TRANSPORTATION

Lane Transit District (tel 541/687-5555 or 687-4265 for deaf or hard-of-hearing) provides nine transit stations located in the Eugene/Springfield area and operates buses 5am–midnight weekdays; 7am–midnight Sat; 8am–8pm Sun. Several park-and-ride lots are located along routes. Fares: adults 80¢, children 5–11 and seniors 40¢. Reduced fares after 7pm and on weekends. Discounts for Medicare cardholders and customers with disabilities.

HOTELS

Eugene Hilton Hotel

66 E 6th Ave, 97401 (Downtown); tel 541/342-2000 or toll free 800/937-6660; fax 541/342-6661. Eugene's only high-rise, full-service hotel is adjacent to city conference center and performing arts center, and convenient to downtown. **Rooms:** 270 rms and stes. Executive level. CI 3pm/CO noon. Nonsmoking rms avail. **Amenities:** A/C, cable TV w/movies. All units w/terraces. **Services:** Masseur. Free shuttle to University of Oregon and Sacred Heart Medical Center. **Facilities:** 2500 2 restaurants, 2 bars (w/entertainment), whirlpool, beauty salon. Eugene's largest convention facilities. Although the pool and outdoor hot tub are very small, the fitness center is relatively large. **Rates:** $112–$190 S; $127–$190 D; $245–$340 ste. Extra person $15. Children under age 18 stay free. Parking: Indoor, free. AE, CB, DC, DISC, MC, V.

Valley River Inn

1000 Valley River Way, PO Box 10088, 97440; tel 541/687-0123 or toll free 800/543-8266; fax 541/683-5121. Adjacent to Valley River Center, off I-105. The area's premier lodging is convenient to the shopping mall and to downtown by a complicated freeway. Located on the city's riverside bike path system. **Rooms:** 257 rms and stes. Executive level. CI 4pm/CO 11am. Nonsmoking rms avail. **Amenities:** A/C, cable TV w/movies, dataport. All units w/terraces, 1 w/whirlpool. **Services:** Babysitting. Turndown service by request. **Facilities:** 800 1 restaurant (*see* "Restaurants" below), 1 bar (w/entertainment), spa, sauna, whirlpool. Day pass to excellent downtown athletic club available for $6. **Rates:** $79–$150 S or D; $160–$300 ste. Extra person $20. Children under age 16 stay free. Min stay special events. Parking: Outdoor, free. Rates vary by view. AE, CB, DC, DISC, MC, V.

MOTELS

Agnus Inn

2121 Franklin Blvd, 97403; tel 541/342-1243 or toll free 800/456-6487; fax 541/342-1243. 4 blocks from University of Oregon. Backing up to the Willamette River, this sprawling complex is convenient to the university. Most rooms are far enough away from the busy street to be quiet. **Rooms:** 81 rms, stes, and effic. CI 3pm/CO 11am. Nonsmoking rms avail. Rooms are large and clean. **Amenities:** A/C, cable

TV w/movies, refrig. Some units w/terraces, some w/fireplaces. **Services:** Facilities: 1 restaurant, 1 bar, sauna, whirlpool. Bikes are available free in summer. Pool area is quite spartan. **Rates:** $36–$45 S; $46–$55 D; $52–$70 ste. Extra person $2. Children under age 12 stay free. Parking: Outdoor, free. Discounts for seniors and students. AE, CB, DC, DISC, MC, V.

Barron's Motor Inn
1859 Franklin Blvd, 97403; tel 541/342-6383 or toll free 800/444-6383; fax 541/342-6383. 2 blocks from University of Oregon. A very pleasant motel, particularly the newer rooms. It backs up to the Willamette River and is close to the university. **Rooms:** 60 rms and stes. CI 3pm/CO 11am. Nonsmoking rms avail. No views, but clean and well appointed. **Amenities:** A/C, cable TV w/movies. Some units w/whirlpools. **Services:** Free newspaper. **Facilities:** 1 restaurant (lunch and dinner only), sauna, whirlpool. You can ride the city's nearby riverside bike path with the free bikes in summer. **Rates (CP):** Peak (summer) $56–$69 S or D; $68–$75 ste. Extra person $10. Children under age 12 stay free. Lower rates off-season. Parking: Outdoor, free. Special rates for groups, bus tours, seniors, and "Frequent Sleepers." AE, DC, DISC, MC, V.

Best Western New Oregon Motel
1655 Franklin Blvd, 97403; tel 541/683-3669 or toll free 800/528-1234; fax 541/484-5556. Adjacent to University of Oregon. This recently renovated motel is a restful stop for freeway travelers. **Rooms:** 128 rms. CI 3pm/CO noon. Nonsmoking rms avail. **Amenities:** A/C, cable TV w/movies, refrig, dataport. Some units w/terraces. **Services:** Complimentary coffee and tea in lobby 24 hours. The front desk offers complimentary toiletries and also rents racquetball equipment. **Facilities:** Sauna, whirlpool, washer/dryer. **Rates:** Peak (July–Sept) $50–$60 S; $65–$75 D. Extra person $2. Lower rates off-season. Parking: Outdoor, free. AE, CB, DC, DISC, ER, JCB, MC, V.

Campus Inn
390 E Broadway, 97401; tel 541/343-3376 or toll free 800/888-6313; fax 541/343-3376. A nicely furnished, clean, safe, budget motel that is convenient to downtown, university, hospital, and recreation. **Rooms:** 58 rms. CI 2pm/CO 11am. Nonsmoking rms avail. **Amenities:** A/C, cable TV w/movies. **Services:** Dataport phone jacks available at front desk. Pet deposit $20. **Rates:** $40–$46 S; $46–$52 D. Extra person $6. Children under age 13 stay free. Parking: Outdoor, free. AE, CB, DC, DISC, MC, V.

Eugene Motor Lodge
476 E Broadway, 97401; tel 541/344-5233 or toll free 800/876-7829; fax 541/344-5233. Edge of downtown near university. An old motor court on a busy street, this place is clean and cheap. Convenient to the university and downtown. **Rooms:** 49 rms and stes. CI open/CO 11am. Nonsmoking rms avail. No views from the rooms, 80% of which are designated nonsmoking. **Amenities:** A/C, cable TV. **Services:** Friendly staff arranges deal with local taxi service to go to airport for half the usual rate. **Facilities:** **Rates:** Peak (Mem Day–Labor Day) $32–$38 S; $36–$42 D; $57 ste. Extra person $4. Children under age 16 stay free. Lower rates off-season. Parking: Outdoor, free. Discounts for seniors, students, and for families of hospital patients. Weekly rates available. AE, CB, DC, DISC, MC, V.

Holiday Inn Eugene
225 Coburg Rd, 97401; tel 541/342-5181 or toll free 800/917-5500; fax 541/342-5164. Just off I-105, N of Ferry St Bridge. Decent motel convenient to freeway. **Rooms:** 148 rms and stes. CI 2pm/CO noon. Nonsmoking rms avail. Rooms next to freeway are noisy, but some rooms face interior pool area and have no outside windows. **Amenities:** A/C, dataport. **Services:** Continental breakfast served Mon-Fri only. **Facilities:** 1 restaurant, 1 bar (w/entertainment), whirlpool, washer/dryer. Poolside video games and pool tables. **Rates (CP):** Peak (May–Sept) $65–$72 S; $71–$78 D; $115 ste. Extra person $6. Children under age 16 stay free. Lower rates off-season. Parking: Outdoor, free. AE, CB, DC, DISC, JCB, MC, V.

Phoenix Inn
850 Franklin Blvd, 97403; tel 541/344-0001 or toll free 800/344-0131; fax 541/686-1288. 2 blocks from University of Oregon. Opened in 1994, this exceptional motel is located along historic Mill Race and is convenient to the hospital and university. Excellent value. **Rooms:** 97 rms and stes. Executive level. CI 3pm/CO noon. Nonsmoking rms avail. Better-than-average rooms, with wood and leather furnishings and a spacious layout. Many accommodations have a tub/shower combo. **Amenities:** A/C, cable TV w/movies, refrig, dataport. Some units w/whirlpools. VCRs and bathrobes provided in suites. **Services:** **Facilities:** Whirlpool, washer/dryer. Pool has a lift for guests with disabilities. **Rates (CP):** $59 S; $64 D; $99–$119 ste. Extra person $5. Children under age 18 stay free. Parking: Outdoor, free. AE, DC, DISC, MC, V.

Red Lion Inn
205 Coburg Rd, 97401; tel 541/342-5201 or toll free 800/547-8010; fax 541/485-2314. North of Ferry Street Bridge, just off I-105. Pleasant, up-to-date motel with clean, comfortable rooms. **Rooms:** 137 rms. CI 3pm/CO 1pm. Nonsmoking rms avail. All rooms open to outside parking. **Amenities:** A/C, satel TV w/movies, dataport. Some units w/terraces. **Services:** **Facilities:** 2 restaurants, 1 bar (w/entertainment), whirlpool. **Rates:** $69–$75 S; $80–$90 D. Extra person $15. Children under age 12 stay free. Parking: Outdoor, free. AE, CB, DC, DISC, JCB, MC, V.

Travelers Inn Motel
540 E Broadway, 97401; tel 541/342-1109 or toll free 800/432-5999. Clean, decent, centrally located budget motel;

convenient to downtown, hospital, university, and recreation. **Rooms:** 34 rms. CI open/CO 11am. Nonsmoking rms avail. Most rooms have shower only; some have tub/shower combo. **Amenities:** A/C, cable TV w/movies, refrig. Some units w/terraces. **Services:** **Facilities:** **Rates:** Peak (June–Oct 15) $33 S; $39 D. Children under age 16 stay free. Lower rates off-season. Parking: Outdoor, free. AE, DC, DISC, MC, V.

INN

The Campbell House

252 Pearl St, 97401; tel 541/343-1119 or toll free 800/264-2519; fax 541/343-2258. Near 5th Street Market District, edge of downtown. This elegant, self-described "city inn" opened in 1993 in a renovated, century-old Victorian home. Charm abounds, with a fireplace in the guest lounge, fresh flowers, and period furniture throughout. The carefully landscaped grounds abut wooded Skinner Butte Park. **Rooms:** 13 rms. CI 3pm/CO noon. No smoking. **Amenities:** A/C, cable TV w/movies, refrig, dataport, VCR, bathrobes. 1 unit w/terrace, some w/fireplaces, 1 w/whirlpool. TVs and VCRs can be hidden away when not in use. Hair dryers in most bathrooms. Honeymoon Suite features a whirlpool, fireplace, and four-poster bed. **Services:** Wine/sherry served. Copy and fax machines; video library of classic movies. Morning coffee delivered to rooms. **Facilities:** 32 Guest lounge. **Rates (BB):** Peak (May–Oct) $70–$225 S or D. Extra person $15. Min stay special events. Lower rates off-season. Higher rates for special events/hols. Parking: Outdoor, free. Romance packages avail Nov–Apr. AE, MC, V.

RESTAURANTS

Ambrosia

174 W Broadway (Downtown); tel 541/342-4141. **Italian.** Exposed-brick walls, stamped-tin ceilings, eclectic furniture, and a huge, ornate, turn-of-the-century bar set the scene. Dishes like pasta, seafood, veal, and chicken are offered along with upscale pizzas baked in a wood-burning oven. (Half-orders for kids are available.) Refreshments include espresso, microbrews, and a large selection of wines from Italy, California, and the Northwest. **FYI:** Reservations not accepted. **Open:** Lunch Mon–Thurs 11:30am–4:30pm, Fri–Sat 11:30am–2:30pm; dinner Sun–Thurs 4:30–10:30pm, Fri–Sat 4:30–11:30pm. **Prices:** Main courses $10–$15. MC, V.

★ Cafe Navarro

454 Willamette St; tel 541/344-0943. Off 5th St, adjacent to train station. **Eclectic.** Chef/owner Jorge Navarro serves generous portions of creative food inspired by a variety of equatorial cuisines: African, Caribbean, and Latin American. On weekend evenings, Jorge pulls out his guitar and, with a violinist, serenades diners. No children's menu, but kids are accommodated with quesadillas and other simple fare. **FYI:** Reservations accepted. Guitar/violin. Beer and wine only. No smoking. **Open:** Breakfast Sat–Sun 9am–2pm; lunch Tues–Sat 11am–2pm; dinner Tues–Sat 5–9:30pm. **Prices:** Main courses $8–$15. MC, V.

★ Café Zenon

898 Pearl St; tel 541/343-3005. 1 block E of mall. **Eclectic.** Lively and fast-paced hangout offering interesting and exquisitely prepared food. With slate floors, wide windows, and close-packed tables, it's a good place to see and be seen. The menu changes daily, and selections take inspiration from cuisines as diverse as Moroccan, West Texan, Thai, and provincial French. No children's menu, but kids are graciously accommodated with plain buttered pasta or other simple fare. Outstanding dessert selection. **FYI:** Reservations not accepted. Beer and wine only. No smoking. **Open:** Breakfast Mon–Sat 8–11am; lunch Mon–Sat 11:30am–5pm; dinner Sun–Thurs 5–10pm, Fri–Sat 5–11pm; brunch Sun 9:30am–2:30pm. **Prices:** Main courses $11–$15. MC, V.

Chanterelle

In Fifthpearl Building, 207 E 5th Ave; tel 541/484-4065. **French.** Named for the prized mushroom found in local woods, this Euro-style dinner house sports 12 tables, white linen table cloths, and tasteful watercolors on the walls. The primarily French menu (escargots bourguignon) has Italian moments (fettuccine Napoli) and occasionally touches down in the chef's native Switzerland (zwiebelsteak). Extensive wine list. **FYI:** Reservations recommended. Beer and wine only. No smoking. **Open:** Tues–Sat 5–9pm. Closed Aug 26–Sept 7/Mar 15–Apr 7. **Prices:** Main courses $13–$23. AE, DC, MC, V.

★ Excelsior Cafe

754 E 13th Ave; tel 541/342-6963. University area. **Eclectic.** The Excelsior opened in a renovated sorority house in 1972, and it has been popular among students and faculty ever since for its fine meals in an intimate setting. Every month, the chef tilts his menu towards a different European region, with dinner entrees usually including meats, seafood, and pasta, plus game such as rabbit or pheasant. Simple children's fare available by request. **FYI:** Reservations recommended. No smoking. **Open:** Lunch Mon–Sat 11:30am–2:30pm; dinner Sun–Thurs 5:30–9pm, Fri–Sat 5:30–10pm; brunch Sun 10am–2pm. **Prices:** Main courses $14–$18. AE, DC, DISC, MC, V.

★ Poppi's Anatolia

992 Willamette St; tel 541/343-9661. **Greek/Indian.** Warm service and authentic, memorable flavors prevail over worn decor and furnishings. Primarily Greek and Indian dishes are featured. Good lunch choices are the excellent Greek salad or the various pita sandwiches. A range of curries is offered at dinner, while an all-Greek menu served on Sunday nights. Reservations for parties of six or more. **FYI:** Reservations not accepted. Beer and wine only. No smoking. **Open:** Peak

(Mem Day–Labor Day) lunch Sun–Fri 11:30am–5pm, Sat 11:30am–3pm; dinner Sun–Thurs 5–9:30pm, Fri–Sat 5–10pm. **Prices:** Main courses $2–$12. MC, V.

Steelhead Brewery and Cafe
In Station Square, 199 E 5th Ave (Market district); tel 541/686-2739. **Eclectic.** Between the music, several TV screens tuned to sports, and the conversations amplified by the tile floors and dark wood paneling, this popular microbrewery is loud and lively. The menu includes a sampling of burgers, fish-and-chips, pasta, and interesting appetizers; of course, the brewery's own half-dozen beers are available on tap. After 5pm, you can order from a creative pizza menu, with the crusts made from barley used in the brewing process. Must be 21 years old. **FYI:** Reservations not accepted. Beer and wine only. **Open:** Sun–Thurs 11:30am–10pm, Fri–Sat 11:30am–11pm. **Prices:** Main courses $4–$8. DISC, MC, V. ♿

SweetWaters
In Valley River Inn, 1000 Valley River Way; tel 541/341-3462. Adjacent to Valley River Center. **Northwest.** Popular with locals and motel guests. All tables have a view of the Willamette River and park beyond. Frequently changing creative menu leaning toward northwest specialties. The well-chosen wine list features almost exclusively Washington, Oregon, and California wines. **FYI:** Reservations recommended. Dancing. Children's menu. **Open:** Breakfast Mon–Sat 6:30–11am, Sun 7:30am–1pm; lunch daily 11:30am–2pm; dinner daily 5:30–9:30pm; brunch Sun 9am–2pm. **Prices:** Main courses $12.50–$20. AE, DC, DISC, MC, V. ♿

ATTRACTIONS

University of Oregon Museum of Natural History
1680 E 15th Ave; tel 541/346-3024. Three main collections concerning anthropology, paleontology, and zoology; two permanent exhibits—the Archeology of Oregon and the Fossil History of Oregon—and a temporary exhibition area allow visitors to explore the past. The museum also offers tours, family days, lectures, workshops, and field trips. **Open:** Wed–Sun noon–5pm. Closed some hols. **Free**

Lane County Historical Museum
740 W 13th Ave; tel 541/687-4239. Museum of local history featuring exhibits on the Oregon Trail and other aspects of early pioneer life, including clothing and household goods. **Open:** Wed–Fri 10am–4pm, Sat noon–4pm. Closed some hols. **$**

University of Oregon Museum of Art
Johnson Lane; tel 541/686-3027. Asian art is the museum's strong point with works from China, Japan, Korea, Cambodia, and Mongolia. Primitive African art, Indian sculptures, Russian icons, and Persian miniatures round out the international collections. Contemporary art of the Northwest is also represented. Changing exhibits throughout the year. **Open:** Wed–Sun noon–5pm. Closed some hols. **Free**

Florence

The City of Rhododendrons, located at the mouth of the Siuslaw River. Explore Old Town or hop aboard a seaplane for a bird's-eye view of the coastline. Northern gateway to Oregon Dunes National Recreation Area. **Information:** Florence Area Chamber of Commerce, 270 US 101, PO Box 26000, Florence, 97439 (tel 541/997-3128).

MOTELS

Best Western Pier Point Inn
85625 US 101 S, PO Box 2235, 97439; tel 541/997-3828 or toll free 800/435-6736; fax 541/997-3828. South of town center. Located on a high bluff with a great view of the Siuslaw River, this well-maintained property offers all the services of a large chain. **Rooms:** 55 rms. CI 4pm/CO 11am. Nonsmoking rms avail. **Amenities:** Cable TV w/movies. No A/C. Some units w/terraces. **Facilities:** 100 ♿ Sauna, whirlpool. **Rates (CP):** Peak (May 1–Sept 4) $99–$109 S or D. Extra person $8. Children under age 12 stay free. Lower rates off-season. Parking: Outdoor, free. Group rates during the off season. AE, CB, DC, DISC, MC, V.

The Driftwood Shores Resort and Conference Center
88416 1st Ave, 97439; tel 541/997-8263 or toll free 800/422-5091; fax 541/997-5857. Bustling with families, this motel is situated on a wide, uncrowded beach. Great for groups. **Rooms:** 135 rms, stes, and effic. CI 4pm/CO 11am. Nonsmoking rms avail. Almost all rooms have kitchenettes. **Amenities:** Cable TV, refrig. No A/C. All units w/terraces, some w/fireplaces. **Services:** VCRs available for rent. **Facilities:** 150 1 restaurant, 1 bar, 1 beach (ocean), volleyball, whirlpool. **Rates:** $73 S or D; $215–$275 ste; $95–$110 effic. Extra person $15. Children under age 13 stay free. Parking: Outdoor, free. Golf package for nearby course. AE, CB, DC, DISC, MC, V.

Park Motel
85034 US 101 S, 97349; tel 541/997-2634 or toll free 800/392-0441. Rustic and lovingly maintained grounds make this place appear to be in its own little park. As homey as any North Woods cabin, this motel can make you forget that you're only 300 feet from the highway. **Rooms:** 17 rms and effic. CI 3pm/CO 11am. Nonsmoking rms avail. **Amenities:** Cable TV, refrig. No A/C. 1 unit w/terrace. **Services:** Pet fee $5/day. **Facilities:** 35 Two fully equipped RV sites. **Rates:** Peak (June–Sept) $49 S; $59–$64 D; $69 effic; $109 cottage/villa. Extra person $5. Children under age 2 stay free. Lower rates off-season. Parking: Outdoor, free. Weekend specials in off season. AE, CB, DC, DISC, MC, V.

RESTAURANTS

Bridgewater Seafood Restaurant
1297 Bay St; tel 541/997-9405. In Old Town wharf area. **Seafood/Steak.** Located in a 1901 building, this Old Town

hangout has ceiling fans, wicker chairs, and knickknack-covered walls. The mostly seafood and steak menu changes regularly. Excellent desserts: strawberry shortcake, homemade cheesecake, zuccatto (raspberries and Amaretto in a pound cake mold). **FYI:** Reservations recommended. Children's menu. **Open:** Peak (June–Sept) daily 11am–10pm. **Prices:** Main courses $10–$15. MC, V.

Fisherman's Wharf
1341 Bay St; tel 541/997-2613. East of US 101. **American.** Sufficient for a late-night or early morning bite, this centrally located coffeehouse features seafood and traditional American fare. **FYI:** Reservations accepted. **Open:** Daily 24 hrs. **Prices:** Main courses $6–$12. MC, V.

ATTRACTION

Sea Lion Caves
91560 OR 101; tel 541/547-3111. Home of a population of sea lions. During fall and winter, the sea lions usually stay inside the cave; during the warmer months they frequent the outside rocks, where they breed and bear their pups. Sea birds—mainly gulls, cormorants, and pigeon guillemots—also populate the area, and there are special platforms for whale watching. Guided tours start at the visitors center/gift shop, continuing along a scenic pathway to the elevator that takes visitors into the 200-foot-deep sea cave. **Open:** June–Aug, daily 8am–dusk; Sept–May, daily 9am–dusk. Closed Dec 25. **$$**

Gleneden Beach

Home of Salishan Lodge, one of Oregon's finest destination resorts. Sprawled over 1,000 acres, the community features an 18-hole golf course, a 750-acre forest, and great views of the surf.

RESORT

Salishan Lodge
US 101, 97388; tel 541/764-3600 or toll free 800/452-2300; fax 541/764-3681. 700 acres. A style-setting resort when it opened in 1965, the Lodge, built onto a wooded hillside, is a collection of low-profile timber buildings constructed throughout with Oregon timber and stone and connected by covered walkways. Although on the coast, it's located across US 101 and a tad too far from the ocean to be considered a beach resort. But the wonderful scenic beach is worth the five-minute drive—especially for beachcombing. **Rooms:** 205 rms. CI 4pm/CO noon. Nonsmoking rms avail. All are large and done in contemporary rustic style with interior walls of rough-hewn wood and brick. Balconies overlook ocean, inlet, or fairways. Siletz Bay rooms have whirlpool tubs and windows on two sides (but, surprisingly, no cross-ventilation). Well-equipped bathrooms with dressing areas. Small closets. **Amenities:** A/C, cable TV w/movies, bathrobes. All units w/minibars, all w/terraces, all w/fireplaces, some w/whirlpools. **Services:** Twice-daily maid svce, car-rental desk, babysitting. Staff of 285. Firewood supplied daily. Cellular phones for rent. **Facilities:** 18 3 3 restaurants (*see* "Restaurants" below), 1 bar (w/entertainment), 1 beach (ocean), games rm, sauna, whirlpool, beauty salon, playground. Exceptional sports facilities enhanced by recent addition of 18-hole "putting course"; 18 holes of golf just $35 in summer (electric carts optional). Miles of jogging and hiking trails. Resort-owned shopping center across US 101. Private covered carports; parking area at beach reserved for resort guests. **Rates:** Peak (July–Oct) $164–$236 S or D. Extra person $15. Children under age 12 stay free. Min stay peak. Lower rates off-season. Parking: Outdoor, free. Rates vary with size, not view, but second floor is better (higher ceilings, better views). Golf, tennis, and wine-lover packages avail. AE, CB, DC, DISC, MC, V.

RESTAURANT

The Dining Room at Salishan Lodge
In Salishan Lodge, US 101; tel 541/764-3600. **Northwest.** At first sight, Salishan Lodge, a sprawling, low-profile, cedar-shingled resort on a wooded hillside, hardly seems like the venue for one of the country's finest wine cellars. But travelers drive from all over to pick and choose among the 15,000 bottles and savor chef Rob Pounding's Chinook salmon smoked with three woods; terrine of corned duck and couscous gratinee with a ragout of fresh mushrooms; or seared pancetta-wrapped sea scallops. The split-level setting and panoramic windows give most tables a view of Siletz Bay, and the rustic ambience is tastefully complemented by fine linens and china. **FYI:** Reservations recommended. Children's menu. Dress code. No smoking. **Open:** Daily 5:30–10pm. **Prices:** Main courses $18–$26. AE, CB, DC, DISC, MC, V.

Gold Beach

Rough-and-tumble Rogue River spills into the sea between Gold Beach and its twin, Wedderburn. Jet boats travel upriver, with possible glimpses of bears, beavers, sea lions, eagles and other wild critters. Fine steelhead and salmon fishing. Forest trails reveal ancient trees, secret coves. **Information:** Gold Beach Visitors Center, 1225 S Ellensburg Ave #3, Gold Beach, 97444 (tel 541/247-7526).

MOTELS

Gold Beach Resort
1330 S Ellensburg Ave, 97444; tel 541/247-7066 or toll free 800/541-0947; fax 541/247-7069. Just S of town, on US 101. Freshly refurbished; large, clean rooms. **Rooms:** 39 rms. CI 2pm/CO 11am. Nonsmoking rms avail. **Amenities:** Cable TV, refrig. No A/C. All units w/terraces. **Services:** Twice-daily maid svce. **Facilities:** 250 1 beach

(ocean), whirlpool. Beach is well lighted at night. **Rates:** Peak (May 15–Sept) $79 S; $89–$99 D. Extra person $8. Lower rates off-season. Parking: Outdoor, free. AE, DC, DISC, MC, V.

Ireland's Rustic Lodges

1120 S Ellensburg Ave, PO Box 774, 97444; tel 541/247-7718. This rustic motel offers large, wood-burning fireplaces and balconies overlooking the ocean waves, so you'll never feel like you're roughing it. Great North Woods atmosphere, without the isolation. Just a short walk to the beach. **Rooms:** 40 rms and effic; 11 cottages/villas. CI 1pm/CO 11am. Nonsmoking rms avail. Like having your own cozy wilderness cabin. **Amenities:** Cable TV w/movies. No A/C or phone. Some units w/terraces, some w/fireplaces. **Services:** Twice-daily maid svce. **Facilities:** 20 1 beach (ocean), playground, washer/dryer. **Rates:** Peak (June–Sept) $50–$66 S or D; $40–$45 effic; $60–$80 cottage/villa. Extra person $10. Lower rates off-season. Parking: Outdoor, free. No CC.

Jot's Resort

94360 Wedderburn Loop, Wedderburn, PO Box J, Gold Beach, 97444; tel 541/247-6676 or toll free 800/367-5687; fax 541/247-6716. Just below Rogue River Bridge. A large complex located on the bank of the Rogue River, with great recreational possibilities nearby. **Rooms:** 140 rms, stes, and effic; 35 cottages/villas. CI 4pm/CO 11am. Nonsmoking rms avail. All rooms overlook the water. **Amenities:** Cable TV, refrig, VCR. No A/C. All units w/terraces, some w/fireplaces. **Services:** Babysitting. Motor-boat rentals, guided deep-sea fishing, and river-running trips. **Facilities:** 250 1 restaurant, 1 bar, games rm, sauna, whirlpool, washer/dryer. Boat moorings available for guests. **Rates:** Peak (June 15–Sept 15) $80 S; $80–$90 D; $115 ste; $100 effic; $120–$165 cottage/villa. Extra person $5. Children under age 12 stay free. Lower rates off-season. Parking: Outdoor, free. AE, CB, DC, DISC, MC, V.

LODGE

Tu Tu' Tun Lodge

96550 North Bank Rogue, 97444; tel 541/247-6664; fax 541/247-0672. Innkeepers Dirk and Laurie Van Zante treat visitors like personal guests. With a massive stone fireplace at its center, the lodge is both architecturally striking and first-rate in its appointments. **Rooms:** 19 rms and stes; 1 cottage/villa. CI 3pm/CO 11am. No smoking. Sophisticated, individually decorated rooms. **Amenities:** A/C, TV, refrig, bathrobes. All units w/terraces, all w/fireplaces. **Services:** Social director, masseur, babysitting. Guided fishing and white-water rafting trips can be arranged. **Facilities:** 4 50 1 restaurant, 1 bar, 1 beach (cove/inlet), games rm, lawn games, washer/dryer. Hiking trails nearby. **Rates:** $125–$195 S or D; $170–$180 ste; $195 cottage/villa. Extra person $10. Children under age 4 stay free. Min stay peak. MAP rates avail. Parking: Outdoor, free. Breakfast and dinner available for an additional $37.50/day. DISC, MC, V.

RESTAURANTS

Captain's Table

1295 S Ellensburg Ave; tel 541/247-6308. S end of town; on US 101. **Seafood/Steak.** The decor here skews toward aging, dark-wood nautical, but the food makes up for the uninspired setting. This is fresh-fish country, and you'll find plenty of selections here: salmon teriyaki, shrimp scampi, plus the catch of the day. A range of steaks is also featured. **FYI:** Reservations not accepted. **Open:** Peak (June–Aug) daily 5–10pm. **Prices:** Main courses $10–$30. MC, V.

The Chowderhead Restaurant

910 S Ellensburg Ave; tel 541/247-0588. On US 101. **Seafood/Northwest.** A simple setting, with large windows overlooking the ocean. The menu not only describes the seafood—it also explains where the local varieties of fish are caught. The Rogue Coast Combo spotlights local seafood bounty, including red snapper, ling cod, salmon, and halibut. **FYI:** Reservations not accepted. Children's menu. **Open:** Peak (June–Sept) daily 11am–10pm. **Prices:** Main courses $10–$30. AE, DISC, MC, V.

Nor'Wester Seafood

10 Harbor Way; tel 541/247-2333. Off US 101. **Seafood/Steak.** A sophisticated local institution, this restaurant by the harbor overlooks the coast through the large windows. Good bets are the prawns and scallops mardi gras, and the pasta and shrimp tapenade. Portions are large, and the cuisine robust. **FYI:** Reservations not accepted. Children's menu. No smoking. **Open:** Peak (July–Sept) daily 5–10pm. Closed Thanksgiving–Christmas. **Prices:** Main courses $12–$20. AE, MC, V.

$ Wong's Cafe

280 N Ellensburg Ave; tel 541/247-7423. Off US 101. **Chinese.** A nice little addition to a region starved for ethnic-cuisine diversity. Try the chow yuk (vegetables, sautéed chicken, barbecued pork, ham, and shrimp) and Kung Pao tofu. Great value. **FYI:** Reservations recommended. Children's menu. No liquor license. No smoking. **Open:** Wed–Fri 11:30am–9:30pm, Sat–Sun 4–9:30pm, Mon 11:30am–9:30pm. **Prices:** Main courses $5–$9. MC, V.

Government Camp

See Mount Hood National Forest

Grants Pass

Oregon's white-water rafting capital. Activities in the area include exploring the caverns at Oregon Caves National

Monument, jet-boat tours, steelhead and salmon fishing, antique shopping, pari-mutuel horse racing, hiking in the nearby Siskiyous, or driving through scenic Illinois Valley. **Information:** Grants Pass Convention and Visitors Bureau, 1501 NE 6th, PO Box 1787, Grants Pass, 97526 (tel 541/476-5510).

MOTELS

Best Western Grants Pass Inn

111 NE Agness Ave, 97526; tel 541/476-1117 or toll free 800/553-ROOM; fax 541/479-4315. Exit 55 off I-5. Clean and convenient to the freeway, this property is popular with businesspeople, but the pool makes it a good choice for families too. **Rooms:** 84 rms, stes, and effic. CI open/CO 11am. Nonsmoking rms avail. Relatively quiet, considering the freeway location. The room for guests with disabilities is especially well designed and includes a roll-in shower. **Amenities:** A/C, dataport. Some units w/whirlpools. **Services:** $5 per pet per night. **Facilities:** 1 restaurant (bkfst only), 1 bar, whirlpool, washer/dryer. Pool and hot tub (both renovated in 1995) are shared with the adjacent Holiday Inn Express. **Rates:** Peak (May 15–Oct 15) $69–$125 S; $79–$125 D; $125 ste; $110 effic. Extra person $5. Children under age 18 stay free. Lower rates off-season. Parking: Outdoor, free. AE, CB, DC, DISC, EC, ER, JCB, MC, V.

Best Western Inn at the Rogue

8959 Rogue River Hwy, 97527; tel 541/582-2200 or toll free 800/238-0700; fax 541/582-1415. Exit 48 off I-5; across river from city of Rogue River. 2 acres. Elegant new facility, conveniently located on I-5 between Medford and Grants Pass. Travelers will appreciate the security of a 24-hour-attended lobby and locked corridors. Well worth the price. **Rooms:** 54 rms, stes, and effic. CI 2pm/CO 11am. Nonsmoking rms avail. Upper-level rooms have views of Rogue River and the nearby wooded hills. **Amenities:** A/C, cable TV w/movies. 1 unit w/terrace, some w/whirlpools. Full of thoughtful touches, such as a night light over the toilet. **Services:** Babysitting. **Facilities:** 60 Whirlpool, washer/dryer. Well-kept exercise room offers step machine, cycle, and free weights. The city park across the road fronts the river, and there are raft rentals and jet-boat excursions nearby. **Rates (CP):** Peak (June 23–Sept 15) $64–$129 S; $74–$129 D; $129–$179 ste; $145 effic. Extra person $5. Children under age 12 stay free. Lower rates off-season. Parking: Outdoor, free. AE, CB, DC, DISC, MC, V.

Grants Pass Thrift Lodge

748 SE 7th St, 97526; tel 541/476-7793 or toll free 800/525-9055; fax 541/479-4812. Between L and M. Basic downtown motel with decent, if a bit noisy, rooms. **Rooms:** 35 rms. CI 1pm/CO 11am. Nonsmoking rms avail. **Amenities:** A/C, cable TV. **Services:** Fax service. **Facilities:** **Rates:** Peak (Apr–Oct) $40–$45 S or D. Extra person $6. Children under age 17 stay free. Lower rates off-season. Parking: Outdoor, free. Weekend rates higher. AE, CB, DC, DISC, MC, V.

Knights' Inn Motel

104 SE 7th St, 97526 (Downtown); tel 541/479-5595 or toll free 800/826-6835; fax 541/479-5256. At G St. Basic and clean property located near a variety of restaurants and businesses. **Rooms:** 32 rms and effic. CI open/CO 11am. Nonsmoking rms avail. Rooms are relatively quiet despite the noisy location. Some accommodations face a dark alleyway. Small but clean kitchenettes, with dishes and pots on request. **Amenities:** A/C, cable TV w/movies. **Services:** **Facilities:** **Rates:** Peak (Mem Day–mid-Sept) $35–$37 S; $40–$44 D; $38–$44 effic. Children under age 12 stay free. Lower rates off-season. Parking: Outdoor, free. AE, DC, DISC, MC, V.

Redwood Motel

815 NE 6th St, 97526; tel 541/476-0878; fax 541/476-1032. 1 mi S of exit 58 off I-5. An oasis set among redwood trees, despite its location on a very busy street. Good value. **Rooms:** 25 rms and effic. CI 2pm/CO 11am. Nonsmoking rms avail. Very clean. Half the rooms have been remodeled recently; older rooms are smaller and darker. Nine units have two bedrooms. Kitchenettes are fully equipped (even dog biscuits are included). **Amenities:** A/C, cable TV w/movies. Some units w/terraces. **Services:** Manager is fishing/raft guide. Complimentary coffee 7am–11pm. Designated lawn areas for pets and for barbecuing. Pet fee $5/night. **Facilities:** Whirlpool, playground, washer/dryer. **Rates (CP):** Peak (May–Sept) $50–$90 S or D; $65–$100 effic. Extra person $5. Children under age 12 stay free. Lower rates off-season. Parking: Outdoor, free. AE, CB, DC, DISC, MC, V.

Riverside Inn Resort & Conference Center

971 SE 6th St, 97526; tel 541/476-6873 or toll free 800/334-4567; fax 541/474-9848. Between 6th and 7th Sts at Rogue River. Set on a bank of the Rogue River, this three-story building has three separate wings. **Rooms:** 174 rms, stes, and effic; 1 cottage/villa. CI 4pm/CO 11am. Nonsmoking rms avail. Rooms in the west wing offer the nicest river views; accommodations in the east wing feature views of a city park. **Amenities:** A/C. Some units w/terraces, some w/fireplaces. **Services:** Babysitting. Security guard patrols property 24 hours. First pet $15/visit; $5 per additional pet. **Facilities:** 300 1 restaurant (bkfst only; *see* "Restaurants" below), 1 bar (w/entertainment), whirlpool. Guests pay reduced rate at adjacent fitness center. **Rates:** Peak (mid-June–mid-Sept) $85–$95 S or D; $120–$175 ste; $140 effic; $350 cottage/villa. Extra person $10. Children under age 12 stay free. Lower rates off-season. Parking: Outdoor, free. AE, CB, DC, DISC, MC, V.

Shilo Inn

1880 NW 6th St, 97526; tel 541/479-8391 or toll free 800/222-2244; fax 541/474-7344. Exit 58 off I-5. Located on a busy street near freeway and fast-food restaurants. Nice, but no views. **Rooms:** 70 rms. CI 2pm/CO noon. Nonsmoking rms avail. Minisuites offer sleeper sofa. **Amenities:** A/C, satel TV, dataport. Refrigerator and microwave in minisuites. **Services:** VCRs for rent. Coffee and popcorn 24 hours in lobby; complimentary *USA Today*. Free dog biscuits and cat food. $7 fee for pets. Fax service. **Facilities:** 15 Sauna, steam rm. Private but very small pool; children's pool is tiny. **Rates (CP):** Peak (mid-May–mid-Sept) $59–$79 S. Extra person $7. Children under age 15 stay free. Lower rates off-season. Parking: Outdoor, free. AE, DC, DISC, EC, JCB, MC, V.

RESORT

Paradise Ranch Inn

7000 Monument Dr, 97526 (North Valley); tel 541/479-4333; fax 541/479-7821. Exit 61 off I-5, then 2 mi N on Monument Dr. 319 acres. Set among willow-lined ponds stocked with trout and covered with waterlilies. Attracts fishing enthusiasts, especially in the fall. **Rooms:** 15 rms and effic; 2 cottages/villas. CI 3pm/CO 11am. Nonsmoking rms avail. Rooms are attractive, but not as exceptional as the beautiful grounds might lead you to believe. They vary, with some having newer, nicer baths. **Amenities:** A/C. No phone or TV. 1 unit w/terrace, 1 w/whirlpool. **Services:** Babysitting. $10 per pet per night. **Facilities:** 9 2 140 1 restaurant (bkfst and dinner only; *see* "Restaurants" below), volleyball, games rm, whirlpool. Restaurant, located in an old farmhouse, has a scenic view of the ponds. **Rates (CP):** Peak (May–Sept) $100 effic; $125 cottage/villa. Extra person $15. Lower rates off-season. MAP rates avail. Parking: Outdoor, free. MC, V.

RESTAURANTS

Legrand's

323 NE E St; tel 541/471-1554. At 9th. **Continental.** Gleaming dark wood tables, two intimate dining rooms, murals of Provence, and a mostly European staff lend this airy bakery/restaurant its sophisticated ambience. Day starters include eggs and omelettes in various dress, while the lunch menu features salads, sandwiches, and small entrees of pasta, seafood, and chicken. Dinner entree choices might be rack of lamb with cumin sauce, or roasted sea bass with herb crust. Pastries, breads, salads, and pâtés (all made on premises) are available to go. **FYI:** Reservations recommended. No smoking. **Open:** Breakfast Fri–Sun 8:30–11am; lunch daily 11am–2pm; dinner Fri–Sat 4–9:30pm, Sun–Thurs 4–8:30pm. **Prices:** Main courses $11–$17. DISC, MC, V.

Paradise Ranch Inn

7000 Monument Dr; tel 541/479-4333. Exit 61 off I-5, 2 mi N. **Continental/Northwest.** Lovely views of the estatelike grounds and ponds make this small, eight-table dining room seem spacious. Seafood and continental specialties head the menu. Expect gracious and attentive service. During nice weather, you can eat out on the deck; in winter, the old farmhouse parlor (with fireplace) is cozy and romantic. **FYI:** Reservations recommended. **Open:** Breakfast daily 8–10am; dinner daily 4:30–8:30pm; brunch Sun 10am–2pm. **Prices:** Main courses $9–$16. MC, V.

Riverside Restaurant & Lounge

In Riverside Inn, 971 SE 6th St; tel 541/471-2003. On Rogue River. **Northwest.** Bi-level restaurant and lounge with views of the Rogue River. The deck is very popular in summer—especially with the all-you-can-eat chicken and ribs barbecue. The regular menu features specialties such as whiskey steak and rosemary chicken. The upper-level dining room closes between 2:30pm and 4:40pm; the lower-level lounge stays open all day but is often inundated with crowds from arriving tour boats. **FYI:** Reservations recommended. Country music/dancing. Children's menu. Dress code. **Open:** Peak (May 15–Oct 15) daily 6:30am–11pm. **Prices:** Main courses $8–$15. AE, DISC, MC, V.

★ Si Casa Flores

In Williams Hwy Shopping Center, 1632 Williams Plaza; tel 541/474-7198. **Mexican.** Regarded as the most authentic Mexican eatery in town, with a menu featuring specialties from Jalisco, Mazatlan, and Guadalajara. Carne asada and platillo de Mazatlan (with shrimp, chicken, and red snapper) rank among the house favorites. The friendly wait staff wears colorful shirts, and all belong to the large, extended Flores family. Covered, heated patio is open year round. **FYI:** Reservations recommended. No smoking. Additional location: 2332 Poplar Dr, Medford (tel 503/857-1770). **Open:** Peak (May–Oct) Fri–Sat 11am–10:30pm, Sun–Thurs 11am–9:30pm. **Prices:** Main courses $7–$11. MC, V.

★ Wild River Brewing & Pizza Company

595 NE E St; tel 541/471-7487. At F St and Mill St. **Pizza/Northwest.** Large ficus plants, copper beer tanks, and hanging tapestries set the mood at this microbrewery-cum-restaurant, where tours and free beer tastings are offered throughout the day. Wild River began operating in 1990, and they currently produce a wide range of brews, from a very light *kolsh* to the dark imperial stout to a barley wine with 8% alcohol. Foodwise, the salads are crisp and fresh and the pizzas (from wood-fired ovens) are noteworthy, topped with everything from sausage to refried beans. Burgers, sandwiches, and pastas round out the menu. **FYI:** Reservations recommended. Beer and wine only. No smoking. Additional location: 249 N Redwood Hwy (US 199), Cave Junction (tel 592-3556). **Open:** Daily 10:30am–11pm. **Prices:** Main courses $5–$8. MC, V.

ATTRACTIONS

Schmidt House Museum
508 SW 5th St; tel 541/479-7827. The Schmidt family, homesteaders who came to America from Germany in the mid-1880s, lived in this home from 1899 to 1978. The house is now occupied by the Josephine County Historical Society; otherwise, few changes have been made to the building's construction and interior decor. Rooms are decorated in period fashion, and most of the furnishings and fixtures are original to the house. A special collection of antique toys and children's belongings is the focus of one room. The garden contains many native Oregon plants and flowers. **Open:** Tues–Fri 1–4pm. Closed some hols. **$**

Grower's Market
4th and T Sts; tel 541/476-5375. The market, a self-supporting cooperative effort to increase agriculture in Josephine County, offers local patrons and tourists a chance to buy farm-fresh produce, flowers from local greenhouses, and a myriad of handcrafted arts, crafts, and homemade foods. Vendors ship their products to over half the states in the country and to foreign countries as well. **Open:** June–Sept, Sat and Tues 9am–1pm; Mar–May, Oct–Nov, Sat 9am–1pm. **Free**

Siskiyou National Forest
200 NE Greenfield Rd; tel 541/471-6500. This forest's 1.1 million acres contain over 600 miles of trails, five National Wilderness Areas, and a wild and scenic river. Hawks, owls, deer, elk and bears live amongst the forest's huge variety of trees and plants and its inspiring scenery such as the natural rock garden wonderland in the **Kalmiopsis Wilderness.** Campgrounds (open Mem Day to Labor Day) are located in quiet, scenic areas and sites are available on a first-come, first-served basis with a 14-day limit. Picnic areas are also available. Commercial outfitters can arrange guided rafting and backpacking trips. Fishing licenses are required to fish the forest's lakes, which are stocked with salmon, steelhead, and trout; and Rogue River, which is famous for its salmon.

The forest may be accessed via I-5 South or North. There are a number of state parks in or near the forest; for more information about these parks, call 503/238-7488. **Open:** Most ranger district offices, Mon–Fri 8am–5pm. **Free**

Harbor

MOTEL

Best Western Beachfront Inn
16008 Boat Basin Rd, PO Box 2729, 97415; tel 541/469-7779 or toll free 800/468-4081; fax 541/469-0283. US 101 to Lower Harbor Road. Located next to the marina, this is the only oceanfront motel in the area. Every room faces the ocean and private balconies offer great views of the Pacific Coast. **Rooms:** 78 rms, stes, and effic. CI 2pm/CO 11am. Nonsmoking rms avail. **Amenities:** Cable TV, refrig. No A/C. All units w/terraces, some w/whirlpools. Microwave. 18 have whirlpools with windows overlooking the ocean. **Services:** **Facilities:** 48 1 restaurant, 1 bar, 1 beach (ocean), whirlpool, washer/dryer. **Rates:** Peak (May 26–Sept) $74–$84 S; $79–$89 D; $160 ste; $84–$105 effic. Extra person $5. Children under age 3 stay free. Min stay special events. Lower rates off-season. Parking: Outdoor, free. AE, DC, DISC, MC, V.

Hells Canyon National Recreation Area

See Wallowa-Whitman National Forest

Hood River

See also Mount Hood National Forest, The Dalles

Brisk Columbia River Gorge winds make this a prime spot for sailboarding, attracting international competitions. The river is can be thick with 'boarders at times. Fine views of Mount Hood and the Hood River Valley are available from Panorama Point. **Information:** Hood River County Chamber of Commerce, Port Marina Park, Hood River, 97031 (tel 541/386-2057).

HOTELS

Columbia Gorge Hotel
4000 Westcliff Dr, 97031; tel 541/386-5566 or toll free 800/345-1921; fax 541/387-5414. Exit 62 off I-84. Built in 1921, this yellow stucco, Spanish-style hotel overlooks a waterfall and the Columbia River. Paths wind through the beautifully landscaped gardens. **Rooms:** 44 rms and stes. CI 3pm/CO noon. Some accommodations have views of the gardens; others look out over the river and green hills of Washington. **Amenities:** Cable TV, bathrobes. No A/C. Some units w/fireplaces. Morning newspaper at the door, evening chocolates, and a rose on the pillow. **Services:** Babysitting. **Facilities:** 150 1 restaurant (*see* "Restaurants" below), 1 bar. **Rates (BB):** $150–$270 S or D; $295–$365 ste. Extra person $30. Children under age 5 stay free. Parking: Outdoor, free. Lower rates apply Sun–Thurs. AE, DISC, MC, V.

Hood River Hotel
102 Oak St, 97031 (Downtown); tel 541/386-1900. Corner of 1st. A renovated, historic brick hotel with an old-fashioned brass elevator, tall windows, ceiling fans, and spacious, cheerful rooms. Located on the town's main thoroughfare. **Rooms:** 41 rms, stes, and effic. CI 4pm/CO noon. Nonsmoking rms avail. Some rooms are noisy because of street traffic and passing trains. **Amenities:** Cable TV. No A/C.

Services: Babysitting. Drinks, coffee, and tea by the fireplace in the lobby. **Facilities:** 1 restaurant, 1 bar (w/entertainment). **Rates:** Peak (Mar–Nov) $59–$85 S; $69–$95 D; $105–$145 ste; $105–$145 effic. Extra person $10. Children under age 12 stay free. Lower rates off-season. AE, DC, DISC, MC, V.

MOTELS

Best Western Hood River Inn

1108 E Marina Way, 97031; tel 541/386-2200 or toll free 800/828-7873; fax 541/386-8905. Off OR 35, by the bridge. This handsome, gray, lodgelike motel overlooks the Columbia River and is close to town. A good choice for groups and business travelers. **Rooms:** 149 rms and stes. CI 4pm/CO noon. Nonsmoking rms avail. Quiet, comfortable, well-appointed rooms; those in the west wing are older and smaller. **Amenities:** A/C, cable TV w/movies. Some units w/terraces, some w/fireplaces, some w/whirlpools. **Services:** Babysitting. **Facilities:** 1 restaurant, 1 bar (w/entertainment), volleyball, washer/dryer. Local windsurfing center offers lessons and rentals to guests. **Rates:** Peak (June–Oct) $73–$93 S; $79–$99 D; $115–$149 ste. Extra person $6. Children under age 18 stay free. Lower rates off-season. Parking: Outdoor, free. Commercial and government rates. AE, DC, DISC, MC, V.

Love's Riverview Lodge

1505 Oak St, 97031; tel 541/386-8719; fax 541/386-6671. Exit 62 off I-84, west of downtown. Two-story hillside motel with partial views of the Columbia River and Mount Adams, in Washington. The newest section, built in 1994, stands back further from the road. **Rooms:** 15 rms. CI 2pm/CO 11am. Nonsmoking rms avail. Nicely kept, reasonably quiet rooms have blond furniture and a pastel decor. **Amenities:** A/C, satel TV w/movies, refrig. Some rooms have microwaves. Hair dryers available on request. **Services:** **Facilities:** Laundromat nearby. **Rates:** Peak (June–Oct) $59–$72 S or D. Extra person $5. Children under age 13 stay free. Lower rates off-season. Parking: Outdoor, free. AE, CB, DC, DISC, MC, V.

Vagabond Lodge

4070 Westcliff Dr, 97031; tel 541/386-2992. Exit 62 off I-84, in Columbia River Gorge. Four buildings scattered along a wooded bluff overlooking the Columbia River. **Rooms:** 41 rms, stes, and effic. CI 1pm/CO 11am. Nonsmoking rms avail. Accommodations vary from standard motel-style rooms to very good quality, restful retreats. The quietest and most appealing rooms are away from the road, facing the river. **Amenities:** Cable TV. No A/C. Some units w/terraces, some w/fireplaces, some w/whirlpools. Some rooms are air conditioned. Alarm clocks provided upon request. **Services:** **Facilities:** Basketball, playground. **Rates:** $45–$65 S or D; $59–$75 ste; $75 effic. Extra person $6. Parking: Outdoor, free. AE, MC, V.

RESTAURANTS

Columbia River Court Dining Room

In Columbia Gorge Hotel, 4000 Westcliff Dr; tel 541/386-5566. Off I-84. **New American.** This gracious restaurant overlooking the Columbia River is well known for its multi-course farm breakfast. The adjacent Valentino Lounge (Rudolph was a regular, as were several other Jazz Age celebrities) is a pleasant place to enjoy an aperitif or after-dinner drink. **FYI:** Reservations recommended. Jazz. Dress code. No smoking. **Open:** Breakfast Mon–Sat 8–11am; lunch Mon–Sat 11:30am–2:30pm; dinner Mon–Fri 4–9pm, Sat–Sun 4–10pm; brunch Sun 8am–2:30pm. **Prices:** Main courses $18–$28. AE, MC, V.

The Mesquitery

1219 12th St; tel 541/386-2002. **Barbecue.** A lively, casual spot with booths, tables, and an open kitchen specializing in mesquite-grilled foods. The bar, called The Shed, is decorated with beer labels and has a large TV and pool table. Large list of draft beers, including microbrews. **FYI:** Reservations not accepted. Blues/jazz/rock. Dress code. No smoking. **Open:** Peak (Mothers Day–Labor Day) lunch Wed–Fri 11:30am–2pm; dinner Wed–Sun 4:30–9:30pm. **Prices:** Main courses $11–$16. AE, MC, V.

Sixth Street Bistro & Loft

509 Cascade St; tel 541/386-5737. On 6th, between Cascade and Oak Streets. **Northwest.** A casual, friendly hillside bistro serving a generally northwest-style cuisine including pasta, seafood, and burgers. Emphasis is on local products. Children's portions are available. Bar stays open until midnight. **FYI:** Reservations accepted. No smoking. **Open:** Peak (June–Oct) daily 11am–9pm. Closed 2 weeks in winter. **Prices:** Main courses $10–$13. MC, V.

★ Stonehedge

3405 Cascade St; tel 541/386-3940. ¼ mile off Cascade St, in West Hood River. **Continental.** Picturesque, low stone walls surround this 1905 historic house set against a wooded hillside. Stained glass, oriental carpets, and lace curtains continue the homelike feeling at this fine restaurant. The menu offers steak, chicken, seafood, duckling, and lamb entrees; lighter dishes are also available. **FYI:** Reservations recommended. Dinner theater. Dress code. No smoking. **Open:** Peak (May–Oct) Wed–Sun 5–10pm. **Prices:** Main courses $14–$19. AE, DC, DISC, MC, V.

ATTRACTIONS

Columbia River Gorge National Scenic Area

Tel 541/386-2333. Spanning nearly 70 miles from Portland to The Dalles, the Columbia River Gorge connects the rain-soaked forests on the west-side of the mountains with the desert-dry "rain shadow" areas of central Oregon. In between these two extremes lie plants and wildflowers that are unique to the area. In 1915 a scenic highway was built through the gorge, and in 1986 much of the area was designated a National Scenic Area to preserve its spectacular natural beauty.

Looming over the gorge are two snow-capped sentinels—**Mount Adams** and **Mount Hood.** Mount Adams, at 12,307 feet in elevation, is the least accessible and least visited of the Cascades; the 11,235-foot tall Mount Hood, on the other hand, is home to five ski areas and a historic mountain lodge. The scenic area is home to many picturesque waterfalls—Latourelle Falls, Shepherd's Dell Falls, Bridalveil Falls, Mist Falls, and Wahkeena Falls, to name a few—but none are more famous than 620-foot tall **Multnomah Falls** (see Troutdale). An interpretive display at the foot of the falls explains the geologic history of the Columbia Gorge, and there are hiking trails connecting Multnomah with Mount Hood National Forest.

Other scenic highlights of the area include the **Bridge of the Gods** (which, according to Native American legend, is built on the site of a natural stone bridge used by the gods) and the **Cascade Locks.** The area around Hood River is especially popular with sailboarders, who take advantage of the river's gusty winds. **Open:** Daily 24 hrs. **Free**

Full Sail Brew Pub & Tasting Room
506 Columbia St; tel 541/386-2247. Produces eight year-round beers and six seasonal brews, including ale, lager, stout, porter, and bock. An English-style pub doubles as a tasting room, where visitors can look out over the Columbia River Gorge. **Open:** Mid-May–mid-Oct, daily noon–8pm; mid-Oct–mid-May, Thurs–Sun noon–8pm. Closed some hols. **Free**

Jacksonville

This gold-rush town is one of only eight US cities named as a National Historic Landmark. Summer Britt Festival draws top jazz, pop, classical artists. **Information:** Jacksonville Chamber of Commerce and Visitors Information, PO Box 33, Jacksonville, 97530 (tel 541/899-8118).

MOTEL

The Stage Lodge
830 N 5th St, PO Box 1316, 97530; tel 541/899-3953 or toll free 800/253-8254; fax 541/899-7556. This motel blends in nicely with Jacksonville's renowned 19th-century buildings. The office closely resembles an old farmhouse originally on the property. Within walking distance to town and Britt Music festival. **Rooms:** 27 rms and stes. CI 2pm/CO 11am. Nonsmoking rms avail. Attractive rooms are spacious with coordinated decor; all accommodations have ceiling fans and armoires. **Amenities:** A/C, cable TV. Some units w/fireplaces, some w/whirlpools. **Services:** **Rates (CP):** Peak (May 15–Sept) $69 S; $74 D; $125 ste. Extra person $5. Children under age 13 stay free. Lower rates off-season. Parking: Outdoor, free. AE, CB, DC, DISC, MC, V.

INN

Jacksonville Inn
175 E California St, PO Box 359, 97530 (Downtown); tel 541/899-1900 or toll free 800/321-9344; fax 541/899-1373. Located in a historic mining town. Offers extremely clean, newly renovated rooms. No elevator. **Rooms:** 8 rms; 1 cottage/villa. CI 3pm/CO 11am. No smoking. Individually decorated. Honeymoon cottage (1 block away) has picket fence and large lawn area. **Amenities:** A/C, cable TV, refrig. 1 unit w/whirlpool. Fresh flowers, mints, note cards, books, magazines, thick towels, original art, and refrigerators that are tucked out of sight. One room has dataport. **Services:** Masseur. Coffee and tea on hall table. Fax available. **Facilities:** 100 1 restaurant (*see* "Restaurants" below), 1 bar, guest lounge w/TV. **Rates (BB):** $60–$110 S; $80–$135 D; $165–$185 cottage/villa. Extra person $10. Parking: Outdoor, free. AE, DC, DISC, MC, V.

RESTAURANTS

($) ★ Bella Union Restaurant & Saloon
170 W California St; tel 541/899-1770. **Italian.** A Jacksonville institution favored for casual lunches or dinners served indoors or on a patio framed by wisteria. This old-time saloon is decorated with large watercolors of Bella Union regulars by artist Leo Meyersdorf. Favorite menu items include caesar salad, rack of lamb, fresh swordfish, plus the pastas and pizzas. All choices are also available to go; picnic baskets available for the Peter Britt Music Festival. **FYI:** Reservations not accepted. Blues/country music/folk/jazz. Children's menu. **Open:** Daily 11:30am–10pm. **Prices:** Main courses $10–$15. AE, DISC, MC, V.

★ Jacksonville Inn Dinner House
175 E California St; tel 541/899-1900. **Continental.** A celebrated eatery located in the historic Gold Rush–era Jacksonville Inn (built in 1861). The exposed sandstone walls of the cavernous lower-level dining room glint with flecks of genuine gold. Executive chef Diane Menzie offers an extensive menu, ranging from prime rib and chinook salmon to several "healthy heart" entrees. The flower-bedecked outdoor patio is also delightful, and the wine cellar houses over 700 selections. **FYI:** Reservations recommended. No smoking. **Open:** Breakfast daily 7:30–10:30am; lunch Tues–Sat 11:30am–2pm; dinner Sun 5–9pm, Mon–Sat 5–10pm; brunch Sun 10am–2pm. **Prices:** Main courses $12–$47. AE, DC, DISC, MC, V.

($) ★ McCully House Inn
240 E California St; tel 541/899-1942. **New American/International.** This local landmark—an elegant 19th-century house set amid Jackson & Perkins test rose gardens—is the perfect venue for sampling chef William Prahl's cuisine. Most items meld local and international influences, and might include pistachio- and almond-crusted lamb chops with wild rice, carmelized onions, and oyster mushrooms; or a chile-

cured sturgeon with white beans, aioli, and leeks. The inn also composes picnic baskets for the Peter Britt Music Festival. **FYI:** Reservations recommended. Children's menu. No smoking. **Open:** Peak (June 15–Sept 7) dinner Wed–Mon 5–8:30pm; brunch Sun 10am–2pm. **Prices:** Main courses $10–$25; prix fixe $30. AE, MC, V.

ATTRACTIONS

Jacksonville Museum of Southern Oregon History
206 N 1st St; tel 541/773-6536. Housed in the former county courthouse, built in 1883. In addition to exhibits on the history of Jacksonville, visitors can browse through a display of 19th century photos by pioneer photographer Peter Britt. Admission ticket is also valid for the adjacent Children's Museum, which is housed in the town's former jail. **Open:** Mem Day–Labor Day, daily 10am–5pm; Labor Day–Mem Day, Tues–Sun 10am–5pm. Closed some hols. **$**

Beekman House
470 E California St; tel 541/773-6536. At the 1876 Beekman House, history comes alive as actors in period costumes portray the family of an early Jacksonville banker. The turn-of-the-century Beekman bank is also open to the public. **Open:** Mem Day–Labor Day, daily 1–5pm. **$**

Jeremiah Nunan House
635 N Oregon St; tel 541/889-1890. Long known as the Catalog House, the Queen Anne–style Nunan home was ordered from a catalog in 1892 and shipped to Jacksonville in 14 boxcars. The house has been completely restored and is furnished with period antiques. **Open:** May–Sept, Wed–Mon 10:30am–5pm; Nov–Dec, Fri–Sun 10:30am –5pm. **$$**

Oregon Belle Mine
California St; tel 541/779-2239. Two-and-a-half-hour tours include a trip through underground tunnels dug in the 1890s, a visit to an ore mill, and a chance to pan for gold. **Open:** June–Sept, daily. **$$$$**

The House of Mystery at the Oregon Vortex
4303 Sardine Creek Rd, Gold Hill; tel 541/855-1543. 10 mi NW of Jacksonville. Originally an assay office for a gold mining company, this house stands on what was known to local Native Americans as "The Forbidden Ground." In 1943, the surrounding area was discovered to be a vortex, or a spherical force field. Visitors, lead through the house by guides who demonstrate various natural phenomena and optical illusions, are free to conduct their own experiments. **Open:** Mar–May and Sept–mid-Oct, 9am–4:15pm; June–Aug, 9am–5:15pm. **$$$**

John Day Fossil Beds National Monument

Forty-million-year-old fossil records indicate that this area, now filled with lava beds and cinder cones, was once a tropical or subtropical forest. An amazing array of tropical plants and animals—from tiny seeds to now-extinct relatives of the rhinoceros and elephant—have been preserved in one of the world's most extensive and unbroken fossil records.

To see fossil plants in their natural state, visit the **Clarno Unit** (60 mi N of US 20). Here, ancient mudflows inundated an entire forest. At the **Painted Hills Unit,** along the John Day River near Mitchell, you won't see any fossils but you will see hills with bands of strikingly colored rock caused by the weathering of volcanic ash under different climatic conditions. At the **Sheep Rock Unit,** on US 26 near Dayville, stop by the visitors center, where you can get a close-up look at some fossils and watch a paleontologist at work. Each of the three units has a picnic area. For more information, contact the John Day Fossil Beds National Monument, 420 W Main St, John Day, OR 97845 (tel 541/575-0721).

Joseph

Thriving art communities have sprung up here and in nearby Enterprise, contrasting with yet complementing the rural flavor. A tramway leads to the summit of 8,256-foot Mount Howard in visit adjacent Wallowa Lake State Park. **Information:** Joseph Chamber of Commerce, PO Box 13, Joseph, 97848 (tel 541/432-1015).

MOTELS

Eagle Cap Chalets
59879 Wallowa Lake Hwy, 97846; tel 541/432-4704; fax 541/432-4704. At the south end of Wallowa Lake, 6 mi from Joseph. Complex of chalet rooms, cabins, and condos tucked against the foot of Mount Howard, near Eagle Cap Wilderness and Wallowa Lake. Cedar-sided buildings are scattered over the property. **Rooms:** 37 rms; 11 cottages/villas. CI 2pm/CO 11am. Nonsmoking rms avail. All accommodations have kitchens. Cabins sleep up to six people. Chalet rooms are the least expensive. **Amenities:** Cable TV. No A/C. Some units w/terraces, some w/fireplaces. All one- and two-bedroom condos, and some cabins, have fireplaces. Fire alarm and phones for deaf or hard-of-hearing guests. **Services:** **Facilities:** Whirlpool, playground. Tram ride up Mount Howard is next to property; hiking trails nearby. **Rates:** Peak (June–Aug) $46–$81 S or D; $53–$91 cottage/villa. Min stay peak. Lower rates off-season. Parking: Outdoor, free. Minimum stay in high season for cabins and condos—no minimum stay in chalet rooms. AE, DC, DISC, MC, V.

Indian Lodge Motel
201 S Main St, 97846; tel 541/432-2651. Small, recently renovated motel with views of the snow-capped Wallowa Mountains. **Rooms:** 16 rms. CI open/CO 11am. Nonsmoking rms avail. Baskets of artificial flowers and framed prints add decorative touches to basic, comfortable rooms filled with dark wood furniture. **Amenities:** A/C, cable TV.

Closet space is limited; some rooms have refrigerators. **Services:** **Facilities:** There's a patch of front lawn, with picnic tables. **Rates:** Peak (June–Sept) $35 S; $43–$46 D. Extra person $5. Children under age 4 stay free. Lower rates off-season. Parking: Outdoor, free. MC, V.

LODGE

Wallowa Lake Lodge

60060 Wallowa Lake Hwy, 97846; tel 541/432-9821; fax 541/432-4885. 6 mi S of Joseph; on the lakeshore. 8 acres. Rustic lodge set in a pine forest on the shore of Wallowa Lake. Built in the 1920s, the lodge boasts a big lobby with a stone fireplace and comfortable couches. Close to a state park and wilderness area. **Rooms:** 22 rms and stes; 8 cottages/villas. CI 2pm/CO 11am. No smoking. Quaint lodge rooms (some with balconies) on second and third floors. Cabins have kitchens. **Amenities:** No A/C, phone, or TV. Some units w/terraces, some w/fireplaces. Cabins have cozy fireplaces; some cabins offer access for guests with disabilities. **Services:** Babysitting. **Facilities:** 50 1 restaurant (bkfst and dinner only), 1 beach (lake shore). Area offers opportunities for hiking, swimming, and bicycling. Nearby gondola ride up Mount Howard. **Rates:** Peak (May–Oct) $70–$80 S or D; $105–$115 ste; $75–$130 cottage/villa. Min stay peak. Lower rates off-season. Parking: Outdoor, free. DISC, MC, V.

ATTRACTION

Wallowa Lake Tramway

59919 Wallowa Lake Hwy; tel 541/432-5331. A spectacular 15-minute ride to the peak of 8,200-foot Mount Howard in the "Oregon Alps." Four-passenger gondolas grant views of four states, the Eagle Cap wilderness, Wallowa Lake, and the Seven Devils. Once at the top, visitors can relax at the Summit Deli and Alpine Patio, or explore the two miles of hiking trails. **Open:** Daily 10am–4pm. **$$$$**

Klamath Falls

This is an entry point to all sorts of outdoor adventure: Winema and Rogue River National Forests, Lake of the Woods, numerous national wildlife refuges, and volcanically formed and strikingly colored Crater Lake. **Information:** Klamath County Dept of Tourism, 1451 Main St, PO Box 1867, Klamath Falls, 97601 (tel 541/884-0666).

MOTELS

UNRATED **Best Western Klamath Inn**

4061 S 6th St, 97603; tel 541/882-1200 or toll free 800/528-1234; fax 541/882-2729. Typical motel, located near county fairgrounds. **Rooms:** 52 rms. CI 3pm/CO noon. Nonsmoking rms avail. **Amenities:** A/C, cable TV, refrig. **Services:** **Facilities:** Whirlpool. **Rates:** $52–$82 S; $56–$82 D. Extra person $10. Children under age 18 stay free. Parking: Outdoor, free. AE, CB, DC, DISC, MC, V.

Comfort Inn

2500 S 6th, 97601; tel 541/884-9999 or toll free 800/228-5050; fax 541/882-4020. At Washburn Way. A newer property in good condition, both well decorated and pleasant. Set back from a busy intersection in a shopping center. Priced on the high end, but worth it. **Rooms:** 61 rms and stes. CI 3pm/CO noon. Nonsmoking rms avail. Large and attractive, furnished with contemporary decor. Everything looks brand new. **Amenities:** A/C, cable TV, refrig. **Services:** **Facilities:** 75 Whirlpool. **Rates:** $55–$85 S; $60–$85 D; $75–$95 ste. Extra person $10. Children under age 18 stay free. Parking: Outdoor, free. AE, CB, DISC, MC, V.

Quality Inn

100 Main St, 97601; tel 541/882-4666 or toll free 800/732-2025; fax 541/883-8795. Family-owned two-story property with a large, attractive lobby. **Rooms:** 81 rms and stes. CI 2pm/CO noon. Nonsmoking rms avail. Rooms are decorated in pleasing colors, with expensive-looking carpets and fabrics. **Amenities:** A/C, cable TV w/movies, VCR. Some units w/whirlpools. **Services:** **Facilities:** 1 restaurant, 1 bar, whirlpool, washer/dryer. **Rates:** $59–$67 S or D; $92 ste. Extra person $5. Children under age 18 stay free. Parking: Outdoor, free. AE, DISC, MC, V.

Red Lion Inn

3612 S 6th St, 97603; tel 541/882-8864 or toll free 800/RED-LION; fax 541/884-2046. Newly redecorated, it's modern, comfortable, and located near the county fairgrounds. Quiet location, set back from street. **Rooms:** 108 rms. CI 2pm/CO noon. Nonsmoking rms avail. Accommodations are large and well maintained, done in wine and gray. **Amenities:** A/C, cable TV w/movies, VCR. **Services:** **Facilities:** 15 1 restaurant, 1 bar, whirlpool. Restaurant is disappointing. **Rates:** $46–$63 S; $48–$63 D. Extra person $10. Children under age 18 stay free. Parking: Outdoor, free. AE, CB, DC, DISC, MC, V.

RESTAURANTS

Chez Nous Restaurant

3927 S 6th St; tel 541/883-8719. **American/Continental.** Set in a Victorian house with a lovely ambience, this always-busy restaurant is the best dining spot in town—and the prices reflect that. Appetizers like onion soup or escargots can be followed by steak Diane, chateaubriand, or chicken cordon bleu, or one of the many fish entrees offered. A packed dessert cart holds a variety of sweets, and the bar has recently been expanded. **FYI:** Reservations recommended. **Open:** Mon–Sat 5–9pm. **Prices:** Main courses $11–$18. AE, CB, DC, DISC, MC, V.

Pappy Gander and Company
237 E Front St, Merrill; tel 541/798-5042. 12 mi S of Klamath Falls. **American.** Located on the banks of the Los River, this friendly local hangout is a popular gathering spot for duck hunters, many of whom record their hunting experiences in the guest book. Levis are the garment of choice, and cowboy hats are worn at the table. We're in the heart of meat-and-potatoes country here, so look for choices such as chicken-fried steak ($6.95), rib eye steak, deep-fried shrimp and seafood. Some nights feature pasta and Mexican specials. **FYI:** Reservations not accepted. Beer and wine only. **Open:** Daily 6am–8pm. **Prices:** Main courses $7–$21. No CC.

RJs at the Lake
28121 Rocky Point Rd; tel 541/356-2287. **American.** Located on a bluff overlooking Pelican Bay (a quiet inlet of Upper Klamath Lake), this restaurant offers spectacular views of the snowy peaks of Mount Harriman and the Mountain Lakes Wilderness. While you're admiring the vistas, you can try the rib-eye steak, teriyaki chicken, or filet mignon wrapped in bacon and served with sautéed mushrooms and onions. **FYI:** Reservations not accepted. **Open:** Breakfast Sat–Sun 9–11am; lunch Thurs–Tues 11am–2pm; dinner Thurs–Tues 5–9pm. Closed Feb–Mar. **Prices:** Main courses $10–$14. MC, V.

Schatzie's Gasthot
3200 US 97 N; tel 541/883-8650. **American/German.** The Bavarian decor at this eight-table restaurant consists of lace curtains, German posters, beer steins, and family snapshots. Tables are smartly set with pink linen and lace cloths, delicately patterned china, and fancy-folded linen napkins. Interesting menu offerings are *pfannenkuchen-auflauf,* a quichelike potato pancake stuffed with broccoli, onions, and mushrooms; *polnishenwurst,* a mild but savory sausage with hot potato salad and sauerkraut; and a dessert called *pfirsich-bowle* (peaches and raisins in spiced rum with whipped cream and toasted nuts). **FYI:** Reservations recommended. Children's menu. Beer and wine only. No smoking. **Open:** Lunch Tues–Fri 11am–2pm; dinner Mon–Sat 4–10pm. **Prices:** Main courses $8–$12. No CC.

Sergio's
327 Main St (Downtown); tel 541/883-8454. Near 3rd St intersection. **Mexican.** Mexican music, decor, and personnel. The owner and 14 employees moved from Bakersfield, CA to start this restaurant in 1994, and they were an instant success. Food is good, service outstanding, and the margaritas are unforgettable. Best item on the menu is the fajitas, delivered on a sizzling platter. **FYI:** Reservations not accepted. **Open:** Daily 11am–9pm. **Prices:** Main courses $7–$12. MC, V.

ATTRACTION

Favell Museum of Western Art and Indian Artifacts
125 W Main; tel 541/882-9996. Thousands of arrowheads, hundreds of miniature guns, and artwork by members of the Cowboy Artists of America and by Native Americans are packed into this family-owned western museum. **Open:** Mon–Sat 9:30am–5:30pm. Closed some hols. **$$**

La Grande

Farming, logging, and a railroad started this Oregon Trail town in the Grande Ronde Valley; Eastern Oregon State College and tourism keep it going. Centerpiece of abundant outdoor recreation in northeastern Oregon: wilderness hiking, hunting, fishing, camping, skiing. **Information:** La Grande-Union County Chamber of Commerce, 1912 4th St #200, La Grande, 97850 (tel 541/536-9771).

MOTEL

Pony Soldier Inn
2612 Island Ave, 97850; tel 541/963-7195 or toll free 800/634-PONY; fax 541/963-4498. Good-quality two-story motel in convenient location. **Rooms:** 150 rms. Executive level. CI 3:30pm/CO noon. Nonsmoking rms avail. Preferred rooms are on second floor overlooking pool and landscaped courtyard. **Amenities:** A/C, cable TV, refrig, dataport, bathrobes. Some units w/terraces. Hair dryers available on request. **Services:** **Facilities:** Whirlpool, washer/dryer. Pool open in summer only. **Rates (CP):** $60 S; $62–$70 D. Extra person $5. Children under age 12 stay free. Parking: Outdoor, free. Corporate rates avail. AE, DC, DISC, MC, V.

Lake Oswego

See Portland

Lakeview

At a mile high, this Great Basin community owes its existence to livestock and logging, but tourism and recreation are creeping into the economy. Hang-gliders flock here to ride powerful thermals above town. There are lakes and reservoirs, a small downhill and cross-country ski area, antelope and deer hunting, and national wildlife refuges at Hart Mountain and Summer Lake.

ATTRACTION

Hart Mountain National Antelope Refuge
18 S G St; tel 541/947-3315. The pronghorn antelope, though not related to the African antelope, is the fastest land

mammal in North America. One of the largest remaining herds roams this area of south-central Oregon. The most accessible location for viewing these graceful creatures is refuge headquarters, located 65 miles northeast of Lakeview. Primitive camping is available at Hot Springs Campground, four miles south of the refuge headquarters. **Open:** Daily 24 hours. **Free**

Lincoln City

Kite fliers love the winds here at this popular resort area. Other recreational opportunities include whale-watching off Cascade Head, and crabbing and fishing in nearby Siletz Bay. Further inland, there's sailing and fishing at Devil's Lake. **Information:** Lincoln City Visitor and Convention Bureau, 801 SW US 101 #1, Lincoln City, 97367 (tel 541/994-8378).

HOTEL

Inn at Spanish Head

4009 SW US 101, 97367; tel 541/996-2161 or toll free 800/452-8127 in the US, 800/547-5235 in Canada; fax 541/996-4089. Just south of business district. The sand's just a few feet away from the ground-floor rooms at this oceanfront hotel. **Rooms:** 120 rms and effic. CI 4pm/CO noon. Nonsmoking rms avail. Accommodations are individually decorated—some more attractively than others. All rooms have kitchenettes. **Amenities:** Cable TV, refrig, bathrobes. No A/C. All units w/terraces. **Services:** Babysitting. **Facilities:** 200 1 restaurant, 1 bar, 1 beach (ocean), games rm, sauna, whirlpool, washer/dryer. **Rates:** $99–$179 S or D; $99–$179 effic. Extra person $15. Children under age 16 stay free. Parking: Outdoor, free. AE, CB, DC, DISC, MC, V.

MOTELS

Best Western Lincoln Sands Inn

535 NW Inlet, 97367; tel 541/994-4227 or toll free 800/445-3234. At 6th St. This beachfront motel is one of the better properties in the area. **Rooms:** 33 effic; 1 cottage/villa. CI 4pm/CO 11am. Nonsmoking rms avail. Large rooms, with separate living room area, hide-a-bed, and full kitchen, are great for families. **Amenities:** Cable TV w/movies, refrig. No A/C. All units w/terraces. **Services:** $10 per pet (under 10 lbs). **Facilities:** 1 beach (ocean), whirlpool. **Rates (CP):** Peak (July–Sept) $140–$160 effic. Extra person $10. Children under age 5 stay free. Min stay special events. Lower rates off-season. Parking: Outdoor, free. Two-for-one in off season. AE, CB, DC, MC, V.

Coho Inn

1635 NW Harbor Ave, 97367; tel 541/994-3684. Off US 101, take NW 17th St to Harbor. Clean, well-maintained, and located in a quiet neighborhood, this motel offers good value for seaside lodgings. **Rooms:** 50 rms, stes, and effic. CI 4pm/CO 11am. Nonsmoking rms avail. **Amenities:** Cable TV w/movies. No A/C. Some units w/terraces, some w/fireplaces. **Services:** **Facilities:** Sauna, whirlpool. **Rates:** Peak (July 1–Sept 15) $66 S or D; $74 ste; $78–$86 effic. Extra person $6. Min stay special events. Lower rates off-season. Parking: Outdoor, free. AE, DISC, MC, V.

Ester Lee Motel

3803 SW Hwy, 97367; tel 541/996-3606. On US 101. Large, cottagelike units are a plus, although the property is past its prime. A good value for families or groups wishing to stay together. **Rooms:** 53 rms, stes, and effic. CI 2pm/CO noon. Nonsmoking rms avail. Sparsely furnished and somewhat faded. **Amenities:** Cable TV, refrig. No A/C. Some units w/fireplaces. **Services:** Fee for pets. **Facilities:** 1 beach (ocean). **Rates:** Peak (July–Aug) $54 S; $59 D; $54 ste; $59–$69 effic. Extra person $5. Children under age 13 stay free. Min stay wknds. Lower rates off-season. Parking: Outdoor, free. DISC, MC, V.

Nordic Motel

2133 NW Inlet Ave, 97367; tel 541/994-2329; fax 541/994-2329. From US 101, go W on 21st St. Rooms are tidy and well maintained; terraces on the bluff above the beach are great spots to watch the sunset. **Rooms:** 52 rms and effic. CI 4pm/CO noon. No smoking. Most have kitchenettes. **Amenities:** Cable TV, refrig. No A/C. 1 unit w/terrace, some w/fireplaces. **Services:** Babysitting. **Facilities:** 35 1 beach (ocean), games rm, sauna, whirlpool. **Rates:** Peak (June 30–Sept 3) $68 S; $72 D; $74–$86 effic. Extra person $5. Children under age 2 stay free. Min stay peak and wknds. Lower rates off-season. Parking: Outdoor, free. Off-season discounts avail. DISC, MC, V.

Shilo Inn

1501 NW 40th Place, 97367; tel 541/994-3655 or toll free 800/222-2244; fax 541/994-2199. US 101, W on 40th Place. A large, well-appointed motel, with many guests thronging through the common areas. It offers direct access to the ocean. **Rooms:** 248 rms and stes. CI 4pm/CO 11am. Nonsmoking rms avail. Rooms are nicely maintained. **Amenities:** Cable TV w/movies, refrig. No A/C. Some units w/terraces, some w/fireplaces. **Services:** Babysitting. Pet fee is $7/night. **Facilities:** 700 1 restaurant, 1 bar (w/entertainment), 1 beach (ocean), sauna, whirlpool, washer/dryer. **Rates:** Peak (May–Oct) $85–$119 S or D; $159–$209 ste. Extra person $12. Children under age 13 stay free. Min stay special events. Lower rates off-season. Parking: Outdoor, free. AE, CB, DC, DISC, MC, V.

Surftides Beach Resort

2945 NW Jetty Ave, 97367; tel 541/994-2191 or toll free 800/452-2159; fax 541/994-2727. Located right on a popular beach. **Rooms:** 123 rms and effic. CI 4pm/CO 11am. Nonsmoking rms avail. Clean and brightly furnished. **Amenities:** Cable TV, refrig, VCR. No A/C. Some units w/minibars, some w/terraces, some w/fireplaces, some w/whirlpools. **Services:** $6 fee for pets. **Facilities:** 1 restaurant, 1 bar, 1 beach (ocean), sauna, whirlpool, washer/dryer. Indoor tennis courts. **Rates:** Peak (June–Sept) $68–$74 S or D; $89–$125 effic. Extra person $6. Min stay wknds. Lower rates off-season. Parking: Outdoor, free. Two-for-one and dinner packages avail in off-season. AE, CB, DC, DISC, MC, V.

RESTAURANTS

Bay House

5911 SW US 101; tel 541/996-3222. 1 mi S of business district. **Northwest.** Chef Greg Meixner presents some of the best food on the Oregon coast in this elegant, sophisticated place with a great bay view. Entree winners are the halibut Parmesan, shellfish pan roast with capellini cakes, and herb-crusted rack of lamb with port demiglacé. 300 choices on the award-winning wine list. **FYI:** Reservations recommended. Children's menu. No smoking. **Open:** Peak (June–Oct) Wed–Sun 5:30–9pm. **Prices:** Main courses $13–$25. AE, DISC, MC, V.

Chameleon Cafe

2145 NW US 101; tel 541/994-8422. **Eclectic.** A great find: fresh, eclectic cuisine with an emphasis on vegetarian and ethnic dishes. Casual and sophisticated, it has the feel of a hip city bistro. The menu offers Mediterranean plates (tabbouleh, falafel, and stuffed grape leaves), angel-hair pasta, and salmon cakes. Crayons are supplied for doodling on the paper table covering. **FYI:** Reservations not accepted. Children's menu. Beer and wine only. No smoking. **Open:** Peak (May–Oct) Mon–Sat 11:30am–9pm. **Prices:** Main courses $5–$10. MC, V.

McMenamin's Lighthouse Brewpub

In Lighthouse Square Mall, 4157 US 101 N, Ste 117; tel 541/994-7238. At Logan Rd. **American.** Part of a Portland area chain. Funky and very informal, the restaurant is a great hangout and takeout spot, with its publike atmosphere, lively music, and good pub-grub. Well-made burgers, fish-and-chips, soups, and salads are available. Brews include Terminator Stout and Port Side Porter. Beer-making equipment can be seen through big windows. **FYI:** Reservations accepted. Children's menu. Beer and wine only. Additional locations: 2927 SW Cedar Hills Blvd, Beaverton (tel 641-0151); 420 NW 3rd St, Corvallis (tel 758-6044). **Open:** Peak (May 1–Sept 15) daily 11am–11pm. **Prices:** Main courses $4–$8. AE, MC, V.

Road's End Dory Cove

5819 Logan Rd; tel 541/994-5180. Off US 101. **Seafood/Steak.** A family-owned and family-frequented restaurant, it is indeed at the end of the road, in a quiet neighborhood. Clam chowder and surf-and-turf items, as well as some "diet" dishes, are served. Extensive dessert selections. **FYI:** Reservations not accepted. Children's menu. Beer and wine only. No smoking. **Open:** Peak (June–Sept 15) daily 11:30am–9pm. Closed Thanksgiving–Christmas. **Prices:** Main courses $9–$16. AE, DISC, MC, V.

Manzanita

People continue to discover this quiet community. A golf resort here is laid out on a sandy peninsula south of Canon Beach. Hiking and biking trails and uncrowded beaches can be found just south at Nehalem Bay.

INN

The Inn at Manzanita

67 Laneda Ave, PO Box 243, 97310; tel 503/368-6754. 2 blocks from beach. 1 acre. From the lush native vegetation lining its walkways to the simple elegance of its rooms, this intimate inn captures the freshness and informality of the Oregon coast. Rooms fill up every weekend, year-round. Very popular for honeymoons and anniversaries; many repeat guests. Unsuitable for children under 16. **Rooms:** 10 rms and effic. CI 4pm/CO noon. No smoking. Rooms are strictly for couples (no extra people). **Amenities:** Cable TV, refrig, VCR, bathrobes. No A/C or phone. All units w/minibars, all w/terraces, all w/whirlpools. Fresh flowers in room every day. Mini-refrigerator stocked with sodas and juices. **Services:** Masseur. Transportation from airstrip at nearby state park by request. **Facilities:** Washer/dryer. Golf course five minutes away, bike rentals up the street, beach two blocks away, good cafes and restaurants within a few minutes walk. **Rates:** $100–$140 D; $125 effic. Min stay peak, wknds, and special events. Parking: Outdoor, free. MC, V.

McMinnville

Located southwest of Portland, in the northern Willamette Valley. Winemakers flock here for the three-day International Pinot Noir Celebration in late July on the Lindfield College campus. **Information:** McMinnville Chamber of Commerce, 417 N Adams St, McMinnville, 97128 (tel 503/472-6198).

MOTELS

Safari Motor Inn

345 N OR 99 W, 97128; tel 503/472-5187 or toll free 800/321-5543; fax 503/434-6380. Clean motel, good for people on a budget. **Rooms:** 90 rms and stes. CI 3pm/CO noon. Nonsmoking rms avail. **Amenities:** A/C. **Services:** **Facilities:** 1 restaurant, whirlpool. Parking area can accommodate RVs and boat trailers. **Rates:** $46 S or D; $56 ste. Extra person $5. Children under age 10 stay free. Parking: Outdoor, free. AE, DISC, MC, V.

Vineyard Inn Best Western

2035 OR 99 W, 97128; tel 503/472-4900 or toll free 800/285-6242; fax 503/434-9157. At jct OR 18 and OR 99 W.

Impeccable and spacious accommodations located close to Yamhill County vineyards, wineries, and tasting rooms. **Rooms:** 65 rms and stes. CI 3pm/CO noon. Nonsmoking rms avail. Bright and airy, all rooms have cozy sitting areas with sofas. **Amenities:** A/C, refrig, dataport. Some units w/whirlpools. **Services:** Social director. Helpful, friendly staff can arrange customized tours of wineries, art galleries, and antiques dealers. **Facilities:** 50 Games rm, whirlpool, washer/dryer. **Rates (CP):** $57–$65 S; $45–$105 D; $80–$105 ste. Extra person $6. Children under age 12 stay free. Parking: Outdoor, free. AE, DISC, MC, V.

ATTRACTION

Yamhill County Historical Museum
605 Market St, Lafayette; tel 503/472-7328. Three historic buildings are part of this small local museum: an old poling church, a farm equipment barn, and a log museum. Together, they house over 5,000 artifacts depicting early life in Yamhill County. Also on display are antique quilts and Native American artifacts. A research library is available for those who wish to trace their family trees. **Open:** June 15 to Sept 1, Wed–Sun 1–4pm; Sept 2 to June 14, Sat–Sun 1–4pm. Closed some hols. **Free**

Medford

See also Ashland, Jacksonville

The commercial hub of southwest Oregon. Scenic Bear Creek is the centerpiece for two city parks with nature trails, bike paths, and picnic areas. Rogue River rafting keeps adventure seekers coming back. The city is surrounded by pear orchards. **Information:** Medford Convention and Visitors Bureau, 101 E 8th St, Medford, 97501 (tel 541/779-4847).

HOTEL

Rogue Regency Inn
2345 Crater Lake Hwy, 97504; tel 541/770-1234 or toll free 800/535-5805; fax 541/770-2466. I-5 N, Medford exit 30. A full service hotel located in North Medford, attracting couples and businesspeople. Good deal. **Rooms:** 122 rms and stes. CI 3pm/CO 11am. Nonsmoking rms avail. Attractive, coordinated decor. **Amenities:** A/C, cable TV w/movies. Some units w/fireplaces, some w/whirlpools. Minisuites offer microwave, refrigerator, and coffeemaker. **Services:** **Facilities:** 180 1 restaurant, 1 bar, whirlpool. Small, intimate lounge with three video games. **Rates:** $71–$81 S or D; $175–$250 ste. Extra person $10. Children under age 18 stay free. Parking: Outdoor, free. AE, CB, DC, DISC, MC, V.

MOTELS

Best Western Medford Inn
1015 S Riverside Ave, 97501; tel 541/773-8266 or toll free 800/626-1900; fax 541/734-5447. Exit 27 off I-5 W on Barnett Rd; right on Riverside. Above-average motel with a mansard-shingled roof and a large fireplace in the lobby. **Rooms:** 112 rms. CI 3pm/CO noon. Nonsmoking rms avail. Rooms have English manor–style decor: cherry-wood furniture with floral upholstery, brass pulls, brass lamps, and complementing framed prints. **Amenities:** A/C, cable TV. Some units w/whirlpools. **Services:** **Facilities:** 43 1 restaurant, 1 bar. Pool is in the midst of a landscaped garden. **Rates:** Peak (May–Oct) $52–$56 S; $58–$66 D. Extra person $6. Children under age 13 stay free. Lower rates off-season. Parking: Outdoor, free. AE, CB, DC, DISC, MC, V.

Best Western Pony Soldier Inn
2340 Crater Lake Hwy, 97504; tel 541/779-2011 or toll free 800/634-PONY-32; fax 541/779-7304. Exit 30 off I-5 N or S on Crater Lake Hwy (OR 62). A standard motel convenient to airport. **Rooms:** 72 rms. CI 2pm/CO noon. Nonsmoking rms avail. **Amenities:** A/C, refrig, dataport. **Services:** Car-rental desk. Coffee and hot chocolate available in lobby 24 hours. Six rooms for guests with pets. **Facilities:** 12 Whirlpool, washer/dryer. Guests get free passes to health club two blocks away. **Rates (CP):** Peak (May 16–Sept 31) $71–$81 S; $77–$87 D. Extra person $5. Children under age 12 stay free. Lower rates off-season. Parking: Outdoor, free. AE, CB, DC, DISC, EC, MC, V.

Cedar Lodge Motor Inn
518 N Riverside Ave, 97501; tel 541/773-7361 or toll free 800/282-3419; fax 541/776-1033. Generally clean, budget-priced motel in a rundown, mid-town neighborhood. **Rooms:** 80 rms and effic. CI 1pm/CO 11am. Nonsmoking rms avail. **Amenities:** A/C, cable TV. Newer rooms have microwaves and refrigerators. **Services:** **Facilities:** 30 **Rates (CP):** Peak (May–Oct) $32–$40 S; $35–$52 D; $45–$65 effic. Extra person $5. Children under age 13 stay free. Lower rates off-season. Parking: Outdoor, free. AE, CB, DC, DISC, MC, V.

Holiday Inn
2300 Crater Lake Hwy, 97504; tel 541/779-3141 or toll free 800/779-STAY; fax 541/779-2623. Just off I-5 in north Medford, in busy commercial district near airport. Uncarpeted concrete stairs are a bit tacky, but the new lobby is attractive. **Rooms:** 164 rms and stes. CI 3pm/CO noon. Nonsmoking rms avail. **Amenities:** A/C, cable TV. Some units w/minibars, 1 w/terrace. **Services:** Car-rental desk. **Facilities:** 1000 1 restaurant, 1 bar (w/entertainment), washer/dryer. Rock 'N Rodeo nightclub has dancing every night; separate room has four pool tables, big-screen TV, and darts. Larger-than-usual indoor pool with large plaster waterfall; raised deck around pool has putting

green. **Rates:** Peak (June–Aug) $55 S; $60 D; $125 ste. Extra person $5. Children under age 18 stay free. Lower rates off-season. Parking: Outdoor, free. AE, DC, DISC, MC, V.

Horizon Motor Inn
1154 E Barnett Rd, 97504; tel 541/779-5085 or toll free 800/452-2255; fax 541/779-5085. Exit 27 off I-5. An older, brick colonial-style property. **Rooms:** 129 rms and stes. CI 2pm/CO noon. Nonsmoking rms avail. Six rooms have wheelchair access for guests with disabilities. **Amenities:** A/C, cable TV. 1 unit w/whirlpool. **Services:** Car-rental desk. **Facilities:** 1 restaurant, 1 bar, sauna, whirlpool. Flower beds and shrubs are uncared for; the indoor whirlpool is dirty; walkways need sweeping. Free use of sports facility four blocks away. **Rates:** Peak (May 1–Oct 15) $50–$65 S; $55–$70 D; $90–$150 ste. Extra person $5. Children under age 18 stay free. Lower rates off-season. Parking: Outdoor, free. AE, CB, DC, MC, V.

RESTAURANTS

Genessee Place
203 Genessee St; tel 541/772-5581. Between Jackson and Main. **Continental.** Housed in a 1910 residence surrounded by gardens, this restaurant is composed of four intimate rooms decorated with lace curtains, original art, and dried flower arrangements. Typical specials include veal piccata, and rack of lamb served with a zesty balsamic-cream sauce. Desserts and fresh breads are created on the premises. There's also a small deli off the back porch (open Mon–Sat, 9am–9pm). **FYI:** Reservations recommended. No smoking. **Open:** Lunch Mon–Sat 11am–2pm; dinner Mon–Sat 5–9pm. **Prices:** Main courses $10–$18. MC, V.

Hungry Woodsman
2001 N Pacific Hwy; tel 541/772-2050. **Seafood/Steak.** A uniquely southern Oregon experience. The decor includes authentic equipment from local lumber mills: huge circular saw blades, massive wood beams, and over-size doors of prime lumber. A chain-sculpted lumberjack greets diners in the lobby, not far from the massive stone fireplace. The menu features large portions of steak, prime rib, and seafood, including chinook salmon and Alaskan king crab. **FYI:** Reservations not accepted. Children's menu. **Open:** Lunch Mon–Fri 11am–2:30pm; dinner Mon–Fri 5–10pm, Sat 5–11pm, Sun 4–9pm. **Prices:** Main courses $9–$50. AE, CB, DC, DISC, MC, V.

La Burrita
2716 Jacksonville Hwy; tel 541/770-5770. Across from Bi-Mart. **Mexican.** Authentic, healthful (no lard or preservatives) Mexican food, served amid piñatas and paintings of rural Mexican scenes. High-quality options include dishes like chimichangas, enchiladas, tacos, and marinated steak; a small Mexican deli and grocery on the premises sells food to go. **FYI:** Reservations accepted. Children's menu. Beer and wine only. No smoking. Additional location: 102 S Main St, Phoenix (tel 503/535-8446). **Open:** Sun–Thurs 9am–8:30pm, Fri–Sat 9am–9pm. **Prices:** Main courses $3–$6. No CC.

Streams—An Oregon Eatery
1841 Barnett Rd; tel 541/776-9090. E of exit 27 off I-5. **Eclectic/Northwest.** Framed, hand-tied fishing flies, Rogue River photos, fishing creels, and hand nets adorn the walls of this ruggedly sophisticated restaurant. Dinner features a wide choice of distinctly Oregon entrees, such as Dungeness crab cakes, fish stews, seafood fettuccine, and brandied pork medallions. **FYI:** Reservations accepted. Children's menu. No smoking. **Open:** Peak (June–Oct) lunch Mon–Fri 11:30am–2pm; dinner daily 5–9pm. **Prices:** Main courses $10–$17. AE, DC, DISC, MC, V.

ATTRACTION

Harry and David Country Village
1314 Center Dr; tel 541/776-2277. Established in the 1930s, Harry and David is well known to locals and gourmets across the country for its excellent gourmet treats, unique Northwest gifts, and fruit baskets featuring locally grown Oregon pears. Their 17,000-square-foot flagship store provides a fun and friendly atmosphere for browsing and shopping, and there are always plenty of tasty, free samples. Free tours can also be arranged. Visitors may want to make a quick stop next door at Jackson & Perkins, which bills itself as the nation's largest rose grower. **Open:** Mon–Sat 9am–9pm, Sun 10am–6pm. Closed Dec 25. **Free**

Merrill

See Klamath Falls

Mount Hood National Forest

MOTEL

Mount Hood Inn
87450 E Government Camp Loop, Government Camp, 97028; tel 503/272-3205 or toll free 800/443-7777. Off US 26. Located at an elevation of about 3,000 feet; close to Ski Bowl and Summit ski areas, making it handy for skiers. The rest of the year, the motel is a good one-night stopover. **Rooms:** 56 rms and stes. CI 3pm/CO noon. Nonsmoking rms avail. Accommodations are clean and comfortable. **Amenities:** A/C, refrig. Some units w/whirlpools. **Services:** **Facilities:** Whirlpool. Ski lockers available on main level. **Rates (CP):** $95–$135 S or D; $115–$135 ste. Extra person $10. Children under age 12 stay free. Parking: Outdoor, free. AE, DISC, MC, V.

LODGE

Timberline Lodge

Timberline Ski Area, Timberline, 97028; tel 503/272-3311 or toll free 800/547-1406; fax 503/272-3710. On Mount Hood, at 6000′ level, 6 mi above Government Camp. Oregon's premier historic mountain lodge dates to 1937, when it was built as part of President Roosevelt's WPA program. The large, comfortable common areas are accented by floor-to-ceiling fireplaces, with cozy locales to hole up with a book and a cup of steaming espresso. **Rooms:** 60 rms and stes. CI 4pm/CO noon. No smoking. Rustic wood furniture complements hand-crafted rugs and comforters. Bedspreads and paintings carry out motif of native flowers, animals, and birds. **Amenities:** TV. No A/C. Some units w/fireplaces. **Services:** Children's program. Ski programs available for entire family. **Facilities:** 300 1 restaurant (*see* "Restaurants" below), 2 bars, sauna, whirlpool. Chairlifts carry both skiers and summer sightseers. Beginners' slope is especially good for kids. **Rates:** $90–$160 S or D; $140–$160 ste. Extra person $15. Children under age 11 stay free. Parking: Outdoor, free. AE, DISC, MC, V.

RESORT

The Resort at the Mountain

68010 E Fairway Ave, Welches, 97067; tel 503/622-3101 or toll free 800/669-7666; fax 503/622-5677. Off US 26, S on Welches Rd. 300 acres. Located in the Cascades at an elevation of 1,300 feet, it's elegant yet casual, and a great place for golf lovers. Scottish theme; staffers wear special resort tartan. **Rooms:** 160 rms, stes, and effic. CI 3pm/CO noon. Nonsmoking rms avail. Deluxe rooms have fireplaces and mini-kitchens. **Amenities:** A/C, refrig, dataport, voice mail. All units w/terraces, some w/fireplaces, some w/whirlpools. **Services:** Twice-daily maid svce, social director, masseur, babysitting. Special events year-round, from jazz music to Christmas carols, plus a schedule of Oregon winemakers dinners. Concierge on duty during summer. **Facilities:** 27 4 2 450 2 restaurants, 2 bars (1 w/entertainment), volleyball, sauna, whirlpool, playground. Tartans Restaurant overlooks golf course; Highlands Restaurant features Northwest cuisine and wines. **Rates:** Peak (June 15–Sept 30) $95–$160 S or D; $180–$240 ste; $150–$195 effic. Extra person $20. Children under age 18 stay free. Lower rates off-season. Parking: Outdoor, free. AE, DISC, MC, V.

RESTAURANT

Cascade Dining Room

In Timberline Lodge, Timberline Ski Area, Timberline; tel 503/272-3700. **Northwest.** Dine in a mountain setting at this historic lodge with views of Mount Jefferson and the Cascade foothills. Rustic ambience: large rock fireplace, thick wood beams, wide plank flooring with wooden pegs. Dinner entrees include Oregon red-curry rabbit, duck confit, fresh salmon, and Northwest-style bouillabaisse. **FYI:** Reservations recommended. Children's menu. No smoking. **Open:** Breakfast daily 8–10am; lunch daily noon–2pm; dinner daily 6–8:30pm; brunch Sun 8–10:30am. **Prices:** Main courses $15–$23. AE, DISC, MC, V.

ATTRACTIONS

Bonneville Lock and Dam

Visitor Center, Exit 40 off I-84, Cascade Locks; tel 503/374-8820. Built and operated by the US Army Corps of Engineers, the project links Oregon and Washington and impounds Lake Bonneville, a 48-mile-long reservoir. The visitors center includes an observation deck, interior displays, and a large theater. Underwater windows provide views of migrating salmon, steelhead trout, shad, and sea lamprey as they fight their way up fish ladders during the summer and early fall. Tourists can also watch the navigation lock in action or get a close-up view of the powerhouse generators. **Open:** July–Aug, daily 8am–8pm; Sept–June, daily 9am–5pm. Closed some hols. **Free**

Mount Hood Brewing Company

87304 E Government Camp Loop, Government Camp; tel 503/272-0102. One of the oldest breweries in Oregon, begun in 1908 in Portland's Sellwood district. After being closed during prohibition, the pub was resurrected in 1991 when the operators of Timberline Lodge decided that the local people needed a place to relax after a hard day of mountain activities. Visitors can tour the brewery and enjoy a hearty meal at the Brew Pub. **Open:** Daily noon–10pm. **Free**

Mount Hood Meadows

OR 35, Mount Hood; tel 503/227-7669. The largest ski resort on Mount Hood, with more than 2,000 skiable acres. There are nine chairlifts that can carry 14,400 skiers per hour. With 2,777 vertical feet and a wide variety of terrains, the ski area is ideal for everyone from beginner to expert. In the day lodge, you can sit and watch the action on the slopes through a 120-foot-long wall of glass. When you're ready to hit the slopes, there are rentals and plenty of instructors to help you improve your form. **Open:** Mid-Nov–mid-May, Mon–Tues 9am–4:30pm, Wed–Sat 9am–10pm, Sun 9am–7pm. **$$$$**

Mount Hood SkiBowl

US 26, Mount Hood; tel 503/222-2695. The closest ski area to Portland and offers 65 runs to challenge skiers of all levels of ability. There are four double-chairlifts and five surface tows. With 1,500 vertical feet, SkiBowl has more expert slopes than any other ski area on the mountain. This also happens to be the largest lighted ski area in the United States. In summer there's an Alpine Slide for exhilarating runs down warm grassy slopes. **Open:** Thanksgiving–Apr, Mon–Thurs 9am–10pm, Fri 9am–11pm, Sat–Sun 8:30am–11pm. **$$$$**

Timberline Ski Area
Jct OR 35 and US 26, Timberline; tel 503/272-3311. High on the slopes of Mount Hood, features seven lifts covering 2,000 vertical feet. After dark, three lifts continue running for those diehards who just can't get enough of the slopes. In addition to the excellent skiing here, there is the stunning **Timberline Lodge,** constructed during the Great Depression of the 1930s as a WPA project. This classic Alpine ski lodge is now listed as a National Historic Landmark. **Open:** Nov–Mar, daily 9am–10pm; Apr–Sept, daily 7am–1:30pm. **$$$$**

Newport

The postcard-perfect Yaquina Head Lighthouse welcomes visitors to Newport, about halfway down Oregon's coastline. The most distinct features of this city are its harbor and the graceful arches of the Yaquina Bay Bridge. **Information:** Greater Newport Chamber of Commerce, 555 SW Coast Hwy, Newport, 97365 (tel 541/265-8801).

HOTELS

Embarcadero Resort Hotel and Marina
1000 SE Bay Blvd, 97365; tel 541/265-8521 or toll free 800/547-4779; fax 541/265-7844. At John Moore Rd. Located right on the marina, this motel offers the atmosphere of a yacht club. **Rooms:** 85 rms and effic. CI 4pm/CO noon. Nonsmoking rms avail. Balconies overlook the harbor and the spectacular Yaquina Bay Bridge. **Amenities:** Cable TV. No A/C. All units w/terraces, some w/fireplaces. **Services:** Mooring for small boats can be arranged through the front desk. **Facilities:** 150 1 restaurant, 1 bar, sauna, whirlpool, washer/dryer. **Rates:** Peak (June–Oct 16) $97 S or D; $129 effic. Lower rates off-season. Parking: Outdoor, free. AE, CB, DC, DISC, MC, V.

Hotel Newport
3019 N Coast Hwy, 97365; tel 541/265-9411 or toll free 800/547-3310; fax 541/265-8773. On US 101, just north of town. Offers the standard amenities, but it's a bit past its prime. Nice ocean views and a short walk to the beaches. **Rooms:** 146 rms and stes. CI 4pm/CO noon. Nonsmoking rms avail. **Amenities:** Cable TV w/movies. No A/C. All units w/terraces. **Services:** VCR and movie rentals. **Facilities:** 50 1 restaurant, 1 bar (w/entertainment), whirlpool. **Rates:** $104–$116 S or D; $155 ste. Extra person $10. Children under age 16 stay free. Parking: Outdoor, free. AE, CB, DC, DISC, MC, V.

Nye Beach Hotel
219 NW Cliff St, 97365; tel 541/265-3334. At Third Ave. Designed and built by its owner in 1992. Set in a quaint neighborhood overlooking the waves below, it provides a delightful alternative to the more-standard accommodations lining the coast. **Rooms:** 18 rms. CI 3pm/CO 11am. No smoking. **Amenities:** Cable TV w/movies. No A/C or phone. All units w/terraces, all w/fireplaces, some w/whirlpools. Down comforters in every room are perfect for cool coastal evenings. **Services:** **Facilities:** 1 restaurant. Informal bistro and outdoor dining patio add to the appealing atmosphere. **Rates:** Peak (Mem Day–Sept) $55–$105 S; $90 D. Min stay wknds. Lower rates off-season. Parking: Outdoor, free. AE, DISC, MC, V.

MOTEL

Puerto Nuevo Inn
544 SW Coast Hwy, 97365; tel 541/265-5767 or toll free 800/999-3068. US 101. This clean, well-maintained property is within a short drive of the historic bayfront shops and restaurants. Good value. **Rooms:** 32 rms, stes, and effic. CI 2pm/CO 11am. Nonsmoking rms avail. **Amenities:** Cable TV w/movies, refrig, VCR. No A/C. Some units w/terraces, some w/fireplaces, some w/whirlpools. Microwave. **Services:** **Facilities:** Whirlpool. **Rates (CP):** Peak (May 15–Oct 15) $42–$54 S; $45–$55 D; $72–$100 ste; $72–$100 effic. Extra person $5. Children under age 10 stay free. Lower rates off-season. Parking: Outdoor, free. AE, DC, DISC, MC, V.

INN

UNRATED **Ocean House Bed and Breakfast**
4920 NW Woody Way, 97365; tel 541/265-6158 or toll free 800/562-2632. At US 101. 1 acre. By opening his home of 30 years to guests, proprietor Bob Garrard has created a wonderful, welcoming inn. Visitors can enjoy incomparable views from the bluff-top garden, with miles of beaches to the south and the Yaquina Headlands and the historic lighthouse to the north. Lots of cozy reading spots around the fireplace. Unsuitable for children under 18. **Rooms:** 4 rms. CI 2pm/CO 11am. No smoking. **Amenities:** No A/C, phone, or TV. Some units w/terraces. **Services:** Afternoon tea served. **Facilities:** Guest lounge w/TV. **Rates (BB):** Peak (Apr 15–Oct 15) $70–$115 D. Extra person $15. Lower rates off-season. Parking: Outdoor, free. MC, V.

RESTAURANTS

★ **Rogue Ales Public House**
748 SW Bay Blvd; tel 541/265-3188. E off US 101. **Italian/Seafood.** With almost 20 different brews to its name, Rogue is the brewing pride of the region. The restaurant grew out of the brewery tasting room. Standard seafood fare and pizza complement the imaginatively named lagers, ales, and porters. **FYI:** Reservations recommended. Comedy. Beer and wine only. **Open:** Peak (May 15–Sept 15) daily 11am–11pm. **Prices:** Main courses $7–$12. AE, CB, DISC, MC, V.

Whale's Tale
452 SW Bay Blvd; tel 541/265-8660. East of US 101. **Seafood/Vegetarian.** Rough-hewn beams and Native American decorations give the place a "Northern Exposure" feel. In addition to seafood specialties there are a few vegetarian

entrees. Leave room for the "Mousse in a Bag" (white chocolate mousse in Belgian chocolate shell topped with fresh berries). Freshly baked breads. Good wine list, great selection of beers. **FYI:** Reservations not accepted. Children's menu. Beer and wine only. No smoking. **Open:** Peak (May 15–Oct 15) Mon–Fri 8am–10pm, Sat–Sun 9am–10pm. Closed Jan. **Prices:** Main courses $9–$17. AE, CB, DC, DISC, MC, V.

ATTRACTION

Oregon Coast Aquarium
2820 Ferry Slip Rd; tel 541/867-3474. A slice of Oregon's rugged coastline, reproduced on the shores of Newport's Yaquina Bay. The aquarium presents more than 190 species in a four-acre outdoor space consisting of cliffs, caves, rocky pools, wave pools, and nature trails and in large indoor exhibit galleries. Highlights include seals, sea lions, sea otters, jellyfish, and a giant Pacific octopus. Inside, visitors can watch sealife from a sea creature's point of view through underwater windows or touch the animals in the touch pool. All facilities, including the cafe and the gift shop, are wheelchair accessible. **Open:** Mem Day–Labor Day, daily 9am–6pm; Labor Day–Mem Day, daily 10am–5pm. Closed Dec 25. **$$$**

Oceanside

Oceanside graces the coast eight miles west of Tillamook along the popular Three Capes Scenic Drive. Nearby Mount Maxwell is a good spot to watch migrating gray whales.

MOTEL

House on the Hill
1816 Maxwell Point Rd, PO Box 187, 97134; tel 503/842-6030. Panoramic views, friendly service, and good furnishings have earned this motel a loyal following. Short walk or drive to the beach. **Rooms:** 17 rms, stes, and effic. CI 2pm/CO 11am. No smoking. All rooms have a view of the ocean—perfect for winter storm watching. **Amenities:** Cable TV, refrig. No A/C or phone. Some units w/terraces. Some units offer microwaves. **Services:** **Facilities:** Room off the lobby includes a telescope for viewing nearby Three Arch Rocks wildlife refuge. **Rates:** Peak (May–Sept) $75–$85 S or D; $90–$110 ste; $80–$110 effic. Extra person $10. Min stay special events. Lower rates off-season. Parking: Outdoor, free. MC, V.

RESTAURANT

★ Roseanna's
1490 Pacific; tel 503/842-7351. **New American/Seafood.** Pink-painted plaster, rough wood paneling, driftwood mobiles, and tables overlooking the ocean give this place the look of a weird beach house. The seafood-oriented menu features fish sautéed with lemon and garlic, or spiced Cajun-style; no deep-fried dishes here. Other options include burgers and salads. Generally closes at 8pm in winter. **FYI:** Reservations not accepted. **Open:** Peak (June–Aug) Mon–Tues 8am–9pm, Wed 11am–5pm, Thurs–Fri 8am–9pm, Sat–Sun 8am–5pm. Closed Dec 18–25. **Prices:** Main courses $11–$16. MC, V.

Ontario

Oregon Trail emigrants first set foot in the state just south of here, near present-day Nyssa; wagon ruts can be seen at nearby Keeney Pass. Lake Owyhee is a popular recreation area. **Information:** Ontario Visitors and Convention Bureau, 88 SW 3rd Ave, Ontario, 97914 (tel 541/889-8012).

HOTEL

Howard Johnson Lodge
1249 Tapadera Ave, 97914; tel 541/889-8621 or toll free 800/525-5333, 800/345-5333 in OR; fax 541/889-8023. Exit 376B off I-84; left on Goodfellow. Clean and smart-looking property is probably the best deal in town. **Rooms:** 98 rms. Executive level. CI 3pm/CO noon. Nonsmoking rms avail. Elegant for the price; nice decor with cushy, deep-green carpets. **Amenities:** A/C, cable TV. All units w/terraces. **Services:** Only place in town with room service. **Facilities:** 1 restaurant, 1 bar, whirlpool. **Rates:** Peak (May–Sept) $49–$57 S; $52–$61 D. Extra person $4. Children under age 18 stay free. Lower rates off-season. Parking: Outdoor, free. AE, CB, DC, DISC, MC, V.

MOTELS

Best Western Inn
251 Goodfellow, 97914; tel 541/889-2600 or toll free 800/828-0364; fax 541/889-2259. Clean property with convenient access to I-84. Rates are competitive with nearby motels. **Rooms:** 61 rms and stes. CI 2pm/CO noon. Nonsmoking rms avail. Brightly decorated. Deluxe suites available. **Amenities:** A/C, cable TV. Some units w/whirlpools. Suites offer small hot tub, VCR. **Services:** **Facilities:** Whirlpool, washer/dryer. **Rates (CP):** Peak (Dec–Mar) $47–$55 S; $51–$69 D; $85–$90 ste. Extra person $5. Children under age 12 stay free. Lower rates off-season. Parking: Outdoor, free. AE, DC, DISC, MC, V.

Motel 6
275 Butler St, 97914; tel 541/889-6617 or toll free 800/440-6000; fax 541/889-8232. Exit 376B off I-84; left on Goodfellow. Predictably clean and basic, with convenient access to I-84. **Rooms:** 126 rms. CI open/CO noon. Nonsmoking rms avail. **Amenities:** A/C, cable TV w/movies. **Services:** **Facilities:** Washer/dryer. Attractive iris garden near the pool. **Rates:** $28 S; $34 D. Extra person $3. Children under age 18 stay free. Parking: Outdoor, free. AE, CB, DC, DISC, MC, V.

Super 8 Motel

266 Goodfellow, 97914; tel 541/889-8282 or toll free 800/800-8000; fax 541/881-1400. Exit 376B off I-84; right turn, then left on Goodfellow. Clean and basic, with convenient access to I-84. **Rooms:** 63 rms and stes. CI 2pm/CO 11am. Nonsmoking rms avail. **Amenities:** A/C, cable TV w/movies. 1 unit w/whirlpool. **Services:** **Facilities:** 60 Basketball, whirlpool, washer/dryer. Only motel in town with an indoor pool. Basketball hoop in corner of parking lot. **Rates (CP):** Peak (Dec–Mar) $45–$50 S; $54–$60 D; $68–$74 ste. Extra person $4. Children under age 12 stay free. Lower rates off-season. Parking: Outdoor, free. AE, CB, DC, DISC, MC, V.

RESTAURANT

Cheyenne Social Club and Midget Mary's Lounge

111 SW 1st St (Downtown); tel 541/889-3777. Take exit 376A, off I-84. **American.** A small-town original and the only non-chain restaurant here. Decor is a mishmash of Victorian and tacky 1970s, complete with kerosene lamps on the tables and less-than-inviting carpeting. The simple menu is limited to few items, though each is quite good. Prime rib and lobster keep bringing patrons back. **FYI:** Reservations recommended. Piano. Children's menu. **Open:** Peak (Oct–Dec) lunch Mon–Fri 11:30am–2pm; dinner Mon–Sat 5:30–10pm. **Prices:** Main courses $11–$36. DC, MC, V.

Otter Rock

Named for a rock, about a half-mile offshore, formerly inhabited by sea otters. The tiny coastal community lies between Cape Foulweather to the north and Newport to the south; Devil's Punchbowl State Park is also nearby.

MOTEL

The Inn at Otter Crest

301 Otter Crest Loop, PO Box 50, 97369; tel 541/765-2111 or toll free 800/452-2101; fax 541/765-2047. W on Otter Crest Loop, off US 101. Surrounded by 35 acres of coastal forest, it offers a peaceful setting—keep an eye out for ducks crossing the road. A tram transports guests up the hill to rooms. **Rooms:** 105 rms and effic. CI 5pm/CO noon. Nonsmoking rms avail. Rooms are clean and well maintained. **Amenities:** Cable TV w/movies, refrig, VCR. No A/C. All units w/terraces, some w/fireplaces, 1 w/whirlpool. **Services:** **Facilities:** 250 1 restaurant, 1 bar, 1 beach (ocean), sauna, whirlpool, washer/dryer. **Rates:** Peak (June 15–Sept 15) $109 S or D; $119–$169 effic. Min stay peak. Lower rates off-season. Parking: Outdoor, free. AE, CB, DC, DISC, MC, V.

Pendleton

This Oregon Trail community at the foot of the Blue Mountains is home of the renowned Pendleton Woolen Mills, as well as the world-famous Pendleton Round-up rodeo held every September. **Information:** Pendleton Chamber of Commerce, 25 SE Dorion St, Pendleton, 97801 (tel 541/276-7411).

MOTELS

Best Western Pendleton Inn

400 SE Nye Ave, 97801; tel 541/276-2135 or toll free 800/528-1234; fax 541/278-2129. Off I-84, one mile from city center. Modern, well-maintained, unfancy hostelry. **Rooms:** 69 rms and stes. Executive level. CI open/CO 11am. Nonsmoking rms avail. Most spacious rooms are in the new wing. **Amenities:** A/C, cable TV. Rooms in new wing have refrigerators. **Services:** **Facilities:** 100 Whirlpool, washer/dryer. **Rates (CP):** Peak (May–Oct) $43–$64 S; $47–$70 D; $80–$114 ste. Children under age 12 stay free. Lower rates off-season. Parking: Outdoor, free. Senior and corporate rates avail. AE, DC, DISC, MC, V.

Chaparral Motel

620 SW Tutuilla, PO Box 331, 97801; tel 541/276-8654; fax 541/276-5805. Far west end of Pendleton. Standard but modern three-story motel, next to the freeway. **Rooms:** 51 rms and effic. CI open/CO 11am. Nonsmoking rms avail. Some rooms newly refurbished, with tasteful fabrics. Views of street or cemetery. **Amenities:** A/C, cable TV. **Services:** Babysitting. Free morning coffee at front desk. **Rates:** $36–$40 S; $43–$49 D; $49 effic. Extra person $5. Children under age 12 stay free. Parking: Outdoor, free. AE, CB, DC, DISC, MC, V.

Red Lion Inn

304 SE Nye Ave, 97801; tel 541/276-6111 or toll free 800/547-8010; fax 541/278-2413. Exit 210 off I-84, 1 mile from city center. This modern motel in ranch country has a duck pond and views of rolling hills and wheat fields. **Rooms:** 170 rms and stes. Executive level. CI Before 6pm/CO noon. Nonsmoking rms avail. Spacious and well appointed. **Amenities:** A/C, cable TV w/movies, dataport, voice mail. Some units w/minibars, some w/terraces, 1 w/whirlpool. Iron and ironing board in each room. **Services:** Prompt room service. **Facilities:** 600 2 restaurants, 1 bar (w/entertainment), whirlpool, beauty salon. Free use of Round-up Athletic Club, including racquetball, indoor pool, basketball, fitness center, and sauna. **Rates:** $71–$86 S; $81–$96 D; $130–$225 ste. Extra person $10. Children under age 18 stay free. Parking: Outdoor, free. Variety of discount and weekend rates avail. AE, DC, DISC, MC, V.

RESTAURANTS

✱ Cimmiyoti's

137 S Main St; tel 541/276-4314. Downtown. **American.** Ranchers in cowboy hats crowd the bar of this friendly place on weekends. The decor consists of red-flocked wallpaper, some rough brick walls, and black vinyl booths (but no windows), while the menu offers steak, lobster, chicken, and spaghetti, along with a long list of coffee drinks. **FYI:** Reservations accepted. Dress code. No smoking. **Open:** Daily 4–11pm. **Prices:** Main courses $9–$17. AE, MC, V.

Raphael's Restaurant & Lounge

233 SE 4th St; tel 541/276-8500. 4 blocks east of Downtown across street from county courthouse. **Eclectic.** An attractive homey restaurant in a historic house, with outdoor dining by a pretty garden and pond in warm weather. Owner Raphael Hoffman, of Nez Perce Indian heritage, also sells Native American art. The intriguing menu has a different theme each month. Game (elk, pheasant, venison, rattlesnake) is a specialty in the fall. Noisy when crowded; the bar is a small afterthought. **FYI:** Reservations recommended. Children's menu. Dress code. **Open:** Lunch Tues–Fri 11:30am–1:30pm; dinner Tues–Sat 5–9pm. **Prices:** Main courses $9–$20. AE, DISC, MC, V.

Portland

See also Beaverton, Troutdale

At the confluence of the Columbia and Willamette Rivers, Portland unfolds beneath the stately watch of Mount Hood, the state's highest peak. A one-time encampment for settlers and traders, Portland has grown into a vibrant urban center big enough to entertain a variety of interests: The highly regarded Oregon Symphony Orchestra is based here, and theater, the visual arts, dance, festivals, microbreweries, and nightlife abound. **Information:** Portland, OR Visitors Association, 26 SW Salmon St, Portland, 97204 (tel 503/275-9750).

PUBLIC TRANSPORTATION

Tri-Met serves the greater Portland area with 16 transit centers, 85 bus routes, and one light rail, called the Max line. Call 238-RIDE for route information. Fares determined by zone, ranging from $1 to $1.30 for adults; lower fares for seniors and youths. Tickets for MAX must be purchased before boarding at any MAX station. Buses can be paid for on board with exact change or with pre-paid tickets. Transfers between buses and MAX are free. Fareless Square is a 300-block area in downtown Portland where MAX and Tri-Met buses are free. Most buses are wheelchair-accessible; look for the wheelchair symbol.

HOTELS

The Benson Hotel

309 SW Broadway, 97205 (Downtown); tel 503/228-2000 or toll free 800/426-0670; fax 503/226-4603. Listed on the National Register of Historic Places. The grand walnut-paneled lobby and lounge with Italian marble floors and a sweeping staircase have been restored to the 1912 original **Rooms:** 290 rms and stes. CI 3pm/CO 1pm. Nonsmoking rms avail. Recently renovated, but despite old-style high ceilings and cornices, neither as spacious nor as elegant as one might expect from the lobby. Some are dreary, others (e.g. corner rooms) brighter—it pays to preview two or three rooms before hanging up your garment bags. One penthouse suite comes with its own baby grand—but a guest shouldn't find a stained shower curtain in a hotel that's just gone through a $20 million renovation. **Amenities:** A/C, cable TV w/movies, dataport, voice mail. All units w/minibars, some w/fireplaces, some w/whirlpools. Two-line speakerphones. Bathrobes. **Services:** VP Twice-daily maid svce, car-rental desk, babysitting. Pleasant, willing, knowledgeable staff. Strollers available for toddlers. **Facilities:** 600 2 restaurants (*see* "Restaurants" below), 2 bars (1 w/entertainment). Small but appealing weight room (open until 10:30pm). Buffet lunch (a good value) in the Lobby Court; afternoon tea beside the antique fireplace. **Rates:** $145–$165 S; $170–$190 D; $185–$600 ste. Extra person $10. Children under age 18 stay free. Parking: Indoor, $12/day. Weekend rates bring junior suites that match the regular price for a double room. AE, CB, DC, DISC, EC, ER, JCB, MC, V.

Best Western Inn at the Convention Center

420 NE Halladay St, 97232; tel 503/233-6331 or toll free 800/528-1234; fax 503/233-2677. At NE Grand. A basic hotel across the street from the Convention Center, and within walking distance to the new Rose Garden Arena, the Coliseum, and Lloyd Center. Right at the light rail line, which can take you downtown in 10 minutes. **Rooms:** 97 rms. CI 4pm/CO noon. Nonsmoking rms avail. South-facing rooms have views of downtown Portland across the Willamette River. **Amenities:** A/C, cable TV w/movies, refrig. Some units w/minibars, 1 w/fireplace. **Services:** **Facilities:** 50 1 restaurant (bkfst and lunch only), washer/dryer. **Rates:** Peak (May–Sept) $60–$70 S; $65–$75 D. Extra person $5. Children under age 12 stay free. Lower rates off-season. Parking: Indoor/outdoor, free. AE, DC, DISC, MC, V.

Courtyard by Marriott Portland Airport

11550 NE Airport Way, 97220; tel 503/252-3200 or toll free 800/321-2211; fax 503/252-8921. Exit 24B off I-205 N. A high quality, attractive lodging catering to business travelers. Less expensive than other airport hotels. **Rooms:** 150 rms and stes. CI 4pm/CO 1pm. Nonsmoking rms avail. **Amenities:** A/C, cable TV w/movies, voice mail.

Services: Car-rental desk, masseur, babysitting. **Facilities:** 1 restaurant, 1 bar, whirlpool, washer/dryer. **Rates:** $54–$75 S; $54–$85 D; $100–$110 ste. Extra person $10. Children under age 17 stay free. Parking: Outdoor, free. AE, DC, DISC, MC, V.

Days Inn City Center
1414 SW 6th Ave, 97201 (Downtown); tel 503/221-1611 or toll free 800/899-0248; fax 503/226-0447. Between Clay and Columbia. A good, inexpensive hotel in the heart of the city. **Rooms:** 173 rms. CI 3pm/CO noon. Nonsmoking rms avail. **Amenities:** A/C, cable TV w/movies, dataport. Complimentary hair dryers available. **Services:** Car-rental desk, masseur, babysitting. Complimentary morning newspaper, plus travelers' "emergency" items, such as toothbrushes and shavers. **Facilities:** 1 restaurant, 1 bar. **Rates:** $59–$66 S; $64–$71 D. Extra person $10. Children under age 12 stay free. Parking: Outdoor, free. AE, CB, DC, DISC, MC, V.

Embassy Suites
9000 SW Washington Square Rd, Tigard, 97223; tel 503/644-4000 or toll free 800/362-2779; fax 503/641-4654. Progress exit off OR 217. Elegant atrium lounge features waterfalls and trees. **Rooms:** 354 stes. CI 3pm/CO noon. Nonsmoking rms avail. All accommodations offer a separate living room with sofa, armchairs, and game table. **Amenities:** A/C, refrig, dataport, VCR, voice mail. Some units w/terraces, some w/whirlpools. Microwave in each room. **Services:** Beverages and cocktails offered 5:30–7:30pm, along with piano music. **Facilities:** 1 restaurant (lunch and dinner only), 1 bar (w/entertainment), games rm, sauna, whirlpool. Spacious meeting rooms. Pool and whirlpool open 24 hours. **Rates (BB):** $137–$500 ste. Children under age 18 stay free. Parking: Outdoor, free. AE, CB, DC, DISC, MC, V.

Governor Hotel
611 SW 10th at Alder, 97205 (Downtown); tel 503/224-3400 or toll free 800/554-3456; fax 503/241-2122. Built in 1909, the property was restored as a luxury hotel in 1992. Lobby has mural depicting the journey of Lewis and Clark. **Rooms:** 100 rms and stes. CI 3pm/CO noon. Nonsmoking rms avail. Rooms are decorated in earth tones; some have views of the city skyline. **Amenities:** A/C, cable TV w/movies, dataport, voice mail, bathrobes. All units w/minibars, some w/terraces, some w/fireplaces, some w/whirlpools. **Services:** Twice-daily maid svce, masseur, babysitting. European-style concierge can arrange for golf or tennis. Multilingual staff. Morning newspaper and overnight shoeshine available. **Facilities:** 2 restaurants (*see* "Restaurants" below), 1 bar, sauna, steam rm, whirlpool, beauty salon. On-site Princeton Athletic Club features indoor track, pool, weight room, steam room, whirlpool, sauna, and aerobics classes ($10 fee for hotel guests). **Rates:** $150–$225 S; $170–$225 D; $185–$500 ste. Extra person $20. Children under age 18 stay free. Parking: Indoor/outdoor, $10–$14/day. AE, CB, DC, DISC, JCB, MC, V.

The Heathman Hotel
1001 SW Broadway at Salmon, 97205 (Downtown); tel 503/241-4100 or toll free 800/551-0011; fax 503/790-7110. A $16 million rehab completed in 1984 revitalized this National Landmark (from 1927), from its Italian Renaissance–style facade to the elevators paneled in Burmese teak to an eclectic collection of artworks from France, Japan, Kenya, and Manhattan. **Rooms:** 151 rms and stes. CI 3pm/CO 2pm. Nonsmoking rms avail. Comfortable and efficient, but in some cases small, slightly dated (1950s rather than '20s), and not always as spiffy as the public areas (some guest quarters have TVs and minibars in cumbersome closets with sliding doors). A special mural painted on the hall's exterior wall enhances the view from many guestrooms. **Amenities:** A/C, cable TV w/movies, dataport, bathrobes. All units w/minibars, some w/fireplaces, some w/whirlpools. Two-line phones. **Services:** Twice-daily maid svce, babysitting. Friendly, helpful staff. Afternoon tea served in elegant Tea Court paneled in gleaming eucalyptus wood; green tea and slippers for Japanese guests. 400-plus movie library on request. **Facilities:** 1 restaurant (*see* "Restaurants" below), 2 bars (1 w/entertainment). Small fitness room (open 5am–10pm; registered guests only) plus guest privileges at nearby athletic club. Library with newspapers and novels, plus shelves of first editions signed by Norman Mailer, Alice Walker, and other authors who've stayed here. Private entrance (popular with performing stars) to concert hall next door **Rates:** $155–$180 S; $175–$200 D; $190–$325 ste. Extra person $20. Children under age 12 stay free. Parking: Indoor, $12/day. Rooms come in three size categories, but since they're all moderately priced to begin with, the top category is worth a few dollars more for the extra space. Weekend and special packages are good value. AE, CB, DC, DISC, EC, ER, JCB, MC, V.

Holiday Inn Portland Airport Hotel
8439 NE Columbia Blvd, 97220 (Portland Int'l Airport); tel 503/256-5000 or toll free 800/HOLIDAY; fax 503/257-4742. Newly remodeled property includes an indoor pool and tiered fountain. **Rooms:** 286 rms and stes. CI 2pm/CO noon. Nonsmoking rms avail. **Amenities:** A/C, satel TV w/movies, dataport. 1 unit w/whirlpool. **Services:** Car-rental desk, masseur, babysitting. **Facilities:** 2 restaurants, 1 bar (w/entertainment), games rm, sauna, whirlpool, washer/dryer. Glass-topped tables and patio chairs curve around the indoor pool, which is in a sunken area in the center of the hotel. **Rates:** $95 S; $101 D; $125–$250 ste. Extra person $6. Children under age 18 stay free. Parking: Outdoor, free. AE, CB, DC, DISC, JCB, MC, V.

Hotel Vintage Plaza
422 SW Broadway, 97205 (Downtown); tel 503/228-1212 or toll free 800/243-0555; fax 503/228-3598. Between Washington and Stark. A smart, classy, newly renovated hotel in the heart of downtown. **Rooms:** 107 rms and stes. CI 3pm/CO noon. Nonsmoking rms avail. "Starlight" rooms feature solarium-style windows, so guests can stargaze from bed. Two-story townhouse suites feature a winding staircase connecting the large living room to the bedroom; they also offer jet-tubs. **Amenities:** A/C, cable TV w/movies, dataport, voice mail, bathrobes. All units w/minibars, some w/terraces, some w/whirlpools. **Services:** Twice-daily maid svce, car-rental desk, masseur, babysitting. VCRs for $25/night. Complimentary morning coffee, juice, breakfast muffins, and newspaper; complimentary wine tasting each evening. Complimentary overnight shoe shine. **Facilities:** 100 1 restaurant (*see* "Restaurants" below), 1 bar. **Rates:** $150–$170 S; $165–$170 D; $195–$210 ste. Extra person $15. Children under age 16 stay free. Parking: Outdoor, $13/day. AE, CB, DC, DISC, EC, ER, JCB, MC, V.

Imperial Hotel
400 SW Broadway, 97205 (Downtown); tel 503/228-7221 or toll free 800/452-2323; fax 503/223-4551. This friendly, comfortable hotel is in the heart of the city and costs about half the price of other downtown lodgings. **Rooms:** 136 rms. CI 3pm/CO 2pm. Nonsmoking rms avail. **Amenities:** A/C, satel TV w/movies. Approximately one-third of the rooms have dataports, refrigerators, and sofas. **Services:** VP Car-rental desk. Free valet parking. **Facilities:** 125 1 restaurant, 1 bar. **Rates:** $70–$85 S; $75–$95 D. Extra person $5. Children under age 12 stay free. Parking: Indoor, free. AE, CB, DC, DISC, MC, V.

Mallory Hotel
729 SW 15th Ave, 97205; tel 503/223-6311 or toll free 800/228-8657; fax 503/223-0522. At Yanhill St. This reasonably priced hotel, just outside of downtown, is a good choice for people who like the roominess of an older hotel—and don't mind the few blemishes that come with it. Very loyal following. **Rooms:** 136 rms and stes. CI 3pm/CO 2pm. Rooms are large with plenty of seating; some look out to the green hills of Forest Park. Some bathrooms have original tile floors, which may be slightly cracked. **Amenities:** A/C, satel TV w/movies, refrig, in-rm safe. **Services:** **Facilities:** 125 1 restaurant, 1 bar. **Rates:** $60–$100 S; $65–$110 D; $110 ste. Extra person $5. Children under age 12 stay free. Parking: Indoor/outdoor, free. AE, CB, DC, DISC, MC, V.

The Mark Spencer Hotel
409 SW 11th Ave, 97205 (Downtown); tel 503/224-3293 or toll free 800/548-7848; fax 503/223-7848. At Stark. Nice, basic hotel on the edge of downtown, one block from famous Powell's bookstore. **Rooms:** 101 stes and effic. CI 3pm/CO noon. Nonsmoking rms avail. Every room has small kitchen. **Amenities:** A/C, cable TV, refrig, dataport. Guests can choose to have direct phone line to their room, which can be answered by the front desk when they go out. **Services:** Car-rental desk, babysitting. In the process of becoming an "eco-hotel" where guests will get a slight discount if they choose to have linens changed less frequently; beds will still be made daily. VCRs for rent. **Facilities:** 100 Beauty salon, washer/dryer. Guest passes to the nearby Princeton Athletic Club for $10. **Rates:** $89–$99 ste; $62–$99 effic. Extra person $10. Children under age 12 stay free. Parking: Indoor/outdoor, $7/day. Weekly and monthly rates avail. AE, CB, DC, DISC, MC, V.

The Portland Hilton Hotel
921 SW 6th Ave, 97204 (Downtown); tel 503/226-1611 or toll free 800/HILTONS; fax 503/220-2565. Between Salmon and Taylor. A nice hotel in the heart of downtown. **Rooms:** 455 rms and stes. Executive level. CI 3pm/CO noon. Nonsmoking rms avail. Accommodations on upper stories look east to the Willamette River and Mt Hood, or west to Portland's West Hills. **Amenities:** A/C, cable TV w/movies, dataport, voice mail. 1 unit w/whirlpool. Refrigerators and hairdryers are available free on request; VCRs for rent. **Services:** VP Car-rental desk, masseur, babysitting. **Facilities:** 1450 2 restaurants (*see* "Restaurants" below), 2 bars (1 w/entertainment), spa, sauna, whirlpool, beauty salon. Athletic club (fee required) features pool, spa, fitness equipment, and aerobics classes. Alexander's rooftop restaurant has vistas of the West Hills. **Rates:** $125–$165 S; $150–$200 D; $600–$800 ste. Extra person $25. Children under age 18 stay free. Parking: Indoor, $12–$15/day. AE, DC, DISC, JCB, MC, V.

Portland Marriott Hotel
1401 SW Front Ave, 97201 (Downtown); tel 503/226-7600 or toll free 800/228-9290; fax 503/226-1789. At Columbia St. The best thing about this hotel it its great location overlooking the Willamette River and the Tom McCall Waterfront Park in downtown Portland. **Rooms:** 503 rms and stes. Executive level. CI 4pm/CO noon. Nonsmoking rms avail. Half the rooms face the river and cost a little more; they must be reserved in advance. **Amenities:** A/C, satel TV w/movies, dataport, voice mail. All units w/terraces. Refrigerators on request. **Services:** VP Car-rental desk, masseur, babysitting. **Facilities:** 2500 2 restaurants, 2 bars (1 w/entertainment), spa, sauna, whirlpool, beauty salon, washer/dryer. **Rates:** Peak (Apr–Oct) $145 S; $165 D; $300–$450 ste. Children under age 18 stay free. Lower rates off-season. Parking: Indoor, $12/day. Discounts for guests who pay in advance. AE, CB, DC, DISC, JCB, MC, V.

Portland Silver Cloud Inn
2426 NW Vaughn St, 97210 (Nob Hill); tel 503/242-2400 or toll free 800/205-6939; fax 503/242-1770. At 24th. An attractive, basic hotel within walking distance of the many shops and restaurants in Portland's Nob Hill neighborhood.

Rooms: 81 rms and stes. CI 2pm/CO noon. Nonsmoking rms avail. Several rooms offer mini-kitchenettes with microwaves. **Amenities:** A/C, cable TV w/movies, refrig, dataport. Some units w/whirlpools. **Services:** Car-rental desk, masseur. Complimentary fruit and coffee in lobby. Room service provided by several nearby restaurants. **Facilities:** 40 Whirlpool, washer/dryer. **Rates (CP):** Peak (June–Aug) $69–$92 S; $75–$98 D; $95 ste. Extra person $6. Children under age 12 stay free. Lower rates off-season. Parking: Indoor/outdoor, free. AE, DC, DISC, MC, V.

Ramada Inn Portland Airport

6221 NE 82nd Ave, 97220 (Portland Int'l Airport); tel 503/255-6511 or toll free 800/2-RAMADA; fax 503/255-8417. Attracts business travelers. **Rooms:** 202 rms and stes. CI 3pm/CO noon. Nonsmoking rms avail. More than half the accommodations are minisuites, complete with couch and table. Two executive suites have an extra living room and a small meeting space. **Amenities:** A/C, cable TV w/movies. Some units w/terraces, some w/whirlpools. Minisuites feature a microwave, wet bar, and refrigerator. Two have whirlpools. **Services:** Car-rental desk. The hotel's airport van has a wheelchair lift. **Facilities:** 600 1 restaurant, 1 bar, spa, sauna, whirlpool, washer/dryer. **Rates:** $74–$89 S or D; $140–$300 ste. Extra person $10. Children under age 18 stay free. Parking: Outdoor, free. Special rates avail. AE, CB, DC, DISC, MC, V.

Red Lion Hotel Columbia River

1401 N Hayden Island Dr, 97217 (Northeast); tel 503/283-2111 or toll free 800/547-8010; fax 503/283-4718. On the Columbia River just off I-5 at exit 308. An attractive hotel, overlooking the Columbia River, within walking distance of Jantzen Beach shopping mall and cinemas. **Rooms:** 367 rms and stes. CI 3pm/CO noon. Nonsmoking rms avail. Many rooms have river views. **Amenities:** A/C, cable TV w/movies, dataport. Some units w/terraces, some w/whirlpools. **Services:** Car-rental desk, masseur. Food is served poolside. **Facilities:** 2 700 2 restaurants, 1 bar (w/entertainment), whirlpool, beauty salon. Hotel shares a boat dock with the Red Lion Jantzen Beach, which is next door. Although the attractive outdoor pool overlooks the Columbia River, it is noisy because of proximity to the I-5 bridge; patio dining is noisy also. Putting green. **Rates:** $102–$108 S; $117–$125 D; $200–$475 ste. Extra person $10–$15. Parking: Outdoor, free. AE, CB, DC, DISC, JCB, MC, V.

Red Lion Hotel Downtown

310 SW Lincoln St, 97201 (Downtown); tel 503/221-0450 or toll free 800/547-8010; fax 503/226-6260. Between 4th and 1st Ave. Pleasant hotel on the edge of downtown Portland's "urban renewal" district. **Rooms:** 235 rms and stes. CI 3pm/CO noon. Nonsmoking rms avail. **Amenities:** A/C, cable TV w/movies, dataport. Some units w/terraces, some w/whirlpools. **Services:** Car-rental desk, masseur, babysitting. **Facilities:** 350 1 restaurant, 1 bar (w/entertainment), washer/dryer. The pleasant outdoor pool is set in a garden with trees and flowers, tables and chairs. **Rates:** Peak (Apr–Oct) $95–$105 S; $110–$120 D; $250–$350 ste. Extra person $15. Children under age 18 stay free. Lower rates off-season. Parking: Outdoor, free. AE, CB, DC, DISC, JCB, MC, V.

Red Lion Hotel Jantzen Beach

909 N Hayden Island Dr, 97217 (Northeast); tel 503/283-4466 or toll free 800/547-8010; fax 503/283-4743. On the Columbia River just off I-5, at exit 308. Another attractive Red Lion property overlooking the Columbia River. Within walking distance to Jantzen Beach shopping mall and cinemas. **Rooms:** 344 rms and stes. CI 3pm/CO noon. Nonsmoking rms avail. Many rooms have river views. **Amenities:** A/C, cable TV w/movies, dataport. All units w/terraces, some w/whirlpools. **Services:** Car-rental desk, masseur. Food is served poolside. **Facilities:** 2 1200 2 restaurants, 1 bar (w/entertainment), whirlpool. Ballroom and pretty outdoor pool both offer river views. Boat dock and helipad. **Rates:** $105–$111 S; $120–$128 D; $205–$480 ste. Extra person $10–$15. Parking: Outdoor, free. AE, CB, DC, DISC, JCB, MC, V.

Red Lion Hotel Lloyd Center

1000 NE Multnomah St, 97232 (Lloyd District); tel 503/281-6111 or toll free 800/547-8010; fax 503/284-8553. More elegant than other hotels in area. Within walking distance of Convention Center, Rose Garden Arena, the Coliseum, Lloyd Center, and light rail line. **Rooms:** 476 rms and stes. CI 3pm/CO noon. Nonsmoking rms avail. **Amenities:** A/C, cable TV w/movies, dataport, in-rm safe. Some units w/terraces, some w/whirlpools. **Services:** VP Babysitting. **Facilities:** 1100 3 restaurants, 2 bars (w/entertainment). Restaurants include Maxi's (Northwest specialties); Eduardo's Cantina (Mexican); and the Coffee Garden (casual). **Rates:** $124–$149 S; $139–$164 D; $250–$535 ste. Extra person $15. Children under age 18 stay free. Parking: Indoor/outdoor, $6/day. AE, MC, V.

RiverPlace Hotel

1510 SW Harbor Way, 97201 (Downtown); tel 503/228-3233 or toll free 800/227-1333; fax 503/295-6161. Near Willamette River. A lovely hotel on Portland's downtown riverfront. It's a great place for people who want to be near shops, restaurants, and Waterfront Park, which hosts concerts and events throughout the summer. **Rooms:** 74 rms, stes, and effic; 10 cottages/villas. CI 4pm/CO 1pm. Nonsmoking rms avail. The best rooms offer a view of the river. Attractively furnished, accommodations are large and comfortable. Ten condo units are also available. **Amenities:** A/C, cable TV w/movies, dataport, voice mail, bathrobes. 1 unit w/terrace, some w/fireplaces, some w/whirlpools. **Services:** VP Twice-daily maid svce, masseur, babysitting. Complimentary morning newspaper and overnight shoeshine. **Facilities:** 1 restaurant (*see* "Restaurants" below), 1 bar (w/entertainment), sauna, whirlpool. For $8/day, guests have access to the Riverplace Athletic Club, a complete fitness facility with two indoor pools, racquet courts, running track, aerobics classes, and more. **Rates (CP):** $155–$195 S; $175–$195 D; $185–$600 ste; $295–$395 effic; $295–$395 cottage/villa. Extra person $20. Children under age 18 stay free. Parking: Indoor, $12/day. AE, CB, DC, DISC, JCB, MC, V.

Riverside Inn
50 SW Morrison St, 97204 (Downtown); tel 503/221-0711 or toll free 800/899-0247; fax 503/274-0312. At Front, across the street from Tom McCall Waterfront Park. The best part of this medium-price hotel is its location. **Rooms:** 139 rms and stes. CI 2pm/CO noon. Nonsmoking rms avail. **Amenities:** A/C, satel TV w/movies, dataport. Some units w/terraces. **Services:** Car-rental desk, masseur, babysitting. **Facilities:** 1 restaurant, 1 bar. Complimentary access to fitness center across the street. **Rates:** $85–$95 S or D; $200 ste. Extra person $10. Children under age 17 stay free. Parking: Indoor/outdoor, free. AE, CB, DC, DISC, MC, V.

Rodeway Inn
1506 NE 2nd Ave, 97232 (Lloyd District); tel 503/231-7665 or toll free 800/222-2244; fax 503/236-6040. At Weidler. A basic, friendly property within walking distance of the new Rose Garden Arena, Coliseum, Convention Center, Lloyd Center, and the light rail line. **Rooms:** 44 rms. CI 2pm/CO noon. Nonsmoking rms avail. All rooms were completely refurbished in 1994. **Amenities:** A/C, satel TV w/movies. **Services:** Babysitting. VCRs for rent, movies free. Free shuttle to train, plane, and bus station. Complimentary coffee, tea, and fruit available in lobby 24 hours; complimentary popcorn; free morning newspaper. **Facilities:** Washer/dryer. **Rates (CP):** Peak (May–Sept) $65–$79 S or D. Extra person $12. Children under age 12 stay free. Lower rates off-season. Parking: Outdoor, free. AE, DC, DISC, MC, V.

Sheraton Portland Airport Hotel
8235 NE Airport Way, 97220; tel 503/281-2500 or toll free 800/325-3535; fax 503/249-7602. ½ mi from Portland Airport. The only hotel actually located on the airport property—a good place for business travelers. **Rooms:** 215 rms and stes. CI 2pm/CO noon. Nonsmoking rms avail. Some rooms overlook pine trees; others, the airport runways—you can watch planes take off and land. Rooms for guests with disabilities include closed-captioned televisions, special telephones, wheelchair facilities, and more. **Amenities:** A/C, satel TV w/movies, dataport, voice mail. All units w/minibars, 1 w/whirlpool. **Services:** Car-rental desk, babysitting. **Facilities:** 2 restaurants, 2 bars, spa, sauna, whirlpool. Attractive indoor pool has an outdoor patio with lounge chairs and a small garden. **Rates:** $115–$120 S; $122–$132 D; $140–$395 ste. Extra person $10. Children under age 18 stay free. Parking: Outdoor, free. AE, CB, DC, DISC, JCB, MC, V.

Shilo Inn Suites Hotel
11707 NE Airport Way, 97220 (Portland Int'l Airport); tel 503/252-7500 or toll free 800/222-2244 in the US, 800/228-4489 in Canada; fax 503/254-0794. Comfortable hotel, with a small meeting area in each room. **Rooms:** 200 stes and effic. CI 2pm/CO noon. Nonsmoking rms avail. All rooms are small suites; there's also one apartment with a large living room and full kitchen. **Amenities:** A/C, cable TV w/movies, refrig, dataport, VCR, voice mail, bathrobes. Microwave; small TV in bathroom. **Services:** Car-rental desk, masseur, babysitting. **Facilities:** 1 restaurant, 1 bar (w/entertainment), spa, sauna, steam rm, whirlpool, washer/dryer. **Rates (CP):** Peak (May–Aug) $99–$144 ste; $245 effic. Extra person $15. Children under age 12 stay free. Lower rates off-season. Parking: Outdoor, free. AE, CB, DC, DISC, JCB, MC, V.

Travelodge Hotel
1441 NE 2nd Ave, 97232 (Lloyd District); tel 503/233-2401 or toll free 800/578-7878; fax 503/238-7016. At Weidler, near Rose Garden Arena. A well-maintained, modern hotel. Conveniently located, without downtown prices. **Rooms:** 236 rms and stes. Executive level. CI 3pm/CO noon. Nonsmoking rms avail. All rooms have view of Mount Hood, Mount St Helens, or Portland. **Amenities:** A/C, cable TV w/movies, dataport. Rooms on executive floor have refrigerators. Rooms for people with disabilities include closed-captioned TV, phones for the deaf or hard-of-hearing, and strobe-detector lights. **Services:** **Facilities:** 1 restaurant, 1 bar. **Rates:** Peak (June–Sept) $61–$77 S; $61–$87 D; $250 ste. Extra person $10. Children under age 18 stay free. Lower rates off-season. Parking: Outdoor, free. AE, DC, DISC, MC, V.

MOTELS

Cameo Motel
4111 NE 82nd Ave, 97220; tel 503/288-5981. At Sandy Blvd; S of Portland Int'l Airport. Located 20 minutes from downtown Portland, this basic, inexpensive motel is near several restaurants and a laundry/dry cleaner. **Rooms:** 40 rms and effic. CI 1pm/CO 11am. Nonsmoking rms avail. **Amenities:** A/C, cable TV w/movies, refrig, dataport. **Services:** Car-rental desk. Complimentary coffee in lobby. **Facilities:** **Rates:** $30 S; $33 D; $45–$52 effic. Extra person $3. Children under age 5 stay free. Parking: Outdoor, free. AE, CB, DC, EC, ER, JCB, MC, V.

Cypress Inn Portland Downtown
809 SW King Ave, 97205 (Southwest); tel 503/226-6288 or toll free 800/752-9991; fax 503/274-0038. 1 block S of Burnside. An inexpensive motel located just outside downtown Portland near Washington Park, the Rose gardens, the Japanese gardens, and the Nob Hill neighborhood. Because

many units are suites with kitchens, it's a good choice for extended stays. **Rooms:** 83 rms and effic. CI 2pm/CO noon. Nonsmoking rms avail. East-side rooms have nice views of the city. Two-bedroom efficiencies have spacious living rooms. **Amenities:** A/C, satel TV w/movies, refrig. Hair dryers available upon request. **Services:** Car-rental desk, babysitting. **Facilities:** Washer/dryer. **Rates (CP):** $49 S; $56 D; $69–$89 effic. Extra person $7. Children under age 12 stay free. Parking: Outdoor, free. AE, CB, DC, DISC, MC, V.

Ho-Jo Inn
3939 NE Hancock St, 97212 (Hollywood); tel 503/288-6891; fax 503/288-1995. An inexpensive motel in the Hollywood district, about 15 minutes from downtown. **Rooms:** 48 rms. CI 2pm/CO noon. Nonsmoking rms avail. All units were being completely refurbished. **Amenities:** A/C, cable TV. **Services:** Car-rental desk. Complimentary morning coffee and doughnuts in lobby. Manager knows all the wonderful things to see in the area; friendly staff. **Facilities:** **Rates:** $38–$42 S; $52 D. Extra person $5. Children under age 12 stay free. Parking: Outdoor, free. AE, CB, DC, DISC, MC, V.

Midtown Motel
1415 NE Sandy Blvd, 97232 (Northeast/Lloyd District); tel 503/234-0316. Near jct of 12th and Burnside. A basic motel near a bus line to downtown, 10 minutes away. **Rooms:** 40 rms. CI 11am/CO 11am. Nonsmoking rms avail. **Amenities:** A/C, cable TV w/movies, refrig. **Services:** Car-rental desk. Coffee and doughnuts 8–11am in the small lobby. **Rates:** $30–$40 S; $35–$48 D. Extra person $5. Parking: Outdoor, free. AE, CB, DC, DISC, MC, V.

INNS

Heron Haus
2545 NW Westover Rd, 97210 (Nob Hill); tel 503/274-1846; fax 503/274-1846. 1 acre. The elegant decor at this lovely Tudor-style B&B includes original parquet flooring. Wonderful location at the foot of Portland's West Hills, near the shops, boutiques, and restaurants of the Nob Hill area. Unsuitable for children under 10. **Rooms:** 6 rms. CI 4pm/CO noon. Rooms are large and beautifully furnished; some rooms look east over the city and include views of Mount Hood and Mount St Helens. **Amenities:** A/C, cable TV w/movies, dataport, bathrobes. Some units w/fireplaces, 1 w/whirlpool. **Services:** Masseur. **Facilities:** Guest lounge. Sun porch overlooks small pool and garden. **Rates (CP):** $85 S; $125–$250 D. Extra person $65. Parking: Outdoor, free. MC, V.

The Lion and the Rose
1517 NE Schuyler, 97212; tel 503/287-9245 or toll free 800/955-1647; fax 503/287-9247. At Irvington and Schuyler. An attractive B&B located in a restored 1906 Queen Anne–style home that was recently designated a historical landmark. Within a 10-minute bus ride to downtown, and near the Convention Center, Rose Garden Arena, Coliseum, and Lloyd Center shopping. **Rooms:** 7 rms (2 w/shared bath). CI 3pm/CO 11am. No smoking. **Amenities:** A/C, bathrobes. No TV. 1 unit w/whirlpool. **Services:** Car-rental desk, afternoon tea and wine/sherry served. **Facilities:** Guest lounge w/TV. Refrigerator stocked with cold drinks. Small garden with gazebo. **Rates (BB):** $80–$120 S or D w/shared bath, $105–$120 S or D w/private bath. Extra person $15. Children under age 6 stay free. Parking: Outdoor, free. AE, MC, V.

Portland's White House
1914 NE 22nd Ave, 97212 (Irvington); tel 503/287-7131. Between Tillamook and Hancock. A comfortable B&B in a historic building. Its location, 10 minutes from downtown, is convenient to bus lines, shopping center, Rose Garden Arena, Coliseum, and Convention Center. Spacious living room for guests. Unsuitable for children under 12. **Rooms:** 6 rms. CI 2pm/CO 11am. No smoking. Garden Room has its own private deck. **Amenities:** No A/C or TV. Some units w/terraces. **Services:** Babysitting, afternoon tea and wine/sherry served. **Facilities:** Guest lounge w/TV. Guests have use of a refrigerator. **Rates (BB):** $87–$103 S; $96–$112 D. Extra person $20. Children under age 7 stay free. Parking: Outdoor, free. MC, V.

RESTAURANTS

Alexander's
In Hilton Hotel, 921 SW 6th Ave (Downtown); tel 503/226-1611. Downtown. **Regional American/Continental.** A spectacular view of mountains and river from the 23rd floor is matched by the presentation of chef David Strout's dazzling creations. Pheasant stuffed with pheasant mousse is a favorite. The adjoining bar has live music and dancing several nights a week. **FYI:** Reservations recommended. Piano/singer. Dress code. **Open:** **Prices:** Main courses $16.95–$20.95. AE, CB, DC, DISC, MC, V.

Atwater's Restaurant and Lounge
In US Bancorp Tower, 111 SW 5th Ave (Downtown); tel 503/275-3600. **Northwest.** In a visually stunning interior on the 30th floor, young chef Mark Gould makes creative waves with Ellensburg lamb as well as ahi tuna with a pepper crust, roasted vegetables, French lentils, and red-wine essence. Unusually fine wine list; monthly tastings and special wine dinners. **FYI:** Reservations accepted. Jazz. Dress code. No smoking. **Open:** Mon–Sat 5:30–9:30pm, Sun 5–8pm. **Prices:** Main courses $15–$24; prix fixe $35–$55. AE, CB, DC, DISC, MC, V.

Avalon Grill
4630 SW Macadam (John's Landing); tel 503/227-4630. Right on Willamette River bank. **Northwest.** Elegant but casual, this airy, multilevel space reflects a 1930s nautical theme. Generally jammed with diners savoring goat cheese and walnut ravioli with Dungeness crab, or lamb glazed with maple syrup and whole grain mustard. Spacious outdoor decks. **FYI:** Reservations recommended. Children's menu.

Dress code. No smoking. **Open:** Lunch Mon–Fri 11:30am–2pm; dinner Sun–Thurs 5–9:30pm, Fri–Sat 5–10:30pm; brunch Sun 10:30am–2pm. **Prices:** Main courses $13.50–$17.75. AE, MC, V.

★ B Moloch Heathman Bakery & Pub
901 SW Salmon St (Downtown); tel 503/227-5700. Just a block from Symphony and Center for Performing Arts. **Northwest.** Lively, airy, drop-in-all-day cafe cheered by bright red columns and flying silk banners. The bar serves beer from Widmer's brewery next door. Chef Christine Dowd, who trained in France, makes terrific game pâtés, salmon crusted in falafel, as well as classic and more upbeat pizzas (with smoked lamb, for example). A favorite place for a lazy breakfast with the newspapers. **FYI:** Reservations not accepted. Dress code. Beer and wine only. No smoking. **Open:** Mon–Thurs 7am–10:30pm, Fri 7am–11:30pm, Sat–Sun 8am–10:30pm. **Prices:** Main courses $13. AE, DISC, MC, V.

Bread & Ink Café
3610 SE Hawthorne (Hawthorne District); tel 503/239-4756. At SE 36th. **Eclectic/Northwest.** One of the first high-quality eateries to open in the now-thriving Hawthorne District. The menu offers excellent Northwest specialties, as well as an eclectic assortment of Mexican and pasta dishes and attractive salads. A good choice for dessert is the tiramisù (espresso- and rum-soaked sponge cake with mascarpone, whipped cream, and shaved chocolate). The dining room is light and airy. **FYI:** Reservations accepted. Beer and wine only. No smoking. **Open:** Breakfast Mon–Fri 7–11:30am, Sat 8am–noon; lunch Mon–Fri 11:30am–5pm, Sat noon–5pm; dinner Mon–Thurs 5–10pm, Fri–Sat 5–11pm, Sun 5–9pm; brunch Sun 9am–2pm. **Prices:** Main courses $11–$16. AE, DISC, MC, V.

★ Bugatti's Ristorante Italiano
18740 Willamette Dr, West Linn; tel 503/636-9555. **Italian.** Lydia Bugatti creates excellent Italian specialties at this warm, friendly trattoria. Her pastas might be tossed with scallops, clams, shrimp, artichoke hearts, or lamb; with sauces infused with garlic, olive oil, or white wine. Other entrees include salmon, steak, and chicken. **FYI:** Reservations recommended. Beer and wine only. No smoking. **Open:** Sun–Thurs 5–9pm, Fri–Sat 5–10pm. **Prices:** Main courses $9–$15. MC, V.

Cafe des Amis
1987 NW Kearney St (Northwest); tel 503/295-6487. **French.** Quietly elegant, cozy, and soothing restaurant located in a wooden cottage in trendy Northwest Portland. Chef Dennis Baker offers a very French menu pared down to seven entrees such as duck with blackberries, lamb shanks with white beans, and poussin with 40 cloves of garlic. Excellent French wines. **FYI:** Reservations recommended. No smoking. **Open:** Mon–Sat 5:30–10pm. **Prices:** Main courses $11–$21. AE, MC, V.

Couch Street Fish House
105 NW 3rd Ave (Old Town); tel 503/223-6173. Between Couch and Davis. **Seafood/Steak.** Located in the Sinnott House, this small, elegant eatery features fine meats as well as seafood . Orchid bouquets grace the tables, which have a view of the open kitchen. Several dishes—such as caesar salad and cherries jubilee—are prepared tableside. Large wine list. Smoking in bar only. **FYI:** Reservations recommended. No smoking. **Open:** Mon–Thurs 5–10pm, Fri–Sat 5–11pm. **Prices:** Main courses $14–$30. AE, CB, DC, DISC, MC, V. VP

Dan & Louis Oyster Bar
208 SW Ankeny St (Downtown); tel 503/227-5906. Between 2nd and 3rd. **Seafood.** A basic, friendly eatery run by the Wachmuth family since 1907. Decor tends toward beer stein and plate collections, mixed with family and seafaring memorabilia. Start with oyster shooters and move on to seafood salads and sandwiches. Bigger appetites might opt for entrees of fish stews or lightly breaded and fried oysters, shrimp, scallops, halibut, cod, or calamari. **FYI:** Reservations accepted. Children's menu. Beer and wine only. **Open:** Sun–Thurs 11am–10pm, Fri–Sat 11am–11pm. **Prices:** Main courses $6–$12. AE, CB, DC, DISC, MC, V.

★ Doris Cafe
325 NE Russell (Elliott); tel 503/287-9249. 6 blocks N of Broadway just off MLK Dr. **Barbecue.** Delicious barbecue served in a light, airy atmosphere. Popular since it opened in a little hole-in-the-wall, seven blocks from the present location. **FYI:** Reservations recommended. Jazz. Children's menu. Beer and wine only. **Open:** Breakfast Sat–Sun 7–10:30am; lunch daily 11am–10pm; dinner daily 11am–10pm; brunch. **Prices:** Main courses $9–$11. AE, DISC, MC, V.

($) ★ Esparza's Tex Mex Cafe
2725 SE Ankeny; tel 503/234-7909. At SE 28th, 1 block S of Burnside. **Tex-Mex.** Excellent food at reasonable prices, served in a decor of old cowboy posters and dangling marionettes. Regular offerings include carne asada, fried catfish, and Joe Esparza's special beef brisket; nightly specials are posted on the blackboard. The cooks smoke all their own meats, and the tortillas are made fresh. Reservations are accepted only for groups of six or more, so the lines can get long. **FYI:** Reservations not accepted. No smoking. **Open:** Peak (June–Aug) Tues–Thurs 11:30am–10pm, Fri–Sat 11:30am–10:30pm. **Prices:** Main courses $6–$10. AE, MC, V.

Esplanade
In RiverPlace Hotel, 1510 SW Harbor Way (Downtown); tel 503/295-6166. At the S end of Tom McCall Waterfront Park. **Regional American.** With its engaging wide-angle view of the Willamette River, this lovely room offers diners visual stimulation beyond the pretty plate set before them. Chef John Zenger presents fine appetizers like rich lobster bisque, spiced pear with prosciutto and brie, or baby spinach with smoked salmon. Entree choices include seafood strudel,

barbecued veal, T-bone steak, pan-seared halibut, and Washington State lamb. **FYI:** Reservations recommended. Piano. No smoking. **Open:** Breakfast Mon–Sat 6:30–11am, Sun 6:30–10am; lunch Mon–Fri 11:30am–2pm; dinner Mon–Sat 5–10pm, Sun 5–9pm; brunch Sun 11am–2pm. **Prices:** Main courses $15–$25. AE, CB, DC, DISC, ER, MC, V.

FuJin
3549 SE Hawthorne Blvd (Hawthorne District); tel 503/231-3753. **Mandarin/Szechuan.** This simple little cafe on a busy shopping street is easy to miss if you aren't careful. (Don't be put off by the neon soft drink sign in the window.) The Vietnamese chef/owner has a gossamer touch with crispy fried eggplant in black bean sauce and delicious crisp string beans. Swift service. **FYI:** Reservations not accepted. Dress code. Beer and wine only. No smoking. **Open:** Mon–Thurs 11am–9:30pm, Fri 11am–10pm, Sat noon–10pm. **Prices:** Main courses $5.50–$8.75. MC, V.

Genoa
2832 SE Belmont St (Southeast); tel 503/238-1464. **Italian.** Four- and seven-course meals just keep flowing from the kitchen of this formal, elegant, Northern Italian bedecked with gorgeous flowers and presided over by expert waiters. Choose from main courses like roast pheasant sauced in apples, quinces, and cherries with mustard and red wine, or poached sturgeon with a sauce of capers and anchovies over polenta and zucchini. **FYI:** Reservations recommended. Beer and wine only. No smoking. **Open:** Mon–Sat 5:30–9:30pm. **Prices:** Prix fixe $40–$48. AE, CB, DC, DISC, MC, V.

Harborside Restaurant
0309 SW Montgomery; tel 503/220-1865. On the S end of Tom McCall Waterfront Park. **Northwest.** An attractive eatery located amid plenty of boutiques and sidewalk action. The menu includes a wide selection of northwest seafood as well as steaks and poultry (including braised ostrich). In nice weather, tables are arrayed along the sidewalk, which overlooks the Willamette River and the marina below. **FYI:** Reservations recommended. Children's menu. **Open:** Lunch Mon–Sat 11:30am–2pm; dinner Mon–Thurs 5–10pm, Fri 5–11pm, Sat 4–11pm, Sun 4–10pm; brunch Sun 10am–3pm. **Prices:** Main courses $7–$23. AE, DC, DISC, MC, V.

($) ★ The Heathman Restaurant
In the Heathman Hotel, 1001 SW Broadway at Salmon (Downtown); tel 503/241-4100. **Northwest.** This 1920s landmark managed to snare one of Manhattan's star chefs, Normandy-born Philippe Boulot, who has revitalized one of the Northwest's most appealing rooms. Popular with theatergoers and concertgoers (who have only a few yards to walk from dining tables to loge seats), the tiered room has picture windows overlooking Broadway and Andy Warhol silkscreen prints adorning the walls; dark wood and brass give it the air of a stylish Paris bistro. A gleaming glass-fronted kitchen offers diners glimpses of Boulot and his brigade preparing roast suckling pig with fricassee of brussels sprouts and hedgehog mushrooms; venison wrapped in applewood smoked bacon; and sauté of Indonesian tiger shrimp and bay scallops in ginger. Personable, knowledgeable servers handle their Oregon wines as though they were precious Montrachets, but the overall tone is casual and neighborly. Lunch is also served in the adjoining Marble Bar. Prices in both are a bargain for a chef of such esteem. **FYI:** Reservations recommended. No smoking. **Open:** Breakfast Mon–Fri 6:30–11am, Sat 6:30am–noon, Sun 6:30am–3pm; lunch Mon–Fri 11am–2pm, Sat–Sun noon–3pm; dinner daily 5–11pm. **Prices:** Main courses $14–$25. AE, CB, DC, DISC, ER, MC, V.

House of Louie
331 NW Davis (Chinatown); tel 503/228-9898. Corner of NW 3rd. **Chinese.** Carved screens of dragons, lions, and birds divide the large dining room of this eatery in the heart of Portland's small Chinatown. The menu runs the gamut of Chinese specialties, with dim sum available all day. **FYI:** Reservations accepted. **Open:** Mon–Thurs 11am–11pm, Fri 11am–1am, Sat 10:30am–1am, Sun 10:30am–11pm. **Prices:** Main courses $5–$17. MC, V.

Hunan
In Morgan's Alley, 515 SW Broadway (Downtown); tel 503/224-8063. **Chinese.** Tucked away behind Broadway, this gem is far larger than it appears. A pretty pink decor, fast service, and very fair prices keep the place packed, especially at lunch when there is a special full meal for $4.95. The sweet and sour soup is one of Portland's bargains. Lamb with mushrooms and broccoli in a dark sauce and mu shu crepe dishes are favorites. **FYI:** Reservations recommended. Dress code. **Open:** Mon–Thurs 11am–9pm, Fri 11am–10pm, Sat noon–10pm, Sun 5–9pm. **Prices:** Main courses $8–$13. MC, V.

★ Il Piatto
2348 SE Ankeny St (Southeast); tel 503/236-4997. **Italian.** Genuine "new age" Italian: offbeat and gently funky, yet hearty and relaxing. Popular for goat cheese torta made with cream, eggs, thyme, garlic, and caramelized nuts. Also try breast of chicken stuffed with tomato pesto, mozzarella, prosciutto in madeira, and cream sauce with polenta. Local opera singers hang out here after performances (you just might be treated to an impromptu aria!). **FYI:** Reservations recommended. Beer and wine only. No smoking. **Open:** Lunch Tues–Fri 11:30am–2:30pm; dinner Sun–Thurs 5:30–10pm, Fri–Sat 5:30–11pm. **Prices:** Main courses $10–$14. MC, V.

Indigine
3725 SE Division St (Richmond); tel 503/238-1470. **Eclectic.** An off-beat place in a tiny wooden cottage with a pleasant deck, run by owner/chef Millie Howe. A bit pricey but guaranteed unusual, with appetizers like mild goat cheese baked in a pepper, and entrees such as Salman's Vindaloo (prawns and spicy pork sausage in a hot, sweet, and sour sauce), or rabbit in a mustard sauce. Popular Saturday night

East Indian feasts. **FYI:** Reservations accepted. Beer and wine only. No smoking. **Open:** Tues–Sat 5:30am–9:30pm. Closed the last week of Aug. **Prices:** Main courses $16–$20. MC, V.

Jake's Famous Crawfish
401 SW 12th Ave (Downtown); tel 503/226-1419. At SW Stark. **Seafood.** Diners can choose from about 20 varieties of fresh fish daily. Favorite dishes include Willapa Bay oysters, New Zealand green-lip mussels, Alaska halibut stuffed with Dungeness crab, bay shrimp and Brie, and ahi tuna with Madeira-orange-soy sauce. Jake's is also known for its chocolate truffle cake. **FYI:** Reservations recommended. Children's menu. Dress code. Additional locations: 611 SW 10th Ave (tel 220-1850); 235 SW 1st Ave (tel 224-7522). **Open:** Lunch Mon–Fri 11:30am–4pm; dinner Mon–Thurs 4–11pm, Fri 4pm–midnight, Sat 5pm–midnight, Sun 5–10pm. **Prices:** Main courses $9–$29. AE, DC, DISC, MC, V.

Lake Grove Bistro
15902 SW Boones Ferry Rd, Lake Oswego (Lake Grove Village); tel 503/636-4384. **French/Italian.** Dine in a fun atmosphere with brilliantly colorful Mediterranean decor. Noted for Gorgonzola sauce on walnut ravioli, flaky quiche crusts, tender salmon, and good tiramisù. You can also eat in the welcoming bar with charming murals. **FYI:** Reservations recommended. Piano. No smoking. Additional location: 8075 SE 13th Ave (tel 234-8259). **Open:** Lunch Tues–Sat 11am–3pm; dinner Tues–Thurs 5–10pm, Fri–Sat 5–11pm, Sun 4:30–9:30pm. **Prices:** Main courses $13–$16. MC, V.

L'Auberge
2601 NW Vaughn; tel 503/223-3302. At 26th Ave. **Regional American/French.** An attractive bistro featuring a variety of dining options, ranging from duck breast in honey-lemon demiglacé to rack of lamb, seafood, and steaks. A four-course prix fixe dinner is offered, as well as lighter bistro entrees (steamed mussels, clams, pasta). Outdoor deck opens for dining in summer; in winter, a well-stoked fire warms the bar, where movie classics are screened on Sunday nights. **FYI:** Reservations recommended. **Open:** Sun–Thurs 5:30pm–midnight, Fri–Sat 5:30pm–1am. **Prices:** Main courses $9–$21; prix fixe $35–$36. AE, CB, DC, DISC, MC, V.

L'Etoile
4627 NE Fremont St (Beaumont-Almeda); tel 503/281-4869. **French.** One of Portland's few French restaurants, l'Etoile reflects panache on and off your dinner plate. Owner/chef John Zweben brilliantly decorates with stencilled stars on the walls, huge vase of flowers at the entry, and star-printed maroon silk swags over a large antique mirror in the bar. Among his creations are honey-glazed Oregon quail stuffed with savory sausage, and sautéed sea scallops in champagne sauce. There is a dazzling wine list. **FYI:** Reservations accepted. Dress code. No smoking. **Open:** Tues–Sat 5:30–9:30pm. Closed 3 weeks after Labor Day. **Prices:** Main courses $19–$25. AE, MC, V.

The London Grill
In Benson Hotel, 309 SW Broadway (Downtown); tel 503/228-2000. **Continental.** This stately, handsome, historic, refurbished dining room is the Grande Olde Dame of Portland, but chef Xavier Bauser astonishes diners with exciting new dishes like medallions of ostrich sautéed in Calvados. Fabulous Sunday buffet brunch features at least seven kinds of shellfish. **FYI:** Reservations recommended. Harp. Dress code. **Open:** Breakfast Mon–Sat 6:30–11:30am, Sun 6:30–8:30am; lunch Mon–Sat 11:30am–2pm; dinner Mon–Thurs 5am–10pm, Fri–Sat 5–11pm, Sun 5–10pm; brunch Sun 9:30am–2pm. **Prices:** Main courses $18.75–$24.75. AE, CB, DC, DISC, ER, MC, V. VP

Macheezmo Mouse
723 SW Salmon St (Downtown); tel 503/228-3491. Between Broadway and Park. **Mexican.** "Healthy fast food" is considered to be an oxymoron, but this place manages to pull it off. The cooks bake, grill, steam—but never fry—the mostly heart-smart food, like burritos with brown rice, black beans, and low-fat cheese. All items can be taken out. A new location near the Portland Airport specializes in food to take on the plane. Many locations in the Portland area. **FYI:** Reservations not accepted. Children's menu. Beer and wine only. No smoking. Additional locations: 1200 NE Broadway (tel 249-0002); 3553 SE Hawthorne (tel 232-6588). **Open:** Mon–Sat 11am–9pm, Sun noon–9pm. **Prices:** Main courses $4–$5. MC, V.

Paley's Place
1204 NW 21st Ave (Northwest); tel 503/243-2403. **French/Northwest.** In this chic little place on Restaurant Row, chef Vitaly Paley makes a truffled risotto crunchy with radicchio. Horseradish-crusted salmon with warm fennel and red cabbage may vie for your attention with house-cured salmon bathed in gin. **FYI:** Reservations recommended. No smoking. **Open:** Peak (May–Sept) Tues–Sat 5:30–11pm. **Prices:** Main courses $10–$16; prix fixe $40–$60. MC, V.

Papa Haydn
701 NW 23rd Ave (Nob Hill); tel 503/228-7317. At Irving. **Northwest.** A bright, lively dining room specializing in pastas and lavish desserts. Fruit sorbets and berry tarts are available seasonally, and if you're *very* lucky the Autumn Meringue will be available—Swiss meringues generously layered with chocolate mousse, then wrapped with wide ribbons of dark chocolate. The gorgeous bar next door, Jo Bar and Rotisserie, is under the same ownership and is a great place to wait for your table. Sandwiches, salads, and desserts are offered for an hour after dinner service finishes. **FYI:** Reservations not accepted. Children's menu. No smoking. Additional location: 5829 SE Milwaukie (tel 232-9440). **Open:** Lunch Tues–Sat 11:30am–5pm; dinner Tues–Thurs 5–10pm, Fri–Sat 5–11pm; brunch Sun 10am–3pm. **Prices:** Main courses $16–$24. AE, MC, V.

Pazzo Ristorante
In Hotel Vintage Plaza, 627 SW Washington St (Downtown); tel 503/228-1515. **Italian.** The Armani-clad set play peasant and come here for fine rustic Northern Italian mood, food, and terrific Italian wines. Chef David Machado does grilled duck breast with braised red cabbage, truffle–celery root puree, and dried-fig sauce, as well as ravioli stuffed with butternut squash in hazelnut butter spiked with marsala. **FYI:** Reservations recommended. Dress code. No smoking. **Open:** Breakfast Mon–Fri 7:30–10:30am, Sat 8–10:30am, Sun 8–11am; lunch Mon–Fri 11:45am–2:30pm, Sat 11:30am–2:30pm, Sun noon–10pm; dinner Mon–Thurs 5–10pm, Fri 5–11pm, Sat 4:30–11pm, Sun noon–10pm. **Prices:** Main courses $11–$17. AE, CB, DC, DISC, ER, MC, V. VP

Plainfield's Mayur Restaurant & Art Gallery
852 SW 21st Ave (Downtown); tel 503/223-2995. 1 block S of Burnside. **Indian.** Exotic cuisine from the subcontinent is the specialty at this art-filled venue. (A gallery of intricate carvings from India is on permanent display.) Try the biryani (a huge mound of cleverly spiced rice made with your choice of beef, lamb, chicken, or vegetables). As in the Mogul courts of Emperor Shah Jahan (builder of the Taj Mahal), your biryani will be served with a covering of silver leaf. **FYI:** Reservations recommended. **Open:** Daily 5:30–10pm. **Prices:** Main courses $9–$18. AE, DISC, MC, V.

★ Ringside West
2165 W Burnside St (Northwest/Nob Hill); tel 503/223-1513. Between 21st and 22nd. **Seafood/Steak.** For over 50 years, perfectly cooked steaks have been served here. James Beard declared the onion rings "the best I've ever had"; seafood is also handled adeptly. The decor (hand-split cedar timbers and a stone fireplace) is a throwback to the 1940s. **FYI:** Reservations recommended. Dress code. Additional location: 14021 NE Glisan (tel 255-0750). **Open:** Mon–Sat 5pm–midnight, Sun 4–11:30pm. **Prices:** Main courses $7–$36. AE, CB, DC, DISC, MC, V. VP ♿

$ Ron Paul Charcuterie
In Macadam Market, 6141 SW Macadam (John's Landing); tel 503/977-0313. 5 blocks S of John's Landing Mall. **Eclectic/Northwest.** Portland's original upscale deli, with food you could serve to the chairman of the board. Alluring takeaway counters, fine wines, and attractive dining areas add up to a cozy neighborhood feeling. Dishes that win raves are Szechuan noodle salad with Oriental vegetables in a spicy peanut-ginger sauce; and Jamaican jerked pork loin with molasses and corn vinaigrette, black beans, and rice. **FYI:** Reservations not accepted. Beer and wine only. No smoking. Additional location: 1441 NE Broadway (tel 284-5347). **Open:** Breakfast Mon–Fri 7:30–11:30am; lunch Mon–Fri 11:30am–5pm, Sat 9am–2pm, Sun 9am–4pm; dinner Mon–Fri 5–10pm, Sat 5–11pm. **Prices:** Main courses $7.95–$14.95. AE, MC, V. ♿

Saigon Kitchen
835 NE Broadway (Northeast/Lloyd District); tel 503/281-3669. **Thai/Vietnamese.** Big, lively, and brisk, with harsh lighting. Large portions of Thai and Vietnamese dishes are served up, like a huge tureen of classic Thai chicken soup with lemongrass, coconut milk, and ground peanuts. Plenty of noodle dishes as well, such as angel-hair pasta with bean sprouts, sweet vinegar sauce, fresh coriander, and chunks of crispy spring roll. **FYI:** Reservations not accepted. Dress code. Beer and wine only. No smoking. Additional locations: 3954 SE Division St (tel 236-2312); 14280 SW Allen Blvd, Beaverton (tel 646-4611). **Open:** Mon–Fri 11am–10pm, Sat–Sun noon–10pm. **Prices:** Main courses $5–$15; prix fixe $8–$15. AE, MC, V.

★ Salty's on the Columbia
3839 NE Marine Dr (Northeast); tel 503/288-4444. **Seafood.** Steak and seafood are served up at this upscale-casual eatery with nautical decor and a fine river view. Dine indoors or on the big deck on such dishes as escargots royale, filbert-encrusted Camembert, and grilled mahimahi with garlic and black bean sauce. **FYI:** Reservations recommended. Children's menu. **Open:** Peak (June–Aug) Mon–Sat 11am–10pm, Sun 11am–9pm. **Prices:** Main courses $14–$22. AE, CB, DC, DISC, MC, V. VP ♿

Thai Orchid Restaurant
2231 W Burnside; tel 503/226-4542. N side, between 22nd and 23rd. **Thai.** Located at the southern edge of Nob Hill, this attractive dining room boasts orchids on the tables, large windows, and plenty of elbow room.Wide variety of Thai favorites, from mild to spicy. **FYI:** Reservations not accepted. Beer and wine only. No smoking. **Open:** Lunch Mon–Fri 11:30am–2pm; dinner Mon–Fri 5–10pm, Sat–Sun 4–10pm. **Prices:** Main courses $7–$12. MC, V.

Three Doors Down
1429 SE 37th Ave (Hawthorne District); tel 503/236-6886. Off Hawthorne Blvd. **Italian.** Intimate and casual. Features northern Italian dishes like seafood fra diavolo (a mix of clams, East Coast scallops and mussels), and shrimps and black olives over linguine in spicy marinara sauce. Amazingly long list of Italian wines. **FYI:** Reservations not accepted. Beer and wine only. No smoking. **Open:** Peak (spring and summer) Tues–Sat 5–10pm, Sun 5–9pm. Closed first two weeks of Jan. **Prices:** Main courses $14–$19. AE, DISC, MC, V. ♿

Waterzoies
2574 NW Thurman St; tel 503/225-0641. **Northwest.** A peaceful, gently sophisticated place where owner/chef Bill McCarty serves marvelous orange-pecan snapper with a crusty edge. Wild mushroom gratinee comes with or without escargots, and waterzoie—a famed Belgian dish—is a top seller. **FYI:** Reservations not accepted. Dress code. No smoking. **Open:** Lunch Tues–Sat 11:30am–2:30pm; dinner Tues–Thurs 5:30–9:30pm, Fri–Sat 5:30–10:30pm; brunch Sun 11am–2:30pm. **Prices:** Main courses $10–$16. MC, V. ♿

Wild Abandon
2411 SE Belmont St (Buckman); tel 503/232-4458. **New American.** Eclectic and amusing with fair prices. Chef Julie Hawkinson stuffs quail with Italian cheese and bosc pears, then arranges them on a bed of spinach. Her love of herbs and fruit inspires unusual treatments such as a sage crème anglaise for a chocolate ganache. Wine list is growing fast. **FYI:** Reservations recommended. Beer and wine only. No smoking. **Open:** Dinner Mon–Thurs 5–10pm, Fri–Sat 5–11pm; brunch Sat–Sun 9am–2pm. **Prices:** Main courses $8–$14. AE, CB, DC, DISC, MC, V.

Wildwood
1221 NW 21st Ave (Northwest); tel 503/248-9663. **Northwest.** The minimalist decor is perfect background for the imaginative food conjured up by chef Cory Shreiber. Try duck breast with caramelized onion griddle cake, morels, and roasted apple; or a crème brûlée with ginger and lemon zest. Great list of Pacific Coast wines. The bar offers light food all day. **FYI:** Reservations recommended. Dress code. No smoking. **Open:** Mon–Thurs 11:30am–10pm, Fri–Sat 11:30am–10:30pm, Sun 10am–8:30pm. **Prices:** Main courses $15–$20. AE, MC, V.

Winterborne
3520 NE 42nd Ave (Beaumont-Almeda); tel 503/249-8486. A few yards off NE Fremont St. **French/Seafood.** The small pale pink room is lined with prints of fish and has twinkling lights. Owner/chef Gilbert Henry serves only six seafood entrees a night including sole Parmesan flecked with fresh lavender. The dense chocolate cake is a winner. **FYI:** Reservations accepted. Dress code. Beer and wine only. No smoking. **Open:** Wed–Sat 5:30–9:30pm. **Prices:** Main courses $13.50–$16.50; prix fixe $18.50. MC, V.

★ Zefiro Restaurant and Bar
NW 21st Ave (Northwest); tel 503/226-3394. **International.** Cool sophistication marks chef Christopher Israel's hip and immensely popular bistro. His innovative Mediterranean cuisine with southeast Asian influences yields such wonderful creations as warm roasted quail topped with preserved plum and flanked by mango slices with a spicy Indonesian dressing. Fine desserts and a superb wine list. **FYI:** Reservations recommended. Dress code. **Open:** Lunch Mon–Sat 11:30am–2:30pm; dinner Mon–Thurs 5:30–10:30pm, Fri–Sat 5:30–11pm. Closed two weeks in Feb. **Prices:** Main courses $13–$17. AE, DC, MC, V. VP

★ Zell's: An American Cafe
1300 SE Morrison St (Downtown); tel 503/239-0196. **New American/American.** A neighborhood classic with a tiled counter and plenty of newspapers to read. Lightest, most original pancakes in town with versions like the "Tropical" (lemon, orange, and pineapple). Daily blackboard specials might include rhubarb German pancake or spicy chicken salad. Excellent coffee. **FYI:** Reservations not accepted. Beer and wine only. No smoking. **Open:** Mon–Sat 7am–2pm, Sun 8am–3pm. **Prices:** Lunch main courses $5.25–$6.95. AE, MC, V.

Zen Restaurant
910 SW Salmon St (Downtown); tel 503/222-3056. Between 9th and 10th. **Japanese.** In addition to a wide selection of sushi, Zen offers all the usual Japanese favorites: tempura, teriyaki, sashimi. The house specialty, Kaiseki, is a full course dinner with courses chosen by the chef and made from the freshest seasonal ingredients. Tatami rooms are available. **FYI:** Reservations recommended. Dress code. **Open:** Lunch Mon–Fri 11:30am–2pm; dinner Mon–Sat 5–10pm. **Prices:** Main courses $10–$50. AE, DC, MC, V.

ATTRACTIONS 

MUSEUMS

Portland Art Museum
1219 SW Park Ave (Downtown); tel 503/226-2811 or toll free 800/789-1830. The region's oldest and largest visual and media arts center, with treasures spanning 35 centuries of Asian, European, and American art. Renowned collection of Native American art features transformation masks (worn during ritual dances), a totem pole, and countless wood carvings. Pre-Columbian and African collections are also notable. The museum's Northwest Film Center presents films five nights a week and is widely acclaimed for its annual Portland International Film Festival. Live music on Wednesday nights (except in summer). **Open:** Tues–Sat 11am–5pm, Sun 1–5pm. Closed some hols. **$$**

Oregon Museum of Science and Industry
1945 SW Water Ave; tel 503/797-4000. Six huge halls contain a wide variety of hands-on exhibits, including several that allow visitors to "touch" a tornado or "ride" an earthquake. Oregon's first Omnimax theater is located here, and the Murdock Sky Theater features astronomy presentations and laser light shows. **Open:** Sat–Wed 9:30am–5:30pm, Thurs–Fri 9:30am–9pm. Closed Dec 25. **$$$**

Oregon History Center
1200 SW Park Ave; tel 503/306-5200. More than 300,000 people a year visit this center, founded in 1965 by the Oregon Historical Society. The museum's permanent collections include more than 80,000 artifacts dealing with sea and land exploration, the Oregon Trail, Native Americans, and Northwest art. There are also interactive video displays, workshops, group tours, traveling exhibits, and a museum store. **Open:** Tues–Sat 10am–5pm, Sun noon–5pm. Closed some hols. **$$**

American Advertising Museum
9 NW 2nd Ave (Skidmore District); tel 503/226-0000. Visitors can learn about the history of advertising in America and see favorite old TV commercials at this unusual museum. One exhibit shows the changes in advertising over several centuries, while another displays all-time best advertising cam-

paigns. There's even a complete series of Burma Shave roadside signs. **Open:** Wed–Fri 11am–5pm, Sat–Sun noon–5pm. Closed some hols. **$$**

Columbia County Historic Museum
Old County Courthouse, St Helens; tel 503/397-3868. 15 mi N of Portland. Housed on the second floor of the old Columbia County Courthouse in St Helens. Exhibits include Native American artifacts, photos of early settlers, and a display on the Lewis and Clark Expedition, which passed by this area in 1805. Windows offer an excellent view of nearby Mount St Helens. **Open:** Fri–Sat noon–4pm. **Free**

Old Aurora Colony Museum
SE corner 2nd and Liberty Sts, Aurora; tel 503/678-5754. 20 mi S of Portland. Site of a communal Christian society that flourished during the 1860s and 1870s. Museum's guided tours and interpretive programs focus on Colony music, quilts and textiles, furniture, and family life. Surrounding buildings include an ox barn, two Colony homes, a communal wash house, and a farm machinery building. Artisans give demonstrations of traditional crafts. Self-guided walking tour brochures available. **Open:** Wed–Sun 12:30–4:30pm. Closed Jan and some hols. **$$**

Children's Museum
3037 SW Second Ave; tel 503/823-2227. Hands-on fun for children 6 months–10 years old. Kids can "operate" on parents and friends in the Medical Center, shop for groceries in Kid City Thriftway, or prepare an international feast in the fully stocked kiddie Bistro. The Children's Cultural Center, located in the museum annex, teaches youngsters about different cultures and traditions. Omokunle Village, a re-creation of a typical Nigerian village, enables children to hear Yoruban music, barter for goods, and try on authentic African garb. **Open:** Daily 9am–5pm. Closed some hols. **$$**

World Forestry Center Museum
4033 SW Canyon Rd; tel 503/228-1367. Learn about the forests in the Pacific Northwest and around the world. Highlights include a Smithsonian exhibition on tropical rain forests, a special exhibition concerning old growth forests, and a petrified wood exhibit created by 200-million-year-old trees. A 70-foot talking tree greets visitors, and the gift shop sells unique wooden gifts. **Open:** Mem Day–Labor Day, daily 9am–5pm; Labor Day–Mem Day, daily 10am–5pm. Closed Dec 25. **$**

PARKS & GARDENS

Metro Washington Park Zoo
4001 SW Canyon Rd; tel 503/226-1561. Tucked in a corner of the Southwest hills, this award-winning zoo is home to animals from all corners of the world-from exotic African rain forests to Alaska to Oregon's Cascade Mountains. The zoo has the largest breeding herd of elephants in captivity; amazingly lifelike habitats including an Alaskan-tundra exhibit with grizzly bears, wolves, and musk oxen; and an African exhibit with a newly added rain forest section. Train carries visitors from one section to another. Petting zoo. **Open:** June–Aug, daily 9:30am–6pm; Sept–May, daily 9:30am–4pm. Closed Dec 25. **$$$**

Japanese Garden Society of Oregon
611 SW Kingston; tel 503/223-4070. Five traditional gardens over 5½ acres, a Japanese Tea House, and a Pavilion combine to recapture the mood of ancient Japan. From the Japanese-style wooden house in the center of the garden, you have a view over Portland to Mount Hood, which is so reminiscent of Mount Fuji that it seems almost as if it were placed there just for the sake of this garden. Tours are offered daily from April through October at 10:45am and 2:30pm. **Open:** Apr–May, Sept, daily 10am–6pm; June–Aug, daily 9am–8pm; Oct–Mar, daily 10am–4pm. Closed some hols. **$$**

Oaks Park
East end of Sellwood Bridge; tel 503/233-5777. Covering more than 44 acres, this amusement park first opened in 1905 to coincide with the Lewis and Clark Exposition. Beneath the shady oaks for which the park is named, visitors will find waterfront picnic sites, miniature golf, music, and rides such as a roller coaster. The largest roller-skating rink in the Northwest is also here. All activities have separate fees. **Open:** Mar–June, Sat–Sun noon–5pm; July–Aug, Tues–Thurs noon– 9pm, Fri–Sat noon–10pm, Sun noon–7pm.

Hoyt Arboretum
4000 SW Fairview Blvd; tel 503/228-8733. Portland's outdoor tree museum features 100-year old native trees and unique plants from six different continents. More than 800 species of trees and shrubs are labeled and displayed on 175 acres, which also include 10 miles of scenic hiking trails. Free, hourlong guided tours of the arboretum are offered every Sat and Sun at 2pm(April–October). The Bristlecone Pine trail and the Oregon Vietnam Veterans Memorial Trail are wheelchair accessible. **Open:** Grounds, daily 6am–10pm; visitor center, daily 9am–3pm. **Free**

The Grotto
Sandy Blvd at NE 85th Ave; tel 503/254-7371. Since its dedication as the Sanctuary of our Sorrowful Mother in 1924, thousands have been drawn to this 62-acre botanical garden each year. The peaceful garden is home to more than 100 statues and shrines, several reflecting ponds, award-winning architecture, and a natural outdoor cathedral—a magnificent rock cave hewed from the base of a 110-foot cliff, which houses a white-marble replica of Michelangelo's famous *Pietà*. The upper-level grounds offer breathtaking panoramic views of the Columbia River Valley, the Cascade Range, and Mount St Helens, while the Meditation Chapel offers a 180° floor-to-ceiling view through a beveled glass wall. **Open:** May–Sept, daily 9am–8pm; Oct–Apr, daily 9am–5pm. Closed some hols. **Free**

Forest Park
Bounded by W Burnside St, Newberry, St Helens, and Skyline Rds; tel 503/823-4492. With 4,800 acres of wilderness this is

the largest forested city park in the United States. There are 50 miles of trails and old fire roads for hiking and jogging. More than 100 species of birds call these forests home, making this park a birdwatcher's paradise. **Open:** Daily sunrise–sunset. **Free**

ENTERTAINMENT VENUES

Portland Center for the Performing Arts

1111 SW Broadway (Downtown); tel 503/248-4335. Four units in the heart of Portland's dining and entertainment district include the **Arlene Schnitzer Concert Hall,** a former 1920s movie palace with original Portland Theater sign and marquee on the outside; its interior has been immaculately restored. Schnitzer is home to the Oregon Symphony. The **New Theater Building,** a sparkling glass jewel box, houses the **Intermediate** (home to the Oregon Shakespeare Festival Portland) and the **Winningstad.** The **Portland Civic Auditorium** was constructed shortly after World War I and completely remodeled in the 1960s; it is home to the Oregon Ballet Theater and the Portland Opera. Guided tours available. **Open:** Office, Mon–Fri 8am–5pm. **$$$$**

Memorial Coliseum

1401 Wheeler St; tel 503/231-8000. The **Portland Trail Blazers,** one of the hottest NBA teams in recent years, pound the boards here between fall and spring. Also, the **Portland Winter Hawks,** a minor-league hockey team, carve up the ice here from October to March. **$$$$**

Pioneer Courthouse Square

701 SW 6th (Downtown); tel 503/223-1613. This popular square, with its tumbling waterfall fountain and free-standing columns, is a local favorite for events ranging from flower displays to concerts to protest rallies. At noon, a mechanical sculpture called the *Weather Machine* forecasts the upcoming 24 hours. Amid a fanfare of music and flashing lights, it sends up clouds of mist and then raises either a sun (clear weather), a dragon (stormy weather), or a blue heron (clouds and drizzle). The square's bricks are also worth a look—each one contains a name or statement, and some are rather curious. **Open:** Daily 6am–midnight. **Free**

WINERIES

Elk Cove Vineyards

27751 NW Olson Rd, Gaston; tel 503/985-7760. 20 mi W of Portland, in Gaston. Enjoy award-winning wines while drinking in inspiring views from the wine-tasting room. The winery, owned and operated by Joe and Pat Campbell, produces estate-bottled pinot noir, riesling, chardonnay, pinot gris, and gewurztraminer. **Open:** Daily 11am–5pm. Closed some hols. **Free**

Oak Knoll Winery

29700 SW Burkhalter Rd, Hillsboro; tel 503/648-8198, or toll free 800/625-5665. 10 mi W of Portland in Hillsboro. This countryside winery does not grow their own vines, but selectively chooses their grapes from local growers. The Vuylsteke family uses only the finest equipment and French oak barrels, which can be viewed inside the winery—a former dairy with hollow tile construction that provides natural temperature control. **Open:** Daily noon–5pm. Closed some hols.

Tualatin Vineyards

10850 NW Seavey Rd, Forest Grove; tel 503/357-5005. 22 mi SW of Portland. Established in 1973 by Bill Fuller, a wine maker from Napa Valley, and Bill Malkmus, an investment banker from San Francisco, the vineyard has received over 60 gold and silver medals for its chardonnays and pinot noirs. Its 85 acres include a tasting room and a picnic area that offers a spectacular view of the vineyard and the Willamette Valley. **Open:** Mon–Fri 10am–4pm, Sat–Sun noon–5pm. Closed Jan and some hols. **Free**

OTHER ATTRACTIONS

Portland Saturday Market

West end of Burnside Bridge/Skidmore Fountain (Old Town); tel 503/222-6072. Every Saturday and Sunday nearly 300 artists and craftspeople can be found selling their exquisite creations here. In addition to dozens of crafts stalls, you'll find flowers, fresh produce, ethnic foods, and lots of free entertainment. One of the best places in Portland to buy one-of-a-kind gifts. **Open:** Sat 10am–5pm, Sun 11am–4:30pm. Closed Dec 25. **Free**

Pittock Mansion

3229 NW Pittock Dr; tel 503/823-3624. Portland pioneers Henry and Georgiana Pittock lived in this 16,000-square-foot chateauesque mansion from 1914 to 1919. Tours allow visitors an intimate look at the home's eclectic architectural design and lavishly decorated interior, including some family artifacts. The lawns are open for strolling, picnicking, and gazing at the sweeping view of mountains, rivers, and the city skyline. Gift shop and restaurant on site. **Open:** Daily noon–4pm. Closed first 3 weeks in Jan and some hols. **$$**

McLoughlin House National Historic Site

713 Center St, Oregon City; tel 503/656-5146. Approximately 12 mi SE of Portland. Home of Dr John McLoughlin, the "father of Oregon." The house has been restored to its appearance during McLoughlin's 1846 to 1857 occupancy, with a third of the original furnishings. The rest of the furnishings are period pieces collected from the Hudson Bay Company (where McLoughlin was Chief Factor) and from local residents. The neighborhood surrounding the house is a local historic district. **Open:** Tues–Sat 10am–4pm, Sun 1–4pm. Closed Jan, some hols. **$**

Portlandia and The Portland Building

1120 SW 5th Ave. The massive kneeling figure of Portlandia holds a trident in one hand and with the other reaches toward the street. The symbol of the city, *Portlandia* is the second-largest hammered-bronze statue in the country (the largest is the Statue of Liberty). Strangely enough, this classically designed figure perches above the entrance to Portland's most controversial building: The Portland Building, considered the first postmodern structure in the country.

Church of Elvis
219 Ankeny St (Old Town). Two blocks from Portland Saturday Market on a narrow little street is Portland's most bizarre attraction: the first 24-hour video psychic and church of Elvis. A window full of kitschy contraptions bearing the visage of the King never fails to stop people in their tracks as they stroll past. The King will absolve you of sin, unless, of course, you have committed the unforgivable sin of believing that Elvis is dead. Great fun if you are a fan of Elvis, tabloids, or the unusual. **Open:** Daily 24 hours. **$**

Cascade Sternwheelers
Portland and Cascade Locks; tel 503/223-3928. The sternwheeler *Columbia Gorge* cruises the Columbia River (mid-June to early October) and the Willamette River (October to mid-June). The trip up the Columbia, with its towering cliffs, includes stops at the Cascade Locks and Bonneville Dam. There are lunch, brunch, dinner, and dance cruises. An annual five-hour cruise back down the Columbia to Portland marks the end of the summer season. Another stern-wheeler, *Cascade Queen*, cruises the scenic Willamette Greenway, a remarkably untouched area just south of the central city. Downriver trips offer glimpses of the downtown Portland skyline. **$$$$**

Port Orford

A natural deep-water harbor and busy fishing center, especially when the salmon run in the nearby Sixes and Elk Rivers. **Information:** Port Orford Chamber of Commerce, PO Box 637, Port Orford, 97465 (tel 541/332-8055).

MOTEL

Castaway By the Sea
545 W 5th St, PO Box 844, 97465; tel 541/332-4502; fax 541/332-9303. Off US 101, take Oregon St. This is an exceptional value for a relaxing seaside stay. **Rooms:** 14 rms and effic. CI 3pm/CO 11am. Nonsmoking rms avail. Enclosed sun porches allow for great views of the harbor and coast. Efficiencies have a three-bed loft. **Amenities:** Cable TV w/movies. No A/C. Some units w/terraces. **Services:** Pet fee $5. **Facilities:** A half-mile path leads to a wide beach on a sandy cove. **Rates:** Peak (June–Oct) $45–$55 S or D; $55–$75 effic. Extra person $10. Min stay peak. Lower rates off-season. Parking: Outdoor, free. MC, V.

Redmond

Rock climbers from around the world pass through this central Oregon town on their way to Smith Rock State Park for some of the most challenging and scenic vertical experiences found anywhere. Eagle Crest Resort (just west of town) has a pair of championship golf courses along the Crooked River. **Information:** Redmond Chamber of Commerce, 446 SW 7th St, Redmond, 97756 (tel 541/923-5191).

MOTEL

Best Western Rama Inn
2630 SW 17th Place, 97756; tel 541/548-8080 or toll free 800/821-0543. US 97 on south end of Redmond. Fairly standard, two-story motel on the strip, but new and clean. Probably the nicest rooms in town. **Rooms:** 49 rms and stes. CI 2pm/CO 11am. Nonsmoking rms avail. Nothing fancy, but functional. No great views. **Amenities:** A/C, cable TV w/movies, refrig, dataport, voice mail. Some units w/whirlpools. **Services:** **Facilities:** Sauna, whirlpool, washer/dryer. Pool and weight room are both small. **Rates (CP):** Peak (May–Oct) $57–$160 S or D; $110–$160 ste. Extra person $10. Children under age 12 stay free. Lower rates off-season. Parking: Outdoor, free. AE, CB, DC, DISC, JCB, MC, V.

RESORT

Eagle Crest Resort
1522 Cline Falls Rd, PO Box 1215, 97756; tel 541/923-2453 or toll free 800/682-4786; fax 541/923-1720. 5 mi W of Redmond; 1 mi off OR 126. 520 acres. A slice of the good life located among the juniper trees of central Oregon. Now a sprawling destination playground, the resort offers views of Mount Jefferson and other Cascade peaks. **Rooms:** 119 rms, stes, and effic; 175 cottages/villas. CI 4pm/CO noon. Nonsmoking rms avail. Condominiums (about 175 at last count) far out-number standard rooms. Condos include spacious, sunny 2- and 3-bedroom units. Forty-one of the 119 hotel rooms have small kitchens. **Amenities:** A/C, cable TV w/movies, refrig, VCR, CD/tape player. Some units w/terraces, some w/fireplaces, some w/whirlpools. **Services:** Social director, masseur, children's program, babysitting. **Facilities:** 36 4 2 170 2 restaurants, 1 bar, basketball, volleyball, games rm, racquetball, squash, sauna, whirlpool, beauty salon, day-care ctr, playground, washer/dryer. Walkers and joggers can use 1½ miles of river trail. Tanning booths available. **Rates:** Peak (June 15–Sept) $80–$85 S; $88–$93 D; $109–$114 ste; $185–$235 effic; $185–$235 cottage/villa. Children under age 13 stay free. Lower rates off-season. Parking: Outdoor, free. Condos require two-night minimum stay; check-in for condos is 6pm. AE, DISC, MC, V.

Reedsport

The community of Reedsport sits along the Umpqua River north of Coos Bay. The area is popular with visitors interested in wildlife viewing and whale watching. **Information:** Reedsport/Winchester Bay Chamber of Commerce, 805 Hwy Ave, PO Box 11, Reedsport, 97467 (tel 541/271-3495).

MOTELS

Anchor Bay
1821 Winchester Ave, 97467; tel 541/271-2149 or toll free 800/767-1821. Off US 101. Standard, serviceable roadside motel. **Rooms:** 21 rms, stes, and effic. CI noon/CO 11am. Nonsmoking rms avail. **Amenities:** Cable TV w/movies, refrig. No A/C. **Services:** **Facilities:** Washer/dryer. **Rates (CP):** Peak (May 15–Oct) $39–$46 S; $53 D; $125 ste; $60–$85 effic. Extra person $5. Children under age 9 stay free. Lower rates off-season. Parking: Outdoor, free. AE, DC, DISC, MC, V.

Best Western Salbasgeon Inn
1400 Highway Ave, 97467; tel 541/271-4831 or toll free 800/528-1234; fax 541/271-4832. Off US 101. Clean and well appointed, this new motel is the best of the national-chain accommodations in town. **Rooms:** 56 rms, stes, and effic. CI 2pm/CO 11am. Nonsmoking rms avail. **Amenities:** A/C, cable TV w/movies. Some units w/minibars, some w/fireplaces, some w/whirlpools. **Services:** **Facilities:** Whirlpool, washer/dryer. **Rates (CP):** Peak (June 15–Aug) $68–$73 S; $78–$88 D; $92–$112 ste; $102–$112 effic. Extra person $5. Lower rates off-season. Parking: Outdoor, free. AE, CB, DC, DISC, MC, V.

Douglas Country Inn
1894 Winchester Ave, 97467; tel 541/271-3686. Standard roadside motel, convenient for coastal travelers. **Rooms:** 23 rms and effic. CI open/CO 11am. Nonsmoking rms avail. **Amenities:** Cable TV, refrig. No A/C. **Services:** Pet fee $5. **Rates:** Peak (June–Sept) $36–$38 S; $38–$42 D; $42–$50 effic. Lower rates off-season. Parking: Outdoor, free. DISC, MC, V.

Sallbasgeon Inn of the Umpqua
45209 OR 38, 97467; tel 541/271-2025. From US 101, go 7 mi E on OR 38. With elk- and waterfowl-viewing areas just down the road, this is a haven for nature lovers. The Umpqua River flows behind the motel, just beyond the large lawn. **Rooms:** 12 rms and effic. CI 3pm/CO 11am. Nonsmoking rms avail. Rooms are clean and well kept—but the best attractions are outdoors. **Amenities:** Cable TV w/movies, refrig. No A/C. **Services:** $5 charge for pets. **Rates:** Peak (July–Sept) $65 S; $79 D; $75–$99 effic. Extra person $5. Lower rates off-season. Parking: Outdoor, free. AE, CB, DC, DISC, MC, V.

Roseburg

Nestled in the Umpqua Valley where two branches of the Umpqua River converge, this timber town is located near seven local wineries. **Information:** Roseburg Visitors and Convention Bureau, 410 SE Spruce, PO Box 1262, Roseburg, 97470 (tel 541/673-7868).

MOTELS

Comfort Inn
1539 NW Mulholland Dr, 97470; tel 541/957-1100 or toll free 800/228-5150; fax 541/957-1100. Exit 125 off I-5. Opened in 1995. Minimal amenities but good service. **Rooms:** 37 rms and stes. CI open/CO 11am. Nonsmoking rms avail. **Amenities:** A/C, cable TV w/movies. 1 unit w/whirlpool. **Services:** Full continental breakfast, with cereals and a variety of baked goods. **Facilities:** Whirlpool, washer/dryer. Very small fitness room has only two pieces of equipment. **Rates (CP):** Peak (June–Sept) $55–$65 S; $60–$95 D; $160 ste. Extra person $10. Children under age 18 stay free. Lower rates off-season. Parking: Outdoor, free. AE, CB, DC, DISC, MC, V.

National 9 Inn
1627 SE Stephans St, 97470; tel 541/672-3354 or toll free 800/524-9999; fax 541/673-3455. Exit 120 off I-5 N; exit 124 off I-5 S. A bare-bones motel at the south end of town. **Rooms:** 12 rms. CI open/CO 11am. Nonsmoking rms avail. Some rooms connect to a second bedroom; some connect to a kitchen unit. **Amenities:** A/C, cable TV w/movies. **Services:** **Rates:** Peak (June–Oct) $32–$38 S; $34–$75 D. Extra person $4. Lower rates off-season. Parking: Outdoor, free. Kitchen units are $10 extra. AE, DISC, MC, V.

Windmill Inn of Roseburg
1450 NW Mulholland Dr, 97470; tel 541/673-0901 or toll free 800/547-4747; fax 541/673-0901. Exit 125 off I-5. Older but well-kept motel convenient to the freeway. **Rooms:** 128 rms and effic. CI 3pm/CO 11am. Nonsmoking rms avail. One efficiency apartment available. **Amenities:** A/C, cable TV w/movies, dataport. Some units w/terraces, 1 w/whirlpool. Microwaves and mini-refrigerators available. **Services:** Complimentary coffee, tea, or hot chocolate, muffin, and newspaper delivered to room each morning. Complimentary fruit and coffee in lobby 24 hours. Fax service. **Facilities:** 1 restaurant, 1 bar, sauna, whirlpool. Motel is two blocks from the city's riverside bike path; free loaner bikes are available. Pool is in lovely, landscaped courtyard setting. **Rates (CP):** Peak (June 15–Sept 15) $68 S; $78–$84 D; $95 effic. Extra person $6. Children under age 19 stay free. Lower rates off-season. Parking: Outdoor, free. Corporate and government rates. Wildlife Safari package avail for nearby game park. AE, CB, DC, DISC, MC, V.

ATTRACTIONS

Douglas County Museum of History and Natural History
Exit 123 off I-5; tel 541/440-4507. Built in 1969, this museum's four wings house Native American tools, prehistoric skeletons and fossils, and displays detailing the hardships of the area's early white settlers. Also on the grounds are the Lavola Bakken Memorial Research Library and the restored 1882 Dillard Oregon and California Railroad Depot. **Open:** Daily 9am–5pm. Closed some hols. **$$**

Wildlife Safari
1790 Safari Rd, Winston; tel 541/679-6761 or toll free 800/355-4848. 3 mi W of Roseburg. Hundreds of exotic animals from around the world inhabit this 600-acre roadside park, where visitors drive through the clusters of lions, tigers, and bears. The park village features restaurant, gift shop, education center, petting zoo, train, and elephant ride. **Open:** Summer, daily 9am–7pm; winter, daily 9am–4pm. **$$$$**

Salem

Capital of Oregon. Historical markers throughout town celebrate the state's past. The Capitol building is built of Vermont marble and its rotunda was recently restored following earthquake damage. The Salem Art Fair and Festival is held here each July and the state fair is held here each August. **Information:** Salem Convention and Visitors Association, 1313 Mill St SE, Salem, 97301 (tel 503/581-4325).

PUBLIC TRANSPORTATION

Salem Area Transit's Cherriots System (tel 503/588-BUSS) operates buses Mon–Fri 6am–6:15pm and Sat 7:45am–5:45pm. On most routes buses run every half-hour; on Sat buses run hourly. Fares: adults 75¢; children 6–17 50¢, seniors and persons with disabilities 35¢; children under 6 ride free. Transfers are free.

HOTEL

Quality Inn Hotel and Convention Center
3301 NE Market St, 97301; tel 503/370-7888 or toll free 800/248-6273; fax 503/370-6305. Just off I-5 at Market St exit. This older property is Salem's only full-service hotel; it has been kept up to date with high-quality furnishings and amenities. Caters to Japanese businesspeople. **Rooms:** 150 rms and stes. CI 3pm/CO 11am. Nonsmoking rms avail. **Amenities:** A/C, cable TV w/movies. Some units w/terraces, some w/whirlpools. Some rooms offer mini-refrigerators and microwaves. **Services:** Masseur. Fax service available. **Facilities:** 500 1 restaurant, 1 bar (w/entertainment), sauna, whirlpool, washer/dryer. Passes for nearby athletic club are $4, free to guests at corporate rate. **Rates:** $66–$73 S; $73–$78 D; $96–$101 ste. Children under age 12 stay free. Parking: Outdoor, free. Romance and winery tour packages avail. AE, CB, DC, DISC, MC, V.

MOTELS

Best Western Pacific Hwy Inn
4646 Portland Rd, 97305; tel 503/390-3200 or toll free 800/528-1234; fax 503/393-7989. off I-5 exit 258, E side of fwy. A secure, pleasantly furnished, clean motel convenient to I-5. **Rooms:** 52 rms. CI open/CO noon. Nonsmoking rms avail. **Amenities:** A/C, cable TV, refrig. **Services:** **Facilities:** 120 Whirlpool, washer/dryer. **Rates (CP):** Peak (May 15–Sept) $59 S; $65 D. Extra person $6. Children under age 2 stay free. Lower rates off-season. Parking: Outdoor, free. AE, CB, DC, DISC, ER, MC, V.

Lamplighter Inn
3195 Portland Rd, 97303; tel 503/585-2900. Take I-5 to exit 258. A spartan, but serviceable, motel for budget-minded travelers. Convenient to state fairgrounds. **Rooms:** 40 rms. CI open/CO 11am. Nonsmoking rms avail. **Amenities:** A/C, satel TV w/movies. **Services:** **Facilities:** **Rates:** Peak (June–Aug) $32 S; $36 D. Extra person $4. Lower rates off-season. Parking: Outdoor, free. Rates rise during State Fair (late Aug–early Sept). AE, DISC, MC, V.

Ramada Inn
200 SE Commercial St, 97301 (Downtown); tel 503/363-4123 or toll free 800/272-6232; fax 503/363-8993. Conveniently located near downtown businesses and restaurants. **Rooms:** 114 rms, stes, and effic. Executive level. CI 2pm/CO noon. Nonsmoking rms avail. **Amenities:** A/C, cable TV. 1 unit w/terrace, some w/whirlpools. **Services:** **Facilities:** 45 1 restaurant (lunch and dinner only), 1 bar (w/entertainment), sauna, whirlpool. **Rates (CP):** Peak (June–Sept) $80–$89 S; $85–$90 D; $85–$145 ste; $115–$130 effic. Extra person $6. Children under age 11 stay free. Lower rates off-season. Parking: Outdoor, free. AE, CB, DC, DISC, MC, V.

Shilo Inn
3304 Market St, 97301; tel 503/581-4001 or toll free 800/222-2244; fax 503/399-9385. Take I-5 to Salem's Market St exit. Newer (1992) motel convenient to I-5 is clean, well furnished, and comfortable. **Rooms:** 90 rms, stes, and effic. CI 2pm/CO noon. Nonsmoking rms avail. **Amenities:** A/C, satel TV w/movies, refrig, dataport, VCR. **Services:** Babysitting. **Facilities:** 102 1 restaurant, sauna, steam rm, whirlpool, washer/dryer. **Rates (CP):** Peak (June 1–Sept 1) $89–$95 S or D; $89–$95 ste; $225–$275 effic. Extra person $10. Children under age 12 stay free. Lower rates off-season. Parking: Indoor/outdoor, free. Senior, corporate, and government rates avail. AE, CB, DC, DISC, MC, V.

RESTAURANTS

Alessandro's Park Plaza Restaurant
In Pringe Park Parking Structure, 325 High St SE; tel 503/370-9951. **Italian.** Alessandro's serves up a rustic yet elegant Italian ambience—with rough-plastered walls and dark-stained exposed beams—in a convenient though somewhat hidden location overlooking a lovely park. You'll find classic Italian dishes such as fettuccine Alfredo and veal piccata. A five-course dinner ($25; $35 including wines) is offered nightly. Oregonian and Italian wines. **FYI:** Reservations recommended. **Open:** Lunch Mon–Fri 11:30am–2pm; dinner Mon–Sat 5:30–9pm. **Prices:** Main courses $8–$16; prix fixe $25–$35. AE, MC, V. ♿

✶ The Night Deposit
195 Commercial St NE (Downtown); tel 503/585-5588. **New American.** Located in a 19th-century brick grocery store, this eatery has a casual, refined atmosphere and a fairly predictable menu—seafood, steak, pasta—with some surprises: raspberry-pistachio chicken, for example. Several menu items have "lite" options, offering smaller portions and a smaller price tag. The Sunday night menu includes traditional favorites like baked ham, grilled liver with onions, and roast turkey. **FYI:** Reservations recommended. Guitar. **Open:** Lunch Mon–Fri 11am–2pm; dinner Sun noon–9pm, Mon–Thurs 5–9pm, Fri–Sat 5–10pm. **Prices:** Main courses $10–$38. AE, DC, MC, V. ♿

ATTRACTIONS

Oregon State Capitol
Court St; tel 503/378-4423. Stark and boxy, the capitol was built in 1938 of white Italian marble. Vaguely neoclassical in styling, the building is topped by a 230-foot-tall gilded statue known as *The Oregon Pioneer*. Inside the building there are murals of historic Oregon scenes. Surrounding the capitol are the expansive Willson Gardens, which show off the best of Oregon landscaping with unusual trees and neatly manicured lawns. Several fountains grace the gardens, including a large contemporary fountain directly in front of the entrance. Tours available. **Open:** Mon–Fri 8am–5pm, Sat 9am–4pm, Sun noon–4pm. Closed some hols. **Free**

Bush House Museum and Bush Barn Art Center
600 Mission St NE; tel 503/581-2228. Originally part of a 100-acre complex built between 1877 and 1882, the Victorian-style Bush House is filled with an extensive collection of 19th-century fine and decorative arts; its conservatory is the oldest greenhouse in Oregon. The adjacent barn, remodeled as an art center in 1965, houses two exhibit galleries. Every summer the Salem Art Fair & Festival, featuring the work of 200 artists and craftspersons, is held in Bush's Pasture Park. **Open:** May–Sept, Tues–Sun noon–5pm; Oct–Apr, Tues–Sun 2–5pm. Closed some hols. **$**

Historic Deepwood Estate
12th and Mission Sts; tel 503/363-1825. Light and airy Queen Anne–style Victorian mansion, built in 1894, with numerous peaked roofs and gables. Set amid six acres of garden and forest, the 13-room home features golden oak moldings, stained-glass windows, a solarium, a 1912 player piano, and a costume collection. A nature trail winds through the adjacent forest. **Open:** May–Sept, Sun–Fri noon–4:30pm; Oct–Apr, Sun–Mon, Wed and Fri 1–4pm. Closed some hols. **$**

Mission Mill Village
1313 Mill St; tel 503/585-7012. This sprawling red building constructed of brick, wood, and corrugated metal has become one of the most fascinating attractions in Salem. Built in 1889, the water powered mill operated until 1962. Today the restored buildings house exhibits on every stage of the wool-making process. In the main mill building the water-driven turbine is still in operation producing electricity for these buildings. Also on these neatly manicured grounds are several old homes, a parsonage, a church, a pioneer herb garden, a cafe, and a collection of shops. **Open:** Daily 10am–5pm. Closed some hols. **$**

Gilbert House Children's Museum
116 Marion St NE; tel 503/371-3631. A C Gilbert was the inventor of the Erector Set, the perennially popular children's toy that has inspired generations of budding engineers, and here in the restored Gilbert house, kids can learn all about engineering, art, music, drama, science, and nature through fun hands-on exhibits. **Open:** Tues–Sat 10am–5pm, Sat noon–4pm. Closed some hols. **$$**

Silver Falls State Park
20024 Silver Falls Hwy, Sublimity; tel 503/873-8681. One of Oregon State Park's "secret treasures," Silver Creek Canyon Trail, which starts at the day-use area near the parking lot and lodge, leads hikers on a spectacular journey past, over, and even behind 10 waterfalls—the highest reaching 178 feet. On return to the rest area, weary nature lovers can grab a treat at the snack bar, enjoy the swimming and play areas, or picnic at a log or stone shelter. **Open:** Daily 8am–dusk **$**

Seaside

Once best-known as the end of the Lewis and Clark Trail, Seaside is now Oregon's largest beach resort community, complete with a two-mile promenade. Spectacular coastal views can be had at nearby Ecola State Park. **Information:** Seaside Convention and Visitors Bureau, 415 1st Ave, Seaside, 97138 (tel 503/738-8585).

HOTELS

🏴🏴🏴 Best Western Ocean View Resort
414 N Prom, 97138; tel 503/738-3334 or toll free 800/234-8439; fax 503/738-3264. On beach, at end of 4th Ave.

This six-year old hotel is just across the dunes from the beach, four blocks north of Broadway. A nice alternative to busier locations on the main drag. **Rooms:** 104 rms, stes, and effic. CI 3pm/CO 11am. Nonsmoking rms avail. Oceanfront rooms have kitchenettes. **Amenities:** Cable TV w/movies, refrig. No A/C. Some units w/terraces, some w/fireplaces, some w/whirlpools. All rooms have microwaves; oceanfront accommodations have gas fireplaces. **Services:** Babysitting. VCRs and movies available for rent. Pets allowed off-season only. **Facilities:** 300 1 restaurant, 1 bar, 1 beach (ocean), lifeguard, whirlpool, washer/dryer. Volleyball net and swing set in sand in front of hotel. **Rates:** Peak (July–Aug) $72–$139 S or D; $235 ste; $157 effic. Extra person $15. Min stay special events. Lower rates off-season. Parking: Outdoor, free. AE, CB, DC, DISC, MC, V.

Sand & Sea Condominiums
475 S Prom, 97138; tel 503/738-8441 or toll free 800/628-2371; fax 503/738-9546. 2 blocks S of Broadway. A high-rise by Seaside standards, this place has only one- and two-bedroom suites. Beachfront location makes this convenient for families. **Rooms:** 60 effic. CI 2pm/CO 11am. Nonsmoking rms avail. Only 27 of the 60 units are available to rent. All accommodations are either oceanfront or south-facing with view of town, Coast Range, and beach. All rental units have full kitchens and very large closets; two-bedroom units have two baths. **Amenities:** Cable TV, refrig, VCR. No A/C. All units w/terraces, all w/fireplaces. Gas fireplaces. **Services:** **Facilities:** 1 beach (ocean), lifeguard, sauna. Lobby and pool are surrounded by a dark, rather grim ground-floor parking area. **Rates:** Peak (Aug) $107–$240 effic. Min stay peak. Lower rates off-season. Parking: Indoor/outdoor, free. MC, V.

MOTELS

Ambassador by the Sea
40 Ave U, 97138; tel 503/738-6382. On beach at south end of town. Located at the quiet south end of town, this complex consists of all privately owned condominiums. About half of the 64 units are available to rent. **Rooms:** 64 rms and effic. CI 3pm/CO 11am. Nonsmoking rms avail. There is one oceanfront unit; the others are no more than a block away from the beach. Each is individually furnished by the owner. Bedmaking was sloppy upon inspection, but units were clean. **Amenities:** Cable TV, refrig. No A/C. Some units w/fireplaces. Some units have VCRs and remote controls for TV. **Services:** Masseuse available by arrangement. **Facilities:** 1 beach (ocean), lifeguard, washer/dryer. Condos are situated on dunes; guests follow path to reach beach. **Rates:** Peak (May 15–Oct 31) $59 S or D; $90–$149 effic. Children under age 16 stay free. Min stay special events. Lower rates off-season. Parking: Outdoor, free. DISC, MC, V.

Colonial Motor Inn
1120 N Holladay Dr, 97138; tel 503/738-6295 or toll free 800/221-3804; fax 503/738-8437. 2 blocks off US 101 at 12th Ave. Quaint nine-unit motel located in a residential neighborhood on the banks of the Necanicum River, four blocks from the beach and a refreshing ten-block walk from busy downtown Seaside. **Rooms:** 9 rms and stes. CI 3pm/CO 11am. Nonsmoking rms avail. Very small rooms have lovely Queen Anne–style furniture. All but one room are nonsmoking. Executive suite is very large with vaulted ceiling, river view, full kitchen, and large bedroom with king-size bed (three night minimum stay). **Amenities:** Cable TV, VCR. No A/C. 1 unit w/terrace, 1 w/fireplace. Executive suite equipped with fireplace, stereo, and computer. **Services:** Complimentary coffee and tea in lobby. **Rates:** Peak (June 15–Sept 15) $76–$110 S or D; $295 ste. Min stay special events. Lower rates off-season. Parking: Outdoor, free. AE, DISC, MC, V.

Hi-Tide Motel
30 Ave G, 97138; tel 503/738-8414 or toll free 800/621-9876; fax 503/738-0875. On the beach, 7 blocks S of Broadway. Pleasing motel located an easy walk from the center of action on Broadway. Situated along the "Prom," an oceanfront walkway. All units are either on the oceanfront or not more than one block away. **Rooms:** 64 rms. CI 3pm/CO noon. Nonsmoking rms avail. All rooms have kitchenettes. **Amenities:** Cable TV w/movies, refrig. No A/C. All units w/fireplaces. Kitchenettes have two-burner stoves and refrigerators. **Services:** **Facilities:** 1 beach (ocean), lifeguard, whirlpool. **Rates:** Peak (May–Oct) $80–$105 S; $85–$115 D. Extra person $5. Children under age 6 stay free. Min stay special events. Lower rates off-season. Parking: Outdoor, free. AE, CB, DC, DISC, MC, V.

Inn on the Prom
361 S Prom, 97138; tel 503/738-5241 or toll free 800/654-2506. On beach, 3 blocks S of Broadway. This slightly funky, very friendly place consists of an old shingled beach house attached to a 25-year old motel unit. Located on the oceanfront "Prom," a block from Broadway. **Rooms:** 24 rms, stes, and effic. CI 3pm/CO 11am. Nonsmoking rms avail. Wide variety of room styles; all have kitchens or kitchenettes "Tub-showers" are actually square, shallow tubs more like a plain shower. 15 units face ocean. **Amenities:** Cable TV. No A/C. Some units w/terraces. Fireplaces are electric. Some units have remote-controlled TVs. **Services:** Babysitting. Only small dogs allowed. **Facilities:** 12 1 beach (ocean), lifeguard. **Rates:** Peak (Mem Day–Labor Day) $65–$95 S or D; $65–$100 ste; $95–$140 effic. Children under age 18 stay free. Min stay special events. Lower rates off-season. Parking: Outdoor, free. Midweek specials in off-season. AE, CB, DC, DISC, MC, V.

Seashore Resort
60 N Prom, 97138; tel 503/738-6368; fax 503/738-8314. On beach at the end of Broadway. This older motel has fairly spartan rooms but a great oceanfront location. **Rooms:** 53 rms. CI 2pm/CO noon. Three-quarters of the rooms have an ocean view, some have kitchens. **Amenities:** Cable TV.

No A/C. Some units w/terraces. **Services:** **Facilities:** 1 beach (ocean), lifeguard, sauna, whirlpool. **Rates:** Peak (May 16–Sept 30) $62–$108 S; $68–$114 D. Extra person $10. Min stay wknds. Lower rates off-season. Parking: Outdoor, free. Senior rates. No minimum stay in off-season. AE, CB, DC, DISC, MC, V.

Shilo Inn Seaside East
900 S Holladay, 97138; tel 503/738-0549 or toll free 800/222-2244; fax 503/738-0532. 1 block off US 101. Located five blocks from the beach, this property offers many of the same amentities as more expensive oceanfront lodgings. **Rooms:** 58 rms. CI 4pm/CO noon. Nonsmoking rms avail. **Amenities:** A/C, cable TV w/movies. Some units w/whirlpools. Most units have refrigerator and microwave; larger two-bedroom suites have an additional two-burner stove and whirlpool. **Services:** Complimentary coffee, tea, and doughnuts in lobby 7–10am. **Facilities:** Sauna, steam rm, whirlpool, washer/dryer. **Rates (CP):** Peak (July–Sept 6) $59–$124 S or D. Extra person $15. Children under age 12 stay free. Lower rates off-season. Parking: Outdoor, free. AE, CB, DC, DISC, ER, JCB, MC, V.

Shilo Inn Seaside Oceanfront Resort
30 N Prom, 97138; tel 503/738-9571 or toll free 800/222-2244; fax 503/738-0674. On the beach at the end of Broadway. Seaside's premier motel has large meeting rooms and pleasant guest rooms. Location is right on Broadway, in front of the part of the public beach with summer lifeguards, a swing set, and volleyball nets. **Rooms:** 112 rms and effic. CI 4pm/CO noon. Nonsmoking rms avail. All oceanfront rooms have full kitchens. Rollaway beds are $20 extra. **Amenities:** Cable TV w/movies, refrig. No A/C. Some units w/terraces, some w/fireplaces. Gas fireplaces. All oceanfront rooms have patio or balcony. **Services:** VCRs and movies for rent. Free morning newspaper. **Facilities:** 400 1 restaurant, 1 beach (ocean), lifeguard, games rm, spa, sauna, steam rm, whirlpool, washer/dryer. Recreational beach vehicles for rent across street. Fitness center has ocean view. **Rates:** Peak (July–Aug) $125–$165 S or D; $170–$220 effic. Extra person $15. Children under age 18 stay free. Lower rates off-season. Parking: Indoor/outdoor, free. AE, CB, DC, DISC, ER, JCB, MC, V.

RESTAURANTS

Dooger's Seafood & Grill
505 Broadway; tel 503/738-3773. 3 blocks off US 101. **American.** Busy, small, and friendly. The menu features sandwiches, burgers, steak, and a wide variety of seafood, mostly deep-fried, sautéed, or prepared Cajun-style. Often open until 10pm on weekends. **FYI:** Reservations not accepted. Children's menu. Beer and wine only. No smoking. Additional location: 1371 S Hemlock, Cannon Beach (tel 436-2225). **Open:** Lunch daily 11am–4pm; dinner daily 11am–9pm. Closed Dec 1–14. **Prices:** Main courses $10–$21. MC, V.

Rob's Family Restaurant
1815 S Holladay; tel 503/738-8722. On US 101 at south end of town. **American.** Small, with formica tables, friendly waitresses, and a familiar menu of sandwiches, steak, and seafood. There are several "smaller portions" on the menu, and dishes can be split for sharing. **FYI:** Reservations not accepted. No liquor license. **Open:** Sun–Thurs 5:30am–8pm, Fri–Sat 5:30am–8:30pm. **Prices:** Main courses $6–$11. No CC.

ATTRACTION

Seaside Aquarium
200 N Promenade; tel 503/738-6211. Underwater viewing tanks hold 20-ray starfish, Wolf and Moray eels, sharks, octopuses, and other forms of sea life. The touch tank gives visitors a chance to explore tide-pool creatures hands-on. The stars of the show are the seals, who will perform for visitors. The aquarium boasts one of the best captive breeding records for harbor seals in the world. **Open:** Mar–Oct, daily 9am–dusk; Nov–Feb, Wed–Sun 9am–dusk. Closed some hols. **$$**

Springfield

See Eugene

Sunriver

A planned resort community built the pine forests near the Deschutes River. Ample opportunities for outdoor recreation, including skiing at nearby Mount Bachelor. Newberry Crater, to the southeast of town, is the central attraction of a national volcanic monument. **Information:** Sunriver Area Chamber of Commerce, PO Box 3246, Sunriver, 97707 (tel 541/593-3581).

RESORT

Sunriver Resort
1 Center Dr, PO Box 3609, 97707; tel 541/593-1221 or toll free 800/547-3922; fax 541/593-5458. West of US 97. 3,300 acres. The oldest and largest destination resort in central Oregon. Families, groups, and conventioneers come here year-round for Sunriver's wide array of outdoor activities and excellent meeting facilities. **Rooms:** 211 rms, stes, and effic; 80 cottages/villas. CI 4pm/CO 11am. Nonsmoking rms avail. More than 100 private homes and condos are part of the complex; units range from simple singles to deluxe condominiums. **Amenities:** A/C, cable TV. All units w/terraces, all w/fireplaces. Some condos include private hot tubs. All rooms feature large, stone fireplaces. **Services:** Car-rental desk, social director, masseur, children's program, babysitting. **Facilities:** 54 28 450 3 restaurants (*see* "Restaurants" below), 1 bar (w/entertainment), basketball, volleyball, games

rm, lawn games, racquetball, squash, spa, sauna, whirlpool, beauty salon, day-care ctr, playground, washer/dryer. Marina, nature center, miniature golf course, and Nordic skiing center with 20 kilometers of groomed trails (in winter). The recently renovated Great Hall is constructed from 511 logs, 40-foot beams, and 159 cubic yards of stone. **Rates:** Peak (June 10–Sept 30) $99–$129 S or D; $175–$195 ste; $175–$195 effic; $148–$274 cottage/villa. Lower rates off-season. Parking: Outdoor, free. AE, CB, DC, DISC, MC, V.

RESTAURANT

The Meadows Restaurant
In Sunriver Resort, PO Box 3609; tel 541/593-1221. 15 miles S of Bend, E of US 97. **Northwest.** Located at the resort's main lodge, this bright dining room with a vaulted ceiling looks out to the middle golf course. A recent emphasis has focused on becoming a more casual family-style restaurant. The Northwest menu includes smoked trout ravioli, linguine with wild mushrooms, and grilled salmon with champagne-shallot butter. **FYI:** Reservations recommended. Rock. Children's menu. No smoking. **Open:** Peak (Mem Day–Labor Day) daily 5:30–9pm. **Prices:** Main courses $9–$21. AE, CB, DC, DISC, MC, V.

ATTRACTION

Sunriver Nature Center & Observatory
River Rd; tel 541/593-4394. The nature center offers a combination of indoor and outdoor exhibits. Inside the main building are displays on natural history, as well as a collection of live animals. Alongside this building is a botanical garden containing plants native to central Oregon, with plaques explaining their history and use. A nature trail leads visitors from the nature center, past the volcanic landscape geology trail and wetland habitat, to the observatory, where a 12.5-inch reflecting telescope offers views of the heavens. **Open:** Winter: Tues 10am–noon, Wed–Sat 10am–4pm; summer: Sun–Tues 9am–4pm, Wed–Sat 9am–5pm. Closed some hols. $

The Dalles

See also Hood River, Mount Hood National Forest

Oregon Trail emigrants made this the end of their overland journey in the 1840s. (From here they proceeded by raft.) Today, cherry orchards dot the hills above this agricultural town, which is popular with sailboarders. **Information:** The Dalles Convention and Visitors Bureau, 404 W 2nd St, PO Box 1053, The Dalles, 97058 (tel 541/296-6616).

MOTELS

The Best Western Tapadera Inn
112 W 2nd St, 97058; tel 541/296-9107 or toll free 800/722-8277; fax 541/296-3002. Corner of 2nd and Liberty, next to City Hall. Caters to business travelers. Located near several fast-food restaurants. **Rooms:** 64 rms. CI 1pm/CO noon. Nonsmoking rms avail. **Amenities:** A/C, cable TV. **Services:** Complimentary coffee available in lobby. **Facilities:** 1 restaurant, 1 bar (w/entertainment). Courtyard pool open seasonally. Guests get complimentary passes to Dalles Athletic Club. **Rates:** Peak (May–Sept) $51 S; $59 D. Extra person $4. Children under age 13 stay free. Lower rates off-season. Parking: Outdoor, free. AE, CB, DC, DISC, MC, V.

Quality Inn
2114 W 6th St, 97058; tel 541/298-5161 or toll free 800/848-9378; fax 541/298-6411. Exit 83 off I-84. Popular motel on old US 30, which parallels I-84. Rustic theme in lobby: twig and cane chairs, light fixtures made from antlers. **Rooms:** 85 rms and effic. CI 2:30pm/CO 11am. Nonsmoking rms avail. Fine art prints and mauve-patterned fabrics give rooms a touch of style. Some units have kitchens. **Amenities:** A/C, cable TV w/movies, refrig. **Services:** **Facilities:** 1 restaurant (*see* "Restaurants" below), 1 bar, whirlpool. Pool open seasonally. Guests have free use of the nearby Dalles Fitness and Court Club. **Rates:** Peak (May–Oct) $54–$76 S or D; $72–$79 effic. Extra person $5. Children under age 18 stay free. Lower rates off-season. Parking: Outdoor, free. AE, DC, DISC, MC, V.

Shilo Inn
3223 Bret Clodfelter Way, 97058; tel 541/298-5502 or toll free 800/222-2244; fax 541/298-4673. Exit 87 off I-84; at The Dalles Bridge jct. Attractive, contemporary motel overlooking the Dalles Dam and the historic buildings of the Native American Lone Pine Settlement. **Rooms:** 112 rms and stes. CI 3pm/CO noon. Nonsmoking rms avail. **Amenities:** A/C, satel TV w/movies, refrig. Some units w/terraces, some w/whirlpools. All rooms have microwaves. Suites and minisuites have wet bars and three phones. **Services:** **Facilities:** 1 restaurant, 1 bar, sauna, whirlpool, washer/dryer. Swimming pool open seasonally. **Rates (CP):** Peak (May–Oct) $55–$79 S or D; $69–$89 ste. Extra person $10. Children under age 13 stay free. Lower rates off-season. Parking: Outdoor, free. AE, CB, DISC, ER, JCB, MC, V.

RESTAURANT

Cousins Restaurant
2114 W 6th St; tel 541/298-2771. Adjacent to Quality Inn on old US 30. **American.** Good down-home cooking and a country-calico atmosphere characterize this friendly eatery. Counter stools are made from milk cans and in one room there is a full-size tractor with a plastic cow in the driver's seat. Meat loaf, pot roast with "taters," and barbecued ribs are good choices. The Gandydancer Saloon has a railroad theme and a model train running on a track above the bar. **FYI:** Reservations not accepted. Children's menu. Dress

code. **Open:** Peak (June–Oct) Sun–Thurs 5:45am–10pm, Fri–Sat 5:45am–11pm. **Prices:** Main courses $8–$11. AE, CB, DC, DISC, MC, V.

Tigard

See Portland

Tillamook

Tillamook is best known for its cheese—the state's largest cheese factory is located here and the Tillamook County Creamery Association (located north of town) attracts nearly a million visitors annually. **Information:** Tillamook Chamber of Commerce, 3705 US 101 N, Tillamook, 97141 (tel 503/842-7525).

MOTEL

Shilo Inn Tillamook

2515 N Main St, 97141; tel 503/842-7971 or toll free 800/222-2244; fax 503/842-7960. on US 101, 1 mi N of downtown. Dependably clean, well-appointed motel convenient to US 101. Set in the midst of Tillamook dairy country, so be prepared for slight cow-pasture odor in morning. **Rooms:** 100 rms and effic. CI 4pm/CO noon. Nonsmoking rms avail. Five rooms have full kitchens; the rest have kitchenettes. **Amenities:** A/C, cable TV w/movies, refrig. Some units w/whirlpools. **Services:** Free coffee in lobby 6am–noon. **Facilities:** 125 1 restaurant, 1 bar (w/entertainment), spa, sauna, steam rm, whirlpool, washer/dryer. "Fish Room" offers complete facilities for cleaning, bagging, and freezing catch. Deli-mart off lobby sells staples, snacks, and souvenirs. **Rates:** Peak (May 16–Sept 15) $85 S or D; $95 effic. Extra person $10. Children under age 13 stay free. Lower rates off-season. Parking: Outdoor, free. Senior and corporate rates avail weekdays. AE, CB, DC, DISC, ER, JCB, MC, V.

RESTAURANT

McClaskey's Restaurant

2102 1st St; tel 503/842-5674. Jct OR 6 and US 101. **American/Seafood.** Conveniently located, clean, and inviting, this family-run restaurant features seafood but offers a wide selection of other choices like burgers, surf-and-turf, clam chowder, and pasta. Closes at 8pm in winter. **FYI:** Reservations accepted. Children's menu. Beer and wine only. No smoking. **Open:** Peak (Apr–Sept) daily 7am–9pm. **Prices:** Main courses $8–$17. MC, V.

ATTRACTIONS

Cape Lookout State Park

13000 Whiskey Creek Rd W; tel 503/842-4981. The tip of this 2½-mile peninsula provides excellent views of passing whales, resident sea lions, the Cape Meares lighthouse, and more than 150 species of birds from the Netarts Bay estuary. Visitors can go clamming or crabbing in the bay, hiking or biking on the trails, camp at one of 195 sites, or stay year-round in a yurt—a weather-resistant, circular domed tent complete with plywood floor, electricity, and a plexiglass skylight. **Open:** Daily 7am–10pm. **$$$$**

Cape Meares State Park

North end of Three Capes Scenic Loop; tel 503/842-4981. This day-use area and wildlife refuge, located at the north end of the beautiful 20-mile Three Capes Scenic Loop, offers hiking trails, bird-watching, and one of the Oregon coast's premier whale-watching sites. Highlights include the "octopus tree," a Sitka spruce with a diameter of more than 10 feet that, as legend has it, is a Native American sacred burial tree; and the Cape Meares Lighthouse, which has lit the way for mariners since 1889. **Open:** Park, daily 7am–10pm; lighthouse, Mar–Apr and Oct Sat–Sun 11am–5pm. **Free**

Timberline

See Mount Hood National Forest

Tolovana Park

See Cannon Beach

Troutdale

The gateway to the Columbia River Gorge National Scenic Area, scene of such attractions as Vista House at Crown Point and the breathtaking 620-foot Multnomah Falls. **Information:** Troutdale Area Chamber of Commerce, PO Box 245, Troutdale, 97060 (tel 503/669-7473).

HOTEL

McMenamins Edgefield

2126 SW Halsey, 97060; tel 503/669-8610 or toll free 800/669-8610; fax 503/665-4209. Exit 16A off I-84. 26 acres. Located in a complex of historic brick buildings, including a theater, a vineyard/winery, a brewery, and an herb garden. **Rooms:** 105 rms. CI 3pm/CO 11am. Three rooms have private baths; the rest share the immaculate bathrooms located on each floor. (Some rooms have sinks.) Rooms have armoires, not closets. **Amenities:** Bathrobes. No A/C, phone, or TV. Some units w/terraces. **Services:** Brewery and winery tours, wine tastings, and a variety of special events. **Facilities:** 250 1 restaurant (*see* "Restaurants" below), 1 bar. **Rates (BB):** $35–$45 S; $65–$85 D. Extra person $15. Children under age 7 stay free. Parking: Outdoor, free. Discounts for extended stays. AE, DISC, MC, V.

RESTAURANT

Black Rabbit Restaurant & Bar
In McMenamins Edgefield, 2126 SW Halsey; tel 503/492-4686. **International.** Once a part of the county poor farm, now a retreat that includes lodging, winery, brewery, and theater. The sizable breakfast menu offers crab and salmon cakes, buttermilk pancakes with berry syrup, omelettes, and corned-beef hash. Dinner entrees include chicken with fennel and lemon crust, mustard-coated rabbit with sage polenta, vegetable lasagna, and New York steak with garlic mashed potatoes. Smaller entrees are also available. **FYI:** Reservations recommended. Children's menu. Dress code. No smoking. **Open:** Breakfast Mon–Sat 7–11:30am, Sun 7am–1:30pm; lunch Mon–Sat 11:30am–2:30pm, Sun 7am–1:30pm; dinner Mon–Sat 5–10pm, Sun 4–9pm. **Prices:** Main courses $12–$17. AE, DISC, MC, V.

ATTRACTION

Multnomah Falls
OR 30 E; tel 503/695-2376. One of the star attractions of the Columbia River Gorge National Scenic Area (see Hood River). At 620 feet from the lip to the lower pool, Multnomah is the tallest waterfall in Oregon and the fourth tallest in the United States. An arched bridge stands directly in front of the falls and is a favorite of photographers. A steep paved trail leads from the foot of the falls up to the top, from which other trails lead off into the Mount Hood National Forest. An interpretive display at the foot of the falls explains the geologic history of the Columbia Gorge. **Open:** Daily 8am–9pm. Closed some hols. **Free**

Wallowa-Whitman National Forest

For lodgings, see Joseph

Visitors to Wallowa-Whitman can engage in a wide range of outdoor activities, from white-water rafting, fishing, and backpacking to downhill and cross-country skiing and snowmobiling. Spanning over two million acres in northeastern Oregon and western Idaho, with an elevation range from 875 feet to 9,845 feet above sea level, the forest encompasses snow-capped mountains, desert-like countryside, wildflower meadows, evergreen forests, and roaring rivers.

Within the forest are **Hells Canyon National Recreation Area** and **Eagle Cap Wilderness.** Few people realize that the Grand Canyon is not the deepest canyon in the United States; Hells Canyon, which was carved by the Snake River and acts as the boundary between Oregon and Idaho, is actually deeper. Bounded on the east by the Seven Devils Mountains and on the west by the Wallowa Mountains, the canyon is 8,000 feet deep in some places. The canyon area offers 900 miles of hiking trails.

Eagle Cap—the largest protected wilderness in the Pacific Northwest, with 47 trailheads, 37 miles of streams, and 53 lakes—is a refuge for many endangered and threatened animals including the bald eagle and the peregrine falcon. There are more big-game species here than in any other forest in Oregon or Washington. Most trails are open from early July to late October.

Campgrounds offer a wide variety of options, from primitive tent sites to ones with modern facilities and lakeshore accommodations. Much of Hells Canyon is only accessible by boat, horse, or on foot; the few roads that lead into the canyon are mostly for four-wheel drive vehicles only. There are, however, driving tours via scenic byways. Access to Eagle Cap Wilderness is easier, with several main routes, the most popular being OR 82 to Wallowa Lake. For more information on the forest, contact the Wallowa Mountains Visitors Center, 88401 Hwy 82, Enterprise, OR 97828 (tel 541/523-6391).

Warm Springs

High Desert canyon town along the Deschutes River. The central community on the Confederated Tribes of Warm Springs Indian Reservation, the largest reservation in Oregon.

RESORT

Kah-Nee-Ta Resort
PO Box K, 97761; tel 541/553-1112 or toll free 800/554-4786; fax 541/553-1071. 11 mi NE of US 26 on Warm Springs reservation. 650 acres. Built in 1972 in a fertile, high desert area on the Confederated Tribes Warm Spring Reservation. Reportedly, the sun shines an average of 300 days per year here. Many rooms afford great views of rimrock bluffs, rolling plains, and colorful sunsets. **Rooms:** 139 rms and stes; 25 cottages/villas. CI 4pm/CO 11:30am. Nonsmoking rms avail. Spacious, tastefully decorated. Also available are 21 teepees and 60 RV spaces. **Amenities:** A/C, VCR. All units w/terraces, some w/fireplaces, some w/whirlpools. **Services:** Social director, masseur, children's program, babysitting. Supervised summer activities for children. **Facilities:** 18 2 600 4 restaurants, 1 bar (w/entertainment), basketball, volleyball, games rm, lawn games, spa, sauna, steam rm, whirlpool, playground, washer/dryer. The village, located in the valley directly below the hillside hotel, contains most of the recreational offerings, including the huge swimming pool, putting green, and mineral bath. **Rates:** $115–$155 S or D; $165–$195 ste; $105–$125 cottage/villa. Extra person $14. Children under age 5 stay free. Min stay wknds. Parking: Outdoor, free. Teepees cost $50–$100/night for as many guests as can squeeze in. RV spaces are $30–$35/night for full hookup. Both are located apart from hotel. AE, CB, DC, DISC, MC, V.

ATTRACTION

The Museum at Warm Springs
2189 OR 26; tel 541/553-3331. Created by the confederated tribes of Oregon and completed in 1993, this is the first Native American museum in the state. Tribal history comes alive as visitors view traditional dwellings, witness a re-enactment of a Wasco wedding, and listen to traditional singing and drumming—all contained in a beautiful, modern complex. There are also walking trails, picnic areas, and an amphitheater. **Open:** Daily 10am–5pm. Closed some hols. **$$**

Warrenton

See Astoria

Wedderburn

See Gold Beach

Welches

See Mount Hood National Forest

West Linn

See Portland

Yachats

Pronounced yah-hots, this coastal hamlet attracts visitors looking to fish, rock-hunt, and picnic on uncrowded beaches. The rocky shoreline is like a natural aquarium, its tidal pools teaming with life. **Information:** Yachats Area Chamber of Commerce, PO Box 728, Yachats, 97498 (tel 541/547-3530).

MOTELS

The Adobe
1555 US 101, PO Box 219, 97498; tel 541/547-3141 or toll free 800/522-3623; fax 541/547-4234. Just N of town on US 101. Clean and well-kept. The Pacific crashes just below the rooms and the stretch of beach is wonderful for tidepooling. Great for families. **Rooms:** 93 rms, stes, and effic; 1 cottage/villa. CI 4pm/CO 11am. Nonsmoking rms avail. **Amenities:** Cable TV w/movies, refrig, VCR. No A/C. Some units w/terraces, some w/fireplaces, some w/whirlpools. **Services:** Babysitting. Pets $5/night. **Facilities:** 20 1 restaurant, 1 bar (w/entertainment), 1 beach (ocean), sauna, whirlpool. **Rates:** Peak (May 18–Sept) $58–$95 S or D; $150 ste; $110–$125 effic; $110–$125 cottage/villa. Extra person $8. Children under age 2 stay free. Min stay peak. Lower rates off-season. Parking: Outdoor, free. Meal coupons avail (off-season only). AE, DC, DISC, MC, V.

Fireside Resort Motel
1881 N US 101, PO Box 313, 97498; tel 541/547-3636 or toll free 800/336-3573; fax 541/547-3152. Just north of town. Great tidepooling 200 feet from the back door. **Rooms:** 44 rms and effic; 3 cottages/villas. CI 2pm/CO 11am. Nonsmoking rms avail. Rooms are clean but have slightly dated decor; many have ocean views. **Amenities:** Cable TV, refrig, voice mail. No A/C. Some units w/terraces, some w/fireplaces, 1 w/whirlpool. **Services:** VCRs and movies for rent. **Facilities:** 1 beach (ocean). **Rates:** Peak (May 15–Sept 15) $55–$73 S; $60–$83 D; $129 effic; $99–$135 cottage/villa. Children under age 5 stay free. Min stay special events. Lower rates off-season. Parking: Outdoor, free. DISC, MC, V.

Oregon House
94288 US 101, 97498; tel 541/547-3329. A quiet set of duplexes offering exceptional value and seaside solitude. A lighted path leads to two miles of isolated beach. **Rooms:** 10 rms and effic; 1 cottage/villa. CI 2pm/CO 11am. No smoking. Individually decorated rooms, with full kitchens. **Amenities:** Refrig. No A/C or TV. Some units w/fireplaces, some w/whirlpools. **Services:** **Rates:** Peak (May 15–Oct 15) $45–$100 S or D; $45 effic; $100 cottage/villa. Extra person $5. Min stay peak. Lower rates off-season. Parking: Outdoor, free. CB, DC, DISC, MC, V.

Shamrock Lodgettes
105 S US 101, PO Box 346, 97498; tel 541/547-3312 or toll free 800/845-5028; fax 541/547-3843. Cozy cabins built in the 1950s account for half the accommodations; other section contains motel-style rooms. **Rooms:** 13 rms and effic; 6 cottages/villas. CI open/CO 11am. Rooms in the motel section are tidy and large, with balconies and cathedral ceilings. Cabins have kitchens. **Amenities:** Cable TV w/movies, refrig. No A/C. All units w/terraces, all w/fireplaces, some w/whirlpools. **Services:** Masseur, babysitting. **Facilities:** Spa, sauna, whirlpool. **Rates:** $67 S or D; $90 effic; $86–$98 cottage/villa. Extra person $7. Children under age 1 stay free. Parking: Outdoor, free. AE, MC, V.

INN

Sea Quest Bed & Breakfast
95354 US 101, PO Box 448, 97948; tel 541/547-3782. 2.2 acres. Located a seashell's throw from the beach, this B&B has two parlors with great views. Unsuitable for children under 14. **Rooms:** 5 rms. CI 3pm/CO 11am. No smoking. All rooms have ocean views. **Amenities:** No A/C, phone, or TV. All units w/terraces, some w/whirlpools. Bring one of the provided telescopes into your room for a closer look at the

beautiful seascapes. **Facilities:** 1 beach (ocean), guest lounge w/TV. **Rates (CP):** $115–$130 D. Parking: Outdoor, free. AE, MC, V.

RESTAURANT

✱ La Serre
160 W 2nd St; tel 541/547-3420. Off US 101. **Seafood/Steak.** Fresh and intelligently prepared, the food covers a range of traditional items such as seafood, pasta, and steak as well as a nightly vegetarian special. An espresso bar also offers pastries. High ceilings, hanging plants, small rooms, and an open kitchen make a welcoming atmosphere. **FYI:** Reservations recommended. Folk. **Open:** Peak (July–Sept) breakfast Sun 9am–noon; dinner Wed–Mon 5:30–9pm. Closed Jan. **Prices:** Main courses $13–$23. AE, MC, V. ♿

ATTRACTION

Cape Perpetua Visitor Center
2400 OR 101 S; tel 541/547-3289. This 2,700-acre scenic area, located along the central Oregon coast, offers 18 miles of hiking trails, camping, beaches, and a picnic area. The area is also popular for deep-sea fishing. Visitors center has exhibits on Native American inhabitants, natural history (shells, plants, animals), and the surrounding tidepools and volcanic rock. **Open:** Summer, daily 9am–5pm; winter, Sat–Sun 10am–4pm. Closed Dec 25. **Free**

SOUTH DAKOTA

Bold Legends, Hidden Wonders

Crystal caves, presidential faces carved in granite, Native American powwows, buffalo roundups, and sky stretching for a hundred miles to the horizon —these are some of the familiar images to be found in South Dakota. Here the famed Black Hills rise above a grass sea, a bounty of forested mountains filled with wildlife, flashing streams, waterfalls, and a history with names that still glitter: Calamity Jane, Wild Bill Hickok, George Custer, Crazy Horse, Sitting Bull.

What is less well known is that this land was once part-jungle, where camels and three-toed horses roamed for millenia—until, that is, they were buried in a rain of volcanic ash. That same ash dusted the dramatic rocky spires and castles of the southern region now known as the Badlands. Meanwhile, beneath the Black Hills lies a vast cave system—only 5% or so of which has been mapped—with twisting passages that are over 60 million years old.

Back above ground, history is preserved in wagon train ruts left by pioneers on the move, while the past brilliance of Native American art and culture shines at many South Dakota galleries and museums. The paintings of Harvey Dunn, many of which hang on the walls of the South Dakota Art Museum in Brookings, capture the pride and strength of the homesteaders who farmed and mined this land in earlier days. And those of us who as children experienced pioneer life through the autobiographical novels of Laura Ingalls Wilder will find visiting the author's homestead, near De Smet, especially rewarding.

This sparsely settled land of dramatic scenery and little surprises is one worth exploring at leisure. Driving off the interstates crisscrossing the state will allow the opportunity to wander the small towns and visit the many parks and lakes. And hopeful-

STATE STATS

CAPITAL
Pierre

AREA
77,047 square miles

BORDERS
North Dakota, Wyoming, Montana, Nebraska, Minnesota, and Iowa

POPULATION
715,000 (1992)

ENTERED UNION
November 2, 1889 (40th state)

NICKNAMES
Coyote State, Sunshine State

STATE FLOWER
Pasque flower

STATE BIRD
Chinese ring-necked pheasant

FAMOUS NATIVES
Tom Brokaw,
Hubert H Humphrey,
Tatanka Iyotake (Sitting Bull)

rommer's #1

ly you'll get to meet some of the friendly farmers, ranchers, and others who make their living from these prairies and plains, and learn why they're so proud to call South Dakota home.

A Brief History

Exploring Sioux Territory At the time Frenchmen François and Louis-Joseph Vérendrye and their party explored part of the area that is now South Dakota in the mid-18th century, the region was inhabited by the agricultural Arikara people and the nomadic Sioux. But it was the warlike Sioux who dominated the area (they had completely driven out the Arikara by the 1830s), this despite the acquisition of South Dakota as part of the Louisiana Purchase in 1803 and the subsequent exploration by the Lewis and Clark expedition. French and American fur traders were active in the region (and nearly wiped out the beaver population along the Missouri River and around other lakes and stream beds in the Dakotas) in the following decades, but it was not until land speculators and farmers from Minnesota, Wisconsin, and Iowa moved here starting in the mid-1850s that there was any appreciable white settlement.

In 1861, the Dakota Territory was established after a treaty with the Sioux had opened up the land between the Big Sioux and Missouri Rivers. Yankton was chosen as the capital. Settlers were discouraged by drought, locust plagues, as well as continuing conflicts with Native Americans, but railroad construction brought the beginning of a great influx of European immigrants starting in the 1870s. Eventually, Norwegians, Swedes, Russians, Germans, Dutch, Scots, Czechs, and Finns made their way over to try their luck at farming, ranching, and other enterprises.

Last Days This first wave of immigration coincided with the discovery of gold in the Black Hills. The inevitable swarm of prospectors who converged on the region was to seal the fate of the Sioux nation. The Sioux had been granted much of the Black Hills by treaty; when they refused to sell mining rights or the land itself, war broke out. Despite the defeat of Custer and his men at the Battle of the Little Bighorn in 1876, the Sioux's hold on their land gradually weakened. The once plentiful buffalo—the sustenance of life for the Plains Indians—had been all but annihilated. The great leader Sitting Bull was killed in 1890. The final act in the tragedy was played out at Wounded Knee Creek, where a confrontation between Minniconjou Sioux and the US Army (stemming from the army's wariness of the explosive popularity of the messianic "ghost dance" movement) ended in a massacre; 146 Sioux, along with 31 soldiers, lost their lives. Native Americans were moved to reservations and many were to head for cities in the region. Today, they make up only 7% of South Dakota's population.

Fun Facts

- The geographic center of the United States (including Alaska and Hawaii) is located west of Castle Rock, in Butte County.
- Homestake Mine in Lawrence County is the largest operating gold mine in the United States.
- Frontier legend Calamity Jane is known for her sharpshooting skill and her rough-and-tumble ways, but she evidently had a caring, compassionate side as well—as when she nursed the sick of Deadwood, SD during the smallpox epidemic there in 1878.
- The world's largest sculpture is located just north of Custer. The 563-foot-high, 600-foot-long monument to the great Sioux leader Crazy Horse, who led the ambush of Custer and his command on the banks of the Little Bighorn River in 1876, is scheduled to be completed before the year 2000.

Forging Ahead From Wounded Knee on, progress in the form of industry and new scientific farming methods was swift and sure. South Dakota was made a state in 1889, with Pierre named capital. By the early 1900s, farming was going well, though slowed by a grasshopper plague in 1930 and, of course, the Great Depression. Work on the four massive presidential visages that now grace Mount Rushmore was begun in 1927, and the monument eventually became one of the leading draws for tourists from around the nation. (The faces of Washington, Jefferson, Lincoln, and Theodore Roosevelt were intended to represent, respectively, the nation's founding, its philosophy, unity, and expansion.) Years later, Korczak Ziolkowki began the long process of sculpting a likeness of Oglala Sioux leader Crazy Horse into the world's largest sculpture.

Upside Down in the Seventies Although generally a politically conservative state, South Dakota politics was dominated largely by liberal Democrat George McGovern in the 1960s and '70s. McGovern, who represented the state in the US House of Representatives before being elected to the Senate three times, was the Democratic nominee for President in 1972, losing to incumbent Richard Nixon in a landslide. In 1973, members of the American Indian Movement briefly occupied a courthouse at Wounded Knee to dramatize their demands for reforms in Indian tribal government. The occupation and ensuing gun battle with federal marshals was a sobering indication of the resentment many Native Americans harbor toward the US government and its history of broken treaties.

The 1980s saw significant economic growth as South Dakota made a shift toward service, finance, and trade industries. Limited casino gambling was legalized in 1989, and tourism is today one of the top generators of income for the state.

A Closer Look

GEOGRAPHY

Residents tend to think of their state as divided by the Missouri River, which runs down its center. The eastern half consists of rolling hills and stretches of nearly flat prairie, while the west tends to have dramatic hills and buttes. But local geographers divide South Dakota into four regions, because each region has different characteristics.

Some 20,000 years ago, huge glaciers moved slowly across **northeast South Dakota,** digging out 120 lake beds that later filled with glacial melt. Small game and waterfowl live along the lakesides. Lake Pelican and the Big Sioux River and the many other lakes have made this area ideal for campers and vacationers who love water. This has proven to be good farmland, and the virgin prairie attracted traders, trappers and, before them, the Sioux and other Native American tribes.

Devils Gulch (leaped by Jesse James on horseback); quartzite canyon walls around lakes; rolling, tree-covered hills; grassy meadows; the pounding waterfalls from which Sioux Falls got its name; clear creeks and streams—these are some of the wonders of **southeastern South Dakota.** Dell Rapids, north of Sioux Falls, has a multilevel rocky set of crags called the Dells. This quartzite canyon was created 12,000 years ago by powerful currents. Hills that rise and fall under coats of gentle green along the **Big Sioux River Valley** are prime grazing land for horses and cattle. More quartzite can be seen along Split Rock Creek. The area has over 175 lakes, both large and small.

On either side of the Missouri River is the **Great Lakes region.** Up the Missouri came Lewis and Clark, the first settlers arriving by steamboat, the riverboat gamblers, the gold rushers. The nickname "Big Muddy" gives an idea of what sections of this river are like. Today, four massive earthen dams have tamed the wild Missouri and created four majestic lakes: Oahe, Sharp, Francis Case, and Lewis and Clark. The area is beautiful, with its grass prairies and cedars. The presence of the big lakes, with sandy beaches and boat launches, along with the river, provide water-related fun year-round. Just north of Chamberlain is the Big Bend of the Missouri, where steamboat riders had a chance to get off and walk a bit while the boat made its way around the bend. The **Ordway Prairie** has been set aside to preserve a bit of the wild grass that once covered the great plains and is now so rare. Wildflowers and waterfowl, pelicans and antelope, deer and beaver commingle here. Farmland is so fertile in this area that it was once the greatest wheat growing area in the world.

In **southwestern South Dakota** lie two very different kinds of land: the pine-forested **Black Hills** and the ghostly **Badlands.** The eerily shaped ridges and hills of the Badlands were whipped into their odd forms by winds and millions of years of water erosion. The faces of Mount Rushmore were carved into the granite of the Black Hills mountains, whose deep pine forests look blackish from a distance. In this magical area are both craggy and smooth rock walls, rushing brooks, waterfalls, lakes, streams, and underground caves with names like Jewel Cave, Crystal Cave, Sitting Bull Crystal Cave, Wind Cave, and Wonderland Cave.

DRIVING DISTANCES

Pierre

171 mi NE of Rapid City
180 mi SW of Aberdeen
194 mi SW of Watertown
226 mi NW of Sioux Falls
245 mi NW of Yankton
410 mi W of Minneapolis, MN

Rapid City

171 mi SW of Pierre
333 mi SW of Aberdeen
341 mi W of Sioux Falls
362 mi SW of Bismarck, ND
380 mi NW of Yankton
581 mi SW of Minneapolis, MN

Sioux Falls

49 mi S of Brookings
66 mi E of Mitchell
85 mi NE of Yankton
197 mi SE of Aberdeen
238 mi SW of Minneapolis, MN
341 mi E of Rapid City

CLIMATE

In South Dakota, the weather changes quickly. A sunny sky can suddenly turn menacing with steel-gray clouds and dancing lightning. Summer days, although they can be quite hot, are not quite as humid as in other midwestern states, and nights can be refreshingly cool. By late September the night air is downright crisp and days are cool. Some extremely cold weather, and the occasional blizzard, should be expected for winter, but interspersed throughout are mild, sunny days. Spring is a mix of rain and sun, though it can snow as late as May.

WHAT TO PACK

Bring a rain jacket and umbrella if you come March through May, and bring warm clothes as well (spring weather is unpredictable). If you plan to hike in the Badlands and Black Hills, bring a windbreaker and sturdy shoes, already broken in, for rocky and steep trails. Pack layers of clothes to keep warm in winter. You'll need a light jacket even in summer, since nights can get chilly.

AVG MONTHLY TEMPS (°F) & RAINFALL (IN)

	Rapid City	Sioux Falls
Jan	22/0.4	14/0.5
Feb	27/0.5	20/0.6
Mar	34/1.0	33/1.6
Apr	45/1.9	47/2.5
May	55/2.7	58/3.0
June	65/3.1	68/3.4
July	72/2.0	74/2.7
Aug	71/1.7	71/2.9
Sept	60/1.2	61/3.0
Oct	49/1.1	49/1.8
Nov	35/0.6	33/1.1
Dec	24/0.5	18/0.7

TOURIST INFORMATION

Request state maps, lists of state parks, and other information from the **South Dakota Tourism Office** at 900 Governors Dr, Pierre, SD 57501 (tel 605/773-3301 or toll free 800/732-5682). The **Office of Indian Affairs,** 118 W Capitol Ave, Pierre, SD 57501 (tel 605/773-3415) will provide information on Native American cultural events and historic sites. The state also has four regional tourism associations: **The Black Hills, Badlands & Lakes Association,** 900 Jackson Blvd, Rapid City, SD 57702 (tel 605/341-1462); **The Dakota Heritage & Lakes Association,** 818 E 41st St, Sioux Falls, SD 57105 (tel 605/336-2602); **The Glacial Lakes & Prairies Association,** PO Box 255 (W US 212 and 3rd St SW), Watertown, SD 57201 (tel 605/886-7305); and **The Great Lakes Association,** PO Box 786 (121 Grand Ave), Pierre, SD 57501 (tel 605/224-4617).

DRIVING RULES AND REGULATIONS

Driver and front seat passengers must wear seat belts; if the passenger is under age five, he or she must wear child restraints. The rural interstate speed limit is 65 mph; 55 mph on open highways. Right turn on red light is permitted, unless a sign prohibits it. Motorcyclists under 18 are required to wear helmets, and all cyclists must wear protective glasses or goggles. Radar detectors are permitted. It is illegal to have an open alcoholic beverage container in any vehicle unless it is in the trunk or otherwise inaccessible by the driver. Licenses may be revoked if drivers refuse a blood-alcohol level test.

RENTING A CAR

The following car rental agencies have offices in the state. The minimum age requirement for renting starts at 19 and varies from company to company. Check with your insurance agent to make sure you are covered when driving a rental car.

- **Avis** (tel toll free 800/331-1212)
- **Budget** (tel 800/527-0700)
- **Dollar** (tel 800/421-6868 or 800/327-7607)
- **Hertz** (tel 800/654-3131)
- **National** (tel 800/328-4567)
- **Thrifty** (tel 800/367-2277)

ESSENTIALS

Area Code: South Dakota's area code is **605.**

Emergencies: For on-the-road emergencies, call the state highway patrol at 605/773-3105.

Liquor Laws: You must be at least 21 years of age to consume alcohol in South Dakota.

Road Info: Call 605/773-3536 for a statewide report.

Smoking: Smoking is restricted at arts and cultural facilities, child care centers, elevators, government buildings, health facilities, courtrooms, aboard public transit, and in schools.

Taxes: The state sales tax is 4%, but communities may add 1–2% for accommodations and alcohol.

Time Zone: The eastern part of the state (including Sioux Falls, Pierre, and Aberdeen) is in the Central time zone, while the west (Rapid City, Badlands National Park) is in the Mountain time zone.

Best of the State

WHAT TO SEE AND DO

Below is a general overview of some of the top sights and attractions in South Dakota. To find out more detailed information, look under "Attractions" under individual cities in the listings portion of this book.

Parks & Recreation Areas In the southwestern part of the state lies **Badlands National Park,** an area shaped into spires, dramatic ravines, stone tables and turrets by 37 million years of wind and water erosion. Fossil beds, bison trails, and occasional display of terrific lightning storms add to its drama. Enter the north unit at Cedar Pass Lodge; the Visitors Center there has maps and information. The **Sage Creek Wilderness Area,** added to the park in 1976, is operated by the Park Service in conjunction with the Sioux of the Pine Ridge Reservation. **Custer National Forest,** near Buffalo, covers over 73,000 acres.

Bear Butte State Park is located on a spot sacred for both the Cheyenne and Sioux people. Sweat lodge ceremonies and vision quests are still held there. **Custer State Park** has lots of opportunities for swimming, paddleboating, and hiking. **Shadehill Recreation Area,** in the northwestern part of the state, features ancient trees, soaring eagles, and a giant reservoir where you can fish, canoe, and swim.

Natural Wonders South Dakota has plenty of awe-inspiring natural sights, from the cascading waterfalls that gave **Sioux Falls** its name, to **Thunderhead Falls,** a roaring underground waterfall inside an old gold mine west of Rapid City, to underground adventures in **Jewel Cave National Monument** and **Wind Cave National Park.** These crystal caves are part of an extensive cave system that is around 60 million years old. Jewel Cave is the fourth-longest cave in the world; many of its caverns have yet to be explored. Guides are on hand to explain the box work, frostwork, moonmilk, scintillites, and other rock formations visible underground.

Manmade Wonders Monumental **Mount Rushmore National Memorial** is probably the most popular destination in South Dakota. Washington's head was the first to be completed by sculptor Gutzon Borglum, back in 1930. Jefferson, Lincoln, and Theodore Roosevelt followed, with noses that span 20 feet and eyes that are 11 feet wide. The **Crazy Horse Memorial,** a massive stone monument being carved from Black Hills granite, honors the great Sioux war leader. The project is so huge (when completed, it will be the largest sculpture in the world) that others now carry on the work of the original sculptor, who has since died. The complex at the monument includes the Indian Museum of North America, representing 80 tribes.

Wildlife Elk, bears, and wolves have pretty much disappeared from this area, killed off by man's westward expansion and overhunting. Millions of buffalo are also gone, although a few thousand roam again thanks to US and state park service programs. Trumpeter swans call across **La Creek National Wildlife Refuge** and migrations of waterbirds, ducks, and geese periodically fill the wide-open sky. In the Badlands, coyotes, bighorn sheep, badgers, bison, deer, and hares populate the landscape and golden eagles soar through the sky. Just south of Hot Springs, a herd of **wild mustangs** run free across the prairie.

Historic Sites & Areas The **Stavkirke,** a replica of 800-year-old Borglund Church in Norway, is located off Rimrock Hwy near Rapid City. The **Prairie Homestead Historic Site,** an original sod house, stands at the east entrance to the Badlands. The names of Wild Bill Hickok and Calamity Jane still echo in the gold-rush town of **Deadwood.** Hickok died here, and both he and Calamity Jane (Martha Jane Burke) are buried in Deadwood's **Mount Moriah Cemetery.** The former home of the *Little House on the Prairie* author Laura Ingalls Wilder, located in De Smet, has been turned into a museum. **Rockerville Ghost Town** near Rapid City is a replica of a late 19th-century mining camp. **Mellette House,** home of the state's first governor, is set on a bluff near Watertown.

Movie fans may want to visit the set of *Dances with Wolves* in **Fort Hays,** just south of Rapid City. The 53,000-acre Houck ranch (where 3,000 buffalo still roam) was also used in the film; the ranch is northwest of Pierre along Hwy 1806. **Stronghold Table** in the Badlands was the site of the famous Sioux Ghost Dances, and visitors can pay tribute to the Ghost Dancers slain at the **Wounded Knee Battlefield.**

Museums The **Black Hills Mining Museum** presents the history and lore of gold mining. The **FMB Museum of American Indian and Pioneer Life and Case Art Gallery** preserves over 100,000 pioneer and tribal artifacts. Mitchell's **Enchanted World Doll Museum** (across from the Corn Palace) displays 4,000 dolls from all over the world. The **Great Plains Zoo and Museum** features a Penguin Pool, a Primate Building, birds and animals from the Australian Outback, and an Asian Cat Habitat. At the **Akta Lakota Museum** in Chamberlain, traditional bead and quillwork are on display. For other interesting historical information on this state's native people you can visit the **W H Over Museum** at the University of South Dakota in Vermillion, where numerous Native American and pioneer artifacts are on display.

Family Favorites **Storybook Land,** at Wylie Park in Aberdeen, is built around storybook characters and themes. A castle with a fountain and a moat stand at its center, and children can take a spin around the carousel, ride the train, or scoot down the waterslide. The park also includes "The Land of Oz" (*Wizard of Oz* creator Frank Baum once lived in Aberdeen).

Families interested in wildlife can spend a week on a working cattle ranch or a dude ranch—check out the **Thompson Ranch** in Buffalo. The **Black Hills Raptor Rehabilitation Center,** located at the Reptile Gardens in Rapid City, helps rehabilitate injured hawks and eagles and educates visitors on why these creatures are of benefit to mankind.

At **Dinosaur Park,** overlooking Rapid City, children can climb around on the lifelike sculptures while parents sit back and enjoy the view. Trail rides and chuck-wagon meals are offered at the **Circle B Ranch** in Rapid City. Families interested in Native American life in the Dakotas might want to attend the **Sisseton-Wahpeton Dakota Nation's Annual Wacipi.** Held every July, dancers come from Canada and from the far corners of the United States to participate.

Shopping The **Corn Palace** in Mitchell has several gift shops featuring Palace memorabilia. Folk-art angels and contemporary designs are part of the shopping tradition at **Cliff Avenue Greenhouse West** in Sioux Falls, a year-round Christmas store. Regional Native American art and crafts are on sale at various locations around the state: the **Northern Plains Gallery** in Sioux Falls, the **Heritage Center** in Pine Ridge, and the **Cultural Heritage Center** in Pierre, among others. The **Tekawitha Fine Arts Center** in Sisseton displays works by 37 Native American artists in 8 galleries; their gift shop features fine Dakota arts and crafts.

EVENTS AND FESTIVALS

- **Oglala Lakota Nation Powwow,** Pine Ridge. Annual cultural event features dancing, food, and Native American arts and crafts. Call 605/867-5821.
- **Black Hills Quilters Guild Annual Show,** Rapid City. See all kinds of fancy stitching and designs used from pioneer days to the present. Summer. Call 605/342-4126.
- **Northern Prairie Storytelling Festival,** Sioux Falls. A wonderful event for both children and adults. Experienced storytellers and novices join in the fun. June. Call 605/331-6710.
- **Kids Rodeo,** Kimball. Rodeo events for youngsters with riding experience to participate in and for other youngsters and adults to watch. Summer. Call 605/778-6939.
- **Fort Sisseton Historical Festival,** Fort Sisseton State Park. Features muzzleloading shooting contests and other demonstrations of history at the fort. First weekend in June. Call 605/698-7261 or toll free 800/244-8860.
- **Laura Ingalls Wilder Pageant,** De Smet. A parade, a play based on one of the author's stories, tours of the cemetery where members of the Ingalls family are buried, and a tour of their homes. Free wagon rides. Last weekend in June and first two weekends in July. Call 605/692-2108.
- **Black Hills Jazz and Blues Festival,** Lead. Great acoustics, great sounds. July. Call 605/394-4101.
- **Old West Days,** Fort Pierre. A tribute to the settlers who took on the wilds of South Dakota. Late summer. Call 605/223-9561.
- **Northern Plains Tribal Arts Show and Market,** Sioux Falls. September. Call 605/334-4060.
- **Great Plains Old Time Fiddling Contest,** Yankton. Dueling violins and fiddles. September. Call 605/665-3636.
- **Victorian Christmas,** Deadwood. Each year, this old Wild West town sponsors an authentic 19th-century-style Christmas display. December. Call 605/578-1876.

SPECTATOR SPORTS

Baseball American Legion baseball with its home-grown heroes is played in Watertown every spring.

Call 605/886-3604 for information on locations and tickets. Little League games are played statewide. Call local chambers of commerce for dates and times.

Basketball The **Jackrabbits** of South Dakota State University and the University of South Dakota's **Coyotes** are fierce intrastate rivals—as you might gather from their names. Both teams are members of the North Central Intercollegiate Conference. South Dakota also has a professional basketball team—the **Skyforce** of the Continental Basketball Association (whose players sometimes get picked up by NBA teams). Call Sioux Falls Arena (tel 605/332-0605) for schedule and ticket information.

Football The state's most exciting games are between the Coyotes and Jackrabbits from the two state universities. Call 605/773-3301 to get dates and locations for these contests.

Motorcycling The annual, weeklong Sturgis Rally & Races is one of the world's biggest motorcycle rallies. Call 605/347-2556 for details.

Rodeos Rodeos are held all over the state. One of the favorites is the **Corn Palace Stampede Rodeo** in Mitchell (call 605/996-5567 for information). Yankton's **Riverboat Days PRCA Rodeo** (tel 605/665-9231) gives a sense of the area's past as well as present. The **Indian National Finals Rodeo** (tel 605/394-4115) is held annually in Rapid City.

ACTIVITIES A TO Z

Ballooning One of the state's most spectacular sights is a sunrise or sunset balloon trip over the Black Hills. Black Hills Balloons, Inc (in Custer) provides plenty of hot air. Pass over the Crazy Horse monument, herds of buffalo, Mount Rushmore, and lots of sparkling lakes and streams. Call 605/673-5075 for information.

Bicycling You can't get it any better than the back country of South Dakota for mountain biking. The state has over 6,000 miles of old fire trails, logging roads, and abandoned railway grades perfect for bikers. Almost all of the 1.2 million acres of the Black Hills National Forest is open to bikers, while Custer State Park offers lots of back trails and more easily passable multi-use trails. The Centennial Trail is over 60 miles long. Rapid City has a nine-mile trail along Rapid Creek and Yankton has two paved bike roads along the waterfront if you want to stay in the city and ride through beautiful sights. US 16A, a 17-mile length of highway connecting Mount Rushmore and Custer State Park, is yet another fine stretch. Call the **Department of Game, Fish, and Parks** (tel 605/773-3391) for information on trails in parks and back country.

Bird Watching In the farmlands of South Dakota, you will see lots of bird life on just about any summer day. Pheasants flap out of their hiding places in deep grass and rise into clear skies. The **Waubay National Wildlife Refuge** near Webster has an observation tower that provides an astonishing bird's-eye view of the area. Call the Webster Chamber of Commerce for information (tel 605/345-4636).

Camping The lunar landscape of the Badlands—particularly dramatic under a full moon and starry sky—has filled many a camper with a sense of absolute wonder. Aside from the odd appearance by a prairie rattlesnake, this is safe and beautiful terrain. For campground information at state parks, call toll free 800/710-CAMP. For camping in national parks, call the main park offices.

Cross-Country Skiing South Dakotans don't like to stay indoors even when the weather gets very cold. Cross-country ski trails network through state parks and recreation areas. Call toll free 800/732-5682 for information on where to find the best areas.

Fishing You can fish year-round in South Dakota (and if you have a four-wheel drive vehicle you can go just about anywhere to do it). Bass, walleye, and smallmouth bass swim the cool waters of Francis Case Lake near Platte. Some spring-fed streams (such as Crow Creek and Spearfish Creek) never freeze and are good trout streams. Three lakes in the Black Hills—Sheridan, Deerfield, and Pactola—are stocked by state fish hatcheries. If it's ice fishing you like, try Blue Dog, Enemy Swim, or Pickerel Lakes. (Lakes are iced over from December through March generally, but check with the Department of Game and Fish before you go.) The **South Dakota Department of Game, Fish, and Parks** (tel 605/773-3485) provides license information.

Golf You haven't really golfed until you've teed off in the Black Hills—just try not to lose the ball in a trout stream or lose your concentration by staring off at Mount Rushmore! Call the state tourism office for a list of the 14 courses in the Black Hills, as well as others throughout the state.

Hiking The most spectacular trails are to be found in the Badlands and the Black Hills. In the Badlands there are six developed hiking trails (all of the park area is open to hikers, trails or not). Call 605/433-5361 for maps and information. Hikers love the **Black Elk Wilderness** and the **Norbeck Wildlife Preserve** in the Black Hills National Forest. Hikers who climb to the top of 7,242-foot-tall **Harney Peak** are treated to a panoramic 60-mile view on a clear day. Call Black Hills National Forest (tel 605/673-2251) for trail maps.

Horseback Riding One of the most interesting trips is to **Stronghold Table,** site of the Sioux Ghost Dances. Horse trails in these hills cut through stunning buttes and rocky cliffs that resemble castles and turrets, and fossil deposits seem to lie around every bend. Call the **Black Hills National Forest** (tel 605/673-2251) for information on horse trails in the Black Hills. You can get outfitted for a horse ride or group ride through the Badlands by calling **Dakota Badlands Outfitters** (tel toll free 800/444-0099).

Mountain Climbing Mountaineers like the short, challenging, granite-faced climbs in the Black Hills. The best and most popular climb is up 865-foot **Devils Tower,** just across the border in Wyoming but easily accessible from South Dakota. **Harney Range** has rocky castles that offer climbs up to 300 feet. Sport shops in nearby Rapid City or Spearfish and other area towns have guidebooks and gear.

Rock Hounding There's copper, silver, quartz, mica, agate, lead, and even gold in "them thar hills"—even today! The Black Hills are a geologist's dream. Collecting is allowed near Kadoka, Scenic, and Fairborn, but not in the Badlands National Park. For information about the state's rocks, call the **South Dakota School of Mines and Technology** (tel 605/394-2467) or the **Buffalo Gap National Grasslands** (tel 605/279-2125).

Skiing So you don't think South Dakota would have any good skiing? Think again. **Terry Peak** and **Deer Mountain** have vertical rises of 600 and 1,000 feet respectively, and the snowfall is deep (up to about 150 inches at times). Both resorts are located just west of Lead and both offer ski shops and rental equipment.

Snowmobiling The Black Hills, with its 270-mile web of groomed trails, is one of the most popular snowmobiling sites in the United States. These trails dip into canyons and network through deep pine. Call 800/445-3474 for information on snow quality and maps of trails.

Water Sports Boaters, sailors, windsurfers, and swimmers enjoy lakes and rivers all over the state. The Missouri River cuts down the center of the state, while the northeastern corner of the state has no fewer than 120 lakes. Every year thousands enjoy everything from paddleboating to inner-tube floats. Call the Division of Tourism at 800/732-5682 for details.

Selected Parks & Recreation Areas

- **Badlands National Park,** PO Box 6, Interior, SD 57750 (tel 605/433-5361)
- **Wind Cave National Park,** RR 1, Box 190, Hot Springs, SD 57747 (tel 605/745-4600)
- **Black Hills National Forest,** RR 2, Box 200, Custer, SD 57730 (tel 605/673-2251)
- **Custer National Forest,** Ranger Station, Camp Crook, SD 57724 (tel 605/797-4432)
- **Bear Butte State Park,** Box 688, Sturgis, SD 57785 (tel 605/347-5240)
- **Custer State Park,** HC 83, Box 70, Custer, SD 57730 (tel 605/255-4515 or 255-4464)
- **Fisher Grove State Park,** RR 1, Box 130, Frankfort, SD 57440 (tel 605/472-1212)
- **Fort Sisseton State Historical Park,** c/o District 2 Park Headquarters, RR 2, Box 94, Lake City, SD 57247 (tel 605/448-5701)
- **Hartford Beach State Park,** RR 1, Box 50, Corona, SD 57227 (tel 605/432-6374)
- **Lake Herman State Park,** RR 3, Box 79, Madison, SD 57042 (tel 605/256-5003)
- **Lake Hiddenwood State Park,** c/o District 14 Headquarters, West Whitlock RA, HC 3, Box 73A, Gettysburg, SD 57442 (tel 605/765-9410)
- **Newton Hills State Park,** RR 1, Box 162, Canton, SD 57013 (tel 605/987-2263)
- **Oakwood Lakes State Park,** RR 2, Box 42, Bruce, SD 57220 (tel 605/627-5441)
- **Palisades State Park,** 15495 485th Ave, Garretson, SD 57030 (tel 605/594-3824)
- **Pickerel Lake Recreation Area,** RR 1, Box 113, Greenville, SD 57239 (tel 605/486-4753)
- **Roy Lake State Park,** RR 2, Box 94, Lake City, SD 57247 (tel 605/448-5701)
- **Sica Hollow State Park,** c/o District 2 Park Headquarters, RR 2, Box 94, Lake City, SD 57247 (tel 605/448-5701)
- **Swan Creek State Recreation Area,** c/o District 14 Park Headquarters, HC 3, Box 73A, Gettysburg, SD 57442 (tel 605/765-9410)
- **Union County State Park,** c/o District 7 Park Headquarters, RR 1, Box 162, Canton, SD 57013 (tel 605/987-2263)

BADLANDS NATIONAL PARK AND THE BLACK HILLS

Start	Rapid City
Finish	Crazy Horse Memorial
Distance	Approximately 140 miles
Time	2 days
Highlights	A national park, a verdant pine forest, two magnificent outdoor sculptures, plus an art gallery focusing on the Northern Plains Indians.

The cowboy-and-Indian way of life—with its history, legends, and present-day vitality—roams proudly through a stretch of geologically diverse land in western South Dakota. Within an hour's drive, you can travel from the windswept mood of Badlands National Park, see the prairie lands, and then stroll under the whispering pine trees of the Black Hills National Forest. This tour will take you closer to the spirit and talent of Native Americans as well as the pioneers and includes a journey to one of the most indelible statements to democracy—Mount Rushmore National Memorial. Although the high-spirited traveler could make this trip in one day, you are advised to take in the western South Dakota experience over two days.

For additional information on lodgings, restaurants, and attractions in the region covered by the tour, look under specific cities in the listings portion of this chapter.

To begin the tour, head east on I-90 out of Rapid City. After about an hour's drive, take exit 131 off I-90 onto SD 240 to begin a drive through the gullies and multicolored canyons of:

1. **Badlands National Park** (tel 605/433-5361). When the Lakota first encountered the mysterious buttes and spires of the Badlands, they aptly named them *mako sica* ("bad land"). Today, the ravaged beauty of the 244,000-acre park still inspires the poet, tourist, New Age philosopher, and artist. Depending on your frame of mind, the Badlands are a stark and eerie moonscape or a land of sun-kissed beauty. No matter the opinion, Badlands National Park stands as an anomaly amid the Great Plains. Sixty-five million years of wind and rain have shaped buttes in sandy sunset hues, rising abruptly from the rolling grasslands. The land has been described as "hell with the fires burned out." Visually, the Badlands are at their finest early or late in the day, when deep shadows define their forms.

   The 32-mile **Badlands Loop** along SD 240 affords some of the finest scenery with points of interest along the way (park entrance fee is $5 per vehicle), or leave the modern highway behind for camping and hiking. Although the Badlands seem barren from a distance, they are teeming with nearly 50 wild grasses and 200 types of wildflowers. The waters that ran through this prairie land millions of years ago attracted huge rhinoceros-like animals and vicious saber-toothed cats. Today, prairie dogs, rattlesnakes, deer, bison, bighorn sheep, and coyotes inhabit the landscape.

   The stunning topography of the Badlands makes a natural site for filming TV commercials and movies. In 1992, the movie *Thunderheart* was shot on the Badlands and Pine Ridge Indian Reservation (on which 120,000 acres of the park lie). More recently, buffalo hunt scenes for Kevin Costner's *Wyatt Earp* were shot near the Badlands in 1994.

   The Ben Reifel Visitor Center at Cedar Pass, 9 miles south of I-90 on SD 240, helps visitors learn more about the area. Evening programs and activities conducted by ranger-naturalists are offered during the summer. The center is open year-round.

   There are three National Grasslands in South Dakota, and you will cross part of the **Buffalo Gap National Grasslands** during the Badlands tour. The United States government bought this patchwork quilt of land—racked by the Great Depression and subsequent cycles of drought and relentless winds—from destitute landowners, with the goal of restoring its all-important natural resource: prairie grass.

   As you finish the Badlands Loop, you will exit SD 240 at I-90. If you take exit 109, you'll find Wall, the tiny town that is considered the window to the west, and the world-famous:

2. **Wall Drug Store,** 510 Main St (tel 605/279-2175). After the dusty Badlands, you might want to stop for a free glass of water at Wall Drug Store. Ever since the Great Depression, the Hustead family has offered its patrons free water and five-cent cups of coffee. Three generations of owners have amassed a historical but whimsical panorama of the Wild West. You can dine on buffalo burgers in the cafeteria—decorated with turn-of-the-century Victorian ceiling lamps, cedar-paneled walls, and the brands of local ranchers—and find South Dakota humor in the "jackalopes" on display. (Jackalopes, if you're wondering, are a taxidermist's cross be-

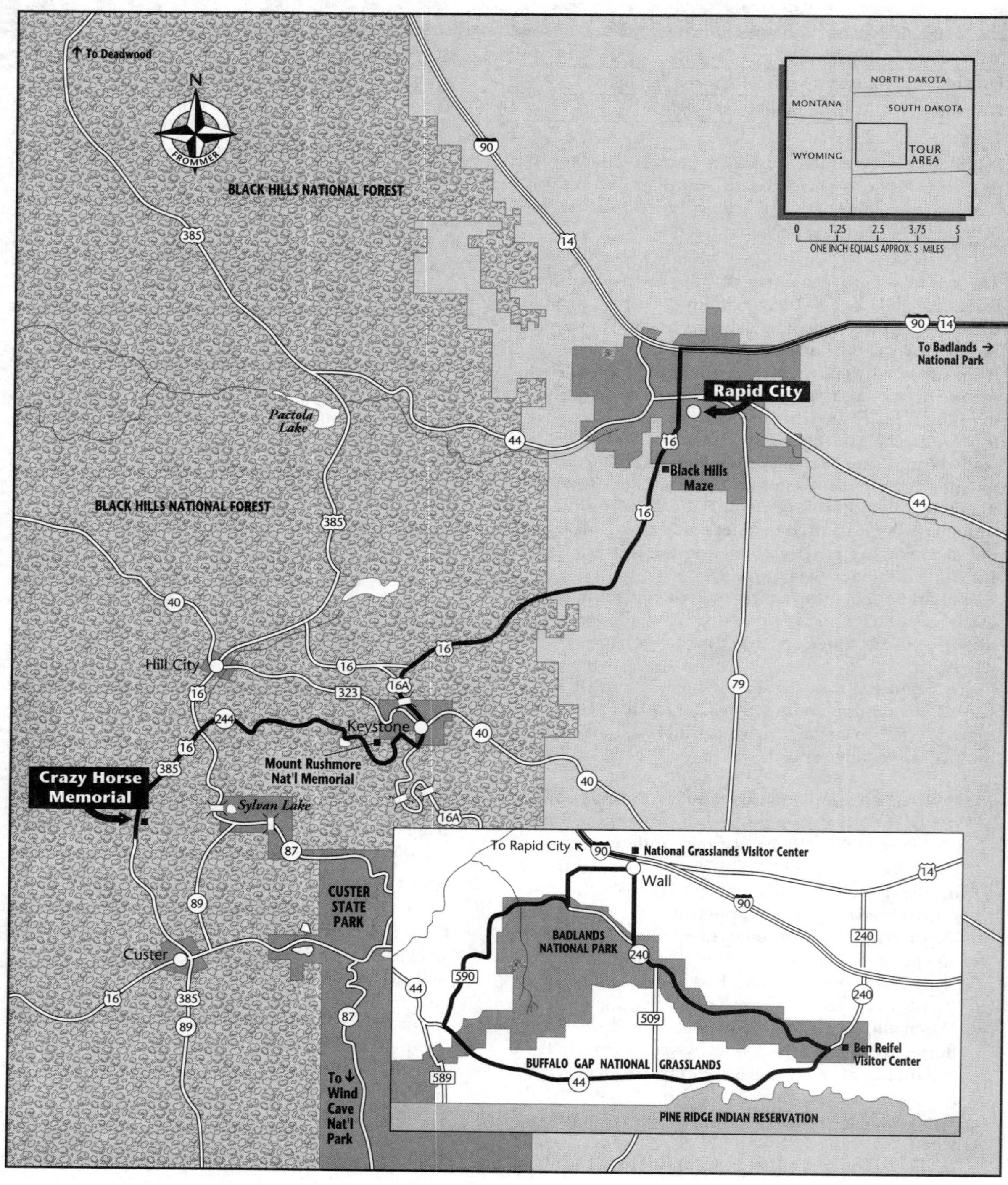

To Deadwood
N
FROMMER
BLACK HILLS NATIONAL FOREST
NORTH DAKOTA
MONTANA
SOUTH DAKOTA
WYOMING
TOUR AREA
0 1.25 2.5 3.75 5
ONE INCH EQUALS APPROX. 5 MILES
To Badlands National Park
Rapid City
Pactola Lake
Black Hills Maze
BLACK HILLS NATIONAL FOREST
Hill City
Keystone
Mount Rushmore Nat'l Memorial
Crazy Horse Memorial
Sylvan Lake
CUSTER STATE PARK
Custer
To Wind Cave Nat'l Park
To Rapid City
National Grasslands Visitor Center
Wall
BADLANDS NATIONAL PARK
Ben Reifel Visitor Center
BUFFALO GAP NATIONAL GRASSLANDS
PINE RIDGE INDIAN RESERVATION

tween the jack rabbit and antelope.)

If you walk two blocks south, you'll find the:

3. **National Grasslands Visitor Center.** Discover the diversity of wildlife and recreation opportunity here. Hands-on exhibits and videos (available year-round) explore the four main ecosystems of the High Plains, and explain why we must respect the resources and creatures of the Great Plains. History buffs also might want to stop by the **Wild West Historical Wax Museum,** 601 Main St. Here, legends like Jesse James, Wyatt Earp, Doc Holliday, and Calamity Jane nearly come to life in realistic settings.

After strolling through Wall, take SD 240 exit 109 to I-90W. The 62-mile drive to Rapid City and the Black Hills National Forest lends quick insight into why farmers and ranchers cherish the prairie spiritually and economically. You can almost feel the cowboy pride rise like dry heat from the vast prairie land during this scenic drive. Regional writer Frederick Manfred extolled the strength—and cruelty—of the heartland more than 50 years ago in *The Golden Bowl.* Today, the visitor can relate to the gracious solitude of endless plains and blue skies Kathleen Norris so deftly describes in *Dakota: A Spiritual Geography.* Nestled in the foothills of the 6,000-square-foot pine forest (which from a distance looks black) is the next stop.

4. **Rapid City** basically remains a rollicking cowtown —with a cosmopolitan twist. For a quick study of the arts scene, take exit 57 off I-90, drive 1.6 miles, then turn left on Omaha St. Drive about ½ mile (to the left is **Memorial Park,** with its fragrant All-American Rose Gardens), then turn right on 6th St. At the corner of Main and 6th Sts is **Prairie Edge Trading Co and Galleries,** Main St (tel 605/342-3086). Here you will see the formidable talents of regional and Native American artists and craftsmen come together in a handsomely restored building. The Native American Gallery features hundreds of hand-crafted, one-of-a-kind items. See a ceremonial shirt finely embroidered with colorful porcupine quills, for instance, or the intricately inlaid pattern on a piece of jewelry. The gallery also houses the Italian Glass Bead Library, where more than 2,600 different styles and colors of beads—from the same companies that supplied fur traders in the 19th century—capture the eye.

Outside the three-story gallery is a haunting statue of a Native American, *He Is, They Are,* by New Mexico sculptor Glenna Goodacre, who also designed the Vietnam Women's Memorial in Washington, DC.

If you want to make an overnight stay in Rapid City, you might want to splurge on a stay at the

Take a Break

The Firehouse Brewing Co, 610 Main St (tel 605/348-1915). A Wilderness Wheat beer, served with a wedge of lemon, is one of the many options on tap at this microbrewery and restaurant. See how this beer and others—from stout to ale—are made in this tastefully restored 1915 firehouse. Regional favorites such as buffalo and prime rib highlight the moderately priced lunch and dinner menus, and live music can be heard on the patio every weekend during the summer. Across the street, **The Uptown Grill,** 615 Main St (tel 605/343-1942), offers a similar atmosphere and menu, but with blues and jazz bands. The bravehearted can join in on jam sessions every Thursday night.

Hotel Alex Johnson, 523 Sixth St (tel 605/342-1210 or toll free 800/888-2539). Listed on the National Register of Historic Places, the grand six-story hotel (built in 1928) was featured in Alfred Hitchcock's *North by Northwest.* Today, it is surrounded by colorful boutiques, antique emporiums, art galleries, a movie theater, and a deli. If a more intimate bed-and-breakfast stay is desired, check into **The Carriage House Bed & Breakfast,** 721 West Blvd (tel 605/343-6415), which offers Victorian charm at a reasonable price.

A visit to the Black Hills would not be complete without seeing one of America's most revered symbols—Mount Rushmore National Memorial. Go west on Main St for one block. Turn left on Mount Rushmore Rd. This eventually will take you outside Rapid City and onto US 16.

Your drive to the Four Faces on US 16 also will bring you through the heart of the verdant 1,247,000-acre:

5. **Black Hills National Forest** (tel 605/673-2251). Like the Badlands, the Black Hills National Forest is a veritable delight for the weekend geologist. The domed mountain region is composed of an ancient crystalline core with deep valleys, surrounded by ridges of sedimentary strata. The forest offers 28 campgrounds, 20 picnic areas, lakes, and endless opportunities for the outdoors enthusiast.

Drive on US 16 for 20 miles. Turn left at the Mount Rushmore exit and take US 16A west for 2.5 miles to Keystone, a quaint town filled with shops and eateries. Go through Keystone and then stay right onto SD 244W. Drive 2 miles to:

6. **Mount Rushmore National Memorial** (tel 605/574-2523). The faces of four great presidents—George Washington, Thomas Jefferson, Abraham

Lincoln, and Theodore Roosevelt—stand out on a 6,000-foot-tall mountain in the Black Hills. Their granite images seem to gaze approvingly over the lush forest.

Sculptor Gutzon Borglum began work on the carving in 1927, at the age of 60. The original plan for Mount Rushmore called for the presidents to be sculpted to the waist. It quickly became obvious that carving the 60-foot heads would be a monumental task in itself, so Borglum concentrated on the faces. Today, the four faces tower 5,500 feet above sea level and are scaled to men who would stand 465 feet tall.

Borglum put 14 years of blood, sweat, and tears into creating the likenesses of the four presidents. Although he died before Mount Rushmore's completion, his son Lincoln finished the mammoth project in 1941. Today, more than two million visitors each year see the Borglums' grand legacy to the four men who contributed so much to America and its people. When President Calvin Coolidge dedicated the project in 1927, he proclaimed Mount Rushmore was "decidedly American in its conception, magnitude, and meaning. It is altogether worthy of our country."

A brand new **Orientation Center,** the first facility you will enter after parking your car, explains the physical layout of the visitor facilities at Mount Rushmore, outlines the different interpretive buildings and programs, and shows the day's schedule of special activities or performances. A four-minute audiovisual presentation, which runs continuously from 8am to 10pm, includes biographies of the four chief executives and a discussion of how Borglum executed each man's portrait on Mount Rushmore's granite cliffs. There's a new grand-entry pavilion as well.

Other noteworthy Rushmore sites are the **Sculptor's Studio,** constructed in 1939, where visitors will find winches, jack hammers, and pneumatic drills dating from the construction days, in addition to Borglum's original model of the monument. Staff give impromptu presentations from 9am to 6pm daily, on topics such as the original location of the Jefferson face (different from where it appears today), the drive to place Susan B Anthony's likeness on Rushmore, and Borglum's aborted plans for an elaborate Hall of Records behind the faces.

Undoubtedly the most spectacular display, however, is the evening lighting ceremony held at 9pm nightly (Memorial Day–Labor Day) in an amphitheater in the pines. Jackets are recommended, as evenings can be cool. The memorial is open year-round and admission is free.

With patriotism still swelling in your heart, turn right onto SD 244. Drive 8.9 miles, then turn right onto US 16W/385N. Drive 3 miles to the next stop:

7. **Hill City,** where you can take a trip back in time with **Black Hills Central Railroad's 1880 Train.** An antique steam locomotive takes you through the Black Hills back country—just like the first pioneers and miners.

Take a Break

Oriana's Bookcafe, 349 Main St (tel 605/574-4878), is a culinary and literary experience. Discuss world events over a morning espresso and the *New York Times,* or browse through the eclectic collection of fiction and nonfiction titles in the afternoon. Residents affectionately consider Oriana's their granola-hippy haven, and yet the three-story eatery appeals to the more refined connoisseur as well—the cheesecake is scrumptious. Prices are moderate.

For a last stop at what many call the Fifth Face in the Black Hills, take US 385 south through Hill City for 9.3 miles, then turn left at:

8. **Crazy Horse Memorial,** 6 miles north of Custer (tel 605/673-4681). Awesome in scale, this mountain-sized sculpture of Lakota leader Crazy Horse astride his warhorse began in 1949, and it remains a work in progress. At the request of several Lakota chiefs, sculptor Korczak Ziolkowski began work on Crazy Horse—refusing any government funds to support the project. Although Ziolkowski died in 1982, his wife Ruth and their children continue the sculptor's dream. When completed, it will stand 563 feet high and 641 feet long. Travelers can view drilling and blasting on the mountain, visit the on-site **Indian Museum of North America**, or dine at the **Laughing Water Restaurant.** Crazy Horse Memorial is open year-round and admission is $6 per adult (under age 6 free), or $15 a carload.

South Dakota Listings

Aberdeen

Nicknamed "The Hub City" in the 1800s, when railroad lines converged here. Still a regional trade center, Aberdeen was once the home of L Frank Baum, author of *The Wizard of Oz.* **Information:** Aberdeen Convention and Visitors Bureau, 516 S Main St, PO Box 1179, Aberdeen, 57402 (tel 605/225-2414).

MOTELS

Best Western Ramkota Inn
1400 8th Ave NW, 57401; tel 605/229-4040 or toll free 800/528-1234; fax 605/229-0480. On US 281. Clean and quiet motel. **Rooms:** 154 rms and stes. CI 2pm/CO noon. Nonsmoking rms avail. A bit bigger than your average room—and a bit nicer, with attractive woodwork and ample drawer space. **Amenities:** A/C, cable TV w/movies. Some units w/terraces, some w/whirlpools. Some rooms have microwaves. **Services:** Car-rental desk, babysitting. **Facilities:** 2000 1 restaurant, 1 bar, games rm, sauna, whirlpool, washer/dryer. Good-size indoor pool and well-regarded restaurant on premises. Located adjacent to 36-hole golf course. **Rates:** $49–$52 S; $57–$60 D; $63–$140 ste. Extra person $6. Children under age 18 stay free. Parking: Outdoor, free. AE, CB, DC, DISC, MC, V.

Breeze Inn Motel
1216 6th Ave SW, 57401; tel 605/225-4222. An older-style motel, worth it only if you want to save some money. **Rooms:** 22 rms. CI 2pm/CO 11am. Nonsmoking rms avail. Rooms vary in size, and are dated but clean. **Amenities:** A/C, cable TV. Some units have microwaves. **Services:** **Facilities:** **Rates:** Peak (June–Oct) $23–$30 S; $28–$31 D. Extra person $1.50. Lower rates off-season. Parking: Outdoor, free. Weekly and monthly rates avail. AE, CB, DC, DISC, MC, V.

Holiday Inn
2727 6th Ave SE, 57401; tel 605/225-3600 or toll free 800/HOLIDAY; fax 605/225-6704. On US 12. Attractive Holiday Inn, located close to a mall and restaurants. **Rooms:** 153 rms and stes. CI 2pm/CO 11am. Nonsmoking rms avail. Good-size rooms are nicely decorated and have paintings on walls. Some poolside accommodations available. **Amenities:** A/C, cable TV. **Services:** Car-rental desk. **Facilities:** 900 1 restaurant, 2 bars (w/entertainment), games rm, sauna, whirlpool. Holidome features exercise room and video game. The bar offers comedy acts and music on the weekends. **Rates:** $52 S; $60 D; $80 ste. Extra person $8. Children under age 18 stay free. Parking: Outdoor, free. Senior and corporate discounts avail. AE, CB, DC, DISC, JCB, MC, V.

Super 8 Motel
2405 6th Ave, 57401; tel 605/229-5005 or toll free 800/800-8000; fax 605/229-5005. On US 12. A bit of hotel history—this was the first Super 8 in the nation, and it's still well maintained and neat. Located near Lakewood Mall and many restaurants. **Rooms:** 108 rms. CI 2pm/CO 11am. Nonsmoking rms avail. Very clean accommodations, some with waterbeds. **Amenities:** A/C, cable TV. Free local calls. **Services:** Car-rental desk. **Facilities:** 30 Sauna, whirlpool, washer/dryer. Nice indoor pool area. **Rates (CP):** Peak (May–Sept) $36–$41 S; $43 D. Extra person $5. Children under age 12 stay free. Lower rates off-season. Parking: Outdoor, free. AE, CB, DC, DISC, MC, V.

RESTAURANTS

The Flame
2 S Main; tel 605/225-2082. **American.** Family-owned for decades, this eatery located in the interesting, old-style downtown area specializes in steaks, seafood, and ribs. **FYI:** Reservations accepted. Children's menu. **Open:** Daily 11am–11pm. **Prices:** Main courses $7–$18. AE, CB, DC, DISC, MC, V.

★ Refuge Oyster Bar and Grill
715 Lancelot Dr; tel 605/229-2681. ½ mi N of Roosevelt exit off SD 12. **Italian.** Locals recommend this place for its ambience, which includes a duck pond out back and mounted fish and animal trophies decorating the bar. The menu highlights reasonably priced Italian dishes, with an emphasis on steaks, seafood, and pastas (such as the shrimp pasta with herbs and pine nuts). **FYI:** Reservations recommended. **Open:** Daily 11am–midnight. **Prices:** Main courses $6–$16. AE, DISC, MC, V.

ATTRACTION

Dacotah Prairie Museum
21 S Main St; tel 605/626-7117. Early pioneer settlers, the railroad, and the original Native American inhabitants of the Dakota prairie are the focus at this museum housed in a historic Romanesque-style building. Exhibits include Native American ceremonial clothing, pioneer artifacts, and railroad memorabilia. The Lamont Gallery features the work of regional and local artists, while a third-floor gallery displays over 55 mounted wildlife specimens from North America, Africa, and Asia. **Open:** Tues–Fri 9am–5pm, Sat–Sun 1–4pm. Closed some hols. **Free**

Badlands National Park

A combination of volcanic ash, a sharp decrease in rainfall, and extreme temperatures—over tens of millions of years—have created the steep canyons, sharp ridges, and other eerie-looking rock formations that are the hallmark of the Dakota Badlands. Although the Badlands were viewed as a dangerous wasteland by 19th-century immigrants from the eastern United States, today the area is recognized as a geologic and ecological wonder worthy of preservation. Mud and clay sediment contains the fossilized remains of prehistoric horses, cats, and even camels. Despite summer highs well above 100°F and frigid winter winds, hundreds of wildflowers and animals still make the Badlands their home. Yucca, cottonwood trees, and wild roses dot the landscape, which is populated by prairie dogs, badgers, coyotes, and a small but hardy band of surviving bison.

The section of ND 240 from Cedar Pass (near the town of Interior) to the Pinnacles entrance features a dozen scenic overlooks as well as a fossil exhibit trail. Stop by the **Ben Reifel Visitor Center,** in the Sage Creek Wilderness Area, for details. The visitors center also has brochures on bird and wildlife watching along the park's self-guided nature trails. In summer, staff naturalists are on hand for guided nature walks. Sage Creek also has two campgrounds and two picnic areas.

The **White River Visitors Center** (in the Stronghold Unit, which is operated with the cooperation of the Pine Ridge Reservation) has special Native American cultural exhibits and a film on Oglala Lakota history. White River is only open during the summer.

Located 30 mi S of the park, off SD 27, is **Wounded Knee National Historic Site.** This site pays tribute to an important turning point in the US government's relationship with Native Americans. In 1890, Chief Big Foot led a band of his followers here after the killing of Sioux spiritual leader Sitting Bull. Exhausted and plagued by sickness, Big Foot agreed to surrender to the Seventh Cavalry. However, before the Native Americans could surrender, the cavalry opened fire, killing 256 unarmed Sioux. This massacre enraged the American public, and it was later decided that the use of brutal force on Native Americans would no longer be tolerated. A monument marks the place of the massacre. (Wounded Knee was also the site of a protest by Oglala Sioux in 1973.)

For further information, contact Superintendent, Badlands National Park, PO Box 6, Interior, SD 57750 (tel 605/433-5361).

RESTAURANT

Cedar Pass Lodge & Restaurant
1 Cedar St; tel 605/433-5460. ½ mile W of Visitor Center. **American.** Enjoy a wide view of the Badlands from this diner decorated with an American Indian motif. Usual diner fare like hamburgers and sandwiches, salads, steaks, chicken, roast beef, and seafood are joined by the unusual—Indian tacos. **FYI:** Reservations not accepted. Beer and wine only. No smoking. **Open:** Peak (June–Aug) daily 8am–6pm. Closed Nov–Mar. **Prices:** Main courses $8–$15. AE, CB, DC, DISC, MC, V.

Beresford

Founded in 1883 when the Chicago & Northwestern Railway announced its plans to build a new depot here. Although close to Sioux City, Beresford retains its small-town pace and charm. **Information:** Beresford Chamber of Commerce, 510 W Oak, Beresford, 57004 (tel 605/763-5864).

RESTAURANT

★ Yesterday's
Jct I-29 and SD 46; tel 605/763-5300. **Diner.** Fifties-style decor—featuring neon-lit posters of Elvis and James Dean—and food are the keynote at this local favorite (it gets extremely busy at lunch). A typical breakfast might include two eggs, two pieces of bacon or sausage, and pancakes for $2.79, while a dinner of Salisbury steak, mashed potatoes and gravy, and vegetables costs less then $5. **FYI:** Reservations accepted. Children's menu. No liquor license. **Open:** Daily 6am–midnight. **Prices:** Main courses $5–$9. AE, DISC, MC, V.

Brookings

Home of South Dakota State University, the largest university in the state. The homesteader's experience is conveyed in Harvey Dunn's paintings at the South Dakota Art Museum, while McCrory Gardens has been called the prettiest 70 acres in South Dakota. **Information:** Brookings Area Convention and Visitors Bureau, 2308 E 6th St, PO Box 431, Brookings, 57006 (tel 605/692-6125).

HOTEL

Holiday Inn

2500 E 6th St, 57006; tel 605/692-9471 or toll free 800/HOLIDAY; fax 605/692-5807. At exit 132 off I-29. A neat facility with comfortable rooms. **Rooms:** 125 rms. CI 2pm/CO 11am. Nonsmoking rms avail. **Amenities:** A/C, cable TV. Some units w/whirlpools. **Services:** **Facilities:** 350 1 restaurant, 1 bar (w/entertainment), games rm, sauna, whirlpool, washer/dryer. Cribs free; rollaway beds $5/night. **Rates:** $49–$59 S or D. Children under age 18 stay free. Parking: Outdoor, free. B&B packages avail. AE, DISC, MC, V.

MOTELS

Best Western Staurolite Inn

2515 E 6th St, 57006; tel 605/692-9421 or toll free 800/582-1234; fax 605/692-9429. Exit 132 off I-29. Beautiful stone walls—inside and out—add to the decor. **Rooms:** 102 rms and stes. CI 2pm/CO 11am. Nonsmoking rms avail. Rooms are large and clean. **Amenities:** A/C, cable TV. Some units w/terraces, some w/whirlpools. **Services:** **Facilities:** 300 1 restaurant, 1 bar, whirlpool. **Rates:** Peak (June–Aug) $45–$60 S or D; $94 ste. Children under age 18 stay free. Lower rates off-season. Parking: Outdoor, free. AE, DISC, MC, V.

Comfort Inn

514 Sunrise Ridge Rd, 57006; tel 605/692-9566 or toll free 800/228-5150; fax 605/692-9511. Exit 132 off I-29. New, clean building with a comfortable lobby. **Rooms:** 53 rms and stes. CI 2pm/CO noon. Nonsmoking rms avail. **Amenities:** A/C, cable TV. Some units w/whirlpools. **Services:** **Facilities:** Games rm, whirlpool. Breakfast room, with TV and microwave, is open all day. **Rates (CP):** Peak (June–Aug) $42–$99 S or D; $89–$99 ste. Children under age 18 stay free. Lower rates off-season. Parking: Outdoor, free. Senior rates avail. AE, DC, DISC, JCB, MC, V.

ATTRACTION

State Agricultural Heritage Museum

925 11th St; tel 605/688-6226. Located on the campus of South Dakota State University. Farm implements and preserved buildings—including tractors and horse-drawn plows, an original homesteader's shack, and a 1910 farmhouse—highlight the development of farming and ranching in the Dakotas. In addition to the museum's permanent exhibits, a variety of special exhibits are featured. Gift shop offers books, postcards, posters, and reproduction items. **Open:** Mon–Sat 10am–5pm, Sun 1–5pm. Closed some hols. **Free**

Chamberlain

Missouri River town named for Selah Chamberlain, director of the Milwaukee railroad when the town was founded in 1880. Legend has it that Native Americans referred to the town as *Makah Tepee,* or mud house, because a hermit had a dugout here. **Information:** Chamberlain Area Chamber of Commerce, 115 W Lawler, PO Box 517, 57325 (tel 605/734-6541).

MOTELS

Best Western Lee's Motor Inn

220 W King, 57325; tel 605/734-5575 or toll free 800/528-1234. Exit 265 off I-90; along SD 16. An older property that has had some remodeling in recent years, but decor is still dated. **Rooms:** 60 rms. CI 2pm/CO 11am. Nonsmoking rms avail. Some units have two bedrooms, with two king beds or one king and one queen. Rooms with recliners available. **Amenities:** A/C, cable TV. **Facilities:** Games rm, sauna, whirlpool. Vehicle plug-ins in winter. Surprisingly nice pool and hot tub in separate building. **Rates:** Peak (June–Aug) $50 S; $55–$100 D. Extra person $5. Children under age 12 stay free. Lower rates off-season. Parking: Outdoor, free. AE, CB, DC, DISC, MC, V.

Oasis Inn

Exit 260 off I-90, PO Box 39, 57365; tel 605/734-6061 or toll free 800/635-3559; fax 605/734-4161. Exit 260 off I-90, turn right and travel 3 mi W. The nicest motel in the area. Within two miles of recreational activities on the Missouri River. Next door to well-known restaurant and truckstop. **Rooms:** 69 rms. CI 2pm/CO 11am. Nonsmoking rms avail. Rooms are large enough for family of four. **Amenities:** A/C, cable TV. Some units w/whirlpools. **Services:** **Facilities:** 10 Sauna, whirlpool. Children's fishing pond. **Rates:** Peak (Mem Day–Labor Day) $50–$60 S or D. Extra person $5. Children under age 16 stay free. Lower rates off-season. Parking: Outdoor, free. AE, CB, DC, DISC, ER, MC, V.

Riverview Inn

128 North St, 57325; tel 605/734-6057. Exit 263 I-90. Basic motel, with a great view of the Missouri River. Tiny lobby. **Rooms:** 29 rms. CI noon/CO 10:30am. Nonsmoking rms avail. Fairly large rooms, but dated decor and linen. **Amenities:** A/C, TV. **Facilities:** Guests can use pool at nearby motel. **Rates:** $30–$65 S or D. Parking: Outdoor, free. $100 fine for having a pet in the room. Closed Nov–Apr. DISC, MC, V.

Super 8

S Main St, 57325; tel 605/734-6548 or toll free 800/800-8000. Exit 263 off I-90. Property with old and new wings, but even accommodations in the dated older section are pleasant. Rooms at the front offer great views down the hill to the Missouri River. **Rooms:** 56 rms and stes. CI 1pm/CO 11am. Nonsmoking rms avail. Rooms are clean and functional. **Amenities:** A/C, cable TV. Some units w/whirlpools. **Services:** Free local calls; no pets allowed. **Facilities:** 20 Sauna, whirlpool. **Rates (CP):** Peak (Mem Day–Labor Day) $29–$46 S; $35–$56 D; $57–$76 ste.

Extra person $2. Children under age 5 stay free. Lower rates off-season. Parking: Outdoor, free. AE, CB, DC, DISC, MC, V.

RESORT

Radisson Resort at Cedar Shore
101 George S Mickelson Shoreline Dr, PO Box 308, 57325; tel 605/734-6376 or toll free 800/456-0038; fax 605/734-6854. Exit 260 off I-90. 200 acres. Opened in 1995, this resort offers complete recreational facilities. Great for fishing, boating, or just relaxing, and close to casinos. **Rooms:** 99 rms and stes. CI 3pm/CO noon. Nonsmoking rms avail. Some accommodations overlook the Missouri River. **Amenities:** A/C, cable TV w/movies, dataport. Some units w/terraces, some w/whirlpools. Lakeside rooms have microwaves and refrigerators. **Services:** Children's program, babysitting. Courtesy van available. **Facilities:** 1 restaurant (*see* "Restaurants" below), 1 bar, 1 beach (lake shore), basketball, games rm, whirlpool, playground, washer/dryer. Surprisingly small indoor pool. Campground and 100-slip marina. **Rates (CP):** $55–$149 S or D; $149 ste. Extra person $7. Children under age 18 stay free. Parking: Outdoor, free. AE, CB, DC, DISC, MC, V.

RESTAURANTS

Al's Oasis
Exit 260 off I-90; tel 605/734-6054. **American.** The most popular menu items at this well-known tourist stop are the buffalo burger and the nickel cup of coffee. There's a campground, motel, gift shop, and grocery next door. **FYI:** Reservations not accepted. Children's menu. **Open:** Peak (June–Aug) daily 6am–10:30pm. **Prices:** Main courses $5–$15. AE, DC, DISC, MC, V.

Bridges
In Radisson Resort at Cedar Shore, 101 George S Mickelson Shoreline Dr; tel 605/734-6376. Exit 260 off I-90, 2½ miles E on US 16. **New American.** Decorated in a stylish western motif, this hangout features common (and not-so-common) South Dakota specialties such as walleye, pheasant, and buffalo. The outdoor dining area affords an excellent view of the Missouri River. **FYI:** Reservations recommended. Piano. Children's menu. **Open:** Sun–Thurs 7am–10pm, Fri–Sat 7am–11pm. **Prices:** Main courses $9–$19. AE, DC, DISC, MC, V.

Casey Drug & Jewelry
In Welcome West Plaza, Exit 263 off I-90; tel 605/734-6530. **American.** Sixties-style drugstore/cafe claims to serve the best cheeseburger in the region—a boast supported by magazine and newspaper clippings on the walls. The food is good but a tad expensive for basic burger and patty-melt items; it's a dime store setting without the dime store prices. Breakfast served all day. **FYI:** Reservations not accepted. Children's menu. Beer and wine only. No smoking. **Open:** Daily 6am–9:30pm. **Prices:** Main courses $5–$8. DISC, MC, V.

ATTRACTION

Akta Lakota Museum
Exit 263 off I-90; tel 605/734-3455 or toll free 800/798-3452. In the Sioux language, *Akta Lakota* means "to honor the people." This museum has attempted to do that by amassing the largest collection of Sioux artifacts and contemporary Lakota art in South Dakota. Other exhibits feature original art, books, films, and other memorabilia depicting the culture of the Lakota. **Open:** May–Sept, Mon–Sat 8am–6pm, Sun 1–5pm; Oct–Apr, Mon–Fri 8am–4:30pm. Closed some hols. **Free**

Crazy Horse Memorial

See Custer

Custer

Beneath the towering granite spires of Custer, one can find clear streams, deep forest, and boundless wildlife. Just a short drive from major Black Hills attractions: Crazy Horse Memorial, Mount Rushmore, Custer State Park. **Information:** Custer County Chamber of Commerce, 447 Crook St, Custer, 57730 (tel 605/673-2244).

MOTEL

Sun-Mark Inn
342 Mt Rushmore Rd, 57730; tel 605/673-4400 or toll free 800/568-5314; fax 605/673-2314. Average two-story motel with no lobby; located in the business district. **Rooms:** 45 rms and stes. CI noon/CO 10am. Nonsmoking rms avail. **Amenities:** A/C, cable TV. Some units w/whirlpools. **Services:** **Facilities:** Whirlpool, washer/dryer. 10% discount at nearby restaurant. **Rates:** Peak (June–Aug) $30–$54 S; $42–$69 D; $85–$125 ste. Extra person $5. Lower rates off-season. Parking: Outdoor, free. Closed Dec–Feb. AE, CB, DC, DISC, MC, V.

RESTAURANT

Skyway Restaurant & Lounge
511 Mt Rushmore Rd (Downtown); tel 605/673-4477. **American.** Traditional American dishes such as steak, seafood, salads, and chicken share the menu with a selection of Mexican items. Wide variety of desserts. Closing hours vary. **FYI:** Reservations not accepted. Children's menu. **Open:** Peak (June–Aug) daily 6:30am–9:30pm. **Prices:** Main courses $8–$14. AE, CB, DC, DISC, MC, V.

ATTRACTIONS

Crazy Horse Memorial
Ave of the Chiefs, Crazy Horse; tel 605/673-4681. 5 mi N of Custer off US 16/385. Boston sculptor Korczak Ziolkowski, who once worked on Mount Rushmore, conceived and began this gigantic equestrian figure, carved with bulldozers and explosives from the granite of Thunderhead Mountain. (After the sculptor died in 1982, his wife, Ruth, and his 10 sons took over the work and expect to complete it around the end of the century.) The work, begun in 1948, has already required the removal of 8 million tons of rock—18 times more than at Mount Rushmore.

The memorial pays tribute to Crazy Horse, chief of the Oglala Sioux and one of those who defeated Lt-Col George Armstrong Custer at the battle of the Little Big Horn. A model in the visitors center gives an idea of the size and shape envisaged for the finished work: the horse's head will be as tall as a 22-story building. The monument is floodlit at night. **Open:** Daily sunrise–sunset. **$$$**

National Museum of Woodcarving
SD 16 W; tel 605/673-4404. All the moving pieces at the museum were created by Dr Niblack, a member of Disneyland's original animation crew. Main gallery features the work of over 70 woodcarvers, including 20 members of the Caricature Carvers of America. Gift shop, carving demonstrations. **Open:** May–mid-Oct, daily 8:30am–8pm. **$$$**

Flintstone Bedrock City
SD 16W; tel 605/673-4079. Stone Age theme park features rides and shows based on the popular TV show and movie. Visitors can ride the Flintmobile, see Mount Rockmore, visit Fred Flintstone's house, then enjoy a brontoburger at the drive-in. Adjacent campground with showers, laundry, play areas, and heated swimming pool. **Open:** Mid-May–Labor Day, daily 9am–8pm. **$$**

Custer State Park

Located 42 mi SW of Rapid City and 5 mi E of Custer. Spread across 73,000 acres, it is one of the largest state parks in the country. A unique aspect of the park is the herd of nearly 1,500 buffalo that roam here; visitors can take safari jeep rides to scout the animals. Other animals in the park include elk, mule deer, mountain goats, bighorn sheep, and coyotes.

Recreational activities include fishing in clear-running streams, rock climbing, horseback riding, hiking, and camping. Three scenic driving tour roads afford views of the Black Hills, Mount Rushmore, and the wildlife in the park. In addition, paddle boats and row boats can be rented at Sylvan Lake and Legion Lake. During evenings in the summer, the **Black Hills Playhouse** presents comedy, drama, and music performances. (Tickets can be purchased at any one of the four resorts located in the park.)

Both the **Peter Norbeck Visitors Center** (located on SD 16A) and the **Wildlife Station Visitors Center** (on the wildlife loop) have displays, books, and videos about the Black Hills area, as well as park staff who can answer questions. For further information, contact the Information Director, HC 83, PO Box 70, Custer, SD 57730 (tel 605/255-4515).

HOTEL

Sylvan Lake Resort
SD 87 (Needles Hwy) & SD 89, 57730; tel 605/574-2561 or toll free 800/658-3530; fax 605/574-4943. This three-story hotel overlooking a lake has a circular lobby decorated with a Native American motif. A variety of cabins are also available. **Rooms:** 35 rms; 31 cottages/villas. CI 10am/CO 2pm. Older hotel rooms have somewhat worn furnishings; newer rooms are beautifully decorated with matching oak furnishings. Some rooms offer views of the lake. A few of the cabins are set up for housekeeping. **Amenities:** A/C, satel TV. Some units w/terraces. **Services:** Babysitting. Pets $5. **Facilities:** 100 1 restaurant, 1 bar (w/entertainment). Hiking trails. Swimming area at lake. **Rates:** $80 S; $90–$125 D; $85–$200 cottage/villa. Extra person $5. Parking: Outdoor, free. Closed Oct–Mar. AE, DISC, MC, V.

LODGES

Blue Bell Lodge & Resort
SD 875, 57730; tel 605/255-4535 or toll free 800/658-3530; fax 605/255-4407. Well-maintained, all-cabin property. **Rooms:** 29 cottages/villas. CI noon/CO 10am. Mixture of new and old cabins. **Amenities:** Satel TV w/movies, refrig. No A/C or phone. Some units w/terraces, some w/fireplaces. Fireplace wood provided. **Services:** VCR rentals. **Facilities:** 100 1 restaurant, 1 bar, playground, washer/dryer. **Rates:** Peak (Oct–Apr) $75–$160 cottage/villa. Extra person $5. Lower rates off-season. Parking: Outdoor, free. AE, DC, DISC, MC, V.

Legion Lake Resort
HCR 83, PO Box 67, 57730; tel 605/255-4521 or toll free 800/658-3530; fax 605/255-4521. All-cabin, lakeside property nestled in the pines of Custer State Park. **Rooms:** 25 cottages/villas. CI 2pm/CO 10am. Cabins are well maintained but furnishings are old. **Amenities:** No A/C, phone, or TV. **Services:** Fishing licenses available at general store. **Facilities:** 1 restaurant, playground. Lodge, gift shop. **Rates:** $65–$100 cottage/villa. Extra person $5. Parking: Outdoor, free. Closed Oct–Apr. AE, DISC, MC, V.

State Game Lodge & Resort
US 16A, 57730; tel 605/255-4541 or toll free 800/658-3530; fax 605/255-4706. Set in a spectacular rustic landscape, this 1922 hotel with wood floors is listed on the National Register of Historic Places. Presidents Coolidge and Eisenhower stayed here. Cabins are also available. **Rooms:** 47 rms; 21 cottages/villas. CI 2pm/CO 10am. Nonsmoking rms avail.

Standard rooms have minimal decor and older furnishings. Suites named after presidents have more interesting furnishings. Some cabins have housekeeping facilities; some are creekside. **Amenities:** A/C, cable TV. 1 unit w/fireplace. **Services:** Babysitting. Cribs cost $5. Pets allowed in cabins only, for $5. **Facilities:** 1 restaurant, 1 bar. Banquet facilities. Jeep rides. **Rates:** $80–$100 D; $65–$250 cottage/villa. Extra person $5. Parking: Outdoor, free. Closed Oct–Apr. AE, DISC, MC, V.

Deadwood

This rambunctious town rejuvenated itself five years ago by legalizing the activity that helped Deadwood prosper a hundred years ago—gambling. Yesteryear's heroes were the likes of Wild Bill Hickok and Calamity Jane. Today's list of movers and shakers includes actor Kevin Costner, who owns the elegant Midnight Star casino with his brother Dan. **Information:** Deadwood/Lead Area Chamber of Commerce, 735 Main St, Deadwood, 57732 (tel 605/578-1876).

HOTELS

The Bullock Hotel

633 Main St, 57732 (Downtown); tel 605/578-1745 or toll free 800/336-1876. Built in 1895 by the area's first sheriff, whose ghost is reputed to still walk the halls. Antiques and Old West memorabilia decorate the lobby. **Rooms:** 28 rms and stes. CI 3pm/CO 11am. Nonsmoking rms avail. Uniquely decorated rooms all feature a Victorian motif. **Amenities:** A/C, cable TV. Some units w/whirlpools. **Services:** Masseur, babysitting. **Facilities:** 1 restaurant, 1 bar. Casino on main level. **Rates:** Peak (May–Sept) $25–$85 S; $40–$95 D; $65–$125 ste. Extra person $5. Children under age 14 stay free. Lower rates off-season. Parking: Outdoor, free. Rates increase $20 per room during annual Harley-Davidson Motorcycle Rally (early Aug). AE, DISC, MC, V.

First Gold Hotel

270 Historic Main St, 57732; or toll free 800/274-1876; fax 605/578-3979. New three-story brick property located on the business loop. No lobby. **Rooms:** 53 rms, stes, and effic. CI 3pm/CO 11am. Nonsmoking rms avail. Some rooms offer a view of the hills and pine trees; accommodations in back of building are quieter. **Amenities:** A/C, cable TV. 1 unit w/whirlpool. **Services:** Car-rental desk, social director, children's program. Airport transportation $15. **Facilities:** 2 restaurants, 2 bars. Casino. **Rates:** Peak (May–Sept) $39–$69 S; $49–$79 D; $79–$109 ste; $109 effic. Extra person $10. Children under age 13 stay free. Lower rates off-season. Parking: Outdoor, free. Rates increase $20/night during annual Harley-Davidson Motorcycle Rally (early Aug). AE, DISC, MC, V.

Historic Franklin Hotel & Gambling Hall

700 Main St, 57732 (Downtown); tel 605/578-2241 or toll free 800/688-1876; fax 605/578-3452. Historic hotel built in 1903 that retains turn-of-the-century feel. Front porch, spacious lobby, hand-operated elevator. **Rooms:** 76 rms, stes, and effic. CI 4pm/CO 11am. Nonsmoking rms avail. Each room is named for a historic figure like William Taft or Buffalo Bill. Wooden floors, antique furniture, and old-fashioned radiators set the tone. **Amenities:** A/C, cable TV. **Services:** Babysitting. **Facilities:** 1 restaurant, 2 bars (1 w/entertainment). **Rates:** Peak (June–Sept) $39–$65 S; $49–$85 D; $92–$155 ste; $92–$155 effic. Lower rates off-season. Parking: Outdoor, free. Rates rise to $85–$95 during annual Harley-Davidson Motorcycle Rally (early Aug). AE, DC, DISC, MC, V.

Mineral Palace

601 Historic Main St, 57732 (Downtown); tel 605/578-2036 or toll free 800/84-PALACE; fax 605/578-2037. New three-story brick hotel with a large lobby, casino, and lounge. **Rooms:** 63 rms and stes. CI 3pm/CO 11am. Nonsmoking rms avail. Rooms are attractively decorated with a floral motif; some overlook Main St. **Amenities:** A/C, cable TV w/movies. Some units w/minibars, 1 w/fireplace, 1 w/whirlpool. **Services:** Babysitting. Turndown service on request. **Facilities:** 1 restaurant, 2 bars (1 w/entertainment), games rm. **Rates:** Peak (June–Aug) $59–$89 S; $69–$99 D; $79–$195 ste. Extra person $5. Children under age 18 stay free. Lower rates off-season. Parking: Indoor/outdoor, free. AE, CB, DC, DISC, MC, V.

MOTELS

Best Western Hickok House

137 Charles St, 57732; tel 605/578-1611 or toll free 800/837-8174; fax 605/578-1855. 6 blocks from downtown. Located on a busy street; noise tends to be excessive. **Rooms:** 46 rms and stes. CI 1pm/CO 11am. Nonsmoking rms avail. Older but clean furnishings. **Amenities:** A/C, cable TV w/movies. Some units w/terraces. Closed-captioned TV and other equipment for the deaf and hard-of-hearing are available in some rooms. **Services:** Babysitting. **Facilities:** 1 restaurant, 1 bar, whirlpool, washer/dryer. Second level features a casino area with slot machines. **Rates:** Peak (June–Sept) $35–$74 S; $40–$89 D; $125–$250 ste. Extra person $5. Lower rates off-season. Parking: Outdoor, free. Rates increase during the annual Harley-Davidson Motorcycle Rally (early Aug). AE, CB, DC, DISC, MC, V.

Cedar Wood Inn

103 Charles St, 57732; tel 605/578-2725 or toll free 800/841-0127. Located on a busy street, this motel has well-maintained grounds. No lobby. **Rooms:** 19 rms. CI 1pm/CO 11am. Nonsmoking rms avail. Small rooms have older furnishings; fairly noisy, but comfortable. **Amenities:** A/C, cable TV. Some units w/terraces, 1 w/fireplace. **Services:**

Facilities: Playground. **Rates:** Peak (May–Sept) $25–$55 S; $30–$75 D. Lower rates off-season. Parking: Outdoor, free. DISC, MC, V.

Deadwood Gulch Resort
US 85 S, PO Box 643, 57732; tel 605/578-1294 or toll free 800/695-1876; fax 605/578-2505. 1¼ miles south of historic Main St. Perfect family getaway located on the south edge of town. **Rooms:** 97 rms. CI 3pm/CO 11am. Nonsmoking rms avail. Clean, cozy rooms, some of which offer views of nearby creek. Mini-suites available. **Amenities:** A/C, cable TV. **Services:** Social director, children's program, babysitting. **Facilities:** 1 restaurant, 3 bars (1 w/entertainment), basketball, games rm, whirlpool, playground. 24-hour gaming hall, children's arcade, general store, gas station, RV campground, family fun park, and creekside lounge. **Rates:** Peak (June–Sept) $45–$95 S or D. Extra person $5. Children under age 18 stay free. Lower rates off-season. Parking: Outdoor, free. AE, DISC, MC, V.

RESTAURANTS

Jakes
In Midnight Star Casino, 677 Main St; tel 605/578-1555. **American.** Historic Deadwood's most posh restaurant. Owned by Kevin Costner, it has a definite hint of Hollywood glamour in the wooden pillars inlaid with glass, cast-iron hand rails, and glass enclosed elevator. Featured are seafood, steaks, and chicken entrees. The peanut-butter pie is a house favorite. Extensive wine list. **FYI:** Reservations recommended. Piano. Children's menu. **Open:** Peak (Mem Day–Labor Day) Sun–Thurs 5:30–9pm, Fri 5–10pm, Sat 5–11pm. **Prices:** Main courses $14–$20; prix fixe $16–$22. AE, MC, V.

Sassy's Restaurant & Lounge
In Goldiggers Hotel & Gaming Estate, 629 Historic Main St (Downtown); tel 605/578-3213. **American.** A daily full breakfast buffet will keep you going until soup, salad, and sandwiches roll out at lunch. Dinner offerings are steak, seafood, pasta, barbecue ribs, and pork chops. Imported beer and wine. **FYI:** Reservations accepted. Piano. Beer and wine only. **Open:** Daily 24 hrs. **Prices:** Main courses $8–$13. AE, DISC, MC, V.

ATTRACTIONS

Adams Museum
54 Sherman St; tel 605/578-1714. This treasure trove of Black Hills history includes the area's first locomotive, a Plesiosaur skeleton, Wild Bill Hickok and Calamity Jane memorabilia, and impressive collections of guns, photographs, minerals, and Native American artifacts. **Open:** May 1-Sept 30, Mon–Sat 9am–6pm, Sun 9am–5pm; Oct 1–Apr 30, Tues–Sat 10am–4pm, Sun noon–4pm. Closed some hols. **$**

Broken Boot Gold Mine
US 14A; tel 605/578-1876 or toll free 800/999-1876. Visitors to the mine, which is operated by the Deadwood-Lead Chamber of Commerce, are shown how early-day miners followed stretches of quartz in quest of pockets of gold. Guided tours and gold panning are available. **Open:** Daily 8am–6pm. **$$**

Hill City

Considered the Heart of the Black Hills. Cherished for its laid-back style, Hill City provides many recreation opportunities—from ice fishing to rock climbing—as well as some of the area's most elegant restaurants.

MOTEL

Best Western Golden Spike Inn
106 Main St, 57745; tel 605/574-2577 or toll free 800/528-1234; fax 605/574-4719. Two-story brick motel at the edge of town. **Rooms:** 61 rms. CI 1pm/CO 11am. Nonsmoking rms avail. All rooms are well appointed. **Amenities:** A/C, cable TV. Some units w/terraces. Some rooms have recliners. **Services:** **Facilities:** 1 restaurant, whirlpool, washer/dryer. Garden area with seating. Cafe and espresso bar in lobby. **Rates:** Peak (June–Aug) $34–$83 S; $40–$95 D. Extra person $4. Lower rates off-season. Parking: Outdoor, free. Rates increase during annual Harley-Davidson Motorcycle Rally (early Aug). Closed Dec–Mar. AE, CB, DC, DISC, MC, V.

LODGE

Palmer Gulch Lodge
SD 244, PO Box 295, 57745; tel 605/574-2525 or toll free 800/233-4331; fax 605/574-2574. A charming, rustic retreat, with new and old cabins dispersed among the pine trees. Property also includes a new, 60-unit motel and tent sites. **Rooms:** 30 cottages/villas. CI 2pm/CO 11am. The two-room cabins have wooden floors and walls, with windows looking out to the hills. **Amenities:** No A/C, phone, or TV. Some units w/fireplaces. Each cabin has a wood-burning stove or fireplace, with free firewood furnished. **Services:** Babysitting. Lots of freebies, including a free Mount Rushmore shuttle, Native American dance performances, hay rides, and more. Paddleboat rentals available. **Facilities:** 1 restaurant, 1 bar (w/entertainment), basketball, volleyball, games rm, whirlpool, playground, washer/dryer. Mini-golf, trail rides, hiking trails. **Rates:** Peak (June–Aug) $66–$150 cottage/villa. Extra person $5. Lower rates off-season. Parking: Outdoor, free. Seventh-night-free program. Closed Oct–Apr. DISC, MC, V.

RESTAURANTS

Alpine Inn
225 Main St; tel 605/574-2749. **American/German.** Known as the "Show Place of Hill City" when it was a hotel in the 1850s, it now serves a German-inspired lunch menu and dinners geared toward beef lovers. The specialty is 6- or 9-ounce filet mignon. **FYI:** Reservations not accepted. Children's menu. Beer and wine only. **Open:** Lunch Mon–Sat 11am–2:30pm; dinner Mon–Sat 5–9:30pm. **Prices:** Main courses $6–$8. No CC.

Oriana's Bookcafe
349 Main St (Downtown); tel 605/574-4878. **Southwestern.** This three-level cafe/bookstore serves Mexican breakfast burritos and croissants to go with your coffee or espresso. Other specialities include enchiladas, black-bean tacos, and various burritos. A fine place to read or just relax. **FYI:** Reservations not accepted. Beer and wine only. No smoking. **Open:** Peak (June–Aug) daily 9am–9pm. **Prices:** Main courses $4–$9. AE, DISC, MC, V.

ATTRACTION

Black Hills Central Railroad "1880 Train"
1880 Circle Dr; tel 605/574-2222. This vintage train follows the original route of the CBG&O railroad, as laid down in the 1880s. The 20-mile round trip winds through Black Hills National Forest and climbs some of the steepest grades in North America. Depot gift shop features railroad books and memorabilia. Phone ahead for train reservations; evening trips scheduled July–August, call for days and times. **Open:** Mid-May–Sept. **$$$$**

Hot Springs

Home to warm waters, woolly mammoths, and wild mustangs. Mineral waters still flow through Hot Springs, while at Mammoth Site, researchers dig for Ice Age animals. Hundreds of wild horses roam freely at the Black Hills Wild Horse Sanctuary. **Information:** Hot Springs Area Chamber of Commerce, 801 S 6th St, Hot Springs, 57747 (tel 605/745-4140).

MOTEL

Best Western Inn by the River
602 W River St, 57747; tel 605/745-4292 or toll free 800/528-1234; fax 605/745-3584. Nestled against a hillside, this older two-story building sits next to a creek. Casual, no-frills accommodations. **Rooms:** 32 rms. CI 1pm/CO 11am. Nonsmoking rms avail. Average-size, minimally decorated rooms all have views of historic buildings across the creek. **Amenities:** A/C, cable TV w/movies. Some units w/terraces. **Services:** **Facilities:** Picnic area across the road. **Rates:** Peak (June–Sept) $38 S or D. Extra person $4. Lower rates off-season. Parking: Outdoor, free. Seniors get 10% discount. AE, CB, DC, MC, V.

RESTAURANT

Dakota Rose
Jct US 18 and SD 79; tel 605/745-6447. **American.** Early American decor, piped-in country music. Prime rib, steaks, seafood, hot sandwiches, and hamburgers are the main offerings. Homemade pies and desserts. **FYI:** Reservations accepted. Children's menu. **Open:** Daily 7am–9pm. **Prices:** Main courses $6–$14; prix fixe $6–$10. AE, CB, DC, DISC, MC, V.

ATTRACTIONS

The Mammoth Site
1800 US 18 By-Pass; tel 605/745-6017. A huge, 26,000-year-old mammoth graveyard, under active excavation by paleontologists, believed to have the largest concentration of Columbian and woolly mammoth bones in the world. Year-round guided tours escort visitors through the now-enclosed sinkhole and past the actual fossils. Visitors can also observe the work of scientists and volunteers as they excavate, map, and preserve the relics. **Open:** May–Aug, daily 8am–8pm; Sept–Apr, daily 9am–5pm. Closed some hols. **$$**

Evans Plunge
1145 N River St; tel 605/745-5165. Water park with a wide array of indoor and outdoor water rides and pools, all fed by natural South Dakota springs. Water slides, Tarzan rings, and kiddie pools. Locker, suit, towel, and life jacket rentals; spa and fitness center available for a small additional fee. **Open:** June–Aug, daily 5:30am–10pm. Reduced hours off-season. **$$$**

Huron

Backdrop for the South Dakota State Fair, this town takes pride in its hometown hospitality, brilliant sunsets, and rich history. Huron's favorite sons and daughters include Hubert Humphrey and former *Charlie's Angels* star Cheryl Ladd. **Information:** Huron Area Convention and Visitors Bureau, 15 4th St SW, Huron, 57350 (tel 605/352-8775).

ATTRACTIONS

Pyle House Museum
376 Idaho Ave SE; tel 605/352-2528. Former home of Gladys Pyle, the first female elected to the US Senate. The Queen Anne–style house was completed in 1894, and now contains 19th-century period antiques, stained glass, carved woodwork, and personal memorabilia. **Open:** Daily 1–4pm. Closed some hols. **$**

Centennial Stone Church
48 4th St SE; tel 605/352-1442. Built in 1887 from native South Dakota granite, this Gothic-style former church now houses Native American artifacts, railroad memorabilia, and an art gallery. One room features a model railroad. **Open:** Mon–Fri 1–5pm, Sat 11am–3pm. Closed some hols. **Free**

Jewel Cave National Monument

For lodgings and dining, see Custer

13 mi W of Custer. Jewel Cave is the fourth-longest explored cave in the world, and the second-longest in the United States, with more than 80 miles of mapped passageways. The monument's **visitors center** houses exhibits explaining the cave's rare calcite crystal formations: dogtooth spar, nailhead spar, helictites, gypsum "flowers," and silvery hydromagnesite "balloons." Some of these formations are unique to Jewel Cave.

Three different cave tours (fee charged) are conducted May–September: a 1¼-hr scenic tour, a 1¾-hr history tour, and a 4–5 hr spelunking tour. Even the shortest tour is quite strenuous. For further information, contact the Superintendent, Jewel Cave National Monument, RR1, PO Box 60 AA, Custer, SD 57730 (tel 605/673-2288).

Kadoka

MOTEL

Best Western H&H Centro Motel

I-90, PO Box 37, 57543; tel 605/837-2287 or toll free 800/837-8011; fax 605/837-2186. Exit 150 or 152 off I-90. Fairly standard—but clean and well-kept. The cast and crew of the movie *Thunderheart* (starring Val Kilmer and Sam Shepard) stayed here during filming. **Rooms:** 40 rms. CI open/CO 11am. Nonsmoking rms avail. **Amenities:** A/C, cable TV w/movies. **Services:** Friendly staff. **Facilities:** 120 1 restaurant (bkfst and dinner only), games rm, spa, whirlpool, playground, washer/dryer. **Rates:** Peak (June–Sept) $30–$60 S; $34–$99 D. Extra person $6. Children under age 13 stay free. Lower rates off-season. Parking: Outdoor, free. Closed Dec 15–Jan. AE, DC, DISC, MC, V.

Keystone

Keystone might have been just another quaint mining ghost town in the Black Hills, except for the sculpting of Mount Rushmore. Today, Keystone's unique atmosphere embodies elements of Mardi Gras, a Sunday picnic, a midway, and an old-fashioned hoedown.

MOTELS

Best Western Four Presidents Motel

250 Winter St, 57751; tel 605/666-4472 or toll free 800/732-9155. Average rooms, in an old three-story building on the main street. **Rooms:** 30 rms. CI 2pm/CO 10am. Nonsmoking rms avail. A bit noisy because of traffic. **Amenities:** A/C, cable TV w/movies. **Services:** **Facilities:** **Rates (CP):** Peak (June–Labor Day) $45–$77 S; $55–$87 D. Extra person $5. Lower rates off-season. Parking: Outdoor, free. Rates increase during annual Harley-Davidson Motorcycle Rally (early Aug). Closed Nov–Mar. AE, CB, DC, DISC, MC, V.

Kelly Inn

US 16A and Cemetery Rd, PO Box 654, 57751; tel 605/666-4483; fax 605/666-4883. 1 block E of US 16A. This new two-story building is located next to a helicopter tour facility, so it is noisy during business hours. **Rooms:** 44 rms. CI open/CO 11am. Nonsmoking rms avail. Rooms have minimal decor, views of hillside and pine trees. **Amenities:** A/C, cable TV. Some units w/terraces. **Services:** Pets cannot be left unattended in rooms. **Facilities:** 40 Sauna, whirlpool. **Rates:** Peak (May–Sept) $60 S; $65 D. Extra person $5. Children under age 4 stay free. Lower rates off-season. Parking: Outdoor, free. AE, CB, DC, DISC, MC, V.

Roosevelt Inn

US 16A (Old Cemetery Rd), PO Box 642, 57751; tel 605/666-4599 or toll free 800/257-8923; fax 605/666-4599. New property located on a main road, next to a helicopter tour company. **Rooms:** 19 rms. CI 2pm/CO 11am. Nonsmoking rms avail. Rooms are small but attractive. **Amenities:** A/C, cable TV w/movies. All units w/terraces. **Services:** **Facilities:** Washer/dryer. Pleasant outdoor deck with canopy. **Rates (CP):** Peak (Mem Day–Labor Day) $49–$79 S or D. Extra person $5. Lower rates off-season. Parking: Outdoor, free. Rates may vary during annual Harley-Davidson Motorcycle Rally (early Aug). Closed Nov–Apr. DISC, MC, V.

RESTAURANTS

Buffalo Room

Mount Rushmore National Memorial; tel 605/574-2515. **Cafeteria.** Located at the base of Mount Rushmore, the restaurant's floor-to-ceiling windows offer a view of the presidents' faces. Cafeteria eats include breakfast fare (waffles, eggs, bacon) and rest-of-the-day choices like roast beef, chicken, and lasagna. The view is the best asset. **FYI:** Reservations not accepted. No liquor license. No smoking. **Open:** Peak (Mem Day–Labor Day) breakfast daily 8–11am; lunch daily 11am–7pm; dinner daily 11am–7pm. **Prices:** Main courses $5. AE, DC, DISC, MC, V.

Ruby House Restaurants

126 Winter St; tel 605/666-4404. **American/Italian.** A traditional old-west saloon eating house replete with all appropriate decorations: swinging doors, velvet wall paper, old wooden floors, etched and stained-glass windows, and waitresses wearing "saloon dresses" and garters. The Italian-American menu offers steaks, chicken, seafood, and pasta. Extensive selection of domestic wines. Live entertainment during summer months. **FYI:** Reservations accepted. Country music/guitar/jazz. Children's menu. **Open:** Peak (Mem Day–Labor

Day) breakfast daily 7–10am; lunch daily 11:30am–4:30pm; dinner daily 4:30–9pm. Closed Nov–Mar. **Prices:** Main courses $10–$18. AE, DISC, MC, V.

ATTRACTION

Big Thunder Gold Mine
604 Blair St; tel 605/666-4847. Visitors are encouraged to pan for their own gold in this historic 1880s Black Hills gold mine. Even the panning supplies are included. Orientation film, guided tours. Gift shop sells gold jewelry and souvenirs. **Open:** May–mid-Oct, daily 8am–8pm. **$$$**

Lead

The chain of gold mines that started in Custer and spread through the Black Hills eventually ended in Lead. Surface mining has changed the look and culture of Lead since those early days, but Homestake Gold Mine is still one of the largest gold producers in this hemisphere. Skiers visiting nearby Deer Mountain and Terry Peak also add to the local economy. **Information:** Deadwood/Lead Area Chamber of Commerce, 735 Main St, Deadwood, 57732 (tel 605/578-1876).

HOTELS

Best Western Golden Hills Resort
900 Miners Ave, 57754; tel 605/584-1800 or toll free 800/528-1234; fax 605/584-3933. Five-story building with a glass facade and a spacious, beautifully furnished lobby. Located on a busy street. **Rooms:** 100 rms and stes. CI 3pm/CO 11am. Nonsmoking rms avail. Large, newly carpeted rooms are decorated with watercolor paintings of local gold mines. **Amenities:** A/C, cable TV. Some units w/whirlpools. **Services:** Social director, babysitting. Airport transportation from Rapid City is $50. **Facilities:** 400 1 restaurant, 1 bar, basketball, games rm, racquetball, spa, sauna, steam rm, whirlpool. Guests get free passes for adjacent YMCA. Snowmobile rentals and trail information available. **Rates:** Peak (June–Sept) $59–$89 S; $69–$99 D; $145–$185 ste. Extra person $10. Children under age 19 stay free. Lower rates off-season. Parking: Outdoor, free. Snowmobile package avail. Rates increase during annual Harley-Davidson Motorcycle Rally (early Aug). AE, CB, DC, DISC, MC, V.

Whitehouse Inn
395 Glendale Dr, 57754; tel 605/584-2000 or toll free 800/654-5323; fax 605/584-2000. Located on a busy street, this four-story hotel has a small but well-maintained lobby. **Rooms:** 71 rms and stes. CI 3pm/CO 11am. Nonsmoking rms avail. Average-size rooms; some have views of the distant hills. **Amenities:** A/C, cable TV w/movies. **Services:** Free shuttle to historic Deadwood. Deposit for pets. **Facilities:** 25 Whirlpool. **Rates (CP):** Peak (June–Sept) $35–$70 S; $45–$75 D; $60–$110 ste. Extra person $10. Children under age 17 stay free. Lower rates off-season. Parking: Outdoor, free. AE, CB, DC, DISC, MC, V.

ATTRACTIONS

Black Hills Mining Museum
323 W Main St; tel 605/584-1605. Guides escort visitors on a simulated underground mine tour, complete with life-size models, historic photographs and maps, timber stopes, carbide lamps, and compressed air locomotives. Visitors can watch a free gold-panning demonstration, or pan by themselves for an additional fee. **Open:** May–Sept, daily 9am–5pm. **$$**

Homestake Surface Tours
160 W Main St; tel 605/584-3110. One of the oldest operating underground gold mines in the United States. An orientation video tells the story of the Black Hills gold rush of the 1870s and explains modern gold mining and refining techniques. A bus tour takes visitors through the mine's surface operations. Free ore samples available upon request. **Open:** June–Aug, Mon–Fri 8am–5pm, Sat–Sun 10am–5pm; Sept–May, Mon–Fri 8am–4pm. Closed some hols. **$$**

Terry Peak Ski Area
Nevada Gulch Lodge; tel 605/584-2165 or toll free 800/456-0521. Five chairlifts, a vertical drop of 1,052 feet, 20 trails, and an average of 150 inches of snow a year provide a variety of skiing opportunities for all skill levels. The top of the mountain provides a clear view of the Black Hills and the neighboring states of Wyoming, Montana, North Dakota, and Nebraska. Snowboarding, ski school, restaurants, rentals. For the latest information on snow conditions, call 605/584-2165 or 800/456-0524. **Open:** Dec–Mar, daily 9am–4pm. **$$$$**

Madison

Tucked between two of South Dakota's finest lakes, Lake Madison and Lake Herman, Madison is a recreational hot spot. Home of Dakota State University.

ATTRACTIONS

Smith-Zimmerman State Museum
221 NE 8th St; tel 605/256-5308. Exhibits here focus on eastern South Dakota history from 1860 to 1940. An original covered wagon and replica claim shanty give visitors a look at homesteading life; there's also a completely refurbished 1880s parlor and a fully restored 1920 Oldsmobile. Changing displays feature household articles, Civil War memorabilia, and period clothing. **Open:** Tues–Thurs 10am–noon and 1–7pm, Fri 10am–noon and 1–5pm. Other times by appointment. Closed some hols. **$**

Prairie Village
SD 34; tel 605/256-3644. More than 40 pioneer-era structures have been moved to this site and restored to their

original appearance. Highlights include a steam carousel built in 1893, several windmills, a working kitchen, a sod house, and a chapel car specifically designed as a "church on rails." Diesel train rides given on the first and third Sundays of each month. **Open:** Mem Day–Labor Day, daily 9am–6pm. **$$**

Milbank

This small dairy community is the birthplace of American Legion baseball, proposed here on July 17, 1925. Site of an authentic, late 19th-century gristmill. **Information:** Milbank Area Chamber of Commerce, 401 Main St, Milbank, 57252 (tel 605/432-6656).

MOTELS

Lantern Motel
SD 15 S, PO Box 281 RR2, 57252; tel 605/432-4591 or toll free 800/627-6075. 5 blocks S of US 12. A basic motel with the feel of a college dormitory. Motel caters to reunion groups and wedding parties, in association with the next-door Lantern Inn. Peeling paint on building's exterior needs attention. **Rooms:** 30 rms. CI open/CO 11am. Nonsmoking rms avail. Newer wing has larger rooms. **Amenities:** A/C, cable TV. **Services:** Babysitting. **Facilities:** Sauna. **Rates (CP):** $28–$34 S; $40–$50 D. Extra person $5. Children under age 12 stay free. Parking: Outdoor, free. AE, CB, DC, DISC, MC, V.

Manor Motel
US 12 E, 57252; tel 605/432-4527 or toll free 800/341-8000. A hidden gem located close to the Big Stone Lake recreation areas. Neat, clean, and cheap. **Rooms:** 30 rms. CI 1pm/CO 11am. Nonsmoking rms avail. Size of the wood-paneled accommodations varies, so check out the different rooms available before you choose one. **Amenities:** A/C, cable TV. Some rooms with dataports. **Services:** Babysitting. **Facilities:** Sauna, whirlpool. **Rates:** $30–$36 S; $40–$48 D. Extra person $3. Children under age 16 stay free. Parking: Outdoor, free. AE, CB, DC, DISC, MC, V.

Super 8
US 12 E, 57252; tel 605/432-9288 or toll free 800/800-8000; fax 605/432-9288. The nearest motel to the Stone Lake recreation areas, it has some maintenance problems. **Rooms:** 39 rms. CI 1pm/CO 11am. Nonsmoking rms avail. Small and quiet. **Amenities:** A/C. Some rooms have microwaves. Dataports available. **Services:** **Facilities:** 50 Sauna, whirlpool, washer/dryer. **Rates (CP):** Peak (May–Sept) $34–$38 S; $44–$49 D. Extra person $6. Children under age 12 stay free. Lower rates off-season. Parking: Outdoor, free. AE, CB, DC, DISC, MC, V.

RESTAURANT

★ Lantern Inn
SD 15 S; tel 605/432-4421. **American.** The appeal of this eatery is enhanced by candles at the tables and a sports bar in the evenings. House specialty is prime rib. **FYI:** Reservations recommended. **Open:** Daily 5:30–10:30pm. **Prices:** Main courses $7–$12; prix fixe $5–$7. AE, CB, DC, DISC, MC, V.

Mitchell

This mainly agricultural town is perhaps best known for its colorful harvest festival held each September. The world's only Corn Palace was started here in 1892 to encourage settlement and prove the richness of eastern South Dakota soil. **Information:** Mitchell Area Chamber of Commerce, 601 N Main St, PO Box 206, Mitchell, 57301 (tel 605/996-5567).

MOTELS

Anthony Motel
1518 W Havens Rd, 57301; tel 605/996-7518 or toll free 800/477-2235; fax 605/996-7251. Exit 330 off I-90, N ½ mi to Havens. An older, basic motel with newly refurbished rooms. Lots of repeat business from travelers who want a quiet place away from fast-food strips. **Rooms:** 34 rms and effic. CI 1pm/CO 11am. Nonsmoking rms avail. Clean but spartan. **Amenities:** A/C, cable TV. **Services:** **Facilities:** Games rm, washer/dryer. **Rates:** Peak (June–Aug) $27–$40 S; $46–$50 D; $46–$49 effic. Children under age 16 stay free. Lower rates off-season. Parking: Outdoor, free. AE, DISC, MC, V.

Best Western Motor Inn
1001 S Burr St, 57301; tel 605/996-5536 or toll free 800/528-1234; fax 605/996-5535. Along SD 37; ¼ mi N from I-90 exit 332. Clean and functional rooms; located near several restaurants. **Rooms:** 77 rms. CI 2pm/CO 11am. Nonsmoking rms avail. **Amenities:** A/C, cable TV. **Services:** One pet allowed per room; no charge. **Facilities:** Whirlpool, washer/dryer. **Rates (CP):** Peak (July 21–Aug 13) $48–$58 S; $58–$68 D. Extra person $5. Children under age 12 stay free. Lower rates off-season. Parking: Outdoor, free. AE, DC, DISC, MC, V.

Coachlight Motel
1000 W Havens St, 57301; tel 605/996-5686. Exit 330 off I-90, N ½ mi to Havens, then E. An older motel catering to hunters and travelers with pets (there are kennels and a pet play area in the back of the property). Fills up fast on many weekends. **Rooms:** 20 rms. CI 11am/CO 11am. Nonsmoking rms avail. Rooms are surprisingly attractive, given the exterior appearance of the building. **Amenities:** A/C, cable TV. **Services:** **Facilities:** **Rates:** Peak (June–Sept) $28–$30 S; $29–$35 D. Lower rates off-season. Parking: Outdoor, free. AE, DISC, MC, V.

Comfort Inn
At jct I-90 and SD 37, PO Box 447, 57301; tel 605/996-1333 or toll free 800/221-2222; fax 605/996-6022. ¼ mi N of exit 332 off I-90. A very nice lobby and staircase lead to the fresh and clean rooms at this newish (1991) motel. **Rooms:** 60 rms. CI 2pm/CO 2pm. Nonsmoking rms avail. **Amenities:** A/C, cable TV. Some units w/whirlpools. **Services:** **Facilities:** Games rm, sauna, whirlpool, washer/dryer. **Rates (CP):** Peak (May–Oct) $49–$64 S or D. Extra person $5. Children under age 18 stay free. Lower rates off-season. Parking: Outdoor, free. AE, DISC, JCB, MC, V.

Days Inn
1506 S Burr, 57301; tel 605/996-6208 or toll free 800/DAYS-INN; fax 605/996-5220. Exit 332 off I-90. Smart, new-looking property located close to I-90 and next door to restaurants. A great place to stop on the way to the Black Hills. **Rooms:** 65 rms. CI 2pm/CO 11am. Nonsmoking rms avail. Nice-size rooms with attractive furnishings. **Amenities:** A/C, cable TV. Some units w/whirlpools. **Services:** **Facilities:** Games rm, whirlpool, washer/dryer. **Rates (CP):** $30–$49 S or D. Extra person $5. Children under age 12 stay free. Parking: Outdoor, free. Senior discounts avail. AE, DC, DISC, MC, V.

Thunderbird Lodge
I-90 and SD 37, 57301; tel 605/996-6645 or toll free 800/341-8000; fax 605/995-5883. Off I-90 exit 332; 1 mi S of downtown. The exterior seems rundown but rooms have been refurbished. Many restaurants within walking distance or a short drive. **Rooms:** 48 rms. CI 2pm/CO 11am. Nonsmoking rms avail. Clean rooms are quiet despite nearby interstate and highway. **Amenities:** A/C, cable TV. **Services:** **Facilities:** Sauna, whirlpool. **Rates:** Peak (Apr 30–Sept 30) $29–$36 S; $38–$50 D. Extra person $5. Children under age 12 stay free. Lower rates off-season. Parking: Outdoor, free. AE, DC, DISC, MC, V.

RESTAURANTS

Chef Louie's
601 E Havens St; tel 605/996-7565. Exit 332 off I-90; at Burr. **American.** Specialties at this 50-year-old local institution focus on steak and seafood, with pheasant available year-round. Beef is aged and handcut on the premises. Various stir-frys offered. Open late during hunting season. **FYI:** Reservations recommended. Children's menu. **Open:** Peak (June–Sept) daily 11am–11pm. **Prices:** Main courses $7–$17. AE, CB, DC, DISC, MC, V.

★ **Town House Cafe and Restaurant**
103-105 N Main St; tel 605/996-4615. 5 blocks S of Corn Palace. **American.** A very functional, very casual downtown cafe and restaurant. American-style meat and potatoes, steaks, and an all-you-can-eat buffet keeps patrons returning. The cafe caters to hunters, and will prepare pheasants brought in by hunters for their dinner. The restaurant is slightly more upscale, but the same menu is offered at both places. **FYI:** Reservations accepted. Children's menu. **Open:** Daily 6am–10pm. **Prices:** Main courses $5–$19. MC, V.

ATTRACTION

World's Only Corn Palace
604 N Main St; tel 605/996-7311 or toll free 800/257-2676. Every year since 1892, the exterior of this downtown auditorium and basketball arena has been decorated with ears of locally grown corn. The colors—red, purple, blue, and brown, as well as the expected yellow—come entirely from naturally grown grains, and the design changes every year. Decorating of the turreted and domed landmark begins in early September and is completed in time for the Corn Palace harvest festival in late September, which is the best time for a visit. **Open:** Mem Day–Labor Day, daily 8am–10pm; May and Sept, daily 8am–5pm; Oct–Apr, Mon–Fri 8am–5pm. Closed some hols. **Free**

Mobridge

The Missouri River gropes its way through Mobridge, making it an ideal place for the outdoors enthusiast. Sitting Bull, who masterminded the Native American victory at the Battle of Little Big Horn, lies buried on a bluff just west of town. **Information:** Mobridge Chamber of Commerce, 212 Main St, Mobridge, 57601 (tel 605/845-2387).

MOTELS

Mo-Rest Motel
US 12 W, 57601; tel 605/845-3668. Very clean, no-nonsense facility located near Missouri River and Lake Oahe. Considered the "Pike Capital of the World," the region attracts fishermen, hunters, and anybody who likes open spaces and blue skies. **Rooms:** 27 rms. CI open/CO 11am. Nonsmoking rms avail. **Amenities:** A/C, cable TV. **Facilities:** Porch swing outside the main office. **Rates:** Peak (May–Sept) $24 S; $40 D. Extra person $4. Lower rates off-season. Parking: Outdoor, free. DISC, MC, V.

Wrangler Motor Inn
820 W Grand Crossing, 57601 (Business District); tel 605/845-3641 or toll free 800/341-8000; fax 605/845-3641. Nicely decorated facility. **Rooms:** 61 rms. CI 2pm/CO 11am. Nonsmoking rms avail. **Amenities:** A/C, cable TV, dataport. New rooms are elegantly furnished. **Services:** Social director, babysitting. **Facilities:** 2 restaurants, 1 bar, games rm, sauna, steam rm, whirlpool. **Rates:** $44–$49 S; $54–$64 D. Extra person $5. Children under age 13 stay free. Parking: Outdoor, free. AE, DC, DISC, MC, V.

RESTAURANTS

Dakota Country Café
122 W Grand Crossing; tel 605/845-7495. **American.** Decorated with country accents and Norman Rockwell prints, this cafe offers traditional items like steak, seafood, buckets of chicken, and fresh-baked pies. Full breakfast menu, daily breakfast specials. **FYI:** Reservations not accepted. Children's menu. No liquor license. **Open:** Daily 6am–8pm. **Prices:** Main courses $4–$10. No CC.

Wheel Restaurant
820 W Grand Crossing; tel 605/845-7474. **American.** Offers panoramic view of the lake created by the Missouri River. American favorites like chicken-fried steak, seafood, various chicken dinners, and sandwiches. Homemade soups and pies. Lunch and Sunday buffets are available regularly; during summer, there is a weekend breakfast buffet. **FYI:** Reservations accepted. Children's menu. No liquor license. **Open:** Daily 6am–10pm. **Prices:** Main courses $5–$14. MC, V.

ATTRACTION

Klein Museum
1820 W Grand Crossing; tel 605/845-7243. Various rooms contain re-creations of doctor, dentist, and lawyer's offices from the pioneer days; there's also a trapper's shack and a pre-electric kitchen. Sioux and Arikara artifacts on display include beadwork, pottery, and tools, while a small art gallery features work by local artists. Gift shop offers Sioux arts and crafts. **Open:** Apr–Oct, Mon and Wed–Fri 9am–noon and 1–5pm, Sat–Sun 1–5 pm. Closed some hols. **$**

Mount Rushmore National Memorial

For lodgings and dining, see Custer, Hill City, Keystone, Rapid City

24 mi SW of Rapid City on US 16. Visited every year by more than 2½ million tourists, Mount Rushmore is one of the best-known monuments in America. The features of presidents George Washington, Thomas Jefferson, Abraham Lincoln, and Theodore Roosevelt, each some 60 foot high, have been carved from a 6,000-foot-tall mountain. These colossal portraits, begun in 1927 by sculptor Gutzon Borglum and completed after his death by son Lincoln, required 14 years of work and the removal of 450,000 tons of rock. After dark, the sight of these enormous granite faces illuminated by floodlights is eerie and captivating.

The **Lincoln Borglum Visitor Center** provides information on the monument and houses a snack bar, a gift shop, and a cafeteria. In summer, nighttime interpretive programs and tours of the sculptor's studio are available. The memorial itself is open daily year round and is lit by floodlights for a scheduled period each night. For more information, contact Mount Rushmore National Memorial, PO Box 268, Keystone, SD 57751 (tel 605/574-2523).

Murdo

Rolling bluffs and endless fields of prairie stretch out in all directions from Murdo, providing habitat for many game animals.

MOTEL

Sioux Motel
302 E 5th St, 57559; tel 605/669-2422. On I-90 and US 83. Located on a busy street on the west edge of town, this older, no-frills motel is attractively kept. **Rooms:** 24 rms. CI noon/CO 10am. Nonsmoking rms avail. Small rooms with clean, sturdy furnishings. **Amenities:** A/C, cable TV w/movies. No phone. Not all rooms have phones. **Services:** Pet fee $5. **Facilities:** Whirlpool, washer/dryer. Vehicle plug-ins in winter. **Rates:** Peak (June–Aug) $23–$36 S; $26–$59 D. Extra person $3. Children under age 11 stay free. Lower rates off-season. Parking: Outdoor, free. DISC, MC, V.

RESTAURANTS

Star Restaurant
103 E 5th St (Downtown); tel 605/669-2411. Off I-90 Business Loop. **American.** 1950s diner serving regional favorites like walleye pike and buffalo. Daily soup and salad bar; dessert. **FYI:** Reservations not accepted. Children's menu. No liquor license. **Open:** Daily 7am–10pm. Closed May–Sept. **Prices:** Main courses $8–$12; prix fixe $7. No CC.

Tee Pee Restaurant
303 5th St (Business District); tel 605/669-2432. **American.** Southwest decor and high ceilings, with soft country music in the background. Burgers, meat loaf, chicken, salads, sandwiches. **FYI:** Reservations accepted. Children's menu. No liquor license. **Open:** Daily 7am–10pm. Closed Oct 30–Apr 1. **Prices:** Main courses $8–$12. No CC.

Piedmont

Home of Stage Barn Crystal Cave, the third-largest cave in South Dakota.

LODGE

Elk Creek Resort & Lodge
HC 80 Box 767, 57769; tel 605/787-4884 or toll free 800/846-2267. Exit 46 off I-90, go ¾ mi N. This all-cabin property is bordered by a stand of pine trees. **Rooms:** 17 cottages/villas. CI 2pm/CO 11am. Nonsmoking rms avail. Generous-size rooms; some cabins have sleeping lofts, and all overlook the surrounding valley and hills. **Amenities:**

A/C, TV, refrig. All units w/terraces. **Services:** Babysitting. Catering available for groups. **Facilities:** Games rm, whirlpool, playground, washer/dryer. Picnic area. **Rates:** Peak (June–Aug) $89–$177 cottage/villa. Extra person $7. Children under age 11 stay free. Lower rates off-season. Parking: Outdoor, free. Rates increase $10/cabin during annual Harley-Davidson Motorcycle Rally (early Aug). AE, DISC, MC, V.

RESTAURANT

Elk Creek Steak House & Lounge
Exit 46 & Elk Creek Rd; tel 605/787-6349. Off I-90. **Seafood/Steak.** Decorated with a country & western theme; the lounge has a dance floor. You can practice your Texas two-step, or cotton-eyed Joe on weekends, when there's live music. Steaks, chicken, seafood. **FYI:** Reservations recommended. Country music/dancing. Children's menu. **Open:** Mon–Thurs 5–10pm, Fri–Sat 5–11pm, Sun 4:30–10pm. **Prices:** Main courses $8–$30; prix fixe $10–$14. AE, DC, DISC, MC, V.

Pierre

Pronounced "peer." This small plains town on the Missouri River, with a population of only some 13,000 people, is the capital of South Dakota. Founded in 1880 as a railroad terminus and named the capital in 1889, the town lies in a farming region. Recreational opportunities are nearby. Most of *Dances with Wolves* was filmed 25 miles north of town, on Houck's Buffalo Ranch. **Information:** Pierre Convention and Visitors Bureau, 800 W Dakota Ave, PO Box 548, Pierre, 57501 (605/224-7361).

MOTELS

Best Western Kings Inn
220 S Pierre St, 57501 (Business District); tel 605/224-5951 or toll free 800/528-1234; fax 605/224-5301. Older facility within walking distance of downtown stores. **Rooms:** 104 rms and stes. CI noon/CO noon. Nonsmoking rms avail. Clean, minimally decorated rooms. **Amenities:** A/C, cable TV w/movies, refrig, dataport. **Services:** **Facilities:** 400 1 restaurant, 2 bars (1 w/entertainment), spa, whirlpool. **Rates (BB):** $31–$43 S; $51 D; $60 ste. Extra person $4. Children under age 13 stay free. Parking: Outdoor, free. AE, DISC, MC, V.

Best Western Ramkota Inn
920 W Sioux Ave, 57501 (Business District); tel 605/224-6877 or toll free 800/528-1234; fax 605/224-1042. Elegant property attracting long-term guests. An especially inviting lobby has lots of cozy chairs and is decorated with a fishing-and-hunting motif. **Rooms:** 151 rms, stes, and effic. CI 2pm/CO noon. Nonsmoking rms avail. Forty rooms have extra closet space and microwaves to accommodate long-term guests while the state legislature is in session. **Amenities:** A/C, cable TV w/movies, refrig. Some units w/terraces, some w/whirlpools. **Services:** Babysitting. **Facilities:** 1200 1 restaurant (*see* "Restaurants" below), 1 bar, games rm, sauna, whirlpool, washer/dryer. **Rates:** $55–$150 S; $61–$150 D; $90–$150 ste; $55–$61 effic. Extra person $6. Children under age 18 stay free. Parking: Outdoor, free. AE, CB, DC, DISC, ER, MC, V.

Days Inn
520 W Sioux Ave, 57501; tel 605/224-0411 or toll free 800/DAYS-INN; fax 605/224-0411. This property has a small, beautifully furnished lobby. **Rooms:** 80 rms. CI noon/CO 11am. Nonsmoking rms avail. Rooms have color-coordinated furnishings; some have hot tubs. **Amenities:** A/C, cable TV w/movies. Some units w/whirlpools. **Services:** Babysitting. $5 charge for pets. **Facilities:** 20 **Rates (CP):** Peak (June–Aug) $35–$38 S; $40–$43 D. Extra person $5. Children under age 18 stay free. Lower rates off-season. Parking: Outdoor, free. Seventh-night-free package. AE, CB, DC, DISC, MC, V.

Governor's Inn
700 W Sioux Ave, 57501; tel 605/224-4200 or toll free 800/341-8000; fax 605/224-4200. Set on a busy street, this nicely painted motel has a well-manicured lawn and a small lobby. **Rooms:** 82 rms and stes. CI 2pm/CO noon. Nonsmoking rms avail. **Amenities:** A/C, cable TV w/movies. Some units w/terraces, some w/whirlpools. **Services:** **Facilities:** 60 Whirlpool, washer/dryer. **Rates:** $38 S; $49 D; $85 ste. Extra person $5. Children under age 19 stay free. Parking: Outdoor, free. Group rates avail. AE, DISC, MC, V.

Iron Horse Inn
205 W Pleasant Dr, 57501 (Business District); tel 605/224-5981; fax 605/224-7125. As its name suggests, this motel sits alongside railroad tracks. The trains still run, and yes, the whistle blows at every nearby intersection—even at 5am. Train memorabilia in the lobby gives a sense of the importance of the railroads to the development of the Plains. **Rooms:** 52 rms. CI 4pm/CO 11am. Nonsmoking rms avail. Clean, bright rooms with nice views. **Amenities:** A/C, cable TV, refrig, dataport. **Services:** Twice-daily maid svce. Wonderfully friendly and helpful staff. **Facilities:** 30 Washer/dryer. **Rates:** $32 S; $40 D. Extra person $4. Parking: Outdoor, free. AE, DC, DISC, MC, V.

RESTAURANT

River Centré Cafe
In Best Western Ramkota Inn, 920 W Sioux Ave (Business District); tel 605/224-6877. **American.** A pleasant, tastefully decorated cafe. The menu features chicken cordon bleu, prime rib, seafood, and salads. Buffets are open during evening hours. **FYI:** Reservations accepted. Children's menu. **Open:** Mon–Fri 6am–10pm, Sat–Sun 7am–10pm. **Prices:** Main courses $4–$14. AE, DC, DISC, MC, V.

ATTRACTION

South Dakota Cultural Heritage Center
900 Governors Dr; tel 605/773-3458. Anchored by *The South Dakota Experience,* a $3 million multimedia exhibition on the history of the state. The first phase, "Moving Up," covers the period from the first white explorers in the mid-1700s to statehood in 1889. Genuine stagecoaches and railroad cars, dioramas, and a video bring those early days to life. The second phase, "Oyate Tawicoh'an: The Ways of the People," explores Native American life before the pioneer settlements of the mid-1800s. (A third phase covering the 20th century is scheduled for completion in 1997.) **Open:** Mon–Fri 9am–4:30pm, Sat–Sun 1–4:30pm. Closed some hols. $

Rapid City

The second-largest city in South Dakota, Rapid City is the gateway to the Black Hills National Forest and the cultural center of the western part of the state. The city is a colorfully eclectic mixture of cowboy chic, Native American heritage, fine arts, funky music, and outdoor adventure. Ellsworth Air Force Base (home of the nation's second-largest fleet of B-1 bombers) is located seven miles east, as is the town of Box Elder. **Information:** Rapid City Convention and Visitors Bureau, PO Box 747, Rapid City, 57709 (tel 605/343-1744).

PUBLIC TRANSPORTATION

Rapid Transit System (RTS or RapidRide) (tel 605/394-6631) provides service throughout Rapid City with five routes. Buses run 6:15am–6:30pm Mon–Fri and 9:15–4:15pm on Sat. No Sun or holiday service. Fare: $1; seniors and persons with disabilties 50¢. Paratranist service available. Exact change required.

HOTELS

Alex Johnson Hotel
523 6th St, 57701 (Downtown); tel 605/342-1210 or toll free 800/888-ALEX; fax 605/342-1210. This downtown hotel, opened in 1928, was built by Alex Carton Johnson, the Vice President of the Chicago & Northwestern Railroad. Now on the National Register of Historic Places, it is known as "a shrine and tribute to the Sioux Indian Nation." The tall brick building features gables, awnings, and carvings of Native American chiefs on the exterior. Movie stars, such as Kevin Costner and Henry Fonda, have considered this their "home away from home" when filming in the Black Hills. **Rooms:** 142 rms and stes. CI 2pm/CO 11am. Nonsmoking rms avail. Rooms are small, clean, and beautifully decorated in a southwestern motif. **Amenities:** A/C, cable TV w/movies. **Services:** VP Masseur. The hotel seems understaffed. **Facilities:** 200 1 restaurant (*see* "Restaurants" below), 2 bars (1 w/entertainment). **Rates:** Peak (July–Sept) $39–$89 S; $45–$99 D; $110–$250 ste. Children under age 18 stay free. Lower rates off-season. Parking: Outdoor, free. AE, DC, DISC, MC, V.

Econo Lodge
625 E Disk Dr, 57701; tel 605/342-6400 or toll free 800/424-4777. 2 blocks N of exit 59 off I-90. This three-floor hotel has easy access to downtown. **Rooms:** 120 rms. CI 2pm/CO noon. Nonsmoking rms avail. Some rooms offer view of grassland. **Amenities:** A/C, cable TV. 1 unit w/whirlpool. **Services:** **Facilities:** Games rm, whirlpool, washer/dryer. Pool has 180-foot waterslide. **Rates:** Peak (May–Aug) $29–$199 S or D. Extra person $7. Lower rates off-season. Parking: Outdoor, free. Rates increase to $299/night during annual Harley-Davidson Motorcycle Rally (early Aug). AE, DISC, MC, V.

Holiday Inn Rushmore Plaza Hotel & Convention Center
505 N 5th St, 57701; tel 605/348-4000 or toll free 800/HOLIDAY; fax 605/348-9777. Next to Rushmore Plaza Civic Center. This five-year-old hotel has a nine-story atrium lobby with a multi-tiered waterfall and glass elevators. **Rooms:** 205 rms and stes. CI 4pm/CO noon. Nonsmoking rms avail. Average-size rooms have new furnishings. Rooms open to balcony-walkway overlooking atrium. **Amenities:** A/C, cable TV w/movies, dataport. 1 unit w/whirlpool. **Services:** Car-rental desk, babysitting. Pets permitted in smoking rooms only. VCR rentals available. UPS next-day package center. **Facilities:** 400 1 restaurant, 1 bar, sauna, steam rm, whirlpool, washer/dryer. Fitness center has new equipment. Beautifully furnished pool area. **Rates:** Peak (June–Aug) $74–$83 S; $89–$103 D; $105–$120 ste. Extra person $15. Children under age 18 stay free. Lower rates off-season. Parking: Outdoor, free. B&B package avail. AE, CB, DC, DISC, JCB, MC, V.

The Inn At Rapid City
445 Mount Rushmore Rd, 57701; tel 605/348-8300 or toll free 800/456-3750; fax 605/348-3833. 2 blocks S of Rushmore Plaza Civic Center. Located in the downtown area, this tired property is slated for a full renovation. Hall carpets are dirty and worn. **Rooms:** 176 rms and stes. Executive level. CI 3pm/CO 11am. Nonsmoking rms avail. **Amenities:** A/C, cable TV w/movies. **Services:** Masseur. **Facilities:** 200 1 restaurant, 1 bar (w/entertainment), games rm, whirlpool, beauty salon. **Rates:** Peak (June–Sept) $57–$103 S; $67–$113 D; $135–$220 ste. Extra person $10. Children under age 18 stay free. Lower rates off-season. Parking: Outdoor, free. Rates rise during annual Harley-Davidson motorcycle rally (early Aug). AE, CB, DC, DISC, MC, V.

MOTELS

Best Western Town 'N Country Inn
2505 Mt Rushmore Rd, 57701; tel 605/343-5383 or toll free 800/528-1234; fax 605/343-9670. "Foot" of US 16; leading

out to Blackhills. Nestled against a hillside, this red-brick building's lobby and surrounding grounds are noisy, but the rooms are quiet. **Rooms:** 100 rms and stes. CI 3pm/CO 11am. Nonsmoking rms avail. Small, clean rooms have new furniture, carpeting, and bathroom tile. **Amenities:** A/C, satel TV w/movies. **Services:** **Facilities:** 20 Whirlpool, playground. Spacious yard with grass, trees, and playground. Outdoor pool is clean but has limited deck space; the unattractive indoor pool is not well maintained. **Rates:** Peak (June–Aug) $35–$77 S; $45–$87 D; $80–$110 ste. Extra person $5. Children under age 12 stay free. Lower rates off-season. Parking: Outdoor, free. AE, CB, DC, DISC, MC, V.

Castle Inn

15 E North St, 57701; tel 605/348-4120 or toll free 800/658-5464. Two-story motel, located in heavily trafficked area, with easy access to nearby shopping center. **Rooms:** 20 rms, stes, and effic. CI 1pm/CO 11am. Nonsmoking rms avail. Older units with older furnishings. All have queen-size beds. Some rooms offer view of distant hills. **Amenities:** A/C, cable TV w/movies. Some units w/terraces. **Services:** Small pets $5/night, cribs $3/night. **Facilities:** **Rates (CP):** Peak (June–Aug) $70 S; $75 D; $60–$160 ste; $35–$85 effic. Extra person $5. Lower rates off-season. Parking: Outdoor, free. Rates increase to $189–$200 during annual Harley-Davidson Motorcycle Rally (early Aug). DISC, MC, V.

Comfort Inn

1550 N LaCrosse St, 57701; tel 605/348-2221 or toll free 800/221-2222; fax 605/348-3110. Exit 59 off I-90 2 block S. Small motel with comfortable lobby. **Rooms:** 71 rms. CI 2pm/CO 11am. Nonsmoking rms avail. **Amenities:** A/C, cable TV. **Services:** **Facilities:** 1 restaurant, games rm, whirlpool. Nicely landscaped pool area. **Rates:** Peak (June–Aug) $34–$99 S; $34–$149 D. Extra person $5. Children under age 18 stay free. Lower rates off-season. Parking: Outdoor, free. Room rates rise to $149 during annual Harley-Davidson motorcycle rally (early Aug). AE, CB, DC, DISC, MC, V.

Days Inn

125 Main St, 57701; tel 605/343-5501 or toll free 800/DAYS-INN; fax 605/343-4313. 3 blocks W of post office. Old building with basic, clean rooms located on a busy street. **Rooms:** 156 rms, stes, and effic. CI 2pm/CO 11am. Nonsmoking rms avail. **Amenities:** A/C, cable TV. **Services:** Babysitting. **Facilities:** 1000 1 restaurant, 2 bars, washer/dryer. **Rates:** Peak (May–Aug) $40–$90 S; $45–$95 D; $125–$150 ste; $50–$100 effic. Extra person $5. Children under age 17 stay free. Lower rates off-season. Parking: Outdoor, free. AE, CB, DC, DISC, MC, V.

Holiday Inn

1902 LaCrosse St, 57701; tel 605/348-1230 or toll free 800/HOLIDAY; fax 605/348-9212. Exit 59 off I-90. Two miles from downtown. Old, but well kept. **Rooms:** 211 rms. CI 2pm/CO noon. Nonsmoking rms avail. **Amenities:** A/C, cable TV w/movies. **Services:** Car-rental desk, babysitting. **Facilities:** 200 1 restaurant, 1 bar, games rm, whirlpool, washer/dryer. Nicely landscaped indoor pool area with good furniture on deck. **Rates:** Peak (June–Aug) $58–$84 S; $68–$94 D. Extra person $10. Children under age 19 stay free. Lower rates off-season. Parking: Outdoor, free. AE, CB, DC, DISC, JCB, MC, V.

Howard Johnson Lodge

2211 LaCrosse St, 57701; tel 605/343-8550 or toll free 800/446-4656; fax 605/343-9107. Exit 59 off I-90 (northwest side of interstate) 1 block E of Rushmore Mall. Easy access to business loop. **Rooms:** 272 rms and stes. Executive level. CI 4pm/CO noon. Nonsmoking rms avail. **Amenities:** A/C. Some units w/terraces. **Services:** Car-rental desk, social director, babysitting. **Facilities:** 1500 1 restaurant, 1 bar (w/entertainment), spa, sauna, whirlpool, playground, washer/dryer. Large patio area around pool. **Rates:** Peak (June–Aug) $40–$80 S; $50–$90 D; $95–$150 ste. Extra person $8. Children under age 18 stay free. Lower rates off-season. Parking: Outdoor, free. AE, CB, DC, DISC, MC, V.

Quality Inn Mt Rushmore

2208 Mount Rushmore Rd, 57701; tel 605/342-3322 or toll free 800/228-5151; fax 605/342-9005. Take I-90 to exit 57. An old but well-kept property on a busy street, this place is best for businesspeople. **Rooms:** 109 rms and effic. CI 3pm/CO 11am. Nonsmoking rms avail. Small rooms. **Amenities:** A/C, cable TV w/movies, refrig. **Services:** Social director, babysitting. **Facilities:** 1 restaurant, 2 bars. Outdoor outlets for winter plug-ins for cars. Pool area noisy and has some maintenance problems. **Rates:** Peak (June–Aug) $29–$89 S; $39–$99 D; $39–$99 effic. Extra person $10. Children under age 18 stay free. Lower rates off-season. Parking: Outdoor, free. Rates increase to $129–$139 a night during the annual Harley-Davidson motorcycle rally (early Aug). AE, DC, DISC, MC, V.

Ramada Inn

1721 LaCrosse St, 57701; tel 605/342-1300 or toll free 800/RAMADA; fax 605/342-0663. ½ block south of exit 59 off I-90 E or W; 3 blocks SE of Rushmore Mall. On a busy street, with a spacious lobby decorated in a hunting motif. **Rooms:** 140 rms and stes. CI 2pm/CO noon. Nonsmoking rms avail. **Amenities:** A/C, cable TV w/movies. **Services:** Babysitting. VCRs available at front desk. **Facilities:** 350 1 restaurant, 1 bar, games rm, whirlpool. Waterslide in nicely kept pool. **Rates:** Peak (May–Aug) $54–$129 S; $59–$139 D; $89–$195 ste. Extra person $10. Children under age 18 stay free. Lower rates off-season. Parking: Outdoor, free. AE, CB, DC, DISC, MC, V.

Rushmore Inn

5410 US 16 (Mount Rushmore Rd), 57702; tel 605/343-4700 or toll free 800/698-1676. 1½ mi S of Rapid City.

Older but well-maintained building located outside of city. **Rooms:** 60 rms. CI 2pm/CO noon. Nonsmoking rms avail. New rooms are more desirable than older ones; some have view of distant Black Hills. **Amenities:** A/C, satel TV w/movies. All units w/terraces. **Services:** **Facilities:** 1 restaurant, 1 bar, playground. Casino. **Rates:** $30–$60 S; $50–$80 D. Children under age 12 stay free. Parking: Outdoor, free. Rates may increase during annual Harley-Davidson Motorcycle Rally (early Aug). Guests staying three or more nights get $5 discount per night on entire stay. AE, CB, DC, DISC, MC, V.

Stables Motel
518 E Omaha, 57701; tel 605/342-9241 or toll free 800/874-6435. 3 blocks N of County Fairgrounds. An old building on a busy street. Nothing more than a place to sleep. **Rooms:** 19 rms and effic. CI 2pm/CO 10am. No smoking. Nonsmoking rms avail. Old furnishings, but clean. **Amenities:** A/C, cable TV. **Services:** **Facilities:** Washer/dryer. Poorly maintained pool. **Rates:** Peak (June–Aug) $24–$65 S; $34–$70 D; $85 effic. Extra person $5. Lower rates off-season. Parking: Outdoor, free. Rates rise during the County Fair and the annual Harley-Davidson motorcycle rally (early Aug). AE, DISC, MC, V.

Sunburst Inn
620 Howard St, 57701; tel 605/343-5434 or toll free 800/456-0061. At exit 58 off I-90 E or W. Three-story motel located in a busy district. **Rooms:** 98 rms. CI 2pm/CO 11am. Nonsmoking rms avail. Somewhat noisy rooms have older but clean furnishings. **Amenities:** A/C, cable TV. **Services:** **Facilities:** **Rates:** Peak (June–Aug) $20–$59 S; $26–$79 D. Extra person $5. Children under age 17 stay free. Lower rates off-season. Parking: Outdoor, free. AE, CB, DC, DISC, MC, V.

Super 8 Lodge
2520 Tower Rd, 57701; tel 605/342-4911 or toll free 800/800-8000; fax 605/342-4911 ext 700. South edge of Rapid City near US 16. A no-frills motel with easy access to Mount Rushmore and surrounding Black Hills area. **Rooms:** 101 rms. CI 11am/CO 11am. Nonsmoking rms avail. **Amenities:** A/C, cable TV. **Services:** **Facilities:** 6 **Rates (CP):** Peak (June–Aug) $27–$77 S; $34–$92 D. Extra person $5. Lower rates off-season. Parking: Outdoor, free. Rates increase $10/night during annual Harley-Davidson Motorcycle Rally (early Aug). AE, DC, DISC, MC, V.

Tip Top Motel
405 St Joseph St, 57701; tel 605/343-3901 or toll free 800/341-8000; fax 605/343-3901. Next to County Courthouse. Old but clean property in busy commercial district. No lobby. **Rooms:** 62 rms and effic. CI noon/CO 11am. Nonsmoking rms avail. Rooms face street traffic or alley behind motel. **Amenities:** A/C, cable TV. **Services:** **Facilities:** 1 bar, washer/dryer. Small microwave and refrigerator in hallway. Lounge area with table and chairs on second floor. **Rates:** Peak (June–Aug) $29–$59 S; $40–$80 D; $56–$83 effic. Extra person $6. Lower rates off-season. Parking: Outdoor, free. AE, CB, DC, DISC, MC, V.

RESTAURANTS

Carini's
324 St Joseph St; tel 605/348-3704. Across from County Courthouse. **Italian.** A mural depicting an Italianate landscape sets the scene for stromboli, spaghetti, manicotti, stuffed shells Florentine, lasagna, and pizza. Lunch buffet on weekdays. **FYI:** Reservations accepted. Children's menu. Beer and wine only. No smoking. **Open:** Peak (June–Sept) lunch Mon–Sat 11am–3pm; dinner Mon–Sat 3–10pm, Sun 4–9pm. **Prices:** Main courses $6–$11; prix fixe $9. AE, DC, DISC, MC, V.

★ **Firehouse Brewing Co**
610 Main St (Downtown); tel 605/348-1915. **Burgers/Pub.** A brewpub in a remodeled 1915 firehouse, with brewing kettles visible through floor-to-ceiling windows. Eclectic pub grub includes English pot pies, pasta, steak, seafood, burgers, burritos, and salads. Famous beer bread. Tasting sampler of current house brews for $3. **FYI:** Reservations not accepted. Children's menu. **Open:** Lunch Mon–Sat 11am–4pm; dinner Mon–Sun 4–9pm. **Prices:** Main courses $7–$14. AE, CB, DC, DISC, MC, V.

Landmark Restaurant
In Alex Johnson Hotel, 523 6th St; tel 605/342-1210. **Regional American.** Located in a historic landmark building, the restaurant has brick walls adorned with American Indian artifacts, pictures, and carvings. The menu offers traditional choices of chicken and beef accompanied by mashed potatoes and gravy. **FYI:** Reservations accepted. Children's menu. **Open:** Breakfast daily 6–11am; lunch daily 11am–2pm; dinner daily 5–10pm; brunch Sun 10am–2pm. **Prices:** Main courses $6.95–$16.95. AE, CB, DC, DISC, MC, V.

Mediterranean Islands Restaurant
523 Main; tel 605/394-7727. **Mediterranean.** This small, cozy, bright restaurant has a pleasant, appetite-inspiring, herb/spice scent floating in the air. Menu choices include salads, pasta, chicken, and lamb, all prepared with Mediterranean influences. **FYI:** Reservations accepted. Beer and wine only. **Open:** Peak (June–Aug) lunch Mon–Fri 11am–2pm, Sat 11am–10pm; dinner Mon–Fri 5–9pm, Sat 11am–10pm. **Prices:** Main courses $7.95–$12.95. AE, MC, V.

Pirates Table
3550 Sturgis Rd; tel 605/341-4842. At W Chicago St. **Seafood/Steak.** In keeping with its name, this restaurant is decorated with a nautical theme: a large mural, paintings of ships, and seascapes that cover the rock walls. Booths and tables are divided by plants for privacy. Seafood, steaks,

prime rib. **FYI:** Reservations not accepted. Children's menu. **Open:** Mon–Thurs 5–8:30pm, Fri–Sat 5–9pm. **Prices:** Main courses $9–$30; prix fixe $9–$12. DISC, MC, V.

Purple Frog Smoke House and Lounge
710 St Joseph (Downtown); tel 605/348-5210. **American.** Decorated with pictures of frogs, statues of frogs, and frog-shaped cast-iron sugar bowls. The menu features burgers and fries, steak, and breaded shrimp. The house specialty is smoked barbecue ribs and, yes, they also serve frogs' legs. **FYI:** Reservations accepted. **Open:** Peak (June–Aug) Tues–Sat 10am–10pm. **Prices:** Main courses $11–$15. AE, DISC, MC, V.

✱ Sixth Street Deli & Bakery
516 6th St; tel 605/342-6660. Across from Alex Johnson Hotel. **Deli.** A fire engine red ceiling, lofty space, and a gently turning ceiling fan set the tone. Menu choices include spinach lasagna, vegetable or meat quiches, soups, pasta salads, and sandwiches. The coffee bar, which serves espresso and pastries, is a favorite local hangout. **FYI:** Reservations not accepted. No liquor license. No smoking. **Open:** Mon–Wed 7am–6pm, Thurs–Sat 7am–8pm, Sun 10am–4pm. **Prices:** Main courses $2–$5. No CC.

✱ The Uptown Grill
615 Main St (Downtown); tel 605/343-1942. Across from Prairie Edge Galleries. **American.** Housed in a recently renovated historic building, and decorated with memorabilia from the 1950s and '60s. Hamburgers, soups, and a variety of salads. Weekend jazz performances make this place popular with locals. **FYI:** Reservations not accepted. Blues/jazz. Beer and wine only. **Open:** Peak (June–Aug) Mon–Wed 11am–midnight, Thurs–Sat 11am–2am. **Prices:** Main courses $6–$17; prix fixe $5–$6. DC, DISC, MC, V.

ATTRACTIONS

Dahl Fine Arts Center
7th and Quincy Sts; tel 605/394-4101. Three galleries with separate exhibits. The Cyclorama Gallery depicts two centuries of US history via a 180-foot, oil-on-canvas panorama enhanced with special lighting and narration; the Dakota Art Gallery features the work of local and regional painters, potters, sculptors, jewelers, hand-cast papermakers, stained glass workers, and basket-makers; and the Central Gallery features world-class contemporary and Native American artwork. **Open:** Sept–May, Mon–Sat 9am–5pm, Sun 1–5pm; June–Aug, Mon–Thurs 9am–7pm, Fri–Sat 9am–5pm, Sun 1–5pm. Closed some hols. **Free**

South Dakota Air and Space Museum
2890 Davis Dr, Box Elder; tel 605/385-5189. Located at the entrance to Ellsworth Air Force Base, one of the largest operational bases in the country. (Tours of the base leave from the museum, daily from mid-May to mid-September, for a nominal fee.) The museum houses 23 vintage aircraft, including a 3/5 scale model of the Honda Stealth Bomber and Gen Eisenhower's personal B-25 bomber from World War II. Other highlights include a UH1F helicopter used in Vietnam and several Minuteman and Titan missiles. Uniforms, aviation gear, and war memorabilia are also displayed. Gift shop. **Open:** May–Sept, daily 8:30am–6pm; Oct–Apr, daily 8:30am–4:30pm. Closed some hols. **Free**

Sioux Indian Museum
515 West Blvd; tel 605/348-0557. One of the highlights of this museum's permanent collection is an extensive display of everyday clothing and ceremonial costumes as worn by Sioux men, women, and children during the past two centuries. Other areas are devoted to decorated horse gear, weaponry, household utensils, teepee decorations, papoose carriers, children's games, and musical instruments. Contemporary Native American arts and crafts are featured in two special exhibition galleries, and are offered for sale in the museum's gift shop. **Open:** June–Sept, Mon–Sat 9am–5pm, Sun 1–5pm; Oct–May, Tues–Sat 10am–5pm, Sun 1–5pm. Closed some hols. **Free**

Museum of Geology
501 E St Joseph St; tel 605/394-2467 or toll free 800/544-8162. Located on the campus of the South Dakota School of Mines and Technology. Permanent collection includes minerals from the Black Hills, Badlands fossils, prehistoric shells, and reptile skeletons. **Open:** Mem Day–Labor Day, Mon–Sat 8am–6pm, Sun noon–6pm; Labor Day–Mem Day, Mon–Fri 8am–5pm, Sat 9am–4pm, Sun 1–4pm. Closed some hols. **Free**

Marine Life Aquarium
6001 S US 16; tel 605/343-7400. Aquarium houses sharks, moray eels, tropical fish, and a family of Megellan penguins. Outdoor arena with sea lion and porpoise shows. **Open:** May 15–Sept 15, daily 8am–7pm. **$$$**

Black Hills Reptile Gardens
US 16; tel 605/342-5873. Located 6 mi S of Rapid City. There's much more than lizards, snakes, turtles, and crocodiles at this 40-acre park. The Wings of Adventure show features hawks, owls, and falcons, while the unique residents of Bewitched Village include Poker Alice, the card-playing chicken. The Sky Dome, filled with tropical plants, is home to the Safari Room, with its colorful finches, doves, and many types of parrots. Kids can ride the miniature horses and giant tortoises. A gift shop sells gifts and souvenirs of all types: rocks and minerals, figurines, T-shirts, jewelry, and more. **Open:** Spring and fall, daily 9am–5pm; summer, daily 7am–8pm. Closed Oct 31–Apr 1. **$$$**

Bear Country USA
US 16; tel 605/343-2290. Drive-through wildlife reserve featuring native North American animals such as bears, wolves, cougar, buffalo, and elk. Visitors stay in their completely closed cars for up-close encounters with the free roaming animals. Barnyard animal petting area; bear cub viewing area. **Open:** May–Oct, daily 8am–dusk. **$$$**

Black Hills Caverns
2600 Cavern Rd; tel 605/343-0542. 4 mi W of Rapid City. Striking cave formations include stalagmites, stalactites, rare frost crystal, amethyst, dogtooth spar, and cave flowers. Three different guided tours (leaving approximately every 20 minutes) are available, ranging in difficulty from easy to strenuous. Gift and rock shop, snack bar, museum, and picnic area. **Open:** May–mid-Oct, daily 8am–8pm. **$$**

Rockerville

Rockerville's turn-of-the-century charm, and its proximity to Custer State Park and Mount Rushmore, make it a popular tourist destination.

RESTAURANT

The Gas Light
13490 Main St; tel 605/343-9276. **Burgers.** Located in the center of an old gold-mining town, the restaurant offers steak, chicken, seafood, and pasta. There is an on-premises saloon, old-fashioned soda parlor, candy shop, and antique shop. **FYI:** Reservations accepted. Children's menu. **Open:** Peak (June–Aug) Wed–Sun 11am–9pm. **Prices:** Main courses $6–$16; prix fixe $7–$11. AE, DISC, MC, V.

Sioux Falls

The largest city in South Dakota, Sioux Falls is a perennial favorite on lists of the most livable cities in America. Named after the Falls of the Big Sioux River, Sioux Falls is now a retail hub and cultural center. The Pettigrew Museum, The Old Courthouse Museum, an historic downtown district, and first-class dining and theater are just a few of the finer points that prove the prairie can indeed be cosmopolitan. **Information:** Sioux Falls Convention and Visitors Bureau, 200 N Phillips, PO Box 1425, Sioux Falls, 57102 (tel 605/336-1620).

HOTELS

Holiday Inn City Center
100 W 8th St, 57102; tel 605/339-2000 or toll free 800/HOLIDAY; fax 605/339-3724. Between Phillips and Main Sts. A full renovation of this conveniently located downtown property is almost complete. **Rooms:** 302 rms and stes. Executive level. CI 3pm/CO noon. Nonsmoking rms avail. Nicely decorated with all-new carpet, bedspreads, and drapes. **Amenities:** A/C, cable TV w/movies, dataport, voice mail. **Services:** VP VCRs available. Transportation to area restaurants. **Facilities:** 1000 1 restaurant, games rm, sauna, whirlpool. Passes to local health club. **Rates:** Peak (June–Aug) $54 S; $58–$64 D; $78–$178 ste. Extra person $6. Children under age 18 stay free. Lower rates off-season. Parking: Indoor/outdoor, free. AE, DC, DISC, MC, V.

Radisson Encore Inn
4300 Empire Place, 57116; tel 605/361-6684 or toll free 800/333-3333; fax 605/361-6684. Exit 77 E off I-29. This beautifully decorated hotel is the most stylish in Sioux Falls. **Rooms:** 106 rms and stes. Executive level. CI 3pm/CO noon. Nonsmoking rms avail. **Amenities:** A/C, cable TV w/movies, dataport, bathrobes. Some units w/whirlpools. **Services:** Twice-daily maid svce. Limo and van services available. **Facilities:** 360 1 restaurant, 1 bar. Passes to local health club. **Rates:** $65–$72 S; $69–$83 D; $175 ste. Extra person $7. Children under age 18 stay free. Parking: Outdoor, free. Corporate rates avail. AE, DC, DISC, MC, V.

MOTELS

Best Western Town House
400 S Main Ave, 57101; tel 605/336-2740 or toll free 800/888-2594; fax 605/336-7846. At 12th St. Convenient downtown location attracts a lot of bus-tour business. Decor needs updating. **Rooms:** 44 rms. CI 2pm/CO noon. Nonsmoking rms avail. **Amenities:** A/C, cable TV. **Services:** **Facilities:** 75 1 restaurant, 1 bar. Good Italian restaurant. **Rates (CP):** Peak (June–Aug) $44–$46 S; $48–$64 D. Extra person $8. Children under age 16 stay free. Lower rates off-season. Parking: Outdoor, free. AE, DC, DISC, MC, V.

Brimark Inn
3200 W Russell St, 57107; tel 605/332-2000 or toll free 800/658-4508; fax 605/332-2000. Exit 8 off I-29 to Easton Service Road 38. Budget-priced, standard motel rooms. **Rooms:** 107 rms. CI 2pm/CO 11am. Nonsmoking rms avail. **Amenities:** A/C, cable TV w/movies. **Services:** **Facilities:** 50 Whirlpool, washer/dryer. Very clean outdoor heated pool. **Rates:** $36–$48 S; $44–$56 D. Parking: Outdoor, free. AE, DISC, MC, V.

Comfort Inn South
3216 S Carolyn Ave, 57106; tel 605/361-2822 or toll free 800/228-5150; fax 605/361-2822. Exit 77 off I-29. Clean, neat, average-size rooms. Near I-29 and shopping mall. **Rooms:** 67 rms. CI 3pm/CO 11am. Nonsmoking rms avail. **Amenities:** A/C, cable TV. **Services:** **Facilities:** 20 Games rm, whirlpool. **Rates (CP):** $44–$61 S; $49–$70 D. Extra person $5. Children under age 18 stay free. Parking: Outdoor, free. AE, DC, DISC, MC, V.

Comfort Suites
3208 Carolyn Ave, 57106; tel 605/362-9711 or toll free 800/221-2222; fax 605/362-9711. Exit 77 off I-29. Extra-large accommodations; attractive lobby. **Rooms:** 61 rms. CI 3pm/CO 11am. Nonsmoking rms avail. All units have sofa and two beds. **Amenities:** A/C, cable TV, refrig. All units have

microwave. **Services:** **Facilities:** Games rm, whirlpool. **Rates (CP):** $66–$76 S or D. Extra person $5. Children under age 17 stay free. Parking: Outdoor, free. AE, DC, DISC, JCB, MC, V.

Days Inn North
5001 N Cliff Ave, 57104; tel 605/331-5959 or toll free 800/325-2525; fax 605/331-5959. Exit 399 off I-90. Standard, budget-priced rooms. **Rooms:** 86 rms. CI 2pm/CO noon. Nonsmoking rms avail. Bathrooms could use more thorough cleaning. **Amenities:** A/C, cable TV. **Services:** **Facilities:** **Rates (CP):** Peak (June–Sept) $45–$53 S; $48–$65 D. Extra person $5. Children under age 12 stay free. Lower rates off-season. Parking: Outdoor, free. AE, DC, DISC, MC, V.

Fairfield Inn
4501 W Empire Plaza, 57116; tel 605/361-2211 or toll free 800/228-2800; fax 605/361-2211. Exit 77 off I-29. Opened in 1994. Convenient to shopping and I-29. **Rooms:** 63 rms. CI 2pm/CO 11am. Nonsmoking rms avail. **Amenities:** A/C, cable TV, dataport. **Services:** **Facilities:** Games rm, whirlpool. Passes to local wellness center. **Rates (CP):** Peak (June–Aug) $52 S; $57 D. Extra person $6. Children under age 17 stay free. Lower rates off-season. Parking: Outdoor, free. AE, DISC, MC, V.

Howard Johnson Hotel
3300 W Russell, 57101; tel 605/336-9000 or toll free 800/446-4656; fax 605/336-9000. Exit 81 off I-29. Basic chain motel. **Rooms:** 200 rms and stes. Executive level. CI noon/CO 11am. Nonsmoking rms avail. **Amenities:** A/C, cable TV w/movies. Some units w/terraces. Morning coffee and newspaper available. **Services:** **Facilities:** 1 restaurant, 1 bar (w/entertainment), games rm, sauna, playground, washer/dryer. **Rates:** $55–$72 S; $55–$76 D; $85 ste. Extra person $6. Children under age 18 stay free. Parking: Outdoor, free. Rates are higher on weekends. 15% discount for senior citizens. AE, DISC, MC, V.

Kelly Inn
3101 W Russell, 57118; tel 605/338-6242 or toll free 800/635-3559; fax 605/338-6242. Exit 81 off I-29 on Service road 38. Clean and comfortable property convenient to I-29, the airport, and convention facilities. **Rooms:** 42 rms. CI 11am/CO 11am. Nonsmoking rms avail. **Amenities:** A/C, cable TV. Some units w/whirlpools. **Services:** Coffee, cocoa, and fruit available in lobby. Extra charge for pets. **Facilities:** Sauna, whirlpool, playground, washer/dryer. Guest privileges at indoor pool (free) and racquetball court (small fee) of nearby hotel. **Rates:** $46 S; $44–$75 D. Extra person $5. Children under age 12 stay free. Parking: Outdoor, free. AE, CB, DC, DISC, MC, V.

Ramada Limited
407 S Lyons Ave, 57107; tel 605/330-0000 or toll free 800/272-6232; fax 605/330-0402. Exit 79 off I-29. Opened in 1994, it's neat and clean—the best facility near the fairgrounds. **Rooms:** 67 rms and stes. CI 3pm/CO 11am. Nonsmoking rms avail. **Amenities:** A/C, cable TV, refrig, dataport. Some units w/whirlpools. All units have microwaves. **Services:** **Facilities:** Whirlpool, washer/dryer. **Rates (CP):** Peak (June–Aug) $55–$65 S; $57–$67 D; $129–$139 ste. Extra person $5. Children under age 18 stay free. Lower rates off-season. Parking: Outdoor, free. AE, CB, DC, DISC, ER, V.

Select Inn
3500 Gateway Blvd, 57106; tel 605/361-1864 or toll free 800/641-1000; fax 605/361-9287. Exit 77 off I-29. An older motel in need of renovation, but sufficient for a budget-minded traveler wanting few frills. **Rooms:** 100 rms and stes. CI 2pm/CO 11am. Nonsmoking rms avail. The best room in the house is the suite, which offers a full kitchen. **Amenities:** A/C, cable TV. **Services:** **Facilities:** **Rates (CP):** $29 S; $35 D; $63 ste. Children under age 12 stay free. Parking: Outdoor, free. AE, CB, DC, DISC, MC, V.

RESTAURANTS

Minervas
301 S Phillips Ave; tel 605/334-0386. **New American.** Known for a varied menu and superior service. Salad bar, pastas, steaks, seafood. **FYI:** Reservations recommended. Children's menu. Additional location: 1716 S Western (tel 334-7491). **Open:** Lunch Mon–Sat 11am–2:30pm; dinner Mon–Thurs 5:30–10pm, Fri 5–10pm, Sat 5–11pm. **Prices:** Main courses $11–$20. AE, DC, DISC, MC, V.

Sioux Falls Brewery
431 N Phillips; tel 605/332-4847. **New American.** Located in a remodeled historic building, this microbrewery/restaurant serves up four different homebrews to accompany the barbecued ribs, prime rib, or coconut-fried shrimp, as well as sandwiches and salads. **FYI:** Reservations recommended. Blues/guitar/jazz/piano. **Open:** Lunch daily 11am–2pm; dinner daily 5–10pm. **Prices:** Main courses $10–$19. AE, DISC, MC, V.

Theo's
601 W 33rd; tel 605/338-6801. 1 block W of Minnesota Ave. **New American.** A modern and stylish bistro offering a wide selection of seafood, pastas, and other items. Rack of lamb is the house specialty. Concerts are occasionally held on the patio. **FYI:** Reservations recommended. Children's menu. **Open:** Lunch Mon–Sat 11am–2pm; dinner Mon–Thurs 5–10pm, Fri–Sat 5–11pm; brunch Sun 10am–2pm. **Prices:** Main courses $11–$20. AE, DISC, MC, V.

ATTRACTIONS

The Old Courthouse Museum
200 W 6th St; tel 605/335-4210. Built in 1890 out of locally quarried Sioux quartzite and completed in 1890, the Courthouse was in use by Minnehaha County until 1962. Twelve years later, the building was restored and reopened as a

museum dedicated to the natural and cultural history of the area. Hallways are embellished with scenic murals; a courtroom and law library on the second floor have been restored to their original appearance. **Open:** Tues–Sat 9am–5pm, Sun 1–5pm. Closed some hols. **Free**

Civic Fine Arts Center
235 W 10th St; tel 605/336-1167. Housed in the historic Carnegie Library (circa 1902), this visual arts center features collections of national, regional, and South Dakota art, including Native American polished blackware bowls, sculpture, and paintings. **Open:** Mon–Fri 9am–5pm, Sat 10am–5pm, Sun 1–5pm. Closed some hols. **Free**

Great Plains Zoo and Delbridge Museum
805 S Kiwanis Ave; tel 605/339-7059. Many unusual animals—from Siberian tigers to black-footed penguins—thrive in the extreme climate of South Dakota, with its hot summers and cold winters. Visitors to this zoo can experience the wild recesses of an African veldt and the serene beauty of the Australian Outback, all in the middle of the North American plains. A "Wild Dogs of America" exhibit and Grizzly Bear Canyon represent the zoo's wild-west surroundings. The **Delbridge Museum** houses a collection of mounted birds and mammals from five continents of the world. **Open:** Apr–Oct, daily 9am–6pm; Nov–Mar, Sat–Sun 10am–4pm. Closed Dec 25. **$$**

Sisseton

MOTEL

I-29 Motel
E SD 10, PO Box 190A Rte 1, 57262; tel 605/698-4314 or toll free 800/341-8000. 1 mile W of I-29. A low-priced motel with appealing, countryside ambience despite being close to the highway. **Rooms:** 29 rms. CI noon/CO 11am. No smoking. Fairly sizeable, neat rooms. **Amenities:** A/C, cable TV. **Services:** **Facilities:** **Rates:** $25–$29 S; $32–$40 D. Extra person $4. Children under age 6 stay free. Parking: Outdoor, free. AE, DC, DISC, MC, V.

Spearfish

Nestled in a broad valley on the northern edge of the Black Hills, Spearfish is naturally busy with events like the Festival in the Park in July and the Christmas Stroll in December. National Forest Scenic Byway (US 14A) meanders through beautiful Spearfish Canyon. **Information:** Spearfish Area Chamber of Commerce, 115 E Hudson, PO Box 550, Spearfish, 57738 (tel 605/642-7310).

MOTELS

Best Western Downtown Spearfish
346 W Kansas St, 57783; tel 605/642-4676 or toll free 800/528-1234; fax 605/642-5314. 3 blocks W of Main St. Older motel located in relatively quiet residential area. **Rooms:** 33 rms. CI 4pm/CO 10am. Nonsmoking rms avail. **Amenities:** A/C, cable TV. **Services:** **Facilities:** Games rm, whirlpool, washer/dryer. **Rates (CP):** Peak (June–Aug) $40–$80 S or D. Extra person $5. Children under age 19 stay free. Lower rates off-season. Parking: Outdoor, free. Rates increase during annual Harley-Davidson Motorcycle Rally (early Aug). AE, CB, DC, DISC, MC, V.

Days Inn
240 Ryan Rd, 57783; tel 605/642-7101 or toll free 800/DAYS-INN; fax 605/642-7120. 1 block E of Main St. Clean, comfortable, lodging. Well maintained. **Rooms:** 50 rms and stes. CI 2pm/CO 11am. Nonsmoking rms avail. Some noise in the west rooms. **Amenities:** A/C, cable TV w/movies. 1 unit w/whirlpool. **Services:** Free coffee in lobby. **Facilities:** Sauna, whirlpool, washer/dryer. **Rates (CP):** Peak (June–Sept) $35–$65 S; $40–$70 D; $65–$80 ste. Extra person $5. Children under age 13 stay free. Lower rates off-season. Parking: Outdoor, free. Snowmobile packages avail. Rates increase during annual Harley-Davidson Motorcycle Rally (early Aug). AE, CB, DC, DISC, MC, V.

Fairfield Inn
2720 1st Ave E, 57783; tel 605/642-3500 or toll free 800/228-2800; fax 605/642-3500. Exit 14 off I-90. Nice motel located east of town. **Rooms:** 57 rms and stes. CI 3pm/CO 11am. Nonsmoking rms avail. Clean and fresh with new furnishings; some rooms offer a view of grasslands and hills. **Amenities:** A/C, cable TV w/movies. 1 unit w/whirlpool. **Services:** Masseur. **Facilities:** 14 Games rm, whirlpool. **Rates (CP):** Peak (May–Labor Day) $40–$65 S; $45–$80 D; $55–$90 ste. Extra person $5. Children under age 19 stay free. Lower rates off-season. Parking: Outdoor, free. AE, CB, DC, DISC, MC, V.

Holiday Inn Northern Black Hills
I-90 and US 14A, 57783; tel 605/642-4683 or toll free 800/HOLIDAY; fax 605/642-4683 ext 101. Exit 14 off I-90. Clean, well-decorated, average-size rooms. Spacious lobby with a French country motif. **Rooms:** 160 rms. CI 4pm/CO noon. Nonsmoking rms avail. Some have view of pool, some have view of rolling hills and grasslands. **Amenities:** A/C, cable TV. Some units w/terraces. Some units have coffeemakers and hair dryers. **Services:** Social director. Fax service. **Facilities:** 700 1 restaurant, 1 bar, games rm, spa, whirlpool, washer/dryer. Well-maintained pool area with large deck and plants; two whirlpools. Children under 12 eat free in restaurant. **Rates:** Peak (June–Aug) $50–$82 S; $57–$89 D. Extra person $7. Children under age 19 stay free. Lower rates off-season. Parking: Outdoor, free.

Senior rates avail. Rates increase during annual Harley-Davidson Motorcycle Rally (early Aug). AE, DC, DISC, JCB, MC, V.

Kelly Inn
540 E Jackson, 57783; tel 605/642-7795 or toll free 800/635-3559; fax 605/642-7795. Exit 12 off I-90. A relatively quiet, comfortable motel with beautifully furnished rooms. **Rooms:** 50 rms. CI noon/CO 11am. Nonsmoking rms avail. **Amenities:** A/C, cable TV w/movies. Some units w/whirlpools. **Services:** Pet fee $5. **Facilities:** Sauna, whirlpool, washer/dryer. Hot tub room with ceramic-tile floor, arched ceiling, and plants. **Rates:** Peak (June–Aug) $35–$55 S; $40–$80 D. Extra person $5. Children under age 13 stay free. Lower rates off-season. Parking: Outdoor, free. AE, CB, DC, DISC, MC, V.

RESTAURANTS

Bay Leaf Café
126 W Hudson (Downtown); tel 605/642-5462. 1 block west of Main St. **American.** A nice surprise, with high ceilings, tile floors, and works by regional artists. Menu choices include specialty omelettes, veggie sandwiches, salads, pastas, chicken, beef, and seafood dishes. Espresso and cappuccino drinks. **FYI:** Reservations accepted. Beer and wine only. No smoking. **Open:** Daily 8am–10pm. **Prices:** Main courses $6–$11; prix fixe $7–$12. AE, DISC, MC, V.

Cedar House Restaurant
130 E Ryan Rd; tel 605/642-2104. North end of Main St. **American.** The cedar-siding walls and a down-home cooking aroma create a casual, welcoming feeling. Menu picks are beef, seafood pasta, and chicken fajitas. **FYI:** Reservations accepted. Children's menu. Beer and wine only. **Open:** Daily 6am–10pm. **Prices:** Main courses $6–$10; prix fixe $7–$10. CB, DC, DISC, MC, V.

ATTRACTIONS

The Black Hills Passion Play
Off I-90; tel 605/642-2646 or toll free 800/622-8383. A reconstruction of the last week of the life of Christ, this Passion Play has been performed in Germany since the Middle Ages and in South Dakota since 1939. The play lasts 2¼ hours and features a cast of 25 professional actors, 150 nonspeaking extras, and scores of live camels, goats, and sheep. Outdoor amphitheater (billed as the world's largest) seats 6,400 people. Gift shop, museum, and backstage tours available; call for details. **Open:** June–Aug, performances at 8pm on Sun, Tues, and Thurs. **$$$$**

Matthews Opera House
614 ½ Main St; tel 605/642-7973. Ornate opera house built in 1906 boasts ornate boxes, gilt moldings, and ceiling murals featuring Edwin Booth, Joseph Jefferson, and William Shakespeare. The theater now houses a year-round performing arts center; call for schedule. **$$$**

Tri State Memorial Museum
831 State St, Belle Fourche; tel 605/892-3654. Natural history exhibits and artifacts from Wyoming, Montana, and South Dakota. Native American arrowheads and beadwork, pioneer farm implements and musical instruments, cowboy saddles, dolls and toys, and an array of prehistoric fossils round out the collection. **Open:** May 15–June 1 and Sept 1–15, daily 2–8pm; June–Aug, daily 8am–8pm. Closed Labor Day. **Free**

Sturgis

For one week each year, this small agricultural community becomes Motorcycle City, USA. The annual Sturgis Rally & Races draws thousands each year, from famous bike-riding celebrities to not-so-famous weekend warriors. **Information:** Sturgis Chamber of Commerce, 606 Anna St, PO Box 504, Sturgis, 57785 (tel 605/347-2556).

MOTELS

Best Western Phil Town Inn
2431 S Junction St, 57785; tel 605/347-3604 or toll free 800/528-1234; fax 605/347-2376. Exit 32 off I-90. Older motel located in busy district near the interstate. **Rooms:** 56 rms and stes. CI 2pm/CO 11am. Nonsmoking rms avail. Some rooms have poolside views. Rooms facing interstate are very noisy. **Amenities:** A/C, cable TV. Some units w/terraces. **Services:** **Facilities:** 200 1 restaurant (*see* "Restaurants" below), 1 bar, games rm, sauna, washer/dryer. **Rates:** Peak (June–Aug) $35–$74 S; $45–$84 D; $55–$94 ste. Extra person $5. Children under age 13 stay free. Lower rates off-season. Parking: Outdoor, free. Rates increase during annual Harley-Davidson Motorcycle Rally (early Aug). AE, CB, DC, DISC, MC, V.

Days Inn
HC 55, PO Box 348, 57785; tel 605/347-3027 or toll free 800/DAYS-INN; fax 605/347-0291. Exit 30 off I-90, hotel on SW side of I-90. New and quiet hotel, with a large lobby and breakfast area. **Rooms:** 53 rms and stes. CI 2pm/CO 11am. Nonsmoking rms avail. Oak furniture. No views from rooms. **Amenities:** A/C, cable TV w/movies. Some units w/terraces, 1 w/whirlpool. **Services:** Coffee available 24 hours. **Facilities:** 30 Games rm, whirlpool, washer/dryer. **Rates (CP):** Peak (June–Aug) $40 S; $45 D; $45–$80 ste. Extra person $5. Children under age 13 stay free. Lower rates off-season. Parking: Outdoor, free. AE, DC, DISC, MC, V.

RESTAURANT

Phil Town Country Kitchen
In Best Western Phil Town Inn, 2431 S Junction; tel 605/347-3604. Exit 32 off I-90 next to Phil Town Inn. **American.** Complete breakfast menu. The rest of the day's offerings are a variety of salads, sandwiches, burgers, steak, chicken,

seafood, and pasta. Nightly dinner specials; desserts such as apple dumpling and "the country's best bread pudding." **FYI:** Reservations not accepted. Children's menu. **Open:** Peak (Apr–Oct) daily 6am–10pm. **Prices:** Main courses $4–$6; prix fixe $5–$11. AE, CB, DC, DISC, MC, V.

ATTRACTION

Bear Butte State Park

SD 79; tel 605/347-5240. 6 mi NE of Sturgis. Originally called *mato paha* ("bear mountain") by the Sioux, Bear Butte is now a registered national landmark. (A 4,000 year old campsite and artifacts dating back 10,000 years have been found nearby.) The park provides opportunities for picnicking, lakeside camping, fishing, boating, and buffalo viewing. There's also a visitors center and an interpretive trail. **Open:** Daily 8am–8pm **$**

Vermillion

For lodgings and dining, see Yankton

A gracious college town offering many cultural treasures, including elegant historic homes, eminent museums, and a picturesque campus. The Shrine to Music Museum showcases more than 5,000 rare musical instruments. **Information:** Vermillion Area Chamber of Commerce, 906 E Cherry St, Vermillion, 57069 (tel 605/624-5571).

ATTRACTION

The Shrine to Music Museum

Clark and Yale Sts (USD Campus); tel 605/677-5306. More than 5,000 rare and antique musical instruments from all corners of the globe and every historical period are on display here. Among the instruments housed in these eight galleries are a zither built in the shape of a crocodile, a hand-painted Persian drum, and a primitive trumpet mask from the South Pacific. **Open:** Mon–Fri 9am–4:30pm, Sat 10am–4:30pm, Sun 2–4:30pm. Closed some hols. **Free**

Wall

Nestled in the shadows of Badlands National Park is the tiny town of Wall. Rich in history and tradition, you can still see the wagon tracks of the pioneers who passed through on the old Deadwood Trail, located near town.

MOTELS

Best Western Plains Motel

712 Glenn St, 57790; tel 605/279-2145 or toll free 800/528-1234; fax 605/279-2977. Clean, older motel with small lobby. **Rooms:** 74 rms. CI noon/CO 11am. Nonsmoking rms avail. Older but clean furnishings. **Amenities:** A/C, cable TV w/movies. Some units w/terraces. All king rooms have recliners. **Services:** **Facilities:** Games rm. **Rates:** Peak (June–Aug) $30–$70 S; $45–$83 D. Extra person $5. Lower rates off-season. Parking: Outdoor, free. Closed Dec–Jan. AE, CB, DC, DISC, MC, V.

Days Inn

Norriss St, Box 424, 57790; tel 605/279-2000 or toll free 800/DAYS-INN; fax 605/279-2004. Located on the south edge of town; somewhat noisy because of interstate traffic. **Rooms:** 32 rms. CI noon/CO 11am. Nonsmoking rms avail. Clean, well-kept rooms have American Indian motif. **Amenities:** A/C, cable TV w/movies. **Services:** **Facilities:** Sauna, whirlpool. Guests can use swimming pool at motel across the street. **Rates:** Peak (Aug) $40–$85 S; $45–$95 D. Extra person $5. Children under age 13 stay free. Lower rates off-season. Parking: Outdoor, free. AE, DISC, MC, V.

Sands Motor Inn

804 Glenn St, 57790; tel 605/279-2121 or toll free 800/341-1000. S edge of town. A good rest stop. **Rooms:** 49 rms and stes. CI 2pm/CO 10:30am. Nonsmoking rms avail. **Amenities:** A/C, cable TV w/movies. **Services:** **Facilities:** **Rates:** Peak (July–Aug) $55–$65 S; $68–$72 D; $115–$125 ste. Extra person $4. Lower rates off-season. Parking: Outdoor, free. Closed Nov 5–Apr 15. AE, DISC, MC, V.

RESTAURANT

Elkton House

I-90 exit 110 and Hwy 240; tel 605/279-2152. **American/Steak.** A basic, no-frills family eatery. The breakfast bar offers eggs, ham, sausage, biscuits and gravy, french toast, and fresh fruit. The nightly buffet features roast chicken, barbecued pork ribs, roast beef, and an assortment of side dishes, as well as a salad bar and soup. **FYI:** Reservations accepted. Children's menu. Beer and wine only. **Open:** Peak (May 15–Sept 15) daily 5:30am–10pm. **Prices:** Main courses $8–$13; prix fixe $8–$13. DISC, MC, V.

ATTRACTION

Wall Drug Store

510 Main St; tel 605/279-2175. According to legend, Wall Drug began booming in the late 1930s when the owners posted signs on the highway advertising free ice water. The store has since grown from a little storefront pharmacy to a sprawling museum of Americana where an 80-foot dinosaur greets visitors, Western art decorates the walls, and buffalo burgers are a specialty. (Ice water, however, is still free.) Also incorporated into the complex are an Apothecary Shoppe and Pharmacy Museum, a Travelers Chapel, and the only working pharmacy in a 6,000-square-mile area. **Open:** June–Aug, daily 6am–10pm; Sept–May, daily 6:30am–6pm. Closed some hols. **Free**

Watertown

As its name suggests, this is a city of lakes. Lake Kampeska and Lake Pelican (formed from melting glaciers), as well as the Big Sioux River, create a vacation mecca. Watertown's rich hunting ground abound with ring-necked pheasants, geese, doves, and deer. **Information:** Watertown Convention and Visitors Bureau, 26 S Broadway, PO Box 1113, Watertown, 57201 (tel 605/886-5814).

MOTELS

Best Western Ramoka Inn
1901 9th Ave SW, 57201; tel 605/886-8011 or toll free 800/528-1234; fax 605/886-3667. On US 212, ½ mi W of Watertown. Even in a town of nice motels, this one's a step above the others—clean, comfortable, and spacious, and reasonably priced for what you get. **Rooms:** 101 rms and stes. Executive level. CI 2pm/CO 11am. Nonsmoking rms avail. Well decorated, with attractive wood furniture. **Amenities:** A/C. Some units w/whirlpools. Some rooms have microwaves. **Services:** Car-rental desk, babysitting. **Facilities:** 600 1 restaurant, 1 bar, games rm, spa, sauna, whirlpool. Wedding chapel in back of motel. **Rates:** $46–$50 S; $55–$60 D; $125–$150 ste. Extra person $6. Children under age 18 stay free. Parking: Outdoor, free. Various discounts avail. AE, CB, DC, DISC, MC, V.

Comfort Inn
800 35th St Circle, 57201; tel 605/886-3010 or toll free 800/221-2222; fax 605/886-3010. Another super-clean motel in Watertown—it opened in 1993 and still looks brand new. A good choice for families. **Rooms:** 60 rms and stes. CI 3pm/CO 11am. Nonsmoking rms avail. Some accommodations offer recliners. **Amenities:** A/C, cable TV w/movies. Some units have microwaves. **Services:** **Facilities:** 60 Games rm, whirlpool, washer/dryer. Minimart on premises. **Rates (CP):** $42–$48 S; $44–$62 D; $54–$110 ste. Extra person $6. Children under age 18 stay free. Parking: Outdoor, free. AE, CB, DC, DISC, JCB, MC, V.

Days Inn
2900 9th Ave, 57201; tel 605/886-3500 or toll free 800/325-2525; fax 605/886-0820. ⅓ mile W of I-29 on US 212. Opened in 1994, it's a super-clean motel just off the highway. The huge lobby has the indoor pool room off to the right. Certainly among the best of the motel bunch in the area. **Rooms:** 56 rms. CI 3pm/CO 11am. Nonsmoking rms avail. Spotless and attractively furnished, the accommodations are fairly spacious, although bathrooms are small. **Amenities:** A/C, cable TV w/movies. Some units w/whirlpools. Some rooms have microwaves. **Services:** Car-rental desk. **Facilities:** 50 1 bar, games rm, spa, sauna, whirlpool, washer/dryer. Burger bar and small pub on premises. **Rates (CP):** Peak (May 15–Sept 15) $30–$40 S; $40–$50 D. Children under age 17 stay free. Lower rates off-season. Parking: Outdoor, free. Senior discounts avail. AE, CB, DC, DISC, JCB, MC, V.

Stones' Inn
3900 9th Ave SE, 57201; tel 605/882-3630 or toll free 800/658-5470; fax 605/886-3022. Exit 177 at jct I-29 and US 212. Very clean and close to I-29, it draws a lot of repeat business and an older clientele. **Rooms:** 34 rms. CI 1pm/CO 11am. Nonsmoking rms avail. Owners say they are fussy about cleanliness, and it shows. **Amenities:** A/C, cable TV w/movies. Fresh bakery rolls in the morning. **Services:** **Facilities:** Restaurant next door is open 24 hours. **Rates (CP):** Peak (Mem Day–Labor Day) $30 S; $40–$60 D. Lower rates off-season. Parking: Outdoor, free. Senior discount avail. AE, CB, DC, DISC, MC, V.

Traveler's Inn
920 14th St SE, 57201; tel 605/882-2243 or toll free 800/568-7074; fax 605/882-0968. On US 212, 2 mi W of I-29. Well-situated motel, with attractive lobby and wooden staircase. **Rooms:** 50 rms. CI 10am/CO 11am. Nonsmoking rms avail. Very neat, fairly large rooms. Second-floor rooms have cathedral ceilings. **Amenities:** A/C. **Services:** Owner will drive guests to airport. **Facilities:** **Rates (CP):** $31–$38 S; $42–$50 D. Extra person $7. Children under age 12 stay free. Parking: Outdoor, free. AE, DC, DISC, MC, V.

ATTRACTION

Dakota Sioux Casino
Sioux Valley Rd; tel 605/882-2051 or toll free 800/658-4717. Owned and operated for the benefit of the Sisseton Wahpeton Dakota Nation, this casino offers Vegas-style blackjack, poker, and slot machines for every budget. Red Velvet Lounge features live entertainment and a restaurant offers full-service dining. **Open:** Daily 24 hours. **Free**

Wind Cave National Park

For lodgings and dining, see Hot Springs

20 mi NE of Hot Springs. Discovered in 1881, the Wind Cave owes its name to the violent winds that blow between the cave and the outside world due to changes in atmospheric pressure. On the inside, it's one of the country's most beautiful natural caverns, lying at a depth of 196 to 328 feet beneath the slopes of the Black Hills. An eight-mile pedestrian walkway runs through the chambers of the cavern. Five different guided cave tours are offered, ranging in length from one hour to four hours; reservations are recommended, especially for the more strenuous tours, and be sure to wear warm clothing and sturdy shoes.

Aboveground, the park offers a campground (open May–September) with 96 sites, an outdoor amphitheater, a picnic area, and two nature trails. Hikers can explore 30 miles of trails, including the southern terminus of the 111-mile Centennial Trail. Trail maps may be picked up at the **visitors center,** which also offers books, slide programs, and exhibits about the cave and other park resources. For more information, contact the Superintendent, Wind Cave National Park, RR1, Box 190-WCNP, Hot Springs, SD 57747 (tel 605/745-4600).

Yankton

The age of river steamers made Yankton a doorway to the West. Today, its historic Victorian homes recall San Francisco, the rolling green hills and bluffs bring Ireland to mind, and the tall masts and elegant harbor dining near the Lewis and Clark Marina suggest Maine. **Information:** Yankton Area Chamber of Commerce, 218 4th St, PO Box 588, Yankton, 57078 (tel 605/665-3636).

MOTELS

Comfort Inn

2118 Broadway, 57078; tel 605/665-8053 or toll free 800/221-2222. Along US 81; north of downtown. Clean, neat property within a few miles of Lewis and Clark Lake, a major water recreation area. Shopping mall and fast-food restaurants nearby. **Rooms:** 45 rms. CI 2pm/CO 11am. Nonsmoking rms avail. **Amenities:** A/C, cable TV. **Services:** **Facilities:** Whirlpool. **Rates (CP):** $38–$59 S or D. Extra person $4. Children under age 18 stay free. Parking: Outdoor, free. AE, DISC, MC, V.

Days Inn

2410 Broadway, 57078; tel 605/665-8717 or toll free 800/329-7466; fax 605/665-8841. On US 81, 2 mi N of downtown. Neat, clean, and quiet. Located near recreation areas at Lewis and Clark Lake. Shopping mall across the street, grocery next door. **Rooms:** 45 rms and stes. CI 1pm/CO 11am. Nonsmoking rms avail. **Amenities:** A/C, cable TV. **Services:** **Facilities:** Sauna, whirlpool. **Rates (CP):** $30–$36 S; $43–$45 D; $50–$60 ste. Extra person $4. Children under age 12 stay free. Parking: Outdoor, free. AE, DC, DISC, MC, V.

Yankton Inn & Convention Center

1607 SD 50E, 57078; tel 605/665-2906 or toll free 800/457-9090. ½ mi E of downtown. Attracts families with kids. **Rooms:** 124 rms. CI 2pm/CO 11am. Nonsmoking rms avail. Standard, adequately furnished rooms; 20 rooms facing pool get noise from children playing in pool area and hallways. **Amenities:** A/C, cable TV. **Services:** **Facilities:** 600 1 restaurant, 1 bar, games rm, racquetball, sauna, whirlpool. 10 minutes from Lewis and Clark Recreation Area. **Rates:** $42–$95 S or D. Extra person $4. Children under age 18 stay free. Parking: Outdoor, free. Romance and family weekend packages avail. AE, DISC, MC, V.

RESORT

Lewis & Clark Resort

43496 Lakeshore Dr, 57078; tel 605/665-2680; fax 605/665-8613. Just off SD 52; 3 mi W of Yankton. 5 acres. Basic cabins and a motel are located on a lakefront state park property, one of the most popular outdoor recreation spots in the region. Next to a marina, restaurant, and bar. **Rooms:** 24 rms; 10 cottages/villas. CI 3pm/CO 11am. Nonsmoking rms avail. Simple rooms are clean and neat. **Amenities:** A/C, cable TV, refrig. No phone. Some units w/terraces. **Services:** **Facilities:** 1 restaurant, 1 bar, 1 beach (lake shore). **Rates:** Peak (May 26–Sept 6) $50–$75 S or D; $100–$140 cottage/villa. Extra person $5. Children under age 12 stay free. Min stay peak. Lower rates off-season. Parking: Outdoor, $6/day. Midweek specials and extended stay rates avail. Closed Nov–Mar. AE, DC, DISC, MC, V.

RESTAURANT

$ ★ Jodean's

US 81 N; tel 605/665-9884. 2 mi N of Yankton; along US 81. **American.** Room decor and general ambience are lacking in this rural eatery, but the quality and quantity of the food keeps patrons coming back for more. Very popular Friday seafood buffet features crab, salmon, and other choices for a very modest price. All meals include the salad and dessert bar. The gift shop has an excellent selection of works by area artisans. **FYI:** Reservations recommended. Children's menu. **Open:** Mon–Thurs 4:30–10pm, Fri–Sat 4:30–11pm, Sun 10:30am–10pm. **Prices:** Main courses $6–$22. AE, CB, DISC, MC, V.

ATTRACTION

Lewis and Clark Recreation Area

RR 1, Box 240; tel 605/668-2985. 4 mi W of Yankton. An NFAA-approved archery course, four miles of equestrian trails, and the boat marinas and sandy beaches at Lewis and Clark Lake offer an abundance of recreational opportunities. A campground contains 380 campsites and cabins, with all the amenities: hot showers, electric hookups, paved pads, and more. Playgrounds, hiking and biking trails, and daily planned activities mean enjoyment for the whole family. $

WASHINGTON

A State of Contrasts

STATE STATS

CAPITAL
Olympia

AREA
68,139 square miles

BORDERS
Idaho, Oregon, British Columbia, and the Pacific Ocean

POPULATION
4,866,692 (1990)

ENTERED UNION
November 11, 1889 (42nd state)

NICKNAME
Evergreen State

STATE FLOWER
Western rhododendron

STATE BIRD
Willow goldfinch

FAMOUS NATIVES
Bing Crosby, Jimi Hendrix, Robert Joffrey

A primordial silence reigns in the Hoh Valley on Washington's Olympic Peninsula. Incessant rains—measured in feet instead of inches—nurture giant hemlocks and cedars. Moss hangs thick from the branches of these trees, dripping water onto giant ferns. Yet only 100 miles away, jumbo jets roll off the assembly line at the Boeing plant and computer whiz kids dream up the next generation of Microsoft programs.

While western Washington, home to Seattle and the San Juan Islands, has given the country espresso, grunge rock, *Free Willy,* and *Northern Exposure,* the east side has provided the country with red delicious apples, wheat, excellent wines, and the massive Grand Coulee Dam. From the peak of 14,410-foot-tall Mount Rainier, it is possible to gaze down into two very different Washington landscapes. To the west lie towering fir trees and shimmering waterways; to the east, a high desert bisected by the Columbia River, the second-largest river in America.

Washington has also brought to the nation's consciousness some of the greatest environmental issues. In western Washington, controversy over the fate of the spotted owl helped draw the battle line between the timber industry and environmentalists, while the nuclear wastes generated by the US Department of Energy's Hanford Site threaten to contaminate a vast area of eastern Washington.

Washington, once the remote and forgotten upper left corner of the nation, has in the past decade emerged into the nation's consciousness as a leader in modern technologies. Seattle has been the launching point of the aviation giant Boeing, computer pioneer Microsoft—even Muzak. Turning to the Pacific Rim for its future, Washington has positioned itself to become one of the nation's most important states.

Frommer's #1

A Brief History

Trade & Tragedy Native American tribes in the Northwest developed a complex culture that included a remarkable artistic aesthetic. The most recognizable expression of native art is the totem pole, which actually developed farther to the north (in what is today British Columbia). Trade was an integral part of this region's native culture, especially along the Columbia River, where life revolved around the life cycle of the salmon. It was the fur trade that fueled early European and American interest in the Northwest. In 1776, the area suddenly became of intense interest to the British, Americans, Spanish, and Russians because of the high demand for sea otter pelts. Not long after European and American explorers and traders began visiting this area, the region's natives began succumbing to introduced diseases such as smallpox, measles, and influenza, for which they had no resistance. Sadly, between the 1780s and the 1830s much of the Northwest's population of Native Americans was wiped out by these diseases.

Discovery & Conflict The increased fur trade brought more exploration of this coast, and in 1787, fur trader James Barkley discovered a wide strait that was dubbed the Strait of Juan de Fuca. The following year, the seizure of a British trading ship by the Spanish nearly led the two nations to war. Capt George Vancouver, on his way to negotiate a settlement to the conflict in 1792, took a detour on his way to meet the Spanish at Nootka Sound. He sailed up the Strait of Juan de Fuca and discovered an inland sea, which he named the Puget Sound after one of his lieutenants. In 1819, the Spanish finally relinquished claims to the region, and with the Russians content with their claim on Alaska, only the British and Americans were left to squabble over the Northwest.

When the sea otter population had been decimated, fur traders headed inland. The Hudson's Bay Company, a British fur trading company, established Fort Vancouver as its Northwest headquarters, near the junction of the Columbia and Willamette Rivers. Fort Vancouver was the most important settlement in the region between 1824 and 1846. These years saw the arrival of several groups of American missionaries as well as a few settlers. By the early 1840s, there was a steady flow of settlers arriving and the British agreed to withdraw to the north of the 49th parallel, which still forms the boundary between Canada and the United States.

This agreement split the two nations' land claims down the middle of the main channel between the mainland and Vancouver Island. However, there was a disagreement over where this channel lay and both countries laid claim to San Juan Island When, in 1859, a British pig was shot in an Amercan garden, tempers on the island flared and the two countries came to the brink of war. It took international arbitration to settle the "Pig War," but the island was finally ceded to the United States.

Fun Facts

- Contrary to popular belief, it rains fewer inches per year in Seattle than it does in New York, Boston, or Washington, DC.
- There used to be seven major hills in Seattle, but now there are only six: Denny Hill was leveled by high-powered water hoses—it was just too steep.
- The average geoduck (pronounced "gooey-duck") clam, harvested from the Puget Sound area, weighs more than five pounds.
- Everett is home to the largest building in the world—a Boeing 747 plant. It could hold almost 100 football fields!
- Ever hear the expression, "Don't take any wooden nickels"? During the Great Depression, the Washington town of Tenino issued wooden money when a local bank closed, freezing the town's assets. Although there weren't any wooden nickels, 25 cent, 50 cent, and one dollar denominations were printed on spruce and cedar chips.

Destination: Seattle The first settlers in the Puget Sound region established a camp at Alki Point, on the west side of Elliott Bay, in 1851. However, they soon abandoned this storm-lashed spot for a more protected location, which they named Seattle in honor of Chief Sealth, a Native American who had befriended the early settlers. The new city grew steadily for the next several decades, its economy fueled by lumber mills. In 1889 (the same year Washington was admitted to the Union) a fire burned most of Seattle to the ground. Four years later, in 1893, the transcontinental railroad finally reached Seattle, but it was the steamship *Portland*, which docked in Seattle in 1897, that would cause more of a stir. This ship brought the first news of the gold strike in the Yukon. The rush was on, and nearly everyone heading to or from the goldfields stopped in Seattle.

Boeing & Beyond Although the timber industry dominated Washington's economy almost from the very start of settlement, the foundation of Seattle's economic diversification was laid in 1916. That was the year that William Boeing launched a small seaplane from the waters of Lake Union. By World War II, the Boeing corporation was the one of the most important airplane manufacturers in the world, producing B-17s and B-29s for the war effort. Boeing is still a major player in the Puget Sound's economy, but it has been partly overshadowed by high-tech neighbor Microsoft.

A Closer Look

GEOGRAPHY

Stretching from the Pacific Ocean to the western ranges of the Rocky Mountains, Washington encompasses a vast and varied landscape. In the far western part of the state are the **Olympic Mountains,** which rise to nearly 8,000 feet. The western slopes of the Olympics are the wettest area in the continental United States—receiving as much as 150 inches of rain each year—while the east side of the peninsula, in the rain shadow of the mountains, gets only a tenth as much rain.

The **Puget Sound** region is the most populous of the state, with Seattle, Tacoma, and Olympia sprawling along the Puget's shore. This area is what most people picture when they think of Washington: green, lush, sparkling waterways, and snow-capped mountains. Lying just to the north of Puget Sound are the **San Juan Islands,** an archipelago of emerald green islands.

Most of the **Cascade Range,** which runs from the Canadian border to the Columbia River gorge, is made of volcanic peaks. Mount Rainier, Mount Baker, and Mount St Helens rise above the green foothills, while in the northern part of the range, the inaccessible North Cascades raise their jagged granite peaks. **Central Washington,** to the east of the Cascade rain shadow, receives significantly less rainfall than much of the state. This region encompasses the state's most productive agricultural regions, including the Okanogan Valley and the Chelan and Wenatchee areas, all of which are known for their apple orchards.

Eastern Washington, which borders Idaho on the east, encompasses the Palouse Hills as well as several mountain ranges. In the southern part of this region lie the Blue Mountains and in the north are the Kettle and Selkirk Mountains, which are western ranges of the Rockies.

DRIVING DISTANCES

Mount Rainier National Park

71 mi NW of Yakima
75 mi N of Mount St Helens
78 mi SE of Tacoma
108 mi SE of Seattle
158 mi NE of Portland, OR
279 mi E of Spokane

Seattle

78 mi S of Anacortes
108 mi NW of Mount Rainier
141 mi S of Vancouver, BC
179 mi NW of Yakima
180 mi N of Portland, OR
281 mi W of Spokane

Spokane

33 mi W of Coeur d'Alene, ID
88 mi E of Grand Coulee Dam
161 mi N of Walla Walla
191 mi W of Missoula, MT
281 mi E of Seattle
423 mi N of Boise, ID

CLIMATE

Despite the image of Washington as a place where people rust or grow webbed feet, the state's climate is as diverse as its geography. The state's legendary rains are caused by moist air that flows in off the Pacific Ocean and Puget Sound. That same moist air also gives the Cascade Range some of the heaviest winter snowfalls in the country. While the western slopes of the Cascade Range and Olympic Mountains are being drenched with moisture, the regions lying to the east of these mountains are receiving only a fraction of that precipitation. This phenomenon is known as the rain-shadow effect and is responsible for the entire eastern half of the state being almost desert dry. On a smaller scale, the rain shadow of the Olympic Mountains leaves Sequim, Port Townsend, and the San Juan Islands much dryer than nearby neighbors around the Puget Sound.

WHAT TO PACK

Of course an umbrella is a good idea, but even better is a rain jacket of some sort, since nights are cool even in the summer. Snow skis in winter and hiking boots in summer are necessities for many visitors. Don't forget your sunglasses, either.

TOURIST INFORMATION

For statewide travel information, contact **Washington State Tourism,** 101 General Administration

Building (PO Box 42500), Olympia, WA 98504-2500 (tel toll free 800/544-1800). For information on national parks, forests, monuments, and historic sites in Washington, contact the **National Park Service/US Forest Service Outdoor Recreation Information Center,** 915 2nd Ave, Rm 442, Seattle, WA 98174 (tel 206/220-7450). For information on state parks, contact **Washington State Parks & Recreation Commission,** 7150 Cleanwater Lane (PO Box 42650), Olympia, WA 98504-2650 (tel 360/902-8563). For information on ferries, contact **Washington State Ferries,** Colman Dock, Seattle, WA 98501 (tel 206/464-6400 or toll free 800/843-3779 in WA).

AVG MONTHLY TEMPS (°F) & RAINFALL (IN)

	Seattle	Spokane
Jan	46/6.0	27/2.5
Feb	50/4.2	32/1.6
Mar	53/3.6	38/1.4
Apr	58/2.4	46/1.1
May	65/1.6	54/1.4
June	69/1.4	62/1.2
July	75/0.7	70/0.5
Aug	74/1.3	68/0.7
Sept	69/2.0	59/0.7
Oct	60/3.4	48/1.1
Nov	52/5.6	35/2.1
Dec	47/6.3	29/2.5

DRIVING RULES AND REGULATIONS

Seat belts are required for driver and all passengers, and car seats are required for children under one year of age. A right turn on red is permitted after coming to a full stop, as is a left turn on red if turning from a one-way street into another one-way street. Drunk driving laws are strictly enforced. Radar detectors are legal.

RENTING A CAR

All the major car rental companies have offices in Washington. You'll find desks for many of these in the arrivals hall of Seattle-Tacoma International Airport. It pays to make car reservations as far in advance as possible; this will usually save you a bit of money.

- **Alamo** (tel toll free 800/327-9633)
- **Avis** (tel 800/331-1212)
- **Budget** (tel 800/527-0700)
- **Dollar** (tel 800/800-4000)
- **Hertz** (tel 800/654-3131)
- **National** (tel 800/227-7368)
- **Thrifty** (tel 800/367-2277)

ESSENTIALS

Area Codes: The area code for the greater Seattle metropolitan area is **206.** The area code for the rest of Washington west of the Cascades is **360.** The area code for Washington east of the Cascades is **509.**

Emergencies: If you need to summon the police, the fire department, or an ambulance from most places in the state, dial 911.

Liquor Laws: The legal drinking age in Washington is 21.

Road Info: For information on pass conditions in the Washington Cascades, you can call the Washington State Department of Transportation at 900/407-7277 (35¢ per minute; in operation October–mid-April).

Taxes: The state sales tax is 6.5%; local sales taxes (which vary) are added on top of this. Hotel-room taxes also vary, with the Seattle room tax at 15.2%.

Time Zone: All of Washington is in the Pacific time zone.

Best of the State

WHAT TO SEE AND DO

Below is a general overview of some of the top sights and attractions in Washington. To find out more detailed information, look under "Attractions" under individual cities in the listings portion of this book.

National & State Parks From ocean shore to desert lakes, Washington has a surprising diversity of parks and recreation areas. Foremost among these are the state's three national parks. **Mount Rainier National Park** preserves one of the most spectacular of the Cascade Range's many volcanic peaks, with glaciers and meadows full of summer wildflowers. **Olympic National Park** boasts alpine meadows, rain forests full of old-growth trees, and miles of rugged and remote shoreline. **North Cascades National Park,** the least accessible and most rugged of these three parks, offers many miles of remote hiking trails. For camping, fishing, and water sports there is the **Coulee Dam National Recreation Area** in north-central Washington.

Mount St Helens National Volcanic Monument and the **Columbia River Gorge National Scenic Area** also provide outdoor recreation and breathtaking scenery. The former preserves landscape devastated by the eruption of Mount St Helens in 1980, while the latter contains the unique, waterfall-filled Columbia Gorge, created by massive floods thousands of years ago.

The state's seven **national forests** also provide thousands of miles of hiking trails, lakes, rivers, campgrounds, and remote wilderness areas. Among the most interesting of these areas are the Glacier Peak Wilderness, the Alpine Lakes Wilderness, the Goat Rocks Wilderness, and Mount Baker Wilderness.

Many Washington **state parks** are centered around lakes, rivers, or beaches. In the north Puget Sound and San Juan Islands, Deception Pass State Park on Whidbey Island and Spencer Spit State Park on Lopez Island provide forested settings and beaches. Fort Worden State Park in Port Townsend also has a popular beach. Moran State Park, on Orcas Island, is the most popular state park in the San Juan Islands and offers lakes, hiking, and mountain biking trails. In the Cascades, Lake Wenatchee and Lake Chelan state parks attract visitors interested in camping and water sports. There are a dozen state parks along the Washington coast, some offering camping and some open for day use only.

Natural Wonders Over the centuries, nature has conspired to produce several unique creations across the state. Several valleys on the west side of the Olympic Peninsula support temperate rain forests, complete with thick mats of moss and trees that grow hundreds of feet tall. Most accessible of these is the Hoh Valley.

In central and eastern Washington, the ice ages left two fascinating legacies. **Lake Chelan** is a 55-mile-long, 1,500-foot-deep glacial lake that is less than 2 miles wide in most places and slices deep into the North Cascade mountains. At its deepest point, the lake bottom is below sea level. Ancient floods created **Dry Falls,** the region's other natural wonder. Thousands of years ago a huge flood of water poured over this now-dry precipice south of Coulee City.

Manmade Wonders When the **Grand Coulee Dam** was completed in 1941, it was the largest manmade structure ever built, and today it is still an impressive sight. With all the waterways in the Puget Sound region, bridge builders have had to be creative. Seattle boasts two floating bridges, including the longest floating bridge in the world. A third floating bridge crosses the Hood Canal on the west side of the sound. Seattle is also the home of the state's most immediately recognizable manmade wonder: the **Space Needle,** built for the 1962 World's Fair.

Wildlife Because there is no hunting allowed within Mount Rainier National Park and Olympic National Park, the deer populations have become quite tame and are very easily observed. On Mount Rainier, marmots are also frequently seen. About 21 miles west of Yakima, elk (and sometimes bighorn sheep) can be seen in winter at the **Oak Creek Game Management Preserve.**

Historic Sites & Monuments Several of Puget Sound's historic towns have been preserved. The largest of these is **Port Townsend,** which in the 1880s was expected to become the region's largest city. Hundreds of Victorian homes and commercial buildings line its streets. Other historic towns in the region include La Conner, surrounded by tulip fields and now a shopping mecca; Coupeville and Langley, two old fishing-and-farming villages on Whidbey Island that now have quite a bit of shopping; Steilacoom, located near Tacoma and Washington's oldest incorporated town; and Port Gamble, a logging company town established in 1853 and still owned by the mill. The tiny community of Oysterville on the Long Beach Peninsula is yet another historic district that is little changed from its days as an oystering town.

In Seattle, the Pioneer Square historic district, which dates to the years shortly after the Seattle Fire of 1889, preserves dozens of brick commercial buildings. However, it is **Pike Place Market,** which dates to 1907, that is the most beloved of Seattle's historic districts. Seattle is also the site of a branch of the **Klondike Gold Rush National Historical Park.**

Several historic military installations can be found around the state. Officers' Row National Historic District in Vancouver and Fort Worden State Park in Port Townsend preserve Victorian officers' quarters, while Fort Vancouver and Fort Nisqually are reconstructions of forts that were built by the Hudson's Bay Company. San Juan National Historic Park on San Juan Island commemorates the little-known "Pig War" of 1859. Out in the eastern part of the state, the Whitman Mission National Historic

Site preserves one of the region's earliest missions, which was the site of a massacre by Cayuse Native Americans in 1847.

Museums The state's foremost art museums are the **Seattle Art Museum** and the affiliated **Seattle Asian Art Museum,** which together present the city's impressive collection of Native American, African, and Asian art. The **Tacoma Art Museum** is known for its collection of art glass by local artist Dale Chihuly, while out in the wilds of south-central Washington is the **Maryhill Museum,** home of an impressive collection of Rodin sculptures and sketches.

Several museums around the state chronicle the region's Native American history. The **Makah Cultural and Research Center,** on the northwest tip of the Olympic Peninsula, is a repository for artifacts unearthed at a site that was buried in mud for over 500 years. Closer to Seattle, the **Suquamish Museum** presents a Native American perspective on Puget Sound history. In central Washington, the **Yakama Indian Nation Cultural Center** in Toppenish documents the heritage of the Yakama people.

Specialty museums around the state include the large and impressive **Museum of Flight** in Seattle, the **Whale Museum** on San Juan Island, and the **Naval Undersea Museum** near Keyport on the Kitsap Peninsula. Various aspects of Columbia River history are documented at the **Columbia Gorge Interpretive Center** in Stevenson and at the **Lewis and Clark Interpretive Center** outside Ilwaco.

Beaches Washington's beaches are divided between those on the rough Pacific Ocean and those on the calmer waters of the Puget Sound and the Strait of Juan de Fuca. Cold water prevents people from spending much time in the water at any of the state's beaches; however, beachcombing, kite flying, fishing, and clamming are all popular. The **Long Beach Peninsula** boasts one of the longest beaches in the United States and supports a thriving summer-vacation business with mile after mile of motels, cabins, and fast-food restaurants. Farther north along the Pacific coast, the beaches become more rugged and remote. Some of the most beautiful of these beaches lie within Olympic National Park. Other popular beaches include Dungeness Spit near Sequim, Fort Worden State Park in Port Townsend, Scenic Beach State Park near Bremerton, and Birch Bay north of Bellingham. In Seattle, Alki Beach and Golden Gardens Park are popular summer sunning spots.

Theme Towns Leavenworth, done over as a Bavarian village, is the most popular of the several theme towns scattered around the state. Others include Winthrop, a Wild West town complete with wooden sidewalks; Poulsbo, a "Viking" town that plays up its Scandinavian heritage and fjordlike setting; Toppenish, a central Washington town that has covered much of its blank wall space with murals; and Lynden, a Dutch farming community with a real Old World–style windmill.

Family Favorites Zoos are always popular with kids, and Washington has several excellent ones worth visiting. The **Woodland Park Zoo** in Seattle and the **Point Defiance Zoo and Aquarium** in Tacoma are the state's two top zoos and have many outstanding and realistic exhibit areas. For a ride-through, wild-animal experience, there's **Northwest Trek Wildlife Park** outside Tacoma. Seattle's **Pacific Science Center** is another perennial favorite of families, as is the **Seattle Aquarium,** which takes a look at the sea life of Puget Sound and other bodies of water, with sea otters among the star attractions.

Washington also has several excursion trains. The *Spirit of Washington* makes its run along the shore of Lake Washington; a little bit farther east, the **Puget Sound & Snoqualmie Railroad** chugs along from North Bend to Snoqualmie. Near Mount Rainier, there is the **Cascadian Dinner Train,** which leaves from Morton. The **Lewis River Excursion Train** starts its run in Battle Ground and travels to Moulton Falls County Park.

Cuisine With so much water all around, it is no surprise that seafood is an important part of Northwest cuisine. Salmon (fresh and smoked), Dungeness crab, farm-raised oysters and mussels, giant geoduck (pronounced "gooey-duck") clams, and razor clams are all mainstays in Washington. These often get combined with the berries and apples that the state produces in great quantities. Washington also produces its own excellent wines. The main wine district is in the eastern part of the state near Yakima, but there are also wineries north of Seattle near the north end of Lake Washington.

EVENTS AND FESTIVALS

- **Northwest Flower & Garden Show,** Seattle. The largest flower and garden show in the Northwest.

Beautiful displays and hundreds of vendors. Held in the Washington State Convention Center. Mid- to late February. Call 206/789-5333.

- **Chinese New Year,** Seattle. Traditional new year's celebration in the International District. Late January or early February (depending on the lunar calendar).
- **Spring Barrel Tasting,** Yakima Valley wineries. Barrels of new wine are tapped. Late April. Call 509/575-1300.
- **Washington State Apple Blossom Festival,** Wenatchee. Dozens of events in celebration of the flowering of the commercial orchards. Late April to early May. Call toll free 800/57-APPLE.
- **Irrigation Festival,** Sequim. Oldest continuous festival in the state, featuring a parade, logging show, arts and crafts. Early May. Call 360/683-6197.
- **Viking Fest,** Poulsbo. A celebration of the town's Scandinavian heritage. Mid-May. Call 360/779-4848.
- **Northwest Folklife Festival,** Seattle. Largest festival of its kind in the United States, featuring craftspeople and folk musicians from around the country. Held in the Seattle Center. Memorial Day weekend. Call 206/684-7300.
- **Port Townsend Blues Festival.** Blues musicians from around the country perform in this restored Victorian seaport. Mid-June. Call toll free 800/733-3608.
- **Fourth of July Fireworks,** near Fort Vancouver National Historic Site in Vancouver. The biggest July 4th fireworks display west of the Mississippi.
- **Seafair,** Seattle. The city's biggest annual event includes everything from a torchlight parade and ethnic festivals to hydroplane races and the Navy's Blue Angels. third weekend in July to first weekend in August. Call 206/728-0123.
- **Pacific Northwest Arts & Crafts Fair,** Bellevue. More than 300 juried arts and crafts vendors and lots of live music. July. Call 206/454-4900.
- **Omak Stampede and World Famous Suicide Run.** Rodeo, Native American encampment, and horse race. Early August. Call 509/826-1983 or toll free 800/225-OMAK.
- **Washington State International Kite Festival,** Long Beach. Kite flying competitions, lighted night fly, fireworks. Late August. Call toll free 800/451-2542.
- **Chief Seattle Days,** Suquamish. Powwow with salmon bake, canoe races, dancing, and crafts. Mid-August. Call 360/598-3311.
- **Bumbershoot,** Seattle. Megafest, held at Seattle Center, featuring lots of rock music and arts and crafts booths. Labor Day weekend. Call 206/682-4386.
- **Ellensburg Rodeo/Kittitas County Fair.** Washington's biggest rodeo and county fair. Labor Day weekend. Call 509/962-7831.
- **Western Washington Fair,** Puyallup. The state fair for the western half of the state, and one of the largest in the country. Third week in September. Call 206/841-5045.

SPECTATOR SPORTS

Baseball The American League's **Seattle Mariners** (tel 206/628-3555) play in the Kingdome. Tickets are available through Ticketmaster (tel 206/628-0888).

Basketball The NBA's **Seattle Supersonics** (tel 206/281-5800) play in the recently renovated and expanded Seattle Center Coliseum. Tickets are available through Ticketmaster (tel 206/628-0888). The **University of Washington Huskies** play at Edmundson Pavilion and do not have as devoted a following as the Huskies football team. However, the UW women's basketball team, which also plays in the Edmundson Pavilion, is one of the best in the country. For ticket and schedule information for both UW teams, call 206/543-2200.

Football The NFL's **Seattle Seahawks** (tel 206/827-9777) play in Seattle's Kingdome and due to their loyal following, tickets are very hard to get. The **University of Washington Huskies** play at Husky Stadium on the UW campus. Their fans are rabidly devoted and tickets are almost impossible to come by. (Many fans beat the traffic jams by coming to games by boat.) For ticket and schedule information, call 206/543-2200.

Hockey Through the fall and winter, the city's minor-league team, the Seattle **Thunderbirds** (tel 206/448-PUCK), carves up the ice at the Seattle Center Arena.

Horse Racing The state's only regularly scheduled horse racing is at **Yakima Meadows** (tel 509/248-4210 or toll free 800/767-2388) at the Central Washington State Fairgrounds in Yakima. The season runs from April to September.

ACTIVITIES A TO Z

Bicycling The San Juan Islands, with their winding

country roads and Puget Sound vistas, are the most popular bicycling area in the state. Of the four main islands (San Juan, Orcas, Lopez, and Shaw), Lopez is the easiest and Orcas the most difficult. Seattle, Tacoma, Spokane, and Yakima all have easy bicycle trails that are either in parks or connect parks. The state's national forests provide miles of logging roads and single-track trails for mountain biking. Among the most popular mountain biking areas is the Methow Valley, on the east side of the North Cascades. For a map and other information on bicycling, contact the Bicycle Program, Washington Department of Transportation, Transportation Building, 310 Maple Park Ave, Olympia, WA 98501 (tel 360/705-7277).

Bird Watching One of the state's best bird-watching excursions is a ride through the San Juan Islands on one of the Washington State Ferries. From these floating observation platforms, birders can spot bald eagles and numerous pelagic birds. Each January, bald eagles flock to the Skagit River, north of Seattle, to feast on salmon. Birders can observe from shore or on a guided raft trip. Migratory shorebirds make annual stops at Bowerman Basin in the Gray's Harbor Wildlife Refuge outside of Hoquiam.

Boardsailing In the Columbia Gorge, winds and current come together to produce some of the best boardsailing conditions in the world. Skilled sailors perform aerial acrobatics as they launch their boards at high speed off the tops of wind-whipped waves. On calmer days and in spots where the wind isn't blowing so hard, there are opportunities for novices to learn the basics. The most popular launching spots are west of the Hood River bridge.

Camping Camping is very popular in the state's three national parks—Mount Rainier, Olympic, and North Cascades. (Camping is on a first-come-first-served basis at all three.) Washington also has 80 state parks with campgrounds—Moran State Park on Orcas Island and Deception Pass State Park are two of the most enjoyable. For information on camping in state parks, contact the Washington State Parks and Recreation Commission, 7150 Cleanwater Lane (PO Box 42650), Olympia, WA 98504-2650 (tel 360/902-8500).

Hiking Washington has an abundance of hiking trails, including the Pacific Crest Trail, which runs along the spine of the Cascades from Canada to the Columbia River. The state's three national parks offer hiking routes through various types of terrain; another popular hike is to the top of Mount St Helens. Lesser known are the hiking trails on Mount Adams, in the southern part of the state. In the Columbia Gorge, the hike up Dog Mountain is strenuous but rewarding. The Alpine Lakes region outside Leavenworth is breathtakingly beautiful, but so popular that permits are required.

Sailing Puget Sound and the waters to its north are a favorite sailing spot. Many companies offer sailing charters through these waters, with the San Juan Islands being home port for many charter companies.

Scuba Diving Though the waters of the Puget Sound are cold, they are generally quite clear and harbor an astounding variety of life, including giant octopi. There are underwater scuba parks at Fort Worden, Kopachuck, Blake Island, Saltwater, and Tolmie state parks. For more information, contact the Washington Scuba Alliance, 120 State Ave #18, Olympia, WA 98501-8212.

Sea Kayaking Sea kayaks differ from river kayaks by being much longer, more stable, and able to carry gear as well as a paddler or two. There are few places in the country that offer better sea kayaking than Washington. The protected waters of the Puget Sound offer numerous spots for a paddle of anywhere from a few hours to a few days. There is even a water trail under development that will link camping spots throughout the sound. The San Juan Islands are by far the most popular sea kayaking spot (several of the islands include state campsites accessible only by boat).

Skiing Washington has numerous ski areas spread across the state, from Hurricane Ridge in the Olympic Mountains to Mount Spokane near the Idaho border. However, the most frequented areas are all within a few hours drive of Seattle. These include, from north to south, Mount Baker, Stevens Pass, Alpental/Ski Acres/Snoqualmie/Hyak, Mission Ridge, Crystal Mountain, and White Pass. Other, more remote ski areas include Mount Spokane, 48 Degrees North, Sitzmark, Loup Loup, Echo Valley, Badger Mountain, and Hurricane Ridge. Many of these ski areas also offer cross-country ski trails.

Water Sports Water sports such as motorboating and water skiing are particularly popular on lakes and reservoirs in eastern Washington. One of the most popular summer water sports destinations is Lake Chelan. Other popular spots include Moses

Selected State Parks & Recreation Areas

- **Mount Rainier National Park,** Tahoma Woods, Star Rte, Ashford, WA 98304-9751 (tel 360/569-2211)
- **North Cascades National Park,** 2105 WA 20, Sedro Woolley, WA 98284 (tel 360/856-5700)
- **Olympic National Park,** 3002 Mount Angeles Rd, Port Angeles, WA 98362 (tel 360/452-0330)
- **Coulee Dam National Recreation Area,** PO Box 37, Coulee Dam, WA 99116 (tel 509/633-0881)
- **Mount Baker National Recreation Area,** Mount Baker–Snoqualmie National Forest, 21905 64th Ave W, Mountlake Terrace, WA 98043 (tel 206/775-9702)
- **Mount St Helens National Volcanic Monument,** 42218 NE Yale Bridge Rd, Amboy, WA 98601 (tel 360/750-3900)
- **Gifford Pinchot National Forest/Mount Adams Wilderness,** 6926 E Fourth Plain Blvd, Vancouver, WA 98668 (tel 360/750-5000)
- **Beacon Rock State Park,** MP 34.83 L State Road 14, Skamania, WA 98648 (tel 509/427-8265)
- **Deception Pass State Park,** 5175 NSH 20, Oak Harbor, WA 98277 (tel 360/675-2417)
- **Fay Bainbridge State Park,** 15446 Sunrise Dr NE, Bainbridge Island, WA 98110 (tel 206/842-3931)
- **Fort Worden State Park,** 200 Battery Way, Port Townsend, WA 98368 (tel 360/385-4730)
- **Lake Chelan State Park,** Rte 1, Box 90, Chelan, WA 98816 (tel 509/687-3710)
- **Lake Wenatchee State Park,** 21588A WA 207, Leavenworth, WA 98826 (tel 509/763-3101)
- **Moran State Park,** Star Rte, Box 22, Eastsound, WA 98245 (tel 360/376-2326)
- **Spencer Spit State Park,** Rte 2, Box 3600, Lopez, WA 98261 (tel 360/468-2251)

Lake and Potholes Reservoir. In the Seattle area, Lake Washington has long been a popular water sports area.

Whale Watching Orca whales, commonly called "killer whales," are frequently seen in Puget Sound and around the San Juan Islands, especially during the summer months. Dozens of companies offer whale-watching trips from the San Juans. It is also possible to spot orcas from the shore at Lime Kiln State Park. Out on Washington's coast, migrating gray whales can be seen March through May. In Westport, there are both viewing areas and companies operating boat excursions to see whales.

White-Water Rafting In the Cascades, some of the popular rafting rivers include the Wenatchee River outside Leavenworth, the Methow River near Winthrop, the Skagit and Skykomish Rivers north of Seattle, and the White Salmon River near Trout Lake. On the Olympic Peninsula, the Queets, Hoh, and Elhwa Rivers are the main rafting rivers.

SEATTLE TO WHIDBEY ISLAND

Start	Seattle
Finish	Langley
Distance	Approximately 100 miles
Time	2–4 days
Highlights	Washington State Ferries; rolling hills of Bainbridge Island; Suquamish Museum; Scandinavian community of Poulsbo; Victorian port of Port Townsend; rural beauty of Whidbey Island and two of its towns, Coupeville and Langley

Starting with a 30-minute ferry trip from the Seattle waterfront to Bainbridge Island, this tour takes you through some of Washington's most scenic territory: Puget Sound, Bainbridge Island, parts of the Kitsap and Olympic peninsulas, and Whidbey Island. Along the way, gently rolling countryside and the rugged, snow-capped Olympic Mountains will be your constant companions.

At the Suquamish Museum, you will hear the recorded voices of tribal members who were displaced from their families and stripped of their heritage and their language when they were sent to white boarding schools in the early 1900s. In Poulsbo, you can sample some delectable Danish pastries and stroll the quaint main street of this one-time fishing village. Crossing the Hood Canal Bridge to the Olympic Peninsula, you'll head to Port Townsend, a town of Victorian mansions once owned by wealthy ship captains. From there, you will take another ferry to Whidbey Island (considered to be the longest island in the continental United States after the Supreme Court judged Long Island in New York to be a peninsula).

For additional information on lodgings, restaurants, and attractions in the region covered by the tour, look under specific cities in the listings portion of this chapter. (Note that Little & Lewis Water Gardens (stop 2) and the Bloedel Reserve (stop 4) are open by appointment only; if you are interested in visiting these places, call ahead.)

From Seattle's waterfront, take a Washington State Ferry to:

1. **Bainbridge Island.** Once there, head out of the ferry terminal and turn left (west) at the intersection of WA 305 and Winslow Way. The Bainbridge Island Chamber of Commerce information center (tel 206/842-3700), located at that intersection, offers maps for sale and free brochures. Continue west on Winslow Way into the village of Bainbridge, once named Winslow. The **Town and Country Thriftway,** 343 Winslow Way E, hosts a farmer's market 9am–1pm on Saturdays where you can buy local produce, plants, herbs, flowers, and crafts. The village has several pleasant shops: **Estelle's Fabric Shop,** 285 Winslow Way E (tel 206/842-2261), stocks fine cottons, silks, rayon fabrics, and an array of fabric ribbons and unusual buttons. The **Eagle Harbor Book Co,** 157 Winslow Way E (tel 206/842-5332), focuses on the work of northwest authors. The **Madrona Restaurant,** Parfitt Way SW and Madison Ave at the marina (tel 206/842-8339), displays photographs of the town at the turn of the century; diners can enjoy views of the water from the outside deck or through the restaurant's large windows.

Take a Break

Stop for a coffee break at **Cafe Nola**, at Madison Ave and Winslow Way W in Bainbridge (tel 206/842-3822). The cafe, which opened in 1995, turns out especially good pastries—such as fresh peach muffins and ginger cream biscuits—made from locally grown, organic ingredients. The cafe's aged-copper counters were designed by a local architect, and the hand-stenciled, butternut squash–colored walls add a touch of elegance. Entrees are $10 to $18.

Return to WA 305. From the intersection with Winslow Way, continue straight (east) on Winslow Way for ¼ mile; make a left (north) onto Ferncliff Ave NE for ¼ mile and a right (east) onto Wing Point Way for ½ mile, until you reach the:

2. **Little & Lewis Water Gardens,** 1940 Wing Point Way NE (tel 206/842-8327), which looks like a corner of Eden, with water dripping and burbling around lush plantings. The artisans here create organically shaped sculptures, bowls, urns, columns, and plaques from concrete, then color and stain them to look as though they were unearthed from antiquity. Items are for sale.

Retrace your route back to the intersection of Winslow Way and WA 305. Head north ¼ mile to:

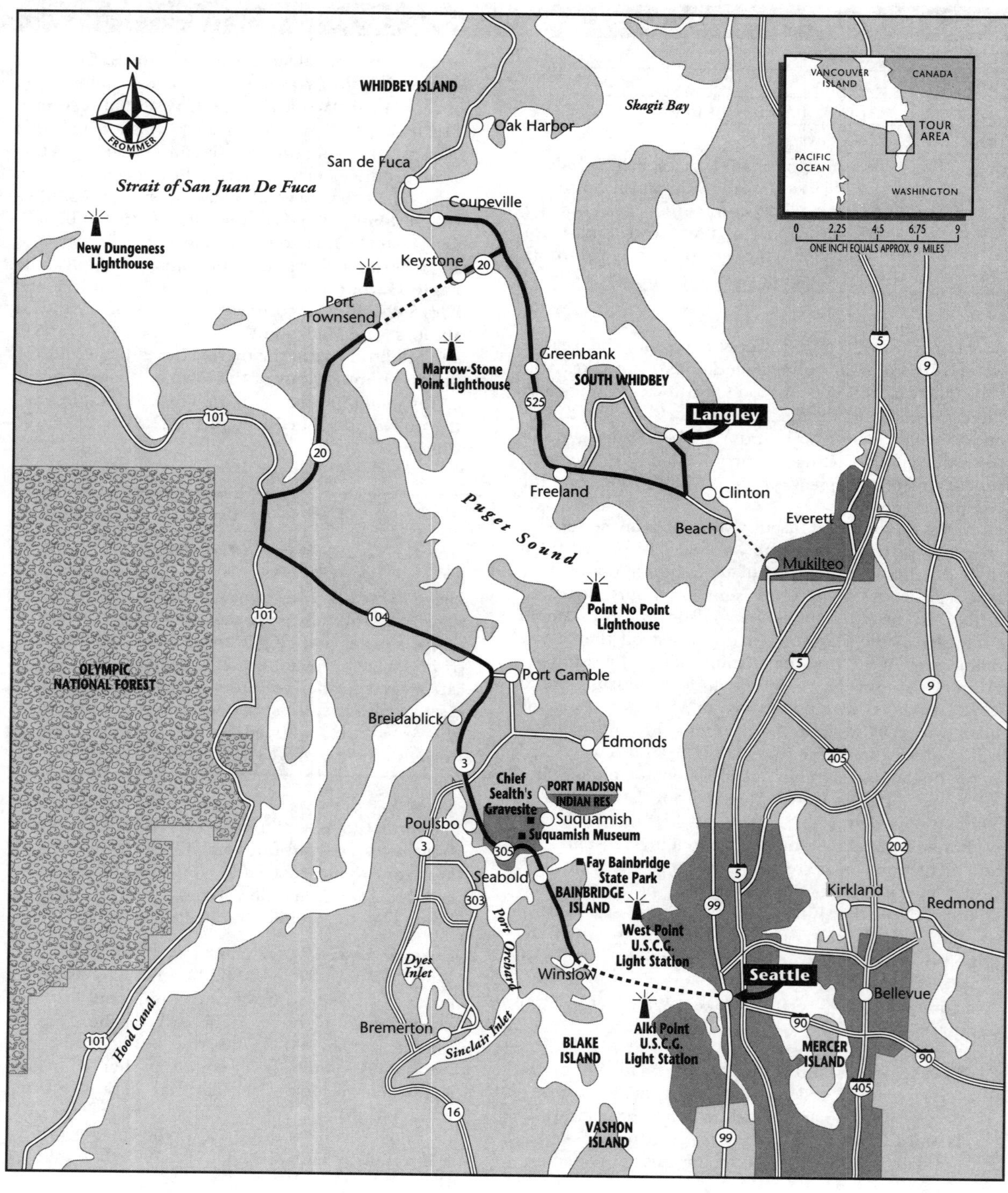
N
FROMMER
WHIDBEY ISLAND
Skagit Bay
VANCOUVER ISLAND
CANADA
TOUR AREA
PACIFIC OCEAN
WASHINGTON
0 2.25 4.5 6.75 9
ONE INCH EQUALS APPROX. 9 MILES
Oak Harbor
San de Fuca
Strait of San Juan De Fuca
Coupeville
New Dungeness Lighthouse
Keystone
Port Townsend
Marrow-Stone Point Lighthouse
Greenbank
SOUTH WHIDBEY
Langley
Freeland
Clinton
Puget Sound
Beach
Everett
Mukilteo
Point No Point Lighthouse
OLYMPIC NATIONAL FOREST
Port Gamble
Breidablick
Edmonds
Chief Sealth's Gravesite
PORT MADISON INDIAN RES.
Suquamish
Poulsbo
Suquamish Museum
Fay Bainbridge State Park
Seabold
BAINBRIDGE ISLAND
Kirkland
Redmond
West Point U.S.C.G. Light Station
Port Orchard
Dyes Inlet
Winslow
Seattle
Bellevue
Hood Canal
Bremerton
Sinclair Inlet
BLAKE ISLAND
Alki Point U.S.C.G. Light Station
MERCER ISLAND
VASHON ISLAND

3. **Bainbridge Island Winery,** WA 305 (tel 206/842-WINE), where the Bentryn family tends its vineyard and makes wine. The winery and a small museum are open Wed–Sun, noon–5pm; tastings are offered.

Continue north on WA 305 about 6 miles and follow the signs to:

4. **Bloedel Reserve,** 7571 NE Dolphin Dr (tel 206/842-7631). Prentice and Virginia Bloedel bought this 150-acre property in 1951. Over the next 30 years, the Bloedels blended the natural setting of second-growth forest, meadows, and wetlands with designs from horticultural professionals. Today the preserve, owned by an independent foundation, includes a native woodland and bird refuge with red-winged blackbirds, ducks, geese, trumpeter swans, and tundra swans. There are also wild flowers, perennials, and more than 15,000 cyclamen, as well as an orchid trail, Japanese garden, reflecting garden, moss garden, and camellia walk. Tours of the estate's mansion are available. The reserve is open by reservation only; no dogs or picnicking allowed.

Retrace your route to WA 305 and continue for 1 mile north across Agate Pass Bridge. Take a right on Suquamish Way NE then go 1½ miles to a small shopping center just outside of the town of Suquamish. Go south on Division St and southeast on McKinstry St about ½ mile to a small park at the foot of McKinstry, the site of:

5. **Old Man House.** Interpretive signage tells the story of Old Man House, a structure started around 1800 as a home, fortress, and festival house. Chief Sealth's father, Schweabe, is credited with the idea of building this large tribal gathering place. Over the years, thousands of Native Americans lived here, with each family's area partitioned by woven mats. (Archeologists estimate that the house was more than 500 feet long, 60 feet wide in the middle, and 40 feet wide at each end.) Eventually, the Native Americans who lived here were moved to reservations, and what little remained of the building was burned in the 1870s. Visitors can see a flat area on the beach where the building stood, looking out to Puget Sound.

Retrace your route back to the shopping center, cross Suquamish Way NE, and turn east on South St for ¼ mile to St Peter Catholic Church, where you can see:

6. **Chief Sealth's gravesite.** Prayer ties dangle from the split-rail fence at the edge of the cemetery. On a knoll ahead, four large timbers support horizontal beams painted with intricate designs of native coastal art. Inside the structure is the headstone to the grave of Chief Sealth, revered leader of the Suquamish and Duwamish tribes, who died in 1866 at age 80. The grave is decorated with cedar boughs, bundles of sage, prayer ties, rocks, and even a poem printed on lined notebook paper.

As you drive out of the exit to South Street, you can see a totem pole looking out to the Sound. After a look through the village of Suquamish, you can retrace your route back to WA 305. From that intersection, proceed ½ mile to:

7. **Suquamish Museum,** 15383 Sandy Hook Rd (tel 360/598-3311). Here, you can experience the Pacific Northwest from the perspective of Chief Seattle and his descendants. The *Eyes of Chief Seattle* permanent exhibit focuses on the history of Puget Sound's Native Americans and their way of life, and includes displays on fishing, canoes, basket making, and food gathering; there's also a longhouse. Through photographs and recorded voices, the multimedia production *Come Forth Laughing: Voices of the Suquamish People* tells the story of the tribe over the last 100 years. Continue on WA 305 for 3½ miles to:

8. **Poulsbo.** Turn left at the first traffic light in town onto Hostmark St and park on or near Front St, which is lined with shops denoting the Scandinavian heritage of this fishing village. During the first 50 years after Poulsbo was founded in the 1880s, most residents continued to speak Norwegian. **Slys Bakery,** 18924 Front St NE (tel 360/779-2798), opened in 1966 and is still operated by the same family. The bakery turns out German sourdough rye, Swedish hearth bread, Danish pumpernickel, Norwegian black bread, potato bread, Poulsbo bread (a popular hearty bread), and several Scandinavian pastries. **Shotwell's Book Store** (tel 360/779-5909) features especially good sections on northwest travel, northwest authors, and children's books. Fiber artists and hobbyists will find a rich array of handspun and novelty yarns at **Victoria's Attic,** 18846 E Front St NE (tel 360/779-3666), and **Lauren's Wild & Wooly,** 19020 Front St (tel toll free 800/743-2100). Self-guided historic walking tour brochures are available from the **Poulsbo Chamber of Commerce,** 19131 8th Ave NE (tel 360/779-4848).

Return to WA 305 and continue through Poulsbo. Turn right on Bond Rd for 1½ miles, then make a left on Foss Rd.

Retrace your route and head north on WA 305. Continue north on WA 3 to the Hood Canal Bridge, cross the bridge to the Olympic Peninsula, and drive 31 miles to Port Townsend via WA 104, US 101, and WA 20.

9. **Port Townsend** is one of only four Victorian seaports on the National Register of Historic Places. Capt George Vancouver discovered the large, safe harbor in 1792 and named it for the English Marquis of Townshend. It took pioneers another 60 years to settle there. Port Townsend's early economy centered around logging and farming, and later shipping. Many of the ships that came into Puget Sound picked up their crews in Port Townsend, and the waterfront area spawned brothels, saloons, and gambling halls. (The more genteel families lived on the bluff, away from the waterfront.) Property values and population soared when word came that the Union Pacific Railroad would be routing its line to Port Townsend, but the railroad terminated in Tacoma instead and the 1890s ended in a bust. Today, the downtown waterfront, now designated a National Historic District, is filled with restored late-19th-century buildings.

Ancestral Spirits Gallery, 921 Washington St (tel 360/385-0078), features paintings, carvings, and jewelry by North America's first people. Many of the elegant mansions on the bluff that were homes of ship captains have been converted to bed-and-breakfast inns. Fort Worden is home of Centrum, an arts and education program, and a convention center, with accommodations in the old officers' quarters. For walking tours of Port Townsend, contact **Guided Historical Tours,** 820 Tyler St (tel 360/385-1967). Information is available from the **Visitor Center,** 2437 E Sims Way (tel 360/385-2722 or toll free 800/499-0047 for a recorded list of weekly events).

If you'd like to make Port Townsend an overnight stop, **the James House,** 1238 Washington St (tel 360/385-1238 or toll free 800/385-1238), is a fine choice. Located in a three-story Victorian mansion built in 1889, this elegant bed-and-breakfast inn features the original handcarved cherry staircase and parquet floors. The 12 guestrooms are individually decorated with period antiques. Your overnight stay includes a full breakfast with fresh-baked scones, fritatta or other egg entree, and fresh fruit.

Take a Break

The **Silverwater,** 237 Taylor St (tel 360/385-6448), features high ceilings and tall windows in a restored brick building in downtown Port Townsend. The eclectic menu of pasta, seafood, and vegetarian entrees appeals to couples and business diners as well as families enjoying a special outing. Entrees cost $8 to $14.

Take the ferry from Port Townsend to Whidbey Island, named for Joseph Whidbey, sailing master for Capt George Vancouver. Continue north on WA 20 to:

10. **Coupeville,** the oldest town on the island. In 1852, Thomas Coupe and his wife Maria filed a land claim on 320 acres. During the 1800s, the town boomed with trade from the Coupeville Wharf in wool, lumber, and farm produce.

Self-guided walking tour brochures of historical buildings, including the Coupe home, are available at the **Island County Historical Society Museum,** Alexander and Front Sts (tel 360/678-3310). **Exclusively Whidbey,** 11 NW Coveland St (tel 360/678-5416), features gifts from Whidbey Island, such as Whidbey's Coffee, Seabolt's smoked salmon, and Scully's Farm Honey.

Take a Break

For a quiet lunch or an enchanting dinner, head for **Christopher's** in Mariner's Court at Front and Alexander Sts (tel 360/678-5480). Young chef Christopher Panek offers a seasonal menu relying on fresh Northwest seafood, vegetables, and herbs. Entrees are $12.50 to $17.50.

Head south on WA 525 toward Greenbank, on Whidbey's "waist." At this narrow point, you can see both Admiralty Inlet on the west and Saratoga Passage to the east, where gray whales visit from March to late May on their way to Alaska. The next stop is:

11. **Whidbey's Loganberry Farm,** 657 Wonn Rd (tel 360/678-7700). In the early 1900s, Finnish immigrants settled here and by 1920 they had planted fields of loganberry vines. Today, you can tour the operation, taste the liqueur, and enjoy a picnic on the property. Just south of Greenbank, follow the signs to:

12. **Meerkerk Rhododendron Gardens,** Resort Rd (tel 360/678-1912). The Seattle Rhododendron Society maintains a 53-acre woodland garden started by Ann and Max Meerkerk in the early 1960s. The gardens include 10 acres of rhododendrons and ornamental trees (peak bloom is in April and May), and 43 acres of woodland, ponds, wildlife habitat, and nature trails.

Retrace your route to WA 525 and continue south. Head north on Bayview Rd and then northeast on Brooks Hill Rd into:

13. Langley. In the 1880s, teenager Jacob Anthes filed a claim for 160 acres of timber land on a bluff above Saratoga Passage. Anthes was the town's first shopkeeper, first postmaster, founder of the school, and developer of roads for early settlers on the island. Most importantly, he supplied wood for steamships on Puget Sound—and so began the town of Langley. The town was dealt a blow when the Great Northern Railroad was extended to Bellingham in 1894 and steamships bypassed Langley, but just a few years later (during the Alaska gold rush of 1898) the town bounced back by supplying lumber for wharves along Puget Sound.

Today, Langley retains its small-town character. Several shops and galleries along First Street attest to the number of artists and artisans living in the area. **Annie Steffen's,** 101 First St (tel 360/221-6535), features handknit and handwoven apparel. Several bed-and-breakfast inns in the area offer quaint accommodations.

Take a Break

The **Garibyan Brothers Cafe Langley,** 113 First St (tel 360/221-3090), is a light and airy bistro serving up some of the finest Mediterranean fare around. Fresh Northwest ingredients are the foundation for entrees such as braised lamb shank wrapped in grilled eggplant, moussaka, and Russian cream. Dinner entrees are $13 to $17.

Washington Listings

Aberdeen

See also Hoquiam

Historic lumbering community located at the confluence of the Chehalis and Wishkah Rivers. Several of the lumber-baron mansions in town have been converted to bed-and-breakfast inns. This is the home port of the tall ship *Lady Washington.* **Information:** Grays Harbor Chamber of Commerce, 506 Duffy St, Aberdeen, 98520 (tel 360/532-1924).

MOTELS

Nordic Inn Convention Center
1700 S Boone St, 98520; tel 360/533-0100 or toll free 800/442-0101; fax 360/533-3229. Clean, well managed property close to airport. **Rooms:** 66 rms. CI 4pm/CO 11am. Nonsmoking rms avail. The old rooms are out of date with cheap fiberglass partitions and veneer-style furniture. **Amenities:** Cable TV, refrig. No A/C. **Services:** **Facilities:** 400 2 restaurants, 1 bar (w/entertainment). Dancing in lounge Tues–Sat. **Rates:** \$45–\$60 S; \$50–\$70 D. Extra person \$10. Children under age 12 stay free. Parking: Outdoor, free. AE, DC, DISC, MC, V.

Olympic Inn Motel
616 W Heron St, 98520; tel 360/533-4200; fax 360/533-6223. At jct US 101 and Alder St. Older motel offers large rooms with modest furnishings. Noisy. **Rooms:** 55 rms, stes, and effic. CI 1pm/CO noon. Nonsmoking rms avail. **Amenities:** Cable TV w/movies, refrig. No A/C. 1 unit w/fireplace. **Services:** Phone for availability of pet rooms. **Facilities:** 75 Washer/dryer. **Rates:** Peak (July 1–Sept 15) \$40–\$65 S; \$50–\$70 D; \$83 ste; \$60–\$88 effic. Extra person \$7. Children under age 16 stay free. Lower rates off-season. Parking: Outdoor, free. AE, CB, DC, DISC, MC, V.

Red Lion Inn
521 W Wishkah, 98520; tel 360/532-5210 or toll free 800/547-8010; fax 360/533-8483. At Michigan. Basic motel located on a busy street, convenient to downtown. Not as upscale as most Red Lion Inns. **Rooms:** 67 rms. CI 2pm/CO noon. Nonsmoking rms avail. **Amenities:** A/C, cable TV. Iron and ironing board in every room. **Services:** **Facilities:** **Rates (CP):** Peak (May–Sept) \$64 S; \$74 D. Extra person \$10. Children under age 18 stay free. Lower rates off-season. Parking: Outdoor, free. AE, CB, DC, DISC, JCB, MC, V.

RESTAURANTS

Billy's Bar and Grill
322 E Heron St; tel 360/533-7144. US 101 and Heron at Chehalis River Bridge. **American.** Known locally for burgers and steaks. Has stained-glass and rich cherry-wood paneled interior. **FYI:** Reservations not accepted. Children's menu. **Open:** Mon–Thurs 11am–11pm, Fri–Sat 11am–midnight, Sun noon–9pm. **Prices:** Main courses \$4.95–\$10.95. AE, DC, MC, V.

Bridges Restaurant
112 N G St; tel 360/532-6563. Corner of 1st and G Sts. **Seafood/Steak.** Family restaurant with quirky library motif in both dining room and bar. House specialties are grilled oysters, oven-broiled salmon, and razor clams. **FYI:** Reservations accepted. Children's menu. No smoking. **Open:** Peak (June–Sept) Mon–Thurs 11am–10pm, Fri–Sat 11am–11pm, Sun 4–11pm. **Prices:** Main courses \$8.95–\$14.95. AE, CB, DC, DISC, MC, V.

ATTRACTION

Grays Harbor Historical Seaport Authority
813 E Heron St; tel 360/532-8612 or toll free 800/200-LADY. Visitors can tour the tall ship *Lady Washington,* a replica of one of the vessels Capt Robert Gray sailed when he first explored the Northwest coast. Heritage education programs, port-to-port cruises, and group charters. **Open:** Daily 10am–5pm. Closed some hols. **\$**

Anacortes

A mid-sized city on Fidalgo Island. Connected by bridges to the mainland, it serves as a ferry terminal for the San Juan Islands. **Information:** Anacortes Chamber of Commerce, 819 Commercial Ave, Suite G, Anacortes, 98221 (tel 360/293-1595).

HOTEL

Majestic Hotel
419 Commercial Ave, 98221; tel 360/293-3355; fax 360/293-5214. At 5th St. Upscale hotel located in an 1889 former meat market. **Rooms:** 23 rms. Executive level. CI 3pm/CO 11am. Nonsmoking rms avail. Individually decorated rooms. **Amenities:** A/C, cable TV w/movies, dataport, VCR. Some units w/minibars, some w/terraces, some w/fireplaces, some w/whirlpools. **Services:** Babysitting. **Facilities:** 60 1 restaurant (lunch and dinner only), 1 bar. The Rose and Crown Pub serves snacks and a variety of beers in an English tavern setting. The Courtyard Bistro specializes in fresh local seafood. **Rates (CP):** Peak (summer) $89–$189 S or D. Extra person $15. Children under age 4 stay free. Lower rates off-season. Parking: Outdoor, free. AE, DISC, MC, V.

MOTELS

Anacortes Inn
3006 Commercial Ave, 98221; tel 360/293-3153 or toll free 800/327-7976; fax 360/293-0209. An attractive place for a family to stay. **Rooms:** 44 rms and effic. CI 2pm/CO 11am. Nonsmoking rms avail. The standard rooms have new carpeting, drapes, and bedspreads. **Amenities:** Cable TV. No A/C. 1 unit w/whirlpool. Most rooms have new refrigerators, and all have small microwaves. **Services:** **Facilities:** Swimming pool is small. **Rates:** Peak (May–Oct 15) $42–$60 S; $44–$72 D; $55–$82 effic. Extra person $5. Children under age 13 stay free. Lower rates off-season. Parking: Outdoor, free. AE, CB, DC, DISC, JCB, MC, V.

Marina Inn
3300 Commercial Ave, 98221; tel 360/293-1100; fax 360/293-1100. At 33rd St. The attractive Marina Inn, opened in 1995, is the newest motel in Anacortes. A good choice for families, couples, and business travelers. **Rooms:** 52 rms and effic. CI 2pm/CO 11am. Nonsmoking rms avail. Rooms are neat and clean. **Amenities:** Cable TV. No A/C. Some units w/whirlpools. Hot tub rooms and kitchen rooms feature king-size beds, microwaves, refrigerators, and wet bars. **Services:** **Facilities:** **Rates (CP):** Peak (May 1–Oct 1) $59–$65 S; $71–$83 D; $73 effic. Extra person $6. Children under age 12 stay free. Lower rates off-season. Parking: Outdoor, free. AE, DC, DISC, MC, V.

Ship Harbor Inn
5316 Ferry Terminal Rd, 98221; tel 360/293-5177 or toll free 800/852-8568 in the US, 800/235-8568 in Canada. Next to Ferry Terminal. This motel, in the trees near the ferry terminal, offers the best view in Anacortes. **Rooms:** 16 rms, stes, and effic; 10 cottages/villas. CI 3pm/CO 11am. Nonsmoking rms avail. **Amenities:** Cable TV, refrig. No A/C. All units w/terraces, some w/fireplaces. Not all TVs have remote control. **Services:** **Facilities:** 120 Playground, washer/dryer. **Rates (CP):** Peak (June–Sept) $65–$95 S or D; $85–$95 ste; $85–$95 effic; $85–$95 cottage/villa. Extra person $5. Children under age 13 stay free. Lower rates off-season. Parking: Outdoor, free. AE, DC, DISC, MC, V.

RESTAURANTS

Calico Cupboard Old Town Cafe and Bakery
901 Commercial Ave; tel 360/293-7315. Adjacent to Visitor Information Center parking lot. **Eclectic.** Emphasizes organically grown and preservative-free ingredients. Grandma's hotcakes, made with oatmeal, cornmeal, and buttermilk, are served with fresh fruit or sausage and syrup. Breads and pastries are displayed in an old-fashioned case. **FYI:** Reservations accepted. Beer and wine only. No smoking. Additional location: 720 S 1st St, La Conner (tel 466-4451). **Open:** Mon–Sat 6:30am–3:30pm, Sun 7am–4:30pm. **Prices:** Lunch main courses $4.25–$7.95. No CC.

Charlie's
Ferry Terminal Rd; tel 360/293-7377. Near the Ferry Terminal. **Seafood/Steak.** Nautical decor and views of the ferry building accent this steak and seafood restaurant. Puget Sound salmon is grilled or poached; scallops Swiss are served in a casserole with a Swiss cheese sauce. Fresh local oysters are prepared various ways. **FYI:** Reservations recommended. Children's menu. **Open:** Sun–Thurs 11:30am–9pm, Fri–Sat 11:30am–10pm. **Prices:** Main courses $9.95–$18.95. AE, DISC, MC, V.

La Petite
3401 Commercial Ave; tel 360/293-4644. At 34th Street. **French.** Aside from some Dutch decorations, the decor is nondescript. Two favorite entrees are chateaubriand, and lamb marinated in sambal and other Indonesian spices served over rice. The dessert *gaaresmelpap* is a farina-based almond pudding with raspberry sauce. **FYI:** Reservations recommended. **Open:** Tues–Sun 5–10pm. **Prices:** Main courses $14.95–$24.50; prix fixe $14.95–$24.50. AE, CB, DC, DISC, MC, V.

Arlington

Located at the foothills of the Cascade Mountains and along the Stillaguamish River, this community offers a wide range of outdoor recreational opportunities. **Information:** Greater Arlington Chamber of Commerce, 120 N Olympic Ave, PO Box 102, Arlington 98223 (tel 360/435-3708).

MOTELS

Arlington Motor Inn
2214 WA 530, 98223; tel 360/652-9595; fax 360/652-9595. Exit 208 off I-5. Tidy but noisy; a popular motel for truckers. **Rooms:** 42 rms. CI open/CO 11am. Nonsmoking rms avail. **Amenities:** A/C, TV. **Services:** **Facilities:** Enclosed whirlpool is a pleasant surprise. **Rates:** Peak (June–

Oct) $43–$46 S; $56–$58 D. Children under age 12 stay free. Lower rates off-season. Parking: Outdoor, free. AE, DC, DISC, MC, V.

Smokey Point Motor Inn
17329 Smokey Point Dr, 98223; tel 360/659-8561; fax 360/658-8703. Exit 206 off I-5. This mom-and-pop motel is difficult to find from the highway, even though you can see the sign from a distance. **Rooms:** 54 rms and stes. CI open/CO 11am. Nonsmoking rms avail. Very dark, dungeonlike rooms have brown shag carpets and shiny, brown-and-gold foil wallpaper. **Amenities:** A/C, satel TV. **Services:** **Facilities:** Sauna, whirlpool, playground. Small pool; lawn area for kids and dogs. **Rates:** Peak (July–Sept) $39–$75 S or D; $75 ste. Extra person $5. Lower rates off-season. Parking: Outdoor, free. AE, DC, DISC, MC, V.

Ashford

Access point for the only year-round entrance to Mount Rainier National Park.

MOTEL

Whittaker's Bunkhouse
30205 WA 706 E, 98304; tel 360/569-2439. This 1912 loggers' and mill-workers' bunkhouse, located just outside the west entrance of Mount Rainier National Park, was completely renovated in 1990 and is a popular place for skiers, mountain climbers, and hikers. Owner Lou Whittaker is a famous mountain climber himself. **Rooms:** 12 rms. CI 4pm/CO noon. No smoking. Rooms are small but cozy. **Amenities:** No A/C, phone, or TV. **Services:** Friendly staff offers tips on hiking, skiing, and climbing Mount Ranier. **Facilities:** 300-foot front porch. Espresso Cafe (muffins and soft drinks) is meeting place for winter climbing seminars and headquarters for Mount Tehama hut-to-hut cross-country ski trail system. **Rates:** Peak (May–Sept) $55–$76 S or D. Children under age 10 stay free. Lower rates off-season. Parking: Outdoor, free. MC, V.

INN

Alexander's Country Inn
37515 WA 706 E, 98304; tel 360/569-2300 or toll free 800/654-7615; fax 360/569-2323. 19 acres. Popular country inn located in a modified Victorian house. **Rooms:** 12 rms and stes; 2 cottages/villas. CI 3pm/CO 11am. No smoking. Accommodations are well-appointed with beautiful antiques. **Amenities:** No A/C, phone, or TV. Some units w/terraces, 1 w/fireplace. Fresh flowers in rooms. **Services:** Wine/sherry served. Friendly staff can provide information about hiking, fishing, and skiing in the area. **Facilities:** 1 restaurant (*see* "Restaurants" below), games rm, whirlpool, washer/dryer, guest lounge. Excellent restaurant. Hot tub overlooks small trout pond. **Rates (BB):** Peak (May–Oct) $75–$89 S or D; $95–$125 ste; $195–$255 cottage/villa. Extra person $15. Children under age 2 stay free. Lower rates off-season. AP rates avail. Parking: Outdoor, free. MC, V.

LODGES

Nisqually Lodge
31609 WA 706, 98304; tel 360/569-8804; fax 360/569-2435. Big, standard motel located several miles from the west entrance of Mount Rainier National Park. **Rooms:** 24 rms. CI 3pm/CO 11am. No smoking. **Amenities:** A/C, TV. Some units w/terraces. **Services:** Babysitting. **Facilities:** Whirlpool, playground. **Rates (CP):** Peak (May–Sept) $67–$77 S or D. Extra person $5–$10. Children under age 2 stay free. Lower rates off-season. Parking: Outdoor, free. AE, DC, MC, V.

Rainier Overland Restaurant & Lodge
31811 WA 706, PO Box S, 98304; tel 360/569-0851; fax 360/569-2033. A small friendly place owned by Kathryn Simonson, wife of climbing guide Eric Simonson. Located five miles from the west entrance to Mount Rainier National Park, the buildings have the bleached-wood look of the Old West. **Rooms:** 8 rms; 1 cottage/villa. CI 4pm/CO noon. No smoking. Simple and clean. Great views of mountains and a broad meadow. **Amenities:** No A/C, phone, or TV. 1 unit w/terrace. **Services:** Babysitting. **Facilities:** 1 restaurant (*see* "Restaurants" below). **Rates:** Peak (May–Oct) $65–$85 S or D; $95–$145 cottage/villa. Extra person $10. Children under age 2 stay free. Lower rates off-season. Parking: Outdoor, free. Closed Nov–Apr. DISC, MC, V.

RESTAURANTS

★ Alexander's Country Inn
37515 WA 706 E; tel 360/569-2300. **American.** This pretty country restaurant has stained-glass windows, lots of pine accents, and booths. Menu specialties include pan-fried trout, salmon, wild-blackberry pie, and strawberry shortcake. **FYI:** Reservations accepted. Children's menu. Beer and wine only. No smoking. **Open:** Peak (May–Oct) daily 7:30am–9:30pm. **Prices:** Main courses $10–$17. MC, V.

Copper Creek Inn
35707 WA 706 E; tel 360/569-2326. **American.** Visitors here enjoy fresh mountain trout, stew, homemade breads, and delicious wild-blackberry pie, served in a western-style setting. **FYI:** Reservations accepted. Children's menu. Beer and wine only. No smoking. **Open:** Peak (June–Sept) daily 8am–8pm. Closed Nov–Jan. **Prices:** Main courses $12–$15. Lunch main courses $5–$7. AE, MC, V.

★ Rainier Overland Restaurant & Lodge
31811 WA 706; tel 360/569-0851. 1 mi E of Ashford, 5 mi from Mount Rainier National Park. **New American.** Log cabin–style restaurant decorated with stained glass, original art by local artists, and mountaineering photos from around

the world. Family-style specialties include a good Monte Cristo sandwich, hearty four-egg omelettes, and the "garden patch"—sautéed vegetables and Swiss cheese in a pita pocket. **FYI:** Reservations accepted. Children's menu. Beer and wine only. **Open:** Peak (May–Oct) daily 6:30am–9pm. Closed Nov–Apr. **Prices:** Main courses $9–$11. DISC, MC, V.

★ Wild Berry Restaurant
37720 WA 706 E; tel 360/569-2628. ½ mi from Nisqually entrance to Mount Rainier National Park. **Northwest.** This rural eatery occupies a log cabin complete with wood stove and nice plants. Menu specialties are veggie chili, wild-berry cornbread, and blackberry pie. Another favorite is the peasant pie: onions, potatoes, turkey, and small white beans in a creamy corn casserole covered with melted cheese. **FYI:** Reservations accepted. Children's menu. Beer and wine only. No smoking. **Open:** Daily 11am–8pm. **Prices:** Main courses $7–$10. MC, V.

ATTRACTION

Northwest Trek Wildlife Park
11610 Trek Dr E, Eatonville; tel 360/832-6117 or toll free 800/433-TREK. 13 mi NW of Ashford. This unique 600-acre wildlife park displays animals without the use of cages or bars. The park features the largest natural outdoor display of grizzly and black bears in North America. At the hands-on discovery center, visitors can touch live amphibians and reptiles, and see thousands of bees in a working beehive. There is a 50-minute, naturalist-guided tram tour and tree-lined paths for walking. Gift shop and cafe. **Open:** Mar–Oct, daily 9:30am–sunset; Nov–Apr, Fri–Sun 10am–3pm. Closed some hols. **$$$**

Auburn

A bedroom community, located east of Tacoma, offering easy access to water sports and mountain recreation. **Information:** Auburn Area Chamber of Commerce, 228 1st St NE, Auburn, 98002 (tel 206/833-0700).

MOTELS

UNRATED **Nendels Valu Inn**
102 15th St NE, 98002; tel 206/833-8007 or toll free 800/833-8007. Clean, well-kept property. **Rooms:** 35 rms. CI 3pm/CO 11am. Nonsmoking rms avail. **Amenities:** A/C, refrig. **Services:** **Facilities:** **Rates (CP):** $48 S; $56 D. Parking: Outdoor, free. AE, CB, DC, DISC, MC, V.

Pony Soldier Inn Best Western
1521 D St NE, 98002; tel 206/939-5950 or toll free 800/634-PONY; fax 206/735-4197. Nice, clean, standard rooms, but this older property is literally at the end of the runway of the municipal airport, so noise could be a problem. **Rooms:** 66 rms. CI 3pm/CO noon. Nonsmoking rms avail. **Amenities:** A/C, cable TV w/movies, refrig. Some units w/minibars, some w/terraces. **Services:** **Facilities:** Sauna, whirlpool. **Rates (CP):** $66–$75 S; $74–$84 D. Extra person $5. Children under age 12 stay free. Parking: Outdoor, free. AE, CB, DC, DISC, MC, V.

Bainbridge Island

Located directly across the Puget Sound from Seattle, Bainbridge Island is one of Washington's main artist communities. **Information:** Bainbridge Island Chamber of Commerce, 590 Winslow Way E, Bainbridge Island, 98110 (tel 206/842-3700).

RESTAURANTS

Cafe Nola
101 Winslow Way E; tel 206/842-3822. At Madison St. **Cafe.** Two sisters own this European-style bakery. One was a caterer in San Francisco; the other was celebrity chef Wolfgang Puck's pastry expert for 12 years. Offerings include fresh peach scones, croissants, potato egg pie and various small sandwiches. Organic farmers grow produce especially for the cafe. **FYI:** Reservations not accepted. No smoking. **Open:** Tues–Sun 8am–5pm. **Prices:** Lunch main courses $3.25–$6.75. No CC.

The Madrona Waterfront Cafe
Parfitt Way SW and Madison Ave; tel 206/842-8339. At Winslow Wharf Marina on Eagle Harbor. **Regional American.** Nice views overlooking the harbor. Much of the fish served is caught locally. The prawns and scallops Espagnol is a spicy seafood entree with Asian and Mediterranean influences. **FYI:** Reservations recommended. Children's menu. **Open:** Daily 11:30am–9pm. **Prices:** Main courses $7.95–$14.95. AE, MC, V.

★ Streamliner Diner
397 Winslow Way E; tel 206/842-8595. **New American.** A breakfast favorite here is the veggie tofu scramble with mushrooms, garlic, green onion, spinach, and oyster sauce served with grilled potatoes and toast. Decorated with period diner kitsch and kids' artwork. **FYI:** Reservations not accepted. No liquor license. No smoking. **Open:** Mon–Fri 7am–3pm, Sat–Sun 8am–2:30pm. **Prices:** Lunch main courses $2.50–$6.95. No CC.

ATTRACTIONS

Bainbridge Island Historical Museum
7650 NE High School Rd; tel 206/842-2773. Housed within a restored one-room schoolhouse (built circa 1908) are photos, videos, and artifacts that interpret island history, folklore, architecture, and natural wonders. **Open:** May–Sept, Sat–Sun 1–4pm. Closed July 4. **Free**

Suquamish Museum
15383 Sandy Hook Rd; tel 206/598-3311. Located on the Port Madison Indian Reservation, this museum is dedicated

to the Suquamish people and Chief Sealth (from whom Seattle derived its name). In addition to exhibits covering Suquamish early history, there are canoe-carving and Native American art demonstrations. The grave of Chief Sealth, the site of a Suquamish village and longhouse, and the Suquamish Fish Hatchery are all nearby. **Open:** Mem Day–Sept, daily 10am–5pm; Oct–May, Fri–Sun 11am–4pm. Closed some hols. **$**

Bloedel Reserve
7571 NE Dolphin Dr; tel 206/842-7631. This 150-acre preserve on the northern end of Bainbridge Island is the ideal place for a stroll amid plants from around the world. Unspoiled, dense Northwest forest covers 84 acres, while the rest of the park contains formal English- and Japanese-style gardens. A bird refuge houses blackbirds, ducks, geese, swans, and herons. Self-guided tour audio tapes and maps available at the visitors center. Tours are by reservation only, and no food is allowed on the grounds. **Open:** Wed–Sun 10am–4pm, by reservation. Closed some hols. **$$$**

Bellevue

The major metropolitan area in eastern King County, Bellevue serves as a transportation and distribution hub and is home to several high-tech industries. The city is linked to Seattle by the Evergreen Point Floating Bridge. **Information:** East King County Convention and Visitors Bureau, 520 112th Ave NE #101W, Bellevue, 98004 (tel 206/455-1926).

HOTELS

Courtyard by Marriott
14615 NE 29th Place, 98007; tel 206/869-5300 or toll free 800/321-2211; fax 206/883-9122. 148th Ave exit off WA 520. Secure, small hotel located at crossroads, but feels residential. Manicured courtyard with patio and indoor pool adds to the sense of separation from the world. **Rooms:** 152 rms and stes. CI 3pm/CO 1pm. Nonsmoking rms avail. **Amenities:** A/C, cable TV w/movies, dataport. Some units w/terraces. All rooms have iron and ironing board. **Services:** Babysitting. Full buffet breakfast served every day, dinner served Mon–Fri. **Facilities:** 50 1 restaurant (bkfst and dinner only), 1 bar, whirlpool, washer/dryer. **Rates:** $84 S; $94 D; $100–$110 ste. Parking: Outdoor, free. AE, DC, DISC, MC, V.

Embassy Suites
3225 158th Ave SE, 98008; tel 206/644-2500 or toll free 800/EMBASSY; fax 206/644-4556. Exit 11A off I-90 E; exit 11 off I-90 W. Attractive five-story atrium hotel. A quarter-mile waterway with two waterfalls runs through the atrium, which also sports Mediterranean-style balconies, palm trees, and giant ferns. **Rooms:** 240 stes. CI 3pm/CO 1pm. Nonsmoking rms avail. Every suite is spacious. Some guests might be disturbed by clatter of waterfalls in lobby. **Amenities:** A/C, refrig, dataport, voice mail. Some units w/terraces, some w/whirlpools. Wet bar, 2 TVs. **Services:** Car-rental desk, social director, babysitting. Nightly reception 5:30–7:30pm with wine and spirits—fine, except promised hors d'oeuvres were popcorn. **Facilities:** 500 1 restaurant, 1 bar (w/entertainment), games rm, spa, sauna, whirlpool, washer/dryer. **Rates (BB):** Peak (June–Aug) $139–$169 ste. Extra person $15. Children under age 17 stay free. Lower rates off-season. Parking: Outdoor, free. AE, CB, DC, JCB, MC, V.

Hyatt Regency Bellevue
900 Bellevue Way NE, 98004 (Downtown); tel 206/462-1234 or toll free 800/233-1234; fax 206/451-3017. At NE 8th. With two small lobbies decorated with rich woods and bouquets of flowers, the Hyatt has the intimate feel of a boutique hotel. Located diagonally across from the Bellevue Square Mall, it attracts mainly a corporate clientele. **Rooms:** 382 rms and stes. Executive level. CI 3pm/CO noon. Nonsmoking rms avail. **Amenities:** A/C, cable TV w/movies, dataport, voice mail. Some units w/terraces, 1 w/whirlpool. Ironing board. Regency Club and Business Plan floors offer a fax in every room, plus work area and dataport. **Services:** VP Twice-daily maid svce, car-rental desk, babysitting. **Facilities:** 600 2 restaurants (*see* "Restaurants" below), 2 bars, beauty salon. **Rates:** $145–$175 S; $160–$190 D; $225–$800 ste. Extra person $25. Children under age 18 stay free. Parking: Indoor, $7/day. Shopper and Romance packages avail. AE, CB, DC, DISC, JCB, MC, V.

Red Lion Hotel Bellevue
300 112th Ave SE, 98004; tel 206/455-1300 or toll free 800/547-8010; fax 206/455-0466. A dramatic entrance opens into seven-story-high vaulted atrium. The Atrium cafe, plus trees, vines, flowers, and plenty of natural light help make a festive atmosphere. **Rooms:** 353 rms and stes. Executive level. CI 3pm/CO noon. Nonsmoking rms avail. Double vanities in baths. **Amenities:** A/C, dataport. All units w/terraces, some w/whirlpools. Irons in every room. **Services:** VP Car-rental desk, babysitting. Free shuttle service to Bellevue Square Mall. **Facilities:** 1200 2 restaurants (*see* "Restaurants" below), 2 bars (1 w/entertainment), whirlpool, beauty salon. **Rates:** $120–$140 S; $135–$155 D; $250–$495 ste. Extra person $15. Children under age 18 stay free. Parking: Outdoor, free. AE, CB, DC, DISC, JCB, MC, V.

Residence Inn by Marriott Seattle East
14455 NE 29th Place, 98007; tel 206/882-1222 or toll free 800/331-3131; fax 206/885-9260. WA 520 to 148th Ave. Looking like a residential condominium, the Residence Inn offers a snug lobby with sunken fireplace pit and vaulted ceiling where people gather for breakfast, reading, or Tues evening cocktails. **Rooms:** 120 stes. CI 4pm/CO noon. Nonsmoking rms avail. Rooms are complete apartments for long-stay guests. **Amenities:** A/C, cable TV w/movies,

refrig, dataport. Some units w/terraces, all w/fireplaces. **Services:** Twice-daily maid svce. Manager's reception and dinner on Tues evenings. **Facilities:** Basketball, volleyball, whirlpool, playground, washer/dryer. Reciprocal sauna and pool arrangement with neighboring Courtyard by Marriott. **Rates (CP):** Peak (Apr–Oct) $97–$198 ste. Lower rates off-season. Parking: Outdoor, free. AE, CB, DC, DISC, MC, V.

West Coast Bellevue Hotel
625 116th Ave NE, 98004; tel 206/455-9444 or toll free 800/426-0670; fax 206/455-2154. At NE 8th. This property's main feature is its prime location off the NE 8th approach to I-405. **Rooms:** 176 rms and stes. CI 3pm/CO noon. Nonsmoking rms avail. **Amenities:** A/C, TV w/movies, dataport. **Services:** Car-rental desk. **Facilities:** 1 restaurant, 1 bar (w/entertainment). **Rates:** Peak (July–Sept) $58–$77 S; $68–$87 D; $77 ste. Extra person $10. Children under age 16 stay free. Lower rates off-season. Parking: Outdoor, free. AE, CB, DC, DISC, MC, V.

MOTELS

La Quinta Inn
10530 NE Northup Way, 98033; tel 206/828-6585 or toll free 800/531-5900; fax 206/822-8722. Between Lake Wash Blvd and 108th Ave NE. Attracts mostly business travelers to the nearby high-tech corridor. Eight blocks from Bellevue Square Shopping Mall. **Rooms:** 118 rms and stes. CI 2pm/CO noon. Nonsmoking rms avail. **Amenities:** A/C, satel TV w/movies, dataport. **Services:** **Facilities:** **Rates (CP):** Peak (May 27–Oct 14) $65–$72 S; $72–$88 D; $110 ste. Extra person $8. Children under age 18 stay free. Lower rates off-season. Parking: Outdoor, free. AE, DC, DISC, MC, V.

Red Lion Inn-Bellevue Center
818 112th Ave NE, 98004; or toll free 800/Red-Lion; fax 206/454-3964. At NE 8th. The location—at Bellevue's crossroads—is the main feature here. **Rooms:** 207 rms, stes, and effic. CI 3pm/CO noon. Nonsmoking rms avail. **Amenities:** A/C, cable TV w/movies, dataport. Some units w/terraces. **Services:** Free shuttle to Bellevue Square. **Facilities:** 2 restaurants, 1 bar (w/entertainment), games rm, whirlpool. **Rates:** Peak (June–Sept) $65–$88 S; $75–$98 D; $119–$150 ste; $119–$150 effic. Extra person $10. Children under age 18 stay free. Lower rates off-season. Parking: Outdoor, free. AE, DC, DISC, JCB, MC, V.

RESTAURANTS

★ Andre's Gourmet Cuisine
14125 NE 20th St; tel 206/747-6551. At 140th NE. **Continental/Asian.** This bistro-style eatery located in a shopping center is popular with the lunch crowd. Andre's specializes in a marriage of Western and Asian cooking. The signature dish—Eurasian pork—combines pork tenderloin with curry, coconut, ginger, onion, and apricot chutney. **FYI:** Reservations recommended. Children's menu. Beer and wine only. No smoking. **Open:** Lunch Mon–Fri 11:30am–3pm; dinner Tues–Thurs 5:30–9:30pm, Fri–Sat 5:30–10pm. **Prices:** Main courses $7–$13. AE, MC, V.

★ Eques Restaurant
In Hyatt Regency Bellevue, 900 Bellevue Way NE (Downtown); tel 206/462-1234. At NE 8th across from Bellevue Sq. **Northwest.** Although the equestrian theme lends a masculine, rich atmosphere, the menu specialties are prepared with light sauces. Perhaps try prawn and Dungeness crab ravioli, or seared sea scallops with rosemary carrot sauce, or Dungeness crab cakes. **FYI:** Reservations recommended. Children's menu. No smoking. **Open:** Breakfast Mon–Sat 6:30–11:30am, Sun 6:30am–3pm; lunch daily 11:30am–3pm; dinner daily 5:30–10:30pm. **Prices:** Main courses $11.25–$19.95. CB, DC, DISC, MC, V. VP

★ Twelve Baskets
825 116th Ave NE; tel 206/455-3684. At 8th. **Coffeehouse/Health.** One of Bellevue's favorite lunch stops, offering tasty and well-priced vegetarian sandwiches, soups, quiches, and yogurt desserts. The decor is simple, almost dorm-style, with plain tables lined up. Always full, this place rates high with its mostly female patrons. **FYI:** Reservations accepted. Children's menu. No liquor license. No smoking. **Open:** Mon–Sat 11am–3pm. **Prices:** Lunch main courses $5.50–$7.25. AE, DC, DISC, MC, V.

Velato's
In Red Lion Hotel Bellevue, 300 112th Ave SE; tel 206/455-1300. At SE 8th. **Italian.** Everything about Velato's is fun and colorful: The multicolored napkins, huge Alice in Wonderland coffee cups, and banners hanging from the ceiling make you feel chipper, as do the food and drink. Tastings of wine and spirits (including small-batch bourbons) complement the flamboyant tableside preparation of several dishes. A special is baked ziti with Dungeness crab, basil, mushrooms, ricotta, and mozzarella. **FYI:** Reservations accepted. Children's menu. **Open:** Lunch Mon–Fri 11am–2pm; dinner daily 5–10pm; brunch Sun 10am–2pm. **Prices:** Main courses $8.50–$15. AE, CB, DC, DISC, MC, V. VP

REFRESHMENT STOP

★ London's Bakehouse
10640 Main St; tel 206/688-8332. at 107th Ave NE. **Bakery.** Master baker Josh London makes 14 types of marvelous, super-healthy breads—Marie Antoinette should have said, "Let them eat raisin-pecan bread at London's Bakehouse." That particular bread, small and compact, has 12 ounces of raisins and pecans, but no oils, sugar, yeasts, or dairy products—just flour, salt, and water. London's bread has been pronounced "Best Hearth Baked Bread" by noted food critic and cookbook author Craig Claiborne. **Open:** Mon–Sat 8am–7pm. MC, V.

Bellingham

A seaside community with the Cascade Mountains as a backdrop. Serves as the access point for the Mount Baker recreation area and the southern port for Alaska's Marine Ferry. **Information:** Bellingham/Whatcom Chamber of Commerce and Industry, 1801 Roeder Ave #140, PO Box 958, Bellingham, 98227 (tel 360/734-1330).

MOTELS

Best Western Heritage Inn

151 E McLeod Rd, 98226; tel 360/647-1912 or toll free 800/528-1234; fax 360/671-3878. Across from Bellis Fair Mall. Colonial-style motel located next to a busy shopping mall. The lush creek flowing at the rear would be heavenly to sit by if it weren't for the noise of the freeway. **Rooms:** 90 rms, stes, and effic. CI 3pm/CO noon. No smoking. Beautifully furnished rooms, with good soundproofing. Two-bedroom condos available half-mile down the road for long-term stays. **Amenities:** A/C, cable TV w/movies. **Services:** Children's program. Complimentary morning newspaper. **Facilities:** 100 Whirlpool, washer/dryer. **Rates (CP):** $64–$77 S; $74–$89 D; $131–$141 ste; $77–$82 effic. Extra person $5. Children under age 14 stay free. Parking: Outdoor, free. AE, CB, DC, DISC, MC, V.

Best Western Inn

714 Lakeway Dr, 98226; tel 360/671-1011 or toll free 800/528-1234; fax 360/676-8519. Exit 253 off I-5 N and S. The only full-service motel/hotel in the area. Live trees in the lobby give the place a holiday feel; however, the 10,000 square feet of meeting space makes for a bustling business atmosphere. **Rooms:** 132 rms and stes. CI 3pm/CO noon. Nonsmoking rms avail. Rooms facing indoor pool don't have natural light, and therefore tend to be dark. **Amenities:** A/C, cable TV w/movies. **Services:** Children's program. Children's program includes gifts and newsletter. **Facilities:** 900 2 restaurants, 1 bar (w/entertainment), games rm, sauna, whirlpool, beauty salon, washer/dryer. **Rates (BB):** Peak (May–Sept) $61–$70 S; $69–$78 D; $95–$105 ste. Extra person $10. Children under age 16 stay free. Lower rates off-season. Parking: Outdoor, free. AE, DC, DISC, MC, V.

Comfort Inn

4282 Meridian St, 98226; tel 360/738-1100 or toll free 800/228-5150; fax 360/738-8123. Exit 256 off I-5 N and S. This clean and comfortable highway motel is close to Bellis Fair, a busy shopping center. **Rooms:** 85 rms, stes, and effic. CI 3pm/CO noon. Nonsmoking rms avail. **Amenities:** A/C, cable TV w/movies, dataport, voice mail. Some units w/whirlpools. **Services:** **Facilities:** 24 Sauna, whirlpool, washer/dryer. **Rates (CP):** Peak (June 1–Sept 1) $47–$56 S; $51–$61 D; $56–$66 ste; $90–$106 effic. Extra person $5. Children under age 18 stay free. Lower rates off-season. Parking: Outdoor, free. Lower rates on some holiday weekends. AE, CB, DC, DISC, EC, JCB, MC, V.

Days Inn

125 E Kellogg Rd, 98226; tel 360/671-6200 or toll free 800/831-6187; fax 360/671-9491. Exit 256 off I-5. Surrounded by major department stores. Rest after shopping by curling up near the fireplace in the cozy lobby or by soaking in the hot tub. **Rooms:** 70 rms, stes, and effic. CI 2pm/CO 11am. Nonsmoking rms avail. **Amenities:** A/C, cable TV w/movies, refrig. Some units w/whirlpools. **Services:** **Facilities:** 55 Whirlpool, washer/dryer. Free passes for nearby golf course. **Rates (CP):** Peak (June–Sept) $54 S; $59 D; $79–$85 ste; $54 effic. Extra person $5. Children under age 18 stay free. Lower rates off-season. Parking: Outdoor, free. AE, CB, DC, DISC, MC, V.

Hampton Inn

3985 Bennett Dr, 98225; tel 360/676-7700 or toll free 800/HAMPTON; fax 360/671-7557. A business traveler's favorite offering spacious, clean, and restful rooms. Handy to the Bellingham airport and only 24 miles from the Canadian border. **Rooms:** 132 rms. CI 2pm/CO noon. Nonsmoking rms avail. **Amenities:** A/C, cable TV w/movies. Some units w/whirlpools. **Services:** Complimentary breakfast includes freshly baked muffins, waffles, cereals, yogurt, juices, and coffee. Free local phone calls. **Facilities:** 50 Whirlpool, washer/dryer. **Rates (CP):** Peak (May–Sept) $62–$79 S; $67–$79 D. Children under age 19 stay free. Min stay special events. Lower rates off-season. Parking: Outdoor, free. AE, CB, DC, DISC, JCB, MC, V.

INN

North Garden Inn

1014 N Garden, 98225; tel 360/671-7828 or toll free 800/922-6414 in the US, 800/367-1676 in Canada. On the National Historic Register, this Queen Anne Victorian home sits high on a hill overlooking Bellingham Bay. Homey atmosphere. Although not really suited for children, they aren't turned away. **Rooms:** 10 rms (2 w/shared bath). CI 3pm/CO 11am. No smoking. Several rooms have views of Bellingham Bay; one room has a grand piano. **Amenities:** Bathrobes. No A/C, phone, or TV. 1 unit w/terrace. **Services:** You won't leave hungry—the full breakfast really means full! Pleasant hosts are attentive to guests needs. **Facilities:** Guest lounge w/TV. **Rates (BB):** $35 S w/shared bath, $54–$69 S w/private bath; $40 D w/shared bath, $59–$74 D w/private bath. Extra person $15. Children under age 6 stay free. Parking: Outdoor, free. AE, DISC, MC, V.

RESTAURANTS

il fiasco

1309 Commercial St; tel 360/676-9136. downtown. **Italian/Mediterranean.** Low-key, elegant atmosphere. A largely downtown business crowd opts for squid, raw oyster, and vegetarian fare. Dinners include lamb chops, duck, and Italian sausage. Extensive wine list. Bistro menu available in bar. **FYI:** Reservations recommended. No smoking. **Open:** Lunch Mon–Fri 11:30am–2:30pm; dinner daily 5:30–9:30pm. **Prices:** Main courses $8.95–$23.95. AE, DC.

Orchard Street Brewery
In Squalicum Corporate Park, 709 W Orchard Dr, ste 1; tel 360/647-1614. 3 blocks S of Bellingham Golf & Country Club. **Eclectic.** Bistro-style food is served in this new cafe with a purple floor. Traditional "peasant food" has a sprinkle of upbeat spice. Menu includes chicken and prawns with creole sauce, and a veggie sandwich on fresh-baked focaccia. **FYI:** Reservations accepted. Beer and wine only. No smoking. **Open:** Breakfast Mon–Fri 7–11:30am; lunch Mon–Fri 11:30am–4pm, Sat–Sun noon–4pm; dinner Sun–Thurs 4–10pm, Fri–Sat 4–11pm. **Prices:** Main courses $5.25–$13.50. AE, MC, V.

Pacific Café
In Mount Baker Theater Complex, 100 N Commercial St (Downtown); tel 360/647-0800. **Eclectic.** When you ask a local person where to eat in Bellingham, he or she will probably steer you here. The location in the old Mount Baker Theater building (currently under restoration) adds a bit of historical flavor to the tasty pastas and seafood, which are prepared with Asian and northwest ingredients.. **FYI:** Reservations recommended. Dress code. Beer and wine only. No smoking. **Open:** Lunch Mon–Fri 11:30am–2pm; dinner Mon–Sat 5:30–8:30pm. **Prices:** Main courses $9–$22. AE, MC, V.

($) Tony's Coffee & Teas
In the Terminal Building, 1101 Harris Ave (Fairhaven); tel 360/738-4710. **Coffeehouse.** This is the oldest surviving building in the old district of Fairhaven, and it has as much flavor as the many spices, fresh-roasted coffees, and specialty teas for sale inside. Wonderful homemade soups and pastry, and generous salads and sandwiches, too. Be prepared—the decor looks as battered as the building. The funky cafe/bistro also sells coffee pots, coffee grinders, espresso machines, teapots, and coffee cups. **FYI:** Reservations not accepted. Beer and wine only. No smoking. **Open:** Daily 7am–10pm. **Prices:** Main courses $3–$8. MC, V.

Blaine

Washington's busiest customs station on the US/Canada border. **Information:** Blaine Community Chamber of Commerce and Visitors Information Center, PO Box 1718, Blaine, 98231 (tel 360/332-6484).

MOTEL

Northwoods Motel
288 D St, 98230; tel 360/332-5603. Exit 276 off I-5 at Canada/US border. Simple and practical property. Huge adjacent parking lot makes it a good choice for truckers. **Rooms:** 29 rms. CI 2pm/CO 11am. Nonsmoking rms avail. Plants and artwork in the single rooms give the place a homey touch, though noise might be somewhat of a problem. **Amenities:** A/C, cable TV. **Services:** Coffee in lobby all morning. Seattle-Tacoma airport shuttle arranged with 24-hour notice. Small pets permitted. **Facilities:** Whirlpool. **Rates (CP):** Peak (July 1–Sept 5) $37–$40 S; $43–$50 D. Extra person $10. Lower rates off-season. Parking: Outdoor, free. AE, MC, V.

RESORT

The Inn at Semi-ah-moo
9565 Semi-ah-moo Pkwy, PO Box 790, 98230; tel 360/371-2000 or toll free 800/770-7992; fax 360/371-5490. Just S of the US/Canada border. 1,100 acres. A sophisticated surprise at the end of a simple country road, this inn is perfect for the golfer and those wanting to experience the rugged, peaceful Pacific Northwest without sacrificing amenities. **Rooms:** 198 rms and stes. CI 4pm/CO noon. Nonsmoking rms avail. **Amenities:** A/C, cable TV, bathrobes. Some units w/terraces, some w/fireplaces. **Services:** Masseur, children's program, babysitting. **Facilities:** 18 300 3 restaurants, 2 bars (1 w/entertainment), 1 beach (bay), basketball, volleyball, games rm, lawn games, racquetball, squash, spa, sauna, steam rm, whirlpool, beauty salon. Arnold Palmer–designed golf course. Trails run through a wildlife preserve. **Rates:** Peak (May–Oct) $150–$225 S or D; $250–$275 ste. Extra person $20. Children under age 17 stay free. Lower rates off-season. Parking: Outdoor, free. Golf packages including meals available.. AE, CB, DC, DISC, MC, V.

Bothell

RESTAURANT

Gerard's Relais de Lyon
17121 Bothell Way NE; tel 206/485-7600. Take I-5 N to exit 171; follow WA 522 about 9 mi. **French.** Worth the trip out of Seattle. Situated among the fir trees, this lovely house is even more charming inside, where a fireplace warms the entryway and an intimate dining room seats only 65. Chef Gerard Parrat, a student of Paul Bocuse, prepares contemporary French cuisine in the classic style. The constantly changing menu includes choices from lobster and fish to lamb, duck, venison, and rabbit. Six- and seven-course prix-fixe dinners are offered, as well as a four-course bistro menu ($20). The award-winning wine list includes nearly 300 domestic and French selections. **FYI:** Reservations recommended. **Open:** Tues–Sun 5–10pm. **Prices:** Main courses $21–$27; prix fixe $20–$52. AE, CB, DC, DISC, MC, V.

Bremerton

The state's major naval shipyard is the northern home port for the Pacific Fleet and the site of several maritime museums. **Information:** Bremerton Area Chamber of Commerce, 837 4th St, PO Box 229, Bremerton, 98337 (tel 360/479-3579).

MOTELS

Best Western Bayview Inn
5640 Kitsap Way, 98312; tel 360/373-7349 or toll free 800/422-5017; fax 360/377-8529. W of downtown. Located on a major arterial road, this is a pleasant, clean facility. There are 12 golf courses within 15 miles. **Rooms:** 143 rms and stes. CI 4pm/CO noon. Nonsmoking rms avail. Rooms are pleasant, and have double sinks. **Amenities:** A/C, satel TV, refrig. Some units w/terraces, some w/whirlpools. **Services:** Car-rental desk. **Facilities:** 600 1 restaurant (lunch and dinner only), 1 bar (w/entertainment), whirlpool, washer/dryer. Pool area feels like a sauna because of poor ventilation. **Rates:** Peak (May–Sept) $62–$67 S; $67–$72 D; $79–$150 ste. Extra person $5. Children under age 17 stay free. Lower rates off-season. Parking: Outdoor, free. AE, CB, DC, DISC, ER, JCB, MC, V.

Dunes Motel
3400 11th St, 98312; tel 360/377-0093 or toll free 800/828-8238. 1 mi N of US 3. In a good location near restaurants and shops, this simple property with small but clean rooms is set back from the main thoroughfare. **Rooms:** 64 rms and effic. CI 1pm/CO 11am. Nonsmoking rms avail. **Amenities:** A/C, cable TV, refrig. **Services:** Car-rental desk. **Facilities:** Spa, whirlpool, washer/dryer. **Rates (CP):** Peak (June 15–Sept 15) $48–$54 S; $54–$64 D; $64–$74 effic. Extra person $5. Children under age 6 stay free. Lower rates off-season. Parking: Outdoor, free. AE, CB, DC, DISC, MC, V.

Mid Way Inn
2909 Wheaton Way, 98310; tel 360/479-2909 or toll free 800/231-0575; fax 360/479-1576. N of Bremerton; on the Kitsap Peninsula. Clean and comfortable rooms. Ideal for people visiting Navy bases in the area; it's also located near a shopping center. **Rooms:** 60 rms and effic. CI noon/CO 11am. Nonsmoking rms avail. **Amenities:** A/C, cable TV, refrig, dataport. **Services:** VP Small pets $10/night. **Facilities:** 18 Washer/dryer. **Rates (CP):** $51 S; $56–$65 D; $54 effic. Extra person $7. Children under age 13 stay free. Parking: Indoor, free. Senior, corporate, military, and weekly rates avail. AE, CB, DC, DISC, MC, V.

Quality Inn
4303 Kitsap Way, 98312; tel 360/405-1111 or toll free 800/776-2291; fax 360/377-0597. A neat, clean motel with lots of pleasant surprises, including recently renovated rooms and a good location close to shopping and restaurants. The wonderful lobby offers a fireplace, and table and chairs for relaxing. **Rooms:** 102 rms, stes, and effic. CI 2pm/CO 11am. No smoking. **Amenities:** A/C, cable TV w/movies, refrig, dataport. Some units w/terraces, some w/whirlpools. **Services:** **Facilities:** 50 Spa, whirlpool, playground, washer/dryer. Attractive fenced-in pool. **Rates (CP):** Peak (Apr–Oct) $59 S; $64 D; $69–$105 ste; $69–$105 effic. Extra person $5. Children under age 18 stay free. Lower rates off-season. Parking: Outdoor, free. AE, CB, DC, DISC, MC, V.

ATTRACTION

Naval Underseas Museum
WA 308, Keyport; tel 360/396-4148. 15 mi NE of Bremerton. Exhibits include a deep-sea exploration and research craft, a Japanese kamikaze torpedo, and a deep-sea rescue vehicle. US Naval history and ship models are also included. **Open:** Tues–Sun 10am–4pm. Closed some hols. **Free**

Carlton

Located in the Methow Valley, between Twisp and Methow on WA 153. This former mining boomtown is now dominated by apple orchards.

MOTEL

Country Town Motel and RV Park
2266 WA 153, PO Box 130, 98814; tel 509/997-3432. Woodsy-style motel with clean and comfortable rooms, right in the heart of horse country. Has big lawn, tiny lobby, and adjacent RV park. **Rooms:** 24 rms and effic. CI 2pm/CO 11am. **Amenities:** A/C, satel TV w/movies. No phone. **Services:** Children's program. Pets allowed at manager's discretion. **Facilities:** Volleyball, games rm, lawn games, whirlpool, playground, washer/dryer. Solar-heated pool; park within walking distance. **Rates:** Peak (May 15–Dec 1) $35–$49 S or D; $40–$54 effic. Extra person $5. Children under age 2 stay free. Min stay special events. Lower rates off-season. Parking: Outdoor, free. No charge for children if extra bed not needed. MC, V.

Cashmere

A bedroom community in the Wenatchee area, noted for its fruit orchards. **Information:** Cashmere Chamber of Commerce, PO Box 834, 98815 (tel 509/782-2191).

MOTEL

Village Inn Motel
229th Cottage Ave, 98815; tel 509/782-3522. Concrete-block motel within walking distance of restaurants and gift shops, and the excellent Chelan County Historical Museum and Pioneer Village. Friendly new owners are currently

upgrading the property. **Rooms:** 21 rms and effic. CI 2pm/CO 11am. Nonsmoking rms avail. Simple rooms. **Amenities:** A/C, cable TV. Some rooms have refrigerators and/or coin-operated vibrating beds. **Services:** **Rates:** Peak (May–Oct) $45–$51 S; $50–$57 D; $57–$64 effic. Extra person $5. Children under age 9 stay free. Min stay special events. Lower rates off-season. Parking: Outdoor, free. AE, DISC, MC, V.

ATTRACTION

Chelan County Historical Society Museum and Pioneer Village
600 Cottage Ave; tel 509/782-3230. The 10,000 square feet of space at this museum contain a comprehensive collection of material from Central Washington, dating back 9,000 years. The Pioneer Village features a railroad depot and section house, schoolhouse, barber shop, general store, cabins, saddle shop, post office, saloon, jail, mission church, print shop, doctor-dentist office, hotel, blacksmith shop, and two outhouses. Donations are requested for admission. **Open:** Mon–Sat 9:30am–5pm, Sun 1–5pm. Closed Nov–Mar, except by appointment. **Free**

Centralia

See also Chehalis

Founded in 1875 by a freed slave; some downtown buildings have murals reflecting the town's heritage. Today, Centralia is best known as a shopping mecca because of its numerous antique stores and a factory outlet mall. **Information:** Lewis County Visitors and Convention Bureau, 500 NW Chamber of Commerce Way, Chehalis, 98532 (tel 360/736-7132).

MOTELS

Ferryman's Inn
1003 Eckerson Rd, 98531; tel 360/330-2094. Exit 82 off I-5. Homey feeling despite limitations of older property **Rooms:** 84 rms and effic. CI 2pm/CO noon. Nonsmoking rms avail. Older style rooms, but very clean. **Amenities:** A/C, cable TV. **Services:** Free candy, cookies, and coffee. **Facilities:** 75 Whirlpool, washer/dryer. Exceptionally clean swimming pool and well-maintained indoor whirlpool. **Rates (CP):** $34–$40 S; $37–$43 D; $40–$50 effic. Extra person $3. Children under age 2 stay free. Parking: Outdoor, free. AE, CB, DC, DISC, MC, V.

Huntley Inn
702 W Harrison Ave, 98531; tel 360/736-2875; fax 360/736-2651. Exit 82 off I-5; 3 blocks east. This 25-year-old property has a cheerful exterior with fresh green shutters framing the windows. Very noisy from both the interstate and busy Harrison Ave. **Rooms:** 87 rms. CI open/CO 11am. Nonsmoking rms avail. Tired interiors, with old bedspreads that refuse to cover the bed neatly. **Amenities:** A/C, cable TV, refrig. Some units w/whirlpools. **Services:** **Facilities:** 15 **Rates (CP):** $35–$40 S or D. Extra person $8. Children under age 12 stay free. Parking: Outdoor, free. Shoppers Specials packages Oct–May. AE, CB, DC, DISC, MC, V.

Chehalis

See also Centralia

Western town with a fine national historic district that includes the oldest church in the state. A steam train offers rail excursions between Chehalis and Centralia. **Information:** Lewis County Visitors and Convention Bureau, 500 NW Chamber of Commerce Way, Chehalis, 98532 (tel 360/736-7132).

MOTEL

Nendels
122 Interstate Ave, 98532; tel 360/748-0101 or toll free 800/648-7138; fax 360/748-7591. I-5 at exit 76. Basic highway motel. **Rooms:** 70 rms and stes. CI 3pm/CO noon. Nonsmoking rms avail. Rooms smell of smoke and bedspreads are stained and worn. **Amenities:** A/C, cable TV w/movies, refrig. **Services:** **Facilities:** 12 Whirlpool. **Rates (CP):** Peak (May 1–Sept 15) $50–$95 S; $55–$100 D; $100–$110 ste. Extra person $5. Children under age 12 stay free. Lower rates off-season. Parking: Outdoor, free. AE, CB, DC, DISC, MC, V.

ATTRACTION

Lewis County Historical Museum
599 NW Front Way; tel 206/748-0831. Housed in this restored railroad depot (circa 1912) are pioneer displays including a blacksmith shop and a general store; as well as Indian artifacts, farming tools, and written family histories of the area's settlers. **Open:** Tues–Sat 9am–5pm, Sun 1–5pm. Closed some hols. **$**

Chelan

See also Manson

Located on glacier-carved Lake Chelan, this central Washington town offers year-round outdoor recreation ranging from water sports to snowmobiling and skiing. It is the access point for the remote up-lake village of Stehekin, reachable only by boat or floatplane. **Information:** Lake Chelan Chamber of Commerce, PO Box 216, Chelan 98816 (tel 509/682-3503).

MOTELS

Caravel Resort
322 W Woodin Ave, PO Box 1509, 98816; tel 509/682-2582 or toll free 800/962-8723; fax 509/682-3551. South end of Lake Chelan. The Caravel sits on Lake Chelan like a floating

hotel. Its prize location is a walk across an old bridge from downtown shops and cafes, and across the street from a tranquil riverfront walkway. **Rooms:** 92 rms, stes, and effic. CI 4pm/CO 11am. Standard rooms all have magnificent views of the lake. **Amenities:** A/C, cable TV. All units w/terraces, some w/fireplaces, some w/whirlpools. Accommodations with the best amenities, including whirlpool suites and penthouse suites with fireplaces, are on the fourth floor. **Services:** Babysitting. **Facilities:** 120 Whirlpool. **Rates:** Peak (June 16–Labor Day) $92–$112 S; $100–$120 D; $125–$138 ste; $125–$250 effic. Extra person $5. Min stay wknds. Lower rates off-season. Parking: Outdoor, free. Housekeeping units rent by the week in summer. AE, DC, DISC, MC, V.

Westview Resort Motel
2312 W Woodin Ave, PO Box 14, 98816; tel 509/682-4396; fax 509/682-2043. On the South Shore of Lake Chelan. Although not apparent from the parking lot, this bright, light, and cheery motel offers heavenly views of Lake Chelan. **Rooms:** 23 rms and stes; 2 cottages/villas. CI 3pm/CO 11am. Nonsmoking rms avail. Rooms are in almost-new condition. **Amenities:** A/C, cable TV, refrig, VCR. All units w/terraces, some w/fireplaces, 1 w/whirlpool. Wet bar, microwave. **Services:** **Facilities:** 40 Whirlpool, washer/dryer. Day use of dock. **Rates:** Peak (May 15–Sept 20) $98 S; $98–$118 D; $145–$175 ste; $135–$155 cottage/villa. Extra person $10. Children under age 2 stay free. Min stay wknds. Lower rates off-season. Parking: Outdoor, free. Romance packages avail. AE, CB, DC, DISC, MC, V.

RESORTS

Campbell's Resort and Conference Center
104 W Woodin Ave, PO Box 278, 98816; tel 509/682-2561; fax 509/682-2177. 9 acres. A sprawling, energetic, family-run resort on the shore of Lake Chelan. Some buildings could use brightening up; however, most of the action is on the lake or in the conference rooms. **Rooms:** 144 rms, stes, and effic; 7 cottages/villas. CI 4pm/CO noon. Nonsmoking rms avail. All rooms face a sandy beach. **Amenities:** A/C, cable TV. All units w/terraces, some w/fireplaces, 1 w/whirlpool. **Services:** Babysitting. **Facilities:** 18 400 2 restaurants, 1 bar, 1 beach (lake shore), volleyball, lawn games, snorkeling, sauna, whirlpool. Original hotel building, completed in 1901, now houses the resort's restaurant. Water sports equipment can be rented nearby. **Rates:** Peak (June 16–Labor Day) $104–$122 S; $136–$168 D; $162–$288 ste; $144–$204 effic; $144–$204 cottage/villa. Extra person $10. Children under age 10 stay free. Lower rates off-season. Parking: Outdoor, free. Desert Canyon golf packages available. AE, CB, DISC, MC, V.

Darnell's Resort Motel
901 Spader Bay Rd, PO Box 506, 98816; tel 509/682-2015 or toll free 800/967-8149. N shore of Lake Chelan. 4 acres. Located on beautiful Lake Chelan, this popular family resort offers weekly rentals and two-bedroom units. Ignore the outdated decor and spend your time outdoors. **Rooms:** 38 rms, stes, and effic. CI 4pm/CO 11am. No smoking. Rooms are somewhat tacky. Smoking on the decks only. **Amenities:** A/C, cable TV, refrig. All units w/terraces, 1 w/fireplace, 1 w/whirlpool. **Services:** Babysitting. **Facilities:** 80 1 beach (lake shore), basketball, volleyball, games rm, lawn games, whirlpool. Boat mooring for $10. Water-ski float, barbecues, bikes, and putters are free. **Rates:** Peak (mid-June–Labor Day) $75 S; $75–$180 D; $140–$180 ste; $140–$155 effic. Extra person $10. Children under age 4 stay free. Min stay wknds. Lower rates off-season. Parking: Outdoor, free. Weekly rates range from $500 for a sleeping loft to $1,850 for a penthouse. Closed Apr–Oct. AE, DISC, MC, V.

ATTRACTIONS

Slidewaters
102 Waterslide Dr; tel 509/682-5751. Popular attractions at this water park, located on a butte overlooking Lake Chelan, include the 400-foot Tubeblaster (with two 360° turns), a turtle slide for toddlers, an inner-tube river ride, and a 60-person hot tub. Arcade, gift shop, picnic area. **Open:** Mem Day–mid-June, Mon–Fri 10am–6pm, Sat–Sun 10am–8pm; mid-June–Labor Day, daily 10am–8pm. **$$$$**

Lake Chelan State Park
Rte 1; tel 509/687-3710. 9 mi W of Chelan. Visitors may enjoy a wide variety of recreational activities on the lake, including swimming, boating, water-skiing, fishing, and scuba diving. On land, there's a 144-site campground and a day-use area with playground, swimming beach, 52 picnic sites, horseshoe pits, and softball diamond. **Open:** Apr–Nov, daily 6:30am–dusk; Dec–March, weekends and hols only. **Free**

Clarkston

Popular with tourists who come for rafting and jet-boating excursions in Hells Canyon on the Snake River. The area is well known for its Native American petroglyphs. **Information:** Clarkston Chamber of Commerce, 502 Bridge St, Clarkston, 99403 (tel 509/758-7712).

MOTELS

Best Western Rivertree Inn
1257 Bridge St, 99403; tel 509/758-9551 or toll free 800/325-8765; fax 509/758-9551. US 12 W; 8 blocks W of Snake River Bridge. Property is located eight blocks from the landscaped, paved path that borders the Snake and Clearwater Rivers—a popular spot for walking, biking, and in-line skating. **Rooms:** 61 rms, stes, and effic. CI 2pm/CO noon. Nonsmoking rms avail. Some rooms have a spiral, wrought-iron stairway leading up to a sleeping loft. Deluxe rooms offer larger bathrooms and bathtubs. **Amenities:** A/C,

cable TV w/movies, refrig. Some units w/terraces, some w/whirlpools. Deluxe accommodations feature dataports, recliners, and VCRs. **Services:** Coffee in lobby 24 hours. **Facilities:** Sauna, whirlpool. Tanning booth on premises. **Rates:** $55–$80 S; $60–$95 D; $90–$130 ste; $63–$88 effic. Extra person $8. Min stay special events. Parking: Outdoor, free. AARP and commercial rates avail. AE, CB, DC, DISC, MC, V.

Motel 6
222 Bridge St, 99403; tel 509/758-1631; fax 509/758-4942. Located downtown on the US 12 business route, this motel is fine for budget-minded travelers needing no special amenities. **Rooms:** 87 rms. CI open/CO noon. Nonsmoking rms avail. **Amenities:** A/C, cable TV w/movies. **Services:** Complimentary morning coffee in lobby. **Facilities:** Washer/dryer. Within walking distance of paved, recreational pathway. **Rates:** Peak (May 25–Oct 12) $36 S; $42 D. Extra person $3. Children under age 18 stay free. Lower rates off-season. Parking: Outdoor, free. Senior discounts avail. AE, DC, DISC, MC, V.

Quality Inn Clarkston
700 Port Dr, 99403 (Port District); tel 509/758-9500 or toll free 800/228-5151; fax 509/758-5580. 3 blocks N of US 12 Business. Located adjacent to the Lewis & Clark Convention Center (on the south bank of the Snake River), this property attracts conventioneers, businesspeople, and local event participants. The large inviting lobby faces the river and is lighted by skylights; a fireplace, large chandelier, lots of plants, and overstuffed chairs add to the decor. **Rooms:** 75 rms. CI 2pm/CO noon. Nonsmoking rms avail. 48 units face the river; 16 rooms open to a patio. **Amenities:** A/C, cable TV w/movies. Some units w/terraces, some w/whirlpools. Some rooms have speaker phones, dataports, jet tubs, and larger tables. **Services:** Complimentary newspaper and coffee in lobby in morning. Fax and copy services available. **Facilities:** 1 restaurant, 1 bar, washer/dryer. Public boat dock adjacent to the motel provides jet-boat pickup for those going to the popular Hells Canyon scenic tours. **Rates:** Peak (May–Sept) $60–$85 S; $65–$85 D. Extra person $5. Children under age 12 stay free. Min stay special events. Lower rates off-season. Parking: Outdoor, free. Senior, commercial, government, and group rates avail. AE, CB, DC, DISC, MC, V.

Copalis Beach

A tourist community noted for its razor clam digging and other coastal recreational opportunities.

RESORT

Iron Springs Resort
WA 109, PO Box 207, 98535; tel 360/276-4230; fax 360/276-4365. 3 mi N of Copalis Beach. 100 acres. An unassuming resort amid spruce trees at the edge of the sea. String quartet performs weekends in summer. **Rooms:** 29 rms and effic; 15 cottages/villas. CI 3pm/CO noon. Spectacular views of the beach. **Amenities:** TV, refrig. No A/C or phone. Some units w/terraces, some w/fireplaces. Most rooms have a wood-burning fireplace or stove. **Services:** **Facilities:** 1 beach (ocean), playground. **Rates:** $60–$96 S or D; $60–$96 effic; $60–$96 cottage/villa. Extra person $10. Parking: Outdoor, free. AE, DISC, MC, V.

Coulee Dam

Located at the base of the Grand Coulee Dam, one of the largest concrete structures in the world. The town is a popular destination for boaters and other water-sports enthusiasts who flock to nearby Coulee Dam National Recreational Area.

MOTEL

Coulee House Motel
110 Roosevelt Way, 99116; tel 509/633-1101 or toll free 800/715-7767; fax 509/633-1416. 1 block E of Coulee Dam Bridge; just off WA 155 N. Popular with tourists and businesspeople. Within walking distance of viewing area for nightly laser-light show (Mem Day–Sept 30) on surface of Grand Coulee Dam. **Rooms:** 61 rms, stes, and effic. CI 3pm/CO 11am. Nonsmoking rms avail. Many rooms have view of Grand Coulee and all are decorated with historic photos and memorabilia from the dam's construction. Two 2-bedroom units. **Amenities:** A/C, cable TV w/movies. Some units w/terraces. One unit has wet bar, full kitchen, and two terraces. **Services:** Complimentary coffee in lobby 6:30am–11pm. Fax, copy, typing, and printer services available. **Facilities:** Whirlpool, washer/dryer. Private whirlpool is available by reservation. **Rates:** Peak (May–Sept) $46–$54 S; $66 D; $74 ste; $58–$66 effic. Extra person $4. Children under age 2 stay free. Lower rates off-season. Parking: Outdoor, free. Commercial and senior rates available. AE, DC, DISC, MC, V.

RESTAURANTS

Melody Restaurant & Lounge
512 River Dr; tel 509/633-1151. Adjacent to Coulee House Motel; ½ block E of Coulee Dam Bridge on WA 155 N. **New American.** This is the only restaurant in town with a view of the Grand Coulee Dam and the nightly laser light show (summer months only). The outdoor dining deck is ringed with flower boxes and rose bushes. Large portions of charbroiled steak and seafood and steak combos at good prices. **FYI:** Reservations accepted. Children's menu. **Open:** Peak (mid-May–Sept) daily 6am–10pm. **Prices:** Main courses $7–$15. AE, DISC, MC, V.

Sage Inn Restaurant
415 Midway Ave, Grand Coulee; tel 509/633-0550. On WA 155 S; 2 mi S of Coulee Dam Visitor Center. **American.** A 37-year-old establishment, popular with both tourists and locals. The breakfast menu is available at all hours. Lunch features a large selection of sandwiches and burgers. House favorites are chicken-fried steak and boneless mountain trout. **FYI:** Reservations not accepted. Karaoke. Children's menu. **Open:** Peak (May–Sept) daily 6am–10pm. **Prices:** Main courses $6–$15. MC, V.

Siam Palace Restaurant
213 Main St, Grand Coulee; tel 509/633-2921. **Chinese/Thai.** Small place offering predominantly Chinese cooking and the familiar combination platters. The Siam chow mein, a blend of Chinese and Thai seasonings on noodles, is a favorite here. Some Thai and American dishes, such as steak and chicken, are also available. **FYI:** Reservations accepted. Beer and wine only. **Open:** Lunch Tues–Fri 11am–2pm; dinner Tues–Sat 4–9pm, Sun 12–9pm. **Prices:** Main courses $6–$10. DISC, MC, V.

Wildlife Restaurant
113 Midway Ave, Grand Coulee; tel 509/633-1160. On WA 155 S, 2 mi S of Grand Coulee Dam Visitor Center. **Eclectic.** Photos of wildlife adorn the walls at this eatery serving a variety of burgers and hot sandwiches; the chicken-fried steak is a favorite. Sauces and soups are made fresh daily. **FYI:** Reservations accepted. Rock. Children's menu. **Open:** Daily 7am–9pm. **Prices:** Main courses $6–$17. DISC, MC, V.

Coupeville

See Whidbey Island

Crystal Mountain

See Mount Rainier National Park

Deer Harbor

See Orcas Island

Eastsound

See Orcas Island

Edmonds

Located on the Puget Sound waterfront. Edmonds is filled with marinas and beaches; there's even an underwater park for scuba divers. **Information:** Edmonds Chamber of Commerce, 120 5th Ave N, PO Box 146, Edmonds, 98020 (tel 206/670-1496).

MOTELS

Edmonds Harbor Inn
130 W Dayton St, 98020; or toll free 800/441-8033; fax 206/672-2880. 1 block S of Edmonds-Kingston ferry at Edmonds Way. Situated within easy walking distance of the City of Edmonds Underwater Park, the most popular dive site in the Pacific Northwest. Also close to waterfront boardwalk and downtown. **Rooms:** 61 rms, stes, and effic. CI 3pm/CO 11am. Nonsmoking rms avail. **Amenities:** A/C, cable TV, refrig. **Services:** **Facilities:** Access to nearby athletic club, where facilities include lap pool, whirlpool, and sauna; costs are $5/person, $8/couple, $10/family. **Rates (CP):** Peak (May 15–Sept 15) $51–$54 S; $60 D; $85–$130 ste; $85–$130 effic. Extra person $5. Children under age 12 stay free. Lower rates off-season. Parking: Outdoor, free. AE, DC, DISC, MC, V.

K & E Motor Inn
23921 WA 99, 98020; tel 206/778-2181; fax 206/778-1516. At 238th St W. Budget motel on a very busy, noisy highway. Close to shopping center and convenient to I-5. **Rooms:** 32 rms. CI open/CO 11am. Nonsmoking rms avail. Smell of stale cigarette smoke in rooms. **Amenities:** A/C, cable TV, refrig. **Services:** **Facilities:** **Rates (CP):** $39 S; $44 D. Extra person $5. Children under age 7 stay free. Parking: Outdoor, free. AE, CB, DISC, MC, V.

Travelodge Seattle North
23825 WA 99, 98026; tel 206/771-8008 or toll free 800/771-8009; fax 206/771-8008. At WA 104. Just a 20-minute drive from Seattle, sandwiched between Blockbuster Video and other small motels on busy WA 99. Clean, relatively new, economical. **Rooms:** 58 rms. CI open/CO 11am. Nonsmoking rms avail. **Amenities:** A/C, cable TV w/movies. **Services:** **Facilities:** Whirlpool. **Rates (CP):** Peak (June–Sept) $54–$59 S; $64–$69 D. Extra person $7. Children under age 17 stay free. Lower rates off-season. Parking: Outdoor, free. AE, CB, DC, DISC, MC, V.

Ellensburg

Noted for combining the flavor of the rural Old West with that of a refined city. The annual Ellensburg rodeo is part of the PRCA (Professional Rodeo Cowboys Association) rodeo circuit, and there are several dude ranches in the area. The town is also the home of Central Washington University. **Information:** Ellensburg Chamber of Commerce, 436 N Sprague St, Ellensburg, 98926 (tel 509/925-2002).

MOTELS

Best Western Ellensburg Inn
1700 Canyon Rd, 98926; tel 509/925-9801 or toll free 800/321-8791; fax 509/925-2093. Exit 109 off I-90. Located next to a noisy truck stop, although rooms have good soundproofing. Easy interstate access. **Rooms:** 105 rms. CI 2pm/CO noon. Nonsmoking rms avail. Decorated in earth tones; artwork on walls depicts rural American landscapes. **Amenities:** A/C, satel TV w/movies. 1 unit w/terrace. One larger unit offers two phones, a balcony, and refrigerator. **Services:** **Facilities:** 300 1 restaurant, 1 bar, sauna, whirlpool, playground. Private courtyard has sun deck and two hot tubs. **Rates (BB):** Peak (May–Oct) $59 S; $64 D. Extra person $5. Children under age 12 stay free. Lower rates off-season. Parking: Outdoor, free. Senior, corporate, government, and group discounts avail. AE, CB, DC, DISC, ER, JCB, MC, V.

Nites Inn, Inc
1200 S Ruby, 98926; tel 509/962-9600. Exit 109 off I-90, then ¼ mi N on Main St. Located one block off a busy thoroughfare, but quieter than most other lodgings in the area. Clean, safe rooms at competitive prices. **Rooms:** 32 rms. CI 4pm/CO 11am. Nonsmoking rms avail. Average decor, with prints depicting rural farm scenes. **Amenities:** A/C, cable TV w/movies. Some rooms have refrigerators and microwaves. **Services:** Complimentary morning coffee in the lobby. Used paperback library with a leave-one, take-one policy. **Facilities:** Washer/dryer. **Rates:** $41 S; $45–$48 D. Extra person $5. Children under age 10 stay free. Parking: Outdoor, free. Senior, government, and corporate discounts avail. AE, CB, DC, MC, V.

Everett

Bordered by the Cascade Mountains on the east, and Puget Sound and the Olympic Mountains on the west. Site of a Boeing assembly plant and Jetty Island, a popular marine wildlife and bird watching spot. **Information:** Everett Area Chamber of Commerce, 1710 W Marine View Dr, PO Box 1086, Everett, 98206 (tel 206/252-5181).

MOTELS

Cypress Inn
12619 4th Ave, 98208; tel 206/347-9099 or toll free 800/752-9991 ext 3; fax 206/348-3048. Inside Mariner Square in S Everett. Basic motel located off I-5. **Rooms:** 70 rms. CI 3pm/CO noon. Nonsmoking rms avail. **Amenities:** A/C, cable TV, refrig. Some units w/whirlpools. **Services:** **Facilities:** 70 Day-care ctr. **Rates (CP):** $60 S; $70–$80 D. Extra person $7. Children under age 12 stay free. Parking: Outdoor, free. AE, DC, DISC, MC, V.

Days Inn
1122 N Broadway, 98201; tel 206/252-8000 or toll free 800/329-7466. Located ½ mile from I-5. Nothing fancy. **Rooms:** 51 rms. CI open/CO 11am. Nonsmoking rms avail. **Amenities:** A/C, cable TV w/movies, refrig. Some units w/whirlpools. **Services:** **Facilities:** Washer/dryer. Good homestyle meals available at Cookbook Restaurant across the street. **Rates (CP):** Peak (June 15–Sept 15) $45–$55 S; $47–$59 D. Extra person $2. Children under age 12 stay free. Lower rates off-season. Parking: Outdoor, free. AE, CB, DISC, MC, V.

Everett Comfort Inn
1602 SE Everett Mall Way, 98208; tel 206/355-1570 or toll free 800/221-2222. At E Mall Dr. Comfortable, modest motel within walking distance of the Everett Mall. **Rooms:** 75 rms. CI 7am/CO 11am. Nonsmoking rms avail. **Amenities:** A/C, cable TV, refrig. **Services:** **Facilities:** 30 **Rates (CP):** Peak (June 15–Labor Day) $46–$54 S; $60–$64 D. Extra person $5. Children under age 18 stay free. Lower rates off-season. Parking: Outdoor, free. AE, CB, DC, DISC, MC, V.

Marina Village Inn
1728 W Marine View Dr, 98201; tel 206/259-4040 or toll free 800/281-7037; fax 206/252-8419. Everett Marina Village, off W Marine View Dr. The only waterfront accommodation in Snohomish County. Has an intimate feeling. **Rooms:** 27 rms and stes. CI 3pm/CO noon. Nonsmoking rms avail. Accommodations are large and lavish. Baths have playful, hand-crafted pottery sinks. **Amenities:** A/C, satel TV w/movies, refrig, bathrobes. Some units w/terraces, some w/whirlpools. **Services:** Social director, babysitting. **Facilities:** 90 Free boat moorage. Cozy library with antique desk and gas fireplace. **Rates (CP):** Peak (June 1–Sept 30) $82–$130 S or D; $140–$229 ste. Extra person $20. Children under age 18 stay free. Lower rates off-season. Parking: Outdoor, free. AE, DC, DISC, MC, V.

Ramada Inn
9602 19th Ave SE, 98208; tel 206/337-9090 or toll free 800/228-2828; fax 206/337-9090. Exit 189 off I-5. Basic, convenient, just off the highway. Very noisy with I-5 and 19th Ave traffic. **Rooms:** 116 rms. CI open/CO noon. Nonsmoking rms avail. **Amenities:** A/C, cable TV w/movies. **Services:** Car-rental desk. **Facilities:** 40 Whirlpool. **Rates (CP):** Peak (May 15–Sept 15) $50–$60 S; $65–$75 D. Extra person $5. Children under age 16 stay free. Lower rates off-season. Parking: Outdoor, free. AE, CB, DC, DISC, JCB, MC, V.

ATTRACTION

Boeing Tour Center
Exit 189 off I-5; tel 206/342-4801. Go 3 ½ mi W on WA 526. Anyone interested in how planes are built will enjoy a free 90-minute tour of the Boeing assembly plant. An observation

window allows visitors to watch the assembly line in operation, there's also a 30-minute video presentation. (Please note that children must be able to see over a 45-inch balcony railing in order to join the tour; however, all children are welcome in the video theater.) **Open:** Mon–Fri 9am–4:30pm. Closed some hols. **$**

Forks

See also Olympic National Park

Timber town located on the west side of the Olympic Peninsula, at the western entrance to Olympic National Forest. Several clean, fast-running rivers attract rafters, kayakers, and fishing enthusiasts. **Information:** Forks Chamber of Commerce, PO Box 1249, Forks, 98331 (tel 360/374-2531).

MOTELS

Forks Motel
432 US 101 S, 98331; tel 360/374-6243 or toll free 800/544-3416; fax 360/374-6760. At E C St. After a day on the beach at La Push, 10 miles away, the motel looks inviting with its outdoor pool and proximity to a cafe and pizza. No frills. **Rooms:** 73 rms, stes, and effic. CI 1:30pm/CO 11am. Nonsmoking rms avail. **Amenities:** A/C, cable TV, refrig. 1 unit w/whirlpool. **Services:** **Facilities:** Washer/dryer. **Rates:** Peak (May 15–Sept 15) $43–$65 S; $48–$70 D; $95–$125 ste; $70 effic. Extra person $5. Children under age 12 stay free. Lower rates off-season. Parking: Outdoor, free. AE, DC, DISC, MC, V.

Pacific Inn Motel
352 US 101 S, 98331; tel 360/374-9400 or toll free 800/235-7344; fax 360/374-9402. Four-year-old motel located 10 miles from the ocean beaches at La Push. **Rooms:** 34 rms. CI 2pm/CO 11am. Nonsmoking rms avail. Bright and cheery furnishings. **Amenities:** A/C, cable TV. **Services:** **Facilities:** 1 restaurant, washer/dryer. **Rates:** Peak (May 15–Sept 30) $43 S; $52 D. Extra person $5. Children under age 12 stay free. Lower rates off-season. Parking: Outdoor, free. AE, DC, DISC, MC, V.

ATTRACTION

Hoh Visitor Center
Off US 101; tel 360/374-6925. The Hoh river valley receives an average of 140 inches of rain per year, making it one of the wettest regions in the continental United States. At the visitors center, you can learn all about the natural forces that cause this tremendous rainfall. To see the effect of so much rain on the landscape, walk the ¾-mile Hall of Mosses Trail. The trees, primarily Sitka spruce, western red cedar, and western hemlock, tower 200 feet tall with limbs of gigantic proportions. These tree limbs are draped with thick carpets of mosses that hold the rain and can add tons of weight to tree branches. Beneath these giants grow sword ferns, trilliums, salmonberries, and other plants that have adapted to this western environment. **Open:** Daily 9am–5pm. **Free**

Friday Harbor

See San Juan Island

Goldendale

Site of Goldendale Observatory State Park, home of the nation's largest public telescope. Other nearby attractions include the Maryhill Museum and Stonehenge Memorial. **Information:** Goldendale Chamber of Commerce, 116A W Main, PO Box 524, Goldendale, 98620 (tel 509/773-3400).

RESORT

Highland Creeks Resort
2120 US 97, 98620; tel 509/773-4026 or toll free 800/458-0174; fax 509/773-4334. In Simcoe Mountains, N of Columbia River Gorge. 100 acres. Romantic resort in a forest setting on the Little Klickitat River. Peaceful—except for the traffic noise from US 97. **Rooms:** 23 rms, stes, and effic. CI 4pm/CO noon. No smoking. Spacious rooms with skylights and hand-carved furniture. Most accommodations overlook the creek or trees. Some rooms have kitchens. **Amenities:** A/C, satel TV w/movies, refrig. Some units w/minibars, all w/terraces, some w/fireplaces, all w/whirlpools. **Services:** Masseur. **Facilities:** 50 1 restaurant (*see* "Restaurants" below), 1 bar, basketball, volleyball. Wineries and miles of hiking trails are nearby, and horseback riding is available through a local ranch. **Rates:** $46–$56 S or D; $105–$180 ste; $149–$169 effic. Extra person $10. Children under age 13 stay free. Min stay special events. Parking: Outdoor, free. AE, MC, V.

RESTAURANT

Highland Creeks Resort Restaurant
2120 US 97; tel 509/773-4026. 9 mi N of Goldendale. **Northwest.** An attractive restaurant in a woodsy setting, with country cuisine to match. A typical appetizer is forest mushrooms with garlic-butter and brandy; entrees include medallions of elk with peppercorn sauce, salmon, and venison sausage with raspberry mustard. A dessert specialty is cheesecake with wild berries. **FYI:** Reservations accepted. Children's menu. Dress code. No smoking. **Open:** Breakfast daily 8–11am; lunch daily 11am–3pm; dinner daily 5–9pm. **Prices:** Main courses $13–$20. AE, MC, V.

ATTRACTION

Maryhill Museum of Art
35 Maryhill Museum Dr; tel 509/773-3733. Built by millionaire Sam Hill, the museum is located on a hill overlooking the

Columbia River. The collection includes sculptures by Rodin, works by European and American painters, Russian icons, and antique chess sets. **Open:** Mar–Nov, daily 9am–5pm. $

Grand Coulee

See Coulee Dam

Greenwater

Small town near the northern entrance to Mount Rainier National Park and Crystal Mountain Ski Resort. Federation Forest State Park and its many nature trails is located here.

RESORT

Alta Crystal Resort
68317 WA 410 E, 98022; tel 360/663-2500. 2 acres. Tucked away in the woods, two miles from the northeast entrance to Mount Rainier National Park and eight miles from Crystal Mountain Ski Resort. **Rooms:** 22 rms, stes, and effic; 2 cottages/villas. CI 2pm/CO 11am. Nonsmoking rms avail. **Amenities:** TV w/movies, refrig. No A/C or phone. Some units w/terraces, some w/fireplaces. **Services:** Social director. **Facilities:** 50 Volleyball, playground, washer/dryer. **Rates:** Peak (Nov 24–Dec 31) $75–$110 S or D; $99–$150 ste; $75–$110 effic; $129–$159 cottage/villa. Extra person $8. Min stay peak. Lower rates off-season. Parking: Outdoor, free. Honeymoon and ski packages avail. AE, MC, V.

RESTAURANT

Naches Tavern
58411 WA 410 E; tel 360/663-2267. **American.** A woodsy country tavern decorated with old road signs, logging gear, and mining equipment. Sandwiches, burgers, and deep-fried mushrooms are quite good, and the milkshakes are terrific. Popular with loggers, skiers, and hikers; because it is a tavern, children aren't allowed. **FYI:** Reservations not accepted. Beer and wine only. **Open:** Mon–Fri 3–11pm, Sat–Sun noon–11pm. **Prices:** Main courses $4–$9. No CC.

Hoquiam

For lodging, see Aberdeen

Historic timber town, settled in 1850. Several lumber-baron homes have been converted to bed-and-breakfast inns. The town hosts the annual Grays Harbor Shorebird Celebration for millions of migrating shorebirds. **Information:** Grays Harbor Chamber of Commerce, 506 Duffy St, Aberdeen, 98520 (tel 360/532-1924).

RESTAURANT

Duffy's
825 Simpson Ave; tel 360/532-1519. At 9th St. **American.** In 1995, this restaurant marked its 50th year of serving seafood, pasta, and fish-and-chips. Famous locally for its pies, especially wild blackberry. **FYI:** Reservations accepted. Additional locations: 1605 Simpson Ave, Aberdeen (tel 532-3842); 1212 E Wishkah, Aberdeen (tel 538-0606). **Open:** Sun–Thurs 6am–10pm, Fri–Sat 6am–11pm. **Prices:** Main courses $7–$15. AE, CB, DC, DISC, MC, V.

ATTRACTIONS

Hoquiam's Castle
515 Chenault Ave; tel 360/533-2005. Built for lumber tycoon Robert Lytle, this house brought a touch of civility to the rugged timber town of Hoquiam when it was completed in 1897. Today, visitors are guided through many of the home's 20 rooms, which are beautifully appointed with Tiffany lamps, stained-glass windows, grandfather clocks, and a 17-piece handcarved dining room set. The music room is furnished with a rosewood grand piano, Tiffany window, and chandelier, and there's a turn-of-the-century saloon on the third floor. **Open:** Summer, daily 10am–5pm; winter, Sat–Sun 11am–5pm. Closed Dec. $$

Arnold Polson Museum
1611 Riverside Ave; tel 360/533-5862. A small museum featuring antique furniture and clothing, Native American artifacts, collectable dolls, and other such remnants of local history. One highlight is the 1870 Howard 60-beat grandfather clock, originally built in Boston. The Burton C Ross Memorial Rose Garden, named for a early timber man, borders the 26-room house. **Open:** June–Sept, Wed–Sun 11am–4pm. Closed some hols. $

Index

Located on the North Fork of the Skykomish River.

INN

Bush House Country Inn
300 5th St, 98256; tel 360/793-2312 or toll free 800/428-BUSH. 3 acres. This three-story inn, built in 1898, is an ideal choice for history buffs. Its crooked floors, tilted walls, and a lace-adorned living room/guest lounge enhance the nostalgic atmosphere. Not suitable for boisterous children. **Rooms:** 11 rms (all w/shared bath). CI 3pm/CO noon. No smoking. Guest quarters are appropriately decorated with fine old furniture. One room has sink and toilet; all others share bath. No closets. **Amenities:** Bathrobes. No A/C, phone, or TV. **Services:** Masseur, afternoon tea served. **Facilities:** 1 restaurant, 1 bar, guest lounge. **Rates (CP):** $59–$80 D w/shared bath. Extra person $15. Children under age 12 stay free. Parking: Outdoor, free. AE, MC, V.

Kelso

See also Longview

Near the north shore of the Columbia River. The January and February annual smelt run up the Cowlitz River draws smelters from throughout the region. **Information:** Kelso Area Chamber of Commerce, 105 Minor Rd, Kelso, 98626 (tel 360/577-8058).

HOTEL

Red Lion Inn–Kelso/Longview
510 Kelso Dr, 98626; tel 360/636-4400 or toll free 800/RED-LION; fax 360/425-3296. Exit 39 off I-5, E on Allen St. Comfortable and spacious rooms; easy access to interstate. **Rooms:** 162 rms and stes. CI 3pm/CO noon. Nonsmoking rms avail. **Amenities:** A/C, cable TV w/movies. Some units w/terraces. **Services:** **Facilities:** 500 2 restaurants, 1 bar (w/entertainment), whirlpool. Especially nice outdoor pool area. Restaurants offer casual, relaxed atmosphere. **Rates:** $74–$84 S; $89–$94 D; $150 ste. Extra person $5. Children under age 12 stay free. Parking: Outdoor, free. AE, CB, DC, DISC, MC, V.

MOTELS

Best Western Aladdin Motor Inn
310 Long Ave, 98626; tel 360/425-9660 or toll free 800/764-7378; fax 360/577-9436. At Cowlitz Way. Although the exterior looks a bit worn, the rooms are clean. A good choice for those on a budget. **Rooms:** 78 rms and effic. CI 3pm/CO noon. Nonsmoking rms avail. **Amenities:** A/C. **Services:** Complimentary coffee in lobby. **Facilities:** **Rates:** $59–$70 S or D; $70 effic. Extra person $5. Children under age 12 stay free. Parking: Outdoor, free. AE, DISC, MC, V.

Comfort Inn
440 Three Rivers Dr, 98626; tel 360/425-4600 or toll free 800/228-5150; fax 360/423-0762. Exit 39 off I-5. A good place to stop if you are traveling between Portland and Seattle on I-5. **Rooms:** 57 rms and stes. CI 3pm/CO noon. Nonsmoking rms avail. Rooms are very clean and comfortable; several minisuites have love seats and whirlpools. **Amenities:** A/C, cable TV w/movies. Some units w/whirlpools. Some minisuites equipped with refrigerators and microwaves. **Services:** **Facilities:** Games rm, whirlpool. Especially nice indoor pool. **Rates (CP):** $65–$100 S or D; $85–$100 ste. Extra person $5. Children under age 18 stay free. Parking: Outdoor, free. AE, DISC, MC, V.

Kelso Inn Motel
505 N Pacific, 98626; tel 360/636-4610; fax 360/636-4773. From I-5 exit 40. Tired and worn '50s-vintage structure. An OK bet for overnights or traveling on the cheap. **Rooms:** 51 rms and effic. CI 3pm/CO noon. Nonsmoking rms avail. Reasonably clean rooms. **Amenities:** A/C, cable TV w/movies. **Services:** **Rates:** $40–$44 S or D; $45–$49 effic. Extra person $3. Children under age 13 stay free. Parking: Outdoor, free. AE, DISC, MC, V.

Kennewick

See also Pasco, Richland

One of the Tri-Cities near the confluence of the Yakima, Snake, and Columbia Rivers. Kennewick's name is derived from a Native American word meaning winter paradise. A convention town with lots of shopping facilities. **Information:** Tri-Cities Convention and Visitors Bureau, 6951 W Grainbridge Blvd, Kennewick, 99336 (tel 509/735-8486).

MOTELS

Cavanaugh's at Columbia Center
1101 N Columbia Center Blvd, 99336; tel 509/783-0611 or toll free 800/843-4667; fax 509/735-3087. Inviting, well-run motel on a knoll in the sprawling Columbia Center complex. Convenient to Tri-Cities Coliseum. A cascading stream runs through the landscaped grounds. **Rooms:** 162 rms. Executive level. CI 3pm/CO noon. Nonsmoking rms avail. Rooms are decorated in soothing tones of green, mauve, and gray, and the sturdy furniture is made of good-quality wood. Courtyard rooms face the pool. **Amenities:** A/C, cable TV. Some units w/minibars. Suites have refrigerators. **Services:** **Facilities:** 1000 1 restaurant, 1 bar (w/entertainment), whirlpool. Guests receive discounted rates at nearby Gold's Gym. **Rates:** Peak (Apr–Oct) $75 S; $85 D; $90–$280 ste. Children under age 17 stay free. Min stay special events. Lower rates off-season. Parking: Outdoor, free. AE, CB, DC, DISC, MC, V.

Clearwater Inn
5616 W Clearwater, 99336; tel 509/735-2242 or toll free 800/424-1145; fax 509/735-2317. 2 mi off US 395. New motel with tasteful interior and small but attractive lobby. Very little landscaping on the grounds. **Rooms:** 59 stes. CI 2pm/CO 11am. Nonsmoking rms avail. Kitchenettes have no cooking or eating utensils, but they are available at front desk. Suites are spacious one-room units. **Amenities:** A/C, cable TV, refrig. Microwave. **Services:** **Facilities:** Washer/dryer. **Rates (CP):** $47–$62 ste. Extra person $5. Children under age 17 stay free. Parking: Outdoor, free. AE, CB, DC, DISC, MC, V.

Comfort Inn
7801 W Quinault, 99336; tel 509/783-8396 or toll free 800/228-5150; fax 509/783-8396. Next to Columbia Center Mall. Perched on a hill above a large shopping complex, the motel is fresh and new, although surrounded by parking lots. **Rooms:** 56 rms and stes. CI 2pm/CO 11am. Nonsmoking rms avail. Rooms are very clean and quiet, with decent-quality furniture and good lighting. **Amenities:** A/C, cable TV. Some units w/whirlpools. Suites have microwaves and refrig-

erators. **Services:** Facilities: Whirlpool, washer/dryer. **Rates (CP):** Peak (May–Sept) $47 S; $53 D; $63–$126 ste. Extra person $10. Children under age 18 stay free. Lower rates off-season. Parking: Outdoor, free. AE, DC, DISC, JCB, MC, V.

Ramada Inn on Clover Island
435 Clover Island, 99336; tel 509/586-0541 or toll free 800/2-RAMADA; fax 509/586-6956. On River Island; in heart of Tri-Cities area. This four-story, stone-aggregate motel popular with business travelers offers an efficient staff, no-frills rooms, and convenient location. **Rooms:** 150 rms and stes. CI 3pm/CO noon. Nonsmoking rms avail. Riverside rooms have the best views and are the most expensive. **Amenities:** A/C, cable TV. Some units w/terraces, some w/whirlpools. **Services:** **Facilities:** 350 1 restaurant, 1 bar, whirlpool. Public boat landing nearby. **Rates:** Peak (Apr–Oct) $65–$95 S; $70–$100 D; $175–$300 ste. Extra person $8. Children under age 18 stay free. Min stay special events. Lower rates off-season. Parking: Outdoor, free. AE, CB, DC, DISC, MC, V.

RESTAURANT

Chez Chaz Bistro & Catering
5011 W Clearwater Ave; tel 509/735-2138. **Continental.** A collection of whimsical salt and pepper shakers is part of the decor in this open, light, casual bistro. Dinner choices include T-bone steak with shallots and mushrooms, salmon baked with hazelnuts and herbs, and raspberry chicken; a pasta dish is always on the menu, too. Lighter meals are posted on a chalkboard. **FYI:** Reservations accepted. Dress code. Beer and wine only. No smoking. **Open:** Mon 9am–3pm, Tues–Thurs 9am–8pm, Fri 9am–9pm, Sat 10am–9pm. **Prices:** Main courses $17–$20. No CC.

Kent

A city with award-winning parks and recreation, and popular local festivals. **Information:** Kent Chamber of Commerce, 524 W Meeker #1, PO Box 128, Kent, 98035 (tel 206/854-1770).

MOTELS

Best Western Choicelodge
24415 Russell Rd, 98032; tel 206/854-8767 or toll free 800/835-3338; fax 206/850-7667. This very nice hotel is in a quiet location on a golf course. **Rooms:** 70 rms and stes. CI noon/CO noon. Nonsmoking rms avail. Rooms have older, worn furniture, but good views. **Amenities:** A/C, cable TV w/movies. Some units w/terraces, some w/whirlpools. Some rooms have refrigerators. **Services:** Babysitting. **Facilities:** 90 Sauna, whirlpool. **Rates (CP):** Peak (June–Sept) $79–$98 S; $89–$150 D; $98–$150 ste. Extra person $5. Children under age 18 stay free. Lower rates off-season. Parking: Outdoor, free. AE, CB, DC, DISC, MC, V.

Days Inn of Kent
1711 W Meeker St, 98444; tel 206/854-1950 or toll free 800/DAYS-INN; fax 206/859-1018. Exit 149A off I-5. Clean and simple rooms in an older building showing signs of aging. **Rooms:** 82 rms, stes, and effic. CI 2pm/CO noon. Nonsmoking rms avail. **Amenities:** A/C, cable TV, refrig, in-rm safe. **Services:** **Facilities:** Washer/dryer. Dark hallways. **Rates (CP):** Peak (June–Aug) $50–$55 S; $60–$65 D; $70–$75 ste; $75–$85 effic. Extra person $5. Children under age 18 stay free. Lower rates off-season. Parking: Outdoor, free. AE, DC, DISC, MC, V.

Kirkland

A boating center located on the shore of Lake Washington, the town is also known for its art galleries and boutiques. **Information:** Greater Kirkland Chamber of Commerce, 356 Parkplace Center, Kirkland, 98033 (tel 206/822-7066).

HOTEL

The Woodmark Hotel at Carillon Point
1200 Carillon Point, 98033; tel 206/822-3700 or toll free 800/822-3700; fax 206/822-3699. 1 mi N of WA 520 on Lake Washington Blvd. The only hotel on Lake Washington. Popular with businesspeople; close to major high-tech companies. Small and intimate, and casually elegant. Expensive, but worthwhile for travelers looking for quiet, style, and convenience. **Rooms:** 100 rms and stes. CI 4pm/CO noon. Nonsmoking rms avail. Many with lake views. **Amenities:** A/C, cable TV w/movies, dataport, VCR, voice mail, bathrobes. All units w/minibars, some w/terraces, 1 w/fireplace, some w/whirlpools. 3″ television/radio in bathrooms. **Services:** VP Babysitting. **Facilities:** 250 1 restaurant, 1 bar (w/entertainment), 1 beach (lake shore), spa. Lobby bar has cozy library motif with fireplace, books, and overstuffed chairs. **Rates:** Peak (June–Oct) $150–$195 S; $165–$210 D; $225–$1,000 ste. Extra person $15. Children under age 18 stay free. Lower rates off-season. Parking: Indoor, $8/day. AE, CB, DC, MC, V.

INN

Shumway Mansion
11410 99th Pl NE, 98033 (Residential); tel 206/823-2303; fax 206/822-0421. 3 blocks from Juanita Beach. This 10,000-square-foot mansion built in 1909 overlooks Juanita Bay of Lake Washington. When there are no social functions booked for the enormous first floor, guests have access to the living room, sun room, dining room, library, and balcony. Close to local wineries. Rates reasonable considering the cheery rooms and huge breakfast. **Rooms:** 8 rms and stes. CI 3pm/

CO 11am. No smoking. Each room is named for a local city and has an animal theme. The Bellevue room is keyed to rabbits, the Issaquah to cows, etc. **Amenities:** No A/C, phone, or TV. 1 unit w/terrace. **Services:** Afternoon tea served. Cookie tray served with coffee each evening. **Facilities:** 60 Free use of nearby fitness center. **Rates (BB):** $65–$95 S; $95 ste. Parking: Outdoor, free. AE, MC, V.

RESTAURANTS

Cafe Juanita
9702 NE 120th Place; tel 206/823-1505. 1 block N of Juanita Dr. **Italian.** Simple decor and wooden chairs counterpoint the lavish, rich food at this long-time northern Italian favorite. Appetizers, usually offered family style, include shellfish from the Hama Hama River on the Olympic Peninsula. Among the entrees are chicken breast served with pistachios and prosciutto in a thick cream sauce, and huge pork chops. A bit hard to find; best to call for directions. **FYI:** Reservations recommended. No smoking. **Open:** Daily 5:30–9:15pm. **Prices:** Main courses $13–$21. AE, MC, V.

Yarraw Bay Grill
1270 Carillon Point; tel 206/889-7497. 1 mi N of WA 520. **Eclectic.** An upscale grill and beach cafe with expansive views of Lake Washington. The Grill offers Lopez Island mussels, Penn Cove select oysters, Atlantic salmon, and northwestern bouillabaisse. The downstairs cafe offers "flavors of the world" theme like Thai or Cuban cuisine. **FYI:** Reservations recommended. Children's menu. No smoking. **Open:** Daily 11am–11pm. **Prices:** Main courses $15–$20. AE, DC, MC, V.

ATTRACTION

Château Ste Michelle Winery
14111 NE 145th, Woodinville; tel 206/488-1133. 10 mi N of Kirkland. Founded in 1934, Château Ste Michelle is the oldest and one of the most acclaimed wineries in Washington. Located on the 87-acre estate of the late Frederick Stimson (a turn-of-the-century Seattle lumber baron), this wooded retreat features formal gardens, trout ponds, and the 11-bedroom summer home of the Stimson family. (The home is listed on the National Register of Historic Places.) Extensive guided tours of the wine cellar (a complimentary tasting included) are given daily on the hour and half hour, from 10am to 4:30pm; the Vintage Reserve Room offers tastes of reserve and single-vineyard wines for a fee. **Open:** Daily 10am–5pm. Closed some hols. **Free**

La Conner

Once a pioneer trading post and fishing port, La Conner now attracts Northwest artists looking for a rural, quiet setting. Fishing trips and marine sightseeing cruises attract vacationers. **Information:** La Conner Chamber of Commerce, PO Box 1610, La Conner, 98257 (tel 360/466-4778).

MOTEL

La Conner Country Inn
107 S 2nd St, PO Box 573, 98257; tel 360/466-3101; fax 360/466-5902. 1 block from City Center. Country-style inn with old-fashioned library, huge stone fireplace, and fresh-cut flowers. **Rooms:** 28 rms. CI 3pm/CO noon. Nonsmoking rms avail. Some rooms have brass beds and pillow shams. Two 2-room suites. **Amenities:** Cable TV w/movies, voice mail. No A/C. All units w/fireplaces. **Services:** Social director. VCRs for rent. Continental breakfast includes homemade scones, cinnamon rolls, muffins, granola, juices, coffee, and tea. **Facilities:** 50 1 restaurant (lunch and dinner only; *see* "Restaurants" below), 1 bar. Microwave in lobby. **Rates (CP):** Peak (Apr–Aug) $81–$130 S or D. Extra person $20. Children under age 12 stay free. Lower rates off-season. Parking: Outdoor, free. Honeymoon and anniversary packages available. AE, DC, DISC, MC, V.

INN

The Heron in La Conner
117 Maple St, PO Box 716, 98257; tel 360/466-4626. 1 acre. Cozy country inn. Pretty lobby has lace curtains, wainscotting, and a stone fireplace. Unsuitable for children under 12. **Rooms:** 12 rms and stes. CI 3pm/CO 11am. No smoking. Rooms in the rear of the inn have views of farm fields and the Cascade Mountains. Few drawers and little counter space in most rooms. **Amenities:** Cable TV. No A/C. Some units w/fireplaces, 1 w/whirlpool. **Services:** Social director, afternoon tea served. Pets permitted at management's discretion. **Facilities:** 8 Whirlpool, guest lounge. Pleasant backyard with flower garden and outdoor hot tub. **Rates (CP):** Peak (Apr–Oct) $69–$83 S or D; $101–$135 ste. Extra person $15. Lower rates off-season. Parking: Outdoor, free. DISC, MC, V.

LODGE

La Conner Channel Lodge
201 N 1st St, PO Box 573, 98257; tel 360/466-1500; fax 360/466-1525. On the Swinomish Channel. A waterfront lodge where you can listen to the sea gulls, smell the salty air, and watch the boats drift by. The lobby is warm and inviting. **Rooms:** 40 rms and stes. CI 3pm/CO noon. No smoking. All rooms are very attractively furnished, and all but five have views of the channel. **Amenities:** Cable TV w/movies, refrig, bathrobes. No A/C. Some units w/terraces, all w/fireplaces, some w/whirlpools. **Services:** Continental breakfast includes home-baked goods, juices, cereal, and fresh fruit. **Facilities:** 20 Wooden pier and outdoor patio. Piano player entertains on Fri and Sat nights. **Rates (CP):** Peak (Apr–Aug) $140–$172 S or D; $175–$222

ste. Extra person $20. Children under age 12 stay free. Lower rates off-season. Parking: Outdoor, free. AE, DC, DISC, MC, V.

RESTAURANTS

Andiamo Ristorante Italiano

505 S 1st St; tel 360/466-9111. **Italian.** Located among the boutiques and specialty gift shops in the heart of La Conner; a couple of upstairs tables have a view of the picturesque waterfront village. To start, olive oil and freshly grated Parmesan cheese are served with crusty bread. Choose from a variety of antipasti plus dishes like Italian ham and potato dumplings. Extensive wine list. **FYI:** Reservations recommended. Beer and wine only. No smoking. **Open:** Lunch Wed–Sun 11:30am–2:30pm; dinner Wed–Sun 5–10pm. **Prices:** Main courses $12–$18. AE, MC, V.

Palmer's Restaurant and Pub

In La Conner Country Inn, 205 E Washington St; tel 360/466-4261. At S 2nd St. **French.** This fairly new, yet firmly established, French restaurant is decorated with belle epoque artwork, pink tablecloths, and fresh flowers. A signature dish is tournedos duet: tenderloin medallions with two sauces, a Bordelaise and a roasted-garlic cream sauce. Half portions are available for children. Smoking is permitted in the friendly downstairs pub, where lunch is served throughout the day. **FYI:** Reservations recommended. No smoking. **Open:** Lunch daily 11:30am–3pm; dinner daily 5–10pm. **Prices:** Main courses $14–$20. AE, MC, V.

ATTRACTIONS

Gaches Mansion

703 S 2nd St; tel 360/466-4288. Elegant mansion constructed in 1891 for the Gaches, one of the area's earliest families. The mansion has been used in the years since as a hospital and apartment house, but has now been restored and furnished with period antiques. A museum on the second floor exhibits work by Northwest artists such as Morris Graves, Mark Tobey, and Guy Anderson. **Open:** Summer, Fri–Sun 1–5pm; winter, Fri–Sun 1–4pm; or by appointment. Closed Jan. $

Skagit County Historical Museum

501 S 4th St; tel 360/466-3365. The commercial and domestic life of the region are chronicled here with displays of antiques donated by local families, video programs on area history, and special programs on local oyster farming, Native Americans, and the Skagit River. **Open:** Tues–Sun 11am–5pm. Closed some hols. $

Viking Cruises

109 N 1st; tel 360/466-2639. Search for orca (killer) and minke whales, seals, dall's porpoises, bald eagles, seabirds, and other Deception Pass marine life aboard the 30-foot jet boat *Viking Explorer,* or enjoy a nature cruise into Skagit Valley's delta in search of waterfowl aboard the 58-foot *Viking Star.* Daily tours from Rosario aboard the *Explorer,* a Coast Guard–certified tech version of Jacques Cousteau's *Speedy Zodiac,* visit three pods of Orca totaling over 90 members. (Tour organizers claim that whales are sighted on 80% of their cruises.) The *Star* departs from La Conner at 10:30am for a 1½ hour excursion featuring bald eagles, great blue heron, loons, and views of the coast and Cascade Mountains. **Open:** Daily 8am–5pm. Closed some hols. $$$$

Langley

See Whidbey Island

Leavenworth

A popular Bavarian-styled village, noted for its fine selection of bed-and-breakfasts. A popular cross-country ski destination town, serviced by the free LINK bus system connecting it with Wenatchee and Chelan. **Information:** Leavenworth Chamber of Commerce, 894 US 2, PO Box 327, Leavenworth, 98826 (tel 509/548-5807).

MOTELS

Enzian Motor Inn

590 US 2, 98826; tel 509/548-5269 or toll free 800/223-8511. 1 block W of downtown. Experience the charm of Europe without the long flight. The impressive lobby has a wood-burning fireplace, a grand piano, and an overhead loft stocked with board games and puzzles. Upper floors have sofas in hallways. Returning guests get preference for reservations for the popular Autumn Leaf Festival and Christmas Lighting Festival. **Rooms:** 104 rms and stes. Executive level. CI 3pm/CO 11am. Nonsmoking rms avail. Rooms have fine Austrian furniture and luxurious down quilts; some face a grassy courtyard and flower garden. Entire third floor consists of suites. **Amenities:** A/C, cable TV. Some units w/terraces, some w/fireplaces, some w/whirlpools. Some TVs have remote controls. **Services:** **Facilities:** 300 Basketball, whirlpool. Table tennis room. **Rates (BB):** $78–$132 S; $82–$112 D; $150–$187 ste. Extra person $10. Children under age 6 stay free. Min stay special events. Parking: Outdoor, free. AE, DC, DISC, MC, V.

Linderhof Motor Inn

690 US 2, 98826; tel 509/548-5283 or toll free 800/828-5680; fax 509/548-6616. A Bavarian-style motel with white stucco accented by green trim, it offers a cozy lobby and even cozier rooms. **Rooms:** 26 rms, stes, and effic. CI 3pm/CO 11am. Nonsmoking rms avail. Pretty bedspreads and pastel shades make accommodations inviting, although drawer space is limited. Rooms with fireplace and whirlpool tub are great for honeymooners. **Amenities:** A/C, cable TV w/movies. Some units w/fireplaces, some w/whirlpools. **Services:** **Facilities:** 40 Whirlpool. Located

near 30 miles of cross-country ski trails. **Rates (CP):** $75–$107 S or D; $105 ste; $105 effic. Extra person $10. Children under age 7 stay free. Min stay special events. Parking: Outdoor, free. Rates vary with occupancy levels. AE, DISC, MC, V.

INNS

Haus Rohrbach Pension

12882 Ranger Rd, 98826; tel 509/548-7024 or toll free 800/548-4477. At the base of Tumwater Mtn; 1½ mi northwest of town. 13 acres. Located in a rural garden set high on a hill, this property offers cozy rooms and suites and splendid views of Leavenworth Valley. A big wooden door with blackened brass hinges opens to a tiny, antiqued entrance and spacious breakfast room. **Rooms:** 12 rms and stes (4 w/shared bath). CI 2pm/CO 11am. No smoking. **Amenities:** A/C, bathrobes. No phone or TV. All units w/terraces, some w/fireplaces, some w/whirlpools. Suites have hot tub, wet bar, heated floor, and gas fireplace. **Services:** Children's program, babysitting. **Facilities:** 18 Whirlpool, guest lounge. In winter, guests can sled down the hill in front of the property. **Rates (BB):** Peak (June–Oct/Thanksgiving–mid-Mar) $55–$70 S w/shared bath, $75–$85 S w/private bath; $65–$80 D w/shared bath, $85–$95 D w/private bath; $140–$160 ste. Extra person $20. Min stay peak. Lower rates off-season. Parking: Outdoor, free. AE, DC, DISC, MC, V.

Pension Anna

926 Commercial St, 98826 (Downtown); tel 509/548-6273 or toll free 800/509-ANNA. Intimate inn with surprisingly spacious rooms. Small details—candles on the windowsills, pink-and-white linen in the breakfast room, overflowing bookshelves—reveal the owner's pride in her establishment. **Rooms:** 15 rms and stes. CI 1pm/CO 11am. No smoking. Each room is uniquely decorated with imported furniture. In 1991, a chapel was moved to the site and transformed into guest quarters. **Amenities:** A/C, cable TV. All units w/terraces, some w/fireplaces, some w/whirlpools. **Services:** Twice-daily maid svce, social director, babysitting, afternoon tea served. **Facilities:** 20 **Rates (BB):** $65 S; $75 D; $140–$165 ste. Extra person $15. Children under age 2 stay free. Min stay special events. Parking: Outdoor, free. AE, CB, DC, DISC, MC, V.

RESTAURANTS

Lorraine's Edel House

In the Edel House Inn, 320 9th St; tel 509/548-4412. 2 blocks S of Front St. **Eclectic/Northwest.** Superb meals served in an elegant old inn steps from the hustle and bustle of Leavenworth. Candles, fresh flowers, and forest views add romance to both indoor and patio dining. Prepared from northwest ingredients with an international spice inflection, dinner choices might be grilled salmon with a Japanese sesame glaze, mesa verde pasta (a medley of vegetables in a spicy cilantro-pesto cream served over jalapeño fettucine), or blackened prime rib. Evening closing hours are flexible. Minimal parking. **FYI:** Reservations recommended. Children's menu. Beer and wine only. No smoking. **Open:** Peak (May–Oct) lunch Mon–Fri 11am–2pm, Sat–Sun 10am–2pm; dinner daily 5–9pm; brunch Sat–Sun 10am–2pm. **Prices:** Main courses $9–$19; prix fixe $6–$11. DISC, MC, V.

Reiner's Gasthaus

829 Front St (Downtown); tel 509/548-5111. **German/Hungarian.** The entrance to this upstairs restaurant is via a narrow stairway, the walls of which are plastered with photos of patrons enjoying themselves. German and Austrian flavors are present in the decor and music, as well as the food. (Things get very festive on the weekends when a strolling musician plays his accordion.) The specialty of the house is *sauerbraten nach frankischer astmit knodel und blaukraut,* a dish where the meat is marinated for five days. No lunch served Tues–Thur from Feb to Apr. **FYI:** Reservations not accepted. Accordionist. Children's menu. Beer and wine only. **Open:** Peak (Apr–Jan) lunch daily 11am–3:30pm; dinner daily 4:30–9pm. **Prices:** Main courses $11–$17. MC, V.

Long Beach

See Long Beach Peninsula

Long Beach Peninsula

This 28-mile-long sandy beach in southwestern Washington is bounded by the Pacific Ocean (on the west) and Willapa Bay (on the east). It comprises six small communities; Long Beach, the largest, boasts a 2,300-foot-long boardwalk. Nahcotta is best known for oyster farming and processing. Neighboring Oysterville was founded in 1854 after the discovery of oyster beds in Willapa Bay; all 80 acres of the town have been placed on the National Register of Historic Places. Ocean Park and Seaview are primarily resort towns. **Information:** Long Beach Peninsula Convention and Visitors Bureau, PO Box 562, Long Beach, 98631 (tel 360/642-2400).

MOTELS

Klipsan Beach Cottages

22617 Pacific Hwy, Ocean Park, 98640; tel 360/665-4888. WA 103, 8 mi N of Long Beach. The cottages offer superb views of the dunes and beach. Homey interiors with full housekeeping allow for a totally private retreat. Reservations required over a year in advance for summer, holidays, and weekends; often available midweek during winter. **Rooms:** 10 effic; 10 cottages/villas. CI 2pm/CO 11am. No smoking. The large cabins have bay windows and a sliding door that opens to a deck. **Amenities:** Cable TV, refrig. No A/C or phone. All units w/terraces, all w/fireplaces. Microwaves and dishwashers. Barbecue on the deck. **Services:** **Facilities:** 1 beach (ocean), volleyball. Rose garden, picnic area, and fountain. **Rates (CP):** $80–$150 effic; $80–$150 cottage/villa. Extra person $3. Min stay wknds. Parking: Outdoor, free. Closed Jan. MC, V.

Nendels Edgewater Inn
409 SW 10th St, PO Box 793, Long Beach, 98631; tel 360/642-2311 or toll free 800/547-0106; fax 360/642-8018. Bare-bones place whose only asset is its proximity to the beach and the Lightship Restaurant, which has a superb view from the third floor. **Rooms:** 84 rms and stes. CI 2pm/CO 11am. No smoking. Nonsmoking rms avail. Minimalist furniture. **Amenities:** Cable TV. No A/C. **Services:** **Facilities:** 100 1 restaurant (*see* "Restaurants" below), 1 bar, 1 beach (ocean), whirlpool. **Rates:** Peak (May 15–Sept 30) $60–$78 S; $68–$93 D; $73–$98 ste. Min stay special events. Lower rates off-season. Parking: Outdoor, free. AE, DISC, MC, V.

INN

Shelburne Country Inn
4415 Pacific Hwy, PO Box 250, Seaview, 98644; tel 360/642-2442; fax 360/642-8904. Jct WA 103 and US 101. 1 acre. Continuously operated as an inn since 1896. The Victorian-style lobby is jammed with antiques and iron lamps, and there's usually a roaring fire in the fireplace. Unsuitable for children under 12. **Rooms:** 15 rms and stes. CI 2:30pm/CO 11am. No smoking. Rooms are large and airy, each with its own theme and colors. Armoires, rocking chairs, and handmade quilts are typical furnishings. **Amenities:** No A/C, phone, or TV. Some units w/terraces. **Services:** Twice-daily maid svce, babysitting. Full, rich country breakfast served family-style in lobby; low-fat or vegetarian preparations can be made on request. **Facilities:** 20 1 restaurant (*see* "Restaurants" below), 1 bar, guest lounge. **Rates (BB):** Peak (June–Sept) $89 S; $95–$135 D; $165 ste. Extra person $10. Min stay wknds. Lower rates off-season. Parking: Outdoor, free. AE, MC, V.

RESORT

Sunset View Resort
256th St, PO Box 309, Ocean Park, 98640; tel 360/665-4494 or toll free 800/272-9199; fax 360/665-6528. 10 mi N of Long Beach on WA 103. 7 acres. Gardens and outdoor facilities enhance this simple lodging. Beautiful landscaping, play areas, and courts for various sports allow guests to be outside nonstop. **Rooms:** 52 rms, stes, and effic. CI 3pm/CO 11:30am. Nonsmoking rms avail. Old furniture. **Amenities:** Cable TV, refrig. No A/C. Some units w/terraces, some w/fireplaces. **Services:** **Facilities:** 100 1 beach (ocean), basketball, volleyball, sauna, whirlpool, playground, washer/dryer. The grounds and play areas are good for families. **Rates (CP):** $59–$94 S or D; $94–$154 ste; $94–$104 effic. Parking: Outdoor, free. Discounts offered in winter. AE, DC, DISC, MC, V.

RESTAURANTS

Lightship Restaurant
In Nendels Edgewater Inn, 409 SW 10th St, Long Beach; tel 360/642-3252. **Northwest.** Good seafood, great view of Long Beach. Choices include local Willapa Bay oyster shooters, crab and shrimp fondue, and "Devils on Horseback" (scallops wrapped in bacon) as well as halibut-and-chips. Chicken, pasta, and steak also served. **FYI:** Reservations accepted. Children's menu. **Open:** Peak (June 15–Sept 15) Mon–Fri 11am–10pm, Sat–Sun 8:30am–10pm. **Prices:** Main courses $11.95–$17.95. AE, CB, DC, DISC, MC, V.

The Shoalwater Restaurant
In Shelburne Country Inn, 4415 Pacific Hwy, Seaview; tel 360/642-4142. US 101 and WA 103 (Pacific Hwy). **Seafood.** Elegant paintings, antiques, and fresh flowers give an air of gracious hospitality. On most tables you will find a copy of *The Shoalwater's Finest Dinners* by the owners, Tony and Ann Kischner and Cheri Walker. The most popular appetizer is Oregon rabbit sausage in wonton wrappers. Two favorite entrees are crab cakes and a delicate, moist baked salmon cooked in vermouth. The charming and intimate Heron and Beaver Pub has a deck overlooking the fragrant herb garden. **FYI:** Reservations recommended. Children's menu. No smoking. **Open:** Peak (May–Sept) lunch Mon–Sat 11:30am–3pm; dinner Mon–Fri 5:30–9pm, Sat–Sun 5–9:30pm; brunch Sun 10am–3pm. Closed Nov 29–Dec 12. **Prices:** Main courses $15–$19. AE, DC, DISC, MC, V.

ATTRACTIONS

Lewis and Clark Interpretive Center
Robert Gray Dr, Ilwaco; tel 360/642-3029. Exhibits chronicle the famous explorers' incredible journey from 1805–1806 (nearby Cape Disappointment, located in Fort Canby State Park, was the end of the western trail). In the past 300 years more than 2,000 vessels and 700 lives have been lost due to the treacherous waters here at the mouth of the Columbia River. The center tells tales of some of these shipwrecks, and the histories of the two nearby lighthouses. **Open:** Daily 10am–5pm. **Free**

Ilwaco Heritage Museum
115 SE Lake St, Ilwaco; tel 360/642-2446. A modern museum with displays on the history of southeast Washington. Exhibits focus on traditional Native American culture as well as the exploration and development of the region. Displays include a mock-up of a pioneer village and the old Ilwaco Railroad depot. **Open:** Mon–Sat 9am–5pm, Sun noon–4pm. Closed some hols. **$**

Fort Canby State Park
Ilwaco; tel 360/642-3078 or toll free 800/562-0990. Located on the south end of the peninsula, this park is on the grounds of a former military installation used to guard the mouth of the Columbia River; many of its bunkers and batteries are still visible. Also within the boundaries of the park are the North Head and Cape Disappointment lighthouses. The latter was built in 1856 and is the oldest lighthouse on the West Coast; it is open for tours. For recreation, the park offers boating (with a boat launch), fishing (both ocean and lake), hiking trails, several picnic areas, and a campground with 250 sites. **Open:** Daily sunrise–sunset. **Free**

Longmire

See Mount Rainier National Park

Longview

See also Kelso

This port city on the Columbia River provides access to the Long Beach Peninsula via scenic WA 4. **Information:** Longview Area Chamber of Commerce, 1563 Olympia Way, Longview, 98632 (tel 360/423-8400).

HOTEL

Monticello Hotel
1405 17th Ave, 98632; tel 360/425-9900; fax 360/425-3424. At jct of Washington Way, 15th Ave, and Circle Dr. Built in 1923 by lumber baron R A Long, the founder of Longview. Much of its original, polished woodwork has been maintained, particularly in the vintage lobby and cocktail lounge. **Rooms:** 22 rms and stes. CI 3pm/CO noon. Nonsmoking rms avail. Rooms in adjacent motel section are currently in the best condition, with mahogany furnishings and dark paneling. Major renovation is planned for hotel section. **Amenities:** A/C, refrig. **Services:** **Facilities:** 1 restaurant (lunch and dinner only). Lovely restaurant serves gourmet lunches, dinners, and Sunday brunch. Elegantly furnished with wingback chairs, the cocktail lounge has the original fireplace with dark mahogany mantel. **Rates:** $34–$110 S; $36–$110 D; $90–$110 ste. Extra person $4. Children under age 12 stay free. Parking: Outdoor, free. AE, DISC, MC, V.

Lopez Island

One of the islands in the San Juan Island group. **Information:** Lopez Island Chamber of Commerce, PO Box 102, Lopez Island, 98261 (tel 360/468-3636).

MOTEL

The Islander Lopez Resort
Fisherman Bay Rd, PO Box 459, 98261; tel 360/468-2233 or toll free 800/736-3434; fax 360/468-3382. ½ mile S of Lopez Village. Clean, attractive motel across from the bay and marina. **Rooms:** 28 rms, stes, and effic. CI 3pm/CO 11am. No smoking. Furnishings are a bit above average, and rooms have outstanding views of the bay. Some standard rooms have a kitchenette. **Amenities:** Satel TV, refrig. No A/C or phone. Some units w/terraces, 1 w/fireplace. "Deluxe" accommodations offer wet bars and microwaves. **Services:** **Facilities:** 1 restaurant, 1 bar, 1 beach (bay), whirlpool, washer/dryer. Enclosed pool area gives sense of privacy. **Rates:** Peak (May 25–Sept 30) $80–$120 S or D; $220–$275 ste; $120 effic. Extra person $10. Lower rates off-season. Parking: Outdoor, free. AE, DISC, MC, V.

RESTAURANTS

★ Bay Cafe
Lopez Rd; tel 360/468-3700. On the waterfront. **Northwest.** On any given night, the rest of Lopez Village on this laid-back island may be empty, but you'll see plenty of cars parked near the Bay Cafe. A taupe-colored false-fronted building houses this very trendy restaurant. A special appetizer is polenta-encrusted Dungeness crab with wild mushroom tapenade and aioli. Entrees include a nice variety of meat, seafood, and vegetarian offerings; sea scallops in Thai green curry with fresh basil, lime, and jasmine rice is especially good. **FYI:** Reservations recommended. Beer and wine only. No smoking. **Open:** Peak (May 21–Sept 15) **Prices:** Prix fixe $13–$19. DISC, MC, V.

Gail's
101 Village Center Building; tel 360/468-2150. **Northwest.** A real find is housed in this white-trimmed gray building. Gail Pollock presents her inventive, eclectic cuisine in an informal dining room furnished with black director's chairs and work of local artists. Shoal Bay (Lopez Island) mussels make a fine appetizer; a popular entree is halibut in black bean sauce steamed in bok choy. Desserts include cheesecake and fruit kuchen. The wine list has almost 150 choices, mostly moderately priced northwest labels. **FYI:** Reservations recommended. Children's menu. Beer and wine only. No smoking. **Open:** Peak (Mem Day–Labor Day) lunch daily 11am–4pm; dinner daily 5:30–9pm. **Prices:** Main courses $13–$20. DISC, MC, V.

Manson

See also Chelan

A small village on Lake Chelan, featuring craft shops and art galleries.

MOTEL

Mountain View Lodge
25 Wapato Point Pkwy, PO Box 337, 98831; tel 509/687-9505 or toll free 800/687-9505; fax 509/687-9505. A pretty mountain setting isn't the only attraction at this sunny motel—the nearby casino is bringing them in by the busload. The small lobby gets cramped at times and the staff can get a bit overwrought. **Rooms:** 30 rms, stes, and effic. CI 3pm/CO 11am. Nonsmoking rms avail. **Amenities:** A/C, cable TV w/movies, refrig. 1 unit w/terrace. Coffeemakers, hair dryers, robes, clocks, extra blankets and pillows on request. **Services:** Social director, children's program, babysitting. **Facilities:** Volleyball, lawn games, whirlpool, playground, washer/dryer. **Rates:** Peak (June 16–Sept 14) $69–$75 S; $83–$89 D; $99–$105 ste; $105 effic. Lower rates off-season. Parking: Outdoor, free. AE, DISC, MC, V.

RESTAURANT

Coyote Cafe
In Mill Bay Casino, E Wapato Lake Rd; tel 509/687-2102. 6 mi from downtown Chelan. **Northwest.** Its location—a casino parking lot—won't win any awards for ambience, but this cafe does have plentiful and reasonably priced basic American food. The restaurant gives out "bonus bucks," senior specials, and discounts to the tourists streaming in. During summer, ribs and salmon sizzle on the outdoor barbecue. **FYI:** Reservations accepted. Children's menu. No liquor license. **Open:** Daily 7am–11pm. **Prices:** Main courses $8–$12. AE, DISC, MC, V.

Moclips

A Pacific Coast community, noted for its sunsets and sandy beaches.

RESORT

Ocean Crest Resort
WA 109, 98562; tel 360/276-4465 or toll free 800/684-8439; fax 360/276-4149. 20 mi N of Ocean Shores on Sunset Beach. 100 acres. There's a full range of accommodations at this oceanside resort. A wonderful boardwalk leads to the beach. **Rooms:** 45 rms, stes, and effic; 1 cottage/villa. CI 3pm/CO 11am. No smoking. Ocean breezes make air conditioning unnecessary. **Amenities:** Cable TV, refrig. No A/C. Some units w/terraces, some w/fireplaces. **Services:** Masseur. Razor clam guns (shovels) available free. **Facilities:** 50 1 restaurant (*see* "Restaurants" below), 1 bar (w/entertainment), 1 beach (ocean), spa, sauna, whirlpool, playground, washer/dryer. **Rates (CP):** Peak (Mar 16–Sept 24) $54–$97 S; $67–$103 D; $85–$118 ste; $85–$108 effic; $67 cottage/villa. Children under age 4 stay free. Lower rates off-season. Parking: Outdoor, free. Three nights for price of one Sun–Thurs. AE, DISC, MC, V.

RESTAURANT

Ocean Crest Resort
WA 109; tel 360/276-4465. 20 mi N of Ocean Shores on Sunset Beach. **Seafood/Steak.** The decor could use an upgrade from plastic to upholstery, but a view of the beach framed by fir trees rescues the ambience. Specialties are Quinault River salmon, delivered fresh each day, and steamer butter clams and Penn Cove mussels. **FYI:** Reservations recommended. Piano. Children's menu. No smoking. **Open:** Peak (Mar 16–Sept 24) breakfast daily 8am–2:30pm; lunch daily 8am–2:30pm; dinner daily 5:30–10pm. **Prices:** Main courses $12.95–$23.95. AE, DISC, MC, V.

Moses Lake

A central Washington city, surrounded by agricultural lands. Moses Lake is part of the state's scenic pothole lakes region, which is noted for its fisheries. **Information:** Moses Lake Area Chamber of Commerce, 324 S Pioneer Way, Moses Lake, 98837 (tel 509/765-7888).

MOTELS

Best Western Hallmark Inn and Resort
3000 Marina Dr, 98837; tel 509/765-9211 or toll free 800/235-4255; fax 509/766-0493. Exit 176 off I-90. Located on the lake, with a private boat dock and beach area. **Rooms:** 162 rms and stes. CI 4pm/CO noon. Nonsmoking rms avail. **Amenities:** A/C, cable TV w/movies, refrig, voice mail. Some units w/terraces, some w/whirlpools. Suites have dataports, large table work areas, additional chairs and couches. **Services:** Car-rental desk, babysitting. Lobby offers VCR, movie, and Super Nintendo rentals. Complimentary morning coffee and copies of *USA Today.* $10 fee for pets. **Facilities:** 2 300 1 restaurant (*see* "Restaurants" below), 1 bar (w/entertainment), 1 beach (lake shore), snorkeling, sauna, steam rm, whirlpool, washer/dryer. **Rates:** Peak (mid-May–mid-Sept) $75–$95 S or D; $105–$130 ste. Extra person $5. Children under age 12 stay free. Lower rates off-season. Parking: Outdoor, free. Rooms with lake view are $10 extra. Several packages avail. AE, CB, DC, DISC, JCB, MC, V.

Shilo Inn
1819 E Kittleson Rd, 98837; tel 509/765-9317 or toll free 800/222-2244; fax 509/765-5058. Jct WA 17 and I-90 exit 179. Motel adjacent to an interstate travel plaza offers easy access to gas, food, and other roadside services. **Rooms:** 100 rms and effic. CI 4pm/CO noon. Nonsmoking rms avail. King rooms have sofa and extra vanity area. Six efficiencies have kitchens (but no ovens). **Amenities:** A/C, cable

TV w/movies, refrig, dataport, voice mail. Larger-than-average rooms have microwaves and wet bars. **Services:** Car-rental desk. Complimentary morning coffee and newspaper in lobby. VCRs and movies for rent. Pet fee $7. **Facilities:** 1 restaurant, 1 bar, games rm, sauna, steam rm, whirlpool, washer/dryer. Four 24-hour restaurants within walking distance. **Rates (CP):** Peak (May 15–Sept 30) $75 S or D; $95 effic. Extra person $6. Children under age 12 stay free. Lower rates off-season. Parking: Outdoor, free. Senior, commercial, government, and trucker discounts; romance and golf packages avail. AE, CB, DC, DISC, ER, JCB, MC, V.

Travelodge of Moses Lake

316 S Pioneer Way, 98837 (Downtown); tel 509/765-8631 or toll free 800/578-7878; fax 509/765-3685. Near 3-way intersection of Pioneer Way, Third Ave, and Broadway. Centrally located motel gets lots of repeat commercial travelers. **Rooms:** 40 rms. CI 2pm/CO noon. Nonsmoking rms avail. Half the rooms have a shower/tub combo. Four two-bedroom units. **Amenities:** A/C, cable TV w/movies, voice mail. Some rooms have refrigerator. **Services:** Twice-daily maid svce. Complimentary coffee and newspaper available in lobby every morning. Menus of local restaurants available for review. **Facilities:** Sauna, whirlpool. **Rates:** Peak (June 1–Sept 5) $44 S; $49 D. Extra person $5. Children under age 14 stay free. Lower rates off-season. Parking: Outdoor, free. Commercial, government, military, and senior rates available. AE, DC, DISC, ER, MC, V.

RESTAURANT

★ Cade's Restaurant & Lounge

In Best Western Hallmark Inn and Resort, 3000 Marina Dr; tel 509/765-9211. **Eclectic.** A bright and airy place with views of Moses Lake. Known locally for its fresh seafood, the house favorite is coquille St Jacques (large scallops, mushrooms, and shallots with a creamy Swiss cheese sauce). Tableside dessert preparation is an eye-catching event. Most dietary requests can be accommodated. **FYI:** Reservations accepted. Children's menu. No smoking. **Open:** Daily 6:30am–10pm. **Prices:** Main courses $8–$32. AE, DC, DISC, MC, V.

Mount Rainier National Park

See also Ashford, Greenwater

The jagged shape of Mount Rainier, the 14,410-foot dormant volcano, was produced by years of glacial activity carving away at its stone face (the mountain still has 26 glaciers). The stately mountain is so much taller than the surrounding Cascades that it seems to loom over Seattle on clear days, even though it's actually 90 miles southeast of the city. The mountain and some 235,400 acres surrounding it are part of the national park, which was established in 1899.

Just past the park's southwest entrance at Nisqually, you'll come to Longmire, the park's main visitors center. Longmire is equipped with a lodge, a museum featuring exhibits on the park's natural and human history, a hiker information center that issues backcountry permits, and a ski-touring center.

The road from Longmire up to the circular **Henry M Jackson Memorial Visitors Center** at Paradise is usually open all-year. (Most other roads in the park close in November.) At an elevation of 5,400 feet, Paradise affords a breathtaking close-up view of the mountain. Many of the park's most scenic hiking trails start or end here.

The **Ohanapecosh Visitors Center,** in the southeastern section of the park, is only open in summer. Here visitors can walk through a forest of old-growth trees, some more than 1,000 years old. Continuing around the mountain, you'll reach the turnoff for **Sunrise Visitors Center.** At 6,400 feet, Sunrise is the highest spot accessible by car and is only open July–Sept. The beautiful old log lodge is surrounded by a picnic area.

From downtown Seattle, the easiest route to Mount Rainier is via I-5 south to exit 127, then take WA 706. The area may also be approached from the northwest via WA 165; from the east via WA 410; and from the south via US 12. For more information about the park, contact the Superintendent, Mount Rainier National Park, Tahoma Woods, Star Rte, Ashford, WA 98304 (tel 360/569-2211).

LODGES

Crystal Mountain Resort

1 Crystal Mountain Blvd, Crystal Mountain, 98022; tel 360/663-2558; fax 360/663-0145. 640 acres. These chalet-style buildings look best in winter surrounded by a lot of snow. **Rooms:** 186 rms, stes, and effic. Executive level. CI 4pm/CO noon. Nonsmoking rms avail. Rooms are pleasant, simple, and comfortable, with Bavarian motif. **Amenities:** Cable TV w/movies, refrig, VCR. No A/C or phone. Some units w/terraces, some w/fireplaces. **Services:** Children's program, babysitting. **Facilities:** 4 2 bars (1 w/entertainment), basketball, volleyball, lawn games, sauna, whirlpool, day-care ctr, playground, washer/dryer. **Rates:** Peak (Nov–Apr) $77–$95 S or D; $95–$105 ste; $110–$125 effic. Extra person $8. Min stay peak. Lower rates off-season. Parking: Outdoor, free. Ski packages avail. Closed Apr 15–June 25/Sept 10–Nov 15. AE, MC, V.

National Park Inn

PO Box 108, Longmire, 98304; tel 360/569-2411; fax 360/569-2770. 6 mi inside Nisqually entrance. Beautifully restored National Park Lodge, built in Cascadia style with rock and large timber logs. **Rooms:** 25 rms. CI 4pm/CO 11am. No smoking. Accommodations are simple, clean, and pleasant. **Amenities:** No A/C, phone, or TV. **Services:**

Facilities: 1 restaurant, games rm. Because the lodge is inside Mount Rainier National Park, there are hundreds of miles of hiking trails nearby. **Rates:** Peak (May 17–Oct) $80–$108 S or D. Extra person $10. Lower rates off-season. AP and MAP rates avail. Parking: Outdoor, free. AE, DC, DISC, MC, V.

Paradise Inn
Stevens Canyon Rd, Paradise, 98398; tel 360/569-2413; fax 360/569-2418. Built in 1917 with huge pieces of timber from the nearby forest. Last renovated in 1990, the outside needs paint but the inside is grand indeed. Wonderful lobby with large fireplaces. If you want to stay at a lodge high on Rainier, this is the place. **Rooms:** 126 rms and stes. CI 4pm/CO 11am. No smoking. Rooms are spare but clean; some have large exposed beams. **Amenities:** No A/C, phone, or TV. **Services:** Babysitting. **Facilities:** 1 restaurant. Guide services located next door for hiking and climbing the mountain. **Rates:** Peak (May–Oct) $62–$88 S or D; $118–$138 ste. Extra person $10. Children under age 2 stay free. Lower rates off-season. Parking: Outdoor, free. Closed Oct–May 15. AE, DC, DISC, MC, V.

Mount St Helens National Volcanic Monument

30 mi E of Silver Lake. Mount St Helens, an active volcano southwest of dormant Mount Rainier, attracted worldwide attention when it erupted on May 18, 1980, killing 57 people. The US government has since designated the area a national monument, and plants and wildlife have reappeared in the formerly devastated landscape.

There are numerous information centers and viewing sites, and it is even possible to climb to the top now, although only a few permits are handed out each day and reservations for weekends must be made far in advance. The main visitors center, located at Silver Lake, includes exhibits on the eruption and its effects on the region. Farther east on WA 504 (at MP 47) is the new **Coldwater Ridge Visitors Center**. This center offers programs and exhibits on the events leading up to and following the eruption. It's located only eight miles from the crater and offers spectacular views. For further information, contact the Monument Headquarters, 42218 NE Yale Bridge Rd, Amboy, WA 98601 (tel 360/247-5473).

Mount Vernon

Best known for its flower bulb farms. Daffodils start the rainbow parade in March, then come the tulips in April and irises in May. The nearby Skagit River is home to a large population of bald eagles, which can be viewed by guided raft float trips. **Information:** Mount Vernon Chamber of Commerce, 220 E College #174, PO Box 1007, Mount Vernon, 98273 (tel 360/428-8547).

RESTAURANT

Farmhouse Inn
1376 Whitney Rd; tel 360/466-4411. At WA 20. **American.** Housed in a rambling barn set in an open field, this place can get very busy, especially in high season. Large portions of roast turkey and prime rib served; special lingonberry butter from Norway available. Parking lot and entrance need better maintenance. **FYI:** Reservations not accepted. Country music/dancing. Children's menu. **Open:** Peak (June–Aug) breakfast Mon–Fri 7–11am, Sat 7–11:15am, Sun 7–11:45am; lunch Mon–Thurs 11am–9pm, Fri–Sat 11am–10pm, Sun noon–9pm; dinner Mon–Thurs 4–9pm, Fri–Sat 4–10pm, Sun 4–9pm. **Prices:** Main courses $6–$14. AE, DISC, MC, V.

ATTRACTION

Breazeale–Padilla Bay Interpretive Center
1043 Bayview-Edison Rd (Bay View); tel 360/428-1558. Overlooking Padilla Bay on 64 acres donated by the Breazeale family, the center houses indoor exhibits, a "hands-on" room, a reference library, and a saltwater aquarium. The bay is the only National Estuarine Research Reserve in Washington State and its 11,000 acres is managed by the Washington State Department of Ecology. Large seagrass meadows—which serve as feeding grounds for migratory black brant, sea goose, and as nursery areas for young fish and crabs—create a beautiful outdoor setting that visitors can enjoy every season of the year. Hiking, bicycling, kayaking, windsurfing, and bird watching are all available. There are two hiking trails; both are wheelchair accessible. **Open:** Wed–Sun 10am–5pm. Closed some hols. **Free**

Neah Bay

Located on the Makah Indian Reservation, on the far northwestern tip of the Olympic Peninsula. Salmon fishing is the most popular recreation. Lake Ozette and its famous boardwalk trails are located about an hour drive south of the town.

ATTRACTION

Makah Museum
WA 112; tel 360/645-2711. Exhibits of 500-year-old Makah tribal artifacts, recovered in 1970 due to tidal erosion. Articles on display include baskets, whaling tools, weapons, boats, and a full-size Makah longhouse. Gift shop sells modern-day Makah crafts. **Open:** Mem Day–mid-Sept, daily 10am–5pm; mid-Sept–Mem Day, Wed–Sun 10am–5pm. Closed Dec 25. **$$**

North Cascades National Park

20 mi E of Sedro Wooley. Some of America's most breathtaking scenery—high jagged peaks, ridges, and slopes, 318 glaciers, and countless cascading waterfalls—can be enjoyed at this 505,000-acre park. Access to the park is by the **North Cascades Scenic Hwy** (WA 20), from Burlington on the West and Twisp on the East. This byway, the most scenic mountain drive in Washington, is closed in the winter and bisects the park, going through most of **Ross Lake National Recreation Area.** Along the way are Gorge, Diablo, and Ross Lakes; spectacular look-out points; picnic areas and rest stops; and trails through old growth forests. The Ross Lake Area's 117,00 acres encompasses all three of Seattle City Light's power projects. Tours of the hydro facilities are regularly scheduled.

Lake Chelan National Recreation Area fills out the southern tip of the park. This natural lake rests in a glacially carved trough at a depth of nearly 1,500 feet. Lodging and meals, postal service, and basic camping supplies are available at the Stehekin Landing. Stehekin is not accessible by car, however, only by hiking, boating, or flying.

Hiking, backpacking, and mountaineering are the most popular activities in the park, which includes several self-guided walking trails. There are a few resorts and lodges within the park and camping at designated sites does not require a permit. Pets are prohibited in all areas except for the Pacific Crest National Trail. The **North Cascades Visitors Center** provides information, interpretive exhibits, a theater and slide program, and book and map sales. For information call or write Superintendent, North Cascades National Park, 2105 WA 20, Sedro Wooley, WA 98284 (tel 206/386-4495).

Ocean Park

See Long Beach Peninsula

Ocean Shores

See also Copalis Beach, Moclips

A planned resort community, with miles of clean beaches, fresh-water lakes, and a PGA golf course. Popular with bird watchers. **Information:** Ocean Shores Chamber of Commerce, 899 Pt Brown Ave, PO Box 382, Ocean Shores, 98569 (tel 360/289-2451).

MOTELS

Cantebury Inn

643 Ocean Shores Blvd, 98569; tel 360/289-3317 or toll free 800/562-6678; fax 360/289-3420. S of Chance á la Mere St; near Convention Center. Efficient motel with large grassy areas for kids to play. **Rooms:** 44 rms, stes, and effic. CI 3pm/CO noon. Nonsmoking rms avail. Compact with dining table and kitchenette. Very functional and comfortable. **Amenities:** Cable TV w/movies, refrig, VCR. No A/C. Some units w/terraces, some w/fireplaces, 1 w/whirlpool. Rooms have microwaves; accommodations on upper floor feature balconies. **Services:** Babysitting. **Facilities:** 45 1 beach (ocean), whirlpool. Large social room and larger-than-usual indoor pool with hot tub. **Rates:** Peak (Apr–Sept) $78–$92 S; $104–$114 D; $130–$150 ste; $78–$92 effic. Extra person $10. Children under age 14 stay free. Min stay wknds and special events. Lower rates off-season. Parking: Outdoor, free. AE, MC, V.

The Grey Gull

Ocean Shores Blvd, PO Box 1417, 98569; tel 360/289-3381; fax 360/289-3673. An attractive three-story motel with a sunken lobby. **Rooms:** 36 rms, stes, and effic. CI 4pm/CO noon. Nonsmoking rms avail. All rooms overlook beach, sand dunes, and pool. **Amenities:** Cable TV, refrig, VCR. No A/C. All units w/terraces, all w/fireplaces. **Services:** **Facilities:** 1 beach (ocean), sauna, whirlpool, washer/dryer. **Rates:** Peak (June–Aug) $110–$129 S or D; $110–$215 ste; $98–$115 effic. Min stay wknds and special events. Lower rates off-season. Parking: Outdoor, free. AE, DC, DISC, MC, V.

Polynesian Condominium Resort

615 Ocean Shores Blvd, 98569; tel 360/289-3361 or toll free 800/562-4836; fax 360/289-0294. The social room facing the beach is the highlight of property. **Rooms:** 72 rms, stes, and effic. CI 5pm/CO noon. Nonsmoking rms avail. Large with lots of seating. **Amenities:** Cable TV, refrig, VCR. No A/C. Some units w/terraces, some w/fireplaces, 1 w/whirlpool. **Services:** Babysitting. **Facilities:** 90 1 restaurant (dinner only), 1 bar (w/entertainment), 1 beach (ocean), basketball, volleyball, games rm, sauna, whirlpool, playground, washer/dryer. **Rates:** Peak (June–Sept) $69 S; $79–$92 D; $104–$165 ste; $69 effic. Extra person $10. Children under age 12 stay free. Min stay wknds. Lower rates off-season. Parking: Outdoor, free. Honeymoon and anniversary packages avail. AE, CB, DC, DISC, MC, V.

Olga

See Orcas Island

Olympia

The capital city of Washington boasts beautifully landscaped parks, a harborside boardwalk, and an attractive historic district. Olympia is also the starting point for the scenic Olympic Highway (US 101), which loops around three sides of the Olympic Peninsula. **Information:** Olympia/Thurston County Chamber of Commerce, 1000 Plum St, PO Box 1427, Olympia, 98507 (tel 360/289-2451).

HOTELS

UNRATED **Holiday Inn Select Olympia**
2300 Evergreen Park Dr SW, 98502; tel 360/943-4000 or toll free 800/551-8500; fax 360/357-6604. Set in a pleasant landscape with large trees. Basic rooms, small lobby, dark hallways. Popular with conventioneers because of its meeting rooms. **Rooms:** 191 rms and stes. CI 3pm/CO noon. Nonsmoking rms avail. **Amenities:** A/C. Some units w/terraces, some w/whirlpools. **Services:** Babysitting. **Facilities:** 1200 1 restaurant, 1 bar (w/entertainment), games rm, whirlpool, washer/dryer. **Rates (BB):** $120–$164 ste. Extra person $10. Children under age 18 stay free. Parking: Outdoor, free. AE, CB, DC, DISC, JCB, MC, V.

Ramada Inn Governor House
621 S Capitol Way, 98501; tel 360/352-7700 or toll free 800/228-2828; fax 360/943-9349. Great views from some rooms on the higher floors. Priced a bit higher than most hotels in the area. **Rooms:** 120 rms, stes, and effic. CI 3pm/CO noon. Nonsmoking rms avail. Spacious rooms. **Amenities:** A/C, satel TV w/movies, voice mail. Some units w/terraces. Some rooms have refrigerators and microwaves. **Services:** **Facilities:** 200 1 restaurant, 1 bar (w/entertainment), sauna, whirlpool. **Rates:** Peak (May–Sept) $125–$160 ste; $120 effic. Children under age 18 stay free. Lower rates off-season. AP and MAP rates avail. Parking: Indoor, $2/day. AE, CB, DC, DISC, MC, V.

West Coast Tyee Hotel
500 Tyee Dr, 98502; tel 360/352-0511 or toll free 800/386-8933; fax 360/943-6448. At exit 102 off I-5. Big rooms, inviting lobby, and a well-cared-for inner courtyard. **Rooms:** 146 rms. Executive level. CI 3pm/CO noon. Nonsmoking rms avail. New furniture; some have sofas. **Amenities:** A/C, cable TV w/movies. Some units w/terraces, some w/fireplaces, some w/whirlpools. **Services:** Car-rental desk, babysitting. **Facilities:** 1200 1 restaurant, 1 bar (w/entertainment), sauna, whirlpool. **Rates:** Peak (June–Aug/Jan–Mar) $59–$85 S; $65–$150 D. Children under age 18 stay free. Lower rates off-season. Parking: Outdoor, free. AE, DC, DISC, MC, V.

MOTELS

UNRATED **Best Western Aladdin Motor Inn**
900 Capitol Way, 98501; tel 360/352-7200 or toll free 800/369-7771; fax 360/352-0846. Clean property, located a block from the Capitol. Small lobby. **Rooms:** 100 rms. CI open/CO noon. Nonsmoking rms avail. **Amenities:** A/C, cable TV w/movies, dataport. Some rooms offer refrigerators and microwaves. **Services:** **Facilities:** 45 1 restaurant, 1 bar (w/entertainment). **Rates:** Peak (June–Sept) $60–$70 S; $66–$76 D. Children under age 12 stay free. Lower rates off-season. Parking: Outdoor, free. AE, CB, DC, DISC, MC, V.

Carriage Inn Motel
1211 S Quince St, 98501; tel 360/943-4710. I-5, exit 105B. Owners offer friendly service. Favorable rates for area. **Rooms:** 62 rms. CI 3pm/CO noon. Nonsmoking rms avail. **Amenities:** A/C, cable TV w/movies, refrig. Some units w/terraces. **Services:** **Facilities:** 1 restaurant (bkfst and dinner only). **Rates:** $45 S; $54–$60 D. Extra person $4. Children under age 12 stay free. Parking: Outdoor, free. AE, DC, DISC, MC, V.

RESTAURANTS

★ **Budd Bay Cafe**
525 N Columbia St; tel 360/357-6963. on the waterfront. **Northwest.** Large windows and a great view of the water, plus nautical-but-not-tacky decor. Good lunch bets are hot seafood salad, salmon, or broiled halibut. Dinner entrees include steaks and chicken in various preparations. On a sunny day, the patio is guaranteed to be crowded. **FYI:** Reservations recommended. Children's menu. Dress code. **Open:** Mon–Thurs 11am–9pm, Fri–Sat 11am–10pm, Sun 10am–9pm. **Prices:** Main courses $7–$25. AE, DC, DISC, MC, V.

Falls Terrace
106 Deschutes Way; tel 360/943-7830. Near Olympia Brewery and Deschutes River. **American.** The main appeal of this restaurant is the terrific view of the Deschutes Falls through the wide windows in the dining room. Steaks are the most popular option. Parking is on a busy street. **FYI:** Reservations recommended. Dress code. **Open:** Peak (June–Sept) Mon–Fri 11am–9pm, Sat 11:30–9pm, Sun 11:30–8pm. **Prices:** Main courses $10–$30. AE, DC, DISC, MC, V.

Gardner's Seafood & Pasta
111 W Thurston Ave; tel 360/786-8466. Near Olympia's wharf. **Seafood.** A cozy but spacious place tucked away next to a farmers market. Considered one of Olympia's premier dining spots (reservations are generally necessary days in advance). For starters you may try the seafood-stuffed mushrooms or the focaccia slathered with pesto. Featured entrees include seafood fettucine and cioppino (fish and shellfish in a light broth). Excellent wine selection. **FYI:** Reservations

recommended. Children's menu. Dress code. Beer and wine only. No smoking. **Open:** Tues–Sat 5–9pm. **Prices:** Main courses $11–$18. AE, MC, V.

Genoas on the Bay
1525 N Washington; tel 360/943-7770. At the end of Olympia Wharf. **Seafood.** Large windows guarantee diners a great view of Budd Inlet. Although the building can be a bit hard to find (hidden behind high stacks of timber waiting for maritime shipment), it's worth the trouble. Extensive selection of seafood and steaks. **FYI:** Reservations accepted. Children's menu. Dress code. **Open:** Lunch Mon–Thurs 11am–4pm; dinner Mon–Thurs 4am–9pm, Fri–Sat 4–10pm, Sun 4:30–9pm; brunch Sun 10:30am–2:30pm. **Prices:** Main courses $10–$25. AE, CB, DC, DISC, MC, V.

Jean-Pierre's Chattery Down
209 5th Ave SE; tel 360/352-8483. **International.** This friendly husband-and-wife-run place feels more like a cottage kitchen than a restaurant. The menu changes often, but typical specials include pork with calvados, Black Angus steak, or pastas tossed with smoked salmon or exotic mushrooms. **FYI:** Reservations recommended. Dress code. Beer and wine only. No smoking. **Open:** Lunch Mon 11am–3pm, Tues 11:30am–3pm, Wed–Fri 11:30am–3pm; dinner Thurs–Sat 5:30–9pm; brunch Sat 9:30am–3pm. **Prices:** Main courses $12–$18. No CC.

La Petite Maison
2005 NW Ascension; tel 360/943-8812. **Northwest.** The chef at this small restaurant is known for producing high-quality dishes using local ingredients. The layout offers spacious, private dining areas as well as intimate nooks and crannies. Frequently changing menu. **FYI:** Reservations recommended. Dress code. Beer and wine only. No smoking. **Open:** Lunch Tues–Fri 11:30am–2pm; dinner Mon–Sat 5:30–9pm. **Prices:** Main courses $14–$19. AE, MC, V.

Raeline's Eatery
212 Legion Way SE; tel 360/352-7160. **Deli.** A clean, well-lighted bistro filled with flowers and plants. Serves mainly sandwiches and is also known for its wonderful cookies. **FYI:** Reservations not accepted. No liquor license. No smoking. **Open:** Peak (June–Aug) Mon–Fri 8am–4pm, Sat 9am–2pm. **Prices:** Lunch main courses $2–$5. No CC.

Spar Cafe & Bar
114 E 4th Ave (Downtown); tel 360/357-6444. **Diner.** Opened in 1935 as a diner for lumbermen and legislators, this eatery/hangout has a long meal counter, tobacco shop, and a wood decor that, together with the poker room and dim lounge, give an authentic "greasy spoon" feel. A great place to grab a cup of "joe" and read the newspaper. **FYI:** Reservations not accepted. Jazz. Children's menu. Dress code. **Open:** Peak (June–Aug) Mon–Thurs 6am–9pm, Fri–Sat 6am–10pm, Sun 6am–9pm. **Prices:** Main courses $6–$10. AE, CB, DC, MC, V.

The Urban Onion
116 Legion Way (Downtown); tel 360/943-9242. Across from park. **New American/Vegetarian.** Here you'll find superb vegetarian meals as well as carnivore-oriented choices. Popular for business lunches because it's two blocks from the Capitol Campus, it's also around the corner from the Washington Performing Arts Center. Terrific ambience, good selection of wines, and fine desserts make it a great place for a pre- or post-performance dinner. **FYI:** Reservations accepted. Jazz. Children's menu. Dress code. No smoking. **Open:** Mon–Thurs 7am–10pm, Fri–Sat 7am–11pm, Sun 8am–9pm. **Prices:** Main courses $8–$12. AE, MC, V.

ATTRACTIONS

State Capital Museum
211 W 21st Ave; tel 360/753-2580. This small museum houses exhibits on the history of Washington both during its territorial days and since statehood. Of particular interest are the exhibits on Northwest Native Americans. The building itself is a Spanish-style mansion that was built for a former mayor of Olympia. **Open:** Tues–Fri 10am–4pm, Sat–Sun noon–4pm. Closed some hols. **$**

Henderson House Museum
602 Deschutes Blvd; tel 360/753-8583. Built in 1905, the Henderson House is now a repository and display center for artifacts and photos pertaining to the history of the Tumwater area. Nearby is another historic home, the Crosby House, which was built in 1858 by one of Bing Crosby's relatives. **Open:** Thurs–Sun noon–4pm. Closed some hols. **Free**

Wolf Haven International
3111 Offut Lake Rd, Tenino; tel 360/264-4695 or toll free 800/448-9653. 7 mi S of Olympia. This 75-acre refuge is run by a nonprofit group dedicated to wolf conservation. Visitors can meet many of the resident wolves on guided tours of the facility, which are given on the hour. From May to September, there are Friday and Saturday evening "howl-ins" featuring storytelling, folk singing, and of course a chance to howl. **Open:** Daily 10am–5pm. **$$**

Olympic National Forest Headquarter's Office
1835 Black Lake Blvd SW; tel 360/956-2400. Surrounding much of **Olympic National Park** (see below), this 632,000-acre national forest includes an incredible variety of climates, plants, and animals. The Quinault district, on the western edge of the park, consists of a lush, temperate rain forest with 300-foot-tall trees and year-round mild temperatures while the mighty Mount Olympus, just a few miles away, gets nearly 20 feet of snow per year and is home to arctic plants like lichens and mosses. The area is home to more than 100 varieties of wildflowers, 200 species of birds, and the largest elk population in the world.

The forest offers 19 campgrounds, five boating sites, and several trails ranging in difficulty from 20-mile treks to ½-mile nature walks. Glacier-fed Quinault Lake is popular for trout and salmon fishing. (Since the lake is managed by the Quinault Indian Nation, visitors need a tribal fishing permit. Ask at local stores or the ranger stations for details.)

The main **visitors center** at Olympia has a large relief map of the area, a book and map store, and interpretive displays. Other ranger offices are located in Hoodsport, Quilcene, Quinault, and Forks. For further information, contact the Supervisor, Olympia National Forest, Federal Building, 1835 Black Lake Blvd SW, Olympia, WA 98502 (tel 360/956-2400). **Open:** Mem Day–Labor Day, daily 8am–4:30pm; Labor Day–Mem Day, Mon–Fri 8am–4:30pm. Closed some hols. **Free**

Olympic National Park

See also Forks, Neah Bay, Port Angeles, Quinault, Sequim

Within this 1,430-square-mile park, covering much of northwestern Washington's Olympic Peninsula, lies an amazing array of ecosystems. The mighty 7,965-foot Mount Olympus crowns a jumble of peaks, many of them over a mile high. Such high elevations mean that the western side of the mountains is constantly deluged with rain—in the west-facing valleys of the Bogachield, Hoh, Clearwater, Queets, and Quinault Rivers, rainfall often exceeds 150 inches per year; it is this constant rain that allows trees here to grow as tall as 200 feet. The combination of high elevations and heavy rainfall have also lead to the formation of over 60 glaciers. The eastern side of the Olympic Mountains is one of the driest areas on the West Coast. A second, smaller unit of the park consists of a 57-mile-long strip of coastline along the western edge of the peninsula.

More than 600 miles of hiking trails provide the only access to most of the park; there are fewer than a dozen park roads, and most of them lead only a few miles into the interior. (However, US 101, which loops around the park's periphery, has been designated the **Olympic Peninsula Scenic Drive.**) The visitors center at Port Angeles offers an orientation slide program, a store selling books and maps, and information on trail and road conditions throughout the park.

From the visitors center, continue another 17 miles on the interior park road to **Hurricane Ridge,** which offers spectacular views. (This area is a popular cross-country skiing spot during the winter.) West of Port Angeles on US 101 is **Lake Crescent,** a glacier-carved lake surrounded by mountains. A one-mile trail leads to the 90-foot-tall **Marymere Falls.** Continue 14 miles further west to **Sol Duc Hot Springs,** long used for healing ceremonies by local Native Americans. Here, visitors will find cabins, a campground, a restaurant, and a snack bar, as well as a six-mile loop trail leading to the scenic **Sol Duc Falls.**

For further information, contact Park Headquarters, Olympic National Park, 600 E Park Ave, Port Angeles, WA 98362 (tel 360/452-0330). There's also a visitors center at Hoh Rain Forest in Forks (see).

LODGE

Kalaloch Lodge

157151 US 101, Forks, 98331; tel 360/962-2271; fax 360/962-3391. 35 mi S of Forks on coast in Olympic National Park. Popular as quiet, romantic getaway. Eight ocean beaches are within five-mile radius. **Rooms:** 58 rms, stes, and effic; 40 cottages/villas. CI 4pm/CO 11am. Large, comfortable rooms with cedar paneling, vaulted ceilings, Haida prints, and ocean treasures. **Amenities:** Refrig. No A/C, phone, or TV. Some units w/terraces, some w/fireplaces, 1 w/whirlpool. Many accommodations have Franklin-style fireplaces. No cooking or eating utensils in efficiencies. **Services:** **Facilities:** 2 restaurants, 1 bar, 1 beach (ocean), volleyball. Gallery Restaurant and Whaler's lounge overlook ocean beach. **Rates (CP):** Peak (June 11–Oct 7) $80 S; $99 D; $110 ste; $109–$119 effic; $103–$150 cottage/villa. Extra person $10. Children under age 5 stay free. Lower rates off-season. Parking: Outdoor, free. Sweetheart packages include three meals, fruit basket, and champagne. AE, MC, V.

RESTAURANT

Kalaloch Lodge

157151 US 101, Forks; tel 360/962-2271. **Seafood.** Dine on fresh salmon prepared a number of ways while enjoying the magnificent ocean view. Dishes include salmon Oscar with crab, asparagus, and béarnaise sauce, and salmon amandine with raspberry sauce. All salmon comes from nearby Quinalt. **FYI:** Reservations recommended. Children's menu. No smoking. **Open:** Peak (June 11–Oct 7) daily 7am–9pm. **Prices:** Main courses $12.95–$17.95. AE, MC, V.

Orcas Island

The largest island in the San Juan Islands group, Orcas Island consists of 57 square miles of rocky bays and steep tree-lined ridges. Site of the cities of Orcas, a charming village with a number of bed-and-breakfasts; and Olga, a quiet community known for its beachcombing, hiking, sea kayaking, and all types of boating.

HOTEL

Orcas Hotel

PO Box 155, Orcas, 98280; tel 360/376-4300; fax 360/376-4399. At Orcas ferry landing. This historic red-and-white hotel is surrounded by trees, gardens, and a picket fence. **Rooms:** 12 rms. CI 1:30pm/CO 11am. No smoking. Individually decorated rooms furnished with antique bureaus, armoires, brass beds, and quilts. Second-floor accommodations have shared baths; those on the third floor have private half-baths. **Amenities:** No A/C, phone, or TV. Some units w/terraces, some w/whirlpools. **Services:** Babysitting. **Facilities:** 1 restaurant, 1 bar. Dining room serves three meals daily in summer only. **Rates (BB):** Peak (June 15–Oct 1) $69–$170 S or D. Extra person $15. Lower rates off-season. Parking: Outdoor, free. AE, DISC, MC, V.

MOTEL

Eastsound Landmark Inn

Rte 1 Box A108-Main St, Eastsound, 98245; tel 360/376-2423. On the west edge of Eastsound. Small condominium development located on a hill at the edge of town. Clean and attractive; perfect for families. **Rooms:** 15 cottages/villas. CI 1pm/CO 11am. Well-lighted, individually decorated rooms have many of the comforts of home, including queen-size beds and full kitchens. **Amenities:** Cable TV, refrig. No A/C. All units w/terraces, all w/fireplaces. All rooms have dishwashers and microwaves. Books and magazines contribute to the homey atmosphere. **Facilities:** Washer/dryer. **Rates:** Peak (May 15–Sept 30) $100–$130 cottage/villa. Extra person $10. Children under age 1 stay free. Min stay peak. Lower rates off-season. Parking: Outdoor, free. AE, DISC, MC, V.

LODGE

Beach Haven Resort

Box 12, Rte 1, Eastsound, 98245; tel 360/376-2288. 3 mi W of Eastsound. This secluded beach-front lodge, located amid 10 acres of old-growth trees, has been a favorite with families since the 1940s. **Rooms:** 16 cottages/villas. CI 4pm/CO 10am. Nonsmoking rms avail. Individually decorated cabins have fully equipped kitchens. Romantic one-bedroom cabins are separate from the family section. **Amenities:** Refrig. No A/C, phone, or TV. All units w/terraces, some w/fireplaces. Bedding, towels, firewood, and cleaning supplies provided. **Services:** Babysitting. **Facilities:** 1 beach (cove/inlet), playground. Play area for kids features a fort, bridge, slides, swings, table tennis, and horseshoes. **Rates:** Peak (mid-June–mid-Sept) $80–$190 cottage/villa. Extra person $10. Min stay. Lower rates off-season. Parking: Outdoor, free. MC, V.

RESORTS

Deer Harbor Resort & Marina

200 Deer Harbor Rd, PO Box 200, Deer Harbor, 98243; tel 360/376-4420; fax 360/376-5523. 7 miles W of ferry landing. 6 acres. Property overlooking the harbor and marina includes motel-style rooms and several cottages. **Rooms:** 12 rms; 13 cottages/villas. CI 4pm/CO 11am. Pleasantly decorated rooms have decks and water views. **Amenities:** Cable TV. No A/C. All units w/terraces, some w/fireplaces, some w/whirlpools. Some rooms have private spas. Cottages and villas have fireplaces and/or wood stoves (wood provided). **Facilities:** 2 restaurants, 1 bar, 1 beach (cove/inlet), whirlpool. **Rates:** Peak (May–Sept) $99–$229 S or D; $129–$229 cottage/villa. Min stay wknds. Lower rates off-season. Parking: Outdoor, free. AE, DISC, MC, V.

Doe Bay Village Resort

Star Rte Box 86, Olga, 98279; tel 360/376-2291; fax 360/376-5809. 12 mi SE of Eastsound. 40 acres. A property with many former incarnations as an artist colony, a health spa, and a "human potential center," Doe Bay now offers a low-cost, extremely basic alternative to the island's higher-priced accommodations. **Rooms:** 22 cottages/villas. CI 1pm/CO 11am. No smoking. Rustic cabins (some with kitchen and bathroom) act as a hostel-style dorm. There are also some tent-cabins, tent sites, and RV hookups. **Amenities:** No A/C, phone, or TV. Some units w/terraces, some w/fireplaces. **Services:** Masseur. **Facilities:** 1 restaurant, 1 beach (cove/inlet), volleyball, sauna, whirlpool. Restaurant open for three meals daily in summer. **Rates:** $41–$92 cottage/villa. Extra person $10.50. Children under age 10 stay free. Min stay wknds. Parking: Outdoor, free. Co-ed dorm with eight beds, $15/night. Camping grounds $12–$16/night. AE, CB, DC, DISC, EC, ER, JCB, MC, V.

UNRATED Rosario Resort & Spa

1 Rosario Way, Eastsound, 98245; tel 360/376-2222 or toll free 800/562-8820; fax 360/376-2289. 20 acres. Built in 1909 as a home for wealthy shipbuilder Robert Moran, this former mansion is accented with teak, mahogany, and parquet floors. **Rooms:** 131 rms and stes. CI 4pm/CO 11am. No smoking. Guest rooms are located a very short walk from the main building. Waterside rooms have great views. **Amenities:** Cable TV, dataport. No A/C. Some units w/terraces, some w/fireplaces. **Services:** Car-rental desk, masseur, babysitting. **Facilities:** 1 restaurant, 2 bars (1 w/entertainment), 1 beach (bay), spa, sauna, whirlpool, beauty salon, playground. Mopeds for rent; two-masted schooner available for day trips; golf at nearby public course. Organ concerts given in second-floor music room. **Rates:** Peak (mid-June–Sept) $95–$175 S or D; $160–$220 ste. Extra person $20. Children under age 12 stay free. Min stay wknds. Lower rates off-season. Parking: Outdoor, free. AE, DC, DISC, MC, V.

RESTAURANTS

★ Bilbo's Festivo

North Beach Rd, Eastsound; tel 360/376-4728. At A St. **Mexican.** Southwestern and regional Mexican cuisine are done very well here. Start with one of the bar offerings featuring 12 different tequilas and 21 various beers, then move on to a fine chile relleno made with pine nuts and grated squash. Mesquite-grilled specialties are served nightly. For dessert, the sopapillas (chilled flourless chocolate cake) and sorbet are excellent. **FYI:** Reservations accepted. Children's menu. No smoking. **Open:** Peak (June–Oct) lunch daily 11:30am–2:30pm; dinner Mon–Fri 5–9pm, Sat 4:30–9pm. **Prices:** Main courses $5–$16. DISC, MC, V.

Christina's
1 Main St, Eastsound; tel 360/376-4904. **New American.** This romantic restaurant looks out to the water from an enclosed second-floor terrace. Innovative entrees include halibut with tomato-ginger chutney served with fresh asparagus, or fillet of beef with garlic mashed potatoes and wild-mushroom ragout. Fine dessert choices are the pear-hazelnut torte with vanilla ice cream or pumpkin flan with cookies. Special Northwest winemaker dinners feature the best vintages. **FYI:** Reservations recommended. **Open:** Peak (June–Sept) daily 5:30–10:30pm. Closed Nov 1–Thanksgiving. **Prices:** Main courses $10–$25. AE, DC, MC, V.

Deer Harbor Inn
Deer Harbor Rd, Deer Harbor; tel 360/376-4110. 9 mi W of ferry landing. **Seafood/Northwest.** Set in a country house complete with white picket fence. Written on a board in the entryway, the menu might feature smoked salmon fettucine, or sautéed prawns over pasta, all garnished with homegrown vegetables. Fresh strawberry shortcake, homemade breads. **FYI:** Reservations recommended. Children's menu. Beer and wine only. No smoking. **Open:** Peak (Mem Day–Labor Day) daily 6–9pm. Closed Dec–Jan. **Prices:** Main courses $9–$20. AE, MC, V.

Paradise

See Mount Rainier National Park

Pasco

See also Kennewick, Richland

One of the "Tri-Cities" situated at the confluence of the Columbia, Snake, and Yakima Rivers. The rivers offer diverse water sports opportunities and irrigate the many vineyards in the area. Nearby Ice Harbor Dam is one of four dams on the lower Snake River that allow river barge navigation from the Pacific Ocean to Lewiston, ID. **Information:** Greater Pasco Area Chamber of Commerce, 1600 N 20th Ave #A-1, PO Box 550, Pasco, 99301 (tel 509/547-9755).

MOTEL

Red Lion Inn
2525 N 20th Ave, 99301; tel 509/547-0701 or toll free 800/547-8010; fax 509/547-4278. 3 blocks from airport, off US 12 and I-82. Attractive three-story brick motel with large, open lobby. Wineries and factory outlets nearby. **Rooms:** 279 rms and stes. CI 3pm/CO noon. Nonsmoking rms avail. All rooms have king- or queen-size beds; many accommodations overlook nicely landscaped pool and courtyard. **Amenities:** A/C, cable TV w/movies, dataport. All units w/terraces, some w/whirlpools. **Services:** **Facilities:** 2100 2 restaurants, 1 bar, whirlpool. Adjacent to 18-hole golf course. **Rates:** $85–$95 S; $95–$105 D; $125–$325 ste. Extra person $10. Children under age 18 stay free. Parking: Outdoor, free. Commercial, government, and senior rates. AE, CB, DC, DISC, ER, JCB, MC, V.

Port Angeles

See also Olympic National Park

The largest city on the north side of the Olympic Peninsula, located between two popular vacation playgrounds: the Olympic Mountains (popular for hiking, biking, and nature viewing) and the Strait of Juan de Fuca (noted for fishing and boating). Port Angeles lies directly across the strait from Victoria, British Columbia. **Information:** Port Angeles Chamber of Commerce, 121 E Railroad Ave, Port Angeles, 98362 (tel 360/452-2363).

MOTELS

Aggie's Port Angeles Inn
602 E Front St, 98362; tel 360/457-0471; fax 360/452-1752. 5 blocks from Victoria ferry. Worn, older motel that caters to families. **Rooms:** 114 rms. CI open/CO noon. Nonsmoking rms avail. **Amenities:** Cable TV. No A/C. Some units w/terraces. **Services:** Babysitting. Free shuttle to Port Angeles Airport and to ferry to Victoria. **Facilities:** 125 1 restaurant, 1 bar (w/entertainment), sauna. **Rates:** Peak (June 15–Oct 15) $45–$55 S; $55–$65 D. Children under age 12 stay free. Lower rates off-season. Parking: Outdoor, free. AE, CB, DC, DISC, MC, V.

Best Western Olympic Lodge
140 Del Guzzi Dr, 98362; tel 360/452-2993 or toll free 800/600-2993; fax 360/452-1497. At Jct US 101. One of the newest lodgings in Port Angeles. Huge, yet cozy lobby with high ceilings, gas fireplace, and fine views of Juan de Fuca Strait, Mount Olympus, and Hurricane Ridge. **Rooms:** 106 rms and stes. CI 4pm/CO 11am. No smoking. All rooms have a bay or mountain view, reclining chairs, and a large desk. **Amenities:** A/C, cable TV. Some units w/terraces, 1 w/whirlpool. Executive king-size rooms have microwaves and refrigerators. **Services:** The staff will help guests plan travel itineraries to Olympic National Park and beyond. **Facilities:** 100 Whirlpool. **Rates:** Peak (June–Sept) $89–$109 S or D; $250 ste. Extra person $10. Children under age 18 stay free. Lower rates off-season. Parking: Outdoor, free. AE, DC, DISC, MC, V.

Red Lion Bayshore Inn
221 N Lincoln, 98362; tel 360/452-9215 or toll free 800/547-8010; fax 360/452-4734. Nothing remarkable, but convenient to Victoria ferry and waterfront shopping at Harbor

Towne Mall. **Rooms:** 187 rms and stes. CI 2pm/CO noon. Nonsmoking rms avail. **Amenities:** A/C, cable TV w/movies. Some units w/minibars, some w/terraces. Each room has iron and ironing board. **Services:** **Facilities:** 1 restaurant, 1 bar, whirlpool. **Rates:** Peak (June 15–Sept 15) $80–$110 S; $95–$125 D; $140 ste. Extra person $10. Children under age 18 stay free. Lower rates off-season. Parking: Outdoor, free. AE, CB, DC, DISC, JCB, MC, V.

LODGE

Lake Crescent Lodge
416 Lake Crescent Rd, 98363; tel 360/928-3211; fax 360/928-3253. Off US 101 on Lake Crescent. A historic lodge built in 1937 in Olympic National Park on Lake Crescent. Popular with folks who want quiet—there are no phones. Guests can hike to nearby Marymere Falls and Mount Storm King. **Rooms:** 52 rms; 4 cottages/villas. CI 4pm/CO 11am. A variety of historic rooms, cottages with rustic stone fireplaces, and motel-style accommodations. Lake views from each room. **Amenities:** No A/C, phone, or TV. Some units w/terraces, some w/fireplaces. Filled woodbox in room. **Services:** Fires are laid. The wake up call is a knock on the door. **Facilities:** 1 restaurant, 1 bar, 1 beach (lake shore). **Rates:** $72–$130 S or D; $107–$119 cottage/villa. Extra person $10. Parking: Outdoor, free. Closed Nov–Apr. AE, DC, MC, V.

RESTAURANTS

C'est Si Bon
23 Cedar Park Dr; tel 360/452-8888. Across from Cedar Park Cinema on US 101. **French.** Charming flower gardens, and terrace with a gazebo, set the scene for fine dining. Chef Michele Juhasz specializes in light sauces for veal, seafood, and chicken. Good, hearty portions of poached chicken breast with a chardonnay sauce or filet mignon with Dungeness crab are entree favorites. The owners plan to build a 60-room hotel, to be called Chateau Mamaison, on five acres of land adjacent to the restaurant. **FYI:** Reservations recommended. **Open:** Tues–Sun 5–11:30pm. **Prices:** Main courses $19–$24. AE, DISC, MC, V.

★ **First Street Haven**
107 E 1st St (Downtown); tel 360/457-0352. At Laurel. **Cafe.** A breakfast-and-lunch-only favorite for years, this small hole-in-the-wall cafe is a place where the waitress knows everybody's name, but newcomers feel instantly welcome. Try the Haven Veggie Browns, a mixture of sautéed green peppers, onions, zucchini, and mushrooms atop homemade hash brown potatoes served with salsa; customize the extravaganza by adding eggs, ham, tomatoes, or melted Swiss cheese. Huge portions. **FYI:** Reservations not accepted. No liquor license. No smoking. **Open:** Mon–Sat 7am–4pm, Sun 8am–2pm. **Prices:** Main courses $5–$7. No CC.

Lake Crescent Lodge
416 Lake Crescent Rd; tel 360/928-3211. Off US 101 on Lake Crescent. **Northwest.** Located in a historic building overlooking Lake Crescent and famed for seafood like king salmon, fresh Hood Canal oysters, and crab Louis made from Dungeness crab. Only eight items on the menu. **FYI:** Reservations not accepted. Children's menu. No smoking. **Open:** Breakfast daily 7:30–10am; lunch daily noon–2pm; dinner daily 6–8:30pm. Closed Nov–Apr. **Prices:** Main courses $10–$18. AE, DC, MC, V.

ATTRACTIONS

The Museum of the Clallam County Historical Society
223 E 4th St; tel 360/417-2364. Located in a Georgian Revival building (circa 1914), the museum focuses primarily on the pioneer and maritime history of the area, with a photographic exhibit comparing local sites today with photos taken 100 years ago. **Open:** June–Aug, Mon–Sat 10am–4pm; Sept–May, Mon–Fri 10am–4pm. Closed some hols. **Free**

Port Angeles Fine Arts Center
1203 E Lauridsen Blvd; tel 360/457-3532. Situated on five wooded acres, this strikingly modern building houses exhibits of contemporary painting, sculpture, photography, drawing, and mixed media. Lectures, concerts, and readings complement changing exhibitions of visual art. **Open:** Thurs–Sun 11am–5pm. Closed some hols. **Free**

Arthur D Fiero Marine Lab
Port Angeles City Pier; tel 360/452-9277 ext 264. Visitors can get a close up look at some of the peninsula's aquatic inhabitants in the lab's tanks, where wolf eel and octopus reside, or in the touch tanks, where starfish and sea cucumbers can be petted and stroked. **Open:** June–Aug, daily 10am–8pm; Sept–May, Sat–Sun noon–4pm. **$**

Port Ludlow

A retirement and resort community on the northeast corner of the Olympic Peninsula.

HOTEL

Inn at Ludlow Bay
1 Heron Rd, PO Box 65460, 98365; tel 360/437-0411; fax 360/437-0310. 8 miles N of Hood Canal Bridge, next to Port Ludlow Marina. Beautifully set on a spit of land jutting into Ludlow Bay, this well-designed boutique hotel, built in 1994, is reminiscent of an estate on the Maine coast. **Rooms:** 37 rms and stes. CI 3pm/CO noon. No smoking. Rooms have views of forest, the Olympic and Cascade Mountains, Mount Baker, or the Port Ludlow marina. Comfortable furnishings. **Amenities:** Cable TV w/movies, refrig, dataport, VCR, bathrobes. No A/C. All units w/minibars, some w/terraces, all w/fireplaces, all w/whirlpools. **Services:**

Masseur, children's program, babysitting. Kids program available at neighboring resort. Seaplane service available from Seattle three times a day. **Facilities:** 27 2 75 1 restaurant (dinner only), 1 bar, 1 beach (bay). **Rates (CP):** $165–$200 S or D; $300–$450 ste. Extra person $35. Children under age 18 stay free. Parking: Outdoor, free. AE, MC, V.

RESORT

Port Ludlow Resort and Conference Center

9483 Oak Bay Rd, 98365; tel 360/437-2222 or toll free 800/732-1239. 8 mi N of Hood Canal Bridge on Puget Sound. 15 acres. Open, spacious resort in a quiet, wooded setting. Facilities are spread out, with some walking distance between beach, pool, condos, marina, and tennis courts. **Rooms:** 74 rms and stes; 67 cottages/villas. CI 4pm/CO noon. Nonsmoking rms avail. Most rooms have views of the bay, woods, or grounds. No elevators in two-story buildings. **Amenities:** Cable TV, VCR. No A/C. Some units w/terraces, some w/fireplaces. **Services:** Children's program. Extensive supervised children's activities for ages 3–12, including arts and crafts, games, beach walks. **Facilities:** 27 2 300 2 restaurants (lunch and dinner only), 1 bar (w/entertainment), 1 beach (bay), basketball, volleyball, games rm, lawn games, squash, sauna, whirlpool, playground, washer/dryer. **Rates:** Peak (May–Sept) $75–$95 S or D; $145–$165 ste; $115–$350 cottage/villa. Extra person $10. Children under age 12 stay free. Lower rates off-season. Parking: Outdoor, free. AE, MC, V.

Port Townsend

A Victorian-styled seaport with lots of turn-of-the-century homes. Nearby Fort Flagler and Fort Worden State Parks are popular with visitors. Served by Washington State Ferries. **Information:** Port Townsend Chamber of Commerce, 2437 E Sims Way, Port Townsend, 98368 (tel 360/385-2722).

MOTEL

Port Townsend Inn

2020 Washington St, 98368; tel 360/385-2211 or toll free 800/822-8696. A neat, clean, good-looking motel, good for families—not many Port Townsend B&Bs take children. **Rooms:** 25 rms and effic. CI 2pm/CO 11am. Nonsmoking rms avail. **Amenities:** Cable TV w/movies, refrig, VCR, bathrobes. No A/C. 1 unit w/whirlpool. Playpens available upon request. **Facilities:** The centrally located hot tub is in a nicely landscaped, attractive gazebo. **Rates (CP):** Peak (May 1–Oct 1) $68–$98 S or D; $78–$98 effic. Lower rates off-season. Parking: Outdoor, free. AE, DISC, MC, V.

INNS

Ann Starrett Mansion

744 Clay St, 98368; tel 360/385-3205 or toll free 800/321-0644; fax 360/385-2976. From downtown take Monroe St up to the bluff and turn left on Clay St. This mansion was built in 1889 by a wealthy contractor, George Starret, as a wedding present for his bride, Ann. It features classic Victorian architecture, frescoed ceilings, plus a free-hung, three-story, spiral staircase leading to a domed turret. "Painted Lady" is an appropriate moniker, given the shrimp-colored exterior with sage-and-cream trim. Unsuitable for children under 14. **Rooms:** 12 rms and stes. CI 3pm/CO 11am. No smoking. Each room is individually decorated. The Drawing Room has a Renaissance revival mahogany bedroom set, an antique tin bathtub, and an Eastlake settee and chair, as well as magnificent views of Mounts Baker and Rainier. Furnishings may be a bit too museum-like for some tastes. **Amenities:** No A/C, phone, or TV. Some units w/terraces, some w/fireplaces, 1 w/whirlpool. **Services:** Afternoon tea and wine/sherry served. **Facilities:** 30 Guest lounge. **Rates (BB):** Peak (June 15–Sept 30) $75–$225 S or D; $225 ste. Extra person $25. Lower rates off-season. Parking: Outdoor, free. AE, DISC, MC, V.

The James House

1238 Washington St, 98368; tel 360/385-1238 or toll free 800/385-1238. ¼ mile from downtown. This three-story Victorian mansion, built in 1889, was the Northwest's first B&B. A hand-carved cherry staircase and the original parquet floors add to the abundant elegance. It remains the standard by which other inns are judged. Unsuitable for children under 12. **Rooms:** 11 rms and stes (2 w/shared bath); 1 cottage/villa. CI 3pm/CO 11am. No smoking. Rooms are individually decorated with period antiques. The bridal suite, with sitting room, balcony, and fireplace, is furnished with its original bed, armoire, and fainting couch. **Amenities:** Bathrobes. No A/C, phone, or TV. Some units w/terraces, some w/fireplaces. **Services:** Afternoon tea and wine/sherry served. **Facilities:** Guest lounge. The two front parlors are perfect for reading or listening to music. **Rates (BB):** Peak (Apr 28–Oct 30) $52 S w/shared bath, $75–$80 S w/private bath; $65 D w/shared bath, $95 D w/private bath; $110–$150 ste; $100–$120 cottage/villa. Extra person $10. Min stay peak. Lower rates off-season. Parking: Outdoor, free. AE, MC, V.

Manresa Castle

7th and Sheridan Sts, PO Box 564, 98368; tel 360/385-5750 or toll free 800/732-1281, 800/732-1281 in WA; fax 360/385-5883. On the bluff above downtown. Built in 1892 in Prussian style, this property was named by Jesuit priests for the birthplace, in Spain, of St Ignatius, the founder of the Catholic order. On the National Register of Historic Places. **Rooms:** 40 rms and stes. CI 4pm/CO 11am. Individually decorated with white iron beds, dust ruffles, and curtains.

Rust-and-brown carpets don't always match rest of decor. Rooms on the north have water view. **Amenities:** Cable TV w/movies. No A/C. Some units w/whirlpools. **Services:** Babysitting. **Facilities:** 80 1 restaurant (bkfst and dinner only; *see* "Restaurants" below), 1 bar. Polished mahogany bar in lounge from the old Savoy Hotel in San Francisco. **Rates:** Peak (May 1–Oct 15) $55–$165 S; $65–$175 D; $100–$175 ste. Extra person $10. Lower rates off-season. Parking: Outdoor, free. Winter getaway package available. DISC, MC, V.

Palace Hotel
1004 Water St, 98368 (Downtown); tel 360/385-0773 or toll free 800/962-0741 in WA; fax 360/385-0780. At Tyler St. The three-story brick building, built in 1889 for a retired sea captain, was operated as a hotel and brothel from 1925 to 1933. Each of the rooms still bears the name of one of the women who worked there. **Rooms:** 15 rms, stes, and effic (3 w/shared bath). CI 2pm/CO 11am. Nonsmoking rms avail. The rooms are individually decorated with reproductions and collectibles; however, the kitchenettes look incongruous with the Victorian theme. Some rooms have antique iron beds and offer views of downtown and the waterfront. **Amenities:** Cable TV, refrig. No A/C or phone. 1 unit w/fireplace, 1 w/whirlpool. Room #3, Marie's Suite, was the madam's and contains the original working fireplace. **Services:** Complimentary breakfast delivered to rooms in a basket. **Facilities:** 25 1 restaurant, guest lounge. **Rates (CP):** Peak (May 1–Oct 15) $45–$65 S or D w/shared bath, $75–$119 S or D w/private bath; $89–$119 ste; $109–$119 effic. Extra person $10. Min stay special events. Lower rates off-season. Higher rates for special events/hols. Parking: Outdoor, free. AE, DISC, MC, V.

LODGE

Fort Warden State Park Conference Center
200 Battery Way, 98368; tel 360/385-4730; fax 360/385-7248. 1 mi N of Port Townsend. Former artillery post turned conference center. Former officers' quarters (some dating to 1904) offer clean and spacious lodging. Good value for families and other groups. It is recommended that visitors make reservations a year in advance. **Rooms:** 25 cottages/villas. CI 3pm/CO 11am. No smoking. Bedrooms in refurbished units have brass headboards and reproduction oak chairs, with Tiffany-style lamps on the bedside table, but the effect is more Salvation Army than antique. **Amenities:** Refrig. No A/C or TV. Some units w/fireplaces. Six-bedroom units have four fireplaces. **Facilities:** 1200 1 restaurant (dinner only), 1 beach (cove/inlet), basketball, volleyball, washer/dryer. **Rates:** $65–$209 cottage/villa. Children under age 4 stay free. Min stay wknds. Parking: Outdoor, free. DISC, MC, V.

RESTAURANTS

★ Fountain Cafe
920 Washington St; tel 360/385-1364. ½ block from the Town Fountain. **Eclectic/Italian/Seafood.** Located at the edge of downtown below a bluff. In summer, people line up outside for a table and the fresh seafood available inside. A special treat is smoked salmon in a cream sauce flavored with a hint of scotch whisky, garnished with caviar, and served with fettucine. Save room for desserts like loganberry and rhubarb fool and hot gingerbread. **FYI:** Reservations not accepted. Beer and wine only. No smoking. **Open:** Peak (June 1–Sept 30) lunch Mon–Thurs 11:30am–3pm; dinner Mon–Thurs 4–9:30pm. **Prices:** Main courses $9.25–$11. AE, MC, V.

★ Lanza's Ristorante & Pizzaria
1020 Lawrence St; tel 360/385-6221. Take Monroe St up the bluff and follow the sign to the uptown area. **Italian.** Start with a robust marinated eggplant salad (with tomatoes, artichoke hearts, red pepper, and orzo) served with roasted garlic and Gorgonzola crostini. The Mediterranean fettuccine features Lanza's own smoked salmon, flaked and sautéed, mixed with chopped walnuts, figs, and spinach in a lemon-butter sauce. All entrees come with organic local vegetables in season. **FYI:** Reservations accepted. Jazz. Children's menu. Beer and wine only. No smoking. **Open:** Peak (June–Sept) Mon–Thurs 5–8:30pm, Fri–Sat 5–9:30pm. **Prices:** Main courses $9–$14. CB, DC, MC, V.

Manresa Castle
7th and Sheridan Sts; tel 360/385-5750. **International.** In a house dating from 1892. Dinner might start with artichoke-tahini pâté served with toast and salsa, while the entree could be spicy Dungeness crab cakes with mustard beurre blanc, or rack of lamb coated with herb mustard and coffee paste. **FYI:** Reservations recommended. No smoking. **Open:** Peak (May 1–Oct 17) Mon–Thurs 5–9pm, Fri–Sat 5–10pm, Sun 9am–2pm. **Prices:** Main courses $14.75–$27; prix fixe $48–$54. DISC, MC, V.

The Silverwater
237 Taylor St; tel 360/385-6448. W of Water St next to the Rose Theater. **Northwest.** The casually elegant ambience, with high ceilings and tall windows, is a good backdrop to the well-prepared pasta, seafood, and vegetarian entrees offered here. One specialty is northwestern Floribunda, which combines several types of fish and shellfish, sauced and served over black pepper linguine. Desserts include chocolate espresso cheesecake and blackberry pie. **FYI:** Reservations recommended. Beer and wine only. No smoking. **Open:** Mon–Sat 11:30am–10pm, Sun 5–10pm. **Prices:** Main courses $7.95–$13.95. MC, V.

ATTRACTION

Port Townsend Marine Science Center
522 Battery Way, Fort Worden State Park; tel 360/385-5582. Aquariums, maps, charts, shells, and marine fossils fill this

center, which stresses both educational and scientific understanding of the marine sciences. Special activities include beach walks, studies of plankton, art programs, and daily interpretive programs. **Open:** Apr–June 14, Sat–Sun noon–4pm; June 15–Aug, Tues–Sun noon–6pm; Sept–Nov, Sat–Sun noon–4pm. $

Poulsbo

Located on fjordlike Liberty Bay in the Puget Sound, this largely Norwegian town is filled with antiques and arts-and-crafts shops. **Information:** Greater Poulsbo Chamber of Commerce, 19131 8th Ave NE, PO Box 1063, Poulsbo, 98370 (tel 360/779-4848).

RESTAURANT

Molly Ward Gardens
27462 Big Valley Rd; tel 360/779-4471. 5 miles north of Poulsbo. **Regional American.** Women in hats and flowing dresses celebrating a birthday: a typical sight at this civilized restaurant located adjacent to a garden and nursery. Soups such as carrot-orange, chilled mango, parsnip, or leek and mushroom are a specialty. Dinner brings loin of lamb with mint sauce and orange-cap potatoes. Tea with three types of sandwiches and dessert is served Thursday afternoon. **FYI:** Reservations recommended. No liquor license. No smoking. **Open:** Tues–Sun 10am–5pm, Fri–Sat 6:30–10pm. **Prices:** Main courses $5–$19. MC, V.

ATTRACTION

Marine Science Center
18743 Front St NE; tel 360/779-5549. The center has living displays, touch tanks, and watershed and tidepool exploration exhibits. **Open:** Tues–Sat 10am–4pm, Sun noon–4pm. Closed some hols. $

Pullman

The home of Washington State University, Pullman is located in the heavily agricultural Palouse region of eastern Washington. **Information:** Pullman Chamber of Commerce, 415 Grand Ave, Pullman, 99163 (tel 509/334-3565).

MOTEL

Quality Inn Paradise Creek
1050 SE Bishop Blvd, 99163; tel 509/332-0500 or toll free 800/669-3212; fax 509/334-4271. Located near Washington State University and University of Idaho at Moscow. **Rooms:** 66 rms and stes. CI 3pm/CO noon. Nonsmoking rms avail. Soft color decor in rooms. **Amenities:** A/C, cable TV, dataport. Some units w/whirlpools. 14 suites have two-person whirlpool tub, 2 TVs, VCR with free movies, king-size bed, wet bar, refrigerator, and dataport. **Services:** Complimentary 24-hour shuttle service between WSU and airport. Complimentary newspapers and 24-hour coffee in lobby; cookies and milk served at 8:30pm. VCR and movies for rent. Nonrefundable $7.50 small-pet fee. **Facilities:** 150 1 restaurant, sauna, whirlpool. Espresso bar in lobby open 24 hours. Free use of Palouse Physical Therapy fitness center, reachable by five-minute walk or free shuttle. **Rates (CP):** $49–$59 S; $59–$65 D; $80–$135 ste. Extra person $7.50. Children under age 18 stay free. Min stay special events. Parking: Outdoor, free. Senior, commercial, government, and group rates; romance and seasonal packages avail. AE, CB, DC, DISC, MC, V.

RESTAURANTS

Hilltop Restaurant
In Hilltop Motel Complex, Davis Way; tel 509/334-2555. **Seafood/Steak.** A casual restaurant popular with locals celebrating special occasions. Diners have a bird's-eye view of the town nestled among rolling hills of farm land. Favorites entrees are prime rib, and grilled king salmon with honey-onion marmalade, served with a creamy-mustard sauce. **FYI:** Reservations accepted. Children's menu. **Open:** Lunch Mon–Fri 11am–2pm; dinner Mon–Thurs 5–9pm, Fri–Sat 5–10pm, Sun 2–9pm; brunch Sun 10am–1:30pm. **Prices:** Main courses $10–$30. AE, DISC, MC, V.

The Seasons Restaurant
215 SE Paradise Ave (Downtown); tel 509/334-1410. **Eclectic.** At first glance, this old wood-framed house with its two flights of worn wooden stairs might not look like a promising dining option, but the wood and stained-glass chandelier, hand-blown glass lamps, and sculpted wood decor of the restarant's interior is worth every step. The menu, which changes twice a month, features seasonal specialties. A notable entree is blackened prime rib with fanned potatoes. **FYI:** Reservations accepted. Beer and wine only. No smoking. **Open:** Tues–Sun 5:30–9pm. **Prices:** Main courses $8–$30. AE, DC, MC, V.

Quinault

See also Olympic National Park

Located on the south shore of Lake Quinault on the Olympic Peninsula. Popular base for visiting the Olympic rain forests; the largest spruce tree in the state is located nearby.

LODGE

Lake Quinault Lodge
345 S Shore Rd, 98575; tel 360/288-2900; fax 360/288-2901. Off US 101 on Lake Quinault. The lodge is situated in the middle of the Quinault Rain Forest in Olympic National Park and is a welcome haven for rain-soaked travelers. Opened in the 1890s as a "Log Hotel," it has a lobby with a stuffed black bear, comfortable rattan sofas, and usually a

roaring fire in the hearth. **Rooms:** 92 rms and stes. CI 3pm/CO 11am. Nonsmoking rms avail. Old-fashioned, but comfortable with a sink in the bedroom. **Amenities:** No A/C, phone, or TV. Some units w/terraces, some w/fireplaces. Four types of accommodations available: lodge, annex (pets allowed), and fireplace rooms (gas) all have view and balcony; lakeside accommodations all have view. **Services:** Babysitting. **Facilities:** 80 1 restaurant (*see* "Restaurants" below), 1 bar, 1 beach (lake shore), volleyball, games rm, sauna, whirlpool. Canoe and rowboat rentals. **Rates:** Peak (June 15–Oct 7) $92–$125 S or D; $170–$220 ste. Extra person $10. Children under age 5 stay free. Lower rates off-season. Parking: Outdoor, free. AE, MC, V.

RESTAURANT

The Roosevelt Room
In Lake Quinault Lodge, 345 S Shore Rd; tel 360/288-2900. **Seafood/Steak.** Seafood sauté and Quinault salmon head the list of favorites on the seafood, steak, and pasta menu. Roosevelt chicken is named in honor of President Franklin Delano Roosevelt. The lounge is popular because of its satellite TV. **FYI:** Reservations recommended. No smoking. **Open:** Breakfast daily 7–11:30am; lunch daily 11:30am–3pm; dinner daily 5–9:30pm. **Prices:** Main courses $10–$20. AE, MC, V.

Renton

This busy industrial city at the south end of Lake Washington serves as a bedroom community for commuters to the greater Seattle area. **Information:** Greater Renton Chamber of Commerce, 300 Rainier Ave N, Renton, 98055 (tel 206/226-4560).

MOTELS

Nendel's Inn Renton
3700 E Valley Rd, 98055; tel 206/251-9591 or toll free 800/547-0106; fax 206/251-0340. Business-type motel close to Sea-Tac International Airport and interstates. **Rooms:** 130 rms, stes, and effic. Executive level. CI 2pm/CO noon. Nonsmoking rms avail. **Amenities:** A/C, refrig, dataport. **Services:** Twice-daily maid svce, car-rental desk. **Facilities:** 45 Whirlpool. Truck parking available. All guests have free access (via free shuttle) to Cascade Health Club, 24 hours, 7 days. **Rates (CP):** Peak (June–Sept) $45–$53 S; $53–$63 D; $78–$68 ste; $63–$68 effic. Extra person $7. Children under age 12 stay free. Lower rates off-season. Parking: Outdoor, free. Bingo, Pike St Market, and entertainment packages avail. AE, CB, DC, DISC, EC, ER, MC, V.

Silver Cloud at Renton
1850 Maple Valley Hwy, 98055; tel 206/226-7600 or toll free 800/551-7207 ext 5; fax 206/271-1296. Highway motel oriented to the business traveler. Rates are very reasonable for the location. **Rooms:** 105 rms and effic. CI 3pm/CO noon. Nonsmoking rms avail. **Amenities:** A/C, cable TV, refrig. Some units w/whirlpools. **Services:** Social director. Public Relations Director welcomes guests and does many concierge jobs. **Facilities:** 55 Whirlpool, washer/dryer. Large well-lighted whirlpool. **Rates (CP):** Peak (June 15–Sept 15) $52–$89 S; $61–$71 D; $120 effic. Extra person $6. Children under age 12 stay free. Lower rates off-season. Parking: Outdoor, free. AE, DC, DISC, MC, V.

Traveler's Inn
4710 Lake Washington NE, 98056; tel 206/228-2858 or toll free 800/633-8300; fax 206/228-3055. I-405 at exit 7. Located between Renton and Bellevue, and adjacent to 44th St Market, a small shopping center. The service road that leads to the motel is difficult to find, and the lobby entrance is poorly distinguished—you have to follow signs from the ice machine. **Rooms:** 116 rms and stes. CI 2pm/CO 11am. Nonsmoking rms avail. **Amenities:** A/C, satel TV. **Services:** **Facilities:** Washer/dryer. **Rates:** Peak (June–Sept) $37 S; $43 D; $58 ste. Extra person $6. Children under age 12 stay free. Lower rates off-season. Parking: Outdoor, free. AE, CB, DC, DISC, MC, V.

RESTAURANT

★ Armando's
919 S 3rd (Downtown); tel 206/228-0759. Corner of Main. **Italian.** A favorite destination and local hangout in south King County. Armondo smokes his own salmon and also prepares salmon and cheese ravioli and manicotti. Features a wood-burning pizza oven. **FYI:** Reservations not accepted. Children's menu. Beer and wine only. **Open:** Mon–Wed 11am–9pm, Thurs–Fri 11am–10pm, Sat 4–10pm, Sun 4–9pm. **Prices:** Main courses $8–$12. AE, MC, V.

Richland

See also Kennewick, Pasco

One of the Tri-Cities located on the Columbia River. Richland was one of the key sites (along with Oak Ridge, TN, Los Alamos, NM, and Chicago) for the development of the atomic bomb. The area is largely agricultural today, with many vineyards and orchards. **Information:** Richland Chamber of Commerce, 515 Lee Blvd, PO Box 637, Richland, 99352 (tel 509/946-1651).

MOTELS

Best Western Tower Inn & Conference Center
1515 George Washington Way, 99352; tel 509/946-4121 or toll free 800/635-3980; fax 509/946-2222. Centrally located, with easy access to highways. Popular for conferences and groups. **Rooms:** 195 rms and stes. CI 4pm/CO noon. Non-

smoking rms avail. Some rooms are located in a six-story tower, others are in a low-rise wing. Some rooms overlook the swimming pool in a large indoor courtyard. **Amenities:** A/C, cable TV w/movies, dataport. Some units w/terraces. **Services:** **Facilities:** 1 restaurant, 1 bar (w/entertainment), sauna, whirlpool, washer/dryer. **Rates:** Peak (June–Sept) $70 S; $80 D; $85–$125 ste. Children under age 18 stay free. Lower rates off-season. Parking: Outdoor, free. AE, CB, DC, DISC, MC, V.

Nendels Inn
615 Jadwin Ave, 99352; tel 509/943-4611 or toll free 800/547-0106; fax 509/946-2271. Two-level motel located on a commercial strip, facing a parking lot and Mexican restaurant. Offers comfortable lodging and ready access to Richland business centers. **Rooms:** 98 rms and effic. CI open/CO noon. Nonsmoking rms avail. Rooms have white walls, dark furniture, and standard motel art. Some have kitchenettes. **Amenities:** A/C, cable TV w/movies, refrig. Some TVs have remote control. **Services:** Coffee is available at all times and there is a microwave for guest use in the small lobby. Pets $5. **Facilities:** Pool open May–Sept. **Rates (CP):** $39 S; $44–$47 D; $50–$53 effic. Extra person $5. Children under age 12 stay free. Parking: Outdoor, free. Personal checks not accepted. AE, DC, DISC, MC, V.

Red Lion Inn Hanford House
802 George Washington Way, 99352; tel 509/946-7611 or toll free 800/RED-LION; fax 509/946-8564. This horseshoe-shaped motel, in the commercial district of town, faces a quiet park on the Columbia River. **Rooms:** 150 rms and stes. Executive level. CI 3pm/CO noon. Nonsmoking rms avail. Rooms facing street are subject to traffic noise; river-facing rooms are quiet. **Amenities:** A/C, cable TV w/movies, dataport. Some units w/terraces. All units have iron and ironing board. Some have wet bars. Phone hookups for the deaf and hard-of-hearing available. **Services:** Prompt room service. **Facilities:** 1 restaurant, 1 bar, whirlpool. Well-landscaped pool area. **Rates:** Peak (June–Sept) $79–$89 S or D; $110–$160 ste. Extra person $10. Children under age 18 stay free. Min stay special events. Lower rates off-season. Parking: Outdoor, free. Corporate and senior rates available; special rates and amenities for frequent guests. AE, CB, DC, DISC, MC, V.

Shilo Inn Rivershore
50 Comstock St, 99352; tel 509/946-4661 or toll free 800/222-2244; fax 509/943-6741. Just off US 12 by Columbia River. Two wings face a green park and the Columbia River. **Rooms:** 150 rms and effic. CI 4pm/CO noon. Nonsmoking rms avail. Rooms have been redone with Southwest-inspired fabrics and cherry-wood furnishings. **Amenities:** A/C, cable TV w/movies, refrig, VCR. Some units w/whirlpools. Microwave. **Services:** Babysitting. Pet charge $7/day. **Facilities:** 1 restaurant, 1 bar, spa, sauna, steam rm, whirlpool, washer/dryer. Marina and park located adjacent to hotel. **Rates:** Peak (May 1–Oct 15) $69–$115 S or D; $105 effic. Extra person $9. Children under age 12 stay free. Min stay special events. Lower rates off-season. Parking: Outdoor, free. AE, CB, DC, DISC, EC, MC, V.

RESTAURANT

Emerald of Siam
In Uptown Shopping Center, 1314 Jadwin Ave; tel 509/946-9328. **Thai.** Authentic Thai food—the owner teaches Thai cooking and culture. Daily lunch buffet is popular, and buffet dinners are offered Fri and Sat. Banquet facilities; discount for children. **FYI:** Reservations accepted. Dress code. Beer and wine only. No smoking. **Open:** Lunch Mon–Fri 11:30am–2pm; dinner Mon–Sat 5–9pm. **Prices:** Main courses $6–$11. MC, V.

Roche Harbor

See San Juan Island

San Juan Island

One of the 172 picturesque islands of the San Juan archipelago, and the site of the infamous 1859 Pig War between Britain and the United States. The island mainly consists of the towns of Friday Harbor and Roche Harbor, both of which have protected harbors and are popular yacht and sailboat moorages. Friday Harbor, a state ferry port, is a hub for marine and land wildlife watching, biking, hiking, and boating. The smaller resort village of Roche Harbor is located on the northwest tip of the island.

MOTEL

The Inns at Friday Harbor
Spring St, PO Box 339, Friday Harbor, 98250; tel 360/378-4000; fax 360/378-5800. Near Argyle St. Property housed in two separate buildings. The location at 410 Spring St contains motel rooms. The all-suite inn, at 680 Spring St, has a lobby with a stone fireplace, wing-back chairs, hardwood floors, area rugs, and bronze sculptures by a local artist. **Rooms:** 138 rms and stes. CI 3pm/CO 11am. Nonsmoking rms avail. Motel rooms are clean and attractive; suites have kitchenettes and private patios looking out to well-landscaped grounds. **Amenities:** Cable TV w/movies, refrig, dataport, voice mail. No A/C. All units w/terraces. **Services:** Car-rental desk, babysitting. **Facilities:** 1 restaurant, 1 bar, games rm, spa, sauna, steam rm, whirlpool, beauty salon, washer/dryer. Pool is kept very clean. **Rates:** Peak (June–Oct) $85–$95 S or D; $108–$188 ste. Children under age 12 stay free. Min stay special events. Lower rates off-season. Parking: Outdoor, free. AE, CB, DC, DISC, MC, V.

INN

Friday Harbor House

130 West St, PO Box 1385, Friday Harbor, 98250; tel 360/378-8455; fax 360/378-8453. Next to the Whale Museum. 1 acre. This three-story, Italian villa–style inn sits atop a bluff overlooking the Friday Harbor Marina. Great for a quiet retreat. Can accommodate families, but not ideal for children. **Rooms:** 20 rms and stes. CI 3pm/CO noon. No smoking. All rooms have sophisticated and understated decor, a selection of books, and European mattresses. Some rooms have a wall of windows opening onto a stunning view of the harbor. **Amenities:** Cable TV w/movies, refrig, dataport, VCR, voice mail, bathrobes. No A/C. Some units w/terraces, all w/fireplaces, all w/whirlpools. Nice cotton thermal-weave robes. Some rooms have whirlpool with harbor view. **Services:** Masseur, babysitting. Guests can order bottles of fine wine delivered to the room. Fresh apples available at front desk. Staff is exceptionally friendly and helpful. **Facilities:** 12 1 restaurant (bkfst and dinner only; *see* "Restaurants" below). On-premises parking is cramped. **Rates (CP):** Peak (May 26–Oct 8) $185 S or D; $325 ste. Extra person $35. Children under age 17 stay free. Min stay wknds. Lower rates off-season. Parking: Outdoor, free. AE, CB, DC, MC, V.

RESORT

Roche Harbor Resort

PO Box 4001, Roche Harbor, 98250; tel 360/378-2155 or toll free 800/451-8910; fax 360/378-6809. 160 acres. Lovely 109-year-old hotel situated on beautiful grounds. The lobby is furnished with a mix of antiques and Craftsman-period oak chairs. **Rooms:** 20 rms; 59 cottages/villas. CI 3pm/CO 11am. Nonsmoking rms avail. The quality and decor of rooms vary widely, so it's best to preview what's offered. Condos (which are 10–25 years old) available for short-term rental. **Amenities:** No A/C or TV. Some units w/terraces, some w/fireplaces. Condos have TV, hotel and cottages do not. **Services:** Babysitting. **Facilities:** 2 150 2 restaurants, 1 bar (w/entertainment), 1 beach (bay), playground. Marina accommodates vessels up to 200 feet. **Rates:** Peak (June 16–Sept 16) $70–$75 S or D; $115–$165 cottage/villa. Lower rates off-season. Parking: Outdoor, free. Closed Nov 1–Mar 15. AE, MC, V.

RESTAURANTS

Duck Soup Inn

3090 Roche Harbor Rd, Friday Harbor; tel 360/378-4878. **New American.** A cozy, countrified eatery, set in a weathered cedar structure, with art on the walls and lovely hooked rugs on the floors. Many of the fresh, local ingredients come from chef Gretchen Allison's own garden. Dinner (which includes soup and salad) might feature duck bruchetta or grilled prawns with mashed sweet potatoes and red-pepper salsa. Homemade sorbets make a light but luscious finale. The chef's winemaker-husband has selected a top quality wine list, with excellent choices in all price ranges. **FYI:** Reservations recommended. Beer and wine only. No smoking. **Open:** Peak (May 28–Oct) Wed–Sun 5:30–9pm. Closed mid-Nov–Mar. **Prices:** Main courses $10–$23. DISC, MC, V.

Friday Harbor House Restaurant

130 West St, Friday Harbor; tel 360/378-8455. **Northwest.** Overlooking manicured gardens, herb pots, the marina, and islands beyond, the restaurant is decorated in an imaginative nautical motif. A dinner might start with pink scallops with tarragon mayonnaise on a bed of arugula. Entrees include broiled Alaskan halibut fillet with lemon and roasted pepper puree, and vegetarian risotto with asparagus, saffron, and morels. Desserts are light, like the fresh fruit tart with lemon curd. **FYI:** Reservations recommended. No smoking. **Open:** Peak (June 21–Sept 21) daily 4–10pm. **Prices:** Main courses $16–$28. AE, CB, DC, MC, V.

Roberto's

205 A St, Friday Harbor; tel 360/378-6333. Behind ferry terminal parking lot at 1st St. **Italian.** This cozy little Italian place with shrimp-colored walls, small tables, and ice-cream parlor chairs offers pastas and entrees à la carte. Starters might be scallops in a sherry, garlic, and brown butter sauce; or mussels steamed in white wine, garlic, red pepper, tomato, and fresh basil. Smoked salmon cannelloni is made with herbed ricotta cheese and garlic-dill cream sauce. Specialties from the alder-wood-burning grill include Sicilian-style swordfish steak with olive oil, oregano, and lemon. Several pastas, too. **FYI:** Reservations recommended. Beer and wine only. No smoking. **Open:** Peak (July 4–Labor Day) daily 5–9:30pm. Closed Jan–Feb. **Prices:** Main courses $10–$11; prix fixe $15–$19. AE, MC, V.

Springtree Cafe

310 Spring St, Friday Harbor; tel 360/378-4848. At Argyle St; 3 blocks from ferry landing. **Seafood/Northwest.** Diners can eat in the peach-colored stucco dining room of this Euro-style bistro, or opt for an outdoor table near a 100-year-old elm. The menu focuses on fresh seafood, Waldron Island produce, and vegetarian fare. A house favorite is a sautéed seafood salad with marinated eggplant, mussels, shrimp, cod, sprouts, and spinach with vinaigrette dressing. You can't go wrong with ginger-shrimp with a sauce of mangos and dark rum. Don't miss a trip to the creatively designed rest room, otherwise-known as the "Caribbean Can." **FYI:** Reservations recommended. Children's menu. Beer and wine only. No smoking. **Open:** Peak (May–Sept) lunch daily 11:30am–2:30pm; dinner daily 5:30–9:30pm. Closed Jan–Mar. **Prices:** Main courses $14–$21. MC, V.

ATTRACTIONS

The Whale Museum

62 First St N, Friday Harbor; tel 360/378-4710. One of the few museums in the United States dedicated entirely to whales. The physiology, growth, reproduction, migration,

communication, and intelligence of these creatures is explored via skeletons, comparative displays, and whale-themed art. **Open:** Mem Day–Sept 30, daily 10am–5pm; Oct 1–Mem Day, daily 11am–4pm. Closed some hols and part of Feb; call ahead. **$**

Waterworks Gallery
315 Spring St, Friday Harbor; tel 360/378-3060. Established ten years ago, this gallery represents some of the finest in Northwest contemporary art. Owner Ruth Offen-Pearson looks for new and intriguing works to fill her gallery, often producing theme shows. Featured artists include Trevor Southey, Mary Ann Rock, Michelle Kirsch, and Monte Dolack. **Open:** Daily 10am–5pm. Closed some hols. **Free**

San Juan National Historic Park
Spring and 1st Sts, Friday Harbor; tel 206/378-2240. This historic park commemorates the not-so-famous Pig War of 1859, which was initiated when a British pig living in Canada crossed the border to eat dinner in an American garden. When the garden owner shot the pig, it sparked off an international incident that almost ended in armed confrontation between Britain and the United States. The park consists of two units: American Camp and British Camp. At both camps, visitors may tour historic buildings that look much as they did in 1859.

San Juan Islands

See Lopez Island, Orcas Island, San Juan Island

Seattle

See also Auburn, Bainbridge Island, Bellevue, Bothell, Edmonds, Kent, Kirkland, Renton, Silverdale, Tacoma; for airport lodgings, see Seattle-Tacoma Int'l Airport

Founded in 1850. Initially, Seattle was built on an island in Elliott Bay and on mud flats below forested bluffs. As the city grew, the bluffs were leveled to provide the dirt used to fill in the wetlands, but much of the town land remained soggy and most streets were mud holes. A fire in 1889 destroyed the downtown business section, and the city was rebuilt on the charred remains. Eight years after the fire, the arrival of the steamship *Portland,* loaded down with a ton of Klondike gold, set Seattle's first economic boom into motion. Today's Seattle is a sprawling, high-rise city—the cultural and entertainment center for western Washington. Its citizens enjoy world-class arts institutions, a natural landscape of breathtaking beauty, and a standard of living bolstered by the aerospace and computer industries. Seattle is a port terminal for the state ferry system and the Clipper Navigation hydroplane to Victoria, Canada. **Information:** Seattle-King County Convention and Visitors Bureau, 520 Pike St #1300, Seattle, 98101 (tel 206/461-5800).

PUBLIC TRANSPORTATION

Seattle's transit system, simply called **Metro**, offers a variety of services including buses, a waterfront streetcar, a monorail, and a metro tunnel for electric buses. Zone-based bus fares (Mon–Fri): adults $1.10–$1.60; children 5–17 75¢; children under 5 ride free. Reduced fares on weekends and non-rush hours. Rides within a limited core area of dowtown Seattle are free to all 6am–7pm. Wheelchair-accessible rides are indicated by wheelchair symbol. For routes, schedules, and assistance call 206/553-3000, or 689-3413 for deaf or hard-of-hearing.

HOTELS

Alexis Hotel Seattle
1007 1st Ave, 98107 (Downtown); tel 206/624-4844 or toll free 800/426-7033; fax 206/621-9009. Boutique hotel two blocks from the ferryboats; now listed on the National Register of Historic Places. Expensive—even given the spacious rooms and sumptuous decor—but the stiff rates don't seem to deter aficionados: The Alexis is busy year-round. **Rooms:** 54 rms and stes. CI 4pm/CO 1pm. Nonsmoking rms avail. On three floors (none with views), larger-than-average (some suites measure 700 square feet) with 55 additional rooms soon to be available. Many different styles—all luxurious—with antiques and designer decor in muted variations of mauve, coral, and green; styled for romance rather than business, although popular with executives and the likes of the Sultan of Brunei. **Amenities:** A/C, cable TV w/movies, dataport, voice mail, bathrobes. All units w/minibars, some w/terraces, some w/fireplaces, some w/whirlpools. Two-line speakerphones; minibars come with Krupps coffeemakers and Aveda Spa Bars (including $20 Euphoric candles); special "amenities package" for pets. **Services:** Twice-daily maid svce, car-rental desk, masseur, babysitting. Staff of 125 is friendly and helpful, despite no-tipping rule. **Facilities:** 2 restaurants (*see* "Restaurants" below), 2 bars (1 w/entertainment), steam rm. Restaurants include the publike Bookstore, just off the hotel lobby, offering light fare (and heavy reading, for guests who browse through the stacks of cookbooks and magazines), and the acclaimed Painted Table. **Rates (CP):** $170–$190 S; $185–$205 D; $220–$350 ste. Extra person $15. Children under age 12 stay free. Parking: Indoor, $15/day. Special packages are worth looking into. AE, DC, DISC, MC, V.

The Camlin Hotel
1619 9th Ave, 98101 (Downtown); tel 206/682-0100 or toll free 800/426-0670; fax 206/682-7415. At Pine. Convenient to Seattle Bus Terminal and Paramount theater. Offers motel-type rooms at a good price, but the place needs some TLC. **Rooms:** 136 rms and stes. CI 2pm/CO noon. Nonsmoking rms avail. Originally an apartment building, so rooms tend to be slightly larger than rooms in most older downtown hotels. **Amenities:** A/C, satel TV w/movies,

voice mail. Some units w/terraces. **Services:** Babysitting. **Facilities:** 1 restaurant (bkfst only), 1 bar (w/entertainment). Seattle's first rooftop restaurant has a great panoramic view, but the furnishings are tired. **Rates:** $74–$94 S; $84–$104 D; $175 ste. Extra person $10. Children under age 16 stay free. Parking: Indoor/outdoor, $9/day. AE, CB, DC, DISC, JCB, MC, V.

The Claremont Hotel

2000 4th Ave, 98121 (Downtown); tel 206/448-8600 or toll free 800/448-8601; fax 206/441-7140. At Virginia. A classic boutique hotel located in a 1920s-era building near Pike Place Market and Seattle Center. The lobby is decorated with marble floors and fine furnishings. **Rooms:** 110 rms, stes, and effic. CI 3pm/CO noon. Nonsmoking rms avail. Most of the rooms are well-furnished apartment/suites, complete with kitchenettes. Small rooms are really quite small, but full suites have a luxurious feel. **Amenities:** TV, refrig, dataport. No A/C. **Services:** Babysitting. **Facilities:** 1 restaurant (lunch and dinner only; *see* "Restaurants" below), washer/dryer. **Rates:** Peak (June–Sept) $79 S; $99–$109 D; $109–$149 ste; $99–$109 effic. Extra person $10. Children under age 16 stay free. Lower rates off-season. Parking: Indoor, $11/day. Extended-stay rates avail. AE, DC, DISC, MC, V.

The Edgewater

Pier 67, 2411 Alaskan Way, 98121 (Waterfront); tel 206/728-7000 or toll free 800/624-0670; fax 206/441-4119. Seattle's only waterfront hotel exudes comfort throughout its lodge-like interior. Superb views of Puget Sound, Washington St ferries, sailboats, and sea lions from the lobby. Five fireplaces throughout public areas. "Storytellers" entertain on holidays. **Rooms:** 233 rms and stes. CI 3pm/CO noon. Nonsmoking rms avail. Cabin-style interiors with knotty pine furniture. **Amenities:** A/C, refrig, dataport, voice mail. All units w/minibars, some w/terraces. **Services:** Twice-daily maid svce, babysitting. **Facilities:** 1 restaurant, 1 bar (w/entertainment). Games tables always ready for chess, checkers, or backgammon. **Rates:** Peak (May–Oct) $119–$190 S; $119–$210 D; $300 ste. Extra person $15. Children under age 18 stay free. Lower rates off-season. Parking: Outdoor, $6/day. Romance, Northwest, and other packages available. AE, DISC, MC, V.

Four Seasons Olympic Seattle

411 University St, 98101 (Downtown); tel 206/621-1700 or toll free 800/332-3442, 800/821-8106 in WA, 800/268-6282 in Canada; fax 206/682-9633. At Rainier Square. Handsomely restored 1924 landmark, now on the National Register of Historic Places and a Four Seasons hotel since 1982. Guests are greeted by the "grand hotel" facade of the 12-story building, with its arched Palladian windows above a carriageway and porte cochere; elevators lead up to a soaring grand luxe lobby of intricately carved oak. **Rooms:** 450 rms and stes. CI 3pm/CO 1pm. Nonsmoking rms avail. All units are spacious and soothingly decorated. Full-size work desk; sitting area with armchair, ottoman, and reading lamp. Large, well-equipped bathrooms. **Amenities:** A/C, cable TV w/movies, dataport, bathrobes. All units w/minibars, some w/whirlpools. Three 2-line speakerphones. **Services:** Twice-daily maid svce, car-rental desk, children's program, babysitting. Alert staff of 575, more than one per room. 24-hour concierge. Overnight laundry, car wash, and detailing. Children's menu, strollers, infant bathtubs; pet amenities (including doorknob signs announcing the presence of a pet inside). Complimentary early morning coffee in the lobby; "bon voyage" box of goodies (perhaps chocolate chip cookies and milk) placed in cars at check-out. **Facilities:** 3 restaurants (*see* "Restaurants" below), 3 bars (1 w/entertainment), sauna, whirlpool, beauty salon. Health club (open 5:30am–10pm; until 11pm Fri–Sat) with glass-pavilioned, 41-foot swimming pool and outdoor patios. Gardenlike atrium for light meals and afternoon tea; elegant dining in Georgian Room. **Rates:** $200–$230 S; $230–$260 D; $250–$1,100 ste. Extra person $20. Children under age 18 stay free. Parking: Indoor, $15/day. Two categories of rooms ("moderate", the lowest, will meet most demands); six categories of suites, including the very practical Four Seasons Executive Suites at $280/double. Weekend rates on request; special packages avail for theater-goers, romantics, honeymooners, families, and gourmets. AE, CB, DC, EC, ER, JCB, MC, V.

Holiday Inn Crowne Plaza

1113 6th Ave, 98101 (Downtown); tel 206/464-1980 or toll free 800/521-2762; fax 206/340-1617. An elegant, high-rise hotel just off I-5 and two blocks from the Washington Convention Center. If you're a seeker of ballplayers' autographs, you might be able to add to your collection—visiting American League teams stay here. **Rooms:** 415 rms and stes. Executive level. CI 4pm/CO noon. Nonsmoking rms avail. Each room features stunning views of Seattle, Elliott Bay, or the mountains. Comfortable furnishings. **Amenities:** A/C, cable TV w/movies, dataport, voice mail. 1 unit w/whirlpool. Iron and ironing board in each room. **Services:** Car-rental desk, babysitting. 24-hour security staff. **Facilities:** 1 restaurant, 1 bar (w/entertainment), spa, sauna, whirlpool. Restaurant has outdoor pavilion for summer dining. **Rates:** Peak (June–Sept) $160 S; $180 D; $250–$500 ste. Extra person $20. Children under age 18 stay free. Lower rates off-season. Parking: Indoor, $14/day. AE, CB, DC, DISC, JCB, MC, V.

Hotel Seattle

315 Seneca St, 98101 (Downtown); tel 206/623-5110 or toll free 800/426-2439, 800/421-6662 in WA; fax 206/623-5110. At 4th Ave. An old, no-frills hotel in the center of town. Rooms need renovation. **Rooms:** 81 rms and stes. CI 2pm/CO noon. Nonsmoking rms avail. A promised renovation will supposedly yield new carpets, beds, furniture, and fixtures. **Amenities:** Satel TV. No A/C. **Services:** **Facilities:** 1 restaurant (bkfst and lunch only), 1 bar.

Rates: $66–$70 S; $72–$76 D; $80–$98 ste. Extra person $6. Children under age 12 stay free. Parking: Outdoor, $11/day. AE, CB, MC, V.

Hotel Vintage Park
1100 5th Ave, 98101 (Downtown); tel 206/624-8000 or toll free 800/624-4433; fax 206/623-0568. At Spring. An intimate, cozy boutique hotel with a European feel. Although expensive, it combines elegance of luxury hotel with ease and comfort of charming bed-and-breakfast. The small, librarylike lobby, furnished with truly comfortable sofas and chairs around a blazing fire, is adjacent to the porte cochere for convenient check-in. **Rooms:** 126 rms and stes. CI 3pm/CO noon. Nonsmoking rms avail. Guest rooms are each named for a Washington State winery and decorated in warm, playful colors with fanciful headboard canopies. **Amenities:** A/C, cable TV w/movies, dataport, voice mail, bathrobes. All units w/minibars, 1 w/fireplace, 1 w/whirlpool. Individual electronic climate-control panels, irons/ironing boards in every room. **Services:** Twice-daily maid svce, babysitting. Complimentary tastings of Washington State wines 6–7pm (Mon–Sat). **Facilities:** 1 restaurant, 1 bar. **Rates:** $170–$200 S; $185–$215 D; $250–$370 ste. Extra person $15. Children under age 13 stay free. Parking: Indoor, $16/day. AE, CB, DC, DISC, JCB, MC, V.

Inn at the Market
86 Pine St, 98101 (Pike Place Market); tel 206/443-3600 or toll free 800/446-4484; fax 206/448-0631. A secret retreat for business and leisure travelers, located amidst bustling Pike Place Market. The inn surrounds a lovely courtyard with fountain, seats, ivy, and flower boxes. The inviting lobby has comfy sofas, brick floors, and lavish fresh flowers. Not inexpensive, but you get your money's worth. **Rooms:** 65 rms and stes. CI 4pm/CO noon. Nonsmoking rms avail. Rooms are huge with floor-to-ceiling bay windows looking out to market or courtyard. Enormous armoires and closets **Amenities:** A/C, cable TV, bathrobes. All units w/minibars. Large minibar fridge adequate for leftovers. **Services:** Twice-daily maid svce, babysitting. Across the courtyard from the celebrated Campagne Restaurant. **Facilities:** 20 **Rates:** Peak (May 1–Oct 15) $135–$300 S or D; $250–$300 ste. Extra person $15. Children under age 16 stay free. Lower rates off-season. Parking: Indoor, $14/day. AE, CB, DC, DISC, JCB, MC, V.

The Inn at Virginia Mason
1006 Spring St, 98104 (First Hill); tel 206/583-6453 or toll free 800/283-6453; fax 206/223-7545. 4 blocks SE of Convention Center. Warm, friendly property located in a well-maintained 1920s-style building adjacent to Virginia Mason Hospital. Also close to shopping and downtown Seattle. **Rooms:** 79 rms and stes. CI 3pm/CO noon. No smoking. Accommodations have nicely styled furniture; those on the upper floor offer views of the city and Mount Rainier. **Amenities:** A/C, cable TV, dataport. Some units w/fireplaces, some w/whirlpools. **Services:** Babysitting. **Facilities:** 300 1 restaurant, washer/dryer. Outdoor roof garden. **Rates:** $90–$145 S or D; $135–$200 ste. Children under age 18 stay free. Parking: Indoor/outdoor, $5/day. AE, CB, DC, DISC, MC, V.

The Madison—A Stouffer Renaissance Hotel
515 Madison St, 98104 (Downtown); tel 206/583-0300 or toll free 800/HOTELS-1; fax 206/622-8635. High-rise chic—that's what you'll find at this big, business-oriented hotel. The second-floor lobby, reached by escalator, features oriental accents and a splendid collection of art-glass by Dale Chihuly—offering a dramatic contrast with the building's austere facade. **Rooms:** 553 rms and stes. Executive level. CI 3pm/CO 1pm. Nonsmoking rms avail. Rooms decorated in floral prints in tones of cinnamon and sage. Corner suites afford excellent views of Puget Sound and Lake Washington. **Amenities:** A/C, cable TV w/movies. Some units w/minibars, some w/terraces, some w/whirlpools. A nice touch here: Complimentary tea, coffee, or hot chocolate delivered five minutes after wake-up call, if desired. **Services:** Babysitting. **Facilities:** 2 restaurants, 1 bar, whirlpool, beauty salon. **Rates:** $154–$214 S or D; $174–$234 ste. Children under age 18 stay free. Parking: Indoor, $13/day. AE, CB, DC, DISC, ER, JCB, MC, V.

Mayflower Park Hotel
405 Olive Way, 98101 (Downtown); tel 206/623-8700 or toll free 800/426-5100; fax 206/382-6996. At 4th. This old world hideaway built in 1927 sparkles with crystal chandeliers, gold leaf, and period antiques. Enjoys an ace location, with direct access to Westlake Shopping Center's 90 stores, bus tunnel, monorail, and market. Two-tiered lobby allows guests to retreat to comfortable sofas upstairs. **Rooms:** 173 rms and stes. CI 3pm/CO noon. Nonsmoking rms avail. Rooms are compact, with English-style furnishings. Although bathrooms are thoroughly updated with big mirrors and good lighting, they retain old-style panache with white-tile floors and pedestal sinks. **Amenities:** A/C, cable TV w/movies. 1 unit w/whirlpool. **Services:** Babysitting. **Facilities:** 100 1 restaurant, 1 bar. Oliver's Lounge is known for its award-winning martinis. **Rates:** $110–$140 S; $120–$165 D; $165–$350 ste. Extra person $10. Children under age 17 stay free. Parking: Indoor, $9/day. Romance Package offered all year; Shoppers Package Thanksgiving–Christmas. AE, DC, DISC, JCB, MC, V.

Meany Tower Hotel
4507 Brooklyn Ave NE, 98105 (University District); tel 206/634-2000 or toll free 800/899-0251; fax 206/547-6029. At 45th. Although the rooms have mismatched furniture and tiny baths, the location in the center of the University District within walking distance of all campus activities compensates for the circa-1931 building's deficits. **Rooms:** 155 rms. CI 2pm/CO noon. Nonsmoking rms avail. Every room has a

view, either of downtown Seattle and Lake Union, or even more exceptional views of Lake Washington. **Amenities:** A/C, satel TV w/movies, dataport. **Services:** **Facilities:** 1 restaurant, 1 bar (w/entertainment), games rm. **Rates:** Peak (June–Sept) $78–$98 S; $88–$108 D. Extra person $10. Children under age 14 stay free. Lower rates off-season. Parking: Outdoor, free. Packages available for Huskies football games, Valentine's Day, and holidays. AE, CB, DC, JCB, MC, V.

Pacific Plaza Hotel

400 Spring St, 98104 (Downtown); tel 206/623-3900 or toll free 800/462-1165; fax 206/623-2059. At 4th. Dates from 1928. Small rooms, but the warm lobby feels like cozy living room. **Rooms:** 160 rms. CI 4pm/CO 11am. Nonsmoking rms avail. **Amenities:** Cable TV w/movies. No A/C. **Services:** Front desk service needs tightening: 8 minutes lapsed before eye contact was made with a guest ready to register. **Facilities:** 2 restaurants (lunch and dinner only), 1 bar. **Rates (CP):** $77–$97 S or D. Children under age 16 stay free. Parking: Indoor, $10/day. AE, DC, DISC, JCB, MC, V.

Pioneer Square Hotel

77 Yesler Way, 98104 (Pioneer Square); tel 206/340-1234 or toll free 800/800-5514; fax 206/467-0707. This reasonably priced hotel is at an interesting locale in the heart of Pioneer Square, just one block from Washington Street ferries and the Victoria Line. Originally opened in 1914 as a "workingman's" hotel, it recently underwent a $2 million renovation. The comfortable lounge is done in rich cherry wood and marble. **Rooms:** 75 rms. CI 3pm/CO 11am. Nonsmoking rms avail. All accommodations are configured differently, so guests have a choice of styles, furnishings, and dimensions. Some have views of Puget Sound. **Amenities:** A/C, cable TV, dataport. Some units w/terraces. **Services:** Babysitting. **Facilities:** 1 bar (w/entertainment). Juice and Java bar adjacent to lobby offering snacks and coffees. **Rates (CP):** Peak (May–Sept) $89–$135 S; $99–$145 D. Extra person $10. Children under age 12 stay free. Lower rates off-season. Parking: Indoor, $12/day. AE, CB, DC, DISC, JCB, MC, V.

Residence Inn by Marriott—Lake Union

800 Fairview Ave N, 98109 (E Lake Union); tel 206/624-6000 or toll free 800/331-3131; fax 206/223-8160. Corner of Valley. Relatively new property with six-story atrium and waterfall. Basically for extended-stay guests. **Rooms:** 234 stes. CI 4pm/CO noon. Nonsmoking rms avail. Attractive rooms have new couches and carpets. **Amenities:** A/C, cable TV w/movies, refrig, dataport, voice mail. All units w/terraces. **Services:** Babysitting. Free shuttle within 2½ miles of hotel. Complimentary dessert and flavored coffee Tues–Thurs. "Manager's reception" Wed eve with unlimited beer, wine, and catered appetizer buffet. **Facilities:** Sauna, steam rm, whirlpool, washer/dryer. Hearth Room library is an inviting spot to read. **Rates (CP):** $150–$270 ste. Parking: Indoor, $9/day. AE, DC, DISC, JCB, MC, V.

The Roosevelt Hotel

1531 7th Ave, 98101; tel 206/621-1200 or toll free 800/426-0670; fax 206/233-0335. At Pine Ave. Blockmates with the new Nike Town and the planned Planet Hollywood, the Roosevelt remains a good value in a great location—1½ blocks from Westlake Mall and Washington Convention Center. **Rooms:** 151 rms and stes. CI 3pm/CO noon. Nonsmoking rms avail. **Amenities:** A/C, cable TV w/movies, dataport, voice mail. Some units w/minibars, some w/whirlpools. **Services:** Babysitting. **Facilities:** 1 restaurant (bkfst only), 1 bar. King Edward, former member of the Inkspots, performs on a baby grand Tues–Sat 8–11pm. **Rates:** $90–$220 S; $100–$220 D; $170–$220 ste. Extra person $10. Children under age 18 stay free. Parking: Indoor, $11/day. Shopping and Romance packages avail. AE, CB, DC, DISC, JCB, MC, V.

Seattle Hilton Hotel

1301 6th Ave, 98101 (Downtown); tel 206/624-0500 or toll free 800/445-8667; fax 206/682-9029. At University St. Main attribute is the hotel's connection to Rainier Square shopping and business center. Worn furniture and dark atmosphere in lobby need attention. **Rooms:** 237 rms and stes. CI 4pm/CO 1pm. Nonsmoking rms avail. **Amenities:** A/C, cable TV w/movies, dataport. Iron and ironing boards in every room. **Services:** Car-rental desk, babysitting. **Facilities:** 2 restaurants, 2 bars (1 w/entertainment). Small and intimate Asgard's Restaurant & Lounge on 29th floor features Northwest cuisine and offers great view of Puget Sound and Lake Union. 20% discount for hotel guests. **Rates:** Peak (May–Sept) $139–$185 S or D; $259–$359 ste. Extra person $10. Children under age 18 stay free. Lower rates off-season. Parking: Indoor, $12/day. AE, CB, DC, DISC, MC, V.

Sheraton Seattle Hotel & Towers

1400 6th Ave, 98101 (Downtown); tel 206/621-9000 or toll free 800/325-3535; fax 206/621-8441. At Union. One of the largest hotels in Seattle and popular for conventions. But rates are high relative to quality of motel-style rooms. **Rooms:** 840 rms and stes. Executive level. CI 3pm/CO noon. Nonsmoking rms avail. Disappointing decor/furnishings. **Amenities:** A/C, cable TV w/movies, dataport, voice mail. All units w/minibars. **Services:** Twice-daily maid svce, babysitting. **Facilities:** 3 restaurants (*see* "Restaurants" below), 2 bars (1 w/entertainment), spa, sauna, whirlpool. Chef Monique Barbeau, co-winner of James Beard Award in 1994, heads the team at Fullers, Sheraton's fine dining restaurant. Pike St Cafe, under renovation, has "lunar" theme and Northwestern food. Bar in large, busy lobby hums after business hours with conversation and live piano music. **Rates:** $190 S; $210 D; $250–$550 ste. Extra person $20. Parking: Indoor/outdoor, $14/day. AE, CB, DC, DISC, JCB, MC, V.

Sixth Avenue Inn

2000 6th Ave, 98121 (Downtown); tel 206/441-8300 or toll free 800/648-6440; fax 206/441-9903. At Virginia. Attractive to families and business travelers, this property is close to shopping, restaurants, theater, Seattle Center, and tour bus services. **Rooms:** 166 rms and stes. CI 3pm/CO noon. Nonsmoking rms avail. Bright, inviting, good-size rooms. **Amenities:** A/C, cable TV w/movies, dataport, voice mail. Rooms have video games and a small bookshelf with books. **Services:** Fax and copy service available. **Facilities:** 35 1 restaurant, 1 bar. **Rates:** Peak (June–Sept) $84 S; $99 D; $135–$150 ste. Extra person $12. Children under age 18 stay free. Lower rates off-season. Parking: Outdoor, free. AE, CB, DC, MC, V.

The Sorrento Hotel

900 Madison St, 98104; tel 206/622-6400 or toll free 800/426-1265; fax 206/343-6155. Just E of downtown. This 1908 veteran on First Hill, designed in vaguely Florentine style with campanile towers and terra cotta trim, rises 17 stories above a fountained courtyard and carriageway. Its octagonal lounge is bedecked with Honduran mahogany and a fireplace topped with pictorial tiles. Although the recent $1.3-million modernization could find space for only one small elevator (an occasional test of patience) the warmth of the staff compensates for most shortcomings. And given the spaciousness of most rooms, rates represent good value, with suites here costing no more than rooms in other hotels of this caliber. **Rooms:** 76 rms and stes. CI 4pm/CO noon. Nonsmoking rms avail. All rooms and suites are of different size (larger than average), shape, and decor; most have antiques to enhance the elegant decor. **Amenities:** A/C, cable TV, dataport, voice mail, bathrobes. All units w/minibars, 1 w/terrace. Two-line speakerphones with voice mail; goosedown pillows; bed warmers with turndown service on chilly nights. **Services:** VP Twice-daily maid svce, car-rental desk, babysitting. 24-hour concierge. Complimentary limo to downtown locations. "Guest history" profiles. Cellular phones and fax machines for rent. **Facilities:** 120 1 restaurant (*see* "Restaurants" below), 1 bar (w/entertainment). Brand-new fitness room plus guest privileges at nearby athletic club. Afternoon tea in Fireside Lounge; all meals in swank Hunt Club. **Rates:** Peak (May–Oct) $145–$180 S or D; $185–$1000 ste. Extra person $15. Children under age 16 stay free. Lower rates off-season. Parking: Indoor, $12/day. "Luxury Leisure" packages offer whimsical items like keepsake pajamas, tiramisu for two, and a stay-in-bed delight. AE, CB, DC, DISC, MC, V.

University Plaza Hotel

400 NE 45th St, 98105 (University/Wallingford); tel 206/634-0100 or toll free 800/343-7040; fax 206/633-2743. W side of I-5 at exit 169. On the outside, this hotel is agreeable but plain; on the inside, its lobby, rooms, and meeting facilities are surprisingly impressive. Located just blocks from the University of Washington, and a mile from downtown. **Rooms:** 135 rms and stes. CI 3pm/CO 11am. Nonsmoking rms avail. Bright, cheerful, well-furnished rooms; many overlook the pool area. **Amenities:** A/C, cable TV w/movies. Some units w/terraces. **Services:** Babysitting. **Facilities:** 300 1 restaurant, 1 bar (w/entertainment), beauty salon. The lounge, which has panoramic views of Seattle and local mountain ranges, offers jazz music every night. **Rates:** Peak (May 15–Oct 15) $84 S; $92 D; $165 ste. Extra person $6. Children under age 12 stay free. Lower rates off-season. Parking: Outdoor, free. Valentine's Day and Christmas packages avail. AE, CB, DC, DISC, MC, V.

The Warwick Hotel

401 Lenora St, 98121 (Downtown); tel 206/443-4300 or toll free 800/426-9280; fax 206/448-1662. At 4th. An elegant property featuring Italian marble and fine woods. Tasteful decorations include antique Asian screens and vases. **Rooms:** 229 rms and stes. CI 3pm/CO noon. Nonsmoking rms avail. Plush, comfortable decor and furnishings. **Amenities:** A/C, cable TV w/movies, refrig, dataport, bathrobes. Some units w/minibars, some w/terraces, some w/whirlpools. **Services:** VP Babysitting. A 24-hour, complimentary van shuttles guests to and from various downtown sites, including the Kingdome and Seattle Center. **Facilities:** 100 1 restaurant, 1 bar (w/entertainment), spa, sauna, whirlpool. **Rates:** Peak (May–Oct) $170 S; $185 D; $350 ste. Extra person $15. Children under age 18 stay free. Lower rates off-season. Parking: Indoor, $11/day. AE, CB, DC, DISC, ER, JCB, MC, V.

Westcoast Vance Hotel

620 Stewart St, 98101 (Downtown); tel 206/441-4200 or toll free 800/426-0670; fax 206/441-8612. At 7th Ave. Small, European-style, centrally located hotel convenient to Westlake Mall and Paramount theater. **Rooms:** 165 rms. CI 2pm/CO noon. Nonsmoking rms avail. Very compact bathrooms with no counter space. **Amenities:** A/C, TV w/movies, dataport, voice mail. **Services:** VP Babysitting. **Facilities:** 1 restaurant, 1 bar. **Rates:** $85–$135 S; $95–$135 D. Extra person $10. Children under age 18 stay free. Parking: Indoor/outdoor, $9/day. Summer packages avail. AE, DC, DISC, JCB, MC, V.

Westin Hotel Seattle

1900 5th Ave, 98101 (Downtown); tel 206/728-1000 or toll free 800/228-3000; fax 206/728-2259. Set in twin circular towers is the largest hotel in Seattle and the most central one to the city's main features, such as the Westlake Center, monorail, and Pike Place Market. Although it has that big-city feel, the Westin also manages to impart warmth and friendliness. **Rooms:** 865 rms and stes. CI 3pm/CO noon. Nonsmoking rms avail. Pie-shaped rooms accentuate views of skyline, mountains, or water. **Amenities:** A/C, cable TV w/movies, dataport, voice mail, in-rm safe, bathrobes. All units w/minibars, some w/whirlpools. Ironing boards and irons. **Services:** Twice-daily maid svce, car-rental desk, masseur, children's program, babysitting. **Facilities:** 3 restaurants (*see* "Restaurants" below), 3 bars, spa, sauna, steam rm, whirlpool, beauty salon. Piano music in lobby every late afternoon and early evening. **Rates:** Peak (Apr–Nov 15) $175–$195 S; $195–$215 D; $240–$1,000 ste. Extra person $25. Children under age 18 stay free. Lower rates off-season. Parking: Indoor, $13/day. Honeymoon, shopping, and holiday getaway packages available. AE, DC, DISC, JCB, MC, V.

MOTELS

Best Western Loyal Inn

2301 8th Ave, 98121; tel 206/682-0200 or toll free 800/528-1234; fax 206/467-8984. At Denny Way. A neatly maintained, pleasant motel with a well-kept exterior. Located close to Seattle Center. **Rooms:** 91 rms and stes. CI 2pm/CO noon. Nonsmoking rms avail. **Amenities:** A/C, cable TV w/movies. **Services:** Pets allowed with approval. **Facilities:** Spa, sauna, whirlpool, washer/dryer. Clean health spa with 24-hour whirlpool and sauna. **Rates (CP):** Peak (June–Sept 15) $79–$108 S; $86–$115 D; $180 ste. Extra person $6. Children under age 12 stay free. Lower rates off-season. Parking: Outdoor, free. AE, CB, DC, DISC, JCB, MC, V.

Days Inn Town Center

2205 7th Ave, 98121 (Downtown); tel 206/448-3434 or toll free 800/225-7169; fax 206/441-6976. Although it looks like an ordinary motel on the outside, it's much nicer than most on the inside. Close to downtown shopping. **Rooms:** 91 rms and stes. CI 3pm/CO noon. Nonsmoking rms avail. Clean and pleasant. **Amenities:** A/C, cable TV, dataport. **Services:** Car-rental desk. Pets allowed at manager's discretion. **Facilities:** 1 restaurant, 1 bar. Children under 12 eat free at restaurant. **Rates:** Peak (May–Sept) $80 S; $85 D; $125 ste. Extra person $7. Children under age 18 stay free. Lower rates off-season. Parking: Outdoor, free. AE, CB, DC, DISC, MC, V.

Kings Inn

2106 5th Ave, 98121 (Downtown); tel 206/441-8833 or toll free 800/546-4760; fax 206/441-0730. At Lenora. No-frills, downtown motel. **Rooms:** 70 rms and stes. CI noon/CO noon. Nonsmoking rms avail. Several units lacked smoke alarms at time of inspection; others had alarms but no batteries. **Amenities:** A/C, cable TV w/movies, VCR. **Services:** **Facilities:** Washer/dryer. Parking spaces in garage are very tight. **Rates:** Peak (July–Sept 15) $45–$55 S; $65–$90 ste. Extra person $5. Children under age 12 stay free. Lower rates off-season. Parking: Indoor/outdoor, free. AE, CB, DC, DISC, ER, JCB, MC, V.

INN

Gaslight Inn

1727 15th Ave, 98122 (Capitol Hill); tel 206/325-3654; fax 206/328-4803. A 1906 Craftsman four-square, originally built as a model home and refurbished in 1985. The inn is beautifully maintained and still contains details such as original oak panels. Good security. Unsuitable for children under 18. **Rooms:** 13 rms, stes, and effic (4 w/shared bath). CI 3pm/CO noon. No smoking. Accommodations are individually decorated with museum-quality antiques; some offer views of downtown Seattle and the Olympic Mountains. Four rooms share baths. **Amenities:** TV, refrig. No A/C. 1 unit w/terrace, some w/fireplaces. **Services:** Masseur. Toiletries available upon request. Local bus stop and airport shuttle stop in front of inn. **Facilities:** Sauna, washer/dryer, guest lounge. **Rates (CP):** $68–$78 D w/shared bath, $88–$98 D w/private bath; $118 ste; $98–$118 effic. Parking: Outdoor, free. AE, MC, V.

RESTAURANTS

Adriatica

1137 Dexter Ave N (South Lake Union); tel 206/285-5000. **Mediterranean.** Perched high on a hill above Lake Union, Adriatica is worth the climb up the steep, narrow stairs. New chef Katherine Mackenzie has a passion for Mediterranean-style food. Pastas and impeccably grilled fresh seafood are a specialty, as is grilled pork tenderloin in a port and cranberry sauce. The bar, on the top floor of the three-story house, is the perfect place to nibble fabulous fried calamari and share a bottle of wine (there are 200 choices). **FYI:** Reservations recommended. **Open:** Daily 5pm–midnight. **Prices:** Main courses $14–$23. AE, CB, DC, MC, V.

★ Al Boccalino

1 Yester Way; tel 206/622-7688. **Italian.** The rustic charm of the decor and the food make this a popular dining spot. Favorite dishes include saddle of lamb in tarragon and brandy sauce, and a daily-special risotto. The all-Italian wine list is superbly matched to the cuisine. **FYI:** Reservations recommended. Beer and wine only. **Open:** Lunch Mon–Fri 11:30am–2pm; dinner Mon–Thurs 5–10pm, Fri–Sat 5–10:30pm. **Prices:** Main courses $10–$22. AE, CB, DC, MC, V.

Cactus

4220 E Madison St (Madison Park); tel 206/324-4140. **Mexican/Southwestern.** Living up to the restaurant's name, the fanciful southwestern decor features giant swags of chile peppers, twinkling lights, and lots of cacti. The food is similarly colorful, fresh, and bold. Entrees include the usual—tacos and enchiladas—plus the unusual—salmon and mussel stew with chipotle peppers and white beans. Tapas are tasty too (especially when accompanied by a glass of sherry), and the Navajo fry bread is well worth a try. **FYI:** Reservations accepted. No smoking. **Open:** Lunch Mon–Sat

11:30am–2:30pm; dinner Sun–Thurs 5–9:30pm, Fri–Sat 5–10pm. **Prices:** Main courses $9–$12. CB, DC, DISC, MC, V.

Cafe Campagne
1600 Post Alley (Pike Place Market); tel 206/728-2233. **French.** Expect classic bistro food stylishly done like rotisserie chicken, steak frites, steamed mussels, and great mashed potatoes. Very popular, but easy to get in at off-peak hours. Delicious takeout is available at the charcuterie counter. **FYI:** Reservations not accepted. No smoking. **Open:** Breakfast Mon–Sat 8–11am; lunch Mon–Sat 11:30am–5pm; dinner Mon–Sat 5–11pm; brunch Sun 8am–3pm. **Prices:** Main courses $6.95–$14.95. AE, CB, DC, MC, V.

Cafe Hue
312 2nd Ave S (Pioneer Square); tel 206/625-9833. **Vietnamese.** Lots of wood and pretty patterned upholstery accent the decor of this spacious restaurant. On the menu you will find many stir-fried dishes and specialties such as barbecue prawns, sliced beef and tomatoes in spicy broth, steamed halibut, and roasted quail or game hen. French pastries are offered for dessert. The largely upscale and Italian wine list works surprisingly well with the Vietnamese cuisine. **FYI:** Reservations accepted. Beer and wine only. **Open:** Mon 11am–9pm, Tues–Fri 11am–10pm, Sat noon–10pm, Sun 11am–2pm. **Prices:** Main courses $5–$14. MC, V.

Cafe Septieme
214 Broadway E (Capitol Hill); tel 206/860-8858. **Eclectic.** A bohemian aura surrounds this shabbily elegant cafe on funky Capitol Hill. It's a place to linger—over coffee and French toast for breakfast, a sausage sandwich and a beer for lunch, a glass of wine and some chevre in the late afternoon, or roast chicken, garlic mashed potatoes, and a bottle of Meursault for dinner. There are always a few vegetarian options, too, like stuffed acorn squash and meatless lasagna. A large counter makes a convivial gathering place for those eating alone. **FYI:** Reservations not accepted. Beer and wine only. **Open:** Mon–Fri 7am–midnight, Sat–Sun 9am–midnight. **Prices:** Main courses $8–$11. MC, V.

Cafe Sophie
1921 1st Ave (Downtown); tel 206/441-6139. **Continental.** Set in a landmark building that once housed one of the first mortuaries in the west. There are three distinctly different rooms: an elegant, Euro-style bar up front; a darkly romantic dining room in the middle; and an inviting, book-lined library in the rear, complete with fireplace. The menu changes three times a year, and leans towards bistro fare at lunch and more formal entrees in the evening. Live jazz on Friday and Saturday; excellent beverage list, with a huge selection of wines, beers, and single malts. **FYI:** Reservations recommended. Jazz. **Open:** Lunch Mon–Sat 11:30am–2:30pm; dinner Mon–Thurs 5:30–9:30pm, Fri–Sat 5:30–10:30pm. **Prices:** Main courses $14–$20. AE, DC, DISC, MC, V.

Campagne Restaurant
86 Pine St (Pike Place Market); tel 206/728-2800. **French.** Chef Tamara Murphy presents classy country French fare at this intimate restaurant and bar. Lavender-fried quail salad, cassoulets, homemade pasta, fresh fish, rabbit, and rack of lamb are just some of the offerings. The wine list is excellent. When the kitchen closes at 10pm, a bar menu is available until midnight, and the bar stays lively until 2am. **FYI:** Reservations recommended. **Open:** Daily 5:30–10pm. **Prices:** Main courses $14–$26. AE, CB, DC, MC, V.

Canlis
2576 N Aurora Ave (Queen Anne Hill); tel 206/283-3313. **American.** Kimono-clad waitresses, a piano bar, and a great view are part of what have made this place a Seattle favorite for 40 years. Thick-cut steaks and sautéed seafood are the house specialties. The wine list is hefty, as are the prices. **FYI:** Reservations recommended. Piano. **Open:** Mon–Sat 5pm–midnight. **Prices:** Main courses $22–$32. AE, CB, DC, MC, V. VP

Chez Shea
94 Pike St, Ste 34 (Pike Place Market); tel 206/467-9990. **Northwest.** Smart, casual dress is recommended for this ultra-romantic, tiny place on the second floor overlooking Pike Place Market. The creative seasonal specialties reflect the abundant offerings in Pike Place and the bounty of the Northwest. The recent addition of Chez's Lounge, featuring a limited menu of Iberian specialties, affords a relaxed dining option. **FYI:** Reservations recommended. No smoking. **Open:** Tues–Sun 5:30–10:30pm. Closed Jan 1–7. **Prices:** Main courses $25–$30; prix fixe $38. AE, MC, V. VP

Dahlia Lounge
1904 4th Ave (Downtown); tel 206/682-4142. **Eclectic/Northwest.** Owner/chef Tom Douglas is often credited with "inventing" Northwest cuisine. Although his style is now all over the map, his ingredients and execution still rank among the best in the area. Crab cakes are the signature dish at his dimly lit, whimsically furnished spot. Although the menu changes weekly, you'll usually find mainstays such as pot stickers stuffed with lobster and shiitake mushrooms, and the sublime pear tart. **FYI:** Reservations recommended. No smoking. **Open:** Lunch Mon–Fri 11:30am–2:30pm; dinner Mon–Thurs 5:30–10pm, Fri–Sat 5:30–11pm, Sun 5–9pm. **Prices:** Main courses $12–$23. AE, CB, DC, DISC, MC, V.

Elliott's
Pier 56 (Waterfront); tel 206/623-4340. **Seafood.** The always lively Elliott's is more than a tourist spot—it's the place to find some of the freshest fish in Seattle. A raw bar features many varieties of local oysters, while Dungeness crab, wild king salmon, and cioppino are specialties on the menu. The restaurant runs the length of the pier. Touches of brass, brightly patterned fabrics, and many booths make the inside cozy when the weather takes a turn for the worse. Smoking allowed only outside and in the bar. **FYI:** Reservations recommended. Children's menu. No smoking. **Open:** Peak

(mid-June–Labor Day) Sun–Thurs 11am–11pm, Fri–Sat 11am–11:30pm. **Prices:** Main courses $15–$28. AE, CB, DC, DISC, MC, V.

The Emerald Suite and Space Needle Restaurant
219 4th Ave (Seattle Center); tel 206/443-2100. **Northwest.** The entire city of Seattle serves as the decor at this slowly rotating landmark 500 feet above the sidewalks. Choose from two locales: the Emerald Suite (an intimate room suited to quiet dining) or the more informal Space Needle Restaurant (good for families). Local ingredients get top billing on a menu that features salmon and other fresh seafood, as well as Ellenburg lamb. A fun treat is the "Lunar Orbiter" dessert—an ice-cream sundae served in a cloud of smoking dry ice. The elevator ride up the Needle is free when you eat here. **FYI:** Reservations recommended. Children's menu. No smoking. **Open:** Daily 8am–midnight. **Prices:** Main courses $15–$30. AE, CB, DC, DISC, ER, MC, V. VP

Emmett Watson's Oyster Bar
1916 Pike Place (Pike Place Market); tel 206/448-7721. **Seafood.** A hole-in-the-wall that serves some of the freshest oysters in town. Salmon soup and fish-and-chips are other good choices. On a sunny day, the handkerchief-size courtyard is pleasant. **FYI:** Reservations not accepted. Beer and wine only. **Open:** Mon–Thurs 11:30am–8pm, Fri–Sat 11:30am–9pm, Sun 11:30am–4pm. **Prices:** Main courses $5–$9. No CC.

Etta's Seafood
2020 Western Ave (Pike Place Market); tel 206/443-6000. **Northwest.** Tom Douglas, owner/chef of the Dahlia Lounge, opened this more casual restaurant in early 1995. Salmon, ling cod, halibut, catfish, lobster, and sturgeon are but a few of the seasonal offerings, and touches of Asia, the Southwest, and the Mediterranean are likely to appear in their preparation. For a splurge try the wok-fried whole Dungeness crab with ginger lemongrass sauce. Non-fish items also available. **FYI:** Reservations recommended. No smoking. **Open:** Daily 11am–midnight. **Prices:** Main courses $8–$21. AE, CB, DC, DISC, MC, V.

Fullers
In Seattle Sheraton Hotel and Towers, 1400 6th Ave (Downtown); tel 206/447-5544. **Eclectic/Northwest.** Award-winning chef Monique Barbeau brings a new exuberance to the bill of fare here. Her extensive travels infuse her cooking with international influences, and there's not a boring dish on the menu. Items include mushroom-stuffed, juniper-spiced quail, saltimbocca with seasonal fish, fire and ice prawn cocktail, and savory-spiced venison. The sleek dining room is rimmed by cozy semicircular booths, suitable for two to four people. **FYI:** Reservations recommended. No smoking. **Open:** Lunch Mon–Fri 11:30am–2pm; dinner Mon–Sat 5:30–10pm. **Prices:** Main courses $18–$24; prix fixe $49. AE, CB, DC, DISC, MC, V. VP

The Georgian Room
In Four Seasons Olympic Seattle, 411 University St (Downtown); tel 206/621-1700. Downtown at Rainier Square. **Pacific Northwest.** Dining rooms don't come much grander than this, even in the Europe that inspired The Georgian Room. The two-story, high '20s masterpiece is now exquisitely restored and bedecked with English Renaissance chandeliers, paneled oak, arched windows, and arched mirrors. Widely spaced tables are separated by dividers and planters. Fortunately, the cuisine matches the grandeur of the room in the skilled hands of Kerry Sear, British-born and -trained but now a devotee of Pacific produce. Hence his signature dish: The Georgian Thick Cut Smoked Salmon, smoked right in the kitchen and served with Washington apples with apple brandy sauce. Other regional accents include Northwest raw oysters on the half-shell and Dungeness crab bisque with baked artichoke among the appetizers; baked halibut with grilled sunchokes and vegetable scrolls with butterbean sauce over smoked eggplant noodles; and local nectarberries for dessert. The wine list is equally imposing, with some prices as high as the ceilings. Service is informed and considerate (servers refer to guests by name, and the maitre d' may recharge a glass of house wine "because the salmon is so large"), and the pianist plays quietly—but purists may bemoan the popping of flashbulbs. **FYI:** Reservations recommended. Piano. Children's menu. Jacket required. **Open:** Breakfast daily 6–11am; dinner Mon–Sat 6–11pm. **Prices:** Main courses $22–$36; prix fixe $50–$65. AE, CB, DC, ER, MC, V. VP

The Hunt Club
In the Sorrento Hotel, 900 Madison St (First Hill); tel 206/622-6400. A few blocks from Downtown. **Northwest.** Turn-of-the-century elegance handsomely restored in four intimate rooms with polished mahogany, louvered shutters, and burgundy banquettes. Festively presented dishes by top chef Eric S Lenard include steamed Lopez Island mussels, Pacific swordfish loin roasted in an almond and bread crust, spiced glazed breast of African pheasant, and rosemary-and-alder-wood-smoked rack of Ellensburg lamb. Fine wine list at moderate prices. Attentive, professional service, but sometimes grating pop music from the '40s and '50s. **FYI:** Reservations recommended. Dress code. **Open:** Breakfast Mon–Fri 7–10am, Sat–Sun 7am–2:30pm; lunch Mon–Fri 11am–2:30pm; dinner Sun–Thurs 5:30–10:30pm, Fri–Sat 5:30–11pm. **Prices:** Main courses $18–$25. AE, DC, MC, V. VP

Huong Binh
1207 S Jackson St (International District); tel 206/720-4907. **Vietnamese.** The very friendly and accommodating owners named their restaurant for the river and mountains of their hometown in central Vietnam, and they strive for authenticity in the cuisine. Specialties include grilled shrimp on sugar cane with rice vermicelli; charbroiled pork with rice noodles; and Saifun noodle soup with seafood, pork, and pork liver. Plastic ivy hangs around the perimeter of the simple dining

room. **FYI:** Reservations not accepted. No liquor license. **Open:** Daily 9am–8pm. **Prices:** Main courses $5–$6. No CC. ♿

Il Bistro
93-A Pike St (Pike Place Market); tel 206/682-3049. **Italian.** This dark, cozy hideaway below Pike Place Market has a great bar, active until 2am almost every night (single-malt scotch a specialty; cigar smokers welcomed). Rustic Italian food, with grilled meats being a good bet, especially rack of lamb. Late-night menu during week. **FYI:** Reservations recommended. No smoking. **Open:** Sun–Thurs 5:30–10pm, Fri–Sat 5:30–11pm. **Prices:** Main courses $10.50–$26.95. AE, CB, DC, MC, V. ♿

I Love Sushi
1001 Fairview Ave N (Lake Union); tel 206/625-9604. **Japanese.** Enjoy very good sushi along with a pretty view of boats bobbing on Lake Union. Try any of the inventive combinations rolled in seaweed wrappers, such as the namesake "I Love Sushi" roll (with eel, shrimp, avocado, cucumber, and flying-fish eggs). The Bellevue location has a lounge with karaoke open until 2am. **FYI:** Reservations accepted. Additional location: 11818 NE 8th, Bellevue (tel 454-5706). **Open:** Lunch Mon–Fri 11:30am–2:30pm; dinner Mon–Thurs 5–10:30pm, Fri–Sat 5–11pm, Sun 5–10pm. **Prices:** Main courses $7–$18. MC, V. ♿

Ivar's Acres of Clams
Pier 54 (Waterfront); tel 206/624-6852. **Seafood.** Of the three waterfront restaurants that bear Seattle legend Ivar Haglund's name, this one is the flashiest. Its Pier 54 location is surrounded by lots of boating and shipping activity, guaranteed to keep the kids entertained (as will the menu masks). The seafood is fresh and reliably prepared, as are the chicken and meat entrees for non–fish lovers. **FYI:** Reservations recommended. Children's menu. **Open:** Peak (Mem Day–Labor Day) daily 11am–11pm. **Prices:** Main courses $11–$19. AE, MC, V. ♿

Ivar's Salmon House
401 NE Northlake Way (Lake Union); tel 206/632-0767. **Seafood.** Sweeping Seattle and Lake Union views complement the house specialty: seasonal fresh salmon, cooked over an open fire pit on green alder wood in the traditional Native American style. Non-seafood items are also available. The building, designed in the manner of the Native American long-house, is so authentic that it was granted landmark status within two years of its opening. Smoking allowed only in the lounge. **FYI:** Reservations recommended. Children's menu. No smoking. **Open:** Peak (June–Labor Day) lunch Mon–Fri 11:30am–4pm, Sat noon–4pm; dinner Mon–Sat 4–11pm, Sun 4–10pm; brunch Sun 10am–2pm. **Prices:** Main courses $12–$20; prix fixe $13–$24. AE, MC, V. ♿

Kamon on Lake Union
1177 Fairview Ave (Lake Union); tel 206/622-4665. **Japanese.** Millions of dollars went into the creation of this restaurant in 1988, and it still retains much of its gloss. The big circular room affords fabulous views of the lake, downtown, and Queen Anne hill. Done in soothing pinks and mauves, the interior features a long sushi bar and teppanyaki bar, as well as a dining room and an outdoor deck. The large menu roams from traditional Japanese fare to pasta with smoked scallops. **FYI:** Reservations recommended. Piano. No smoking. **Open:** Peak (May–Sept) lunch Mon–Fri 11:30am–2:30pm; dinner Mon–Thurs 5–10pm, Fri–Sat 5–11pm, Sun 5–9:30pm. **Prices:** Main courses $12–$27. AE, CB, DC, MC, V. ♿

Kaspar's
19 W Harrison St (Lower Queen Anne); tel 206/298-0123. **Northwest.** An elegant, spacious spot offering one of the most gracious dining experiences in Seattle. Swiss-born chef/owner Kaspar Donier excels in preparing the bounty of the Northwest using classic, European culinary techniques. International influences abound, and Donier is as adept with delicate fish as he is with heartier dishes like lamb shanks. Save room for dessert: they are all delicious and made in-house. Menu changes seasonally. Bar open 4:30–10pm. **FYI:** Reservations recommended. No smoking. **Open:** Tues–Thurs 5–9pm, Fri–Sat 5–10pm. **Prices:** Main courses $14–$19. AE, MC, V. VP ♿

Lampreia
2400 1st Ave (Belltown); tel 206/443-3301. **Eclectic.** Chef/owner Scott Carlsberg embraces a minimalist approach to both cooking and presentation. A stickler for using the freshest, best-quality ingredients (including organically grown produce), he created a brief four-course menu to showcase his fine efforts and abilities: appetizers, intermezzo, main course, and a cheese course comprise the selections. The menu changes monthly but usually features lamb, beef, game, and fish. An expertly chosen wine list is well matched to the cuisine, as is the understated but elegant decor. **FYI:** Reservations recommended. No smoking. **Open:** Tues–Sat 5:30–10pm. **Prices:** Main courses $18–$23; prix fixe $28–$32. AE, MC, V. ♿

Le Gourmand
425 NW Market St (Ballard); tel 206/784-3463. **French.** The newly remodeled dining room at Le Gourmand is reminiscent of the French countryside, with a large mural depicting an alder grove and wildflowers. The decor provides a soothing setting for the deeply satisfying food: roasted rack of lamb with chestnuts and pears, poached king salmon fillet with gooseberries and dill, and blintzes filled with goat cheese in a chive butter sauce. **FYI:** Reservations recommended. Beer and wine only. No smoking. **Open:** Wed–Sat 5:30pm–midnight. **Prices:** Prix fixe $18–$28. AE, MC, V. ♿

($) Macheezmo Mouse
425 Queen Anne Ave N; tel 206/282-9904. **Tex-Mex.** A fast-growing Northwest chain offering healthy, no-frills Tex-Mex. All foods are baked, grilled, or steamed—never fried—and

no animal fats or tropical oils are used. Burritos, enchiladas, quesadillas, and salads make up the bulk of the menu. The fresh, tasty ingredients are brightened by lively salsas. Bright, hard surfaces, paper plates and cups make this a good place to take kids. **FYI:** Reservations not accepted. Children's menu. Beer and wine only. No smoking. Additional location: 701 5th Ave (tel 382-1730). **Open:** Mon–Sat 11am–10pm, Sun noon–10pm. **Prices:** Main courses $4–$6. MC, V.

Macrina Bakery & Cafe
2408 1st Ave (Belltown); tel 206/448-4032. **Mediterranean.** Regarded as one of Seattle's best bread makers, Leslie Mackie has expanded her bakery to include a Mediterranean-style taverna. Breakfast consists of baked goods, granola, and yogurt, while lunch features *meze*—a Middle Eastern word meaning "little dishes." On the dinner menu, choices might include duck confit or grilled quail with raclette crostini and thyme-potato gnocchi in a wild mushroom and tomato sauce. **FYI:** Reservations accepted. Beer and wine only. No smoking. **Open:** Breakfast Mon–Fri 7–11am, Sat 7am–noon; lunch Mon–Fri 11am–3pm, Sat noon–4pm; dinner Wed–Sat 6–9:30pm. **Prices:** Main courses $9–$14; prix fixe $17–$23. MC, V.

Marco's Supperclub
2510 1st Ave (Belltown); tel 206/441-7801. **Eclectic.** The eclectic decor—dark wood, textured cement table tops, and assorted bric-a-brac—gives Marco's a cozy if slightly demented feeling. Inventive menu items include jerk chicken; Japanese-inspired tuna over soba noodles; grilled sea scallops in a salad with red curry dressing; and papardelle topped with grilled endive, red onion and radicchio. The wine list is short, but has lots of unusual choices that are wonderfully matched to the menu. **FYI:** Reservations recommended. Children's menu. **Open:** Dinner Sun–Thurs 5:30–11pm, Fri–Sat 5:30pm–midnight; brunch Sun 10am–2pm. **Prices:** Main courses $9–$15. AE, MC, V.

McCormick & Schmick's
1103 1st Ave (Downtown); tel 206/623-5500. **Seafood.** Dark wood paneling, white linen, flickering lanterns, bow-tied waiters, and secluded booths add to this restaurant's old-fashioned atmosphere. The fresh seafood, however, is prepared in a contemporary, West Coast style. There's a new menu each day, with dozens of choices. During Happy Hour, a bar menu features food items for $1.95. **FYI:** Reservations recommended. **Open:** Mon–Fri 11:30am–11pm, Sat 5–11pm, Sun 5–10pm. **Prices:** Main courses $9–$20. AE, CB, DC, DISC, MC, V.

McCormick's Fish House and Bar
722 4th Ave (Downtown); tel 206/682-3900. **Seafood.** Done in classic fish-house style, with maple-top tables and mahogany booths, McCormick's boasts over 36 varieties of fresh Northwest seafood. The menu changes daily to take advantage of the fresh catch. A special $1.95 bar menu is offered daily from 3:30pm to 6:30pm, and 10pm to midnight. **FYI:** Reservations recommended. Children's menu. **Open:** Mon–Thurs 11:30am–11pm, Fri 11:30am–midnight, Sat 4:30pm–midnight, Sun 4:30–11pm. **Prices:** Main courses $10–$20. AE, CB, DC, DISC, MC, V.

Metropolitan Grill
818 2nd Ave (Downtown); tel 206/624-3287. **Steak.** Steaks are the highlight at this dimly lit, clubby restaurant where the high-backed booths ensconce lawyers, brokers, and other high-stakes players from the nearby financial district. Steaks and chops are thick, well aged, and done to order; to complement your choice, you might want to try the savory herbed au jus offered by your waiter. After dinner, belly up to the bar or enjoy a good cigar with a snifter of cognac. **FYI:** Reservations recommended. **Open:** Lunch Mon–Fri 11am–3:30pm; dinner Mon–Fri 5–11pm, Sat 4:30–11pm, Sun 4:30–10pm. **Prices:** Main courses $11–$30. AE, CB, DC, DISC, MC, V. VP

Nikko
In Westin Hotel Seattle, 1900 5th Ave (Downtown); tel 206/322-4641. **Japanese.** Along with a decor dominated by natural woods carved into bold geometric patterns, Nikko offers a full panoply of traditional and modern Japanese dishes. Chefs take advantage of fresh local seafood to create exquisitely prepared sushi, teppanyaki, sukiyaki, and more. Diners can settle in at the sushi bar or in the dining or tatami rooms. The wine list includes 20 sakes and plum wines; Japanese beers and Northwest microbrews are also offered. **FYI:** Reservations recommended. **Open:** Peak (May–Sept) Mon–Sat 5:30–10:30pm. **Prices:** Main courses $15–$20. AE, CB, DC, MC, V. VP

The Painted Table
In Alexis Hotel Seattle, 1007 1st Ave (Downtown); tel 206/624-4844. **Eclectic.** Hand-painted platters on the tables, original art on the walls, flourishes of art deco on the lamps and furnishings—and a creative touch in the kitchen. Among chef Tim Kelley's provocative dishes are grilled five-spice Oregon quail, lemongrass-cured salmon with pickled lotus root, vegetable radiatoni pasta, and Mongolian barbecue loin pork with egg noodle and scallion cake. Unfortunately, the unfocused service doesn't do justice to the kitchen. **FYI:** Reservations recommended. Piano. No smoking. **Open:** Breakfast Mon–Fri 6:30–10am, Sat–Sun 7:30am–midnight; lunch Mon–Fri 11:30am–2pm; dinner daily 5:30–10pm. **Prices:** Main courses $11.95–$19.95; prix fixe $45. AE, DC, DISC, MC, V. VP

Paragon
2125 Queen Anne Ave N (Queen Anne Hill); tel 206/283-4548. **New American.** Modeled after the Paragon Bar & Grill in San Francisco, Seattle's version is an informal neighborhood restaurant with music four to five nights a week. The front of the handsome space is dominated by a large mirrored bar; whimsical rusty metal sculptures and "aged" plaster wall treatments highlighted by a 20-foot mixed-media mural make

a dramatic setting for wall-to-wall crowds. The main dining room is in the rear and seats about 65. Crispy calamari salad, shrimp kataifi with sweet chili sauce, and seared ahi tuna niçoise salad are dishes to try. Serious diners may want to eat early to avoid the late night madness. Bar is open until 2am. **FYI:** Reservations not accepted. Blues/jazz/reggae/rock. **Open:** Mon–Sat 5:30–10pm, Sun 10am–2pm. **Prices:** Main courses $9–$12. MC, V.

Pescatore
5300 NW 34th Ave (Ballard); tel 206/784-1733. **Italian/Seafood.** Stunningly decorated eatery featuring magnificent views of the boat traffic along the canal from practically every table. The covered and heated patio is a definite plus, given Seattle's unpredictable weather, but the food sometimes has a hard time living up to the spectacular surroundings. Pasta, wood-fired pizzas, and caesar salad are all good choices, although side dishes can be undistinguished. Hopefully, time will smooth out the rough edges. **FYI:** Reservations recommended. Children's menu. No smoking. **Open:** Lunch Mon–Sat 11am–3pm; dinner Mon–Thurs 3–10pm, Fri–Sat 3–10:30pm, Sun 4–10pm; brunch Sun 9am–2pm. **Prices:** Main courses $9–$22. AE, DISC, MC, V. VP

Pirosmani
2216 Queen Anne Ave N; tel 206/285-3360. **Mediterranean/Georgian.** Chef and co-owner Laura Dewell spent a year in Georgia (formerly part of the USSR) and came back steeped in its culture and eager to present its cuisine. The restaurant is decorated with reproductions of paintings by Georgian artist Niko Pirosmani, who painted murals in restaurants in exchange for meals. The food here would make him feel right at home. Good choices are khinkali (pork and beet dumplings seasoned with mint, onion, green pepper, and paprika) and khachapuri (round bread filled with mozzarella and feta cheese). Other notable entrees include duck Satsivi and tuna with muhammara sauce. **FYI:** Reservations recommended. Beer and wine only. No smoking. **Open:** Tues–Sat 5:30–10pm. **Prices:** Main courses $16–$22. AE, CB, DC, DISC, MC, V.

Pizzeria Pagliacci
426 Broadway Ave E (Capitol Hill); tel 206/324-0730. **Italian.** Seattle's East Coast–style pizzeria. The ingredients are fresh and the dough is made in-house. Salads, calzones, and lasagna are available, too. **FYI:** Reservations not accepted. Beer and wine only. No smoking. Additional locations: 4529 University Way NE (tel 632-0421); 550 Queen Anne Ave N (tel 285-1232). **Open:** Sun–Thurs 11am–11pm, Fri–Sat 11am–1am. **Prices:** Main courses $8–$17. MC, V.

Place Pigalle
81 Pike Place (Pike Place Market); tel 206/624-1756. **Eclectic.** Tucked behind Pike Place Market, Place Pigalle occupies a perch overlooking Elliott Bay and the Olympic Mountains. Seafood is the focus of a menu that changes seasonally, and also includes meat and game specialties. (Mussels Pigalle and calamari dijonnaise are perennial favorites.) The tiny bar stocks more than 200 brands, including a vast selection of eaux de vie. **FYI:** Reservations recommended. **Open:** Lunch Mon–Fri 11:30am–3pm, Sat 11am–3:30pm; dinner Mon–Thurs 5:30–10pm, Fri 6–11pm, Sat 6–10:30pm. **Prices:** Main courses $15–$20. MC, V. VP

Ponti Seafood Grill
3014 3rd Ave N (Fremont); tel 206/284-3000. **Seafood.** Spacious, canalside restaurant tucked under the Fremont Bridge. Chef Alvin Binuya displays a delicate hand with seafood and is fond of introducing Asian, Italian, and Southwest flavors. Typical offerings include Dungeness crabmeat ravioli; and lobster stew with mussels, coconut milk, tomato, ginger, and cilantro pesto. A few meat and poultry selection are offered. The wine list is extensive and international in scope. **FYI:** Reservations recommended. Children's menu. No smoking. **Open:** Lunch Mon–Sat 11:30am–2:30pm; dinner Sun–Thurs 5–10pm, Fri–Sat 5–11pm; brunch Sun 10am–2:30pm. **Prices:** Main courses $14–$24. AE, CB, DC, MC, V. VP

Queen City Grill
2201 1st Ave (Belltown); tel 206/443-0975. **Northwest.** Simple preparation highlights the fresh Northwest ingredients used here. Cozy, high-backed booths create an intimate ambience at some tables, although the bar (which dominates half the room) is usually packed. Seafood is done particularly well here. Bar open until 2am. **FYI:** Reservations recommended. **Open:** Mon–Fri 11:30am–11pm, Sat–Sun 4:30pm–midnight. **Prices:** Main courses $10–$20. AE, CB, DC, DISC, MC, V.

★ Ray's Boathouse
6049 NW Seaview Ave (Ballard); tel 206/789-3770. **Seafood.** One of the most spectacular water views of any Seattle restaurant. An institution for over 20 years, Ray's is famous for serving the freshest fish, simply prepared. Ray's Cafe (on the second floor) includes a lounge, outdoor deck, and a more casual dining area. Special three-course "Early Bite" menu (Mon–Fri 5–6pm) is an inexpensive way to enjoy early sunsets. An extensive, award-winning wine list focuses on Northwest producers. **FYI:** Reservations recommended. No smoking. **Open:** Lunch daily 11:30am–2:30pm; dinner Mon–Thurs 5–10pm, Fri 5–10:30pm, Sat 4:30–10:30pm, Sun 4:30–10pm. **Prices:** Main courses $10.95–$19.95. AE, CB, DC, DISC, MC, V. VP

Reiner's
1106 8th Ave (Downtown); tel 206/624-2222. **International.** This intimate dining room has all the trappings of a grand European-style hotel dining room. Be prepared to be pampered by Reiner Greubel and wife Flavia, who preside over the kitchen and front of the house, respectively. Specialties include house smoked salmon, crab cakes, rack of lamb, calves' liver, and sweetbreads. **FYI:** Reservations recommend-

ed. No smoking. **Open:** Tues–Thurs 5–9pm, Fri–Sat 5–10pm. Closed Jan. **Prices:** Main courses $15–$22. AE, MC, V.

Rover's
2808 E Madison (Madison Valley); tel 206/325-7442. **French.** Highly regarded owner/chef Thierry Rautureau combines classic French technique and Northwest style to produce a visually stunning contemporary cuisine. The main menu features foie gras, game, lobster, and fish, and the prix fixe menu is both a tour de force and a great value. The small wine list offers several half-bottles. Expect a long wait for courtyard dining in fine weather. **FYI:** Reservations recommended. Beer and wine only. No smoking. **Open:** Tues–Sat 5:30–10pm. **Prices:** Main courses $23–$26. AE, DC, MC, V.

★ Saleh al Lago
6804 E Green Lake Way N (Green Lake); tel 206/524-4044. **Italian.** Genial host Saleh Joudah works the bright, multilevel dining room the old-fashioned way, hopping from table to table to greet old friends and newcomers alike. The food here is rich and wonderful: Fine choices are vitello quatro formaggi; mushroom-stuffed ravioli in roasted-garlic and tomato butter; sautéed calamari; and the various risotti. **FYI:** Reservations recommended. No smoking. **Open:** Lunch Mon–Fri 11:30am–1:30pm; dinner Mon–Sat 5:30–9:30pm. **Prices:** Main courses $14–$19. AE, CB, DC, MC, V.

Siam on Broadway
616 Broadway (Capitol Hill); tel 206/324-0892. **Thai.** A countryside ambience pervades this pretty dining room done in pinks, blues, and mauves and lined with vivid tropical-fish tanks. The extensive menu offers traditional Thai dishes prepared to your chosen degree of hotness. Favorites are Siam Special orange beef, and classic pad thai. Homemade coconut ice cream for dessert. **FYI:** Reservations accepted. Beer and wine only. No smoking. Additional location: 1880 Fairview Ave E (tel 323-8101). **Open:** Mon–Thurs 11:30am–10pm, Fri 11:30am–11pm, Sat 5–11pm, Sun 5–10pm. **Prices:** Main courses $6–$10. AE, MC, V.

Sostanza
1927 43rd Ave N (Madison Park); tel 206/324-9701. **French/Italian.** The roaring fire in the main dining room sets off the pumpkin-colored walls and rustic decor of this neighborhood eatery. The frequently changing menu takes advantage of seasonal ingredients. Fresh seafood, meat, game, pasta, risotto, and free-range chicken are usually among the selections. **FYI:** Reservations recommended. Beer and wine only. No smoking. **Open:** Lunch Mon–Fri 11:30am–2:30pm; dinner Mon–Sat 5:30–10:30pm. **Prices:** Prix fixe $18–$26. AE, MC, V.

Szmania's
3321 W McGraw St (Magnolia); tel 206/284-7305. **Continental/German.** A casual neighborhood place with an open kitchen for a convivial feel. The German-born chef specializes in continental cuisine with Northwest and Pacific Rim overtones. King salmon in potato crust with olive pesto is a signature dish, as is Jaegerschnitzel with spatzle. Meals can be served at the bar. **FYI:** Reservations recommended. Children's menu. No smoking. **Open:** Lunch Tues–Fri 11:30am–2pm; dinner Tues–Thurs 5–9:30pm, Fri–Sat 5–10pm, Sun 5–9:30pm. **Prices:** Main courses $9–$20. AE, CB, DC, MC, V.

Trattoria Mitchelli
84 Yesler Way (Pioneer Square); tel 206/623-3883. **Italian.** This bohemian restaurant in Pioneer Square—Seattle's "old town"—attracts a motley crowd who enjoy dining on the veal and pasta dishes. Breakfast ranges from ham and eggs to Italian specialties. Reservations accepted for parties of six or more; smoking allowed in the bar only. **FYI:** Reservations not accepted. Children's menu. No smoking. **Open:** Mon 7am–11pm, Tues–Fri 7am–4am, Sat 8am–4am, Sun 8am–11pm. **Prices:** Main courses $6–$13. AE, DISC, MC, V.

Un Deux Trois
1329 1st Ave (Pike Place Market); tel 206/233-0123. **Cafe/French.** Sun-drenched Provençale colors heighten the cheery atmosphere of this pretty cafe near Pike Place Market. The menu includes continental-style breakfasts and sturdier bistro fare for lunch and dinner. Roast chicken flavored with pancetta and herbes de Provence is delightfully moist inside and crisp outside; salads are inventive and fresh-tasting. Dinner entrees may include poached salmon, beef tenderloin, or even grilled lamb or rabbit pot pie. For dessert, crème brûlée or a plate of fresh fruit and cheese is the perfect finish. **FYI:** Reservations accepted. Beer and wine only. No smoking. **Open:** Peak (June–Aug) Mon–Thurs 9:30am–9:30pm, Fri–Sat 9:30am–10:30pm, Sun 11am–9pm. **Prices:** Main courses $9–$16. AE, MC, V.

Wild Ginger Asian Restaurant & Satay Bar
1400 Western Ave (Downtown); tel 206/623-4450. **Southeast Asian.** Located near Pike Place Market, this is considered by many to be the best Asian restaurant in Seattle. Polished mahogany warms the large open space that includes a dining area, satay bar, and liquor bar. Satay—meaning foods that are skewered and grilled—are a specialty, with over a dozen selections typically available. Entrees also include various curries, fragrant crispy duck, and Dungeness crab prepared several ways. Attracts an animated late-night bar crowd. **FYI:** Reservations recommended. Jazz. **Open:** Lunch Mon–Sat 11:30am–3pm; dinner Mon–Thurs 5–11pm, Fri 5pm–midnight, Sat 4:30pm–midnight, Sun 4:30–11pm. **Prices:** Main courses $8–$17. AE, CB, DC, DISC, MC, V.

ATTRACTIONS

TOP ATTRACTIONS

Seattle Center
305 Harrison St; tel 206/684-7200. Built for Seattle's World's Fair in 1962, this 74-acre amusement park and

cultural center stands on the north edge of downtown at the end of the monorail line. The most visible landmark in the city—the Space Needle—provides an outstanding panorama of the city from its observation deck. The center also includes Fun Forest (with plenty of rides and games for kids), the Pacific Science Center, the Seattle Center Opera House (home of the Seattle Opera Association, Pacific Northwest Ballet, and the Seattle Symphony), Seattle Repertory Theatre, and the Coliseum (where the NBA Supersonics hold court during basketball season). **Open:** Mem Day–Labor Day, Mon–Sat 11am–8pm, Sun 11am–7pm; Labor Day–Mem Day, Sun–Thurs 9am–9pm, Fri–Sat 9am–midnight. Closed Dec 25. **Free**

The Space Needle
219 4th Ave N; tel 206/443-2111 or toll free 800/937-9582. Erected for the 1962 World's Fair, this 600-foot-tall tower is the most popular tourist attraction in Seattle. At 518 feet above ground level, the views from the observation deck are stunning. Displays identify more than 60 sites and activities in the Seattle area. Two revolving restaurants. **Open:** Daily 8am–midnight. **$$$**

MUSEUMS

Museum of Flight
9404 E Marginal Way S; tel 206/764-5720. A cavernous repository of some of history's most famous planes, including a replica of the Wright Brothers' first glider. This six-story glass-and-steel building holds most of the museum's permanent collection. Highlights include "Apollo," a comprehensive exhibit on the US space program; and the Challenger Learning Center, a participatory educational program. Viewing area lets visitors watch planes take off and land at the adjacent airport. **Open:** Fri–Wed 10am–5pm, Thurs 10am–9pm. **$$$**

Museum of History and Industry
2700 24th Ave E; tel 206/324-1126. Re-created storefronts provide glimpses into the lives of Seattle residents of a hundred years ago. There's also a Boeing mail plane from the 1920s; an exhibit on the Great Fire of 1880; a collection of toys, games, and model ships; and various touring exhibitions. Admission is free on Tuesdays. **Open:** Daily 10am–5pm. Closed some hols. **$$$**

Seattle Aquarium
Pier 59, Waterfront Park; tel 206/386-4320. From the underwater viewing dome, visitors get a fish's-eye view of life beneath the waves. There's a coral-reef tank populated with sharks, a Touch Tank that allows visitors to touch sea stars and featherduster worms, an exhibit on pollution in Puget Sound, and an interactive tide-pool exhibit and discovery lab. In late summer and early autumn, salmon return to spawn in the aquarium's salmon ladder. **Open:** Mem Day–Labor Day, daily 10am–7pm; Labor Day–Mem Day, daily 10am–5pm. **$$$**

Pacific Science Center
200 2nd Ave N; tel 206/443-2001. Dozens of hands-on exhibits—addressing the biological sciences, physics, and chemistry—allow kids to learn how their bodies work, blow giant bubbles, put on shows, build a dam, and play in a rocketship. The Tech Zone allows visitors to experience virtual reality, create and star in their own coffee commercial, and play tic-tac-toe with a 10-foot-tall robot. Recent temporary exhibits have included "The World of Giant Insects" and "Star Trek: Federation Science." There's also a planetarium and an IMAX theater (additional admission fee for each). **Open:** Mon–Fri 10am–5pm, Sat–Sun 10am–6pm. Closed some hols. **$$$**

Seattle Art Museum
Volunteer Park; tel 206/625-8901. Some find this museum's limestone, terra cotta and marble facade tastelessly bland, while others claim it is refreshingly minimalist. No matter what you think of the five-story building (designed by noted architects Robert Venturi and Denise Scott), it makes a perfect backdrop for the museum's most public work of art: Jonathon Borofsky's *Hammering Man,* a giant black-steel sculpture.

Inside, you'll find one of the nation's premier collections of Northwest Coast Native American art and artifacts, and equally large collections of African and Asian art. The top floor houses the museum's collection of European and American art, Northwest modern art, and photography and prints. Library, gift shop, cafe, guided tours. **Open:** Tues–Wed 10am–5pm, Thurs 10am–9pm, Fri–Sun 10am–5pm. Closed Dec 25. **$$$**

Burke Museum
17th Ave NE and NE 45th St; tel 206/543-5590. Located on the northwest corner of the University of Washington campus, this museum features exhibits on the natural and cultural heritage of the Pacific Rim. It is noteworthy primarily for its Northwest Native American art collection, including ceremonial masks, baskets, and six full-size canoes. An ethnobotanical garden displays plants used by Northwestern tribes. **Open:** Daily 10am–5pm. Closed some hols. **$**

Charles and Emma Frye Art Museum
704 Terry Ave (First Hill); tel 206/622-9250. Most of the paintings in this small museum date from the second half of the 19th century and are primarily by European artists, but there are also selected works by 19th-century Americans and the prolific Wyeth family. **Open:** Mon–Sat 10am–5pm, Sun noon–5pm. Closed some hols. **Free**

Wing Luke Asian Museum
407 7th Ave S (International District); tel 206/623-5124. Asian American culture, art, and history are explored at this museum in the heart of the International District. The emphasis is on the lives of immigrants in the Northwest; special exhibits help explain Asian customs to non-Asians. **Open:** Tues–Fri 11am–4:30pm, Sat–Sun noon–4pm. Closed some hols. **$**

Seattle Asian Art Museum
1400 E Prospect St (Capitol Hill); tel 206/654-3100. Located in the former home of the Seattle Art Museum (see above) in Volunteer Park. Thematic displays of Japanese, Chinese, Korean, Indian, Himalayan, and Southeast Asian art. Japanese-style tea garden (open weekends only), gift shop, cafe. A ticket purchased at this museum or at the Seattle Art Museum is good at the other museum within a two-day period. (Both museums offer free admission on the first Tuesday of each month.) **Open:** Tues–Wed 10am–5pm, Thurs 10am–9pm, Fri–Sun 10am–5pm. Closed Dec 25. **$$$**

Klondike Gold Rush National Historical Park
117 S Main St (Pioneer Square); tel 206/553-7220. Would-be miners heading up to the Klondike in the 1890s made Seattle their outfitting center. When they struck it rich up north, they headed back to Seattle—the first outpost of civilization—to unload their gold. This entire cycle made Seattle doubly rich and helped turn it into a prosperous city.

The visitors center, housed in Seattle's first bank building, contains artifacts and photographs chronicling America's last great gold rush, as well as videos and gold-panning demonstrations. Film buffs can even catch a free screening of Charlie Chaplin's great film *The Gold Rush* the first Sunday of each month. (Another unit of the park is located in Skagway, AK.) **Open:** Visitors center, daily 9am–5pm. Closed some hols. **Free**

The Center for Wooden Boats
1010 Valley St; tel 206/382-BOAT. Dedicated to the preservation of historic wooden boats, the center is unique in that many exhibits can be rented and taken out on Lake Union. There are rowboats and large and small sailboats, with rates ranging from $6–$15 per hour. Individual sailing instruction also available. **Open:** June–Aug, daily 11am–7pm; Sept–May, Wed–Mon noon–6pm. **$$$**

Ye Olde Curiosity Shop
Per 54, Alaskan Way; tel 206/682-5844. Crowded shop and erstwhile museum packed with Siamese-twin calves, a natural mummy, shrunken heads, and the like. **Open:** Sun–Thurs 9:30am–6pm, Fri–Sat 9am–9pm. **Free**

PARKS & GARDENS

Japanese Gardens
1502 Lake Washington Blvd; tel 206/684-4725. Located in the Washington Park Arboretum. This 3½-acre garden features a cherry orchard, brooks and streams, and a lake rimmed with Japanese irises and filled with *koi* fish. A special Tea Garden encloses a Tea House where, on the third Sunday of each month, visitors can attend a traditional Japanese tea ceremony. **Open:** Daily 10am–6pm. **$**

Washington Park Arboretum
2300 Arboretum Dr E; tel 206/325-4510. Within this 200-acre park, there are quiet trails surrounded by more than 5,000 varieties of plants, trees, and shrubs. The north end, a marshland housing ducks and herons, is popular with kayakers and canoeists. **Open:** Daily 8am–sunset. **Free**

Woodland Park Zoo
5500 Phinney Ave N; tel 206/684-4800. The impressive new elephant habitat here includes a tropical forest, pool, Thai logging camp, and an elephant house designed to resemble a Thai Buddhist temple. A lush tropical rain forest exhibit includes two separate gorilla habitats, and the African savannah habitat is equally grand. The zoo also includes a Family Farm, where kids can marvel at animal babies. **Open:** Mar 15–Oct 14, daily 9:30am–6pm; Oct 15–May 14 daily 9:30am–4pm. **$$$**

Volunteer Park
E Prospect St and 14th Ave E; tel 206/684-4743. Surrounded by the elegant mansions of Capitol Hill, this is a popular spot for sunbathing and playing Frisbee. A stately conservatory houses a large collection of tropical plants (including palm trees, orchids, and cacti) and a water tower offers gorgeous views of the city. **Open:** Daily sunrise–sunset. **Free**

OTHER ATTRACTIONS

Fifth Avenue Theatre
1308 5th Ave; tel 206/625-1900. First opened in 1926 as a vaudeville house, the theater is a loose re-creation of the imperial throne room in Beijing's Forbidden City. When vaudeville lost popularity, the opulent setting was used as a movie theater. After a renovation was undertaken in 1980, the theater once again opened as a venue for live stage performances. Since then, both national touring shows and the resident musical-theater company perform for Seattle audiences. Call for schedule. **$$$$**

Smith Tower Observatory
506 2nd Ave (Pioneer Square); tel 206/622-4004. Not as popular as the Space Needle, but still worth a trip. Great views of the city can be had from the top of this old-fashioned, 42-story skyscraper (which was the tallest building west of the Mississippi when it was built in 1914), plus there's the ride up in the brass-and-copper elevator with glass doors and an elevator operator. The observation deck is also known as the Chinese Room because its interior is made from Chinese hand-carved teakwood. **Open:** Daily 10am–10pm. Closed some hols. **$**

Tillicum Village
Blake Island Marine State Park; tel 206/443-1244. Northwest Native American culture comes alive at Tillicum Village, where locally produced, hand-carved totem poles stand vigil outside a huge cedar longhouse. Guests can enjoy a meal of alder-smoked salmon while watching traditional masked dances, then explore the surrounding forests and beaches. **Open:** May–Oct, daily. Call for schedule. **$$$$**

Hiram M Chittenden Locks
3015 NW 54th St; tel 206/783-7059. Mostly used by small boats, the locks are a popular spot for salmon watching. People watch salmon jumping up the cascades of a fish ladder as they return to spawn in the stream where they were born, and windows below the waterline give an even closer look. (The best months for salmon viewing are July and August.) **Open:** June–Aug, Mon–Fri 8am–8pm, Sat 9am–4pm; Sept–Dec and Mar–May, daily 8am–5pm. Closed some hols. **Free**

Pike Place Market
1st and Pike Sts (Downtown); tel 206/682-7453. Pike Place Market, founded in 1907, almost fell prey to a major redevelopment project in the early 1970s. However, a grass-roots movement to save the seven-acre market culminated in its being declared a National Historic District. Today the market is once again bustling, but the hundreds of farmers and fishmongers who set up shop here are only a small part of the attraction. There are excellent restaurants, booths selling the work of more than 200 local craftspeople and artists, and street performers to serenade the crowds. An information booth, below the large Pike Place Market sign, provides a free map and restaurant guide. **Open:** Market, Mon–Sat 9am–6pm, Sun 11am–5pm. Individual shop hours vary. Closed some hols. **Free**

GUIDED TOURS

Seattle Underground Tours
610 1st Ave; tel 206/682-1511. When a fire raged through downtown Seattle in 1889, city authorities had to start all over again. Part of their solution was to build on top of the old city, but today's visitors can still see parts of old Seattle on this fascinating 1½ hour tour. **$$$$**

Argosy/Seattle Harbor Tours
Pier 55, Ste 201; tel 206/623-1445. Learn about the history and geography of Seattle while enjoying magnificent views. Three different tours, ranging from 1 to 2½ hours in length, cover the city. The Seattle Harbor Tour includes downtown Seattle and the city skyline, the Lake Washington Tour cruises past beautiful waterfront homes with Mount Rainier as the backdrop, and the Locks Tour circles the entire Seattle peninsula, going through the **Hiram M Chittenden Locks** (see above). Longer four-hour cruises to **Tillicum Village** (see above) are also available. **Open:** Daily. Call for schedule. **$$$$**

Let's Go Sailing
Pier 56 (Waterfront); tel 206/624-3931. Tours of the Harbor and Elliott Bay on the 70-foot performance yacht *Obsession*. Harbor sailing excursions last 1½ hours and depart at approximately 11am, 1:30pm, and 4pm daily, while 2½ hour Sunset Sails depart generally between 6pm and 7pm daily (depending on sunset time). **Open:** May–Oct, daily 11am–7pm. **$$$$**

Seattle–Tacoma Int'l Airport

See also Renton

HOTELS

Hampton Inn
19445 International Blvd, Seattle, 98188; tel 206/878-1700 or toll free 800/HAMPTON; fax 206/824-0720. Just S of Sea-Tac Airport. Very well-maintained property set back from WA 99, although noise from adjacent airport can hardly be avoided. **Rooms:** 131 rms. CI 1pm/CO noon. Nonsmoking rms avail. Comfortable and clean. **Amenities:** A/C, cable TV w/movies, dataport. Free in-room movies. **Services:** Free local phone calls. **Facilities:** 30 **Rates (CP):** Peak (May–Sept 5) $69–$71 S; $79–$81 D. Children under age 18 stay free. Lower rates off-season. Parking: Outdoor, free. Senior discounts avail. AE, DC, DISC, MC, V.

Holiday Inn Seattle—Renton
800 Rainier Ave S, Renton, 98055 (Renton Village); tel 206/226-7700 or toll free 800/521-1412; fax 206/271-2315. 5 mi E of Sea-Tac Airport at WA 167 and I-405. Although considered the quietest airport property, this is located in a busy, noisy intersection. The biggest asset is the mix of full-service facilities, including bars and restaurants, and efficient check-in. **Rooms:** 188 rms and stes. CI 3pm/CO 1pm. Nonsmoking rms avail. The 30 spacious rooms with king-size beds and sofas are popular with corporate travelers. **Amenities:** A/C, satel TV, dataport, voice mail. **Services:** **Facilities:** 300 2 restaurants, 2 bars (w/entertainment), whirlpool. Attractive pool and whirlpool in small courtyard. Panoramic view of South End Valley from Penthouse Lounge. **Rates:** Peak (May–Sept) $99–$109 S; $109–$119 D; $130–$140 ste. Extra person $10. Children under age 14 stay free. Lower rates off-season. Parking: Outdoor, free. Sweetheart packages avail. AE, CB, DC, DISC, JCB, MC, V.

Radisson Hotel
17001 Pacific Hwy S, Seattle, 98188; tel 206/244-6000 or toll free 800/333-3333; fax 206/248-1601. At 170th St. Older airport property with mature landscaping; court gardens offer pleasant, green respite after travel. **Rooms:** 165 rms and stes. Executive level. CI 3pm/CO noon. Nonsmoking rms avail. Spacious quarters, all with sofa and lots of counterspace. **Amenities:** A/C, cable TV w/movies, dataport, voice mail. Some units w/terraces. **Services:** Car-rental desk, masseur, babysitting. **Facilities:** 400 1 restaurant, 1 bar (w/entertainment), spa, sauna. **Rates:** Peak (June 15–Sept 15) $119–$139 S; $129–$149 D; $175 ste. Extra person $10. Children under age 18 stay free. Lower rates off-season. Parking: Outdoor, free. AE, CB, DC, DISC, JCB, MC, V.

UNRATED **Red Lion Hotel Seattle Airport**
18740 Pacific Hwy S, Seattle, 98188; tel 206/246-8600 or toll free 800/547-8010; fax 206/242-9727. Located on a busy street three blocks from the airport. **Rooms:** 850 rms and stes. CI 3pm/CO noon. Nonsmoking rms avail. **Amenities:** A/C, cable TV w/movies, refrig, dataport, voice mail. Some units w/terraces. **Services:** Car-rental desk, babysitting. **Facilities:** 2200 3 restaurants, 2 bars (w/entertainment), games rm, sauna, whirlpool, beauty salon. **Rates:** $59–$79 S; $67–$89 D; $450–$650 ste. Extra person $5. Children under age 18 stay free. Parking: Outdoor, free. AE, DC, DISC, MC, V.

Seattle Marriott Hotel
3201 S 176th St, Seattle, 98188; tel 206/241-2000 or toll free 800/643-5479; fax 206/248-0789. 1 block E of WA 99 at 176th St. This Marriott comes with an enormous atrium with fir and hemlock trees and a totem pole, as well as a large lap pool, a cafe, sitting areas, and a lounge. **Rooms:** 460 rms and stes. Executive level. CI 3pm/CO 1pm. Nonsmoking rms avail. **Amenities:** A/C, cable TV w/movies, dataport, voice mail. 1 unit w/fireplace. Ironing board and iron. **Services:** Twice-daily maid svce, car-rental desk, babysitting. **Facilities:** 650 1 restaurant, 1 bar, games rm, spa, sauna, whirlpool. **Rates:** Peak (June–Sept) $124 S or D; $195–$450 ste. Lower rates off-season. Parking: Outdoor, free. Weekend specials include a full breakfast for two. AE, CB, DC, DISC, ER, JCB, MC, V.

Westcoast Sea-Tac Hotel
182210 Pacific Hwy S, Seattle, 98188; tel 206/246-5535 or toll free 800/426-0670; fax 206/246-5535. Bland building, severely limited parking. **Rooms:** 146 rms and stes. Executive level. CI open/CO noon. Nonsmoking rms avail. **Amenities:** A/C, voice mail. Some units w/minibars. **Services:** VP **Facilities:** 200 1 restaurant, 1 bar (w/entertainment), sauna, steam rm, whirlpool. **Rates:** Peak (May–Sept) $200 ste. Extra person $10. Children under age 18 stay free. Lower rates off-season. Parking: Outdoor, free. AE, DC, DISC, MC, V.

MOTEL

UNRATED **Sea-Tac Airport Travelodge**
2900 S 192nd St, Seattle, 98188; tel 206/241-9292 or toll free 800/578-7878; fax 206/242-0681. A well-kept, three-story building with no elevator. **Rooms:** 104 rms. CI 3pm/CO noon. Nonsmoking rms avail. **Amenities:** A/C, cable TV w/movies. Some units w/terraces. Some rooms have refrigerator. **Services:** Car-rental desk. **Facilities:** Sauna. **Rates:** Peak (July–Sept 3) $34–$45 S; $39–$50 D. Children under age 12 stay free. Lower rates off-season. Parking: Outdoor, free. AE, CB, DC, DISC, JCB, MC, V.

Seaview

See Long Beach Peninsula

Sequim

See also Olympic National Park

A small coastal town known for the Dungeness Recreation Area, a 5½-mile-long natural sandspit jutting out into the Strait of Juan de Fuca. **Information:** Sequim-Dungeness Valley Chamber of Commerce, 1192 E Washington, PO Box 907, Sequim, 98382 (tel 360/683-6197).

MOTELS

Best Western Sequim Bay Lodge
268522 US 101, 98382; tel 360/683-0691 or toll free 800/622-0691; fax 360/683-3748. 3 mi E of Sequim. Convenient to 7 Cedars Casino and close to Sequim State Park. **Rooms:** 54 rms and stes. CI 3pm/CO 11am. Nonsmoking rms avail. **Amenities:** A/C, cable TV w/movies. Some units w/minibars, all w/terraces, some w/fireplaces, some w/whirlpools. 70% of rooms are air-conditioned. **Services:** Continental breakfast available Oct-Mar. Shuttle service to Sequim and 7 Cedars Casino-schedule varies seasonally. **Facilities:** 40 1 restaurant, 1 bar. 9-hole putting green. **Rates:** Peak (May–Sept) $67 S; $77 D; $87–$135 ste. Extra person $6. Children under age 18 stay free. Lower rates off-season. Parking: Outdoor, free. Golf packages with Dungeness Golf Course. AE, CB, DC, DISC, ER, JCB, MC, V.

Holiday Inn Express
1095 E Washington, 98382; tel 360/683-1775 or toll free 800/683-1775; fax 360/683-2698. E end of Sequim on US 101. The newest motel in Sequim, and the only one with an indoor swimming pool. Popular with groups and tourists due to proximity to Dungeness Wildlife Refuge and Olympic Game Farm. **Rooms:** 60 rms. Executive level. CI 3pm/CO noon. Nonsmoking rms avail. **Amenities:** A/C, cable TV w/movies. Some units w/whirlpools. Guests who stay five nights or more get use of microwave and small refrigerator. **Services:** **Facilities:** 30 Whirlpool, washer/dryer. **Rates (CP):** Peak (June–Labor Day) $69–$79 S or D. Extra person $10. Children under age 19 stay free. Lower rates off-season. Parking: Outdoor, free. AE, CB, DC, DISC, JCB, MC, V.

Sequim West Inn
740 W Washington St, 98382; tel 360/683-4144 or toll free 800/528-4527; fax 360/683-6452. At the W end of Sequim on US 101. Basic motel with warmly decorated rooms. Constantly upgrading exterior in southwest motif. Motel also rents mobile homes for vacationers. **Rooms:** 21 rms and stes. CI open/CO 11am. Nonsmoking rms avail. Refreshing decor with wood accents. **Amenities:** Cable TV, refrig. No

A/C. Ceiling fans, plus microwave and built-in refrigerator in small alcove near bedroom. **Services:** **Facilities:** Washer/dryer. RV park adjoins motel. **Rates:** Peak (May–Sept) $64–$71 S; $75 D; $95 ste. Lower rates off-season. Parking: Outdoor, free. Golf packages avail. AE, DC, DISC, MC, V.

RESTAURANTS

El Cazador
In Landmark Mall, 531 W Washington (Midtown); tel 360/683-4788. At 5th St. **Mexican.** Located at the base of a landmark grain elevator, this simple, no-frills Mexican has good prices and generous portions. Known for blueberry margaritas and fajitas. **FYI:** Reservations accepted. Children's menu. Additional location: 6051 60th NW, Oak Harbor (tel 206/675-6114). **Open:** Peak (May–Sept) Mon–Sat 11am–11pm, Sun noon–10pm. **Prices:** Main courses $3.50–$11.25. AE, DISC, MC, V.

Riptide
380 E Washington; tel 360/683-7244. E edge of town on US 101. **Seafood.** Basic family restaurant with adjoining sports bar. Known for reasonably priced seafood like crab cakes and fish-and-chips. **FYI:** Reservations accepted. Children's menu. **Open:** Sun–Thurs 7am–12am, Fri–Sat 7am–2am. **Prices:** Main courses $7–$15. AE, CB, DC, MC, V.

Silverdale

Located on the Kitsap Peninsula in the Puget Sound, near the US Navy's Trident Submarine Base. **Information:** Silverdale Chamber of Commerce, PO Box 1218, Silverdale, 98383 (tel 360/692-6800).

HOTEL

Silverdale on the Bay Resort Hotel
3073 Bucklin Hill Rd, 98383; tel 360/698-1000 or toll free 800/544-9799; fax 360/692-0932. N end of Dyes Inlet. 3 acres. A pleasant new lodging, in a rapidly growing area, offering scenic views and proximity to shopping areas. **Rooms:** 151 rms and stes. CI 3pm/CO noon. Nonsmoking rms avail. Most rooms have balconies featuring fine views of Dyes Inlet. **Amenities:** A/C, cable TV w/movies. Some units w/terraces, some w/fireplaces. **Services:** Car-rental desk, babysitting. **Facilities:** 500 1 restaurant, 1 bar (w/entertainment), 1 beach (cove/inlet), basketball, volleyball, games rm, lawn games, spa, sauna, whirlpool. Espresso bar off lobby. **Rates:** Peak (May 16–Oct 15) $75–$85 S; $85–$105 D; $195–$325 ste. Extra person $10. Children under age 18 stay free. Lower rates off-season. Parking: Outdoor, free. Romance and B&B packages avail. AE, CB, DC, DISC, ER, JCB, MC, V.

Skykomish

The chief western gateway to the Cascade Mountains. Nearby Wallace Falls State Park offers camping and other outdoor activities.

MOTEL

Sky River Inn
333 River Dr E, PO Box 280, 98228; tel 360/677-2261. Clean clapboard motel located along Skykomish River. Perfect for outdoors enthusiasts. Stevens Pass ski area is 16 miles away. **Rooms:** 17 rms, stes, and effic; 1 cottage/villa. CI 2pm/CO 11am. Some rooms have river view. No nonsmoking rooms—most need airing. **Amenities:** A/C, cable TV w/movies, refrig. Some units w/terraces. Not all TVs have remote control. **Services:** **Facilities:** **Rates:** Peak (Nov–Mar; May–Sept) $50–$53 S; $62–$71 D; $62–$71 ste; $56–$76 effic; $82–$91 cottage/villa. Extra person $3. Min stay peak. Lower rates off-season. Parking: Outdoor, free. AE, DISC, MC, V.

Snoqualmie

Transcontinental I-90 crosses the Cascade Mountains at Snoqualmie Pass, the home of four ski resorts and numerous guided snowshoe treks and cross-country ski trail heads. Summer recreation includes nature hikes and mountain biking.

LODGE

Salish Lodge
37807 SE Fall City–Snoqualmie Rd (WA 202), PO Box 1109, 98065; tel 206/888-2556 or toll free 800/826-6124; fax 206/888-2533. Perched atop 268-foot-high Snoqualmie Falls, this lodge combines excellent service, elegant dining, and spa luxury with old-fashioned country comforts. Highly romantic. **Rooms:** 91 rms and stes. Executive level. CI 4pm/CO noon. Nonsmoking rms avail. Look for homey touches such as wicker and Shaker furnishings, down comforters, and overstuffed pillows. **Amenities:** A/C, cable TV w/movies, dataport, bathrobes. All units w/minibars, some w/terraces, all w/fireplaces, all w/whirlpools. **Services:** VP Twice-daily maid svce, masseur, babysitting. In-room massages available. **Facilities:** 150 2 restaurants (*see* "Restaurants" below), 1 bar (w/entertainment), basketball, volleyball, spa, sauna, steam rm, whirlpool. New $1.2 million spa offers a range of massage treatments, as well as water therapy rooms, facials, manicures, and more. There's a cozy library where guests can read in front of a fireplace. Guests can hike to the foot of the falls or enjoy complimentary use of mountain bikes. **Rates:** Peak (June–Sept) $180–$295 S or D; $295–$575 ste. Extra person $25. Children under age 18 stay free. Lower rates off-season. Parking: Outdoor, free. AE, CB, DC, DISC, JCB, MC, V.

RESTAURANT

Salish Lodge Restaurant
37807 SE Fall City–Snoqualmie Rd (WA 202); tel 206/888-2556. **Northwest.** Large windows overlook 268-foot-high Snoqualmie Falls and intimate booths and individual tables give diners the feeling of privacy and warmth. The dinner menu highlights seafood and game. You may want to begin with crab cakes loaded on a crisp potato tower, then move on to entrees such as lightly smoked salmon or roasted pheasant stuffed with wild mushrooms. A six-course "Country Celebration Breakfast" features selections like king salmon and Dungeness crab. The wine list offers over 700 labels, including 100 different champagnes. **FYI:** Reservations recommended. Children's menu. No smoking. **Open:** Peak (June–Sept) daily 7am–10pm. **Prices:** Main courses $18–$29. AE, CB, DC, DISC, MC, V.

ATTRACTION

The Pass–Alpental, Snoqualmie, Ski Acres, Hyak
Mercer Island; tel 206/232-8182. The Pass's grand resort complex covers four different ski areas with a total of more than 12 miles of skiing. Serviced by 23 lifts and boasting a vertical lift of 14,000 feet, the Pass offers something for everyone. A comprehensive ski school, NASTAR racing, mitey mite and junior racing, and a nighttime racing league are available for skiiers, while snowboarders enjoy Snoqualmie's snowboard park and Hyak's half pipe. Other services include child care, shuttles, ski check, overnight parking, eight food and beverage locations, and equipment rental. Call 206/236-1600 for the latest information on snow conditions.

Summer at the Pass offers a multitude of hiking and mountain biking trails, with bike rental and instruction available. **Open:** Call for schedule. Open year-round. **$$$$**

Spokane

Built near the site of Spokane House, the first non-Native American settlement in the Pacific Northwest. In its early years, Spokane acted as a railroad link between the gold fields of Idaho and the Columbia River Basin; it is now the largest city in eastern Washington. The 1974 World's Fair was held on several islands in the Spokane River; the area has since been turned into the 100-acre Riverfront Park. Nearby Veradale, once an agricultural area, is now one of Spokane's suburbs. **Information:** Spokane Convention and Visitors Bureau, 926 W Sprague, Spokane, 99204 (tel 509/624-1341).

PUBLIC TRANSPORTATION

Spokane Transit provides service throughout Spokane. Route and schedule information is available at The Bus Shop at 510 W Riverside Ave or by calling 509/328-RIDE, or 456-4327 (TDD). Fares: 75¢; paratransit service 35¢; children under 5 ride free. Exact change required. Transfers are free.

HOTELS

Cavanaugh's Inn at the Park
303 N River Dr, 99201 (Downtown); tel 509/326-8000 or toll free 800/THE-INNS; fax 509/325-7329. Next to Spokane River and Riverfront Park. An elegant property in the heart of town. The well-appointed lobby is part of a large atrium complete with trees, flowering plants, a fireplace, overstuffed chairs, and an espresso cart. **Rooms:** 402 rms, stes, and effic. Executive level. CI 3pm/CO noon. Nonsmoking rms avail. Pool-side rooms are available. **Amenities:** A/C, cable TV w/movies, voice mail. Some units w/minibars, some w/terraces, some w/fireplaces, some w/whirlpools. Executive Wing rooms offer wet bars, honor bars. Deluxe suites have balconies and fireplaces. All suites have fluffy bathrobes. **Services:** Car-rental desk, social director, babysitting. **Facilities:** 800 2 restaurants (*see* "Restaurants" below), 2 bars (1 w/entertainment), sauna, whirlpool. Beautifully landscaped outdoor pool area has waterfall, water slide, and pool-side bar. Wild hoary marmots, which have homesteaded in burrows under the sculpted rock pool complex, are fun to watch and photograph. **Rates:** Peak (May 1–Oct 31) $80–$135 S; $90–$145 D; $170–$850 ste. Extra person $5. Children under age 16 stay free. Lower rates off-season. Parking: Outdoor, free. Rates vary by view and location. Golf, theater, and special holiday packages offered. AE, DC, DISC, ER, MC, V.

Courtyard by Marriott
401 Riverpoint Blvd, 99202 (Downtown); tel 509/456-7600 or toll free 800/321-2211; fax 509/456-0969. S bank of Spokane River; E of Division St Bridge. Caters to business folks and offers attractive room views. Centennial Trail is at back door. **Rooms:** 149 rms and stes. CI 4pm/CO 1pm. Nonsmoking rms avail. Interior rooms overlook the beautifully landscaped courtyard; exterior rooms offer views of the river and city. **Amenities:** A/C, satel TV w/movies, dataport. Some units w/terraces. **Services:** Car-rental desk, social director, babysitting. **Facilities:** 40 1 restaurant (bkfst and dinner only), 1 bar, whirlpool, washer/dryer. **Rates:** Peak (May 1–Nov 5) $79–$89 S or D; $99–$109 ste. Children under age 18 stay free. Min stay wknds. Lower rates off-season. Parking: Outdoor, free. Rates vary according to view. AE, CB, DC, DISC, MC, V.

The Ridpath, A Westcoast Hotel
515 W Sprague Ave, PO Box 2176, 99210 (City Center); tel 509/838-2711 or toll free 800/426-0670; fax 509/747-6970. Between Stevens and Howard Sts. Travelers wanting full service and central location stay here. Situated four blocks from convention center, three blocks from Riverfront Park, half-block from Skywalk shopping complex. **Rooms:** 344 rms and stes. Executive level. CI 3pm/CO 1pm. Nonsmoking rms

avail. Hunter green and burgundy color scheme, live plants, and solid walnut furnishings. **Amenities:** A/C, cable TV w/movies, dataport, bathrobes. Some units w/minibars, some w/terraces, all w/fireplaces, some w/whirlpools. Nintendo in all rooms. **Services:** Car-rental desk, babysitting. Pet fee deposit $200. **Facilities:** 1000 2 restaurants, 2 bars (1 w/entertainment), beauty salon, washer/dryer. Full catering and banquet facilities and services available. **Rates:** Peak (May 1–Oct 1) $85–$125 S; $95–$135 D; $125–$150 ste. Extra person $10. Children under age 18 stay free. Lower rates off-season. Parking: Indoor/outdoor, free. Golf, theater, shopping, and B&B packages offered. AE, CB, DC, DISC, MC, V.

Sheraton Spokane Hotel
322 N Spokane Falls Court, 99201 (Downtown); tel 509/455-9600 or toll free 800/848-9600; fax 509/455-6285. Next to Convention Center. On southern bank of Spokane River, next to Spokane Opera House and close to the financial district. Near Centennial Trail for biking, walking, and in-line skating. **Rooms:** 367 rms and stes. Executive level. CI 3pm/CO 1pm. Nonsmoking rms avail. City, park, and river views available. **Amenities:** A/C, cable TV w/movies, voice mail. 1 unit w/fireplace. All rooms have Lodge Net system for Nintendo, movies, and trivia games. **Services:** Car-rental desk, babysitting. **Facilities:** 1500 2 restaurants, 3 bars (2 w/entertainment), sauna, beauty salon. Indoor pool has lift chair for swimmers with disabilities. **Rates:** $98–$108 S; $108–$118 D; $120–$450 ste. Extra person $10. Children under age 18 stay free. Parking: Outdoor, free. Golf, entertainment, and shopper's packages. AE, CB, DC, DISC, EC, ER, JCB, MC, V.

UNRATED **Shilo Inn**
923 3rd Ave, 99204 (Downtown); tel 509/838-6630 or toll free 800/222-2244. Between 2nd and 3rd Aves. Basic motel undergoing full refurbishment of rooms and bathrooms. **Rooms:** 105 rms and stes. CI 2pm/CO noon. Nonsmoking rms avail. **Amenities:** A/C, satel TV w/movies, refrig, dataport. **Services:** Babysitting. **Facilities:** 300 Whirlpool, washer/dryer. **Rates:** $55–$59 S or D; $89 ste. Children under age 13 stay free. Parking: Outdoor, free. AE, CB, DC, DISC, ER, JCB, MC, V.

MOTELS

Best Western Thunderbird Inn
120 W 3rd Ave, 99204 (Downtown); tel 509/747-2011 or toll free 800/57-TBIRD; fax 509/747-9170. 1 block W of Division St exit off I-90. On a major thoroughfare with lots of fast food restaurants. Attracts families in town for sports events. Near several hospitals. **Rooms:** 89 rms. CI 1pm/CO noon. Nonsmoking rms avail. All rooms have recliner. **Amenities:** A/C, cable TV w/movies. 1 unit w/whirlpool. **Services:** Coffee in lobby 24 hours. Pet fee deposit is $25. **Facilities:** Whirlpool. **Rates (CP):** $45 S; $56 D. Extra person $5. Children under age 16 stay free. Parking: Outdoor, free. Golf package avail. AE, CB, DC, DISC, MC, V.

Cavanaugh's River Inn
700 N Division St, 99202 (Downtown); tel 509/326-5577 or toll free 800/THE-INNS; fax 509/326-1120. E of Division St bridge, N side of Spokane River. Large motel complex; attracts those attending regional sports competitions. **Rooms:** 241 rms and stes. CI 3pm/CO noon. Nonsmoking rms avail. Pool-side rooms available. **Amenities:** A/C, cable TV w/movies. Some units w/minibars. **Services:** Babysitting. **Facilities:** 1 250 1 restaurant, 1 bar (w/entertainment), volleyball, sauna, whirlpool, playground. Guests can use nearby fitness center. **Rates:** $75–$85 S or D; $130–$160 ste. Extra person $5. Children under age 18 stay free. Parking: Outdoor, free. Wedding, theater, and golf packages offered. AE, DC, DISC, ER, MC, V.

Comfort Inn Valley
905 N Sullivan Rd, Veradale, 99037 (Spokane Valley); tel 509/924-3838 or toll free 800/221-2222; fax 509/921-6976. I-90 and Sullivan Rd, S side of fwy. Adequate for one-night stay for travelers passing through Spokane. Right off I-90 on a busy street, but well sound-proofed. **Rooms:** 76 rms, stes, and effic. Executive level. CI 3pm/CO 11am. One of the buildings has all nonsmoking rooms. **Amenities:** A/C, cable TV. Some units w/terraces, some w/fireplaces, some w/whirlpools. **Services:** $15 nonrefundable pet fee. **Facilities:** 50 Sauna, whirlpool, washer/dryer. **Rates (CP):** Peak (May 1–Oct 31) $63–$125 S or D; $79–$125 ste; $79–$89 effic. Extra person $5. Children under age 18 stay free. Lower rates off-season. Parking: Outdoor, free. Golf packages available. AE, CB, DC, DISC, ER, JCB, MC, V.

Hampton Inn Spokane
2010 S Assembly Rd, 99204 (West Spokane); tel 509/747-1100 or toll free 800/HAMPTON; fax 509/747-8722. Exit 277 off I-90 W; exit 277A off I-90 E. Located at western edge of town. Exceptionally well landscaped entrance drive. **Rooms:** 131 rms and stes. CI 4pm/CO noon. Nonsmoking rms avail. **Amenities:** A/C, satel TV w/movies, dataport. Some units w/terraces, some w/fireplaces, some w/whirlpools. Suites have wet bars, VCRs, bath robes. **Services:** Car-rental desk. **Facilities:** 120 1 restaurant (lunch only), whirlpool, washer/dryer. Pool open 24 hours. **Rates (CP):** $63–$83 S; $73–$93 D; $155–$195 ste. Children under age 18 stay free. Parking: Outdoor, free. AE, CB, DC, DISC, MC, V.

Quality Inn Oakwood
7919 N Division St, 99208 (North Gate); tel 509/467-4900 or toll free 800/4-CHOICE; fax 509/467-4933. Located at the northern edge of town, about a mile from the huge Northtown Mall. Clean and comfortable. **Rooms:** 92 rms and

stes. CI 4pm/CO noon. Nonsmoking rms avail. **Amenities:** A/C, cable TV w/movies. 1 unit w/fireplace, some w/whirlpools. **Services:** Babysitting. Coffee in lobby 24 hours; lemonade and cookies available 7–11pm. **Facilities:** 1 restaurant, 1 bar, whirlpool, washer/dryer. Pool open 24 hours. **Rates (CP):** $63–$68 S; $68–$73 D; $125–$170 ste. Extra person $5. Children under age 18 stay free. Parking: Outdoor, free. Honeymoon package offered. AE, DC, DISC, ER, MC, V.

Quality Inn Valley Suites
8923 E Mission Ave, 99212 (Spokane Valley); tel 509/928-5218 or toll free 800/777-7355; fax 509/928-5218. Attractive to business travelers because of its location between downtown and suburban business complexes. **Rooms:** 127 rms, stes, and effic. Executive level. CI 3pm/CO 11am. Nonsmoking rms avail. Various theme rooms available—Marilyn Monroe Suite, Galaxy Suite, Honeymoon Suite, and Royal Suite. **Amenities:** A/C, cable TV w/movies, refrig. All units w/minibars, some w/terraces, some w/fireplaces, some w/whirlpools. **Services:** Masseur, babysitting. **Facilities:** 1 restaurant (dinner only), 1 bar, sauna, whirlpool, beauty salon, washer/dryer. **Rates (CP):** Peak (Apr 15–Sept 15) $79–$300 S; $89–$300 D; $160–$300 ste; $79–$99 effic. Children under age 18 stay free. Lower rates off-season. Parking: Outdoor, free. Honeymoon packages available. AE, CB, DC, DISC, ER, JCB, MC, V.

Ramada Inn
Airport Rd, Spokane Int'l Airport, 99219 (West Spokane); tel 509/838-5211 or toll free 800/2-RAMADA; fax 509/838-1074. Appeals to business travelers. Spacious lobby offers quiet public areas for informal meetings. **Rooms:** 161 rms, stes, and effic. Executive level. CI 2pm/CO noon. Nonsmoking rms avail. Two suites adjoin the indoor pool and offer 24-hour pool access. **Amenities:** A/C, satel TV w/movies. Some units w/terraces, some w/whirlpools. **Services:** Car-rental desk. **Facilities:** 2 restaurants (*see* "Restaurants" below), 1 bar (w/entertainment), whirlpool, playground. Nice large courtyard and pool area, but noisy because of plane traffic. **Rates (CP):** $56–$80 S; $69–$120 D; $125–$145 ste; $145 effic. Extra person $8. Children under age 18 stay free. Parking: Outdoor, free. AE, CB, DC, DISC, ER, JCB, MC, V.

Suntree Inn
211 S Division St, 99202 (Downtown); tel 509/838-6630 or toll free 800/888-6630; fax 509/624-2147. 1 block N of Division St exit off I-90. On a busy thoroughfare with lots of traffic, but the rooms are quiet and comfortable. **Rooms:** 80 rms. Executive level. CI 3pm/CO 1pm. Nonsmoking rms avail. **Amenities:** A/C, cable TV w/movies. **Services:** **Facilities:** Whirlpool, washer/dryer. Hot tub open 24 hours. **Rates (CP):** Peak (Apr 1–Sept 30) $45–$50 S; $50–$55 D. Extra person $5. Children under age 18 stay free. Lower rates off-season. Parking: Outdoor, free. "Frequent Traveler" discounts available. AE, DC, DISC, MC, V.

RESTAURANTS

Clinkerdagger Restaurant
In the Flour Mill, 621 W Mallon St (Downtown); tel 509/328-5965. Across from Spokane Arena. **American.** An Old English ambience with views of the Spokane River make this place a destination for romantic couples. Steaks, seafood, and pasta entrees will be prepared in any style, based on fair market prices, if enough notice is given. **FYI:** Reservations recommended. No smoking. **Open:** Lunch Mon–Sat 11:15am–2:30pm; dinner Mon–Thurs 5–9pm, Fri–Sat 5–10pm, Sun 4–9pm. **Prices:** Main courses $11.95–$19.95. AE, DC, DISC, MC, V.

Coyote Cafe
702 W 3rd Ave (Downtown); tel 509/747-8800. At Wall St. **Tex-Mex.** Upbeat and casual with low prices and good service. The spartan cafe is decorated with Mexican pepper and tomato cans to lend a Southwest feeling. Known locally for fajitas and barbecue baby-back ribs. Forty-eight sauces are made daily from scratch. **FYI:** Reservations accepted. Children's menu. No smoking. **Open:** Sun–Mon 11:30am–9pm, Tues–Thurs 11:30am–10pm, Fri–Sat 11:30am–11pm. **Prices:** Main courses $5–$11. AE, MC, V.

Milford's Fish House and Oyster Bar
719 N Monroe Ave (Downtown); tel 509/326-7251. W Broadway Ave. **Seafood.** Spokane's first fish house, located in an 1895 building. The specialty is crawfish tails baked with Pacific shrimp and Florida rock prawns in a southern-style pie plate, served with Cajun spiced cream sauce. **FYI:** Reservations recommended. Children's menu. No smoking. **Open:** Dinner Mon 4–9pm, Tues–Sat 5–10pm, Sun 4–9pm. **Prices:** Main courses $13.50–$18.50. MC, V.

Mustard Seed Oriental Cafe
W 245 Spokane Falls Blvd (Downtown); tel 509/747-2689. Across from Spokane Convention Center. **Japanese.** Contemporary Japanese cooking is offered in a casual family atmosphere. The prices are low and the portions generous. The half-priced menu served 10pm–1am Thurs–Sat makes this a popular late-night spot. Located across from the Spokane Opera House and the Convention Center. **FYI:** Reservations accepted. Additional location: 9806 E Sprague Ave (tel 926-3194). **Open:** Lunch Mon–Fri 11:15am–2:30pm, Sat 11:30am–5pm; dinner Mon–Wed 5–10pm, Thurs–Sat 5pm–1am, Sun 4–10pm. **Prices:** Main courses $7.95–$12.25. AE, DC, DISC, MC, V.

The Onion
320 W Riverside Ave (Downtown); tel 509/747-3852. At Bernard St. **Eclectic.** Families and young couples come here for standard cafe soups, salads, sandwiches, and burgers at moderate prices. This place was once called The Union.

According to local tradition, a former owner wanted to upgrade the clientele after a remodeling. To save money on a new sign, he just closed the opening on the "U" to make it an "O". The magnificent oak back bar and brass fixtures are still there. **FYI:** Reservations accepted. Children's menu. No smoking. Additional location: 7522 N Division St (tel 482-6100). **Open:** Daily 11:15am–1am. **Prices:** Main courses $3.50–$19.50. AE, DC, DISC, MC, V.

✱ Patsy Clark's
2208 W 2nd Ave (Browne Addition); tel 509/838-8300. 6 blocks W of Maple Street bridge access. **New American.** Chef Michael Scroggie's restaurant is in a historic 1898 mansion with twelve dining rooms. The menu, which specializes in wild game, changes seasonally. The extensive Sunday brunch offers fresh seafoods, crepe and omelette bars, and pastries. **FYI:** Reservations recommended. Piano. Children's menu. **Open:** Lunch Mon–Fri 11:30am–1:30pm; dinner Sun–Thurs 5–9pm, Fri–Sat 5–10pm; brunch Sun 10am–1:30pm. **Prices:** Main courses $12.95–$18.95. AE, CB, DC, DISC, MC, V. VP

Remington's Restaurant & Lounge
In Ramada Inn, Airport Rd, Spokane Int'l Airport (West Spokane); tel 509/838-5211. **American.** A bright and cheery atmosphere welcomes travelers seeking refuge from the overpriced fare that's offered at the airport. Entrees include prime rib and veal saltimbocca with a mixture of prosciutto, turkey, mozzarella, and oregano sautéed with mushrooms and marsala wine. **FYI:** Reservations recommended. Blues/country music/rock. No smoking. **Open:** Breakfast daily 6–11am; lunch daily 11am–2pm; dinner daily 5–11pm. **Prices:** Main courses $12.95–$17.95. AE, CB, DC, DISC, MC, V.

Riverview Thai Restaurant
In the Flour Mill, 621 W Mallon St (Downtown); tel 509/325-8370. Across from Spokane Arena. **Thai.** Typical hot and spicy Thai fare with appropriate decor and background music. The small dining room overlooks the Spokane River, and its location in the historic Flour Mill across from the new Spokane Arena makes this a popular spot for quick dinners before performances and events. **FYI:** Reservations accepted. No smoking. **Open:** Lunch Mon–Fri 11:30am–2pm, Sat noon–4pm; dinner Mon–Fri 5–9pm, Sat 4–9pm, Sun 5–8:30pm. **Prices:** Main courses $5.95–$10.50. AE, DC, DISC, MC, V.

✱ Rock City
In the Fernwell Building, 505 W Riverside Ave (Downtown); tel 509/455-4400. **Italian.** Self-described as "Seriously Fun Italian—Rockin' America." Pizzas are baked in a wood-fired oven and varieties range from barbecue and smoked chicken to Thai. Extensive menu, low prices. **FYI:** Reservations accepted. Children's menu. No smoking. **Open:** Daily 11am–10pm. **Prices:** Main courses $5.95–$13.95. AE, CB, DC, DISC, MC, V.

Rosso's Ristorante
In Red Lion Inn, 1100 N Sullivan Rd, Veradale (Spokane Valley); tel 509/924-9000. At I-90 and Sullivan Rd on south side of fwy. **Italian.** A little like sitting in the courtyard of a villa in Tuscany, gazing out at the surrounding vineyard. House specialties are filet mignon, scampi Provençale, and veal scaloppine. **FYI:** Reservations recommended. Country music/dancing/jazz/rock. Children's menu. Dress code. **Open:** Peak (May–Sept) lunch Mon–Fri 11:30am–1:30pm; dinner Mon–Sat 5–10pm; brunch Sun 9am–2pm. **Prices:** Main courses $7.95–$15.95. AE, CB, DC, DISC, ER, MC, V.

Sully's
259 W Spokane Falls Blvd (Downtown); tel 509/456-7410. Across from Spokane Opera House and Convention Center. **Continental/Italian.** Quiet and intimate, this place is popular for pre-theater dining and after-theater cocktails. Noted for its lamb entrees, many of which are named for favorite customers. **FYI:** Reservations recommended. Piano. No smoking. **Open:** Lunch Mon–Fri 11am–2pm; dinner Mon–Thurs 5–10pm, Fri–Sat 5–11pm. **Prices:** Main courses $9.95–$22.95. AE, MC, V.

✱ Upstairs Downtown Rustic Cuisine
In Bennett Block of Skywalk Shopping Complex, Howard and Main (Downtown); tel 509/747-9830. **New American.** Noted for its bright and airy European country atmosphere. The menu changes seasonally and all stocks and soups are made from scratch, with herbs and spices specially ordered to ensure their freshness. **FYI:** Reservations recommended. Beer and wine only. No smoking. **Open:** Lunch Mon–Sat 11:30am–3pm; dinner Tues–Sat 5–9pm. **Prices:** Main courses $10–$16.75. AE, MC, V.

Windows of the Seasons
In Cavanaugh's Inn at the Park, 303 N River Dr (Downtown); tel 509/328-9526. Next to Spokane River and Riverfront Park. **American.** A local favorite for special and formal occasions, it offers tables overlooking the Spokane River and Riverfront Park. The cloth-covered chairs, columns, high ceiling, elegant table settings, and soft colors present an old world charm. Signature dishes include roast rack of lamb with Hunan glaze, and beef tournedos Jack Daniels. Some menu items are identified as being approved by the Heart Institute of Spokane. **FYI:** Reservations recommended. Children's menu. **Open:** Breakfast Mon–Thurs 6:30–9am; lunch Mon–Thurs 11:30am–2pm; dinner Mon–Thurs 5:30–10pm, Fri–Sat 5–11pm, Sun 4–9pm; brunch Sun 9am–2pm. **Prices:** Main courses $13.95–$22.95. AE, CB, DC, DISC, MC, V. VP

ATTRACTIONS

Cheney Cowles Museum & Campbell House
2316 W 1st Ave; tel 509/456-3932. Displays depicting the history of the Spokane area, including many Native American and pioneer artifacts. A fine-arts gallery features up-and-

coming regional and national artists. Adjacent to the museum is **Campbell House,** a restored 1898 Tudor-style home with period antiques and decorative arts. **Open:** Tues–Sat 10am–5pm, Wed 10am–9pm, Sun 1–5pm. Closed some hols. **$**

Bing Crosby Collection
Gonzaga University; tel 509/328-4220. The famous actor/singer's alma mater is home to the Crosbyana Room, located in the school's Crosby Student Center (near Dakota St and Desmet Ave). Crosby's Best Actor Oscar (for the 1944 film *Going My Way*), gold and platinum records, and many other awards and trophies are on display here. The school also owns the **Bing Crosby Birthplace,** where visitors are welcome to view Crosby family memorabilia, along with photos of Bing and his college classmates. **Open:** Crosby Student Center: Sept–May, Mon–Fri 7:30am–midnight, Sat–Sun 11am–midnight; June–Aug, Mon–Fri 8:30am–4:30pm. Closed some hols. **Free**

Walk in the Wild Zoo
E 12600 Euclid Ave (Spokane Valley); tel 509/924-7220. 10 mi E of downtown Spokane. This 81-acre zoo contains more than 120 animals from five continents. There's a petting zoo for the young ones, and the zoo can be visited on cross-country skis during the winter months. **Open:** Summer, daily 10am–6pm; fall–spring, call for hours. Closed Dec 25. **$$**

Manito Park and Botanical Gardens
4 W 21st Ave; tel 509/625-6622. 2 mi SW of downtown Spokane. Spacious 90-acre park offering picnic area, playground, and wading pool, in addition to the botanical gardens. Garden highlights include Northwest-native perennials, a tropical greenhouse, a Japanese garden, Rose Hill (with more than 1,500 roses representing 150 varieties), and a formal European-style garden. **Open:** Daily 8am–dusk. Closed some hols. **Free**

Riverfront Park
507 N Howard St; tel 509/625-6602 or toll free 800/336-PARK. Set on an island in the middle of the Spokane River, this 100-acre park was created for the 1974 World's Fair Expo. Today, the park houses a restored 1909 carousel (with hand-carved horses), an IMAX theater, a weekend arts and crafts fair, and summertime concerts. The **Gondola Skyride** provides a spectacular view of Spokane Falls, while a family-fun center includes kiddie rides, miniature golf, and arcade games. Separate admission charged for each attraction or ride; park admission is free. **Open:** Apr 1–Mem Day, Sat–Sun 11am–8pm; Mem Day–Labor Day, daily 11am–8pm. **Free**

Stevenson

Historic Columbia River town. Provides access to Gifford Pinchot National Forest and Mount St Helens National Monument. **Information:** Skamania County Chamber of Commerce, 167 NW 2nd St, PO Box 1037, Stevenson, 98648 (tel 509/427-8911).

LODGE

Skamania Lodge
1131 Skamania Lodge Way, PO Box 189, 98648; tel 509/427-7700 or toll free 800/221-7117; fax 509/427-2547. 1 mi W of Stevenson, in the Columbia River Gorge. Built to blend in with its stunning natural environment, this resort and conference center features lots of wood and wide windows. Large room off the lobby has a stone fireplace. **Rooms:** 195 rms and stes. Executive level. CI 4pm/CO noon. Nonsmoking rms avail. Accommodations characterized by warm wood, contemporary furnishings, Pendleton fabrics, river and forest views. **Amenities:** A/C, cable TV w/movies, bathrobes. All units w/minibars, some w/terraces, some w/fireplaces, 1 w/whirlpool. Some accommodations have wet bars. **Services:** Social director, masseur, babysitting. **Facilities:** 18 2 1000 1 restaurant (*see* "Restaurants" below), 1 bar, volleyball, games rm, lawn games, spa, sauna, whirlpool, playground. Fitness center has one outdoor and three indoor whirlpools. Walking paths meander through the ground and adjacent woods. **Rates:** Peak (May–Oct) $95–$190 S or D; $185–$265 ste. Extra person $15. Children under age 12 stay free. Lower rates off-season. Parking: Outdoor, free. AE, DC, DISC, MC, V.

RESTAURANT

Skamania Lodge Restaurant
In Skamania Lodge, 1131 Skamania Lodge Way; tel 509/427-7700. **Northwest.** Enjoy sweeping views of the Columbia River Gorge's forested cliffs from this fine, casual restaurant. Breads, meats, fish, and pizza are prepared in a wood-burning oven in the open kitchen. There is a buffet on Friday nights, and in summer barbecues are held on the lawn. The adjacent lounge serves light meals from a more limited menu. **FYI:** Reservations recommended. Children's menu. Dress code. No smoking. **Open:** Breakfast daily 7–10:45am; lunch daily 11am–1pm; dinner daily 5–10pm; brunch Sun 10am–3pm. **Prices:** Main courses $12–$20. AE, DC, DISC, MC, V.

Tacoma

From the town's inception in 1869, it was destined to be a place where the rails would meet the sails. Today's mechanized shipping industry continues to handle an increasing growth of ship-to-rail and rail-to-ship cargo transfers, making the city the sixth-largest container port in North America. In recent years, downtown Tacoma has experienced an artistic renaissance, as historic buildings have been revamped as theaters and performing arts venues. **Information:** Tacoma-Pierce County Visitor Convention Bureau, PO Box 1754, Tacoma, 98401 (tel 206/627-2836).

PUBLIC TRANSPORTATION

Pierce Transit (tel 206/581-8000) offers 50 bus routes serving greater Pierce County and King, Thurston, and Kitsap counties. Fares: local service 75¢, seniors and persons with disabilities 35¢; Olympia express $1.50; Seattle express $2. Children under 6 ride free. Exact change required. All local service is wheelchair accessible.

HOTELS

Best Western Executive Inn

5700 Pacific Hwy E, 98424; tel 206/922-0080 or toll free 800/938-8500; fax 206/922-6439. Exit 137 off I-5. This large convention property is surrounded by more parking lot than grassy lawns, but the interior is clean and without a motel feel. **Rooms:** 139 rms and stes. CI 3pm/CO noon. Nonsmoking rms avail. Rooms are attractive with clean, modern furnishings. **Amenities:** A/C, cable TV w/movies. 1 unit w/minibar. **Services:** Car-rental desk. **Facilities:** 900 1 restaurant, 1 bar (w/entertainment), whirlpool. **Rates (CP):** $70–$75 S; $125–$150 ste. Extra person $8. Children under age 18 stay free. AP and MAP rates avail. Parking: Outdoor, free. AE, CB, DC, DISC, MC, V.

La Quinta Inn

1425 E 27th St, 98421; tel 206/383-0146 or toll free 800/531-5900; fax 206/627-3280. Off I-5, Portland Ave exit. A large building set next to the freeway and surrounded by asphalt. **Rooms:** 158 rms and effic. CI 1pm/CO noon. Nonsmoking rms avail. Rooms are small, with mediocre furniture. **Amenities:** A/C, cable TV w/movies, voice mail. Some units w/terraces. **Services:** Car-rental desk. **Facilities:** 450 1 restaurant, 1 bar (w/entertainment), whirlpool. **Rates (CP):** $56–$62 S; $63–$69 D. Children under age 18 stay free. Parking: Outdoor, free. AE, CB, DC, DISC, MC, V.

Sheraton Tacoma Hotel

1320 Broadway Plaza, 98402; tel 206/572-3200 or toll free 800/845-8466; fax 206/591-4110. Beautiful building in Tacoma's business district. Rooms are priced a bit high, though some do offer a great view of Mount Rainier. **Rooms:** 319 rms and stes. Executive level. CI 2pm/CO noon. Nonsmoking rms avail. **Amenities:** A/C, cable TV w/movies. Some units w/minibars, some w/whirlpools. **Services:** VP Social director, babysitting. **Facilities:** 50 1 restaurant (dinner only), 1 bar (w/entertainment), spa, sauna, steam rm, whirlpool, beauty salon. **Rates (CP):** $99–$123 S or D; $300–$400 ste. Extra person $10. Children under age 18 stay free. Lower rates off-season. AP and MAP rates avail. Parking: Outdoor, $5/day. AE, CB, DC, DISC, MC, V.

MOTELS

Best Western Lakewood Motor Inn

6125 Motor Ave SW, 98499; tel 206/584-2212 or toll free 800/528-1234; fax 206/588-5546. Located in a quiet residential neighborhood, it's a bit hard to find. The property is nicely landscaped with green lawns around the buildings and hanging baskets of flowers in outside corridors. Reasonable rates. **Rooms:** 78 rms. CI 3pm/CO noon. Nonsmoking rms avail. Rooms have nice furniture and attractive pictures. **Amenities:** A/C, cable TV w/movies, refrig, dataport. Some units w/terraces. **Services:** Car-rental desk, babysitting. **Facilities:** 25 Beauty salon, washer/dryer. Guests have access to nearby YMCA. **Rates (CP):** $48–$90 S; $55–$110 D. Extra person $7. Children under age 18 stay free. Parking: Outdoor, free. AE, CB, DC, DISC, MC, V.

Best Western Tacoma Inn

8726 Hosmer St, 98444; tel 206/535-2880 or toll free 800/528-1234; fax 206/537-8379. Clean, well-cared-for property near I-5. **Rooms:** 147 rms, stes. CI 2pm/CO noon. Nonsmoking rms avail. **Amenities:** A/C, cable TV w/movies. Some units w/terraces, some w/whirlpools. **Services:** **Facilities:** 250 1 restaurant, 1 bar (w/entertainment), whirlpool, playground, washer/dryer. Putting green. **Rates:** $62 S; $68 D. Extra person $8. Children under age 12 stay free. Parking: Outdoor, free. AE, CB, DC, DISC, MC, V.

Days Inn Tacoma

6802 S Tacoma Mall Blvd, 98409; tel 206/475-5900 or toll free 800/329-7466; fax 206/475-3540. Near Tacoma Mall. This well-kept property has a nice inner courtyard away from highway noise. **Rooms:** 123 rms, stes, and effic. CI 2pm/CO noon. Nonsmoking rms avail. Rooms are airy and well lighted. **Amenities:** A/C, cable TV w/movies, refrig, dataport. **Services:** Car-rental desk. **Facilities:** 40 1 restaurant, 1 bar (w/entertainment). **Rates:** Peak (May 25–Sept) $48–$65 S; $53–$75 D; $85–$95 ste; $65 effic. Extra person $10. Children under age 12 stay free. Lower rates off-season. Parking: Outdoor, free. AE, DC, DISC, MC, V.

Econo Lodge North

3518 Pacific Hwy E, 98424; tel 206/922-0550 or toll free 800/424-4777; fax 206/922-3203. Exit 136 off I-5. Generic motel off a busy street, several blocks from I-5. No lobby. Fast-food restaurants nearby. Rates generally lower than other motels in area. **Rooms:** 83 rms. CI 11am/CO 11am. Nonsmoking rms avail. **Amenities:** A/C, cable TV w/movies. Some units w/terraces. **Services:** **Facilities:** **Rates:** Peak (May–Oct) $40 S; $45 D. Extra person $4. Children under age 12 stay free. Lower rates off-season. Parking: Outdoor, free. AE, CB, DC, DISC, MC, V.

Howard Johnson Lodge

8702 S Hosmer St, 98444; tel 206/535-3100 or toll free 800/I-GO-HOJO; fax 206/539-6497. Clean, well-kept property located off a busy street near the freeway. **Rooms:** 143 rms, stes, and effic. CI 3pm/CO noon. Nonsmoking rms avail. **Amenities:** A/C, cable TV w/movies, dataport. Some units w/terraces. **Services:** Car-rental desk, babysitting. **Facilities:** 35 Playground. Guest passes to local health club are $5. **Rates (CP):** Peak (May 15–Sept 15) $49–$64 S; $59–$69 D; $100 ste; $100 effic. Children under age 12 stay free. Min stay special events. Lower rates off-season. Parking: Outdoor, free. AE, CB, DC, DISC, MC, V.

RESTAURANTS

Fujiya
In Broadway Plaza, 1125 Court C; tel 206/627-5319. **Japanese.** A very popular lunch spot with a sushi bar; small, but nicely decorated with Japanese art on the walls. Familiar assortment of hot and cold dishes. **FYI:** Reservations accepted. Dress code. Beer and wine only. No smoking. **Open:** Lunch Mon–Fri 11:30am–2pm; dinner Mon–Sat 5:30–9pm. **Prices:** Main courses $12–$16. AE, MC, V.

The Pacific Rim Restaurant
100 S 9th St; tel 206/627-1009. Across from the Waterfront. **Regional American.** Located across the street from a nice park. The interior has dark wood fixtures and walls covered with entertainment posters. Menu choices include lobster, pizza, burgers, and salads; there are always at least six microbrews on tap. **FYI:** Reservations recommended. Blues/jazz/reggae. Children's menu. Dress code. **Open:** Mon–Fri 11am–9pm, Sat–Sun 11am–10pm. **Prices:** Main courses $9–$13. AE, DC, DISC, MC, V.

✱ Southern Kitchen
1716 6th Ave; tel 206/627-4282. **Southern.** As soon as you open the bright-red painted screen door, you'll feel as if you're in grandma's kitchen—if you grew up in the South. Tables are stocked with plenty of napkins and several varieties of hot sauce, primed for the fried specialties. The cobbler is a fine choice for dessert. A hearty southern breakfast is served, complete with grits and biscuits and gravy. **FYI:** Reservations accepted. Children's menu. Dress code. No liquor license. No smoking. **Open:** Mon–Sat 7am–8pm. **Prices:** Main courses $4–$8. AE, DISC, MC, V.

ATTRACTIONS

Tacoma Art Museum
1123 Pacific Ave; tel 206/272-4258. Small but far-reaching permanent collection features works by such artists as Degas, Renoir, Corot, Pissarro, Hopper, and Lichtenstein. The museum's greatest claim to fame is the Dale Chihuly Retrospective Gallery, the only comprehensive public display of the glass artist's work. Additionally, there are exhibits of Japanese woodblock prints, Chinese imperial robes, Native American arts, and Soviet art. **Open:** Tues–Sat 10am–5pm, Sun noon–5pm. $

Washington State Historical Society Museum
315 N Stadium Way; tel 206/593-2830. Whether a visitor to this museum is new to the area or has lived here for years, they should find the exhibit "Washington: Home, Frontier, Crossroads" a fascinating exploration of Washington's history. From a varied natural history and geography to ancient Native American cultures that found time for diverse artistic expression to settlers and pioneers struggling for a new life in a new land, this exhibit succeeds in its evocative presentation of the state's history. **Open:** Tues–Sat 10am–5pm, Sun 1–5pm. $

Children's Museum of Tacoma
925 Court C; tel 206/627-2436. Features hands-on displays and special exhibits such as "Body Basics," an exhibit that allows children to interactively explore the mysteries of the human body. The adventure begins as visitors enter a larger-than-life mouth over a padded tongue passageway that leads them to other parts of the body. **Open:** Tues–Fri 10am-5pm, Sat 10am–4pm, Sun noon–4pm. Closed some hols. **$$**

Point Defiance Zoo & Aquarium
5400 N Pearl; tel 206/591-5337. You won't see any lions or giraffes or African elephants at this zoo. Only animals that inhabit the Pacific Rim are kept here: Asian elephants, monkeys, apes, lizards, polar bears, beluga whales, sea lions, walruses, penguins, puffins, and the like. Exhibits include a North Pacific aquarium, a Northwest tide pool, and a tropical coral reef aquarium containing more than 40 sharks. At the farm zoo, visitors can pet a llama. **Open:** Sept–May, daily 10am–4pm; June–Aug, daily 10am–7pm. Closed some hols. **$$$**

WW Seymour Botanical Conservatory
316 S G St; tel 206/591-5330. Located in Wright Park. This elegant Victorian conservatory, constructed in 1908, is one of only three of its kind on the West Coast. More than 200 species of exotic plants are housed within the huge greenhouse, which contains more than 12,000 panes of glass. **Open:** Daily 8am–4:30pm. **Free**

Twisp

Located in the Methow Valley, at the confluence of the Twisp and Methow Rivers. A popular stop for water-sport enthusiasts and those driving through on the North Cascades Scenic Highway (WA 20). **Information:** Twisp Chamber of Commerce, PO Box 686, Twisp, 98856 (tel 509/997-2926).

MOTEL

Idle-a-While Motel
505 N WA 20, PO Box 667, 98856; tel 509/997-3222. Property includes a string of white cabins and a one-story building containing motel-style rooms. A good alternative to the limited and higher-priced lodging in Winthrop. **Rooms:** 16 rms and effic; 9 cottages/villas. CI 1pm/CO 11am. Nonsmoking rms avail. Humdrum decor. **Amenities:** A/C, TV. **Services:** Babysitting. Dogs are the only pets allowed. VCR and movie rental. Coffee in lobby. **Facilities:** 1 Basketball, lawn games, sauna, whirlpool, playground. Picnic area with barbecue pits. Kids can play on the grassy knoll in front. **Rates:** Peak (May–Nov) $37–$45 S; $42–$45

D; $42–$69 effic; $42–$69 cottage/villa. Extra person $4. Min stay special events. Lower rates off-season. Parking: Outdoor, free. DISC, MC, V.

Vancouver

Located on the north bank of the Columbia River across from Portland, OR. Originally founded in 1824 as Fort Vancouver by the Hudson's Bay Company. Home of Pearson Field, the oldest operating airfield (established in 1905) in the United States. **Information:** Vancouver/Clark County Visitors and Convention Services, 404 E 15th St #11, Vancouver, 98663 (tel 360/693-1313).

HOTEL

Red Lion Inn at the Quay

100 Columbia St, 98660 (Downtown); tel 360/694-8341 or toll free 800/547-8010; fax 360/694-2023. Many rooms overlook the landscaped pool area, others offer good views of the colorful boats on the Columbia River. **Rooms:** 160 rms and stes. CI 3pm/CO noon. Nonsmoking rms avail. Rooms are spacious and comfortable. **Amenities:** A/C, refrig, dataport. Some units w/terraces, some w/whirlpools. **Services:** VP **Facilities:** 900 1 restaurant, 1 bar (w/entertainment). **Rates:** Peak (Apr–Oct) $108–$220 S; $113–$225 D; $220–$225 ste. Extra person $5. Children under age 12 stay free. Lower rates off-season. Parking: Outdoor, free. AE, DISC, MC, V.

MOTELS

Best Western Ferryman's Inn

7901 NE 6th Ave, 98665 (Hazel Dell); tel 360/574-2151 or toll free 800/528-1234; fax 360/574-9644. Rooms are clean and generously sized, but have outdated colors and faded wallpaper. Outdoor pool is too close to rooms—can get noisy at times. **Rooms:** 134 rms. CI 3pm/CO noon. Nonsmoking rms avail. **Amenities:** A/C, cable TV w/movies. **Services:** **Facilities:** 175 Washer/dryer. **Rates (CP):** $59–$63 S or D. Extra person $3–$5. Children under age 12 stay free. Parking: Outdoor, free. AE, DISC, MC, V.

Comfort Suites

4714 NE 9th Ave, 98662; tel 360/253-3100 or toll free 800/221-2222; fax 360/253-7998. From I-5, exit 2. Clean and comfortable. Located adjacent to a large mall. **Rooms:** 66 rms and stes. CI 3pm/CO noon. Nonsmoking rms avail. **Amenities:** A/C, dataport. Some units w/whirlpools. **Services:** Complimentary coffee and tea available 24 hours. **Facilities:** 30 Whirlpool. **Rates (CP):** $68–$75 S; $73–$80 D; $80 ste. Extra person $5. Children under age 18 stay free. Parking: Outdoor, free. AE, DC, DISC, MC, V.

Residence Inn by Marriott

8005 NE Parkway Dr, 98662; tel 360/253-4800 or toll free 800/331-3131; fax 360/256-4758. Exit 2 off WA 500. Accommodations, clustered in groups of eight, are located in low-rise, contemporary wooden structures, which are connected by well-lighted walkways that wend through the parklike grounds. **Rooms:** 120 rms and effic. CI 3pm/CO noon. Nonsmoking rms avail. All accommodations are comfortable suites of various sizes. All have fully equipped kitchens. **Amenities:** A/C, refrig, dataport. Some units w/terraces, all w/fireplaces. Basket on the kitchen counter filled with coffee, tea, sugar, and microwave popcorn. **Services:** The comfortable Gatehouse has a fireplace and tables adorned with fresh flowers; continental breakfast and afternoon snacks (fruit and desserts) are served here daily. Manager's reception every Wednesday, 5–6:30pm. Grocery shopping service available. **Facilities:** 1 25 Basketball, whirlpool, washer/dryer. Outdoor barbecue equipment available. **Rates (CP):** $119–$145 S or D; $119–$145 effic. Extra person $15. Children under age 18 stay free. Parking: Outdoor, free. "Weekend getaway" rates avail. AE, DISC, MC, V.

Shilo Inn–Hazel Dell

13206 NE WA 99, 98686 (Hazel Dell area); tel 360/573-0511 or toll free 800/222-2244; fax 360/573-0396. Exit 7 off I-5. Good bet for families attending local baseball games, Clark County Fair, or local car races. Exterior boasts pretty shrubs and hanging flower baskets, and the pool area is lovely. **Rooms:** 66 rms, stes, and effic. CI 3pm/CO noon. Nonsmoking rms avail. **Amenities:** A/C, satel TV w/movies, refrig. **Services:** Complimentary coffee, fruit, popcorn, and morning newspaper. **Facilities:** Sauna, steam rm, whirlpool, washer/dryer. **Rates (CP):** $55–$79 S or D; $80–$85 ste; $80–$85 effic. Extra person $5. Children under age 16 stay free. Parking: Outdoor, free. AE, DISC, MC, V.

RESTAURANT

Pinot Ganache

In Vancouver Marketplace, 1004 Washington St (Downtown); tel 360/695-7786. **International.** Coolly elegant mecca in this rather basic town. The chrome, black, and gray interior is highlighted by attractive fresh flowers. Asian chicken salad is prepared with a sharp soy-accented vinaigrette. The tart key lime pie is superb, and New York cheesecake can be bought whole or by the slice for takeout. Popular after-movies stop for desserts, wine, and good coffee. **FYI:** Reservations recommended. Jazz. Beer and wine only. No smoking. **Open:** Peak (Nov–Jan) lunch Tues–Sat 11am–3pm; dinner Tues–Sat 5–10pm. **Prices:** Main courses $11–$19. AE, DISC, MC, V.

ATTRACTIONS

Fort Vancouver National Historic Site

612 E Reserve St; tel 360/696-7655. Built in 1825 by the Hudson's Bay Company, Fort Vancouver was a stopping point for fur trappers, mountain men, missionaries, explor-

ers, and settlers throughout the mid-19th century. Today, visitors to the fort can visit several reconstructed buildings, which are furnished as they might have been when the HBC was the only "authority" in the region. Among the buildings within the fort are a blacksmith's shop, trading post, doctor's residence, and infirmary. The visitors center provides a 15-minute orientation video. **Open:** Mid-May–mid-Sept, daily 9am–5pm; mid-Sept–mid-May, daily 9am–4pm. Closed some hols. **$**

Officers Row National Historic District
E Evergreen Blvd. After the British gave up Fort Vancouver and moved north to Victoria, British Columbia, Vancouver became the site of the Vancouver Barracks US military post. Stately homes were built for the officers of this post, and these buildings are now preserved as a historic district. Most homes are private, but the George C Marshall House (tel 206/693-3103) is open to the public. This Victorian-style building was the commanding officer's quarters. **Open:** Mon–Fri 9am–5pm. **Free**

Pearson Air Museum
1105 E 5th St; tel 206/694-7026. Pearson Field, on the far side of Fort Vancouver from Officer's Row, was established in 1905 and is the oldest operating airfield in the United States. Dozens of vintage aircraft, including several World War I-era biplanes and the plane that made the first transpacific flight, are on display in a large hangar. **Open:** Wed–Sun noon–5pm. **$**

Veradale

See Spokane

Walla Walla

Located in an agricultural valley surrounded by the Blue Mountains. Walla Walla's name is derived from a Native American word meaning many waters. Site of the Dr Marcus Whitman Mission, the first settler's home in the Pacific Northwest. **Information:** Walla Walla Area Chamber of Commerce, 29 E Sumach, PO Box 644, Walla Walla, 99362 (tel 509/525-0850).

MOTELS

Comfort Inn
520 N 2nd Ave, 99362; tel 509/525-2522 or toll free 800/4-CHOICE; fax 509/522-2565. City Center exit off US 12. Located across the street from the former train depot. Inviting lobby—with brick fireplace, TV, and soft sofas—is decorated with a railroad theme. **Rooms:** 61 rms, stes, and effic. Executive level. CI 3pm/CO 1pm. Nonsmoking rms avail. **Amenities:** A/C, cable TV. Some units w/whirlpools. **Services:** **Facilities:** 40 Sauna, whirlpool, washer/dryer. **Rates (CP):** Peak (May–Sept) $56 S; $62 D; $125 ste; $68–$80 effic. Extra person $8. Children under age 18 stay free. Lower rates off-season. Parking: Outdoor, free. AE, DC, DISC, MC, V.

Pony Soldier Motor Inn
325 E Main, 99362; tel 509/529-4360 or toll free 800/634-PONY; fax 509/529-7463. Between Tukanon and Palouse Streets. Located near the Whitman College campus. High-ceilinged lobby with big windows and plants. **Rooms:** 85 rms and effic. Executive level. CI 4pm/CO noon. Nonsmoking rms avail. White concrete-block rooms are enlivened by wicker and wood furnishings and tasteful art on the walls. **Amenities:** A/C, cable TV. Some units w/terraces, some w/whirlpools. Some units have microwaves and coffeemakers. **Services:** Babysitting. **Facilities:** 12 Spa, sauna, whirlpool, washer/dryer. Exceptionally attractive indoor tiled spa with skylight. **Rates (CP):** $64 S; $69 D; $83–$87 effic. Extra person $5. Children under age 12 stay free. Min stay special events. Parking: Outdoor, free. Corporate and senior rates. AE, DC, DISC, MC, V.

INN

Green Gables Inn
922 Bonsella, 99362; tel 509/525-5501. Next to Whitman College, off US 12. Gracious, gabled mansion located on a quiet corner next to the Whitmore College campus. Large living room has two fireplaces, TV, and piano; beautifully landscaped, tree-lined grounds. **Rooms:** 5 rms; 1 cottage/villa. CI 3pm/CO 11am. No smoking. Individually furnished with verve and charm, rooms are named after places in the book *Anne of Green Gables*. The carriage house has been set aside as a cottage for families. **Amenities:** A/C, cable TV, refrig, bathrobes. No phone. Some units w/terraces, 1 w/fireplace, 1 w/whirlpool. **Services:** Afternoon tea served. A full breakfast enhanced by sterling place settings and crystal glasses is served by candlelight. Coffee and tea available all day. **Facilities:** Guest lounge w/TV. Tandem bicycle available. **Rates (BB):** $65–$90 S or D; $75–$100 cottage/villa. Extra person $15. Children under age 1 stay free. Min stay special events. Higher rates for special events/hols. Parking: Outdoor, free. AE, DISC, MC, V.

RESTAURANT

★ Merchants Ltd
21 E Main St (Downtown); tel 509/525-0900. Off 2nd St. **Deli.** A casual deli with a blackboard menu and hanging-plant decor. Excellent sandwiches, salads, and bakery items; Wednesday night features a special spaghetti dinner. **FYI:** Reservations accepted. Dress code. Beer and wine only. No smoking. **Open:** Mon–Fri 6am–6pm, Sat 6am–4:30pm, Sun 7am–noon. **Prices:** Lunch main courses $4–$7. MC, V.

ATTRACTION

Fort Walla Walla Museum

755 Myra Rd; tel 509/525-7703. Five exhibit buildings arranged in a broken wagon-wheel design are the anchor of this 15-acre complex, where household artifacts and horse-drawn equipment illustrate the lifestyle of the 19th-century pioneer-farmer. In Pioneer Village, 14 historic buildings display family heirlooms, tools, and household items used by pioneers and settlers. **Open:** Tues–Sun 10am–5pm. Closed some hols. **$**

Wenatchee

This central Washington city, positioned on the banks of the Columbia and Wenatchee Rivers, is known as the apple capital of the world—cherries, pears, and other fruits are grown here as well. The LINK bus system transports bikers (in the summer) and skiers (in the winter) between Wenatchee, Leavenworth, and Chelan. **Information:** Wenatchee Area Chamber of Commerce, 2 S Chelan, PO Box 850, Wenatchee, 98807 (tel 509/662-2116).

HOTEL

West Coast Wenatchee Center Hotel

201 N Wenatchee Ave, 98801 (Downtown); tel 509/662-1234 or toll free 800/426-0670; fax 509/662-0782. With direct access to the convention center, this classy hotel attracts many business-oriented guests. The lobby is bedecked with comfortable sofas and a marble fireplace, and a tray of apples for guests adds a nice touch. If this property was in a major city, rates would be much higher; the two-room luxury suites are a steal. **Rooms:** 147 rms and stes. Executive level. CI 3pm/CO noon. Nonsmoking rms avail. River, city, and mountain views, custom-made furniture and armoires make each room unique. Executive suites on the top floor will please the most finicky. **Amenities:** A/C, cable TV w/movies, dataport, voice mail. Some units w/whirlpools. Hair dryers on request. **Services:** Babysitting. Small pets allowed, $50 deposit. Staff is helpful and very friendly **Facilities:** 1 restaurant (*see* "Restaurants" below), 1 bar (w/entertainment), games rm, whirlpool. **Rates (BB):** Peak (Apr 15–Oct 31) $87–$92 S; $97–$102 D; $150–$200 ste. Extra person $10. Children under age 18 stay free. Min stay special events. Lower rates off-season. Parking: Outdoor, free. AE, CB, DC, DISC, EC, ER, JCB, MC, V.

MOTELS

Chieftain Motel and Restaurant

1005 N Wenatchee Ave, PO Box 1905, 98807; tel 509/663-8141 or toll free 800/572-4456 in WA; fax 509/663-8176. A big, not-too-attractive, bare-bones place. Three large two-story units are located on the main street, next to fast-food restaurants and other motels. OK for groups on a budget. **Rooms:** 105 rms and stes. CI open/CO noon. Nonsmoking rms avail. Rooms are a bit on the dark side but not unpleasant. **Amenities:** A/C, cable TV w/movies. Some units w/terraces. All rooms have double vanities, most have patios. **Services:** **Facilities:** 1 restaurant, 1 bar (w/entertainment), volleyball, whirlpool. Banquet room, ski-waxing room. Restaurant claims it sells the most prime rib in the Northwest. **Rates:** $55 S; $65–$80 D; $80 ste. Parking: Outdoor, free. Children can stay free in rooms with double queen beds. AE, DC, DISC, MC, V.

Four Seasons Inn

11 W Grant Rd, East Wenatchee, 98802; tel 509/884-6611 or toll free 800/223-6611; fax 509/884-6611. Large grey-stone-and-shingle motel located on the bank of the Columbia River. Lively atmosphere. **Rooms:** 100 rms, stes, and effic. CI 3pm/CO noon. Nonsmoking rms avail. Rooms have splendid views of the mountains and the river. Decor is rather passé. **Amenities:** A/C, cable TV w/movies. Some units w/terraces. Suite has cooking facilities. **Services:** Small dogs allowed for $5 fee. **Facilities:** 2 restaurants, 1 bar, sauna, whirlpool. Putting green under construction. **Rates:** Peak (Mar 15–Oct 15) $39–$49 S; $45–$57 D; $75–$185 ste; $75 effic. Extra person $5. Children under age 13 stay free. Lower rates off-season. Parking: Outdoor, free. Ski packages avail. AE, DC, DISC, MC, V.

Red Lion Inn Wenatchee

1225 N Wenatchee Ave, 98801; tel 509/663-0711 or toll free 800/547-8010; fax 509/662-8175. One of the better-quality chain motels in town, with recently renovated lobby, restaurant, and lounge. Attracts mostly businesspeople, but summer brings tourists as well. **Rooms:** 149 rms and stes. CI 3pm/CO 1pm. Nonsmoking rms avail. Rooms have view of courtyard or pool. **Amenities:** A/C, cable TV w/movies, dataport. All units w/terraces. VCRs on request. **Services:** Fax service available. **Facilities:** 2 restaurants, 1 bar (w/entertainment), games rm, whirlpool. **Rates:** Peak (mid-May–mid-Sept) $59–$99 S; $69–$109 D; $150 ste. Extra person $10. Children under age 17 stay free. Lower rates off-season. Parking: Outdoor, free. AE, DC, DISC, MC, V.

Rivers Inn

580 Valley Mall Pkwy, East Wenatchee, 98802; tel 509/884-1474 or toll free 800/922-3199; fax 509/884-9471. Flowering potted plants add color to the brown and gray siding of this handy motel located across from the Wenatchee Valley Mall. The lobby has a nice seating area. **Rooms:** 55 rms. CI 3pm/CO 11am. Nonsmoking rms avail. Some rooms overlook the pool and flower pots, others face the highway. **Amenities:** A/C, cable TV. Some units w/terraces. Refrigerators in some rooms. **Services:** VCRs and movies for rent. **Facilities:** Whirlpool. **Rates (CP):** $47–$58 S; $42–$62 D. Extra person $5. Children under age 12 stay free. Parking: Outdoor, free. AE, DC, DISC, MC, V.

RESTAURANT

Wenatchee Roaster and Ale House
In West Coast Wenatchee Center Hotel, 201 N Wenatchee Ave (Downtown); tel 509/662-1234. **American.** The decor is bright and brazen, with hanging banners and lots of colors. A menu for all appetites offers both low-calorie and low-fat dishes as well as various preparations of lamb, beef, chicken, turkey, and pork. All-clam clam chowder and some of the best prime rib in the city are highlights. Senior discounts; kids under 5 eat free. A private dining room with a fireplace seats five. The bar's worth a peek, even if you're a teetotaller. **FYI:** Reservations recommended. Children's menu. **Open:** Breakfast daily 6:30–11am; lunch daily 11:30am–4pm; dinner daily 4–10pm; brunch Sun 10am–2pm. **Prices:** Main courses $6–$19. AE, CB, DC, DISC, ER, MC, V.

Whidbey Island

The largest island in the Puget Sound, noted for its farmland, forests, and picturesque shoreline. It comprises the small communities of Clinton, Coupeville, Freeland, Greenbank, Langley, and Oak Harbor. Coupeville is one of Washington's oldest towns, while Langley (often referred to as the bed-and-breakfast capital of the Puget Sound) is a popular weekend getaway for Seattle residents. The largest community on the island—Oak Harbor—is named for the abundance of white oak trees in the area. Evidence of a rich Dutch heritage is visible in its windmills and tulip beds.

MOTEL

The Coupeville Inn
200 NW Coveland St, PO Box 370, Coupeville, 98239; tel 360/678-6668 or toll free 800/247-6162; fax 360/678-3059. Close to historic Front St. Reasonable rates; good for families and seniors. **Rooms:** 24 rms; 1 cottage/villa. CI 3pm/CO 11am. Nonsmoking rms avail. Fairly standard rooms, but clean and bright. **Amenities:** Cable TV. No A/C. Some units w/terraces. **Services:** **Facilities:** 40 **Rates (CP):** Peak (May 1–Sept 31) $54–$95 S or D; $120 cottage/villa. Extra person $10. Children under age 1 stay free. Min stay wknds. Lower rates off-season. Parking: Outdoor, free. AE, CB, DC, DISC, MC, V.

INNS

Captain Whidbey Inn
2072 W Captain Whidbey Inn Rd, Coupeville, 98239; tel 360/678-4097 or toll free 800/366-4097; fax 360/678-4097. From Main St in Coupeville go 2 mi W on NW Coveland St (which becomes Madronna); follow the signs. 15 acres. Picturesque 1907 inn built from madrone logs. Sits on 15 acres of woodland overlooking Penn Cove. **Rooms:** 25 rms (12 w/shared bath); 7 cottages/villas. CI 4pm/CO noon. Nonsmoking rms avail. Rooms in the lodge are small, with sound insulation almost nonexistent; they share two attractive bathrooms, one for men, the other for women. Lagoon rooms are more spacious and quiet. Some calico duvet covers and curtains look a bit faded. **Amenities:** Bathrobes. No A/C, phone, or TV. Some units w/terraces, some w/fireplaces. Cottages have fireplace or wood stove, and some have full kitchens. **Services:** Babysitting. **Facilities:** 15 1 restaurant (dinner only; *see* "Restaurants" below), 1 bar, 1 beach (cove/inlet), guest lounge. **Rates (BB):** $75–$135 S w/shared bath, $115–$135 S w/private bath; $85–$145 D w/shared bath, $125 D w/private bath; $145 ste; $150–$195 cottage/villa. Extra person $15. Children under age 5 stay free. Min stay peak. Parking: Outdoor, free. Two-night minimum stay on weekends July–Aug. AE, DC, DISC, MC, V.

The Harrison House Inn
201 Cascade Ave, Langley, 98260; tel 360/221-5801; fax 360/221-5804. At 2nd St. 1 acre. The newest hostelry in Langley is run by veteran innkeepers John and Kathleen Harrison. Unsuitable for children under 12. **Rooms:** 15 rms and effic; 1 cottage/villa. CI 3pm/CO 11am. No smoking. Spacious rooms are colorfully decorated. Second-story rooms feature cathedral ceilings. Some rooms have view of Saratoga Passage. **Amenities:** Cable TV, bathrobes. No A/C. Some units w/terraces, all w/fireplaces. Gas fireplaces with attractive mantles. **Services:** Wine/sherry served. **Facilities:** 12 Guest lounge w/TV. **Rates (CP):** $125–$165 S or D; $235 effic. Extra person $25. Parking: Outdoor, free. MC, V.

Inn at Langley
400 1st St, Langley, 98260; tel 360/221-3033; fax 360/221-3033. Near Anthes St. 2 acres. This gracious, contemplative place to unwind is well worth the rates. The architecture melds Craftsman, Asian, and Northwest styles. Unsuitable for children under 12. **Rooms:** 24 rms and stes (all w/shared bath). CI 3pm/CO noon. No smoking. Spacious rooms decorated in soft tones become a backdrop for the fabulous view of Saratoga Passage. A wall of windows opens onto a private deck lined with plants and cushioned seating. **Amenities:** Cable TV w/movies, refrig, dataport, VCR, voice mail, bathrobes. No A/C. All units w/terraces, all w/fireplaces, all w/whirlpools. Bathrooms feature Jacuzzi-style tubs with a sliding screen so you can see the quarry-tile fireplace. **Facilities:** 17 1 restaurant (dinner only; *see* "Restaurants" below), 1 bar, 1 beach (cove/inlet), guest lounge. **Rates (CP):** $169 S w/shared bath, $169–$249 S or D; $249 ste. Extra person $35. Min stay wknds. Parking: Outdoor, free. MC, V.

RESTAURANTS

Cafe Raven
197 2nd St, Langley; tel 360/221-3211. Between Anthes St and Cascade Ave. **Regional American.** The sign outside depicts the stylized Coastal Indian representation of a raven. Inside, the cafe has a somewhat 1960s counterculture feel, with reggae music on the stereo, kids' art on the walls, and

notices for consumer co-op members on the counter. The menu features sesame-seed waffles with real maple syrup and bananas or blueberries; items like spinach-feta quiche, sandwiches, and scones round out the menu. **FYI:** Reservations not accepted. Beer and wine only. No smoking. **Open:** Mon–Fri 7am–4pm, Sat 8am–4pm, Sun 8am–3pm. **Prices:** Lunch main courses $5–$7. No CC.

Captain's Galley
10 Front St, Coupeville; tel 360/678-0241. Just W of Main St. **American.** Built over the water with a superb view of Penn Cove. Seafood appetizers include oysters, mussels, clams, and crab. A special entree is chicken dijonnaise—chicken strips sautéed with mushrooms, garlic, tomatoes, tarragon, and leeks finished with a mustard-cream sauce. Other chicken dishes, plus beef, seafood, and pasta, are offered. **FYI:** Reservations recommended. **Open:** Peak (Mem Day–Labor Day) daily 11am–10pm. **Prices:** Main courses $12.50–$15.95. MC, V.

★ The Captain Whidbey Inn
2072 W Captain Whidbey Inn Road, Coupeville; tel 360/678-4097. **Seafood/Northwest.** The dining room in this 1907 inn looks out to the mussel beds of Penn Cove. For appetizers, consider those very mussels or the smoked salmon cheesecake with grain-mustard vinaigrette and spring onion oil. Among the entrees is Tyee spinach salad made with island spinach and tossed with alder-smoked duck breast, dressed with a kiln-dried tomato vinaigrette, then served with a warm goat cheese polenta tart. **FYI:** Reservations recommended. No smoking. **Open:** Peak (July 4–mid-Sept) lunch daily noon–3pm; dinner Sun–Fri 6–9:30pm, Sat 5:30–9:30pm. **Prices:** Main courses $18–$24. AE, DC, DISC, MC, V.

Christopher's
23 Front St, Coupeville; tel 360/678-5480. In Mariner's Court at Alexander St. **Northwest.** Owner/chef Christopher Panek presents his inventive cuisine in a light and airy dining room. Broiled local oysters are prepared with prosciutto and provolone and served with sun-dried tomatoes and pickled peppers. Sautéed medallions of pork tenderloin are dressed with Whidbey's loganberry wine and cream reduction. At least two vegetarian choices are on the seasonal menu. **FYI:** Reservations recommended. Beer and wine only. No smoking. **Open:** Lunch Fri 11:30am–2pm; dinner Wed–Sun 5–9pm. Closed 2 weeks in Dec. **Prices:** Main courses $13–$18. AE, DC, DISC, MC, V.

Country Kitchen
400 1st St, Langley; tel 360/221-3033. Between Anthes and Park Sts. **Northwest.** Looks like a small Asian-inspired temple, with strong architectural lines, a reflecting pond, and herb garden. Chef Stephen Nogal presents such fare as mussels in a black bean sauce, breast of duck sauced with a reduction of pan juices and loganberries, and Columbia River spring salmon baked with apples, leeks, and chanterelles. One sitting per night for the 2½-hour, five-course, prix fixe meal. Guests can tour the 2,500-bottle wine cellar. **FYI:** Reservations recommended. Dress code. Beer and wine only. No smoking. **Open:** Peak (mid-May–mid-Sept) Fri–Sat 7–10pm, Sun 6–9pm. Closed Jan 1–22. **Prices:** Prix fixe $45. AE, MC, V.

Dog House Backdoor Restaurant
230 1st St, Langley; tel 360/321-9996. Near Anthes. **American.** Great views of the Saratoga Passage are available at this eatery focusing on homemade low-salt food—from clam strips and nachos to fish-and-chips, the house specialty. Nearly forty bottled beers and a dozen northwest microbrews are on tap, including Whidbey ale, made just a stone's throw away. **FYI:** Reservations not accepted. **Open:** Daily 11am–9pm. **Prices:** Main courses $3.25–$7.10. No CC.

★ Garibyan Brothers Cafe Langley
113 1st St, Langley; tel 360/221-3090. East of Anthes St. **Mediterranean/Northwest.** Arshavir and Shant Garibyan meld the cuisines of their native Armenia with those of the Mediterranean and the Northwest. You can start with Penn Cove mussels, hummus, or babaganoush on pita bread before taking on Dungeness crab cakes with tri-colored bell pepper concasse, or braised lamb shank wrapped with grilled eggplant and served with a spicy sauce. Dessert favorites are baklava and Russian cream with raspberry sauce. **FYI:** Reservations recommended. Beer and wine only. No smoking. **Open:** Peak (June–Dec) **Prices:** Main courses $13–$17. AE, MC, V.

Star Bistro Cafe and Bar
201½ 1st St, Langley; tel 360/221-2627. East of Anthes St; on the 2nd floor. **Northwest.** Open and airy, with splendid views of Saratoga Passage. The menu features Northwest ingredients prepared with Italian overtones. For starters try the local Penn Cove mussels served with rice vinegar mignonette sauce. Pasta lovers may opt for roasted eggplant over penne with goat cheese, rosemary, and a warm vinaigrette. Salmon often appears on the seasonal menu. **FYI:** Reservations accepted. Beer and wine only. **Open:** Sun noon–8pm, Mon 11:30am–2:30pm, Tues–Thurs 11:30am–8:30pm, Fri–Sat 11:30am–10pm. **Prices:** Main courses $6.95–$17.95. AE, MC, V.

Toby's Tavern
8 NW Front St, Coupeville; tel 360/678-4222. Between Grace and Main Sts. **American.** A tavern since 1938, housed in the historic Whidbey Mercantile Exchange (circa 1890) and offering a great view of Penn Cove. Burgers, broiled fresh salmon, cod, and halibut as well as grilled oysters are served up. Seven microbrews on tap and 50 bottled beers available. **FYI:** Reservations not accepted. Beer and wine only. **Open:** Daily 11am–9pm. **Prices:** Main courses $3.75–$12.95. MC, V.

ATTRACTIONS

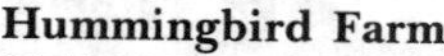

Hummingbird Farm
2041 N Zylstra Rd, Oak Harbor; tel 360/679-5044 or toll free 800/201-8335. Three large display gardens feature perennials and herbs, and the nursery features a large selection of herbs, rare perennials, and a unique selection of annual bedding plants that can be grown for drying. Four-acre rowing field with touring perimeter. Gift shop offers a full selection of botanical gifts, garden furniture, and dried flowers. **Open:** Mon–Sat 9:30am–5:30pm, Sun 11am–5pm. Closed some hols. **Free**

Whidbeys Greenbank Farm
765 E Wonn Rd, Greenbank; tel 360/678-7700. Home of Whidbeys, the only liqueur produced in Washington. Visitors can stroll the farm's 100 acres—the largest loganberry farm in the world. Picnic tables are scattered throughout the grounds and gourmet fixings can be purchased at the farm's shop. Complimentary tasting bar. **Open:** Daily 10am–5pm. Closed some hols. **Free**

Deception Pass State Park
5175 N WA 20, Oak Harbor; tel 360/675-2417. The most popular state park in Washington. What draws the crowds are miles of beaches, quiet coves, freshwater lakes, dark forests, hiking trails, camps, and scenic views of Deception Pass, the churning channel between Whidbey and Fidalgo Islands. **Open:** Daily dawn–dusk. **Free**

Winthrop

This historic Old West town in the Methow Valley serves as the eastern terminus of the North Cascades Scenic Highway (WA 20). Winthrop's 1890s ambience is accented by false-fronted buildings, wooden sidewalks, and old-fashioned street lights. **Information:** Winthrop Chamber of Commerce, PO Box 39, Winthrop, 98862 (tel 509/996-2125).

HOTEL

The Duck Brand/The Farmhouse Inn
248 Riverside N, PO Box 238, 98862 (Downtown); tel 509/996-2192 or toll free 800/996-2192. The Duck Brand is built on a hill, its tiered wooden facade fitting in perfectly with the rest of the western-theme village; the Farmhouse Inn, about a mile away, is exactly that. Both places offer rustic rooms, with just the bare necessities. **Rooms:** 12 rms. CI 2pm/CO noon. No smoking. **Amenities:** A/C, TV. No phone. Some units w/terraces. **Facilities:** 1 restaurant (*see* "Restaurants" below), whirlpool. **Rates:** Peak (May–Sept) $35–$55 S; $45–$65 D. Extra person $6. Lower rates off-season. Parking: Outdoor, free. AE, MC, V.

MOTELS

Hotel Rio Vusta
N Cascades Hwy (WA 20), PO Box 815, 98862 (Downtown); tel 509/996-3535. Guests at this Old West–style motel can settle into a comfy lawn chair on the river bank, or watch the sunset from the deck of their room. **Rooms:** 16 rms. CI 3pm/CO 11am. No smoking. Rooms decorated with colorful fabrics. Poor soundproofing means guests can hear neighbors' activities through the walls and ceiling. Extra sink and roomy counter in bedroom. Smoking permitted on decks. **Amenities:** A/C, cable TV w/movies. All units w/terraces. Cable TV in high season only. **Services:** Lobby closed 11pm–9am; no incoming guest phone calls during those hours. **Facilities:** Whirlpool. **Rates:** Peak (May–Sept) $80 S; $85 D. Extra person $5. Children under age 1 stay free. Min stay special events. Lower rates off-season. Parking: Outdoor, free. MC, V.

The Virginian
808 N Cascades Hwy (WA 20), PO Box 237, 98862; tel 509/996-2535 or toll free 800/854-2834. Rustic log cabins and a motel nestled along the banks of the Methow River. This is a place for families, and outdoors fans who don't want to sacrifice any amenities. **Rooms:** 32 rms, stes, and effic; 7 cottages/villas. CI 3pm/CO noon. Nonsmoking rms avail. Upper-level rooms have river or mountain views; decor in standard, lower-level rooms is a bit dark. **Amenities:** A/C, TV w/movies. No phone. Some units w/terraces, 1 w/fireplace. **Services:** Small pets allowed in some rooms. **Facilities:** 1 restaurant, 1 bar, volleyball, lawn games, whirlpool, playground. Cross-country skiing at the doorstep; hiking and hunting nearby. Restaurant is nonsmoking. **Rates:** Peak (Mem Day–Sept) $55–$85 S or D; $230 ste; $95 effic; $75 cottage/villa. Extra person $10. Children under age 5 stay free. Min stay special events. Lower rates off-season. Parking: Outdoor, free. AE, DISC, MC, V.

LODGE

Sun Mountain Lodge
Lake Patterson Rd, PO Box 1000, 98862; tel 509/996-2211 or toll free 800/572-0493; fax 509/996-3133. 8 miles off WA 20 on Sun Mountain; follow signs. 2,000 acres. This palatial hideaway, located high on a hill beyond the farms and ranches, features both wild and groomed grounds, superb views of the mountains and valley below, and a most impressive lobby. **Rooms:** 78 rms and stes; 13 cottages/villas. CI 4pm/CO noon. Nonsmoking rms avail. All but a few of the elegant rooms have stunning views. Limited number of rooms available for smokers. New rooms being added. **Amenities:** A/C. No TV. Some units w/minibars, some w/terraces, some w/fireplaces. Although you won't find a TV behind the armoire doors, you will likely find reading material or extra blankets. **Services:** Twice-daily maid svce, social director, children's program, babysitting. Foot reflexologist

available. **Facilities:** 1 restaurant, 1 bar (w/entertainment), 1 beach (lake shore), volleyball, games rm, lawn games, whirlpool, playground, washer/dryer. TV lounge near lobby. **Rates:** Peak (June 30–Sept 3) $145–$175 S or D; $250 ste; $150–$250 cottage/villa. Extra person $16. Children under age 12 stay free. Min stay wknds. Lower rates off-season. Parking: Outdoor, free. AE, MC, V.

RESTAURANT

Duck Brand Restaurant and Hotel
248 Riverside (Downtown); tel 509/996-2192. **Californian/Mexican.** A fun place, somewhat messy in decor, but with a happy staff and good food. During busy summer months, the outdoor patio, which hangs over a bank, is full of locals and tourists. There's plenty to choose from on the menu—Mexican fajitas, teriyaki chicken, burgers, pastas. The adjacent bakery, which was once the saloon belonging to town founder Guy Waring, supplies pies, rolls, and biscotti. **FYI:** Reservations not accepted. Beer and wine only. No smoking. **Open:** Peak (May–Sept) daily 7am–10pm. **Prices:** Main courses $8–$15. AE, MC, V.

Yakima

Located in the Yakima River Valley, this town is best known as a gateway to the vineyards, vegetable farms, and fruit tree orchards of central Washington. **Information:** Greater Yakima Chamber of Commerce, 19 N 9th St, PO Box 1490, Yakima, 98907 (tel 509/248-2021).

HOTEL

Cavanaugh's at Yakima Center
607 E Yakima Ave, 98901 (Downtown); tel 509/248-5900 or toll free 800/THE-INNS; fax 509/575-8975. Take I-82 to exit 33. Located next to Yakima Convention Center, this property attracts businesspeople and convention-goers. **Rooms:** 152 rms and stes. CI 3pm/CO noon. Nonsmoking rms avail. Deluxe rooms with new furnishings. **Amenities:** A/C, cable TV w/movies. Some units w/terraces, some w/whirlpools. Four different types of suites contain extra amenities such as whirlpools, wet bars, and refrigerators. **Services:** Pet fee is $10. **Facilities:** 1 restaurant, 1 bar (w/entertainment). Espresso bar in lobby. Banquet rooms available. **Rates:** $50–$79 S; $60–$89 D; $125–$200 ste. Extra person $10. Children under age 12 stay free. Parking: Outdoor, free. Corporate discounts and special packages avail. AE, CB, DC, DISC, ER, MC, V.

MOTELS

Holiday Inn
9 N 9th St, 98901 (Downtown); tel 509/452-6511 or toll free 800/HOLIDAY; fax 509/457-4931. Take I-82 to exit 33, 2 blocks W. Located one block from Yakima Convention Center and near commercial district. **Rooms:** 170 rms, stes, and effic. CI 4pm/CO noon. Nonsmoking rms avail. Contemporary-style furnishings; king-size beds available. **Amenities:** A/C, cable TV w/movies, dataport. Some units w/terraces, 1 w/whirlpool. Business rooms offer larger work area and a recliner. **Services:** Car-rental desk. Complimentary coffee in lobby; poolside food and beverage service. Fax, copy, and typing services available. **Facilities:** 1 restaurant, 1 bar, games rm, whirlpool, washer/dryer. Guests can use the nearby YMCA for $5. **Rates:** $65–$75 S; $75–$85 D; $195 ste; $65–$85 effic. Extra person $10. Children under age 18 stay free. Parking: Outdoor, free. Extra charge for poolside rooms. Discounts for seniors, groups, and commercial travelers. AE, CB, DC, DISC, JCB, MC, V.

Quality Inn Yakima Valley
12 Valley Mall Blvd, 98903 (Union Gap); tel 509/248-6924 or toll free 800/448-5544; fax 509/575-8470. Exit 36 off I-82; across from Valley Mall. A ten-minute drive from the Sun Dome and the Yakima Convention Center; within walking distance of six restaurants. Direct access to Yakima Greenway, a paved, recreational pathway along the Yakima River. **Rooms:** 86 rms and stes. Executive level. CI 3pm/CO 11am. Nonsmoking rms avail. **Amenities:** A/C, cable TV w/movies, dataport. Refrigerators available upon request. 17 executive rooms offer king-size beds, coffee makers, morning newspaper delivery, large work areas, speaker phones, and dataports. **Services:** Twice-daily maid svce, car-rental desk. VCR and movies for rent at front desk. Fax and copy machine available. **Facilities:** Games rm, washer/dryer. Complimentary passes for nearby YMCA. **Rates (CP):** $46–$52 S; $56–$66 D; $85 ste. Extra person $8. Children under age 18 stay free. Parking: Outdoor, free. Golf, wine tour, and romance packages avail. Special Sun night rate. Senior and commercial rates. AE, DC, DISC, JCB, MC, V.

Sun Country Inn
1700 N 1st St, 98901; tel 509/248-5650 or toll free 800/559-3675; fax 509/457-6486. Exit 31 off I-82; ¼ mi S. Attracts repeat corporate clientele looking for clean, safe rooms at competitive prices. Easy access off interstate. **Rooms:** 70 rms, stes, and effic. CI 3pm/CO 11am. Nonsmoking rms avail. Rooms open to parking lot. Two completely furnished apartments are generally rented by week or month. **Amenities:** A/C, cable TV w/movies. Six kitchenette units with stove (no oven) and microwave. **Services:** Complimentary coffee and tea 24 hours. Free morning newspaper, fax machine, and copier in lobby. **Facilities:** Sauna, washer/dryer. **Rates (CP):** Peak (Mar 1–Nov 15) $52 S; $57–$66 D; $55 ste; $45–$50 effic. Extra person $5. Children under age 16 stay free. Lower rates off-season.

Parking: Outdoor, free. Commercial, government, senior, and group rates offered. Guests staying 10 nights receive 11th night free. AE, CB, DC, DISC, JCB, MC, V.

INN

Birchfield Manor Country Inn

2018 Birchfield Rd, 98901; tel 509/452-1960 or toll free 800/375-3420. 2½ miles E on WA 24, exit 34 off I-82. 9 acres. Rural property, located next to a wildlife preserve. Gracious older building has five upstairs rooms, while six more modern rooms are in adjoining building. Unsuitable for children under 12. **Rooms:** 11 rms. CI 3pm/CO 11am. No smoking. Older rooms are individually decorated. All rooms have panoramic views of nearby vineyards. **Amenities:** A/C. No phone or TV. Some units w/terraces, some w/fireplaces, some w/whirlpools. Deluxe rooms are larger and may have fireplaces, private patios/decks, two-person whirlpools, and sauna. Guests in deluxe rooms receive basket filled with Northwest products and the inn's handcrafted chocolates. TVs and phones available upon request. **Services:** Afternoon tea served. Snacks and beverages available by prior arrangement. **Facilities:** 40 1 restaurant (bkfst and dinner only; *see* "Restaurants" below), whirlpool, guest lounge w/TV. **Rates (BB):** $60–$165 S; $70–$175 D. Extra person $20. MAP rates avail. Parking: Outdoor, free. Romance, wine tour, and getaway packages avail. AE, DC, MC, V.

RESTAURANTS

Birchfield Manor Restaurant

In Birchfield Manor Country Inn, 2018 Birchfield Rd; tel 509/452-1960. Exit 34 off I-82; 2 mi E. **Northwest.** Located in the Birchfield Manor Country Inn (originally the mansion of the owner of a large sheep ranch), this restaurant offers only one seating per night. Owner/chef Wil Masset taught courses in classical cuisine at several Seattle colleges for 14 years. He uses locally grown produce and products to make such dishes as mushroom-stuffed salmon baked in a pastry crust. The wine list has 200 choices from 80 central Washington wineries. **FYI:** Reservations recommended. Beer and wine only. No smoking. **Open:** Dinner Thurs 7pm, Fri 7pm, Sat 6pm, Sat 8:45pm. **Prices:** Main courses $20–$27. AE, DC, MC, V.

✱ Gasparetti's Gourmet

1013 N 1st St; tel 509/248-0628. Exit 31 (First St) off I-82. **Northern Italian.** This Yakima landmark has been serving locals for 30 years. A large fresco, glass sculptures, big bouquets of fresh flowers, stained-glass windows, and lots of greenery set the stage in the nonsmoking main dining room. Chef John Gasparetti specializes in fresh seafood, veal, and pasta, although a house favorite is filet mignon with Gorgonzola-and-pecan sauce. The award-winning, extensive wine list features Northwest vineyards. In the adjacent Bar Giovanni, smoking is permitted and there are choices from both a lunch-style or dinner menu. **FYI:** Reservations recommended. **Open:** Lunch Tues–Fri 11:30am–2:30pm; dinner Tues–Sat 4:30–11pm. **Prices:** Main courses $10–$25. AE, DISC, MC, V.

✱ Grant's Brewery Pub

32 N Front St (Downtown); tel 509/575-2922. **Pub.** This beautiful, oak-paneled, Scottish-style pub in a historic railroad station was the first microbrewery in Washington and is a standard-setter for others in the state. It features locally brewed ales, beers, and such traditional lunch favorites as Scotch egg (hard-boiled egg wrapped in pork sausage, breaded and deep-fried) served with a special mustard, and British banger (an English-style beef-and-pork sausage) served with bread and mustard. Many salads and sandwiches. **FYI:** Reservations accepted. Blues/jazz. Beer and wine only. No smoking. **Open:** Mon–Thurs 11:30am–midnight, Fri–Sat 11:30am–1am, Sun 11:30am–8:30pm. **Prices:** Main courses $3–$6. MC, V.

The Greystone

5 N Front St (Downtown); tel 509/248-9801. **Northwest.** In 1898, this building housed a brothel and bar; today, patrons come for fine dining and for the "Cheers"-like atmosphere in the lounge. A generally turn-of-the-century style prevails both in decor and the waitstaff's uniforms. The signature dish is rack of lamb, marinated in apple juice and seasonings. An extensive wine list highlights central Washington labels. **FYI:** Reservations accepted. Dress code. No smoking. **Open:** Tues–Sat 6–10pm. **Prices:** Main courses $10–$28. AE, MC, V.

ATTRACTIONS

Yakima Valley Museum

2105 Tieton Dr; tel 509/248-0747. Historical displays chronicle the valley's natural history, Native American culture, early pioneer life, and the roots and development of the Valley's fruit industry. There's a superb collection of horse-drawn vehicles, a tribute to Supreme Court Justice William O Douglas, and an interactive children's center. Nearby is the Gilbert House, a late Victorian farmhouse filled with period furnishings. **Open:** Mon–Fri 10am–5pm, Sat–Sun noon–5pm. Closed some hols. **$**

Central Washington Agricultural Museum

4508 Main St, Union Gap; tel 509/457-8735. Hundreds of pieces of antique farm equipment are housed here, in 18 large display buildings. Among the items on display are a McCormick Deering tractor, a portable hop-picking machine, and a pea picker, as well as horse-drawn machinery and a steam engine used to power a sawmill. **Open:** Daily 9am–5pm. **Free**

The Wild and Woolly West

Wyoming has always been a state of pioneering firsts. In the 19th century, Buffalo Bill Cody started his own town here, and the wagon wheels of westward emigrants cut so deeply into the Wyoming sandstone that the tracks are still visible today. Fort Laramie, in the southeast portion of the state, was established as the first trading post in this part of the country, in order to outfit those pioneers. Wyoming was also the first state to grant the vote to women (the territorial legislature made it law in 1869, a full 50 years before the rest of the country), the first state to have a woman judge, and the first to elect a female governor. Even though African Americans make up just 2% of its population, Wyoming was the first state to send an African American woman as its representative to the Miss America Pageant.

Of course, Wyoming's natural beauty is first-rate as well. Yellowstone, designated as the country's first national park in 1872, draws visitors by the millions with its geysers, dramatic waterfalls, and eerie rock formations. Devils Tower—one of the first landmarks the Oregon Trail pioneers saw as they left the Great Plains and entered the Rocky Mountains—was America's first national monument. (The core of an extinct volcano, the mysterious tower was also used in the film *Close Encounters of the Third Kind.*) The Grand Tetons draw mountain climbers, hikers, and skiers.

Farming and ranching in this land was—and is—tough work, and some 13 million people in the West have given it up in the last 50 years. Wyoming—a huge state with a total population smaller than that of Milwaukee—has suffered its share of this exodus, which has taken a toll on its spirit. Still, cattle and sheep continue to graze on remaining ranches, and sugar beets and wheat ripen on farmland.

STATE STATS

CAPITAL
Cheyenne

AREA
97,914 square miles

BORDERS
South Dakota, Nebraska, Colorado, Utah, and Montana

POPULATION
453,588 (1990)

ENTERED UNION
July 10, 1890 (44th state)

NICKNAME
Equality State

STATE FLOWER
Indiana paintbrush

STATE BIRD
Meadowlark

FAMOUS NATIVES
Jackson Pollock, Nellie Taylor Ross, James Bridger

But despite a growing tourist industry and the rapid development of resorts like Jackson Hole and Teton Village, there are still parts of the state that are so rugged that it's entirely possible that no man or woman has tread on them—only the wolves and the bears and the bobcats and mountain lions continue to stake their claims. These sections of wild and wooly Wyoming are likely to remain, as a legacy for future generations to discover.

A Brief History

The Plains Indians Paleo-Indians first moved into this region around 18,000 BC, and for centuries they reigned over the Great Plains. The Plains Indians' largely nomadic lives revolved around the mighty buffalo, whose vast herds they followed across the plains. The arrival of horses and guns (courtesy of the Spanish) in the New World during the 17th and 18th centuries made hunting the buffalo immeasurably easier, and tribes flourished as a result. Warriors grew in significance as raiding parties attacked other tribes and snatched horses, and each of the tribes struggled for dominion over the buffalo hunting grounds. During the 1700s, Indians from the Great Lakes and Canadian plains had migrated to Wyoming and by the 1850s, the Sioux, Cheyenne, Arapaho, Crow, Shoshone, Bannock, and Ute either occupied or were in control of various regions of Wyoming.

Trappers, Traders & the Trail In the fateful year of 1743, French fur trappers came hunting for beaver pelt (to satisfy the wealthy people back east longing for beaver hats), and traders soon trailed behind. Sixty years later, Wyoming became part of the enormous chunk of land known as the Louisiana Purchase ("purchase" being loosely defined here, since the native residents were not exactly selling anything). Trapper John Colter's tales of his travels in northwestern Wyoming in 1807–1808 lured a steady stream of other trappers and traders into the area.

In 1834, Fort William (later known as Fort Laramie) was established as a trading post, making it the state's first permanent white settlement. (It was later transformed into a military post.) Fort Bridger was built a few years later by trapper Jim Bridger, a western entrepreneur who led gold prospectors over the Bridger Trail. The Oregon Trail opened in 1839 and by the 1840s, caravans were making their way along the 2,000-mile route, with fur-trading posts acting as stations along the route. By 1870, some 350,000 people—those escaping economic depression in the East, Mormons fleeing religious persecution, gold-seekers rushing headlong to the California hills, and those simply looking for a new start on life—had traversed the mountain passes of Wyoming on the way West. It was the largest peacetime migration in the nation's history.

Fun Facts

- Wyoming—the Equality State—was the first state to explicitly grant women the right to vote. Governor John Campbell signed the suffrage bill into law in 1869. It was also the first state to elect a woman governor, Nellie Tayloe Ross, who served from 1925 to 1927.
- Wyoming, although it is the ninth-largest state in area, has the smallest population—even smaller than Alaska's.
- There are more pronghorn antelope than people in Wyoming.
- The city of Cody, named for US cavalry scout and Wild West showman Buffalo Bill Cody, is certainly the "Rodeo Capital of the World"—rodeos are staged here day and night.
- The first "yellow pages" telephone directory was published in Cheyenne in 1883.

The War for Survival Of course, as white migration into the area increased, so too did conflict with Native Americans who sought to protect their vital buffalo hunting grounds from incursions by settlers. A great council called at Fort Laramie in 1851 drew thousands of Plains Indians from various tribes and generated an agreement that permitted settlers to use the Oregon Trail across tribal lands in Wyoming. But the treaty, whose unstated goal was to transform the Plains Indians from hunters into farmers, did not last long. Outbreaks of violence soon occurred both among the tribes and with westward emigrants. It wasn't long before whites had expanded their goal from getting safely through Native American lands to dispossessing tribes of them entirely.

Wars with the Sioux, Cheyenne, Arapaho, and other tribes persisted throughout the 1860s and 1870s (particularly with the Sioux in the Powder River valley), but by the late 1870s Native American resistance against the US Army had all but ceased. The Plains tribes were dispatched to reservations or displaced from the region altogether. They who had lived off the land and its great buffalo herds for so long had suddenly been killed off or pushed aside by the fiercely determined newcomers.

Railroads & Ranchers By 1868, Wyoming had been organized into a US territory, with Cheyenne—which had mushroomed along the railroad line—as its capital. In that same year, the Wyoming sector of the Union Pacific Railroad was completed. The railroads not only increased settlement sharply but led to the decimation of the buffalo, as "sportsmen" (shooting from the safety of the train) killed them by the thousands. By the middle of the 1880s, settlers had homesteads in the Teton range, and even Jackson Hole (long a sacred tribal hunting ground) was no longer exclusively Native American territory.

Cattlemen increasingly poured into Wyoming during this time as well. Now that Native Americans no longer posed a threat, cattle could safely be led into the area, and they were—by the millions. Rustling, however, soonbecamewidespread. To combat it, the powerful and feared Wyoming Stock Growers Association was established, which in turn formed vigilante groups to enforce the cattle barons' own brand of justice. The conflict reached its frenzied height in the Johnson County cattle war of 1892. The influx of sheep in the late 1890s led to further violent encounters, as cattle and sheep ranchers hotly contested the precious grasslands.

Progressive Politics Wyoming achieved statehood in 1890, and a liberal state con stitution—in keeping with Wyoming's frontier ideals—was adopted. The progressive movement took hold firmly in the new state. In 1915, after a bitter fight, progressive forces overcame the clout of the railroad and other powerful interests to establish a state utilities commission; also in that year, a workers' compensation law was passed. In 1924, Wyoming became the first state to elect a woman governor—Nellie Tayloe Ross—an event perhaps not so surprising given the fierce independence Wyoming's women had developed over the years. They had, after all, worked just as hard as men on the ranches and homesteads, sometimes running them on their own for decades after husbands and fathers died.

DRIVING DISTANCES

Casper

153 mi S of Sheridan
180 mi NW of Cheyenne
214 mi SE of Cody
226 mi NE of Rock Springs
267 mi SE of Yellowstone
363 mi S of Miles City, MT

Laramie

49 mi NW of Cheyenne
207 mi E of Rock Springs
222 mi E of Green River
359 mi SE of Cody
380 mi SE of Yellowstone
383 mi SE of Jackson

Cheyenne

180 mi SE of Casper
271 mi E of Green River
393 mi SE of Cody
429 mi SE of Yellowstone
549 mi W of Sioux City, IA
818 mi SW of Minneapolis, MN

Boom, Bust & Rebound Richly endowed with natural resources—oil, coal, natural gas, copper, uranium—Wyoming has enjoyed energy booms at various times throughout this century. The state's first oil well was drilled in 1884, and production climbed over the decades until reaching a peak in 1970. After the 1973 Arab oil embargo, soaring energy prices turned Wyoming oil and mining towns upside down, bringing in new workers and spurring all kinds of development. The inevitable bust came in 1982 and the state paid dearly: population decresed over 3% in the 1980s. Fortunately, Wyoming's economy rebounded by the end of the decade, and in recent years efforts have been made to diversify.

A Closer Look

GEOGRAPHY

Wyoming's name is derived from a Delaware Indian word that describes a land shaped into mountains and valleys, rising and falling. The word captures the look of the state—a plateau broken by 11 mountain ranges—exactly. Here, the Great Plains meet the Rocky Mountains at the Continental Divide; rivers to the east of the Divide empty into the Missouri River Basin, while those to the west join the Columbia. Mountain ranges to the east and south of the Divide include the **Medicine Bow, Laramie,** and **Sierra Madre;** to the north lie the **Big Horns.**

The dramatic, 867-foot-tall volcanic core known as **Devils Tower** is located in the far northeast corner of the state. Oregon Trail pioneers used it as a landmark and meeting place en route to their destination. (Today, I-90 passes right by the monument; the highway designers recognized a direct route when they saw one.) Directly across the state from Devils Tower is **Yellowstone National Park,** with its thousands of geothermal wonders, and the majestic **Grand Teton Mountains.**

While the mountain ranges and stunning rock formations give the state its drama, the **lowlands** of central Wyoming, with their varied grasses and rolling farmland and lakes and rivers, give it a gentle quiet. Water is plentiful all over the state. Names of Wyoming's rivers are famous: Belle Fourche, Yellowstone, Shoshone, Little Missouri, Snake, and Green River. Jackson Lake, Yellow Lake, Bighorn Lake and the Flaming Gorge Reservoir are favorite play spots for vistors who converge on the state from every direction, year-round.

For millions of years, water and heat have carved away at the landscape now included in **Yellowstone National Park.** Heat from under the rocks continually changes the rocky slopes and shapes as the stone sloughs off and is carried away by streams and by the **Yellowstone River.** Spectacular waterfalls—**Upper Falls, Lower Falls, Tower Falls, Gibbon Falls**—drop hundreds of feet over sheer cliffs, as hundreds of geysers burst forth from under rock that was literally blown out of the earth by volcanic eruptions about 600,000 years ago. One of the less active geysers, **Steamboat,** is also the most powerful, shooting water up to 350 feet into the air. Before the eruptions, for millions of years, redwood trees blanketed the area and some of their petrified remains can still be found today.

AVG MONTHLY TEMPS (°F) & RAINFALL (IN)

	Cheyenne	Jackson
Jan	27/0.4	16/1.6
Feb	29/0.4	20/1.0
Mar	34/1.0	26/1.0
Apr	43/1.4	37/1.1
May	52/2.4	47/1.7
June	61/2.1	54/1.7
July	68/2.1	61/0.8
Aug	66/1.7	59/1.2
Sept	57/1.3	51/1.2
Oct	47/0.7	41/1.1
Nov	35/0.5	28/1.1
Dec	28/0.4	18/1.7

CLIMATE

Because of its high mean elevation (almost 7,000 feet above sea level), Wyoming's climate is relatively cool and dry. The lower elevations have their highest amount of precipitation in May and June, while the mountain regions get theirs in the winter (in the form of snowfall). Springtime is wet and sometimes brings surprising dips in temperature after a string of warm days. Summer daytime temperatures can climb to 85°F, but rarely higher, and evenings can even get quite chilly. Autumn is cool, and winter can be downright hazardous—if you have not yet driven across Wyoming in a blizzard, don't! Devastating winds blow snow horizontally and visibility is just about zero. What's worse, they can actually occur at any time from November to June.

WHAT TO PACK

Higher elevations get a lot of sun during the day and can get cold at night, so bring a warm jacket, thick gloves, caps and sun goggles, and sunscreen (for use in both winter and summer). Long johns are also a good idea. You will need layers of clothes; sweatshirts and at least a windbreaker, even in summer, are helpful in keeping off the edge of an evening chill. Moisture cream and lip balm help in the arid climate.

If you plan to do much hiking around Yellowstone or Grand Teton or any of the more rugged areas, be sure to bring well broken in, sturdy hiking boots. If you plan to backpack, bring rain gear and a plastic container for water. In the warmer seasons it's wise to pack tick repellent, long pants, and socks. You might also consider a snake bite kit if you plan to hike extensively.

TOURIST INFORMATION

The **Wyoming Division of Tourism** (tel 307/777-7777 or toll free 800/225-5996) has maps and calendars of events, and can direct you to detailed information about campground, fishing, and scenic locations. They will also be happy to send you a map of the state's travel information centers, most of which are located along I-80 and I-90. For specific information on parks and historical sites, contact the **Division of Parks and Historic Sites,** 2301 Central Ave, Cheyenne, WY 82002 (tel 307/777-6323). For information about fishing licenses and good locations to view wildlife, call **Wyoming Game and Fish** (tel 307/777-4600).

DRIVING RULES AND REGULATIONS

Drivers can get a learner's permit and probationary license at age 15; at age 16 they can be issued a full license. Speed limits are 65 mph on a four-lane divided highway or rural interstate, 55 mph on the open highway. Speed is checked by radar. Seat belts are required for front seat passengers and child restraints are mandatory for children age 3 and younger (or those weighing less than 40 pounds). A right turn on a red light is permitted unless prohibited by signs. Motorcycle riders must wear helmets if they are under 19 years of age.

RENTING A CAR

The following rental agencies have offices in Wyoming. Before you leave, check with your insurance company to see if you are insured while driving a rental car. Most companies provide this service; if not, the agencies can sell you insurance.

- **Alamo** (Jackson Hole only; tel 800/327-9633)
- **Avis** (tel 800/331-1212)
- **Budget** (Jackson Hole only; tel 800/527-0700)
- **Dollar** (tel 800/421-6868)
- **Hertz** (tel 800/654-3131)
- **National** (tel 800/328-4567)
- **Thrifty** (Jackson Hole only; tel 800/367-2277)

ESSENTIALS

Area Code: The entire state is in the **307** area code.

Emergencies: When on the road, report accidents or get help by calling the Wyoming Highway Patrol at 800/442-9090.

Liquor Laws: You must be 21 years of age to consume alcohol in this state.

Road Info: Several cities around the state have their own road conditions numbers that you can call. Some key ones: Cody (tel 307/587-9966), Jackson (tel 307/733-9966), Green River (tel 307/875-9966), Casper (tel 307/237-8411), Cheyenne (tel 307/635-9966), Laramie (tel 307/742-8981).

Smoking: Wyoming restricts smoking in government buildings.

Taxes: There is no general sales tax, but there is a 9-cent tax on gas and diesel fuel.

Time Zone: Wyoming is in the Mountain time zone.

Best of the State

WHAT TO SEE AND DO

Below is a general overview of some of the top sights and attractions in Wyoming. To find out more detailed information, look under "Attractions" under individual cities in the listings portion of this book.

Yellowstone National Park Besides its dramatic geysers and beautiful rocky walls and waterfalls, Yellowstone has other claims to fame, such as **Yellowstone Lake** (North America's largest alpine lake) and over 1,200 miles of hiking trails (the **Old Faithful Geyser Loop** being one of the most popular). Formed by cataclysmic volcanic eruptions, the area is still constantly changing because of underground water and heat and the nature of the rock itself. The abundant wildlife includes bears, coyotes, bobcats, mountain lions, moose, elk, and many smaller animals such as porcupine, skunks, and beavers.

Grand Teton National Park Unlike Yellowstone, the Grand Tetons were formed by what is called fault-block mountain formation rather than volcanic eruptions. A national park in 1929, the area was expanded to include the **Jackson Hole National Monument** in 1940. This 500-square-mile park has several lakes, including the 16-mile-long **Jackson Lake** (with mountains towering some 7,000 feet above the lake's west shore) and over 200 miles of scenic trails. Moose and buffalo have been seen grazing within sight of lodges. Campsites are available, and you can rent horses, boats, canoes, skis, or whatever you need to get around. Guided float trips and rock climbing expeditions are very popular. The 25,000-acre **National Elk Refuge,** along the park's southern border, is the winter habitat of thousands of elk; visitors can ride in horse-drawn sleighs to see the elk up close.

State Parks The warm-water lakes and rivers of **Guernsey State Park** are popular for swimming and water skiing, while **Bear River State Park,** along I-80 near Evanston, is perfect for a quick bike ride, hike, or picnic. **Keyhole State Park,** on the western edge of the Black Hills, has a reservoir for water play. Eagles and antelope as well as deer have been seen in this area.

Natural Wonders You could say that every part of Wyoming is a natural wonder, from **Devils Tower** in the east to the geysers at Yellowstone, to the breathing alpine meadows at Grand Teton. But there are other sights to behold, including the hundreds of wild horses at the **Pryor Mountain Wild Horse Range,** northeast of Lovell, and the glorious **Wind River Canyon,** a 2,000-foot-deep gorge. At the canyon's north end is **Hot Springs State Park** where the largest hot springs in the world are located. The awe-inspiring **Saratoga Valley,** with its healing hot springs, lies between Medicine Bow and the Sierra Madre Mountains. The loop highway into **Flaming Gorge** will provide literally hundreds of visual thrills: colorful buttes, eroded and whipped into strange shapes by wind and rain; startlingly blue waters; and the twisty spires of the Gorge's **Firehole Canyon.** Also amazing is **Fossil Butte National Monument,** which rises above Twin Creek Valley. On these 8,200 acres are gloriously colored rocks and numerous limestone fossil deposits. Dominating the scene is a 1,000-foot escarpment that towers above the arid plains.

Manmade Wonder It is hard in Wyoming for anything manmade to compete with Mother Nature, yet there's at least one worthy sight: the **Medicine Wheel,** not far from Lovell. This stone circle, some 70 feet across with 28 spokes radiating from its center, was probably used by Native Americans as a calendar or in a rite-of-passage ceremony—but no one knows for certain.

Wildlife The once vast herds of buffalo that blanketed the Plains are now gone, but a sizable herd of 2,600 has been restored to Yellowstone. Grizzly and black bears are of course famous there, and wolves are being introduced into one of their former habitats. Deep in the grasslands and forests, and in some of the rockier elevations, live coyotes, foxes, prairie dogs, and a few elk herds. More than 60 species of animals and 200 species of birds—from chickadees to osprey to pelicans, trumpeter swans, wild turkey, and eagles—inhabit Wyoming. In its rivers and lakes swim 22 species of game fish. River otters swim in all the rivers, especially the Snake and Yellowstone. Those little animals with big ears you might see in Yellowstone and Grand Teton are called pikas; they're related to another common Wyoming animal, the jackrabbit.

Historic Sites & Areas Over 300 miles of wagon-wheels ruts were carved into Wyoming's earth and sandstone during the heyday of the Oregon Trail. One of the best places to see the ruts is the **Oregon Trail Ruts National Historic Landmark,** located south of Guernsey.

Lots of American history comes together in **Fort Laramie,** once called Fort William, the region's first trading post and later a stopover for the Pony Express. **Fort Caspar** (located in the city of Casper) was also a frontier trading post. **Independence Rock,** west of Casper, was irresistible to pioneers—they had to carve their names into it, as they did at **Names Hill,** south of La Barge, and at **Register Cliff,** south of Guernsey.

You can see Native American petroglyphs and pictographs at **Medicine Lodge** near Hyattville. In **South Pass City,** the cry of "Gold!" led hundreds to try their luck. This former boomtown, which now features 20 restored historic buildings, was also the birthplace of the fight for women's suffrage. **Trail Town,** on the western edge of Cody, preserves the **Hole-in-the-Wall Cabin** for posterity, since Butch Cassidy and the Sundance Kid and the rest of the notorious Wild Bunch are no longer around to do it themselves.

Museums Even Old West entrepreneur Buffalo Bill Cody could not have foreseen that the **Buffalo Bill Historical Center** in Cody would become one of the most important museums of the West. It contains the Whitney Gallery of Western Art, the Plains Indian Museum, the Buffalo Bill Museum, and the Cody Firearms Museum. In Douglas, the **Wyoming Pioneers' Museum** contains pioneer and Native American artifacts. If you have ever wanted to know what it takes to make a mountain man, a visit to the **Museum of Mountain Men** in Pinedale would surely enlighten. The **Frontier Days Old West Museum** in Cheyenne displays over 200 Old West coaches and carriages, as well as plenty of exhibits on railroad and Native American history. The history of the region's cattle ranching, an extensive collection on Native American life in the region, and nearly one million other artifacts of state history are the focus of displays at the **Wyoming State Museum** in Cheyenne. The **Indian Heritage Center** on the Wind River Reservation and the **Riverton Museum** both contain fine displays of how Native Americans have for centuries lived and worked and practiced their arts and religions on this land.

Family Favorites The **Great Plains Wildlife Institute** gives both children and adults a chance to learn about the Wyoming wilderness. Wildlife biologists lead tours and teach how to mark elk calves and prairie dogs with tags so they can be studied. The curious can have a look at some old Wyoming residents, the dinosaurs, in the old coal town of Rock Springs at the **Western Wyoming Community College,** then head out to White Mountain, north of town, to look at pictographs on the rocky walls. You can also see dinosaurs at the **University of Wyoming Geological Museum** in Laramie. The **Big Wind Powwow,** held each June in Crowheart, includes dances, native costumes, crafts, and good food. Check with the Division of Tourism for exact dates and locations of other powwows, which are held all over the state.

EVENTS AND FESTIVALS

- **Winter Carnival,** Encampment. Dog sled races and other snowy events. February. Call 307/745-7339.
- **Devils Tower Volksmarch,** Devils Tower. This "peoples' walk" is a healthy adventure and a good way to meet people. May. Call 307/283-1611.
- **Cowboy Poetry Music Festival,** Rock Springs. Features some of the best cowboy poets and musicians from around the country. May. Call 307/362-3771.
- **Days of '49,** Greybull. A reenactment of gold-rush events. Early June. Call 307/765-2100.
- **Mountain Man Rendezvous,** Laramie. Find out if you have what it takes to be a mountain man. June. Call 307/745-7339.
- **Annual Chugwater Chili Cook-off,** Chugwater. Yep, there are some great chili cooks in these here hills. Live bands. June. Call 307/777-7777, or the nearby Wheatland Chamber of Commerce (tel 307/322-2322).
- **Grand Teton Music Festival,** Teton Village. One of the great events of the state for classical music and nature lovers. Late June to mid-August. Call toll free 800/959-4863.
- **Woodchoppers Jamboree,** Encampment. Wood cutting competitions, live music. Late June. Call the Laramie Chamber of Commerce at 307/745-7339.
- **Legend of Rawhide,** Lusk. A reenactment of the days of the Old West. Early July. Call 307/334-2950.
- **Professional Women's Rodeo,** Laramie. A rough-and-tough bunch of rides and tricky roping events. July. Call 307/745-7339.
- **Cheyenne Indian Center Pow Wow,** Cheyenne. Dancing, native costume, and lots of insight into the customs of local Native Americans. July. Call 307/638-3388.
- **Beartrap Summer Bluegrass Festival,** Casper. Great bluegrass music. Street dances. July. Call 307/234-5311.
- **Cheyenne Frontier Days,** Cheyenne. Largest outdoor rodeo in the world (in terms of cash prizes). Big-name rodeo stars, big-time country music. Late July. Call 307/778-7200.
- **Jackson Hole Wildlife Film Festival,** Jackson. A top draw to the state, with films and outdoor events. September. Call 307/733-3316.
- **Jackson Hole Fall Arts Festival,** Jackson. For a couple of weeks, Jackson goes all out for art. Crafts, too. Mid-September to early October. Call 307/733-3316.
- **Annual Native American Craft Market,** Lander. Fall. Call 307/332-3892.

SPECTATOR SPORTS

College Athletics The University of Wyoming in Laramie sponsors the state's only NCAA Division I football and basketball teams. The football Cowboys take to the field at War Memorial Stadium. Call 307/766-4850 for both football and basketball tickets.

Horse Racing The thoroughbred season at **Wyoming Downs,** north of Evanston, runs from May to September. Call toll free 800/842-8722.

Pole/Peddle/Paddle Races Every year, Jackson Hole hosts a unique 32-mile triathlon consisting of a downhill ski run and a 10km cross-country ski loop, followed by a 19-mile bike ride and a 9-mile boat ride down the Snake. Call 307/733-6433 for information on participating or watching.

Rodeos Two of the most complete displays of rodeo expertise and shenanigans can be seen at annual July rodeos in Cheyenne and Casper. For information about dates and times of rodeos all over the state, request a Calendar of Events from the Division of Tourism (tel 307/777-7777).

ACTIVITIES A TO Z

Bicycling This territory is made for the mountain bike. Yellowstone is a popular area, since some of its trails are set aside for bike and foot traffic only (check park maps). You can rent a bike easily in Cody, Jackson, and West Yellowstone. **Backroads Bicycle Touring** is a good outfit to connect with if you would like to tour any Western national park (tel 510/527-1555). You can also join in the fun at the Rendezvous Mountain Bike Race in September in Jackson; call the **Jackson Chamber of Commerce** (tel 307/733-3316) for details. The Wyoming Bicycle Guidance Map is available by writing to Bicycle Coordinator, Box 1708, Cheyenne, WY 82003-1708.

Bird Watching Eagles, ospreys, owls, pheasant, migratory birds, falcons, and about 200 other species of birds fly the skies of Wyoming. For information about where to look for which birds, you can contact the **National Audubon Society** (tel 203/

869-2017) or the **Wyoming Game and Fish Department** (tel 307/777-4600).

Boating Wyoming is full of lakes and rivers. The most popular ones are in Yellowstone National Park; boating permits are required (call park office for details). Be aware that the wind is as unpredictable as the weather if you choose to sail. You could find yourself in a gusty storm after starting out under sunny skies.

Camping Campgrounds fill quickly all summer long, especially in the western portions of the state. For some areas of Yellowstone you cannot reserve a campsite, so the best idea is to arrive early in the day and stake your claim. Sites are doled out on a first-come, first-served basis. Rangers and visitor information centers will advise in any of the state parks or either of the national parks on where to camp and how to take care of yourself around bears and other wildlife—be sure to pay attention to their instructions. For the Yellowstone campsites that offer reservations and to reserve space in other Wyoming campsites, call the **US Forest Service** (tel toll free 800/280-2267) or **Mistix** (tel toll free 800/365-2267).

Cattle Drives Yes, you too can become a cowhand. Choose a day or a week at some of the local ranches and round up stray calves, shear sheep, bond with your horse, and ride through cedar forests and open range. Sleep under the stars after trading stories around the campfire. Call 800/444-DUDE for dude ranch vacations in the west, or try a couple of Wyoming favorites: the **7D Ranch** near Cody (tel 307/587-3997) or **T Cross Ranch** in Dubois (tel 307/455-2206).

Fishing Wyoming lakes and rivers contain 22 species of game fish. You can't go wrong in the **Yellowstone River, Shoshone Lake,** or **Flaming Gorge Lake,** or practically anywhere else. Of course, the farther away from civilization, the better your chances at a rainbow trout or any of the fish your heart and stomach really crave. Call **Wyoming Game and Fish** (tel 307/777-4600) for information on licenses and the best locales.

Golf Many towns, even the smaller ones, have at least one golf course. Cheyenne and Casper have five and three respectively. Greens are often in the middle of, or within view of, spectacular mountain or prairie vistas. Check municipal listings for course numbers and locations, or contact the **Wyoming Golf Association** (tel 307/568-3304) for further information. Jackson holds an **Annual Ice Breaker Best Ball Golf Tournament** every May, and Lusk hosts an invitational in July.

Hiking Wyoming's **Sierra Club** (tel 307/455-2161) will head you in the right direction for the best hikes; trails are plentiful in both national and state parks. (Call 307/344-7381 for hiking information in Yellowstone; 739-3399 for Grand Teton.) Always check on the length of the trail before you set out, and remember that you are hiking in a high-altitude area. (High altitudes can cause flulike symptoms that can get more serious as you ascend. If you start to feel nauseous, turn around.)

Womantrek (tel toll free 800/477-TREK) offers hiking, biking, and rafting adventures for women only.

Horseback Riding Check with state parks for information on the best-marked trails. Riding some of the overused horses in Yellowstone can be a disappointment, even if an outfitter comes highly recommended. Sometimes the horses are just plain tired, and you may soon feel you are abusing these animals with yet another trip. Backcountry tours of the Bridger-Teton wilderness leave from Jackson. Call the **Jackson Chamber of Commerce** (tel 307/733-3316) for information.

Llama Treks Suppose you want to climb to higher altitudes without having to pack the gear yourself? Llama treks are the answer. There are treks to Green Lake and the Big Horns, as well as other areas on the state. Call 307/777-7777 for further information.

Rock Climbing Devils Tower is one of the most popular climbs in the state—or anywhere else for that matter. The rubble at the base discourages a few potential climbers, though some are just as happy to putter around in those rocks while their friends make the ascent. Be sure to get yourself properly outfitted for a climb. Call 307/283-1611 to get assistance on Devils Tower climbs.

Skiing Wyoming has terrific ski areas. Three popular sites are **Jackson Hole** (tel 307/733-2292), with a vertical drop of 4,139 feet; **Snow King** (tel 307/733-5200); and **Grand Targhee Nordic Center** (tel 307/353-2304). For more ski locations and information, check with the Division of Tourism (tel 307/777-7777).

Selected Parks & Recreation Areas

- **Yellowstone National Park,** PO Box 168, Yellowstone, WY 82190 (tel 307/344-7381)
- **Grand Teton National Park,** Moose, WY 83012-0170 (tel 307/739-3999)
- **Bighorn National Forest,** 1969 S Sheridan Ave, Sheridan, WY 82801 (tel 307/672-0751)
- **Black Hills National Forest,** PO Box 680, Sundance, WY 82729 (tel 307/283-1361)
- **Bridger-Teton National Forest,** Box 1888, Jackson, WY 83001 (tel 307/739-5500)
- **Medicine Bow National Forest,** 2468 Jackson St, Laramie, WY 82070-6535 (tel 307/745-8971)
- **Shoshone National Forest,** PO Box 2140, Cody, WY 82414 (tel 307/527-6241)
- **Bighorn Canyon National Recreation Area,** PO Box 487, Lovell, WY 82431 (tel 307/548- 2251)
- **Flaming Gorge National Recreation Area,** PO Box 278, Manila, UT 84046 (tel 801/784- 3445)
- **Bear River State Park,** 601 Bear River Dr, Evanston, WY 82930 (tel 307/789-6540)
- **Big Sandy State Park,** 131 South Pass Main, South Pass City, WY 82520 (tel 307/332-3684)
- **Boysen State Park,** 15 Ash Boysen Rte, Shoshone, WY 82649 (tel 307/876-2796)
- **Buffalo Bill State Park,** 47 Lakeside Rd, Cody, WY 82414 (tel 307/587-9227)
- **Glendo State Park,** Box 398 (397 Glendo Park Rd), Glendo, WY 82213 (tel 307/735-4433)
- **Guernsey State Park,** PO Box 429, Guernsey, WY 82214 (tel 307/836-2334)
- **Hot Springs State Park,** 220 Park St, Thermopolis, WY 82443 (tel 307/864-2176)
- **Keyhole State Park,** 353 Mckean Rd, Moorcroft, WY 82721 (tel 307/756-3596)
- **Seminoe State Park,** Seminoe Dam Rte, Sinclair, WY 82334 (tel 307/328-0115)
- **Sinks Canyon State Park,** 3079 Sinks Canyon Rd, Lander, WY 82520 (tel 307/332-6333)

Snowmobiling See Wyoming's backcountry on a snowmobile! The state has 1,300 miles of regularly groomed trails. National forests are an especially popular locale, as are state parks. Call the Division of Tourism for the latest on snow conditions, and to get directions to the best snowmobile areas.

Wagon-Train Rides Get off the beaten path and onto more rugged terrain on a wagon-train ride. Gather at the chuckwagon for dinner and then sing along around the campfire. The wagons creak along, accompanied by rolling sagebrush and a wide-open Wyoming sky. Ride through ghost towns, past herds of antelope, buffalo, and elk.

White-Water Rafting One of the most exciting things to do in this part of the world—some people travel to Wyoming just to ride the rapids. Jackson Hole has some of the best outfitters to take you on the Snake River, leaving as often as five times a day. The Shoshone also offers exciting rafting. Some guided trips include cookouts and overnight camping. Call the state's **Division of Tourism** (tel 307/777-7777) for details.

YELLOWSTONE AND THE GRAND TETONS

Start	Jackson Hole
Finish	Cody
Distance	276 miles
Time	2–3 days
Highlights	Western-style resorts; glacial lakes; hot springs, mud pots, geysers, and other geothermal wonders; one of the tallest waterfalls in America; hometown of Buffalo Bill

This scenic driving tour takes you through two of the nation's best-known national parks: **Grand Teton National Park** and **Yellowstone National Park.** The route begins and ends at two true Western towns—Jackson Hole and Cody—and in between, it passes through some of the country's most amazing natural phenomena. Along the way you'll see the magnificent panorama of the Grand Tetons with their lovely glacial lakes and wildlife; Yellowstone National Park offers additional wildlife sightings, a magnificent lake and mountains, fantastic geysers, colorful pools and mysterious bubbling mud pots, ethereal terraces, and a spectacular canyon complete with breathtaking waterfalls and rivers.

For additional information on lodgings, restaurants, and attractions in the region covered by the tour, look under specific cities in the listings portion of this chapter.

The tour begins in the western part of the state, in the booming tourist mecca of:

1. **Jackson Hole.** When it was founded at the turn of the century, Jackson was little more than a cow town, with an open square and a fence, where tired fur traders would make pit-stops on their travels between Wyoming and Idaho. Now it's a small metropolis of shops, art galleries, lodgings, and restaurants. Start your tour at the town square: a shady park with elk-antler arches opening onto the surrounding shopping area and wooden planked sidewalks. Here you might witness a staged reenactment of an old-fashioned cowboy shootout. Thirsty travelers might want to stop at the **Million Dollar Cowboy Bar,** on the town square, where patrons can "saddle up" to the bar (the barstools are made from actual saddles), listen to live music, or dance the two-step.

   The very active Jackson Hole Ski Area is located northwest of town. The hub of the area is Teton Village, a Swiss-style compound housing Wyoming's principal ski resort. Summer attractions include the Grand Teton Festival Orchestra, with its two-month-long schedule of performances, and Old West Days, featuring parades, rodeos, Native American dances, and cowboy poetry.

   On your way out of Jackson, you might want to pay a visit to the 5,000-square-foot **National Museum of Wildlife Art,** located three miles north of town on US 89/191. You can also pick up some picnic supplies en route to the next stop.

> ### Take a Break
> Stop in at **Dornan's,** 13 miles north of Jackson at #10 Moose Street in Moose (tel 307/733-2415). They have an incredible wine store, with over 20,000 bottles of wine to choose from, and a deli selling picnic supplies for your scenic journey.

From Jackson Hole, take US 89/191 for 12 miles north along the Snake River to Moose Junction and:

2. **Grand Teton National Park.** Back in the Roaring Twenties, some idealists opposed to the commercialization of forests and lakes sought out John D Rockefeller Jr as a benefactor for their cause. Rockefeller managed to save the land by buying it—some 30,000 acres, encompassing the entire valley and most of the lakes—and donating it to the federal government. Pay your park entrance fee ($10/car for a seven-day pass) at **Moose Junction,** which will gain you entrance to both Grand Teton and Yellowstone. The park ranger can provide you with a map of the area.

   From here, take Teton Park Road; you will pass Jenny Lake, the first (and most accessible) of a string of dazzling blue glacial lakes. Here you can go mountain climbing, hike to Hidden Falls, go horseback riding, or camp out. You will also be treated to spectacular views of the "Cathedral Group" of the Grand Tetons. (There are numerous, well-marked turnouts in both parks for viewing/photo-taking opportunities.)

   From Jenny Lake, drive 9 miles to Jackson Lake Dam and continue along Teton Park Road towards Colter Bay. There are several turnouts along the

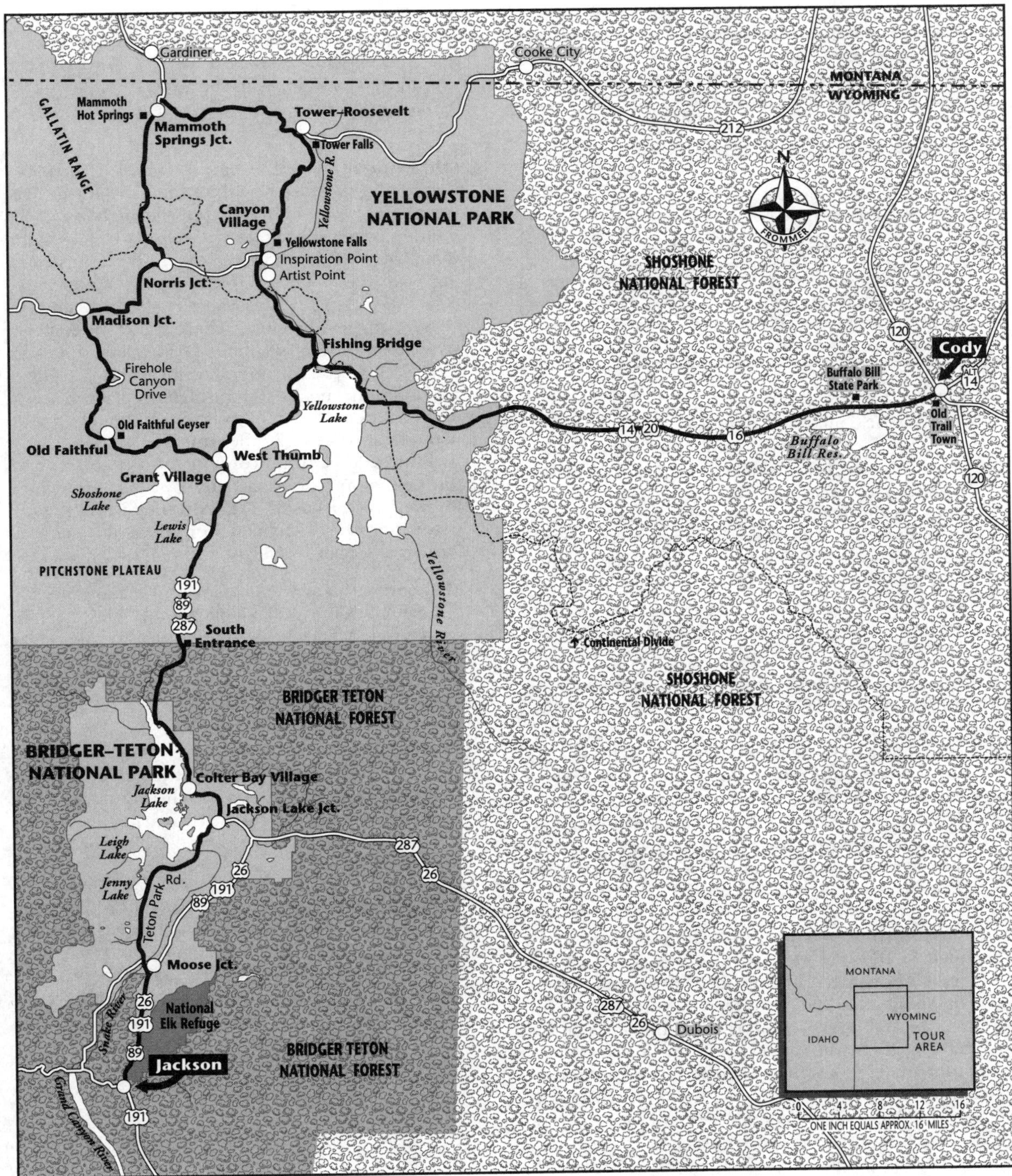

Gardiner
Cooke City
MONTANA
WYOMING
Mammoth Hot Springs
Mammoth Springs Jct.
GALLATIN RANGE
Tower-Roosevelt
Tower Falls
212
Yellowstone R.
YELLOWSTONE NATIONAL PARK
Canyon Village
Yellowstone Falls
Inspiration Point
Artist Point
Norris Jct.
Madison Jct.
SHOSHONE NATIONAL FOREST
FROMMER
N
Fishing Bridge
120
Cody
ALT 14
Buffalo Bill State Park
Firehole Canyon Drive
Yellowstone Lake
Old Faithful Geyser
Old Faithful
14
20
16
Old Trail Town
Buffalo Bill Res.
West Thumb
Grant Village
Shoshone Lake
Lewis Lake
PITCHSTONE PLATEAU
191
89
287
South Entrance
Yellowstone River
Continental Divide
SHOSHONE NATIONAL FOREST
BRIDGER TETON NATIONAL FOREST
BRIDGER-TETON NATIONAL PARK
Colter Bay Village
Jackson Lake
Jackson Lake Jct.
Leigh Lake
Jenny Lake
Teton Park Rd.
26
Moose Jct.
National Elk Refuge
Snake River
Jackson
Grand Canyon River
BRIDGER TETON NATIONAL FOREST
Dubois
MONTANA
WYOMING
IDAHO
TOUR AREA
0 4 8 12 16
ONE INCH EQUALS APPROX. 16 MILES

northerly route; Oxbow Bend Turnout and Willow Flats Turnout both offer views of wildlife, especially elk and Canada geese. If you're ready for an overnight stop, you might try **Jackson Lake Lodge** (tel 307/543-2811), located inside the park, which offers grand views across Willow Flats towards Mount Moran. Room rates range from moderate to expensive.

Take a Break

Stop in for a cappuccino or soda fountain treat in the **Pioneer Grill** at Jackson Lake Lodge. If you'd rather have a full meal, the **Mural Room** offers grand views and serves three meals a day.

From here, take the Jackson Lake Junction (US 89/191) for 6 miles to Colter Bay. This road travels alongside Jackson Lake, the biggest and grandest lake in Grand Teton. Make a stop at **Colter Bay Village,** a complex with a visitor center, marina, shops, restaurants, lodging, and the quite wonderful **Indian Arts Museum,** which features an extensive collection of Native American artifacts ranging from war bonnets and paintings to weaving and beadwork.

From Colter Bay, head north 23 miles on US 89/191 to:

3. **Yellowstone National Park (south entrance).** The park covers over two million acres, so it would be wise to be selective in your driving stops; otherwise, you could easily spend months here. The driving route known as the Grand Loop, which gives a good overview of the park, travels through Grant Village, West Thumb, Old Faithful, Madison, Junction, Norris, Mammoth Hot Springs, Tower Junction, and Canyon before ending at Fishing Bridge. This 145-mile drive, with stops, could take about 1½ days.

   Yellowstone was the first national park, established in 1872. It was named for the high yellow-rock cliffs rising up along the Yellowstone River. The Minnetaree Indians referred to the river as *Mi tsi a da zi* ("rock yellow river"); the French fur trappers then translated this to "yellow rock," or Yellowstone. It has been estimated that prehistoric hunters lived here as many as 11,000 years ago, and humans have inhabited the area for most of the 8,500 years since the last Ice Age.

   After entering the park, turn off at **Grant Village** for a view of the east side of Yellowstone Lake, which has numerous campgrounds, picnic areas, boat ramps, and a ranger station. Next, return to the main road, which provides ample opportunity for wildlife sightings, like moose, elk, grizzly bears, bison, and bald eagle. But park rangers will warn you to keep your distance, as several visitors a year are injured by animals in the park.

   At West Thumb, follow the two-lane highway for 17 miles to:

4. **Old Faithful.** One of five geyser basins in the park, this is the world's best known. The geyser has regular eruption intervals approximately every 79 minutes, when spectators are rewarded by the sight of an over-100-foot-tall fountain of roaring, steaming water. The **Old Faithful Visitor Center** (tel 307/545-2750) features exhibits that explain and predict geyser eruptions. There's also the impressive **Old Faithful Inn,** built of logs and stones in 1903–1904. The six-story interior hall boasts intricate log work and an 85-foot-high fireplace made of 500 tons of stone; the Inn is said to be the largest native-log structure in the world.

   From Old Faithful, continue north. En route to the next stop, you'll pass the Upper, Lower, and Midway Geyser Basins. (The Morning Glory Pool, a noted thermal pool named for its deep blue color, is located at Upper Geyser.) Continue for 16 miles to:

5. **Madison and Norris.** At Madison Junction there is a small museum and campground. The 14-mile route from Madison to Norris features numerous hot-spring pools, geysers, and other thermal areas, including Back Basin and Porcelain Basin. Awaiting visitors at the Norris Geyser Basin is a dramatic landscape of active and colorful mud pots, a blue hot-spring pool, roaring steam vents, and some small water-geysers. If you don't have time to visit every geyser basin in the park, this route provides the best overview and the widest variety.

   From Norris, travel through 21 miles of forests and low hills to:

6. **Mammoth Hot Springs,** the Park's headquarters. Here, visitors can view travertine terraces of limestone deposited by hot water coming up from below the earth's crust. Be sure to take the one-way **Mammoth Terrace Drive,** a narrow and windy one-lane roller coaster of a driving loop that circles round the hot spring terraces. Stop at the **Horace Albright Visitor Center** (tel 307/344-2263), which houses exhibits on Yellowstone's history and early exploration.

   From Mammoth Hot Springs, travel 18 miles east until you reach:

7. **Tower-Roosevelt.** On the left is Tower Falls, a 132-foot waterfall running off into the Yellowstone River canyon; the 10,317-foot-tall Mount Washburn stands on the right. Continue 19 miles south

from Tower to Canyon over Dunraven Pass. The Pass has a lookout point at the top which can only be reached by trail, although a road goes part of the way to the summit from the north side. (Note: Always be sure to check road conditions in the park; Dunraven Pass can be closed due to late snow/ weather conditions.)

Take a Break

Ride horse-drawn wagons or horses through breathtaking scenery to **Roosevelt's Old West Cookout,** an outdoor steak dinner at the Roosevelt Lodge (tel 307/344-7311). The cost is $24 to $36 for adults and $16 to $24 for children (including ride and meal). The cookouts are offered from early June to late August; reservations are recommended.

From Tower-Roosevelt, drive 19 miles to:

8. **Canyon.** Canyon Village boasts an Information Center, lodging, dining, gift shops, and other facilities. The Canyon itself has an Upper Falls (which take the Yellowstone River down 109 feet) and a Lower Falls (at 308 feet, Lower Falls is twice as tall as Niagara). Both falls can be seen from lookouts on a 2½-mile loop road that leads to Inspiration Point. Another loop road leads to Artist's Point. (If you're not faint of heart, take the hiking trail on the side of the Canyon for a spectacular, ringside view of the Lower Falls.)

   Continuing on your driving tour, you'll pass through the Hayden Valley. Known for its roaming bison, elk, and deer, the meadows and sagebrush flats of Hayden Valley stretch between the Canyon and Yellowstone Lake. Glaciers from the Ice Age created the lake bed and now the Yellowstone River flows through the valley, leaving marshes that are home to blue heron, swan, and Canada geese. Moose and grizzly bears occupy the woods and river as well, but are solitary in nature and therefore more difficult to spot.

   Following the Yellowstone River's twisting path, drive 16 miles south towards Yellowstone Lake; on the left you will see:

9. **Fishing Bridge,** which crosses the river at Yellowstone Lake's outlet. Fishing has been prohibited here since 1973, but the bridge was once filled with hopeful anglers. A **visitors center** (tel 307/242-2450) features exhibits about the bird life, fish, and geology of the Yellowstone Lake area. There's also an RV park here.

   At this point, depending on your time, you can either return to Jackson via the Grand Loop Road along Lake Yellowstone, or drive 27 miles east and exit Yellowstone through the east gate.

Take a Break

If you're not returning to Jackson, you may want to make a brief, two-mile detour to the gracious and historic **Lake Yellowstone Hotel** (tel 307/ 344-7311) before heading out of the Park. Drinks are available in the lobby lounge, or you can order a full meal in the **Dining Room.** Lunch entrees are $4 to $7; dinner entrees are $11 to $17. Dinner reservations required.

After leaving the east entrance of Yellowstone, take US 14/20/16 east along the north fork of the Shoshone River towards the Wapiti Valley and Cody. Teddy Roosevelt called this drive "the most scenic 50 miles in the world." On the road you will see magnificent rock formations (don't miss the "Holy City"), pass through Shoshone Canyon, and tunnel through Rattlesnake Mountain. You can see fantastic views of **Buffalo Bill Dam,** a National Historic Civil Engineering Landmark that was the highest arch structure of its kind when it was completed in 1910. On top of the 350-foot-tall dam is the **Buffalo Bill Dam Visitor Center** (tel 307/ 527-6076), where you can catch a spectacular view of the Shoshone Canyon. This portion of the tour also passes through the **Shoshone National Forest,** America's first national forest. President Benjamin Harrison set aside these nearly 2.5 million acres of timberland as the Yellowstone Park Timberland Reserve in 1891.

After traveling approximately 43 miles, you'll reach:

10. **Cody,** founded in 1896 by the legendary Col William "Buffalo Bill" Cody. Also known as the "Rodeo Capital of the World," there's plenty worth checking out in this historic town. One of the town's main attractions is the **Buffalo Bill Historical Center,** 720 Sheridan Ave (tel 307/587-4771), famous for its displays and artifacts from the early settlement of the West. The Center consists of several different museums: The **Buffalo Bill Museum** displays memorabilia from Buffalo Bill's life as a buffalo hunter, scout, showman, and soldier; the **Plains Indian Museum** focuses on the art, culture, and history of these tribes; and the **Whitney Gallery of Western Art** features the work of Charles M Russell, Frederick Remington, Thomas Moran, and many other Western artists. The **Cody Firearms Museum** contains approximately 6,000 firearms

and other materials that document the development of projectile weapons in the United States.

Cody has plenty of other activities to choose from. The **Cody Nightly Rodeo** (tel 307/587-5155) has performances at 8:30pm from June through August. Stroll through **Trail Town,** an authentic "frontier town" with Native American and pioneer artifacts (including the cabin used by Butch Cassidy and the Sundance Kid in the late 19th century). And don't forget to pack your cowboy boots for a night of dancing at **Cassie's Supper Club,** 214 Yellowstone Hwy (tel 307/527-5200), where the locals enjoy a rip-roaring time dancing to live country and rock bands.

If you're tuckered out enough to want to spend the night, you might want to consider the Cody Guest Houses (tel 307/587-6000 or toll free 800/587-6560), which consist of four different accommodations—a three-bedroom Victorian house, a four-bedroom Western house, and two one-bedroom cottages. Owners Daren and Kathy Singer go out of their way to ensure a pleasant stay and offer guidance to Cody's attractions and restaurants. Rates are moderate to expensive.

Wyoming Listings

Alpine

So named because of its idyllic mountain scenery, Alpine is still a small rural community of farmers and ranchers. The town was originally settled by Mormons heading west.

HOTEL

Alpen Haus

Alpine Jct Hwy, PO Box 258, 83128; tel 307/654-7545 or toll free 800/343-6755; fax 307/654-7587 ext 331. Jct US 26/89. Located in an isolated area about 45 minutes from Jackson, this motel features Austrian-style architecture and hand-painted murals. **Rooms:** 44 rms. CI 4pm/CO 11am. Nonsmoking rms avail. Rooms are comfortable and well decorated; some on the east side offer lovely views of the surrounding hills. **Amenities:** Satel TV w/movies, refrig. No A/C. Some units w/terraces. **Services:** Masseur, children's program, babysitting. VCRs, and a very large selection of movies, available. **Facilities:** 100 1 restaurant, 1 bar (w/entertainment), volleyball, games rm, lawn games, whirlpool, playground, washer/dryer. Large park with playground and gazebo; 13 full-service RV sites. Ice cream shop, market, and gas station adjacent. **Rates:** $35–$90 S; $54–$97 D. Extra person $7. Children under age 12 stay free. Parking: Outdoor, free. Snowmobile package avail. AE, DC, DISC, MC, V.

MOTEL

Best Western Flying Saddle Lodge

US 89/26, PO Box 227, 83128; tel 307/654-7561 or toll free 800/528-1234; fax 307/654-7563. ½ mi N of Alpine Junction. A nondescript concrete building in an isolated location close to the highway, but it does have pretty views of the Snake River. Rates, high for location, are commensurate with quality of accommodations and helpfulness of staff. **Rooms:** 20 rms and stes; 6 cottages/villas. CI 3pm/CO 11am. Nonsmoking rms avail. Large, clean, and comfortable, and decorated in country theme. Ralph Lauren linens. Suites have sitting area with hide-a-bed couch. **Amenities:** A/C, satel TV w/movies. Some units w/terraces, some w/whirlpools. Some rooms have refrigerators. Suites feature VCRs and robes. **Services:** **Facilities:** 1 restaurant (bkfst and dinner only), 1 bar, whirlpool. **Rates:** $60–$145 S or D; $135–$145 ste; $145 cottage/villa. Extra person $5. Parking: Outdoor, free. Rooms with whirlpool $5 extra. Closed Oct 15–May 26. AE, CB, DC, DISC, MC, V.

Bighorn Canyon National Recreation Area

5 mi E of Lovell, off US 14A. Bighorn Canyon, created by the Bighorn River as it cuts its way between the Pryor and Bighorn Mountains, spans nearly 100 miles across the border of Montana and Wyoming. The completion of Yellowtail Dam, in Fort Smith, Montana, led to the creation of 71-mile-long Bighorn Lake. The lake is a popular site for boating, fishing, waterskiing, and swimming. A commercial marina at the Lovell end of the lake offers boat rentals and tour boat excursions; the Ok-A-Beh marina at the north end provides a boat launch, snack bar, and camp store. The park has a total of five campgrounds and four picnic areas.

An orientation film describing activities throughout the park is shown at the solar-heated visitors center in Lovell, while exhibits at the Yellowtail Visitors Center (in Hardin, MT, off I-90) focus on the surrounding Crow reservation and the Yellowtail Dam. Backcountry hiking permits are available at both centers.

The **Mason-Lovell Ranch**, also located in the canyon, was one of the largest cattle ranches in Wyoming Territory during the 1870s and 1880s. Rangers lead guided tours (starting at the Lovell visitors center) of the ranch's bunkhouse, blacksmith shop, and married employees' cabin.

For more information contact the Superintendent, Bighorn Canyon National Monument, Box 458, Fort Smith, MT 59035 (tel 406/666-2412).

Buffalo

Settled by Scotch and Irish immigrants, who hired Basques as sheepherders; many descendants of the original Basques still ranch here. Gateway to the Big Horn Mountains, on the famous Cloud Peak Skyway at the convergence of I-90 and I-25. **Information:** Buffalo Chamber of Commerce, 55 N Main St Buffalo, 82834 (tel 307/684-5544).

MOTEL

Super 8 Motel

655 E Hart St, 82834; tel 307/684-2531 or toll free 800/800-8000; fax 307/684-7954. At the jct of I-90 and I-25. The owner takes pride in her property and has fixed it up with several nice touches that move this motel well beyond the basics. **Rooms:** 48 rms and stes. CI 11am/CO 11am. Nonsmoking rms avail. Clean and cheerful rooms with emerald-green carpeting. Live plants and historic photos adorn each room. Family suites will sleep six comfortably. **Amenities:** A/C, cable TV. **Services:** Friendly, outgoing, and efficient staff. **Facilities:** 1 restaurant, 1 bar. TV lobby on second floor for smokers. Miniature golf, carousel, ferris wheel, and ice-cream shop located in the complex; the walking path along Clear Creek also begins here. **Rates:** Peak (June–Sept) $24–$36 S; $28–$43 D; $48–$79 ste. Extra person $2. Children under age 12 stay free. Lower rates off-season. Parking: Outdoor, free. Commercial rates, special packages avail. AE, CB, DC, DISC, MC, V.

INN

UNRATED Cloud Peak Inn

590 N Burritt Ave, 82834; tel 307/684-5794; fax 307/684-7653. Located on a tree-lined street in a quiet residential area, this comfortable 1912 Craftsman-style house is full of period antiques. Small ballroom on third floor is a unique touch. **Rooms:** 5 rms (2 w/shared bath). CI 4pm/CO 11am. No smoking. Each accommodation is uniquely decorated. The Cloud Peak Room has a private balcony, wicker furniture, and a rich floral carpet echoing the hand-painted flowers on its ceiling. **Amenities:** Bathrobes. No A/C, phone, or TV. 1 unit w/terrace. Beautiful linens in each room. **Services:** Social director, masseur, children's program, afternoon tea and wine/sherry served. Hearty, multicourse breakfasts. **Facilities:** 25 Lawn games, whirlpool, washer/dryer, guest lounge w/TV. Lovely kitchen opens to greenroom with whirlpool. Large TV room. **Rates (BB):** Peak (May 15–Sept 15) $35–$50 S w/shared bath, $45–$70 S w/private bath; $45–$55 D w/shared bath, $50–$75 D w/private bath. Lower rates off-season. Parking: Outdoor, free. Special weekend theme-packages include murder-mystery parties. AE, MC, V.

RESORT

Paradise Guest Ranch

Hunter Creek Rd, PO Box 790, 82834; tel 307/684-7876; fax 307/684-9054. 160 acres. An all-cabin guest ranch located in the breathtaking Big Horn Mountains. Good value, given the facilities and activities included. Fishing streams nearby. **Rooms:** 18 cottages/villas. CI 3pm/CO 10am. New, or beautifully renovated, log cabins—each with one, two, or three bedrooms—are tastefully decorated in western/cowboy motif. Everything is modern and comfortable, with cozy chairs in front of the fireplace and a private porch from which you can watch for wildlife. All units offer a kitchen (though all meals are served in the ranch dining room). **Amenities:** Refrig. No A/C, phone, or TV. All units w/terraces, all w/fireplaces, 1 w/whirlpool. Washer/dryer. **Services:** Social director, masseur, children's program, babysitting. Children's programs include a kids' rodeo and supervised overnight camp-out, as well as family singalongs. **Facilities:** 50 1 restaurant, 1 bar (w/entertainment), volleyball, games rm, lawn games, whirlpool, playground, washer/dryer. Helpful staff will match your riding abilities with the correct horse; all guests have their "own" horse for the week. Organized activities include cookouts, pack trips, guided fishing expeditions, hay rides, a talent show, and square dancing. **Rates (AP):** $1,115–$1,375 cottage/villa. Min stay. Parking: Outdoor, free. Rates are weekly (Sun–Sun), and include all meals and scheduled activities. Closed Oct–Mem Day. No CC.

RESTAURANTS

Colonel Bozeman's

655 E Hart; tel 307/684-5555. East edge of Buffalo next to I-90 and I-25. **Eclectic.** Comfortable and friendly, this eatery prides itself on its steaks and burgers, and serves northern Wyoming's largest selection of microbrews. The stockade-look decor includes historical memorabilia and artwork. "Buffalo Room" tavern is intimate and private with high booths. **FYI:** Reservations recommended. Children's menu. Dress code. **Open:** Breakfast daily 6–11am; lunch daily 11am–4pm; dinner daily 5–10pm. **Prices:** Main courses $5–$15; prix fixe $5–$9. AE, CB, DC, DISC, MC, V.

Stagecoach Inn

845 Fort St; tel 307/684-2507. Take US 16 W; on the western edge of town. **American/Steak.** Owner Dick Grabherr is especially proud of the prime rib and seafood Newburg pot pie served in his eatery, which is decorated with western memorabilia and antiques. **FYI:** Reservations accepted. Children's menu. **Open:** Lunch Mon–Sat 11:30am–2pm; dinner Mon–Sat 5–9pm. Closed Nov. **Prices:** Main courses $9–$17; prix fixe $9. DISC, MC, V.

ATTRACTIONS

Jim Gatchell Museum

100 Fort; tel 307/684-9331. Two downtown buildings house more than 10,000 artifacts which focus on Native Americans, pioneers, and soldiers. Among the more unusual items on display are a pair of Cheyenne medicine rattles used in the Dance of Victory after Custer's defeat at Little Big Horn, a

shell from Custer's handgun, and an arrowhead that belonged to Red Cloud. **Open:** June–Aug, daily 9am–8pm; May, Sept–Oct, Mon–Fri 9am–5pm. Closed some hols. $

Fort Phil Kearney State Historic Site
528 Wagon Box Rd, Story; tel 307/684-7629. 13 mi N of Buffalo. From 1866 to 1868, Fort Phil Kearny was the site of several violent battles between the US Army and the Sioux, Cheyenne, and Arapaho. Today, the grounds contain a visitors center with interpretive exhibits, a self-guided walking trail through the remains of 20 of the fort's buildings, and a memorial to the Native Americans who died here. **Open:** May 15–Oct 1, daily 8am–6pm; Oct 1–Nov 31, Wed–Sun noon–4pm; Apr 1–May 15, noon–4pm. $

Canyon

See Yellowstone National Park

Casper

Started as a cattle shipping point, Casper is one of the largest cities in Wyoming and was once a hub for oil production in the state. Home of Casper College and the famous Casper Drum and Bugle Corp. Casper Mountain, just south of town, is a popular site for downhill skiiing, cross-country skiing, and snowmobiling. **Information:** Casper Area Convention and Visitors Bureau, PO Box 399, Casper, 82602 (tel 307/234-5311).

HOTEL

Casper Hilton Inn
I-25 at Polar Rd, PO Box 224, 82601; tel 307/266-6000 or toll free 800/HILTONS; fax 307/473-1010. Like so many Wyoming Plains establishments, this property has a bland exterior. However, Hilton put a lot of effort into the interior: lots of tropical greenery, a rambling lobby, and an "outdoor" cafe by the pool make things quite pleasant. **Rooms:** 229 rms and stes. Executive level. CI 3pm/CO noon. Nonsmoking rms avail. **Amenities:** A/C, satel TV w/movies, dataport. Some units w/whirlpools. **Services:** Babysitting. **Facilities:** 850 2 restaurants, 1 bar, games rm, whirlpool, beauty salon. **Rates:** $61–$66 S; $71–$76 D; $130–$175 ste. Extra person $10. Children under age 18 stay free. Parking: Outdoor, free. AE, CB, DC, DISC, MC, V.

MOTELS

Best Western East Motel
2325 E Yellowstone St, 82601; tel 307/234-3541 or toll free 800/675-4242; fax 307/266-5850. Exit 187 off I-25. Set in an industrial neighborhood of car dealers, welding shops, and truck traffic. Dull brick exterior and minimal landscaping, but renovations have improved the look of many of the rooms. **Rooms:** 40 rms. CI noon/CO 11am. Nonsmoking rms avail. Rooms in new wing are clean and spacious, though bland. **Amenities:** A/C, satel TV w/movies. **Services:** **Facilities:** Large, unlandscaped pool sheltered with corrugated plastic. **Rates (CP):** Peak (May 15–Sept 15) $50–$84 S; $55–$85 D. Extra person $5. Children under age 12 stay free. Lower rates off-season. Parking: Outdoor, free. AE, CB, DC, DISC, EC, MC, V.

Hampton Inn
400 W F St, 82601; tel 307/235-6668 or toll free 800/426-7866; fax 307/235-2027. Exit I-25 at Poplar St N. Attractively furnished property located in the northwest part of town. Pervasive smell of popcorn in the rambling lobby and corridors. **Rooms:** 122 rms. CI 11am/CO 11am. Nonsmoking rms avail. **Amenities:** A/C, cable TV w/movies. **Services:** Special effort is made to serve guests with disabilities. **Facilities:** 40 1 restaurant (lunch and dinner only), sauna. **Rates (CP):** Peak (May 26–Aug) $64 S or D. Children under age 18 stay free. Lower rates off-season. Parking: Outdoor, free. AE, DC, DISC, MC, V.

Parkway Plaza
123 W E St, 82601; tel 307/235-1777 or toll free 800/270-STAY; fax 307/235-8068. Off Poplar St; just S of I-25. Once the largest convention center in the state, this property is finally making a comeback after years of decline. A top-to-bottom renovation is underway; for now, guests should ask for rooms in the "tower" section. Lobby features striking wrought-iron curved stairways. **Rooms:** 226 rms, stes, and effic. CI 3pm/CO noon. Nonsmoking rms avail. Some rooms on first floor have large, sliding glass doors opening onto grassy courtyards. **Amenities:** A/C, cable TV w/movies. Some units w/terraces, some w/whirlpools. **Services:** VP Babysitting. **Facilities:** 1200 1 restaurant, 1 bar, games rm, sauna, whirlpool, beauty salon, washer/dryer. Off-track betting parlor adjacent to the bar. **Rates:** Peak (June–Aug) $48–$55 S; $55–$62 D; $120–$225 ste. Extra person $6. Children under age 13 stay free. Lower rates off-season. AP rates avail. Parking: Outdoor, free. AE, CB, DC, DISC, MC, V.

RESTAURANTS

Armor's
3422 S Energy Lane; tel 307/235-3000. Off US 220. **New American/Steak.** Patrons enjoy getting spiffed up to come here. The overall atmosphere is quiet and refined: One dining room is decorated in tones of grays and blues, the other is darker with high-sided wooden booths and hanging plants offering additional privacy. Seafood and steak are the best items. Specialties include Coho salmon, blackened prime rib, and veal duxelles (white wine–mushroom sauce). **FYI:** Reservations recommended. Children's menu. **Open:** Mon–Sat 5–10pm, Sun 5–9pm. **Prices:** Main courses $8–$23. AE, CB, DC, DISC, MC, V. VP

El Jarro Family Restaurant
500 W F Ave; tel 307/577-0538. **Mexican.** Comprised of several split-level dining rooms, the pleasant clutter of the decor (old steamer trunks, braids of garlic, and colorful serapes) lends this eatery a friendly, intimate, festive atmosphere. However, it can be fairly noisy. Chimichangas are the house specialty; those who avoid fried foods might try flautas or fajitas. Portions are generous and seasonings are mild. **FYI:** Reservations accepted. Children's menu. Additional location: 621 SE Wyoming Blvd (tel 235-8500). **Open:** Brunch. **Prices:** Main courses $5–$10. AE, MC, V.

ATTRACTIONS

Fort Caspar Museum and Historic Site
4001 Fort Casper Rd; tel 307/265-0610. Reconstructed fort, originally built in 1862. Interpretive center features Native American and military artifacts, and displays about the Pony Express, the Oregon Trail, and Mormon immigrants. **Open:** Summer, Mon–Sat 9am–7pm, Sun noon–7pm; winter, Mon–Fri 8am–5pm, Sun 1–4pm. Closed some hols. **Free**

Nicolaysen Art Museum
400 E Collins; tel 307/235-5247. The permanent collection focuses on the work of German-American illustrator Carl Link, as well as Native American paintings, pottery, and rugs. A children's area has a painting center and its own art gallery. **Open:** Mon–Sat 10am–5pm, Thurs until 8pm. Closed some hols. **$**

Tate Mineralogical Museum
125 College Dr; tel 307/268-2110. Located on the campus of Casper College. Displays in the museum include fossils, minerals, several meteorites, petrified wood, and Indian artifacts. **Open:** June–Aug, Mon–Fri 10am–5pm; Sept–May, Mon–Fri 10am–2pm. **Free**

Werner Wildlife Museum
405 E 15th St, Casper College; tel 307/235-2108. Displays of mounted animals native to Wyoming including antelope, deer, bears, and bison. A trophy room has exotic mounted animals from around the world. **Open:** June–Aug, Mon–Fri 10am–5pm; Sept–May, Mon–Fri 10am–2pm . **Free**

Cheyenne

Cheyenne started life as a bawdy railroad and livestock town, then became the state capital after the Union Pacific Railroad came through. Home to Cheyenne Frontier Days, one of the first rodeos. F E Warren Air Force Base is also located here. **Information:** Cheyenne Area Convention and Visitors Bureau, 309 W Lincolnway, PO Box 765, Cheyenne, 82003 (tel 307/778-3133).

HOTELS

Holiday Inn
204 W Fox Farm Rd, 82007; tel 307/638-4466 or toll free 800/HOLIDAY; fax 307/638-3677. Central Ave S exit off I-80; turn right on Fox Farm Rd. Renovations have made the spacious lobby more attractive; unfortunately, the rooms have not yet caught up. Although convenient to the interstate, the hotel is on the opposite side of town from the state capitol building. **Rooms:** 236 rms and stes. CI 2pm/CO noon. Nonsmoking rms avail. Nondescript, but clean and nicely furnished. Dark drapes and furnishings make the rooms look gloomy. **Amenities:** A/C, cable TV w/movies. **Services:** Children's program, babysitting. **Facilities:** 1000 1 restaurant, 1 bar (w/entertainment), games rm, sauna, whirlpool. **Rates:** Peak (June–Aug) $55–$70 S; $65–$80 D; $90–$125 ste. Children under age 6 stay free. Lower rates off-season. Parking: Outdoor, free. Rates rise sharply during annual Frontier Days Rodeo (last two weeks in July); reserve far in advance. AE, DC, EC, JCB, MC, V.

Little America Hotel and Resort
2800 W Lincolnway, 82001; tel 307/775-8400 or toll free 800/235-6383; fax 307/775-8425. At jct I-80 and I-25. 80 acres. This hotel, together with two others in the chain (in Salt Lake City, UT and Evanston, WY), was built to serve interstate traffic but has evolved into a luxurious lodging. Along with the Hitching Post in Cheyenne, it's a favorite of the movers and shakers in town. Pine groves have been planted everywhere—a significant amenity in windswept, barren southern Wyoming. **Rooms:** 188 rms and stes. Executive level. CI 3pm/CO noon. Nonsmoking rms avail. Tastefully furnished, luxurious rooms have serene views of the grounds. **Amenities:** A/C, refrig. All units w/terraces, some w/fireplaces. Large, 31″ TVs. **Services:** VP Twice-daily maid svce, babysitting. A special effort is made to serve guests with disabilities; room configurations can be changed according to individual needs. The public address system in the banquet facilities offers devices for the deaf or hard-of-hearing. **Facilities:** 18 500 2 restaurants, 1 bar, washer/dryer. Few people play the golf course because of high winds. **Rates:** Peak (June–Sept) $65–$89 S; $75–$99 D; $99–$120 ste. Extra person $10. Children under age 12 stay free. Lower rates off-season. Parking: Outdoor, free. AE, CB, DC, DISC, MC, V.

MOTELS

Best Western Hitching Post Inn
1700 W Lincolnway, 82001; tel 307/638-3301 or toll free 800/528-1234; fax 307/778-7194. Lincolnway exit off I-25, go ½ mi N. A self-contained little world catering to convention-goers, politicians, lobbyists, and businesspeople. Although the grounds are well kept, the wind keeps everyone inside. Additions to the facility are tentacle-like; it's a long

walk from the farthest wing to the lobby, and signage is confusing. **Rooms:** 166 rms and stes. CI 3pm/CO noon. Nonsmoking rms avail. Rooms are large, clean, and nicely appointed. **Amenities:** A/C, cable TV w/movies, refrig, voice mail. Some units w/terraces. **Services:** Car-rental desk, social director, masseur, babysitting. **Facilities:** 4 600 3 restaurants, 2 bars (w/entertainment), games rm, spa, sauna, whirlpool, playground, washer/dryer. The pool is long enough for lap swimming. Even during the week, as many as three different entertainers might be performing in various parts of the motel. A singer/guitarist performs evenings in a sitting area adjacent to the lobby. **Rates:** Peak (June 1–Sept 15) $55–$75 S; $60–$80 D; $100–$200 ste. Extra person $10. Children under age 18 stay free. Lower rates off-season. Parking: Outdoor, free. Rates rise sharply during annual Frontier Days Rodeo (last two weeks in July); reserve far in advance. AE, CB, DC, DISC, MC, V.

Days Inn

2360 W Lincolnway, 82001; tel 307/778-8877 or toll free 800/DAYS-INN; fax 307/778-8697. At the I-25 Lincolnway exit. No frills, just easy interstate access and a clean bed. **Rooms:** 72 rms. CI 3pm/CO noon. Nonsmoking rms avail. **Amenities:** A/C, cable TV w/movies. **Services:** **Facilities:** 35 Sauna, whirlpool. **Rates (CP):** Peak (May 15–Sept 15) $50–$57 S; $55–$62 D. Extra person $5. Children under age 17 stay free. Lower rates off-season. Parking: Outdoor, free. Rates rise sharply during annual Frontier Days Rodeo (last two weeks in July); reserve far in advance. AE, CB, DC, DISC, JCB, MC, V.

La Quinta Inn

2410 W Lincolnway, 82001; tel 307/632-7117 or toll free 800/531-5900; fax 307/638-7807. Practical, well-kept place, located next to the interstate along with a cluster of other lodgings catering to pass-through travelers. **Rooms:** 105 rms and stes. CI 3pm/CO noon. Nonsmoking rms avail. Two nicely decorated suites can be arranged to accommodate meetings or family stays. **Amenities:** A/C, cable TV w/movies, dataport. **Services:** **Facilities:** 30 Health club two blocks away is available to guests. **Rates (CP):** Peak (May 15–Oct 1) $51 S; $59 D; $71–$87 ste. Extra person $8. Children under age 18 stay free. Lower rates off-season. Parking: Outdoor, free. Rates rise sharply during annual Frontier Days Rodeo (last two weeks in July); reserve far in advance. AE, CB, DC, DISC, MC, V.

RESTAURANTS

Lexies

216 E 17th St; tel 307/638-8712. 2 blocks E of Center St, 1 block N of Lincolnway. **American.** Homelike setting, with attractive wainscoting and eclectic art, consisting of several rooms of a late-Victorian house. The breakfast crowd goes for the eggs Benedict and the soft and fluffy omelettes; the coffee, alas, is pedestrian. Friendly service. **FYI:** Reservations accepted. **Open:** Mon–Sat 7am–3am. **Prices:** Lunch main courses $4–$7. AE, CB, DC, DISC, ER, MC, V.

Los Amigos

620 Central Ave; tel 307/638-8591. ½ mi from Lincolnway/Central Jct. **Mexican.** It isn't the decidedly ordinary food that attracts families and groups of young people to this festive working class hangout; it's the friendly service, low prices, and a chance to stay late over a pitcher of margaritas or Mexican beer. **FYI:** Reservations accepted. Children's menu. **Open:** Mon–Thurs 11am–8:30pm, Fri–Sat 11am–9pm. **Prices:** Main courses $5–$9. AE, CB, DC, DISC, MC, V.

★ **Poor Richard's**

2233 E Lincolnway; tel 307/635-5114. 1 mi E of Central Ave. **American.** One of the top dining choices among movers and shakers in the state's capital. Although the dining room is usually packed, booths and soft lighting offer a sense of privacy. Menu highlights include champagne veal and lobster sautéed with asparagus and red peppers, and angel-hair pasta with mushrooms and prosciutto in a light cream sauce. **FYI:** Reservations recommended. **Open:** Lunch Mon–Fri 11am–2:30pm; dinner Sun–Thurs 5–10pm, Fri–Sat 5–11pm; brunch Sat 11am–2:30pm. **Prices:** Main courses $8–$16. AE, CB, DC, DISC, MC, V.

ATTRACTIONS

Wyoming State Capitol Building

200 W 24th St; tel 307/777-7220. The interior of this Corinthian structure, built in 1887, is punctuated with artwork depicting Wyoming culture, past and present. Both the Senate and House of Representatives chambers contain large murals (by Wyoming native Allen True) depicting industry, pioneer life, law, and transportation in the state; chamber ceilings are inlaid with Tiffany stained-glass windows depicting the official state seal. Mounted bison and elk specimens are on display in the lobby. Guided tours are conducted June–August from 8am–5pm. **Open:** Mon–Fri 8am–5pm. Closed some hols. **Free**

Historic Governors' Mansion

300 E 21st St; tel 307/777-7878. Used from 1905–1976, the mansion was the residence of 19 of Wyoming's first families. Visitors can tour the mansion, which houses the work of prominent Wyoming furniture makers, historical photographs, and period furnishings from the early 1900s. **Open:** Tues–Sat 9am–5pm. Closed some hols. **Free**

Wyoming State Museum

2301 Central Ave; tel 307/777-7022. This 100-year-old museum contains more than half a million items relating to Wyoming's history, including prehistoric fossils, early photographs, fine arts (including works by Allen True, Harry Jackson, and Joseph Henry Sharp) and Native American artifacts. Gift shop. **Open:** June–Aug, Mon–Fri 8:30am–5pm, Sat 9am–4pm, Sun noon–4pm; Sept–May, Mon–Fri 8:30am–5pm, Sat noon–4pm. Closed some hols. **Free**

Cheyenne Frontier Days Old West Museum
4501 N Carey Ave; tel 307/778-7290. Located on the grounds of Frontier Park Arena, site of Cheyenne Frontier Days, this museum has an impressive collection of memorabilia from the world's largest outdoor rodeo and the cowboys and cowgirls who made it famous. Saddles, classic Western clothing, a collection of more than 125 horse-drawn vehicles, Native American artifacts, and paintings by Western artists are also featured. **Open:** Summer, Mon–Fri 8am–6pm, Sat–Sun 10am–5pm. Call ahead for winter hours. Closed some hols. **$**

Cody

Buffalo Bill Cody's hometown and namesake, now the home of the Buffalo Bill Historical Center. Famous for its nightly rodeos in the summer. Cody is also a gateway to Yellowstone National Park. **Information:** Cody County Visitors and Convention Council, 836 Sheridan Ave, PO Box 2777, Cody, 82414 (tel 307/587-2297).

HOTELS

Holiday Inn Convention Center
1701 Sheridan Ave, 82414 (Downtown); tel 307/587-5555 or toll free 800/527-5544; fax 307/527-7757. At 17th. A clean, modern, dependable property catering to conventioneers in the winter and tourists in the summer. The only convention hotel in town. **Rooms:** 190 rms and stes. CI 2pm/CO noon. Nonsmoking rms avail. Better-than-average furnishings include teak headboards and night stands. **Amenities:** A/C, cable TV. Most rooms have two phones (one in bathroom). **Services:** Babysitting. **Facilities:** 500 3 restaurants, 1 bar. Wonderful gift shop open in summer only. **Rates:** Peak (May–Sept) $50–$120 S; $56–$126 D; $150–$156 ste. Extra person $6. Children under age 19 stay free. Lower rates off-season. Parking: Outdoor, free. B&B plan avail. AE, CB, DC, DISC, JCB, MC, V.

The Irma Hotel
1192 Sheridan Ave, 82414; tel 307/587-4221 or toll free 800/745-IRMA; fax 307/587-4221 ext 21. Historic two-story hotel built in 1902 by Buffalo Bill Cody (for $80,000) and named for his daughter. The original cherrywood bar, made in France at a cost of $100,000, is much photographed by tourists. **Rooms:** 40 rms and stes. CI 3pm/CO 11am. Nonsmoking rms avail. Accommodations vary from charming original rooms (furnished with antiques but equipped with modern bathroons) to slightly garish modern rooms. Look for period details, such as ceiling fans and pull-chain toilets. **Amenities:** A/C, cable TV. Some units w/terraces. **Services:** **Facilities:** 100 1 restaurant (*see* "Restaurants" below), 1 bar. **Rates:** Peak (June–Oct 1) $75 S; $80 D; $103 ste. Extra person $8. Children under age 12 stay free. Lower rates off-season. Parking: Outdoor, free. AE, CB, DC, DISC, MC, V.

MOTELS

Best Western Sunset Motor Inn
1601 8th St, 82414; tel 307/587-4265 or toll free 800/624-2727; fax 307/587-9029. 2 blocks S of Buffalo Bill Historical Center. Very nice, recently refurbished one-story property. Although it's located on a main highway into town, the setting is very tranquil, with lawns and cottonwood trees. The attractive lobby features leather chairs, tile floors, and a huge photo of Buffalo Bill. **Rooms:** 102 rms and stes. CI 2pm/CO 10am. Nonsmoking rms avail. Standard rooms are ordinary; attractive deluxe rooms have reproduction antique furnishings. **Amenities:** A/C. Some units w/terraces. **Services:** Coffee in lobby 6–10am. **Facilities:** 1 restaurant, whirlpool, playground, washer/dryer. **Rates:** Peak (June 12–Aug 26) $84 S; $94 D; $109–$130 ste. Extra person $3. Lower rates off-season. Parking: Outdoor, free. AE, CB, DC, DISC, MC, V.

Buffalo Bill Village Cabin Resort
1701 Sheridan Ave, 82414 (Downtown); tel 307/587-5544 or toll free 800/527-5544; fax 307/527-7757. Corner of US 14/16/20. Cute, western-style property located in a historic building. The uniformed staff even wears jeans and bandannas. Located close to town, it shares a compound with the Comfort Inn and Holiday Inn. **Rooms:** 83 cottages/villas. CI noon/CO 11am. Nonsmoking rms avail. All accommodations are in cabins, some of which are over 60 years old. They're clean, albeit slightly funky. **Amenities:** A/C, cable TV. **Services:** Babysitting. Friendly staff can help you make reservations for Yellowstone National Park hotels. **Facilities:** The Sasparilla Saloon has a snack bar and serves shakes, ice cream, and hot drinks, but no alcohol. **Rates:** $45–$90 cottage/villa. Children under age 19 stay free. Parking: Outdoor, free. Closed Oct–Apr. AE, CB, DC, DISC, JCB, MC, V.

The Burl Inn
1213 17th St, 82414; tel 307/587-2084 or toll free 800/388-2084; fax 307/587-3031. At US 14/16/20. Locally owned and operated motel located on the main road into town. **Rooms:** 40 rms. CI open/CO 10am. Nonsmoking rms avail. Notable for unique decor—lamps, headboards, credenzas, and bedside tables are all handmade from burl wood by the owner. The wood—mostly pine, but some cedar too—came from the Big Horn Mountains. **Amenities:** A/C, cable TV w/movies. 1 unit w/whirlpool. **Services:** Babysitting. Very friendly staff. **Facilities:** **Rates (CP):** Peak (June 16–Labor Day) $70–$85 S or D. Extra person $5. Children under age 2 stay free. Lower rates off-season. Parking: Outdoor, free. AE, DISC, MC, V.

Comfort Inn
1601 Sheridan Ave, 82414 (Downtown); tel 307/587-5556 or toll free 800/527-5544; fax 307/527-7757. Located downtown in the Buffalo Bill Village Resort, this modern and comfortable motel greets guests with an attractive lobby decorated with cowboy lamps, an antler chandelier, and an antique sideboard. Even the registration desk has a carving of Buffalo Bill and Sitting Bull. **Rooms:** 75 rms and stes. CI 2pm/CO noon. Nonsmoking rms avail. Clean, airy, and simple rooms with oak dressers and headboards. **Amenities:** A/C, cable TV. **Services:** Babysitting. Continental breakfast (cereals, bagels, doughnuts) served at the atmospheric Sasparilla Saloon next door. **Facilities:** Guests can use pool at the adjoining Holiday Inn. **Rates (CP):** Peak (May–Sept) $50–$119 S; $56–$125 D; $60–$129 ste. Extra person $6. Children under age 19 stay free. Lower rates off-season. Parking: Outdoor, free. AE, CB, DC, DISC, JCB, MC, V.

Days Inn of Cody
724 Yellowstone Ave, 82414; tel 307/527-6604 or toll free 800/DAYS-INN; fax 307/527-7341. This above-average, newer motel has an uninspired external architecture but clean and thoughtfully-decorated interiors. The spacious lobby has sofas, a kiva-style fireplace, and ceiling fans. **Rooms:** 52 rms and stes. CI 2pm/CO 11am. Nonsmoking rms avail. Rooms are large and nicely furnished with white-washed pine furniture. Honeymoon suite, with red, heart-shaped whirlpool tub. **Amenities:** A/C, cable TV. Some units w/whirlpools. **Services:** **Facilities:** Whirlpool, washer/dryer. Very attractive indoor pool with showers and men's and women's changing rooms. **Rates (CP):** Peak (June–Sept) $95–$105 S; $105–$115 D; $120–$140 ste. Extra person $6. Children under age 13 stay free. Lower rates off-season. Parking: Outdoor, free. AE, CB, DC, DISC, MC, V.

Kelly Inn
2513 Greybull Hwy, 82414; tel 307/527-5505 or toll free 800/635-3559; fax 307/527-5505. near Cody airport. Clean, attractive, quiet, well-maintained motel. Located on the east end of town near Cody's Vietnam War Memorial. **Rooms:** 50 rms. CI open/CO 11am. Nonsmoking rms avail. Some rooms are extremely large; Lake View rooms offer lovely views. **Amenities:** A/C. Some units w/whirlpools. **Services:** **Facilities:** Sauna, whirlpool, washer/dryer. **Rates:** Peak (June–Sept 15) $65 S; $78 D. Extra person $5. Children under age 12 stay free. Lower rates off-season. Parking: Outdoor, free. AE, DC, DISC, MC, V.

INN

UNRATED **Cody Guest Houses**
1513 and 1519 Beck, 1405 and 1415 Rumsey, 82414; tel 307/587-6000 or toll free 800/587-6560. 2 acres. The nicest and most unique lodgings in Cody, consisting of a three-bedroom Victorian house, a four-bedroom western-style lodge, four one-bedroom western "cottages" and a one-bedroom executive suite. All are located in a downtown residential neighborhood. **Rooms:** 7 cottages/villas. CI 3pm–8pm/CO 11am. No smoking. Houses and cottages are all thoughtfully and authentically decorated with brass beds, claw-foot bathtubs, and antiques. Built circa 1906, the Victorian house features a dining room, kitchen, and parlor. No children permitted in Victorian house. **Amenities:** Refrig. No A/C. All units w/terraces, 1 w/fireplace, some w/whirlpools. Victorian house equipped with whirlpool. Houses stocked with milk, juice, coffee, tea, bread, and jellies. **Services:** Babysitting. Owners Daren and Kathy Singer go out of their way to serve guests—they'll even come in and prepare dinners. Kathy is also a talented photographer who specializes in Victorian-style portraits. **Facilities:** 20 **Rates:** Peak (May–Oct) $85–$250 cottage/villa. Extra person $25. Lower rates off-season. Parking: Outdoor, free. Weekly rates avail. AE, DISC, MC, V.

LODGES

Absaroka Mountain Lodge
1231 E Yellowstone Hwy, Wapiti, 82450; tel 307/587-3963; fax 307/587-3963. 12 mi E of Yellowstone. 6.5 acres. In the language of the Crow people, *absaroka* means "home place." This historic, family-owned and -operated mountain lodge sits on 6½ acres along Gun Barrel Creek, all surrounded by the 2.4 million acres of Shoshone National Forest. A good value for peace and quiet. **Rooms:** 16 cottages/villas. CI 2pm/CO 11am. The log cabins date back to the early 1920s and are simply furnished but comfortable. Family cabins can sleep up to six people; most have showers only, and one has a kitchenette. Choose #12 if you want privacy; it's set the furthest back. **Amenities:** No A/C, phone, or TV. Some units w/terraces. **Services:** Babysitting. Definitely animal friendly—resident dogs and cats are available for walks or as bedmates. Naturalist gives weekly talks. **Facilities:** 30 1 restaurant (bkfst and dinner only), 1 bar, basketball, volleyball, games rm, lawn games, playground. Extensive fishing and riding facilities, including a corral with 32 horses. Chuck wagon barbecues on Wed evenings in summer (extra fee). **Rates:** Peak (June–Nov) $53–$102 cottage/villa. Extra person $6–$10. Lower rates off-season. Parking: Outdoor, free. Closed Oct 1–23/Thanksgiving–May. DISC, MC, V.

Cody's Ranch Resort
2604-F Yellowstone Hwy, 82414 (Wapiti Valley); tel 307/587-6271. 26 mi W of Cody; 26 mi from E Entrance of Yellowstone. Down-home lodge and cabins, featuring a strong emphasis on horseback riding. Barbara Cody, the owner since 1971, was married to Buffalo Bill Cody's grandson. **Rooms:** 1 rms; 13 cottages/villas. CI open/CO 10am. Nonsmoking rms avail. Accommodations are decorated with cowboy art; some have hand-carved furniture dating to the 1940s. No TVs or phones in cabins. **Amenities:** No A/C, phone, or TV. 1 unit w/terrace. **Services:** Social

director, children's program, babysitting. **Facilities:** 1 restaurant, 1 bar. 70 horses and 17 different trails to ride; up to 4 hours riding daily. Horse-drawn wagon rides. Riding available to the public by the hour, half-day, or day. **Rates (AP):** Peak (June 10–Aug) $140 S; $280 D; $140 cottage/villa. Extra person $65–85. Min stay peak. Lower rates off-season. Parking: Outdoor, free. Three-night minimum stay in high season. DISC, MC, V.

Elephant Head Lodge

1170 Yellowstone Hwy, Wapiti, 82450 (Wapiti Valley); tel 307/587-3980; fax 307/527-7922. 11½ mi E of Yellowstone. Built as a guest lodge in 1910 by Buffalo Bill Cody's niece, this place is located in the heart of the Shoshone National Forest. Good value. **Rooms:** 11 cottages/villas. CI noon/CO noon. The cozy cabins are thoughtfully decorated; some feature lodgepole pine bed frames, wicker furniture, and patchwork quilts. **Amenities:** No A/C, phone, or TV. Some units w/terraces, 1 w/fireplace. **Services:** Social director, babysitting. **Facilities:** 1 restaurant, 1 bar, volleyball, lawn games, playground. Nightly movies in lounge; large video library. Trail rides by the hour or day, hiking, rock climbing, and nature walks. **Rates:** Peak (June–Sept 20) $58–$106 cottage/villa. Lower rates off-season. AP rates avail. Parking: Outdoor, free. Closed Oct–May 15. AE, DISC, MC, V.

Pahaska Teepee Resort

183 Yellowstone Hwy, 82414; tel 307/527-7701 or toll free 800/628-7791; fax 307/527-4019. Motel-style lodge located near the east entrance of Yellowstone National Park. Buffalo Bill's original hunting lodge, located on the grounds, is now a small historical museum; tours are free and the guide is excellent. **Rooms:** 19 rms and effic; 23 cottages/villas. CI 4pm/CO 11am. Nonsmoking rms avail. Rooms next to the highway are noisy; A-frames (farther back) are dated; log cabins are large and comfortable. **Amenities:** No A/C, phone, or TV. Some units w/terraces, 1 w/fireplace, 1 w/whirlpool. **Services:** Babysitting. **Facilities:** 1 restaurant, 1 bar, volleyball, lawn games. Fishing pond. Tacky gift shop. **Rates:** Peak (June 20–Aug 23) $73–$94 S or D; $119 effic; $73–$94 cottage/villa. Lower rates off-season. Parking: Outdoor, free. "Family reunion" cabin with 7 bedrooms, 11 beds, 8 bathrooms, and fireplace for $3,500/week. AE, CB, MC, V.

RESTAURANTS

Cassie's Supper Club

214 Yellowstone Ave; tel 307/527-5500. **Seafood/Steak.** Dating back to the 1920s, this one-time "house of ill fame" and speakeasy (bootleg whiskey was brewed and bottled in the cellar) has been remodeled and expanded several times, but the original building still remains. Local hunters have donated numerous animal-head trophies, which hang in the club; the dining room is decorated in western/Victorian style. The kitchen specializes in excellent steaks and lobsters, but pasta, chicken, and seafood also figure on the menu. The out-of-this-world desserts are made by the owner's mother. Huge portions. **FYI:** Reservations recommended. Blues/country music/dancing/rock. **Open:** Lunch Mon–Sat 11am–2pm; dinner Mon–Sat 5–10pm. **Prices:** Main courses $9–$50. AE, DISC, MC, V.

Franca's Italian Dining

1421 Rumsey Ave; tel 307/587-5354. **Italian.** Italian-born Franca Facchetti proudly presents her northern Italian cuisine in the lovely ambience of a 1920s house. Different fixed menus each night offer four courses. Although main dishes are veal, chicken, beef, and pork, vegetarians are nicely accommodated. Wine list boasts more than 100 selections. Franca's husband, Joseph, operates a small art gallery in back. **FYI:** Reservations recommended. No smoking. **Open:** Peak (June–Sept) Wed–Sun 6–10pm. Closed Mar–Apr. **Prices:** Main courses $15–$27; prix fixe $12.50–$27. No CC.

The Irma Hotel Grill & Silver Saddle Lounge

1192 Sheridan Ave; tel 309/587-4221. **American.** The most atmospheric restaurant in town. Sit at the counter, booths, or tables in the cavernous dining room, or check out the famous $100,000 cherrywood bar hand-carved in France. House specialties include buffalo burgers, steaks, prime rib, and seafood; there's also a soup and salad bar. **FYI:** Reservations recommended. Children's menu. **Open:** Peak (June–Aug) daily 6am–10pm. **Prices:** Main courses $10–$17. AE, CB, DC, DISC, MC, V.

La Comida

1385 Sheridan Ave; tel 307/587-9556. **American/Mexican.** The husband-and-wife owners, John and Karen Gibbons, have created a popular Mexican-American restaurant with a casual atmosphere. The watercolors of Mexico that adorn the walls were painted by Karen's grandmother. Menu favorites include chicken breast with green chiles, Swiss cheese, and cream; plus the usual tacos and enchiladas. Desserts such as flan and margarita mud pie have been featured in gourmet magazines. **FYI:** Reservations recommended. Children's menu. **Open:** Peak (June–Sept) daily 11am–10pm. **Prices:** Main courses $5–$15. AE, DISC, MC, V.

Proud Cut Saloon

1227 Sheridan Ave; tel 307/527-6905. **American.** A friendly, atmospheric western bar and restaurant with a copper-top bar, tin ceiling, historic photos, and animal trophies. For lunch, you can order tasty burgers and sandwiches; dinner offers choices like steak, fried shrimp, and grilled chicken. Prime rib featured Fri–Sat. Save room for the homemade desserts, such as cheesecake or peanut butter pie. Those under 21 can eat in the back room or patio only. **FYI:** Reservations recommended. **Open:** Mon–Sat 10am–11pm, Sun noon–10pm. **Prices:** Main courses $8–$15. AE, DC, DISC, MC, V.

ATTRACTIONS

Buffalo Bill Historical Center
720 Sheridan Ave; tel 307/587-4771. Four-museum complex surrounds a central orientation gallery. The **Buffalo Bill Museum** is home to the personal collections of William Frederick "Buffalo Bill" Cody and memorabilia from his Wild West show, including guns, costumes, and show posters. A lower-level gallery houses special exhibitions. The **Whitney Gallery of Western Art** boasts a large collection of paintings, sculptures, and prints depicting the West from the early 19th-century to the present. Featured artists include George Catlin, Thomas Moran, Frederic Remington, and N C Wyeth. The **Plains Indian Museum** illustrates the culture and artistry of the Arapaho, Cheyenne, Kiowa, Comanche, Sioux, and other tribes, while one of the largest collections of American firearms in the world—more than 5,000 pieces—is housed at the **Cody Firearms Museum.** Self-guided audio tours are available; ask at the orientation gallery. **Open:** June–Aug, daily 7am–8pm; May and Sept, daily 8am–8pm; Oct, daily 8am–5pm; Apr, Tues–Sun 8am–5pm; Mar and Nov, Tues–Sun 10am–3pm. **$$$**

Old Trail Town
1831 Demaris Dr; tel 307/587-5302. Authentic turn-of-the-century houses have been re-erected on the original site of Cody. Among the buildings in this open-air museum are a saloon, a general store, a school, and a forge. **Open:** Daily 8am–8pm. **$**

Shoshone National Forest
Supervisor's office, 225 W Yellowstone Ave; tel 307/527-6241. The first national forest in the United States, established by presidential proclamation in 1891, encompasses 2.4 million acres and extends along a 180-mile strip from the Montana border to the Wind River Mountains. The diverse topography of glaciers, lakes, exposed rock, meadows, and woodlands provides homes for great black bears, coyotes, bald eagles, elk, moose, and antelopes. More than 1,500 miles of trails offer hiking and horseback riding opportunities, 50 campgrounds. **Open:** Daily 24 hours. **Free**

Devils Tower National Monument

Monument entrance located 27 mi NW of Sundance, WY; 33 mi NE of Moorcroft, WY; and 52 mi SW of Belle Fourche, SD on WY 110. The first national monument, created in 1906 by President Theodore Roosevelt, is anchored by an 867-foot tall "tower" formed by the core of an ancient volcano. The ghostly rock formation was used as a landmark by westward pioneers, who eventually made a sport of climbing it. Annually, more than 5,000 people come here just to climb on its massive columns.

The monument's visitors center (open April–October) has displays on the Tower's history and geology. In summer months, guided walks, campfire programs, and climbing demonstrations are available; ask at visitors center. There are five nature trails, a campground (open April–October, depending on weather), and a picnic area. Visitors who want to climb the Tower must register with a ranger before setting out. For more information, contact the Superintendent, Devils Tower National Monument, PO Box 8, Devils Tower, WY 82714 (tel 307/467-5283).

Douglas

Hosts the Wyoming State fair every August. Named for Stephen Douglas, Abraham Lincoln's opponent in the Lincoln-Douglas debates. **Information:** Douglas Area Chamber of Commerce, 43 W Center, Douglas, 82633 (tel 307/358-2950).

MOTEL

UNRATED **Holiday Inn**
1450 Riverbend Dr, 82633; tel 307/358-9790 or toll free 800/HOLIDAY; fax 307/358-6251. At I-25 exit 59. Grassy inner courtyard with flowers and a sitting area. **Rooms:** 118 rms. CI 3pm/CO 11am. Nonsmoking rms avail. **Amenities:** A/C, satel TV w/movies. Some rooms have hair dryers. **Services:** **Facilities:** 1 restaurant, 1 bar, games rm, sauna, whirlpool, washer/dryer. Children under 12 eat free with adults in hotel restaurant. **Rates:** Peak (Mem Day–Labor Day) $57 S; $65 D. Extra person $8. Children under age 19 stay free. Lower rates off-season. Parking: Outdoor, free. AE, CB, DC, DISC, EC, ER, JCB, MC, V.

ATTRACTION

Wyoming Pioneer Memorial Museum
400 West Center; tel 307/358-9288. Located on the Wyoming State Fairgrounds. Extensive collections of pioneer artifacts feature saddles and firearms, home furnishings, vintage clothing, early photographs, dolls, quilts, and other memorabilia. The museum has also acquired a collection of 19th- and 20th-century Western art. The Johnson Gallery is devoted to Native American decorative arts, sculpture, artifacts—even a full-size teepee used in *Dances with Wolves.* **Open:** Summer, Mon–Fri 8am–5pm, Sat 1–5pm; winter, Mon–Fri 8am–5pm. Closed some hols. **Free**

Dubois

This small community was once a center for producing railroad ties. Although the local economy was based on the timber industry until the 1980s, Dubois is now mainly a ranching and tourist area. **Information:** Dubois Chamber of Commerce, 616 W Ramshorn, PO Box 632, Dubois, 82513 (tel 307/455-2556).

MOTELS

Black Bear Country Inn

505 N Ramshorn, 82513; tel 307/455-2344 or toll free 800/873-BEAR. W side of US 287/26; at center of town. A large sculpted bear marks the entrance of this very basic lodging near the Wind River. Attractive to hunters who need a bed and not much else. **Rooms:** 16 rms and effic. CI open/CO 11am. Nonsmoking rms avail. Many of the rooms have been somewhat refurbished but the bathrooms need quite a bit of work. **Amenities:** Cable TV, refrig. No A/C. Some units w/terraces. **Services:** Very generous owners (stay more than a day and they will loan you the keys to their Jeep) can arrange horseback rides and other outdoor activities. **Rates:** Peak (July–Aug) $40 S; $44 D; $65 effic. Extra person $3. Children under age 12 stay free. Lower rates off-season. Parking: Outdoor, free. Closed Dec–Apr. AE, CB, DC, DISC, MC, V.

Stagecoach Motor Inn

103 E Ramshorn, PO Box 216, 82513; tel 307/455-2303 or toll free 800/455-5090. At jct US 26 and US 287. Pretty Horse Creek runs behind this clean motel, set away from the Main St traffic. **Rooms:** 50 rms and effic. CI open/CO 11am. Nonsmoking rms avail. Accommodations vary in size, modernity, and allure; newer accommodations are much handsomer than the old ones. Two-bedroom efficiencies are very nice for groups. **Amenities:** Cable TV, refrig. No A/C. Some units w/terraces. **Services:** Babysitting. Steaks and other western fare are served up at nightly barbecue cookouts in summer. The owners (John Suda and family) are reputable hunting guides and outfitters. **Facilities:** 30 Playground. Trees and lawns surround the roomy swimming pool, accented by an elk-antler arch and a recreated stagecoach. There's a horseshoe pit, and also an enclosed area for pets. **Rates:** Peak (June–Aug) $38–$46 S; $50–$60 D; $65–$90 effic. Extra person $5. Children under age 4 stay free. Lower rates off-season. Parking: Outdoor, free. AE, DC, DISC, MC, V.

RESTAURANT

Old Yellowstone Garage

110 N Ramshorn; tel 307/455-3666. Along US 26/287. **Italian.** Decidedly rustic Dubois offers a surprise culinary treat: sophisticated Northern Italian fare (much of it prepared in an open brick oven) presented with artifice but no pretense. Stereotypes are gone forever when you see rugged, Stetson-wearing cowboys gleefully dipping bread in basil-infused olive oil, savoring shrimp pasta, and devouring large sautéed mushrooms. When weather allows, there is outdoor pit barbecue service. **FYI:** Reservations accepted. **Open:** Peak (Mem Day–Sept) lunch daily 11:30am–2:30pm; dinner daily 6–10pm. Closed Dec–Apr. **Prices:** Main courses $13–$18. AE, DISC, MC, V.

Evanston

Evanston was founded in 1868 during the building of the Union Pacific Railroad. Depot Square preserves the history of the town. **Information:** Bear River Travel Information Center, 601 Bear River Dr, Evanston, 82930 (tel 307/789-6547).

HOTEL

Weston Plaza Hotel

1983 Harrison Dr, 82930; tel 307/789-0783 or toll free 800/255-9840; fax 307/789-7186. Exit 3 (Harrison Dr) off I-80; turn left. Attractive motel and a good value. **Rooms:** 101 rms. CI noon/CO 11am. Nonsmoking rms avail. Large, comfortable, and well appointed. **Amenities:** A/C, satel TV. Some units w/terraces. **Services:** **Facilities:** 200 1 restaurant, 1 bar, whirlpool. Pool open 6am–10pm. **Rates:** Peak (May 15–Sept 15) $47 S; $52 D. Extra person $5. Children under age 16 stay free. Lower rates off-season. Parking: Outdoor, free. AE, DC, DISC, MC, V.

MOTELS

Best Western Dunmar Inn

1601 Harrison Dr, 82930; tel 307/789-3770 or toll free 800/654-6509; fax 307/789-3758. On the W side of town. All units are in clusters of low houses at this extremely good-looking property. Prices are a bit higher than elsewhere, but represent good value. The large lobby offers plush easy chairs and greenery, as well as a stuffed bear and mountain lion. **Rooms:** 166 rms and stes. CI open/CO noon. Nonsmoking rms avail. **Amenities:** A/C, satel TV. **Services:** Babysitting. **Facilities:** 200 1 restaurant (*see* "Restaurants" below), 1 bar (w/entertainment). **Rates:** Peak (May 26–Sept 30) $66–$78 S; $78–$90 D; $95–$195 ste. Extra person $6. Children under age 18 stay free. Lower rates off-season. Parking: Outdoor, free. AE, CB, DC, DISC, JCB, MC, V.

Weston Super Budget Inn

1936 Harrison Dr, 82930; tel 307/789-2810 or toll free 800/255-9840; fax 307/789-5506. On the W end of business I-80. Basic lodgings for a modest price. **Rooms:** 112 rms. CI open/CO 11am. Nonsmoking rms avail. **Amenities:** A/C, cable TV. Some units w/whirlpools. **Services:** Babysitting. **Facilities:** 100 1 restaurant, 2 bars (1 w/entertainment), washer/dryer. Pool along 9th fairway of golf course—set internal radar to "duffer alert." **Rates:** Peak (May 15–Sept 15) $30–$40 S; $35–$140 D. Extra person $5. Children under age 15 stay free. Lower rates off-season. Parking: Outdoor, free. AE, CB, DC, DISC, MC, V.

RESTAURANT

★ Dunmar's Legal Tender Dining and Lounge
In Best Western Dunmar Inn, 1601 Harrison Dr; tel 307/789-3770. **American.** Don't be surprised if it's standing room only—especially on summer weekends—at this popular local gathering place. The menu highlights steaks; other popular entree choices include halibut, marinated chicken, and fried shrimp. Country and western music Sat–Sun in the downstairs Wyoming Hall. **FYI:** Reservations recommended. Children's menu. **Open:** Daily 5:30am–10pm. **Prices:** Main courses $9–$25. AE, DC, DISC, MC, V.

Gillette

Called the Energy Capital of the Nation by locals, this prairie town is rich in coal. An early 1960s oil boom made this area one of the richest in the state. The Cam-plex center hosts everything from rodeos to concerts. **Information:** Gillette Convention and Visitors Bureau, 314 S Gillette Ave, Gillette, 82716 (tel 307/686-0040).

HOTEL

Holiday Inn
2009 S Douglas Hwy, 82718; tel 307/686-3000 or toll free 800/686-3368; fax 307/686-4018. This white-brick structure boasts a sparkling, tasteful interior, with muted colors and silk flowers adorning the lobby. Near a convention facility which hosts ballets, symphonies, craft fairs, and rodeos. **Rooms:** 158 rms and stes. Executive level. CI 2pm/CO noon. Nonsmoking rms avail. Smallish, newly decorated rooms have new mattresses and linens. **Amenities:** A/C, refrig, dataport, VCR. Some units w/terraces, 1 w/whirlpool. Suites equipped with dataports, refrigerators, coffeemakers, silk flower arrangements, and telephones in bathrooms. **Services:** Social director. Small pets allowed. Guest Director can arrange mine tours, Durham Buffalo Ranch tours, and buffalo barbecues for groups. **Facilities:** 500 1 restaurant, 3 bars (1 w/entertainment), games rm, sauna, whirlpool, playground, washer/dryer. Banquet facilities; charming gift shop. **Rates:** Peak (June–Aug) $62–$77 S or D; $100–$130 ste. Extra person $8. Children under age 19 stay free. Lower rates off-season. Parking: Outdoor, free. New Year's Eve and honeymoon packages avail. AE, DC, DISC, MC, V.

MOTEL

Best Western Towers West Lodge
109 N US Hwy 14/16, 82716; tel 307/686-2210 or toll free 800/762-7375; fax 307/682-5105. At the western edge of town. A modern brick structure on the west side of town, this property has an inviting lobby with a fireplace, overstuffed chairs, and a couch. **Rooms:** 190 rms and stes. CI 6pm/CO noon. Nonsmoking rms avail. Rooms are small but newly redecorated. **Amenities:** A/C, cable TV w/movies, dataport. Some units w/whirlpools. Some rooms have dataports. **Services:** Masseur, babysitting. **Facilities:** 300 1 restaurant, 1 bar (w/entertainment), games rm, sauna, whirlpool, washer/dryer. Vehicle plug-ins in winter. 24-hour convenience store. Banquet rooms. **Rates:** Peak (May 30–Sept 15) $44–$75 S; $49–$80 D; $100–$150 ste. Extra person $5. Children under age 18 stay free. Lower rates off-season. Parking: Outdoor, free. Senior rates avail. AE, DC, DISC, MC, V.

RESTAURANT

$ ★ The Prime Rib Restaurant
1205 S WY 59; tel 307/682-2944. E of downtown Gillette; N of I-90. **Italian/Steak.** Occasionally, the cuisine of a guest chef is featured, but this place is most known for its prime rib. The traditionally decorated room, done in hunter green and dark wood, is filled with wine racks. The award-winning wine list boasts more than 350 choices. **FYI:** Reservations recommended. Country music/folk/jazz/karaoke. Children's menu. **Open:** Lunch Mon–Fri 11am–5pm; dinner Mon–Fri 5–9pm, Sat–Sun 4–9pm. **Prices:** Main courses $7–$22; prix fixe $10–$13. AE, MC, V.

ATTRACTION

Campbell County Rockpile Museum
900 W 2nd; tel 307/682-5723. Located next to a large rockpile formation that has been used as a landmark since early settlement days. This museum's permanent collections feature relics of ranch and cowboy life, including clothing, blacksmithing tools, farm equipment, firearms, and a genuine chuck wagon. A hands-on area allows visitors to weigh themselves on a railroad luggage scale or ring up purchases on an old-time cash register. **Open:** June–Aug, Mon–Sat 9am–8pm, Sun 12:30–6:30pm; Sept–May, Mon–Sat 9am–5pm. Closed some hols. **Free**

Grand Teton National Park

See also Jackson Hole

13 mi N of Jackson on US 89, just south of Yellowstone. Grand Teton's impressive mountain range numbers 31 peaks rising above 10,825 foot; the highest, Grand Teton, itself soars to 13,770 foot. The mountains owe their name to the romantic (or perhaps humorous) imagination of the 19th century French-Canadian trappers, who saw in these pointed, snow-capped peaks a likeness to a woman's breast.

With the torrential Snake River, deep forests, lakes full of fish, and remote mountain peaks, Grand Teton encompasses some of the most beautiful natural landscapes in the United States. More than 187 miles of marked trails offer an unlimited choice of hiking or skiing excursions, according to the season. Winters are long and snowy (the mean temperature is 5°F) while summers are short, cool, and sunny. The lake water is always too cold for swimming. About 500 black and grizzly bears, about 30,000 elk, and about 2,500 buffalo populate the park.

Along with pristine lodges (open mid-May to September) located in the park, beautiful camping and mobile-home spots are available, but campers must adhere to strict regulations. Several commercial outfitters specialize in various park adventures from llama and covered wagon trips to rafting trips on the Snake River, mountain biking, and mountain climbing expeditions. The park is open year-round, although services vary according to season. For more information contact the park's superintendent, PO Box 170, Moose, WY 83012 (tel 307/733-2880). Visitors centers are located at Colter Bay, Jenny Lake, and Moose.

LODGES

Colter Bay Village

US 89, Colter Bay, PO Box 240, 83013; tel 307/543-2811. Rustic lodging in a great setting on the shores of Jackson Lake. **Rooms:** 274 cottages/villas. CI 4pm/CO 11am. Nonsmoking rms avail. Funky but serviceable log or knotty-pine cabins with linoleum floors and hook rugs. Some of the cabins were built elsewhere in the valley and moved to their current location. Tent cabins (two walls wood, two walls canvas) are also available—guests supply own bedding or sleeping bags. **Amenities:** No A/C, phone, or TV. **Services:** Babysitting. **Facilities:** 2 restaurants, 1 bar, 1 beach (lake shore), washer/dryer. Full-service marina rents canoes and powerboats. Near hiking trails. **Rates:** $27–$99 cottage/villa. Extra person $7.50. Children under age 12 stay free. Parking: Outdoor, free. Tent cabins are $22 per couple per night. Closed early Oct–mid-May. AE, DC, MC, V.

Jenny Lake Lodge

North Jenny Lake Loop Rd, PO Box 240, 83013; tel 307/733-4647. Elegant yet rural (the property once belonged to John D Rockefeller), this lodge provides the loveliest accommodations in the park. Updated log cabins, renowned cuisine, incredible views. **Rooms:** 37 cottages/villas. CI 4pm/CO 11am. No smoking. Comfortably furnished with hook rugs and patchwork quilts and enhanced by all the comforts and amenities, the log cabins offer a rustic-but-glamorous experience. **Amenities:** Bathrobes. No A/C, phone, or TV. All units w/terraces, some w/fireplaces, some w/whirlpools. Rooms are stocked with Crabtree & Evelyn toiletries; rocking chairs on the porches, plus walking sticks and umbrellas. **Services:** Twice-daily maid svce, babysitting. **Facilities:** 1 restaurant (*see* "Restaurants" below). Free horseback riding and use of bicycles. No pool or spa, but near hiking, fishing, and river swimming. **Rates (MAP):** $255–$465 cottage/villa. Extra person $100. Children under age 12 stay free. Parking: Outdoor, free. Closed early Oct–late May. AE, DC, MC, V.

RESORTS

Jackson Lake Lodge

US 89 W, PO Box 240, 83013; tel 307/543-2811 or toll free 800/628-9988. Full-service property offering a spectacular lobby and dramatic views of the Tetons across Willow Flats. Very busy in summer. **Rooms:** 37 rms and stes; 348 cottages/villas. CI 4pm/CO 11am. Nonsmoking rms avail. Accommodations vary from hotel-style in main building to motel-style "cottages." Views from either can be spectacular or nonexistent. "Moose Pond" rooms are nicest. **Amenities:** A/C, dataport. No TV. Some units w/terraces. **Services:** Social director, masseur, babysitting. Wonderful summer staff of enthusiastic, friendly young people from all across the country. **Facilities:** 300 2 restaurants, 1 bar (w/entertainment). Activities desk, hiking trails, barbecue, quiet reading/card room, medical clinic, gift shop. **Rates:** $89–$155 S or D; $300–$450 ste; $112–$162 cottage/villa. Extra person $9. Children under age 12 stay free. Parking: Outdoor, free. Closed mid-Oct–mid-May. AE, DC, MC, V.

Signal Mountain Lodge

Teton Park Rd, PO Box 50, Moran, 83013; tel 307/543-2831; fax 307/543-2569. 40 acres. Located on Jackson Lake within Grand Teton National Park, it offers great views and a full-service marina. Popular with locals from Jackson, as well as tourists. Good value. **Rooms:** 79 rms, stes, and effic. CI 3pm/CO 11am. Nonsmoking rms avail. Accommodations vary from motel-type "country rooms" to lakefront suites. Log cabins are especially cozy, with rustic, lodgepole furnishings. All are comfortable and clean. **Amenities:** No A/C or TV. All units w/terraces, some w/fireplaces. **Services:** In addition to guided fishing trips on the lake, scenic float trips are offered twice a day. **Facilities:** 75 2 restaurants, 1 bar, 1 beach (lake shore). Many types of boats available for rent, from canoes to pontoons. Terrific gift shop. **Rates:** $69–$150 S or D; $140–$150 ste; $140–$150 effic. Extra person $8. Children under age 12 stay free. Parking: Outdoor, free. Summer reservations are accepted 11 months in advance. Closed mid-Oct–mid-May. AE, DISC, MC, V.

RESTAURANT

Jenny Lake Lodge Restaurant

Interloop Rd; tel 307/733-4647. **Regional American.** The dining room continues the upscale theme of the mountain-lodge resort with a log-pole interior and black-painted twig chairs; window tables have views of the Cathedral Group of the Teton range. Every night, a different six-course, prix-fixe dinner is served, concentrating on Rocky Mountain regional cuisine: buffalo and other game from the Rockies, lamb from

Idaho, and local salmon. The Sunday dinner buffet is especially popular. Although the restaurant primarily caters to hotel guests, nonguests are welcome on a space-available basis. **FYI:** Reservations recommended. Guitar. Dress code. No smoking. **Open:** Closed early Oct–late May. **Prices:** Prix fixe $36. AE, DC, MC, V.

Grant Village

See Yellowstone National Park

Green River

See also Rock Springs

Close to Flaming Gorge National Recreation Area. Green River is a mining community that produces trona, a mineral used in products such as glass and baking soda. Green River claims to have the mildest climate in the state. **Information:** Green River Chamber of Commerce, 1450 Uinta Dr, Green River, 82935 (tel 307/875-5711).

ATTRACTIONS

Sweetwater County Historical Museum
80 W Flaming Gorge Way; tel 307/872-6435. Exhibits depict the area's history as a coal mining and railroad town, with special emphasis on the European and Asian immigrants who came here during the late 19th-century boom years. Large collections of Native American artifacts and historic photos. **Open:** July–Aug, Mon–Fri 9am–5pm, Sat 1–5pm; Sept–June, Mon–Fri 9am–5pm. Closed some hols. **Free**

Flaming Gorge National Recreation Area
Manila; tel 801/784-3445. The completion of Flaming Gorge Dam more than 30 years ago lead to the creation of the 91-mile-long Lake Flaming Gorge. The National Recreational Area, occupying northeastern Utah and southwestern Wyoming, is very popular with fishing enthusiasts, with Mackinaw trout, Kokanee salmon, smallmouth bass, and several varieties of trout being the most common catches. (Several years ago, a 51-pound Mackinaw was caught in the lake.) **Buckboard Marina** (tel 307/875-6927), 25 miles south of Green River, offers boat rentals and launching ramps.

Other recreational opportunities include camping (there are nine campgrounds in the Wyoming section of the park), hiking, birdwatching, mountain biking, cross-country skiing, wildlife viewing, and boat tours of the Green River. Guided interpretive programs are offered during the summer months. Green River Visitors Center, located just south of Green River on WY 530, is open year-round. For further information, contact District Ranger, PO Box 278, Manila, UT 84046 (tel 801/784-3445). **Open:** Daily dawn–dusk. **Free**

Greybull

MOTEL

Yellowstone Motel
247 Greybull Ave (US 14 E), 82426; tel 307/765-4456; fax 307/765-2108. Well-maintained older motel. **Rooms:** 34 rms and stes. CI 11am/CO 10am. Nonsmoking rms avail. Large rooms good for families. One suite has cooking facilities. **Amenities:** A/C, cable TV. **Services:** Social director, babysitting. Complimentary van to nearby ranch for buffalo barbecues and covered-wagon rides. **Facilities:** Putting green. Skiing within 25 miles, dinosaur dig 7 miles away, wild horse range 35 miles away. **Rates:** Peak (Mem Day–Sept 15) $30–$36 S; $40–$56 D; $60–$80 ste. Extra person $6. Children under age 6 stay free. Lower rates off-season. Parking: Outdoor, free. Senior and corporate rates avail. AE, DC, DISC, MC, V.

Jackson Hole

See also Grand Teton National Park

Tourism is the largest industry in this beautiful spot near the Grand Tetons—everything from symphonies and art galleries to white-water rafting and mountain hiking is available. The historic town square is noted for its antler archways. **Information:** Jackson Hole Visitors Council, 532 N Cache, PO Box 982, Jackson, 83001 (tel 307/733-7606).

PUBLIC TRANSPORTATION

Southern Teton Rapid Transit (START) (tel 307/733-4521) serves the towns of Jackson, Teton Village, and Hoback. Green Line, which connects Teton Village and Jackson, runs daily 7am–7:45pm; Blue Line, which connects Jackson and Hoback, runs Mon–Fri 7am–7:45pm. Fares: $1; seniors and children under 8 ride free. Exact change required.

HOTELS

Alpenhof
3255 W McCollister, PO Box 288, Teton Village, 83023; tel 307/733-3242 or toll free 800/732-3244; fax 307/739-1516. From WY 22, take WY 390 N, 12 mi N of Jackson Hole. Four-story, chalet-style lodge offers a bit of Switzerland at the base of the Tetons. Expensive, but this is prime ski-resort country. **Rooms:** 42 rms and stes. CI 3pm/CO 11am. Nonsmoking rms avail. Standard rooms offer dated furnishings and mountain views. Deluxe rooms feature hand-carved Bavarian furniture. **Amenities:** Bathrobes. No A/C. Some units w/minibars, some w/terraces, some w/fireplaces, some w/whirlpools. Eiderdown comforters and pretty linens. Fruit basket upon check-in. The romantic Alpine Room boasts a whirlpool and a fireplace. **Services:** Twice-daily maid svce, masseur, babysitting. **Facilities:** 2 restaurants, 1 bar, games rm, sauna, whirlpool, washer/

dryer. Outdoor, heated pool is open year-round and offers views of the Tetons. Large whirlpool can accommodate 8–10 people. **Rates (CP):** Peak (Dec 23–Jan 5) $108–$360 S or D; $402 ste. Extra person $10. Min stay peak. Lower rates off-season. Parking: Outdoor, free. Ask about "value season" rates. Closed Apr 7–May 20/Oct 8–Nov. AE, DC, DISC, MC, V.

Best Western Inn at Jackson Hole
3345 W McCollister Dr, PO Box 328, Teton Village, 83025; tel 307/733-2311 or toll free 800/842-7666; fax 307/733-0844. 12 mi from Jackson. This clean, dependable, four-story shingle building, which sits at the base of Rendezvous Mountain, contains the nicest rooms in Teton Village. A good value. **Rooms:** 83 rms and effic. CI 4pm/CO 11am. Nonsmoking rms avail. Attractively furnished with lodgepole or cane furniture with muted tones of mauve and gray. Loft rooms feature a spiral staircase. **Amenities:** Cable TV, voice mail. No A/C. Some units w/terraces, some w/fireplaces. Bathrobes. Loft rooms have two phones. **Services:** Masseur, babysitting. **Facilities:** 60 2 restaurants, 1 bar, sauna, whirlpool, washer/dryer. Small pond stocked with fish in summer. **Rates:** Peak (July–Aug/Dec 25–Mar) $100–$150 S or D; $125–$200 effic. Extra person $10. Children under age 14 stay free. Min stay peak. Lower rates off-season. AP and MAP rates avail. Parking: Outdoor, free. AE, CB, DC, DISC, EC, ER, JCB, MC, V.

Best Western Lodge at Jackson Hole
80 Scott Lane, PO Box 30436, Jackson, 83001; tel 307/739-9703 or toll free 800/458-3866; fax 307/739-9168. The distinctive lodgepole-pine exterior, with hand-carved bears and raccoons, delights children. An attractive lobby features a high ceiling and fireplace. Good value, especially in off-season. **Rooms:** 154 rms. CI 4pm/CO 11am. Nonsmoking rms avail. Attractively furnished with armoires instead of closets. **Amenities:** A/C, dataport, VCR, voice mail, in-rm safe. All units w/minibars, some w/fireplaces, some w/whirlpools. Most rooms offer a two-person whirlpool. **Services:** Masseur, babysitting. **Facilities:** 50 1 restaurant (bkfst and dinner only), 1 bar, games rm, sauna, whirlpool, washer/dryer. Guest privileges at Jackson Hole Athletic Club across highway. **Rates (CP):** Peak (July–Aug) $179 S or D. Extra person $10. Children under age 14 stay free. Lower rates off-season. Parking: Outdoor, free. AE, CB, DC, DISC, EC, ER, JCB, MC, V.

Snow King Resort
400 E Snow King Ave, PO Box SKI, Jackson, 83001; tel 307/733-5200 or toll free 800/522-5464; fax 307/733-4086. The largest hotel and conference center in Jackson sits at the base of Snow King Mountain. Definitely a convention hotel—commercial in feeling and expensive. **Rooms:** 204 rms and stes; 50 cottages/villas. CI 4pm/CO noon. Nonsmoking rms avail. The rooms in the main hotel are a bit weary; much better are the 50 new condo units, beautifully decorated with western furnishings. **Amenities:** A/C, voice mail. Some units w/terraces. **Services:** Car-rental desk, social director, masseur, babysitting. Complimentary shuttle to/from Teton Village in winter. **Facilities:** 2300 1 restaurant, 1 bar (w/entertainment), games rm, sauna, whirlpool, beauty salon, washer/dryer. Miniature golf, alpine slide. **Rates:** Peak (May 27–Sept 30) $170 S; $180 D; $340 ste; $270–$420 cottage/villa. Extra person $10. Children under age 13 stay free. Lower rates off-season. MAP rates avail. Parking: Outdoor, free. AE, DC, DISC, MC, V.

The Wort Hotel
50 N Glenwood St, PO Box 69, Jackson, 83001 (Downtown); tel 307/733-2190 or toll free 800/322-2727; fax 307/733-2067. At Broadway. This historic yet very up-to-date hotel (rebuilt in 1989) presents spacious and beautifully appointed accommodations. Original western art is displayed throughout. Two lobby lounges offer cozy, comfortable seating. **Rooms:** 60 rms and stes. CI 4pm/CO 11am. Nonsmoking rms avail. Lodgepole-pine bed frames, paisley polished-cotton quilts, pillow shams. **Amenities:** A/C, cable TV w/movies, dataport, voice mail. 1 unit w/whirlpool. **Services:** VP Twice-daily maid svce, masseur, babysitting. **Facilities:** 125 1 restaurant (*see* "Restaurants" below), 1 bar (w/entertainment), whirlpool. The Silver Dollar Bar is inlaid with 2,032 uncirculated 1921 silver dollars. **Rates:** Peak (June–Sept) $160 S or D; $195–$295 ste. Extra person $15. Children under age 12 stay free. Lower rates off-season. AP and MAP rates avail. Parking: Outdoor, free. AE, DC, DISC, JCB, MC, V.

MOTELS

Best Western Parkway Inn
125 N Jackson St, Jackson, PO Box 494, Jackson Hole, 83001 (Downtown); tel 307/733-3143 or toll free 800/247-8390; fax 307/733-0955. Located three blocks from the center of town, this place attracts individuals and families. Lobby decorated with antiques. **Rooms:** 50 rms and stes. CI 3pm/CO 11am. Nonsmoking rms avail. Most rooms individually decorated with antique furniture, armoires, oak desks, and dressers. Cottage suites are separate from main building. People walking by can look into ground-floor rooms. **Amenities:** A/C, cable TV. Some units w/terraces. **Services:** Car-rental desk, masseur, babysitting. Poor phone service. **Facilities:** Spa, sauna, whirlpool. Fitness center with 32-foot lap pool. **Rates:** Peak (Mem Day–Labor Day) $85–$120 S or D; $99–$145 ste. Extra person $5. Min stay peak. Lower rates off-season. Parking: Outdoor, free. Ski packages avail. Closed Nov. AE, CB, DC, DISC, EC, ER, JCB, MC, V.

Days Inn of Jackson Hole
1280 W Broadway, PO Box 2986, Jackson, 83001; tel 307/733-0033 or toll free 800/DAYS-INN; fax 307/733-0044. New three-story motel on the outskirts of town. Located next to a shopping center. **Rooms:** 90 rms. CI 3pm/CO 11am.

Nonsmoking rms avail. Surprisingly attractive decor with a western motif. Suites are individually decorated with lodgepole-pine furniture, iron lariat bedside lamps, and handcarved tables, dressers, and nightstands. **Amenities:** A/C, cable TV w/movies, in-rm safe. 1 unit w/terrace, some w/fireplaces, some w/whirlpools. Microwaves, mini-refrigerators, dataports in some rooms. Suites have two-person whirlpool and fireplace. **Services:** Babysitting. VCRs available. Free local calls. In winter, boot and glove dryer, vehicle plug-ins, and ski tuning are available. **Facilities:** Sauna, whirlpool. **Rates (CP):** Peak (June–Sept) $99–$189 S or D. Extra person $5. Children under age 12 stay free. Lower rates off-season. Parking: Outdoor, free. AE, CB, DC, DISC, MC, V.

Motel 6
1370 W Broadway, Jackson, 83001; tel 307/733-1620; fax 307/734-9175. Off US 89. Bare-bones basic lodging; good value for an expensive resort town. **Rooms:** 155 rms. CI 4pm/CO noon. Nonsmoking rms avail. Rooms in the front are noisy. **Amenities:** A/C. **Services:** Complimentary coffee, hot chocolate, apple cider on weekday mornings; pastries on weekends. **Facilities:** Washer/dryer. Barbecue area with picnic tables in courtyard. **Rates:** Peak (May 25–Oct). Extra person $2. Children under age 17 stay free. Lower rates off-season. Parking: Outdoor, free. AE, CB, DC, DISC, JCB, MC, V.

Painted Buffalo Inn
400 W Broadway, PO Box 2547, Jackson, 83001; tel 307/733-4340 or toll free 800/AT-TETON; fax 307/733-7953. 3 blocks from town square. Attractive, locally owned downtown motel. **Rooms:** 140 rms. CI 4pm/CO 11am. Nonsmoking rms avail. Basic, clean accommodations. Several suites are being added; management also plans to redecorate with new western-style furniture. **Amenities:** A/C, cable TV. **Services:** Masseur. **Facilities:** Beauty salon. **Rates (CP):** Peak (May 15–Oct 1) $95 S; $105 D. Extra person $5. Children under age 18 stay free. Lower rates off-season. Parking: Outdoor, free. AE, DC, DISC, MC, V.

The Virginian Lodge
750 W Broadway Ave, Jackson, PO Box 1052, Jackson Hole, 83001; tel 307/733-2792 or toll free 800/262-4999; fax 307/733-0281. Off US 89. 5 acres. Located at the base on the mountains, this western-style motor lodge appeals to tour groups, conventions, and families. Priced a bit high for what's offered. **Rooms:** 158 rms, stes, and effic. CI 3pm/CO 11am. Nonsmoking rms avail. Somewhat funky rooms. Suites offer four-person whirlpool tubs. **Amenities:** A/C. Some units w/whirlpools. **Services:** Babysitting. **Facilities:** 1 restaurant, 1 bar (w/entertainment), games rm, beauty salon, washer/dryer. **Rates:** Peak (Mem Day–Sept 15) $105 S; $110 D; $135–$175 ste; $175 effic. Extra person $10. Children under age 13 stay free. Lower rates off-season. Parking: Outdoor, free. AE, CB, DC, DISC, MC, V.

INNS

UNRATED **The Alpine House Bed & Breakfast**
285 N Glenwood St, PO Box 20245, Jackson, 83001; tel 307/739-1570 or toll free 800/753-1421. An excellent choice near Jackson Square, set in a Swiss chalet-style building. It's light, airy, and absolutely spotless. Owners Hans and Nancy Johnstone both competed for the United States in the Olympics: He was on the Nordic combined ski team in 1988; she was on the biathlon team in 1992. Unsuitable for children under 5. **Rooms:** 7 rms. CI 4pm CI 4–6pm/CO 11am. No smoking. The spacious rooms all have small balconies and private baths, as well as heated floors. Decor features pine antique furnishings, down comforters, and pretty linens. **Amenities:** No A/C, phone, or TV. All units w/terraces. Complimentary wine and cheese served in afternoon. **Services:** Babysitting, afternoon tea and wine/sherry served. Rates include a delicious, homemade breakfast. Can arrange backcountry and cross-country ski tours, guided winter mountaineering trips, and ice-climbing instruction. **Facilities:** Guest lounge. **Rates (BB):** Peak (July–Aug) $100 S; $110 D. Extra person $20. Children under age 8 stay free. Lower rates off-season. Parking: Outdoor, free. Downhill ski packages avail. A one-bedroom apartment is avail for $125 per night. MC, V.

Rusty Parrot Lodge
175 N Jackson St, PO Box 1657, Jackson, 83001; tel 307/733-2000 or toll free 800/458-2004; fax 307/733-5566. 2 blocks from main square. 1 acre. A gem offering western elegance and plenty of charm. The lobby is attractively decorated with historical photos and original art. 100% nonsmoking. Unsuitable for children under 12. **Rooms:** 33 rms and stes. CI 4pm/CO 11am. No smoking. Individually decorated accommodations reflect a contemporary cowboy motif, with lodgepole-pine bed frames and cowboy lamps. Some rooms feature denim and red fabrics; others have white eyelet duvet covers for the goose-down comforters. Bathrooms are large. **Amenities:** A/C, cable TV w/movies, bathrobes. Some units w/terraces, some w/fireplaces, some w/whirlpools. Two rooms (one with hand-painted murals and a small water garden) offer superb spa services, including include massages, aromatherapy, and herbal wraps. **Services:** Car-rental desk, masseur, babysitting, afternoon tea served. Family owned and managed. Rates include a full "Jackson" breakfast—stuffed pork chops, trout amandine, chicken sausage, granola, fresh-baked goodies, and juice. Free afternoon tea and cookies; free local phone calls. **Facilities:** Whirlpool, guest lounge w/TV. Hot tub on outdoor deck. **Rates (BB):** Peak (late May–early Oct) $165–$215 S or D; $450 ste. Extra person $25. Min stay peak. Lower rates off-season. Higher rates for special events/hols. Parking: Outdoor, free. AE, CB, DC, DISC, MC, V.

LODGES

Moose Head Dude Ranch

US 89, Moose, 83012; tel 307/733-3141; fax 307/739-9097. 120 acres. Set on 120 acres, this family-owned and -operated dude ranch is also family oriented. The comfortable log cabin lodge offers sitting rooms with views, fireplaces, Native American–style rugs, and animal-head trophies. No smoking permitted in cabins or lodge. Wonderful owner, Louise Davenport, is outspoken and helpful. Reserve far in advance because it is sold out every year. **Rooms:** 14 cottages/villas. CI open/CO open. Uniquely decorated cabins boast wood-burning stoves, lodgepole-pine furnishings, and great linens. **Amenities:** Refrig. No A/C, phone, or TV. All units w/terraces, some w/fireplaces, 1 w/whirlpool. **Services:** Social director, babysitting. **Facilities:** 1 restaurant, volleyball, games rm, lawn games, washer/dryer. Lodge lounge has TV and VCR; a library with books, games, and a piano; and family-style dining. Ranch has 50 horses; trail rides are offered twice daily. Ponds stocked with trout for catch-and-release fishing. **Rates (AP):** $185 cottage/villa. Extra person $185. Children under age 2 stay free. Min stay. Parking: Outdoor, free. Five-night minimum stay required. Rates are per adult, per night, based on double occupancy. Rates for children: $100 per child, aged 6 and under. A two-bedroom family house (sleeps 5–6) is available for $1,050 per night. Closed Sept–mid-June. No CC.

R Lazy S Ranch

7800 N Moose Wilson Rd, PO Box 308, Teton Village, 83025; tel 307/733-2655. Situated on 350 gorgeous, tranquil acres at the base of the Tetons, this dude ranch offers fabulous views, birdsong, very western corrals, and aspens rustling in the breeze. No children under 7 allowed. **Rooms:** 14 cottages/villas. CI 11am/CO noon. Log cabins boast porches (some with swings) and have handmade patchwork quilts on beds; some have bunk beds in extra rooms. **Amenities:** No A/C, phone, or TV. All units w/terraces, some w/fireplaces. Boot cleaners. **Services:** Children's program. **Facilities:** 1 restaurant, volleyball, games rm, washer/dryer. Picnic tables; library. **Rates (AP):** $900–$1,200 cottage/villa. Min stay. Parking: Outdoor, free. Rates are per person/per week. Closed Oct–mid-June. No CC.

Spotted Horse Ranch

Star Rte 43, Jackson, 83001; tel 307/733-2097 or toll free 800/528-2084. Set on 63 acres next to the Hoback River, this family-owned and -operated guest ranch has been in business for over 30 years. Located adjacent to tranquil Teton National Forest, known for its varied wildlife. Great river views from the dining room. **Rooms:** 11 cottages/villas. CI 10am/CO 10am. Cabins are plain, almost dormitory style, with limited storage space. Somewhat funky accommodations can accommodate the whole family. **Amenities:** No A/C, phone, or TV. All units w/terraces, 1 w/fireplace. **Services:** Social director, babysitting. **Facilities:** 34 1 bar, volleyball, lawn games, sauna, whirlpool, washer/dryer. River rafting and white-water trips available. Cookouts, swing dancing. Over 400 movies available; nightly show. **Rates (AP):** Peak (July–Aug) $306 cottage/villa. Extra person $116–$153. Children under age 3 stay free. Min stay. Lower rates off-season. Parking: Outdoor, free. Three-day minimum stay required. A 4-person cabin runs $492/night. Rates include meals and activities. Families traveling with more than 4 people receive 10% discount on weekly stay. Closed Sept 24–May. MC, V.

RESORTS

Jackson Hole Racquet Club Resort

3535 N Moose-Wilson Rd, Jackson, 83001; tel 307/733-3990 or toll free 800/443-8616; fax 307/733-5551. 8 mi from Jackson; 4 mi N of jct WY 22/390. 250 acres. Situated at the base of the Tetons, these individually owned condos provide accommodations ranging in size from studios to four-bedroom layouts. Good value. **Rooms:** 120 stes and effic. CI 4pm/CO 11am. Decor varies greatly. The newest (and best) units are decorated with country-pine furnishings and attractive upholsteries. They also feature fully stocked kitchens and washer/dryer combos. **Amenities:** Cable TV, refrig. No A/C. All units w/terraces, all w/fireplaces. Wood-burning fireplaces in the newer units; free firewood in winter. **Services:** Masseur, babysitting. Free shuttle in winter to Jackson Hole Ski Area (five minutes away). **Facilities:** 5 100 1 restaurant (dinner only), 1 bar, racquetball, spa, sauna, whirlpool, beauty salon, day-care ctr, playground, washer/dryer. Two-level athletic club; aerobics classes. The complex is adjoined by an 18-hole, Arnold Palmer–designed golf course. **Rates:** Peak (July–Aug) $149–$349 ste; $149–$345 effic. Children under age 18 stay free. Min stay peak. Lower rates off-season. Parking: Outdoor, free. Houses rent for $355–$375 per day. AE, DISC, MC, V.

Lost Creek Ranch

US 89, 83012; tel 307/733-3435; fax 307/733-1954. 8 mi N of Moose, 22 mi N of Jackson on US 89. 110 acres. Very posh family-owned and -managed guest ranch, built in the 1920s but kept up-to-date. Elegant lodge, decorated with western art and Native American artifacts, offers spectacular views of the Tetons. Property reached via 2½-mile entrance drive. **Rooms:** 10 cottages/villas. CI 3pm/CO 10am. Each log cabin houses two units, each attractively furnished with an upscale western motif. Although this is the most expensive and exclusive guest ranch in the area, you can hear your next-door neighbors. **Amenities:** Refrig. No A/C, phone, or TV. All units w/terraces, some w/fireplaces. Fruit basket upon arrival. Living room suites feature wood-burning fireplaces. **Services:** Twice-daily maid svce, social director, babysitting. Phone messages not delivered to rooms, but left at front desk. Each guest assigned a horse. Disposable cameras provided at check-in; photos are developed for you at end of week. Staff of 38 serves 52 guests. **Facilities:**

1 restaurant, 1 bar (w/entertainment), basketball, volleyball, games rm, whirlpool. Activities include a float trip down the Snake River, excursions to museums, Yellowstone National Park, rodeo in Jackson, cookouts. **Rates (AP):** \$3,735–\$8,475 cottage/villa. Extra person \$825/wk. Children under age 6 stay free. Parking: Outdoor, free. One-week stay required (Sun–Sun). Rates are per cabin/per week: \$3,735 (1–2 people in a 2-unit cabin), \$8,475 (1–4 people in a living room cabin). Closed mid-Sept–early June. No CC.

Spring Creek
1800 Spirit Dance Rd, PO Box 3154, Jackson, 83001 (East Gros Ventre Butte); tel 307/733-8833 or toll free 800/443-6139; fax 307/733-1524. 4 mi W of Jackson. 1,000 acres. A top choice for woodsy elegance, set on 1,000 acres within a wildlife sanctuary. **Rooms:** 36 rms and stes; 62 cottages/villas. CI 4pm/CO 11am. Nonsmoking rms avail. Hotel rooms, spacious condominiums, lodges. All have mountain views and lodgepole furnishings. Studios and condos have fully equipped kitchens. **Amenities:** Cable TV w/movies, refrig, bathrobes. No A/C. All units w/terraces, all w/fireplaces. Ski racks. **Services:** Twice-daily maid svce, car-rental desk, social director, children's program, babysitting. Fire wood delivered to rooms. **Facilities:** 1 restaurant, 1 bar, volleyball, lawn games, whirlpool. Outdoor hot tub for eight people located by duck pond. Indoor equestrian center. Fly fishing in summer, ice skating in winter. **Rates:** Peak (June–Oct 8) \$200 S or D; \$240 ste; \$375–\$750 cottage/villa. Extra person \$15. Children under age 12 stay free. Min stay. Lower rates off-season. Parking: Outdoor, free. Winter, spring, and fall rates include full breakfast for two. Luxury houses for up to eight people also available for \$950 per night. AE, CB, DC, DISC, EC, MC, V.

RESTAURANTS

Bar-J Chuckwagon
Teton Village Rd, Wilson; tel 800/905-BAR-J. **Barbecue.** At this huge country-western dinner theater, the whole family can tank up on ranch grub before enjoying a show performed by actual wranglers from the Bar-J Ranch. Plenty of roast beef, baked beans, potato salad, homemade bread, and spice cake gets washed down by lemonade and coffee (the only drinks available). Guests can dine family style at long wooden tables. Dinner is served at 7:30, and the show runs 8:30–9:45pm. **FYI:** Reservations recommended. Country music. No liquor license. No smoking. **Open:** Daily 5:30–9:45pm. Closed Oct–May 25. **Prices:** Prix fixe \$13. AE, MC, V.

Bar-T-Five Covered Wagon Cookout & Wild West Show
Cache Creek Rd, Jackson; tel 307/733-5386. At the mouth of Cache Creek Canyon. **American/Barbecue.** Diners climb aboard a covered wagon for the ride to a beautiful creekside location in Cache Creek Canyon. The hearty, old-time chuck wagon cookout includes roast beef, chicken, corn on the cob, baked beans, and salad. After dinner, you can whoop it up with singing cowboys, Indians, and mountain men. Price for dinner and show is \$24 for adults, \$19 for kids 9–14, \$16 for kids 4–8, and free for kids under 3. In winter, the evening includes dinner and a sleigh ride up the canyon (\$39 for adults; \$20 for kids under 10). Two shows nightly (5:30pm and 6:30pm in summer; 5pm and 7pm in winter). **FYI:** Reservations recommended. Country music. No liquor license. **Open:** Peak (May–Sept/Dec 15–Mar 31) daily 5:30–9pm. Closed Oct–Dec 15. **Prices:** Prix fixe \$24–\$39. AE, DISC, MC, V.

The Blue Lion
160 N Millward, Jackson; tel 307/733-3912. 2 blocks NW of town square. **New American.** Set in a converted home, this local bistro serves wonderful food in an intimate-yet-casual setting. Start off with the southwestern pheasant cakes, which are rolled in cornmeal, sautéed until golden brown, then served with chipotle mayonnaise. The house specialty is roast rack of lamb accompanied by a jalapeño-mint sauce. There are only 12 tables, so reserve well in advance. Excellent, extensive wine list. **FYI:** Reservations recommended. No smoking. **Open:** Peak (June 15–Sept 15) daily 5:30–10pm. **Prices:** Main courses \$15–\$25. AE, DISC, MC, V.

Bubba's Bar-B-Que Restaurant
515 W Broadway, Jackson; tel 307/733-2288. **Barbecue.** This funky joint is always packed. Diners can load up on combo platters of beef, fowl, and ribs or take a trip to the unlimited salad bar. Desserts include terrific bread pudding and homemade pies; fresh-from-the-oven oatmeal cookies are passed out free to the entire dining room. **FYI:** Reservations not accepted. Children's menu. BYO. **Open:** Peak (May 26–Sept) daily 7am–9pm. **Prices:** Main courses \$4–\$11. DISC, MC, V.

The Bunnery
130 N Cache St, Jackson; tel 307/733-5474. **Cafe.** The pastries, muffins, pies, tarts, and cakes at this casual coffee-shop-cum-bakery are popular with locals and tourists alike. Breads are baked fresh daily and span the range of sweet, sourdough, herbed, potato flour, rye, and focaccia. The house signature bread, called "OSM," is made from oats, sunflower, and millet. Hearty breakfast omelettes yield to sandwiches at lunch. Dinner available during summer only. **FYI:** Reservations not accepted. Children's menu. Beer and wine only. No smoking. **Open:** Peak (June 15–Sept 15) daily 7am–9:30pm. **Prices:** Main courses \$5–\$12. MC, V.

Dornans
10 Moose St, Moose; tel 307/733-2415. Off US 191. **Regional American.** This popular hangout with a wood, stone, and glass interior has a double identity. From September to May, it's a gourmet eatery with an award-winning chef (Alton Russell, of Lost Creek Ranch) in residence. Russell fields entrees such as noisettes of venison and leek-and-mushroom-stuffed swordfish. The 20,000-bottle wine cellar is the largest

in the region. In summer, Dornan's goes casual, serving up family-style chuckwagon dinners with all-you-can-eat barbecue short ribs, roast beef, and more ($11 per person). A deli offers sandwiches to go plus a great selection of cheese. There's a hootenanny each Monday night. **FYI:** Reservations recommended. **Open:** Peak (June–Aug) **Prices:** Main courses $11–$22. MC, V.

The Granary

In Spring Creek Resort, 1800 Spirit Dance Rd, Jackson; tel 307/733-8833. 4 mi from downtown. **Regional American.** A casually elegant, special-occasion eatery located in a bilevel wood-and-glass structure with spectacular views of the Tetons. The bar area is cozy, with a fireplace and copper bar; try one of their specialty drinks. On the menu, you'll find choices such as elk, rack of lamb, and pastas—even kangaroo medallions—along with several featured food-and-wine pairings. **FYI:** Reservations recommended. Children's menu. **Open:** Breakfast daily 7:30–10am; lunch Mon–Sat noon–2pm; dinner daily 6–10pm; brunch Sun noon–2pm. **Prices:** Main courses $17–$29. AE, CB, DC, DISC, MC, V.

★ Jedediah's House of Sourdough

135 E Broadway Ave, Jackson; tel 307/733-5671. ½ block from town square. **American.** Housed in a log cabin decorated with historical photos of Jackson and old news clippings, this eatery is popular for breakfast and stays packed all day. Full-size breakfasts come with unlimited silver-dollar-size sourdough pancakes or biscuits and gravy. The jam is homemade, and the "cowboy coffee" is guaranteed to get you started in the morning. Lunch offers the entire breakfast menu, plus soups, salads, and sandwiches. **FYI:** Reservations not accepted. Beer and wine only. No smoking. **Open:** Daily 7am–2pm. Closed April 1–7. **Prices:** Lunch main courses $5–$7. AE, DISC, MC, V.

Lame Duck Restaurant

680 E Broadway, Jackson; tel 307/733-4311. Near Elk Refuge entrance. **Asian.** Pan-Asian cuisine in a festive atmosphere. Sushi, stir-fry, and daily specials provide relief from the usual red-meat oriented Wyoming cooking. The house special is crispy duck. A large beverage menu presents specialty fruit drinks, sake, imported beers, and even "mocktails" for nondrinkers. **FYI:** Reservations accepted. Children's menu. No smoking. **Open:** Daily 5–10pm. **Prices:** Main courses $6–$15. AE, MC, V.

Louie's Steak House

175 N Center St, Jackson; tel 307/733-6803. 1 block off Jackson town square. **Steak.** For top-quality steak, this place offers the best value in town. It is located in a two-story house; patrons wait in the living room for their tables to be ready. The menu features Wyoming Wellington (fillet of beef surrounded with mushroom pâté, then baked in a pastry casing and served with bordelaise sauce). Other entrees include chicken, rack of lamb, quail, salmon, and shrimp. **FYI:** Reservations recommended. Children's menu. No smoking. **Open:** Daily 5:30–10pm. Closed Nov–Dec/May 1–May 26. **Prices:** Main courses $9–$21. AE, DC, DISC, MC, V.

★ Mangy Moose Saloon and Restaurant

Teton Village, Jackson; tel 307/733-4913. 12 mi from Jackson Hole. **Eclectic.** A two-story, western-style lodge strewn with posters, flags, antiques, and model airplanes. (The namesake moose dangles from the ceiling in the bar.) It's a popular place for families, who tank up on ribs, pastas, seafood, or selections from the salad bar. Two dance floors—upstairs and downstairs—and a bar that hops on weekends, when bands perform. **FYI:** Reservations not accepted. Reggae/rock. Children's menu. No smoking. **Open:** Peak (July–Aug) daily 5–10pm. Closed mid-Apr–May. **Prices:** Main courses $9–$17. AE, MC, V.

Nani's Genuine Pasta House

In El Rancho Motel, 240 N Glenwood St, Jackson; tel 307/733-3888. **Italian.** A gourmet Italian eatery with a cheerful red, white, and green exterior and a dark and intimate interior that only holds about 10 tables. The chef prepares handmade ravioli, seafood stew, and other regional Italian favorites. Italian wines are available by the glass. **FYI:** Reservations accepted. No smoking. **Open:** Tues–Sat 5:30–10pm. Closed Apr, Nov. **Prices:** Main courses $12–$17. MC, V.

Off Broadway Grille

30 King St, Jackson; tel 307/733-9777. **New American/Seafood.** A small, casual place, one block off the town square, where large bay windows enhance the light and airy decor. The seasonally changing menu may feature wild game–stuffed manicotti, or *nam pla* shrimp and scallops served over Oriental noodles. Wines are well selected and reasonably priced. **FYI:** Reservations accepted. No smoking. **Open:** Peak (May 26–Sept) daily 5:30–10pm. Closed Apr 15–May 26/Oct 15–Dec 25. **Prices:** Main courses $12–$18. MC, V.

The Range

225 N Cache, Jackson; tel 307/733-5481. 1½ blocks N of town square. **Regional American.** A fast-paced, festive, and somewhat noisy dining room is arranged around an exhibition-style kitchen so that diners can watch the chef prepare original dishes. The menu changes daily, but might include sautéed breast of wild turkey, red trout, or buffalo tenderloin. The wine list features over 100 domestic, French, and Italian selections. **FYI:** Reservations accepted. Children's menu. No smoking. **Open:** Lunch daily 11am–5pm; dinner daily 5–11pm. **Prices:** Main courses $12–$25. AE, MC, V.

Silver Dollar Bar and Grill

In the Wort Hotel, 50 N Glenwood, Jackson; tel 307/733-2190. ½ block from town square; at Broadway. **Regional American.** Western memorabilia and photos documenting films shot in the area characterize this hotel dining room. An inventive menu features venison sausage with vegetables in a peppercorn sauce, topped with poached eggs and hollandaise; and Belgian waffles with Wyoming huckleberry syrup.

Dinner choices might be elk medallions sautéed in raspberry demiglacé, or rack of Wyoming lamb with a fig and port wine sauce. **FYI:** Reservations accepted. Piano. Children's menu. **Open:** Peak (mid-June–Sept) daily 6:30am–10pm. **Prices:** Main courses $13–$20. AE, DC, DISC, MC, V.

The Strutting Grouse
In Jackson Hole Golf & Tennis Club, 5000 Spring Gulch Rd, Jackson; tel 307/733-7788. 6 mi N of Jackson off US 80. **Regional American.** The atmosphere is upscale casual, with stone walls, a fireplace, an interesting display of local art, and a collection of Native American headdresses. From the outdoor patio, you can enjoy views of the Tetons and the golf course. In addition to steaks, salads, and trout, the menu features bison medallions and venison sausage. **FYI:** Reservations recommended. Guitar. Children's menu. Dress code. **Open:** Peak (June 15–Sept 15) lunch daily 11:30am–2:30pm; dinner Tues–Sun 5:30–9pm. Closed Sept 26–May 20. **Prices:** Main courses $13–$20. AE, DC, MC, V.

Sweetwater Restaurant
King and Pearl Sts, Jackson (Downtown); tel 307/733-3553. **Eclectic.** Located in a converted 1915 pioneer log cabin, the Sweetwater offers both charming atmosphere and good value. On the menu, you'll find fresh salads, homemade soups, and a bevy of mesquite-grilled specialties from ruby trout to New York strip steak. There's a smattering of Greek entrees too, including moussaka and shrimp with feta cheese. Small but reasonably priced wine list. Weekend brunch served in the winter. **FYI:** Reservations recommended. Children's menu. No smoking. **Open:** Peak (Mem Day–Labor Day) lunch daily 11:30am–3pm; dinner daily 5:30–10pm; brunch Sat–Sun 10am–2pm. **Prices:** Main courses $11–$18. AE, DISC, MC, V.

Vista Grande
Teton Village Rd, Jackson; tel 307/733-6964. **Mexican.** Mexican motifs, tile floor, high-back chairs, and impressive views of the mountains. Dine on combination platters, fajitas, seafood chimichangas. Comfortable bar serves good margaritas. **FYI:** Reservations not accepted. Children's menu. **Open:** Daily 5:30–9:30pm. Closed Nov 14–30. **Prices:** Main courses $7–$11. AE, MC, V.

ATTRACTIONS

Jackson Hole Ski & Summer Resort
7658 N Teewinot Chairlift Rd, Teton Village; tel 307/733-2292 or toll free 800/443-6931. Jackson Hole has a reputation as one of the toughest ski areas in the country. Its 62 trails and bowls (half of the trails are black diamond, 40% are intermediate, and 10% are beginner) range from groomed trails to dangerous cliffs, and the highest of its two mountains boasts a vertical rise of 4,139 feet—the highest in the United States. There are nine lifts (one tram, one quad, one triple, five doubles, one surface), as well as facilities for snowboarding, a ski school, and 22 cross-country trails. "Jackson Hole Ski Three" lift tickets include the neighboring **Grand Targhee** and **Snow King** ski resorts (one-resort-per-day limit).

From Memorial Day to early October, the aerial tram to the top of Rendezvous Peak offers scenic rides, and the mountain is used for mountain biking, hiking, and rock climbing. Hiking equipment can be rented at Merrill Hiking Center. **Open:** Ski season: daily 9am–4pm. Call for summer hours. Closed some hols. **$$$$**

Jackson Hole Museum
105 N Glenwood, Jackson; tel 307/733-2414. Displays and collections of firearms, tools, and photographs used by the Native Americans, trappers, and cattlemen who made the valley their home. **Open:** Mid-May–mid-Oct, Mon–Sat 9:30am–6pm, Sun 10am–5pm. **$**

Teton County Historical Center
105 Mercill Ave, Jackson; tel 307/733-9605. Research facility with fur trade exhibit and Native American artifacts. **Open:** May–Aug, Mon–Fri 9am–5pm. **Free**

Wildlife of the American West Art Museum
110 N Center St, Jackson; tel 307/733-5771. Displays more than 250 paintings and sculptures of North American wildlife. Artists represented in the collection include Ernest Thompson Seton, George Catlin, C M Russell, Conrad Schwiering, and Carl Rungius. **Open:** June–Aug, Mon–Sat 10am–6pm, Sun 1–6pm; Sept–Oct and Dec–Mar, May, Tues–Sat 10am–5pm, Sun 1–5pm. Closed some hols. **$**

National Elk Refuge
Tel 307/733-9212. To reach the refuge head 1 mi E on Broadway, follow signs on dirt road for 4 miles. The 25,000-acre winter home of more than 7,500 elk, one of the largest herds in North America. In summer, the elk migrate to higher ground and trumpeter swans take over the area. A visitors center has displays, books, and pamphlets, plus a slide show on elk and the refuge. Horse-drawn sleigh rides, leaving from the visitors center, offer a unique way to ride among the thousands of elk without disturbing their natural habitat. **Open:** Dec–Mar, daily 10am–4pm. **$$$**

Lewis and Clark Expeditions
145 W Gill St, Jackson; tel 307/733-5771. Guided and self-guiding white-water float trips down the Grand Canyon of the Snake River. Tours last three to six hours. **Open:** June–mid-Sept. **$$$$**

Kemmerer

MOTEL

Fairview Motel
61 US 30, 83101; tel 307/877-3938 or toll free 800/247-3938; fax 307/877-3938 ext 202. Two-story L-shaped property with plenty of parking. Nicely appointed rooms. **Rooms:** 61 rms. CI open/CO 11am. Nonsmoking rms avail.

Amenities: Cable TV w/movies. No A/C. **Services:** **Facilities:** Picnic tables on the lawn in summer. **Rates:** Peak (Apr–Oct) $32–$36 S; $44–$54 D. Extra person $5. Lower rates off-season. Parking: Outdoor, free. AE, CB, DC, DISC, MC, V.

ATTRACTION

Fossil Butte National Monument
Off US 30; tel 307/877-4455. 14 mi W of Kemmerer. Now a semi-arid landscape filled with sagebrush and other desert grasses, this area was once the site of an ancient lake. The wildlife of 50 million years ago lives on in remarkably preserved and detailed fossils of bats, snakes, insects, birds, plants, and more than 20 species of freshwater fish. (Many of the fossilized fish, for example, still have their teeth, scales, and skin.)

The monument visitors center, at the south end of the park, has fossil displays and an artist's re-creation of what Fossil Lake may have looked like. Ranger-conducted walks and summertime "porch programs" provide an introduction to the geology of the area. Two park trails give visitors the opportunity to climb the butte and view fossil quarries and the current flora and fauna in the park. A picnic area is available, and cross-country hiking is allowed. **Open:** June–Aug, daily 8am–7pm; Sept–May, daily 8am–4:30pm. Closed some hols. **Free**

Lake Village

See Yellowstone National Park

Lander

Site of the Wind River Indian Reservation, home to the Shoshone and Arapahoe peoples. Hometown of cowboy Stub Farlow, whose silhouette appears on Wyoming license plates. **Information:** Lander Area Chamber of Commerce, 160 N 1st St, Lander, 82520 (tel 307/332-3892).

MOTELS

Holiday Lodge
210 McFarlane Dr, 82520; tel 307/332-2511 or toll free 800/624-1974; fax 307/332-2256. At frontage road at jct US 287 and WY 789. This motel sits on a ledge above the Popo Agie River, which you can hear when the room windows are open. **Rooms:** 40 rms and effic. CI open/CO 11am. Nonsmoking rms avail. One-third of the rooms have been refurbished, but all suffer from sloppy paint trim. Seven kitchenette units available. **Amenities:** A/C, cable TV, refrig. **Services:** Pet fee $5/night. **Facilities:** Whirlpool, washer/dryer. **Rates:** Peak (Apr–Sept) $35 S; $40–$45 D; $40–$50 effic. Extra person $3. Children under age 12 stay free. Lower rates off-season. Parking: Outdoor, free. AE, CB, DC, DISC, MC, V.

Prong Horn Lodge
150 E Main St, 82520; tel 307/332-3940 or toll free 800/BUD-HOST; fax 307/332-2651. At jct WY 789 and US 26. Although there's a lot of asphalt out front, this is the biggest and best-kept motel in town, enhanced by some small but attractive flower beds, a handsome elk statue, and the Little Popo Agie River running by. **Rooms:** 55 rms, stes, and effic. CI open/CO 11am. Nonsmoking rms avail. New wing has the best rooms, with two sinks and views of the mountains from the balconies. Older units are smaller but have new furniture. Three suites have fully equipped kitchens. **Amenities:** A/C, cable TV. Some units w/terraces. All accommodations have 25-inch TVs. Some rooms have refrigerators, which are also available by request. **Services:** **Facilities:** 2 restaurants, whirlpool. Restaurants include a coffee shop (with a liquor license) and a Cambodian restaurant with beautiful views of the mountains. **Rates:** Peak (May–Oct 1) $39 S; $42–$48 D; $55 ste; $55 effic. Extra person $5. Children under age 12 stay free. Lower rates off-season. Parking: Outdoor, free. AE, CB, DC, DISC, MC, V.

ATTRACTION

Fremont County Pioneer Museum
630 Lincoln St; tel 307/332-4137. Exhibits chronicle the story of the Pony Express, Wyoming's role as the first government in the world to grant voting rights to women, and the Native American and military history of the area. **Open:** June 1–mid-Sept, Mon–Fri 10am–5pm, Sat 1–4pm; mid-Sept–May 31, Wed–Fri 1–5pm, Sat 1–4pm. Closed some hols. **Free**

Laramie

Home of the University of Wyoming, the state's only four-year university. A gateway to Medicine Bow National Forest, and mountains to the west of town attract lots of skiers. **Information:** Laramie Area Chamber of Commerce, 800 S 3rd St, PO Box 1166, Laramie, 82070 (tel 307/745-7339).

MOTELS

Foster's Country Corner
1561 Snowy Range Rd, 82070; tel 307/742-8371 or toll free 800/528-1234; fax 307/742-0884. Exit 311 off I-80; W on Snowy Range Rd. Although this motel is located at a busy intersection on the interstate and has no views to speak of, the restaurant and the indoor pool raise it a notch above more basic motels. **Rooms:** 112 rms. CI 2pm/CO noon. Nonsmoking rms avail. Rooms face the parking area, and are simple but clean. If you like extra space, ask to see the two reasonably priced larger rooms. **Amenities:** A/C, cable

TV, refrig. **Services:** Facilities: 1 restaurant, 1 bar, whirlpool. Large indoor pool is usable all year. Small curio shop in lobby sells toiletries and bathing suits. **Rates:** Peak (May 1–Sept 15) $46–$52 S; $52–$58 D. Extra person $6. Children under age 13 stay free. Lower rates off-season. Parking: Outdoor, free. AE, CB, DC, DISC, EC, JCB, MC, V.

Holiday Inn
231 Soldier Springs Rd, 82070; tel 307/742-6611 or toll free 800/526-5245; fax 307/745-8371. Jct I-80 and US 287. Reasonably attractive exterior and lobby, but corridors of rooms seem to extend randomly off the lobby. **Rooms:** 100 rms. CI 2pm/CO noon. Nonsmoking rms avail. Average-size rooms are clean but nondescript. **Amenities:** A/C, cable TV. **Services:** **Facilities:** 400 1 restaurant, 1 bar, whirlpool, washer/dryer. **Rates:** Peak (May 1–Sept 15) $60 S; $68 D. Extra person $8. Children under age 18 stay free. Lower rates off-season. Parking: Outdoor, free. AE, CB, DC, DISC, JCB, MC, V.

Laramie Inn
421 Boswell Dr, 82070; tel 307/742-3721 or toll free 800/642-4212; fax 307/742-5473. Located near the interstate, it recently renovated some rooms and now provides a limited number of excellent rooms in a town that generally offers poor lodgings. First-rate restaurant too. **Rooms:** 80 rms. CI 4pm/CO 11am. Nonsmoking rms avail. The new rooms feature good quality carpeting and attractive antique-reproduction furniture. They're also larger than their predecessors, with a sitting area and table. **Amenities:** A/C, satel TV w/movies. **Services:** Babysitting. **Facilities:** 2 restaurants, 1 bar. Domenic's Italian Restaurant is one of the best places to eat in Laramie. **Rates:** Peak (June–Oct 15) $48–$58 S; $58–$68 D. Children under age 16 stay free. Lower rates off-season. Parking: Outdoor, free. Rates rise during Frontier Days in nearby Cheyenne. AE, CB, DC, DISC, MC, V.

ATTRACTIONS

Laramie Plains Museum
603 Ivinson Ave; tel 307/742-4448. For years after its completion in 1882, this handsome Victorian mansion was the most elegant house in town. Today, visitors can view its beveled, leaded glass windows, restored drawing room with period antiques and fine appointments, and well-outfitted kitchen with century-old appliances. Interestingly, a one-room schoolhouse on the grounds is still used by area teachers. **Open:** Mid-June–Aug, Mon–Sat 9am–7pm, Sun 1–4pm. Reduced hours off-season. Closed some hols. **$$**

University of Wyoming Art Museum
2111 Willett Dr; tel 307/766-6622. Located in the ultramodern Centennial Complex, designed by noted architect Antoine Predock. This museum's permanent collection of over 6,000 items, housed in nine galleries, is especially strong in European and American paintings, prints, and drawings; 19th-century Japanese prints; 18th- and 19th-century Persian and Indian miniature paintings; 20th-century photography; and African and Native American artifacts. **Open:** Tues–Fri 10am–5pm, Sat 11am–5pm, Sun 10am–3pm. Closed some hols. **$$**

University of Wyoming Geological Museum
NW corner of UW campus; tel 307/766-4218. Permanent collection contains more than 120,000 rocks, minerals, and fossils, with special emphasis on fossils from the West. The remains of prehistoric dinosaurs, crocodiles, shells, and ocean-going lizards (Wyoming was once covered by a sea) are among the displays. **Open:** Mon–Fri 8am–5pm, Sat–Sun 10am–3pm. Call ahead to confirm weekend hrs. Closed some hols. **Free**

Medicine Bow National Forest
2468 Jackson St; tel 307/745-8971. Covering close to 1.1 million acres in southeastern Wyoming, the forest is traversed by scenic WY 130; I-80 follows the unusual rock formations of the Pole Mountain Unit. The Snowy Range Division supports an active timber harvesting industry in addition to providing watershed and outdoor recreation opportunities. Wildlife in the park include elk, mule deer, black bear, coyotes, and mountain lions. Trout fishing, picnic grounds, camping, winter sports areas. **Open:** Daily dawn–dusk. **Free**

Wyoming Territorial Park and Scenic Railroad
975 Snowy Range Rd; tel 307/745-6161 or toll free 800/845-2287. Experience the jails, rails, and Old West trails of 19th-century Wyoming. The **Wyoming Territorial Prison** has exhibits on many of its famous occupants, including Butch Cassidy. The **National US Marshals Museum** features displays such as "The Gunmen: Romance and Reality" and "Lawmen and the Courts," and houses collections of marshal's badges and firearms. Tour guides are on hand at both facilities to answer your questions. At **Wyoming Frontier Town,** townsfolk demonstrate various crafts such as blacksmithing, dress making, and weaving, while the **Horse Barn Dinner Theater** is home of the musical revue *Raising the Roof.*

The **Wyoming Scenic Railroad** re-creates the romance of rail travel in vintage coach cars. The nearly six-hour round-trip journey passes through 108 miles of the high plains, past historic mining towns and into the majestic Snowy Range Mountains. Phone 307/742-9162 for schedules and additional information. **Open:** May–Oct, call for schedule. **$$$**

Lusk

A ranching community that was once a stage stop between the gold fields of South Dakota and Cheyenne, WY. *Legend of Rawhide,* an annual outdoor show of western history held in July, includes a cast of some 200 area volunteers. A bit of Lusk's colorful past is evident at the grave of local madam

Old Mother Featherleg, who is buried between two of her best clients. **Information:** Niobrara Chamber of Commerce, 322 S Main, PO Box 457, Lusk, 82225 (tel 307/334-2950).

MOTELS

Best Western Pioneer Court
731 S Main St, PO Box 87, 82225; tel 307/334-2640 or toll free 800/528-1234; fax 307/334-2642. S edge of town; on US 20 and 85. Below-average property; some renovations underway. **Rooms:** 30 rms. CI 1pm/CO 11am. Nonsmoking rms avail. **Amenities:** A/C, cable TV. **Services:** **Facilities:** **Rates:** Peak (June 15–Sept) $38–$40 S; $58–$60 D. Extra person $4. Lower rates off-season. Parking: Outdoor, free. AE, DC, DISC, EC, MC, V.

Covered Wagon Motel
730 S Main St, PO Box 236, 82225; tel 307/334-2836 or toll free 800/341-8000; fax 307/334-2836 ext 357. S edge of town on US 20/85. Very nice indeed after renovation that added an indoor pool and brought in new carpets and furnishings. Very clean property; manager is a stickler for detail. **Rooms:** 51 rms. CI 3pm/CO 11am. Nonsmoking rms avail. Large, comfortable, well decorated rooms offer lots of desk and drawer space. **Amenities:** A/C, cable TV w/movies, dataport. 1 unit w/whirlpool. **Services:** Babysitting. **Facilities:** 50 Basketball, sauna, steam rm, whirlpool, playground, washer/dryer. **Rates (CP):** Peak (July 6–Aug 31) $42–$69 S; $49–$73 D. Extra person $10. Lower rates off-season. Parking: Outdoor, free. AE, CB, DC, DISC, MC, V.

ATTRACTION

Stagecoach Museum and Bookstore
322 S Main St; tel 307/334-3444. The main floor of the museum consists of four re-created pioneer rooms—kitchen, dining room, parlor, and bedroom—as well as an old-fashioned post office. A transportation building houses one of the stagecoaches used to haul gold on the famous Cheyenne–Black Hills Stage and Express Line. (The only other Black Hills coach in existence today is in the Smithsonian Institution in Washington, DC.) Other stagecoaches, covered wagons, buggies, and horse-drawn firefighting equipment are also on display. **Open:** June, Mon–Fri 1–5pm; July–Aug, Tues–Sat 1–8pm, Sun 2–8pm; Sept–May Mon–Wed 1–5pm. Closed some hols. $

Mammoth Hot Springs

See Yellowstone National Park

Moose

See Jackson Hole

Moran

See Grand Teton National Park

Rawlins

Sheep and cattle ranchers abound here. John Candlish, inventor of the sheep wagon, made his first one here to help out the many herders who were living outside year-round as they watched their flocks. The historic Frontier Prison was established here in 1890, and Rawlins is still the site of the state penitentiary. **Information:** Rawlins-Carbon County Chamber of Commerce, 519 W Cedar, PO Box 1331, Rawlins, 82301-1331 (tel 307/324-4111).

MOTELS

Best Western Cottontree Inn
23rd at Spruce, PO Box 387, 82301; tel 307/324-2737 or toll free 800/662-6886; fax 307/324-5011. Off I-80. Superior motel, with more facilities and services than most properties in town. Recently completed a major upgrade. **Rooms:** 122 rms. CI 2pm/CO noon. Nonsmoking rms avail. **Amenities:** A/C, cable TV w/movies. **Services:** VCRs available for rent. **Facilities:** 100 1 restaurant, 1 bar, sauna. Big pool is quite attractive. **Rates:** Peak (July 1–Aug 31) $61–$66 S; $66–$74 D. Extra person $5. Children under age 13 stay free. Lower rates off-season. Parking: Outdoor, free. AE, CB, DC, DISC, MC, V.

Rawlins Days Inn
2222 E Cedar St, 82301; tel 307/324-6615 or toll free 800/DAYS-INN. At jct I-80/US 287. Set between railroad tracks and the interstate. The lobby and corridors are a drab gray. **Rooms:** 121 rms and stes. CI open/CO noon. Nonsmoking rms avail. Although comfortable, rooms are a bit dark. **Amenities:** A/C, cable TV w/movies. **Services:** X **Facilities:** 500 1 restaurant (lunch and dinner only), 1 bar, games rm, playground, washer/dryer. A large open area next to the pool offers a small playground and an expanse of grass. **Rates (CP):** Peak (May 15–Sept 30) $50–$55 S; $55–$60 D; $75 ste. Extra person $5. Children under age 19 stay free. Lower rates off-season. Parking: Outdoor, free. Rates rise during annual Frontier Days Rodeo (last two weeks in July), held in Cheyenne (even though Cheyenne is two hours away). AE, CB, DC, DISC, MC, V.

Weston Inn
1801 E Cedar St, 82301; tel 307/324-2783 or toll free 800/333-STAY, 800/255-9840 in WY; fax 307/328-1011. Just off I-80. Basic motel, popular with work crews on nearby construction projects. Rambling, poorly lit corridors. **Rooms:** 112 rms. CI 11am/CO 11am. Nonsmoking rms avail. Some rooms are in poor condition: duct tape on the windows and air conditioner, Masonite patching on the wall, plywood under the box spring. **Amenities:** A/C, cable TV.

Services: Pool is set in central courtyard with spacious lawn area. **Facilities:** 1 bar, washer/dryer. **Rates (CP):** Peak (June–Sept) $35 S; $40 D. Children under age 14 stay free. Lower rates off-season. Parking: Outdoor, free. Special rates avail for groups staying long term. AE, DC, DISC, MC, V.

Riverton

Farming community occupying land which belonged to the Shoshone and Arapaho tribes, who gave it up in 1904 (most of the land was restored to the reservation in 1939). In the 1950s, the discovery of uranium in the nearby Gas Hills brought an economic boom to Riverton. **Information:** Riverton Chamber of Commerce, 1st and Main, Depot Bldg, Riverton, 82501 (tel 307/856-4801).

MOTELS

Holiday Inn

900 E Sunset, 82501; tel 307/856-8100 or toll free 800/527-5544; fax 307/856-0266. On E side of US 26 (Main St) on N side of town. Property is attractively arranged around a grassy inner courtyard. **Rooms:** 120 rms. Executive level. CI 2pm/CO noon. Nonsmoking rms avail. Rooms are clean and simple, but the furniture is a little tired. **Amenities:** A/C, cable TV. Some units w/terraces. **Services:** Babysitting. **Facilities:** 1 restaurant, 1 bar, whirlpool, beauty salon, washer/dryer. Guest privileges at the Teton Athletic Club. Children under 12 eat free with parents in hotel restaurant. **Rates:** Peak (May–July) $55 S; $65 D. Extra person $6. Children under age 18 stay free. Lower rates off-season. Parking: Outdoor, free. AE, CB, DC, DISC, MC, V.

Sundowner Station Motel

1616 N Federal Blvd, 82501; tel 307/856-6503 or toll free 800/874-1116; fax 307/856-2879. On US 26. Located near a busy highway, but the noise does not penetrate within. **Rooms:** 60 rms. CI open/CO 11am. Nonsmoking rms avail. Clean and well kept, but bathrooms are small, with little counter space. Rooms facing the inner courtyard and pool are nicest. **Amenities:** A/C. All units w/terraces. **Services:** **Facilities:** 1 restaurant, 1 bar, sauna, whirlpool. Restaurant, serving standard American, is popular with locals. **Rates:** $42–$46 S; $48–$56 D. Extra person $4. Children under age 12 stay free. Parking: Outdoor, free. AE, CB, DC, DISC, MC, V.

Tomahawk Motor Lodge

208 E Main St, 82501; tel 307/856-9205 or toll free 800/637-7378; fax 307/856-2879. From Riverton's Main St (US 26/789) turn W on Federal (US 26/287); drive 6 blocks. Downtown location is convenient for businesspeople. Short walk away from several restaurants. **Rooms:** 32 rms. CI 3pm/CO 11am. Nonsmoking rms avail. Rooms are clean and well-furnished, but have sparse decorations; exposed ceiling beams are a nice touch. **Amenities:** A/C, cable TV w/movies, refrig. **Services:** **Facilities:** Complimentary passes to Teton Athletic Club. **Rates:** Peak (July–Sept) $30–$35 S; $35–$44 D. Extra person $5. Children under age 12 stay free. Lower rates off-season. Parking: Outdoor, free. AE, CB, DC, DISC, MC, V.

ATTRACTION

Riverton Museum

700 E Park Ave; tel 307/856-2665. Small, local history museum with artifacts from the early 20th-century homesteaders who established the town. Re-creations of typical Old West buildings—general store, bank, post office, saloon, church, beauty shop—are presented along with quilts, clothing, and exhibits relating to the adjacent Wind River Indian Reservation, home of the Eastern Shoshoni and Northern Arapaho tribes. **Open:** Tues–Sat 10am–4pm. **Free**

Rock Springs

See also Green River

Historic mining town built directly over coal mines, resulting in a street system which followed the paths the miners took while walking to the job. Located here are the largest coal reserves west of the Mississippi River, as well as a wild-horse holding facility. **Information:** Rock Springs Chamber of Commerce, 1897 Dewar Dr, PO Box 398, Rock Springs, 82901 (tel 307/362-3771).

MOTELS

Best Western Outlaw Inn

1630 Elk St, 82901; tel 307/362-6623 or toll free 800/528-1234; fax 307/362-2633. N of I-80. Angular-shaped property built around a huge atrium with an indoor pool. Well-furnished rooms are a cut above average, but a bit pricey. **Rooms:** 100 rms and stes. CI open/CO noon. Nonsmoking rms avail. **Amenities:** A/C, cable TV. **Services:** **Facilities:** 1 restaurant, 1 bar (w/entertainment), beauty salon. **Rates:** Peak (May 15–Sept 30) $64 S; $74 D; $85 ste. Extra person $7. Lower rates off-season. Parking: Outdoor, free. AE, CB, DC, DISC, MC, V.

Comfort Inn

1670 Sunset Dr, 82901; tel 307/382-9490 or toll free 800/221-2222; fax 307/382-7333. Exit 102 off I-80; go S. Very attractive H-shaped property. The lobby sports a mammoth fireplace and mounted big-game animals. **Rooms:** 104 rms, stes. CI open/CO 11am. No smoking. Nonsmoking rms avail. **Amenities:** A/C, cable TV. 1 unit w/terrace. **Services:** Children's program, babysitting. Complimentary drinks Mon–Fri, 5–7pm. **Facilities:** Spa, whirlpool, beauty salon, playground, washer/dryer. Large grassy area, with a log-climbing gym for the kids. **Rates (CP):**

Peak (Apr–Sept) $45 S; $50 D; $70 ste. Extra person $5. Children under age 18 stay free. Lower rates off-season. Parking: Outdoor, free. AE, DC, DISC, JCB, MC, V.

The Inn at Rock Springs
2518 Foothill Blvd, 82901; tel 307/362-9600 or toll free 800/442-9692; fax 307/362-8846. Exit 102 off I-80. Warm, inviting motel. Huge lobby features fireplace, large-screen TV, overstuffed chairs and sofas, and a stuffed Kodiak bear. **Rooms:** 150 rms and stes. Executive level. CI 2pm/CO noon. Nonsmoking rms avail. Rooms are attractively appointed; framed art on the walls. **Amenities:** A/C, cable TV. Some units w/terraces, 1 w/whirlpool. **Services:** **Facilities:** 300 1 restaurant (*see* "Restaurants" below), 1 bar, games rm, whirlpool. **Rates:** Peak (June–Sept) $58 S; $64 D; $72–$135 ste. Extra person $6. Children under age 18 stay free. Lower rates off-season. Parking: Outdoor, free. AE, DC, DISC, MC, V.

La Quinta Inn
2717 Dewar Dr, 82520; tel 307/362-1770 or toll free 800/531-5900; fax 307/362-2830. Exit 102 off I-80. Basic motel close to interstate, restaurant, and shopping. **Rooms:** 130 rms. CI open/CO noon. Nonsmoking rms avail. Minimal decor; some rooms have bare walls. **Amenities:** A/C. **Services:** **Facilities:** 80 Pool area subject to highway noise. **Rates (CP):** $43 S; $51 D. Extra person $8. Children under age 12 stay free. Parking: Outdoor, free. AE, CB, DC, DISC, MC, V.

RESTAURANTS

The Log Inn
12 Purple Sage Rd; tel 307/362-7166. Exit 99 off I-80. **Steak.** Built in 1934, this log structure houses the oldest and best known of Rock Springs' several beef and seafood establishments. In addition to steaks and prime rib, the restaurant is highly regarded for its shrimp fettuccine and deep-fried lobster tail. **FYI:** Reservations recommended. **Open:** Mon–Sat 5:30–10pm, Sun 5–9pm. **Prices:** Main courses $10–$16. AE, CB, DC, DISC, MC, V.

Red Desert Restaurant
In the Inn at Rock Springs, 2518 Foothills Blvd; tel 307/382-3303. Exit 102 off I-80. **American.** Basic selection of sandwiches and steaks. Ambience is pleasing and prices reasonable, but the wine list needs a little work. A small but comfortable lounge features big-screen TV, jukebox, and darts. **FYI:** Reservations accepted. Children's menu. **Open:** Mon–Thurs 6:30am–9pm, Fri–Sat 6:30am–9:30pm, Sun 6:30am–8pm. **Prices:** Main courses $6–$19. AE, DISC, MC, V.

ATTRACTION

Rock Springs Historical Museum
201 B St; tel 307/362-3138. Located in former City Hall, built in 1894. Exhibits highlight the city's history as a coal-mining (the UP Coal Company was headquartered here) and railroad town. In the basement, visitors can tour the town's original jail. **Open:** Summer, Tues–Sat 11am–5:30pm; winter, Wed–Sat noon–5pm. Closed some hols. **Free**

Saratoga

Gateway to the Snowy Range and Sierra Madre Mountains. Famous for its golf course, the Old Baldy. **Information:** Saratoga-Platte Valley Chamber of Commerce, 114 S 1st St, PO Box 1095, Saratoga, 82331 (tel 307/326-8855).

MOTELS

Hacienda Motel
WY 130 S, PO Box 960, 82331; tel 307/326-5751. Spotlessly clean, newer motel, adjacent to the airport. No frills. **Rooms:** 32 rms, stes, and effic. CI noon/CO noon. Nonsmoking rms avail. "Suites" are just larger rooms. **Amenities:** A/C, satel TV, refrig. **Services:** Babysitting. **Facilities:** Parking for large vehicles. **Rates:** Peak (Mem Day–Oct) $32–$42 S; $39–$52 D; $49–$62 ste; $35–$43 effic. Extra person $6. Children under age 12 stay free. Lower rates off-season. Parking: Outdoor, free. AE, DC, MC, V.

Sage & Sand Motel
311 S 1st, 82331; tel 307/326-8339. Off WY 130. This no-frills, thin-walled place offers undecorated rooms that look out on the parking area. **Rooms:** 17 rms and effic. CI open/CO 11am. Like walking into the 1960s: older TVs, stand-alone sinks with no counter space. Closets are big and deep. Efficiencies are clean, but appliances are older models. Some of the accommodations offer a second room, and as many as three or four beds. **Amenities:** Cable TV. No A/C. **Services:** Managed like a small town with good neighbors: a note on the door one day said "Rooms are open, find one you like—see you in the morning." **Rates:** $29 S; $36–$42 D; $36–$49 effic. Extra person $5. Parking: Outdoor, free. Efficiencies with a stove cost the same as regular rooms. AE, DC, MC, V.

Silver Moon Motel
1412 E Bridge, 82331; tel 307/326-5974. Large building set next to the freeway and surrounded by lots of asphalt. The motel is just a short walk from the Platte River, famous for its trout fishing. Good choice for hunters and fishermen who just want a clean bed. **Rooms:** 14 rms and effic. CI open/CO 11am. Rooms are small and contain mediocre furniture. **Amenities:** Cable TV. No A/C. **Services:** **Facilities:** **Rates:** Peak (May 15–Oct) $26 S; $28 D; $38 effic. Children under age 12 stay free. Lower rates off-season. Parking: Outdoor, free. AE, MC, V.

RESORT

Saratoga Inn
602 E Pic Pike Rd, PO Box 869, 82331; tel 307/326-5261; fax 307/326-5109. 205 acres. Under new ownership, this resort is being completely redone, with completion scheduled for spring 1996. **Rooms:** 56 rms and stes. CI 1pm/CO 11am. Nonsmoking rms avail. **Amenities:** Cable TV w/movies, VCR. No A/C. Some units w/terraces. **Services:** Babysitting. Horseback riding can be arranged. **Facilities:** 1 restaurant, 1 bar (w/entertainment), volleyball, spa, whirlpool. Swimming pool and hot tub both fed by waters from an on-site mineral spring. RV hookups available. **Rates:** Peak (May 15–Oct) $46–$61 S; $53–$65 D; $60–$82 ste. Extra person $5. Children under age 12 stay free. Lower rates off-season. Parking: Outdoor, free. Prices expected to increase when renovations are finished. AE, DISC, MC, V.

RESTAURANT

Wolf Hotel Restaurant
101 E Bridge St; tel 307/326-5525. Off WY 130. **Regional American.** Prime rib, accompanied by a commodious salad bar, is the house favorite. Specialties like barbecue ribs are served nightly. The decor is like a step back in time: unfinished brick walls adorned with turn-of-the-century art prints and posters. The front dining room is bustling with families and fishing parties fresh off the Platte River's "Miracle Mile"; the rear dining room is quieter. A compact saloon features a 10-seat bar and a few tables. **FYI:** Reservations accepted. Children's menu. **Open:** Lunch Mon–Sat 11:30am–2pm; dinner Mon–Sat 6–9pm, Sun 5–9pm. **Prices:** Main courses $11–$19. AE, DC, MC, V.

Sheridan

Home of the WYO Theater, the oldest operating vaudeville theater in the state. Coal mining and ranching are the main employers in this frontier town. **Information:** Sheridan County Chamber of Commerce, PO Box 707, Sheridan, 82801 (tel 307/326-8855).

MOTELS

Best Western Sheridan Center Motor Inn
612 N Main St, PO Box 4008, 82801 (Historic Downtown); tel 307/674-7421 or toll free 800/528-1234; fax 307/672-3018. This large facility extends across Main St; a "skybridge" joins the two halves together. Lobby is decorated with a Victorian/Old West motif. **Rooms:** 138 rms. CI 3pm/CO noon. Nonsmoking rms avail. Room decor echoes turn-of-the-century feeling of lobby. **Amenities:** A/C, cable TV. Some units w/terraces. **Services:** Babysitting. Summer entertainment includes Indian dancers, cloggers, polka dancers, and barbecues. **Facilities:** 350 2 restaurants, 1 bar, games rm, sauna, whirlpool. Guests can use local YMCA. **Rates (CP):** Peak (June–Sept) $35–$58 S; $40–$68 D. Extra person $5. Children under age 12 stay free. Lower rates off-season. Parking: Outdoor, free. Winter weekend ski and snowmobile packages avail. AE, CB, DC, DISC, JCB, MC, V.

Mill Inn Motel
2161 Coffeen Ave, 82801; tel 307/672-6401; fax 307/672-6401. Exit 25 off I-90. Located in a renovated flour mill at the eastern edge of town. **Rooms:** 45 rms and effic. CI noon/CO 11am. Nonsmoking rms avail. Rooms are simple, clean, light, and airy; some have snazzy red shower/tub combo. Two-bedroom condo available for extended stays. Honeymoon suite has heart-shaped tub. **Amenities:** A/C, cable TV. 1 unit w/whirlpool. **Services:** **Facilities:** 25 **Rates (CP):** Peak (June–Sept) $29–$59 S or D; $110 effic. Extra person $3. Lower rates off-season. Parking: Outdoor, free. AE, DISC, MC, V.

LODGE

Eaton's Guest Ranch
270 Eaton Ranch Rd, 82801; tel 307/655-9285; fax 307/655-9269. 18 mi W of Sheridan. Located at the base of the mountains, this guest ranch (and working cattle ranch) has been in operation since 1904. According to owner Frank Eaton, some families have been guests here for five generations. Although horseback riding is the main attraction, there are many other activities offered. Reservations required. **Rooms:** 51 cottages/villas. CI 2pm/CO 1pm. Clean and airy, they feature a western decor and modern bathrooms. Living rooms are comfortable, with plump sofas and chairs. Large closets will hold all your gear. **Amenities:** Refrig. No A/C, phone, or TV. Some units w/terraces, some w/fireplaces. **Services:** Social director, children's program. **Facilities:** 65 1 restaurant, volleyball, games rm, washer/dryer. Trail rides, led by enthusiastic and knowledgeable staff, are suited for all levels of riders. After fishing for rainbow trout in Wolf Creek, the chef will cook your catch for dinner. Beautiful pool area secluded in the pines. Team-roping contests, barbecues, weekly dances, and get-acquainted parties. Children under 6 not permitted to ride. **Rates (AP):** Peak (June 15–Sept 4) $850–$925 cottage/villa. Min stay. Lower rates off-season. Parking: Outdoor, free. Rates are per adult, per week, and include meals, accommodations, use of a saddle horse, and all guest activities. Rates for children: $650–$725 ages 6–17; $450–$525 ages 3–5. Children under 2 free. Closed Oct–May. DISC, MC, V.

RESTAURANTS

Ciao Bistro
120 N Main; tel 307/672-2838. In the center of historical Sheridan. **New American/Italian.** Chef/owner Kevin Kobielusz serves a melange of northern Italian and California grill cuisine in his lovely, upscale 30-seat restaurant. Lunch is

mostly salads and sandwiches. A favorite dinner appetizer is shrimp prepared with butter, garlic, tequila, and lime; entree choices are large, composed salads, pastas, chicken, veal, and beef dishes. Housemade breads and desserts. Small but well-chosen wine list. **FYI:** Reservations recommended. No smoking. **Open:** Peak (June–Sept) lunch Tues–Sat 11:30am–2pm; dinner Tues–Sat 6–9pm; brunch. Closed Feb 15–Mar 15. **Prices:** Main courses $9–$20; prix fixe $9–$14. MC, V.

Golden Steer
2071 N Main St; tel 307/674-9334. **Regional American.** Chef Elena Barber has been preparing high-quality filet mignon and prime rib for her loyal clientele for over 25 years. As a counterpart to beef, there is also Australian lobster, coldwater lobster, and Alaskan crab. Senior menu; takeout; banquet facilities. **FYI:** Reservations recommended. Piano. Children's menu. **Open:** Peak (Mem Day–Labor Day) lunch Mon–Fri 11am–2pm; dinner daily 4–10pm. **Prices:** Main courses $8–$50; prix fixe $9–$15. AE, CB, DC, DISC, MC, V.

ATTRACTIONS

Bighorn National Forest
Tel 307/672-0751. This national forest contains more than one million acres of scenic terrain, offering many opportunities for fishing (many different varieties of trout are especially plentiful), hiking, bird and wildlife viewing, and horseback riding. Cross-country skiing, ice skating, and snowmobiling are popular winter pursuits. Medicine Mountain (in the SW section of the forest) is the site of an ancient Native American "medicine wheel" rock formation.

There are a total of 36 campgrounds and picnic areas. Ranger stations located in Buffalo, Greybull, Lovell, Sheridan, and Worland. For more information, contact the Supervisor, Bighorn National Forest, 1969 S Sheridan Ave, Sheridan, WY 82801 (tel 307/672-0751). **Free**

Trail End State Historic Site
400 Clarendon Ave; tel 307/674-4589. Located on 3½ landscaped acres, this historic mansion built by John Kendrick (Wyoming governor, 1915-1917) is one of the few examples of Flemish revival architecture in the western United States. All the woodworking in the house was custom-made and many then-modern features (intercom, laundry chute, dumbwaiter, elevator) were installed. Visitors may tour most of the rooms; highlights include the Navajo-motif bedroom, the marble fireplace in the dining room, and the third-floor ballroom with its Tiffany-style chandelier **Open:** June–Aug, daily 9am–6pm; Apr–May and Sept 1–Dec 14, daily 1–4pm. Closed some hols. **Free**

Teton Village

See Jackson Hole

Thermopolis

Gateway to Hot Springs State Park, home of the largest mineral hot springs in the world. Mouth of scenic Wind River Canyon is just south of town. **Information:** Thermopolis-Hot Springs Chamber of Commerce, 111 N 5th St, PO Box 768, Thermopolis, 82443 (tel 307/864-3192).

MOTELS

Best Western Moonlighter Motel
600 Broadway, 82443; tel 307/864-2321 or toll free 800/528-1234. Jct US 20. Located at the busiest intersection in downtown Thermopolis, this property feels barren on the exterior but the rooms are pleasingly furnished and well-kept. **Rooms:** 26 rms. CI 1pm/CO 11am. Nonsmoking rms avail. A crescent-shaped block of rooms surrounds the pool. **Amenities:** A/C, cable TV w/movies. **Services:** **Facilities:** **Rates:** Peak (July–Aug) $58–$60 S; $61–$71 D. Extra person $3. Lower rates off-season. Parking: Outdoor, free. AE, CB, DC, DISC, EC, JCB, MC, V.

Holiday Inn of the Waters
115 Park, PO Box 1323, 82443; tel 307/864-3131 or toll free 800/HOLIDAY. At entrance to Hot Springs State Park, on the right. Hot-spring terraces and a beautiful park surround this motel on the banks of the Big Horn River. The owner is a big-game hunter and his trophies and photos are everywhere—you might dine with a mounted wildebeest staring at you. Located within Hot Springs State Park, setting for the world's largest mineral hot springs. **Rooms:** 80 rms. CI 3pm/CO noon. Nonsmoking rms avail. Nicely furnished rooms feature brass beds, antiques, and wall art ranging from paintings of mountain lions to photos of orcas. **Amenities:** A/C, cable TV w/movies, dataport, VCR. Some units w/terraces. **Services:** Masseur, babysitting. **Facilities:** 250 2 restaurants, 1 bar, volleyball, games rm, racquetball, spa, sauna, steam rm, whirlpool, washer/dryer. Fully equipped health club with tanning booths, two racquetball courts, a full-time masseur, and mineral baths from the local hot springs. Good restaurant and pleasant multilevel bar offer both indoor and outdoor dining; in summer, kids under 12 eat free. **Rates:** Peak (June 15–Aug) $58–$96 S; $69–$104 D. Extra person $6. Children under age 19 stay free. Lower rates off-season. Parking: Outdoor, free. AE, DC, DISC, JCB, MC, V.

ATTRACTIONS

Hot Springs State Park
US 20 and WY 789; tel 307/864-2176. The park is built around what is believed to be the world's largest single mineral hot spring. **Big Spring** pours forth 2,575 gallons per minute of steaming mineral water at a constant 135° F. From the perpetual fountain, water is channeled into pools to be cooled and then piped into bathhouses for public use. Two swimming plunges and the **State Bath House** provide indoor

and outdoor swimming opportunities. Open year-round, the plunges offer mineral water swimming and all types of recreation equipment. A small herd of buffalo roam the red hills of the park. Picnic area, playground. **Open:** Daily 6am–10pm. **Free**

Hot Springs Historical Museum
700 Broadway; tel 307/864-5183. Period room displays, the cherrywood bar from the Hole-in-the-Wall Saloon (hangout of Butch Cassidy and the Sundance Kid), Native American artifacts, and an antique railroad caboose are among this museum's highlights. There are several seasonal displays and art shows each year, including the August "Outlaw Trail Ride," when wanna-be gunslingers can have a drink at the Hole-in-the-Wall before heading out on horseback to Butch and Sundance's hideout. **Open:** Tues–Sat 8am–5pm. Closed some hols. **$**

Torrington

This farming community produces a variety of grains and vegetables. Rich in wildlife, there's a pheasant rearing facility nearby. **Information:** Goshen County Chamber of Commerce, 350 W 21st Ave, Torrington, 82240 (tel 307/352-3879).

MOTELS

King's Inn
1555 S Main St, 82240 (Downtown); tel 307/532-4011 or toll free 800/532-4011; fax 307/532-7202. New owners plan partial redecoration of this spacious, clean facility. **Rooms:** 51 rms. CI 2pm/CO 11am. Nonsmoking rms avail. Each room uniquely decorated. **Amenities:** A/C, cable TV w/movies. **Services:** Pets at manager's discretion. Pet fee $4. **Facilities:** 380 1 restaurant, 1 bar, whirlpool. **Rates:** Peak (Apr–Nov) $40–$50 S or D. Extra person $8. Children under age 12 stay free. Lower rates off-season. Parking: Outdoor, free. AE, CB, DC, DISC, MC, V.

Super 8 Motel
1548 S Main, 82240; tel 307/532-7118 or toll free 800/800-8000; fax 307/532-7118. S of US 26. Clean and comfortable and located in the heart of downtown, this motel offers personalized service. **Rooms:** 56 rms and stes. CI 1pm/CO 11am. Nonsmoking rms avail. Good accommodations for guests with disabilities. **Amenities:** A/C, cable TV w/movies, refrig, VCR. VCRs available on request. **Services:** **Facilities:** Washer/dryer. Truck and trailer parking. **Rates (CP):** Peak (Apr–Sept) $36–$40 S; $45–$50 D; $55–$60 ste. Extra person $4. Lower rates off-season. Parking: Outdoor, free. AE, CB, DC, DISC, MC, V.

ATTRACTIONS

Homesteaders Museum
495 Main St; tel 307/532-5612. Located in the old 1925 Union Pacific depot, at the center of several major pioneer routes including the Oregon Trail, the Mormon Trail, the Cheyenne–Deadwood stage route, and the Pony Express route. Displays include a fully furnished homestead shack, saddles and rodeo memorabilia, Union Pacific Caboose Gallery of railroad memorabilia and photos, and the Potter collection of Native American arrowheads, knives, and other tools. **Open:** Summer, Mon–Sat 10am–4:30pm, Sun 1–4pm; winter, Mon–Fri 10am–4pm. Closed some hols. **Free**

Fort Laramie National Historic Site
WY 160, Fort Laramie; tel 307/837-2221. In 1849, the government bought this former fur-trading post for use as a resupply point for the emigrants and gold-seekers pouring through along the Oregon Trail. When the Sioux objected to so many people passing through their lands, negotiations between tribal leaders and government representatives were held at the fort. The camp eventually became a military outpost and many treaty councils were held here from the 1860s to the 1880s, although the fort itself was only attacked once.

Today, nearly a dozen structures—including the guardhouse, captain's quarters, surgeon's quarters, and cavalry barracks—have been restored and refurbished. The park visitors center, housed in the fort's former commissary, features a museum with a 20-minute orientation film and exhibits detailing the history of the Sioux, the wagon trains, and the Pony Express. Rangers are on hand to give tours of the grounds during the summer; self-guided tours are available all year. **Open:** Summer, daily 8am–6pm; winter, daily 8am–4:30pm. Closed some hols. **$**

Wapiti

See Cody

Wilson

See Jackson Hole

Yellowstone National Park

The main entrance to the park is 59 mi N of Jackson via US 89; east entrance, 53 mi W of Cody via US 20; north entrance, 85 mi SE of Bozeman via I-90 and US 89. A masterpiece of unspoiled nature with an astonishing variety of scenery gathered together in one place. With its boiling geysers, hot springs, steep canyons, mud volcanoes, frozen lakes, deep pine forests, dizzying waterfalls, and fossilized trees, Yellowstone is an untamed cross section of the North American continent—and one which, geologists tell us, has been three billion years in the making.

The whole great volcanic plateau—60 miles long, 56 miles wide, and rising some 7,870 feet above sea level—is stitched together by 250 miles of impeccably surfaced roads and more than 1,000 miles of marked trails. The park possesses no fewer than 10,000 hot springs and almost 200 geysers bubbling up from the bowels of the earth. To the amazement of many visitors, some geysers like the famous **Old Faithful** spew their columns of steam and boiling water dozens of feet into the air with clockwork regularity (every 72 minutes); others lie dormant for weeks, or years, before bursting forth again. All around lies an ominous landscape of evil-smelling fumaroles, multicolored pools, and boiling cauldrons of bubbling, sulfurous mud.

Yet only a few miles away is the golden splendor of the **Grand Canyon of the Yellowstone,** with two dizzying falls, the 308-foot Lower Falls (1½ times the height of Niagara) and the 109-foot Upper Falls; and the azure-blue waters of Yellowstone Lake, 138 square miles and 308 feet deep.

The catastrophic 1988 fires consumed 780,000 of the 2.2 million acres of the park. The recovery process has added a new dimension to the park, as fire-blackened trees now stand in fields of lush grass, shrubs, and wildflowers.

Several different driving tours traverse the park area. The **Buffalo Bill Highway,** 80 miles between Fishing Bridge, Yellowstone Lake, and Cody along US 20, is a two-hour drive that includes **Shoshone Canyon, Sylvan Pass,** and the **Absaroka Mountains. Canyon Rim Scenic Road,** 1 mile east or 2½ miles south of Canyon Village on Grand Loop Rd, is a scenic drive of about 5 miles, with view of gorges and falls from **Inspiration Point, Lookout Point, Artist Point,** and **Grandview Point. Grand Loop Road,** 22 miles north of the southern entrance to the park, is Yellowstone's busiest road, its 142-mile "figure 8" linking all of the park's scenic sights and tourist attractions.

For more information about the park, contact the Yellowstone National Park Headquarters, PO Box 168, Yellowstone, WY 82190 (tel 307/344-2107).

HOTELS

Lake Lodge

Yellowstone Lake, Lake Village, PO Box 165, Yellowstone National Park, 82190; tel 307/344-7311; fax 307/344-7456. Surrounded by a lovely wooded setting, this property features a fabulous Craftsman-style log lobby with a huge stone fireplace and hickory furniture. Located within walking distance of Lake Yellowstone Hotel. **Rooms:** 186 cottages/villas. CI open/CO 11am. Nonsmoking rms avail. The rest of the hotel does not live up to the standard of the lobby. Western cabins have 1960s-style decor: orange Formica, paneling, and wallpaper. The Frontier cabins are a better value; some have original sinks and toilets. **Amenities:** No A/C, phone, or TV. **Services:** **Facilities:** 1 restaurant, 1 bar, washer/dryer. **Rates:** $41–$80 cottage/villa. Extra person $8. Children under age 11 stay free. Parking: Outdoor, free. Closed Oct–mid-June. AE, DC, DISC, JCB, MC, V.

Lake Yellowstone Hotel & Cabins

On the shore of Lake Yellowstone, Lake Village, PO Box 165, Yellowstone National Park, 82190; tel 307/344-7311; fax 307/344-7456. Originally built in 1891 (additions date to the 1920s), this gracious and lovely hotel sits above Lake Yellowstone. Although it's the oldest hotel in Yellowstone National Park, the rooms are very up to date. Both Calvin Coolidge and Warren Harding slept in the Presidential Suite. Don't be surprised to see buffalo grazing on the front lawn. **Rooms:** 194 rms and stes; 102 cottages/villas. CI open/CO 11am. Nonsmoking rms avail. Attractive rooms feature white-iron bed frames, wicker and pine furnishings, and nicely appointed bathrooms with lots of counter space. Opt for a lakeside room if possible. Clean and simple Frontier cabins are less expensive. Rooms in the hotel and annex have phones, cabins do not. **Amenities:** No A/C or TV. **Services:** Fishing, sightseeing tours, and cruises can be arranged. **Facilities:** 2 restaurants (*see* "Restaurants" below), 1 bar (w/entertainment). **Rates:** $77–$118 S or D; $320 ste; $59 cottage/villa. Extra person $8. Children under age 11 stay free. Parking: Outdoor, free. Closed early Oct–mid-May. AE, DC, DISC, JCB, MC, V.

Mammoth Hot Springs Hotel

Loop Rd, Mammoth Hot Springs, PO Box 165, Yellowstone National Park, 82190; tel 307/344-7901; fax 307/344-7456. 5 mi from N entrance. Built in the 1880s, but only one wing of the original structure remains. Located adjacent to Mammoth Hot Springs Terraces. Hotel-style rooms and cabins available. **Rooms:** 96 rms and stes; 126 cottages/villas. CI open/CO 11am. Nonsmoking rms avail. Hotel rooms range from the historic (with claw-foot bathtubs and Arts and Crafts–style dressers) to the ordinary (with 1950s-era furnishings). Bungalow-style cabins have porches and basic necessities, but they're a great deal at $30–$44. **Amenities:** No A/C, phone, or TV. Hotel rooms have phones, cabins do not. **Services:** Activities desk can arrange bus tours, horseback or stagecoach rides, or old-west cookouts. **Facilities:** 2 restaurants, 1 bar. Built in 1937, the art deco "Map Room" features a wall map of the United States crafted from 15 types of wood. Horseback riding and fishing nearby. **Rates:** $47–$103 S or D; $30–$106 cottage/villa. Extra person $8. Children under age 11 stay free. Parking: Outdoor, free. Closed Mar–Apr/Oct–Nov. AE, DC, DISC, JCB, MC, V.

Old Faithful Inn

Loop Rd, Old Faithful, 82190; tel 307/344-7901; fax 307/344-7456. Located within splashing distance of Old Faithful itself, this historic gem (built 1903–1904) is a miracle of log construction, completely made of local timber and often called the largest log hotel in existence. The lobby alone is worth a visit, soaring 85 feet at its peak and with a massive fireplace made from 500 tons of stone. The clock, copper light fixtures, and hardware were all designed by architect Robert C Reamer. **Rooms:** 359 rms and stes. CI open/CO 11am. Nonsmoking rms avail. A wide range of accommodations are available, some with views of Old Faithful. The "old house" section has rustic, log-cabin rooms which share baths—these can get noisy. Originally built in 1928, the west wing rooms have been spectacularly remodeled with Craftsman-design pine furnishings and copper lamps. **Amenities:** No A/C or TV. Some units w/minibars. **Services:** **Facilities:** 2 restaurants, 1 bar (w/entertainment). **Rates:** $44–$108 S or D; $210–$270 ste. Extra person $8. Children under age 11 stay free. Parking: Outdoor, free. Closed mid-Oct–early May. AE, DC, DISC, JCB, MC, V.

LODGES

Canyon Lodge and Cabins

Loop Rd, Canyon, PO Box 165, Yellowstone National Park, 82190; tel 307/344-7901; fax 307/344-7456. Near Grand Canyon of the Yellowstone River. Despite the drab, 1960s-style architecture of the main buildings, this is a fine base for exploring the Canyon area of Yellowstone. Good value. **Rooms:** 609 rms. CI open/CO 11am. Nonsmoking rms avail. Frontier cabins are a bit funky—simple but spacious with worn, stained carpeting and passé orange chairs—but they're quiet, comfortable and a good deal at $45. Slightly nicer but less endearing, the Western cabins offer pine-paneled, motel-ish quarters. Located in a new three-story, mountain chalet-style building, Cascade Lodge rooms are very pretty, with lodgepole-pine furniture, pine dressers, and modern baths complete with heat lamps and Swiss Institute toiletries. Porches with benches offer views of the trees. **Amenities:** No A/C, phone, or TV. **Services:** Activities desk. **Facilities:** 3 restaurants (*see* "Restaurants" below), 1 bar. Excellent gift shop; good food in the restaurants. **Rates:** $45–$87 S or D. Extra person $8. Children under age 11 stay free. Parking: Outdoor, free. Closed mid-Sept–early June. AE, DC, DISC, JCB, MC, V.

Grant Village

West Thumb section of Yellowstone Lake, Grant Village, PO Box 165, Yellowstone National Park, 82190; tel 307/344-7311. The "newest" (1983) facility in Yellowstone, this well-kept secret mainly accommodates bus tours. Attractive condo-style wooden buildings occupy a nice setting near Lake Yellowstone. **Rooms:** 300 rms. CI open/CO 11am. Nonsmoking rms avail. Well-furnished standard rooms have pretty bedspreads, wooden dressers, and functional bathrooms. **Amenities:** No A/C or TV. **Services:** Activities desk. **Facilities:** 12 2 restaurants (*see* "Restaurants" below), 1 bar. Self-service steak house has fabulous views overlooking Lake Yellowstone. **Rates:** $64–$77 S or D. Extra person $8. Children under age 11 stay free. Parking: Outdoor, free. Closed late Sept–late May. AE, DC, DISC, JCB, MC, V.

RESTAURANTS

Canyon Lodge Dining Room

In Canyon Lodge and Cabins, Loop Rd, Canyon; tel 307/344-7901. **Seafood/Steak/Pasta.** Despite the uninspired, 1960s-type decor, the food is quite good here. Choices like excellent caesar salad, grilled swordfish, steak, seafood, and pasta are all served with fresh vegetables. Service is prompt and thoughtful, and there's a good wine selection, with several wines available by the glass. Box lunches are available; there's also a less expensive, self-serve cafeteria next door. **FYI:** Reservations recommended. Children's menu. No smoking. **Open:** Breakfast daily 7–10:30am; lunch daily 11:30am–2:30pm; dinner daily 5:30–10pm. Closed Sept 12–June 2. **Prices:** Main courses $11–$17. AE, CB, DC, DISC, MC, V.

Grant Village Dining Room

West Thumb section of Yellowstone Lake, Grant Village; tel 307/242-3499. **Eclectic.** Set in a large contemporary shingle building, with a big deck offering lake views. Breakfast options include fruit, eggs, omelettes, and french toast, as well as an all-you-can-eat buffet. Lunch presents the usual assortment of burgers, sandwiches, pizzas, and salads, and dinner choices include eclectic appetizers, steaks, seafood, chicken, and pasta. Menu lists a wine recommendation for each entree. The Seven Stool Saloon—which has exactly that, plus a few tables—is open Mon–Sat 5–11pm, Sun 5–10pm. **FYI:** Reservations recommended. Children's menu. No smoking. **Open:** Breakfast daily 6:30–10am; lunch daily 11:30am–2:30pm; dinner daily 5:30–10pm. Closed late Sept–May. **Prices:** Main courses $11–$17. AE, DC, DISC, MC, V.

Lake Yellowstone Hotel Dining Room

On the shore of Lake Yellowstone, Lake Village; tel 307/344-7311. **Regional American.** This restaurant with a 1920s feel occupies a long, narrow room with leaded windows that permit glimpses of the lake through the trees. You may wish to start off with drinks in the lobby lounge, with its lovely views and music from a pianist or string quartet. The morning breakfast buffet is a good deal; trout stands out among dinner entrees. Gets very busy (and noisy) at time, with service ranging from excellent to tentative depending on the crowds. Reservations required for dinner. **FYI:** Reservations recommended. Piano/string quartet. Children's menu. No smoking. **Open:** Breakfast daily 6:30–10:30am; lunch daily 11:30am–2:30pm; dinner daily 5–10pm. Closed Oct–mid-May. **Prices:** Main courses $11–$17. AE, DC, DISC, MC, V.

Index

Listings are arranged alphabetically, followed by a code indicating the type of establishment, and then by city, state, and page number. The codes for type of establishment are defined as follows: (H) = Hotel, (M) = Motel, (I) = Inn, (L) = Lodge, (RE) = Resort, (R) = Restaurant, (RS) = Refreshment Stop, (A) = Attraction.

D

E

F

G

H

M

N

Q

R

S

T

U

V

10 % OFF
TIME & MILEAGE

CRUISE AMERICA
RV RENTAL & SALES

For national reservations and information:

1-800-327-7799

The most comprehensive line of Recreational vehicles you'll find anywhere.

Save 10% at Thousands of Choice Hotels Worldwide!

Call 1-800-4-CHOICE and request the "America On Wheels Discount #00055607." You'll save 10% on each night's stay at participating Comfort, Quality, Clarion, Sleep, Econo Lodge & Rodeway Inns, Hotels and Suites!

UP TO $100.00 OFF

Save up to $100.00 off when you buy your airline ticket from Travel Discounters.

Call 1-800-355-1065 and give code AOW in order to receive the discount. See reverse side for discount prices.

May not be used in conjunction with any other discount or promotion. Offer expires 12/31/97.

$5.00 Off Per Night

With over 500 locations in the US, Canada and Mexico, Travelodge always offers a clean, comfortable room at a great rate. And you'll also enjoy all these services **free**: fresh brewed in-room coffee, a morning newspaper, cable TV and no long distance access charges.

And if you present this certificate upon check-in we'll take $5.00 off the regular room rate for each night of your stay at a Travelodge location. It just makes sense to stay with us and save.

For reservations, call 1-800-578-7878 or your travel agent and ask for the 5CPN discount.

Terms and Conditions

- Offer includes 10% discount off all time and mileage charges on Cruise America or Cruise Canada vehicles only.
- Offer not available in conjunction with other discount offers or promotional rates.
- Excludes rental charges, deposits, sales tax, amd fuels.
- Normal rental conditions and customer qualification procedures apply.
- Members must reserve through Central Reservations only, at least one week in advance of pick up and mention membership affiliation at time of reservation.

  For reservations, call: 1-800-327-7799 US and Canada
- By acceptance and use of this offer, member agrees to the above conditions.
- Offer expires December 31, 1997.

Save 10% **Save 10%**

Offer expires December 31, 1997.

Savings are subject to certain restrictions and availability.
Valid for flights on most airlines.

Minimum Ticket Price	Save
$200.00	$25.00
$250.00	$50.00
$350.00	$75.00
$450.00	$100.00

Terms and Conditions

1. Advance reservations required.
2. Coupon must be presented at check-in.
3. Coupon cannot be combined with any other special offers, discounted rates.
4. Subject to availability.
5. Valid through December 31, 1997.
6. No photo copies allowed.

Travelodge®

For reservations, call 1-800-578-7878 or your travel agent and ask for the 5CPN discount.

All reservations must be made by calling our toll free reservation system, Superline. Any reservation requiring a guarantee must be guaranteed with the corporate V.I.P. identification number and the individual traveler's major credit card. If a guaranteed reservation is made and subsequently neither used nor cancelled, the corporate traveler will be billed for the one night's room charge plus tax.

expires December 31, 1997

Redeemable at participating Dollar® locations only.

This coupon entitles you to a one class upgrade from a compact or economy car to the next higher car group at no extra charge. Simply make a reservation for a compact or economy class car, then present this coupon to any Dollar rental agent when you arrive. You'll receive an upgrade to the next car class at no additional charge. Upgrade subject to vehicle availability. Renter must meet Dollar age, driver and credit requirements. This coupon must be surrendered at time of rental and may not be used in conjunction with any other offer and has no cash value. **EXPIRES 12/15/97.**

For worldwide reservations, call your travel agent or
800-800-4000

Mention code "afbg2" when you place your first order and receive 15% OFF

Offer expires December 31, 1997

PO Box 5485-AF2, Santa Barbara, CA 93150

Magellan's

10% OFF

- Available at participating properties.
- This coupon cannot be combined with any other special discount offer.
- Limit one coupon per room, per stay. Expires December 31, 1997.
- Not valid during blackout periods or special events.
- Void where prohibited.
- No reproductions accepted.

1-800-DAYS INN

AMERICA ON WHEELS

THE COMPLETE GUIDE TO WORRY-FREE TRAVEL ON THE ROAD!

Country Relics Village

Stanhope, Iowa

$1 off regular admission
"Stroll into the Past"

Expires December 7, 1997

TAKE 10% OFF

America's Most Entertaining Harbor Cruises

CRUISE, DINE, DANCE AND ENJOY A SPECTACULAR VIEW ON AMERICA'S MOST CELEBRATED HARBORS, ALL FOR ONE DISCOUNT PRICE!

– SEE REVERSE FOR DETAILS –

SPIRIT CRUISES

Something different. Something fun.

BOSTON ▪ CHICAGO ▪ NEW YORK ▪ NEW JERSEY ▪ NORFOLK
PHILADELPHIA ▪ SEATTLE ▪ WASHINGTON, DC

Good for $2.00 off Adult Admission or Family Pass

A 15-acre pioneer village with church, town hall, general store, school, and furnished homes. Specialty museums filled with airplanes, cars, farm machinery, and Native American artifacts.

For museum hours and special events schedules, call:
1-800-700-5317

BONANZAVILLE
Cass County Historical Society

Bonanzaville U.S.A.
Pioneer Village and Museums
I-94 Exit 343
West Fargo, North Dakota

Country Relics Village, Highway 17, North, Stanhope, Iowa **(515) 826-3491.**
Located on a working family farm, a population of 49 "dummies" and visitor participation brings life daily to the eleven building complex, May through October, 9 a.m. – 5 p.m. and for ten evenings, 5 – 8 p.m. following Thanksgiving for the annual Christmas Stroll. Come, "Stroll into the Past", place your dot on our maps. Located near Boone, Ames, Story City, or Webster City.

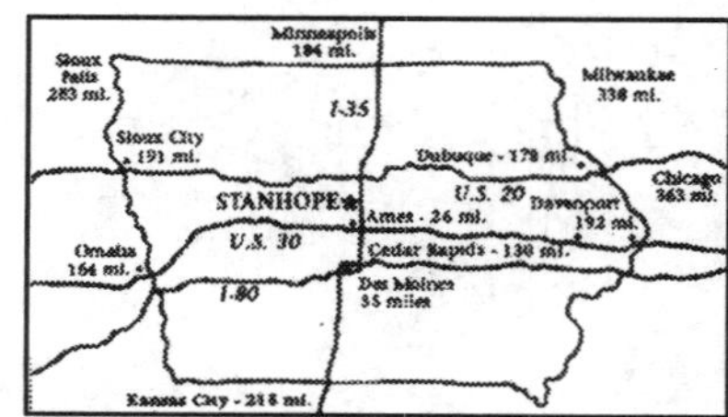

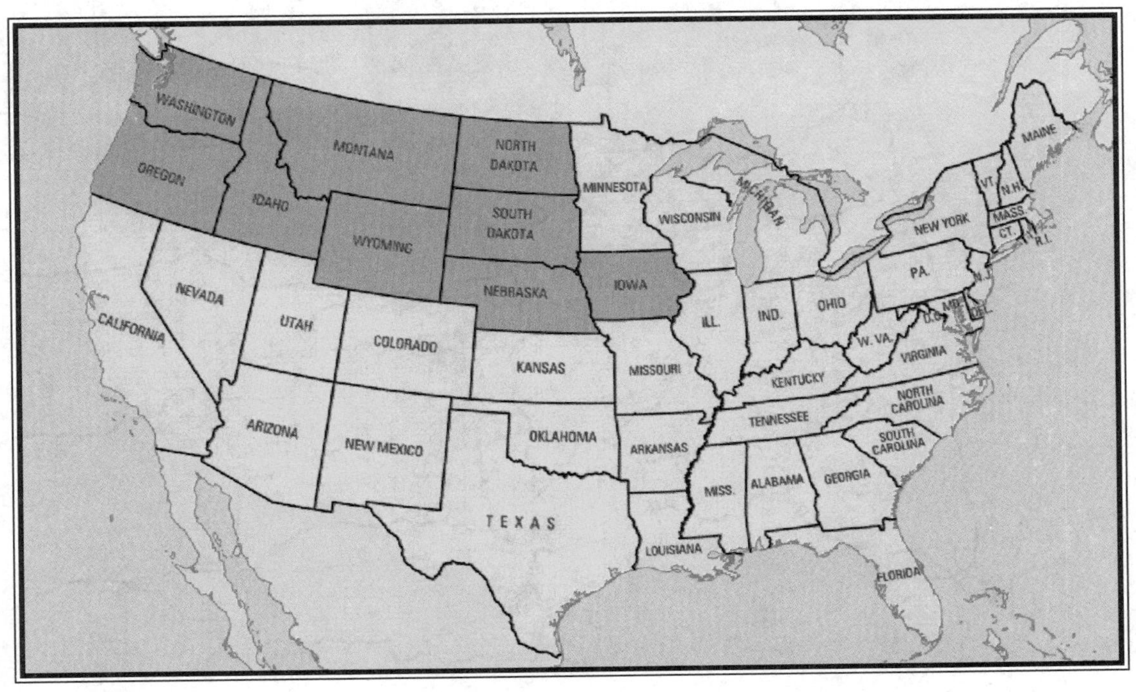
WASHINGTON
OREGON
IDAHO
MONTANA
NORTH DAKOTA
SOUTH DAKOTA
WYOMING
NEBRASKA
IOWA
MINNESOTA
WISCONSIN
MICHIGAN
NEW YORK
MAINE
VT.
N.H.
MASS.
CT.
R.I.
PA.
N.J.
MD.
DEL.
D.C.
OHIO
IND.
ILL.
W. VA.
VIRGINIA
KENTUCKY
NORTH CAROLINA
TENNESSEE
SOUTH CAROLINA
GEORGIA
ALABAMA
MISS.
FLORIDA
LOUISIANA
ARKANSAS
MISSOURI
KANSAS
OKLAHOMA
TEXAS
NEW MEXICO
COLORADO
UTAH
ARIZONA
NEVADA
CALIFORNIA

CONTENTS

BRITISH COLUMBIA
ALBERTA
SASKATCHEWAN
MANITOBA
CANADA
UNITED STATES
PACIFIC OCEAN
WASHINGTON
OREGON
CALIFORNIA
NEVADA
IDAHO
MONTANA
WYOMING
UTAH
COLORADO
ARIZONA
NEW MEXICO
NORTH DAKOTA
SOUTH DAKOTA
NEBRASKA
TEXAS
MEXICO
BAJA CALIFORNIA
SONORA
CHIHUAHUA
COAHUILA
DURANGO
NUEVO LEON
Vancouver
Calgary
Seattle
Spokane
Portland
Salem
Eugene
Boise
Helena
Billings
Bismarck
Pierre
Salt Lake City
Reno
Sacramento
San Francisco
Oakland
San Jose
Fresno
Las Vegas
LOS ANGELES
San Diego
Tijuana
Phoenix
Tucson
Albuquerque
Santa Fe
El Paso
Ciudad Juárez
Denver
Cheyenne
Colorado Springs
Amarillo
Lubbock
Oklahoma City
Wichita
Chihuahua
Hermosillo
Monterrey
Torreón
Great Basin
Columbia Plateau
Edwards Plateau
GREAT BASIN NAT'L PARK
YELLOWSTONE NAT'L PARK
GLACIER NAT'L PARK
GRAND CANYON NAT'L PARK
ROCKY MTN. NP
Mt. Rainier 14,410 ft. (4,392 m)
Mt. Shasta 14,162 ft. (4,317 m)
Mt. Whitney 14,494 ft. (4,418 m)
Mt. Elbert 14,433 ft. (4,399 m)
Pikes Pk. 14,110 ft. (4,301 m)
Isla de Guadalupe (MEX.)

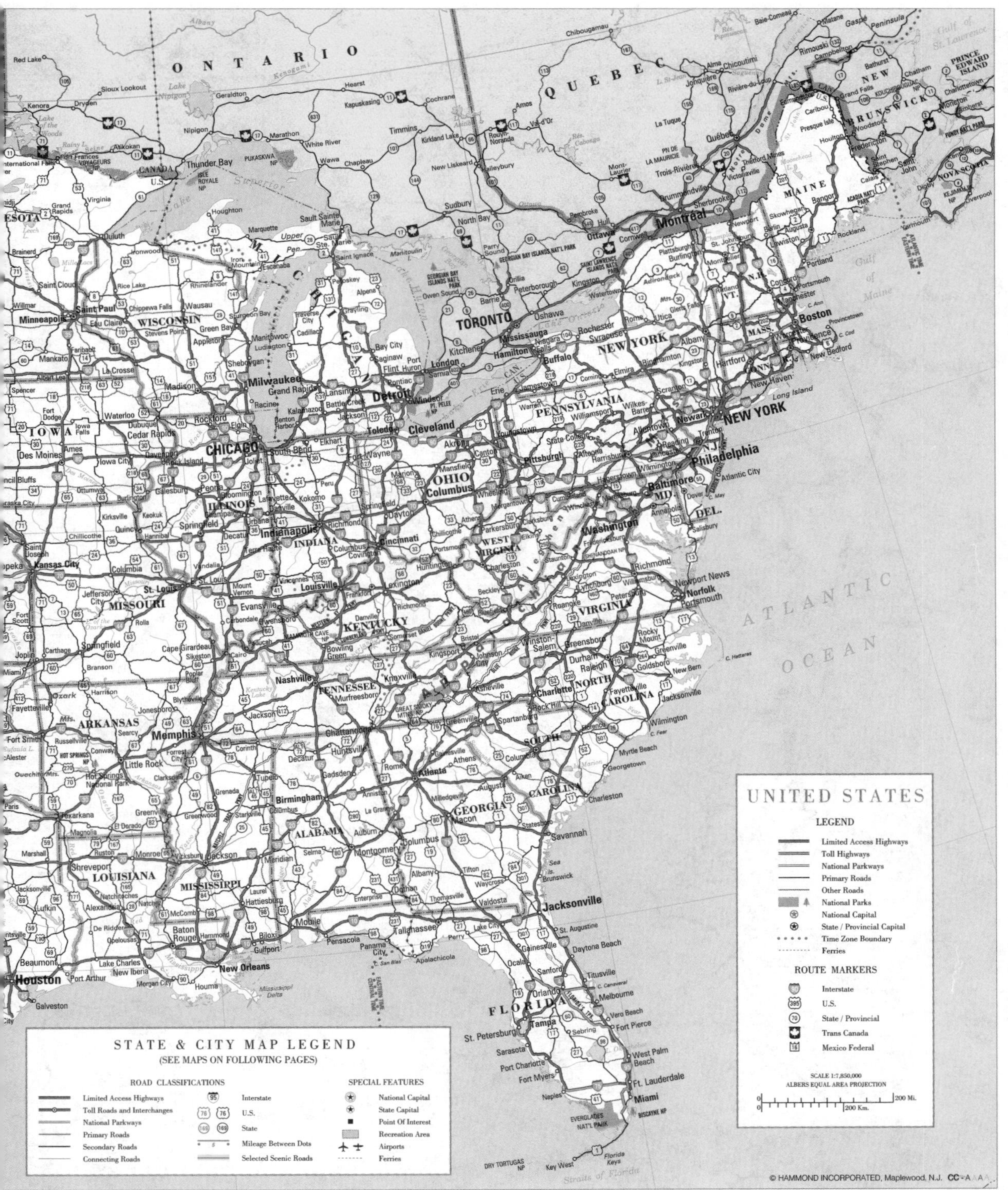
UNITED STATES
LEGEND
Limited Access Highways
Toll Highways
National Parkways
Primary Roads
Other Roads
National Parks
National Capital
State / Provincial Capital
Time Zone Boundary
Ferries
ROUTE MARKERS
Interstate
U.S.
State / Provincial
Trans Canada
Mexico Federal
SCALE 1:7,850,000
ALBERS EQUAL AREA PROJECTION
200 Mi.
200 Km.
STATE & CITY MAP LEGEND
(SEE MAPS ON FOLLOWING PAGES)
ROAD CLASSIFICATIONS
Limited Access Highways
Toll Roads and Interchanges
National Parkways
Primary Roads
Secondary Roads
Connecting Roads
Interstate
U.S.
State
Mileage Between Dots
Selected Scenic Roads
SPECIAL FEATURES
National Capital
State Capital
Point Of Interest
Recreation Area
Airports
Ferries
ONTARIO
QUEBEC
NEW BRUNSWICK
NOVA SCOTIA
PRINCE EDWARD ISLAND
MAINE
N.H.
VT.
MASS.
CONN.
NEW YORK
PENNSYLVANIA
N.J.
DEL.
MD.
WEST VIRGINIA
VIRGINIA
NORTH CAROLINA
SOUTH CAROLINA
GEORGIA
FLORIDA
ALABAMA
MISSISSIPPI
LOUISIANA
ARKANSAS
TENNESSEE
KENTUCKY
OHIO
INDIANA
ILLINOIS
MICHIGAN
WISCONSIN
IOWA
MISSOURI
ATLANTIC OCEAN
Gulf of Maine
Gulf of St. Lawrence
Straits of Florida
Mississippi Delta
CHICAGO
NEW YORK
Philadelphia
Washington
Boston
Montreal
TORONTO
Detroit
Cleveland
Pittsburgh
Baltimore
Atlanta
Memphis
Nashville
Jacksonville
Miami
New Orleans
Houston
St. Louis
Kansas City
Indianapolis
Cincinnati
Louisville
Milwaukee
Minneapolis
St. Paul
Buffalo
Columbus
Charlotte
Richmond
Norfolk
Tampa
© HAMMOND INCORPORATED, Maplewood, N.J.

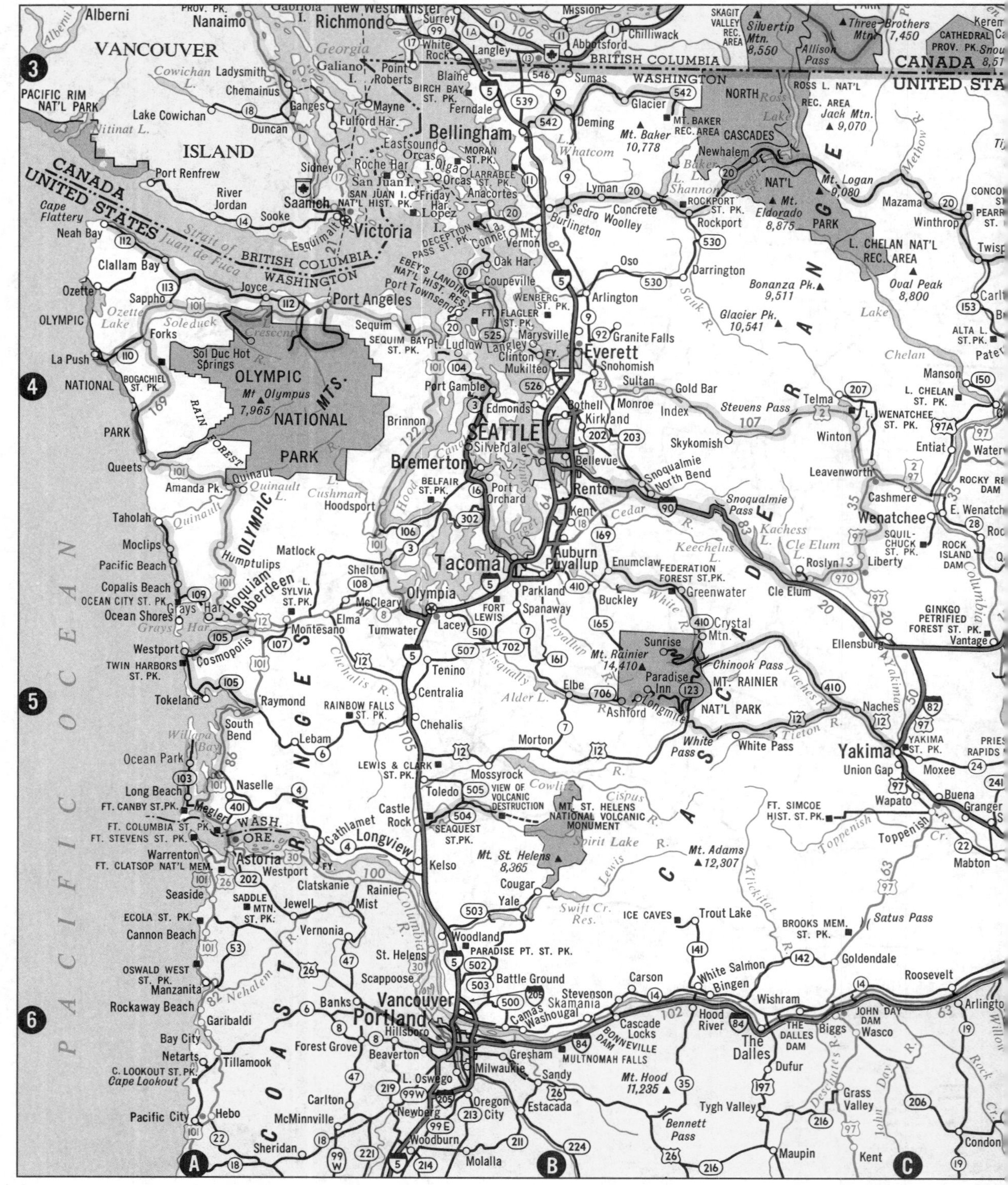

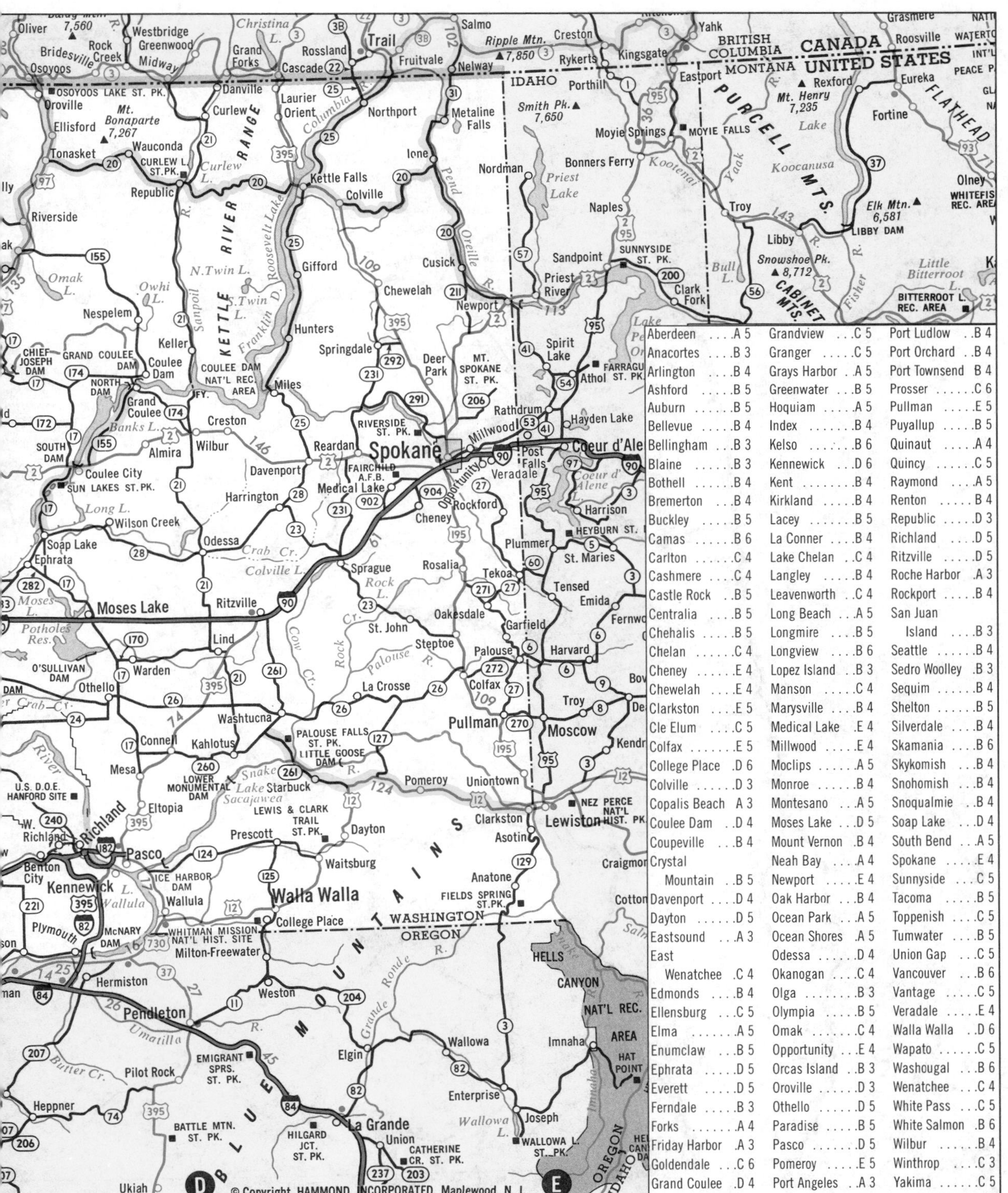

Place	Key
Aberdeen	A 5
Anacortes	B 3
Arlington	B 4
Ashford	B 5
Auburn	B 5
Bellevue	B 4
Bellingham	B 3
Blaine	B 3
Bothell	B 4
Bremerton	B 4
Buckley	B 5
Camas	B 6
Carlton	C 4
Cashmere	C 4
Castle Rock	B 5
Centralia	B 5
Chehalis	B 5
Chelan	C 4
Cheney	E 4
Chewelah	E 4
Clarkston	E 5
Cle Elum	C 5
Colfax	E 5
College Place	D 6
Colville	D 3
Copalis Beach	A 3
Coulee Dam	D 4
Coupeville	B 4
Crystal Mountain	B 5
Davenport	D 4
Dayton	D 5
Eastsound	A 3
East Wenatchee	C 4
Edmonds	B 4
Ellensburg	C 5
Elma	A 5
Enumclaw	B 5
Ephrata	D 5
Everett	D 5
Ferndale	B 3
Forks	A 4
Friday Harbor	A 3
Goldendale	C 6
Grand Coulee	D 4
Grandview	C 5
Granger	C 5
Grays Harbor	A 5
Greenwater	B 5
Hoquiam	A 5
Index	B 4
Kelso	B 6
Kennewick	D 6
Kent	B 4
Kirkland	B 4
Lacey	B 5
La Conner	B 4
Lake Chelan	C 4
Langley	B 4
Leavenworth	C 4
Long Beach	A 5
Longmire	B 5
Longview	B 6
Lopez Island	B 3
Manson	C 4
Marysville	B 4
Medical Lake	E 4
Millwood	E 4
Moclips	A 5
Monroe	B 4
Montesano	A 5
Moses Lake	D 5
Mount Vernon	B 4
Neah Bay	A 4
Newport	E 4
Oak Harbor	B 4
Ocean Park	A 5
Ocean Shores	A 5
Odessa	D 4
Okanogan	C 4
Olga	B 3
Olympia	B 5
Omak	C 4
Opportunity	E 4
Orcas Island	B 3
Oroville	D 3
Othello	D 5
Paradise	B 5
Pasco	D 5
Pomeroy	E 5
Port Angeles	A 3
Port Ludlow	B 4
Port Orchard	B 4
Port Townsend	B 4
Prosser	C 6
Pullman	E 5
Puyallup	B 5
Quinault	A 4
Quincy	C 5
Raymond	A 5
Renton	B 4
Republic	D 3
Richland	D 5
Ritzville	D 5
Roche Harbor	A 3
Rockport	B 4
San Juan Island	B 3
Seattle	B 4
Sedro Woolley	B 3
Sequim	B 4
Shelton	B 5
Silverdale	B 4
Skamania	B 6
Skykomish	B 4
Snohomish	B 4
Snoqualmie	B 4
Soap Lake	D 4
South Bend	A 5
Spokane	E 4
Sunnyside	C 5
Tacoma	B 5
Toppenish	C 5
Tumwater	B 5
Union Gap	C 5
Vancouver	B 6
Vantage	C 5
Veradale	E 4
Walla Walla	D 6
Wapato	C 5
Washougal	B 6
Wenatchee	C 4
White Pass	C 5
White Salmon	B 6
Wilbur	B 4
Winthrop	C 3
Yakima	C 5

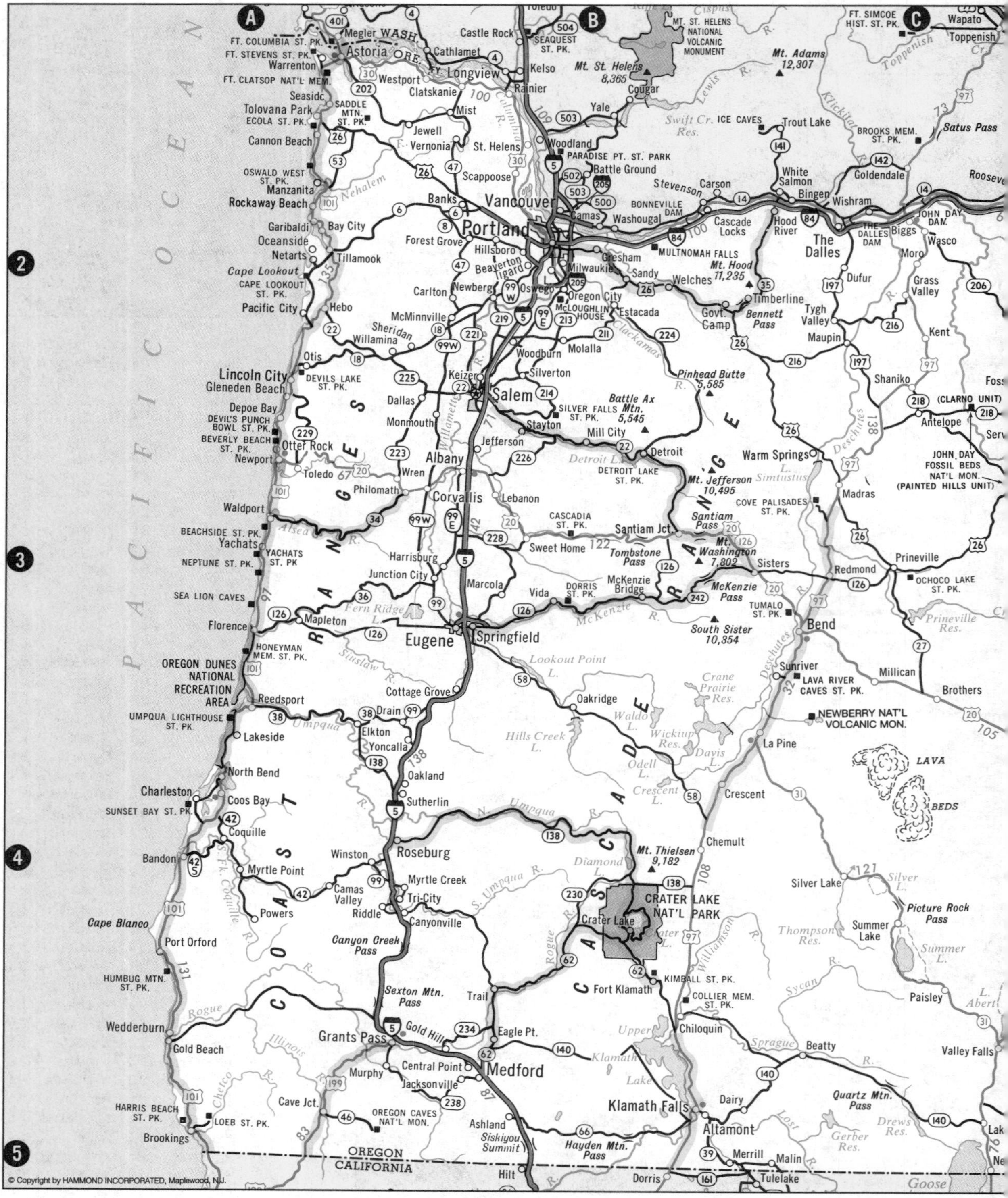

A B C

2 3 4 5

PACIFIC OCEAN

Ft. Columbia St. Pk.
Ft. Stevens St. Pk.
Megler
WASH.
ORE.
Astoria
Warrenton
Ft. Clatsop Nat'l Mem.
Westport
Cathlamet
Longview
Kelso
Castle Rock
Seaquest St. Pk.
Clatskanie
Rainier
Seaside
Saddle Mtn. St. Pk.
Tolovana Park
Ecola St. Pk.
Cannon Beach
Mist
Jewell
Vernonia
St. Helens
Oswald West St. Pk.
Manzanita
Nehalem
Rockaway Beach
Scappoose
Banks
Vancouver
Portland
Garibaldi
Bay City
Oceanside
Netarts
Tillamook
Forest Grove
Hillsboro
Beaverton
Tigard
Cape Lookout
Cape Lookout St. Pk.
Pacific City
Hebo
Carlton
Newberg
Oswego
McMinnville
Sheridan
Willamina
Oregon City
McLoughlin House
Estacada
Otis
Lincoln City
Devils Lake St. Pk.
Gleneden Beach
Depoe Bay
Devil's Punch Bowl St. Pk.
Beverly Beach St. Pk.
Otter Rock
Newport
Toledo
Waldport
Beachside St. Pk.
Yachats
Yachats St. Pk.
Neptune St. Pk.
Sea Lion Caves
Florence
Mapleton
Honeyman Mem. St. Pk.
Oregon Dunes National Recreation Area
Reedsport
Umpqua Lighthouse St. Pk.
Lakeside
North Bend
Charleston
Coos Bay
Sunset Bay St. Pk.
Coquille
Bandon
Myrtle Point
Powers
Cape Blanco
Port Orford
Humbug Mtn. St. Pk.
Wedderburn
Gold Beach
Harris Beach St. Pk.
Loeb St. Pk.
Brookings
Keizer
Salem
Dallas
Monmouth
Albany
Wren
Philomath
Corvallis
Lebanon
Harrisburg
Junction City
Eugene
Springfield
Fern Ridge L.
Cottage Grove
Drain
Elkton
Yoncalla
Oakland
Sutherlin
Roseburg
Winston
Camas Valley
Myrtle Creek
Tri-City
Riddle
Canyonville
Canyon Creek Pass
Sexton Mtn. Pass
Grants Pass
Gold Hill
Murphy
Central Point
Jacksonville
Medford
Cave Jct.
Oregon Caves Nat'l Mon.
Ashland
Siskiyou Summit
Hilt
OREGON
CALIFORNIA
Woodburn
Silverton
Molalla
Silver Falls St. Pk.
Stayton
Mill City
Jefferson
Detroit
Detroit L.
Detroit Lake St. Pk.
Battle Ax Mtn. 5,545
Cascadia St. Pk.
Sweet Home
Santiam Jct.
Santiam Pass
Tombstone Pass
Marcola
Vida
Dorris St. Pk.
McKenzie Bridge
McKenzie Pass
Lookout Point L.
Oakridge
Hills Creek L.
Waldo L.
Odell L.
Crescent L.
Wickiup Res.
Crane Prairie Res.
Davis L.
Diamond L.
Mt. Thielsen 9,182
Crater Lake
Crater Lake Nat'l Park
Kimball St. Pk.
Fort Klamath
Collier Mem. St. Pk.
Trail
Eagle Pt.
Upper Klamath L.
Chiloquin
Klamath Falls
Hayden Mtn. Pass
Altamont
Merrill
Malin
Dorris
Tulelake
Dairy
Mt. St. Helens National Volcanic Monument
Mt. St. Helens 8,365
Cougar
Yale
Swift Cr. Res.
Ice Caves
Mt. Adams 12,307
Trout Lake
Woodland
Paradise Pt. St. Park
Battle Ground
Camas
Washougal
Stevenson
Carson
Bonneville Dam
Cascade Locks
Multnomah Falls
Hood River
White Salmon
Bingen
Wishram
Goldendale
Brooks Mem. St. Pk.
Satus Pass
Ft. Simcoe Hist. St. Pk.
Wapato
Toppenish
Roosevelt
John Day Dam
The Dalles Dam
Biggs
The Dalles
Wasco
Moro
Gresham
Milwaukie
Sandy
Welches
Mt. Hood 11,235
Timberline
Govt. Camp
Bennett Pass
Dufur
Grass Valley
Tygh Valley
Maupin
Kent
Shaniko
Fossil
Pinhead Butte 5,585
Clarno Unit
Antelope
John Day Fossil Beds Nat'l Mon. (Painted Hills Unit)
Warm Springs
Mt. Jefferson 10,495
Madras
Cove Palisades St. Pk.
Mt. Washington 7,802
Sisters
Redmond
Prineville
Ochoco Lake St. Pk.
Prineville Res.
Tumalo St. Pk.
Bend
South Sister 10,354
Sunriver
Lava River Caves St. Pk.
Millican
Brothers
Newberry Nat'l Volcanic Mon.
La Pine
Lava Beds
Crescent
Chemult
Silver Lake
Picture Rock Pass
Summer Lake
Thompson Res.
Paisley
L. Abert
Beatty
Valley Falls
Quartz Mtn. Pass
Drews Res.
Gerber Res.
Goose L.
COAST RANGES
CASCADE RANGE

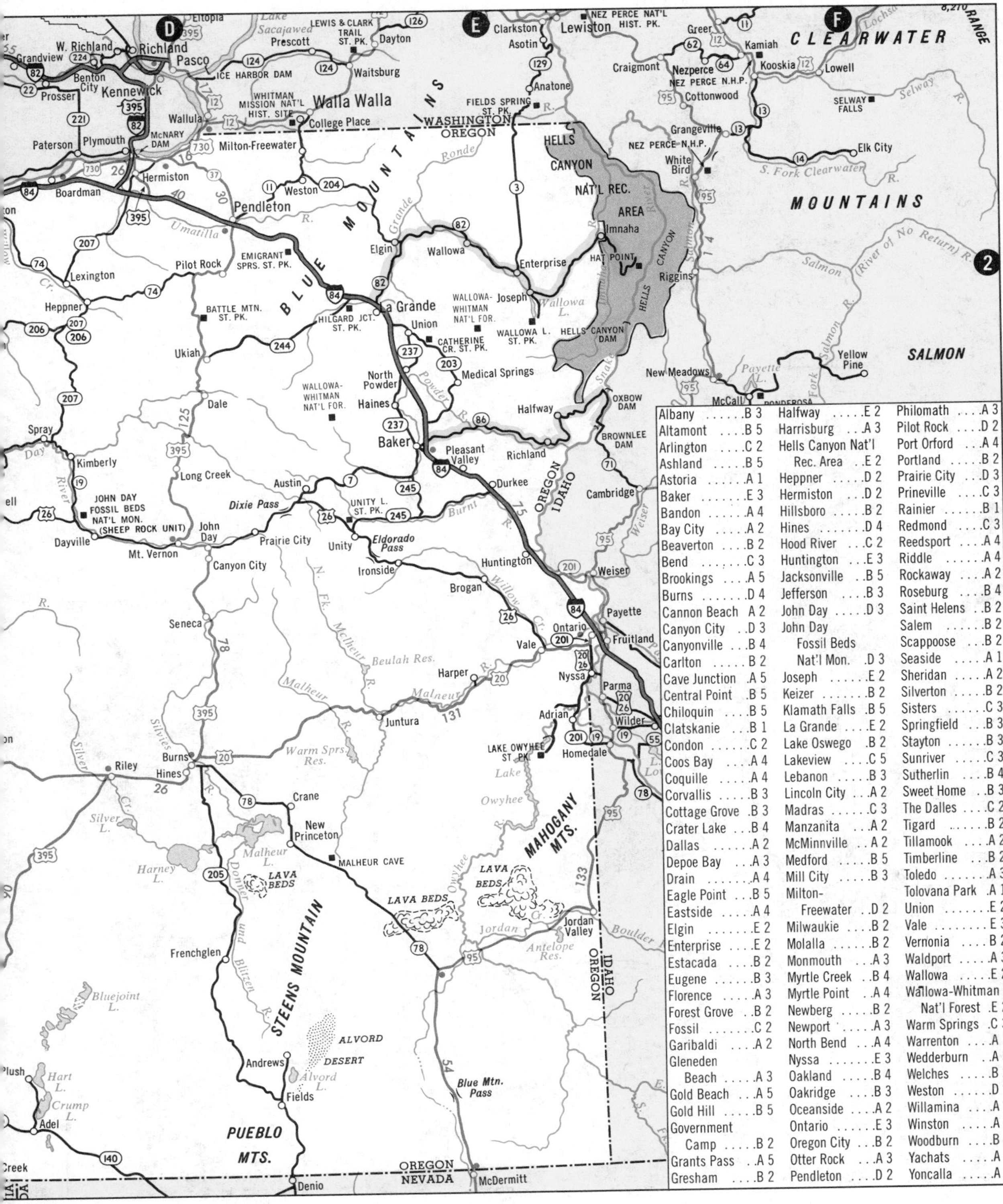

Albany . . . B 3
Altamont . . . B 5
Arlington . . . C 2
Ashland . . . B 5
Astoria . . . A 1
Baker . . . E 3
Bandon . . . A 4
Bay City . . . A 2
Beaverton . . . B 2
Bend . . . C 3
Brookings . . . A 5
Burns . . . D 4
Cannon Beach A 2
Canyon City . . D 3
Canyonville . . B 4
Carlton . . . B 2
Cave Junction . A 5
Central Point . B 5
Chiloquin . . . B 5
Clatskanie . . . B 1
Condon . . . C 2
Coos Bay . . . A 4
Coquille . . . A 4
Corvallis . . . B 3
Cottage Grove . B 3
Crater Lake . . B 4
Dallas . . . A 2
Depoe Bay . . A 3
Drain . . . A 4
Eagle Point . . B 5
Eastside . . . A 4
Elgin . . . E 2
Enterprise . . . E 2
Estacada . . . B 2
Eugene . . . B 3
Florence . . . A 3
Forest Grove . . B 2
Fossil . . . C 2
Garibaldi . . . A 2
Gleneden Beach . . . A 3
Gold Beach . . A 5
Gold Hill . . . B 5
Government Camp . . . B 2
Grants Pass . . A 5
Gresham . . . B 2
Halfway . . . E 2
Harrisburg . . A 3
Hells Canyon Nat'l Rec. Area . . E 2
Heppner . . . D 2
Hermiston . . D 2
Hillsboro . . . B 2
Hines . . . D 4
Hood River . . C 2
Huntington . . E 3
Jacksonville . . B 5
Jefferson . . . B 3
John Day . . . D 3
John Day Fossil Beds Nat'l Mon. . D 3
Joseph . . . E 2
Keizer . . . B 2
Klamath Falls . B 5
La Grande . . . E 2
Lake Oswego . B 2
Lakeview . . . C 5
Lebanon . . . B 3
Lincoln City . . A 2
Madras . . . C 3
Manzanita . . A 2
McMinnville . . A 2
Medford . . . B 5
Mill City . . . B 3
Milton-Freewater . D 2
Milwaukie . . . B 2
Molalla . . . B 2
Monmouth . . A 3
Myrtle Creek . . B 4
Myrtle Point . . A 4
Newberg . . . B 2
Newport . . . A 3
North Bend . . A 4
Nyssa . . . E 3
Oakland . . . B 4
Oakridge . . . B 3
Oceanside . . . A 2
Ontario . . . E 3
Oregon City . . B 2
Otter Rock . . A 3
Pendleton . . . D 2
Philomath . . . A 3
Pilot Rock . . . D 2
Port Orford . . A 4
Portland . . . B 2
Prairie City . . D 3
Prineville . . . C 3
Rainier . . . B 1
Redmond . . . C 3
Reedsport . . . A 4
Riddle . . . A 4
Rockaway . . . A 2
Roseburg . . . B 4
Saint Helens . . B 2
Salem . . . B 2
Scappoose . . . B 2
Seaside . . . A 1
Sheridan . . . A 2
Silverton . . . B 2
Sisters . . . C 3
Springfield . . B 3
Stayton . . . B 3
Sunriver . . . C 3
Sutherlin . . . B 4
Sweet Home . . B 3
The Dalles . . . C 2
Tigard . . . B 2
Tillamook . . . A 2
Timberline . . . B 2
Toledo . . . A 3
Tolovana Park . A 1
Union . . . E 2
Vale . . . E 3
Vernonia . . . B 2
Waldport . . . A 3
Wallowa . . . E 2
Wallowa-Whitman Nat'l Forest . E 2
Warm Springs . C 3
Warrenton . . . A 1
Wedderburn . . A 5
Welches . . . B 2
Weston . . . D 2
Willamina . . . A 2
Winston . . . A 4
Woodburn . . . B 2
Yachats . . . A 3
Yoncalla . . . A 4

IDAHO
Aberdeen C 6
American Falls C 6
Arco B 5
Ashton C 5
Blackfoot C 6
Boise A 5
Bonners Ferry A 2
Buhl B 6
Burley B 6
Caldwell A 5
Coeur d'Alene A 3
Cottonwood A 4
Driggs C 5
Emmett A 5
Filer B 6
Glenns Ferry B 6
Gooding B 6
Grangeville A 4
Hagerman B 6
Hailey B 5
Idaho Falls C 6
Jerome B 6
Kamiah A 4
Kellogg A 3
Ketchum B 5
Kimberly B 6
Lava Hot Springs C 6
Lewiston A 4
Malad City C 6
McCall A 5
Montpelier C 6
Moscow A 4
Mountain Home A 6
Nampa A 5
Orofino A 4
Payette A 5
Pocatello C 6
Preston C 6
Priest River A 3
Rexburg C 5
Rigby C 5
Rupert B 6
Saint Anthony C 5
Saint Maries A 3
Salmon B 4
Sandpoint A 3
Sawtooth Nat'l Rec. Area B 5
Shoshone B 6
Soda Springs C 6
Sun Valley B 5
Twin Falls B 6
Wallace A 3
Weiser A 5
Wendell B 6
MONTANA
(See map on p.9)
Anaconda C 4
Baker F 4
Belgrade C 4
Bigfork B 3
Big Sky C 4
Big Timber D 4
Billings D 4
Boulder C 4
Bozeman C 4
Browning C 2
Butte C 4
Chester C 2
Chinook D 2
Choteau C 3
Circle E 3
Columbia Falls B 3
Columbus D 4
Conrad C 3
Cooke City D 4
Culbertson F 3
Cut Bank C 2
Darby B 4
Dayton B 3
Deer Lodge C 4
Dillon C 4
East Glacier C 2
East Helena C 4
Ennis C 4
Essex B 2
Eureka B 2
Fairview F 3
Flathead Lake B 3
Forsyth E 4
Fort Benton D 3
Fort Peck E 3
Gallatin Gateway C 4
Gardiner C 4
Glacier Nat'l Park B 2
Glasgow E 3
Glendive F 3
Great Falls C 3
Hamilton B 4
Hardin E 4
Harlem D 2
Harlowton D 4
Havre D 3
Helena C 4
Kalispell B 3
Laurel D 4
Lewistown D 3
Libby B 3
Little Bighorn Battlefield Nat'l Mon. E 4
Livingston D 4
Malta E 3
Miles City E 4
Missoula B 3
Moiese B 3
Nevada City C 4
North Havre D 2
Philipsburg B 4
Plentywood F 2
Polson B 3
Poplar F 3
Red Lodge D 5
Ronan B 3
Roundup D 4
Scobey E 2
Shelby C 2
Sidney F 3
Superior B 3
Terry F 3
Thompson Falls B 3
Three Forks C 4
Townsend C 4
Virginia City C 4
Walkerville C 4
West Glacier B 2
West Yellowstone C 5
Whitefish B 3
White Sulphur Springs C 4
Wisdom B 4
Wolf Point E 3
CANADA
UNITED STATES
BR. COLUMBIA
WASHINGTON
OREGON
NEVADA
UTAH
WYOMING
MONTANA
IDAHO
Spokane
Coeur d'Alene
Lewiston
Boise
Nampa
Pocatello
Idaho Falls
Twin Falls
Missoula
CLEARWATER MTS.
SALMON RIVER MTS.
BITTERROOT RANGE
HELLS CANYON NAT'L REC. AREA
SAWTOOTH NAT'L REC. AREA
CRATERS OF THE MOON NAT'L MON.
LAVA BEDS
Borah Pk. 12,662
YELLOWSTONE NATIONAL PARK

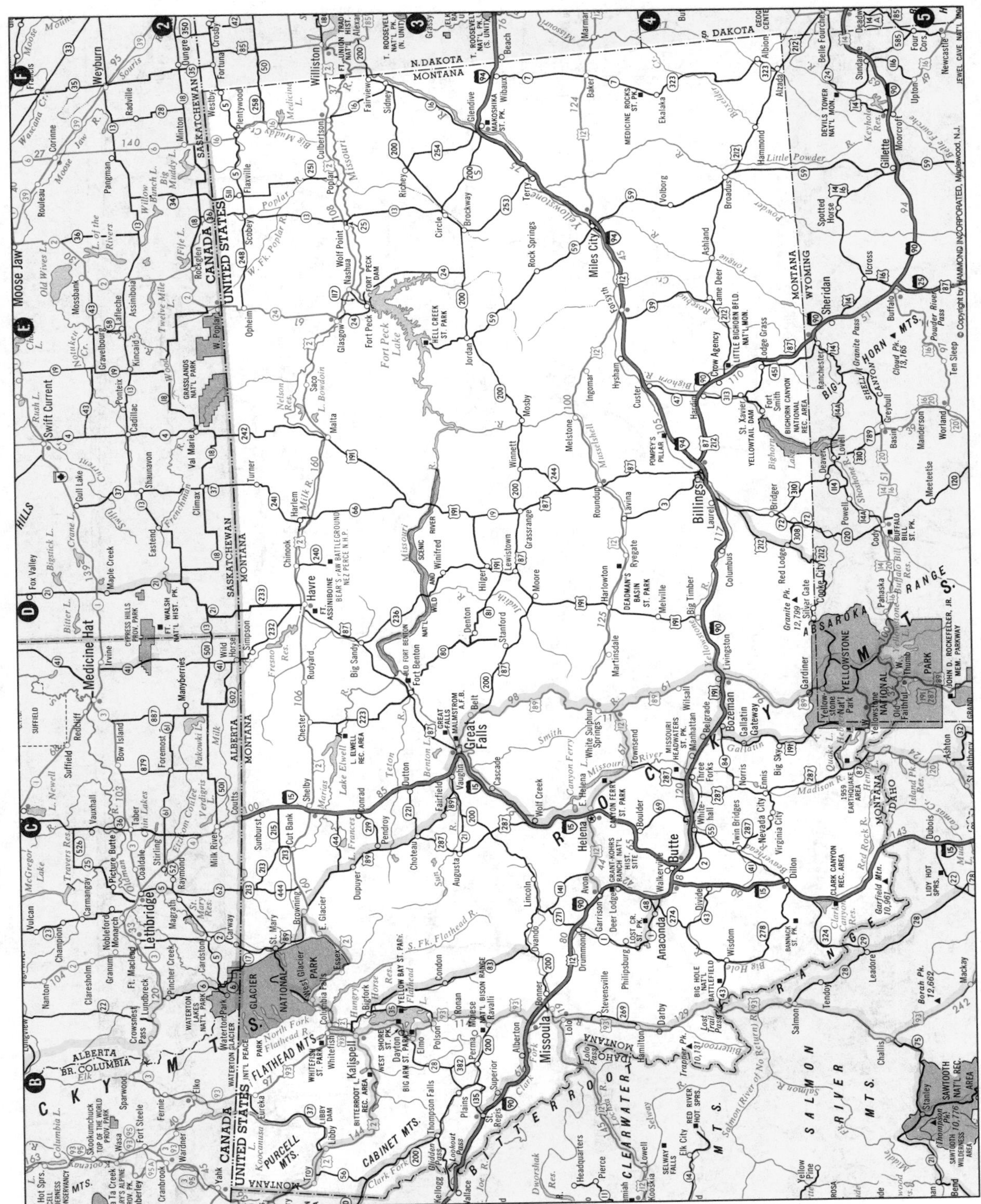

MONTANA
N. DAKOTA
S. DAKOTA
WYOMING
IDAHO
CANADA
UNITED STATES
SASKATCHEWAN
ALBERTA
BR. COLUMBIA
Helena
Billings
Great Falls
Missoula
Butte
Bozeman
Kalispell
Havre
Miles City
Glendive
Lewistown
Livingston
Anaconda
Sidney
Glasgow
Shelby
Dillon
Hardin
Forsyth
Whitefish
Medicine Hat
Lethbridge
Moose Jaw
Swift Current
Weyburn
Williston
Sheridan
Gillette
Cody
GLACIER NATIONAL PARK
YELLOWSTONE NATIONAL PARK
Fort Peck Lake
Missouri R.
Yellowstone R.
Milk R.
Bighorn R.
Powder R.
FLATHEAD MTS.
CABINET MTS.
PURCELL MTS.
BITTERROOT RANGE
ABSAROKA RANGE
BIG HORN MTS.
SALMON RIVER MTS.
CLEARWATER MTS.
ROCKY MTS.
LITTLE BIGHORN BFLD. NAT'L MON.
BIGHORN CANYON NATIONAL REC. AREA
POMPEY'S PILLAR
© Copyright by HAMMOND INCORPORATED, Maplewood, N.J.

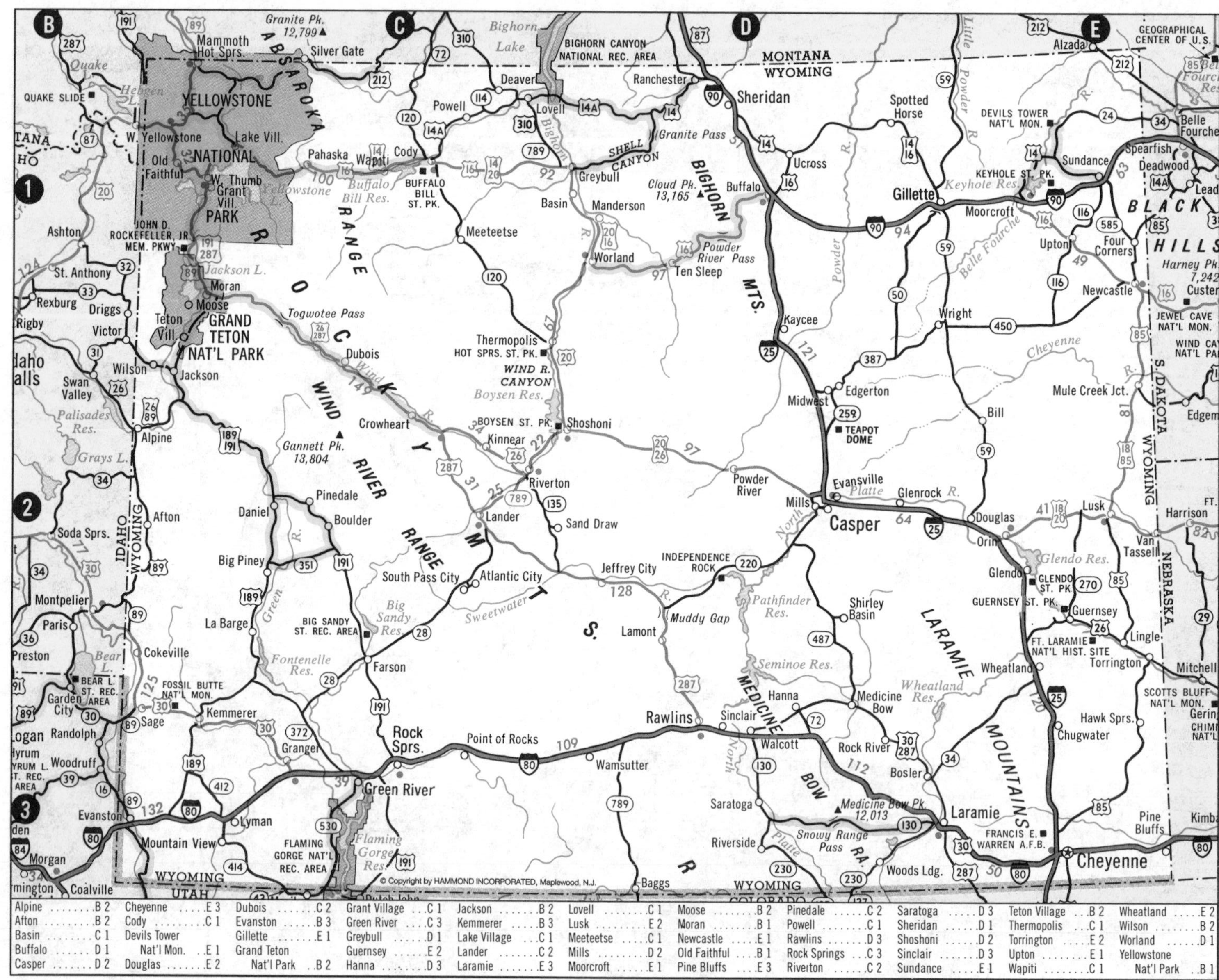
© Copyright by HAMMOND INCORPORATED, Maplewood, N.J.
Alpine ....B 2
Afton ....B 2
Basin ....C 1
Buffalo ....D 1
Casper ....D 2
Cheyenne ....E 3
Cody ....C 1
Devils Tower Nat'l Mon. ....E 1
Douglas ....E 2
Dubois ....C 2
Evanston ....B 3
Gillette ....E 1
Grand Teton Nat'l Park ....B 2
Grant Village ....C 1
Green River ....C 3
Greybull ....D 1
Guernsey ....E 2
Hanna ....D 3
Jackson ....B 2
Kemmerer ....B 3
Lake Village ....C 1
Lander ....C 2
Laramie ....E 3
Lovell ....C 1
Lusk ....E 2
Meeteetse ....C 1
Mills ....D 2
Moorcroft ....E 1
Moose ....B 2
Moran ....B 1
Newcastle ....E 1
Old Faithful ....B 1
Pine Bluffs ....E 3
Pinedale ....C 2
Powell ....C 1
Rawlins ....D 3
Rock Springs ....C 3
Riverton ....C 2
Saratoga ....D 3
Sheridan ....D 1
Shoshoni ....D 2
Sinclair ....D 3
Sundance ....E 1
Teton Village ....B 2
Thermopolis ....C 1
Torrington ....E 2
Upton ....E 1
Wapiti ....C 1
Wheatland ....E 2
Wilson ....B 2
Worland ....D 1
Yellowstone Nat'l Park ....B 1

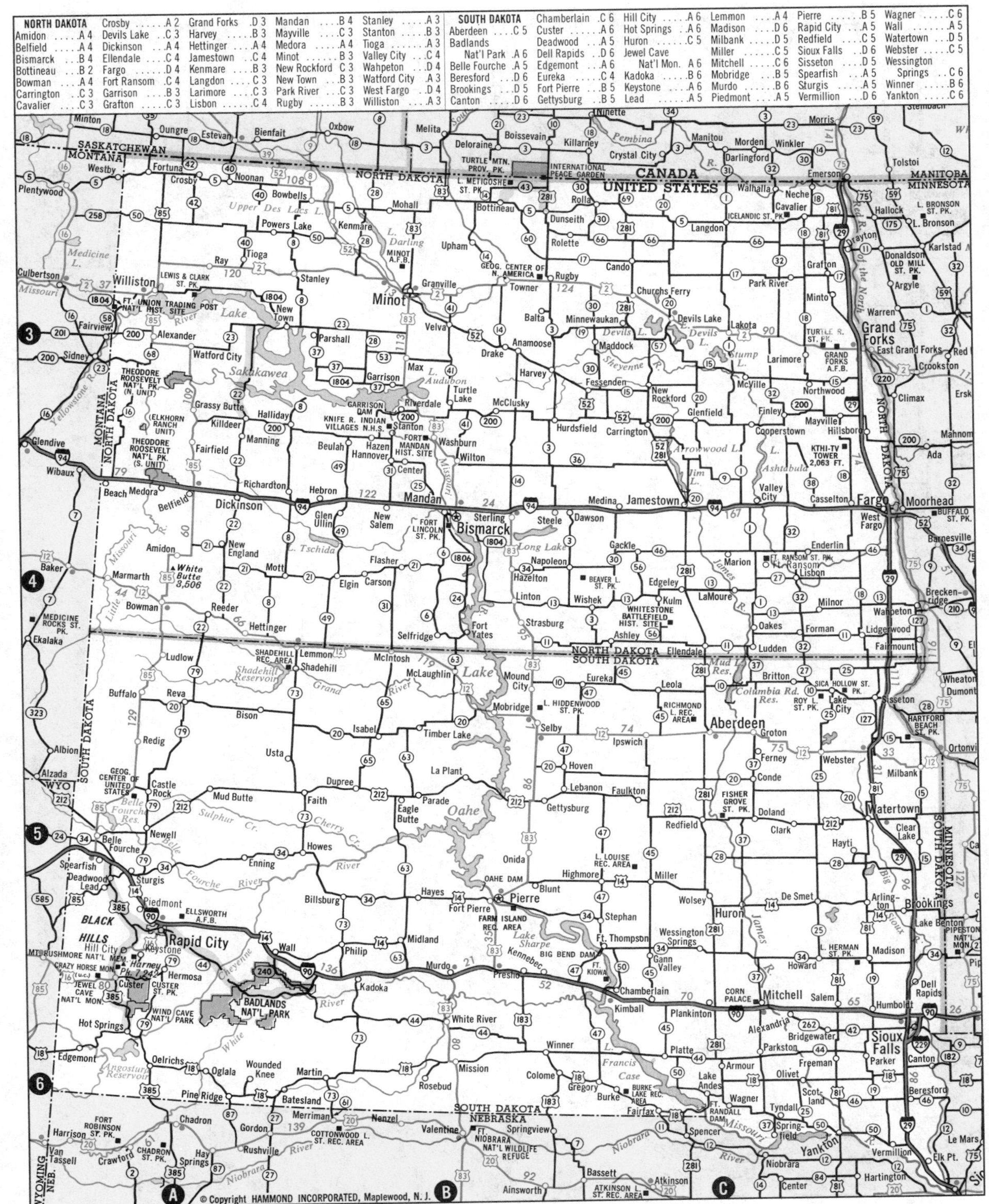

NORTH DAKOTA	
Amidon	A 4
Belfield	A 4
Bismarck	B 4
Bottineau	B 2
Bowman	A 4
Carrington	C 3
Cavalier	C 3
Crosby	A 2
Devils Lake	C 3
Dickinson	A 4
Ellendale	C 4
Fargo	D 4
Fort Ransom	C 4
Garrison	B 3
Grafton	C 3
Grand Forks	D 3
Harvey	B 3
Hettinger	A 4
Jamestown	C 4
Kenmare	B 3
Langdon	C 3
Larimore	C 3
Lisbon	C 4
Mandan	B 4
Mayville	C 3
Medora	A 4
Minot	B 3
New Rockford	C 3
New Town	B 3
Park River	C 3
Rugby	B 3
Stanley	A 3
Stanton	B 3
Tioga	A 3
Valley City	C 4
Wahpeton	D 4
Watford City	A 3
West Fargo	D 4
Williston	A 3

SOUTH DAKOTA	
Aberdeen	C 5
Badlands Nat'l Park	A 6
Belle Fourche	A 5
Beresford	D 6
Brookings	D 5
Canton	D 6
Chamberlain	C 6
Custer	A 6
Deadwood	A 5
Dell Rapids	D 6
Edgemont	A 6
Eureka	C 4
Fort Pierre	B 5
Gettysburg	B 5
Hill City	A 6
Hot Springs	A 6
Huron	C 5
Jewel Cave Nat'l Mon.	A 6
Kadoka	B 6
Keystone	A 6
Lead	A 5
Lemmon	A 4
Madison	D 6
Milbank	D 5
Miller	C 5
Mitchell	C 6
Mobridge	B 5
Murdo	B 6
Piedmont	A 5
Pierre	B 5
Rapid City	A 5
Redfield	C 5
Sioux Falls	D 6
Sisseton	D 5
Spearfish	A 5
Sturgis	A 5
Vermillion	D 6
Wagner	C 6
Wall	A 5
Watertown	D 5
Webster	C 5
Wessington Springs	C 6
Winner	B 6
Yankton	C 6

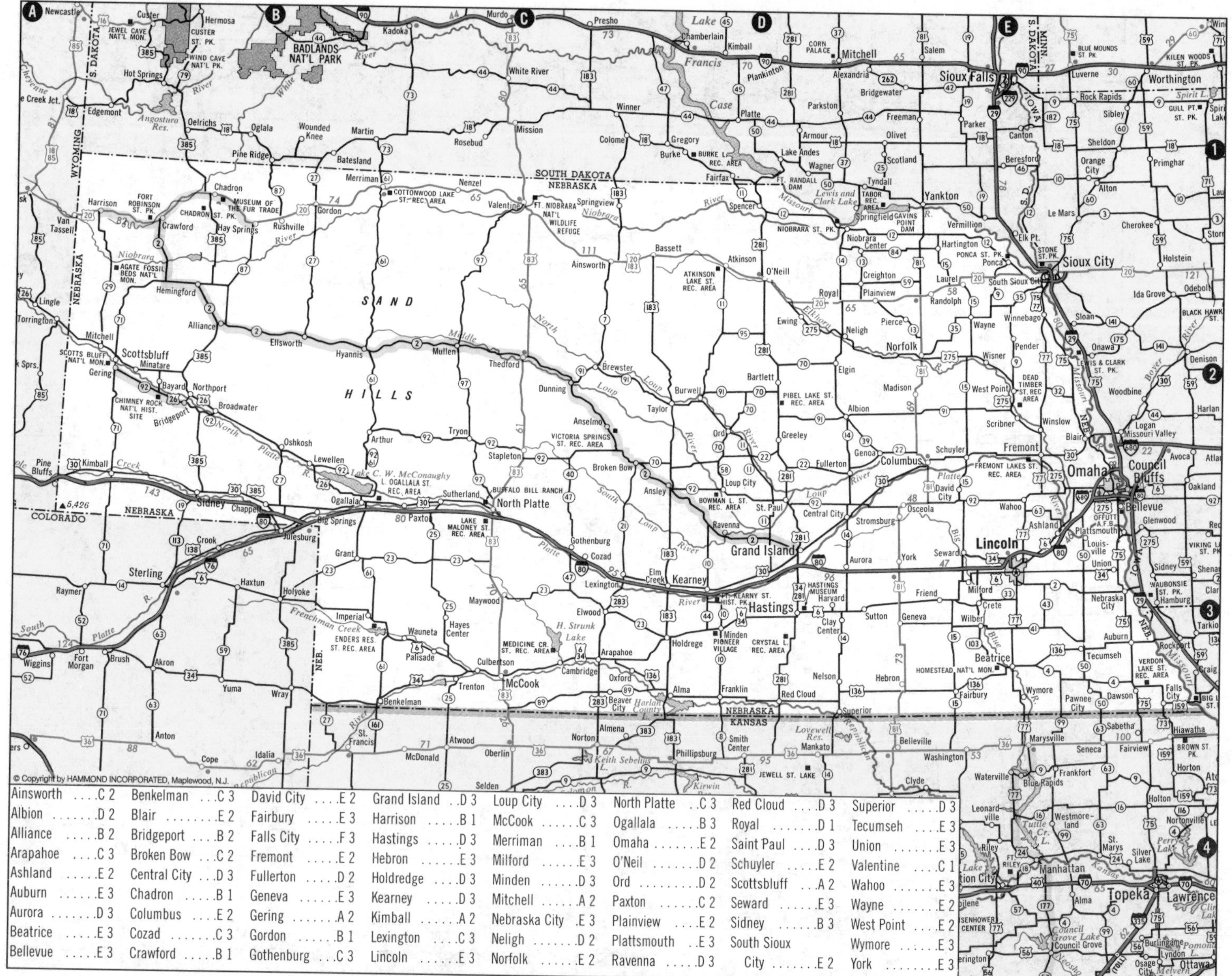
© Copyright by HAMMOND INCORPORATED, Maplewood, N.J.
Ainsworth ....C 2
Albion ....D 2
Alliance .....B 2
Arapahoe .....C 3
Ashland ......E 2
Auburn ....E 3
Aurora ....D 3
Beatrice .....E 3
Bellevue .....E 3
Benkelman ...C 3
Blair ....E 2
Bridgeport ....B 2
Broken Bow ...C 2
Central City ..D 3
Chadron .....B 1
Columbus ....E 2
Cozad ....C 3
Crawford .....B 1
David City ....E 2
Fairbury .....E 3
Falls City .....F 3
Fremont .....E 2
Fullerton .....D 2
Geneva ....E 3
Gering ....A 2
Gordon ....B 1
Gothenburg ...C 3
Grand Island ..D 3
Harrison .....B 1
Hastings .....D 3
Hebron ....E 3
Holdredge ....D 3
Kearney ......D 3
Kimball ....A 2
Lexington ....C 3
Lincoln ....E 3
Loup City ....D 3
McCook ....C 3
Merriman ....B 1
Milford ....E 3
Minden ....D 3
Mitchell ......A 2
Nebraska City .E 3
Neligh ....D 2
Norfolk ....E 2
North Platte ..C 3
Ogallala ....B 3
Omaha ....E 2
O'Neil ....D 2
Ord ....D 2
Paxton ....C 2
Plainview ....E 2
Plattsmouth ..E 3
Ravenna .....D 3
Red Cloud ....D 3
Royal ....D 1
Saint Paul ....D 3
Schuyler .....E 2
Scottsbluff ....A 2
Seward ....E 3
Sidney ....B 3
South Sioux City ....E 2
Superior .....D 3
Tecumseh .....E 3
Union ....E 3
Valentine ....C 1
Wahoo ....E 3
Wayne ....E 2
West Point ....E 2
Wymore ......E 3
York ....E 3

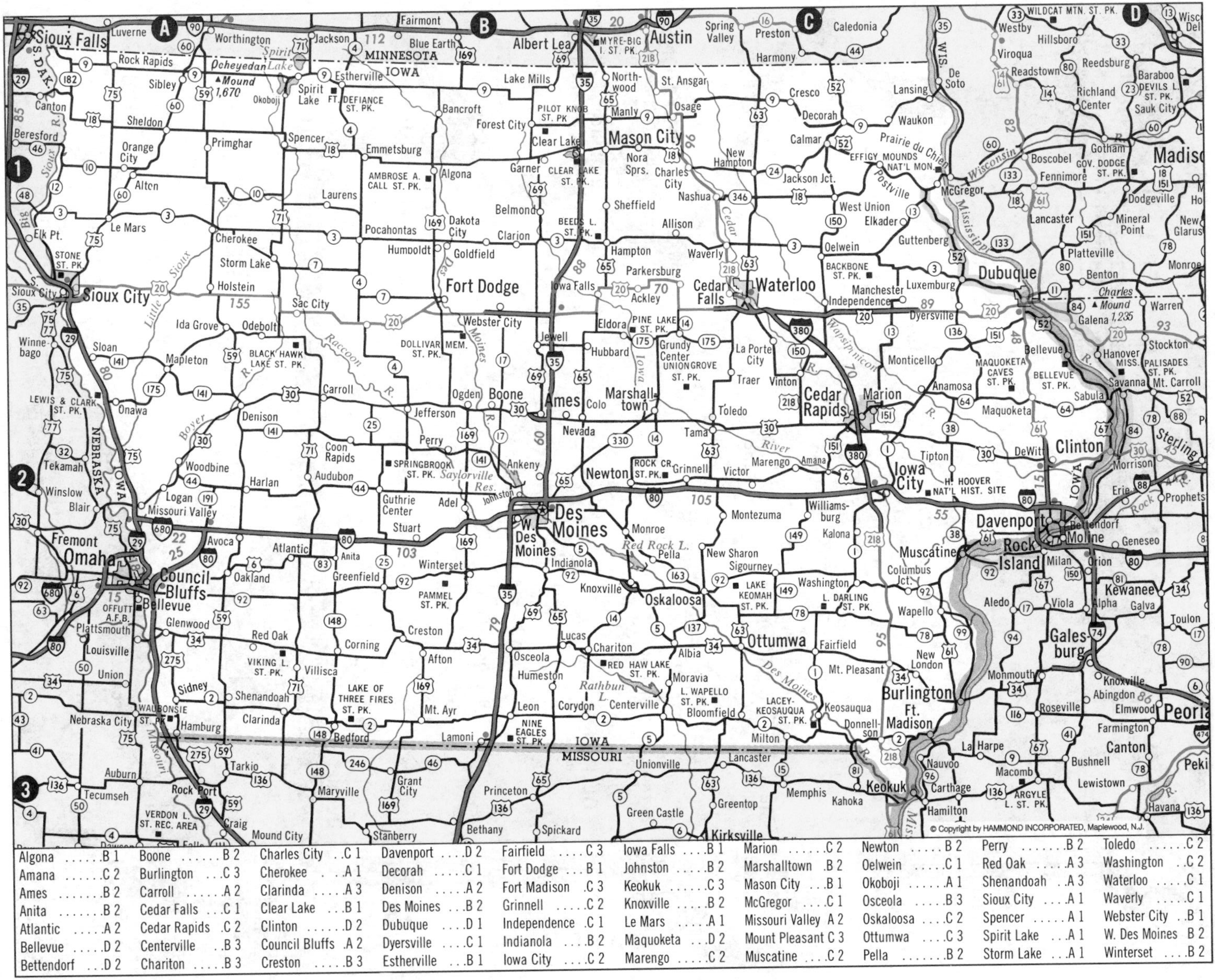

Place	Grid	Place	Grid	Place	Grid	Place	Grid	Place	Grid	Place	Grid	Place	Grid	Place	Grid	Place	Grid	Place	Grid
Algona	B 1	Boone	B 2	Charles City	C 1	Davenport	D 2	Fairfield	C 3	Iowa Falls	B 1	Marion	C 2	Newton	B 2	Perry	B 2	Toledo	C 2
Amana	C 2	Burlington	C 3	Cherokee	A 1	Decorah	C 1	Fort Dodge	B 1	Johnston	B 2	Marshalltown	B 2	Oelwein	C 1	Red Oak	A 3	Washington	C 2
Ames	B 2	Carroll	A 2	Clarinda	A 3	Denison	A 2	Fort Madison	C 3	Keokuk	C 3	Mason City	B 1	Okoboji	A 1	Shenandoah	A 3	Waterloo	C 1
Anita	B 2	Cedar Falls	C 1	Clear Lake	B 1	Des Moines	B 2	Grinnell	C 2	Knoxville	B 2	McGregor	C 1	Osceola	B 3	Sioux City	A 1	Waverly	C 1
Atlantic	A 2	Cedar Rapids	C 2	Clinton	D 2	Dubuque	D 1	Independence	C 1	Le Mars	A 1	Missouri Valley	A 2	Oskaloosa	C 2	Spencer	A 1	Webster City	B 1
Bellevue	D 2	Centerville	B 3	Council Bluffs	A 2	Dyersville	C 1	Indianola	B 2	Maquoketa	D 2	Mount Pleasant	C 3	Ottumwa	C 3	Spirit Lake	A 1	W. Des Moines	B 2
Bettendorf	D 2	Chariton	B 3	Creston	B 3	Estherville	B 1	Iowa City	C 2	Marengo	C 2	Muscatine	C 2	Pella	B 2	Storm Lake	A 1	Winterset	B 2

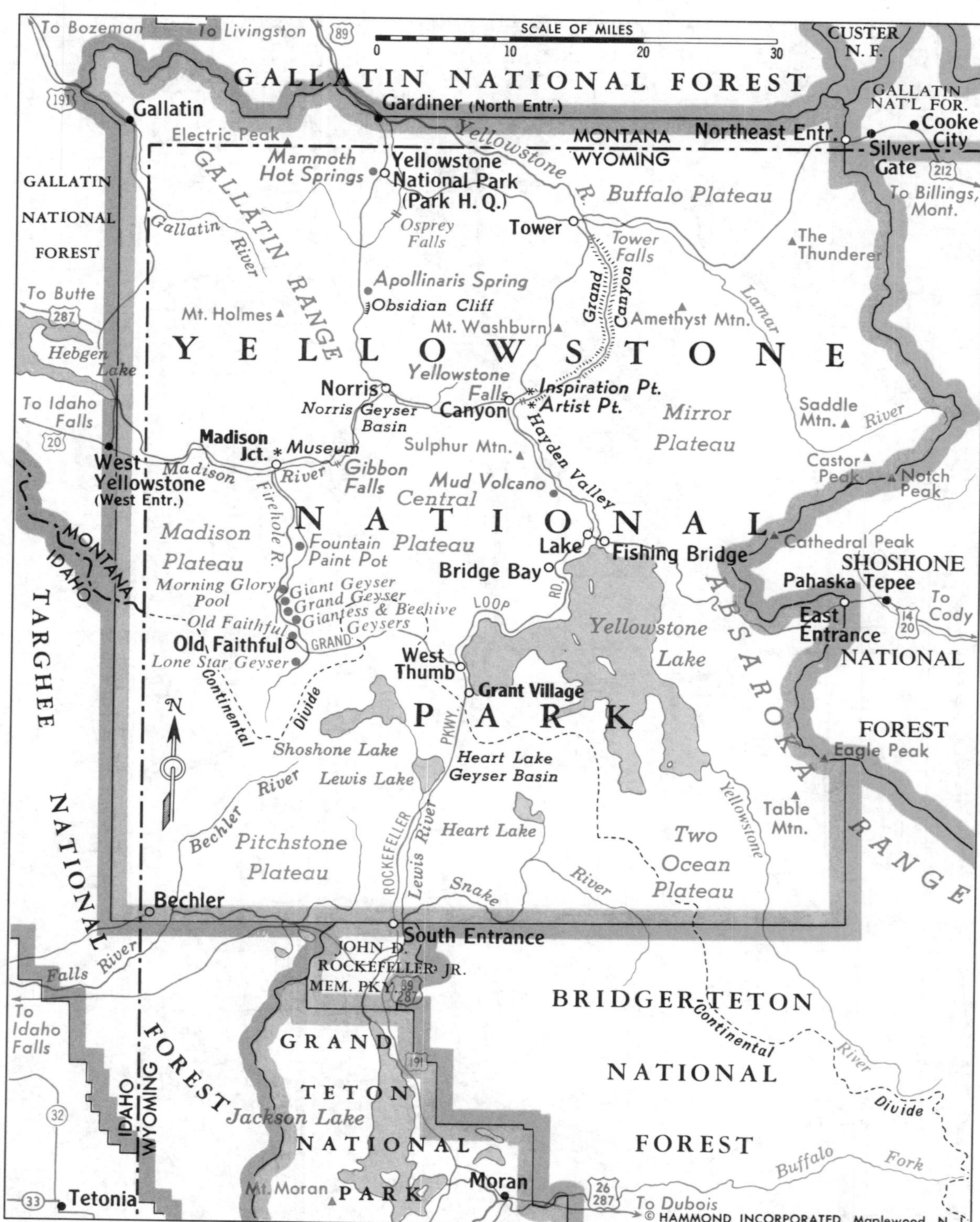

SCALE OF MILES
0 10 20 30
GALLATIN NATIONAL FOREST
To Bozeman
To Livingston
89
CUSTER N. F.
GALLATIN NAT'L FOR.
Cooke City
Silver Gate
212
To Billings, Mont.
191
Gallatin
Gardiner (North Entr.)
Northeast Entr.
MONTANA
WYOMING
Electric Peak
Mammoth Hot Springs
Yellowstone National Park (Park H. Q.)
Yellowstone R.
Buffalo Plateau
GALLATIN NATIONAL FOREST
GALLATIN RANGE
Gallatin River
Osprey Falls
Tower
Tower Falls
The Thunderer
To Butte
287
Apollinaris Spring
Obsidian Cliff
Mt. Holmes
Mt. Washburn
Grand Canyon
Amethyst Mtn.
Lamar
Hebgen Lake
YELLOWSTONE
Yellowstone Falls
Norris
Inspiration Pt.
Artist Pt.
To Idaho Falls
20
Norris Geyser Basin
Canyon
Mirror Plateau
Saddle Mtn.
River
Madison Jct.
Museum
Sulphur Mtn.
Hayden Valley
West Yellowstone (West Entr.)
Madison River
Gibbon Falls
Castor Peak
Notch Peak
Mud Volcano
Central Plateau
Firehole R.
NATIONAL
MONTANA
IDAHO
Madison Plateau
Fountain Paint Pot
Lake
Fishing Bridge
Cathedral Peak
SHOSHONE
Bridge Bay
Pahaska Tepee
To Cody
14 20
Morning Glory Pool
Giant Geyser
Grand Geyser
Giantess & Beehive Geysers
LOOP
RD.
East Entrance
Old Faithful
Old Faithful
GRAND
Yellowstone Lake
NATIONAL
Lone Star Geyser
West Thumb
Grant Village
Continental Divide
TARGHEE
PARK
PKWY.
FOREST
Shoshone Lake
Heart Lake Geyser Basin
Eagle Peak
ABSAROKA RANGE
Lewis Lake
Bechler River
Table Mtn.
Yellowstone
Pitchstone Plateau
ROCKEFELLER
Lewis River
Heart Lake
Two Ocean Plateau
River
Snake
Bechler
South Entrance
NATIONAL
Falls River
JOHN D. ROCKEFELLER JR. MEM. PKY.
89 287
BRIDGER-TETON
To Idaho Falls
Continental Divide
River
GRAND
TETON
NATIONAL
191
32
IDAHO
WYOMING
FOREST
Jackson Lake
NATIONAL
FOREST
Buffalo Fork
Mt. Moran
PARK
Moran
26 287
To Dubois
33
Tetonia

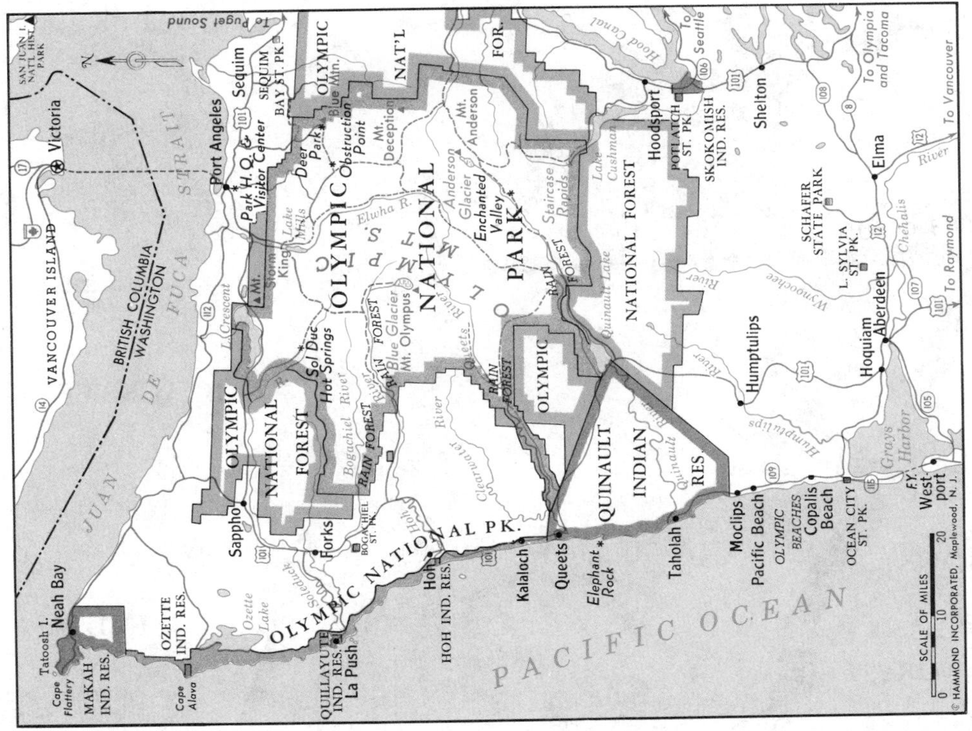
PACIFIC OCEAN
JUAN DE FUCA STRAIT
VANCOUVER ISLAND
BRITISH COLUMBIA
WASHINGTON
Victoria
SAN JUAN I. NAT'L HIST. PARK
To Puget Sound
Port Angeles
Sequim
SEQUIM BAY ST. PK.
Park H.Q. & Visitor Center
Deer Park
Obstruction Point
Blue Mtn.
Mt. Deception
Mt. Anderson
Anderson Glacier
Enchanted Valley
Staircase Rapids
Lake Cushman
Hood Canal
Hoodsport
POTLATCH ST. PK.
SKOKOMISH IND. RES.
Shelton
To Seattle
To Olympia and Tacoma
To Vancouver
Elma
SCHAFER STATE PARK
L. SYLVIA ST. PK.
Aberdeen
Hoquiam
To Raymond
Chehalis River
Wynoochee River
Humptulips
Grays Harbor
Westport
OCEAN CITY ST. PK.
Copalis Beach
OLYMPIC BEACHES
Pacific Beach
Moclips
Taholah
QUINAULT INDIAN RES.
Quinault Lake
Elephant Rock
Queets
Kalaloch
Hoh
HOH IND. RES.
OLYMPIC NATIONAL PK.
OLYMPIC NATIONAL PARK
OLYMPIC NATIONAL FOREST
OLYMPIC MTS.
RAIN FOREST
Mt. Olympus
Blue Glacier
Sol Duc Hot Springs
Lake Crescent
Mt. Storm King
Lake Mills
Elwha R.
Bogachiel River
BOGACHIEL ST. PK.
Forks
Sappho
Clearwater River
Queets River
La Push
QUILLAYUTE IND. RES.
Ozette Lake
OZETTE IND. RES.
Cape Alava
Neah Bay
Tatoosh I.
Cape Flattery
MAKAH IND. RES.
SCALE OF MILES
0 10 20
© HAMMOND INCORPORATED, Maplewood, N. J.

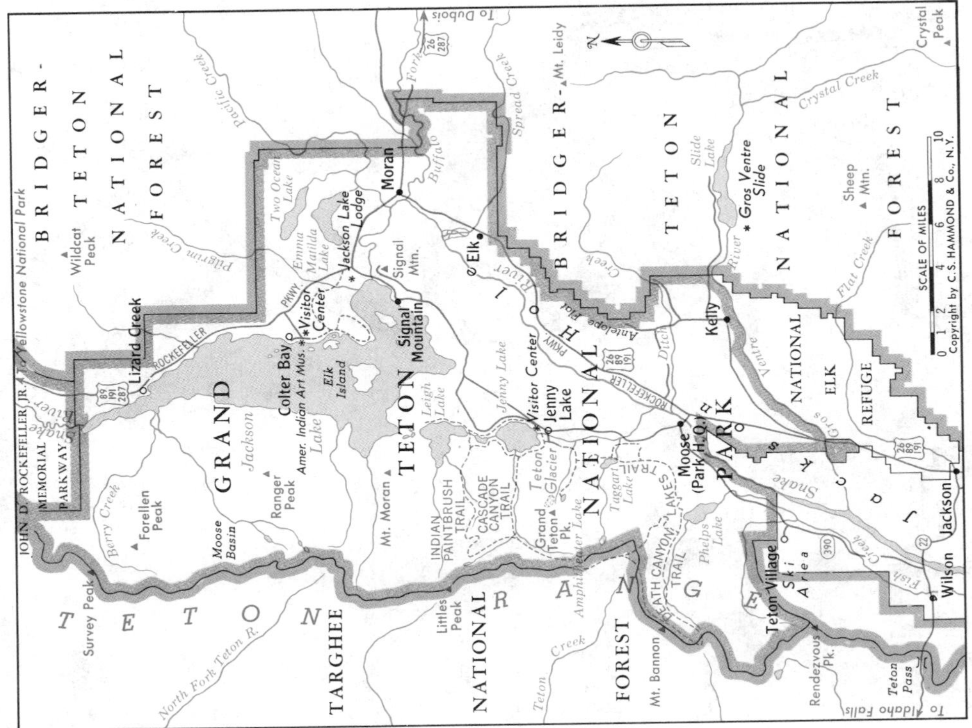
GRAND TETON NATIONAL PARK
JOHN D. ROCKEFELLER, JR. MEMORIAL PARKWAY
Yellowstone National Park
BRIDGER-TETON NATIONAL FOREST
TARGHEE NATIONAL FOREST
TETON RANGE
Survey Peak
Lizard Creek
Wildcat Peak
Snake River
Jackson Lake
Colter Bay
Amer. Indian Art Mus.
Visitor Center
Elk Island
Jackson Lake Lodge
Moran
Two Ocean Lake
Emma Matilda Lake
Signal Mtn.
Signal Mountain
Pilgrim Creek
Pacific Creek
Buffalo Fork
To Dubois
Mt. Leidy
Spread Creek
Elk
Forellen Peak
Moose Basin
Ranger Peak
Mt. Moran
Leigh Lake
Jenny Lake
Visitor Center
INDIAN PAINTBRUSH TRAIL
CASCADE CANYON TRAIL
Teton Glacier
Grand Teton Pk.
Taggart Lake
LAKES TRAIL
DEATH CANYON TRAIL
Phelps Lake
Moose (Park H.Q.)
Antelope Flat
Kelly
Gros Ventre Slide
Slide Lake
Sheep Mtn.
Crystal Creek
Crystal Peak
Flat Creek
NATIONAL ELK REFUGE
Gros Ventre River
Jackson
Wilson
Teton Village
Ski Area
Rendezvous Pk.
Teton Pass
To Idaho Falls
Littles Peak
Mt. Bannon
North Fork Teton R.
Teton Creek
Fish Creek
SCALE OF MILES
0 1 2 4 6 8 10
Copyright by C.S. HAMMOND & Co., N.Y.

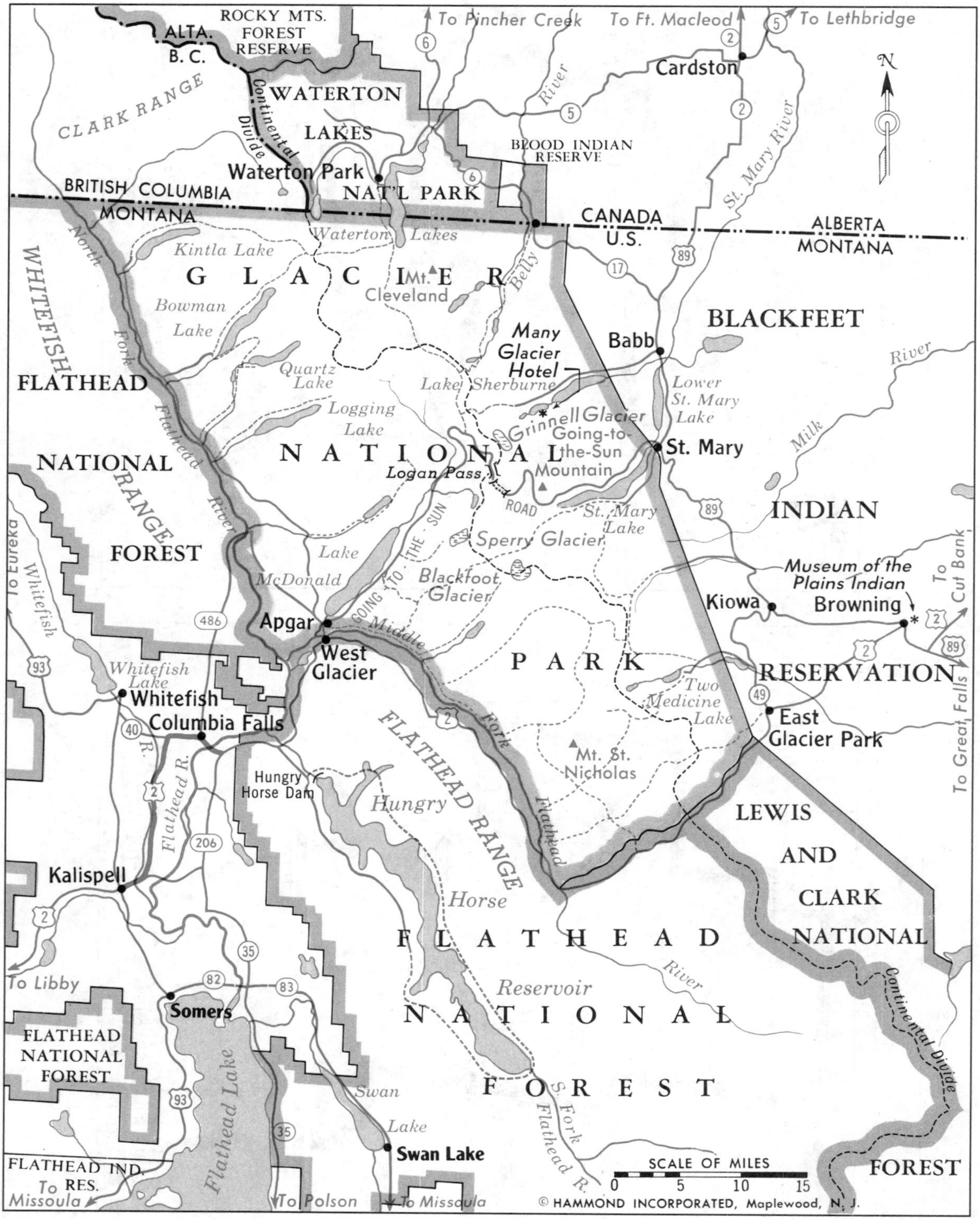
ROCKY MTS. FOREST RESERVE
ALTA.
B. C.
To Pincher Creek
To Ft. Macleod
To Lethbridge
Cardston
CLARK RANGE
WATERTON LAKES NAT'L PARK
Continental Divide
Waterton Park
River
BLOOD INDIAN RESERVE
St. Mary River
BRITISH COLUMBIA
MONTANA
CANADA
U.S.
ALBERTA
MONTANA
Waterton Lakes
Kintla Lake
GLACIER NATIONAL PARK
Mt. Cleveland
Belly
North Fork
WHITEFISH RANGE
Bowman Lake
Many Glacier Hotel
Babb
BLACKFEET INDIAN RESERVATION
River
FLATHEAD NATIONAL FOREST
Quartz Lake
Lake Sherburne
Lower St. Mary Lake
Logging Lake
Grinnell Glacier
Going-to-the-Sun Mountain
St. Mary
Milk
Flathead River
Logan Pass
GOING-TO-THE-SUN ROAD
St. Mary Lake
Sperry Glacier
Lake McDonald
Blackfoot Glacier
Museum of the Plains Indian
Browning
Kiowa
To Cut Bank
To Eureka
Whitefish
Apgar
West Glacier
Middle Fork Flathead
Two Medicine Lake
Whitefish Lake
Whitefish
Columbia Falls
East Glacier Park
To Great Falls
R.
Flathead R.
Hungry Horse Dam
FLATHEAD RANGE
Mt. St. Nicholas
LEWIS AND CLARK NATIONAL FOREST
Hungry Horse Reservoir
Kalispell
FLATHEAD NATIONAL FOREST
River
To Libby
Somers
Continental Divide
FLATHEAD NATIONAL FOREST
Flathead Lake
Swan Lake
Swan Lake
S. Fork Flathead R.
SCALE OF MILES
0 5 10 15
FLATHEAD IND. RES.
To Missoula
To Polson
To Missoula
FOREST
© HAMMOND INCORPORATED, Maplewood, N. J.